THE NEW
CAVALCADE

The New
CAVALCADE

African American Writing from 1760 to the Present

Volume I

Edited by
ARTHUR P. DAVIS,
J. SAUNDERS REDDING,
and JOYCE ANN JOYCE

HOWARD UNIVERSITY PRESS
Washington, D.C., 1991

Howard University Press, Washington, D.C. 20017

Originally published as
Cavalcade: Negro American Writing from 1760 to the Present
Copyright © 1971 by
Arthur P. Davis and Saunders Redding

Manufactured in the United States of America

This book is printed on acid-free paper.

10 9 8 7 6 5 4 3 2

Library of Congress Cataloging-in-Publication Data

The New cavalcade : African American writing from 1760 to the present /
edited by Arthur P. Davis, J. Saunders Redding, and Joyce Ann Joyce.
    p.   cm.
Rev. ed. of : Cavalcade. 1971.
Includes bibliographical references and indexes.
    1. American literature—Afro-American authors. 2. Afro-Americans—
Literary collections. I. Davis, Arthur Paul, 1904–   . II. Redding, J.
Saunders (Jay Saunders), 1906–   . III. Joyce, Joyce Ann, 1949–
IV. Title: Cavalcade.
PS508.N3N48   1991
810.8'0896073—dc20

Volume I
ISBN 0-88258-130-9, cloth
ISBN 0-88258-133-3, paperback
ISBN 0-88258-132-5, set, hardback
ISBN 0-88258-135-X, set, paperback
                                                              90-29285
                                                                   CIP

CONTENTS

PART 2
Freedom Fighters: 1830–1865

PART 4
The New Negro Renaissance and Beyond:
1910–1954

PREFACE

The original *Cavalcade* was published in 1971 and was for a generation of students a popular text. Much has happened, however, in the field of African American literature since 1971. There has been a dramatic upsurge in publications by new authors; there has been a reaction to the black revolution, which climaxed during the late sixties and early seventies; there have been new and important national honors for African American writers; and perhaps most important of all, there has come into prominence a cadre of black female authors—authors who, in some cases, have brought to African American literature a new critical outlook. And there are other factors that make a new edition of *Cavalcade* necessary: the death of certain authors, a new type of critical approach, new works written by authors originally in the text, new sources of bibliography, and several other changes brought about by time. Because of the great number of changes that have occurred and because of the recent proliferation of African-American-related books, the editors felt it necessary to make the edition a two-volume text, which we are certain will make it more convenient for a year course in African American studies.

The purpose of this anthology is to provide a representative selection of as much as possible of the best prose and poetry written by African Americans since 1760. While it has been our primary aim to make these choices on the basis of literary merit, we have also tried to cover as many areas of black life in America as was consistent with our first objective. We believe that this collection gives a fairly comprehensive picture of the black experience in America for more than two hundred years.

In making our selections we have tried within reason to avoid duplicating the material in other anthologies. However, to avoid all of the selections in other works would be unwise; to do so would leave out of our book some of the best work done by black writers in America. Since there is a "classic" African American literature just as there is a classic canon of English or French or any other established literature, we inevitably have some duplications. But we also have included many works not found in other collections.

Whenever feasible, we have given whole works rather than excerpts. A few entries, however, have been far too long to include in their entirety in an anthology of this size, and we have used parts of the works—parts which we believe can stand alone. We have done the same for plays, and naturally we have used chapters from novels and autobiographies. In every case we have seen to it that the selection can stand alone and is fairly representative of the author's general matter and manner. Whenever we left out short sections of a work, we have indicated this omission with the conventional ellipses; for longer omissions, we have used ornaments. When novels or autobiographies have chapter titles, we have used them, noting the work from which the excerpt was taken. When there are no titles, we simply note the work from which the selection was taken.

This anthology is designed for use as a text in African American literature courses or as a supplementary text in American literature courses. The introductions to the six sections in volumes I and II provide, we believe, a background sufficient to give meaning and perspective to the offerings in each section. The bibliographical data at the end of the headnotes and in the "Selected Bibliography" should be helpful to student and teacher alike, serving, we hope, as springboards for additional study.

In preparing this volume, we have examined and consulted practically all of the anthologies, collections, and critical works on African American literature extant, and in some ways we are indebted to all of them. We wish, however, to acknowledge a special indebtedness to the following works: *The Negro in Literature and Art* (third edition) and *Early Negro American Writers* by Benjamin Brawley; *To Make a Poet Black* by J. Saunders Redding; *The Negro Author* by Vernon Loggins; *Dictionary of American Negro Biography*, edited by Rayford W. Logan and Michael R. Winston; *Dictionary of Literary Biography, Volume 33, Afro-American Fiction Writers After 1955; Dictionary of Literary Biography, Volume 41: Afro-American Poets Since 1955; Dictionary of Literary Biography, Volume 50, Afro-American Writers Before the Harlem Renaissance; Dictionary of Literary Biography, Volume 51, Afro-American Writers from the Harlem Renaissance to 1940,* all of which were edited by Trudier Harris and Thadious M. Davis.

An anthology of this size needs so much bibliographical, critical, and other kinds of help, from colleagues, fellow scholars, and friends, it is practically impossible to thank all of them here. We must, therefore, settle for a chosen few, especially those who have helped to bring out *The New Cavalcade*; among them Fay Acker, senior editor of the Howard University Press, who, through her guidance, made our job easier; Cynthia Lewis and Iris Eaton, also of Howard University Press, who handled the numerous permissions requests for both volumes of *The New Cavalcade*; Janell Walden

Agyeman, who researched information for the headnotes; Kamili Anderson, who prepared the bibliographies; Rhonda Williams and Lisa McCullough, who worked on headnotes; Professor Eugene Hammond and Janet Duncan of the University of Maryland; Kathy Johnson and Laurie Wilshusen of the University of Nebraska; and O. Rudolph Aggrey, director of the Howard University Press, who encouraged and supported, in every way possible, this project. We cannot thank individually all of the members of the famous Moorland-Spingarn Research Center who helped us almost daily for a long period. It is a great library with a highly efficient and helpful staff. We are also deeply indebted to Ethelbert E. Miller, supervisor of Howard University's African American Resource Center, for his help in securing source material for our book.

The reader will note that *The New Cavalcade* now has three editors rather than the original two, Arthur P. Davis and J. Saunders Redding. Professor Redding died in 1988. Prior to his death, however, Professors Davis and Redding had decided to add a third editor, some scholar who had a deep knowledge about contemporary criticism and the recent great upsurge in publications by African American women. The new editor is Dr. Joyce A. Joyce, professor of English at the University of Nebraska. Professor Joyce's work complements the critical outlook of the two original editors, and she brings a contemporary balance to *The New Cavalcade*. Professor Redding's sensibility remains in the headnotes, introductions, and selections he chose. We are proud to have worked with him on this volume.

ARTHUR P. DAVIS

JOYCE ANN JOYCE

GENERAL INTRODUCTION

n this enlarged and updated revision of *Cavalcade* (orginially published
n 1971), now *The New Cavalcade*, we have worked with a twofold purpose
n mind: to show the evolution of African American writing as literary art
nd to provide the historical context that gives meaning to this writing as
he expression of the black American's special experience in the nation.
)ur work covers the more than two hundred years of this literature's
xistence and is designed primarily for the student of African-American
iterature.

It has been our purpose to give not only a comprehensive account of
he development of the literature, but, as far as humanly possible, a bal-
nced and impartial account as well. No author has been left out because
ve disagree with his critical attitudes, his politics, or his stand on certain
ssues. By the same token, no author has been included because he happens
o think as we do. Our selections, for example, represent practically every
najor African American critic from Alain Locke to Henry Louis Gates, Jr.,
nd their varying and often strongly conflicting critical stands. *Our* criticism
s found in the headnotes and chapter introductions.

The term "African American writing" as used in the title requires an
xplanation that goes beyond the obvious one of a body of writing by
lack Americans. Some Negro writers like William Stanley Braithwaite,
nne Spencer, and Frank Yerby "write like whites." The entire stock of
heir referents is white, Anglo-Saxon American derived. Most black Amer-
can writers, however, create out of a dual consciousness: African and
merican. The writers are twin-rooted, and while one root is nourished
y the myths, customs, culture, and values traditional in the Western world,
he other feeds hungrily on the experiential reality of blackness. These
vriters have a special vision. They are persuaded by a special mission. In
heir work they combine the sermon and the liturgy, the reality and the
ream, the *is* and the *ought to be*. Their writing is intended to appeal as
nuch to the cognitive as to the affective side of man's being.

The question of what to call ourselves has become an issue for *The
lew Cavalcade*. Frankly, it has been an issue since Emancipation. The

popular name at first was, seemingly, colored (as in NAACP), then came negro (with a lower case "n"), then Negro (with an upper case "N"), then Afro-American, then Black (with a capital "B"), then black (with a small "b"), and now African American.

When *Cavalcade* was originally published, *Negro* was still widely accepted, although after the social and literary changes of the sixties *black* gradually became the popular designation. For some older scholars and laypersons, *black* was an ugly term, and they hung on to *Negro* or used *Afro-American*. The editors of *The New Cavalcade* tended to use the term *African-American*; however, we felt free to use *Negro*, *black*, and *Afro-American*. In short, we have no desire to enter into any controversy over what to call ourselves. It is a decision that the people will make, as they have always done. We are simply trying, as stated previously, to give a comprehensive view of colored, Negro, black, Afro-American, and African American literature.

Though *The New Cavalcade* is comprehensive, the basis on which works were chosen for inclusion is primarily literary merit. This excluded the work of some writers who have a certain historical importance and who, therefore, are subjects of comment in the introductions. When other than an author's best is included, we do so because it represents a critical phase of his or her development.

For the purposes of a historical survey, it seemed sensible to divide the chronology of African American writing into six periods. They are designated and dated: "Pioneer Writers (1760–1830)"; "Freedom Fighters (1830–1865)"; "Accommodation and Protest (1865–1910)"; "The New Negro Renaissance and Beyond (1910–1954)"; "Integration versus Black Nationalism (1954 to c. 1970)"; and "The African American Literary Revival: The 1970s to the Present." Each period is prefaced by a critical introduction; there is a brief biobibliographical headnote for each author and Selected Bibliography at the end of each volume.

The editors have exercised discretion in matters of spelling, punctuation, and capitalization in those works which were carelessly printed and edited in the eighteenth century and the early decades of the nineteenth. After that time, the editors have generally followed the texts as published.

Though the editors designed *The New Cavalcade* primarily as a book for students and scholars, they hope it is something more. They hope that it is a book that the general public may read with pleasure and profit.

A. P. D.

J. S. R.

J. A. J.

THE NEW
CAVALCADE

PART 1

Pioneer Writers: 1760–1830

THE HISTORY of African American writing begins approximately a century and a half after the first black people were landed at Jamestown in the English colony of Virginia in 1619. Whereas the colonial period was marked by cultural and political advancement of the white colonists, leading to their independence, this same period fixed the social position of African Americans, fastened upon them an aggregate of character qualities that were not always reflective of proved attributes, and created for them a repertoire of cultural and social roles that they seemed destined to play forever. Whether free man or slave, the African American was forced into a markedly inferior status which was said to be justified by his "natural" character; and his character was variously and simultaneously described as "savage," "irrepressibly comic," "lecherous," "childish," "sullen," and "without a redeeming human trait."

These attributions and the rationalizations they supported were passionately touted in the South, and the passion increased as such notions were challenged by the philosophy of the Enlightenment and the political concepts of human equality and the natural rights of man. Though the characterizations were considered less valid in the North, they were not rejected there. North and South, blacks had become stereotyped by the middle of the eighteenth century.

The stereotype represented an accommodation of religious and moral scruples to the white man's material interests. It was the answer to questions that had troubled rational men since the beginning of the modern slave era, and that were—as diaries, letters, and essays of the period indicate—particularly pervasive in colonial times: How can slavery be justified? Can black men be excluded from the brotherhood of Christianity? Is slavery right in the eyes of God?

Although hundreds of historical incidents document the fact that blacks responded to the denial of their humanity in a variety of ways, a careful survey of African American writing suggests that the variety of responses can be subsumed under three basic attitudes and their corresponding modes of behavior: accommodation, protest, and escape. These are the attitudes

3

that were established almost at the beginning and were structured into the body of myths and "traditions" that symbolize them. From the first, blacks had a choice of either accommodating to, protesting against, or escaping from a way of life that was cruelly exploitative and inexcusably demeaning. For the illiterate black man the response was direct and physical. He accommodated by projecting the harmless aspects of the black stereotype; he protested by committing acts of violence; he escaped by running away.

But responses were not so clear cut for sophisticated, literate blacks. Jupiter Hammon was among the first of those who left records. He accommodated. He said what seemed to be acceptable. In his one extant prose piece, "An Address to the Negroes of the State of New York," he states, "As for myself . . . I do not wish to be free." But when one reads the servant's replies in "A Dialogue Intitled the Kind Master and the Dutiful Servant," one suspects that Hammon is double-talking, and doing it so artfully and with such subtly pointed irony as not only to reduce the masters' admonitions to absurdity but to constitute a statement of protest against them.

Phillis Wheatley, a much better poet than her older contemporary Hammon, seems also to have combined accommodation and protest, especially in such pieces as "To the Right Honorable William, Earl of Dartmouth" and "To the University of Cambridge, in New-England." But again and again she returned to the mode of escape. It was expressed in her frequently implied rejection of the knowledge that the color of her skin determined her experience—that it set bounds and was prescriptive. Escape often lay in pretending that she was like everyone else in the circle of white acquaintances with which the Wheatley family surrounded her and pretending that she was emotionally involved only in their concerns, directed by their biases, and committed to their tastes. And, to an amazing degree, she did absorb their late-Puritan culture: she was intensely moralistic and religious and considered restraint one of the highest of virtues. Wheatley modeled her work after Alexander Pope and used the heroic couplet, classical allusions, neatness, and precision. Vernon Loggins in *The Negro Author* states, "[Wheatley's] work is sophisticated rather than primitive, artificial rather than spontaneous, polished rather than crude. . . . It is in spirit and in execution little different from the sentimental poems turned out, both in England and in America, by numerous skillful versifiers of the eighteenth century who knew well the neoclassical rules for writing poetry and who followed them with studied care."[1]

Until very recently, scholars have believed that Jupiter Hammon's "An Evening Thought . . ." (1760) was the first known poetical publication by

---

[1] Vernon Loggins, *The Negro Author: His Development in America* (New York: Columbia University Press, 1931), 16.

an American Negro; but, in light of a contemporary discovery, Hammon and the year 1760 must give precedence to Lucy Terry and the year 1746. In that year, she published a broadside, ballad-type poem entitled "Bars Fight." The twenty-eight-line piece describes in starkly realistic and colorful detail a bloody Indian raid on the settlers in Deerfield, Massachusetts, on August 25, 1746. All that we know about Lucy Terry is that she was a slave who belonged to Ebenezer Wells of Deerfield. This is the entire poem:

> August 'twas the twenty-fifth
> Seventeen hundred forty-six
> The Indians did in ambush lay
> Some very valient men to slay
> The names of whom I'll not leave out
> Samuel Allen like a hero fout
> And though he was so brave and bold
> His face no more shall we behold
> Eleazer Hawks was killed outright
> Before he had time to fight
> Before he did the Indians see
> Was shot and killed immediately
> Oliver Amsden he was slain
> Which caused his friends much grief and pain.
> Simeon Amsden they found dead
> Not many rods off from his head.
> Adonijah Gillet, we do hear
> Did lose his life which was so dear
> John Saddler fled across the water
> And so [sic] excaped the dreadful slaughter
> Eunice Allen [sic] see the Indians comeing
> And hoped to save herself by running
> And had not her petticoats stopt [sic] her
> The awful creatures had not cotched [sic] her
> And tommyhawked her on the head
> And left her on the ground for dead.
> Young Samuel Allen, Oh! lack-a-day
> Was taken and carried to Canada.

George Moses Horton, the last of the pioneer poets, was a considerably more complex person and poet than either Phillis Wheatley or Jupiter Hammon. Scarcely typical of his poetry are the lines from "On Liberty and Slavery" which first brought him to general notice in 1829.

> Alas! and am I born for this,
>   To wear this slavish chain?
> Deprived of all created bliss,
>   Through hardship, toil and pain!

After the publication of *The Hope of Liberty*, from which he expected to earn enough to buy his freedom and a passage to Africa, Horton contented himself for more than thirty years with the place he occupied and the reputation he acquired in Chapel Hill, North Carolina. His knack for composing verses on a variety of subjects at a moment's notice gave him the status of a "character" at the university, where he fulfilled poetic commissions for the students. "For twenty-five cents he would supply a poem of moderate warmth, but if a gentleman wished to send a young lady an expression of exceptional fervor, fifty cents would be the fee."[2] But not all the commissions were for love verses. Some of his brightest pieces were purely comic, as in "The Creditor to His Proud Debtor."

> My duck bill boots would look as bright,
> Had you in justice served me right.
> Like you, I then could step as light
>   Before a flaunting maid.
> As nicely could I clear my throat,
> And to my tights my eyes devote;
> But I'd leave you bare, without a coat
>   For which you have not paid.

Horton's verses are refreshing after the solemnity of Phillis Wheatley's work and the religious common-meter hymn doggerel of Jupiter Hammon. His rhythms are seldom monotonous, and his verse structure is varied. He was a troubadour, a purveyor of gossip, a maker of quips, with a special penchant for ridicule. He dealt, often light-heartedly, with love, the fickleness of women and fortune, the curse of drink, and the elusiveness of fame. Of the slave poets, Horton was by far the most imaginative and the freest.

As art, early Negro autobiographical writing is less important than early Negro poetry, but as history it is more important and had a larger contemporary audience. After all, autobiographical writing centers on the experiences of "real life," and the mind of eighteenth-century and postcolonial America had a great affinity for the true. It saw little connection between imagination and experience and cared less for imaginative insight than for the surface rendering of reality. Literary "art" was suspect. It was typical that William Lloyd Garrison, the abolitionist, counseled Frederick Douglass to *tell* his story and expressed an impatience with literary and intellectual embellishments.

The author of the first black American autobiography, then, need not have apologized for the "capacities and conditions" of his life, nor for the

---

[2] Benjamin Brawley, *Early Negro American Writers* (Chapel Hill: University of North Carolina Press, 1935), 110.

language in which he sets them forth. *A Narrative of the Uncommon Sufferings and Surprising Deliverance of Briton Hammon, a Negro Man* is a booklet of fourteen pages. Published in Boston in 1760, it describes episodes in Hammon's roundabout journey from New England to Jamaica to the British Isles and back. In the course of his journey Hammon suffers shipwreck, is held captive by Indians in Florida, and is imprisoned by Spaniards. But the telling falls flat. Hammon makes no attempt at description or character delineation and provides no insights. The *Narrative* deserves mention only because it is the first in a genre that by the middle of the nineteenth century became the most popular form of Negro expression.

While Briton Hammon, who lacked intellectual sophistication, owed nothing to tradition, John Marrant did. He most certainly knew *Pilgrim's Progress*, and he was probably acquainted with Jeremy Taylor's *Holy Living and Holy Dying*. Two of Marrant's three works are autobiographical, but only the title of the first reveals the fact that the author was a Negro. *A Narrative of the Lord's Wonderful Dealings with J. Marrant, a Black* (London, 1785) and *Journal of John Marrant* (London, 1789) tell of miraculous conversions followed by equally miraculous escapes (which symbolize God's mercy) from all sorts of natural cataclysms (which symbolize God's power and wrath) and man-created disasters (which symbolize humanity's wickedness). Marrant's third book, *Sermon*, is just that—a long narrative sermon that retells, with wildly imaginative elaborations, the Old Testament.

The most important autobiography of the period was written by an African, Olaudah Equiano, who was only briefly a slave in America. His autobiography, *The Interesting Narrative of the Life of Olaudah Equiano, or Gustavus Vassa, the African* (London, 1789) principally relates his experiences as a slave in foreign lands and is notable for several reasons. It ran to eight editions in five years. It is a great antislavery document and conveys a wealth of firsthand impressions and information about slavery, which, as Vassa makes brilliantly clear, was one thing in Africa, another in England, and something altogether different in America, but an evil everywhere. *The Narrative* is also an absorbing travel book. Vassa was taken to many places, and his descriptions of people, manners, and customs are powerfully evocative of the realities of eighteenth-century life in several parts of the world. No autobiography of the period matches Vassa's for clarity, honesty, and truth.

But most of the autobiographical writings of this time were essays of protest, and the Negro authorship of several of them is questionable. Some dedicated white abolitionists were not above writing "slave narratives" and issuing them as the authentic work of blacks. There is grave doubt, for instance, that "Petition of an African," which was published in an antislavery journal called *American Museum*, was written by a Negro woman as claimed. Similar doubts are attached to "An Essay on Slavery," signed "Othello," which was also printed in *American Museum* in 1788.

Other autobiographical writers are easily identified as Negroes. One of these was Benjamin Banneker. An engineer, mathematician, and astronomer, Banneker served on the commission that laid out the streets of the nation's capital. In a letter of protest to Thomas Jefferson, he cited his own achievements as evidence against the "train of absurd and false ideas which so generally prevail with respect to the Negro." Other blacks, who certainly did not think of themselves as writers, produced pamphlets and tracts, letters, and petitions which were widely circulated. David Walker's *Appeal*, published in 1829, aroused the slaveholding South to such a pitch of anger and fear as to persuade the governor of Virginia to prepare a special legislative message about it, and the mayor of Savannah, Georgia, to request that the mayor of Boston suppress it. Walker stressed the blatant hypocrisy of American Christianity; earlier writers, among them Benjamin Banneker, struck at the national hypocrisy of a government which could wage a war to give whites their freedom from tyranny without considering freedom from slavery for its black "citizens." Even Jupiter Hammon, in his mild accommodationist way, pointed out this inconsistency.

By the end of the period, George Moses Horton was the only generally recognized writer who remained an accommodationist. Escape in the Phillis Wheatley sense was unthinkable. Protest was the mode and the theme. For all the variations in degrees of talent, in intellect, in "ways of seeing," and in style, protest united Briton Hammon and John Marrant, Gustavus Vassa, Benjamin Banneker, and David Walker. Whether they were as optimistic as Hammon or as desperate as Walker, these authors believed that their writing could help change the lives of blacks for the better. This was their commitment—to contribute to an amelioration of the black race's lot. If in their pursuit of this goal they did not produce literary art, they did reaffirm the values and the ideals of freedom, equality, and justice—ideals that blacks were seldom credited with appreciating and understanding.

Phillis Wheatley

(c. 1753–1784)

PRACTICALLY ALL that is known of the early life of Phillis Wheatley is found in the following letter, written in 1772 by her master, John Wheatley, and printed in her *Poems on Various Subjects* (1773):

> Phillis was brought from *Africa to America,* in the Year 1761, between Seven and Eight years of age. Without any assistance from School Education, and by only what she was taught in the Family, she, in sixteen Months Time from her Arrival, attained the English Language, to which she was an utter Stranger before, to such a Degree, as to read any, the most difficult Parts of the Sacred Writings, to the great Astonishment of all who heard her.
>
> As to her Writing, her own Curiosity led her to it; and this she learnt in so short a Time, that in the Year 1765, she wrote a letter to the Rev. Mr. Occam, the *Indian* Minister, while in *England.*
>
> She has a great Inclination to learn the Latin Tongue, and has made some Progress in it. This Relation is given by her Master who bought her, and with whom she now lives.

John Wheatley, a prosperous Boston tailor, purchased the frail little African to be a companion for his wife Susannah. The Wheatleys soon made Phillis a member of the family. Under their instruction, especially that of Mary, Wheatley's daughter, Phillis became not only a well-educated young girl but also something of a local celebrity. By 1766, at the age of twelve or thirteen, she was writing verses. In 1770 she published her first poem, "An Elegiac Poem on the Death of George Whitefield," which "appeared in at least six different editions in Boston, Philadelphia, and New York, within a few months."[1] In 1771 she received an unusual honor for a slave by becoming a "baptized communicant" of Boston's Old South Meeting House.

The high point in Phillis Wheatley's life came in 1773, when the Wheatleys sent her to London for her health. There Phillis met the Countess of Huntingdon, the patroness of George Whitefield and other Methodists, who introduced the girl to many distinguished Londoners. The Lord Mayor gave Phillis a copy of the 1770 folio edition of *Paradise Lost;* the Earl of Dartmouth presented her with a copy of Smollett's 1770 translation of *Don Quixote.* Phillis was urged to stay in England long enough to be presented at Court, but learning that Mrs. Wheatley was ill, she returned to Boston. Before she

---

[1] Vernon Loggins, *The Negro Author* (New York: Columbia University Press, 1931), 16.

left London, however, Phillis arranged for the publication of her only book, *Poems on Various Subjects, Religious and Moral*, which appeared in 1773 with a "Dedication" to the gracious Countess of Huntingdon.

Mrs. Wheatley died in March 1774, Mr. Wheatley died in 1778. In the same year Phillis, now a "free Negro," married a Negro named John Peters. He was a jack-of-all-trades who was apparently not so successful as he was versatile. At various times he supposedly worked as a baker, grocer, lawyer, and physician. Phillis and John Peters had three children, but their marriage seems not to have been a happy one.

In 1776 Phillis Wheatley wrote a poem entitled "To His Excellency General Washington" and sent the general a manuscript copy. The poem was subsequently published in the April 1776 issue of the *Pennsylvania Magazine, or American Monthly Museum*. Washington courteously thanked the black poet in a letter, dated February 28, 1776, and invited her to visit him at Cambridge, where she was graciously received by the general and his fellow officers.

After the Revolution, Phillis Wheatley drew up "Proposals" for another book of poems and published them originally in the October 30, 1779, *Evening Post and General Advertiser*. But the volume itself was never published, and of the items included in her "Proposals" only five are now extant.

Before the winter of 1783–84, Phillis lost her two older children. Her husband was in jail, and she had to earn her living by working in a "cheap boarding house." She died at the age of thirty-two on December 5, 1784. Her last child died soon enough afterward to be buried with her.

Phillis Wheatley left forty-six known poems. Of these, eighteen are elegies, several of them probably written at the request of friends. They are "correct," typical eighteenth-century elegies using the religious imagery common to this type of poem. She wrote six poems inspired by public acts like the repeal of the Stamp Act and Washington's appointment as commander in chief. It is possible that had she lived longer she would have written more of this type of poem. But not all of Phillis Wheatley's poetry is occasional; she created versified selections from the Bible ("Goliath of Gath") and an adaptation from the sixth book of Ovid's *Metamorphoses*. In addition, she composed typically eighteenth-century poems on abstractions like "Imagination," "Recollection," and "Virtue" and wrote companion poems on "Morning" and "Evening" which show Milton's influence. Her poem in blank verse, "To the University of Cambridge, in New-England," probably also was influenced by Milton.

Phillis Wheatley's poetic master was Alexander Pope, and she was second to none of her contemporaries in capturing the music and cadence of her mentor. In an age of imitators of Pope, she was among the best.

For the most recent study of Phillis Wheatley, see John C. Shields, ed., *The Collected Works of Phillis Wheatley* (1988). The entry written by Saunders Redding, in Rayford W. Logan and Michael R. Winston, eds., *Dictionary of American Negro Biography* (1982) provides comprehensive commentary, as does the article by Kenny J. Williams in the *Dictionary of Literary Biography, Volume 50*. The impact of Wheatley's critical reception upon criticism of African American writing produced since the eighteenth century is examined by Henry Louis Gates, Jr., in his *Figures in Black: Words, Signs, and the "Racial" Self* (1987). Other important sources of comment on Wheatley include Julian D. Mason, Jr., ed., *The Poems of Phillis Wheatley* (1966); Benjamin Brawley, *The Negro in Literature and Art*, (3rd ed., 1929); Brawley, *Early Negro American Writers* (1935); J. Saunders Redding, *To Make a Poet Black* (1939); and Vernon Loggins, *The Negro Author* (1931). For "interpretive essays on the life and poetry" of Wheatley see *Bid the Vassal Soar* (1974) by Merle A. Richmond; for an excellent anthology of essays and comments, see William H. Robinson, *Critical Essays on Phillis Wheatley* (1982). Jean Wagner, the French critic, comments on Wheatley's life and work in his study *Black Poets of the United States: From Paul Laurence Dunbar to Langston Hughes* (1973), and see June Jordan's excellent essay in *Wild Women in the Whirlwind* (1990).

All of the following poems come from *The Poems of Phillis Wheatley*.

TO THE UNIVERSITY OF CAMBRIDGE, IN NEW-ENGLAND

While an intrinsic ardor prompts to write,
The muses promise to assist my pen;
'Twas not long since I left my native shore
The land of errors, and *Egyptian* gloom:
Father of mercy, 'twas thy gracious hand
Brought me in safety from those dark abodes.

Students, to you 'tis giv'n to scan the heights
Above, to traverse the ethereal space,
And mark the systems of revolving worlds.
Still more, ye sons of science ye receive
The blissful news by messengers from heav'n,
How *Jesus'* blood for your redemption flows.
See him with hands out-stretcht upon the cross;
Immense compassion in his bosom glows;
He hears revilers, nor resents their scorn;
What matchless mercy in the Son of God!

When the whole human race by sin had fall'n,
He deign'd to die that they might rise again,
And share with him in the sublimest skies,
Life without death, and glory without end.

Improve your privileges while they stay,
Ye pupils, and each hour redeem, that bears
Or good or bad report of you to heav'n.
Let sin, that baneful evil to the soul,
By you be shunn'd, nor once remit your guard;
Suppress the deadly serpent in its egg.

Ye blooming plants of human race devine,
An *Ethiop* tells you 'tis your greatest foe;
Its transient sweetness turns to endless pain,
And in immense perdition sinks the soul.

ON BEING BROUGHT FROM AFRICA TO AMERICA

'Twas mercy brought me from my *Pagan* land,
Taught my benighted soul to understand
That there's a God, that there's a *Savior* too:
Once I redemption neither sought nor knew.
Some view our sable race with scornful eye,
"Their colour is a diabolic die."
Remember, *Christians, Negroes,* black as *Cain,*
May be refin'd, and join th' angelic train.

ON THE DEATH OF THE REV. MR. GEORGE WHITEFIELD. 1770

Hail, happy saint, on thine immortal throne,
Possest of glory, life, and bliss unknown;
We hear no more the music of thy tongue,
Thy wonted auditories cease to throng.
Thy sermons in unequall'd accents flow'd,
And ev'ry bosom with devotion glow'd;
Thou didst in strains of eloquence refin'd
Inflame the heart, and captivate the mind.
Unhappy we the setting sun deplore,
So glorious once, but ah! it shines no more.

Behold the prophet in his tow'ring flight!
He leaves the earth for heav'ns unmeasur'd height,
And worlds unknown receive him from our sight.
There *Whitefield* wings with rapid course his way,
And sails to *Zion* through vast seas of day.
Thy pray'rs, great saint, and thine incessant cries
Have pierc'd the bosom of thy native skies.
Thou moon hast seen, and all the stars of light,
How he has wrestled with his God by night.
He pray'd that grace in ev'ry heart might dwell,
He long'd to see *America* excel;
He charg'd its youth that ev'ry grace divine
Should with full lustre in their conduct shine;
That Savior, which his soul did first receive,
The greatest gifts that ev'n a God can give,
He freely offer'd to the num'rous throng,
That on his lips with list'ning pleasure hung.

"Take him, ye wretched, for your only good,
"Take him ye starving sinners, for your food;
"Ye thirsty, come to this life-giving stream,
"Ye preachers, take him for your joyful theme;
"Take him my dear *Americans*, he said,
"Be your complaints on his kind bosom laid:
"Take him, ye *Africans,* he longs for you,
"*Impartial Savior* is his title due:
"Wash'd in the fountain of redeeming blood,
"You shall be sons, and kings, and priests to God."

Great *Countess,** we *Americans* revere
Thy name, and mingle in thy grief sincere;
New England deeply feels, the *Orphans* mourn,
Their more than father will no more return.

But, though arrested by the hand of death,
Whitefield no more exerts his lab'ring breath,
Yet let us view him in th' eternal skies,
Let ev'ry heart to this bright vision rise;
While the tomb safe retains its sacred trust,
Till life divine re-animates his dust.

---

*The Countess of Huntingdon, to whom Mr. Whitefield was chaplain.

AN HYMN TO THE MORNING

Attend my lays, ye ever honour'd nine,
Assist my labours, and my strains refine;
In smoothest numbers pour the notes along,
For bright *Aurora* now demands my song.

   Aurora hail, and all the thousand dies,
Which deck thy progress through the vaulted skies:
The morn awakes, and wide extends her rays,
On ev'ry leaf the gentle zephyr plays;
Harmonious lays the feather'd race resume,
Dart the bright eye, and shake the painted plume.

   Ye shady groves, your verdant gloom display
To shield your poet from the burning day:
Calliope awake the sacred lyre,
While thy fair sisters fan the pleasing fire:
The bow'rs, the gales, the variegated skies
In all their pleasures in my bosom rise.

   See in the east th' illustrious king of day!
His rising radiance drives the shades away—
But Oh! I feel his fervid beams too strong,
And scarce begun, concludes th' abortive song.

AN HYMN TO THE EVENING

Soon as the sun forsook the eastern main
The pealing thunder shook the heav'nly plain;
Majestic grandeur! From the zephyr's wing,
Exhales the incense of the blooming spring,
Soft purl the streams, the birds renew their notes,
And through the air their mingled music floats.

   Through all the heav'ns what beauteous dies are spread!
But the west glories in the deepest red;
So may our breasts with ev'ry virtue glow,
The living temples of our God below!

   Fill'd with the praise of him who gives the light;
And draws the sable curtains of the night,
Let placid slumbers sooth each weary mind,
At mourn to wake more heav'nly, more refin'd;

So shall the labours of the day begin
More pure, more guarded from the snares of sin.

Night's leaden sceptre seals my drousy eyes,
Then cease, my song, till fair *Aurora* rise.

ON IMAGINATION

Thy various works, imperial queen, we see,
How bright their forms! how deck'd with pomp by thee!
Thy wond'rous acts in beauteous order stand,
And all attest how potent is thine hand.

From *Helicon's* refulgent heights attend,
Ye sacred choir, and my attempts befriend:
To tell her glories with a faithful tongue,
Ye blooming graces, triumph in my song.

Now here, now there, the roving *Fancy* flies,
Till some lov'd object strikes her wand'ring eyes,
Whose silken fetters all the senses bind,
And soft captivity involves the mind.

Imagination! who can sing thy force?
Or who describe the swiftness of thy course?
Soaring through air to find the bright abode,
Th' empyreal palace of the thund'ring God,
We on thy pinions can surpass the wind,
And leave the rolling universe behind:
From star to star the mental optics rove,
Measure the skies, and range the realms above.
There in one view we grasp the mighty whole,
Or with new worlds amaze th' unbounded soul.

Though *Winter* frowns to *Fancy's* raptur'd eyes
The fields may flourish, and gay scenes arise;
The frozen deeps may break their iron bands,
And bid their waters murmur o'er the sands.
Fair *Flora* may resume her fragrant reign,
And with her flow'ry riches deck the plain;
Sylvanus may diffuse his honours round,
And all the forest may with leaves be crown'd:
Show'rs may descend, and dews their gems disclose,
And nectar sparkle on the blooming rose.

Such is thy pow'r, nor are thine orders vain,
O thou the leader of the mental train:
In full perfection all thy works are wrought,
And thine the sceptre o'er the realms of thought.
Before thy throne the subject-passions bow,
Of subject-passions sov'reign ruler Thou,
At thy command joy rushes on the heart,
And through the glowing veins the spirits dart.

Fancy might now her silken pinions try
To rise from earth, and sweep th' expanse on high;
From *Tithon's* bed now might *Aurora* rise,
Her cheeks all glowing with celestial dies,   }
While a pure stream of light o'erflows the skies. }
The monarch of the day I might behold,
And all the mountains tipt with radiant gold,
But I reluctant leave the pleasing views,
Which *Fancy* dresses to delight the *Muse;*
Winter austere forbids me to aspire,
And northern tempests damp the rising fire;
They chill the tides of *Fancy's* flowing sea,
Cease then, my song, cease the unequal lay.

TO HIS EXCELLENCY GENERAL WASHINGTON

The following LETTER *and* VERSES, *were written by the famous* Phillis Wheatley, *The African Poetess, and presented to his Excellency* Gen. Washington.

SIR.
I have taken the freedom to address your Excellency in the enclosed poem, and entreat your acceptance, though I am not insensible of its inaccuracies. Your being appointed by the Grand Continental Congress to be Generalissimo of the armies of North America, together with the fame of your virtues, excite sensations not easy to suppress. Your generosity, therefore, I presume, will pardon the attempt. Wishing your Excellency all possible success in the great cause you are so generously engaged in. I am,
Your Excellency's most obedient humble servant,
PHILLIS WHEATLEY.

Providence, Oct. 26, 1775.
His Excellency Gen. Washington.

Celestial choir! enthron'd in realms of light,
  Columbia's scenes of glorious toils I write.
While freedom's cause her anxious breast alarms,
She flashes dreadful in refulgent arms.
See mother earth her offspring's fate bemoan,
And nations gaze at scenes before unknown!
See the bright beams of heaven's revolving light
Involved in sorrows and the veil of night!
  The goddess comes, she moves divinely fair,
Olive and laurel binds her golden hair:
Wherever shines this native of the skies,
Unnumber'd charms and recent graces rise.
  Muse! bow propitious while my pen relates
How pour her armies through a thousand gates,
As when Eolus heaven's fair face deforms,
Enwrapp'd in tempest and a night of storms;
Astonish'd ocean feels the wild uproar,
The refluent surges beat the sounding shore;
Or thick as leaves in Autumn's golden reign,
Such, and so many, moves the warrior's train.
In bright array they seek the work of war,
Where high unfurl'd the ensign waves in air.
Shall I to Washington their praise recite?
Enough thou know'st them in the fields of fight.
Thee, first in peace and honours,—we demand
The grace and glory of thy martial band.
Fam'd for thy valour, for thy virtues more,
Hear every tongue thy guardian aid implore!
  One century scarce perform'd its destined round,
When Gallic powers Columbia's fury found;
And so may you, whoever dares disgrace
The land of freedom's heaven-defended race!
Fix'd are the eyes of nations on the scales,
For in their hopes Columbia's arm prevails.
Anon Britannia droops the pensive head,
While round increase the rising hills of dead.
Ah! cruel blindness to Columbia's state!
Lament thy thirst of boundless power too late.
  Proceed, great chief, with virtue on thy side,
Thy ev'ry action let the goddess guide.
A crown, a mansion, and a throne that shine,
With gold unfading, WASHINGTON! be thine.

Jupiter Hammon

(1711–1806)

A SLAVE of the Lloyd family of Lloyd's Neck, Long Island, Jupiter Hammon served three generations of that family. The Lloyds were evidently considerate masters: they helped their talented slave to publish his verses; they also allowed him to get an education sufficient to write pious religious verse and prose tracts, and they seemingly encouraged his activities as a slave preacher. During the American Revolution, Hammon moved with his masters to Hartford, Connecticut, where he remained during the war, publishing there most of his best-known poetical works, including "An Evening Thought: Salvation by Christ with Penitential Cries" (1761); *An Address to Miss Phillis Wheatly* [sic], *Ethiopian Poetess in Boston* (1778); *An Essay on Ten Virgins* (1779)—a work not yet found, but thought to be in verse; "A Poem for Children" (1782); and "The Kind Master and Dutiful Servant" (1782), published as part of a prose work, *An Evening's Improvement*. His prose works published in Hartford include two evangelical tracts: *A Winter Peace* (1782) and *An Evening's Improvement*. In 1786, for "Members of the African Society in New York," he published *Address to the Negroes of the State of New York*.

The "accommodationist" tone of this last-named work,[1] probably accounts for Jupiter Hammon's neglect during the Abolitionist era, when every effort was made to collect evidence of blacks' intellectual ability. Even though Hammon preferred not to "shake the boat," he like other blacks of his generation saw the hypocrisy of a nation fighting a war for its freedom and remaining blind to slavery within its borders.

Oscar Wegelin's *Jupiter Hammon, American Negro Poet* (1915) was among the first works to publicize Hammon's worth. A fuller treatment is found in Stanley A. Ransom, Jr.'s *America's First Negro Poet: The Complete Works of Jupiter Hammon of Long Island* (1970). See also *Early Black American Poets* (1969), edited by William Henry Robinson; William H. Robinson's entry in *Dictionary of American Negro Biography*; and Sondra A. O'Neale's article in *Dictionary of Literary Biography, Volume 51*. There is also a short biography by Benjamin Brawley in *Dictionary of American Biography*. Hammon is a subject in Bernard W. Bell's study "African-American Writers,"

---

[1] See the introduction to Chapter 1.

in *American Literature 1764–1789: The Revoluntionary Years,* ed. Everett Emerson (1977).

The following poems come from *America's First Negro Poet.*

AN ADDRESS TO MISS PHILLIS WHEATLY

I

O come you pious youth! adore
   The wisdom of thy God,
In bringing thee from distant shore,
   To learn His holy word.
Eccles. xii.

II

Thou mightst been left behind
   Amidst a dark abode;
God's tender mercy still combin'd,
   Thou hast the holy word.
Psal. cxxxv, 2, 3.

III

Fair wisdom's ways are paths of peace,
   And they that walk therein,
Shall reap the joys that never cease,
   And Christ shall be their king.
Psal. i, 1, 2; Prov. iii, 7.

IV

God's tender mercy brought thee here;
   Tost o'er the raging main;
In Christian faith thou hast a share,
   Worth all the gold of Spain.
Psal. ciii, 1, 3, 4.

V

While thousands tossed by the sea,
   And others settled down,

From *America's First Negro Poet: The Complete Works of Jupiter Hammon of Long Island,* edited and with an introduction by Stanley A(ustin) Ransom, Jr. (Port Washington, New York: Kennikat Press, Ira J. Friedman Division, 1970).

God's tender mercy set thee free,
  From dangers that come down.

Death.

VI

That thou a pattern still might be,
  To youth of Boston town,
The blessed Jesus set thee free,
  From every sinful wound.

2 Cor. v, 10.

VII

The blessed Jesus, who came down,
  Unvail'd his sacred face,
To cleanse the soul of every wound,
  And give repenting grace.

Rom. v, 21.

VIII

That we poor sinners may obtain,
  The pardon of our sin;
Dear blessed Jesus now constrain,
  And bring us flocking in.

Psal. xxxiv, 6, 7, 8.

IX

Come you, Phillis, now aspire,
  And seek the living God,
So step by step thou mayst go higher,
  Till perfect in the word.

Matth. vii, 7, 8.

X

While thousands mov'd to distant shore,
  And others left behind,
The blessed Jesus still adore,
  Implant this in thy mind.

Psal. lxxxix, 1.

XI

Thou hast left the heathen shore;
  Thro' mercy of the Lord.

Among the heathen live no more,
  Come magnify thy God.
                          Psal. xxxiv, 1, 2, 3.

XII

I pray the living God may be,
  The shepherd of thy soul;
His tender mercies still are free,
  His mysteries to unfold.
                          Psal. lxxx, 1, 2, 3.

XIII

Thou, Phillis, when thou hunger hast,
  Or pantest for thy God;
Jesus Christ is thy relief,
  Thou hast the holy word.
                          Psal. xiii, 1, 2, 3.

XIV

The bounteous mercies of the Lord,
  Are hid beyond the sky,
And holy souls that love His word,
  Shall taste them when they die.
                          Psal. xvi, 10, 11.

XV

These bounteous mercies are from God,
  The merits of His Son;
The humble soul that loves His word,
  He chooses for his own.
                          Psal. xxxiv, 15.

XVI

Come, dear Phillis, be advis'd,
  To drink Samaria's flood;
There nothing that shall suffice
  But Christ's redeeming blood.
                          John iv, 13, 14.

XVII

While thousands muse with earthly toys;
  And range about the street,

Dear Phillis, seek for heaven's joys,
Where we do hope to meet.
Matth. vi, 33.

XVIII

When God shall send his summons down,
And number saints together,
Blest angels chant, (triumphant sound),
Come live with me forever.
Psal. cxvi, 15.

XIX

The humble soul shall fly to God,
And leave the things of time,
Start forth as 'twere at the first word,
To taste things more divine.
Matth. v, 3, 8.

XX

Behold! the soul shall waft away.
Whene'er we come to die,
And leave its cottage made of clay,
In twinkling of an eye.
Cor. xv, 51, 52, 53.

XXI

Now glory be to the Most High,
United praises given,
By all on earth, incessantly,
And all the host of heav'n.
Psal. cl, 6.

AN ADDRESS TO THE NEGROES OF THE STATE OF NEW YORK

When I am writing to you with a design to say something to you for your good, and with a view to promote your happiness, I can with truth and sincerity join with the apostle Paul, when speaking of his own nation the Jews, and say that "I have great heaviness and continual sorrow in my heart for my brethren, my kinsmen according to the flesh." Yes my dear brethren, when I think of you, which is very often, and of the poor, despised and miserable state you are in, as to the things of this world, and when I think of your ignorance and stupidity, and the great wickedness of the most of you, I am pained to the heart. It is at times almost too much for human nature to bear, and I am obliged to turn my thoughts from the subject or endeavour to still my mind, by considering that it is permitted thus to be by that God who governs all things, who seteth up one and pulleth down another. While I have been thinking on this subject, I have frequently had great struggles in my own mind, and have been at a loss to know what to do. I have wanted exceedingly to say something to you, to call upon you with the tenderness of a father and friend, and to give you the last, and I may say dying advice, of an old man, who wishes your best good in this world, and in the world to come. But while I have had such desires, a sense of my own ignorance and unfitness to teach others has frequently discouraged me from attempting to say anything to you; yet when I thought of your situation, I could not rest easy.

When I was at Hartford in Connecticut, where I lived during the war, I published several pieces which were well received, not only by those of my own colour, but by a number of the white people, who thought they might do good among their servants. This is one consideration, among others, that emboldens me now to publish what I have written to you. Another is, I think you will be more likely to listen to what is said, when you know it comes from a Negro, one of your own nation and colour, and therefore can have no interest in deceiving you, or in saying anything to you, but what he really thinks is your interest and duty to comply with. My age, I think, gives me some right to speak to you, and reason to expect you will hearken to my advice. I am now upwards of seventy years old, and cannot expect, though I am well, and able to do almost any kind of business, to live much longer. I have passed the common bounds set for man, and must soon go the way of all the earth. I have had more experience in the world than the most of you, and I have seen a great deal of the vanity and wickedness of it. I have great reason to be thankful that my lot has been so much better than most slaves have had. I suppose I have had more advantages and privileges than most of you who are slaves have ever known, and I believe more than many white people have enjoyed, for which I desire to bless God, and pray that he may bless those who have given them to me. I do not, my dear friends, say these things about myself to make you think that I am wiser or better than others; but that you might hearken, without prejudice, to what I have to say to you on the following particulars.

→ 1st. Respecting obedience to masters. Now whether it is right, and lawful, in the sight of God, for them to make slaves of us or not, I am certain that while we are slaves, it is our duty to obey our masters, in all their lawful commands, and mind them unless we are bid to do that which we know to be sin, or forbidden in God's word. The apostle Paul says, "Servants be obedient to them that are your masters according to the flesh, with fear and trembling in singleness in your heart as unto Christ: Not with eye service, as men pleasers, but as the servants of Christ doing the will of God from the heart: With good will doing service to the Lord, and not to men: Knowing that whatever thing a man doeth the same shall he receive of the Lord, whether he be bond or free."—Here is a plain command of God for us to obey our masters. It may seem hard for us, if we think our masters wrong in holding us slaves, to obey in all things, but who of us dare dispute with God! He has commanded us to obey, and we ought to do it cheerfully, and freely. This should be done by us, not only because God commands, but because our own peace and comfort depend upon it. As we depend upon our masters, for what we eat and drink and wear, and for all our comfortable things in this world, we cannot be happy, unless we please them. This we cannot do without obeying them freely, without muttering or finding fault. If a servant strives to please his master and studies and takes pains to do it, I believe there are but few masters who would use such a servant cruelly. Good servants frequently make good masters. If your master is really hard, unreasonable and cruel, there is no way so likely for you to convince him of it, as always to obey his commands, and try to serve him, and take care of his interest, and try to promote it all in your power. If you are proud and stubborn and always finding fault, your master will think the fault lies wholly on your side, but if you are humble, and meek, and bear all things patiently, your master may think he is wrong, if he does not, his neighbours will be apt to see it, and will befriend you, and try to alter his conduct. If this does not do, you must cry to him, who has the hearts of all men in his hands, and turneth them as the rivers of waters are turned.

→ 2d. The particular I would mention, is honesty and faithfulness. You must suffer me now to deal plainly with you, my dear brethren, for I do not mean to flatter, or omit speaking the truth, whether it is for you, or against you. How many of you are there who allow yourselves in stealing from your masters. It is very wicked for you not to take care of your masters goods, but how much worse is it to pilfer and steal from them, whenever you think you shall not be found out. This you must know is very wicked and provoking to God. There are none of you so ignorant, but that you must know that this is wrong. Though you may try to excuse yourselves, by saying that your masters are unjust to you, and though you may try to quiet your consciences in this way, yet if you are honest in owning the truth you must think it is as wicked, and on some accounts more wicked to steal from your masters, than from others.

We cannot certainly, have any excuse either for taking anything that belongs to our masters without their leave, or for being unfaithful in their business. It is our duty to be faithful, *not with eye service as men pleasers.* We have no right to stay when we are sent on errands, any longer than to do the business we were sent upon. All the time spent idly, is spent wickedly, and is unfaithfulness to our masters. In these things I must say, that I think many of you are guilty. I know that many of you endeavour to excuse yourselves, and say that you have nothing that you can call your own, and that you are under great temptations to be unfaithful and take from your masters. But this will not do, God will certainly punish you for stealing and for being unfaithful. All that we have to mind is our own duty. If God has put us in bad circumstances, that is not our fault and he will not punish us for it. If any are wicked in keeping us so, we cannot help it, they must answer to God for it. Nothing will serve as an excuse to us for not doing our duty. The same God will judge both them and us. Pray then my dear friends, fear to offend in this way, but be faithful to God, to your masters, and to your own souls. . . .

I will conclude what I have to say with a few words to those negroes who have their liberty. The most of what I have said to those who are slaves may be of use to you, but you have more advantages, on some accounts, if you will improve your freedom, as you may do, than they. You have more time to read God's holy word, and to take care of the salvation of your souls. Let me beg of you to spend your time in this way, or it will be better for you, if you had always been slaves. If you think seriously of the matter, you must conclude, that if you do not use your freedom, to promote the salvation of your souls, it will not be of any lasting good to you. Besides all this, if you are idle, and take to bad courses, you will hurt those of your brethren who are slaves, and do all in your power to prevent their being free. One great reason that is given by some for not freeing us, I understand, is that we should not know how to take care of ourselves, and should take to bad courses. That we should be lazy and idle, and get drunk and steal. Now all those of you, who follow any bad courses, and who do not take care to get an honest living by your labour and industry, are doing more to prevent our being free, than anybody else. Let me beg of you then for the sake of your own good and happiness, in time, and for eternity, and for the sake of your poor brethren, who are still in bondage to lead quiet and peaceable lives in all Godliness and honesty, and may God bless you, and bring you to his kingdom, for Christ's sake, Amen.

Benjamin Banneker

(1731–1806)

REMEMBERED BEST for his contribution to the survey in 1791 of Federal Territory, a tract which is now the District of Columbia, Benjamin Banneker is sometimes called the first "Negro man of science." Vernon Loggins describes him as "astronomer, almanac-maker, mechanician, surveyor, botanist, zoologist, philosopher, wit, letter writer, versifier." Loggins is somewhat generous in his labels, but whatever one calls Banneker, this self-taught mathematician and astronomer was a gifted, highly respected, and unusual person. Born in 1731 in Baltimore County, Maryland, Banneker was the son of freed-slave parents. His father, Robert, married Mary Banneky, who was the daughter of Bannka (or Banneka), a freed slave, and of Molly Welsh, an English indentured servant who, when she had completed her service, bought two slaves, gave both freedom, and married one of them. The daughter of this union was Benjamin Banneker's mother. Banneker's father, having only one name, Robert, took his wife's last name when he married.

Banneker's father, an industrious man, bought a one-hundred-acre farm on which he raised tobacco. Benjamin Banneker grew up on this farm and lived there the rest of his life. His English grandmother taught him how to read, using the Bible she had brought with her from England. Once he knew how to read, Banneker taught himself mathematics and other related subjects. When he was twenty-one, he made the necessary calculations and then carved from wood a striking clock that became a local wonder because he had never seen a clock. And more surprising, the clock worked throughout Banneker's life.

Around 1771 five Ellicott brothers, Quakers from Pennsylvania, moved into Banneker's neighborhood. These thrifty, hard-working, and intelligent men built a full-fledged community in Baltimore County, and they became not only good neighbors, but also good friends of Banneker. A son of one brother introduced the latter to the study of astronomy, lending him texts and instruments which he taught himself to use expertly. Another member of that family, Major Andrew Ellicott, after learning that Banneker had taught himself surveying, enlisted Banneker's service for a short while in carrying out a commission given him by George Washington to survey Federal Territory, now the District of Columbia.

Through the Ellicotts, Banneker's work with calculating the ephemeris (a table which shows the position of a heavenly body on a number of dates

..rly sequence) was brought to the attention of the Pennsylvania and
..yland abolition societies. Under the societies' sponsorship *Benjamin
Banneker's Pennsylvania, Delaware, Maryland and Virginia Almanack and
Ephemeris, for the Year of our Lord, 1792* was published. Just before this
publication, Banneker sent a copy of his ephemeris to Thomas Jefferson,
then secretary of state. The letter that accompanied the document follows.
Jefferson acknowledged both documents; the two letters were later printed
in Banneker's published 1793 almanac, along with "A Plan of Peace-Office
for the United States," which follows. Because it was so unusual for a Negro
to produce such works, Banneker's almanacs (he furnished only the ephemeris and eclipse projections for them) became internationally known, and
Banneker himself was often used by the abolitionists to show the Negro's
capabilities and potentialities.

The best biographical material on Banneker is found in Silvia A. Bedini's
The Life of Benjamin Banneker (1972). Bedini also wrote the excellent entry
found in *Dictionary of American Negro Biography*. Benjamin Brawley's *Early
Negro American Writers* (1935) and Vernon Loggins's *The Negro Author*
(1931) both give valuable information on early sources, biographical and
bibliographical, for the scholar interested in this talented pioneer Negro
scientist.

The following selections are found in *Early Negro American Writers.*

LETTER TO THE SECRETARY OF STATE
Maryland, Baltimore County, August 19, 1791.

Sir,
I am fully sensible of the greatness of the freedom I take with
you on the present occasion; a liberty which seemed scarcely allowa-
ble, when I reflected on that distinguished and dignified station in
which you stand, and the almost general prejudice which is so prevalent in the world against those of my complexion.

It is a truth too well attested, to need proof here, that we are a
race of beings, who have long laboured under the abuse and censure
of the world; that we have long been looked upon with an eye of
contempt; and considered rather as brutish than human, and
scarcely capable of mental endowments.

I hope I may safely admit, in consequence of the report which
has reached me, that you are a man far less inflexible in sentiments
of this nature, than many others; that you are measurably friendly,
and well disposed towards us; and that you are willing to lend your

From *Early Negro American Writers* by Benjamin Brawley, University of North Carolina
Press, © 1935, also Books for Libraries, © 1968.

aid and assistance for our relief from those many distresses, and numerous calamities, to which we are reduced.

If this is founded in truth, I apprehend you will embrace every opportunity to eradicate that train of absurd and false ideas and opinions, which so generally prevail with respect to us: and that your sentiments are concurrent with mine, which are, that one universal Father hath given being to us all; that He hath not only made us all of one flesh, but that He hath also, without partiality, afforded us all the same sensations, and endowed us all with the same faculties, and that, however variable we may be in society or religion, however diversified in situation or in colour, we are all of the same family, and stand in the same relation to Him.

If these are sentiments of which you are fully persuaded, you cannot but acknowledge, that it is the indispensable duty of those who maintain for themselves the rights of human nature, and who profess the obligations of Christianity, to extend their powers and influence to the relief of every part of the human race, from whatever burden or oppression they may unjustly labour under, and this, I apprehend, a full conviction of the truth and obligation of these principles should lead all to.

I have long been convinced, that if your love for yourselves, and for those inestimable laws which preserved to you the rights of human nature, was founded on sincerity, you could not but be solicitous, that every individual, of whatever rank or distinction, might with you equally enjoy the blessings thereof; neither could you rest satisfied short of the most active effusion of your exertions, in order to their promotion* from any state of degradation, to which the unjustifiable cruelty and barbarism of men may have reduced them.

I freely and cheerfully acknowledge, that I am of the African race, and in that colour which is natural to them, of the deepest dye; and it is under a sense of the most profound gratitude to the Supreme Ruler of the Universe, that I now confess to you, that I am not under that state of tyrannical thraldom, and inhuman captivity, to which many of my brethren are doomed, but that I have abundantly tasted of the fruition of those blessings, which proceed from that free and unequalled liberty with which you are favoured; and which I hope you will willingly allow you have mercifully received, from the immediate hand of that Being from whom proceedeth every good and perfect gift.

Suffer me to recall to your mind that time, in which the arms of the British crown were exerted, with every powerful effort, in order

---

*Thus.

to reduce you to a state of servitude: look back, I entreat you, on the variety of dangers to which you were exposed; reflect on that period in which every human aid appeared unavailable, and in which even hope and fortitude wore the aspect of inability to the conflict, and you cannot but be led to a serious and grateful sense of your miraculous and providential preservation; you cannot but acknowledge, that the present freedom and tranquillity which you enjoy, you have mercifully received, and that it is the peculiar blessing of heaven.

This, Sir, was a time you clearly saw into the injustice of a state of Slavery, and in which you had just apprehensions of the horrors of its condition. It was then that your abhorrence thereof was so excited, that you publicly held forth this true and invaluable doctrine, which is worthy to be recorded and remembered in all succeeding ages: "We hold these truths to be self-evident, that all men are created equal; that they are endowed by their Creator with certain inalienable rights, and that among these are life, liberty, and the pursuit of happiness."

Here was a time in which your tender feelings for yourselves had engaged you thus to declare; you were then impressed with proper ideas of the great violation of liberty, and the free possession of those blessings, to which you were entitled by nature; but, sir, how pitiable it is to reflect, that although you were so fully convinced of the benevolence of the Father of Mankind and of his equal and impartial distribution of these rights and privileges which he hath conferred upon them, that you should at the same time counteract his mercies, in detaining by fraud and violence, so numerous a part of my brethren under groaning captivity and cruel oppression, that you should at the same time be found guilty of that most criminal act, which you professedly detested in others, with respect to yourselves.

Your knowledge of the situation of my brethren is too extensive to need a recital here; neither shall I presume to prescribe methods by which they may be relieved, otherwise than by recommending to you and all others, to wean yourselves from those narrow prejudices which you have imbibed with respect to them, and as Job proposed to his friends, 'put your soul in their soul's stead'; thus shall your hearts be enlarged with kindness and benevolence towards them; and thus shall you need neither the direction of myself or others, in what manner to proceed herein.

And now, sir, although my sympathy and affection for my brethren hath caused my enlargement thus far, I ardently hope, that your candour and generosity will plead with you in my behalf, when I state that it was not originally my design; but having taken up my pen in order to present a copy of an almanac which I have calculated for the succeeding year, I was unexpectedly led thereto.

This calculation is the production of my arduous study, in my advanced stage of life; for having long had unbounded desires to become acquainted with the secrets of nature, I have had to gratify my curiosity herein through my own assiduous application to astronomical study, in which I need not recount to you the many difficulties and disadvantages which I have had to encounter.

And although I had almost declined to make my calculation for the ensuing year, in consequence of the time which I had alloted for it being taken up at the federal territory, by the request of Mr. Andrew Ellicott, yet I industriously applied myself thereto, and hope I have accomplished it with correctness and accuracy. I have taken the liberty to direct a copy to you, which I humbly request you will favourably receive; and although you may have the opportunity of perusing it after its publication, yet I desire to send it to you in manuscript previous thereto, that thereby you might not only have an earlier inspection, but that you might also view it in my own handwriting.

And, now, sir, I shall conclude, and subscribe myself, with the most profound respect,

Your most obedient humble servant,

Benjamin Banneker.

A PLAN OF PEACE-OFFICE FOR THE UNITED STATES

Among the many defects which have been pointed out in the federal constitution by its antifederal enemies, it is much to be lamented that no person has taken notice of its total silence upon the subject of an office of the utmost importance to the welfare of the United States, that is, an office for promoting and preserving perpetual peace in our country.

It is to be hoped that no objection will be made to the establishment of such an office, while we are engaged in a war with the Indians, for as the War-Office of the United States was established in time of peace, it is equally reasonable that a Peace-Office should be established in time of war.

The plan of this office is as follows:

I. Let a Secretary of Peace be appointed to preside in this office, who shall be perfectly free from all the present absurd and vulgar European prejudices upon the subject of government; let him be a genuine republican and a sincere Christian, for the principles of republicanism and Christianity are no less friendly to universal and perpetual peace, than they are to universal and equal liberty.

II. Let a power be given to this Secretary to establish and maintain free schools in every city, village, and township of the United States; and let him be made responsible for the talents, principles, and morals of all his schoolmasters. Let the youth of our country be carefully instructed in reading, writing, and arithmetic, and in the doctrines of a religion of some kind; the Christian religion should be preferred to all others; for it belongs to this religion exclusively to teach us not only to cultivate peace with all men, but to forgive, nay more—to love our very enemies. It belongs to it further to teach us that the Supreme Being alone possesses a power to take away human life, and that we rebel against his laws whenever we undertake to execute death in any way whatever upon any of his creatures.

III. Let every family in the United States be furnished at the public expense, by the Secretary of this office, with a copy of an American edition of the Bible. This measure has become the more necessary in our country, since the banishment of the Bible, as a school-book, from most of the schools in the United States. Unless the price of this book be paid for by the public, there is reason to fear that in a few years it will be met with only in courts of justice or in magistrates' offices; and should the absurd mode of establishing truth by kissing this sacred book fall into disuse, it may probably, in the course of the next generation, be seen only as a curiosity on a shelf in Mr. Peale's museum.[†]

IV. Let the following sentences be inscribed in letters of gold over the door of every home in the United States:

THE SON OF MAN CAME INTO THE WORLD,
NOT TO DESTROY MEN'S LIVES, BUT TO SAVE THEM.

V. To inspire a veneration for human life, and an horror at the shedding of human blood, let all those laws be repealed which authorize juries, judges, sheriffs, or hangmen to assume the resentments of individuals, and to commit murder in cold blood in any case whatever. Until this reformation in our code of penal jurisprudence takes place, it will be in vain to attempt to introduce universal and perpetual peace in our country.

VI. To subdue that passion for war which education, added to human depravity, has made universal, a familiarity with the instruments of death, as well as all military shows, should be carefully

---

[†]Charles Wilson Peale (1741–1827) was an American painter born in Maryland. He studied with J. S. Copley in Boston and Benjamin West in London. In the course of the Revolution he painted many portraits of Washington and other officers. In 1785 the discovery of the bones of a mastodon gave him the idea of founding a museum, which he opened in Philadelphia in 1802. He was also instrumental in founding the Pennsylvania Academy of Fine Arts, the first of its kind in the United States.

avoided. For which reason, militia laws should everywhere be repealed and military dresses and military titles should be laid aside: reviews tend to lessen the horrors of a battle by connecting them with the charms of order; militia laws generate idleness and vice, and thereby produce the wars they are said to prevent; military dresses fascinate the mind of young men, and lead them from serious and useful professions; were there no uniforms, there would probably be no armies; lastly, military titles feed vanity, and keep up ideas in the mind which lessen a sense of the folly and miseries of war.

In the seventh and last place, let a large room, adjoining the federal hall, be appointed for transacting the business and preserving all the records of this office. Over the door of this room let there be a sign, on which the figures of a lamb, a dove, and an olive-branch should be painted, together with the following inscriptions in letters of gold:

PEACE ON EARTH—GOOD-WILL TO MAN.
AH! WHY SHOULD MEN FORGET THAT THEY ARE BRETHREN?

Within this apartment let there be a collection of plough-shares and pruning-hooks made out of swords and spears; and on each of the walls of the apartment the following pictures as large as life:

1. A lion eating straw with an ox, and an adder playing upon the lips of a child.

2. An Indian boiling his venison in the same pot with a citizen of Kentucky.

3. Lord Cornwallis and Tippo Saib, under the shade of a sycamore tree in the East Indies, drinking Madeira wine out of the same decanter.

4. A group of French and Austrian soldiers dancing, arm in arm, under a bower erected in the neighborhood of Mons.

5. A St. Domingo planter, a man of color, and a native of Africa, legislating together in the same colonial assembly.

To complete the entertainment of this delightful apartment, let a group of young ladies, clad in white robes, assemble every day at a certain hour, in a gallery to be erected for the purpose, and sing odes, and hymns, and anthems in praise of the blessings of peace.

One of these songs should consist of the following beautiful lines of Mr. Pope:

> Peace o'er the world her olive wand extends,
> And white-rob'd innocence from heaven descends,
> All crimes shall cease, and ancient frauds shall fail,
> Returning justice lifts aloft her scale.

Gustavus Vassa (Olaudah Equiano)

(c. 1745–1797)

ACCORDING TO his own statement Gustavus Vassa was born in what is now the interior of eastern Nigeria, probably in 1745. His language was Ibo, and his people came under the nominal jurisdiction of the king of Benin. Captured by local raiders when he was about ten or eleven, Vassa was taken to the coast and sold to slavers bound for the West Indies.

After a few days in the islands, he was shipped to Virginia, served as a slave there, and eventually became the property of a Captain Pascal. This man gave him the name Gustavus Vassa, which remained with him the rest of his life. Vassa traveled widely with Captain Pascal, serving under him during Wolfe's campaign in Canada and with Admiral Boscawen in the Mediterranean during the Seven Years' War. On these trips Vassa, an intelligent youngster, learned a great deal, including English. After leaving Pascal he spent some time in England, went to school, and acquired the skills to become a shipping clerk and an amateur navigator.

With his next master, Robert King, a Quaker from Philadelphia, Vassa traveled often between America and the West Indies. He evidently had a chance to make money on his own, because in 1766 he bought his freedom from Mr. King for £40. Then twenty-one and a free man, Vassa continued his life as a seaman, crossing the Atlantic several more times; on one occasion he went with a scientific expedition to the Arctic.

In the meantime Vassa had been converted to Methodism; he had also become an abolition speaker and traveled through the British Isles lecturing against slavery.

In 1786 Vassa was appointed commissary for Slaves for the Black Poor Going to Sierra Leone, a project to colonize freed slaves in Africa. Because Vassa felt that the men in charge of the mission were both dishonest and prejudiced, he spoke out against them and consequently was relieved of his post as commissary. He later volunteered to go to Africa as a missionary but was rejected.

On April 7, 1792, Gustavus Vassa married Susan (or Susanna) Cullen. The notice of this wedding which appeared in *The Gentleman's Magazine* refers to him as "Gustavus Vassa the African, well known as the champion and advocate for procuring the suppression of the slave trade."

In 1789 Vassa published *The Interesting Narrative of the Life of Olaudah Equiano, or Gustavus Vassa, the African,* a work which became—with good reason—a best seller of the day. The narrative was a valuable antislavery document and was used by abolition forces on both sides of the Atlantic. It was also a highly readable travel book of the type popular in the eighteenth century. The author includes some wonders—crowing snakes and neighing seahorses—but he never strays too far from common sense.

Most American scholars interested in black literature claim Gustavus Vassa as the first important writer of African American autobiography. Although he did spend some time in Philadelphia, in Virginia, and in other places in this country, he is at best an "honorary" American black writer. Actually he belongs in the eighteenth-century tradition of travel writing, one with which we associate Defoe and Swift. It does no harm, however, to claim him as an autobiographer. He is certainly a worthy addition to early African American literature. According to *The Gentleman's Magazine,* Gustavus Vassa died in London on April 30, 1797. (Other dates have also been given.)

For comment on Gustavus Vassa and an excellent reprint (and abridgment) of his work, see Paul Edwards, ed., *Equiano's Travels* (1967). Edwards also brought out in 1969 a two-volume facsimile reprint of the first edition of Vassa's work. The following volumes contain valuable comments on Vassa: Vernon Loggins, *The Negro Author,* and Benjamin Brawley, *Early Negro American Writers.* See also Marion L. Starkey, *Striving to Make It My Home: The Story of Americans from Africa* (1964) and Arna Bontemps, ed., *Great Slave Narratives* (1969), in which one finds an abridged version of Vassa's autobiography.

More recent commentary on Vassa's achievement may be found in Angelo Constanzo's study, *Olaudah Equiano and the Beginnings of Black Autobiography* (1987). See also *The Journey Back* by Houston Baker, Jr. (1981), *From Behind the Veil: A Study of Afro-American Narrative* by Robert Stepto (1979), and R. Victoria Arana's "Culture Shock and Revolution in Gustavus Vassa's *Narrative,*" *Delos,* 1:2.

The following selections come from chapters 1 and 2 of *Equiano's Travels.*

FROM **EQUIANO'S TRAVELS**

I believe it is difficult for those who publish their own memoirs to escape the imputation of vanity; nor is this the only disadvantage under which they labor: it is also their misfortune that what is uncommon is rarely, if ever, believed, and what is obvious we are apt to turn from with disgust, and to charge the writer with impertinence. People generally think those memoirs only worthy to be read or remembered which abound in great or striking events; those, in short, which in a high degree excite either admiration or pity: all others they consign to contempt and oblivion. It is therefore, I confess, not a little hazardous in a private and obscure individual, and a stranger too, thus to solicit the indulgent attention of the public; especially when I own I offer here the history of neither a saint, a hero, nor a tyrant. I believe there are few events in my life, which have not happened to many: it is true the incidents of it are numerous; and, did I consider myself an European, I might say my sufferings were great: but when I compare my lot with that of most of my countrymen, I regard myself as a *particular favorite of heaven,* and acknowledge the mercies of Providence in every occurrence of my life. If, then, the following narrative does not appear sufficiently interesting to engage general attention, let my motive be some excuse for its publication. I am not so foolishly vain as to expect from it either immortality or literary reputation. If it affords any satisfaction to my numerous friends, at whose request it has been written, or in the smallest degree promotes the interests of humanity, the ends for which it was undertaken will be fully attained, and every wish of my heart gratified. Let it therefore be remembered, that, in wishing to avoid censure, I do not aspire to praise.

That part of Africa, known by the name of Guinea, to which the trade for slaves is carried on, extends along the coast above 3400 miles, from Senegal to Angola, and includes a variety of kingdoms. Of these the most considerable is the kingdom of Benin, both as to extent and wealth, the richness and cultivation of the soil, the power of its king, and the number and warlike disposition of the inhabitants. It is situated nearly under the line, and extends along the coast about 170 miles, but runs back into the interior part of Africa to a distance hitherto, I believe, unexplored by any traveller; and seems only terminated at length by the empire of Abyssinia, near 1500 miles from its beginning. This kingdom is divided into many provinces or districts: in one of the most remote and fertile of which, I was born, in the year 1745, situated in a charming fruitful vale, named Essala. The distance of this province from the capital of Benin and the sea coast must be very considerable: for I had never heard of white men or Europeans, nor of the sea; and our subjection to the king of Benin was little more than nominal; for every transaction of the government, as far as my slender observation extended, was conducted by the chief or elders of the place. The manners and government of a people who have little commerce with other countries, are generally very simple; and the history of what passes in one family or village, may serve as a specimen of the whole nation. My father was one of those elders or chiefs I have spoken of, and was styled Embrenche; a term, as I remember, importing the highest distinction, and signifying in our language a *mark* of grandeur. This mark is conferred on the person entitled to it, by cutting the skin

across at the top of the forehead, and drawing it down to the eyebrows: and while it is in this situation applying a warm hand, and
rubbing it until it shrinks up into a thick *weal* across the lower part
of the forehead. Most of the judges and senators were thus marked;
my father had long borne it: I had seen it conferred on one of my
brothers, and I also was *destined* to receive it by my parents. Those
Embrenche or chief men, decided disputes and punished crimes; for
which purpose they always assembled together. The proceedings
were generally short: and in most cases the law of retaliation prevailed. I remember a man was brought before my father, and the
other judges, for kidnapping a boy; and, although he was the son of
a chief or senator, he was condemned to make recompense by a man
or woman slave. Adultery, however, was sometimes punished with
slavery or death; a punishment which I believe is inflicted on it
throughout most of the nation of Africa: so sacred among them is
the honor of the marriage bed, and so jealous are they of the fidelity
of their wives. Of this I recollect an instance—a woman was convicted before the judges of adultery, and delivered over, as the custom was, to her husband, to be punished. Accordingly he
determined to put her to death: but it being found, just before her
execution, that she had an infant at her breast; and no woman being
prevailed on to perform the part of a nurse, she was spared on account of the child. The men, however, do not preserve the same
constancy to their wives, which they expect from them; for they indulge in a plurality, though seldom in more than two. Their mode of
marriage is thus:—both parties are usually betrothed when young by
their parents (though I have known the males to betroth themselves.) On this occasion a feast is prepared, and the bride and
bridegroom stand up in the midst of all their friends, who are assembled for the purpose, while he declares she is henceforth to be
looked upon as his wife, and that no other person is to pay any addresses to her. This is also immediately proclaimed in the vicinity,
on which the bride retires from the assembly. Some time after, she is
brought home to her husband, and then another feast is made, to
which the relations of both parties are invited: her parents then deliver her to the bridegroom, accompanied with a number of blessings, and at the same time they tie round her waist a cotton string of
the thickness of a goose-quill, which none but married women are
permitted to wear: she is now considered as completely his wife; and
at this time the dowry is given to the new married pair, which generally consists of portions of land, slaves, and cattle, household
goods, and implements of husbandry. These are offered by the
friends of both parties; besides which the parents of the bridegroom
present gifts to those of the bride, whose property she is looked

upon before marriage; but after it she is esteemed the sole property
of her husband. The ceremony being now ended, the festival begins,
which is celebrated with bonfires, and loud acclamations of joy, accompanied with music and dancing. . . .

As we live in a country where nature is prodigal of her favors,
our wants are few and easily supplied; of course we have few manu-
factures. They consist for the most part of calicoes, earthen ware, ornaments, and instruments of war and husbandry.—But these make
no part of our commerce, the principal articles of which, as I have
observed, are provisions. In such a state, money is of little use; however, we have some small pieces of coin, if I may call them such.
They are made something like an anchor, but I do not remember
either their value or denomination. We have also markets, at which I
have been frequently with my mother. These are sometimes visited
by stout mahogany-colored men from the south-west of us: we call
them *Oye-Eboe,* which term signifies red men living at a distance.—
They generally bring us fire-arms, gunpowder, hats, beads, and dried
fish. The last we esteemed a great rarity, as our waters were only
brooks and springs. These articles they barter with us for odoriferous
woods and earth, and our salt of wood ashes. They always carry
slaves through our land; but the strictest account is exacted of their
manner of procuring them before they are suffered to pass. Sometimes indeed, we sold slaves to them, but they were only prisoners
of war, or such among us as had been convicted of kidnapping, or
adultery, and some other crimes, which we esteemed heinous. This
practice of kidnapping induces me to think, that, notwithstanding all
our strictness, their principal business among us was to trepan our
people. I remember too, they carried great sacks along with them,
which not long after, I had an opportunity of fatally seeing applied
to that infamous purpose.

Our land is uncommonly rich and fruitful, and produces all
kinds of vegetables in great abundance.—We have plenty of Indian
corn, and vast quantities of cotton and tobacco. Our pine apples
grow without culture; they are about the size of the largest sugar-
loaf, and finely flavored. We have also spices of different kinds, particularly pepper; and a variety of delicious fruits which I have never
seen in Europe; together with gums of various kinds, and honey in
abundance. All our industry is exerted to improve these blessings of
nature. Agriculture is our chief employment; and every one, even the
children and women, are engaged in it. Thus we are all habituated to
labor from our earliest years. Every one contributes something to the
common stock; and, as we are unacquainted with idleness, we have
no beggars. The benefits of such a mode of living are obvious. The
West India planters prefer the slaves of Benin or Eboe, to those of

any other part of Guinea, for their hardiness, intelligence, integrity, and zeal. Those benefits are felt by us in the general healthiness of the people, and in their vigor and activity; I might have added, too, in their comeliness. Deformity is indeed unknown amongst us, I mean that of shape. Numbers of the natives of Eboe now in London, might be brought in support of this assertion: for, in regard to complexion, ideas of beauty are wholly relative. I remember while in Africa to have seen three negro children who were tawny, and another quite white, who were universally regarded by myself, and the natives in general, as far as related to their complexions, as deformed.—Our women, too, were in my eye at least, uncommonly graceful, alert, and modest to a degree of bashfulness; nor do I remember to have heard of an instance of incontinence amongst them before marriage.—They are also remarkably cheerful. Indeed, cheerfulness and affability are two of the leading characteristics of our nation.

Our tillage is exercised in a large plain or common, some hours' walk from our dwellings, and all the neighbors resort thither in a body. They use no beasts of husbandry; and their only instruments are hoes, axes, shovels, and beaks, or pointed iron, to dig with. Sometimes we are visited by locusts, which come in large clouds, so as to darken the air, and destroy our harvest. This, however, happens rarely, but when it does, a famine is produced by it. I remember an instance or two wherein this happened. This common is often the theatre of war; and therefore when our people go out to till their land, they not only go in a body, but generally take their arms with them for fear of a surprise; and when they apprehend an invasion, they guard the avenues to their dwellings, by driving sticks into the ground, which are so sharp at one end as to pierce the foot, and are generally dipt in poison. From what I can recollect of these battles, they appear to have been irruptions of one little state or district on the other, to obtain prisoners or booty. Perhaps they were incited to this, by those traders who brought the European goods I mentioned, amongst us. Such a mode of obtaining slaves in Africa is common; and I believe more are procured this way, and by kidnapping, than any other. When a trader wants slaves, he applies to a chief for them, and tempts him with his wares. It is not extraordinary, if on this occasion he yields to the temptation with as little firmness, and accepts the price of his fellow creatures' liberty, with as little reluctance as the enlightened merchant.—Accordingly he falls on his neighbors, and a desperate battle ensues. If he prevails and takes prisoners, he gratifies his avarice by selling them; but, if his party be vanquished, and he falls into the hands of the enemy, he is put to death; for, as he has been known to foment their quarrels, it is thought dangerous to let him survive, and no ransom can save him, though all other prisoners may be redeemed. We have fire-arms, bows and arrows, broad two-edged swords and javelins: we have shields also which cover a man from head to foot. All are taught the use of these weapons; even our women are warriors, and march boldly out to fight along with the men.—Our whole district is a kind of militia: on a certain signal given, such as the firing of a gun at night, they all rise in arms and rush upon their enemy. It is perhaps something remarkable, that when our people march to the field a red flag or banner is borne before them. I was once a witness to a battle in our common. We had been all at work in it one day as usual, when our people were suddenly attacked. I climbed a tree at some distance, from which I beheld the fight. There were many women as well as men on both sides; among others my mother was there, and armed with a broad sword. After fighting for a considerable time with great fury, and many had been killed, our people obtained the victory, and took their enemy's Chief a prisoner. He was carried off in great triumph, and, though he offered a large ransom for his life, he was put to death. A virgin of note among our enemies, had been slain in the battle, and her arm was exposed in our marketplace, where our trophies were always exhibited.—The spoils were divided according to the merit of the warriors. Those prisoners which were not sold or redeemed, we kept as slaves: but how different was their condition from that of the slaves in the West Indies! With us, they do no more work than other members of the community, even their master; their food, clothing and lodging were nearly the same as theirs, (except that they were not permitted to eat with those who were free-born;) and there was scarce any other difference between them, than a superior degree of importance which the head of a family possesses in our state, and that authority which, as such, he exercises over every part of his household. Some of these slaves have even slaves under them as their own property, and for their own use.

As to religion, the natives believe that there is one Creator of all things, and that he lives in the sun, and is girted round with a belt that he may never eat or drink; but, according to some he smokes a pipe, which is our own favorite luxury. They believe he governs events, especially our deaths or captivity; but, as for the doctrine of eternity, I do not remember to have ever heard of it: some, however, believe in the transmigration of souls in a certain degree. Those spirits, which are not transmigrated, such as their dear friends or relations, they believe always attend them, and guard them from the bad spirits or their foes. For this reason they always before eating, as I have observed, put some small portion of the meat, and pour some

of their drink, on the ground for them; and they often make oblations of the blood of beasts or fowls at their graves. I was very fond
of my mother, and almost constantly with her. When she went to
make these oblations at her mother's tomb, which was a kind of
small solitary thatched house, I sometimes attended her.—There she
made her libations, and spent most of the night in cries and lamentations. I have been often extremely terrified on these occasions. The
loneliness of the place, the darkness of the night, and the ceremony
of libation, naturally awful and gloomy, were heightened by my
mother's lamentations; and these concurring with the doleful cries of
birds, by which these places were frequented, gave an inexpressible
terror to the scene.

⊙⋙⊙

. . . The first object which saluted my eyes when I arrived on the
coast, was the sea, and a slave ship, which was then riding at anchor, and waiting for its cargo. These filled me with astonishment,
which was soon converted into terror, when I was carried on board.
I was immediately handled, and tossed up to see if I were sound, by
some of the crew; and I was now persuaded that I had gotten into a
world of bad spirits, and that they were going to kill me. Their complexions, too, differing so much from ours, their long hair, and the
language they spoke, (which was very different from any I had ever
heard) united to confirm me in this belief. Indeed, such were the
horrors of my views and fears at the moment, that, if ten thousand
worlds had been my own, I would have freely parted with them all
to have exchanged my condition with that of the meanest slave in
my own country. When I looked round the ship too, and saw a large
furnace of copper boiling, and a multitude of black people of every
description chained together, every one of their countenances expressing dejection and sorrow, I no longer doubted of my fate; and,
quite overpowered with horror and anguish, I fell motionless on the
deck and fainted. When I recovered a little, I found some black people about me, who I believed were some of those who had brought
me on board, and had been receiving their pay; they talked to me in
order to cheer me, but all in vain. I asked them if we were not to be
eaten by those white men with horrible looks, red faces, and long
hair. They told me I was not: and one of the crew brought me a
small portion of spiritous liquor in a wine glass, but, being afraid of
him, I would not take it out of his hand. One of the blacks therefore, took it from him and gave it to me, and I took a little down my
palate, which, instead of reviving me, as they thought it would,
threw me into the greatest consternation at the strange feeling it pro-

duced, having never tasted any such liquor before. Soon after this, the blacks who brought me on board went off, and left me abandoned to despair.

I now saw myself deprived of all chance of returning to my native country, or even the least glimpse of hope of gaining the shore, which I now considered as friendly; and I even wished for my former slavery in preference to my present situation, which was filled with horrors of every kind, still heightened by my ignorance of what I was to undergo. I was not long suffered to indulge my grief; I was soon put down under the decks, and there I received such a salutation in my nostrils as I had never experienced in my life; so that, with the loathsomeness of the stench, and crying together, I became so sick and low that I was not able to eat, nor had I the least desire to taste any thing. I now wished for the last friend, death, to relieve me; but soon, to my grief, two of the white men offered me eatables; and, on my refusing to eat, one of them held me fast by the hands and laid me across, I think the windlass, and tied my feet, while the other flogged me severely. I had never experienced any thing of this kind before, and although not being used to the water, I naturally feared that element the first time I saw it, yet, nevertheless, could I have got over the nettings, I would have jumped over the side, but I could not; and besides, the crew used to watch us very closely who were not chained down to the decks, lest we should leap into the water; and I have seen some of these poor African prisoners most severely cut, for attempting to do so, and hourly whipped for not eating. This indeed was often the case with myself. In a little time after, amongst the poor chained men, I found some of my own nation, which in a small degree gave ease to my mind. I inquired of these what was to be done with us? they gave me to understand, we were to be carried to these white people's country to work for them. I then was a little revived, and thought, if it were no worse than working, my situation was not so desperate; but still I feared I should be put to death, the white people looked and acted, as I thought, in so savage a manner; for I had never seen among any people such instances of brutal cruelty; and this not only shown towards us blacks, but also to some of the whites themselves. One white man in particular I saw, when we were permitted to be on deck, flogged so unmercifully with a large rope near the foremast, that he died in consequence of it; and they tossed him over the side as they would have done a brute. This made me fear these people the more; and I expected nothing less than to be treated in the same manner. I could not help expressing my fears and apprehensions to some of my countrymen; I asked them if these people had no country, but lived in this hollow place? (the ship) they told me they did

not, but came from a distant one. 'Then,' said I, 'how comes it in all
our country we never heard of them?' They told me because they
lived so very far off. I then asked where were their women? had they
any like themselves? I was told they had. 'And why,' said I, 'do we
not see them?' They answered, because they were left behind. I
asked how the vessel could go? they told me they could not tell; but
that there was cloth put upon the masts by help of the ropes I saw,
and then the vessel went on; and the white men had some spell or
magic they put in the water when they liked, in order to stop the
vessel. I was exceedingly amazed at this account, and really thought
they were spirits. I therefore wished much to be from amongst them,
for I expected they would sacrifice me; but my wishes were vain—
for we were so quartered that it was impossible for any of us to
make our escape.

While we stayed on the coast I was mostly on deck; and one day,
to my great astonishment, I saw one of these vessels coming in with
the sails up. As soon as the whites saw it, they gave a great shout, at
which we were amazed; and the more so, as the vessel appeared
larger by approaching nearer. At last, she came to an anchor in my
sight, and when the anchor was let go, I and my countrymen who
saw it, were lost in astonishment to observe the vessel stop—and
were now convinced it was done by magic. Soon after this the other
ship got her boats out, and they came on board of us, and the people of both ships seemed very glad to see each other.—Several of the
strangers also shook hands with us black people, and made motions
with their hands, signifying I suppose, we were to go to their country, but we did not understand them.

At last, when the ship we were in, had got in all her cargo, they
made ready with many fearful noises, and we were all put under
deck, so that we could not see how they managed the vessel. But
this disappointment was the least of my sorrow. The stench of the
hold while we were on the coast was so intolerably loathsome, that
it was dangerous to remain there for any time, and some of us had
been permitted to stay on the deck for the fresh air; but now that
the whole ship's cargo were confined together, it became absolutely
pestilential. The closeness of the place, and the heat of the climate,
added to the number in the ship, which was so crowded that each
had scarcely room to turn himself, almost suffocated us. This produced copious perspirations, so that the air soon became unfit for
respiration, from a variety of loathsome smells, and brought on a
sickness among the slaves, of which many died—thus falling victims
to the improvident avarice, as I may call it, of their purchasers. This
wretched situation was again aggravated by the galling of the chains,
now became insupportable; and the filth of the necessary tubs, into

which the children often fell, and were almost suffocated. The shrieks of the women, and the groans of the dying, rendered the whole a scene of horror almost inconceivable. Happily perhaps, for myself, I was soon reduced so low here that it was thought necessary to keep me almost always on deck; and from my extreme youth I was not put in fetters. In this situation I expected every hour to share the fate of my companions, some of whom were almost daily brought upon deck at the point of death, which I began to hope would soon put an end to my miseries. Often did I think many of the inhabitants of the deep much more happy than myself. I envied them the freedom they enjoyed, and as often wished I could change my condition for theirs. Every circumstance I met with, served only to render my state more painful, and heightened my apprehensions, and my opinion of the cruelty of the whites.

One day they had taken a number of fishes; and when they had killed and satisfied themselves with as many as they thought fit, to our astonishment who were on deck, rather than give any of them to us to eat, as we expected, they tossed the remaining fish into the sea again, although we begged and prayed for some as well as we could, but in vain; and some of my countrymen, being pressed by hunger, took an opportunity, when they thought no one saw them, of trying to get a little privately; but they were discovered, and the attempt procured them some very severe floggings. One day, when we had a smooth sea and moderate wind, two of my wearied countrymen who were chained together, (I was near them at the time,) preferring death to such a life of misery, somehow made through the nettings and jumped into the sea; immediately, another quite dejected fellow, who, on account of his illness, was suffered to be out of irons, also followed their example; and I believe many more would very soon have done the same, if they had not been prevented by the ship's crew, who were instantly alarmed. Those of us that were the most active, were in a moment put down under the deck, and there was such a noise and confusion amongst the people of the ship as I never heard before, to stop her, and get the boat out to go after the slaves. However two of the wretches were drowned, but they got the other, and afterwards flogged him unmercifully, for thus attempting to prefer death to slavery. In this manner we continued to undergo more hardships than I can now relate, hardships which are inseparable from this accursed trade. Many a time we were near suffocation from the want of fresh air, which we were often without for whole days together. This, and the stench of the necessary tubs, carried off many.

During our passage, I first saw flying fishes, which surprised me very much; they used frequently to fly across the ship, and many of them fell on the deck. I also now first saw the use of the quadrant; I had often with astonishment seen the mariners make observations with it, and I could not think what it meant. They at last took notice of my surprise; and one of them, willing to increase it, as well as to gratify my curiosity, made me one day look through it. The clouds appeared to me to be land, which disappeared as they passed along. This heightened my wonder; and I was now more persuaded than ever, that I was in another world, and that every thing about me was magic. At last, we came in sight of the island of Barbadoes, at which the whites on board gave a great shout, and made many signs of joy to us. We did not know what to think of this; but as the vessel drew nearer, we plainly saw the harbor, and other ships of different kinds and sizes, and we soon anchored amongst them, off Bridgetown. Many merchants and planters now came on board, though it was in the evening. They put us in separate parcels, and examined us attentively. They also made us jump, and pointed to the land, signifying we were to go there. We thought by this, we should be eaten by these ugly men, as they appeared to us; and, when soon after we were all put down under the deck again, there was much dread and trembling among us, and nothing but bitter cries to be heard all the night from these apprehensions, insomuch, that at last the white people got some old slaves from the land to pacify us. They told us we were not to be eaten, but to work, and were soon to go on land, where we should see many of our country people. This report eased us much. And sure enough, soon after we were landed, there came to us Africans of all languages.

We were conducted immediately to the merchant's yard, where we were all pent up together, like so many sheep in a fold, without regard to sex or age. As every object was new to me, every thing I saw filled me with surprise. What struck me first, was, that the houses were built with bricks and stories, and in every other respect different from those I had seen in Africa; but I was still more astonished on seeing people on horseback. I did not know what this could mean; and, indeed, I thought these people were full of nothing but magical arts. While I was in this astonishment, one of my fellow-prisoners spoke to a countryman of his, about the horses, who said they were the same kind they had in their country. I understood them, though they were from a distant part of Africa; and I thought it odd I had not seen any horses there; but afterwards, when I came to converse with different Africans, I found they had many horses amongst them, and much larger than those I then saw.

We were not many days in the merchant's custody, before we were sold after their usual manner, which is this:—On a signal given, (as the beat of a drum,) the buyers rush at once into the yard where the slaves are confined, and make choice of that parcel they like best. The noise and clamor with which this is attended, and the eagerness visible in the countenances of the buyers, serve not a little to increase the apprehension of terrified Africans, who may well be supposed to consider them as the ministers of that destruction to which they think themselves devoted. In this manner, without scruple, are relations and friends separated, most of them never to see each other again. I remember, in the vessel in which I was brought over, in the men's apartment, there were several brothers, who, in the sale, were sold in different lots; and it was very moving on this occasion, to see and hear their cries at parting. O, ye nominal Christians! might not an African ask you—Learned you this from your God, who says unto you, Do unto all men as you would men should do unto you? Is it not enough that we are torn from our country and friends, to toil for your luxury and lust of gain? Must every tender feeling be likewise sacrificed to your avarice? Are the dearest friends and relations, now rendered more dear by their separation from their kindred, still to be parted from each other, and thus prevented from cheering the gloom of slavery, with the small comfort of being together, and mingling their sufferings and sorrows? Why are parents to lose their children, brothers their sisters, or husbands their wives? Surely, this is a new refinement in cruelty, which, while it has no advantage to atone for it, thus aggravates distress, and adds fresh horrors even to the wretchedness of slavery.

George Moses Horton

(1797–c. 1883)

BORN IN NORTHAMPTON COUNTY, North Carolina, probably in 1797 (slaves rarely knew the exact date of their birth), George Moses was the property of a family of small plantation owners named Horton. When George was a few years old, the master moved to another plantation near the University of North Carolina at Chapel Hill. Here George Moses Horton grew up and became locally famous as a poet.

In an autobiographical sketch written in 1845, Horton tells us that while working as a cowboy, he decided that he would learn to read. By having school children tell him letters, he accomplished this task and read well before he learned to write. Moved by reading "Wesley's old hymns and other pieces of poetry from various authors," the slave boy then decided that he would be a poet.

During his late teens, Horton began visiting the campus of the University of North Carolina on his free time, taking farm products to sell to the students. Soon, however, he began peddling not farm produce but acrostics and love poems (usual charge, 25¢) for undergraduates to send to their girl friends. At first Horton had to dictate the verses, not yet knowing how to write. Eventually he was allowed to give up all farm work and "hire himself out" for fifty cents a day, an arrangement often made for slaves who had skills that were in demand. He became a "comic" campus orator, a writer of love letters as well as verses for the students, and, for several generations of North Carolina students, a kind of legend in his own time.

Aided by Caroline Hentz, the Yankee wife of one of the university's professors, Horton "achieved" his first publication in 1828. On April 8 of that year, Mrs. Hentz had two of his poems printed in her hometown paper, the *Lancaster* (Massachusetts) *Gazette*. Later she persuaded the *Raleigh Register* to publish a few of Horton's poems with a short biography of the slave. These verses were reprinted by other southern papers and by northern periodicals like *Freedom's Journal* and Garrison's *Liberator*. Some of Horton's verses also appeared in *The Southern Literary Messenger*.

In the meantime, the poet's southern friends attempted to secure Horton's freedom by compiling and selling a book of his poems, called *The Hope of Liberty*, which was printed in 1829 in Raleigh. The plan was not successful, for the book did not sell well, and not enough money came from it. But *The Hope of Liberty* made its way to Cincinnati, where it was read by an abolitionist who had it reprinted in 1837 under the title *Poems by a Slave*. (A third reprint was appended in 1838 to *A Memoir and Poems of Phillis Wheatley*.) The next volume of Horton's poems was underwritten by the president, faculty, students, and the poet's friends at the University of North Carolina. Printed in 1845 in Hillsborough, North Carolina, it was entitled *The Poetical Works of George M. Horton, the Colored Bard of North Carolina*. Horton wrote an autobiographical sketch to serve as a preface to the work.

Perhaps before this last publication, George married a slave belonging to a local farmer. The couple had two children, but from the evidence of several of his poems on the subject, the marriage was not successful.

The Yankees came to Horton's section of North Carolina in 1865, and the poet found a new friend and enthusiastic sponsor in twenty-eight-year-old Captain Will H. S. Banks of the Ninth Michigan Cavalry Volunteers. Under Captain Banks's guidance and editorship, Horton published his last work, *Naked Genius*, in 1865 in Raleigh. There were 132 poems in this volume (42 of them, however, came from *The Poetical Works*, 1845). Many of the new poems, probably suggested by Banks, dealt with Civil War incidents and Civil War heroes like Grant, Sherman, and Lincoln.

Last records of George Moses Horton find him in Philadelphia in 1866. He probably died there in the year 1883.

Horton was a prolific and facile versifier, one who was willing to write about anything—no matter how sublime or trivial—that touched him. One is struck by his range of reading (he knew Milton, Byron, and other English poets), and by his mastery of several poetic forms. He freely uses the ode, blank verse, the heroic couplet, and various stanzaic patterns. Although his subject matter ranges far and wide, Horton had certain themes which he tended to overwork, among them the varieties of love, the transitoriness of life, and the woes of marriage. He must have had a very disagreeable time with his wife, because he never tires of describing the troubles a bad wife can cause. In his later poems he admonishes free blacks to make the most of their newly acquired liberty, to be honest and industrious. Understandably, he retained his love for North Carolina and wrote several touching poems about his regret at leaving his native land; in fact, George Moses Horton never became actually anti-South.

Like many poets of his generation, Horton too often wrote on abstract themes like "Memory," "Prosperity," and "Liberty"; he attempted too many noble flights; and he used mythological characters far too often. But he could handle the language realistically and make humorous folk comparisons. Unfortunately, he did so all too rarely.

For an account of the life and works of George Moses Horton, see Richard Walser's *The Black Poet* (1966); see also William Carroll's University of North Carolina dissertation and book, *Naked Genuis: The Poetry of George Moses Horton* (1977) and M. A. Richmond's *Bid the Vassal Soar*

(1974). W. Edward Farrison's article "George Moses Horton: Poet for Freedom," *CLA Journal* (March 1971), James A. Emanuel's entry in *Dictionary of Negro Biography*, and William Carroll's entry in *Dictionary of Literary Biography, Volume 50* should be consulted.

AN ACROSTIC FOR JULIA SHEPARD

Joy, like the morning, breaks from one divine—
Unveiling streams which cannot fail to shine.
Long have I strove to magnify her name
Imperial, floating on the breeze of fame.

Attracting beauty must delight afford,
Sought of the world and of the Bards adored;
Her grace of form and heart-alluring powers
Express her more than fair, the queen of flowers.

Pleasure, fond nature's stream, from beauty sprung,
And was the softest strain the Muses sung,
Reverting sorrows into speechless Joys,
Dispelling gloom which human peace destroys.

THE CREDITOR TO HIS PROUD DEBTOR

Ha! tott'ring Johnny strut and boast,
But think of what your feathers cost;
Your crowing days are short at most,
    You bloom but soon to fade.
Surely you could not stand so wide,
If strictly to the bottom tried [*sic*];
The wind would blow your plume aside,
    If half your debts were paid.
        Then boast and bear the crack,
        With the Sheriff at your back,

Huzza for dandy Jack,
My jolly fop, my Jo—

The blue smoke from your segar flies,
Offensive to my nose and eyes,
The most of people would be wise,
    Your presence to evade.
Your pockets jingle loud with cash,
And thus you cut a foppish dash,
But alas! dear boy, you would be trash,
    If your accounts were paid.
        Then boast and bear the crack, &c.

My duck bill boots would look as bright,
Had you in justice served me right,
Like you, I then could step as light,
    Before a flaunting maid.
As nicely could I clear my throat,
And to my tights, my eyes devote;
But I'd leave you bare, without a coat,
    For which you have not paid.
        Then boast and bear the crack, &c.

I'd toss myself with a scornful air,
And to a poor man pay no care,
I could rock cross-legged in my chair,
    Within the cloister shade.
I'd gird my neck with a light cravat,
And creaming wear my bell-crown hat;
But away my down would fly at that,
    If once my debts were paid.
        Then boast and bear the crack,
        With the Sheriff at your back,
        Huzza for dandy Jack,
        My jolly fop, my Jo—

GEORGE MOSES HORTON, MYSELF

I feel myself in need
    Of the inspiring strains of ancient lore,
My heart to lift, my empty mind to feed,
    And all the world explore.

I know that I am old
    And never can recover what is past,

But for the future may some light unfold
  And soar from ages blast.

I feel resolved to try,
  My wish to prove, my calling to pursue,
Or mount up from the earth into the sky,
  To show what Heaven can do.

My genius from a boy,
  Has fluttered like a bird within my heart;
But could not thus confined her powers employ,
  Impatient to depart.

She like a restless bird,
  Would spread her wings, her power to be
    unfurl'd,
And let her songs be loudly heard,
  And dart from world to world.

ON LIBERTY AND SLAVERY

Alas! and am I born for this,
  To wear this slavish chain?
Deprived of all created bliss,
  Through hardship, toil and pain!

How long have I in bondage lain,
  And languished to be free!
Alas! and must I still complain—
  Deprived of liberty.

Oh, Heaven! and is there no relief
  This side the silent grave—
To soothe the pain—to quell the grief
  And anguish of a slave?

Come Liberty, thou cheerful sound,
  Roll through my ravished ears!
Come, let my grief in joys be drowned,
  And drive away my fears.

Say unto foul oppression, Cease:
  Ye tyrants rage no more,
And let the joyful trump of peace,
  Now bid the vassal soar.

Soar on the pinions of that dove
  Which long has cooed for thee,
And breathed her notes from Afric's grove,
  The sound of Liberty.

Oh, Liberty! thou golden prize,
  So often sought by blood—
We crave thy sacred sun to rise,
  The gift of nature's God!

Bid Slavery hide her haggard face,
  And barbarism fly:
I scorn to see the sad disgrace
  In which enslaved I lie.

Dear Liberty! upon thy breast,
  I languish to respire;
And like the Swan unto her nest,
  I'd to thy smiles retire.

Oh, blest asylum—heavenly balm!
  Unto thy boughs I flee—
And in thy shades the storm shall calm,
  With songs of Liberty!

TO ELIZA

  Eliza, tell thy lover why
Or what induced thee to deceive me?
  Fare thee well—away I fly—
I shun the lass who thus will grieve me.

  Eliza, still thou art my song,
Although by force I may foresake thee;
  Fare thee well, for I was wrong
To woo thee while another take thee.

  Eliza, pause and think awhile—
Sweet lass! I shall forget thee never:
  Fare thee well! although I smile,
I grieve to give thee up for ever.

  Eliza, I shall think of thee—
My heart shall ever twine about thee;

Fare thee well—but think of me,
Compell'd to live and die without thee.
"Fare thee well!—and if for ever,
Still for ever fare thee well!"

JEFFERSON IN A TIGHT PLACE
The Fox Is Caught

The blood hounds, long upon the trail,
Have rambled faithful, hill and dale;
But mind, such creatures never fail,
    To run the rebel down.
His fears forbid him long to stop,
Altho' he gains the mountain top,
He soon is made his tail to drop,
    And fleets to leave the hounds.

Alas! he speeds from place to place,
Such is the fox upon the chase;
To him the mud is no disgrace,
    No lair his cause defends.
He leaves a law and seeks a dell,
And where to fly 'tis hard to tell;
He fears before to meet with hell,
    Behind he has no friends.

But who can pity such a fox,
Though buried among the rocks;
He's a nuisance among the flocks,
    And sucks the blood of geese.
He takes advantage of the sheep,
His nature is at night to creep,
And rob the flocks while the herdsmen sleep,
    When dogs can have no peace.

But he is now brought to a bay,
However fast he run away,
He knows he has not long to stay,
    And assumes a raccoon's dress.
Found in a hole, he veils his face,
And fain would take a lady's place,
But fails, for he has run his race.
    And falls into distress.

The fox is captured in his den,
The martial troops of Michigan,
May hence be known the fleetest men,
    For Davis is their prey.
Great Babylon has fallen down,
A King is left without a crown,
Stripped of honors and renown,
    The evening ends the day.

THE SLAVE

What right divine has mortal man received,
    To domineer with uncontroll'd command?
What philosophic wight has thus believed
    That Heaven entailed on him the weaker band?

If Africa was fraught with weaker light,
    Whilst to the tribes of Europe more was given,
Does this impart to them a lawful right
    To counterfeit the golden rule of Heaven?

Did sovereign justice give to robbery birth,
    And bid the fools to theft their rights betray,
To spread the seeds of slavery o'er the earth,
    That you should hold them as your lawful prey?

Why did Almighty God the land divide
    And bid each nation to maintain her own,
Rolling between the deep, the wind and tide,
    With all their rage to make this order known?

The sad phylactory bound on rebel Cain,
    For killing Abel is in blood reveal'd,
For which the soldier falls among the slain,
    A victim on the sanguinary field.

Thus, in the cause of vile and sordid gain,
    To gratify their lust is all the plea;
Like Cain you've your consanguine brother slain,
    And robbed him of his birthright—Liberty.

Why do ye not the Ishmaelites enslave,
    Or artful red man in his rude attire,
As well as with the Black man, split the wave,
    And to his progeny with rage aspire?

Because the brood-sow's left side pigs were black,
  Whose sable tincture was by nature struck,
Are you by justice bound to pull them back
  And leave the sandy colored pigs to suck?

Or can you deem that God does not intend
  His kingdom through creation to display,
The sacred right of nature to defend,
  And show to mortals who shall bear the sway?

Then suffer Heaven to vindicate the cause,
  The wrong abolish and the right restore;
To make a sacrifice of cruel laws,
  And slavish murmurs will be heard no more.

SLAVERY

Slavery, thou peace-disturbing thief,
  We can't but look with frowns on thee,
Without the balm which gives relief,
  The balm of birthright—Liberty.

Thy wing has been for ages furl'd,
  Thy vessel toss'd from wave to wave,
By stormy winds 'mid billows hurl'd—
  Such is the fate of every slave.

A loathesome burden we are to bear,
  Through sultry bogs we trudging go;
Thy rusty chains we frown to wear,
  Without one inch of wealth to show.

Our fathers from their native land
  Were dragged across the brackish deep,
Bound fast together, hand in hand,
  O! did the God of nature sleep?

When sadly thro' the almond grove
  The pirate dragged them o'er the sod,
Devoid of pity and of love,
  They seemed as left without a God.

Are we not men as well as they,
  Born to enjoy the good of earth,
Brought in creation from the clay,
  To reap a blessing from our birth?

Alas! how can such rebels thrive,
  Who take our lives and wealth away,
Since all were placed on earth to live
  And prosper by the light of day?

The maledictions of our God
  Pervade the dwindling world we see;
He hurls the vengeance with his rod,
  And thunders, let the slave be free!

SNAPS FOR DINNER, SNAPS FOR BREAKFAST AND SNAPS FOR SUPPER

Come in to dinner, squalls the dame,
  You need it now perhaps;
But hear the husband's loud exclaim,
  I do not like your snaps;
'Tis snaps when at your breakfast meal,
  And snaps when at your spinning wheel,
Too many by a devilish deal,
  For all your words are snaps.

Why do you tarry, tell me why?
  The chamber door she taps;
Eat by yourself, my dear, for I
  Am surfeited with snaps;
For if I cough it is the cry,
  You always snap at supper time,
I'd rather lave in vats of lime,
  Than face you with your snaps.

How gladly would I be a book,
  To your long pocket flaps,
That you my face may read and look,
  And learn the worth of snaps;
I'm sorry that I learning lack
  To turn you to an almanac;
Next year I'll hang you on the rack,
  And end the date of snaps.

Snaps: Stringbeans; the pun-filled relationship between the wife's words and the vegetable she serves is exploited fully by the poet. William Carroll's note from *Naked Genius*. Reprinted by permission of William Carroll.

LETTER TO MR. HORACE GREELEY

Sept. 11, 1852
Chapel Hill, N.C.

TO MR. GREELEY

Sir,
From the information of the president of the University of North Carolina, to wit, the honorable D. L. Swain, who is willing to aid me himself, I learn that you are a gentleman of philanthropic feeling. I therefore thought it essential to apply to your beneficent hand for some assistance to remove the burden of hard servitude. Notwithstanding, sir, there are many in my native section of country who wish to bring me out, and there are others far too penurious which renders it somewhat dubious with regard to my extrication. It is evident that you have heard of me by the fame of my work in poetry, much of which I am now too closely confined to carry out and which I feel a warm interest to do; and, sir, by favoring me with a bounty of 175 dollars, I will endeavor to reward your generosity with my productions as soon as possible. I am the only public or recognized poet of color in my native state or perhaps in the union, born in slavery but yet craving that scope and expression whereby my literary labor of the night may be circulated throughout the whole world. Then I forbid that my productions should ever fall to the ground, but rather soar as an eagle above the towering mountains and thus return as a triumphing spirit to the bosom of its God who gave it birth, though now confined in these loathsome fetters. Please assist the lowering vassal arise and live a glad denizen the remnant of his days and as one of active utility.

Yours respect.
George M. Horton
of color

"Letter to Mr. Horace Greeley." Title supplied by editors.

David Walker

(1785–1830)

AS THE CHILD of a slave father and a free mother, David Walker was "born free" in Wilmington, North Carolina. Not much is known about his early life; in his *Appeal* he remarks that he had traveled widely in the United States, especially the South.

On the basis of his own observations and reading, Walker concluded that American slavery was the worst form of slavery in the history of mankind. So, sometime in the 1820s, he decided to flee from the South and its hateful institution. He landed in Boston and by 1827 was the owner of an "old clothes shop" on Brattle Street near the wharves.

Also in that year David Walker added his voice and pen to the abolition movement and began writing for the pioneer *Freedom's Journal*, which had just been established in New York by Samuel Cornish and John Russwurm, the founders of African American journalism. In this connection Walker tried to publicize the work of George Moses Horton and to help the slave buy his freedom.

Walker's *Appeal, in Four Articles; together with a Preamble, to the Coloured Citizens of the World, but in Particular and Very Expressly, to Those of the United States of America* was published in 1829. Reaction to the work was immediate and sensational, especially in the South. The mayor of Savannah, Georgia, wrote to Mayor Harrison Gray Otis of Boston demanding that the book be suppressed. Otis refused, and the governor of Virginia, who had made a similar demand, was told that Walker had not violated any Massachusetts law. It was rumored that in certain sections of the South a reward of $1,000 had been offered for Walker dead and of $10,000 for him alive. Even those who sympathized with the black man's cause and worked for it—Harriet Martineau, Benjamin Lundy, and William Lloyd Garrison—were appalled by the violence expressed in the *Appeal*. Garrison's attitude changed, however, and he later printed most of the *Appeal* in his *Liberator*.

Concerned about Walker's safety, his friends urged him to go to Canada, but he refused to run. "Somebody must die in this cause," he told them. "I may be doomed to the stake and the fire, or to the scaffold tree, but it is not in me to falter if I can promote the work of emancipation." Accordingly, he revised the *Appeal* and brought out second and third editions within approximately a year. And, probably as a result of his writing, he did die for the cause: on June 28, 1830, he was found dead near the door of his shop. He seemed to have been poisoned, although this fact, also, is not known for certain. In any case, the rumor that he was murdered has never been quieted.

For a discussion of Walker's work and importance and for reprints of the *Appeal*, see Charles M. Wiltse, ed., *David Walker's Appeal* (1965). See also Sterling Stuckey's *The Ideological Origins of Black Nationalism* (1972), in which one finds the complete text of Walker's *Appeal*. Stuckey considers Walker "the first major ideologist of black nationalism" in America. Stuckey also wrote an excellent appraisal of Walker for *Dictionary of American Negro Biography*. Other works of importance are Herbert Aptheker's *One Continual Cry* (1965), Vernon Loggins's *The Negro Author* (1931), and Clement Eaton's "A Dangerous Pamphlet," *Journal of Southern History* (August 1935), which gives the effect of the *Appeal* on the South.

The following selections from the *Appeal* come from articles 2 and 3 of the third edition (1830).

OUR WRETCHEDNESS IN CONSEQUENCE OF IGNORANCE

Ignorance, my brethren, is a mist, low down into the very dark and almost impenetrable abyss in which, our fathers for many centuries have been plunged. The Christians, and enlightened of Europe, and some of Asia, seeing the ignorance and consequent degradation of our fathers, instead of trying to enlighten them, by teaching them that religion and light with which God had blessed them, they have plunged them into wretchedness ten thousand times more intolerable, than if they had left them entirely to the Lord, and to add to their miseries, deep down into which they have plunged them tell them, that they are an *inferior* and *distinct race* of beings, which they will be glad enough to recall and swallow by and by. Fortune and misfortune, two inseparable companions, lay rolled up in the wheel of events, which have from the creation of the world, and will continue to take place among men until God shall dash worlds together.

When we take a retrospective view of the arts and sciences—the wise legislators—the Pyramids, and other magnificent buildings—the turning of the channel of the river Nile, by the sons of Africa or of Ham, among whom learning originated, and was carried thence into Greece, where it was improved upon and refined. Thence among the Romans, and all over the then enlightened parts of the world, and it has been enlightening the dark and benighted minds of men from then, down to this day. I say, when I view retrospectively, the renown of that once mighty people, the children of our great progenitor I am indeed cheered. Yea further, when I view that mighty son of Africa, HANNIBAL, one of the greatest generals of antiquity, who defeated and cut off so many thousands of the white Romans or murderers, and who carried his victorious arms, to the very gate of Rome, and I give it as my candid opinion, that had Carthage been well united and had given him good support, he would have carried that cruel and barbarous city by storm. But they were disunited, as the coloured people are now, in the United States of America, the reason our natural enemies are enabled to keep their feet on our throats.

Beloved brethren—here let me tell you, and believe it, that the Lord our God, as true as he sits on his throne in heaven, and as true as our Savior died to redeem the world, will give you a Hannibal, and when the Lord shall have raised him up, and given him to you for your possession, O my suffering brethren! remember the divisions and consequent sufferings of *Carthage* and of *Hayti*. Read the history particularly of Hayti, and see how they were butchered by the whites, and do you take warning. The person whom God shall give you, give him your support and let him go his length, and behold in him the salvation of your God. God will indeed, deliver you through him from your deplorable and wretched condition under the Christians of America. I charge you this day before my God to lay no obstacle in his way, but let him go.

The whites want slaves, and want us for their slaves, but some of them will curse the day they ever saw us. As true as the sun ever shone in its meridian splendor, my colour will root some of them out of the very face of the earth. They shall have enough of making slaves of, and butchering, and murdering us in the manner which they have. No doubt some may say that I write with a bad spirit, and that I being a black, wish these things to occur. Whether I write with a bad or a good spirit, I say if these things do not occur in their proper time, it is because the world in which we live does not exist, and we are deceived with regard to its existence.—It is immaterial however to me, who believe, or who refuse—though I should like to see the whites repent peradventure God may have mercy on them, some however, have gone so far that their cup must be filled.

But what need have I to refer to antiquity, when Hayti, the glory of the blacks and terror of tyrants, is enough to convince the most avaricious and stupid of wretches—which is at this time, and I am sorry to say it, plagued with that scourge of nations, the Catholic religion; but I hope and pray God that she may yet rid herself of it, and adopt in its stead the Protestant faith; also, I hope that she may keep peace within her borders and be united, keeping a strict look out for tyrants, for if they get the least chance to injure her, they will avail themselves of it, as true as the Lord lives in heaven. But one thing which gives me joy is, that they are men who would cut off to a man, before they would yield to the combined forces of the whole world—in fact, if the whole world was combined against them, it could not do any thing with them, unless the Lord delivers them up.

Ignorance and treachery one against the other—a grovelling servile and abject submission to the lash of tyrants, we see plainly, my brethren, are not the natural elements of the blacks, as the Americans try to make us believe; but these are misfortunes which God has suffered our fathers to be enveloped in for many ages, no doubt in consequence of their disobedience to their Maker, and which do, indeed, reign at this time among us, almost to the destruction of all other principles: for I must truly say, that ignorance, the mother of treachery and deceit, gnaws into our very vitals. Ignorance, as it now exists among us, produces a state of things, Oh my Lord! too horrible to present to the world. Any man who is curious to see the full force of ignorance developed among the coloured people of the United States of America, has only to go into the southern and western states of this confederacy, where, if he is not a tyrant, but has the feelings of a human being, who can feel for a fellow creature, he may see enough to make his very heart bleed! He may see there, a son take his mother, who bore almost the pains of death to give him birth, and by the command of a tyrant, strip her as naked as she came into the world, and apply the cow-hide to her, until she falls a victim to death in the road! He may see a husband take his dear wife, not unfrequently in a pregnant state, and perhaps far advanced, and beat her for an unmerciful wretch, until his infant falls a lifeless lump at her feet! Can the Americans escape God Almighty? If they do, can he be to us a God of Justice? God is just, and I know it—for he has convinced me to my satisfaction—I cannot doubt him. My observer may see fathers beating their sons, mothers their daughters, and children their parents, all to pacify the passions of unrelenting tyrants. He may also, see them telling news and lies, making mischief one upon another. These are some of the productions of ignorance, which he will see practiced among my dear brethren, who are held in unjust slavery and wretchedness, by avaricious and unmerciful tyrants, to whom, and their hellish deeds, I would suffer my life to be taken before I would submit. And when my curious observer comes to take notice of those who are said to be free, (which assertion I deny) and who are making some frivolous pretentions to common sense, he will see that branch of ignorance among the slaves assuming a more cunning and deceitful course of procedure.—He may see some of my brethren in league with tyrants, selling their own brethren into *hell upon earth,* not dissimilar to the exhibitions

in Africa, but in a more secret, servile and abject manner. Oh
Heaven! I am full!!! I can hardly move my pen!!!! and as I expect
some will try to put me to death, to strike terror into others, and to
obliterate from their minds the notion of freedom, so as to keep my
brethren the more secure in wretchedness, where they will be permitted to stay but a short time (whether tyrants believe it or not)—I
shall give the world a development of facts, which are already witnessed in the courts of heaven. My observer may see some of those
ignorant and treacherous creatures (coloured people) sneaking about
in the large cities, endeavouring to find out all strange coloured people, where they work and where they reside, asking them questions,
and trying to ascertain whether they are runaways or not, telling
them, at the same time, that they always have been, are, and always
will be, friends to their brethren; and, perhaps, that they themselves
are absconders, and a thousand such treacherous lies to get the better information of the more ignorant!!! There have been and are at
this day in Boston, New-York, Philadelphia, and Baltimore, coloured
men, who are in league with tyrants, and who receive a great portion of their daily bread, of the moneys which they acquire from the
blood and tears of their more miserable brethren, whom they scan-
dously delivered into the hands of our *natural enemies*!!!!!! . . .

OUR WRETCHEDNESS IN CONSEQUENCE OF THE PREACHERS OF THE RELIGION OF JESUS CHRIST

Religion, my brethren, is a substance of deep consideration among
all nations of the earth. The Pagans have a kind, as well as the Mahometans, the Jews and the Christians. But pure and undefiled religion, such as was preached by Jesus Christ and his apostles, is hard
to be found in all the earth. God, through his instrument, Moses,
handed a dispensation of his Divine will, to the children of Israel
after they had left Egypt for the land of Canaan or of Promise, who
through hypocrisy, oppression and unbelief, departed from the
faith.—He then, by his apostles, handed a dispensation of his, together with the will of Jesus Christ, to the Europeans in Europe,
who, in open violation of which, have made *merchandise* of us, and
it does appear as though they take this very dispensation to aid them
in their *infernal* depredations upon us. Indeed, the way in which religion was and is conducted by the Europeans and their descendants,
one might believe it was a plan fabricated by themselves and the *devils* to oppress us. But hark! My master has taught me better than to
believe it—he has taught me that his gospel as it was preached by

himself and his apostles remains the same, notwithstanding Europe
has tried to mingle blood and oppression with it.

It is well known to the Christian world, that Bartholomew Las
Casas, that very very notoriously avaricious Catholic priest or
preacher, and adventurer with Columbus, in his second voyage, proposed to his countrymen, the Spaniards in Hispaniola to import the
Africans from the Portuguese settlement in Africa, to dig up gold
and silver, and work their plantations for them, to effect which, he
made a voyage thence to Spain, and opened the subject to his master, Ferdinand then in declining health, who listened to the plan: but
who died soon after, and left it in the hand of his successor, Charles
V. This wretch ("Las Casas, the Preacher,") succeeded so well in his
plans of oppression, that in 1503, the first blacks had been imported
into the new world. Elated with this success, and stimulated by sordid avarice only, he importuned Charles V. in 1511, to grant permission to a Flemish merchant, to import 4000 blacks at one time. Thus
we see, through the instrumentality of a pretended preacher of the
gospel of Jesus Christ our common master, our wretchedness first
commenced in America—where it has been continued from 1503, to
this day, 1829. A period of three hundred and twenty-six years. But
two hundred and nine, from 1620 [1619]—when twenty of our fathers were brought into Jamestown, Virginia, by a Dutch man of war,
and sold off like brutes to the highest bidders; and there is not a
doubt in my mind, but that tyrants are in hope to perpetuate our
miseries under them and their children until the final consummation
of all things—But if they do not get dreadfully deceived, it will be
because God has forgotten them.

The Pagans, Jews and Mahometans try to make proselytes to
their religions, and whatever human beings adopt their religions they
extend to them their protection. But Christian Americans not only
hinder their fellow creatures, the Africans, but thousands of them
*will absolutely beat a coloured person nearly to death, if they catch him
on his knees, supplicating the throne of grace.* This barbarous cruelty
was by all the heathen nations of antiquity, and is by the Pagans,
Jews and Mahometans of the present day, left entirely to Christian
Americans to inflict on the Africans and their descendants, that their
cup which is nearly full may be completed. I have known tyrants or
usurpers of human liberty in different parts of this country to take
their fellow creatures, the coloured people, and beat them until they
would scarcely leave life in them; what for? Why they say "The
black devils had the audacity to be found *making prayers and supplications to the God who made them!!!!*" Yes, I have known small collections of coloured people to have convened together, for no other
purpose than to worship God Almighty, in spirit and in truth, to the

best of their knowledge; when tyrants, calling themselves *patrols*, would also convene and wait almost in breathless silence for the poor coloured people to commence singing and praying to the Lord our God, as soon as they had commenced, the wretches would burst in upon them and drag them out and commence beating them as they would rattle-snakes—many of whom, they would beat so unmercifully, that they would hardly be able to crawl for weeks and sometimes for months. Yet the American ministers send out missionaries to convert the heathen, while they keep us and our children sunk at their feet in the most abject ignorance and wretchedness that ever a people was afflicted with since the world began. Will the Lord suffer this people to proceed much longer? Will he not stop them in their career? Does he regard the heathens abroad, more than the heathens among the Americans? Surely the Americans must believe that God is partial, notwithstanding his Apostle Peter, declared before Cornelius and others that he has no respect to persons, but in every nation he that feareth God and worketh righteousness is accepted with him.—"The word," said he, "which God sent unto the children of Israel, preaching peace, by Jesus Christ, (he is Lord of all.") Have not the Americans the Bible in their hands? Do they believe it? Surely they do not. See how they treat us in open violation of the Bible!! They no doubt will be greatly offended with me, but if God does not awaken them, it will be, because they are superior to other men, as they have represented themselves to be. Our divine Lord and Master said, "all things whatsoever ye would that men should do unto you, do ye even so unto them." But an American minister, with the Bible in his hand, holds us and our children in the most abject slavery and wretchedness. Now I ask them, would they like for us to hold them and their children in abject slavery and wretchedness? No, says one, that never can be done—you are too abject and ignorant to do it—you are not men—you were made to be slaves to us, to dig up gold and silver for us and our children. Know this, my dear sirs, that although you treat us and our children now, as you do your domestic beast—yet the final result of all future events are known but to God Almighty alone, who rules in the armies of heaven and among the inhabitants of the earth, and who dethrones one earthly king and sits up another, as it seemeth good in his holy sight. We may attribute these vicissitudes to what we please, but the God of armies and of justice rules in heaven and in earth, and the whole American people shall see and know it yet, to their satisfaction. I have known pretended preachers of the gospel of my Master, who not only held us as their natural inheritance, but treated us with as much rigor as any Infidel or Deist in the world— just as though they were intent only on taking our blood and groans to glorify the Lord Jesus Christ. The wicked and ungodly, seeing their preachers treat us with so much cruelty, they say: our preachers, who must be right, if any body are, treat them like brutes, and why cannot we?—They think it is no harm to keep them in slavery and put the whip to them, and why cannot we do the same!—They being preachers of the gospel of Jesus Christ, if it were any harm, they would surely preach against their oppression and do their utmost to erase it from the country; not only in one or two cities, but one continual cry would be raised in all parts of this confederacy, and would cease only with the complete overthrow of the system of slavery, in every part of the country. But how far the American preachers are from preaching against slavery and oppression, which have carried their country to the brink of a precipice; to save them from plunging down the side of which, will hardly be affected, will appear in the sequel of this paragraph, which I shall narrate just as it transpired. I remember a Camp Meeting in South Carolina, for which I embarked in a Steam Boat at Charleston, and having been five or six hours on the water, we at last arrived at the place of hearing, where was a very great concourse of people, who were no doubt, collected together to hear the word of God, (that some had collected barely as spectators to the scene, I will not here pretend to doubt, however, that is left to themselves and their God.) Myself and boat companions, having been there a little while, we were all called up to hear; I among the rest went up and took my seat—being seated, I fixed myself in a complete position to hear the word of my Saviour and to receive such as I thought was authenticated by the Holy Scriptures; but to my no ordinary astonishment, our Reverend gentleman got up and told us (coloured people) that slaves must be obedient to their masters—must do their duty to their masters or be whipped—the whip was made for the backs of fools, &c. Here I pause for a moment, to give the world time to consider what was my surprise, to hear such preaching from a minister of my Master, whose very gospel is that of peace and not of blood and whips, as this pretended preacher tried to make us believe. What the American preachers can think of us, I aver this day before my God, I have never been able to define. They have newspapers and monthly periodicals, which they receive in continual succession, but on the pages of which, you will scarcely ever find a paragraph respecting slavery, which is ten thousand times more injurious to this country than all the other evils put together, and which will be the final overthrow of its government, unless something is very speedily done; for their cup is nearly full.—Perhaps they will laugh at or make light of this; but I tell you Americans! that unless you speedily alter your course, *you* and your *Country are gone!!!!!!* For God Almighty will tear up the very face of the earth!!! Will not that very remarkable passage of Scripture be fulfilled on Christian Americans? Hear it Americans!! "He that is unjust, let him be unjust still:—and he which is filthy, let him be filthy still: and he that is righteous, let him be righteous still: and he that is holy, let him be holy still." I hope that the Americans may hear, but I am afraid that they have done us so much injury, and are so firm in the belief that our Creator made us to be an inheritance to them for ever, that their hearts will be hardened, so that their destruction may be sure. This language, perhaps is too harsh for the American's delicate ears, But Oh Americans! Americans!! I warn you in the name of the Lord, (whether you will hear, or forbear,) to repent and reform, or you are ruined!!! Do you think that our blood is hidden from the Lord, because you can hide it from the rest of the world, by sending out missionaries, and by your charitable deeds to the Greeks, Irish, &c.? Will he not publish your secret crimes on the house top? Even here in Boston, pride and prejudice have got to such a pitch, that in the very houses erected to the Lord, they have built little places for the reception of coloured people, where they must sit during meeting, or keep away from the house of God, and the preachers say nothing about it—much less go into the hedges and highways seeking the lost sheep of the house of Israel, and try to bring them in to their Lord and Master. There are not a more wretched, ignorant, miserable, and abject set of beings in all the world, than the blacks in the Southern and Western sections of this country, under tyrants and devils. The preachers of America cannot see them, but they can send out missionaries to convert the heathens, notwithstanding. Americans! unless you speedily alter your course of proceeding, if God Almighty does not stop you, I say it in his name, that you may go on and do as you please for ever, both in time and eternity—never fear any evil at all!!!!!!!!

PART 2

Freedom Fighters: 1830–1865

THE YEARS covered in this section were the most crucial in the history of our country—crucial for black and white alike. They saw a great nation bitterly divided into two camps over the issue of slavery. They were tense and explosive years that ended in a civil war which united the nation and gave nominal freedom to slaves.

In this prelude to the Civil War, the South began to become alarmed at the restlessness of its great slave population. Slaves increasingly showed their deep resentment through escape (often via the Underground Railroad); through their slave narratives, written by them or dictated after they reached the North; through their fiery and incendiary pamphlets; and through violence in the form of insurrections. Although we make token use of the best known of these uprisings—those led by Denmark Vesey, Gabriel Prosser, and Nat Turner—there were many others, a great many others as Herbert Aptheker showed in his study *American Negro Slave Revolts* (1943, 1969). These attacks on the "peculiar institution" brought from southern slaveholders increased harshness in the treatment of the chattel.

The troubles of the South were augmented during the 1830s by the proliferation of abolition forces in the North and to a limited extent in the South. Some of America's ablest and best-known literary, journalistic, religious, and humanitarian leaders became active in the Abolition movement and did yeoman service in it. A case could be made for the movement as the high point in America's moral history. Among the leaders of this great liberal and humanitarian revolution were William Lloyd Garrison (whose *Liberator* was the strongest voice of the movement), Harriet Beecher Stowe (whose *Uncle Tom's Cabin* crystallized the antislavery sentiment of the nation), John Greenleaf Whittier (whose verses helped to popularize the abolitionist position), Charles G. Finney (who was the moving spirit of the religious revival that swept the North and whose efforts enlisted the help of Theodore D. Weld and the Tappan brothers), and John Brown (whose martyrdom at Harpers Ferry symbolized the extent to which the moral and humanitarian elements in the North would go to rid the country of slavery). Negroes, too, were a vital part of this great movement. All of the authors in this chapter wrote against slavery, and one of Abolition's great leaders—and in all probability one of the movement's greatest speakers—was Frederick Douglass.

From the 1830s to the Civil War, American blacks lived with the overriding condition of slavery. It was the reality that bound even those who were born free and lived in the North. Black writers of this period were, as might be expected, especially responsive to this reality, and in much of their work argument takes precedence over art, again as to be expected. Very few writers avoided racial involvement; Daniel A. Payne's little poetic work *Pleasures and Other Miscellaneous Poems* is one of the exceptions. These men and women were primarily preachers, teachers, and activists whose concept of duty was "uplifting a down-trodden race." They organized conventions and addressed them; they established schools and taught in them; they founded churches and preached in them; and a number of them used creative literature as an instrument in their job of uplifting a race.

Among the few poets of this era, we find George B. Vashon, a teacher, who left two major poems: "Vincent Oge," an ambitious piece, celebrating the life and death of a Haitian, and "A Life-Day," telling the tragic story of the marriage of a white man to a beautiful mulatto girl who had been his slave. We also find James M. Whitfield, who published a thin book of verse, *America and Other Poems*. The title poem—and a few others—are of such high quality that his early death was, in retrospect, a real loss to American poetry.

Among the early novelists, William Wells Brown was more dedicated to a literary career than were any of his black contemporaries. Brown produced one of the first novels written by an American Negro, the first Negro play, and the first Negro book of travel. He also published three volumes of history, and a book of autobiographical sketches. Up until quite recently, scholars claimed that Brown's *Clotel* (1853) was the first novel by an American Negro; but after the research and discoveries made by Professor Henry Louis Gates, Jr., and his associates at Yale University, Brown's position has been clarified. Professor Gates discovered, among other documents, a hitherto unknown novel by a Negro woman, entitled *Our Nig* (1859), written by one Harriet E. Wilson. The date makes it the first novel so far by a black woman and the first to be published in America. Brown's *Clotel* and Frank J. Webb's *The Garies and Their Friends* (1857) were both published in London. *Our Nig* was republished in 1983 with a fascinating fifty-five page introduction by Gates (see the headnote for Harriet Wilson.)

Two other novelists of the period concern us here. The first is Frank J. Webb, mentioned previously. His *The Garies and Their Friends* (London, 1857) deals with Negro life in the North, mainly in Philadelphia. Technically a better novel than *Clotel*, it contains an unusual number of "firsts" in Negro fiction (see Webb's headnote). The second novelist, Martin R. Delany, is far better known for activities other than fiction writing. His unfinished novel, *Blake: or; The Huts of America*, appeared serially in the 1859 *Anglo-African Magazine*. A precursor of later militant and nationalistic works by black authors, *Blake* tells the story of a "heroic slave" trying to organize his fellow bondsmen.

Because most of the speeches and sermons of this period were extemporaneous, few have come down to us. Contemporary opinion, however, suggests that the oratory of Henry Highland Garnet, Josiah Henson, and Samuel Ringgold Ward was as eloquent and moving as the white antislavery oratory of Wendell Phillips, the editorials of William Lloyd Garrison, and the poetry of John Greenleaf Whittier. We also know that of the countless antislavery pamphlets written and published during the era none was as incendiary as Garnet's *An Address to the Slaves of the United States of America*.

With the exception of James M. Whitfield, all the black authors of this period either wrote autobiographies or were the subjects of biographical works, and some of these—particularly Daniel Payne's autobiography—make very interesting reading. But none achieves the literary stature of Frederick Douglass's autobiographical writings. Judged by all acknowledged standards, *Narrative of the Life of Frederick Douglass, My Bondage and My Freedom*, and *Life and Times* are classics of American autobiographical writing.

No one knows when Negro folk literature began to develop, but it had become a separate great body of expression by the middle years of the nineteenth century. Undoubtedly some of it, like the animal tales, derives from Africa, but a large portion originated in the American South. Scholars have shown that many verses found in the spirituals may be traced to the late eighteenth-century Watts-Wesley hymns of the period. Musicologists have pointed out that some of the music of the spirituals may be traced to European origins. Other commentators have insisted that the spirituals have a predominantly West African origin. The controversy over the makeup of the spirituals has been with us since Thomas Wentworth Higginson, greatly impressed by the singing of the black soldiers in his regiment, recorded several spirituals for an article in the *Atlantic Monthly* (1867); and the problem is far too complex to consider here in any depth. Suffice it to say that any one who has heard Negro spirituals *sung by Negroes* knows that, whatever the mixture of original elements, "the black and unknown bards of long ago" transformed these elements into an original and unique contribution to American culture and to world music. Most present-day scholars agree on this, just as they agree on the *American* rather than the *all-black* origins of jazz.

In *Scenes in the Life of Harriet Tubman* (1869), the biography of a runaway slave who became a conductor on the Underground Railroad, we notice an early use of folk material. Sarah H. Bradford, a proper Yankee writer, tells us that Harriet often "created" spirituals to inform potential runaways of her presence and her plans. The use of this folk literature as secret communication among slaves was crucial to their survival. The rhetoric, the idioms, and the images it employs are distinctly black American.

Most folk literature was probably the result of group or community effort, and the variety of versions of any one folk piece is probably a consequence of faulty memory and oral transmission. These factors certainly account for the differing versions of folk pieces of the post–Civil War period and the period of tremendous urbanization (1885–1900), when the "John Henry" ballad, "Frankie and Johnnie," and countless other urban folk songs and sayings came into being. The original composers, whether individuals or groups, were illiterate and could not record their compositions.

Although Negro folk songs and sayings are, like the sophisticated writings of the period, invariably race conscious and evoke the hard realities of the special black experience, and although they too are coded, in a kind of "thieves' jargon," they achieve universal relevance. The materials of Negro folk literature—myth, legend, belief—are allegoric and parabolic. They illustrate attitudes, emotional states, and experiences that are common to all people.

William Wells Brown

(c. 1816–1884)

WILLIAM WELLS BROWN—one of the first African Americans to write a novel, the first to write a play, the first to write a book of travels, and among the first to write history—was born near Lexington, Kentucky. The son of a white father and a mulatto mother, he was one of seven children. According to rumor, Brown's mother was the daughter of Daniel Boone, and his father was thought to be a relative of their master.

Serving under several masters, William Wells Brown did many kinds of work, some of it unusual for a slave. At one time he was hired out to Elijah P. Lovejoy's newspaper office in St. Louis. Under his last master, a riverboat captain, Brown traveled up and down the Ohio and Mississippi rivers. He tried twice to escape. The first time, he took his mother with him, and although the two reached Illinois they were captured and returned to the master. As punishment Brown's mother was sold "down South"; the incident was a terrible blow to the young boy, who felt that he was responsible. His second escape attempt was successful. Having been taken by his master to Cincinnati, Brown simply walked away. On his way north he was helped by a Quaker named Wells Brown, whose name he adopted.

As a free man Brown worked on steamboats on Lake Erie and was able to help many fugitive slaves to their freedom. He finally settled in Buffalo, brushed up on the "letters" he had somehow learned earlier, and improved remarkably his facility with the language. In 1847 Brown was invited to join the Massachusetts Anti-Slavery Society. Although he lacked the genius of Frederick Douglass, William Wells Brown became a faithful and effective speaker and writer for abolition both here and in England, and for the temperance cause, prison reform, and woman's suffrage.

A prolific author, Brown produced the following major works: *Narrative of William W. Brown, a Fugitive Slave* (1847; revised 1848 and 1849); *Three Years in Europe; or, Places I Have Seen and People I Have Met* (London, 1852; enlarged and reprinted in 1855 as *The American Fugitive in Europe*); *Clotel; or, The President's Daughter: A Narrative of Slave Life in the United States* (London, 1853; revised and reprinted under different names in 1860–61, 1864, and 1867); *The Escape; or, A Leap for Freedom: A Drama in Five Acts* (1858); *The Black Man: His Antecedents, His Genius, and His Achievements* (1863); *The Negro in the American Rebellion: His Heroism and His Fidelity* (1867); *The Rising Son; or, The Antecedents and the Advancement of the Colored Race* (1874); and *My Southern Home; or, The South and Its People* (1880).

Brown's *Clotel* is still thought to be the first novel published by an African American. *Clotel* was published in London in 1853. The first novel to be published in America (also the first to be published by a Negro woman), we now believe, is *Our Nig* (1859), by Harriet E. Wilson (see the headnote for Wilson).

The monumental and definitive *William Wells Brown, Author and Reformer* (1969) by W. Edward Farrison is an outstanding achievement in American scholarship. Farrison's introduction to and annotations in Brown's *The Negro in the American Rebellion: His Heroism and His Fidelity* (1867) and Farrison's entry in *Dictionary of American Negro Biography* are both valuable additions to the scholarship on William Wells Brown. So are the comments in *The Negro Author* by Vernon Loggins and in J. Noel Heermance's *William Wells Brown and "Clotelle": A Portrait of the Artist in the First Negro Novel* (with an introduction by Arthur P. Davis), published in 1969. Brown's contributions are also examined in *The Afro-American Novel* by Bernard W. Bell (1987). See also Josephine Brown's *Biography of an American Bondman, By His Daughter* (1856).

The novel selections come from chapters 1 and 2 of *Clotelle* (1867 version). The selection from *My Southern Home* comes from the 1880 publication.

FROM **CLOTELLE**

With the growing population in the Southern States, the increase of mulattoes has been very great. Society does not frown upon the man who sits with his half-white child upon his knee whilst the mother stands, a slave, behind his chair. In nearly all the cities and towns of the Slave States, the real negro, or clear black, does not amount to more than one in four of the slave population. This fact is of itself the best evidence of the degraded and immoral condition of the relation of master and slave. Throughout the Southern States, there is a class of slaves who, in most of the towns, are permitted to hire their time from their owners, and who are always expected to pay a high price. This class is the mulatto women, distinguished for their fascinating beauty. The handsomest of these usually pay the greatest amount for their time. Many of these women are the favorites of men of property and standing, who furnish them with the means of compensating their owners, and not a few are dressed in the most extravagant manner.

When we take into consideration the fact that no safeguard is thrown around virtue, and no inducement held out to slave-women to be pure and chaste, we will not be surprised when told that immorality and vice pervade the cities and towns of the South to an extent unknown in the Northern States. Indeed, many of the slave-women have no higher aspiration than that of becoming the finely-dressed mistress of some white man. At negro balls and parties, this class of women usually make the most splendid appearance, and are eagerly sought after in the dance, or to entertain in the drawing-room or at the table.

A few years ago, among the many slave-women in Richmond, Virginia, who hired their time of their masters, was Agnes, a mulatto owned by John Graves, Esq., and who might be heard boasting that she was the daughter of an American Senator. Although nearly forty years of age at the time of which we write, Agnes was still exceedingly handsome. More than half white, with long black hair and deep blue eyes, no one felt like disputing with her when she urged her claim to her relationship with the Anglo-Saxon.

In her younger days, Agnes had been a housekeeper for a young slave-holder, and in sustaining this relation had become the mother of two daughters. After being cast aside by this young man, the slave-woman betook herself to the business of a laundress, and was considered to be the most tasteful woman in Richmond at her vocation.

Isabella and Marion, the two daughters of Agnes, resided with their mother, and gave her what aid they could in her business. The mother, however, was very choice of her daughters, and would allow them to perform no labor that would militate against their lady-like appearance. Agnes early resolved to bring up her daughters as ladies, as she termed it.

As the girls grew older, the mother had to pay a stipulated price for them per month. Her notoriety as a laundress of the first class enabled her to put an extra charge upon the linen that passed through her hands; and although she imposed little or no work upon her daughters, she was enabled to live in comparative luxury and have her daughters dressed to attract attention, especially at the negro balls and parties.

Although the term "negro ball" is applied to these gatherings, yet a large portion of the men who attend them are whites. Negro balls and parties in the Southern States, especially in the cities and towns, are usually made up of quadroon women, a few negro men, and any number of white gentlemen. These are gatherings of the most democratic character. Bankers, merchants, lawyers, doctors, and their clerks and students, all take part in these social assemblies upon terms of perfect equality. The father and son not unfrequently meet and dance *vis a vis* at a negro ball.

It was at one of these parties that Henry Linwood, the son of a wealthy and retired gentleman of Richmond, was first introduced to Isabella, the oldest daughter of Agnes. The young man had just returned from Harvard College, where he had spent the previous five years. Isabella was in her eighteenth year, and was admitted by all who knew her to be the handsomest girl, colored or white, in the city. On this occasion, she was attired in a sky-blue silk dress, with deep black lace flounces, and bertha of the same. On her well-moulded arms she wore massive gold bracelets, while her rich black hair was arranged at the back in broad basket plaits, ornamented with pearls, and the front in the French style (*a la Imperatrice*), which suited her classic face to perfection.

Marion was scarcely less richly dressed than her sister.

Henry Linwood paid great attention to Isabella, which was looked upon with gratification by her mother, and became a matter of general conversation with all present. Of course, the young man escorted the beautiful quadroon home that evening, and became the favorite visitor at the house of Agnes.

It was on a beautiful moonlight night in the month of August, when all who reside in tropical climates are eagerly gasping for a breath of fresh air, that Henry Linwood was in the garden which surrounded Agnes' cottage, with the young quadroon by his side. He drew from his pocket a newspaper wet from the press, and read the following advertisement:—

> NOTICE.—Seventy-nine negroes will be offered for sale on Monday, September 10, at 12 o'clock, being the entire stock of the late John Graves. The negroes are in an excellent condition, and all warranted against the common vices. Among them are several mechanics, able-bodied field-hands, plough-boys, and women with children, some of them very prolific, affording a rare opportunity for any one who wishes to raise a strong and healthy lot of servants for their own use. Also several mulatto girls of rare personal qualities,—two of these very superior.

Among the above slaves advertised for sale were Agnes and her two daughters. Ere young Linwood left the quadroon that evening, he promised her that he would become her purchaser, and make her free and her own mistress.

Mr. Graves had long been considered not only an excellent and upright citizen of the first standing among the whites, but even the slaves regarded him as one of the kindest of masters. Having inherited his slaves with the rest of his property, he became possessed of them without any consultation or wish of his own. He would neither buy nor sell slaves, and was exceedingly careful, in letting them out, that they did not find oppressive and tyrannical masters. No slave speculator ever dared to cross the threshold of this planter of the Old Dominion. He was a constant attendant upon religious worship, and was noted for his general benevolence. The American Bible Society, the American Tract Society, and the cause of Foreign Missions, found in him a liberal friend. He was always anxious that his slaves should appear well on the Sabbath, and have an opportunity of hearing the word of God.

⟨✶⟩

As might have been expected, the day of sale brought an unusually large number together to compete for the property to be sold. Farmers, who make a business of raising slaves for the market, were there, and slave-traders, who make a business of buying human beings in the slave-raising States and taking them to the far South, were also in attendance. Men and women, too, who wished to purchase for their own use, had found their way to the slave sale.

In the midst of the throng was one who felt a deeper interest in the result of the sale than any other of the bystanders. This was young Linwood. True to his promise, he was there with a blank bank-check in his pocket, awaiting with impatience to enter the list as a bidder for the beautiful slave.

It was indeed a heart-rending scene to witness the lamentations of these slaves, all of whom had grown up together on the old homestead of Mr. Graves, and who had been treated with great kindness by that gentleman, during his life. Now they were to be separated, and form new relations and companions. Such is the precarious condition of the slave. Even when with a good master, there is no certainty of his happiness in the future.

The less valuable slaves were first placed upon the auction-block, one after another, and sold to the highest bidder. Husbands and wives were separated with a degree of indifference that is unknown in any other relation in life. Brothers and sisters were torn from each other, and mothers saw their children for the last time on earth.

It was late in the day, and when the greatest number of persons were thought to be present, when Agnes and her daughters were brought out to the place of sale. The mother was first put upon the auction-block, and sold to a noted negro trader named Jennings. Marion was next ordered to ascend the stand, which she did with a trembling step, and was sold for $1200.

All eyes were now turned on Isabella, as she was led forward by the auctioneer. The appearance of the handsome quadroon caused a deep sensation among the crowd. There she stood, with a skin as fair as most white women, her features as beautifully regular as any of her sex of pure Anglo-Saxon blood, her long black hair done up in the neatest manner, her form tall and graceful, and her whole appearance indicating one superior to her condition.

The auctioneer commenced by saying that Miss Isabella was fit to deck the drawing-room of the finest mansion in Virginia.

"How much, gentlemen, for this real Albino!—fit fancy-girl for any one! She enjoys good health, and has a sweet temper. How much do you say?"

"Five hundred dollars."

"Only five hundred for such a girl as this? Gentlemen, she is worth a deal more than that sum. You certainly do not know the value of the article you are bidding on. Here, gentlemen, I hold in my hand a paper certifying that she has a good moral character."

"Seven hundred."

"Ah, gentlemen, that is something like. This paper also states that she is very intelligent."

"Eight hundred."

"She was first sprinkled, then immersed, and is now warranted to be a devoted Christian, and perfectly trustworthy."

"Nine hundred dollars."

"Nine hundred and fifty."

"One thousand."

"Eleven hundred."

Here the bidding came to a dead stand. The auctioneer stopped, looked around, and began in a rough manner to relate some anecdote connected with the sale of slaves, which he said had come under his own observation.

At this juncture the scene was indeed a most striking one. The laughing, joking, swearing, smoking, spitting, and talking, kept up a continual hum and confusion among the crowd, while the slave-girl stood with tearful eyes, looking alternately at her mother and sister and toward the young man whom she hoped would become her purchaser.

"The chastity of this girl," now continued the auctioneer, "is pure. She has never been from under her mother's care. She is virtuous, and as gentle as a dove."

The bids here took a fresh start, and went on until $1800 was reached. The auctioneer once more resorted to his jokes, and concluded by assuring the company that Isabella was not only pious, but that she could make an excellent prayer.

"Nineteen hundred dollars."

"Two thousand."

This was the last bid, and the quadroon girl was struck off, and became the property of Henry Linwood.

This was a Virginia slave-auction, at which the bones, sinews, blood, and nerves of a young girl of eighteen were sold for $500; her moral character for $200; her superior intellect for $100; the benefits supposed to accrue from her having been sprinkled and immersed, together with a warranty of her devoted Christianity, for $300; her ability to make a good prayer for $200; and her chastity for $700 more. This, too, in a city thronged with churches, whose tall spires look like so many signals pointing to heaven, but whose ministers preach that slavery is a God-ordained institution!

The slaves were speedily separated, and taken along by their respective masters. Jennings, the slave-speculator, who had purchased Agnes and her daughter Marion, with several of the other slaves, took them to the county prison, where he usually kept his human cattle after purchasing them, previous to starting for the New Orleans market.

Linwood had already provided a place for Isabella, to which she was taken. The most trying moment for her was when she took leave of her mother and sister. The "Good-by" of the slave is unlike that of any other class in the community. It is indeed a farewell forever. With tears streaming down their cheeks, they embraced and commended each other to God, who is no respecter of persons, and before whom master and slave must one day appear.

FROM **MY SOUTHERN HOME**

Paying a flying visit to Tennessee, I halted at Columbia, the capital of Maury County. At Redgerford Creek, five miles distant from Columbia, lives Joe Budge, a man with one hundred children. Never having met one with such a family, I resolved to make a call on the gentleman and satisfy my own curiosity.

This distinguished individual is seventy-one years old, large frame, of unadulterated blood, and spent his life in slavery up to the close of the war.

"How many children have you, Mr. Budge?" I asked.

"One hundred, ser," was the quick response.

"Are they all living?"

"No, ser."

"How many wives had you?"

"Thirteen, ser."

"Had you more than one wife living at any time?"

"O, yes, ser, nearly all of dem ware livin' when de war broke out."

"How was this, did the law allow you to have more than one wife at a time?"

"Well, yer see, boss, I waren't under de law, I ware under marser."

"Were you married to all of your wives by a minister?"

"No, ser, only five by de preacher."

"How did you marry the others?"

"Ober de broomstick an' under de blanket."

"How was that performed?"

"Wel, yer see, ser, dey all 'sembles in de quarters, an' a man takes hold of one en' of de broom an' a 'oman takes hole of tudder en', an' dey holes up de broom, an' de man an' de 'oman dats gwine to get married jumps ober an' den slips under a blanket, dey put out de light an' all goes out an' leabs em dar."

"How near together were your wives?"

"Marser had fore plantations, an' dey live 'bout on 'em, dem dat warn't sold."

"Did your master sell some of your wives?"

"O! yes, ser, when dey got too ole to bare children. You see, marser raised slaves fer de market, an' my stock ware called mighty good, kase I ware very strong, an' could do a heap of work."

"Were your children sold away from you?"

"Yes, ser, I see three of 'em sole one day fer two thousand dollars a-piece; yer see dey ware men grown up."

"Did you select your wives?"

"Dunno what you mean by dat word."

"Did you pick out the women that you wanted?"

"O! no, ser, I had nuthin ter say 'bout dat. Marser allers get 'em, an' pick out strong, hearty young women. Dat's de reason dat de planters wanted to get my children, kase dey ware so helty."

"Did you never feel that it was wrong to get married in such a light manner?"

"No, ser, kase yer see I toted de witness wid me."

"What do you mean by that?"

"Why, ser, I had religion, an' dat made me feel dat all ware right."

"What was the witness that you spoke of?"

"De change of heart, ser, is de witness dat I totes in my bosom; an' when a man's got dat, he fears nuthin, not eben de debble himsef."

"Then you know that you've got the witness?"

"Yes, ser, I totes it right here." And at this point, Mr. Budge put his hand on his heart, and looked up to heaven.

"I presume your master made no profession of religion?"

"O! yes, ser, you bet he had religion. He ware de fustest man in de church, an' he ware called mighty powerful in prayer."

"Do any of your wives live near you now, except the one that you are living with?"

"Yes, ser dar's five in dis county, but dey's all married now to udder men."

"Have you many grand-children?"

"Yes, ser, when my 'lations am all tergedder, dey numbers 'bout fore hundred, near as I ken get at it."

"Do you know of any other men that have got as many children as you?"

"No, ser, dey calls me de boss daddy in dis part of de State."

Having satisfied my curiosity, I bade Mr. Budge "good-day."

Martin R. Delany

(1812–1885)

A PIONEERING black nationalist, early magazine publisher, physician, the first black high-ranking field officer in the United States Army, novelist, explorer, and politician, Martin R. Delany was born free in Charlestown [then], Virginia. Delany could trace his lineage back to an African chieftain more convincingly than most of the many blacks who have made that claim. William Lloyd Garrison described him as "black as jet and a fine fellow of great energy and spirit." Frederick Douglass, with whom Delany worked for a while on *The North Star*, said that "when I, Fred Douglass, pray, I thank God for making me a man, but Delany thanks God for making him a *black* man." In one sense, Delany was really the father of the "black is beautiful" attitude of the 1960s.

When Delany was ten his parents moved to Chambersburg, Pennsylvania. His schooling began there. He later attended the Medical School of Harvard College, then under Oliver Wendell Holmes, but in less than a month the white students protested his presence. He was allowed to finish the term and then expelled. After further apprenticeship-type study, he became a practicing physician, first in Pittsburgh and later in Canada.

In 1839 Delany traveled extensively in what is now Louisiana and Texas and in other states in the Southwest, gathering materials to be used in his novel, *Blake*. In 1843 he began publishing in Pittsburgh *The Mystery*; this newspaper seems to have appeared regularly until 1847, when Delany became an assistant to Douglass, who was publishing *The North Star* in Rochester, New York.

In 1852 Delany published his best work, *The Condition, Elevation, Emigration, and Destiny of the Colored People of the United States, Politically Considered*. His primary objective was to encourage blacks to leave the United States for Central America. When attacked by abolitionists for his colonizing sympathies, Delany recanted, and in 1854 printed a speech entitled "Political Destiny of the Colored Race on the American Continent," which explained his former position. The 1852 work also contains short biographical sketches of the outstanding "literary and professional colored men and women" of Delany's era.

In the first issue of the *Anglo-African Magazine* (January 1959), several chapters of Delany's only novel, *Blake; or, The Huts of America*, appeared; others followed in later issues until there were twenty-four chapters in the *Anglo-African*. It was not until 1970 that the complete novel was published.

A descriptive announcement in the 1959 publication gives a general idea of the plot: "The scene is laid in Mississippi, the plot extending into Cuba; the hero being an educated West India Black, who deprived of his liberty by fraud when young and brought to the United States, in mature age, at the instance of his wife being sold from him, sought revenge through the medium of a deep laid secret organization."

A many-sided man, Delany was one of the first to advocate industrial education for blacks; he wrote several scientific works; he went exploring in Africa and later wrote *The Official Report of the Niger Valley Exploring Party*. He was commissioned as a major by President Abraham Lincoln, and sent to Charleston, South Carolina, where he raised two regiments of former slaves before the Civil War was over. In his late years, he became an important political figure in Reconstruction South Carolina.

An early treatment of Delany may be found in Vernon Loggins's, *The Negro Author* (1931) and in Benjamin Brawley's *Negro Builders and Heroes* (1937). Two important studies came out in 1971: *Martin R. Delany: The Beginnings of Black Nationalism* by Victor Ullman and *The Making of an Afro-American: Martin Robinson Delany* by Dorothy Sterling. During the period roughly between 1969 and 1972 several other studies and reprints were published, among them Sterling Stuckey's *The Ideological Origins of Black Nationalism* (1972), which contains Delany's *The Political Destiny of the Colored Race*. See also *The African Dream: Martin R. Delany and the Emergence of Pan-African Thought* by Cyril E. Griffith (1975) and Bernard W. Bell's *The Afro-American Novel and Its Traditon* (1987).

The following first three selections are from *Blake*; the last from *The Condition, Elevation, Emigration, and Destiny of the Colored People of the United States, Politically Considered* (1852, 1969). It is a chapter that gives a valuable list of outstanding pre-Civil War African Americans and of many of their publications.

HENRY AT LARGE

On leaving the plantation carrying them hanging upon his arm, thrown across his shoulders, and in his hands Henry had a bridle, halter, blanket, girt, and horsewhip, the emblems of a faithful servant in discharge of his master's business.

By shrewdness and discretion such was his management as he passed along, that he could tell the name of each place and proprietor, long before he reached them. Being a scholar, he carefully kept a record of the plantations he had passed, that when accosted by a white, as an overseer or patrol, he invariably pretended to belong to a back estate, in search of his master's race horse. If crossing a field, he was taking a near cut; but if met in a wood, the animal was in the forest, as being a great leaper no fence could debar him, though the forest was fenced and posted. The blanket a substitute for a saddle, was in reality carried for a bed. . . .

Reaching Alexandria with no obstruction, his first secret meeting was held in the hut of aunt Dilly. Here he found them all ready for an issue.

"An dis you chile?" said the old woman, stooping with age, sitting on a low stool in the chimney corner; "dis many day, I heahn on yeh!" though Henry had just entered on his mission. From Alexandria he passed rapidly on to Latuer's making no immediate stops, preferring to organize at the more prominent places.

This is a mulatto planter, said to have come from the isle of Guadaloupe. Riding down the road upon a pony at a quick gallop, was a mulatto youth a son of the planter, an old black man on foot keeping close to the horse's heels.

"Whose boy are you?" enquired the young mulatto, who had just dismounted, the old servant holding his pony.

"I'm in search of master's race horse."

"What is your name?" farther enquired the young mulatto.

"Gilbert sir."

"What do you want?"

"I am hungry sir."

"Dolly," said he to an old black woman at the woodpile; "show this man into the negro quarter, and give him something to eat; give him a cup of milk. Do you like milk my man?"

"Yes sir, I have no choice when hungry; anything will do."

"Da is none heah but claubah, maus Eugene," replied the old cook.

"Give him that," said the young master. "You people like that kind of stuff I believe; our negroes like it."

"Yes sir," replied Henry, when the lad left.

"God knows'e needn' talk 'bout wat we po' black folks eat, case da don' ghin us nothin' else but dat an' caun bread." muttered the old woman.

"Dont they treat you well, aunty?" enquired Henry.

"God on'y knows my chile, wat we suffeh."

"Who was that old man who ran behind your master's horse?"

"Dat Nathan, my husban'."

"Do they treat him well, aunty?"

"No chile, wus an' any dog, da beat' im foh little an nothin'."

"Is uncle Nathan religious?"

"Yes chile ole man an' I's been sahvin' God dis many day, fo yeh baun! Wen any on 'em in de house get sick, den da sen foh 'uncle Nathan' come pray foh dem; 'uncle Nathan' mighty good den!"

"Do you know that the Latuers are colored people?"

"Yes, chile; God bless yeh soul yes! Case huh mammy ony dead two-three yehs, an' she black as me."

"How did they treat her?"

"Not berry well; she nus da children; and eat in a house arter all done."

"What did Latuer's children call her?"

"Da call huh 'mammy,' same like wite folks children call de nus."

"Can you tell me aunty why they treat you people so badly, knowing themselves to be colored, and some of the slaves related to them?"

"God bless yeh hunny, de wite folks, dese plantehs make 'em so; da run heah, an' tell 'em da mus'n treat deh neggehs, well, case da spile 'em."

"Do the white planters frequently visit here?"

"Yes, hunny, yes, da heah some on 'em all de time eatin' an' drinkin' long wid de old man; da on'y tryin' get wat little 'e got, dat all! Da 'tend to be great frien' de ole man; but laws a massy hunny, I doh mine dese wite folks no how!"

"Does your master ever go to their houses and eat with them?"

"Yes chile, some time'e go, but den half on 'em got nothin' fit to eat; da hab fat poke an' bean, caun cake an' sich like, dat all da got, some on 'em."

"Does Mr. Latuer give them better at his table?"

"Laws hunny, yes; yes'n deed chile? 'E got mutton—some time whole sheep mos'—fowl, pig, an' ebery tum ting a nuddeh, 'e got so much ting dah, I haudly know wat cook fus."

"Do the white planters associate with the family of Latuer?"

"One on 'em, ten 'e coatin de dahta; I dont recon 'e gwine hab heh. Da cah fool long wid 'Toyeh's gals dat way."

"Whose girls, Metoyers?"

"Yes chile."

"Do you mean the wealthy planters of that name?"

"Dat same chile."

"Well, I want to understand you: You don't mean to say that they are colored people."

"Yes, hunny, yes; da good culed folks any body. Some five-six boys' an five-six gals on 'em; da all rich."

"How do they treat their slaves?"

"Da boys all mighty haud maustas, da gals all mighty good; sah-vants all like em."

"You seem to understand these people very well aunty. Now please tell me what kind of masters there are generally in the Red river country."

"Haud 'nough chile, haud 'nough, God on'y knows!"

"Do the colored masters treat theirs generally worse than the whites?"

"No hunny, 'bout da same."

"That's just what I want to know. What are the usual allowances for slaves?"

"Da 'low de fiel' han' two suit a yeah foh umin one long linen coat,* make suit, an' foh man, pantaloon an' jacket."

"How about eating?"

"Half peck meal ah day foh family uh fo!"

"What about weekly privileges? Do you have Saturday to your-selves?"

"Laud hunny, no! no chile, no! Da do'n 'low us no time, 'tall. Da 'low us ebery uddeh Sunday wash ouh close; dat all de time we git."

"Then you don't get to sell anything for yourselves?"

"No, hunny, no? Da don' 'low pig, chicken, tucky, goose, bean, pea, tateh, nothin' else."

"Well anuty, I'm glad to meet you, and as evening's drawing nigh, I must see your husband a little, then go."

"God bless yeh chile whah ebeh yeh go! Yeh ain' arteh no race-hos, dat yeh aint."

"You got something to eat my man, did you?" enquired the lad Eugene, at the conclusion of his interview with uncle Nathan.

"I did sir, and feasted well!" replied Henry in conclusion; "Good bye!" and he left for the next plantation suited to his objects.

"God bless de baby!" said old aunt Dolly as uncle Nathan entered the hut, referring to Henry.

"Ah, chile!" replied the old man with tears in his eyes; "My yeahs has heahn dis day!"

SOLICITUDE AND AMUSEMENT

. . . "Well, Judge as you wish to become a southerner, you must first 'see the sights,' as children say, and learn to get used to them. I wish you to ride out with me to Captain Grason's, and you'll see some rare sport; the most amusing thing I ever witnessed," suggested Franks.

"What is it?" enquired the Major.

"The effect is lost by previous knowledge of the thing," replied he. "This will suit you Armsted, as you're fond of negro jokes."

---

*Coat—a term used by slaves for frock.

"Then Colonel let's be off," urged the Major.

"Off it is!" replied Franks, as he invited the gentlemen to take a seat in the carriage already at the door.

"Halloo, halloo, here you are Colonel! Why major Armsted, old fellow, 'pon my word!" saluted Grason, grasping Armsted by the hand as they entered the porch.

"Judge Ballard! sir," said Armsted.

"Just in time for dinner gentlemen! Be seated," invited he holding the Judge by the hand. Welcome to Mississippi sir! What's up gentlemen?"

"We've come out to witness some rare sport the Colonel has been telling us about," replied the major.

"Blamed if I don't think the Colonel will have me advertised as a showman presently! I've got a queer animal here; I'll show him to you after dinner," rejoined Grason: "Gentlemen, help yourself to brandy and water."

Dinner over, the gentlemen walked into the pleasure grounds, in the rear of the mansion.

"Nelse, where is Rube? Call him!" said Grason to a slave lad, brother to the boy he sent for.

Shortly there came forward, a small black boy about eleven years of age, thin visage, projecting upper teeth, rather ghastly consumptive look, and emaciated condition. The child trembled with fears as he approached the group.

"Now gentlemen," said Grason, "I'm going to show you a sight!" having in his hand a long whip, the cracking of which he commenced, as a ring master in the circus.

The child gave him a look never to be forgotten; a look beseeching mercy and compassion. But the decree was made, and though humanity quailed in dejected supplication before him, the command was imperative, with no living hand to stay the pending consequences. He must submit to his fate, and pass through the ordeal of training.

"Wat maus gwine do wid me now? I know wat maus gwine do," said this miserable child; "he gwine make me see sights!" when going down on his hands and feet, he commenced trotting around like an animal.

"Now gentlemen, look!" said Grason; "he'll whistle, sing songs, hymns, pray, swear like a trooper, laugh, and cry, all under the same state of feelings."

With a peculiar swing of the whip, bringing the lash down upon a certain spot on the exposed skin, the whole person being prepared for the purpose, the boy commenced to whistle almost like a thrush; another cut changed it to a song, another to a hymn, then a pitiful prayer, then he gave utterance to oaths which would make a Christian shudder, after which he laughed outright; then from the fullness of his soul he cried:

"O, maussa, I's sick! Please stop little!" casting up gobs of hemorrhage.[†]

Franks stood looking on with unmoved muscles. Armsted stood aside whittling a stick; but when Ballard saw, at every cut the flesh turn open in gashes streaming down with gore, till at last in agony he appealed for mercy, he involuntary found his hand with a grasp on the whip, arresting its further application.

"Not quite a southerner yet Judge, if you can't stand that!" said Franks on seeing him wiping away the tears.

"Gentlemen help yourself to brandy and water. The little negro don't stand it nigh so well as formerly. He used to be a trump!"

"Well Colonel," said the Judge; "as I have to leave for Jackson this evening, I suggest that we return to the city."

The company now left Grason's, Franks for the enjoyment of home, Ballard and Armsted for Jackson, and the poor boy Reuben from hemorrhage of the lungs, that evening left time for eternity.

⚬⚬⚬

Busying about the breakfast for herself and other servants about the house—the white members of the family all being absent—mammy Judy for a time lost sight of the expected arrival. Soon however, a hasty footstep arrested her attention, when on looking around it proved to be Henry who came smiling up the yard.

"How'd you do mammy! how's Mag' and the boy?" inquired he, grasping the old woman by the hand.

She burst into a flood of tears, throwing herself upon him.

"What is the matter!" exclaimed Henry, "is Maggie dead?"

"No chile," with increased sobs she replied, "much betteh she wah."

"My God! has she disgraced herself?"

"No chile, may be betteh she dun so, den she bin heah now an' not sole. Maus Stephen sell eh case she!—I dun'o, reckon dat's da reason!"

"What!—Do you tell me mammy she had better disgraced herself than been sold! By the—!"

"So, Henry! yeh ain' gwine swah! hope yeh ain' gwine lose yeh 'ligion? Do'n do so; put yeh trus' in de Laud, he is suffishen fah all!"

"Don't tell me about religion! What's religion to me? My wife is

---

[†]This is a true Mississippi scene.

sold away from me by a man who is one of the leading members of
the very church to which both she and I belong! Put my trust in the
Lord! I have done so all my life nearly, and of what use is it to me?
My wife is sold from me just the same as if I did n't. I'll—"

"Come, come, Henry, yeh mus'n talk so; we is po' weak an' bline
cretehs, an' cah see de way uh da Laud. He move' in a mystus way,
his wundahs to puhfaum."

"So he may, and what is all that to me? I don't gain anything by
it, and—"

"Stop, Henry, stop! ain' de Laud bless yo' soul? ain' he take yeh
foot out de miah an' clay, an' gib yeh hope da uddah side dis vale ub
teahs?"

"I'm tired looking the other side; I want a hope this side of the
vale of tears. I want something on this earth as well as a promise of
things in another world. I and my wife have been both robbed of
our liberty, and you want me to be satisfied with a hope of heaven. I
won't do any such thing; I have waited long enough on heavenly
promises; I'll wait no longer. I—"

"Henry, wat de mauttah wid yeh? I neveh heah yeh talk so fo'—
yeh sin in de sight ub God; yeh gone clean back, I reckon. De good
Book tell us, a tousan' yeahs wid man, am but a day wid de Laud.
Boy, yeh got wait de Laud own pinted time."

"Well mammy, it is useless for me to stand here and have the
same gospel preached into my ears by you, that I have all my life
time heard from my enslavers. My mind is made up, my course is
laid out, and if life last, I'll carry it out. I'll go out to the place to-
day, and let them know that I have returned."

"Sho boy! what yeh gwine do, bun house down? Bettah put yeh
trus' in de Laud!" concluded the old woman.

"You have too much religion mammy for me to tell you what I
intend doing," said Henry in conclusion.

After taking up his little son, impressing on his lips and cheeks
kisses for himself and tears for his mother, the intelligent slave left
the abode of the care-worn old woman, for that of his master at the
cotton place.

Henry was a black—a pure negro—handsome, manly and intelligent, in size comparing well with his master, but neither so fleshy
nor heavy built in person. A man of good literary attainments—unknown to Col. Franks, though he was aware he could read and
write—having been educated in the West Indies, and decoyed away
when young. His affection for wife and child was not excelled by
colonel Franks for his. He was bold, determined and courageous, but
always mild, gentle and courteous, though impulsive when an occasion demanded his opposition.

Going immediately to the place, he presented himself before his master. Much conversation ensued concerning the business which had been entrusted to his charge, all of which was satisfactorily transacted, and full explanations concerning the horses, but not a word was uttered concerning the fate of Maggie, the Colonel barely remarking "your mistress is unwell."

After conversing till a late hour, Henry was assigned a bed in the great house, but sleep was far from his eyes. He turned and changed upon his bed with restlessness and anxiety, impatiently awaiting a return of the morning.

Early on Tuesday morning in obedience to his master's orders, Henry was on his way to the city, to get the house in readiness for the reception of his mistress, Mrs. Franks having much improved in three or four days. Mammy Judy had not yet risen when he knocked at the door.

"Hi Henry! yeh heah ready! huccum yeh git up so soon; arter some mischif I reckon? Do'n reckon yeh arter any good!" saluted mammy Judy.

"No mammy," replied he; "no mischief, but like a good slave such as you wish me to be, come to obey my master's will, just what you like to see."

"Sho boy! none yeh nonsens'; huccum I want yeh bey maus Stephen? Git dat nonsens' in yeh head las' night long so, I reckon! Wat dat yeh gwine do now?"

"I have come to dust and air the mansion for their reception. They have sold my wife away from me, and who else would do her work?" This reply excited the apprehension of mammy Judy.

"Wat yeh gwine do Henry? yeh arter no good; yeh ain' gwine 'tack maus Stephen is yeh?"

"What do you mean mammy, strike him?"

"Yes! reckon yeh ain' gwine him 'im?"

"Curse—!"

"Henry, Henry, membeh wat ye 'fess! fah de Laud sake, yeh ain gwine take to swahin?" interrupted the old woman.

"I make no profession mammy. I once did believe in religion, but now I have no confidence in it. My faith has been wrecked on the stony hearts of such pretended Christians as Stephen Franks, while passing through the stormy sea of trouble and oppression! and—"

"Hay, boy! yeh is gittin high! yeh call maussa 'Stephen?'"

"Yes, and I'll never call him 'master' again, except when compelled to do so."

"Bettah g'long ten' t' de house fo' wite folks come, an' nebeh mine talkin' 'bout fightin' 'long wid maus Stephen. Wat yeh gwine do wid wite folks? Sho!"

"I don't intend to fight him, mammy Judy, but I'll attack him concerning my wife, if the words be my last! Yes, I'll—!" and pressing his lips to suppress the words, the outraged man turned away from the old slave mother, with such feelings as only an intelligent slave could realize.

The orders of the morning were barely executed, when the carriage came to the door. The bright eyes of the foot boy Tony sparkled when he saw Henry approaching the carriage.

"Well Henry! ready for us?" enquired his master.

"Yes sir," was the simple reply. "Mistress!" he saluted, politely bowing as he took her hand to assist her from the carriage.

"Come Henry, my man, get out the riding horses," ordered Franks after a little rest.

"Yes sir."

A horse for the Colonel and lady each, was soon in readiness at the door, but none for himself, it always having been the custom in their morning rides, for the maid and man-servant to accompany the mistress and master.

"Ready did you say?" enquired Franks on seeing but two horses standing at the stile.

"Yes sir."

"Where's the other horse?"

"What for sir?"

"What for? yourself to be sure!"

"Colonel Franks!" said Henry, looking him sternly in the face, "when I last rode that horse in company with you and lady, *my wife* was at my side, and I will not now go without her! Pardon me—my life for it, I won't go!"

"Not another word you black imp!" exclaimed Franks, with an uplifted staff in a rage, "or I'll strike you down in an instant!"

"Strike away if you will sir, I dont care—I wont go without my wife!"

"You impudent scoundrel! I'll soon put an end to your conduct! I'll put you on the auction block, and sell you to the negro traders."

"Just as soon as you please sir, the sooner the better, as I dont want to live with you any longer!"

"Hold your tongue sir, or I'll cut it out of your head! you ungrateful black dog! Really things have come to a pretty pass, when I must take impudence off my own negro! By gracious!—God forgive me for the expression—I'll sell every negro I have first! I'll dispose of him to the hardest negro trader I can find!" said Franks in a rage.

"You may do your mightiest, colonel Franks. I'm not your slave, nor never was, and you know it! and but for my wife and her people, I never would have staid with you till now. I was decoyed away when young, and then became entangled in such domestic relations as to induce me to remain with you; but now the tie is broken! I know that the odds are against me, but never mind!"

"Do you threaten me, sir! Hold your tongue, or I'll take your life instantly, you villain!"

"No sir, I dont threaten you, colonel Franks, but I do say that I wont be treated like a dog. You sold my wife away from me, after always promising that she should be free. And more than that, you sold her because—! and now you talk about whipping me. Shoot me, sell me, or do anything else you please, but dont lay your hands on me, as I will not suffer you to whip me!"

Running up to his chamber, colonel Franks seized a revolver, when Mrs. Franks grasping hold of his arm exclaimed—

"Colonel! what does all this mean?"

"Mean, my dear? It's rebellion! a plot—this is but the shadow of a cloud that's fast gathering around us! I see it plainly, I see it!" responded the Colonel, starting for the stairs.

"Stop Colonel!" admonished his lady, "I hope you'll not be rash. For Heaven's sake, do not stain your hands in blood!"

"I do not mean to, my dear! I take this for protection!" Franks hastening down stairs, when Henry had gone into the back part of the premises.

"Dah now! dah now!" exclaimed mammy Judy as Henry entered the kitchen, "see wat dis gwine back done foh yeh! Bettah put yo' trus' in de Laud! Henry, yeh gone clean back t'de wuhl ghin, yeh knows it!"

"You're mistaken mammy, I do trust the Lord as much as ever, but I now understand him better than I use to, that's all. I dont intend to be made a fool of any longer by false preaching."

"Henry!" interrogated daddy Joe, who apprehending difficulties in the case, had managed to get back to the house, "yeh gwine lose all yo' ligion? Wat yeh mean boy!"

"Religion!" replied Henry rebukingly, "that's always the cry with black people. Tell me nothing about religion when the very man who hands you the bread at communion, has sold your daughter away from you!"

"Den yeh 'fen' God case man 'fen' yeh! Take cah Henry, take cah! mine wat yeh 'bout; God is lookin' at yeh, an' if yeh no' willin' trus' 'im, yeh need'n call on 'im in time o' trouble."

"I dont intend, unless He does more for me then than He has done before. 'Time of need!' If ever man needed his assistance, I'm sure I need it now."

"Yeh do'n know wat yeh need; de Laud knows bes'. On'y trus' in 'im, an' 'e bring yeh out mo' nah conkah. By de help o' God I's heah dis day, to gib yeh cumfut!"

"I have trusted in Him daddy Joe, all my life, as I told mammy Judy this morning, but—"

"Ah boy, yeh's gwine back! Dat on't do Henry, dat on't do!"

"Going back from what? my oppressor's religion! If I could only get rid of his inflictions as easily as I can his religion, I would be this day a free man, when you might then talk to me about 'trusting.'"

"Dis Henry, am one uh de ways ob de Laud; 'e fus 'flicks us an' den he bless us."

"Then it's a way I dont like."

"Mine how yeh talk, boy!"

> " 'God moves in a myst'us way
> His wundahs to pehfaum,' an—' "

"He moves too slow for me daddy Joe; I'm tired waiting so—"

"Come Henry, I hab no sich talk like dat! yeh is gittin' rale weaked; yeh gwine let de debil take full 'session on yeh! Take cah boy, mine how yeh talk!"

"It is not wickedness, daddy Joe; you dont understand these things at all. If a thousand years with us is but a day with God, do you think that I am required to wait all that time?"

"Dont Henry, dont! de wud say 'Stan' still an' see de salbation.' "

"That's no talk for me daddy Joe, I've been 'standing still' long enough; I'll 'stand still' no longer."

"Den yeh no call t' bey God wud? Take cah boy, take cah!"

"Yes I have, and I intend to obey it, but that part was intended for the Jews, a people long since dead. I'll obey that intended for me."

"How yeh gwine bey it?"

" 'Now is the accepted time, to-day is the day of salvation.' So you see, daddy Joe, this is very different to standing still."

"Ah boy, I's feahed yeh's losen yeh 'ligion!"

"I tell you once for all daddy Joe, that I'm not only 'losing,' but I have altogether lost my faith in the religion of my oppressors. As they are our religious teachers, my estimate of the thing they give, is no greater than it is for those who give it."

With elbows upon his knees, and face resting in the palms of his hands, daddy Joe for some time sat with his eyes steadily fixed on the floor, whilst Ailcey who for a part of the time had been an auditor to the conversation, went into the house about her domestic duties.

"Never mind Henry! I hope it will not always be so with you. You have been kind and faithful to me and the Colonel, and I'll do anything I can for you!" sympathetically said Mrs. Franks, who hav-

ing been a concealed spectator of the interview between Henry and
the old people, has just appeared before them.

Wiping away the emblems of grief which stole down his face,
with a deep toned voice, upgushing from the recesses of a more than
iron-pierced soul, he enquired—

"Madam, what can you do! Where is my wife?" To this, Mrs.
Franks gave a deep sigh. "Never mind, never mind!" continued he,
"yes, I will mind, and by—!"

"O! Henry, I hope you've not taken to swearing! I do hope you
will not give over to wickedness! Our afflictions should only make
our faith the stronger."

" 'Wickedness!' Let the righteous correct the wicked, and the
Christian condemn the sinner!"

"That is uncharitable in you Henry! as you know I have always
treated you kindly, and God forbid that I should consider myself any
less than a Christian! and I claim as much at least for the Colonel,
though like frail mortals he is liable to err at times."

"Madam!" said he with suppressed emotion—starting back a pace
or two—"do you think there is anything either in or out of hell so
wicked, as that which colonel Franks has done to my wife, and now
about to do to me? For myself I care not—my wife!"

"Henry!" said Mrs. Franks, gently placing her hand upon his
shoulder, "there is yet a hope left for you, and you will be faithful
enough I know, not to implicate any person; it is this: Mrs. Van
Winter, a true friend of your race, is shortly going to Cuba on a
visit, and I will arrange with her to purchase you through an agent
on the day of your sale, and by that means you can get to Cuba,
where probably you may be fortunate enough to get the master of
your wife to become your purchaser."

"Then I have two chances!" replied Henry.

Just then Ailcey thrusting her head in the door, requested the
presence of her mistress in the parlor.

Henry passed directly around and behind the house.

"See, ole man, see! reckon 'e gwine dah now!" whispered mammy
Judy, on seeing Henry pass through the yard without going into the
kitchen.

"Whah?" enquired daddy Joe.

"Dun'o out yandah, whah 'e gwine way from wite folks!" she replied.

The interview between Franks and the trader Harris was not over
half an hour duration, the trader retiring, Franks being prompt and
decisive in all of his transactions, making little ceremony.

So soon as the front door was closed, Ailcey smiling bore into
the kitchen a half pint glass of brandy, saying that her master had
sent it to the old people.

The old man received it with compliments to his master, pouring it into a black jug in which there was both tansy and garlic, highly recommending it as a 'bitters' and certain antidote for worms, for which purpose he and the old woman took of it as long as it lasted, though neither had been troubled with that particular disease since the days of their childhood.

"Wat de gwine do wid yeh meh son?" enquired mammy Judy as Henry entered the kitchen.

"Sell me to the soul-drivers! what else would they do?"

"Yeh gwin 'tay 'bout till de git yeh?"

"I shant move a step! and let them do their—!"

"Maus wants to see yeh in da front house Henry," interrupted Ailcey, he immediately obeying the summons.

"Heah dat now!" said mammy Judy, as Henry followed the maid out of the kitchen.

"Carry this note sir, directly to captain Jack Harris!" ordered Franks, handing to Henry a sealed note. Receiving it, he bowed politely, going out of the front door, directly to the slave prison of Harris.

"Eh heh! I see," said Harris on opening the note; "colonel Frank's boy; walk in here;" passing through the office into a room which proved to be the first department of the slave-prison. "No common negro I see! you're a shade higher. A pretty deep shade too! Can read, write cipher; a good religious fellow, and has a Christian and sir name. The devil you say! Who's your father? Can you preach?"

"I have never tried," was the only reply.

"Have you ever been a member of Congress?" continued Harris with ridicule.

To this Henry made no reply.

"Wont answer hey! beneath your dignity. I understand that you're of that class of gentry who dont speak to common folks! You're not quite well enough dressed for a gentleman of your cloth. Here! Mr. Henry, I'll present you with a set of ruffles: give yourself no trouble sir, as I'll dress you! I'm here for that purpose," said Harris, fastening upon the wrists of the manly bondman, a heavy pair of handcuffs.

"You hurt my wrist!" admonished Henry

"New clothing will be a little tight when first put on. Now sir!" continued the trader, taking him to the back door and pointing into the yard at the slave gang there confined; "as you have been respectably dressed, walk out and enjoy yourself among the ladies and gentleman there; you'll find them quite a select company."

Shortly after this the sound of the bell-ringer's voice was heard— a sound which usually spread terror among the slaves: "Will be sold this afternoon at three o'clock by public outcry, at the slave-prison

of captain John Harris, a likely choice negro-fellow, the best trained
body servant in the state, trained to the business by the most accomplished lady and gentleman negro-trainers in the Mississippi Valley.
Sale positive without a proviso."

"Dah, dah! did'n eh tell yeh so? Ole man, ole man! heah dat
now! Come heah. Dat jis what I been tellin on im, but 'e uden blieve
me!"

LITERARY AND PROFESSIONAL COLORED MEN AND WOMEN

Dr. James McCune Smith, a graduate of the Scientific and Medical
Schools of the University of Glasgow, has for the last fifteen years,
been a successful practitioner of medicine and surgery in the city of
New York. Dr. Smith is a man of no ordinary talents, and stands
high as a scholar and gentleman in the city, amidst the *literati* of a
hundred seats of learning.

In 1843, when the character of the colored race was assailed to
disparagement, by the representative of a combination of maligners,
such was the influence of the Doctor, that the citizens at once
agreed to give their presence to a fair public discussion of the subject—the Comparative Anatomy and Physiology of the races. This
discussion was kept up for several evenings, attended by large and
fashionable assemblages of ladies and gentlemen, until it closed.
Doctor Smith, in the estimation of the audience, easily triumphed
over his antagonist, who had made this a studied subject. The Doctor is the author of several valuable productions, and in 1846, a very
valuable scientific paper, issued from the press in pamphlet form, on
the "Influence of Climate on Longevity, with special reference to Life
Insurance." This paper, we may surmise, was produced in refutation
of the attempt at a physiological disquisition on the part of Hon.
John C. Calhoun, United States Senator, on the colored race, which
met with considerable favor from some quarters, until the appearance of Dr. Smith's pamphlet—since when, we have heard nothing
about Calhoun's learned argument. It may be well to remark, that
Senator Calhoun read medicine before he read law, and it would
have been well for him if he had left medical subjects remain where
he left them, for law. We extract a simple note of explanation without the main argument, to show with what ease the Doctor refutes
an absurd argument: "The reason why the proportion of mortality is
not a measure of longevity, is the following:—The proportion of
mortality is a statement of how many persons die in a population;
this, of course, does not state the age at which those persons die. If

1 in 45 die in Sweden, and 1 in 22 in Grenada, the ages of the dead might be alike in both countries; here the greater mortality might actually accompany the greater longevity.". . .

About three months since, at a public meeting of scientific gentlemen, for the formation of a "Statistic Institute," Doctor Smith was nominated as one of five gentlemen, to draught a constitution. This, of course, anticipated his membership to the Institution. He, for a number of years, has held the office of Physician to the Colored Orphan Asylum, an excellent institution, at which he is the only colored officer. The Doctor is very learned.

Rev. Samuel Ringgold Ward was, for several years, pastor of a white congregation, in Courtlandville, N.Y., of the Congregational persuasion, and editor of an excellent newspaper, devoted to the religious elevation of that denomination. Mr. Ward is a man of great talents—his fame is widespread as an orator and man of learning, and needs no encomium from us. His name stood on nomination for two or three years, as Liberty-party candidate for Vice President of the United States. Mr. Ward has embraced the legal profession, and intends to practise law. Governor Seward said of him, that he "never heard true eloquence until he heard Samuel R. Ward speak." Mr. Ward has recently left the United States, for Canada West, and is destined to be a great statesman.

Rev. Henry Highland Garnett, was also the pastor of a white congregation, in Troy, N.Y. Mr. Garnett is a graduate of Oneida Institute, a speaker of great pathetic eloquence, and has written several valuable pamphlets. In 1844, Mr. Garnett appeared before the Judiciary Committee of the Legislature at the capital, in behalf of the rights of the colored citizens of the State, and in a speech of matchless eloquence, he held them for four hours spell-bound.

He has also been co-editor of a newspaper, which was conducted with ability. As a token of respect, the "Young Men's Literary Society of Troy," elected him a life-member—and he was frequently solicited to deliver lectures before different lyceums. Mr. Garnett left the United States in the summer of 1849, and now resides in England, where is is highly esteemed.

Rev. James William Charles Pennington, D.D., a clergyman of New York city, was born in Maryland,—left when young—came to Brooklyn—educated himself—studied divinity—went to Hartford, Conn.;—took charge of a Presbyterian congregation of colored people—went to England—returned—went to the West Indies—returned—was called to the Shiloh Presbyterian Colored Congregation—was sent a Delegate to the Peace Congress at Paris, in 1849, preached there, and attended the National Levee at the mansion of the Foreign Secretary of State, Minister De Tocqueville;

and had the degree of *Doctor of Divinity* conferred on him by the ancient time-honored University of Heidelberg, in Germany.

Dr. Pennington is very learned in theology, has fine literary attainments, and has written several useful pamphlets, and contributed to science, by the delivery of lectures before several scientific institutions in Europe.

He has, by invitation, delivered lectures before the "Glasgow Young Men's Christian Association;" and "St. George's Biblical, Literary, and Scientific Institute," London. In one of the discourses, the following extract will give an idea of the style and character of the speaker:—"One of the chief attributes of the mind is a desire for freedom; but it has been the great aim of slavery to extinguish that desire."

"To extinguish this attribute would be to extinguish mind itself. Every faculty which the master puts forth to subdue the slave, is met by a corresponding one in the latter." . . . "Christianity is the highest and most perfect form of civilization. It contains the only great standard of the only true and perfect standard of civilization. When tried by this standard, we are compelled to confess, that we have not on earth, one strictly civilized nation; for so long as the sword is part of a nation's household furniture, it cannot be called strictly civilized; and yet there is not a nation, great or small, black or white, that has laid aside the sword." . . . The Doctor has been editor of a newspaper, which was ably conducted. He belongs to the Third Presbytery of New York, and stands very high as a minister of the Gospel, and gentleman.

Charles Lenox Remond, Esq., of Salem, Massachusetts, is among the most talented men of the country. Mr. Remond is a native of the town he resides in, and at an early age, evinced more than ordinary talents. At the age of twenty-one, at which time (1832) the cause of the colored people had just begun to attract public attention, he began to take an interest in public affairs, and was present for the first time, at the great convention of colored men, of that year, at which the distinguished colonization gentlemen named in another part of this work, among them, Rev. R. R. Gurley, and Elliot Cresson, Esqs., were present. At this convention, we think, Mr. Remond made his virgin speech. From that time forth he became known as an orator, and now stands second to no living man as a declaimer. This is his great forte, and to hear him speak, sends a thrill through the whole system, and a tremor through the brain.

In 1835, he went to England, making a tour of the United Kingdom, where he remained for two years, lecturing with great success; and if we mistake not was presented the hospitality of one of the towns of Scotland, at which he received a token of respect, in a code of resolutions adopted expressive of the sentiments of the people, signed by the town officers, inscribed to "Charles Lenox Remond, Esq.," a form of address never given in the United Kingdom, only where the person is held in the highest esteem for their attainments; the "Mr." always being used instead.

In Syracuse, N.Y., resides George Boyer Vashon, Esq., A.M., a graduate of Oberlin Collegiate Institute, Attorney at Law, Member of the Syracuse Bar. Mr. Vashon, is a ripe scholar, an accomplished Essayist, and a chaste classic Poet; his style running very much in the strain of Byron's best efforts. He probably takes Byron as his model, and Childe Harold, as a sample, as in his youthful days, he was a fond admirer of George Gordon Noel Byron, always calling his whole name, when he named him. His Preceptor in Law, was the Honorable Walter, Judge Forward, late Controller, subsequently, Secretary of the Treasury of the United States, and recently *Charge de Affaires* [sic] to Denmark, now President of the Bench of the District Court of the Western District of Pennsylvania.

Mr. Vashon was admitted to the Bar of the city of New York, in the fall of 1847, to practise in all the Courts of the State. He immediately subsequently, sailed to the West Indies, from whence he returned in the fall of 1850. He has contributed considerably to a number of the respectable journals of the country.

Miss Eliza Greenfield the Black Swan, is among the most extraordinary persons of the present century. Being raised in obscurity, inured to callings far beneath her propensity, and unsuited to her taste, she had a desire to cultivate her talents, but no one to encourage her. Whenever she made the effort, she was discouraged—perhaps ridiculed; and thus discouraged, she would shrink again from her anxious task. She knew she could sing, and knew she could sing unlike any body else; knew she sung better than any whom she had heard of the popular singers, but could not tell why others could not think with, and appreciate her. In this way it seems she was thrown about for three years, never meeting with a person who could fully appreciate her talents; and we have it from her own lips, that not until after the arrival of Jenny Lind and Parodi in the country, was she aware of the high character of her own talents. She knew she possessed them, because they were inherent, inseparable with her being. She attended the Concerts of Mad'll. [sic] Jenny Lind, and Operas of Parodi, and at once saw the "secret of their success"—they possessed talents, that no other popular singers mastered.

She went home; her heart fluttered; she stole an opportunity when no one listened, to mock or gossip; let out her voice, when *ecce!* she found her strains *four* notes *above* Sweden's favored Nightingale; she descended, when lo! she found her tones *three* notes *be-*

low! she thanked God with a "still small voice;" and now, she ranks second in point of voice, to no vocalist in the world. Miss Greenfield, if she only be judicious and careful, may become yet, in point of popularity, what Miss Lind was. The Black Swan, is singing to fine fashionable houses, and bids fair to stand unrivalled in the world of Song.

William C. Nell, of Rochester, N.Y., formerly of Boston, has long been known as a gentleman of chaste and lofty sentiments, and a pure philanthropist. Mr. Nell, in company with Mr. Frederick Douglass, was present by invitation, and took his seat at table, at the celebration of Franklin's Birth Day, by the Typographical and Editorial corps of Rochester. In 1850, being again residing in Boston, he was nominated and ran for the Legislature of Massachusetts, by the Free Soil party of Essex county. Mr. Nell stood even with his party vote in the District.

He recently issued from the Boston press a Pamphlet, on the colored men who served in the wars of the United States of 1776, and 1812. This pamphlet is very useful as a book of reference on this subject, and Mr. Nell, of course does not aim at a full historical view. The circumstances under which it was got out, justify this belief. He was collecting materials in the winter of 1850–'51, when he was taken down to his bed with a severe attack of disease of one of his lungs, with which he lingered, unable to leave his room for weeks. In the spring, recovering somewhat his health, so as to go out—during this time, he had the little pamphlet published, as a means of pecuniary aid, promising another part to be forthcoming some subsequent period, which the writer hopes may soon be issued. Mr. Nell, is an excellent man, and deserves the patronage of the public.

Rev. Daniel A. Payne, commenced his literary career in Charleston, South Carolina, where he taught school for some time. In 1833 or 1834, he came North, placing himself in the Lutheran Theological Seminary, at Gettysburg, under the tutorage of the learned and distinguished Dr. Schmucker, where he finished his education as a Lutheran clergyman. To extend his usefulness, he joined the African Methodist Connexion, and for several years resided in Baltimore, where he taught an Academy for colored youth and maidens, gaining the respect and esteem of all who had the fortune to become acquainted with him. He is now engaged travelling and collecting information, for the publication of a history of one of the colored Methodist denominations in the United States. Mr. Payne is a pure and chaste poet, having published a small volume of his productions in 1850, under the title of "Pleasures and other Miscellaneous Poems, by Daniel A. Payne," issued from the press of Sherwood and Company, Baltimore, Maryland.

John B. Russworm, a gentleman of splendid talents, graduated at Bowdoin College, many years ago. Mr. Russworm was a class-mate of Honorable John P. Hale, United States Senator, and after leaving College as his first public act, commenced the publication of a newspaper, for the elevation of colored Americans, called "Freedom's Journal." Subsequently to the publication of his paper, Mr. Russworm became interested in the Colonization scheme, then in its infancy, and went to Liberia; after which he went to Bassa Cove, of which place he was made governor, where he died in 1851.

Henry Bibb, an eloquent speaker, for several years, was the principal traveling lecturer for the Liberty Party of Michigan. Mr. Bibb, with equal advantages, would equal many of those who fill high places in the country, and now assume superiority over him and his kindred. He fled an exile from the United States, in 1850, to Canada, to escape the terrible consequences of the Republican Fugitive Slave Law, which threatened him with a total destruction of liberty. Mr. Bibb established the "Voice of the Fugitive," a newspaper, in Sandwich, Canada West, which is managed and conducted with credit.

James M. Whitfield, of Buffalo, New York, though in an humble position, (for which we think he is somewhat reprehensible,) is one of the purest poets in America. He has written much for different newspapers; and, by industry and application—being already a good English scholar—did he but place himself in a favorable situation in life, would not be second to John Greenleaf Whittier, nor the late Edgar A. Poe.

Sojourner Truth

(c. 1797–1883)

BORN A SLAVE in Ulster County, New York, Isabella Baumfree (or Bome-free) was sold many times in the course of the next eighteen years. During this time she married a fellow slave and had five children, all but one of whom were taken away and probably sold into slavery.

Freed under the New York State Emancipation Act of 1827, Isabella took her only remaining child and moved to New York City, where she joined a religious cult. The group involved her in a sordid scandal—including a charge of murder. She sued her accuser for libel and was exonerated; the judgment of $125 which she won was an exceptional triumph for a slave.

Isabella Baumfree was deeply religious and inclined toward mysticism; she saw visions and heard voices. Following one such experience she announced that a spirit had commanded her to go forth "to declare the truth to the people," and that she was no longer Isabella, but "Sojourner Truth." For the next thirty years she roamed the land, turning up at antislavery gatherings, woman's rights conventions, and religious revivals. Bidden or unbidden, Sojourner Truth always spoke, sometimes rising from her seat in the audience to counter remarks and arguments with which she disagreed. Though uneducated, she was a moving and dramatic speaker. Her fame spread throughout the East and Midwest and into Canada. She was in the forefront of many movements and the disciple of many "radical" ideas. When Lincoln received her late in 1861, she urged upon him the enlistment of free blacks to fight in defense of the Union.

After the war Sojourner Truth remained in demand as a speaker, but she felt that her work was done. Friends and admirers helped her to buy a small house in Battle Creek, Michigan, where she died in 1883.

For an excellent and authoritative article on Sojourner Truth, see the entry by Jacqueline De St. Bernard in *Dictionary of American Literary Biography*, also Bernard's *Journey Towards Freedom: The Story of Sojourner Truth* (1967), and the entry by J. Saunders Redding in *Notable American Women, 1607–1950* (1971–3). In *Her Name Was Sojourner Truth* (1962), Hertha Pauli, making use of Olive Gilbert's work on the original *Narrative of Sojourner Truth* (1850), extended considerably our knowledge of this "freedom fighter." In 1983, Mark Dunster published a twelve-page drama titled "Sojourner Truth: A Play." Also see Gloria Joseph's article, "Sojourner

Truth: Archetypal Black Feminist" in *Wild Women in the Whirlwind* (1989), edited by Joanne Braxton and Audrée McLaughlin.

The following selection is representative of Sojourner Truth's dramatic speeches; its delivery was highlighted by her ripping open her dress to expose her breasts. There is no exact copy of this speech, which was given at a woman's rights convention in Akron, Ohio, in 1852. The following selection is based on fragments that have survived and were put in this form by Arthur Huff Fauset in his *Sojourner Truth: God's Faithful Pilgrim* (1938), the first modern biographical work on this fascinating woman.

"AND ARN'T I A WOMAN?"*

As Sojourner made her way to the platform, a hissing sound of disapproval rushed through the room—the kind of sound which in America only a Negro is likely to experience and understand; a sound which says, "You don't belong. You have nothing to do with this."

Unmindful and unafraid, the old black woman moved on, with slowness and solemnity, to the front. Then she laid her old bonnet at her feet and, fastening her great, speaking eyes upon the chairman, she sought permission to address the group.

There she stands before the chairman, with all those hissing sounds rushing through her ears. Does she know an ounce of fear? What!

. . . After a half century of locking horns with a hundred varieties of demoniacal opposition. . . . what mattered one more crowd? Who were these people anyway that they imagined they could make laws just to suit themselves—ministers, thugs, and barbarians? They with their laws about Negroes, laws about women, laws about property and about everything under the sun. . . . There was only one Lawgiver. He could make these picayune creatures fly, law or no law. He was on *her* side; assuredly He was *not* on their side.

She stands before the lady in the chair, looking with confident, unafraid, expectant eyes. That lady cannot refuse her petition to speak; she cannot help herself if she wants to.

The chairman turns to the audience and announces with befitting simplicity, "Sojourner Truth has a word. I beg of you to listen for a few moments."

---

*Title supplied by editors.

With electrical rapidity the air cleared. The hubbub gave way to absolute silence.

Here was was something unusually strange. Queer. Unheard of. Almost inconceivable. *Impossible.*

But there she was, a black woman, unwanted, even despised. Still it will be something rare to see what she will make out of the few minutes which have been given over to her.

Every eye fixes on the tall angular form. Her chin high, her eyes gleaming, yet seeming more a part of some faraway body than of that quiet poised person in whose head they shine, she stands for an instant and appraises her audience. Then slowly, with measured accent, quietly, and in that low deeply placed tone of voice which has made her name a byword in hundreds of cities and hamlets, she begins to hurl the darts of wit and intelligence which are to leave these listeners forever changed creatures. It is one of the few times that a speech of Sojourner's has come down to us in its pristine form, so that we know exactly the kind of language and dialect she employed, and what it was in her speeches that brought people of the highest grade of intelligence and training under her spell.

"Well, chillun," she began with that familiarity which came to her so readily, whether she was addressing God or man, "whar dar is so much racket, dar must be something out o' kilter."

The audience waited with unfeigned curiosity for the resolution which her statement implied.

"I t'ink dat 'twixt de niggers of de Souf an' de women at de Norf' all a-talkin' 'bout rights, de white men will be in a fix pretty soon.

"But what's all dis here talkin' about?"

She wheeled round in the direction of one of the previous speakers. He, probably, was none too pleased to have her attention focussed on him.

"Dat man ober dar say dat women needs to be helped into carriages, and lifted ober ditches, and to have de best place everywhere. . . . Nobody eber helped *me* into carriages, or ober mud puddles, or give *me* any best place!"

She raised herself to her full height and in a voice as rumbling as thunder roared, "And arn't *I* a woman?"

A low murmur advanced through the crowd.

"Look at me," she continued. "Look at my arm."

She bared her right arm to the shoulder and dramatically demonstrated its great muscular power.

"I have plowed and planted and gathered into barns"—her voice was singing into the ether—"and no man could head me—and arn't *I* a woman?"

The murmur became more vocal.

"I have born'd five childrun and seen 'em mos' all sold off into slavery, and when I cried out with mother's grief, none but Jesus heard . . . and arn't *I* a woman?"

Notice the studied emphasis of her assertion of femininity. The oratorical genius of her race is symbolized by this unlettered woman's speech.

Sojourner perceived that the throng had been snared by her persuasive, ungrammatical rhetoric. She felt the power in her dramatic utterance, and she realized that she had smashed that vague and hypocritical symbolism which unthinking white men invariably create when they choose to boast about their deference to the opposite sex.

It was time now to launch out in another quarter.

"Den dey talks 'bout dis t'ing in de head—what dis dey call it?"

"Intellect," whispers someone near by.

"Dat's it, honey—intellect. . . . Now, what's dat got to do wit women's rights or niggers' rights?"

Then came one of those classic aphorisms which distinguish the creative thinker and orator from the mere spellbinder.

"If my cup won't hold but a pint, and yourn holds a quart, wouldn't ye be mean not to let me have my little half-measure full?"

Now the crowd, fickle as always, is delirious. It rocks the church with applause and cheers, and echoes its approval of her words by pointing scornful fingers at the minister whom a few minutes ago it had applauded for sentiments in exactly the opposite key.

"Den dat little man in black dar," she continued, referring to another minister (she can afford now to be droll and even derisive), "he say women can't have as much rights as man, 'cause Christ warn't a woman. . . . Whar did your Christ come from?" she thundered at him, her arms outstretched, her eyes shooting fire. This was a lightning thrust. The throng sat perfectly quiet.

Then, raising her voice as high as it was possible for her to do, she repeated the query.

"*Whar did your Christ come from?*"

She hesitated a moment, poised over the audience like a bird hovering just before a final swoop down upon its prey, then thundered, "From God and a woman! Man had nothing to do with him!"

The audience was overwhelmed. It could not endure so much logic and oratory at one time. Pandemonium broke loose.

But Sojourner was not quite through. She turned finally to the man who had made a deprecating gesture at Eve, and rebuked him.

"If de fust woman God ever made was strong enough to turn the world upside down, all alone—dese togedder ought to be able to turn it back and get it rightside up again; and now dey is asking to do it, de men better let 'em."

Amidst deafening cheering and stamping, Sojourner Truth, who had arisen to catcalls and hisses, could hardly make herself heard as she shouted in conclusion. "Bleeged to ye for hearin' on me; and now ole Sojourner hain't got nothing more to say."

Harriet E. Wilson

(1827 or 1828–?)

MOST OF WHAT we now know about Harriet E. Wilson, the author of *Our Nig*, is to be found in the 1983 landmark edition of this work, a work "resurrected" and edited by Henry Louis Gates, Jr. Because of its thoroughness and its distinction as a model of present-day literary scholarship, this edition should be consulted by the reader interested in Harriet E. Wilson and her novel. The title of this book, originally published in 1859, is indeed a full title: *Our Nig; or, Sketches from the Life of a Free Black, in a Two-Story White House, North. Showing that Slavery's Shadows Fall Even There*—by "Our Nig."

Our Nig, which has all of the tear-jerking qualities of nineteenth-century sentimental fiction, is—among other things—a strong statement on the anti-black attitude found all too often in the North. By no means a literary masterpiece, the novel is important. To it can be attibuted two "firsts"— the first novel by an American black to be *published* in America; the first to be written and published by a black woman. See the headnotes in this volume for William Wells Brown and for Frank J. Webb.

For additional critical comment on Wilson's pioneering work see Henry L. Gates's article on Wilson in *Dictionary of Literary Biography, Volume 50*. See also the following studies for further comment on Wilson's achievement: Bernard W. Bell's *The Afro-American Novel and Its Tradition* (1987); Hazel V. Carby's *Reconstructing Womanhood: The Emergence of the Afro-American Woman Novelist* (1987); and Gates's *Figures in Black* (1987).

The selections that follow are from chapter 2 of *Our Nig*, in which Frado (Nig), the central character, is abandoned and left in the hands of a cruel mistress, and chapter 6, which gives examples of Frado's brutal treatment. Frado, incidentally, is the offspring of a racially mixed marriage.

MY FATHER'S DEATH

Misery! we have known each other,
Like a sister and a brother,
Living in the same lone home
Many years—we must live some
Hours or ages yet to come.

SHELLEY

Jim, proud of his treasure,—a white wife,—tried hard to fulfill his
promises; and furnished her with a more comfortable dwelling, diet,
and apparel. It was comparatively a comfortable winter she passed
after her marriage. When Jim could work, all went on well. Industrious, and fond of Mag, he was determined she should not regret
her union to him. Time levied an additional charge upon him, in the
form of two pretty mulattos, whose infantile pranks amply repaid the
additional toil. A few years, and a severe cough and pain in his side
compelled him to be an idler for weeks together, and Mag had thus
a reminder of by-gones. She cared for him only as a means to sub-
serve her own comfort; yet she nursed him faithfully and true to
marriage vows till death released her. He became the victim of consumption. He loved Mag to the last. So long as life continued, he
stifled his sensibility to pain, and toiled for her sustenance long after
he was able to do so.

A few expressive wishes for her welfare; a hope of better days for
her; an anxiety lest they should not all go to the "good place;" brief
advice about their children; a hope expressed that Mag would not be
neglected as she used to be; the manifestation of Christian patience;
these were *all* the legacy of miserable Mag. A feeling of cold desolation came over her, as she turned from the grave of one who had
been truly faithful to her.

She was now expelled from companionship with white people;
this last step—her union with a black—was the climax of repulsion.

Seth Shipley, a partner in Jim's business, wished her to remain in
her present home; but she declined, and returned to her hovel again,
with obstacles threefold more insurmountable than before. Seth accompanied her, giving her a weekly allowance which furnished most
of the food necessary for the four inmates. After a time, work failed;
their means were reduced.

How Mag toiled and suffered, yielding to fits of desperation,
bursts of anger, and uttering curses too fearful to repeat. When both
were supplied with work, they prospered; if idle, they were hungry
together. In this way their interests became united; they planned for
the future together. Mag had lived an outcast for years. She had
ceased to feel the gushings of penitence; she had crushed the sharp
agonies of an awakened conscience. She had no longings for a purer
heart, a better life. Far easier to descend lower. She entered the
darkness of perpetual infamy. She asked not the rite of civilization
or Christianity. Her will made her the wife of Seth. Soon followed
scenes familiar and trying.

"It's no use," said Seth one day; "we must give the children away,
and try to get work in some other place."

"Who'll take the black devils?" snarled Mag.

"They're none of mine," said Seth; "what you growling about?"

"Nobody will want any thing of mine, or yours either," she replied.

"We'll make 'em, p'r'aps," he said. "There's Frado's six years old, and pretty, if she is yours, and white folks'll say so. She'd be a prize somewhere," he continued, tipping his chair back against the wall, and placing his feet upon the rounds, as if he had much more to say when in the right position.

Frado, as they called one of Mag's children, was a beautiful mulatto, with long, curly black hair, and handsome, roguish eyes, sparkling with an exuberance of spirit almost beyond restraint.

Hearing her name mentioned, she looked up from her play, to see what Seth had to say of her.

"Wouldn't the Bellmonts take her?" asked Seth.

"Bellmonts?" shouted Mag. "His wife is a right she-devil! and if—"

"Hadn't they better be all together?" interrupted Seth, reminding her of a like epithet used in reference to her little ones.

Without seeming to notice him, she continued, "She can't keep a girl in the house over a week; and Mr. Bellmont wants to hire a boy to work for him, but he can't find one that will live in the house with her; she's so ugly, they can't."

"Well, we've got to make a move soon," answered Seth; "if you go with me, we shall go right off. Had you rather spare the other one?" asked Seth, after a short pause.

"One's as bad as t' other," replied Mag. "Frado is such a wild, frolicky thing, and means to do jest as she's a mind to; she won't go if she don't want to. I don't want to tell her she is to be given away."

"I will," said Seth. "Come here, Frado?"

The child seemed to have some dim foreshadowing of evil, and declined.

"Come here," he continued; "I want to tell you something."

She came reluctantly. He took her hand and said: "We're going to move, by-'m-bye; will you go?"

"No!" screamed she; and giving a sudden jerk which destroyed Seth's equilibrium, left him sprawling on the floor, while she escaped through the open door.

"She's a hard one," said Seth, brushing his patched coat sleeve. "I'd risk her at Bellmont's."

They discussed the expediency of a speedy departure. Seth would first seek employment, and then return for Mag. They would take with them what they could carry, and leave the rest with Pete Greene, and come for them when they were wanted. They were long in arranging affairs satisfactorily, and were not a little startled at the close of their conference to find Frado missing. They thought approaching night would bring her. Twilight passed into darkness, and she did not come. They thought she had understood their plans, and had, perhaps, permanently withdrawn. They could not rest without making some effort to ascertain her retreat. Seth went in pursuit, and returned without her. They rallied others when they discovered that another little colored girl was missing, a favorite playmate of Frado's. All effort proved unavailing. Mag felt sure her fears were realized, and that she might never see her again. Before her anxieties became realities, both were safely returned, and from them and their attendant they learned that they went to walk, and not minding the direction soon found themselves lost. They had climbed fences and walls, passed through thickets and marshes, and when night approached selected a thick cluster of shrubbery as a covert for the night. They were discovered by the person who now restored them, chatting of their prospects, Frado attempting to banish the childish fears of her companion. As they were some miles from home, they were kindly cared for until morning. Mag was relieved to know her child was not driven to desperation by their intentions to relieve themselves of her, and she was inclined to think severe restraint would be healthful.

The removal was all arranged; the few days necessary for such migrations passed quickly, and one bright summer morning they bade farewell to their Singleton hovel, and with budgets and bundles commenced their weary march. As they neared the village, they heard the merry shouts of children gathered around the schoolroom, awaiting the coming of their teacher.

"Halloo!" screamed one, "Black, white and yeller!" "Black, white and yeller," echoed a dozen voices.

It did not grate so harshly on poor Mag as once it would. She did not even turn her head to look at them. She had passed into an insensibility no childish taunt could penetrate, else she would have reproached herself as she passed familiar scenes, for extending the separation once so easily annihilated by steadfast integrity. Two miles beyond lived the Bellmonts, in a large, old fashioned, two-story white house, environed by fruitful acres, and embellished by shrubbery and shade trees. Years ago a youthful couple consecrated it as home; and after many little feet had worn paths to favorite fruit trees, and over its green hills, and mingled at last with brother man in the race which belongs neither to the swift or strong, the sire became grey-haired and decrepid, and went to his last repose. His aged consort soon followed him. The old homestead thus passed into the hands of a son, to whose wife Mag had applied the epithet "she-devil," as may be remembered. John, the son, had not in his family arrangements departed from the example of the father. The pastimes of his boyhood were ever freshly revived by witnessing the games of his own sons as they rallied about the same goal his youthful feet had often won; as well as by the amusements of his daughters in their imitations of maternal duties.

At the time we introduce them, however, John is wearing the badge of age. Most of his children were from home; some seeking employment; some were already settled in homes of their own. A maiden sister shared with him the estate on which he resided, and occupied a portion of the house.

Within sight of the house, Seth seated himself with his bundles and the child he had been leading, while Mag walked onward to the house leading Frado. A knock at the door brought Mrs. Bellmont, and Mag asked if she would be willing to let that child stop there while she went to the Reed's house to wash, and when she came back she would call and get her. It seemed a novel request, but she consented. Why the impetuous child entered the house, we cannot tell; the door closed, and Mag hastily departed. Frado waited for the close of day, which was to bring back her mother. Alas! it never came. It was the last time she ever saw or heard of her mother.

VARIETIES

"Hard are life's early steps; and but
that youth is buoyant, confident, and
strong in hope, men would behold
its threshold and despair."

The sorrow of Frado was very great for her pet, and Mr. Bellmont by great exertion obtained it again, much to the relief of the child. To be thus deprived of all her sources of pleasure was a sure way to exalt their worth, and Fido became, in her estimation, a more valuable presence than the human beings who surrounded her.

James had now been married a number of years, and frequent requests for a visit from the family were at last accepted, and Mrs. Bellmont made great preparations for a fall sojourn in Baltimore. Mary was installed housekeeper—in name merely, for Nig was the only moving power in the house. Although suffering from their joint severity, she felt safer than to be thrown wholly upon an ardent, passionate, unrestrained young lady, whom she always hated and felt it hard to be obliged to obey. The trial she must meet. Were Jack or Jane at home she would have some refuge; one only remained; good Aunt Abby was still in the house.

She saw the fast receding coach which conveyed her master and mistress with regret, and begged for one favor only, that James would send for her when they returned, a hope she had confidently cherished all these five years.

She was now able to do all the washing, ironing, baking, and the common *et cetera* of house-hold duties, though but fourteen. Mary left all for her to do, though she affected great responsibility. She would show herself in the kitchen long enough to relieve herself of some command, better withheld; or insist upon some compliance to her wishes in some department which she was very imperfectly acquainted with, very much less than the person she was addressing; and so impetuous till her orders were obeyed, that to escape the turmoil, Nig would often go contrary to her own knowledge to gain a respite.

Nig was taken sick! What could be done? The *work*, certainly, but not by Miss Mary. So Nig would work while she could remain erect, then sink down upon the floor, or a chair, till she could rally for a fresh effort. Mary would look in upon her, chide her for her laziness, threaten to tell mother when she came home, and so forth.

"Nig!" screamed Mary, one of her sickest days, "come here, and sweep these threads from the carpet." She attempted to drag her weary limbs along, using the broom as support. Impatient of delay, she called again, but with a different request. "Bring me some wood, you lazy jade, quick." Nig rested the broom against the wall, and started on the fresh behest.

Too long gone. Flushed with anger, she rose and greeted her with, "What are you gone so long, for? Bring it in quick, I say."

"I am coming as quick as I can," she replied, entering the door.

"Saucy, impudent nigger, you! is this the way you answer me?" and taking a large carving knife from the table, she hurled it, in her rage, at the defenceless girl.

Dodging quickly, it fastened in the ceiling a few inches from where she stood. There rushed on Mary's mental vision a picture of bloodshed, in which she was the perpetrator, and the sad consequences of what was so nearly an actual occurrence.

"Tell anybody of this, if you dare. If you tell Aunt Abby, I'll certainly kill you," said she, terrified. She returned to her room, brushed her threads herself; was for a day or two more guarded, and so escaped deserved and merited penalty.

Oh, how long the weeks seemed which held Nig in subjection to Mary; but they passed like all earth's sorrow and joys. Mr. and Mrs. B. returned delighted with their visit, and laden with rich presents for Mary. No word of hope for Nig. James was quite unwell, and would come home the next spring for a visit.

This, thought Nig, will be my time of release. I shall go back with him.

From early dawn until after all were retired, was she toiling, overworked, disheartened, longing for relief.

Exposure from heat to cold, or the reverse, often destroyed her health for short intervals. She wore no shoes until after frost, and snow even, appeared; and bared her feet again before the last vestige of winter disappeared. These sudden changes she was so illy guarded against, nearly conquered her physical system. Any word of complaint was severely repulsed or cruelly punished.

She was told she had much more than she deserved. So that manual labor was not in reality her only burden; but such an incessant torrent of scolding and boxing and threatening, was enough to deter one of maturer years from remaining within sound of the strife.

It is impossible to give an impression of the manifest enjoyment of Mrs. B in these kitchen scenes. It was her favorite exercise to enter the apartment noisily, vociferate orders, give a few sudden blows to quicken Nig's pace, then return to the sitting room with *such* a satisfied expression, congratulating herself upon her thorough housekeeping qualities.

She usually rose in the morning at the ringing of the bell for breakfast; if she were heard stirring before that time, Nig knew well there was an extra amount of scolding to be borne.

No one now stood between herself and Frado, but Aunt Abby. And if *she* dared to interfere in the least, she was ordered back to her "own quarters." Nig would creep slyly into her room, learn what she could of her regarding the absent, and thus gain some light in the thick gloom of care and toil and sorrow in which she was immersed.

The first of spring a letter came from James, announcing declining health. He must try northern air as a restorative; so Frado joyfully prepared for this agreeable increase of the family, this addition to her cares.

He arrived feeble, lame, from his disease, so changed Frado wept at his appearance, fearing he would be removed from her forever. He kindly greeted her, took her to the parlor to see his wife and child, and said many things to kindle smiles on her sad face.

Frado felt so happy in his presence, so safe from maltreatment! He was to her a shelter. He observed, silently, the ways of the house a few days; Nig still took her meals in the same manner as formerly, having the same allowance of food. He, one day, bade her not remove the food, but sit down to the table and eat.

"She *will*, mother," said he, calmly, but imperatively; I'm deter-

mined; she works hard; I've watched her. Now, while I stay, she is
going to sit down *here*, and eat such food as we eat."

A few sparks from the mother's black eyes were the only reply;
she feared to oppose where she knew she could not prevail. So Nig's
standing attitude, and selected diet vanished.

Her clothing was yet poor and scanty; she was not blessed with a
Sunday attire; for she was never permitted to attend church with her
mistress. "Religion was not meant for niggers," *she* said; when the
husband and brothers were absent, she would drive Mrs. B. and
Mary there, then return, and go for them at the close of the service,
but never remain. Aunt Abby would take her to evening meetings,
held in the neighborhood, which Mrs. B. never attended; and impart
to her lessons of truth and grace as they walked to the place of
prayer.

Many of less piety would scorn to present so doleful a figure;
Mrs. B. had shaved her glossy ringlets; and, in her coarse cloth gown
and ancient bonnet, she was anything but an enticing object. But
Aunt Abby looked within. She saw a soul to save, an immortality of
happiness to secure.

These evenings were eagerly anticipated by Nig; it was such a
pleasant release from labor.

Such perfect contrast in the melody and prayers of these good
people to the harsh tones which fell on her ears during the day.

Soon she had all their sacred songs at command, and enlivened
her toil by accompanying it with this melody.

James encouraged his aunt in her efforts. He had found the *Saviour*, he wished to have Frado's desolate heart gladdened, quieted,
sustained, by *His* presence. He felt sure there were elements in her
heart which, transformed and purified by the gospel, would make
her worthy the esteem and friendship of the world. A kind, affectionate heart, native wit, and common sense, and the pertness she
sometimes exhibited, he felt if restrained properly, might become
useful in originating a self-reliance which would be of service to her
in after years.

Yet it was not possible to compass all this, while she remained
where she was. He wished to be cautious about pressing too closely
her claims on his mother, as it would increase the burdened one he
so anxiously wished to relieve. He cheered her on with the hope of
returning with his family, when he recovered sufficiently.

Nig seemed awakened to new hopes and aspirations, and realized
a longing for the future, hitherto unknown.

To complete Nig's enjoyment, Jack arrived unexpectedly. His
greeting was as hearty to herself as to any of the family.

"Where are your curls, Fra?" asked Jack, after the usual salutation.

"Your mother cut them off."

"Thought you were getting handsome, did she? Same old story, is
it; knocks and bumps? Better times coming; never fear, Nig."

How different this appellative sounded from him; he said it in
such a tone, with such a rogueish look!

She laughed, and replied that he had better take her West for a
housekeeper.

Jack was pleased with James's innovations of table discipline, and
would often tarry in the dining-room, to see Nig in her new place at
the family table. As he was thus sitting one day, after the family had
finished dinner, Frado seated herself in her mistress' chair, and was
just reaching for a clean dessert plate which was on the table, when
her mistress entered.

"Put that plate down; you shall not have a clean one; eat from
mine," continued she. Nig hesitated. To eat after James, his wife or
Jack, would have been pleasant; but to be commanded to do what
was disagreeable by her mistress, *because* it was disagreeable, was
trying. Quickly looking about, she took the plate, called Fido to
wash it, which he did to the best of his ability; then, wiping her
knife and fork on the cloth, she proceeded to eat her dinner.

Nig never looked toward her mistress during the process. She
had Jack near; she did not fear her now.

Insulted, full of rage, Mrs. Bellmont rushed to her husband, and
commanded him to notice this insult; to whip that child; if he would
not do it, James ought.

James came to hear the kitchen version of the affair. Jack was
boiling over with laughter. He related all the circumstances to James,
and pulling a bright, silver half-dollar from his pocket, he threw it at
Nig, saying, "There, take that; 't was worth paying for."

James sought his mother; told her he "would not excuse or palliate Nig's impudence; but she should not be whipped or be punished at all. You have not treated her, mother, so as to gain her love;
she is only exhibiting your remissness in this matter."

She only smothered her resentment until a convenient opportunity offered. The first time she was left alone with Nig, she gave her
a thorough beating, to bring up arrearages; and threatened, if she
ever exposed her to James, she would "cut her tongue out."

James found her, upon his return, sobbing; but fearful of revenge,
she dared not answer his queries. He guessed their cause, and longed
for returning health to take her under his protection.

Henry Highland Garnet

(1815–1881)

A FASCINATING and many-sided man, Henry Highland Garnet at various times in his life was a minister, cabin boy, farm laborer, teacher, college president, operator on the Underground Railroad, missionary to Jamaica, promoter of African colonization, newspaper publisher, United States minister and consul general to Liberia, and above all else, a great antislavery orator.

Garnet was born on a plantation on Maryland's Eastern Shore, an area that spawned other noted fugitive slaves like Frederick Douglass and Harriet Tubman. Using the stratagem of attending a funeral, Garnet's father drove his family and other slaves in a covered wagon to freedom via the Underground Railroad in Wilmington, Delaware, and later to New York City.

In the latter city, Garnet had several classmates who were later to become outstanding persons, among them Patrick Reason, a pioneer Negro painter; Charles L. Reason, poet and teacher; Ira Aldridge, the famous actor; James McCune Smith, a surgeon; and Samuel Ringgold Ward, a Congregationalist minister.[1] After being run out of a school in Canaan, New Hampshire, because of his race, Garnet finished his education at the famous Oneida Institute, New York. Never a strong man physically, Garnet had to have a leg amputated because of a disease. He died in Monrovia, Liberia, in 1881.

Although he was an able and scholarly minister, Garnet preferred to preach abolition rather than orthodox Christian gospel. The blacks of his generation thought of him as a black Tom Paine; but many of them, including Frederick Douglass, thought that Garnet spoke "too much of violence."

In 1843 Garnet gave a speech before the landmark National Negro Convention, meeting in Buffalo, New York. The speech was so fiery, so revolutionary it was rejected by the blacks attending the convention on the grounds that it was too "warlike," that it "encouraged insurrection," and that if the convention adopted it, the lives of the delegates from the border states would be endangered when they returned. The speech was

---

[1]For additional information on James McCune Smith and Samuel Ringgold Ward, see the excerpts from *The Condition, Elevation, Emigration, and Destiny of the Colored People of the United States, Politically Considered,* in this volume.

not printed until 1848, when at "the instigation and expense" of John Brown, it was published in a volume (along with a reprint of *Walker's Appeal*) and called "An Address to the Slaves of the United States of America." In this address, Garnet took perhaps the strongest approach to the abolition of slavery of his generation. He told slaves that it was their *Christian* duty, one demanded by God himself, to rise up in rebellion and overthrow slavery.

Only two other speeches by Garnet have come down to us: "The Past and the Present Condition, and the Destiny of the Colored Race" (1848) and "A Memorial Discourse; Delivered in the Hall of the House of Representatives, Washington, D.C. on Sabbath, February 12, 1865."

For biographical material on Garnet, see the early work by his classmate, James McCune Smith: "The Sketch of the Life and Labors of Rev. Henry Highland Garnet" (1865). For more recent studies, see *Henry Highland Garnet: A Voice of Black Radicalism in the Nineteenth Century* (1977) by Joel Schor; *Let Your Motto Be Resistance* (1972) by Earl Ofari; *Black Abolitionists* (1969) by Benjamin Quarles; and *They Who Would Be Free: Blacks' Search for Freedom, 1830–1861* (1974) by Jane H. Pease and William H. Pease. See also Vernon Loggins's *The Negro Author*, and see especially Earl Ofari's article in *Dictionary of American Negro Biography*.

The following selection comes from *An Address to the Slaves of the United States of America*, reprinted along with *David Walker's Appeal* in the 1969 Arno Press/New York Times series.

AN ADDRESS TO THE SLAVES
OF THE UNITED STATES OF AMERICA

BRETHREN AND FELLOW CITIZENS:

Your brethren of the north, east and west have been accustomed to meet together in National Conventions, to sympathize with each other, and to weep over your unhappy condition. In these meetings we have addressed all classes of the free, but we have never until this time, sent a word of consolation and advice to you. We have been contented in sitting still and mourning over your sorrows, earnestly hoping that before this day, your sacred liberties would have been restored. But, we have hoped in vain. Years have rolled on, and tens of thousands have been borne on streams of blood, and tears, to the shores of eternity. While you have been oppressed, we have also been partakers with you; nor can we be free while you are enslaved. We therefore write to you as being bound with you.

Many of you are bound to us, not only by the ties of a common humanity, but we are connected by the more tender relations of parents, wives, husbands, children, brothers, and sisters, and friends. As such we most affectionately address you.

Slavery has fixed a deep gulf between you and us, and while it shuts out from you the relief and consolation which your friends would willingly render, it afflicts and persecutes you with a fierceness which we might not expect to see in the fiends of hell. But still the Almighty Father of Mercies has left to us a glimmering ray of hope, which shines out like a lone star in a cloudy sky. Mankind are becoming wiser, and better—the oppressor's power is fading, and you, every day, are becoming better informed, and more numerous. Your grievances, brethren, are many. We shall not attempt, in this short address, to present to the world, all the dark catalogue of this nation's sins, which have been committed upon an innocent people. Nor is it indeed, necessary, for you feel them from day to day, and all the civilized world look upon them with amazement.

Two hundred and twenty-seven years ago, the first of our injured race were brought to the shores of America. They came not with glad spirits to select their homes, in the New World. They came not with their own consent, to find an unmolested enjoyment of the blessings of this fruitful soil. The first dealings which they had with men calling themselves Christians, exhibited to them the worst features of corrupt and sordid hearts; and convinced them that no cruelty is too great, no villainy, and no robbery too abhorrent for even enlightened men to perform, when influenced by avarice, and lust. Neither did they come flying upon the wings of Liberty, to a land of freedom. But, they came with broken hearts, from their beloved native land, and were doomed to unrequited toil, and deep degradation. Nor did the evil of their bondage end at their emancipation by death. Succeeding generations inherited their chains, and millions have come from eternity into time, and have returned again to the world of spirits, cursed, and ruined by American Slavery.

The propagators of the system, or their immediate ancestors very soon discovered its growing evil, and its tremendous wickedness, and secret promises were made to destroy it. The gross inconsistency of a people holding slaves, who had themselves "ferried o'er the wave," for freedom's sake, was too apparent to be entirely overlooked. The voice of Freedom cried, "emancipate your Slaves." Humanity supplicated with tears, for the deliverance of the children of Africa. Wisdom urged her solemn plea. The bleeding captive plead his innocence, and pointed to Christianity who stood weeping at the cross. Jehovah frowned upon the nefarious institution, and thunderbolts, red with vengeance, struggled to leap forth to blast the guilty wretches who maintained it. But all was vain. Slavery had stretched its dark wings of death over the land, the Church stood silently by—

the priests prophesied falsely, and the people loved to have it so. Its throne is established, and now it reigns triumphantly.

Nearly three millions of your fellow citizens, are prohibited by law, and public opinion, (which in this country is stronger than law), from reading the Book of Life. Your intellect has been destroyed as much as possible, and every ray of light they have attempted to shut out from your minds. The oppressors themselves have become involved in the ruin. They have become weak, sensual, and rapacious. They have cursed you—they have cursed themselves—they have cursed the earth which they have trod. In the language of a Southern statesman, we can truly say, "even the wolf, driven back long since by the approach of man, now returns after the lapse of a hundred years, and howls amid the desolations of slavery."

The colonists threw the blame upon England. They said that the mother country entailed the evil upon them, and that they would rid themselves of it if they could. The world thought they were sincere, and the philanthropic pitied them. But time soon tested their sincerity. In a few years, the colonists grew strong and severed themselves from the British Government. Their Independence was declared, and they took their station among the sovereign powers of the earth. The declaration was a glorious document. Sages admired it, and the patriotic of every nation reverenced the Godlike sentiments which it contained. When the power of Government returned to their hands, did they emancipate the slaves? No; they rather added new links to our chains. Were they ignorant of the principles of Liberty? Certainly they were not. The sentiments of their revolutionary orators fell in burning eloquence upon their hearts, and with one voice they cried, LIBERTY OR DEATH. O, what a sentence was that! It ran from soul to soul like electric fire, and nerved the arm of thousands to fight in the holy cause of Freedom. Among the diversity of opinions that are entertained in regard to physical resistance, there are but a few found to gainsay that stern declaration. We are among those who do not.

SLAVERY! How much misery is comprehended in that single word. What mind is there that does not shrink from its direful effects? Unless the image of God is obliterated from the soul, all men cherish the love of Liberty. The nice discerning political economist does not regard the sacred right, more than the untutored African who roams in the wilds of Congo. Nor has the one more right to the full enjoyment of his freedom than the other. In every man's mind the good seeds of liberty are planted, and he who brings his fellow down so low, as to make him contented with a condition of slavery, commits the highest crime against God and man. Brethren, your oppressors aim to do this. They endeavor to make you as much like brutes as possible. When they have blinded the eyes of your mind—when they have embittered the sweet waters of life—when they have shut out the light which shines from the word of God—then, and not till then has American slavery done its perfect work.

To such degradation it is sinful in the extreme for you to make voluntary submission. The divine commandments, you are in duty bound to reverence, and obey. If you do not obey them you will surely meet with the displeasure of the Almighty. He requires you to love him supremely, and your neighbor as yourself—to keep the Sabbath day holy—to search the Scriptures—and bring up your children with respect for his laws, and to worship no other God but him. But slavery sets all these at naught and hurls defiance in the face of Jehovah. The forlorn condition in which you are placed does not destroy your moral obligation to God. You are not certain of Heaven, because you suffer yourselves to remain in a state of slavery, where you cannot obey the commandments of the Sovereign of the universe. If the ignorance of slavery is a passport to heaven, then it is a blessing, and no curse, and you should rather desire its perpetuity than its abolition. God will not receive slavery, nor ignorance, nor any other state of mind, for love, and obedience to him. Your condition does not absolve you from your moral obligation. The diabolical injustice by which your liberties are cloven down, neither God, nor angels, or just men, command you to suffer for a single moment. Therefore it is your solemn and imperative duty to use every means, both moral, intellectual, and physical, that promise success. If a band of heathen men should attempt to enslave a race of Christians, and to place their children under the influence of some false religion, surely, heaven would frown upon the men who would not resist such aggression, even to death. If, on the other hand, a band of Christians should attempt to enslave a race of heathen men and to entail slavery upon them, and to keep them in heathenism in the midst of Christianity, the God of heaven would smile upon every effort which the injured might make to disenthral themselves.

Brethren, it is as wrong for your lordly oppressors to keep you in slavery, as it was for the man thief to steal our ancestors from the coast of Africa. You should therefore now use the same manner of resistance, as would have been just in our ancestors, when the bloody foot prints of the first remorseless soul thief was placed upon the shores of our fatherland. The humblest peasant is as free in the sight of God, as the proudest monarch that ever swayed a sceptre. Liberty is a spirit sent out from God, and like its great Author, is no respector of persons.

Brethren, the time has come when you must act for yourselves. It is an old and true saying, that "if hereditary bondmen would be free, they must themselves strike the blow." You can plead your own cause, and do the work of emancipation better than any others. The nations of the old world are moving in the great cause of universal freedom, and some of them at least, will ere long, do you justice. The combined powers of Europe have placed their broad seal of disapprobation upon the African slave trade. But in the slave holding parts of the United States, the trade is as brisk as ever. They buy and sell you as though you were brute beasts. The North has done much—her opinion of slavery in the abstract is known. But in regard to the South, we adopt the opinion of the New York Evangelist—"We have advanced so far, that the cause apparently waits for a more effectual door to be thrown open than has been yet." We are about to point you to that more effectual door. Look around you, and behold the bosoms of your loving wives, heaving with untold agonies! Hear the cries of your poor children! Remember the stripes your fathers bore. Think of the torture and disgrace of your noble mothers. Think of your wretched sisters, loving virtue and purity, as they are driven into concubinage, and are exposed to the unbridled lusts of incarnate devils. Think of the undying glory that hangs around the ancient name of Africa:—and forget not that you are native-born American citizens, and as such, you are justly entitled to all the rights that are granted to the freest. Think how many tears you have poured out upon the soil which you have cultivated with unrequited toil, and enriched with your blood; and then go to your lordly enslavers, and tell them plainly, that YOU ARE DETERMINED TO BE FREE. Appeal to their sense of justice, and tell them that they have no more right to oppress you, than you have to enslave them. Entreat them to remove the grievous burdens which they have imposed upon you, and to remunerate you for your labor. Promise them renewed diligence in the cultivation of the soil, if they will render to you an equivalent for your services. Point them to the increase of happiness and prosperity in the British West Indies, since the act of Emancipation. Tell them in language which they cannot misunderstand, of the exceeding sinfulness of slavery, and of a future judgment, and of the righteous retributions of an indignant God. Inform them that all you desire, is FREEDOM, and that nothing else will suffice. Do this, and forever after cease to toil for the heartless tyrants, who give you no other reward but stripes and abuse. If they then commence the work of death, they, and not you, will be responsible for the consequences. You had far better all die—*die immediately*, than live slaves, and entail your wretchedness upon your posterity. If you would be free in this generation, here is your only hope. However much you and all of us may desire it, there is not much hope of Redemption without the shedding of blood. If you must bleed, let it all come at once—rather, *die freemen, than live to be slaves.* It is impossible, like the children of Israel, to make a grand Exodus from the land of bondage. THE PHARAOHS ARE ON BOTH SIDES OF THE BLOOD-RED WATERS! You cannot remove en masse, to the dominions of the British Queen—nor can you pass through Florida, and overrun Texas, and at last find peace in Mexico. The propagators of American slavery are spending their blood and treasure, that they may plant the black flag in the heart of Mexico, and riot in the halls of the Montezumas. In the language of the Rev. Robert Hall, when addressing the volunteers of Bristol, who were rushing forth to repel the invasion of Napoleon, who threatened to lay waste the fair homes of England, "Religion is too much interested in your behalf, not to shed over you her most gracious influences."

You will not be compelled to spend much time in order to become inured to hardships. From the first moment that you breathed the air of heaven, you have been accustomed to nothing else but hardships. The heroes of the American Revolution were never put upon harder fare, than a peck of corn, and a few herrings per week. You have not become enervated by the luxuries of life. Your sternest energies have been beaten out upon the anvil of severe trial. Slavery has done this, to make you subservient to its own purposes; but it has done more than this, it has prepared you for any emergency. If you receive good treatment, it is what you could hardly expect; if you meet with pain, sorrow, and even death, these are the common lot of the slaves.

Fellow-men! patient sufferers! behold your dearest rights crushed to the earth! See your sons murdered, and your wives, mothers, and sisters, doomed to prostitution! In the name of the merciful God! and by all that life is worth, let it no longer be a debateable question, whether it is better to choose LIBERTY or DEATH!

In 1822, Denmark Veazie, of South Carolina, formed a plan for the liberation of his fellow men. In the whole history of human efforts to overthrow slavery, a more complicated and tremendous plan was never formed. He was betrayed by the treachery of his own people, and died a martyr to freedom. Many a brave hero fell, but History, faithful to her high trust, will transcribe his name on the same monument with Moses, Hampden, Tell, Bruce, and Wallace, Touissaint L'Overteur, Lafayette and Washington. That tremendous movement shook the whole empire of slavery. The guilty soul thieves were overwhelmed with fear. It is a matter of fact, that at that time, and in consequence of the threatened revolution, the slave states talked strongly of emancipation. But they blew but one blast of the trumpet of freedom, and then laid it aside. As these men became quiet, the slaveholders ceased to talk about emancipation: and now, behold your condition to-day! Angels sigh over it, and humanity has long since exhausted her tears in weeping on your account!

The patriotic Nathaniel Turner followed Denmark Veazie. He was goaded to desperation by wrong and injustice. By Despotism, his name has been recorded on the list of infamy, but future generations will number him among the noble and brave.

Next arose the immortal Joseph Cinque, the hero of the Amistad. He was a native African, and by the help of God he emancipated a whole ship-load of his fellow men on the high seas. And he now sings of liberty on the sunny hills of Africa, and beneath his native palm trees, where he hears the lion roar, and feels himself as free as that king of the forest. Next arose Madison Washington, that bright star of freedom, and took his station in the constellation of freedom. He was a slave on board the brig Creole, of Richmond, bound to New Orleans, that great slave mart, with a hundred and four others. Nineteen struck for liberty or death. But one life was taken, and the whole were emancipated, and the vessel was carried into Nassau, New Providence. Noble men! Those who have fallen in freedom's conflict, their memories will be cherished by the true hearted, and the God-fearing, in all future generations; those who are living, their names are surrounded by a halo of glory.

We do not advise you to attempt a revolution with the sword, because it would be INEXPEDIENT. Your numbers are too small, and moreover the rising spirit of the age, and the spirit of the gospel, are opposed to war and bloodshed. But from this moment cease to labor for tyrants who will not remunerate you. Let every slave throughout the land do this, and the days of slavery are numbered. You cannot be more oppressed than you have been—you cannot suffer greater cruelties than you have already. RATHER DIE FREEMEN, THAN LIVE TO BE SLAVES. Remember that you are THREE MILLIONS.

It is in your power so to torment the God-cursed slaveholders, that they will be glad to let you go free. If the scale was turned and black men were the masters, and white men the slaves, every destructive agent and element would be employed to lay the oppressor low. Danger and death would hang over their heads day and night. Yes, the tyrants would meet with plagues more terrible than those of Pharaoh. But you are a patient people. You act as though you were made for the special use of these devils. You act as though your daughters were born to pamper the lusts of your masters and overseers. And worse than all, you tamely submit, while your lords tear your wives from your embraces, and defile them before your eyes. In

the name of God we ask, are you men? Where is the blood of your
fathers? Has it all run out of your veins? Awake, awake; millions of
voices are calling you! Your dead fathers speak to you from their
graves. Heaven, as with a voice of thunder, calls on you to arise
from the dust.

Let your motto be RESISTANCE! RESISTANCE! RESISTANCE!—No oppressed people have ever secured their liberty without resistance.
What kind of resistance you had better make, you must decide by
the circumstances that surround you, and according to the suggestion of expediency. Brethren, adieu. Trust in the living God. Labor
for the peace of the human race, and remember that you are three
millions.

Frank J. Webb

(Dates Unknown)

WE DO NOT KNOW very much about the life of Frank J. Webb, the author of *The Garies and Their Friends*, the second novel by an American black. The first, *Clotel* by William Wells Brown, was published in 1853; Webb's work came out in 1857, and like Brown's was published in London. Henry Louis Gates's discovery of earlier fiction and the resurrection of Harriet E. Wilson's *Our Nig*, originally published in 1859, have forced us to be more careful about designating "firsts" in African American fiction. Since *Our Nig* was published in America, we now say it was the first novel published by a Negro in America; also the first by a black woman.

The little that we know about Webb comes from one main source: the preface to *The Garies and Their Friends*, written by Harriet Beecher Stowe. She states that Webb was "a coloured young man" born and reared in Philadelphia, adding that "the incidents related [in the novel] are mostly true ones," and that "the majority are faithfully drawn from real life." Mrs. Stowe liked the novel and considered it an example of "what the *free people do attain*, and what they can do in spite of all social obstacles."

The Garies and Their Friends is a better-written work than Brown's pioneering *Clotel*, and it may be credited with several literary "firsts." It is the first fictional work to treat seriously the "mixed marriage" problem; it was among the first African American novels to include a lynch mob; among the first to treat ironically (as Charles Chesnutt was to do later) the problems of the "color line"; and among the first to make "passing for white" a major theme, as several novelists were to do during the New Negro (Harlem) Renaissance of the 1920s. A fascinating and in some ways an unusual novel, Webb's work should be better known than it is. In two respects *The Garies* is closer in content to *Our Nig* than to *Clotel*. Both deal with Negroes in the North and the prejudice they found there; both deal with interracial or "mixed" marriages.

For critical comment on *The Garies and Their Friends* and on Webb, see Vernon Loggins, *The Negro Author*; Benjamin Brawley, *Early Negro American Writers* (1935); Hugh M. Gloster, *Negro Voices in Fiction* (1948); and the 1969 Arno Press and The New York Times edition of *The Garies and Their Friends*, with an introduction by Arthur P. Davis and a preface by Harriet Beecher Stowe. The entry by Gregory L. Candela in *Dictionary of Literary Biography, Volume 50* and *The Afro-American Novel and Its Tradition* (1987) by Bernard W. Bell should also be examined.

The selection that follows comes from Chapter XIII of *The Garies and Their Friends*, Arno Press and The New York Times edition, 1969.

HOPES CONSUMMATED

To Emily Winston we have always accorded the title of Mrs. Garie; whilst, in reality, she had no legal claim to it whatever.

Previous to their emigration from Georgia, Mr. Garie had, on one or two occasions, attempted, but without success, to make her legally his wife.

He ascertained that, even if he could have found a clergyman willing to expose himself to persecution by marrying them, the ceremony itself would have no legal weight, as a marriage between a white and a mulatto was not recognized as valid by the laws of the state; and he had, therefore, been compelled to dismiss the matter from his mind, until an opportunity should offer for the accomplishment of their wishes.

Now, however, that they had removed to the north, where they would have no legal difficulties to encounter, he determined to put his former intention into execution. Although Emily had always maintained a studied silence on the subject, he knew that it was the darling wish of her heart to be legally united to him; so he unhesitatingly proceeded to arrange matters for the consummation of what he felt assured would promote the happiness of both. He therefore wrote to Dr. Blackly, a distinguished clergyman of the city, requesting him to perform the ceremony, and received from him an assurance that he would be present at the appointed time.

Matters having progressed thus far, he thought it time to inform Emily of what he had done. On the evening succeeding the receipt of an answer from the Rev. Dr. Blackly—after the children had been sent to bed—he called her to him, and, taking her hand, sat down beside her on the sofa.

"Emily," said he, as he drew her closer to him, "my dear, faithful Emily! I am about to do you an act of justice—one, too, that I feel will increase the happiness of us both. I am going to marry you, my darling! I am about to give you a lawful claim to what you have already won by your faithfulness and devotion. You know I tried, more than once, whilst in the south, to accomplish this, but, owing to the cruel and unjust laws existing there, I was unsuccessful. But now, love, no such difficulty exists; and here," continued he, "is an answer to the note I have written to Dr. Blackly, asking him to come next Wednesday night, and perform the ceremony.—You are willing, are you not, Emily?" he asked.

"Willing!" she exclaimed, in a voice tremulous with emotion— "willing! Oh, God! if you only knew how I have longed for it! It has been my earnest desire for years!" and, bursting into tears, she leaned, sobbing, on his shoulder.

After a few moments she raised her head, and, looking searchingly in his face, she asked: "But do you do this after full reflection on the consequences to ensue? Are you willing to sustain all the odium, to endure all the contumely, to which your acknowledged union with one of my unfortunate race will subject you? Clarence! it will be a severe trial—a greater one than any you have yet endured for me—and one for which I fear my love will prove but a poor recompense! I have thought more of these things lately; I am older now in years and experience. There was a time when I was vain enough to think that my affection was all that was necessary for your happiness; but men, I know, require more to fill their cup of content than the undivided affection of a woman, no matter how fervently beloved. You have talents, and, I have sometimes thought, ambition. Oh, Clarence! how it would grieve me, in after-years, to know that you regretted that for me you had sacrificed all those views and hopes that are cherished by the generality of your sex! Have you weighed it well?"

"Yes, Emily—well," replied Mr. Garie; "and you know the conclusion. My past should be a guarantee for the future. I had the world before me, and chose you—and with you I am contented to share my lot; and feel that I receive, in your affection, a full reward for any of the so-called sacrifices I may make. So, dry your tears, my dear," concluded he, "and let us hope for nothing but an increase of happiness as the result."

After a few moments of silence, he resumed: "It will be necessary, Emily, to have a couple of witnesses. Now, whom would you prefer? I would suggest Mrs. Ellis and her husband. They are old friends, and persons on whose prudence we can rely. It would not do to have the matter talked about, as it would expose us to disagreeable comments."

Mrs. Garie agreed perfectly with him as to the selection of Mr. and Mrs. Ellis; and immediately despatched a note to Mrs. Ellis, asking her to call at their house on the morrow.

When she came, Emily informed her, with some confusion of manner, of the intended marriage, and asked her attendance as witness, at the same time informing her of the high opinion her husband entertained of their prudence in any future discussion of the matter.

"I am really glad he is going to marry you, Emily," replied Mrs. Ellis, "and depend upon it we will do all in our power to aid it. Only yesterday, that inquisitive Mrs. Tiddy was at our house, and, in conversation respecting you, asked if I knew you to be married to Mr. Garie. I turned the conversation somehow, without giving her a direct answer. Mr. Garie, I must say, does act nobly towards you. He must love you, Emily, for not one white man in a thousand would make such a sacrifice for a coloured woman. You can't tell how we all like him—he is so amiable, so kind in his manner, and makes everyone so much at ease in his company. It's real good in him, I declare, and I shall begin to have some faith in white folks, after all.—Wednesday night," continued she; "very well—we shall be here, if the Lord spare us;" and, kissing Emily, she hurried off, to impart the joyful intelligence to her husband.

The anxiously looked for Wednesday evening at last arrived, and Emily arrayed herself in a plain white dress for the occasion. Her long black hair had been arranged in ringlets by Mrs. Ellis, who stood by, gazing admiringly at her.

"How sweet you look, Emily—you only want a wreath of orange blossoms to complete your appearance. Don't you feel a little nervous?" asked her friend.

"A little excited," she answered, and her hand shook as she put back one of the curls that had fallen across her face. Just then a loud ringing at the door announced the arrival of Dr. Blackly, who was shown into the front parlour.

Emily and Mrs. Ellis came down into the room where Mr. Garie was waiting for them, whilst Mr. Ellis brought in Dr. Blackly. The reverend gentleman gazed with some surprise at the party assembled. Mr. Garie was so thoroughly Saxon in appearance, that no one could doubt to what race he belonged, and it was equally evident that Emily, Mrs. Ellis, and her husband, were coloured persons.

Dr. Blackly looked from one to the other with evident embarrassment, and then said to Mr. Garie, in a low, hesitating tone:—

"I think there has been some mistake here—will you do me the favour to step into another room?"

Mr. Garie mechanically complied, and stood waiting to learn the cause of Dr. Blackly's strange conduct.

"You are a white man, I believe?" at last stammered forth the doctor.

"Yes, sir; I presume my appearance is a sufficient guarantee of that," answered Mr. Garie.

"Oh yes, I do not doubt it, and for that reason you must not be surprised if I decline to proceed with the ceremony."

"I do not see how my being a white man can act as a barrier to its performance," remarked Mr. Garie in reply.

"It would not, sir, if all the parties were of one complexion; but I do not believe in the propriety of amalgamation, and on no consideration could I be induced to assist in the union of a white man or woman with a person who has the slightest infusion of African blood in their veins. I believe the negro race," he continued, "to be marked out by the hand of God for servitude; and you must pardon me if I express my surprise that a gentleman of your evident intelligence should seek such a connection—you must be labouring under some horrible infatuation."

"Enough, sir," replied Mr. Garie, proudly; "I only regret that I did not know it was necessary to relate every circumstance of appearance, complexion, &c. I wished to obtain a marriage certificate, not a passport. I mistook you for a *Christian minister*, which mistake you will please to consider as my apology for having troubled you;" and thus speaking, he bowed Dr. Blackly out of the house. Mr. Garie stepped back to the door of the parlour and called out Mr. Ellis.

"We are placed in a very difficult dilemma," said he, as he was joined by the latter. "Would you believe it? that prejudiced old sinner has actually refused to marry us."

"It is no more than you might have expected of him—he's a thorough nigger-hater—keeps a pew behind the organ of his church for coloured people, and will not permit them to receive the sacrament until all the white members of his congregation are served. Why, I don't see what on earth induced you to send for him."

"I knew nothing of his sentiments respecting coloured people. I did not for a moment have an idea that he would hesitate to marry us. There is no law here that forbids it. What can we do?" said Mr. Garie, despairingly.

"I know a minister who will marry you with pleasure, if I can only catch him at home; he is so much engaged in visiting the sick and other pastoral duties."

"Do go—hunt him up, Ellis. It will be a great favour to me, if you can induce him to come. Poor Emily—what a disappointment this will be to her," said he, as he entered the room where she was sitting.

"What is the matter, dear?" she asked, as she observed Garie's anxious face. "I hope there is no new difficulty."

Mr. Garie briefly explained what had just occurred, and informed her, in addition, of Mr. Ellis having gone to see if he could get Father Banks, as the venerable old minister was called.

"It seems, dear," said she, despondingly, "as if Providence looked unfavourably on our design; for every time you have attempted it, we have been in some way thwarted;" and the tears chased one another down her face, which had grown pale in the excitement of the moment.

"Oh, don't grieve about it, dear; it is only a temporary disappointment. I can't think all the clergymen in the city are like Dr. Blackly. Some one amongst them will certainly oblige us. We won't despair; at least not until Ellis comes back."

They had not very long to wait; for soon after this conversation footsteps were heard in the garden, and Mr. Ellis entered, followed by the clergyman.

In a very short space of time they were united by Father Banks, who seemed much affected as he pronounced his blessing upon them.

"My children," he said, tremulously, "you are entering upon a path which, to the most favoured, is full of disappointment, care, and anxieties; but to you who have come together under such peculiar circumstances, in the face of so many difficulties, and in direct opposition to the prejudices of society, it will be fraught with more danger, and open to more annoyances, than if you were both of one race. But if men revile you, revile not again; bear it patiently for the sake of Him who has borne so much for you. God bless you, my children," said he, and after shaking hands with them all, he departed.

Mr. and Mrs. Ellis took their leave soon after, and then Mrs. Garie stole upstairs alone into the room where the children were sleeping. It seemed to her that night that they were more beautiful than ever, as they lay in their little beds quietly slumbering. She knelt beside them, and earnestly prayed their heavenly Father that the union which had just been consummated in the face of so many difficulties might prove a boon to them all.

"Where have you been, you runaway?" exclaimed her husband as she re-entered the parlour. "You stayed away so long, I began to have all sorts of frightful ideas—I thought of the 'mistletoe hung in the castle hall,' and of old oak chests, and all kind of terrible things. I've been sitting here alone ever since the Ellises went: where have you been?"

"Oh, I've been upstairs looking at the children. Bless their young hearts! they looked so sweet and happy—and how they grow! Clarence is getting to be quite a little man; don't you think it time, dear, that he was sent to school? I have so much more to occupy my mind here than I had in Georgia, so many household duties to attend to, that I am unable to give that attention to his lessons which I feel is requisite. Besides, being so much at home, he has associated with that wretched boy of the Stevens's, and is growing rude and noisy; don't you think he had better be sent to school?"

"Oh yes, Emily, if you wish it," was Mr. Garie's reply. "I will search out a school to-morrow, or next day;" and taking out his watch, he continued, "it is near twelve o'clock—how the night has flown away—we must be off to bed. After the excitement of the evening, and your exertions of to-day, I fear that you will be indisposed to-morrow."

Clarence, although over nine years old, was so backward in learning, that they were obliged to send him to a small primary school which had recently been opened in the neighbourhood; and as it was one for children of both sexes, it was deemed advisable to send little Em with him.

"I do so dislike to have her go," said her mother, as her husband proposed that she should accompany Clarence; "she seems so small to be sent to school. I'm afraid she won't be happy."

"Oh! don't give yourself the least uneasiness about her not being happy there, for a more cheerful set of little folks I never beheld. You would be astonished to see how exceedingly young some of them are."

"What kind of a person is the teacher?" asked Mrs. Garie.

"Oh! she's a charming little creature; the very embodiment of cheerfulness and good humour. She has sparkling black eyes, a round rosy face, and can't be more than sixteen, if she is that old. Had I had such a teacher when a boy, I should have got on charmingly; but mine was a cross old widow, who wore spectacles and took an amazing quantity of snuff, and used to flog upon the slightest pretense. I went into her presence with fear and trembling. I could never learn anything from her, and that must be my excuse for my present literary short-comings. But you need have no fear respecting Em getting on with Miss Jordan: I don't believe she could be unkind to any one, least of all to our little darling."

"Then you will take them down in the morning," suggested Mrs. Garie; "but on no account leave Emily unless she wishes to stay."

James Monroe Whitfield

(1822–1871)

NOT A GREAT DEAL is known about the life of James Monroe Whitfield. Earlier scholars say that he was born in Massachusetts, one specifies Boston; but Joan R. Sherman, writing in 1974, claims that he was born in New Hampshire in 1822. These scholars and Sherman also differ on Whitfield's terminal date, but they and Sherman agree that Whitfield as a young man moved to Buffalo, New York, where he worked as a barber. Outside of barbering, the work by which he made his living, Whitfield pursued three major activities: writing poetry, working with the Prince Hall Masons in California and Nevada, and promoting colonization as a "way out" for the African American.

In 1853 Whitfield published his best-known work, *America and Other Poems*, which he dedicated to Martin R. Delany. Like Delany, Whitfield was seemingly an investigator for the colonization movement. Delany went to Africa, looking for suitable sites on which to plant colonies of American blacks; Whitfield, we believe, as commissioner went to Central America in 1859 for the same purpose, staying for two years. Before leaving the country, Whitfield had contributed many poems to Douglass's *North Star* and *Frederick Douglass' Paper*. He had also written a brilliant series of letters espousing and defending colonization against Douglass and others who opposed it.

Returning to the West Coast in 1861, Whitfield took up once more his barbering trade, worked with the California Prince Hall Masons as grand master, joined in political debates, and wrote poems. If Whitfield were alive today, he would be called an "activist." His "America" and other works which appeared in abolition papers like Douglass's *North Star* are strong and well-written statements of protest, surprisingly so when one considers his lack of formal education. As Joan R. Sherman has said, he "became a major propagandist for black independence and racial retributive justice. . . . Whitfield's poetry of protest and despair are among the most robust and convincing of his time."[1]

For biographical information, one will find Vernon Loggins's *The Negro Author* helpful. Joan R. Sherman's *Invisible Poets* (1974) has a documented biography, critical comments on Whitfield's works, and a bibliography.

---

[1] Rayford W. Logan and Michael R. Winston, *Dictionary of American Negro Biography* (New York: W. W. Norton and Company, 1982), 650.

130

See also Sherman's article on Whitfield in *Dictionary of American Negro Biography* and Doris L. Laryea's entry in *Dictionary of Literary Biography, Volume 50.*

"America," "How Long?," and "The North Star" are found originally in *America and Other Poems* (1853), and later found in Benjamin Brawley's *Early Negro American Writers.*

AMERICA

America, it is to thee,
Thou boasted land of liberty,—
It is to thee I raise my song,
Thou land of blood, and crime, and wrong.
It is to thee, my native land,
From which has issued many a band
To tear the black man from his soil,
And force him here to delve and toil;
Chained on your blood-bemoistened sod,
Cringing beneath a tyrant's rod,
Stripped of those rights which Nature's God
   Bequeathed to all the human race,
Bound to a petty tyrant's nod,
   Because he wears a paler face.
Was it for this that freedom's fires
Were kindled by your patriot sires?
Was it for this they shed their blood,
On hill and plain, on field and flood?
Was it for this that wealth and life
Were staked upon that desperate strife,
Which drenched this land for seven long years
With blood of men, and women's tears?
When black and white fought side by side,
   Upon the well-contested field,—
Turned back the fierce opposing tide,
   And made the proud invader yield—
When, wounded, side by side they lay,
   And heard with joy the proud hurrah
From their victorious comrades say
   That they had waged successful war,
The thought ne'er entered in their brains
That they endured those toils and pains,
To forge fresh fetters, heavier chains

For their own children, in whose veins
Should flow that patriotic blood,
So freely shed on field and flood.
Oh, no; they fought, as they believed,
    For the inherent rights of man;
But mark, how they have been deceived
    By slavery's accursed plan.
They never thought, when thus they shed
    Their heart's best blood, in freedom's cause,
That their own sons would live in dread,
    Under unjust, oppressive laws:
That those who quietly enjoyed
    The rights for which they fought and fell,
Could be the framers of a code,
    That would disgrace the fiends of hell!
Could they have looked, with prophet's ken,
    Down to the present evil time,
    Seen free-born men, uncharged with crime,
Consigned unto a slaver's pen,—
Or thrust into a prison cell,
With thieves and murderers to dwell—
While that same flag whose stripes and stars
Had been their guide through freedom's wars
As proudly waved above the pen
Of dealers in the souls of men!
Or could the shades of all the dead,
    Who fell beneath that starry flag,
Visit the scenes where they once bled,
    On hill and plain, on vale and crag,
By peaceful brook, or ocean's strand,
    By inland lake, or dark green wood,
Where'er the soil of this wide land
    Was moistened by their patriot blood,—
And then survey the country o'er,
    From north to south, from east to west,
And hear the agonizing cry
Ascending up to God on high,
From western wilds to ocean's shore,
    The fervent prayer of the oppressed;
The cry of helpless infancy
    Torn from the parent's fond caress
By some base tool of tyranny,
    And doomed to woe and wretchedness;
The indignant wail of fiery youth,

Its noble aspirations crushed,
Its generous zeal, its love of truth,
   Trampled by tyrants in the dust;
The aerial piles which fancy reared,
   And hopes too bright to be enjoyed,
Have passed and left his young heart seared,
   And all its dreams of bliss destroyed.
The shriek of virgin purity,
   Doomed to some libertine's embrace,
Should rouse the strongest sympathy
   Of each one of the human race;
And weak old age, oppressed with care,
   As he reviews the scene of strife,
Puts up to God a fervent prayer,
   To close his dark and troubled life,
The cry of fathers, mothers, wives,
   Severed from all their hearts hold dear,
And doomed to spend their wretched lives
   In gloom, and doubt, and hate, and fear;
And manhood, too, with soul of fire,
And arm of strength, and smothered ire,
Stands pondering with brow of gloom,
Upon his dark unhappy doom,
Whether to plunge in battle's strife,
And buy his freedom with his life,
And with stout heart and weapon strong,
Pay back the tyrant wrong for wrong
Or wait the promised time of God,
   When his Almighty ire shall wake,
And smite the oppressor in his wrath,
And hurl red ruin in his path,
And with the terrors of his rod,
   Cause adamantine hearts to quake.
Here Christian writhes in bondage still,
   Beneath his brother Christian's rod,
And pastors trample down at will,
   The image of the living God.
While prayers go up in lofty strains,
   And pealing hymns ascend to heaven,
The captive, toiling in his chains,
   With tortured limbs and bosom riven,
Raises his fettered hand on high,
   And in the accents of despair,
To him who rules both earth and sky,

Puts up a sad, a fervent prayer,
To free him from the awful blast
  Of slavery's bitter galling shame—
Although his portion should be cast
  With demons in eternal flame!
Almighty God! 'tis this they call
  The land of liberty and law;
Part of its sons in baser thrall
  Than Babylon or Egypt saw—
Worse scenes of rapine, lust and shame,
  Than Babylonian ever knew,
Are perpetrated in the name
  Of God, the holy, just, and true;
And darker doom than Egypt felt,
May yet repay this nation's guilt.
Almighty God! thy aid impart,
And fire anew each faltering heart,
And strengthen every patriot's hand,
Who aims to save our native land.
We do not come before thy throne,
  With carnal weapons drenched in gore,
Although our blood has freely flown,
  In adding to the tyrant's store.
Father! before thy throne we come,
  Not in the panoply of war,
With pealing trump, and rolling drum,
  And cannon booming loud and far;
Striving in blood to wash out blood,
  Through wrong to seek redress for wrong;
For while thou'rt holy, just and good,
  The battle is not to the strong;
But in the sacred name of peace,
  Of justice, virtue, love and truth,
We pray, and never mean to cease,
  Till weak old age and fiery youth
In freedom's cause their voices raise,
And burst the bonds of every slave;
Till, north and south, and east and west,
The wrongs we bear shall be redressed.

HOW LONG?

How long, O gracious God! how long,
    Shall power lord it over right?
The feeble, trampled by the strong,
    Remain in slavery's gloomy night?
In every region of the earth,
    Oppression rules with iron power;
And every man of sterling worth,
    Whose soul disdains to cringe or cower
Beneath a haughty tyrant's nod,
And, supplicating, kiss the rod
That, wielded by oppression's might,
Smites to the earth his dearest right,—
The right to speak, and think, and feel,
    And spread his uttered thoughts abroad,
To labor for the common weal,
    Responsible to none but God,—
Is threatened with the dungeon's gloom,
The felon's cell, the traitor's doom,
And treacherous politicians league
    With hireling priests, to crush and ban
All who expose their vile intrigue,
    And vindicate the rights of man.
How long shall Afric' raise to thee
    Her fettered hand, O Lord! in vain,
And plead in fearful agony
    For vengeance for her children slain?
I see the Gambia's swelling flood,
    And Niger's darkly rolling wave,
Bear on their bosoms, stained with blood,
    The bound and lacerated slave;
While numerous tribes spread near and far,
Fierce, devastating, barbarous war,
Earth's fairest scenes in ruin laid,
To furnish victims for that trade,
Which breeds on earth such deeds of shame,
As fiends might blush to hear or name.
I see where Danube's waters roll,
    And where the Magyar vainly strove,
With valiant arm and faithful soul,
    In battle for the land he loved,—
A perjured tyrant's legions tread

The ground where Freedom's heroes bled,
And still the voice of those who feel
Their country's wrongs, with Austrian steel.
I see the "Rugged Russian Bear"
Lead forth his slavish hordes, to war
Upon the right of every State
Its own affairs to regulate;
To help each despot bind the chain
Upon the people's rights again,
And crush beneath his ponderous paw
All constitutions, rights, and law.
I see in France,—O burning shame!—
The shadow of a mighty name,
Wielding the power her patriot bands
Had boldly wrenched from kingly hands,
With more despotic pride of sway
Than ever monarch dared display.
The Fisher, too, whose world-wide nets
     Are spread to snare the souls of men,
By foreign tyrants' bayonets
     Established on his throne again,
Blesses the swords still reeking red
     With the best blood his country bore,
And prays for blessings on the head
     Of him who wades through Roman gore.
The same unholy sacrifice
Where'er I turn bursts on mine eyes,
Of princely pomp, and priestly pride,
     The people trampled in the dust,
Their dearest, holiest rights denied,
     Their hopes destroyed, their spirit crushed;
But when I turn the land to view,
     Which claims, par excellence, to be
The refuge of the brave and true,
     The strongest bulwark of the free,
The grand asylum for the poor
     And trodden down of every land,
Where they may rest in peace, secure,
     Nor fear the oppressor's iron hand,—
Worse scenes of rapine, lust, and shame,
Than e'er disgraced the Russian name,
Worse than the Austrian ever saw,
Are sanctioned here as righteous law.

Here might the Austrian butcher* make
Progress in shameful cruelty,
Where women-whippers proudly take
The meed and praise of chivalry.
Here might the cunning Jesuit learn,
Though skilled in subtle sophistry,
And trained to persevere in stern
Unsympathizing cruelty,
And call that good, which, right or wrong,
Will tend to make his order strong:
He here might learn from those who stand
High in the gospel ministry,
The very magnates of the land
In evangelic piety,
That conscience must not only bend
To everything the church decrees,
But it must also condescend,
When drunken politicians please
To place their own inhuman acts
Above the "higher law" of God,
And on the hunted victim's tracks
Cheer the malignant fiends of blood,
To help the man-thief bind the chain
Upon his Christian brother's limb,
And bear to slavery's hell again
The bound and suffering child of Him
Who died upon the cross, to save
Alike, the master and the slave.
While all the oppressed from every land
Are welcomed here with open hand,
And fulsome praises rend the heaven
For those who have the fetters riven
Of European tyranny,
And bravely struck for liberty;
And while from thirty thousand fanes
Mock prayers go up, and hymns are sung,
Three million drag their clanking chains,
"Unwept, unhonored, and unsung:"
Doomed to a state of slavery,
Compared with which the darkest night

*Haynau.

Of European tyranny,
  Seems brilliant as the noonday light.
While politicians void of shame,
  Cry this is law and liberty,
The clergy lend the awful name
  And sanction of the Deity,
To help sustain the monstrous wrong,
And crush the weak beneath the strong.
Lord, thou hast said the tyrant's ear
  Shall not be always closed to thee,
But that thou wilt in wrath appear,
  And set the trembling captive free.
And even now dark omens rise
  To those who either see or hear,
And gather o'er the darkening skies
  The threatening signs of fate and fear;
Not like the plagues which Egypt saw,
  When rising in an evil hour,
A rebel 'gainst the "higher law,"
  And glorying in her mighty power,—
Saw blasting fire, and blighting hail,
Sweep o'er her rich and fertile vale,
And heard on every rising gale
Ascend the bitter mourning wail;
And blighted herd, and blasted plain,
Through all the land the first-born slain,
Her priests and magi made to cower
In witness of a higher power,
And darkness like a sable pall
  Shrouding the land in deepest gloom,
Sent sadly through the minds of all,
  Forebodings of approaching doom.
What though no real shower of fire
  Spreads o'er this land its withering blight,
Denouncing wide Jehovah's ire,
  Like that which palsied Egypt's might;
And though no literal darkness spreads
  Upon the land its sable gloom,
And seems to fling around our heads
  The awful terrors of the tomb?
Yet to the eye of him who reads
  The fate of nations past and gone,
And marks with care the wrongful deeds
  By which their power was overthrown,—

Worse plagues than Egypt ever felt
   Are seen wide-spreading through the land,
Announcing that the heinous guilt
   On which the nation proudly stands,
Has risen to Jehovah's throne,
   And kindled his Almighty ire,
And broadcast through the land has sown
   The seeds of a devouring fire;
Blasting with foul pestiferous breath
   The fountain springs of mortal life,
And planting deep the seeds of death,
   And future germs of deadly strife;
And moral darkness spreads its gloom
   Over the land in every part,
And buries in a living tomb
   Each generous prompting of the heart.
Vice in its darkest, deadliest stains,
   Here walks with brazen front abroad,
And foul corruption proudly reigns
   Triumphant in the church of God,
And sinks so low the Christian name
In foul degrading vice and shame,
That Moslem, Heathen, Atheist, Jew,
   And men of every faith and creed,
To their professions far more true,
   More liberal both in word and deed,
May well reject with loathing scorn
   The doctrines taught by those who sell
Their brethren in the Saviour born,
   Down into slavery's hateful hell;
And with the price of Christian blood
Build temples to the Christian's God,
And offer up as sacrifice,
   And incense to the God of heaven,
The mourning wail, and bitter cries,
   Of mothers from their children riven;
Of virgin purity profaned
   To sate some brutal ruffian's lust,
Millions of godlike minds ordained
   To grovel ever in the dust,
Shut out by Christian power and might
From every ray of Christian light.
How long, O Lord! shall such vile deeds
   Be acted in thy holy name,

And senseless bigots o'er their creeds
   Fill the whole world with war and flame?
How long shall ruthless tyrants claim
   Thy sanction to their bloody laws,
And throw the mantle of thy name
   Around their foul, unhallowed cause?
How long shall all the people bow
   As vassals of the favored few,
And shame the pride of manhood's brow,—
   Give what to God alone is due,
Homage to wealth and rank and power,
Vain shadows of a passing hour?
Oh, for a pen of living fire,
   A tongue of flame, an arm of steel!
To rouse the people's slumbering ire,
   And teach the tyrants' hearts to feel.
O Lord! in vengeance now appear,
   And guide the battles for the right,
The spirits of the fainting cheer,
   And nerve the patriot's arm with might;
Till slavery's banished from the world,
And tyrants from their power hurled;
And all mankind, from bondage free,
Exult in glorious liberty.

THE NORTH STAR

Star of the North! whose steadfast ray
   Pierces the sable pall of night,
Forever pointing out the way
   That leads to freedom's hallowed light:
The fugitive lifts up his eye
To where thy rays illume the sky.

That steady, calm, unchanging light,
   Through dreary wilds and trackless dells,
Directs his weary steps aright
   To the bright land where freedom dwells;
And spreads, with sympathizing breast,
Her aegis over the oppressed;

Written for *The North Star*, a newspaper edited by Frederick Douglass.

Though other stars may round thee burn,
  With larger disk and brighter ray,
And fiery comets round thee turn,
  While millions mark their blazing way;
And the pale moon and planets bright
Reflect on us their silvery light.

Not like that moon, now dark, now bright,
  In phase and place forever changing;
Or planets with reflected light,
  Or comets through the heavens ranging;
They all seem varying in our view,
While thou art ever fixed and true.

So may that other bright North Star,
  Beaming with truth and freedom's light,
Pierce with its cheering ray afar,
  The shades of slavery's gloomy night;
And may it never cease to be
The guard of truth and liberty.

William Still

(1821–1902)

THE YOUNGEST of eighteen children, William Still was born near Medford in Burlington County, New Jersey. Still's father was originally named Levi Steel. A former slave who had bought his own freedom, Levi Steel changed his last name to Still in order to protect his wife, who had escaped from bondage in Maryland.

During William Still's early years, he worked at many jobs, but finally became a helper (janitorial and clerical) in the office of the Pennsylvania Society for the Abolition of Slavery. In this new position he met and helped hundreds of blacks who had escaped slavery via the Underground Railroad. Among the fugitives was his own brother, Peter Still, who had escaped from Alabama. (Peter Still is the subject of Mrs. Kate Pickard's biography *The Kidnapped and the Ransomed.*) William Still was especially useful to the Philadelphia Underground Station. He took refugees to his own home, where he fed and sheltered them. John Brown's wife and several of Brown's followers were protected by Still. Though largely self-taught, William Still soon recognized that there was a veritable treasure-trove for a writer in the stories told by the hundreds of ex-slaves who came through the office in which he worked. He therefore began to write down all of the anecdotes and experiences the Underground passengers told him. Realizing that these records could be dangerous to many escaped slaves, he stored them in the loft of a cemetery building. Still collected this material between 1850 and 1860, but did not publish it until 1872, when it appeared in a 780-page volume with this explicit and exhaustively long title: *The Underground Rail Road. A Record of Facts, Authentic Narratives, Letters, etc., Narrating the Hardships, Hair-Breadth Escapes and Death Struggles of the Slaves in Their Efforts for Freedom as Related by Themselves, and Others, or Witnessed by the Author; Together with Sketches of Some of the Largest Stockholders, and Most Liberal Aiders and Advisers of the Road.*

A unique publication, *The Underground Rail Road* was the most popular work of its kind, running to three editions. It is a rich storehouse of intimate and detailed information about slavery. Dramatic, sensational, occasionally tragic, the work, though factual, has the appeal of swiftly moving fiction. Still felt that blacks themselves should write such works to show the world their intellectual capabilities.

In later life, William Still became, among many other things, a pioneer "civil rights" fighter against segregation in Philadelphia, the organizer of

142

one of the early YMCA's for blacks, a successful businessman, a "social worker" who helped the poor, and the organizer of a "social, civil, and statistical association" whose purpose was to collect and preserve data on blacks (a project which anticipated Carter G. Woodson's organization, the Association for the Study of Negro Life and History, now the Association for the Study of Afro-American Life and History).

The 1872 edition of *The Underground Rail Road* has a biographical sketch of Still by James P. Boyd. The Still papers are in the Historical Society of Pennsylvania. Lurey Khan's *One Day, Levin . . . He Be Free: William Still and the Underground Railroad* (1972) and Larry Gara's excellent entry on William Still in *Dictionary of American Negro Biography* should be consulted.

The selections that follow come from *The Underground Rail Road.*

WILLIAM AND ELLEN CRAFT
Female Slave in Male Attire, Fleeing as a Planter, with her Husband as her Body Servant

A quarter of a century ago, William and Ellen Craft were slaves in the State of Georgia. With them, as with thousands of others, the desire to be free was very strong. For this jewel they were willing to make any sacrifice, or to endure any amount of suffering. In this state of mind they commenced planning. After thinking of various ways that might be tried, it occurred to William and Ellen, that one might act the part of master and the other the part of servant.

Ellen being fair enough to pass for white, of necessity would have to be transformed into a young planter for the time being. All that was needed, however, to make this important change was that she should be dressed elegantly in a fashionable suit of male attire, and have her hair cut in the style usually worn by young planters. Her profusion of dark hair offered a fine opportunity for the change. So far this plan looked very tempting. But it occurred to them that Ellen was beardless. After some mature reflection, they came to the conclusion that this difficulty could be very readily obviated by having the face muffled up as though the young planter was suffering badly with the face or toothache; thus they got rid of this trouble. Straightway, upon further reflection, several other very serious difficulties stared them in the face. For instance, in traveling, they knew that they would be under the necessity of stopping repeatedly at hotels, and that the custom of registering would have to be conformed to, unless some very good excuse could be given for not doing so.

Here they again thought much over matters, and wisely concluded that the young man had better assume the attitude of a gentleman very much indisposed. He must have his right arm placed carefully in a sling; that would be a sufficient excuse for not registering, etc. Then he must be a little lame, with a nice cane in the left hand; he must have large green spectacles over his eyes, and withal he must be very hard of hearing and dependent on his faithful servant (as was no uncommon thing with slave-holders), to look after all his wants.

William was just the man to act this part. To begin with, he was very "likely-looking;" smart, active and exceedingly attentive to his young master—indeed he was almost eyes, ears, hands and feet for him. William knew that this would please the slave-holders. The young planter would have nothing to do but hold himself subject to his ailments and put on a bold air of superiority; he was not to deign to notice anybody. If, while traveling, gentlemen, either politely or rudely, should venture to scrape acquaintance with the young planter, in his deafness he was to remain mute; the servant was to explain. In every instance when this occurred, as it actually did, the servant was fully equal to the emergency—none dreaming of the disguises in which the Underground Rail Road passengers were traveling.

They stopped at a first-class hotel in Charleston, where the young planter and his body servant were treated, as the house was wont to treat the chivalry. They stopped also at a similar hotel in Richmond, and with like results.

They knew that they must pass through Baltimore, but they did not know the obstacles that they would have to surmount in the Monumental City. They proceeded to the depot in the usual manner, and the servant asked for tickets for his master and self. Of course the master could have a ticket, but "bonds will have to be entered before you can get a ticket," said the ticket master. "It is the rule of this office to require bonds for all negroes applying for tickets to go North, and none but gentlemen of well-known responsibility will be taken," further explained the ticket master.

The servant replied, that he knew "nothing about that"—that he was "simply traveling with his young master to take care of him—he being in a very delicate state of health, so much so, that fears were entertained that he might not be able to hold out to reach Philadelphia, where he was hastening for medical treatment," and ended his reply by saying, "my master can't be detained." Without further parley the ticket master very obligingly waived the old "rule," and furnished the requisite tickets. The mountain being thus removed, the young planter and his faithful servant were safely in the cars for the city of Brotherly Love.

Scarcely had they arrived on free soil when the rheumatism departed—the right arm was unslung—the toothache was gone—the beardless face was unmuffled—the deaf heard and spoke—the blind saw—and the lame leaped as an hart, and in the presence of a few astonished friends of the slave, the facts of this unparalleled Underground Rail Road feat were fully established by the most unquestionable evidence.

The constant strain and pressure on Ellen's nerves, however, had tried her severely, so much so, that for days afterwards, she was physically very much prostrated, although joy and gladness beamed from her eyes, which bespoke inexpressible delight within.

Never can the writer forget the impression made by their arrival. Even now, after a lapse of nearly a quarter of a century, it is easy to picture them in a private room, surrounded by a few friends—Ellen in her fine suit of black, with her cloak and high-heeled boots, looking, in every respect, like a young gentleman; in an hour after having dropped her male attire, and assumed the habiliments of her sex the feminine only was visible in every line and feature of her structure.

Her husband, William, was thoroughly colored, but was a man of marked natural abilities, of good manners, and full of pluck, and possessed of perceptive faculties very large.

It was necessary, however, in those days, that they should seek a permanent residence, where their freedom would be more secure than in Philadelphia; therefore they were advised to go to headquarters, directly to Boston. There they would be safe, it was supposed, as it had then been about a generation since a fugitive had been taken back from the old Bay State, and through the incessant labors of William Lloyd Garrison, the great pioneer, and his faithful coadjutors, it was conceded that another fugitive slave case could never be tolerated on the free soil of Massachusetts. So to Boston they went.

On arriving, the warm hearts of abolitionists welcomed them heartily, and greeted and cheered them without let or hindrance. They did not pretend to keep their coming a secret, or hide it under a bushel; the story of their escape was heralded broadcast over the country—North and South, and indeed over the civilized world. For two years or more, not the slightest fear was entertained that they were not just as safe in Boston as if they had gone to Canada. But the day the Fugitive Bill passed, even the bravest abolitionist began to fear that a fugitive slave was no longer safe anywhere under the stars and stripes, North or South, and that William and Ellen Craft were liable to be captured at any moment by Georgia slave hunters. Many abolitionists counselled resistance to the death at all hazards. Instead of running to Canada, fugitives generally armed themselves and thus said, "Give me liberty or give me death."

William and Ellen Craft believed that it was their duty, as citizens of Massachusetts, to observe a more legal and civilized mode of conforming to the marriage rite than had been permitted them in slavery, and as Theodore Parker had shown himself a very warm friend of their's, they agreed to have their wedding over again according to the laws of a free State. After performing the ceremony, the renowned and fearless advocate of equals rights (Theodore Parker), presented William with a revolver and a dirk-knife, counselling him to use them manfully in defence of his wife and himself, if ever an attempt should be made by his owners or anybody else to re-enslave them. . . .

HENRY BOX BROWN
Arrived by Adams' Express

Although the name of Henry Box Brown has been echoed over the land for a number of years, and the simple facts connected with his marvelous escape from slavery in a box published widely through the medium of anti-slavery papers, nevertheless it is not unreasonable to suppose that very little is generally known in relation to this case.

Briefly, the facts are these, which doubtless have never before been fully published—

Brown was a man of invention as well as a hero. In point of interest, however, his case is no more remarkable than many others. Indeed, neither before nor after escaping did he suffer one-half what many others have experienced.

He was decidedly an unhappy piece of property in the city of Richmond, Va. In the condition of a slave he felt that it would be impossible for him to remain. Full well did he know, however, that it was no holiday task to escape the vigilance of Virginia slave-hunters, or the wrath of an enraged master for committing the unpardonable sin of attempting to escape to a land of liberty. So Brown counted well the cost before venturing upon this hazardous undertaking. Ordinary modes of travel he concluded might prove disastrous to his hopes; he, therefore, hit upon a new invention altogether, which was to have himself boxed up and forwarded to Philadelphia direct by express. The size of the box and how it was to be made to fit him most comfortably, was of his own ordering. Two feet eight inches deep, two feet wide, and three feet long were the exact dimensions of the box, lined with baize. His resources with regard to food and water consisted of the following: One bladder of water and a few small biscuits. His mechanical implement to meet the death-struggle for fresh air, all told, was one large gimlet. Satisfied that it would be far better to peril his life for freedom in this way than to remain under the galling yoke of Slavery, he entered his box, which was safely nailed up and hooped with five hickory hoops, and was then addressed by his next friend, James A. Smith, a shoe dealer, to Wm. H. Johnson, Arch street, Philadelphia, marked, "This side up with care." In this condition he was sent to Adams' Express office in a dray, and thence by overland express to Philadelphia. It was twenty-six hours from the time he left Richmond until his arrival in the City of Brotherly Love. The notice, "This side up, &c.," did not avail with the different expressmen, who hesitated not to handle the box in the usual rough manner common to this class of men. For a while they actually had the box upside down, and had him on his head for miles. A few days before he was expected, certain intimation was conveyed to a member of the Vigilance Committee that a box might be expected by the three o'clock morning train from the South, which might contain a man. One of the most serious walks he ever took—and they had not been a few—to meet and accompany passengers, he took at half past two o'clock that morning to the depot. Not once, but for more than a score of times, he fancied the slave would be dead. He anxiously looked while the freight was being unloaded from the cars, to see if he could recognize a box that might contain a man; one alone had that appearance, and he confessed it really seemed as if there was the scent of death about it. But on inquiry, he soon learned that it was not the one he was looking after, and he was free to say he experienced a marked sense of relief. That same afternoon, however, he received from Richmond a telegram, which read thus, "Your case of goods is shipped and will arrive tomorrow morning."

At this exciting juncture of affairs, Mr. McKim, who had been engineering this important undertaking, deemed it expedient to change the programme slightly in one particular at least to insure greater safety. Instead of having a member of the Committee go again to the depot for the box, which might excite suspicion, it was decided that it would be safest to have the express bring it direct to the Anti-Slavery Office.

But all apprehension of danger did not now disappear, for there was no room to suppose that Adams' Express office had any sympathy with the Abolitionist or the fugitive, consequently for Mr. McKim to appear personally at the express office to give directions with reference to the coming of a box from Richmond which would be directed to Arch street, and yet not intended for that street, but for the Anti-Slavery office at 107 North Fifth street, it needed of course no great discernment to foresee that a step of this kind was wholly impracticable and that a more indirect and covert method would have to be adopted. In this dreadful crisis Mr. McKim, with his usual good judgment and remarkably quick, strategical mind, especially in matters pertaining to the U. G. R. R., hit upon the following plan, namely, to go to his friend, E. M. Davis, who was then extensively engaged in mercantile business, and relate the circumstances. Having daily intercourse with said Adams' Express office, and being well acquainted with the firm and some of the drivers, Mr. Davis could, as Mr. McKim thought, talk about "boxes, freight, etc.," from any part of the country without risk. Mr. Davis heard Mr. McKim's plan and instantly approved of it, and was heartily at his service.

"Dan, an Irishman, one of Adams' Express drivers, is just the fellow to go to the depot after the box," said Davis. "He drinks a little too much whiskey sometimes, but he will do anything I ask him to do, promptly and obligingly. I'll trust Dan, for I believe he is the very man." The difficulty which Mr. McKim had been so anxious to overcome was thus pretty well settled. It was agreed that Dan should go after the box next morning before daylight and bring it to the Anti-Slavery office direct, and to make it all the more agreeable for Dan to get up out of his warm bed and go on this errand before day, it was decided that he should have a five dollar gold piece for himself. Thus these preliminaries having been satisfactorily arranged, it only remained for Mr. Davis to see Dan and give him instructions accordingly, etc.

Next morning, according to arrangement, the box was at the Anti-Slavery office in due time. The witnesses present to behold the resurrection were J. M. McKim, Professor C. D. Cleveland, Lewis Thompson, and the writer.

Mr. McKim was deeply interested; but having been long identified with the Anti-Slavery cause as one of its oldest and ablest advocates in the darkest days of slavery and mobs, and always found by the side of the fugitive to counsel and succor, he was on this occasion perfectly composed.

Professor Cleveland, however, was greatly moved. His zeal and earnestness in the cause of freedom, especially in rendering aid to passengers, knew no limit. Ordinarily he could not too often visit these travelers, shake them too warmly by the hand, or impart to them too freely of his substance to aid them on their journey. But now his emotion was overpowering.

Mr. Thompson, of the firm of Merrihew & Thompson—about the only printers in the city who for many years dared to print such incendiary documents as anti-slavery papers and pamphlets—one of the truest friends of the slave, was composed and prepared to witness the scene.

All was quiet. The door had been safely locked. The proceedings commenced. Mr. McKim rapped quietly on the lid of the box and called out, "All right!" Instantly came the answer from within, "All right, sir!"

The witnesses will never forget that moment. Saw and hatchet quickly had the five hickory hoops cut and the lid off, and the marvelous resurrection of Brown ensued. Rising up in his box, he reached out his hand, saying, "How do you do, gentlemen?" The little assemblage hardly knew what to think or do at the moment. He was about as wet as if he had come up out of the Delaware. Very soon he remarked that, before leaving Richmond he had selected for his arrival-hymn (if he lived) the Psalm beginning with these words: "*I waited patiently for the Lord, and He heard my prayer.*" And most touchingly did he sing the psalm, much to his own relief, as well as to the delight of his small audience.

He was then christened Henry Box Brown, and soon afterwards was sent to the hospitable residence of James Mott and E. M. Davis, on Ninth street, where, it is needless to say, he met a most cordial reception from Mrs. Lucretia Mott and her household. Clothing and creature comforts were furnished in abundance, and delight and joy filled all hearts in that stronghold of philanthropy.

As he had been so long doubled up in the box he needed to promenade considerably in the fresh air, so James Mott put one of his broad-brim hats on his head and tendered him the hospitalities of his yard as well as his house, and while Brown promenaded the yard flushed with victory, great was the joy of his friends.

Charlotte L. Forten

(1838–1914)

CHARLOTTE FORTEN was born in Philadelphia; her mother and her father, a wealthy sailmaker, were free blacks. The Forten family had been actively involved in the black man's cause for two generations, and their Philadelphia home was described as a "mecca for abolitionists." Eventually Charlotte herself counted John Greenleaf Whittier, William Lloyd Garrison, and Wendell Phillips among her friends.

Charlotte Forten received some of her education at home, but most of her training was acquired at the Salem, Massachusetts, Normal School, where she was graduated in 1856. She was extremely sensitive to the plight of the black man—a cause to which her family contributed enormous physical and intellectual energy and a considerable share of its wealth. Charlotte Forten's *Journal* frequently alludes to racial prejudice, discrimination, and injustice; her tone is often one of bitter irony, occasionally hinting at despair. "How *can* I be a Christian when so many in common with myself, for no crime suffer so cruelly, so unjustly? It seems vain to try, even to hope."

Charlotte Forten was also sensitive to the pleasures of warm friendship, to nature's beauty, and to the ideals her parents had instilled in her. She read widely and insatiably, wrote "occasional" poems, and taught enthusiastically—first white pupils in Salem, and then black students in her aunt's school in Philadelphia.

At the start of the Civil War Forten grew restless. When Union forces secured Port Royal Harbor and General Thomas W. Sherman urged "that suitable instructors be sent to the Negroes," the young woman volunteered. For two years she taught on St. Helena Island, one of the Sea Islands off the coast of South Carolina. It was her last regular teaching post, but also the most unusual and rewarding.

In 1864 Forten returned to Philadelphia. She wrote a few magazine pieces, which were published in the *Atlantic Monthly*, and translated Erckmann-Chatrian's *Madame Therese; or, the Volunteers of '92*. In 1878 she married Francis J. Grimké, a minister who later won distinction as a spokesman for black people.

Charlotte Forten's *Journal*, which she kept sporadically from 1854 to 1864, is an unusual record and an important historical document. The manuscript diaries of Forten are now in Howard University's Manuscript Division, Moorland-Spingarn Research Center. The best-known account of Forten's life may be found in the introduction to *The Journal of Charlotte L. Forten*, edited by Ray Billington in 1953. For a comment on Billington's *Journal* pointing out certain "errors of fact" in the work, see Gloria C. Oden, "The Journal of Charlotte L. Forten: The Salem-Philadelphia Years (1854–1862) Reexamined," *Essex Institute Historical Collections* 119: 2 (April 1983).

For additional comment, see Edmund Wilson's *Patriotic Gore* (1962) and Joan R. Sherman's *Invisible Poets*. The *Journal* was published in paperback in 1961 and in 1967 by Collier Books; *The Journals of Charlotte Forten Grimké*, edited by Brenda Stevenson, appeared in 1988. The entry in *Dictionary of American Negro Biography*, written by Rayford W. Logan, is a superb summary of the life of this unusual woman. The Trudier Harris entry in *Dictionary of Literary Biography, Volume 50* features facsimiles of selected poetry and journal entries by Forten.

An American Playhouse production, "Charlotte Forten's Mission: An Experiment in Freedom," which was aired on national television on February 25, 1985, and starred Melba Moore, points to the continuing popular interest in Forten's life and work.

The following selections were taken from *The Journal of Charlotte Forten, A Free Negro in the Slave Era*.

FROM **THE JOURNAL OF CHARLOTTE FORTEN**

. . . *Monday, July 16, 1855. Examination day.*—*No further comment is needed.*

Tuesday, July 17. I breathe freely,—our trial is over, and happy are we to escape from the hot, crowded school-room;—for it has been densely crowded all day. This evening the scholars had a pleasant meeting in the school house and the last farewells were said. . . .

Wednesday, Aug. 1. Went with Aunt M[argaretta] and a party of friends to the celebration at Abington. Our much-loved Garrison was not there,—His absence could not fail to be felt. But Mr. Phillips and other able speakers were there and many eloquent speeches were made. We had a pleasant sail on the beautiful pond attached to the Grove;—and passed altogether a delightful day.

Sunday, Aug. 12. Had a delightful ride to Reading, to an anti-slavery meeting. The road is beautiful and our Penn[sylvania] friends warmly admired scenery which the eastern part of the Keystone

State cannot boast of. Mr. Garrison and Mr. Phillips spoke very beautifully. To our great regret we were obliged to leave while Mr. P[hillips] was speaking. Our ride home was extremely pleasant. . . .

Friday, Aug. 17. My eighteenth birthday.—Spent the afternoon and evening very pleasantly at Mrs. Putnam's. Miss Brown was there, I think I shall like her. Her father's fondness for her is rather too demonstrative. I guess she is a sensible girl. I enjoy talking with her about her European life.—She is pleasant and communicative, and though coming lastly from England has, I think, lived in France too much to acquire a great deal of that reserve which characterizes the manners of the English.

Sunday, Aug. 26. Spent the evening at Mrs. Putnam's. Mr. Nell was there. We amused ourselves with making conundrums, reading and reciting poetry. . . .

Wednesday, Sept. 12. To-day school commenced.—Most happy am I to return to the companionship of my studies,—ever my most valued friends. It is pleasant to meet the scholars again; most of them greeted me cordially, and were it not for the thought that *will* intrude, of the want of *entire sympathy* even of those I know and like best, I should greatly enjoy their society. There is one young girl and only one—Miss [Sarah] B[rown] who I believe thoroughly and heartily appreciates anti-slavery,—*radical* anti-slavery, and has no prejudice against color. I wonder that every colored person is not a misanthrope. Surely we have everything to make us hate mankind. I have met girls in the schoolroom[—] they have been thoroughly kind and cordial to me,—perhaps the next day met them in the street—they feared to recognize me; these I can but regard now with scorn and contempt,—once I liked them, believing them incapable of such meanness. Others give the most distant recognition possible.—I, of course, acknowledge no such recognitions, and they soon cease entirely. These are but trifles, certainly, to the great, public wrongs which we as a people are obliged to endure. But to those who experience them, these apparent trifles are most wearing and discouraging; even to the child's mind they reveal volumes of deceit and heartlessness, and early teach a lesson of suspicion and distrust. Oh! it is hard to go through life meeting contempt with contempt, hatred with hatred, fearing, with too good reason, to love and trust hardly any one whose skin is white,—however lovable, attractive and congenial in seeming. In the bitter, passionate feelings of my soul again and again there rises the questions "When, oh! when shall this cease?" "Is there no help?" "How long oh! how long must we continue to suffer—to endure?" Conscience answers it is wrong, it is ignoble to despair; let us labor earnestly and faithfully to acquire knowledge, to break down the barriers of prejudice and oppression.

Let us take courage; never ceasing to work,—hoping and believing that if not for us, for another generation there is a better, brighter day in store,—when slavery and prejudice shall vanish before the glorious light of Liberty and Truth; when the rights of every colored man shall everywhere be acknowledged and respected, and he shall be treated as a *man* and a *brother!*

September. This evening Miss B[rown] and I joined the Female Anti-Slavery Society. I am glad to have persuaded her to do so. She seems an earnest hearted girl, in whom I cannot help having some confidence. I can only hope and pray that she will be true, and courageous enough to meet the opposition which every friend of freedom must encounter. . . .

Friday, October 19. Walked to Marblehead with some of the girls to attend the teachers' meeting. . . . In the evening . . . listened to a very beautiful lecture from Rev. Mr. Huntingdon,—his subject was "Unconscious Tuition." But I felt a want, for among the many true and beautiful sentiments which he uttered not the faintest indication that he was even aware of the existence of that cruel and disgraceful system which refuses all teachings—all that can elevate and improve to millions of the inhabitants of this *glorious* (?) republic. Had a pleasant walk to Salem in the moonlight. . . .

Sunday, Oct. 21. The twentieth anniversary of the day on which beloved Garrison was mobbed and insulted in the streets of Boston. To-day on the very spot where that little band of noble-hearted women so heroically maintained the right, the dauntless Pioneer of our glorious cause stands with many true-hearted co-workers, surrounded by hundreds of eager, sympathizing listeners. The men who dragged him with a rope around his neck through the streets of Boston,—to their own shame—not his—would blush to confess it to-day. And even his bitter enemies are forced, despite themselves, to respect his self-sacrificing unfaltering devotion to Liberty and Truth. Dear, honored friends, I cannot be with you in your gathering to-day, but the light of your loved countenances,—the tones of your eloquent voices fall upon my grateful heart. This evening my necessary absence from the meeting in Boston, upon which my thoughts have dwelt all day, was somewhat compensated for by listening to an excellent and very interesting lecture from Rev. S. Johnson of Lynn. *The first of our course.—*

Sunday, Oct. 28. This has indeed been one of the happiest days of my life.—Wendell Phillips, Mr. Hovey, and Miss Holley and Miss P[hillips] have spent it with us,—could it fail to be a happy one? Mr. Phillips is the most fascinating person I ever saw. That graceful affability which characterizes the truly great, he embodies, with all that is truly good and noble. Mr. Hovey is exceedingly entertaining.

He has travelled much; and presented Mrs. R[emond] with a precious relic—a piece of mosaic pavement from the Baths of Caracalla, Rome, built sixteen hundred years ago. How strange it seems that sixteen centuries ago this stone was laid—almost incredible! While gazing on such relics a strange influence from the mighty, mysterious Past comes over us—conjuring up visions of that olden time, long past, but never to be forgotten; for the soul of man rests not in the *Present*, nor soars only in the great *Future*, which imagination paints for it, but also does it love to dwell in the deep, soul-stirring memories of the Past. Mr. Phillips' lecture was worthy of himself—I can bestow no higher praise upon it. Oh! it is a source of some consolation to feel—to know that some of the noblest minds—the greatest intellects of the age are enlisted in our behalf.—

Friday, Nov. 1. This evening heard Charles Sumner for the first time. He said many excellent things, but I cannot agree with very many of his views—particularly with his reverence for the Constitution and the Union. I believe, though greatly mistaken he yet has a warm, true heart, and certainly he is an elegant and eloquent orator. Though very different from, and inferior to Mr. Phillips, in my opinion.—. . .

Sunday, Dec. 23. This evening had the very great pleasure of hearing dear Mr. May speak on anti-slavery. It was one of the best lectures I have ever heard. And I thanked him with my whole heart for the beautiful and well deserved tribute which he paid Mr. Garrison, who is so very greatly unappreciated and misrepresented. He compared him to the fountain in the Black Forest of Germany where the mighty Danube—the great "anti-slavery stream" has its source; and failed not to mention the numerous valuable tributaries who have contributed to its mass of waters—ever receiving a new impulse from the great Fountain Head. He had a large, and extremely attentive audience.—

Christmas Day, 1855. Alone; I do not know when I have been alone before on Christmas—never, I think.—Wrote a long letter to Aunt M[argaretta] while I was writing, Mrs. Gilliard came in and insisted on my accompanying her home. I spent part of the day and took dinner there. . . . Went to hear Ralph Waldo Emerson, who lectured on Beauty. I liked his originality, though his manner is not particularly interesting. Altogether we were much pleased with the lecture.

Sunday, Dec. 30. Yesterday, Mrs. Remond, who has been attending the Boston Bazaar, came home. . . . Heard read, and read partly myself—"Caste" which is an interesting anti-slavery, anti-prejudice story.

This evening listened to an excellent lecture before our Society, from Mr. Frothingham. . . .

Sunday, Jan. 27 [*1856*]. (Wrote a hymn for examination.) The last few weeks have been but successions of constant study, with but little variation. I have heard but one lecture—that of Mr. Parker,—which was, of course, excellent. His subject was the "Productive Industry of the Age" and he contrasted it with the military achievements of the "olden time"; and strikingly showed the beneficial effects of the industry of our age. Every time I listen to this wonderful man, I become more deeply impressed with the magnificence of his intellect and the sincere goodness and nobleness of his heart. This evening Mr. Hodges gave us a very good anti-slavery lecture. For the first time Mrs. Remond was obliged to introduce the lecturer it was a great trial to her, but she did it well ne'ertheless. . . .

Saturday, Feb. 2. This evening our beloved Mr. Garrison and his wife arrived.—Most gladly did we welcome them. The Remonds and Putnams spent the evening with us, and we had a delightful time. Mr. Garrison was very genial as he always is, and sang delightfully.

Sunday, Feb. 3. This has been one of the happiest days of my life. More and more do I love and admire that great and good man. His wife is a lovely woman; it is indeed delightful to see so happy and noble a couple. This evening, Mr. Garrison gave us one of the best lectures I ever heard him deliver. Always interesting to me, to-night he was unusually entertaining. Just before the lecture Mr. Innis announced the fact of Mr. Banks' election, which was received with tumultuous applause. Mr. G[arrison] spoke beautifully of the "*Banks* of Massachusetts impeding the onward progress of the waves of southern despotism."—

Monday, Feb. 4. This morning Mr. and Mrs. G[arrison] left. They kindly invited me to pay them a visit, which I will be glad to do. This was the first time they have stayed with us since I have been here. And the pleasure, the very great pleasure which I experienced from their visit, will prevent me from soon forgetting it.—

Friday, Feb. 8. Next week we shall have our examination. I dread it, and do most heartily wish it was over!

Tuesday, Feb. 12. The last day of our examination. Thank Heaven it is over at last! I am completely tired out, and need rest, both in body and mind. We have got along very well—I could say pleasantly on the last afternoon, were it not for a few unpleasant remarks of Mr. Russell. The best way is to forget them as soon as possible. The exercises of the graduating class, on this afternoon were very interesting.

Wednesday, Feb. 13. I should be sorry that we have vacation were

it not that I need rest. This morning Mr. R[emond] left for
Phila[delphia]. I felt very anxious to go, but it was impossible. We
met at the school house, and formed a Normal Association. . . .

Saturday, Mar. 1. . . . I would gladly go out and enjoy to the full
the clear, bracing air and the bright sunlight; but I was *wise* enough
to take a severe cold and must pay the penalty by keeping a close
prisoner on this delightful day. I have just heard that my beloved
friend Miss Shepard is much better, and I feel better and happier for
knowing it. A few evenings since attended a pleasant surprise party
at Mrs. P[utnam]'s. Several of the company were dressed as ladies of
the olden time, and very comical they looked in short skirts, high-
heeled shoes, huge collars, and combs which are miniature steeples.
I was persuaded to dress in full Bloomer costume, which I have
since had good cause to regret, however. . . .

Thursday, March 6. Received a long and pleasant letter from
Sarah Brown. I was very glad to hear from her, and shall send her
some anti-slavery tracts when I write. She is a most agreeable and
good-hearted girl, interested in anti-slavery; but I do most earnestly
hope to see her more so.—

Monday, Mar. 10. This evening went to see 'Hamlet.' It is the first
play of Shakespeare's that I [have] ever seen and I enjoyed it very
much. I suppose if I had ever seen any better acting than Mr. Marshall's I should not have been so much pleased. The tragedy I have
always liked very much; and many parts of it are as familiar as
household words.—

Tuesday, Mar. 11. Went to hear the Misses Hall—the 'Singing
Sisters.' They sang very sweetly. One of them has a particularly fine
voice.—On returning home found a very old friend of our family,—
Mr. Coffin,—the former teacher of my father and uncles. I have seldom met any one who possessed such extensive and varied knowledge, and yet from his perfectly unassuming, and perhaps unrefined
manner, a stranger would never suspect it. He is exceedingly entertaining, and, as I know him to be a radical abolitionist I like him
very much. His daughter has just entered our Normal School. . . .

Sunday, March 16. . . . To-day we had our election for those who
are to write our poem, valedictory, and dissertation. Miss Pitman
was chosen to write the dissertation; Lizzie Church the valedictory,
and my unworthy self to write the poem; I most respectfully declined, but every one insists upon my doing it; so I suppose I must
make the attempt. But it is a most formidable undertaking for me,
and one which, I greatly fear, is quite beyond my powers. . . .

Wednesday, April 2. This afternoon I had a long conversation
with Mr. Edwards. He spoke very kindly to me, far more so than I
deserve, and urged me to come back next term. When I very ear-

nestly assured him that it was quite impossible, he asked me why in
such a manner that I could not avoid telling him frankly. He said he
would see if something could not be done. I said nothing, but I
know too well that nothing *can* be done. Indeed though I very much
wish to spend another term here, I desire nothing so much as some
employment which shall enable me to pay my debts.—I hope I shall
be fortunate enough to obtain some situation as a teacher. . . .

 Saturday, May 11. All day I have been worrying about that poem.
That troublesome poem which has yet to be commenced. Oh! that I
could become suddenly inspired and write as only great poets can
write. Or that I might write a beautiful poem of two hundred lines
in my sleep as Coleridge did. Alas! in vain are all such longings. I
must depend upon *myself* alone. And what can that self produce?
Nothing, nothing but *doggerel*! This evening read Plutarch's Lycur-
gus.

 Friday, May 24. To-day Mr. Purvis arrived. I think he looks
poorly. Felt glad to see him. We have vacation this week instead of
next, for which I am sorry, because next week the Boston meetings
take place.

 Wednesday, May 29. Went up to Boston this afternoon with Mr.
Purvis, Mrs. P[urvis] and Miss L[ucy] R[emond]. We went to the
Pillsbury Festival, which was a very brilliant and successful one. . . .
Excellent speeches were made by our best speakers. Mr. P[hillips]
was as usual eloquent and fascinating. Mr. Pillsbury spoke for a little
while with deep feeling; his health is not entirely restored. I like him
much. Had the happiness of seeing Mrs. Chapman for the first time.
I think her the most beautiful woman I ever saw. Also the very great
pleasure of seeing Mrs. Chase of R[hode] I[sland] to whom I wrote
applying for the situation of governess. Her reply was a *very* kind
letter. I love her for it. She is a lovely looking woman, I shall be
glad to have such a friend. . . .

◌⟡✕✕⟡◌

 . . . *Tuesday Night.* T'was a strange sight as our boat approached the
landing at Hilton Head. On the wharf was a motley assemblage,—
soldiers, officers, and "contrabands" of every hue and size. They
were mostly black, however, and certainly the most dismal specimens I ever saw. H[ilton] H[ead] looks like a very desolate place;
just a long low, sandy point running out into the sea with no visible
dwellings upon it but the soldiers' white roofed tents.

 Thence, after an hour's delay, during which we signed a paper,
which was virtually taking the oath of allegiance, we left the "United
States," most rocking of rockety propellers,—and took a steamboat

for Beaufort. On board the boat was General Saxton to whom we
were introduced. I like his face exceedingly. And his manners were
very courteous and affable. He looks like a thoroughly *good* man.—
From H[ilton] H[ead] to B[eaufort] the same low long line of sandy
shore bordered by trees. Almost the only object of interest to me
were the remains of an old Huguenot Fort, built many, many years
ago.

Arrived at B[eaufort] we found that we had yet not reached our
home. Went to Mr. French's, and saw there Reuben T[omlinson],
whom I was very glad to meet, and Mrs. Gage, who seemed to be in
rather a dismal state of mind. B[eaufort] looks like a pleasant place.
The houses are large and quite handsome, built in the usual Southern style with verandahs around them, and beautiful trees. One magnolia tree in Mr. F[rench's] yard is splendid,—quite as large as some
of our large shade trees, and, with the most beautiful foliage, a dark
rich glossy green.

Went into the Commissary's Office to wait for the boat which
was to take us to St. Helena's Island which is about six miles from
B[eaufort]. 'Tis here that Miss Towne has her school, in which I am
to teach, and that Mr. Hunn will have his store. While waiting in the
Office we saw several military gentleman [*sic*], *not* very creditable
specimens, I sh'ld say. The little Commissary himself . . . is a perfect
little popinjay, and he and a Colonel somebody who didn't look any
too sensible, talked in a very smart manner, evidently for our espe-
cial benefit. The word "nigger" was plentifully used, whereupon I set
them down at once as not gentleman [*sic*]. Then they talked a great
deal about rebel attacks and yellow fever, and other alarming things,
with significant nods and looks at each other. We saw through them
at once, and were not at all alarmed by any of their representations.
But if they are a fair example of army officers, I sh'ld pray to see as
little of them as possible.

To my great joy found that we were to be rowed by a crew of
negro boatmen. Young Mr. F[rench] whom I like—accompanied us,
while Mr. H[unn] went with a flat to get our baggage. The row was
delightful. It was just at sunset—a grand Southern sunset; and the
gorgeous clouds of crimson and gold were reflected in the waters below, which were smooth and calm as a mirror. Then, as we glided
along, the rich sonorous tones of the boatmen broke upon the evening stillness. Their singing impressed me much. It was so sweet and
strange and solemn. "Roll, Jordan, Roll" was grand, and another

> *"Jesus make de blind to see*
> *Jesus make de deaf to hear*
> *   "   "   "   cripple walk*
> *Walk in, dear Jesus,"*

and the refrain

"No man can hender me."

It was very, very impressive. I want to hear these men sing Whittier's "Song of the Negro Boatmen." I am going to see if it can't be brought about in some way.

It was nearly dark when we reached St. Helena's, where we found Miss T[owne]'s carriage awaiting us, and then we three and our driver, had a long drive along the lonely roads in the dark night. How easy it w'ld have been for a band of guerillas—had any chanced that way—to seize and hang us. But we feared nothing of the kind. We were in a jubilant state of mind and sang "John Brown" with a will as we drove through the pines and palmettos. Arrived at the Superintendent's house we were kindly greeted by him and the ladies and shown into a lofty *ceilinged* parlor where a cheerful wood fire glowed in the grate, and we soon began to feel quite at home in the very heart of Rebeldom; only that I do not at all realize yet that we are in S[outh] C[arolina]. It is all a strange wild dream, from which I am constantly expecting to awake. But I can write no more now. I am tired, and still feel the motion of the ship in my poor head. Good night, dear A!

Wednesday, Oct. 29. A lovely day, but rather cool, I sh'ld think, for the "sunny South." the ship still seals [*sic*] in my head, and everything is most unreal, yet I went to drive. We drove to Oaklands, our future home. It is very pleasantly situated, but the house is in rather a dilapidated condition, as are most of the houses here, and the and the [*sic*] yard and garden have a neglected look, when it is cleaned up, and the house made habitable I think it will be quite a pleasant place. There are some lovely roses growing there and quantities of ivy creeping along the ground, even under the house, in wild luxuriance.—The negroes on the place are very kind and polite. I think I shall get on amicably with them.

⋐✖✖✖⋑

[*Monday, July 6, 1863*] . . . After school, though very tired, did not neglect my invitation to tea with the officers of the 54th. Drove down to Land's End. . . . Met Col. G[illmore] who went with us. Were just in time to see the Dress Parade. Tis a splendid looking reg[iment]—an honor to the race. Then we went with Col. Shaw to tea. Afterward sat outside the tent, and listened to some very fine singing from some of the privates. Their voices blended beautifully. "Jubilo" is one of the best things I've heard lately.

I am more than ever charmed with the noble little Col. [Shaw].

What purity, what nobleness of soul, what exquisite gentleness in that beautiful face! As I look at it I think "The bravest are the tenderest." I can imagine what he must be to his mother. May his life be spared to her! Yesterday at the celebration he stood, leaning against our carriage and speaking of mother, so lovingly, so tenderly. He said he wished she c'ld be there. If the reg[iment] were going to be stationed there for some time he sh'ld send for her. "But you know," he said "we might be suddenly ordered away, and then she w'ld have nobody to take care of her." I do think he is a wonderfully lovable person. Tonight, he helped me on my horse, and after carefully arranging the folds of my riding skirt, said, so kindly, "Good-bye. If I don't see you again down here I hope to see you at our house." But I hope I shall have the pleasure of seeing him many times even down here. He and his men are eager to be called into active service.

Major H[allowell] rode with L[izzie] and me to Col. G[illmore]'s tent. . . . The rest of the party played whist till a very late hour but I was thoroughly exhausted. Lay down part of the time. And part of the time sat close to the water's edge, and watched the boats, and the gleaming lights over the water, and the rising moon. A deep peace was over everything—not a sound to be heard but the low, musical murmur of the waves as they kissed the shore.

Wednesday, July 8. Mr. T[omlinson] came over and drove down to Land's End for Lieut. [James] W[alton] who is still quite ill. The reg[iment] has gone. Left this morning. My heart-felt prayers go with them—for the men and for their noble, noble young Colonel. God bless him! God keep him in His care, and grant that his men may do nobly and prove themselves worthy of him!

Monday, July 20. For nearly two weeks we have waited, oh how anxiously for news of our reg[iment] which went, we know to Morris Is[land] to take part in the attack on Charleston. To-night comes news, oh, so sad, so heart sickening. It is too terrible, too terrible to write. We can only hope it may not all be true. That our noble, beautiful young Colonel is killed, and the reg[iment] cut to pieces! I cannot, cannot believe it. And yet I know it may be so. But oh, I am stunned, sick at heart. I can scarcely write. There was an attack on Fort Wagner. The 54th put in advance; fought bravely, desperately, but was finally overpowered and driven back after getting into the Fort. Thank Heaven! they fought bravely! And oh, I still must hope that our colonel, *ours* especially he seems to me, is not killed. But I can write no more to-night.

Beaufort, July 21. Came to town to-day hearing that nurses were sadly needed. Went to Mrs. L[ander]'s. Found Col. H[igginson] and Dr. R[ogers] there. Mrs. L[ander] was sure I sh'ld not be able to endure the fatigues of hospital life even for a few days, but I thought differently, and the Col. and Dr. were both on my side. So at last Mrs. L[ander] consented and made arrangements for my entering one of the hospitals to-morrow.

It is sad to see the Col. [T. W. Higginson] at all feeble. He is usually so very strong and vigorous. He is going North next week. The Dr. [Seth Rogers] is looking very ill. He is quite exhausted. I shall not feel at peace until he is safe in his northern home. The attachment between these two is beautiful, both are so thoroughly good and noble. And both have the rarest charm of manner.

Wednesday, July 22. My hospital life began to-day. Went early this morning with Mrs. L[ander] and Mrs. G[?], the Surgeon's wife, saw that the Dr. had not finished dressing the wounds, and while I waited below Mrs. [Rufus] S[axton] gave me some sewing to do— mending the pantaloons and jackets of the poor fellows. (They are all of the 54th) It was with a full heart that I sewed up bullet holes and bayonet cuts. Sometimes I found a jacket that told a sad tale— so torn to pieces that it was far past mending. After awhile I went through the wards. As I passed along I thought "Many and low are the pallets, but each is the face of a friend." And I was surprised to see such cheerful faces looking up from the beds. Talked a little with some of the patients and assisted Mrs. G. in distributing medicines. Mrs. L[ander] kindly sent her carriage for me and I returned home, weary, but far more pleasantly impressed than I had thought possible, with hospital life.

Thursday, July 23. Said farewell to Col. H[igginson] who goes North in the Arago to-day. Am very sorry that Dr. R[ogers] c'ld not go with him, not having been able to get his papers. He is looking so ill. It makes me very anxious. He goes to Seaside for a few days. I hope the change, and Mrs. H[unn]'s kind care will do him good.

Took a more thorough survey of the hospital to-day. It is a large new brick building—quite close to the water,—two-storied, many windowed, and very airy—in every way well adapted for a hospital.

Yesterday I was employed part of the time in writing letters for the men. It was pleasant to see the brave, cheerful, uncomplaining spirit which they all breathed. Some of the poor fellows had come from the far west—even as far as Michigan. Talked with them much to-day. Told them that we had heard that their noble Colonel [Shaw] was not dead, but had been taken prisoner by the rebels. How joyfully their wan faces lighted up! They almost started from their couches as the hope entered their souls. Their attachment to their gallant young colonel is beautiful to see. How warmly, how enthusiastically they speak of him. "He was one of the best little men in the world," they said. "No one c'ld be kinder to a set of men than he was to us." Brave grateful hearts! I hope they will ever prove worthy of such a leader. And God grant that he may indeed be living. But I fear, I greatly fear it may be but a false report.

One poor fellow here interests me greatly. He is very young, only nineteen, comes from Michigan. He is very badly wounded—in both legs, and there is a ball—in the stomach—it is thought that it cannot be extracted. This poor fellow suffers terribly. His groans are pitiful to hear. But he utters no complaint, and it is touching to see his gratitude for the least kindness that one does him. Mrs. G[?] asked him if he w'ld like her to write to his home. But he said no. He was an only son, and had come away against his mother's will. He w'ld not have her written to until he was better. Poor fellow! that will never be in this world.

Another, a Sergeant, suffers great pain, being badly wounded in the leg. But he too lies perfectly patient and uncomplaining. He has such a good, honest face. It is pleasant to look at it—although it is black. He is said to be one of the best and bravest men in the regiment.

When I went in this morning and found my patients so cheerful some of them even quite merry, I tho't it c'ld not be possible that they were badly wounded. Many, indeed have only flesh wounds. But there are others—and they among the most uncomplaining— who are severely wounded;—some dangerously so. Brave fellows! I feel it a happiness, an honor, to do the slightest service for them. True they were unsuccessful in the attack on Fort Wagner. But that was no fault of theirs. It is the testimony of all that they fought bravely as man can fight, and that it was only when completely overwhelmed by superior numbers that they were driven back.

Friday, July 24. To-day the news of Col. Shaw's death is confirmed. There can no longer be any doubt. It makes me sad, sad at heart. They say he sprang upon the parapet of the fort and cried "Onward, my brave boys, onward"; then fell, pierced with wounds. I know it was a glorious death. But oh, it is hard, very hard for the young wife, so late a bride, for the invalid mother, whose only and most dearly loved son he was,—that heroic mother who rejoiced in the position which he occupied as colonel of a colored regiment. My heart bleeds for her. His death is a very sad loss to us. I recall him as a much loved friend. Yet I saw him but a few times. Oh what must it be to the wife and the mother. Oh it is terrible. It seems very, very hard that the best and the noblest must be the earliest called away. Especially has it been so throughout this dreadful war. . . .

Frederick Douglass

(1817?–1895)

FREDERICK AUGUSTUS WASHINGTON BAILEY (DOUGLASS) was the most famous African American in the antislavery movement and one of the most famous in the post–Civil War struggle for black equality and civil rights. Born (of an unknown white father) to a slave on the Eastern Shore of Maryland, he learned early the oppressive cruelty of slavery. During one brief period, however, a kind mistress encouraged the boy to learn to read and write. When he was twenty-one Frederick Bailey used his knowledge to forge papers which enabled him to escape. New York City attracted him, but he lingered just long enough to be joined by Anna Murray, a free black woman from Baltimore, who became his wife.

Frederick Bailey's work as an antislavery crusader began in New Bedford, Massachusetts. Taking the name Douglass, he soon became a leader of the black community in New England. At an antislavery convention in Nantucket in 1841, William Lloyd Garrison heard Douglass speak and, impressed by the ex-slave's intelligence and bearing, persuaded Douglass to become an agent for the Massachusetts Anti-Slavery Society. For the next four years Douglass lectured extensively and with such impact that many doubted the truth of his assertions that he was a self-taught ex-slave. To quiet such doubts, he wrote the *Narrative of the Life of Frederick Douglass, an American Slave* (1845). The book was so explicitly factual and became so popular that it exposed him to the hazard of seizure and reenslavement. Douglass fled to England, where he began to envision freedom as not only physical liberty but social equality and opportunity as well. With money raised by English friends, Douglass bought his freedom.

Returning to the States, Douglass broke with Garrison. The old abolitionist was advocating a policy of New England's seceding from the Union, but this act would leave slavery to flourish in the South, and Douglass would not support it. To avoid open factionalism and the disruption of the antislavery crusade, he moved to Rochester, New York. Here he established his paper, *The North Star* (in 1850 called *Frederick Douglass' Paper*), and vigorously plunged back into the abolition movement. The struggle was difficult, and sometimes Douglass was overcome by despair. During one of his most pessimistic lectures, Sojourner Truth rose in the audience and asked, "Frederick, is God dead?"

But in spite of bitter disappointment, especially after enactment of the Fugitive Slave Law in 1850, Douglass fought on. He lectured everywhere.

His Rochester home was a station on the Underground Railroad. He engaged in politics, first as a member of the Liberty party and later as a Lincoln Republican. He was an intimate of the "extreme abolitionists"—although he did try to dissuade John Brown from his heroic, mad, and ill-fated attempt at insurrection.

When war broke out, Douglass joined Sojourner Truth in urging Lincoln to enlist blacks in the Union army, and when Lincoln yielded in 1862, Douglass helped to recruit two Massachusetts black regiments and enlisted his own sons. The end of the war found him organizing blacks to work against discrimination and segregation. Douglass's political prominence was such that he was appointed United States marshal for the District of Columbia under President Grant, recorder of deeds under President Hayes, and minister to Haiti under President Arthur.

As Benjamin Quarles states in *Dictionary of American Negro Biography*, "Frederick Douglass cast a long shadow because of his sense of humanity and his willingness to battle for his convictions. He is remembered too for his remarkable social insights. No one, for example, pointed out more insistently than he that the status of the Negro was the touchstone of American democracy, its inevitable and ultimate test."

In addition to the landmark 1845 *Narrative of the Life of Frederick Douglass, an American Slave* (reprinted 1982 with an introduction by Houston A. Baker, Jr.), Douglass published the following autobiographies: *My Bondage and My Freedom* (1855) and *The Life and Times of Frederick Douglass* (1881, updated 1892). For the fullest and most authoritative works on Douglass, see Benjamin Quarles, *Frederick Douglass* (1948); Phillip S. Foner, *Frederick Douglass* (1964); and Nathan Irvin Huggins, *Slave and Citizen: The Life of Frederick Douglass* (1980). In 1979 the Yale University Press published the first volume of a planned fourteen-volume edition of *The Frederick Douglass Papers*, edited by John W. Blassingame. For an interesting discussion of the literary merits of Douglass's autobiographical writings, see Marion Wilson Starling's comments in *The Slave Narrative: Its Place in American History* (1988). See also Henry Louis Gates, Jr.'s discussion of Douglass's autobiographies in *Figures in Black: Words, Signs, and the "Racial" Self* (1987).

The first selection comes from *The Life and Times of Frederick Douglass*, now ranked as an American classic. The second is "The Fourth of July" speech given in Rochester, New York on July 5, 1852, and comes from *Rhetoric of Black Revolution* by Arthur L. Smith.

FROM THE LIFE AND TIMES OF FREDERICK DOUGLASS

In the summer of 1841 a grand anti-slavery convention was held in Nantucket, under the auspices of Mr. Garrison and his friends. I had taken no holiday since establishing myself in New Bedford, and feeling the need of a little rest, I determined on attending the meeting, though I had no thought of taking part in any of its proceedings. Indeed, I was not aware that any one connected with the convention so much as knew my name. Mr. William C. Coffin, a prominent Abolitionist in those days of trial, had heard me speaking to my colored friends in the little school-house on Second street, where we worshipped. He sought me out in the crowd and invited me to say a few words to the convention. Thus sought out, and thus invited, I was induced to express the feelings inspired by the occasion, and the fresh recollection of the scenes through which I had passed as a slave.

It was with the utmost difficulty that I could stand erect, or that I could command and articulate two words without hesitation and stammering. I trembled in every limb. I am not sure that my embarrassment was not the most effective part of my speech, if speech it could be called. At any rate, this is about the only part of my performance that I now distinctly remember. The audience sympathized with me at once, and from having been remarkably quiet, became much excited.

Mr. Garrison followed me, taking me as his text, and now, whether *I* had made an eloquent plea in behalf of freedom, or not, his was one, never to be forgotten. Those who had heard him oftenest and had known him longest, were astonished at his masterly effort. For the time he possessed that almost fabulous inspiration often referred to, but seldom attained, in which a public meeting is transformed, as it were, into a single individuality, the orator swaying a thousand heads and hearts at once and, by the simple majesty of his all-controlling thought, converting his hearers into the express image of his own soul. That night there were at least a thousand Garrisonians in Nantucket!

At the close of this great meeting I was duly waited on by Mr. John A. Collins, then the general agent of the Massachusetts Anti-Slavery Society, and urgently solicited by him to become an agent of that society and publicly advocate its principles. I was reluctant to take the proffered position. I had not been quite three years from slavery and was honestly distrustful of my ability, and I wished to be excused. Besides, publicity might discover me to my master, and many other objections presented themselves. But Mr. Collins was not to be refused, and I finally consented to go out for three months, supposing I should in that length of time come to the end of my story and my consequent usefulness.

Here opened for me a new life—a life for which I had had no preparation. Mr. Collins used to say when introducing me to an audience, I was a "graduate from the peculiar institution, with my diploma *written on my back.*" The three years of my freedom had been spent in the hard school of adversity. My hands seemed to be furnished with something like a leather coating, and I had marked out for myself a life of rough labor, suited to the hardness of my hands, as a means of supporting my family and rearing my children.

Young, ardent and hopeful, I entered upon this new life in the full gush of unsuspecting enthusiasm. The cause was good, the men engaged in it were good, the means to attain its triumph, good. Heaven's blessings must attend all, and freedom must soon be given to the millions pining under a ruthless bondage. My whole heart went with the holy cause, and my most fervent prayer to the Almighty Disposer of the hearts of men was continually offered for its early triumph. In this enthusiastic spirit I dropped into the ranks of freedom's friends and went forth to the battle. For a time I was made to forget that my skin was dark and my hair crisped. For a time I regretted that I could not have shared the hardships and dangers endured by the earlier workers for the slave's release. I found, however, full soon that my enthusiasm had been extravagant, that hardships and dangers were not all over, and that the life now before me had its shadows also, as well as its sunbeams.

Among the first duties assigned me on entering the ranks was to travel in company with Mr. George Foster to secure subscribers to the *Anti-Slavery Standard* and the *Liberator*. With him I traveled and lectured through the eastern counties of Massachusetts. Much interest was awakened—large meetings assembled. Many came, no doubt from curiosity to hear what a Negro could say in his own cause. I was generally introduced as a "chattel"—a "thing"—a piece of Southern property—the chairman assuring the audience that *it* could speak. *Fugitive slaves* were rare then, and as a fugitive slave lecturer, I had the advantage of being a "bran new fact"—the first one out.

Up to that time, a colored man was deemed a fool who confessed himself a runaway slave, not only because of the danger to which he exposed himself of being retaken, but because it was a confession of a very low origin. Some of my colored friends in New Bedford thought very badly of my wisdom in thus exposing and degrading myself. The only precaution I took at the beginning, to prevent Master Thomas from knowing where I was and what I was about, was the withholding my former name, my master's name, and the name of the State and county from which I came.

During the first three or four months my speeches were almost exclusively made up of narrations of my own personal experience as a slave. "Let us have the facts," said the people. So also said Friend George Foster, who always wished to pin me down to a simple narrative. "Give us the facts," said Collins, "we will take care of the philosophy." Just here arose some embarrassment. It was impossible for me to repeat the same old story month after month and keep up my interest in it. It was new to the people, it is true, but it was an old story to me; and to go through with it night after night was a task altogether too mechanical for my nature. "Tell your story, Frederick," would whisper my revered friend, Mr. Garrison, as I stepped upon the platform.

I could not always follow the injunction, for I was now reading and thinking. New views of the subject were being presented to my mind. It did not entirely satisfy me to *narrate* wrongs; I felt like *denouncing* them. I could not always curb my moral indignation for the perpetrators of slaveholding villainy long enough for a circumstantial statement of the facts which I felt almost sure everybody must know. Besides, I was growing and needed room.

"People won't believe you ever were a slave, Frederick, if you keep on this way," said friend Foster. "Be yourself," said Collins, "and tell your story." "Better have a little of the plantation speech than not," was said to me; "it is not best that you seem too learned." These excellent friends were actuated by the best of motives and were not altogether wrong in their advice; and still I must speak just the word that seemed to *me* the word to be spoken *by* me.

At last the apprehended trouble came. People doubted if I had ever been a slave. They said I did not talk like a slave, look like a slave, or act like a slave, and that they believed I had never been south of Mason and Dixon's line. "He don't tell us where he came from, what his master's name was, or how he got away; besides, he is educated, and is in this a contradiction of all the facts we have concerning the ignorance of the slaves." Thus I was in a pretty fair way to be denounced as an impostor. The committee of the Massachusetts Anti-Slavery Society knew all the facts in my case and agreed with me thus far in the prudence of keeping them private; but going down the aisles of the churches in which my meetings were held, and hearing the outspoken Yankees repeatedly saying, "He's never been a slave, I'll warrant you," I resolved that at no distant day, and by such a revelation of facts as could not be made by any other than a genuine fugitive, I would dispel all doubt.

In a little less than four years, therefore, after becoming a public lecturer, I was induced to write out the leading facts connected with my experience in slavery, giving names of persons, places, and dates, thus putting it in the power of any who doubted, to ascertain the truth or falsehood of my story. This statement soon became known in Maryland, and I had reason to believe that an effort would be made to recapture me.

It is not probable that any open attempt to secure me as a slave could have succeeded further than the obtainment by my master of the money value of my bones and sinews. Fortunately for me, in the four years of my labors in the Abolition cause I had gained many friends who would have suffered themselves to be taxed to almost any extent to save me from slavery. It was felt that I had committed the double offense of running away and exposing the secrets and crimes of slavery and slaveholders. There was a double motive for seeking my re-enslavement—avarice and vengeance; and while, as I have said, there was little probability of successful recapture, if attempted openly, I was constantly in danger of being spirited away at a moment when my friends could render me no assistance.

In traveling about from place to place, often alone, I was much exposed to this sort of attack. Anyone cherishing the desire to betray me could easily do so by simply tracing my whereabouts through the Anti-Slavery journals, for my movements and meetings were made through these in advance. My friends Mr. Garrison and Mr. Phillips had no faith in the power of Massachusetts to protect me in my right to liberty. Public sentiment and the law, in their opinion, would hand me over to the tormentors. Mr. Phillips especially considered me in danger, and said, when I showed him the manuscript of my story, if in my place he would "throw it into the fire." Thus the reader will observe that the overcoming of one difficulty only opened the way for another, and that though I had reached a free State, and had attained a position of public usefulness, I was still under the liability of losing all I had gained.

THE FOURTH OF JULY

Mr. President, Friends and Fellow Citizens:

He who could address this audience without a quailing sensation, has stronger nerves than I have. I do not remember ever to have appeared as a speaker before any assembly more shrinkingly, nor with greater distrust of my ability, than I do this day. A feeling has crept over me quite unfavorable to the exercise of my limited powers of speech. The task before me is one which requires much previous thought and study for its proper performance. I know that apologies of this sort are generally considered flat and unmeaning. I trust, however, that mine will not be so considered. Should I seem at ease, my appearance would much misrepresent me. The little experience I have had in addressing public meetings, in country school houses, avails me nothing on the present occasion.

The papers and placards say that I am to deliver a Fourth of July Oration. This certainly sounds large, and out of the common way, for me. It is true that I have often had the privilege to speak in this beautiful Hall, and to address many who now honor me with their presence. But neither their familiar faces, nor the perfect gage I think I have of Corinthian Hall seems to free me from embarrassment.

The fact is, ladies and gentlemen, the distance between this platform and the slave plantation, from which I escaped, is considerable—and the difficulties to be overcome in getting from the latter to the former are by no means slight. That I am here to-day is, to me, a matter of astonishment as well as of gratitude. You will not, therefore, be surprised, if in what I have to say I evince no elaborate preparation, nor grace my speech with any high sounding exordium. With little experience and with less learning, I have been able to throw my thoughts hastily and imperfectly together; and trusting to your patient and generous indulgence, I will proceed to lay them before you.

This, for the purpose of this celebration, is the Fourth of July. It is the birthday of your National Independence, and of your political freedom. This, to you, is what the Passover was to the emancipated people of God. It carries your minds back to the day, and to the act of your great deliverance; and to the signs, and to the wonders, associated with that act, and that day. This celebration also marks the beginning of another year of your national life; and reminds you that the Republic of America is now 76 years old. I am glad, fellow-citizens, that your nation is so young. Seventy-six years, though a good old age for a man, is but a mere speck in the life of a nation. Three score years and ten is the allotted time for individual men; but nations number their years by thousands. According to this fact, you are, even now, only in the beginning of your national career, still lingering in the period of childhood. I repeat, I am glad this is so. There is hope in the thought, and hope is much needed, under the dark clouds which lower above the horizon. The eye of the reformer is met with angry flashes, portending disastrous times; but his heart may well beat lighter at the thought that America is young, and that she is still in the impressible stage of her existence. May he not hope that high lessons of wisdom, of justice and of truth, will yet give direction to her destiny? Were the nation older, the patriot's heart might be sadder, and the reformer's brow heavier. Its future might be shrouded in gloom, and the hope of its prophets go out in sorrow. There is consolation in the thought that America is young. Great streams are not easily turned from channels, worn deep in the course of ages. They may sometimes rise in quiet and stately majesty, and inundate the land, refreshing and fertilizing the earth with their mysterious properties. They may also rise in wrath and fury, and bear away, on their angry waves, the accumulated wealth of years of toil and hardship. They, however, gradually flow back to the same old channel, and flow on as serenely as ever. But, while the river may not be turned aside, it may dry up, and leave nothing behind but the withered branch, and the unsightly rock, to howl in the abyss-sweeping wind, the sad tale of departed glory. As with rivers so with nations. . . .

Fellow-citizens, pardon me, allow me to ask, why am I called upon to speak here to-day? What have I, or those I represent, to do with your national independence? Are the great principles of political freedom and of natural justice, embodied in that Declaration of Independence, extended to us? and am I, therefore, called upon to bring our humble offering to the national altar, and to confess the benefits and express devout gratitude for the blessings resulting from your independence to us?

Would to God, both for your sakes and ours, that an affirmative answer could be truthfully returned to these questions! Then would my task be light, and my burden easy and delightful. For who is there so cold, that a nation's sympathy could not warm him? Who so obdurate and dead to the claims of gratitude, that would not thankfully acknowledge such priceless benefits? Who so stolid and selfish, that would not give his voice to swell the hallelujahs of a nation's jubilee, when the chains of servitude had been torn from his limbs? I am not that man. In a case like that, the dumb might eloquently speak, and the "lame man leap as an hart."

But such is not the state of the case. I say it with a sad sense of the disparity between us. I am not included within the pale of this glorious anniversary! Your high independence only reveals the immeasurable distance between us. The blessings in which you, this day, rejoice, are not enjoyed in common. The rich inheritance of justice, liberty, prosperity and independence, bequeathed by your fathers, is shared by you, not by me. The sunlight that brought light and healing to you, has brought stripes and death to me. This Fourth of July is yours, not mine. You may rejoice, I must mourn. To drag a man in fetters into the grand illuminated temple of liberty, and call upon him to join you in joyous anthems, were inhuman mockery and sacrilegious irony. Do you mean, citizens, to mock me, by asking me to speak today? If so, there is a parallel to your conduct. And let me warn you that it is dangerous to copy the example of a nation whose crimes, towering up to heaven, were thrown down by the breath of the Almighty, burying that nation in irrevocable ruin! I can to-day take up the plaintive lament of a peeled and woe-smitten people!

> By the rivers of Babylon, there we sat down. Yea! we wept when we remembered Zion. We hanged our harps upon the willows in the midst thereof. For there, they that carried us away captive, required of us a

song; and they who wasted us required of us mirth, saying, Sing us one of the songs of Zion. How can we sing the Lord's song in a strange land? If I forget thee, O Jerusalem, let my right hand forget her cunning. If I do not remember thee, let my tongue cleave to the roof of my mouth.

Fellow-citizens, above your national, tumultuous joy, I hear the mournful wail of millions; whose chains, heavy and grievous yesterday, are, to-day, rendered more intolerable by the jubilee shouts that reach them. If I do forget, if I do not faithfully remember those bleeding children of sorrow this day, "may my right hand forget her cunning, and may my tongue cleave to the roof of my mouth!" To forget them, to pass lightly over their wrongs, and to chime in with the popular theme, would be treason most scandalous and shocking, and would make me a reproach before God and the world. My subject, then, fellow-citizens, is AMERICAN SLAVERY. I shall see this day and its popular characteristics from the slave's point of view. Standing there identified with the American bondman, making his wrongs mine, I do not hesitate to declare, with all my soul, that the character and conduct of this nation never looked blacker to me than on this 4th of July! Whether we turn to the declarations of the past, or to the professions of the present, the conduct of the nation seems equally hideous and revolting. America is false to the past, false to the present, and solemnly binds herself to be false to the future. Standing with God and the crushed and bleeding slave on this occasion, I will, in the name of humanity which is outraged, in the name of liberty which is fettered, in the name of the constitution and the Bible which are disregarded and trampled upon, dare to call in question and to denounce, with all the emphasis I can command, everything that serves to perpetuate slavery—the great sin and shame of America! "I will not equivocate; I will not excuse"; I will use the severest language I can command; and yet not one word shall escape me that any man, whose judgment is not blinded by prejudice, or who is not at heart a slaveholder, shall not confess to be right and just.

But I fancy I hear some one of my audience say, "It is just in this circumstance that you and your brother abolitionists fail to make a favorable impression on the public mind. Would you argue more, and denounce less; would you persuade more, and rebuke less; your cause would be much more likely to succeed." But, I submit, where all is plain there is nothing to be argued. What point in the anti-slavery creed would you have me argue? On what branch of the subject do the people of this country need light? Must I undertake to prove that the slave is a man? That point is conceded already. No-body doubts it. The slaveholders themselves acknowledge it in the enactment of laws for their government. They acknowledge it when they punish disobedience on the part of the slave. There are seventy-two crimes in the State of Virginia which, if committed by a black man (no matter how ignorant he be), subject him to the punishment of death; while only two of the same crimes will subject a white man to the like punishment. What is this but the acknowledgment that the slave is a moral, intellectual, and responsible being? The manhood of the slave is conceded. It is admitted in the fact that Southern statute books are covered with enactments forbidding, under severe fines and penalties, the teaching of the slave to read or to write. When you can point to any such laws in reference to the beasts of the field, then I may consent to argue the manhood of the slave. When the dogs in your streets, when the fowls of the air, when the cattle on your hills, when the fish of the sea, and the reptiles that crawl, shall be unable to distinguish the slave from a brute, then will I argue with you that the slave is a man!

For the present, it is enough to affirm the equal manhood of the Negro race. Is it not astonishing that, while we are ploughing, planting, and reaping, using all kinds of mechanical tools, erecting houses, constructing bridges, building ships, working in metals of brass, iron, copper, silver and gold; that, while we are reading, writing and ciphering, acting as clerks, merchants and secretaries, having among us lawyers, doctors, ministers, poets, authors, editors, orators and teachers; that, while we are engaged in all manner of enterprises common to other men, digging gold in California, capturing the whale in the Pacific, feeding sheep and cattle on the hill-side, living, moving, acting, thinking, planning, living in families as husbands, wives and children, and, above all, confessing and worshipping the Christian's God, and looking hopefully for life and immortality beyond the grave, we are called upon to prove that we are men!

Would you have me argue that man is entitled to liberty? that he is the rightful owner of his own body? You have already declared it. Must I argue the wrongfulness of slavery? Is that a question for Republicans? Is it to be settled by the rules of logic and argumentation, as matter beset with great difficulty, involving a doubtful application of the principle of justice, hard to be understood? How should I look to-day, in the presence of Americans, dividing, and subdividing a discourse, to show that men have a natural right to freedom? speaking of it relatively and positively, negatively and affirmatively. To do so, would be to make myself ridiculous, and to offer an insult to your understanding. There is not a man beneath the canopy of heaven that does not know that slavery is wrong for him.

What, am I to argue that it is wrong to make men brutes, to rob them of their liberty, to work them without wages, to keep them ignorant of their relations to their fellow men, to beat them with sticks, to flay their flesh with the lash, to load their limbs with irons, to hunt them with dogs, to sell them at auction, to sunder their families, to knock out their teeth, to burn their flesh, to starve them into obedience and submission to their masters? Must I argue that a system thus marked with blood, and stained with pollution, is wrong? No! I will not. I have better employment for my time and strength than such arguments would imply.

What, then, remains to be argued? Is it that slavery is not divine; that God did not establish it; that our doctors of divinity are mistaken? There is blasphemy in the thought. That which is inhuman, cannot be divine! Who can reason on such a proposition? They that can, may; I cannot. The time for such argument is passed.

At a time like this, scorching irony, not convincing argument, is needed. O! had I the ability, and could I reach the nation's ear, I would, to-day, pour out a fiery stream of biting ridicule, blasting reproach, withering sarcasm, and stern rebuke. For it is not light that is needed, but fire; it is not the gentle shower, but thunder. We need the storm, the whirlwind, and the earthquake. The feeling of the nation must be quickened; the conscience of the nation must be roused; the propriety of the nation must be startled; the hypocrisy of the nation must be exposed; and its crimes against God and man must be proclaimed and denounced.

What, to the American slave, is your 4th of July? I answer; a day that reveals to him, more than all other days in the year, the gross injustice and cruelty to which he is the constant victim. To him, your celebration is a sham; your boasted liberty, an unholy license; your national greatness, swelling vanity; your sounds of rejoicing are empty and heartless; your denunciation of tyrants, brass fronted impudence; your shouts of liberty and equality, hollow mockery; your prayers and hymns, your sermons and thanksgivings, with all your religious parade and solemnity, are to Him, mere bombast, fraud, deception, impiety, and hypocrisy—a thin veil to cover up crimes which would disgrace a nation of savages. There is not a nation on the earth guilty of practices more shocking and bloody than are the people of the United States, at this very hour.

Go where you may, search where you will, roam through all the monarchies and despotisms of the Old World, travel through South America, search out every abuse, and when you have found the last, lay your facts by the side of the everyday practices of this nation, and you will say with me, that, for revolting barbarity and shameless hypocrisy, America reigns without a rival.

Take the American slave-trade, which we are told by the papers, is especially prosperous just now. Ex-Senator Benton tells us that the price of men was never higher than now. He mentions the fact to show that slavery is in no danger. This trade is one of the peculiarities of American institutions. It is carried on in all the large towns and cities in one-half of this confederacy; and millions are pocketed every year by dealers in this horrid traffic. In several states this trade is a chief source of wealth. It is called (in contradistinction to the foreign slave-trade) "the internal slave-trade." It is, probably, called so, too, in order to divert from it the horror with which the foreign slave-trade is contemplated. That trade has long since been denounced by this government as piracy. It has been denounced with burning words from the high places of the nation as an execrable traffic. To arrest it, to put an end to it, this nation keeps a squadron, at immense cost, on the coast of Africa. Everywhere, in this country, it is safe to speak of this foreign slave-trade as a most inhuman traffic, opposed alike to the laws of God and of man. The duty to extirpate and destroy it, is admitted even by our DOCTORS OF DIVINITY. In order to put an end to it, some of these last have consented that their colored brethren (nominally free) should leave this country, and establish themselves on the western coast of Africa! It is, however, a notable fact that, while so much execration is poured out by Americans upon all those engaged in the foreign slave-trade, the men engaged in the slave-trade between the states pass without condemnation, and their business is deemed honorable.

Behold the practical operation of this internal slave-trade, the American slave-trade, sustained by American politics and American religion. Here you will see men and women reared like swine for the market. You know what is a swine-drover? I will show you a man-drover. They inhabit all our Southern States. They perambulate the country, and crowd the highways of the nation, with droves of human stock. You will see one of these human flesh jobbers, armed with pistol, whip, and bowie-knife, driving a company of a hundred men, women, and children, from the Potomac to the slave market at New Orleans. These wretched people are to be sold singly, or in lots, to suit purchasers. They are food for the cottonfield and the deadly sugar-mill. Mark the sad procession, as it moves wearily along, and the inhuman wretch who drives them. Hear his savage yells and his blood-curdling oaths, as he hurries on his affrighted captives! There, see the old man with locks thinned and gray. Cast one glance, if you please, upon that young mother, whose shoulders are bare to the scorching sun, her briny tears falling on the brow of the babe in her arms. See, too, that girl of thirteen, weeping, yes! weeping, as she thinks of the mother from whom she has been torn! The drove moves tardily. Heat and sorrow have nearly consumed their strength; suddenly you hear a quick snap, like the discharge of a rifle; the fetters clank, and the chain rattles simultaneously; your ears are saluted with a scream, that seems to have torn its way to the centre of your soul! The crack you heard was the sound of the slave-whip; the scream you heard was from the woman you saw with the babe. Her speed had faltered under the weight of her child and her chains! that gash on her shoulder tells her to move on. Follow this drove to New Orleans. Attend the auction; see men examined like horses; see the forms of women rudely and brutally exposed to the shocking gaze of American slave-buyers. See this drove sold and separated forever; and never forget the deep, sad sobs that arose from that scattered multitude. Tell me, citizens, WHERE, under the sun, you can witness a spectacle more fiendish and shocking. Yet this is but a glance at the American slave-trade, as it exists, at this moment, in the ruling part of the United States.

I was born amid such sights and scenes. To me the American slave-trade is a terrible reality. When a child, my soul was often pierced with a sense of its horrors. I lived on Philpot Street, Fell's Point, Baltimore, and have watched from the wharves the slave ships in the Basin, anchored from the shore, with their cargoes of human flesh, waiting for favorable winds to waft them down the Chesapeake. There was, at that time, a grand slave mart kept at the head of Pratt Street, by Austin Woldfolk. His agents were sent into every town and county in Maryland, announcing their arrival, through the papers, and on flaming "hand-bills," headed CASH FOR NEGROES. These men were generally well dressed men, and very captivating in their manners; ever ready to drink, to treat, and to gamble. The fate of many a slave has depended upon the turn of a single card; and many a child has been snatched from the arms of its mother by bargains arranged in a state of brutal drunkenness.

The flesh-mongers gather up their victims by dozens, and drive them, chained, to the general depot at Baltimore. When a sufficient number has been collected here, a ship is chartered for the purpose of conveying the forlorn crew to Mobile, or to New Orleans. From the slave prison to the ship, they are usually driven in the darkness of night; for since the anti-slavery agitation, a certain caution is observed.

In the deep, still darkness of midnight, I have been aroused by the dead, heavy footsteps, and the piteous cries of the chained gangs that passed our door. The anguish of my boyish heart was intense; and I was often consoled, when speaking to my mistress in the morning, to hear her say that the custom was very wicked; that she hated to hear the rattle of the chains and the heart-rending cries. I was glad to find one who sympathized with me in my horror.

Fellow-citizens, this murderous traffic is, to-day, in active operation in this boasted republic. In the solitude of my spirit I see clouds of dust raised on the highways of the South; I see the bleeding footsteps; I hear the doleful wail of fettered humanity on the way to the slave-markets, where the victims are to be sold like horses, sheep, and swine, knocked off to the highest bidder. There I see the tenderest ties ruthlessly broken, to gratify the lust, caprice and rapacity of the buyers and sellers of men. My soul sickens at the sight.

> Is this the land your Fathers loved,
> The freedom which they toiled to win?
> Is this the earth whereon they moved?
> Are these the graves they slumber in?

But a still more inhuman, disgraceful, and scandalous state of things remains to be presented. By an act of the American Congress, not yet two years old, slavery has been nationalized in its most horrible and revolting form. By that act, Mason and Dixon's line has been obliterated; New York has become as Virginia; and the power to hold, hunt, and sell men, women and children, as slaves, remains no longer a mere state institution, but is now an institution of the whole United States. The power is co-extensive with the star-spangled banner, and American Christianity. Where these go, may also go the merciless slave-hunter. Where these are, man is not sacred. He is a bird for the sportsman's gun. By that most foul and fiendish of all human decrees, the liberty and person of every man are put in peril. Your broad republican domain is hunting ground for men. Not for thieves and robbers, enemies of society, merely, but for men guilty of no crime. Your lawmakers have commanded all good citizens to engage in this hellish sport. Your President, your Secretary of State, your lords, nobles, and ecclesiastics enforce, as a duty you owe to your free and glorious country, and to your God, that you do this accursed thing. Not fewer than forty Americans have, within the past two years, been hunted down and, without a moment's warning, hurried away in chains, and consigned to slavery and excruciating torture. Some of these have had wives and children, dependent on them for bread; but of this, no account was made. The right of the hunter to his prey stands superior to the right of marriage, and to all rights in this republic, the rights of God included! For black men there is neither law nor justice, humanity nor religion. The Fugitive Slave Law makes MERCY TO THEM A CRIME; and bribes the judge who tries them. An American JUDGE GETS TEN DOLLARS FOR EVERY VICTIM HE CONSIGNS to slavery, and five, when he fails to do so. The oath of any two villains is sufficient, under this hell-black enactment, to send the most pious and exemplary black man into the remorseless jaws of slavery! His own testimony is nothing.

He can bring no witnesses for himself. The minister of American justice is bound by the law to hear but one side; and that side is the side of the oppressor. Let this damning fact be perpetually told. Let it be thundered around the world that in tyrant-killing, king-hating, people-loving, democratic, Christian America the seats of justice are filled with judges who hold their offices under an open and palpable bribe, and are bound, in deciding the case of a man's liberty, to hear only his accusers!

In glaring violation of justice, in shameless disregard of the forms of administering law, in cunning arrangement to entrap the defenseless, and in diabolical intent this Fugitive Slave Law stands alone in the annals of tyrannical legislation. I doubt if there be another nation on the globe having the brass and the baseness to put such a law on the statute-book. If any man in this assembly thinks differently from me in this matter, and feels able to disprove my statements, I will gladly confront him at any suitable time and place he may select.

I take this law to be one of the grossest infringements of Christian Liberty, and, if the churches and ministers of our country were not stupidly blind, or most wickedly indifferent, they, too, would so regard it.

At the very moment that they are thanking God for the enjoyment of civil and religious liberty, and for the right to worship God according to the dictates of their own consciences, they are utterly silent in respect to a law which robs religion of its chief significance and makes it utterly worthless to a world lying in wickedness. Did this law concern the "mint, anise, and cummin"—abridge the right to sing psalms, to partake of the sacrament, or to engage in any of the ceremonies of religion, it would be smitten by the thunder of a thousand pulpits. A general shout would go up from the church demanding repeal, repeal, instant repeal!—And it would go hard with that politician who presumed to solicit the votes of the people without inscribing this motto on his banner. Further, if this demand were not complied with, another Scotland would be added to the history of religious liberty, and the stern old convenanters would be thrown into the shade. A John Knox would be seen at every church door and heard from every pulpit, and Fillmore would have no more quarter than was shown by Knox to the beautiful, but treacherous, Queen Mary of Scotland. The fact that the church of our country (with fractional exceptions) does not esteem "the Fugitive Slave Law" as a declaration of war against religious liberty, implies that that church regards religion simply as a form of worship, an empty ceremony, and not a vital principle, requiring active benevolence, justice, love, and good will towards man. It esteems sacrifice above

mercy; psalm-singing above right doing; solemn meetings above
practical righteousness. A worship that can be conducted by persons
who refuse to give shelter to the houseless, to give bread to the hungry, clothing to the naked, and who enjoin obedience to a law forbidding these acts of mercy is a curse, not a blessing to mankind.
The Bible addresses all such persons as "scribes, pharisees, hypo-
crites, who pay tithe of mint, anise, and cummin, and have omitted
the weightier matters of the law, judgment, mercy, and faith."

But the church of this country is not only indifferent to the
wrongs of the slave, it actually takes sides with the oppressors. It has
made itself the bulwark of American slavery, and the shield of American slave-hunters. Many of its most eloquent Divines, who stand as
the very lights of the church, have shamelessly given the sanction of
religion and the Bible to the whole slave system. They have taught
that man may, properly, be a slave; that the relation of master and
slave is ordained of God; that to send back an escaped bondman to
his master is clearly the duty of all the followers of the Lord Jesus
Christ; and this horrible blasphemy is palmed off upon the world for
Christianity.

For my part, I would say, welcome infidelity! welcome atheism!
welcome anything! in preference to the gospel, as preached by those
Divines! They convert the very name of religion into an engine of
tyranny and barbarous cruelty, and serve to confirm more infidels, in
this age, than all the infidel writings of Thomas Paine, Voltaire, and
Bolingbroke put together have done! These ministers make religion a
cold and flinty-hearted thing, having neither principles of right action nor bowels of compassion. They strip the love of God of its
beauty and leave the throne of religion a huge, horrible, repulsive
form. It is a religion for oppressors, tyrants, man-stealers, and thugs.
It is not that "pure and undefiled religion" which is from above, and
which is "first pure, then peaceable, easy to be entreated, full of
mercy and good fruits, without partiality, and without hypocrisy."
But a religion which favors the rich against the poor; which exalts
the proud above the humble; which divides mankind into two classes, tyrants and slaves; which says to the man in chains, stay there;
and to the oppressor, oppress on; it is a religion which may be professed and enjoyed by all the robbers and enslavers of mankind; it
makes God a respecter of persons, denies his fatherhood of the race,
and tramples in the dust the great truth of the brotherhood of man.
All this we affirm to be true of the popular church, and the popular
worship of our land and nation—a religion, a church, and a worship
which, on the authority of inspired wisdom, we pronounce to be an
abomination in the sight of God. In the language of Isaiah, the
American church might be well addressed,

Bring no more vain oblations; incense is an abomination unto me: the new moons and Sabbaths, the calling of assemblies, I cannot away with; it is iniquity, even the solemn meeting. Your new moons, and your appointed feasts my soul hateth. They are a trouble to me; I am weary to bear them; and when ye spread forth your hands I will hide mine eyes from you. Yea! when ye make many prayers, I will not hear. YOUR HANDS ARE FULL OF BLOOD; cease to do evil, learn to do well; seek judgment; relieve the oppressed; judge for the fatherless; plead for the widow.

The American church is guilty, when viewed in connection with what it is doing to uphold slavery; but it is superlatively guilty when viewed in its connection with its ability to abolish slavery.

The sin of which it is guilty is one of omission as well as of commission. Albert Barnes but uttered what the common sense of every man at all observant of the actual state of the case will receive as truth, when he declared that "There is no power out of the church that could sustain slavery an hour, if it were not sustained in it."

Let the religious press, the pulpit, the Sunday School, the conference meeting, the great ecclesiastical, missionary, Bible and tract associations of the land array their immense powers against slavery, and slave-holding; and the whole system of crime and blood would be scattered to the winds, and that they do not do this involves them in the most awful responsibility of which the mind can conceive.

In prosecuting the anti-slavery enterprise, we have been asked to spare the church, to spare the ministry; but how, we ask, could such a thing be done? We are met on the threshold of our efforts for the redemption of the slave, by the church and ministry of the country, in battle arrayed against us; and we are compelled to fight or flee. From what quarter, I beg to know, has proceeded a fire so deadly upon our ranks, during the last two years, as from the Northern pulpit? As the champions of oppressors, the chosen men of American theology have appeared—men honored for their so-called piety, and their real learning. The LORDS of Buffalo, the SPRINGS of New York, the LATHROPS of Auburn, the COXES and SPENCERS of Brooklyn, the GANNETS and SHARPS of Boston, the DEWEYS of Washington, and other great religious lights of the land have, in utter denial of the authority of HIM by whom they professed to be called to the ministry, deliberately taught us, against the example of the Hebrews, and against the remonstrance of the Apostles, that we ought to obey man's law before the law of God.

My spirit wearies of such blasphemy; and how such men can be supported, as the "standing types and representatives of Jesus Christ," is a mystery which I leave others to penetrate. In speaking of the American church, however, let it be distinctly understood that

I mean the great mass of the religious organizations of our land.
There are exceptions, and I thank God that there are. Noble men
may be found, scattered all over these Northern States, of whom
Henry Ward Beecher, of Brooklyn; Samuel J. May, of Syracuse; and
my esteemed friend (Rev. R. R. Raymond) on the platform, are shining examples; and let me say further, that, upon these men lies the
duty to inspire our ranks with high religious faith and zeal, and to
cheer us on in the great mission of the slave's redemption from his
chains.

One is struck with the difference between the attitude of the
American church towards the anti-slavery movement, and that occupied by the churches in England towards a similar movement in that
country. There, the church, true to its mission of ameliorating, ele-
vating and improving the condition of mankind, came forward
promptly, bound up the wounds of the West Indian slave, and restored him to his liberty. There, the question of emancipation was a
high religious question. It was demanded in the name of humanity,
and according to the law of the living God. The Sharps, the Clark-
sons, the Wilberforces, the Buxtons, and the Burchells, and the
Knibbs were alike famous for their piety and for their philanthropy.
The anti-slavery movement there was not an anti-church movement,
for the reason that the church took its full share in prosecuting that
movement: and the anti-slavery movement in this country will cease
to be an anti-church movement, when the church of this country
shall assume a favorable instead of a hostile position towards that
movement.

Americans! your republican politics, not less than your republican union, are flagrantly inconsistent. You boast of your love of liberty, your superior civilization, and your pure Christianity, which
the whole political power of the nation (as embodied in the two
great political parties) is solemnly pledged to support and perpetuate
the enslavement of three millions of your countrymen. You hurl
your anathemas at the crowned headed tyrants of Russia and Austria
and pride yourselves on your Democratic institutions, while you
yourselves consent to be the mere tools and body-guards of the tyrants of Virginia and Carolina. You invite to your shores fugitives of
oppression from abroad, honor them with banquets, greet them with
ovations, cheer them, toast them, salute them, protect them, and
pour out your money to them like water; but the fugitives from your
own land you advertise, hunt, arrest, shoot, and kill. You glory in
your refinement and your universal education; yet you maintain a
system as barbarous and dreadful as ever stained the character of a
nation—a system begun in avarice, supported in pride, and perpetuated in cruelty. You shed tears over fallen Hungary, and make the

sad story of her wrongs the theme of your poets, statesmen, and orators, till your gallant sons are ready to fly to arms to vindicate her
cause against the oppressor; but, in regard to the ten thousand
wrongs of the American slave, you would enforce the strictest silence, and would hail him as an enemy of the nation who dares to
make those wrongs the subject of public discourse! You are all on
fire at the mention of liberty for France or for Ireland; but are as
cold as an iceberg at the thought of liberty for the enslaved of America. You discourse eloquently on the dignity of labor; yet, you sustain a system which, in its very essence, casts a stigma upon labor.
You can bare your bosom to the storm of British artillery to throw
off a three-penny tax on tea; and yet wring the last hard earned far-
thing from the grasp of the black laborers of your country. You profess to believe "that, of one blood, God made all nations of men to
dwell on the face of all the earth," and hath commanded all men,
everywhere, to love one another; yet you notoriously hate (and glory
in your hatred) all men whose skins are not colored like your own.
You declare before the world, and are understood by the world to
declare that you "hold these truths to be self-evident, that all men
are created equal; and are endowed by their Creator with certain inalienable rights; and that among these are, life, liberty, and the pursuit of happiness;" and yet, you hold securely, in a bondage which,
according to your own Thomas Jefferson, "is worse than ages of that
which your fathers rose in rebellion to oppose," a seventh part of the
inhabitants of your country.

Fellow-citizens, I will not enlarge further on your national inconsis-
tencies. The existence of slavery in this country brands your republicanism as a sham, your humanity as a base pretense, and your
Christianity as a lie. It destroys your moral power abroad: it corrupts
your politicians at home. It saps the foundation of religion; it makes
your name a hissing and a bye-word to a mocking earth. It is the
antagonistic force in your government, the only thing that seriously
disturbs and endangers your Union. It fetters your progress; it is the
enemy of improvement; the deadly foe of education; it fosters pride,
it breeds insolence; it promotes vice; it shelters crime; it is a curse to
the earth that supports it; and yet you cling to it as if it were the
sheet anchor of all your hopes. Oh! be warned! a horrible reptile is
coiled up in your nation's bosom; the venomous creature is nursing
at the tender breast of your youthful republic; for the love of God,
tear away, and fling from you the hideous monster, and let the
weight of twenty millions crush and destroy it forever! . . .

Allow me to say, in conclusion, notwithstanding the dark picture
I have this day presented, of the state of the nation, I do not despair
of this country. There are forces in operation which must inevitably

work the downfall of slavery. "The arm of the Lord is not short-ened," and the doom of slavery is certain. I, therefore, leave off where I began, with hope. While drawing encouragement from "the Declaration of Independence," the great principles it contains, and the genius of American Institutions, my spirit is also cheered by the obvious tendencies of the age. Nations do not now stand in the same relation to each other that they did ages ago. No nation can now shut itself up from the surrounding world and trot round in the same old path of its fathers without interference. The time was when such could be done. Long established customs of hurtful character could formerly fence themselves in, and do their evil work with so-cial impunity. Knowledge was then confined and enjoyed by the privileged few, and the multitude walked on in mental darkness. But a change has now come over the affairs of mankind. Walled cities and empires have become unfashionable. The arm of commerce has borne away the gates of the strong city. Intelligence is penetrating the darkest corners of the globe. It makes its pathway over and un-der the sea, as well as on the earth. Wind, steam, and lightning are its chartered agents. Oceans no longer divide, but link nations to-gether. From Boston to London is now a holiday excursion. Space is comparatively annihilated.—Thoughts expressed on one side of the Atlantic are distinctly heard on the other.

The far off and almost fabulous Pacific rolls in grandeur at our feet. The Celestial Empire, the mystery of ages, is being solved. The fiat of the Almighty, "Let there be Light," has not yet spent its force. No abuse, no outrage whether in taste, sport or avarice, can now hide itself from the all-pervading light. The iron shoe, and crippled foot of China must be seen in contrast with nature. Africa must rise and put on her yet unwoven garment. "Ethiopia shall stretch out her hand unto God."

PART 3

Accommodation and Protest: 1865–1910

THE NORTH'S military victory in the Civil War did not bring about change in the ways change was expected. Malice remained, not exorcised by President Lincoln's splendid words; charity, which he prayed for, did not appear. Between the agrarian-gentleman, whose ingrained attitudes and habits of mind dominated southern thought, and the industrialist-banker, whose money power determined northern polity, bitterness was not relieved. In fact, it was intensified, and the tide of enmity was freshened by the Reconstruction Act of 1867, for which northerners were held largely responsible. North and South, blacks were caught in that tide. Their situation was not new, nor was their reaction.

In the South, American blacks were still subject to the whims of the white world. A few blacks benefited from the activities of the Freedmen's Bureau, which helped to ease the transition from slavery to freedom; and a few were privileged to attend Yankee missionary schools, which were built somewhat less quickly than they were burned down by southern whites who opposed education for former slaves. It is true that between 1869 and 1874 southern blacks did vote in sufficient strength to have influence in some state legislatures and to send sixteen fellow blacks to the national Congress. But the terrorist activities of the Ku Klux Klan and other groups brought an effective end to black voting even before federal troops, charged with protecting the right to vote, were withdrawn.

Blacks in the North fared scarcely better. Few could afford schooling, even where free schools were provided—and they were not provided everywhere until the end of the century. Jobs were difficult to get and keep, for there was increasing competition with whites, who often mobbed black workers. Although the right to vote was generally acknowledged, few blacks were sophisticated enough to see the value of exercising that right.

The great majority of blacks in both the North and the South accepted segregation and discrimination, believing, as Booker T. Washington persuaded them to believe, that as they approached the white world's standards, they would win the white world's tolerance, and "things" would be better. A handful of blacks protested. As their eloquent spokesman W. E. B.

Du Bois wrote, "We demand every single right that belongs to a free born American, political, civil, and social; and until we get these rights we will never cease to protest and assail the ears of America."

An infinitesimal number of blacks reacted to the conditions of African American life by trying to escape them. While the imaginative writing of the period sets forth these varying attitudes and reactions symbolically, polemical writing states them straightforwardly. Between 1865 and 1910, an appreciable number of black writers, using both approaches, published significant works. Among the novelists are Charles W. Chesnutt, Paul Laurence Dunbar, Sutton Griggs, and a small number of lesser-known writers, including the recently discovered Harriet E. Wilson. The poets include Dunbar, William Stanley Braithwaite, and a number of dialect poets. The principal writers of autobiography/biography were Booker T. Washington, John M. Langston, and Frederick Douglass. The best-known historians of the period were George Washington Williams and William C. Nell.

Charles W. Chesnutt, the first black novelist of imposing stature, published three novels and two volumes of short stories. With the exception of his earliest stories, which began appearing in the *Atlantic Monthly* in 1887 and were later collected under the title *The Conjure Woman*, all of his work is in the protest tradition. Chesnutt's special theme was the African American of mixed blood, the "tragic mulatto"; he was the first black author to deal in depth with the problem of the "color line" within the race, and the first to make imaginative capital of racism's consequences to the white man. In *The Marrow of Tradition* and *The Colonel's Dream*, which were both constructed around incidents from real life, Chesnutt's artistic control occasionally slips, and he makes didactic digressions that interrupt the story and add nothing to the theme. His short stories are free of this fault, and so is *The House behind the Cedars*, his first novel, and his best.

None of the fiction of Paul Laurence Dunbar matches the best of Charles Chesnutt. Three of Dunbar's four novels neither deal with racial themes nor present blacks as major characters. Dunbar's best novel, *The Sport of the Gods*, begins as a realistic depiction of black life in New York but finally becomes a commitment to the southern white apologist's point of view. Indeed, it might have been written by Thomas Nelson Page or Maurice Thompson, both of whom were widely read southern apologists.

While Dunbar's prose fiction was popular in his own time, it is his dialect poetry for which he is best known today. His poetry, of course, did no violence to the acceptable notions of black life and character or mind and spirit. The widely held opinion of Dunbar the poet was best expressed by William Dean Howells, who was probably the most highly regarded of contemporary critics: "In nothing is [Dunbar's] essentially refined and delicate art so well shown as in those pieces, which . . . describe the range between appetite and emotion . . . which is the range of the race. He reveals in these a finely ironic perception of the Negro's limitations." Dunbar must have had this judgment in mind when, just prior to his death at the age of thirty-four, he wrote the lines that might very well have served as his epitaph:

> He sang of love when life was young,
> And Love itself was in his ways,
> But Ah, the world, it turned to praise
> A jingle in a broken tongue.

Sutton Griggs was a prolific and historically important novelist. Although he had less talent than Dunbar, he nevertheless vacillated between accommodation and militant protest, and his work reveals the ambivalence of many black intellectuals during that troubled period. *Imperium in Imperio*, for instance, advocates militant black nationalism, while *Unfettered* and *Pointing the Way* recommend an alliance between "upper class" blacks and Bourbon whites. Griggs, like Chesnutt, had contempt for poor whites. Because this was the one attitude from which he did not waver, his novels, whatever their story lines and themes, are bitter attacks upon the white poor—those "misguided souls [who] said and did all things, which [they] deemed necessary to leave behind . . . the greatest heritage of hatred the world has ever known."

There was little propaganda in the poetry of the time, and hard-line protest was out. Some poets have been designated as mockingbirds. Albery Whitman was one of these: he was by turns a "black Longfellow," a "black Byron," a "black Spenser." Lacking originality, Whitman's work was not truly significant, and he is remembered only for his versatility and for having composed the longest poem ever written by a Negro, "Not a Man and Yet a Man."

A small host of other poets were imitators, too, but they imitated the dialect poetry of Paul Dunbar. James Edwin Campbell and Daniel Webster Davis were fairly good as imitators, and Davis's only collection, *Wey Down Souf*, bears comparison with Dunbar's *Candle-Ligh'ing Time*. J. Mord Allen's *Rhymes, Tales, and Rhymed Tales* are noteworthy only in that they prove him more industrious than most of his contemporaries. Not much can be said for John Wesley Holloway's *From the Desert*; or for either of Ray Garfield Dandridge's two slim volumes, *Zalka Petruzza and Other Poems* and *The Poet and Other Poems*. George Marion McClellan refused to write dialect poetry. James D. Corrothers was probably the first American black poet to pursue African themes.

The best non-dialect poet of the period was William Stanley Braithwaite. Proud of his yearly anthologies of magazine verse, and of his position as a staff writer on the *Boston Transcript*, Braithwaite rejected the fact of his black heritage. In his autobiography, *The House of Falling Leaves*, he wrote, "I am descended from a long line of English gentlemen." And this was true enough, if one considered only his father's line of descent; his mother was a West Indian black. As a poet, Braithwaite was a Pre-Raphaelite, and his work was haunting, mystical, romantic.

Certain autobiographical works and other prose pieces bridge the emotional gap between the pre–Civil War slave narratives and the racial apostasy of Braithwaite. An example of this type of literature is Elizabeth Keckley's *Behind the Scenes; or Thirty Years a Slave and Four Years in the White House*. John Mercer Langston, who was briefly dean of the law school at the predominantly black Howard University and even more briefly a member of Congress, wrote *From a Virginia Plantation to the National Capital* as a declaration of pride in his race. Then there is *Up from Slavery*. If certain of its episodes are suspect, its spirit and thrust are not. If Booker Washington lied and accommodated, he did so for a cause, and the cause was black advancement. This was also Frederick Douglass's cause, and his *Life and Times*, which was published in its final version in 1892, states it eloquently.

Two black historians deserve mention. Associated with Garrison on *The Liberator* and with Douglass on *The North Star*, William C. Nell was encouraged by John Greenleaf Whittier to do historical research. *The Colored Patriots of the American Revolution* is a work of careful scholarship and the first historical study by an African American to deserve the respect of the academic community. But *The Colored Patriots* was twice surpassed by George Washington Williams's books, *History of the Negro Race in America from 1619 to 1880* and *A History of the Negro Troops in the War of the Rebellion*, which are still used as source books by reputable academic historians.

The customary view of black Reconstruction politicians is that they were both ignorant and venal, and that Congress reached its lowest level while these blacks were in office. This, of course, is a biased view, a view based upon racial antagonism rather than facts. By and large black members of Congress during Reconstruction were neither venal nor ignorant. As in all sessions of Congress then and now there were a few members not quite honest and not well educated, but they were the exception, not the general rule. Black congressmen did speak out bluntly for black rights and governmental reform. *This* was their crime; this lead to the general condemnation of all black members of Congress and officeholders. A look at the record will show that several of the blacks were better educated than their white colleagues. The two senators, Hiram R. Revels and B. K. Bruce, both from Mississippi, were educated men. Robert Brown Elliott of South Carolina was a graduate of Eton. John Mercer Langston of Virginia, who had studied at Oberlin, was a distinguished lawyer long before he went to

Congress, and there were others equally well qualified. The last of these Reconstruction (and post-Reconstruction) congressmen was George H. White of North Carolina, a graduate of Howard University. His farewell speech to Congress, delivered on January 29, 1901, was often quoted during the first decades of this century.

Booker T. Washington

(1856–1915)

DURING HIS PUBLIC CAREER Booker Taliaferro Washington was the most popular and most influential Negro leader in the United States. Northern philanthropists like Andrew Carnegie subsidized him; Republican politicians like William Howard Taft and Theodore Roosevelt admired him, used him, and in turn were used by Washington; most southerners accepted him because of his accommodationist philosophy; and the black-man-in-the-street revered Booker T. and felt that his conservative you-must-crawl-before-you-can-walk message was the "way out" for African Americans. Black intellectuals like William Monroe Trotter, fiery editor of the *Boston Guardian*, and W. E. B. Du Bois fought Washington vigorously, even though Du Bois tried at first to work with him. Washington's black opponents objected not only to his "Uncle Tom" philosophy but also to the "Tuskegee Machine," which they felt had too much influence and power in bolstering Booker T. and in directing the course of black life in America. On the surface, Washington seemed to be a simple man with commonsense ideas expressed in down-to-earth terms. Booker T. Washington, however, as his opponents soon found out, was a complex character, a master of behind-the-scenes manipulation, and a superb salesman of his own philosophy.

Born on the Burrough's Plantation near Hale's Ford, Virginia, Booker T. Washington was the son of a slave woman and a white father. In 1865 the Washingtons moved to Malden, West Virginia, and Booker worked at odd jobs there until he heard of Hampton Normal and Industrial Institute (now Hampton University). With $1.50 in his pocket, he set out for the famous school.

After graduation from Hampton in 1875, Washington taught in Malden, then left for Washington, D.C., for a year's study at Wayland Seminary (now a part of Virginia Union University). In 1879 he returned to Hampton, where he took charge of a group of Native American students and organized Hampton's first night school. In 1881 he was sent to Tuskegee, Alabama, to start a new school of the Hampton type. Within a very short time, Washington built in the backwoods of Alabama one of America's best-known educational centers.

Although it is alleged that Booker T. Washington was "assisted" by others in many if not all of his works, he was a prolific author-editor. He published three autobiographies; one of them, *Up from Slavery* (1901), became an American classic often compared with Benjamin Franklin's autobiography. It was also for many years one of the most popular and most frequently reprinted books by an American black writer. One of his works, *The Negro in the South* (1907), was co-authored with Du Bois.

Though not an orator in the old-fashioned, thundering sense of that term, Booker T. Washington was one of the most popular and effective speakers of his generation. Relying heavily on concrete images, parable-like anecdotes ("cast down your buckets where you are"), and folk humor, usually at the expense of blacks, his speeches became an American institution. Among the best are the two that immediately follow and another he delivered in Boston in 1897 at the unveiling of the Robert Gould Shaw monument. In 1896, Harvard, the first New England college to give an honorary degree to a black, conferred upon Washington a Master of Arts degree. Booker T. Washington died in 1915 and was buried at Tuskegee. More than seven thousand people attended his funeral.

For a full and searching analysis of the great educator's life and for an equally helpful bibliography, see Emma Low Thornbrough's article in *Dictionary of American Negro Biography*. The Booker T. Washington Papers in the Library of Congress are also a most valuable source for scholars interested in Washington's life. For his speeches, see E. Davidson Washington, ed., *Selected Speeches of Booker T. Washington* (1932). See also Hugh Hawkins, ed., *Booker T. Washington and His Critics* (1962), and August Meier's *Negro Thought in America, 1880–1915: Racial Ideologies in the Age of Booker T. Washington* (1963).

Louis R. Harlan is editor of *The Booker T. Washington Papers* (1972–), which appears in thirteen volumes. See also Harlan's two-volume biography, *Booker T. Washington: The Making of a Black Leader, 1856–1901* (1972), and his *Booker T. Washington: The Wizard of Tuskegee, 1901–1915* (1983).

Among the most recent evaluations of Washington's writings are "The Lost Life of the Negro, 1859–1919: Black Literary and Intellectual Life before the Renaissance" by Wilson J. Moses, in *Black American Literature Forum* 21, no. 1–2 (Spring–Summer 1987), and Houston A. Baker, Jr.'s *Modernism and the Harlem Renaissance* (1987).

The first selection is taken from *Up from Slavery*; the two speeches come from Carter G. Woodson's *Negro Orators and Their Orations* (1925).

THE STRUGGLE FOR AN EDUCATION

One day, while at work in the coal-mine, I happened to overhear two miners talking about a great school for coloured people somewhere in Virginia. This was the first time that I had ever heard anything about any kind of school or college that was more pretentious than the little coloured school in our town.

In the darkness of the mine I noiselessly crept as close as I could to the two men who were talking. I heard one tell the other that not only was the school established for the members of my race, but that opportunities were provided by which poor but worthy students could work out all or a part of the cost of board, and at the same time be taught some trade or industry.

As they went on describing the school, it seemed to me that it must be the greatest place on earth, and not even Heaven presented more attractions for me at that time than did the Hampton Normal and Agricultural Institute in Virginia, about which these men were talking. I resolved at once to go to that school, although I had no idea where it was, or how many miles away, or how I was going to reach it; I remembered only that I was on fire constantly with one ambition, and that was to go to Hampton. This thought was with me day and night.

After hearing of the Hampton Institute, I continued to work for a few months longer in the coal-mine. While at work there, I heard of a vacant position in the household of General Lewis Ruffner, the owner of the salt-furnace and coal-mine. Mrs. Viola Ruffner, the wife of General Ruffner, was a "Yankee" woman from Vermont. Mrs. Ruffner had a reputation all through the vicinity for being very strict with her servants, and especially with the boys who tried to serve her. Few of them had remained with her more than two or three weeks. They all left with the same excuse: she was too strict. I decided, however, that I would rather try Mrs. Ruffner's house than remain in the coal-mine, and so my mother applied to her for the vacant position. I was hired at a salary of $5 per month.

I had heard so much about Mrs. Ruffner's severity that I was almost afraid to see her, and trembled when I went into her presence. I had not lived with her many weeks, however, before I began to understand her. I soon began to learn that, first of all, she wanted everything kept clean about her, that she wanted things done promptly and systematically, and that at the bottom of everything she wanted absolute honesty and frankness. Nothing must be sloven or slipshod; every door, every fence, must be kept in repair.

I cannot now recall how long I lived with Mrs. Ruffner before going to Hampton, but I think it must have been a year and a half. At any rate, I here repeat what I have said more than once before, that the lessons that I learned in the home of Mrs. Ruffner were as valuable to me as any education I have ever gotten anywhere since. Even to this day I never see bits of paper scattered around a house or in the street that I do not want to pick them up at once. I never see a filthy yard that I do not want to clean it, a paling off of a fence that I do not want to put it on, an unpainted or unwhitewashed house that I do not want to paint or whitewash it, or a button off one's clothes, or a grease-spot on them or on a floor, that I do not want to call attention to it.

From fearing Mrs. Ruffner I soon learned to look upon her as one of my best friends. When she found that she could trust me she did so implicitly. During the one or two winters that I was with her she gave me an opportunity to go to school for an hour in the day during a portion of the winter months, but most of my studying was done at night, sometimes alone, sometimes under some one whom I could hire to teach me. Mrs. Ruffner always encouraged and sympathized with me in all my efforts to get an education. It was while living with her that I began to get together my first library. I secured a dry-goods box, knocked out one side of it, put some shelves in it, and began putting into it every kind of book that I could get my hands upon, and called it my "library."

Notwithstanding my success at Mrs. Ruffner's I did not give up the idea of going to the Hampton Institute. In the fall of 1872 I determined to make an effort to get there, although, as I have stated, I had no definite idea of the direction in which Hampton was, or of what it would cost to go there. I do not think that any one thoroughly sympathized with me in my ambition to go to Hampton unless it was my mother, and she was troubled with a grave fear that I was starting out on a "wild-goose chase." At any rate, I got only a half-hearted consent from her that I might start. The small amount of money that I had earned had been consumed by my stepfather and the remainder of the family, with the exception of a very few dollars, and so I had very little with which to buy clothes and pay my travelling expenses. My brother John helped me all that he could, but of course that was not a great deal, for his work was in the coal mine, where he did not earn much, and most of what he did earn went in the direction of paying the household expenses.

Perhaps the thing that touched and pleased me most in connection with my starting for Hampton was the interest that many of the older coloured people took in the matter. They had spent the best days of their lives in slavery, and hardly expected to live to see the time when they would see a member of their race leave home to attend a boarding school. Some of these older people would give me a nickel, others a quarter, or a handkerchief.

Finally the great day came, and I started for Hampton. I had only a small, cheap satchel that contained what few articles of clothing I could get. My mother at the time was rather weak and broken in health. I hardly expected to see her again, and thus our parting was all the more sad. She, however, was very brave through it all. At that time there were no through trains connecting that part of West Vir-

ginia with eastern Virginia. Trains ran only a portion of the way, and
the remainder of the distance was travelled by stage-coaches.

The distance from Malden to Hampton is about five hundred
miles. I had not been away from home many hours before it began
to grow painfully evident that I did not have enough money to pay
my fare to Hampton. One experience I shall long remember. I had
been travelling over the mountains most of the afternoon in an old-
fashioned stage-coach, when, late in the evening, the coach stopped
for the night at a common, unpainted house called a hotel. All the
other passengers except myself were whites. In my ignorance I supposed that the little hotel existed for the purpose of accommodating
the passengers who travelled on the stage-coach. The difference that
the colour of one's skin would make I had not thought anything
about. After all the other passengers had been shown rooms and
were getting ready for supper, I shyly presented myself before the
man at the desk. It is true I had practically no money in my pocket
with which to pay for bed or food, but I had hoped in some way to
beg my way into the good graces of the landlord, for at that season
in the mountains of Virginia the weather was cold, and I wanted to
get indoors for the night. Without asking as to whether I had any
money, the man at the desk firmly refused to even consider the matter of providing me with food or lodging. This was my first experience in finding out what the colour of my skin meant. In some way
I managed to keep warm by walking about, and so got through the
night. My whole soul was so bent upon reaching Hampton that I did
not have time to cherish any bitterness toward the hotel-keeper.

By walking, begging rides both in wagons and in the cars, in
some way, after a number of days, I reached the city of Richmond,
Virginia, about eighty-two miles from Hampton. When I reached
there, tired, hungry, and dirty, it was late in the night. I had never
been in a large city, and this rather added to my misery. When I
reached Richmond, I was completely out of money. I had not a single acquaintance in the place, and, being unused to city ways, I did
not know where to go. I applied at several places for lodging, but
they all wanted money, and that was what I did not have. Knowing
nothing else better to do, I walked the streets. In doing this I passed
by many food-stands where fried chicken and half-moon apple pies
were piled high and made to present a most tempting appearance. At
that time it seemed to me that I would have promised all that I expected to possess in the future to have gotten hold of one of those
chicken legs or one of those pies. But I could not get either of these,
nor anything else to eat.

I must have walked the streets till after midnight. At last I became so exhausted that I could walk no longer. I was tired, I was
hungry, I was everything but discouraged. Just about the time when

I reached extreme physical exhaustion, I came upon a portion of a street where the board sidewalk was considerably elevated. I waited for a few minutes, till I was sure that no passers-by could see me, and then crept under the sidewalk and lay for the night upon the ground, with my satchel of clothing for a pillow. Nearly all night I could hear the tramp of feet over my head. The next morning I found myself somewhat refreshed, but I was extremely hungry, because it had been a long time since I had had sufficient food. As soon as it became light enough for me to see my surroundings I noticed that I was near a large ship, and that this ship seemed to be unloading a cargo of pig iron. I went at once to the vessel and asked the captain to permit me to help unload the vessel in order to get money for food. The captain, a white man, who seemed to be kind-hearted, consented. I worked long enough to earn money for my breakfast, and it seems to me, as I remember it now, to have been about the best breakfast that I have ever eaten.

My work pleased the captain so well that he told me if I desired I could continue working for a small amount per day. This I was very glad to do. I continued working on this vessel for a number of days. After buying food with the small wages I received there was not much left to add to the amount I must get to pay my way to Hampton. In order to economize in every way possible, so as to be sure to reach Hampton in a reasonable time, I continued to sleep under the same sidewalk that gave me shelter the first night I was in Richmond. Many years after that the coloured citizens of Richmond very kindly tendered me a reception at which there must have been two thousand people present. This reception was held not far from the spot where I slept the first night I spent in that city, and I must confess that my mind was more upon the sidewalk that first gave me shelter than upon the reception, agreeable and cordial as it was.

When I had saved what I considered enough money with which to reach Hampton, I thanked the captain of the vessel for his kindness, and started again. Without any unusual occurrence I reached Hampton, with a surplus of exactly fifty cents with which to begin my education. To me it had been a long, eventful journey; but the first sight of the large, three-story, brick school building seemed to have rewarded me for all that I had undergone in order to reach the place. If the people who gave the money to provide that building could appreciate the influence the sight of it had upon me, as well as upon thousands of other youths, they would feel all the more encouraged to make such gifts. It seemed to me to be the largest and most beautiful building I had ever seen. The sight of it seemed to give me new life. I felt that a new kind of existence had now begun—that life would now have a new meaning. I felt that I had reached the promised land, and I resolved to let no obstacle prevent me from putting forth the highest effort to fit myself to accomplish the most good in the world.

As soon as possible after reaching the grounds of the Hampton Institute, I presented myself before the head teacher for assignment to a class. Having been so long without proper food, a bath, and change of clothing, I did not, of course, make a very favourable impression upon her, and I could see at once that there were doubts in her mind about the wisdom of admitting me as a student. I felt that I could hardly blame her if she got the idea that I was a worthless loafer or tramp. For some time she did not refuse to admit me, neither did she decide in my favour, and I continued to linger about her, and to impress her in all the ways I could with my worthiness. In the meantime I saw her admitting other students, and that added greatly to my discomfort, for I felt, deep down in my heart, that I could do as well as they, if I could only get a chance to show what was in me.

After some hours had passed, the head teacher said to me: "The adjoining recitation-room needs sweeping. Take the broom and sweep it."

It occurred to me at once that here was my chance. Never did I receive an order with more delight. I knew that I could sweep, for Mrs. Ruffner had thoroughly taught me how to do that when I lived with her.

I swept the recitation-room three times. Then I got a dusting-cloth and I dusted it four times. All the woodwork around the walls, every bench, table, and desk, I went over four times with my dusting-cloth. Besides, every piece of furniture had been moved and every closet and corner in the room had been thoroughly cleaned. I had the feeling that in a large measure my future depended upon the impression I made upon the teacher in the cleaning of that room. When I was through, I reported to the head teacher. She was a "Yankee" woman who knew just where to look for dirt. She went into the room and inspected the floor and closets; then she took her handkerchief and rubbed it on the woodwork about the walls, and over the table and benches. When she was unable to find one bit of dirt on the floor, or a particle of dust on any of the furniture, she quietly remarked, "I guess you will do to enter this institution."

I was one of the happiest souls on earth. The sweeping of that room was my college examination, and never did any youth pass an examination for entrance into Harvard or Yale that gave him more genuine satisfaction. I have passed several examinations since then, but I have always felt that this was the best one I ever passed. . . .

AN ADDRESS DELIVERED AT THE OPENING OF THE COTTON
STATES' EXPOSITION IN ATLANTA, GEORGIA, SEPTEMBER, 1895

Mr. President and Gentlemen of the Board of Directors and Citizens:
One-third of the population of the South is of the Negro race. No
enterprise seeking the material, civil, or moral welfare of this section
can disregard this element of our population and reach the highest
success. I but convey to you, Mr. President and Directors, the sentiment of the masses of my race when I say that in no way have the
value and manhood of the American Negro been more fittingly and
generously recognized than by the managers of this magnificent Exposition at every stage of its progress. It is a recognition that will do
more to cement the friendship of the two races than any occurrence
since the dawn of freedom.

Not only this, but the opportunity here afforded will awaken
among us a new era of industrial progress. Ignorant and inexperienced, it is not strange that in the first years of our new life we began at the top instead of at the bottom; that a seat in Congress or
the State Legislature was more sought than real estate or industrial
skill; that the political convention or stump speaking had more attractions than starting a dairy farm or truck garden.

A ship lost at sea for many days suddenly sighted a friendly vessel. From the mast of the unfortunate vessel was seen a signal,
"Water, water; we die of thirst!" The answer from the friendly vessel
at once came back: "Cast down your bucket where you are." A second time the signal, "Water, water; send us water!" ran up from the
distressed vessel, and was answered: "Cast down your bucket where
you are." The captain of the distressed vessel, at last heeding the injunction, cast down his bucket, and it came up full of fresh, sparkling water from the mouth of the Amazon River. To those of my
race who depend upon bettering their condition in a foreign land, or
who underestimate the importance of cultivating friendly relations
with the Southern white man, who is his next door neighbor, I
would say: "Cast down your bucket where you are"—cast it down in
making friends in every manly way of the people of all races by
whom we are surrounded.

Cast it down in agriculture, mechanics, in commerce, in domestic
service, and in the professions. And in this connection it is well to
bear in mind that whatever other sins the South may be called to
bear, when it comes to business, pure and simple, it is in the South

---

Negro Orators and Their Orations. Copyright © 1925 by The Associated Publishers, Inc.,
published by The Association for the Study of Afro-American Life and History.

that the Negro is given a man's chance in the commercial world, and in nothing is this Exposition more eloquent than in emphasizing this chance. Our greatest danger is, that in the great leap from slavery to freedom we may overlook the fact that the masses of us are to live by the productions of our hands, and fail to keep in mind that we shall prosper in proportion as we learn to dignify and glorify common labor, and put brains and skill into the common occupations of life; shall prosper in proportion as we learn to draw the line between the superficial and the substantial, the ornamental gewgaws of life and the useful. No race can prosper till it learns that there is as much dignity in tilling a field as in writing a poem. It is at the bottom of life we must begin, and not at the top. Nor should we permit our grievances to overshadow our opportunities.

To those of the white race who look to the incoming of those of foreign birth and strange tongue and habits for the prosperity of the South, were I permitted I would repeat what I say to my own race, "Cast down your bucket where you are." Cast it down among the 8,000,000 Negroes whose habits you know, whose fidelity and love you have tested in days when to have proved treacherous meant the ruin of your firesides. Cast down your bucket among these people who have, without strikes and labor wars, tilled your fields, cleared your forests, builded your railroads and cities, and brought forth treasures from the bowels of the earth, and helped make possible this magnificent representation of the progress of the South. Casting down your bucket among my people, helping and encouraging them as you are doing on these grounds, and, with education of head, hand and heart, you will find that they will buy your surplus land, make blossom the waste places in your fields, and run your factories. While doing this, you can be sure in the future, as in the past, that you and your families will be surrounded by the most patient, faithful, law-abiding, and unresentful people that the world has seen. As we have proved our loyalty to you in the past, in nursing your children, watching by the sick bed of your mothers and fathers, and often following them with tear-dimmed eyes to their graves, so in the future, in our humble way, we shall stand by you with a devotion that no foreigner can approach, ready to lay down our lives, if need be, in defense of yours, interlacing our industrial, commercial, civil, and religious life with yours in a way that shall make the interests of both races one. In all things that are purely social we can be as separate as the fingers, yet one as the hand in all things essential to mutual progress.

There is no defense or security for any of us except in the highest intelligence and development of all. If anywhere there are efforts tending to curtail the fullest growth of the Negro, let these efforts be turned into stimulating, encouraging, and making him the most useful and intelligent citizen. Effort or means so invested will pay a thousand per cent interest. These efforts will be twice blessed— blessing him that gives and him that takes.

There is no escape through law of man or God from the inevitable:

> The laws of changeless justice bind
> Oppressor with oppressed;
> And close as sin and suffering joined
> We march to fate abreast.

Nearly sixteen millions of hands will aid you in pulling the load upwards or they will pull against you the load downwards. We shall constitute one-third and more of the ignorance and crime of the South, or one-third its intelligence and progress; we shall contribute one-third to the business and industrial prosperity of the South, or we shall prove a veritable body of death, stagnating, depressing, retarding every effort to advance the body politic.

Gentlemen of the Exposition, as we present to you our humble effort at an exhibition of our progress, you must not expect overmuch. Starting thirty years ago with ownership here and there in a few quilts and pumpkins and chickens (gathered from miscellaneous sources), remember the path that has led from these to the invention and production of agricultural implements, buggies, steam engines, newspapers, books, statuary, carving, paintings, the management of drug stores and banks has not been trodden without contact with thorns and thistles. While we take pride in what we exhibit as a result of our independent efforts, we do not for a moment forget that our part in this exhibition would fall far short of your expectations but for the constant help that has come to our educational life, not only from the Southern States, but especially from Northern philanthropists, who have made their gifts a constant stream of blessing and encouragement.

The wisest among my race understand that the agitation of questions of social equality is the extremest folly, and that progress in the enjoyment of all the privileges that will come to us must be the result of severe and constant struggle rather than of artificial forcing. No race that has anything to contribute to the markets of the world is long in any degree ostracized. It is important and right that all privileges of the law be ours, but it is vastly more important that we be prepared for the exercise of those privileges. The opportunity to earn a dollar in a factory just now is worth infinitely more than the opportunity to spend a dollar in an opera house.

In conclusion, may I repeat that nothing in thirty years has given us more hope and encouragement, and drawn us so near to you of the white race, as this opportunity offered by the Exposition; and here bending, as it were, over the altar that represents the results of the struggles of your race and mine, both starting practically empty-handed three decades ago, I pledge that, in your effort to work out the great and intricate problem which God has laid at the doors of the South, you shall have at all times the patient, sympathetic help of my race; only let this be constantly in mind that, while from representations in these buildings of the products of field, of forest, of mine, of factory, letters, and art, much good will come, yet far above and beyond material benefits will be the higher good, that let us pray God will come, in a blotting out of sectional differences and racial animosities and suspicions, in a determination to administer absolute justice, in a willing obedience among all classes to the mandates of law. This, coupled with our material prosperity, will bring into our beloved South a new heaven and a new earth.

ADDRESS DELIVERED AT THE HARVARD ALUMNI DINNER
IN 1896

Mr. President and Gentlemen: It would in some measure relieve my embarrassment if I could, even in a slight degree, feel myself worthy of the great honor which you do me today. Why you have called me from the Black Belt of the South, from among my humble people, to share in the honors of this occasion, is not for me to explain; and yet it may not be inappropriate for me to suggest that it seems to me that one of the most vital questions that touch our American life is how to bring the strong, wealthy and learned into helpful touch with the poorest, most ignorant and humblest, and at the same time make the one appreciate the vitalizing, strengthening influence of the other. How shall we make the mansions on yon Beacon Street feel and see the need of the spirits in the lowliest cabin in Alabama cotton fields or Louisiana sugar bottoms? This problem Harvard University is solving, not by bringing itself down, but by bringing the masses up.

If through me, an humble representative, seven millions of my people in the South might be permitted to send a message to Harvard—Harvard that offered up on death's altar young Shaw, and Russell, and Lowell, and scores of others, that we might have a free and united country—that message would be, "Tell them that the sacrifice was not in vain. Tell them that by habits of thrift and economy, by way of the industrial school and college, we are coming. We are crawling up, working up, yea, bursting up. Often through oppression, unjust discrimination and prejudice, but through them all we are coming up, and with proper habits, intelligence and property, there is no power on earth that can permanently stay our progress."

If my life in the past has meant anything in the lifting up of my people and the bringing about of better relations between your race and mine, I assure you from this day it will mean doubly more. In the economy of God there is but one standard by which an individual can succeed—there is but one for a race. This country demands that every race shall measure itself by the American standard. By it a race must rise or fall, succeed or fail, and in the last analysis mere sentiment counts for little. During the next half century and more, my race must continue passing through the severe American crucible. We are to be tested in our patience, our forbearance, our perseverance, our power to endure wrong, to withstand temptations, to economize, to acquire and use skill; in our ability to compete, to succeed in commerce, to disregard the superficial for the real, the appearance for the substance, to be great and yet small, learned and yet simple, high and yet the servant of all. This, this is the passport to all that is best in the life of our Republic, and the Negro must possess it, or be debarred.

While we are thus being tested, I beg of you to remember that wherever our life touches yours, we help or hinder. Wherever your life touches ours, you make us stronger or weaker. No member of your race in any part of our country can harm the meanest member of mine without the proudest and bluest blood in Massachusetts being degraded. When Mississippi commits crime, New England commits crime, and in so much, lowers the standard of your civilization. There is no escape—man drags man down, or man lifts man up.

In working out our destiny, while the main center of activity must be with us, we shall need, in a large measure in the years that are to come as we have in the past, the help, the encouragement, the guidance that the strong can give the weak. Thus helped, we of both races in the South soon shall throw off the shackles of racial and sectional prejudice and rise, as Harvard University has risen and as we all should rise, above the clouds of ignorance, narrowness and selfishness, into that atmosphere, that pure sunshine, where it will be our highest ambition to serve man, our brother, regardless of race or previous condition.

George Washington Williams

(1849–1891)

SOLDIER, CLERGYMAN, journalist, lawyer, politician, explorer of the Congo, American envoy and historian, George Washington Williams had a very colorful and many-sided career. Born in Bedford Springs, Pennsylvania, of humble parents who moved to two other towns in the state, Williams had little or no formal education during his early years, several of which were spent in a "house of refuge." When he was fourteen, he used his uncle's name and enlisted in the Union army in 1863. He saw service in several battles and was wounded. He finally joined the famous Tenth Cavalry, remaining with this outfit until given a medical discharge in 1868. According to John Hope Franklin, the legend has not been confirmed that after the Civil War Williams joined the Mexican army and rose to the rank of lieutenant colonel.

From 1868 to 1874, George Washington Williams's civilian life was as varied as his army career. He was in and out of several seminaries and schools, including Howard University. He became a Baptist minister, then a journalist in Washington, D.C., and in Cincinnati, and then a government worker. He passed the Ohio bar and became a lawyer in 1877 and was later elected to the Ohio legislature. Williams was subsequently appointed American envoy to Haiti, and later served the Belgian government in the Congo. He died in Blackpool, England, while still connected with the Belgian government.

In 1883 Williams published *History of the Negro Race in America, from 1619 to 1880*; in 1887, *A History of the Negro Troops in the War of the Rebellion*. The first was brought out by G. B. Putnam's Sons and the second by Harper and Brothers, two of the best publishing companies of Williams's day.

Although too oratorical on occasion, Williams was basically a scholar, collecting and presenting his materials with a scholar's concern for clarity, accuracy, and objectivity. According to John Hope Franklin, Williams's works, judged by the standards of today's historical scholarship, "are substantial and reliable sources of information and bear up surprisingly well under careful scrutiny."

For a modern evaluation of this pioneer historian, see the article in *Dictionary of American Negro Biography*, written by John Hope Franklin; see also two other articles by Franklin—"George Washington Williams, Historian" (*Journal of Negro History*, January 1946) and *George Washington*

Williams and Africa (Department of History, Howard University, 1971); also reprinted in *Historical Judgments Reconsidered* (1988).

FROM **A HISTORY OF THE NEGRO TROOPS IN THE WAR OF THE REBELLION**

South Carolina had set the other States a dangerous example in her attempts at nullification under President Jackson's administration, and was not only first in seceding, but fired the first shot of the slave-holders' rebellion against the laws and authority of the United States Government. It was eminently fitting, then, that the first shot fired at slavery by Negro soldiers should be aimed by the ex-slaves of the haughty South Carolina rebels. It was poetic justice that South Carolina Negroes should have the priority of obtaining the Union uniform, and enjoy the distinction of being the first Negro soldiers to encounter the enemy in battle. And the honor belongs to Massachusetts in furnishing a graduate of Harvard College, Thomas Wentworth Higginson, as the first colonel to lead the First South Carolina Negro Regiment of Volunteers.

Before Colonel Higginson assumed command of this regiment, in fact before it was organized as a regiment, Company A did its first fighting on Saint Helena Island. From the 3d to the 10th of November, 1862, Company A, under Captain Trowbridge, participated in the expedition along the coasts of Georgia and East Florida. The expedition was under the command of Lieutenant-colonel Oliver T. Beard, of the Forty-eighth New York Infantry. Of their fighting quality Colonel Beard in his report says:

"The colored men fought with astonishing coolness and bravery. For alacrity in effecting landings, for determination, and for bush-fighting I found them all I could desire—more than I had hoped. They behaved bravely, gloriously, and deserve all praise."

From the 13th to the 18th of November three companies of the First South Carolina Colored Volunteers participated in an expedition from Beaufort, South Carolina, to Doboy River, Georgia. In his report of the expedition General Rufus Saxton says:

"It gives me pleasure to bear witness to the good conduct of the Negro troops. They fought with the most determined bravery. Although scarcely one month since the organization of this regiment was commenced, in that short period these untrained soldiers have captured from the enemy an amount of property equal in value to the cost of the regiment for a year. They have driven back equal numbers of rebel troops, and have destroyed the salt-works along the whole line of this coast."

On the 23d of January, 1863, by order of Major-general Hunter, Colonel Higginson sailed in transports from Beaufort, South Carolina, to make a raid into Georgia and Florida. No strategic blow was to be struck, no important manœuvre was to be executed. But there were two objects in view. Negro regiments were to be recruited in the Department, but the enemy, in retiring before the Union forces, had taken with him all effective Negroes. It was one of the objects of the expedition to secure Negro recruits in the enemy's country. The second object of the expedition was to obtain the far-farmed lumber which was to be had by a bold dash into the enemy's country. These two objects were of sufficient importance to justify the expedition, but Colonel Higginson cherished another idea that had not been canvassed at headquarters. This First South Carolina Volunteers was the only organized regiment of Negro troops in the army of the United States at this time. The tentative effort of General Hunter in raising this regiment the year before had met the inexorable disapproval of the President, and had drawn the fierce fire of the enemies of the Negro. Colonel Higginson knew that if he could get his black soldiers in battle once, the question of their employment in unlimited numbers would be finally settled. So, while he went ostensibly for recruits and lumber, his main aim was to find the enemy and engage him. His force consisted of four hundred and sixty-two officers and men. The vessels that bore the expedition were the *Ben de Ford*, Captain Hallet, carrying several six-pound guns; the *John Adams*, an army gun-boat, carrying a thirty-pound Parrott gun, two ten-pound Parrotts, and an eight-inch howitzer; the *Planter*, carrying a ten-pound Parrott gun and two howitzers. The *Ben de Ford* was the largest, and carried most of the troops. It was the "flag-ship" of the expedition, in a manner. Major John D. Strong was in command on the *John Adams*, and Captain Charles T. Trowbridge commanded the troops on the *Planter*. For prudential reasons, each vessel sailed at a different hour for St. Simon's, on the coast of Georgia.

On the night of the 26th of January Colonel Higginson found himself on the right track; the enemy he was looking for was not far away. Of his purpose Colonel Higginson says: "That night I proposed to make a sort of trial trip up stream as far as Township Landing, some fifteen miles, there to pay our respects to Captain Clark's company of cavalry, whose camp was reported to lie near by. This was included in Corporal Sutton's programme, and seemed to me more inviting and far more useful to the men than any amount of mere foraging. The thing really desirable appeared to be to get them under fire as soon as possible, and to teach them, by a few small successes, the application of what they had learned in camp."

Back from the river and five miles from Township Landing the much-desired enemy was bivouacked. A troop of skirmishers was landed behind the bend below the landing, with orders to march upon the town and surround it. When the troops arrived by water the town was in possession of the force that had proceeded by land. Colonel Higginson had brought along a good supply of the Emancipation Proclamation to distribute among the Negroes, and these were rather assuring to many who had been led to believe that the "Yankees would sell them into Cuba."

After making a selection of one hundred of the best soldiers in the expedition, Colonel Higginson took up his line of march for the enemy's camp shortly after midnight. The moon shone brightly, but the command soon reached the resinous pines, and clouds of shadows hid it. The column moved on in silence until, when about two miles from its base, the advance-guard came suddenly upon the rebel cavalry and exchanged shots. Colonel Higginson gave orders to fix bayonets, and prepared to receive the enemy kneeling, and the enemy delivered his fire over the heads of the intrepid black soldiers. "My soldiers," says Colonel Higginson, "in turn fired rapidly—too rapidly, being yet beginners—and it was evident that, dim as it was, both sides had opportunity to do some execution.

"I could hardly tell whether the fight had lasted ten minutes or an hour, when, as the enemy's fire had evidently ceased or slackened, I gave the order to cease firing. But it was very difficult at first to make them desist: the taste of gunpowder was too intoxicating. One of them was heard to mutter indignantly, 'Why de cunnel order *cease* firing, when de Secesh blazin' away at de rate of ten dollar a day?' "

The enemy beat a precipitate retreat, and left Colonel Higginson's Negro troops in undisputed possession of the field. The dead and wounded were tenderly taken up by their more fortunate comrades, and the command returned to Township Landing without being again assailed by the enemy. Of the wounded, Surgeon Seth Rogers wrote: "One man killed instantly by a ball through the heart and seven wounded, one of whom will die. Braver men never lived. One man with two bullet-holes through the large muscles of the shoulders and neck brought off from the scene of action, two miles distant, two muskets, and not a murmur has escaped his lips. Another, Robert Sutton, with three wounds—one of which, being on the skull, may cost him his life—would not report himself till compelled to do so by his officers. While dressing his wounds he quietly talked of what they had done and of what they yet could do. To-day I have had the colonel *order* him to obey me. He is perfectly quiet and cool, but takes this whole affair with the religious bearing of a man who realizes that freedom is sweeter than life. Yet another soldier did not report himself at all, but remained all night on guard, and possibly I should not have known of his having had a buckshot in his shoulder if some duty requiring a sound shoulder had not been required of him to-day."

The engagement in which Colonel Higginson's Negro soldiers had courageously and unflinchingly met and returned the enemy's fire was called the "*Battle of the Hundred Pines.*" It decided no important military question, but, under the circumstances, it was of great importance to Negro soldiership throughout the entire country. It was one of the first stand-up fights that ex-slaves had had with their late masters, and their splendid bravery was at once a vindication and a prophecy of valor upon other fields that were yet to be fought for freedom. . . .

The Department of the South up to this time had done little effective military service. Most of the Sea Islands had fallen into the control of the Union forces, but the way to Charleston, both by land and water, was guarded by forts, fortifications, and torpedoes. Fort Wagner was a strongly mounted and thoroughly garrisoned earthwork extending across the north end of the island; it was within twenty-six hundred yards of Fort Sumter. The reduction of this fortress left but little work to subdue Cumming's Point, and thus siege guns could be brought within one mile of Fort Sumter, and the city of Charleston—the heart of the rebellion—would be within extreme shelling distance. In this assault the Fifty-fourth Massachusetts was to participate. It had sustained a loss of fourteen killed, seventeen wounded, and thirteen missing while on James Island, and having had a taste of war, was eager for more. It was eminently proper, too, that this Northern Negro regiment from stalwart old Massachusetts should have its fighting qualities tested in South Carolina before a haughty and formidable fortress, from under whose guns the most splendid valor of white troops had recoiled. Before the trying hour they had been subjected to tests not only of martial pluck, but of endurance, hunger, heat, and thirst. At the close of the engagement on the morning of the 16th these Negro soldiers were set in motion from James to Morris Island. The first shock of battle had burst upon them in the ominous silence of the early morning. All day they marched over the island under the exhausting heat of a July sun in Carolina, with the uncertain sand slipping under their weary tread. All night the march was continued through darkness and rain, amid thunder and lightning, over swollen streams, broken dikes, and feeble, shuddering, narrow causeways. Now a halt for no apparent reason, and then the column moved forward to lead in the dance of death. This dreary, weary, and exhausting march was continued till

six o'clock in the morning of the 18th, when the Fifty-fourth
reached Morris Island. . . .

As the day wore away it seemed certain, from the Union standpoint, that the garrison must yield or perish. Through a field-glass
Wagner seemed little less than an unrecognizable mass of ruins, a
mere heap of sand. It seemed as if the approaches to the bomb-
proofs were choked with sand, and that most of the heavy guns were
disabled and the fort practically dismantled. Its reduction seemed
now near at hand, and the bombardment had facilitated the work of
the infantry who were to consummate its reduction by a dash at the
point of the bayonet. Towards evening the breaching siege guns and
monitors slacked their fire. Soon the beach was filled with life.
Couriers dashed in every direction, and the troops were now being
disposed for an assault. At 6 P.M. the Fifty-fourth Regiment reached
General Geo. C. Strong's headquarters, about the middle of the island, wet and weary, hungry and thirsty; but there was no time for
rest or refreshments. Onward the Negro regiment marched several
hundred yards farther, and proudly took its place at the head of the
assaulting column. General Strong and Colonel Shaw addressed it
briefly, and with burning words of eloquent patriotic sentiment
urged the men to valorous conduct in the approaching assault. Both
officers were inspired; the siren of martial glory was sedulously lur-
ing them to the bloody and inhospitable trenches of Wagner. There
was a tremor in Colonel Shaw's voice and an impressiveness in his
manner. He was young and beautiful, wealthy and refined, and his
heroic words soon flowered into action—bravest of the brave, leader
of men! The random shot and shell that screamed through the ranks
gave the troops little annoyance. The first brigade consisted of the
Fifty-fourth Massachusetts, Colonel Robert Gould Shaw; the Sixth
Connecticut, Colonel Chatfield; the Forty-eighth New York, Colonel
Barton; the Third New Hampshire, Colonel Jackson; the Seventy-
sixth Pennsylvania, Colonel Strawbridge; and the Ninth Maine, Colonel Emory. After about thirty minutes' halt, General Strong gave the
order for the charge, and the column advanced quickly to its perilous work. The ramparts of Wagner flashed with small-arms, and all
the large shotted guns roared with defiance. Sumter and Cumming's
Point delivered a destructive cross-fire, while the howitzers in the
bastions raked the ditch; but the gallant Negro regiment swept
across it and gained the parapet. Here the flag of this regiment was
planted; here General Strong fell mortally wounded; and here the
brave, beautiful, and heroic Colonel Shaw was saluted by death and
kissed by immortality. The regiment lost heavily, but held its ground
under the most discouraging circumstances. The men had actually
gained the inside of the fort, where they bravely contended with a
desperate and determined enemy. The contest endured for about an

hour, when the regiment, shattered and torn, with nearly all of its officers dead or wounded, was withdrawn under the command* of Captain Luis F. Emilio. He formed a new line of battle about seven hundred yards from the fort, and awaited orders for another charge. He despatched a courier to the commanding officer of the second brigade that had gone to the front, stating that he was in supporting position, and was ready and willing to do what he could. Word came that the enemy was quiet and that the Fifty-fourth was not needed. Captain Emilio then occupied the rifle-pits flanking the Union artillery which he found unoccupied, and being out of musket range, organized his men as best he could. The national colors of the regiment which he had brought back from the scene of the battle he sent to the rear with the wounded color-sergeant, William H. Carney, as they could not serve as a rallying point in the deep darkness. . . .

The appalling list of casualties shows how bravely this Negro regiment had done its duty, and the unusually large number of men missing proves that the regiment had fought its way into the fort, and if properly supported, Wagner would have been captured. Colonel Shaw led about six hundred enlisted men and twenty-two officers into this action. Of the enlisted men thirty-one were killed, one hundred and thirty-five wounded, and ninety-two missing. Of the twenty-two officers participating three were killed and eleven were wounded. Nearly half of the enlisted men were killed, wounded, or missing, while more than one-half of the officers were either killed or wounded.

From a purely military stand-point the assault upon Fort Wagner was a failure, but it furnished the severest test of Negro valor and soldiership. It was a mournful satisfaction to the advocates of Negro soldiers to point the doubting, sneering, stay-at-home Negro-haters to the murderous trenches of Wagner. The Negro soldier had seen his red-letter day, and his title to patriotic courage was written in his own blood. Pleased with the splendid behavior of the regiment in particular and the special courage of several enlisted men, General Gillmore awarded a medal to the following soldiers of the Fifty-fourth: Sergeant Robert J. Simmons, Company B; Sergeant William H. Carney, Company C; Corporal Henry F. Peal, Company F; and Private George Wilson, Company A.

---

*Several histories of the war have given Lieutenant Higginson the honor of leading the regiment from the parapets of Wagner. This is an error. Lieutenant Higginson was not in this action, but on detail at the other end of the island. *Captain Luis F. Emilio* was the officer who commanded at the close of the battle.—G. W. W.

But it would be unjust to forget the gallant color-sergeant John Wall who fell in the outer trench. He was a brave and competent soldier, but after the United States colors had been taken up and borne to the top of the parapet, henceforth history seems to have kept her jealous eye upon Sergeant William H. Carney, the heroic self-appointed successor to Sergeant John Wall. Sergeant Carney planted his flag upon the ramparts of the rebel fort, and after having received three severe wounds, brought it to the rear stained with his own blood—

> Glares the volcanic breath,
> Breaks the red sea of death,
> From Wagner's yawning hold,
> On the besiegers bold.
>   Twice vain the wild attack,
>   Inch by inch, sadly slow,
>   Fights the torn remnant back,
>   Face to the foe.
>
> Yet free the colors wave,
> Borne by yon Afric brave,
> In the fierce storm wind higher;
> But, ah! one flashing fire:
>   He sinks! the banner falls
>   From the faint, mangled limb,
>   And droop to mocking walls
>   Those star-folds dim.
>
> Stay, stay the taunting laugh!
> See! now he lifts the staff,
> Clinched in his close-set teeth,
> Crawls from dead heaps beneath,
>   Crowned with his starry robe,
>   Till he the ranks has found:
>   "Comrades, the dear old flag
>   Ne'er touched the ground."
>
> O man so pure, so grand,
> Sidney might clasp thy hand!
> O brother! black thy skin,
> But white the pearl within!
>   Man, who to lift thy race
>   Worthy, thrice worthy art,
>   Clasps thee, in warm embrace
>   A Nation's heart.

At the battle of Thermopylæ three hundred Spartans held the pass against an enormous army, and yet history has made Leonidas representative of them all. Many brave soldiers fell in the forlorn assault upon Fort Wagner, but when some great painter has patriotic inspiration to give this battle an immortal representation, Colonel Shaw will be the central figure; and America will only remember one name in this conflict for all time to come—Colonel Robert Gould Shaw! This was a noble and precious life, but it was cheerfully consecrated to human freedom and the regeneration of the nation. He had good blood, splendid training, wide experience for one so young, and had inherited strong antislavery sentiments. When he had fallen, a flag of truce called for his body. A rebel officer responded, "We have buried him with his niggers." It was thought thus to cast indignity upon the hero dead, but it was a failure. The colonel and his men were united in life, and it was fitting that they should not be separated in death. In this idea his father joined, and the following letter exhibits his feelings:

> *Brigadier-general Gillmore, commanding Department of the South:*
> Sir,—I take the liberty to address you because I am informed that efforts are to be made to recover the body of my son, Colonel Shaw, of the Fifty-fourth Massachusetts Regiment, which was buried at Fort Wagner. My object in writing is to say that such efforts are not authorized by me or any of my family, and that they are not approved by us. We hold that a soldier's most appropriate burial-place is on the field where he has fallen. I shall therefore be much obliged, General, if, in case the matter is brought to your cognizance, you will forbid the desecration of my son's grave, and prevent the disturbance of his remains or those buried with him. With most earnest wishes for your success, I am, sir, with respect and esteem,
>
> > Your most obedient servant,
> > FRANCIS GEORGE SHAW.
> New York, *August 24, 1863.*

Instead of dishonoring the remains of Colonel Shaw by burying him with his brave black soldiers, the intended ignominy was transformed into a beautiful bow of promise that was to span forever the future of the race for which he gave his life. He was representative of all that was good in American life; he had wealth, high social position, and the broadest culture. From his exalted station he chose to fight with and for Negro troops—not only to lead them in conflict, but to die for them and the Republic; and although separated from them in civil life, nevertheless he united the rich and the poor, the learned and the unlearned, the white and black, in his military apotheosis.

"They buried him with his niggers!"
  Together they fought and died;
There was room for them all where they laid him
  (The grave was deep and wide),
For his beauty and youth and valor,
  Their patience and love and pain;
And at the last day together
  They shall all be found again.

"They buried him with his niggers!"
  Earth holds no prouder grave;
There is not a mausoleum
  In the world beyond the wave
That a nobler tale has hallowed
  Or a purer glory crowned,
Than the nameless trench where they buried
  The brave so faithful found.

"They buried him with his niggers!"
  A wide grave should it be.
They buried more in that shallow trench
  Than human eye could see.
Ay, all the shames and sorrows
  Of more than a hundred years
Lie under the weight of that Southern soil
  Despite those cruel sneers.

"They buried him with his niggers!"
  But the glorious souls set free
Are leading the van of the army
  That fights for liberty.
Brothers in death, in glory
  The same palm-branches bear,
And the crown is as bright o'er the sable brows
  As over the golden hair. . . .

Frances Ellen Watkins Harper

(1825–1911)

BORN OF FREE PARENTS in Baltimore, Maryland, Frances Ellen Watkins was educated first at home, and after the loss of her parents, at a school for free Negroes run by her uncle, the Reverend William Watkins. In 1845, according to William Still, with whom she later worked on the Underground Railroad, Watkins published an early collection of prose and poetry, *Forest Leaves*. No copy of this early work has yet been found. From 1850 to 1852, Watkins taught sewing at the A.M.E. Union Seminary, which was near Columbus, Ohio, but she soon left for a better teaching position in York, Pennsylvania. In 1854, reacting to a new and harsh anti-black law in Maryland, she pledged herself to the antislavery cause. Because of her success as a speaker (in her talks she often included portions of her own poems), she was employed by the Maine Antislavery Movement and lectured extensively.

In 1860 Watkins married Fenton Harper and moved to a farm near Columbus, Ohio. The Harpers had one child, who died at an early age. Mr. Harper died soon after, and Frances Harper returned to the antislavery lecture program and in addition toured the South speaking for the Women's Christian Temperance Union (WCTU). A pioneer feminist in essence, Harper advocated higher and fairer standards of domestic morality and better education for women. She worked with the American Women Suffrage Association for a while, but by 1869 was doing more for black suffrage than for women's. During her last years, however, she returned to the WCTU.

Harper was a very popular poet and fiction writer. *Poems on Miscellaneous Subjects* (1854; enlarged 1857) was reprinted many times; finally, with an introduction by William Lloyd Garrison, it went to its twentieth edition. *Moses: A Story of the Nile* (1869; enlarged 1889) became the major part of her *Idylls of the Bible* (1901). *Poems*, at first a small volume in 1871, had grown to ninety pages in 1895. *Sketches of Southern Life* (1872) was enlarged in 1896. These statistics come from William Still, mentioned earlier.

Harper's verse was conventional and, measured by the standards of her era, competent. Its subject matter varied with the periods through which she lived and the particular group with which she was currently connected. She wrote about the evils of drink, women's rights, and the double standard of morality. She put into verse biblical stories, classical myths, and oriental legends, but returned again and again to the black cause. Her novel, *Iola Leroy; or, Shadows Uplifted* (1892), is a "race" novel.

For biographical and critical comment on Frances Ellen Watkins Harper, see the articles by Daniel Walden in *Dictionary of American Negro Biography* and by Maryemma Graham in *Dictionary of Literary Biography, Volume 50*; see also Vernon Loggins's *The Negro Author* (1931), Benjamin Brawley, *Early Negro American Writers* (1935), Louis Filler, *Notable American Women* (1971), and most important, William Still, *The Underground Rail Road* (1872).

For more recent evaluations see the following: *Black Feminist Criticism: Perspectives on Black Women Writers* (1985) by Barbara Christian; Paula Gidding's *When and Where I Enter: The Impact of Black Women on Race and Sex in America* (1984); and *Invisible Poets* by Joan R. Sherman (1974). See also *Reconstructing Womanhood: The Emergence of the Afro-American Woman Novelist* by Hazel V. Carby (1987) and *Invented Lives: Narratives of Black Women, 1860–1960* by Mary Helen Washington (1987).

The selections that follow come from Harper's most popular poetic volumes: *Poems on Miscellaneous Subjects*; *Poems*; and *Sketches of Southern Life*.

THE SLAVE AUCTION

The sale began—young girls were there,
  Defenceless in their wretchedness,
Whose stifled sobs of deep despair
  Revealed their anguish and distress.

And mothers stood with streaming eyes,
  And saw their dearest children sold;
Unheeded rose their bitter cries,
  While tyrants bartered them for gold.

And woman, with her love and truth—
  For these in sable forms may dwell—
Gaz' on the husband of her youth,
  With anguish none may paint or tell.

And men, whose sole crime was their hue,
  The impress of their Maker's hand,
And frail and shrinking children, too,
  Were gathered in that mournful band.

Ye who have laid your love to rest,
  And wept above their lifeless clay,

Know not the anguish of that breast,
    Whose lov'd are rudely torn away.

Ye may not know how desolate
    Are bosoms rudely forced to part,
And how a dull and heavy weight
    Will press the life-drops from the heart.

THE DYING BONDMAN

Life was trembling, faintly trembling
On the bondman's latest breath,
And he felt the chilling pressure
Of the cold, hard hand of Death.

He had been an Afric chieftain,
Worn his manhood as a crown;
But upon the field of battle
Had been fiercely stricken down.

He had longed to gain his freedom,
Waited, watched and hoped in vain,
Till his life was slowly ebbing—
Almost broken was his chain.

By his bedside stood the master,
Gazing on the dying one,
Knowing by the dull grey shadows
That life's sands were almost run.

"Master," said the dying bondman,
"Home and friends I soon shall see;
But before I reach my country,
Master write that I am free;

"For the spirits of my fathers
Would shrink back from me in pride,
If I told them at our greeting
I a slave had lived and died;—

"Give to me the precious token,
That my kindred dead may see—
Master! write it, write it quickly!
Master! write that I am free!"

At his earnest plea the master
Wrote for him the glad release,
O'er his wan and wasted features
Flitted one sweet smile of peace.

Eagerly he grasped the writing;
"I am free!" at last he said.
Backward fell upon the pillow,
He was free among the dead.

BURY ME IN A FREE LAND

Make me a grave where'er you will,
In a lowly plain, or a lofty hill;
Make it among earth's humblest graves,
But not in a land where men are slaves.

I could not rest if around my grave
I heard the steps of a trembling slave;
His shadow above my silent tomb
Would make it a place of fearful gloom.

I could not rest if I heard the tread
Of a coffle gang to the shambles led,
And the mother's shriek of wild despair
Rise like a curse on the trembling air.

I could not sleep if I saw the lash
Drinking her blood at each fearful gash,
And I saw her babes torn from her breast,
Like trembling doves from their parent nest.

I'd shudder and start if I heard the bay
Of bloodhounds seizing their human prey,
And I heard the captive plead in vain
As they bound afresh his galling chain.

If I saw young girls from their mothers' arms
Bartered and sold for their youthful charms,
My eye would flash with a mournful flame,
My death-paled cheek grow red with shame.

I would sleep, dear friends, where bloated might
Can rob no man of his dearest right;

My rest shall be calm in any grave
Where none can call his brother a slave.

I ask no monument, proud and high,
To arrest the gaze of the passers-by;
All that my yearning spirit craves,
Is bury me not in a land of slaves.

A DOUBLE STANDARD

Do you blame me that I loved him?
   If when standing all alone
I cried for bread a careless world
   Pressed to my lips a stone.

Do you blame me that I loved him,
   That my heart beat glad and free,
When he told me in the sweetest tones
   He loved but only me?

Can you blame me that I did not see
   Beneath his burning kiss
The serpent's wiles, nor even hear
   The deadly adder hiss?

Can you blame me that my heart grew cold
   The tempted, tempter turned;
When he was feted and caressed
   And I was coldly spurned?

Would you blame him, when you draw from me
   Your dainty robes aside,
If he with gilded baits should claim
   Your fairest as his bride?

Would you blame the world if it should press
   On him a civic crown;
And see me struggling in the depth
   Then harshly press me down?

Crime has no sex and yet to-day
   I wear the brand of shame;
Whilst he amid the gay and proud
   Still bears an honored name.

Can you blame me if I've learned to think
  Your hate of vice a sham,
When you so coldly crushed me down
  And then excused the man?

Would you blame me if to-morrow
  The coroner should say,
A wretched girl, outcast, forlorn,
  Has thrown her life away?

Yes, blame me for my downward course,
  But oh! remember well,
Within your homes you press the hand
  That led me down to hell.

I'm glad God's ways are not our ways,
  He does not see as man;
Within His love I know there's room
  For those whom others ban.

I think before His great white throne,
  His throne of spotless light,
That whited sepulchres shall wear
  The hue of endless night.

That I who fell, and he who sinned,
  Shall reap as we have sown;
That each the burden of his loss
  Must bear and bear alone.

No golden weights can turn the scale
  Of justice in His sight;
And what is wrong in woman's life
  In man's cannot be right.

LEARNING TO READ

Very soon the Yankee teachers
  Came down and set up school;
But, oh! how the Rebs did hate it,—
  It was agin' their rule.

Our masters always tried to hide
  Book learning from our eyes;

Knowledge did'nt agree with slavery—
　'Twould make us all too wise.

But some of us would try to steal
　A little from the book,
And put the words together,
　And learn by hook or crook.

I remember Uncle Caldwell,
　Who took pot liquor fat
And greased the pages of his book,
　And hid it in his hat,

And had his master ever seen
　The leaves upon his head,
He'd have thought them greasy papers,
　But nothing to be read.

And there was Mr. Turner's Ben,
　Who heard the children spell,
And picked the words right up by heart,
　And learned to read 'em well.

Well, the Northern folks kept sending
　The Yankee teachers down;
And they stood right up and helped us,
　Though Rebs did sneer and frown.

And, I longed to read my Bible,
　For precious words it said;
But when I begun to learn it,
　Folks just shook their heads,

And said there is no use trying,
　Oh! Chloe, you're too late;
But as I was rising sixty,
　I had no time to wait.

So I got a pair of glasses,
　And straight to work I went,
And never stopped till I could read
　The hymns and Testament.

Then I got a little cabin
　A place to call my own—
And I felt as independent
　As the queen upon her throne.

Elizabeth Keckley

(c.1818–1907)

ELIZABETH KECKLEY was born a slave in Dinwiddie, Virginia, and remained in bondage for thirty years. She belonged to the Burwell family of Dinwiddie, and when quite young was taken by members of that family to St. Louis, Missouri, where she soon learned to be an expert seamstress and dressmaker. Following her trade, she helped to support the seven members of that family and her own son, George, whose father was white. From her savings, supplemented by loans from her customers, Keckley was able to buy her own freedom and that of her son. For a short time she was married to a ne'er-do-well black, named James Keckley. Her son, however, was the great joy of her life and a source of pride, and, when he was killed as a Union soldier in the Civil War, the source of her deepest grief.

After repaying the money borrowed from her customers, Mrs. Keckley learned to read and write, spent some time in Baltimore, and finally settled in Washington, D.C. In the capital, before and during the Civil War, she became a popular "society" dressmaker. Among her customers were Mrs. Jefferson Davis, Mrs. E. M. Stanton, and Mrs. Stephen A. Douglas. For Mrs. Abraham Lincoln, she was friend and confidante as well as dressmaker, the one to whom Mrs. Lincoln turned the night of her husband's assassination. To President Lincoln, Elizabeth was "Madame Keckley."

After the war and after the publication of her book *Behind the Scenes; or, Thirty Years as a Slave, and Four Years in the White House* (1868), her friendship with Mrs. Lincoln cooled noticeably and her popularity as a society dressmaker waned. After a very brief career as a teacher of domestic science, she dropped from public notice. Mrs. Keckley died in the Home for Destitute Women and Children in Washington. She had been for many years a member of the historic 15th Street Presbyterian Church, and her funeral was conducted by Francis J. Grimké, the scholar-pastor of that church.

Keckley's *Behind the Scenes* belongs to Lincolniana as well as to African American literature, and its authorship became a matter of controversy. Benjamin Quarles felt that the book was ghostwritten (Keckley freely acknowledged that her printer corrected her grammar); Grimké felt that she was capable of writing her own work; John E. Washington (see the material that follows) felt that Keckley was the author; and there were others who took sides. Among those who sought to discredit the work was the un-

217

known author of a vicious and crude parody entitled *Behind the Seams; by a Nigger Woman Who Took in Work from Mrs. Lincoln and Mrs. Davis.* Published in New York in 1868, the work's preface was signed "Betsey (x) Kickley (Nigger)."

For a comprehensive essay on Elizabeth Keckley's life and work, see the entry by Rayford W. Logan in *Dictionary of American Negro Biography.* See also John E. Washington's *They Knew Lincoln* (1942) and Bejamin Quarles's biographical sketch in *Notable American Women. Behind the Scenes* was republished in 1988 by Oxford University Press with an introduction by James Olney.

The following selection comes from *Behind the Scenes* (1868).

FROM **BEHIND THE SCENES**

In March, 1867, Mrs. Lincoln wrote to me from Chicago that, as her income was insufficient to meet her expenses, she would be obliged to give up her house in the city, and return to boarding. She said that she had struggled long enough to keep up appearances, and that the mask must be thrown aside. "I have not the means," she wrote, "to meet the expenses of even a first-class boarding-house, and must sell out and secure cheap rooms at some place in the country. It will not be startling news to you, my dear Lizzie, to learn that I must sell a portion of my wardrobe to add to my resources, so as to enable me to live decently, for you remember what I told you in Washington, as well as what you understood before you left me here in Chicago. I cannot live on $1,700 a year, and as I have many costly things which I shall never wear, I might as well turn them into money, and thus add to my income, and make my circumstances easier. It is humiliating to be placed in such a position, but, as I am in the position, I must extricate myself as best I can. Now, Lizzie, I want to ask a favor of you. It is imperative that I should do something for my relief, and I want you to meet me in New York, between the 30th of August and the 5th of September next, to assist me in disposing of a portion of my wardrobe."

I knew that Mrs. Lincoln's income was small, and also knew that she had many valuable dresses, which could be of no value to her, packed away in boxes and trunks. I was confident that she would never wear the dresses again, and thought that, since her need was urgent, it would be well enough to dispose of them quietly, and believed that New York was the best place to transact a delicate business of the kind. She was the wife of Abraham Lincoln, the man who had done so much for my race, and I could refuse to do nothing for her, calculated to advance her interests. I consented to render Mrs. Lincoln all the assistance in my power, and many letters passed between us in regard to the best way to proceed. It was finally arranged that I should meet her in New York about the middle of September. While thinking over this question, I remembered an incident of the White House. When we were packing up to leave Washington for Chicago, she said to me, one morning:

"Lizzie, I may see the day when I shall be obliged to sell a portion of my wardrobe. If Congress does not do something for me, then my dresses some day may have to go to bring food into my mouth, and the mouths of my children."

I also remembered of Mrs. L. having said to me at different times, in the years of 1863 and '4, that her expensive dresses might prove of great assistance to her some day.

"In what way, Mrs. Lincoln? I do not understand," I ejaculated, the first time she made the remark to me.

"Very simple to understand. Mr. Lincoln is so generous that he will not save anything from his salary, and I expect that we will leave the White House poorer than when we came into it; and should such be the case, I will have no further need for an expensive wardrobe, and it will be policy to sell it off."

I thought at the time that Mrs. Lincoln was borrowing trouble from the future, and little dreamed that the event which she so dimly foreshadowed would ever come to pass.

I closed my business about the 10th of September, and made every arrangement to leave Washington on the mission proposed. On the 15th of September I received a letter from Mrs. Lincoln, post-marked Chicago, saying that she should leave the city so as to reach New York on the night of the 17th, and directing me to precede her to the metropolis, and secure rooms for her at the St. Denis Hotel in the name of Mrs. Clarke, as her visit was to be *incog*. The contents of the letter were startling to me. I had never heard of the St. Denis, and therefore presumed that it could not be a first-class house. And I could not understand why Mrs. Lincoln should travel, without protection, under an assumed name. I knew that it would be impossible for me to engage rooms at a strange hotel for a person whom the proprietors knew nothing about. I could not write to Mrs. Lincoln, since she would be on the road to New York before a letter could possibly reach Chicago. I could not telegraph her, for the business was of too delicate a character to be trusted to the wires that would whisper the secret to every curious operator along the line. In my embarrassment, I caught at a slender thread of hope, and tried to derive consolation from it. I knew Mrs. Lincoln to be indecisive about some things, and I hoped that she might change her mind in regard to the strange programme proposed, and at the last moment despatch me to this effect. The 16th, and then the 17th of September passed, and no despatch reached me, so on the 18th I made all haste to take the train for New York. After an anxious ride, I reached the city in the evening, and when I stood alone in the streets of the great metropolis, my heart sank within me. I was in an embarrassing situation, and scarcely knew how to act. I did not know where the St. Denis Hotel was, and was not certain that I should find Mrs. Lincoln there after I should go to it. I walked up to Broadway, and got into a stage going up town, with the intention of keeping a close look-out for the hotel in question. A kind-looking gentleman occupied the seat next to me, and I ventured to inquire of him:

"If you please, sir, can you tell me where the St. Denis Hotel is?"

"Yes; we ride past it in the stage. I will point it out to you when we come to it."

"Thank you, sir."

The stage rattled up the street, and after a while the gentleman looked out of the window and said:

"This is the St. Denis. Do you wish to get out here?"

"Thank you. Yes, sir."

He pulled the strap, and the next minute I was standing on the pavement. I pulled a bell at the ladies' entrance to the hotel, and a boy coming to the door, I asked:

"Is a lady by the name of Mrs. Clarke stopping here? She came last night, I believe."

"I do not know. I will ask at the office;" and I was left alone.

The boy came back and said:

"Yes, Mrs. Clarke is here. Do you want to see her?"

"Yes."

"Well, just walk round there. She is down here now."

I did not know where "round there" exactly was, but I concluded to go forward.

I stopped, however, thinking that the lady might be in the parlor with company; and pulling out a card, asked the boy to take it to her. She heard me talking, and came into the hall to see herself.

"My dear Lizzie, I am so glad to see you," she exclaimed, coming forward and giving me her hand. "I have just received your note"—I had written her that I should join her on the 18th—"and have been trying to get a room for you. Your note has been here all day, but it was never delivered until to-night. Come in here, until I find out about your room;" and she led me into the office.

The clerk, like all modern hotel clerks, was exquisitely arrayed, highly perfumed, and too self-important to be obliging, or even courteous.

"This is the woman I told you about. I want a good room for her," Mrs. Lincoln said to the clerk.

"We have no room for her, madam," was the pointed rejoinder.

"But she must have a room. She is a friend of mine, and I want a room for her adjoining mine."

"We have no room for her on your floor."

"That is strange, sir. I tell you that she is a friend of mine, and I am sure you could not give a room to a more worthy person."

"Friend of yours, or not, I tell you we have no room for her on your floor. I can find a place for her on the fifth floor."

"That, sir, I presume, will be a vast improvement on my room. Well, if she goes to the fifth floor, I shall go too, sir. What is good enough for her is good enough for me."

"Very well, madam. Shall I give you adjoining rooms, and send your baggage up?"

"Yes, and have it done in a hurry. Let the boy show us up. Come, Elizabeth." and Mrs. L. turned from the clerk with a haughty glance, and we commenced climbing the stairs. I thought we should never reach the top; and when we did reach the fifth story, what accommodations! Little three-cornered rooms, scantily furnished. I never expected to see the widow of President Lincoln in such dingy, humble quarters.

"How provoking!" Mrs. Lincoln exclaimed, sitting down on a chair when we had reached the top, and panting from the effects of the climbing. "I declare, I never saw such unaccommodating people. Just to think of them sticking us away up here in the attic. I will give them a regular going over in the morning."

"But you forget. They do not know you. Mrs. Lincoln would be treated differently from Mrs. Clarke."

"True, I do forget. Well, I suppose I shall have to put up with the annoyances. Why did you not come to me yesterday, Lizzie? I was almost crazy when I reached here last night, and found you had not arrived. I sat down and wrote you a note—I felt so badly—imploring you to come to me immediately."

This note was afterwards sent to me from Washington. It reads as follows:

> *"St. Denis Hotel, Broadway, N.Y.*
> *"Wednesday, Sept. 17th.*
>
> "MY DEAR LIZZIE:—I arrived *here* last evening in utter despair *at not* finding you. I am frightened to death, being here alone. Come, I pray you, by *next* train. Inquire for
>
> "MRS. CLARKE,
> *"Room 94, 5th or 6th Story.*

"House so crowded could not get another spot. I wrote you especially to meet me here last evening; it makes me wild to think of being here alone. Come by *next train*, without fail.

> "Your friend,
> "MRS. LINCOLN.

"I am booked Mrs. Clarke; inquire for *no other person. Come, come, come.* I will pay your expenses when you arrive here. I shall not leave here or change my room until you come.

> "Your friend, M. L.

"Do not leave this house without seeing me.

> *"Come!"*

I transcribe the letter literally.

In reply to Mrs. Lincoln's last question, I explained what has already been explained to the reader, that I was in hope she would change her mind, and knew that it would be impossible to secure the rooms requested for a person unknown to the proprietors or attachés of the hotel.

The explanation seemed to satisfy her. Turning to me suddenly, she exclaimed:

"You have not had your dinner, Lizzie, and must be hungry. I nearly forgot about it in the joy of seeing you. You must go down to the table right away."

She pulled the bell-rope, and a servant appearing, she ordered him to give me my dinner. I followed him down-stairs, and he led me into the dining-hall, and seated me at a table in one corner of the room. I was giving my order, when the steward came forward and gruffly said:

"You are in the wrong room."

"I was brought here by the waiter," I replied.

"It makes no difference; I will find you another place where you can eat your dinner."

I got up from the table and followed him, and when outside of the door, said to him:

"It is very strange that you should permit me to be seated at the table in the dining-room only for the sake of ordering me to leave it the next moment."

"Are you not Mrs. Clarke's servant?" was his abrupt question.

"I am with Mrs. Clarke."

"It is all the same; servants are not allowed to eat in the large dining-room. Here, this way; you must take your dinner in the servants' hall."

Hungry and humiliated as I was, I was willing to follow to any place to get my dinner, for I had been riding all day, and had not tasted a mouthful since early morning.

On reaching the servants' hall we found the door of the room locked. The waiter left me standing in the passage while he went to inform the clerk of the fact.

In a few minutes the obsequious clerk came blustering down the hall:

"Did you come out of the street, or from Mrs. Clarke's room?"

"From Mrs. Clarke's room," I meekly answered. My gentle words seemed to quiet him, and then he explained:

"It is after the regular hour for dinner. The room is locked up, and Annie has gone out with the key."

My pride would not let me stand longer in the hall.

"Very well," I remarked, as I began climbing the stairs, "I will tell Mrs. Clarke that I cannot get any dinner."

He looked after me, with a scowl on his face:

"You need not put on airs! I understand the whole thing."

I said nothing, but continued to climb the stairs, thinking to myself: "Well, if you understand the whole thing, it is strange that you should put the widow of ex-President Abraham Lincoln in a three-cornered room in the attic of this miserable hotel."

When I reached Mrs. Lincoln's rooms, tears of humiliation and vexation were in my eyes.

"What is the matter, Lizzie?" she asked.

"I cannot get any dinner."

"Cannot get any dinner! What do you mean?"

I then told her of all that had transpired below.

"The insolent, overbearing people!" she fiercely exclaimed. "Never mind, Lizzie, you shall have your dinner. Put on your bonnet and shawl."

"What for?"

"What for! Why, we will go out of the hotel, and get you something to eat where they know how to behave decently:" and Mrs. Lincoln already was tying the strings to her bonnet before the glass.

Her impulsiveness alarmed me.

"Surely, Mrs. Lincoln, you do not intend to go out on the street to-night?"

"Yes I do. Do you suppose I am going to have you starve, when we can find something to eat on every corner?"

"But you forget. You are here as Mrs. Clarke and not as Mrs. Lincoln. You came alone, and the people already suspect that everything is not right. If you go outside of the hotel to-night, they will accept the fact as evidence against you."

"Nonsense; what do you suppose I care for what these low-bred people think? Put on your things."

"No, Mrs. Lincoln, I shall not go outside of the hotel to-night, for I realize your situation, if you do not. Mrs. Lincoln has no reason to care what these people may say about her as Mrs. Lincoln, but she should be prudent, and give them no opportunity to say anything about her as Mrs. Clarke."

It was with difficulty I could convince her that she should act with caution. She was so frank and impulsive that she never once thought that her actions might be misconstrued. It did not occur to her that she might order dinner to be served in my room, so I went to bed without a mouthful to eat.

The next morning Mrs. Lincoln knocked at my door before six o'clock:

"Come, Elizabeth, get up, I know you must be hungry. Dress yourself quickly and we will go out and get some breakfast. I was unable to sleep last night for thinking of you being forced to go to bed without anything to eat."

I dressed myself as quickly as I could, and together we went out and took breakfast, at a restaurant on Broadway, some place between 609 and the St. Denis Hotel. I do not give the number, as I prefer leaving it to conjecture. Of one thing I am certain—the proprietor of the restaurant little dreamed who one of his guests was that morning.

After breakfast we walked up Broadway, and entering Union Square Park, took a seat on one of the benches under the trees, watched the children at play, and talked over the situation. Mrs. Lincoln told me: "Lizzie, yesterday morning I called for the *Herald* at the breakfast table, and on looking over the list of diamond brokers advertised, I selected the firm of W. H. Brady & Co., 609 Broadway. After breakfast I walked down to the house, and tried to sell them a lot of jewelry. I gave my name as Mrs. Clarke. I first saw Mr. Judd, a member of the firm, a very pleasant gentleman. We were unable to agree about the price. He went back into the office, where a stout gentleman was seated at the desk, but I could not hear what he said. [I know now what was said, and so shall the reader, in parentheses. Mr. Brady has since told me that he remarked to Mr. Judd that the woman must be crazy to ask such outrageous prices, and to get rid of her as soon as possible.] Soon after Mr. Judd came back to the counter, another gentleman, Mr. Keyes, as I have since learned, a silent partner in the house, entered the store. He came to the counter, and in looking over my jewelry discovered my name inside of one of the rings. I had forgotten the ring, and when I saw him looking at the name so earnestly, I snatched the bauble from him and put it into my pocket. I hastily gathered up my jewelry, and started out. They asked for my address, and I left my card, Mrs. Clarke, at the St. Denis Hotel. They are to call to see me this forenoon, when I shall enter into negotiations with them."

Scarcely had we returned to the hotel when Mr. Keyes called, and Mrs. Clarke disclosed to him that she was Mrs. Lincoln. He was

much elated to find his surmise correct. Mrs. L. exhibited to him a
large number of shawls, dresses, and fine laces, and told him that
she was compelled to sell them in order to live. He was an earnest
Republican, was much affected by her story, and denounced the in-
gratitude of the government in the severest terms. She complained to
him of the treatment she had received at the St. Denis, and he advised her to move to another hotel forthwith. She readily consented,
and as she wanted to be in an out-of-the-way place where she would
not be recognized by any of her old friends, he recommended the
Earle Hotel in Canal street.

On the way down to the hotel that morning she acceded to a
suggestion made by me, and supported by Mr. Keyes, that she con-
fide in the landlord, and give him her name without registering, so
as to ensure the proper respect. Unfortunately, the Earle Hotel was
full, and we had to select another place. We drove to the Union
Place Hotel, where we secured rooms for Mrs. Clarke, Mrs. Lincoln
changing her mind, deeming it would not be prudent to disclose her
real name to any one. After we had become settled in our new quarters, Messrs. Keyes and Brady called frequently on Mrs. Lincoln, and
held long conferences with her. They advised her to pursue the
course she did, and were sanguine of success. Mrs. Lincoln was very
anxious to dispose of her things, and return to Chicago as quickly
and quietly as possible; but they presented the case in a different
light, and, I regret to say, she was guided by their counsel. "Pooh,"
said Mr. Brady, "place your affairs in our hands, and we will raise
you at least $100,000 in a few weeks. The people will not permit the
widow of Abraham Lincoln to suffer; they will come to her rescue
when they know she is in want."

The argument seemed plausible, and Mrs. Lincoln quietly acceded
to the proposals of Keyes and Brady.

We remained quietly at the Union Place Hotel for a few days. On
Sunday Mrs. Lincoln accepted the use of a private carriage, and accompanied by me, she drove out to Central Park. We did not enjoy
the ride much, as the carriage was a close one, and we could not
throw open the window for fear of being recognized by some one of
the many thousands in the Park. Mrs. Lincoln wore a heavy veil so
as to more effectually conceal her face. We came near being run into,
and we had a spasm of alarm, for an accident would have exposed
us to public gaze, and of course the masquerade would have been at
an end. On Tuesday I hunted up a number of dealers in second-
hand clothing, and had them call at the hotel by appointment. Mrs.
Lincoln soon discovered that they were hard people to drive a bargain with, so on Thursday we got into a close carriage, taking a bundle of dresses and shawls with us, and drove to a number of stores
on Seventh Avenue, where an attempt was made to dispose of a por-

tion of the wardrobe. The dealers wanted the goods for little or nothing, and we found it a hard matter to drive a bargain with them. Mrs. Lincoln met the dealers squarely, but all of her tact and shrewdness failed to accomplish much. I do not care to dwell upon this portion of my story. Let it answer to say, that we returned to the hotel more disgusted than ever with the business in which we were engaged. There was much curiosity at the hotel in relation to us, as our movements were watched, and we were regarded with suspicion. Our trunks in the main hall below were examined daily, and curiosity was more keenly excited when the argus-eyed reporters for the press traced Mrs. Lincoln's name on the cover of one of her trunks. The letters had been rubbed out, but the faint outlines remained, and these outlines only served to stimulate curiosity. Messrs. Keyes and Brady called often, and they made Mrs. Lincoln believe that, if she would write certain letters for them to show to prominent politicians, they could raise a large sum of money for her. They argued that the Republican party would never permit it to be said that the wife of Abraham Lincoln was in want; that the leaders of the party would make heavy advances rather than have it published to the world that Mrs. Lincoln's poverty compelled her to sell her wardrobe. Mrs. L.'s wants were urgent, as she had to borrow $600 from Keyes and Brady, and she was willing to adopt any scheme which promised to place a good bank account to her credit. At different times in her room at the Union Hotel she wrote the following letters:

"*Chicago, Sept. 18, 1867.*

"MR. BRADY, *Commission Broker, No. 609*
Broadway, New York:
"I have this day sent to you personal property, which I am compelled to part with, and which you will find of considerable value. The articles consist of four camels' hair shawls, one lace dress and shawl, a parasol cover, a diamond ring, two dress patterns, some furs, etc.
"Please have them appraised, and confer by letter with me.
Very respectfully,
"MRS. LINCOLN."

"Chicago,_____.

"MR. BRADY, *No. 609 Broadway, N.Y. City:*
"* * * * DEAR SIR:—The articles I am sending you to dispose of were gifts of dear friends, which only *urgent necessity* compels me to part with, and I am especially anxious that they shall not be sacrificed.
"The circumstances are peculiar, and painfully embarrassing; therefore I hope you will endeavor to realize as much as possible for them. Hoping to hear from you, I remain, very respectfully,
"MRS. A. LINCOLN."

"Sept. 25, 1867.

"W. H. BRADY, ESQ.:—My great, great sorrow and loss have made me painfully sensitive, but as my feelings and pecuniary comforts were never regarded or even recognized in the midst of my overwhelming bereavement—*now* that I am pressed in a most startling manner for means of subsistence, I do not know why I should shrink from an opportunity of improving my trying position.

"Being assured that all you do will be appropriately executed, and in a manner that will not startle me very greatly, and excite as little comment as possible, again I shall leave all in your hands.

"I am passing through a very painful ordeal, which the country, in remembrance of my noble and devoted husband, should have spared me.

"I remain, with great respect, very truly,

"MRS. LINCOLN.

"P.S.—As you mention that my goods have been valued at over $24,000, I will be willing to make a reduction of $8,000, and relinquish them for $16,000. If this is not accomplished, I will continue to sell and advertise largely until every article is sold.

"I must have means to live, at least in a medium comfortable state.

"M. L."

The letters are dated Chicago, and addressed to Mr. Brady, though every one of them was written in New York; for when Mrs. L. left the West for the East, she had settled upon no definite plan of action. Mr. Brady proposed to show the letters to certain politicians, and ask for money on a threat to publish them if his demands, as Mrs. Lincoln's agent, were not complied with. When writing the letter I stood at Mrs. Lincoln's elbow, and suggested that they be couched in the mildest language possible.

"Never mind, Lizzie," she said; "anything to raise the wind. One might as well be killed for a sheep as a lamb."

Pauline Hopkins

(1856–1930)

A VERSATILE AND TALENTED PERSON, Pauline Elizabeth Hopkins deserves to be better known than she is today. She was, among other things, an editor of an important Negro magazine, a publisher, a journalist, a novelist and writer of short stories, and a producer of a musical drama in which she sang one of the stellar parts. These were pursuits followed by very few women, white or black, of her generation.

Born in Portland, Maine, Pauline Hopkins was the daughter of Northrup and Sarah (Allen) Hopkins. Her mother, who was born in Exeter, New Hampshire, belonged to a well-known New England African American family, one that included the outstanding clergyman and abolitionist Nathaniel Paul. She was also the grandniece of the poet James Whitfield.

During her early years Pauline Hopkins lived in Boston and attended the public schools of that city. At the age of fifteen she won a prize for her essay "The Evils of Intemperance and Their Remedies" in a contest sponsored by William Wells Brown. The prize inspired her to seek a writing career after graduation from high school. In 1880 Hopkins created and produced a musical presentation called "Hopkins' Coloured Troubadors in the Great Musical Drama, Escape from Slavery." The cast consisted of such well-known performers as Sam Lucas and the Hyers Sisters, a sixty-member chorus, members of her family, and the author-producer herself, billed as "Boston's Colored Soprano." This musical drama ran to five performances.

In 1892 Hopkins won widespread praise for her illustrated lecture on Toussaint L'Ouverture, presented in the famous Tremont Temple for the Robert A. Bell Boston Post of the Grand Army of the Republic. In 1900 she published her first novel, *Contending Forces: A Romance Illustrative of Negro Life North and South*. The work dealt with middle-class Negro life of her generation. She promoted the book by reading portions of it to women's clubs throughout the nation.

Because of the success of this novel, Hopkins was asked to serve as editor of and contributor to the *Colored American*, one of the best-known periodicals of its day. Coming into existence in 1900, it was the first Negro magazine of the twentieth century devoted to the "development of Afro-American art and literature." Pauline Hopkins wrote for the magazine's first issue a short story entitled "The Mystery within Us." For subsequent issues, she wrote three long serials: "Hagar's Daughters: A Story of Southern

Caste Prejudice" (March 1901 to March 1902); "Winona: A Tale of Negro Life in the South and Southwest" (May 1902 to October 1902); and "Of One Blood; or, The Hidden Self" (November 1902 to November 1903). These novels and some of her short stories dealt largely with interracial relationships. In addition to these works of fiction, Hopkins also wrote biographical sketches of "Famous Men of the Negro Race" and "Famous Women of the Negro Race."

According to Dorothy Porter, "the illustrated *Colored American Magazine* [under Hopkins's editorship] is a major source for the literature, science, music, arts, religions, facts, and traditions of the Negro race during four years." On the grounds of poor health, Hopkins left the *Colored American* in 1904. The real reason was probably the purchase of the magazine by accommodationist Fred R. Moore, with money furnished by Booker T. Washington, who was then trying to gain control over newspapers owned by blacks.

After leaving the *Colored American*, Hopkins engaged in several activities: she wrote briefly for the *Voice of the Negro*, founded her own publishing firm, contributed articles to and edited the *New Era*, and wrote several biographies of distinguished black and white abolitionists like Henry Highland Garnet and William Lloyd Garrison. After living in obscurity for more than a decade, Pauline Elizabeth Hopkins died in 1930.

For excellent articles on Pauline Hopkins, see Dorothy Porter's entry in *Dictionary of American Negro Biography* and Jane Campbell's entry in *Dictionary of Literary Biography, Volume 50*. See also Hugh M. Gloster, *Negro Voices in American Fiction* (1948); Ann Allen Shockley, "Pauline Elizabeth Hopkins: A Biographical Excursion into Obscurity," *Phylon* 33 (Spring 1972); Abby A. Johnson and Ronald M. Johnson, "Away from Accommodation: Radical Editors and Protest Journalism, 1900–1910," *Journal of Negro History* (October 1977); and Claudia Tate, "Pauline Hopkins: Our Literary Foremother," in *Conjuring: Black Women, Fiction, and Literary Tradition*, ed. Marjorie Pryse and Hortense J. Spillers (1985). For the most recent commentary see Mary Helen Washington, *Invented Lives* (1987) and Hazel V. Carby, *Reconstructing Womanhood* (1987).

The following selection comes from *Contending Forces*, originally published in 1900, reprinted in 1975 by AMS Press.

BRO'R ABR'M JIMSON'S WEDDING
A Christmas Story

It was a Sunday in early spring the first time that Caramel Johnson dawned on the congregation of _____ Church in a populous New England City.

The Afro-Americans of that city are well-to-do, being of a frugal nature, and considering it a lasting disgrace for any man among them, desirous of social standing in the community, not to make himself comfortable in this world's goods against the coming time, when old age creeps on apace and renders him unfit for active business.

Therefore the members of the said church had not waited to be exhorted by reformers to own their unpretentious homes and small farms outside the city limits, but they vied with each other in efforts to accumulate a small competency urged thereto by a realization of what pressing needs the future might bring, or that might have been because of the constant example of white neighbors, and a due respect for the dignity which *their* foresight had brought to the superior race.

Of course, these small Vanderbilts and Astors of a darker hue must have a place of worship in accord with their worldly prosperity, and so it fell out that _____ church was the richest plum in the ecclesiastical pudding, and greatly sought by scholarly divines as a resting place for four years,—the extent of the time-limit allowed by conference to the men who must be provided with suitable charges according to the demands of their energy and scholarship.

The attendance was unusually large for morning service, and a restless movement was noticeable all through the sermon. How strange a thing is nature; the change of the seasons announces itself in all humanity as well as in the trees and flowers, the grass, and in the atmosphere. Something within us responds instantly to the touch of kinship that dwells in all life.

The air, soft and balmy, laden with rich promise for the future, came through the massive, half-open windows, stealing in refreshing waves upon the congregation. The sunlight fell through the colored glass of the windows in prismatic hues, and dancing all over the lofty star-gemmed ceiling, painted the hue of the broad vault of heaven, creeping down in crinkling shadows to touch the deep garnet cushions of the sacred desk, and the rich wood of the altar with a hint of gold.

The offertory was ended. The silvery cadences of a rich soprano voice still lingered on the air, "O, Worship the Lord in the beauty of holiness." There was a suppressed feeling of expectation, but not the faintest rustle as the minister rose in the pulpit, and after a solemn pause, gave the usual invitation:

"If there is anyone in this congregation desiring to unite with this church, either by letter or on probation, please come forward to the altar."

The words had not died upon his lips when a woman started from her seat near the door and passed up the main aisle. There was a sudden commotion on all sides. Many heads were turned—it takes so little to interest a church audience. The girls in the choir-box leaned over the rail, nudged each other and giggled, while the men said to one another, "She's a stunner, and no mistake."

The candidate for membership, meanwhile, had reached the altar railing and stood before the man of God, to whom she had handed her letter from a former Sabbath home, with head decorously bowed as became the time and the holy place. There was no denying the fact that she was a pretty girl; brown of skin, small of feature, with an ever-lurking gleam of laughter in eyes coal black. Her figure was slender and beautifully moulded, with a seductive grace in the undulating walk and erect carriage. But the chief charm of the sparkling dark face lay in its intelligence, and the responsive play of facial expression which was enhanced by two mischievous dimples pressed into the rounded cheeks by the caressing fingers of the god of Love.

The minister whispered to the candidate, coughed, blew his nose on his snowy clerical handkerchief, and, finally, turned to the expectant congregation:

"Sister Chocolate Caramel Johnson—"

He was interrupted by a snicker and a suppressed laugh, again from the choir-box, and an audible whisper which sounded distinctly throughout the quiet church,—

"I'd get the Legislature to change that if it was mine, 'deed I would!" then silence profound caused by the reverend's stern glance of reproval bent on the offenders in the choir-box.

"Such levity will not be allowed among the members of the choir. If it occurs again, I shall ask the choir master for the names of the offenders and have their places taken by those more worthy to be gospel singers."

Thereupon Mrs. Tilly Anderson whispered to Mrs. Nancy Tobias that, "them choir gals is the mos' deceivines' hussies in the church, an' for my part, I'm glad the pastor called 'em down. That sister's too good lookin' for 'em, an' they'll be after her like er pack o' houn's, min' me, Sis' Tobias."

Sister Tobias ducked her head in her lap and shook her fat sides in laughing appreciation of the sister's foresight.

Order being restored the minister proceeded:

"Sister Chocolate Caramel Johnson brings a letter to us from our sister church in Nashville, Tennessee. She has been a member in good standing for ten years, having been received into fellowship at ten years of age. She leaves them now, much to her regret, to pursue the study of music at one of the large conservatories in this city, and they recommend her to our love and care. You know the contents of the letter. All in favor of giving Sister Johnson the right hand of fellowship, please manifest the same by a rising vote." The whole congregation rose.

"Contrary minded? None. The ayes have it. Be seated, friends. Sister Johnson, it gives me great pleasure to receive you into this church. I welcome you to its joys and sorrows. May God bless you. Brother Jimson?" (Brother Jimson stepped from his seat to the pastor's side.) "I assign this sister to your class. Sister Johnson, this is Brother Jimson, your future spiritual teacher."

Brother Jimson shook the hand of his new member, warmly, and she returned to her seat. The minister pronounced the benediction over the waiting congregation; the organ burst into richest melody. Slowly the crowd of worshippers dispersed.

Abraham Jimson had made his money as a janitor for the wealthy people of the city. He was a bachelor, and when reproved by some good Christian brother for still dwelling in single blessedness always offered as an excuse that he had been too busy to think of a wife, but that now he was "well fixed," pecuniarily, he would begin to "look over" his lady friends for a suitable companion.

He owned a house in the suburbs and a fine brick dwelling-house in the city proper. He was a trustee of prominence in the church, in fact, its "solid man," and his opinion was sought and his advice acted upon by his associates on the Board. It was felt that any lady in the congregation would be proud to know herself his choice.

When Caramel Johnson received the right hand of fellowship, her aunt, the widow Maria Nash, was ahead in the race for the wealthy class-leader. It had been neck-and-neck for a while between her and Sister Viney Peters, but, finally it had settled down to Sister Maria with a hundred to one, among the sporting members of the Board, that she carried off the prize, for Sister Maria owned a house adjoining Brother Jimson's in the suburbs, and property counts these days.

Sister Nash had "no idea" when she sent for her niece to come to B. that the latter would prove a rival; her son Andy was as good as engaged to Caramel. But it is always the unexpected that happens. Caramel came, and Brother Jimson had no eyes for the charms of other women after he had gazed into her coal black orbs, and watched her dimples come and go.

Caramel decided to accept a position as housemaid in order to help defray the expenses of her tuition at the conservatory, and Brother Jimson interested himself so warmly in her behalf that she soon had a situation in the home of his richest patron where it was handy for him to chat with her about the business of the church, and the welfare of her soul, in general. Things progressed very smoothly until the fall, when one day Sister Maria had occasion to call, unexpectedly, on her niece and found Brother Jimson basking in her smiles while he enjoyed a sumptuous dinner of roast chicken and fixings.

To say that Sister Maria was "set way back" would not accurately describe her feelings; but from that time Abraham Jimson knew that he had a secret foe in the Widow Nash.

Before many weeks had passed it was publicly known that Brother Jimson would lead Caramel Johnson to the altar "come Christmas." There was much sly speculation as to the "widder's gittin' left," and how she took it from those who had cast hopeless glances toward the chief man of the church. Great preparations were set on foot for the wedding festivities. The bride's trousseau was a present from the groom and included a white satin wedding gown and a costly gold watch. The town house was refurnished and a trip to New York was in contemplation.

"Hump!" grunted Sister Nash when told the rumors, "there's no fool like an ol' fool. Car'mel's a han'ful he'll fin', ef he gits her."

"I reckon he'll git her all right, Sis' Nash," laughed the neighbor, who had run in to talk over the news.

"I've said my word an' I ain't goin' change it, Sis'r. Min' me, I says, *ef he gits her*, an, I mean it."

Andy Nash was also a member of Brother Jimson's class; he possessed, too, a strong sweet baritone voice which made him a great value to the choir. He was an immense success in the social life of the city, and had created sad havoc with the hearts of the colored girls; he could have his pick of the best of them because of his graceful figure and fine easy manners. Until Caramel had been dazzled by the wealth of her elderly lover, she had considered herself fortunate as the lady of his choice.

It was Sunday, three weeks before the wedding that Andy resolved to have it out with Caramel.

"She's been hot an' she's been col', an' now she's luke warm, an' today ends it before this gent-man sleeps," he told himself as he stood before the glass and tied his pale blue silk tie in a stunning knot, and settled his glossy tile at a becoming angle.

Brother Jimson's class was a popular one and had a large membership; the hour spent there was much enjoyed, even by visitors. Andy went into the vestry early resolved to meet Caramel if possible. She was there, at the back of the room sitting alone on a settee. Andy immediately seated himself in the vacant place by her side. There were whispers and much head-shaking among the few early worshippers, all of whom knew the story of the young fellow's romance and his disappointment.

As he dropped into the seat beside her, Caramel turned her large eyes on him intently, speculatively, with a doubtful sort of curiosity suggested in her expression, as to how he took her flagrant desertion.

"Howdy, Car'mel?" was his greeting without a shade of resentment.

"I'm well; no need to ask how you are," was the quick response. There was a mixture of cordiality and coquetry in her manner. Her eyes narrowed and glittered under lowered lids, as she gave him a long side-glance. How could she help showing her admiration for the supple young giant beside her? "Surely," she told herself, "I'll have long time enough to git sick of old rheumatics," her pet name for her elderly lover.

"I ain't sick much," was Andy's surly reply.

He leaned his elbow on the back of the settee and gave his recreant sweetheart a flaming glance of mingled love and hate, oblivious to the presence of the assembled class-members.

"You ain't over friendly these days, Car'mel, but I gits news of your capers 'roun' 'bout some of the members."

"My—Yes?" she answered as she flashed her great eyes at him in pretended surprise. He laughed a laugh not good to hear.

"Yes," he drawled. Then he added with sudden energy, "Are you goin' to tie up to old Rheumatism sure 'nuff, come Chris'mas?"

"Come Chris'mas, Andy, I be. I hate to tell you but I have to do it."

He recoiled as from a blow. As for the girl, she found a keen relish in the situation: it flattered her vanity.

"How comes it you've changed your mind, Car'mel, 'bout you an' me? You've tol' me often that I was your first choice."

"We—ll," she drawled, glancing uneasily about her and avoiding her aunt's gaze, which she knew was bent upon her every movement, "I did reckon once I would. But a man with money suits me best, an' you ain't got a cent."

"No more have you. You ain't no better than other women to work an' help a man along, is you?"

The color flamed an instant in her face turning the dusky skin to a deep, dull red.

"Andy Nash, you always was a fool, an' as ignerunt as a wil' Injun. I mean to have a sure nuff brick house an' plenty of money. That makes people respec' you. Why don' you quit bein' so shifless and save your money. You ain't worth your salt."

"Your head's turned with pianorer-playin' an' livin' up North. Ef you'll turn *him* off an' come back home, I'll turn over a new leaf, Car'mel," his voice was soft and persuasive enough now.

She had risen to her feet; her eyes flashed, her face was full of pride.

"I won't. I've quit likin' you, Andy Nash."

"Are you in earnest?" he asked, also rising from his seat.

"Dead earnes'."

"Then there's no more to be said."

He spoke calmly, not raising his voice above a whisper. She stared at him in surprise. Then he added as he swung on his heel preparatory to leaving her:

"You ain't got him yet, my gal. But remember, I'm waitin' for you when you need me."

While this whispered conference was taking place in the back of the vestry, Brother Jimson had entered, and many an anxious glance he cast in the direction of the couple. Andy made his way slowly to his mother's side as Brother Jimson rose in his place to open the meeting. There was a commotion on all sides as the members rustled down on their knees for prayer. Widow Nash whispered to her son as they knelt side by side:

"How did you make out, Andy?"

"Didn't make out at all, mammy; she's as obstinate as a mule."

"Well, then, there's only one thing mo' to do."

Andy was unpleasant company for the remainder of the day. He sought, but found nothing to palliate Caramel's treachery. He had only surly, bitter words for his companions who ventured to address him, as the outward expression of inward tumult. The more he brooded over his wrongs the worse he felt. When he went to work on Monday morning he was feeling vicious. He had made up his mind to do something desperate. The wedding should not come off. He would be avenged.

Andy went about his work at the hotel in gloomy silence unlike his usual gay hilarity. It happened that all the female help at the great hostelry was white, and on that particular Monday morning was the duty of Bridget McCarthy's watch to clean the floors. Bridget was also not in the best of humors, for Pat McClosky, her special company, had gone to the priest's with her rival, Kate Connerton, on Sunday afternoon, and Bridget had not yet got over the effects of a strong rum punch taken to quiet her nerves after hearing the news.

Bridget had scrubbed a wide swath of the marble floor when Andy came through with a rush order carried in scientific style high above his head, balanced on one hand. Intent upon satisfying the guest who was princely in his "tips," Andy's unwary feet became entangled in the maelstrom of brooms, scrubbing-brushes and pails. In an instant the "order" was sliding over the floor in a general mix-up.

To say Bridget was mad wouldn't do her state justice. She forgot herself and her surroundings and relieved her feelings in elegant Irish, ending a tirade of abuse by calling Andy a "wall-eyed, bandy-legged nagur."

Andy couldn't stand that from "common, po' white trash," so calling all his science into play he struck out straight from the shoulder with his right, and brought her a swinging blow on the mouth, which seated her neatly in the five-gallon bowl of freshly made lobster salad which happened to be standing on the floor behind her.

There was a wail from the kitchen force that reached to every department. It being the busiest hour of the day when they served dinner, the dish-washers and scrubbers went on a strike against the "nagur who struck Bridget McCarthy, the baste,"* mingled with cries of "lynch him!" Instantly the great basement floor was a battle ground. Every colored man seized whatever was handiest and ranged himself by Andy's side, and stood ready to receive the onslaught of the Irish brigade. For the sake of peace, and sorely against his inclinations, the proprietor surrendered Andy to the police on a charge of assault and battery.

On Wednesday morning of the eventful week, Brother Jimson wended his way to his house in the suburbs to collect the rent. Unseen by the eye of man, he was wrestling with a problem that had shadowed his life for many years. No one on earth suspected him unless it might be the widow. Brother Jimson boasted of his consistent Christian life—rolled his piety like a sweet morsel beneath his tongue, and had deluded himself into thinking that *he* could do no sin. There were scoffers in the church who doubted the genuineness of his pretentions, and he believed that there was a movement on foot against his power led by Widow Nash.

Brother Jimson groaned in bitterness of spirit. His only fear was that he might be parted from Caramel. If he lost her he felt that all happiness in life was over for him, anxiety gave him a sickening feeling of unrest. He was tormented, too, by jealousy; and when he was called upon by Andy's anxious mother to rescue her son from the clutches of the law, he had promised her fair enough, but in reality resolved to do nothing but—tell the judge that Andy was a dangerous character whom it was best to quell by severity. The pas-

---

*"Baste" is "beast" as Hopkins tries to imitate an Irish brogue.

tor and all the other influential members of the church were at court
on Tuesday, but Brother Jimson was conspicuous by his absence.

Today Brother Jimson resolved to call on Sister Nash, and as he
had heard nothing of the outcome of the trial, make cautious inquiries concerning that, and also sound her on the subject nearest his
heart.

He opened the gate and walked down the side path to the back
door. From within came the rhythmic sound of a rubbing board.
The brother knocked, and then cleared his throat with a preliminary
cough.

"Come," called a voice within. As the door swung open it revealed the spare form of the widow, who with sleeves rolled above
her elbows stood at the tub cutting her way through piles of foaming
suds.

"Mornin', Sis' Nash! How's all?"

"That you, Bro'r Jimson? How's yourself? Take a cheer an' make
yourself to home."

"Cert'nly, Sis' Nash, don' care ef I do," and the good brother
scanned the sister with an eagle eye. "Yas'm I'm purty tol'rable these
days, thank God. Bleeg'd to you, Sister, I jes' will stop an res' myself
befo' I repair myself back to the city." He seated himself in the most
comfortable chair in the room, tilted it on the two back legs against
the wall, lit his pipe and with a grunt of satisfaction settled back to
watch the white rings of smoke curl about his head.

"These are mighty ticklish times, Sister. How's you continue on
the journey? Is you strong in the faith?"

"I've got the faith, my brother, but I ain't on no mountain top
this week. I'm way down in the valley; I'm jes' coaxin' the Lord to
keep me sweet," and Sister Nash wiped the ends from her hands and
prodded the clothes in the boiler with the clothes-stick, added fresh
pieces and went on with her work.

"This is a worl' strewed with wrecks an' floatin' with tears. It's
the valley of tribulation. May your faith continue. I hear Jim Jinkins
has bought a farm up Taunton way."

"Wan'ter know!"

"Doctor tells me Bro'r Waters is comin' after Chris-mus. They do
say as how he's stirrin' up things turrible; he's easin' his min' on this
lynchin' business, an' it's high time—high time."

"Sho! Don' say so! What you reck'n he's goin tell us now,
Brother Jimson?"

"Suthin' 'stonishin', Sister; it'll stir the country from end to end.
Yes'm the Council is powerful strong as an organization."

"Sho! sho!" and the "thrub, thrub" of the board could be heard a
mile away.

The conversation flagged. Evidently Widow Nash was not in a talkative mood that morning. The brother was disappointed.

"Well, it's mighty comfort'ble here, but I mus' be goin'."

"What's your hurry, Brother Jimson?"

"Business, Sister, business," and the brother brought his chair forward preparatory to rising. "Where's Andy? How'd he come out of that little difficulty?"

"Locked up."

"You don' mean to say he's in jail?"

"Yes, he's in jail 'tell I git's his bail."

"What might the sentence be, Sister?"

"Twenty dollars fine or six months at the Islan'." There was silence for a moment, broken only by the "thrub, thrub" of the washboard, while the smoke curled upward from Brother Jimson's pipe as he enjoyed a few last puffs.

"These are mighty ticklish times, Sister. Po' Andy, the way of the transgressor is hard."

Sister Nash took her hands out of the tub and stood with arms akimbo, a statue of Justice carved in ebony. Her voice was like the trump of doom.

"Yes; an' men like you is the cause of it. You leadin' men with money an' chances don' do your duty. I arst you, I arst you fair, to go down to the jedge an' bail that po' chile out. Did you go? No; you hard-faced old devil, you lef him be there, an' I had to git the money from my white folks. Yes, an I'm breakin' my back now, over that pile of clo's to pay that twenty dollars. Um! all the trouble comes to us women."

"That's so, Sister; that's the livin' truth," murmured Brother Jimson furtively watching the rising storm and wondering where the lightning of her speech would strike next.

"I tell you that it is our receiptfulness to each other is the reason we don' prosper an' God's a-punishin' us with fire an' with sward 'cause we's so jealous an' snaky to each other."

"That's so, Sister; that's the livin' truth."

"Yes, sir; a nigger's boun' to be a nigger 'tell the trump of doom. You kin skin him, but he's a nigger still. Broad-cloth, biled shirts an' money won' make him more or less, no, sir."

"That's so, Sister; that's jes' so."

"A nigger can't holp himself. White folks can run agin the law all the time an' they never gits caught, but a nigger! Every time he opens his mouth he puts his foot in it—got to hit that po' white trash gal in the mouth an' git jailed an' leave his po'r ol' mother to work her fingers to the secon' jint to get him out. Um!"

"These are mighty ticklish times, Sister. Man's boun' to sin; it's his nat'ral state. I hope this will teach Andy humility of the sperit."

"A little humility'd be good for yourself, Abra'm Jimson." Sister Nash ceased her sobs and set her teeth hard.

"Lord, Sister Nash, what compar'son is there 'twixt me an' a worthless nigger like Andy? My business is with the salt of the earth, an' so I have dwelt ever since I was consecrated."

"Salt of the earth! But ef the salt have los' its saver how you goin' salt it ergin? No, sir, you cain't do it; it mus' be cas' out an' trodded under foot of men. That's who's goin' happen you Abe Jimson, hyar me? An' I'd like to trod on you with my foot, an' every ol' good fer nuthin' bag o' salt like you," shouted Sister Nash. "You're a snake in the grass; you done stole the boy's gal an' then try to git him sent to the Islan'. You cain't deny it, fer the jedge done tol' me all you said, you ol' rhinoceros-hided hypercrite. Salt of the earth! You!"

Brother Jimson regretted that Widow Nash had found him out. Slowly he turned, settling his hat on the back of his head.

"Good mornin', Sister Nash. I ain't no hard feelin's agains' you. I too near to the kingdom to let trifles jar me. My bowels of compassion yearns over you, Sister, a pilgrim an' a stranger in this unfriendly worl'."

No answer from Sister Nash. Brother Jimson lingered.

"Good mornin', Sister." Still no answer.

"I hope to see you at the weddin', Sister."

"Keep on hopin', I'll be there. That gal's my own sister's chile. What in time she wants of a rheumatic ol' sap-head like you for, beats me. I wouldn't marry you for no money, myself; no, sir; it's my belief that you've done goophered her."

"Yes, Sister; I've hearn tell of people refusin' befo' they was ask'd," he retorted, giving her a sly look.

For answer the widow grabbed the clothes-stick and flung it at him in speechless rage.

"My, what a temper it's got," remarked Brother Jimson soothingly as he dodged the shovel, the broom, the coal-hod and the stove-covers. But he sighed with relief as he turned into the street and caught the faint sound of the washboard now resumed.

To a New Englander the season of snow and ice with its clear biting atmosphere, is the ideal time for the great festival. Christmas morning dawned in royal splendor; the sun kissed the snowy streets and turned the icicles into brilliant stalactites. The bells rang a joyous call from every steeple, and soon the churches were crowded with eager worshippers—eager to hear again the oft-repeated, the wonderful story on which the heart of the whole Christian world feeds its faith and hope. Words of tender faith, marvellous in their simplicity fell from the lips of a world-renowned preacher, and touched the hearts of the listening multitude:

"The winter sunshine is not more bright and clear than the atmosphere of living joy, which stretching back between our eyes and that picture of Bethlehem, shows us its beauty in unstained freshness. And as we open once again those chapters of the gospel in which the ever fresh and living picture stands, there seems from year to year always to come some newer, brighter meaning into the words that tell the tale.

"St. Matthew says that when Jesus was born in Bethlehem the wise men came from the East to Jerusalem. The East means man's search after God; Jerusalem means God's search after man. The East means the religion of the devout soul; Jerusalem means the religion of the merciful God. The East means Job's cry, 'Oh, that I knew where I might find him!' Jerusalem means 'Immanuel—God with us.' "

Then the deep-toned organ joined the grand chorus of human voices in a fervent hymn of praise and thanksgiving:

> Lo! the Morning Star appeareth,
> O'er the world His beams are cast;
> He the Alpha and Omega,
> He, the Great, the First the Last!
> Hallelujah! hallelujah!
> Let the heavenly portal ring!
> Christ is born, the Prince of glory!
> Christ the Lord, Messiah, King!

Everyone of prominence in church circles had been bidden to the Jimson wedding. The presents were many and costly. Early after service on Christmas morning the vestry room was taken in hand by leading sisters to prepare the tables for the supper, for on account of the host of friends bidden to the feast, the reception was to be held in the vestry.

The tables groaned beneath their loads of turkey, salads, pies, puddings, cakes and fancy ices.

Yards and yards of evergreen wreaths encircled the granite pillars; the altar was banked with potted plants and cut flowers. It was a beautiful sight. The main aisle was roped off for the invited guests with white satin ribbons.

Brother Jimson's patrons were to be present in a body, and they had sent the bride a solid silver service, so magnificent that the sisters could only sigh with envy.

The ceremony was to take place at seven sharp. Long before that hour the ushers in full evening dress were ready to receive the guests. Sister Maria Nash was among the first to arrive, and even the Queen of Sheba was not arrayed like unto her. At fifteen minutes before the hour, the organist began an elaborate instrumental performance. There was an expectant hush and much head-turning when the music changed to the familiar strains of the "Wedding March." The minister took his place inside the railing ready to receive the party. The groom waited at the altar.

First came the ushers, then the maids of honor, then the flower girl—daughter of a prominent member—carrying a basket of flowers which she scattered before the bride, who was on the arm of the best man. In the bustle and confusion incident to the entrance of the wedding party no one noticed a group of strangers accompanied by Andy Nash enter and occupy seats near the door.

The service began. All was quiet. The pastor's words fell clearly upon the listening ears. He had reached the words:

"If any man can show just cause, etc.," when like a thunder-clap came a voice from the back part of the house—an angry excited voice, and a woman of ponderous avoirdupois advanced up the aisle.

"Hol' on that, pastor, hol' on! A man cain't have but one wife 'cause it's agin' the law. I'm Abe Jimson's lawful wife, an' hyars his six children—all boys—to pint out their daddy." In an instant the assembly was in confusion.

"My soul," exclaimed Viney Peters, "the ol' serpent! An' to think how near I come to takin' up with him. I'm glad I ain't Car'mel."

Sis'r Maria said nothing, but a smile of triumph lit up her countenance.

"Brother Jimson, is this true?" demanded the minister, sternly. But Abraham Jimson was past answering. His face was ashen, his teeth chattering, his hair standing on end. His shaking limbs refused to uphold his weight; he sank upon his knees on the steps of the altar.

But now a hand was laid upon his shoulder and Mrs. Jimson hauled him upon his feet with a jerk.

"Abe Jimson, you know me. You run'd 'way from me up North fifteen year ago, an' you hid yourself like a groun' hog in a hole, but I've got you. There'll be no new wife in the Jimson family this week. I'm yer fus' wife and I'll be yer las' one. Git up hyar now, you mis'able sinner an' tell the pastor who I be." Brother Jimson meekly obeyed the clarion voice. His sanctified air had vanished; his pride humbled into the dust.

"Pastor," came in trembling tones from his quivering lips. "These are mighty ticklish times." He paused. A deep silence followed his words. "I'm a weak-kneed, mis'able sinner. I have fallen under temptation. This is Ma' Jane, my wife, an' these hyar boys is my sons, God forgive me."

The bride, who had been forgotten now, broke in:

"Abraham Jimson, you ought to be hung. I'm going to sue you for breach of promise." It was a fatal remark. Mrs. Jimson turned upon her.

"You will, will you? Sue him, will you? I'll make a choc'late Car'mel of you befo' I'm done with you, you 'ceitful hussy, hoodooin' hones' men from thar wives."

She sprang upon the girl, tearing, biting, rendering. The satin gown and gossamer veil were reduced to rags. Caramel emitted a series of ear-splitting shrieks, but the biting and tearing went on. How it might have ended no one can tell if Andy had not sprang over the backs of the pews and grappled with the infuriated woman.

The excitement was intense. Men and women struggled to get out of the church. Some jumped from the windows and others crawled under the pews, where they were secure from violence. In the midst of the melee, Brother Jimson disappeared and was never seen again, and Mrs. Jimson came into the possession of his property by due process of law.

In the church Abraham Jimson's wedding and his fall from grace is still spoken of in eloquent whispers.

In the home of Mrs. Andy Nash a motto adorns the parlor walls worked in scarlet wool and handsomely framed in gilt. The text reads: "Ye are the salt of the earth; there is nothing hidden that shall not be revealed."

Sutton E. Griggs

(1872–1933)

SUTTON ELBERT GRIGGS was the author of more than thirty works, among them five published novels: *Imperium in Imperio: A Study of the Negro Race Problem* (1899); *Overshadowed: A Novel* (1901); *Unfettered* (1902); *The Hindered Hand: or, The Reign of the Repressionist* (1905); and *Pointing the Way* (1908), all published largely at his own expense. As a novelist he shared a weakness common to many other black authors of his era; he was too much concerned with the race problem and too little with the art of fiction. His technical shortcomings are therefore many and obvious; but in spite of them his writing is significant. An early though vacillating militant, the first black to write a political novel of any consequence, one of the first to "glorify black pigmentation" in his characters, and a strong defender of his race against the vicious attacks of southern apologists like Thomas Dixon and Thomas Nelson Page, Griggs used themes which foreshadowed those used by later and better writers. Robert A. Bone, author of *The Negro Novel in America*, considers Griggs a representative figure, one who in his vacillating between militancy and accommodation reflects "the political dilemma of the black intellectual prior to World War I." As he grew older, Griggs's many political-racial writings became increasingly conservative. He was occasionally referred to as the "Negro Apostle to the White Race."

Born in Chatfield, Texas, Sutton Griggs attended Bishop College in his native state and was an outstanding student. In 1893 he completed a theological course at Richmond Theological Seminary (now a part of Virginia Union University), becoming an ordained Baptist minister. His first pastorate was in Berkley, Virginia, where he remained for two years. For the next twenty years, Griggs was corresponding secretary of the education department of the National Baptist Convention in Nashville, Tennessee. After leaving that office, he held several pastorates in various parts of the country. Just before his death, Griggs went to Houston, Texas, to establish the National Religious and Civic Institute, a school sponsored by the Baptists of that city. He died while working on that project.

For additional comment on Griggs as a novelist, see Hugh M. Gloster, *Negro Voices in Fiction* (1948), and Gloster, "Sutton E. Griggs, Novelist of the New Negro," *Phylon* 4, no. 4. (1943). For Griggs's political and social ideas, see his own *Wisdom's Call* (1909) and *Life's Demands; or, According to Law* (1916). Recent commentary includes the entry in *Dictionary of*

American Negro Biography, written by Arnold Rampersad; a comprehensive article by Betty E. Taylor Thompson in *Dictionary of Literary Biography, Volume 50*, and *The Afro-American Novel and Its Tradition* by Bernard W. Bell (1987). See also James Robert Payne, "Griggs and Corrothers: Historical Reality and Black Fiction," *Explorations in Ethnic Studies* 6 (January 1983); and Robert E. Fleming's "Sutton E. Griggs: Militant Black Novelist," *Phylon* (March 1973).

The following selection comes from *The Hindered Hand*, originally published in 1905, reprinted in 1970 by AMS Press.

THE BLAZE

Little Melville Brant stamped his foot on the floor, looked defiantly at his mother, and said, in the whining tone of a nine-year old child,

"Mother, I want to go."

"Melville, I have told you this dozen times that you cannot go," responded the mother with a positiveness that caused the boy to feel that his chances were slim.

"You are always telling me to keep ahead of the other boys, and I can't even get up to some of them," whined Melville plaintively.

"What do you mean?" asked the mother.

"Ben Stringer is always a crowing over me. Every time I tell anything big he jumps in and tells what he's seen, and that knocks me out. He has seen a whole lots of lynchings. His papa takes him. I bet if my papa was living he would take me," said Melville.

"My boy, listen to your mother," said Mrs. Brant. "Nothing but bad people take part in or go to see those things. I want mother's boy to scorn such things, to be way above them."

"Well, I ain't. I want to see it. Ben Stringer ain't got no business being ahead of me," Melville said with vigor.

The shrieking of the train whistle caused the fever of interest to rise in the little boy.

"There's the train now, mother. Do let me go. I ain't never seen a darky burned."

"Burned!" exclaimed Mrs. Brant in horror.

Melville looked up at his mother as if pitying her ignorance.

"They are going to burn them. Sed Lonly heard his papa and Mr. Corkle talking about it, and it's all fixed up."

"My Heavenly Father!" murmured Mrs. Brant, horror struck.

The cheering of the multitude borne upon the air was now heard.

"Mother, I must go. You can beat me as hard as you want to after I do it. I can't let Ben Stringer be crowing over me. He'll be there."

Looking intently at his mother, Melville backed toward the door. Mrs. Brant rushed forward and seized him.

"I shall put you in the attic. You shall not see that inhuman affair."

To her surprise Melville did not resist, but meekly submitted to being taken upstairs and locked in the attic.

Knowing how utterly opposed his mother was to lynchings he had calculated upon her refusal and had provided for such a contingency. He fastened the attic door on the inside and took from a corner a stout stick and a rope which he had secreted there. Fastening the rope to the stick and placing the stick across the small attic window he succeeded in lowering himself to the ground. He ran with all the speed at his command and arrived at the railway station just in time to see the mob begin its march with Bud and Foresta toward the scene of the killing of Sidney Fletcher.

Arriving at the spot where Fletcher's body had been found, the mob halted and the leaders instituted the trial of the accused.

"Did you kill Mr. Sidney Fletcher?" asked the mob's spokesman of Bud.

"Can I explain the matter to you, gentlemen," asked Bud.

"We want you to tell us just one thing; did you kill Mr. Sidney Fletcher?"

"He tried to kill me," replied Bud.

"And you therefore killed him, did you?"

"Yes, sir. That's how it happened."

"You killed him, then?" asked the spokesman.

"I shot him, and if he died I suppose I must have caused it. But it was in self-defense."

"You hear that, do you. He has confessed," said the spokesman to his son who was the reporter of the world-wide news agency that was to give to the reading public an account of the affair.

"Well, we are ready to act," shouted the spokesman to the crowd.

Two men now stepped forward and reached the spokesman at about the same time.

"I got a fine place, with everything ready. I knew what you would need and I arranged for you," said one of the men.

"My place is nearer than his, and everything is as ready as it can be. I think I am entitled to it," said the other.

"You want the earth, don't you?" indignantly asked the first applicant of the second.

Ignoring this thrust the second applicant said to the spokesman,

"You know I have done all the dirty work here. If you all wanted anybody to stuff the ballot box or swear to false returns, I have been your man. I've put out of the way every biggety nigger that you sent me after. You know all this."

"You've been paid for it, too. Ain't you been to the legislature? Ain't you been constable? Haven't you captured prisoners and held 'um in secret till the governor offered rewards and then you have brung 'em forward? You have been well paid. But me, I've had none of the good things. I've done dirty work, too, don't you forget it. And now I want these niggers hung in my watermelon patch, so as to keep darkies out of nights, being as they are feart of hants, and you are here to keep me out of that little favor."

The dispute waxed so hot that it was finally decided that it was best to accept neither place.

"We want this affair to serve as a warning to darkies to never lift their hands against a white man, and it won't hurt to perform this noble deed where they will never forget it. I am commander to-day and I order the administration of justice to take place near the Negro church."

"Good! Good!" was the universal comment.

The crowd dashed wildly in the direction of the church, all being eager to get places where they could see best. The smaller boys climbed the trees so that they might see well the whole transaction. Two of the trees were decided upon for stakes and the boys who had chosen them had to come down. Bud was tied to one tree and Foresta to the other in such a manner that they faced each other. Wood was brought and piled around them and oil was poured on very profusely.

The mob decided to torture their victims before killing them and began on Foresta first. A man with a pair of scissors stepped up and cut off her hair and threw it into the crowd. There was a great scramble for bits of hair for souvenirs of the occasion. One by one her fingers were cut off and tossed into the crowd to be scrambled for. A man with a corkscrew came forward, ripped Foresta's clothing to her waist, bored into her breast with the corkscrew and pulled forth the live quivering flesh. Poor Bud her helpless husband closed his eyes and turned away his head to avoid the terrible sight. Men gathered about him and forced his eyelids open so that he could see all.

When it was thought that Foresta had been tortured sufficiently, attention was turned to Bud. His fingers were cut off one by one and the corkscrew was bored into his legs and arms. A man with a club struck him over the head, crushing his skull and forcing an eyeball to hang down from the socket by a thread. A rush was made toward Bud and a man who was a little ahead of his competitors snatched the eyeball as a souvenir.

After three full hours had been spent in torturing the two, the spokesman announced that they were now ready for the final act. The brother of Sidney Fletcher was called for and was given a match. He stood near his mutilated victims until the photographer present could take a picture of the scene. This being over the match was applied and the flames leaped up eagerly and encircled the writhing forms of Bud and Foresta.

When the flames had done their work and had subsided, a mad rush was made for the trees which were soon denuded of bark, each member of the mob being desirous, it seemed, of carrying away something that might testify to his proximity to so great a happening.

Little Melville Brant found a piece of the charred flesh in the ashes and bore it home.

"Ben Stringer aint got anything on me now," said he as he trudged along in triumph.

Entering by the rear he caught hold of the rope which he had left hanging, ascended to the attic window and crawled in.

The future ruler of the land!

On the afternoon of the lynching Ramon Mansford alighted from the train at Maulville in search of Bud and Foresta. He noted the holiday appearance of the crowd as it swarmed around the depot awaiting the going of the special trains that had brought the people to Maulville to see the lynching, and, not knowing the occasion that had brought them together, said within himself:

"This crowd looks happy enough. The South is indeed sunny and sunny are the hearts of its people."

At length he approached a man, who like himself seemed to be an onlooker. Using the names under which Mrs. Harper told him that Bud and Foresta were passing, he made inquiry of them. The man looked at him in amazement.

"You have just got in, have you?" Asked the man of Ramon.

"Yes," he replied.

"Haven't you been reading the papers?" further inquired the man.

"Not lately, I must confess; I have been so absorbed in unraveling a murder mystery (the victim being one very dear to me) that I have not read the papers for the last few days."

"We burned the people to-day that you are looking for."

"Burned them?" asked Ramon incredulously.

"Yes, burned them."

"The one crime!" gasped Ramon.

"I understand you," said the man. "You want to know how we square the burning of a woman with the statement that we lynch for one crime in the South, heh?"

The shocked Ramon nodded affirmatively.

"That's all rot about one crime. We lynch niggers down here for anything. We lynch them for being sassy and sometimes lynch them on general principles. The truth of the matter is the real 'one crime' that paves the way for a lynching whenever we have the notion, is the crime of being black."

"Burn them! The one crime!" murmured Ramon, scarcely knowing what he said. With bowed head and hands clasped behind him he walked away to meditate.

"After all, do not I see to-day a gleam of light thrown on the taking away of my Alene? With murder and lawlessness rampant in the Southland, this section's woes are to be many. Who can say what bloody orgies Alene has escaped? Who can tell the contents of the storm cloud that hangs low over this section where the tragedy of the ages is being enacted? Alene, O Alene, my spirit longs for thee!"

Ramon took the train that night—not for Almaville, for he had not the heart to bear the terrible tidings to those helpless, waiting, simple folks, the parents of Bud and Foresta. He went North feeling that some day somehow he might be called upon to revisit the South as its real friend, but seeming foe. And he shuddered at the thought.

Charles W. Chesnutt

(1858–1932)

THE BEST NEGRO FICTION WRITER before Richard Wright, Charles Waddell Chesnutt wrote usually about some aspects of the American "color line," whether within the race or between the races. A "volunteer Negro" himself, that is one who could easily "pass for white" and who was offered two promising opportunities to do so, Chesnutt remained with "his" people and devoted his life to the black's fight for equality. Unlike Dunbar, he was a "protest" writer, attacking in his fiction the portrayal of American blacks given by such nationally popular southern writers as Joel Chandler Harris, Thomas Dixon, Thomas Nelson Page, and others.

Born in Cleveland, Ohio, of free parents who had left their home in Fayetteville, North Carolina, because of pressures put on free blacks, Chesnutt was eight years old when his father in 1866 decided to take his family back to Fayetteville. There he attended the public rural school, his only formal education; there he finally became a teacher himself and was offered the principalship of a state normal school. Possessing a brilliant mind and an indomitable will, Chesnutt taught himself Latin, German, French, mathematics, and subsequently stenography and law. After his marriage in 1878, he became tired of the South and decided to leave for greener pastures. In 1883 he spent a year in New York City as a court stenographer and journalist. The following year he moved his family back to Cleveland. There he became a successful legal stenographer and lawyer, having passed in 1807 the Ohio bar at the top of his "class"; at this time his writing career began.

After several minor works of his were printed in minor publications, Chesnutt's "The Goophered Grapevine" was accepted by the *Atlantic Monthly* in 1887 and "Po Sandy" in 1888. These two short stories were the opening door to the nation's top publishing opportunities, but the door was not yet fully opened. Chesnutt by 1889 had finished his first novel, which was called initially *Rena Walden*; it was turned down because of its subject: interracial marriage. The publishers were saying in effect: short stories about folk material are all right for a black author, but the interracial marriage theme—No! After several rewrites, the book was eventually published in 1900 with the title *The House behind the Cedars*.

In 1899, with the help of Walter Hines Page, editor of the *Atlantic Monthly*, Chesnutt's *The Conjure Woman*, seven southern folklore stories, was published by Houghton Mifflin. In the same year *The Wife of His Youth and Other Stories of the Color Line,* a second volume of stories, was brought out. Two novels followed: *The Marrow of Tradition* (1901), based on the Wilmington Riot, and *The Colonel's Dream* (1905), one of Chesnutt's bitterest protest works. One of his best short stories, "Baxter's Procrustes," was published in the *Atlantic* (June 1904). It had nothing to do with race. Charles W. Chesnutt was given the Spingarn Medal in 1928 for his "pioneer work as a literary artist." He published his last work in 1931, an article for the *Colophon* called "Post Bellum—Pre-Harlem." Chesnutt died in 1932.

Charles W. Chesnutt is not as popular among readers and scholars as he should be. Post-1960s generations do not understand fully the conditions, particularly the color-line emphasis, about which he writes so consistently and dramatically. However, his works helped to make possible the freedom (however limited) which blacks now have in America. As a strong writer of protest fiction, as a pioneer in opening doors for blacks to the nation's major periodicals and publishing firms, as a skillful user of folk material, especially in his short stories, and as a fighter for civil rights in his private and public life, Chesnutt deserves much more recognition than he now has. Any scholar interested in the black's position in America from roughly 1890 to 1920 could benefit greatly from an in-depth reading of Chesnutt's works.

For comment on Charles W. Chesnutt's life and writings see the full-length critical biography by Frances R. Keller, *An American Crusade: The Life of Charles Waddell Chesnutt* (1977); see also the biography by his daughter, Helen M. Chesnutt, *Charles Waddell Chesnutt: Pioneer of the Color Line* (1952). This work contains *inter alia* many letters showing Chesnutt's intimacy with such people as George W. Cable, Walter Hines Page, Mark Twain, Booker T. Washington, and others. Sylvia Lyons Render's edition of *The Short Fiction of Charles W. Chesnutt* (1974, 1980) has an excellent introduction. The entry in *Dictionary of American Negro Biography* by John W. Wideman gives among other fine things "necessarily short descriptions of Chesnutt's major works," which are quite useful. The most recent evaluation of Chesnutt's literary achievement is *The Literary Career of Charles W. Chesnutt* by William L. Andrews (1980). *Charles W. Chesnutt: A Reference Guide* by Curtis W. Ellison and E. W. Metcalf, Jr., was published in 1977. Additional recent commentary can be found in Bernard W. Bell's *The Afro-American Novel and Its Tradition* (1987).

"The Goophered Grapevine" was originally published in *The Conjure Woman* by Houghton Mifflin Company in 1899. "The Wife of His Youth" comes originally from *The Wife of His Youth and Other Stories of the Color Line,* also published in 1899 by Houghton Mifflin. Both stories are found in Sylvia Lyons Render's *The Short Fiction of Charles W. Chesnutt* (1974).

THE GOOPHERED GRAPEVINE

Some years ago my wife was in poor health, and our family doctor, in whose skill and honesty I had implicit confidence, advised a change of climate. I shared, from an unprofessional standpoint, his opinion that the raw winds, the chill rains, and violent changes of temperature that characterized the winters in the region of the Great Lakes tended to aggravate my wife's difficulty, and would undoubtedly shorten her life if she remained exposed to them. The doctor's advice was that we seek, not a temporary place of sojourn, but a permanent residence, in a warmer and more equable climate. I was engaged at the time in grape-culture in northern Ohio, and, as I liked the business and had given it much study, I decided to look for some other locality suitable for carrying it on. I thought of sunny France, of sleepy Spain, of Southern California, but there were objections to them all. It occurred to me that I might find what I wanted in some one of our own Southern States. It was a sufficient time after the war for conditions in the South to have become somewhat settled; and I was enough of a pioneer to start a new industry, if I could not find a place where grape-culture had been tried. I wrote to a cousin who had gone into the turpentine business in central North Carolina. He assured me, in response to my inquiries, that no better place could be found in the South than the State and neighborhood where he lived; the climate was perfect for health, and, in conjunction with the soil, ideal for grape-culture; labor was cheap, and land could be bought for a mere song. He gave us a cordial invitation to come and visit him while we looked into the matter. We accepted the invitation, and after several days of leisurely travel, the last hundred miles of which were up a river on a side-wheel steamer, we reached our destination, a quaint old town, which I shall call Patesville, because, for one reason, that is not its name. There was a red brick market-house in the public square, with a tall tower, which held a four-faced clock that struck the hours, and from which there pealed out a curfew at nine o'clock. There were two or three hotels, a court-house, a jail, stores, offices, and all the appurtenances of a county seat and a commercial emporium; for while Patesville numbered only four or five thousand inhabitants, of all shades of complexion, it was one of the principal towns in North Carolina, and had a considerable trade in cotton and naval stores. This business activity was not immediately apparent to my unaccustomed eyes. Indeed, when I first saw the town, there brooded over it a calm that seemed almost sabbatic in its restfulness, though I learned later on that underneath its somnolent exterior the deeper currents of life—love and hatred, joy and despair, ambition and avarice, faith and friendship—flowed not less steadily than in livelier latitudes.

We found the weather delightful at that season, the end of summer, and were hospitably entertained. Our host was a man of means and evidently regarded our visit as a pleasure, and we were therefore correspondingly at our ease, and in a position to act with the coolness of judgment desirable in making so radical a change in our lives. My cousin placed a horse and buggy at our disposal, and himself acted as our guide until I became somewhat familiar with the country.

I found that grape-culture, while it had never been carried on to any great extent, was not entirely unknown in the neighborhood. Several planters thereabouts had attempted it on a commercial scale, in former years, with greater or less success; but like most Southern industries, it had felt the blight of war and had fallen into desuetude.

I went several times to look at a place that I thought might suit me. It was a plantation of considerable extent, that had formerly belonged to a wealthy man by the name of McAdoo. The estate had been for years involved in litigation between disputing heirs, during which period shiftless cultivation had well-nigh exhausted the soil. There had been a vineyard of some extent on the place, but it had not been attended to since the war, and had lapsed into utter neglect. The vines—here partly supported by decayed and broken-down trellises, there twining themselves among the branches of the slender saplings which had sprung up among them—grew in wild and unpruned luxuriance, and the few scattered grapes they bore were the undisputed prey of the first comer. The site was admirably adapted to grape-raising; the soil, with a little attention, could not have been better; and with the native grape, the luscious scuppernong, as my main reliance in the beginning, I felt sure that I could introduce and cultivate successfully a number of other varieties.

One day I went over with my wife to show her the place. We drove out of the town over a long wooden bridge that spanned a spreading mill-pond, passed the long whitewashed fence surrounding the county fair-ground, and struck into a road so sandy that the horse's feet sank to the fetlocks. Our route lay partly up hill and partly down, for we were in the sand-hill county; we drove past cultivated farms, and then by abandoned fields grown up in scrub-oak and short-leaved pine, and once or twice through the solemn aisles of the virgin forest, where the tall pines, well-nigh meeting over the narrow road, shut out the sun, and wrapped us in cloistral solitude. Once, at a cross-roads, I was in doubt as to the turn to take, and we sat there waiting ten minutes—we had already caught some of the native infection of restfulness—for some human being to come along, who could direct us on our way. At length a little negro girl appeared, walking straight as an arrow, with a piggin full of water on her head. After a little patient investigation, necessary to overcome the child's shyness, we learned what we wished to know, and at the end of about five miles from the town reached our destination.

We drove between a pair of decayed gateposts—the gate itself had long since disappeared—and up a straight sandy lane, between two lines of rotting rail fence, partly concealed by jimson-weeds and briers, to the open space where a dwelling-house had once stood, evidently a spacious mansion, if we might judge from the ruined chimneys that were still standing, and the brick pillars on which the sills rested. The house itself, we had been informed, had fallen a victim to the fortunes of war.

We alighted from the buggy, walked about the yard for a while, and then wandered off into the adjoining vineyard. Upon Annie's complaining of weariness I led the way back to the yard, where a pine log, lying under a spreading elm, afforded a shady though somewhat hard seat. One end of the log was already occupied by a venerable-looking colored man. He held on his knees a hat full of grapes, over which he was smacking his lips with great gusto, and a pile of grape-skins near him indicated that the performance was no new thing. We approached him at an angle from the rear, and were close to him before he perceived us. He respectfully rose as we drew near, and was moving away, when I begged him to keep his seat.

"Don't let us disturb you," I said. "There is plenty of room for us all."

He resumed his seat with somewhat of embarrassment. While he had been standing, I had observed that he was a tall man, and, though slightly bowed by the weight of years, apparently quite vigorous. He was not entirely black, and this fact, together with the quality of his hair, which was about six inches long and very bushy, except on the top of his head, where he was quite bald, suggested a slight strain of other than negro blood. There was a shrewdness in his eyes, too, which was not altogether African, and which, as we afterwards learned from experience, was indicative of a corresponding shrewdness in his character. He went on eating the grapes, but did not seem to enjoy himself quite so well as he had apparently done before he became aware of our presence.

"Do you live around here?" I asked, anxious to put him at his ease.

"Yas, suh. I lives des ober yander, behine de nex' san'-hill, on de Lumberton plank-road."

"Do you know anything about the time when this vineyard was cultivated?"

"Lawd bless you, suh, I knows all about it. Dey ain' na'er a man in dis settlement w'at won' tell you ole Julius McAdoo 'uz bawn en raise' on dis yer same plantation. Is you de Norv'n gemman w'at's gwine ter buy de ole vimya'd?"

"I am looking at it," I replied; "but I don't know that I shall care to buy unless I can be reasonably sure of making something out of it."

"Well, suh, you is a stranger ter me, en I is a stranger ter you, en we is bofe strangers ter one anudder, but 'f I 'uz in yo' place, I would n' buy dis vimya'd."

"Why not?" I asked.

"Well, I dunno whe'r you b'lieves in cunj'in' er not,—some er de w'ite folks don't, er says dey don't,—but de truf er de matter is dat dis yer ole vimya'd is goophered."

"Is what?" I asked, not grasping the meaning of this unfamiliar word.

"Is goophered,—conju'd, bewitch'."

He imparted this information with such solemn earnestness, and with such an air of confidential mystery, that I felt somewhat interested, while Annie was evidently much impressed, and drew closer to me.

"How do you know it is bewitched?" I asked.

"I would n' spec' fer you ter b'lieve me 'less you know all 'bout de fac's. But ef you en young miss dere doan' mine' lis'nin' ter a ole nigger run on a minute er two w'ile you er restin', I kin 'splain to you how it all happen'."

We assured him that we would be glad to hear how it all happened, and he began to tell us. At first the current of his memory—or imagination—seemed somewhat sluggish; but as his embarrassment wore off, his language flowed more freely, and the story acquired perspective and coherence. As he became more and more absorbed in the narrative, his eyes assumed a dreamy expression, and he seemed to lose sight of his auditors, and to be living over again in monologue his life on the old plantation.

"Ole Mars Dugal' McAdoo," he began, "bought dis place long many years befo' de wah, en I 'member well w'en he sot out all dis yer part er de plantation in scuppernon's. De vimes growed monst'us fas', en Mars Dugal' made a thousan' gallon er scuppernon' wine eve'y year.

"Now, ef dey's an'thing a nigger lub, nex' ter 'possum, en chick'n, en watermillyums, it 's scuppernon's. Dey ain' nuffin dat kin stan' up side'n de scuppernon' for sweetness; sugar ain't a suckumstance ter scuppernon'. W'en de season is nigh 'bout ober, en de grapes begin ter swivel up des a little wid de wrinkles er ole age,—w'en de skin git sof' en brown,—den de scuppernon' make you smack yo' lip en roll yo' eye en wush fer mo'; so I reckon it ain' very 'stonishin' dat niggers lub scuppernon'.

"Dey wuz a sight er niggers in de naberhood er de vimya'd. Dere wuz ole Mars Henry Brayboy's niggers, en ole Mars Jeems McLean's niggers, en Mars Dugal's own niggers; den dey wuz a settlement er free niggers en po' buckrahs down by de Wim'l'ton Road, en Mars Dugal' had de only vimya'd in de naberhood. I reckon it ain' so much so nowadays, but befo' de wah, in slab'ry times, a nigger did n' mine goin' fi' er ten mile in a night, w'en dey wuz sump'n good ter eat at de yuther een'.

"So atter a w'ile Mars Dugal' begin ter miss his scuppernon's. Co'se he 'cuse' de niggers er it, but dey all 'nied it ter de las'. Mars Dugal' sot spring guns en steel traps, en he en de oberseah sot up nights once't er twice't, tel one night Mars Dugal'—he 'uz a monst'us keerless man—got his leg shot full er cow-peas. But somehow er nudder dey could n' nebber ketch none er de niggers. I dunner how it happen, but it happen des like I tell you, en de grapes kep' on a-goin' des de same.

"But bimeby ole Mars Dugal' fix' up a plan ter stop it. Dey wuz a conjuh 'oman livin' down 'mongs' de free niggers on de Wim'l'ton Road, en all de darkies fum Rockfish ter Beaver Crick wuz feared er her. She could wuk de mos' powerfulles' kin' er goopher,—could make people hab fits, er rheumatiz, er make 'em des dwinel away en die; en dey say she went out ridin' de niggers at night, fer she wuz a witch 'sides bein' a conjuh 'oman. Mars Dugal' hearn 'bout Aun' Peggy's doin's, en begun ter 'flect whe'r er no he could n' git her ter he'p him keep de niggers off'n de grapevimes. One day in de spring er de year, ole miss pack' up a basket er chick'n en poun'-cake, en a bottle er scuppernon' wine, en Mars Dugal' tuk it in his buggy en driv ober ter Aun' Peggy's cabin. He tuk de basket in, en had a long talk wid Aun' Peggy.

"De nex' day Aun' Peggy come up ter de vimya'd. De niggers seed her slippin' 'roun', en dey soon foun' out what she 'uz doin' dere. Mars Dugal' had hi'ed her ter goopher de grapevimes. She sa'ntered 'roun' 'mongs' de vimes, en tuk a leaf fum dis one, en a grape-hull fum dat one, en a grape-seed fum anudder one; en den a little twig fum here, en a little pinch er dirt fum dere,—en put it all in a big black bottle, wid a snake's toof en a speckle' hen's gall en some ha'rs fum a black cat's tail, en den fill' de bottle wid scuppernon' wine. W'en she got de goopher all ready en fix', she tuk'n went out in de woods en buried it under de root uv a red oak tree, en den come back en tole one er de niggers she done goopher de grapevimes, en a'er a nigger w'at eat dem grapes 'ud be sho ter die inside'n twel' mont's.

"Atter dat de niggers let de scuppernon's 'lone, en Mars Dugal'
did n' hab no 'casion ter fine no mo' fault; en de season wuz mos'
gone, w'en a strange gemman stop at de plantation one night ter see
Mars Dugal' on some business; en his coachman, seein' de scuppernon's growin' so nice en sweet, slip 'roun' behine de smoke-house,
en et all de scuppernon's he could hole. Nobody did n' notice it at
de time, but dat night, on de way home, de gemman's hoss runned
away en kill' de coachman. W'en we hearn de noos, Aun' Lucy, de
cook, she up 'n say she seed de strange nigger eat'n' er de scuppernon's behine de smoke-house; en den we knowed de goopher had
b'en er wukkin'. Den one er de nigger chilluns runned away fum de
quarters one day, en got in de scuppernon's, en died de nex' week.
W'ite folks say he die' er de fevuh, but de niggers knowed it wuz de
goopher. So you k'n be sho de darkies did n' hab much ter do wid
dem scuppernon' vimes.

"W'en de scuppernon' season 'uz ober fer dat year, Mars Dugal'
foun' he had made fifteen hund'ed gallon er wine; en one er de niggers hearn him laffin' wid de oberseah fit ter kill, en sayin' dem fifteen hund'ed gallon er wine wuz monst'us good intrus' on de ten
dollars he laid out on de vimya'd. So I 'low ez he paid Aun' Peggy
ten dollars fer to goopher de grapevimes.

"De goopher did n' wuk no mo' tel de nex' summer, we'n 'long
to'ds de middle er de season one er de fiel' han's died; en ez dat lef'
Mars Dugal' sho't er han's, he went off ter town fer ter buy anudder.
He fotch de noo nigger home wid 'im. He wuz er ole nigger, er de
color er a gingy-cake, en ball ez a hoss-apple on de top er his head.
He wuz a peart ole nigger, do', en could do a big day's wuk.

"Now it happen dat one er de niggers on de nex' plantation, one
er ole Mars Henry Brayboy's niggers, had runned away de day befo',
en tuk ter de swamp, en ole Mars Dugal' en some er de yuther nabor
w'ite folks had gone out wid dere guns en dere dogs fer ter he'p 'em
hunt fer de nigger; en de han's on our own plantation wuz all so
flusterated dat we fuhgot ter tell de noo han' 'bout de goopher on de
scuppernon' vimes. Co'se he smell de grapes en see de vimes, an atter dahk de fus' thing he done wuz ter slip off ter de grapevimes
'dout sayin' nuffin to nobody. Nex' mawnin' he tole some er de niggers 'bout de fine bait er scuppernon' he et de night befo'.

"W'en dey tole 'im 'bout de goopher on de grapevimes, he 'uz dat
tarrified dat he turn pale, en look des like he gwine ter die right in
his tracks. De oberseah come up en axed w'at 'uz de matter; en w'en
dey tole 'im Henry be'n eatin' er de scuppernon's, en got de goopher
on 'im, he gin Henry a big drink er w'iskey, en 'low dat de nex' rainy
day he take 'im ober ter Aun' Peggy's, en see ef she would n' take de
goopher off'n him, seein' ez he did n' know nuffin erbout it tel he
done et de grapes.

"Sho nuff, it rain de nex' day, en de oberseah went ober ter Aun' Peggy's wid Henry. En Aun' Peggy say dat bein' ez Henry did n' know 'bout de goopher, en et de grapes in ign'ance er de conse-q'ences, she reckon she mought be able fer ter take de goopher off'n him. So she fotch out er bottle wid some conjuh medicine in it, en po'd some out in a go'd fer Henry ter drink. He manage ter git it down; he say it tas'e like whiskey wid sump'n bitter in it. She 'lowed dat 'ud keep de goopher off'n him tel de spring; but w'en de sap begin ter rise in de grapevimes he ha'ter come en see her ag'in, en she tell him w'at e's ter do.

"Nex' spring, w'en de sap commence' ter rise in de scuppernon' vime, Henry tuk a ham one night. Whar 'd he git de ham? *I* doan know; dey wa'n't no hams on de plantation 'cep'n' w'at 'uz in de smoke-house, but *I* never see Henry 'bout de smoke-house. But ez I wuz a-sayin', he tuk de ham ober ter Aun' Peggy's; en Aun' Peggy tole 'im dat w'en Mars Dugal' begin ter prune de grapevimes, he mus' go en take 'n scrape off de sap whar it ooze out'n de cut een's er de vimes, en 'n'int his ball head wid it; en ef he do dat once't a year de goopher would n' wuk agin 'im long ez he done it. En bein' ez he fotch her de ham, she fix' it so he kin eat all de scuppernon' he want.

"So Henry 'n'int his head wid de sap out'n de big grapevime des ha'f way 'twix' de quarters en de big house, en de goopher nebber wuk agin him dat summer. But de beatenes' thing you eber see happen ter Henry. Up ter dat time he wuz ez ball ez a sweeten' 'tater, but des ez soon ez de young leaves begun ter come out on de grape-vimes, de ha'r begun ter grow out on Henry's head, en by de middle er de summer he had de bigges' head er ha'r on de plantation. Befo' dat, Henry had tol'able good ha'r 'round' de aidges, but soon ez de young grapes begun ter come, Henry's ha'r begun to quirl all up in little balls, des like dis yer reg'lar grapy ha'r, en by de time de grapes got ripe his head look des like a bunch er grapes. Combin' it did n' do no good; he wuk at it ha'f de night wid er Jim Crow,* en think he git it straighten' out, but in de mawnin' de grapes 'ud be dere des de same. So he gin it up, en tried ter keep de grapes down by havin' his ha'r cut sho't.

"But dat wa'n't de quares' thing 'bout de goopher. When Henry come ter de plantation, he wuz gittin' a little ole an stiff in de j'ints. But dat summer he got des ez spry en libely ez any young nigger on de plantation; fac', he got so biggity dat Mars Jackson, de oberseah, ha' ter th'eaten ter whip 'im, if he did n' stop cuttin' up his didos en

---

*A small card, resembling a currycomb in construction, and used by negroes [sic] in the rural districts instead of a comb.

behave hisse'f. But de mos' cur'ouses' thing happen' in de fall, when de sap begin ter go down in de grapevimes. Fus', when de grapes 'uz gethered, de knots begun ter straighten out'n Henry's ha'r; en w'en de leaves begin ter fall, Henry's ha'r 'mence' ter drap out; en when de vimes 'uz bar', Henry's head wuz baller 'n it wuz in de spring, en he begin ter git ole en stiff in de j'ints ag'in, en paid no mo' 'tention ter de gals dyoin' er de whole winter. En nex' spring, w'en he rub de sap on ag'in, he got young ag'in, en so soopl en libely dat none er de young niggers on de plantation could n' jump, ner dance, ner hoe ez much cotton ez Henry. But in de fall er de year his grapes 'mence' ter straighten out, en his j'ints ter git stiff, en his ha'r drap off, en de rheumatiz begin ter wrastle wid'im.

"Now, ef you 'd 'a' knowed ole Mars Dugal' McAdoo, you 'd 'a' knowed dat it ha' ter be a mighty rainy day when he could n' fine sump'n fer his niggers ter do, en it ha' ter be a mighty little hole he could n' crawl thoo, en ha' ter be a monst'us cloudy night when a dollar git by him in de dahkness; en w'en he see how Henry git young in de spring en ole in de fall, he 'lowed ter hisse'f ez how he could make mo' money out'n Henry dan by wukkin' him in de cotton-fiel'. 'Long de nex' spring, atter de sap 'mence' ter rise, en Henry 'n'int 'is head en sta'ted fer ter git young en soopl, Mars Dugal' up 'n tuk Henry ter town, en sole 'im fer fifteen hunder' dollars. Co'se de man w'at bought Henry did n' know nuffin 'bout de goopher, en Mars Dugal' did n' see no 'casion fer ter tell 'im. Long to'ds de fall, w'en de sap went down, Henry begin ter git ole ag'in same ez yuzhal, en his noo marster begin to git skeered les'n he gwine ter lose his fifteen-hunder'-dollar nigger. He sent fer a mighty fine doctor, but de med'cine did n' 'pear ter do no good; de goopher had a good holt. Henry tole de doctor 'bout de goopher, but de doctor des laff at 'im.

"One day in de winter Mars Dugal' went ter town, en wuz santerin' 'long de Main Street, when who should he meet but Henry's noo marster. Dey said 'Hoddy,' en Mars Dugal' ax 'im ter hab a seegyar; en atter dey run on awhile 'bout de craps en de weather, Mars Dugal' ax 'im, sorter keerless, like ez ef he des thought of it,—

" 'How you like de nigger I sole you las' spring?'

"Henry's marster shuck his head en knock de ashes off'n his seegyar.

" 'Spec' I made a bad bahgin when I bought dat nigger. Henry done good wuk all de summer, but sence de fall set in he 'pears ter be sorter pinin' away. Dey ain' nuffin pertickler de matter wid 'im— leastways de doctor say so—'cep'n' a tech er de rheumatiz; but his ha'r is all fell out, en ef he don't pick up his strenk mighty soon, I spec' I 'm gwine ter lose 'im.'

"Dey smoked on awhile, en bimeby ole mars say, 'Well, a bah-gin's a bahgin, but you en me is good fren's, en I doan wan 'ter see you lose all de money you paid fer dat nigger; en ef wa't you say is so, en I ain't 'sputin' it, he ain't wuf much now. I 'spec's you wukked him too ha'd dis summer, er e'se de swamps down here don't agree wid de san'-hill nigger. So you des lemme know, en ef he gits any wusser I 'll be willin' ter gib yer five hund'ed dollars fer 'im, en take my chances on his livin'.'

"Sho 'nuff, when Henry begun ter draw up wid de rheumatiz en it look like he gwine ter die fer sho, his noo marster sen' fer Mars Dugal', en Mars Dugal' gin him what he promus, en brung Henry home ag'in. He tuk good keer uv 'im dyoin' er de winter,—give 'im w'iskey ter rub his rheumatiz, en terbacker ter smoke, en all he want ter eat,—'caze a nigger w'at he could make a thousan' dollars a year off'n did n' grow on eve'y huckleberry bush.

"Nex' spring, w'en de sap ris en Henry's ha'r commence' ter sprout, Mars Dugal' sole 'im ag'in, down in Robeson County dis time; en he kep' dat sellin' business up fer five year er mo'. Henry nebber say nuffin 'bout de goopher ter his noo marsters, 'caze he know he gwine ter be tuk good keer uv de nex' winter, w'en Mars Dugal' buy him back. En Mars Dugal' made 'nuff money off'n Henry ter buy anudder plantation ober on Beaver Crick.

"But 'long 'bout de een' er dat five year dey come a stranger ter stop at de plantation. De fus' day he 'uz dere he went out wid Mars Dugal' en spent all de mawnin' lookin' ober de vimya'd, en atter din-ner dey spent all de evenin' playin' kya'ds. De niggers soon 'skiver' dat he wuz a Yankee, en dat he come down ter Norf C'lina fer ter l'arn de w'ite folks how to raise grapes en make wine. He promus Mars Dugal' he c'd make de grapevimes b'ar twice't ez many grapes, en dat de noo winepress he wuz a-sellin' would make mo' d'n twice't ez many gallons er wine. En ole Mars Dugal' des drunk it all in, des 'peared ter be bewitch' wid dat Yankee. W'en de darkies see dat Yan-kee runnin' 'roun' de vimya'd en diggin' under de grapevimes, dey shuk dere heads, en 'lowed dat dey feared Mars Dugal' losin' his min'. Mars Dugal' had all de dirt dug away fum under de roots er all de scuppernon' vimes, an' let 'em stan' dat away fer a week er mo'. Den dat Yankee made de niggers fix up a mixtry er lime en ashes en manyo, en po' it 'roun' de roots er de grapevimes. Den he 'vise Mars Dugal' fer ter trim de vimes close't, en Mars Dugal' tuck 'n done eve'ything de Yankee tole him ter do. Dyoin' all er dis time, mind yer, dis yer Yankee wuz libbin' off'n de fat er de lan', at de big house, en playin' kya'ds wid Mars Dugal' eve'y night; en dey say Mars Dugal' los' mo'n a thousan' dollars dyoin' er de week dat Yan-kee wuz a-ruinin' de grapevimes.

"W'en de sap ris nex' spring, ole Henry 'n'inted his head ez yuzhal, en his ha'r 'mence' ter grow des de same ez it done eve'y year. De scuppernon' vimes growed monst's fas', en de leaves wuz greener en thicker dan dey eber be'n dyoin' my rememb'ance; en Henry's ha'r growed out thicker dan eber, en he 'peared ter git younger 'n younger, en soopler 'n soopler; en seein' ez he wuz sho't ter han's dat spring, havin' tuk in consid'able noo groun', Mars Dugal' 'cluded he would n' sell Henry 'tel he git de crap in en de cotton chop'. So he kep' Henry on de plantation.

"But 'long 'bout time fer de grapes ter come on de scuppernon' vimes, dey 'peared ter come a change ober 'em; de leaves withered en swivel' up, en de young grapes turn' yaller, en bimeby eve'ybody on de plantation could see dat de whole vimeya'd wuz dyin'. Mars Dugal' tuk 'n water de vimes en done all he could, but 't wa'n' no use; dat Yankee had done bus' de watermillyum. One time de vimes picked up a bit, en Mars Dugal' 'lowed dey wuz gwine ter come out ag'in; but dat Yankee done dug too close under de roots, en prune de branches too close ter de vime, en all dat lime en ashes done burn' de life out'n de vimes, en dey des kep' a-with'in' en a-swivelin'.

"All dis time de goopher wuz a-wukkin'. When de vimes sta'ted ter wither, Henry 'mence' ter complain er his rheumatiz; en when de leaves begin ter dry up, his ha'r 'mence' ter drap out. When de vimes fresh' up a bit, Henry 'd git peart ag'in, en when de vimes wither' ag'in, Henry 'd git ole ag'in, en des kep' gittin' mo' en mo' fitten fer nuffin; he des pined away, en pined away, en fine'ly tuk ter his cabin; en when de big vime whar he got de sap ter 'n'int his head withered en turned yaller en died, Henry died too,—des went out sorter like a cannel. Dey did n't 'pear ter be nuffin de matter wid 'im, 'cep'n' de rheumatiz, but his strenk des dwinel' away 'tel he did n' hab ernuff lef' ter draw his bref. De goopher had got de under holt, en th'owed Henry dat time fer good en all.

"Mars Dugal' tuk on might'ly 'bout losin' his vimes en his nigger in de same year; en he swo' dat ef he could git holt er dat Yankee he'd wear 'im ter a frazzle, en den chaw up de frazzle; en he'd done it, too, for Mars Dugal' 'uz a monst'us brash man w'en he once git started. He sot de vimya'd out ober ag'in, but it wuz th'ee er fo' year befo' de vimes got ter b'arin' any scuppernon's.

"W'en de wah broke out, Mars Dugal' raise' a comp'ny, en went off ter fight de Yankees. He say he wuz mighty glad dat wah come, en he des want ter kill a Yankee fer eve'y dollar he los' 'long er dat grape-raisin' Yankee. En I 'spec' he would 'a' done it, too, if de Yankees had n' s'picioned sump'n, en killed him fus'. Atter de s'render ole miss move' ter town, de niggers all scattered 'way fum de plantation, en de vimya'd ain' be'n cultervated sence."

"Is that story true?" asked Annie doubtfully, but seriously, as the old man concluded his narrative.

"It's des ez true ez I 'm a-settin' here, miss. Dey 's a easy way ter prove it: I kin lead de way right ter Henry's grave ober yander in de plantation buryin'-groun'. En I tell yer w'at, marster, I would n' 'vise you to buy dis yer ole vimya'd, 'case de goopher 's on it yit, en dey ain' no tellin' w'en it's gwine ter crap out."

"But I thought you said all the old vines died."

"Dey did 'pear ter die, but a few un 'em come out ag'in, en is mixed in 'mongs' de yuthers. I ain' skeered ter eat de grapes, 'caze I knows de old vimes fum de noo ones; but wid strangers dey ain' no tellin' w'at mought happen. I would n' 'vise yer ter buy dis vimya'd."

I bought the vineyard, nevertheless, and it has been for a long time in a thriving condition, and is often referred to by the local press as a striking illustration of the opportunities open to Northern capital in the development of Southern industries. The luscious scuppernong holds first rank among our grapes, though we cultivate a great many other varieties, and our income from grapes packed and shipped to the Northern markets is quite considerable. I have not noticed any developments of the goopher in the vineyard, although I have a mild suspicion that our colored assistants do not suffer from want of grapes during the season.

I found, when I bought the vineyard, that Uncle Julius had occupied a cabin on the place for many years, and derived a respectable revenue from the product of the neglected grapevines. This, doubtless, accounted for his advice to me not to buy the vineyard, though whether it inspired the goopher story I am unable to state. I believe, however, that the wages I paid him for his services as coachman, for I gave him employment in that capacity, were more than an equivalent for anything he lost by the sale of the vineyard.

THE WIFE OF HIS YOUTH

1

Mr. Ryder was going to give a ball. There were several reasons why this was an opportune time for such an event.

Mr. Ryder might aptly be called the dean of the Blue Veins. The original Blue Veins were a little society of colored persons organized in a certain Northern city shortly after the war. Its purpose was to establish and maintain correct social standards among a people whose social condition presented almost unlimited room for improvement. By accident, combined perhaps with some natural affin-

ity, the society consisted of individuals who were, generally
speaking, more white than black. Some envious outsider made the
suggestion that no one was eligible for membership who was not
white enough to show blue veins. The suggestion was readily
adopted by those who were not of the favored few, and since that
time the society, though possessing a longer and more pretentious
name, had been known far and wide as the "Blue Vein Society," and
its members as the "Blue Veins."

The Blue Veins did not allow that any such requirement existed
for admission to their circle, but, on the contrary, declared that
character and culture were the only things considered; and that if
most of their members were light-colored, it was because such persons, as a rule, had better opportunities to qualify themselves for
membership. Opinions differed, too, as to the usefulness of the society. There were those who had been known to assail it violently as a
glaring example of the very prejudice from which the colored race
had suffered most; and later, when such critics had succeeded in getting on the inside, they had been heard to maintain with zeal and
earnestness that the society was a life-boat, an anchor, a bulwark
and a shield,—a pillar of cloud by day and of fire by night, to guide
their people through the social wilderness. Another alleged prerequi-
site for Blue Vein membership was that of free birth; and while there
was really no such requirement, it is doubtless true that very few of
the members would have been unable to meet it if there had been. If
there were one or two of the older members who had come up from
the South and from slavery, their history presented enough romantic
circumstances to rob their servile origin of its grosser aspects.

While there were no such tests of eligibility, it is true that the
Blue Veins had their notions on these subjects, and that not all of
them were equally liberal in regard to the things they collectively
disclaimed. Mr. Ryder was one of the most conservative. Though he
had not been among the founders of the society, but had come in
some years later, his genius for social leadership was such that he
had speedily become its recognized adviser and head, the custodian
of its standards, and the preserver of its traditions. He shaped its social policy, was active in providing for its entertainment, and when
the interest fell off, as it sometimes did, he fanned the embers until
they burst again into a cheerful flame.

There were still other reasons for his popularity. While he was
not as white as some of the Blue Veins, his appearance was such as
to confer distinction upon them. His features were of a refined type,
his hair was almost straight; he was always neatly dressed; his manners were irreproachable, and his morals above suspicion. He had
come to Groveland a young man, and obtaining employment in the

office of a railroad company as messenger had in time worked himself up to the position of stationery clerk, having charge of the distribution of the office supplies for the whole company. Although the lack of early training had hindered the orderly development of a naturally fine mind, it had not prevented him from doing a great deal of reading or from forming decidedly literary tastes. Poetry was his passion. He could repeat whole pages of the great English poets; and if his pronunciation was sometimes faulty, his eye, his voice, his gestures, would respond to the changing sentiment with a precision that revealed a poetic soul and disarmed criticism. He was economical, and had saved money; he owned and occupied a very comfortable house on a respectable street. His residence was handsomely furnished, containing among other things a good library, especially rich in poetry, a piano, and some choice engravings. He generally shared his house with some young couple, who looked after his wants and were company for him; for Mr. Ryder was a single man. In the early days of his connection with the Blue Veins he had been regarded as quite a catch, and young ladies and their mothers had manœuvered with much ingenuity to capture him. Not, however, until Mrs. Molly Dixon visited Groveland had any woman ever made him wish to change his condition to that of a married man.

Mrs. Dixon had come to Groveland from Washington in the spring, and before the summer was over she had won Mr. Ryder's heart. She possessed many attractive qualities. She was much younger than he; in fact, he was old enough to have been her father, though no one knew exactly how old he was. She was whiter than he, and better educated. She had moved in the best colored society of the country, at Washington, and had taught in the schools of that city. Such a superior person had been eagerly welcomed to the Blue Vein Society, and had taken a leading part in its activities. Mr. Ryder had at first been attracted by her charms of person, for she was very good looking and not over twenty-five; then by her refined manners and the vivacity of her wit. Her husband had been a government clerk, and at his death had left a considerable life insurance. She was visiting friends in Groveland, and, finding the town and the people to her liking, had prolonged her stay indefinitely. She had not seemed displeased at Mr. Ryder's attentions, but on the contrary had given him every proper encouragement; indeed, a younger and less cautious man would long since have spoken. But he had made up his mind, and had only to determine the time when he would ask her to be his wife. He decided to give a ball in her honor, and at some time during the evening of the ball to offer her his heart and hand. He had no special fears about the outcome, but, with a little touch of romance, he wanted the surroundings to be in harmony with his own feelings when he should have received the answer he expected.

Mr. Ryder resolved that this ball should mark an epoch in the social history of Groveland. He knew, of course,—no one could know better,—the entertainments that had taken place in past years, and what must be done to surpass them. His ball must be worthy of the lady in whose honor it was to be given, and must, by the quality of its guests, set an example for the future. He had observed of late a growing liberality, almost a laxity, in social matters, even among members of his own set, and had several times been forced to meet in a social way persons whose complexions and callings in life were hardly up to the standard which he considered proper for the society to maintain. He had a theory of his own.

"I have no race prejudice," he would say, "but we people of mixed blood are ground between the upper and the nether millstone. Our fate lies between absorption by the white race and extinction in the black. The one doesn't want us, but may take us in time. The other would welcome us, but it would be for us a backward step. 'With malice towards none, with charity for all,' we must do the best we can for ourselves and those who are to follow us. Self-preservation is the first law of nature."

His ball would serve by its exclusiveness to counteract leveling tendencies, and his marriage with Mrs. Dixon would help to further the upward process of absorption he had been wishing and waiting for.

2

The ball was to take place on Friday night. The house had been put in order, the carpets covered with canvas, the halls and stairs decorated with palms and potted plants; and in the afternoon Mr. Ryder sat on his front porch, which the shade of a vine running up over a wire netting made a cool and pleasant lounging place. He expected to respond to the toast "The Ladies" at the supper, and from a volume of Tennyson—his favorite poet—was fortifying himself with apt quotations. The volume was open at "A Dream of Fair Women." His eyes fell on these lines, and he read them aloud to judge better of their effect:—

> At length I saw a lady within call,
>   Stiller than chisell'd marble, standing there;
> A daughter of the gods, divinely tall,
>   And most divinely fair.

He marked the verse, and turning the page read the stanza beginning,—

> O sweet pale Margaret,
> O rare pale Margaret.

He weighed the passage a moment, and decided that it would not do. Mrs. Dixon was the palest lady he expected at the ball, and she was of a rather ruddy complexion, and of lively disposition and buxom build. So he ran over the leaves until his eye rested on the description of Queen Guinevere:—

> She seem'd a part of joyous Spring:
> A gown of grass-green silk she wore,
> Buckled with golden clasps before;
> A light-green tuft of plumes she bore
> Closed in a golden ring.
>
> She look'd so lovely, as she sway'd
> The rein with dainty finger-tips,
> A man had given all other bliss,
> And all his worldly worth for this,
> To waste his whole heart in one kiss
> Upon her perfect lips.

As Mr. Ryder murmured these words audibly, with an appreciative thrill, he heard the latch of his gate click, and a light footfall sounding on the steps. He turned his head, and saw a woman standing before his door.

She was a little woman, not five feet tall, and proportioned to her height. Although she stood erect, and looked around her with very bright and restless eyes, she seemed quite old; for her face was crossed and recrossed with a hundred wrinkles, and around the edges of her bonnet could be seen protruding here and there a tuft of short gray wool. She wore a blue calico gown of ancient cut, a little red shawl fastened around her shoulders with an old-fashioned brass brooch, and a large bonnet profusely ornamented with faded red and yellow artificial flowers. And she was very black,—so black that her toothless gums, revealed when she opened her mouth to speak, were not red, but blue. She looked like a bit of the old plantation life, summoned up from the past by the wave of a magician's wand, as the poet's fancy had called into being the gracious shapes of which Mr. Ryder had just been reading.

He rose from his chair and came over to where she stood.

"Good-afternoon, madam," he said.

"Good-evenin', suh," she answered, ducking suddenly with a quaint curtsy. Her voice was shrill and piping, but softened somewhat by age. "Is dis yere whar Mistuh Ryduh lib, suh?" she asked, looking around her doubtfully, and glancing into the open windows, through which some of the preparations for the evening were visible.

"Yes," he replied, with an air of kindly patronage, unconsciously flattered by her manner, "I am Mr. Ryder. Did you want to see me?"

"Yas, suh, ef I ain't 'sturbin' of you too much."

"Not at all. Have a seat over here behind the vine, where it is cool. What can I do for you?"

" 'Scuse me, suh," she continued, when she had sat down on the edge of a chair, " 'scuse me, suh, I 's lookin' for my husban'. I heered you wuz a big man an' had libbed heah a long time, an' I 'lowed you would n't min' ef I 'd come roun' an' ax you ef you 'd ever heered of a merlatter man by de name er Sam Taylor 'quirin' roun' in de chu'ches ermongs' de people fer his wife 'Liza Jane?"

Mr. Ryder seemed to think for a moment.

"There used to be many such cases right after the war," he said, "but it has been so long that I have forgotten them. There are very few now. But tell me your story, and it may refresh my memory."

She sat back farther in her chair so as to be more comfortable, and folded her withered hands in her lap.

"My name is 'Liza," she began, " 'Liza Jane. W'en I wuz young I us'ter b'long ter Marse Bob Smif, down in ole Missoura. I wuz bawn down dere. W'en I wuz a gal I wuz married ter a man named Jim. But Jim died, an' after dat I married a merlatter man named Sam Taylor. Sam wuz freebawn, but his mammy and daddy died, an' de w'ite folks 'prenticed him ter my marster fer ter work fer 'im 'tel he wuz growed up. Sam worked in de fiel', an' I wuz de cook. One day Ma'y Ann, ole miss's maid, came rushin' out ter de kitchen, an' says she, ' 'Liza Jane, ole marse gwine sell yo' Sam down de ribber.'

" ' 'Go way f'm yere,' says I; 'my husban' 's free!'

" 'Don' make no diff'ence. I heerd ole marse tell ole miss he wuz gwine take yo' Sam 'way wid 'im ter-morrow, fer he needed money, an' he knowed whar he could git a t'ousan' dollars fer Sam an' no questions axed.'

"W'en Sam come home f'm de fiel' dat night, I tole him 'bout ole marse gwine steal 'im, an' Sam run erway. His time wuz mos' up, an' he swo' dat w'en he wuz twenty-one he would come back an' he'p me run erway, er else save up de money ter buy my freedom. An' I know he'd 'a' done it, fer he thought a heap er me, Sam did. But w'en he come back he did n' fin' me, fer I wuz n' dere. Ole marse had heerd dat I warned Sam, so he had me whip' an' sol' down de ribber.

"Den de wah broke out, an' w'en it wuz ober de cullud folks wuz scattered. I went back ter de ole home; but Sam wuz n' dere, an' I could n' l'arn nuffin' 'bout 'im. But I knowed he 'd be'n dere to look fer me an' had n' foun' me, an' had gone erway ter hunt fer me.

"I 's be'n lookin' fer 'im eber sence," she added simply, as though twenty-five years were but a couple of weeks, "an' I knows he 's be'n lookin' fer me. Fer he sot a heap er sto' by me, Sam did, an' I know he's be'n huntin' fer me all dese years,—'less'n he 's be'n sick er sump'n, so he could n' work, er out'n his head, so he could n' 'member his promise. I went back down de ribber, fer I 'lowed he 'd gone down dere lookin' fer me. I 's be'n ter Noo Orleens, an' Atlanty, an' Charleston, an' Richmon'; an' w'en I 'd be'n all ober de Souf I come ter de Norf. Fer I knows I 'll fin' 'im some er dese days," she added softly, "er he 'll fin' me, an' den we 'll bofe be as happy in freedom as we wuz in de ole days befo' de wah." A smile stole over her withered countenance as she paused a moment, and her bright eyes softened into a far-away look.

This was the substance of the old woman's story. She had wandered a little here and there. Mr. Ryder was looking at her curiously when she finished.

"How have you lived all these years?" he asked.

"Cookin', suh. I 's a good cook. Does you know anybody w'at needs a good cook, suh? I 's stoppin' wid a cullud fam'ly roun' de corner yonder 'tel I kin git a place."

"Do you really expect to find your husband? He may be dead long ago."

She shook her head emphatically. "Oh no, he ain' dead. De signs an' de tokens tells me. I dremp three nights runnin' on'y dis las' week dat I foun' him."

"He may have married another woman. Your slave marriage would not have prevented him, for you never lived with him after the war, and without that your marriage does n't count."

"Would n' make no diff'ence wid Sam. He would n' marry no yuther 'ooman 'tel he foun' out 'bout me. I knows it," she added. "Sump'n 's be'n tellin' me all dese years dat I 's gwine fin' Sam 'fo' I dies."

"Perhaps he's outgrown you, and climbed up in the world where he wouldn't care to have you find him."

"No, indeed, suh," she replied, "Sam ain' dat kin' er man. He wuz good ter me, Sam wuz, but he wuz n' much good ter nobody e'se, fer he wuz one er de triflin'es' han's on de plantation. I 'spec's ter haf ter suppo't 'im w'en I fin' im, fer he nebber would work 'less'n he had ter. But den he wuz free, an' he did n' git no pay fer his work, an' I don' blame 'im much. Mebbe he's done better sence he run erway, but I ain' 'spectin' much."

"You may have passed him on the street a hundred times during the twenty-five years, and not have known him; time works great changes."

She smiled incredulously. "I 'd know 'im 'mongs' a hund'ed men.

Fer dey wuz n' no yuther merlatter man like my man Sam, an' I could n' be mistook. I 's toted his picture roun' wid me twenty-five years."

"May I see it?" asked Mr. Ryder. "It might help me to remember whether I have seen the original."

As she drew a small parcel from her bosom he saw that it was fastened to a string that went around her neck. Removing several wrappers, she brought to light an old-fashioned daguerreotype in a black case. He looked long and intently at the portrait. It was faded with time, but the features were still distinct, and it was easy to see what manner of man it had represented.

He closed the case, and with a slow movement handed it back to her.

"I don't know of any man in town who goes by that name," he said, "nor have I heard of any one making such inquiries. But if you will leave me your address, I will give the matter some attention, and if I find out anything I will let you know."

She gave him the number of a house in the neighborhood, and went away, after thanking him warmly.

He wrote the address on the fly-leaf of the volume of Tennyson, and, when she had gone, rose to his feet and stood looking after her curiously. As she walked down the street with mincing step, he saw several persons whom she passed turn and look back at her with a smile of kindly amusement. When she had turned the corner, he went upstairs to his bedroom, and stood for a long time before the mirror of his dressing-case, gazing thoughtfully at the reflection of his own face.

3

At eight o'clock the ballroom was a blaze of light and the guests had begun to assemble; for there was a literary programme and some routine business of the society to be gone through with before the dancing. A black servant in evening dress waited at the door and directed the guests to the dressing-rooms.

The occasion was long memorable among the colored people of the city; not alone for the dress and display, but for the high average of intelligence and culture that distinguished the gathering as a whole. There were a number of school-teachers, several young doctors, three or four lawyers, some professional singers, an editor, a lieutenant in the United States army spending his furlough in the city, and others in various polite callings; these were colored, though most of them would not have attracted even a casual glance because of any marked difference from white people. Most of the ladies were in evening costume, and dress coats and dancing pumps were the rule among the men. A band of string music, stationed in an alcove behind a row of palms, played popular airs while the guests were gathering.

The dancing began at half past nine. At eleven o'clock supper was served. Mr. Ryder had left the ballroom some little time before the intermission, but reappeared at the supper-table. The spread was worthy of the occasion, and the guests did full justice to it. When the coffee had been served, the toast-master, Mr. Solomon Sadler, rapped for order. He made a brief introductory speech, complimenting host and guests, and then presented in their order the toasts of the evening. They were responded to with a very fair display of after-dinner wit.

"The last toast," said the toast-master, when he reached the end of the list, "is one which must appeal to us all. There is no one of us of the sterner sex who is not at some time dependent upon woman, —in infancy for protection, in manhood for companionship, in old age for care and comforting. Our good host has been trying to live alone, but the fair faces I see around me to-night prove that he too is largely dependent upon the gentler sex for most that makes life worth living,—the society and love of friends,—and rumor is at fault if he does not soon yield entire subjection to one of them. Mr. Ryder will now respond to the toast,—The Ladies."

There was a pensive look in Mr. Ryder's eyes as he took the floor and adjusted his eye-glasses. He began by speaking of woman as the gift of Heaven to man, and after some general observations on the relations of the sexes he said: "But perhaps the quality which most distinguishes woman is her fidelity and devotion to those she loves. History is full of examples, but has recorded none more striking than one which only to-day came under my notice."

He then related, simply but effectively, the story told by his visitor of the afternoon. He gave it in the same soft dialect, which came readily to his lips, while the company listened attentively and sympathetically. For the story had awakened a responsive thrill in many hearts. There were some present who had seen, and others who had heard their fathers and grandfathers tell, the wrongs and sufferings of this past generation, and all of them still felt, in their darker moments, the shadow hanging over them. Mr. Ryder went on:—

"Such devotion and confidence are rare even among women. There are many who would have searched a year, some who would have waited five years, a few who might have hoped ten years; but for twenty-five years this woman has retained her affection for and her faith in a man she has not seen or heard of in all that time.

"She came to me to-day in the hope that I might be able to help her find this long-lost husband. And when she was gone I gave my fancy rein, and imagined a case I will put to you.

"Suppose that this husband, soon after his escape, had learned that his wife had been sold away, and that such inquiries as he could make brought no information of her whereabouts. Suppose that he was young, and she much older than he; that he was light; and she was black; that their marriage was a slave marriage, and legally binding only if they chose to make it so after the war. Suppose, too, that he made his way to the North, as some of us have done, and there, where he had larger opportunities, had improved them, and had in the course of all these years grown to be as different from the ignorant boy who ran away from fear of slavery as the day is from the night. Suppose, even, that he had qualified himself, by industry, by thrift, and by study, to win the friendship and be considered worthy the society of such people as these I see around me to-night, gracing my board and filling my heart with gladness; for I am old enough to remember the day when such a gathering would not have been possible in this land. Suppose, too, that, as the years went by, this man's memory of the past grew more and more indistinct, until at last it was rarely, except in his dreams, that any image of this bygone period rose before his mind. And then suppose that accident should bring to his knowledge the fact that the wife of his youth, the wife he had left behind him,—not one who had walked by his side and kept pace with him in his upward struggle, but one upon whom advancing years and a laborious life had set their mark,—was alive and seeking him, but that he was absolutely safe from recognition or discovery, unless he chose to reveal himself. My friends, what would the man do? I will presume that he was one who loved honor, and tried to deal justly with all men. I will even carry the case further, and suppose that perhaps he had set his heart upon another, whom he had hoped to call his own. What would he do, or rather what ought he to do, in such a crisis of a lifetime?

"It seemed to me that he might hesitate, and I imagined that I was an old friend, a near friend, and that he had come to me for advice; and I argued the case with him. I tried to discuss it impartially. After we had looked upon the matter from every point of view, I said to him, in words that we all know:—

> This above all: to thine own self be true,
> And it must follow, as the night the day,
> Thou canst not then be false to any man.

Then, finally, I put the question to him, 'Shall you acknowledge her?'

"And now, ladies and gentlemen, friends and companions, I ask you, what should he have done?"

There was something in Mr. Ryder's voice that stirred the hearts of those who sat around him. It suggested more than mere sympathy with an imaginary situation; it seemed rather in the nature of a personal appeal. It was observed, too, that his look rested more especially upon Mrs. Dixon, with a mingled expression of renunciation and inquiry.

She had listened, with parted lips and streaming eyes. She was the first to speak: "He should have acknowledged her."

"Yes," they all echoed, "he should have acknowledged her."

"My friends and companions," responded Mr. Ryder, "I thank you, one and all. It is the answer I expected, for I knew your hearts."

He turned and walked toward the closed door of an adjoining room, while every eye followed him in wondering curiosity. He came back in a moment, leading by the hand his visitor of the afternoon, who stood startled and trembling at the sudden plunge into this scene of brilliant gayety. She was neatly dressed in gray, and wore the white cap of an elderly woman.

"Ladies and gentlemen," he said, "this is the woman, and I am the man, whose story I have told you. Permit me to introduce to you the wife of my youth."

Kelly Miller

(1863–1939)

ONE OF THE MOST POPULAR and highly respected figures of his era, Kelly Miller was a moderate who took a stand somewhere between Booker T. Washington and W. E. B. Du Bois, but nearer to the latter. An outstanding and progressive educator, a tremendously popular lecturer, a prolific writer of books, pamphlets, and journalistic articles, most of them on racial themes, Miller was associated throughout the major portion of his life with Howard University, which was often referred to as "Kelly Miller's University." Dean Miller made a great contribution to Howard; he helped to lay the educational foundation upon which the present great institution was built; he helped to make Howard an internationally recognized center for the study of black and African literature, art, and culture.

Born in Winnsboro, South Carolina, the son of a free father and a slave mother, Miller was educated in the first local school for blacks established in his town during Reconstruction. A missionary, discovering young Kelly's aptitude for mathematics, placed the bright youngster in 1878 in a northern Presbyterian mission school in the region. In 1880 he entered the Preparatory Department at Howard University. From 1882 to 1885 he was a student in the university's college, earning his living as a clerk in the U.S. pension office.

Through his connection with the pension office, Miller was able to study advanced mathematics privately for a year. This arrangement was made by Simon Newcomb, then a well-known astronomer and a professor at Johns Hopkins. With Newcomb's recommendation, Kelly Miller became in 1887 the first black student to enter Johns Hopkins, where for two years he studied mathematics, physics, and astronomy.

After a brief period as a teacher in Washington, D.C.'s prestigious M Street High School, he was appointed professor of mathematics at Howard University. During his tenure at Howard (1890–1934), Miller changed his major interest from mathematics to sociology, and for ten years (1915–25) was head of the university's department of sociology. From 1907 to 1919, Kelly Miller was dean of Howard's college of arts and sciences. Unfortunately, his last years at Howard were filled with controversy.

As a journalist and pamphleteer, Miller not only wrote for most of the nation's best-known black newspapers but also for such national periodicals as *Dial, Nineteenth Century, Atlantic Monthly, Journal of Social Science, Educational Review*, and others. Among his best-known pamphlets were

As to the Leopard's Spots: An Open Letter to Thomas Dixon, Jr. (1905) and *The Disgrace of Democracy: An Open Letter to President Woodrow Wilson* (1917), a work which sold 250,000 copies, also a work which stated dramatically the attitude of most blacks toward President Wilson. To the white world he was a great statesmen; to American blacks he was the one who made Princeton a "lily-white" university, the one who brought Jim Crow to the federal government in Washington. Wilson was president of Princeton from 1902–1910; of the United States from 1913–1921. During his tenure at Princeton, Wilson put all the black students out; federal buildings were segregated during his administration.

Among Kelly Miller's most important book publications are *Race Adjustment* (1908), *Out of the House of Bondage* (1914), *An Appeal to Conscience* (1918), and *The Everlasting Stain* (1924).

For a full and impressive discussion of Kelly Miller's life, work, and influence, see the article in *Dictionary of American Negro Biography*, written by Michael R. Winston. See also a biographical sketch by E. Franklin Frazier in *Dictionary of American Biography*, *Supplement* 2 (1958); Carter G. Woodson, "Kelly Miller," *Journal of Negro History* (January 1940); and August Meier, "The Racial and Educational Philosophy of Kelly Miller, 1895–1915," *Journal of Negro Education* (Spring 1960).

FROM AS TO THE LEOPARD'S SPOTS
An Open Letter to Thomas Dixon, Jr.

September, 1905

Mr. Thomas Dixon, Jr.,

Dear Sir:—

I am writing you this letter to express the attitude and feeling of ten millions of your fellow citizens toward the evil propagandism of race animosity to which you have lent your great literary powers. Through the widespread influence of your writings you have become the chief priest of those who worship at the shrine of race hatred and wrath. This one spirit runs through all your books and published utterances, like the recurrent theme of an opera. As the general trend of your doctrine is clearly epitomized and put forth in your contribution to the *Saturday Evening Post* of August 19, I beg to consider chiefly the issues therein raised. You are a white man born in the midst of the civil war, I am a Negro born during the same stirring epoch. You were born with a silver spoon in your mouth, I was born with an iron hoe in my hand. Your race has inflicted accumulated injury and wrong upon mine, mine has borne yours only service and good will. You express your views with the most scathing frankness; I am sure, you will welcome an equally candid expression from me.

Permit me to acknowledge the personal consideration which you have shown me. You will doubtless recall that when I addressed The Congregational Ministers, of New York City, some year or more ago, you asked permission to be present and listened attentively to what I had to say, although as might have been expected, you beat a precipitous retreat when luncheon was announced. In your article in the *Post* you make several references to me and to other colored men with entire personal courtesy. So far as I know you have never varied from this rule in your personal dealings with members of my race. You are merciless, however, in excoriating the race as a whole, thus keenly wounding the sensibilities of every individual of that blood. I assure you that this courtesy of personal treatment will be reciprocated in this letter, however sharply I may be compelled to take issue with the views you set forth and to deplore your attitude. I shall endeavor to indulge in no bitter word against your race nor against the South, whose exponent and special pleader you assume to be.

I fear that you have mistaken personal manners, the inevitable varnish of any gentleman of your antecedents and rearing, for friendship to a race which you hold in despite. You tell us that you are kind and considerate to your personal servants. It is somewhat strange that you should deem such assurance necessary, any more than it is necessary for you to assure us that you are kind to and fond of your horse or your dog. But when you write yourself down as "one of their best friends," you need not be surprised if we retort the refrain of the ritual: "From all such proffers of friendship, good Lord deliver us."

Your fundamental thesis is that "no amount of education of any kind, industrial, classical or religious, can make a Negro a white man or bridge the chasm of the centuries which separates him from the white man in the evolution of human history." This doctrine is as old as human oppression. Calhoun made it the arch stone in the defense of Negro slavery—and lost.

This is but a recrudescence of the doctrine which was exploited and exploded during the antislavery struggle. Do you recall the school of proslavery scientists who demonstrated beyond doubt that the Negro's skull was too thick to comprehend the substance of

Aryan knowledge? Have you not read in the discredited scientific books of that period, with what triumphant acclaim it was shown that the Negro's shape and size of skull, facial angle, and cephalic configuration rendered him forever impervious to the white man's civilization? But all enlightened minds are now as ashamed of that doctrine as they are of the onetime dogma that the Negro had no soul. We become aware of mind through its manifestations. Within forty years of only partial opportunity, while playing as it were in the back yard of civilization, the American Negro has cut down his illiteracy by over fifty per cent; has produced a professional class, some fifty thousand strong, including ministers, teachers, doctors, lawyers, editors, authors, architects, engineers, and all higher lines of listed pursuits in which white men are engaged; some three thousand Negroes have taken collegiate degrees, over three hundred being from the best institutions in the North and West established for the most favored white youth; there is scarcely a first-class institution in America, excepting some three or four in the South, that is without colored students who pursue their studies generally with success, and sometimes with distinction; Negro inventors have taken out four hundred patents as a contribution to the mechanical genius of America; there are scores of Negroes who, for conceded ability and achievements, take respectable rank in the company of distinguished Americans.

It devolves upon you, Mr. Dixon, to point out some standard, either of intelligence, character, or conduct to which the Negro can not conform. Will you please tell a waiting world just what is the psychological difference between the races? No reputable authority, either of the old or the new school of psychology, has yet pointed out any sharp psychic discriminant. There is not a single intellectual, moral, or spiritual excellence attained by the white race to which the Negro does not yield an appreciative response. If you could show that the Negro was incapable of mastering the intricacies of Aryan speech, that he could not comprehend the intellectual basis of European culture, or apply the apparatus of practical knowledge, that he could not be made amenable to the white man's ethical code or appreciate his spiritual motive, then your case would be proved. But in default of such demonstration, we must relegate your eloquent pronouncement to the realm of generalization and prophecy, an easy and agreeable exercise of the mind in which the romancer is ever prone to indulge.

The inherent, essential, and unchangeable inferiority of the Negro to the white man lies at the basis of your social philosophy. You disdain to examine the validity of your fondly cherished hope. You follow closely in the wake of Tom Watson, in the June number of his homonymous magazine. You both hurl your thesis of innate racial inferiority at the head of Booker T. Washington. You use the same illustrations, the same arguments, set forth in the same order of recital, and for the most part in identical language. This seems to be an instance of great minds, or at least of minds of the same grade, running in the same channel.

These are your words: "What contribution to human progress have the millions of Africa who inhabit this planet made during the past four thousand years? Absolutely nothing." These are the words of Thomas Watson spoken some two months previous: "What does civilization owe to the Negro race? Nothing! Nothing!! Nothing!!!" You answer the query with the most emphatic negative noun and the strongest qualifying adjective in the language. Mr. Watson, of a more ecstatic temperament, replies with the same noun and six exclamation points. One rarely meets, outside of yellow journalism, with such lavishness of language, wasted upon a hoary dogma. A discredited dictum that has been bandied about the world from the time of Canaan to Calhoun, is revamped and set forth with as much ardor and fervency of feeling as if discovered for the first time and proclaimed for the illumination of a waiting world.

But neither boastful asseveration on your part nor indignant denial on mine will affect the facts of the case. That Negroes in the average are not equal in developed capacity to the white race, is a proposition which it would be as simple to affirm as it is silly to deny. The Negro represents a backward race which has not yet taken a commanding part in the progressive movement of the world. In the great cosmic scheme of things, some races reach the limelight of civilization ahead of others. But that temporary forwardness does not argue inherent superiority is as evident as any fact of history. An unfriendly environment may hinder and impede the one, while fortunate circumstances may quicken and spur the other. Relative superiority is only a transient phase of human development. You tell us that "The Jew has achieved a civilization—had his poets, prophets, priests, and kings, when our Germanic ancestors were still in the woods cracking cocoanuts and hickory-nuts with the monkeys." Fancy some learned Jew at that day citing your query about the contribution of the Germanic races to the culture of the human spirit, during the thousands of years of their existence! Does the progress of history not prove that races may lie dormant and fallow for ages and then break suddenly into prestige and power? Fifty years ago you doubtless would have ranked Japan among the benighted nations and hurled at their heathen heads some derogatory query as to their contribution to civilization. But since the happenings at Mukden and Port Arthur, and Portsmouth, I suppose that you are ready to change your mind. Or maybe since the Jap has proved himself "a first-class fighting man," able to cope on equal terms with the best breeds in Europe, you will claim him as belonging to the white race, notwithstanding his pig eye and yellow pigment.

The Negro enters into the inheritance of all the ages on equal terms with the rest, and who can say that he will not contribute his quota of genius to enrich the blood of the world?

The line of argument of every writer who undertakes to belittle the Negro is a well-beaten path. Liberia and Haiti are bound to come in for their share of ridicule and contemptuous handling. Mr. Watson calls these experiments freshly to mind, lest we forget. We are told all about the incapacity of the black race for self-government, the relapse into barbarism and much more of which we have heard before; and yet when we take all the circumstances into account, Haiti presents to the world one of the most remarkable achievements in the annals of human history. The panegyric of Wendell Phillips on Toussaint L'Ouverture is more than an outburst of rhetorical fancy; it is a just measure of his achievements in terms of his humble environment and the limited instrumentalities at his command. Where else in the course of history has a slave, with the aid of slaves, expelled a powerfully intrenched master class, and set up a government patterned after civilized models and which without external assistance or reinforcement from a parent civilization, has endured for a hundred years in face of a frowning world? When we consider the difficulties that confront a weak government, without military or naval means to cope with its more powerful rivals, and where commercial adventurers are ever and anon stirring up internal strife, thus provoking the intervention of stronger governments, the marvel is that the republic of Haiti still endures, the only self-governing state of the Antilles. To expect as effective and proficient government to prevail in Haiti as at Washington would be expecting more of the black men in Haiti than we find in the white men of South America. And yet, I suspect that the million Negroes in Haiti are as well governed as the corresponding number of blacks in Georgia, where only yesterday eight men were taken from the custody of the law and lynched without judge or jury. It is often charged that these people have not maintained the pace set by the old master class, that the plantations are in ruin and that the whole island wears the aspect of dilapidation. Wherever a lower people overrun the civilization of a higher, there is an inevitable lapse toward the level of the lower. When barbarians and semi-civilized hordes of northern Europe overran the southern peninsulas, the civilization of the world was wrapped in a thousand years of darkness. Relapse inevitably precedes the rebound. Is there anything in the history of Haiti contrary to the law of human development?

You ask: "Can you change the color of the Negro's skin, the kink of his hair, the bulge of his lip, or the beat of his heart, with a spelling book or a machine?" This rhetorical outburst does great credit to your literary skill, and is calculated to delight the simple; but analysis fails to reveal in it any pregnant meaning. Since civilization is not an attribute of the color of skin, or curl of hair, or curve of lip, there is no necessity for changing such physical pecularities, and if there was, the spelling book and the machine would be very unlikely instruments for its accomplishment. But why, may I ask, would you desire to change the Negro's heart throb, which already beats at a normal human pace? You need not be so frantic about the superiority of your race. Whatever superiority it may possess, inherent or acquired, will take care of itself without such rabid support. Has it ever occurred to you that the people of New England blood, who have done and are doing most to make the white race great and glorious in this land, are the most reticent about extravagant claims to everlasting superiority? You protest too much. Your loud pretensions, backed up by such exclamatory outbursts of passion, make upon the reflecting mind the impression that you entertain a sneaking suspicion of their validity.

Your position as to the work and worth of Booker T. Washington is pitiably anomalous. You recite the story of his upward struggle with uncontrolled admiration: "The story of this little ragged, barefooted pickaninny, who lifted his eyes from a cabin in the hills of Virginia, saw a vision and followed it, until at last he presides over the richest and most powerful institution in the South, and sits down with crowned heads and presidents, has no parallel even in the Tales of the Arabian Nights." You say that his story appeals to the universal heart of humanity. And yet in a recent letter to the *Columbia States*, you regard it as an unspeakable outrage that Mr. Robert C. Ogden should walk arm in arm with this wonderful man who "appeals to the heart of univeral humanity," and introduce him to the lady clerks in a dry goods store. Your passionate devotion to a narrow dogma has seriously impaired your sense of humor. The subject of your next great novel has been announced as "The Fall of Tuskegee." In one breath you commend the work of this great institution, while in another you condemn it because it does not fit into your preconceived scheme in the solution of the race problem. The Tuskegee ideal: "to make Negroes producers, lovers of labor, independent, honest, and good" is one which you say that only a fool or a knave can find fault with, because, in your own words, "it rests squarely upon the eternal verities." Over against this you add with all the condemnatory emphasis of italics and exclamation point: "*Tuskegee is not a servant training school!*" And further: "Mr. Washington is not training Negroes to take their places in the industries of the South in which white men direct and control them. He is not training students to be servants and come at the beck and call of any man. He is training them to be masters of men, to be independent, to own and operate their own industries, plant their own fields, buy and sell their own goods." All of which you condemn by imperative inference ten times stronger than your faint and forced verbal approval. It is a heedless man who wilfully flaunts his little philosophy in the face of "the eternal verities." When the wise man finds that his prejudices are running against fixed principles in God's cosmic plan, he speedily readjusts them in harmony therewith. Has it never occurred to you to reexamine the foundation of the faith, as well as the feeling, that is in you, since you admit that it runs afoul of the "eternal verities?"

⊙᙭⊙

You quote me as being in favor of the amalgamation of the races. A more careful reading of the article referred to would have convinced you that I was arguing against it as a probable solution of the race problem. I merely stated the intellectual conviction that two races cannot live indefinitely side by side, under the same general regime without ultimately fusing. This was merely the expression of a belief, and not the utterance of a preference nor the formulation of a policy. I know of no colored man who advocates amalgamation as a feasible policy of solution. You are mistaken. The Negro does not "hope and dream of amalgamation." This would be self-stultification with a vengeance. If such a policy were allowed to dominate the imagination of the race, its women would give themselves over to the unrestrained passion of white men, in quest of tawny offspring, which would give rise to a state of indescribable moral debauchery. At the same time you would hardly expect the Negro, in derogation of his common human qualities, to proclaim that he is so diverse from God's other human creatures as to make the blending of the races contrary to the law of nature. The Negro refuses to become excited or share in your frenzy on this subject. The amalgamation of the races is an ultimate possibility, though not an immediate probability. But what have you and I to do with ultimate questions, anyway? Our concern is with duty, not destiny.

But do you know, Mr. Dixon, that you are probably the foremost promoter of amalgamation between the two races? Wherever you narrow the scope of the Negro by preaching the doctrine of hate, you drive thousands of persons of lighter hue over to the white race carrying more or less Negro blood in their train. The blending of the races is less likely to take place if the self-respect and manly opportunity of the Negro are respected and encouraged, than if he is to be forever crushed beneath the level of his faculties for dread of the fancied result. Hundreds of the composite progeny are daily crossing the color line and carrying as much of the despised blood as an albicant skin can conceal without betrayal. I believe that it was Congressman Tillman, brother of the more famous Senator of that name, who stated on the floor of the constitutional convention of South Carolina, that he knew of four hundred white families in that State who had a taint of Negro blood in their veins. I personally know, or know of, fifty cases of transition in the city of Washington. It is a momentous thing for one to change his caste. The man or woman who affects to deny, ignore, or scorn the class with whom he previously associated is usually deemed deficient in the nobler qualities of human nature. It is not conceivable that persons of this class would undergo the self-degradation and humiliation of soul necessary to cross the great "social divide" unless it be to escape for themselves and their descendants an odious and despised status. Your oft expressed and passionately avowed belief that the progressive development of the Negro would hasten amalgamation is not borne out by the facts of observation. The refined and cultivated class among colored people are as much disinclined to such unions as the whites themselves. I am sorry that you saw fit to characterize Frederick Douglass as "a bombastic vituperator." You thereby gave poignant offense to ten millions of his race who regard him as the best embodiment of their possibilities. Besides millions of your race rate him among the foremost and best beloved of Americans. How would you feel if some one should stigmatize Jefferson Davis or Robert E. Lee in such language, these beau ideals of your Southern heart? But I will not undertake to defend Frederick Douglass against your calumniations. I am frank to confess that I do not feel that he needs it. The point I have in mind to make about Mr. Douglass is that he has a hold upon the affection of his race, not on account of his second marriage, but in spite of it. He seriously affected his standing with his people by that marriage.

It seems to me, Mr. Dixon, that this frantic abhorrence of amalgamation is a little late in its appearance. Whence comes this stream of white blood, which flows with more or less spissitude, in the veins of some six out of ten million Negroes? The Afro-American is hardly a Negro at all, except constructively; but a new creature. Who brought about this present approachment between the races? Do you not appreciate the inconsistency in the attitude and the action on the part of many of the loudmouthed advocates of race purity? It is said that old Father Chronos devoured his offspring in order to forestall future complications. But we do not learn that he put a bridle upon his passion as the surest means of security. The most effective service you can render to check the evil of amalgamation is to do missionary work among the males of your own race. This strenuous advocacy of race purity in face of proved proneness for miscegenation affords a striking reminder of the lines of Hudibras:—

> The self-same thing they will abhor,
> One way, and long another for. . . .

Your proposed solution of the race problem by colonizing the Negroes in Liberia reaches the climax of absurdity. It is difficult to see how such a proposition could emanate from a man of your reputation. Did you consult Cram's Atlas about Liberia? Please do so. You will find that it has an area of 48,000 square miles and a population of 1,500,000, natives and immigrants. The area and population are about the same as those of North Carolina, which, I believe, is your native State. When you tell us that this restricted area, without commerce, without manufacture, without any system of organized industry, can support every Negro in America, in addition to its present population, I beg mildly to suggest that you recall your plan for revision before submitting it to the judgment of a critical world. Your absolute indifference to and heedlessness of the facts, circumstances, and conditions involved in the scheme of colonization well befit the absurdity of the general proposition.

The solution of the race problem in America is indeed a grave and serious matter. It is one that calls for statesmanlike breadth of view, philanthropic tolerance of spirit, and exact social knowledge. The whole spirit of your propaganda is to add to its intensity and aggravation. You stir the slumbering fires of race wrath into an uncontrollable flame. I have read somewhere that Max Nordau, on reading *The Leopard's Spots*, wrote to you suggesting the awful responsibility you had assumed in stirring up enmity between race and race. Your teachings subvert the foundations of law and established order. You are the high priest of lawlessness, the prophet of anarchy. Rudyard Kipling places this sentiment in the mouth of the reckless stealer of seals in the Northern Sea: "There's never a law of God nor man runs north of fifty-three." This description exactly fits the brand of literature with which you are flooding the public. You openly urge your fellow citizens to override all law, human and divine. Are

you aware of the force and effect of these words? "Could fatuity
reach a sublimer height than the idea that the white man will stand
idly by and see the performance? What will he do when put to the
test? He will do exactly what his white neighbor in the North does
when the Negro threatens his bread—kill him!" These words breathe
out hatred and slaughter and suggest the murder of innocent men
whose only crime is quest for the God-given right to work. You poison the mind and pollute the imagination through the subtle influence of letters. Are you aware of the force and effect of evil
suggestion when the passions of men are in a state of unstable equilibrium? A heterogeneous population, where the elements are, on
any account, easily distinguishable, is an easy prey for the promoter
of wrath. The fuse is already prepared for the spark. The soul of the
mob is stirred by suggestion of hatred and slaughter, as a famished
beast at the smell of blood. The rabble responds so much more
readily to an appeal to passion than to reason. To wantonly stir up
the fires of race antipathy is as execrable a deed as flaunting a red
rag in the face of a bull at a summer's picnic, or raising a false cry of
"fire" in a crowded house. Human society could not exist one hour
except on the basis of law, which holds the baser passions of men in
restraint.

In our complex situation it is only the rigid observance of law reenforced by higher moral restraint that can keep these passions in
bound. You speak about giving the Negro a "square deal." Even
among gamblers, a "square deal" means to play according to the
rules of the game. The rules which all civilized States have set for
themselves are found in the Ten Commandments, the Golden Rule,
the Sermon on the Mount, and the organic law of the land. You acknowledge no such restraints when the Negro is involved, but waive
them all aside with frenzied defiance. You preside at every crossroad
lynching of a helpless victim; wherever the midnight murderer rides
with rope and torch, in quest of the blood of his black brother, you
ride by his side; wherever the cries of the crucified victim go up to
God from the crackling flame, behold you are there; when women
and children, drunk with ghoulish glee, dance around the funeral
pyre and mock the death groans of their fellow man and fight for
ghastly souvenirs, you have your part in the inspiration of it all.
When guilefully guided workmen in mine and shop and factory,
goaded by a real or imaginary sense of wrong, begin the plunder and
pillage of property and murder of rival men, your suggestion is justi-
fier of the dastardly doings. Lawlessness is gnawing at the very vitals
of our institutions. It is the supreme duty of every enlightened mind
to allay rather than spur on this spirit. You are hastening the time
when there is to be a positive and emphatic show of hands—not of

white hands against black hands, God forbid; not of Northern hands against Southern hands, heaven forfend; but a determined show of those who believe in law and God and constituted order, against those who would undermine and destroy the organic basis of society, involving all in a common ruin. No wonder Max Nordau exclaimed: "God, man, are you aware of your responsibility!"

But do not think, Mr. Dixon, that when you evoke the evil spirit, you can exorcise him at will. The Negro in the end will be the least of his victims. Those who become inoculated with the virus of race hatred are more unfortunate than the victims of it. Voltaire tells us that it is more difficult and more meritorious to wean men of their prejudices than it is to civilize the barbarian. Race hatred is the most malignant poison that can afflict the mind. It freezes up the fount of inspiration and chills the higher faculties of the soul. You are a greater enemy to your own race than you are to mine.

I have written you thus fully in order that you may clearly understand how the case lies in the Negro's mind. If any show of feeling or bitterness of spirit crops out in the treatment or between the lines, it is wholly without vindictive intent; but is the inevitble outcome of dealing with issues that verge upon the deepest human passion.

Yours truly,
KELLY MILLER.

FROM **THE DISGRACE OF DEMOCRACY**
An Open Letter to President Woodrow Wilson

Woodrow Wilson believes, or believed, that he could hold a restless world in poise by the soothing balm of pleasing phraseology. His single-track, double-acting mind moves with equal celerity, sometimes with and sometimes against the onsweeping current which he seeks to guide and control. He is no whit abashed at the tangle of moral paradoxes in which he frequently finds himself enmeshed. He follows the lead of events only long enough to gauge their tendency and trend in order that he might make himself appear to guide them. He frequently reverses his course, and proceeds to the new goal with utter disregard of logical sequence or ethical consistency. It is utterly impossible to tell whether he undergoes a genu-

ine conversion of heart or a prudent shift of mind. The same lack of
consecutiveness and consistency appears in every great issue which
he has been called upon to handle. Elected the first time upon a
platform which condemned renomination, he has accepted a second
term and is conniving at a third with convenient forgetfulness. He
forced his Party to change its declared attitude on the Panama Canal
by threats of calamity which he alone foresaw. Habitually opposed to
national female suffrage, after the propaganda had gained significant
proportions, as belated entrant, he now outruns the other disciples.
He kept the Nation out of war while the Presidential campaign was
on, and without additional provocation plunged it into war when the
election was over. After Germany had committed every atrocity with
which she has subsequently been charged, he issued a proclamation
to the American people urging them to refrain from discussing the
moral issues involved lest they disturb the serenity and composure
of the German mind. At first an ardent advocate of the Washington
policy of no entangling foreign alliances, he sits at the head of the
Council Table and ties his country to alliances which are unentan-
gleable. The apostle of new freedom for mankind ignores its application to the freedman in America. The High Priest of Democracy in
Germany becomes the obligated beneficiary of oligarchy in Georgia.
He has played at peace and war successively with Huerta, Villa and
Carranza, and yet our Southern neighbor remains untranquillized
and defiant. In one breath he declares that politics should be ad-
journed during the progress of the war, with another he urges the
country to return a Democratic Congress as more easily pliant to his
imperious will. As head of the Nation he congratulated the Republican Governor of Massachusetts upon his victorious stand for law and
order, and as head of the Democratic Party he felicitates the successful Governor of his own State and Party, who won the election on
the declaration that he would make the Nation as wet as water, thus
subverting all law and order. The highest world exponent of derived
powers, he swiftly overleaps all precedents in the assumption of un-
authorized power. Elected President of the United States, he makes
himself the Chief Magistrate of Mankind. He reverses the world
motto: his charity begins abroad rather than at home. He believes in
Democracy for humanity but not for Mississippi. Abraham Lincoln's
gospel of freedom was immediate; Woodrow Wilson's is remote. The
one believed in the freedom of the Negro; the other in the freedom
of Nations. President Lincoln wrought for the United States of America; Woodrow Wilson for the United States of the World. The former never uttered one insincere or uncertain word; the utterances of
the latter rarely escape the imputation of moral ambiguity. By marvelous assumption of superior insight, he propounds preachments

and compounds idealistic theories as infallible solvents of all social
ills. He retires into the secrecy of his inner consciousness and
evolves his famous Fourteen Points—the new "tetra decalogue,"
which he was the first to violate and ignore. The advocate of open
covenants openly arrived at proceeds to the Peace Conference en-
shrouded in the sacredness and secrecy of Sinai, and returns with
the League of Nations written upon the tablet of his own conception
with the finger of finality. Although the newly conceived League of
Nations transcends the Constitution and Declaration of Independence, "anathema, maranatha" be upon the head of that impious
statesman who would add or subtract one jot or one tittle from the
law oracularly vouchsafed by the ordained lawgiver of the world.

President Wilson is indeed the greatest phrase-maker of the age,
although each preceding phrase is apt to have its meaning nullified
by a quickly succeeding one. "The Nations should be permitted to
shed all the blood they please"; "we are too proud to fight"; "there
must be peace without victory," have already taken their places in
the limbo of innocuous desuetude. Such lofty expressions as "to
make the world safe for democracy"; "overriden peoples must have a
voice in the Governments which they uphold"; "the only way to stop
men from agitation against grievances is to remove the grievances"
still await vindication in light of sanctioned and condoned practices.
To the Negro these phrases seem to possess the sinister suggestion
of hollow mockery under the guise of Holy Democracy. Mr. Wilson
would strengthen the chain by ignoring the weakest links. His abstract doctrine breaks down at the point of concrete application. The
Negro question, the most aggravating moral issue of American life, is
avoided or thrust aside as hopelessly impossible. He has handled this
issue with less positiveness and moral aggression than any president
since James Buchanan. Under pressure of political exigency or military exaction he has indited several of his customary notes on this
question, but their luke-warmness indicates that they might have
been written with the left hand as the easiest riddance of a disagreeable issue. On promise of political support, he pledged Bishop Wal-
ters the full recognition of the Negro's claims. Shortly after election
he sent the name of a Negro as Register of the Treasury. His Southern partizans protested. The nomination was withdrawn. The promise has been ignored. It must be said that the President's change of
attitude or shift of mind is usually in the direction of progress,
aggression and courage; on the Negro question it is in the direction
of timidity, negation, and reaction. President Wilson appears to be at
once the greatest radical and the greatest conservator of the age. Under such leadership the American people—white and black—must
face the issues which now confront the world.

James Edwin Campbell

(1867–1896)

EDUCATOR, JOURNALIST, and pioneer writer of dialect poetry, James Edwin Campbell was born in Pomeroy, Meigs County, Ohio. He attended Pomeroy High School, graduating in 1884. After studying Latin and German in high school, he became a teacher in the black schools of Rutland, Ohio, and was so successful he was offered the principalship of a white school, which he refused.

Entering politics, Campbell soon became a very popular and effective speaker and a force in the Republican politics of Ohio and West Virginia. In 1887 Campbell became editor of the *West Virginia Enterprise*, which was published in Kanawha County, West Virginia; he also brought out in the same year his first book of poems, *Driftings and Gleanings*.

Campbell returned to education in 1890, becoming principal of Langston School in Point Pleasant, West Virginia, and in 1891 he became the first principal of the West Virginia Collegiate Institute, the oldest state-supported institution of higher learning for blacks in that state. He also helped to organize the West Virginia Teachers Association.

Leaving West Virginia for Chicago in 1893, Campbell joined the staff of the *Chicago Times-Herald*. He also wrote poems which appeared in several other newspapers, joined a poetry club which issued the *Four O'Clock Magazine*, and met Paul Laurence Dunbar. In 1895, his peak year, he published his best-known work, *Echoes from the Cabin and Elsewhere*. The dialect poetry of Campbell made use of a South Carolina Gullah dialect which is quite different from that of Dunbar and much harder for present-day readers to understand. Critics, however, find that it is much closer to African and West Indian origins than the dialect verse of Dunbar. Some critics also feel that Campbell's "folk" poems are a little more realistic and cynical than those of the Great Master of Dialect, whom he preceded.

For Jean Wagner, writing in his *Black Poets* (1973), "Campbell remains the most attractive and most interesting of Dunbar's contemporaries." Lorenzo Thomas, who has supplied an impressive entry in *Dictionary of Literary Biography, Volume 50*, describes the essence of Campbell's work as "an energetic optimism that very accurately reflects the generally hopeful and cautiously militant temperament of Black Americans at the end of the nineteenth century."

For perhaps the fullest biographical data on Campbell, see the *Cleveland Gazette* (January 20, 1891). Also see the article by Frank R. Levstik in

Dictionary of American Negro Biography. For his role in education, see Carter G. Woodson, *Early Negro Education in West Virginia* (1921). And for his acquaintance with Paul Laurence Dunbar, see Addison Gayle, Jr., *Oak and Ivy: A Biography of Paul Laurence Dunbar* (1971). See also Eugene Redmond, *Drumvoices: The Mission of Afro-American Poetry* (1976), and Joan R. Sherman, *Invisible Poets* (1974).

All of Campbell's poems are reprinted from James Weldon Johnson, ed., *The Book of American Negro Poetry.*

NEGRO SERENADE

O, de light-bugs glimmer down de lane,
   Merlindy! Merlindy!
O, de whip'-will callin' notes ur pain—
   Merlindy, O, Merlindy!
O, honey lub, my turkle dub,
   Doan' you hyuh my bawnjer ringin',
While de night-dew falls an' de ho'n owl calls
   By de ol' ba'n gate Ise singin'.

O, Miss 'Lindy, doan' you hyuh me, chil',
   Merlindy! Merlindy!
My lub fur you des dribe me wil'—
   Merlindy, O, Merlindy!
I'll sing dis night twel broad day-light,
   Ur bu's' my froat wid tryin',
'Less you come down, Miss 'Lindy Brown,
   An' stops dis ha't fum sighin'!

DE CUNJAH MAN

O chillen, run, de Cunjah man,
Him mouf ez beeg ez fryin' pan,
Him yurs am small, him eyes am raid,
Him hab no toof een him ol' haid,
Him hab him roots, him wu'k him trick,
Him roll him eye, him mek you sick—
   De Cunjah man, de Cunjah man,
   O chillen, run, de Cunjah man!

Him hab ur ball ob raid, raid ha'r,
Him hide it un' de kitchen sta'r,

Mam Jude huh pars urlong dat way,
An' now huh hab ur snaik, de say.
Him wrop ur roun' huh buddy tight,
Huh eyes pop out, ur orful sight—
   De Cunjah man, de Cunjah man,
   O chillen, run, de Cunjah man!

Miss Jane, huh dribe him f'um huh do',
An' now huh hens woan' lay no mo';
De Jussey cow huh done fall sick,
Hit all done by de Cunjah trick.
Him put ur root un' 'Lijah's baid,
An' now de man he sho' am daid—
   De Cunjah man, de Cunjah man,
   O chillen, run, de Cunjah man!

Me see him stan' de yudder night
Right een de road een white moon-light;
Him toss him arms, him whirl him 'roun',
Him stomp him foot urpon de groun';
De snaiks come crawlin', one by one,
Me hyuh um hiss, me break an' run—
   De Cunjah man, de Cunjah man,
   O chillen, run, de Cunjah man!

OL' DOC' HYAR

Ur ol' Hyar lib in ur house on de hill,
He hunner yurs ol' an' nebber wuz ill;
He yurs dee so long an' he eyes so beeg,
An' he laigs so spry dat he dawnce ur jeeg;
He lib so long dat he know ebbry tings
'Bout de beas'ses dat walks an' de bu'ds dat sings—
                Dis Ol' Doc' Hyar,
                Whar lib up dar
Een ur mighty fine house on ur mighty high hill.

He doctah fur all de beas'ses an' bu'ds—
He put on he specs an' he use beeg wu'ds,
He feel dee pu's' den he look mighty wise,
He pull out he watch an' he shet bofe eyes;
He grab up he hat an' grab up he cane,
Den—"blam!" go de do'—he gone lak de train,

                              Dis Ol' Doc' Hyar,
                              Whar lib up dar
Een ur mighty fine house on ur mighty high hill.

Mistah Ba'r fall sick—dee sont fur Doc' Hyar,
"O, Doctah, come queeck, an' see Mr. B'ar;
He mighty nigh daid des sho' ez you b'on!"
"Too much ur young peeg, too much ur green co'n,"
Ez he put on he hat, said Ol' Doc' Hyar;
"I'll tek 'long meh lawnce, an' lawnce Mistah B'ar,"
                              Said Ol' Doc' Hyar,
                              Whar lib up dar
Een ur mighty fine house on ur mighty high hill.

Mistah B'ar he groaned, Mistah B'ar he growled,
W'ile de ol' Miss B'ar an' de chillen howled;
Doctah Hyar tuk out he sha'p li'l lawnce,
An' pyu'ced Mistah B'ar twel he med him prawnce
Den grab up he hat an' grab up he cane
"Blam!" go de do' an' he gone lak de train,
                              Dis Ol' Doc' Hyar,
                              Whar lib up dar
Een ur mighty fine house on ur mighty high hill.

But de vay naix day Mistah B'ar he daid;
Wen dee tell Doc' Hyar, he des scratch he haid:
"Ef pahsons git well ur pahsons git wu's,
Money got ter come een de Ol' Hyar's pu's;
Not wut folkses does, but fur wut dee know
Does de folkses git paid"—an' Hyar larfed low,
                              Dis sma't Ol' Hyar,
                              Whar lib up dar
Een de mighty fine house on de mighty high hill!

WHEN OL' SIS' JUDY PRAY

When ol' Sis' Judy pray,
De teahs come stealin' down my cheek,
De voice ur God widin me speak';
I see myse'f so po' an' weak,
Down on my knees de cross I seek,
When ol' Sis' Judy pray.

When ol' Sis' Judy pray,
De thun'ers ur Mount Sin-a-i
Comes rushin' down f'um up on high—
De Debbil tu'n his back an' fly
While sinnahs loud fur pa'don cry,
When ol' Sis' Judy pray.

When ol' Sis' Judy pray,
Ha'd sinnahs trimble in dey seat
Ter hyuh huh voice in sorro 'peat:
(While all de chu'ch des sob an' weep)
"O Shepa'd, dese, dy po' los' sheep!"
When ol' Sis' Judy pray.

When ol' Sis' Judy pray,
De whole house hit des rock an' moan
Ter see huh teahs an' hyuh huh groan;
Dar's somepin' in Sis' Judy's tone
Dat melt all ha'ts dough med ur stone
When ol' Sis' Judy pray.

When ol' Sis' Judy pray,
Salvation's light comes pourin' down—
Hit fill de chu'ch an' all de town—
Why, angels' robes go rustlin' 'roun',
An' hebben on de Yurf am foun',
When ol' Sis' Judy pray.

When ol' Sis' Judy pray,
My soul go sweepin' up on wings,
An' loud de chu'ch wid "Glory!" rings,
An' wide de gates ur Jahsper swings
Twel you hyuh ha'ps wid golding strings,
When ol' Sis' Judy pray.

COMPENSATION

O, rich young lord, thou ridest by
With looks of high disdain;
It chafes me not thy title high,
Thy blood of oldest strain.
The lady riding at thy side
Is but in name thy promised bride,
    Ride on, young lord, ride on!

Her father wills and she obeys,
The custom of her class;
'Tis Land not Love the trothing sways—
For Land he sells his lass.
Her fair white hand, young lord, is thine,
Her *soul*, proud fool, her *soul* is mine,
    Ride on, young lord, ride on!

No title high my father bore;
The tenant of thy farm,
He left me what I value more:
Clean heart, clear brain, strong arm
And love for bird and beast and bee
And song of lark and hymn of sea,
    Ride on, young lord, ride on!

The boundless sky to me belongs,
The paltry acres thine;
The painted beauty sings thy songs,
The lavrock lilts me mine;
The hot-housed orchid blooms for thee,
The gorse and heather bloom for me,
    Ride on, young lord, ride on!

George Henry White

(1852–1918)

THE LAST of the "post-Reconstruction" members of Congress, George White was born in Rosindale, North Carolina, in 1852. During his life he was a "teacher, lawyer, member of Congress, real estate dealer, banker, and founder of an all-Negro town." Of mixed ancestry—Negro, Indian, and Irish—he was the last former slave to serve in Congress as well as the last post-Reconstruction black member of the House of Representatives. After attending public schools, White spent four years (1873–77) studying at Howard University. Elected to Congress in 1896, reelected in 1898, White, then the only black member of Congress, considered himself a spokesman for all blacks and a defender of attacks on his people made by his colleagues in Congress. On January 20, 1901, White proposed the first antilynching bill. The speech that follows, "A Speech in Defense of the Negro Race," is typical of White's technique in answering the southern congressmen who routinely maligned blacks. White's best-known speech was his last speech in Congress, made January 21, 1901, in which he pointed out the achievements of blacks despite the incredible handicaps imposed upon them by law and custom.

Biographical material on White is found in George W. Reid's entry in *Dictionary of American Negro Biography*. See also Samuel Denny, *The Negro in Congress, 1870–1901* (1940), which is largely negative in its appraisals; and Maurine Christopher, *Black Americans in Congress* (1971), which Reid finds "more detailed and commendatory." See also *Negro Orators and Their Orations*, ed. Carter G. Woodson (1925), for examples of George Henry White's skill at the podium. The following speech is taken from that source.

A SPEECH IN DEFENSE OF THE NEGRO RACE

I want to enter a plea for the colored man, the colored woman, the colored boy, and the colored girl of this country. I would not thus digress from the question at issue and detain the House in a discus-

sion of the interests of this particular people at this time but for the
constant and the persistent efforts of certain gentlemen upon this
floor to mold and rivet public sentiment against us as a people and
to lose no opportunity to hold up the unfortunate few who commit
crimes and depredations and lead lives of infamy and shame, as
other races do, as fair specimens of representatives of the entire colored race. And at no time, perhaps, during the Fifty-sixth Congress
were these charges and countercharges, containing, as they do, slan-
derous statements, more persistently magnified and pressed upon the
attention of the nation than during the consideration of the recent
reapportionment bill, which is now a law. As stated some days ago
on this floor by me, I then sought diligently to obtain an opportunity to answer some of the statements made by gentlemen from different States, but the privilege was denied me; and I therefore must
embrace this opportunity to say, out of season, perhaps, that which I
was not permitted to say in season.

In the catalogue of members of Congress in this House perhaps
none has been more persistent in his determination to bring the
black man into disrepute and, with a labored effort, to show that he
was unworthy of the right of citizenship than my colleague from
North Carolina, Mr. Kitchin. During the first session of this Congress, while the constitutional amendment was pending in North
Carolina, he labored long and hard to show that the white race was
at all times and under all circumstances superior to the Negro by
inheritance if not otherwise, and the excuse for his party supporting
that amendment, which has since been adopted, was that an illiterate
Negro was unfit to participate in making the laws of a sovereign
State and the administration and execution of them; but an illiterate
white man living by his side, with no more or perhaps not so much
property, with no more exalted character, no higher thoughts of civilization, no more knowledge of the handicraft of government, had by
birth, because he was white, inherited some peculiar qualification,
clear, I presume, only in the mind of the gentleman who endeavored
to impress it upon others, that entitled him to vote, though he knew
nothing whatever of letters. It is true, in my opinion, that men
brood over things at times which they would have exist until they
fool themselves and actually, sometimes honestly, believe that such
things do exist.

I would like to call the gentleman's attention to the fact that the
Constitution of the United States forbids the granting of any title of
nobility to any citizen thereof, and while it does not in letters forbid
the inheritance of this superior caste, I believe in the fertile imagination of the gentleman promulgating it, his position is at least in conflict with the spirit of that organic law of the land. He insists and, I

believe, has introduced a resolution in this House for the repeal of the fifteenth amendment to the Constitution. As an excuse for his peculiar notions about the exercise of the right of franchise by citizens of the United States of different nationality, perhaps it would not be amiss to call the attention of this House to a few facts and figures surrounding his birth and rearing. To begin with, he was born in one of the counties in my district, Halifax, a rather significant name.

I might state as a further general fact that the Democrats of North Carolina got possession of the State and local government since my last election in 1898, and that I bid adieu to these historic walls on the fourth day of next March, and that the brother of Mr. Kitchin will succeed me. Comment is unnecessary. In the town where this young gentleman was born, at the general election last August for the adoption of the constitutional amendment, and the general election for state and county officers, Scotland Neck had a registered white vote of 395, most of whom of course were Democrats, and a registered colored vote of 534, virtually if not all of whom were Republicans, and so voted. When the count was announced, however, there were 831 Democrats to 75 Republicans; but in the town of Halifax, the same county, the result was much more pronounced.

In that town the registered Republican vote was 345, and the total registered vote of the township was 539, but when the count was announced it stood 990 Democrats to 41 Republicans, or 492 more Democratic votes counted than were registered votes in the township. Comment here is unnecessary, nor do I think it necessary for anyone to wonder at the peculiar notion my colleague has with reference to the manner of voting and the method of counting these votes, nor is it to be a wonder that he is a member of this Congress, having been brought up and educated in such wonderful notions of dealing out fair-handed justice to his fellow-man.

It would be unfair, however, for me to leave the inference upon the minds of those who hear me that all of the white people of the State of North Carolina hold views with Mr. Kitchin and think as he does. Thank God, there are many noble exceptions to the example he sets, that, too, in the Democratic party; men who have never been afraid that one uneducated, poor, depressed Negro could put to flight and chase into degradation two educated, wealthy, thrifty white men. There never has been, nor ever will be, any Negro domination in that State, and no one knows it any better than the Democratic party. It is a convenient howl, however, often resorted to in order to consummate a diabolical purpose by scaring the weak and gullible whites into support of measures and men suitable to the demagogue and the ambitous office seeker, whose crave for office overshadows and puts to flight all other considerations, fair or unfair.

As I stated on a former occasion, this young statesman has ample time to learn better and more useful knowledge than he has exhibited in many of his speeches upon this floor, and I again plead for him the statute of youth for the wild and spasmodic notions which he has endeavored to rivet upon his colleagues and this country. But I regret that Mr. Kitchin is not alone upon this floor in these peculiar notions advanced.

It is an undisputed fact that the Negro vote in the State of Alabama, as well as most of the other Southern States, has been effectively suppressed, either one way or the other—in some instances by constitutional amendment and State legislation, in others by cold-blooded fraud and intimidation, but whatever the method pursued, it is not denied, but frankly admitted in the speeches in this House, that the black vote has been eliminated to a large extent. Then, when some of us insist that the plain letter of the Constitution of the United States, which all of us have sworn to support, should be carried out, as expressed in the second section of the fourteenth amendment thereof, to wit:

> Representatives shall be apportioned among the several States according to their respective numbers, counting the whole number of persons in each State, excluding Indians not taxed. But when the right to vote at any election for the choice of electors for President and Vice-President of the United States, Represenatives in Congress, the executive and judicial officers of a State, or the members of a legislature thereof, is denied to any of the male inhabitants of such State, being twenty-one years of age, and citizens of the United States, or in any way abridged, except for participation in rebellion, or other crime, the basis of representation therein shall be reduced in proportion which the number of such male citizens shall bear to the whole number of male citizens twenty-one years of age in such State.

That section makes the duty of every member of Congress plain, and yet the gentleman from Alabama (Mr. Underwood) says that the attempt to enforce this section of the organic law is the throwing down of firebrands, and notifies the world that this attempt to execute the highest law of the land will be retaliated by the South, and the inference is that the Negro will be even more severely punished than the horrors through which he has already come.

Let me make it plain: The divine law, as well as most of the State laws, says in substance: "He that sheddeth man's blood, by man shall his blood be shed." A highwayman commits murder, and when the officers of the law undertake to arrest, try, and punish him commensurate with the enormity of his crime, he straightens himself up to his full height and defiantly says to them: "Let me alone; I will not be arrested, I will not be tried, I'll have none of the execution of your laws, and in the event you attempt to execute your laws upon me, I will see to it that many more men, women, or children are murdered."

Here's the plain letter of the Constitution, the plain, simple, sworn duty of every member of Congress; yet these gentlemen from the South say, "Yes, we have violated your Constitution of the nation; we regard it as a local necessity; and now, if you undertake to punish us as the Constitution prescribes, we will see to it that our former deeds of disloyalty to that instrument, our former acts of disfranchisement and opposition to the highest law of the land will be repeated many fold."

Not content with all that has been done to the black man, not because of any deeds that he has done, Mr. Underwood advances the startling information that these people have been thrust upon the whites of the South, forgetting, perhaps, the horrors of the slave trade, the unspeakable horrors of the transit from the shores of Africa by means of the middle passage to the American clime; the enforced bondage of the blacks and their descendants for two and a half centuries in the United States, now, for the first time perhaps in the history of our lives, the information comes that these poor, helpless, and in the main inoffensive people were thrust upon our Southern brethren.

Individually, and so far as my race is concerned, I care but little about the reduction of Southern representation, except in so far as it becomes my duty to aid in the proper execution of all the laws of the land in whatever sphere in which I may be placed. Such reduction in representation, it is true, would make more secure the installment of the great Republican party in power for many years to come in all its branches, and at the same time enable the great party to be able to dispense with the further support of the loyal Negro vote; and I might here parenthetically state that there are some members of the Republican party today—"lily whites," if you please—who, after receiving the unalloyed support of the Negro vote for over thirty years, now feel that they have grown a little too good for association with him politically, and are disposed to dump him overboard. I am glad to observe, however, that this class constitutes a very small percentage of those to whom we have always looked for friendship and protection.

I wish to quote from another Southern gentleman, not so young as my other friends, and who always commands attention in this House by his wit and humor, even though his speeches may not be edifying and instructive. I refer to Mr. Otey, of Virginia, and quote from him in a recent speech on this floor, as follows:

> Justice is merely relative. It can exist between equals. It can exist among homogeneous people—among equals. Among heterogeneous people it never has and, in the very nature of things, it never will obtain. It can exist among lions, but between lions and lambs, never. If justice were absolute, lions must of necessity perish. Open his ponderous jaws and find the strong teeth which God has made expressly to chew lamb's flesh! When the Society for the Prevention of Cruelty to Animals shall overcome this difficulty, men may hope to settle the race question along sentimental lines, not sooner.
>
> These thoughts on the Negro are from the pen, in the main, of one who has studied the Negro question, and it was after I heard the gentleman from North Carolina, and after the introduction of the Crumpacker bill, that they occurred to me peculiarly appropriate.

I am wholly at sea as to just what Mr. Otey had in view in advancing the thoughts contained in the above quotation, unless he wished to extend the simile and apply the lion as a white man and the Negro as a lamb. In that case we will gladly accept the comparison, for of all animals known in God's creation the lamb is the most inoffensive, and has been in all ages held up as a badge of innocence. But what will my good friend of Virginia do with the Bible, for God says that He created all men of one flesh and blood? Again, we insist on having one race—the lion clothed with great strength, vicious, and with destructive propensities, while the other is weak, good natured, inoffensive, and useful—what will he do with all the heterogeneous intermediate animals, ranging all the way from the pure lion to the pure lamb, found on the plantations of every Southern State in the Union?

I regard his borrowed thoughts, as he admits they are, as very inaptly applied. However, it has perhaps served the purpose of which he intended it—the attempt to show the inferiority of the one and the superiority of the other. I fear I am giving too much time in the consideration of these personal comments of members of Congress, but I trust I will be pardoned for making a passing reference to one more gentleman—Mr. Wilson of South Carolina—who, in the early part of this month, made a speech, some parts of which did great credit to him, showing, as it did, capacity for collating, arranging, and advancing thoughts of others and of making a pretty strong argument out of a very poor case.

If he had stopped there, while not agreeing with him, many of us would have been forced to admit that he had done well. But his purpose was incomplete until he dragged in the reconstruction days and held up to scorn and ridicule the few ignorant, gullible, and perhaps purchasable Negroes who served in the State legislature of South Carolina over thirty years ago. Not a word did he say about the unscrupulous white men, in the main bummers who followed in the wake of the Federal Army and settled themselves in the Southern States, and preyed upon the ignorant and unskilled minds of the colored people, looted the States of their wealth, brought into lowest disrepute the ignorant colored people, then hied away to their Northern homes for ease and comfort the balance of their lives, or joined the Democratic party to obtain social recognition, and have greatly aided in depressing and further degrading those whom they had used as tools to accomplish a diabolical purpose.

These few ignorant men who chanced at that time to hold office are given as a reason why the black man should not be permitted to participate in the affairs of the Government which he is forced to pay taxes to support. He insists that they, the Southern whites, are the black man's best friend, and that they are taking him by the hand and trying to lift him up; that they are educating him. For all that he and all Southern people have done in this regard, I wish in behalf of the colored people of the South to extend our thanks. We are not ungrateful to friends, but feel that our toil has made our friends able to contribute the stinty pittance which we have received at their hands.

I read in a Democratic paper a few days ago, the Washington *Times*, an extract taken from a South Carolina paper, which was intended to exhibit the eagerness with which the Negro is grasping every opportunity for educating himself. The clipping showed that the money for each white child in the State ranged from three to five times as much per capita as was given to each colored child. This is helping us some, but not to the extent that one would infer from the gentleman's speech. . . . With all these odds against us, we are forging our way ahead, slowly, perhaps, but surely. You may tie us and then taunt us for a lack of bravery, but one day we will break the bonds. You may use our labor for two and a half centuries and then taunt us for our poverty, but let me remind you we will not always remain poor. You may withhold even the knowledge of how to read God's word and learn the way from earth to glory and then taunt us for our ignorance, but we will remind you that there is plenty of room at the top, and we are climbing.

After enforced debauchery, with the many kindred horrors incident to slavery, it comes with ill grace from the perpetrators of these deeds to hold up the shortcomings of some of our race to ridicule and scorn.

> The new man, the slave who has grown out of the ashes of thirty-five years ago, is inducted into the political and social system, cast into the

arena of manhood, where he constitutes a new element and becomes a competitor for all its emoluments. He is put upon trial to test his ability to be counted worthy of freedom, worthy of the elective franchise; and after thirty-five years of struggling against almost insurmountable odds, under conditions but little removed from slavery itself, he asks fair and just judgment, not of those whose prejudice has endeavored to forestall, to frustrate his every forward movement, rather those who have lent a helping hand, that he might demonstrate the truth of the fatherhood of God and the brotherhood of man.[1]

---

[1] *Congressional Record*, 56th Cong., 2nd Session, 1634–1638.

Paul Laurence Dunbar

(1872–1906)

POET, SHORT STORY WRITER, NOVELIST, and writer of articles, dramatic sketches, plays, and song lyrics, Dunbar was the most popular black author of his generation. He was also the best writer of dialect verse, and his mastery in this genre accounted in large measure for this singular popularity.

The son of ex-slave parents, Dunbar was born in Dayton, Ohio. His father was an escaped slave who returned from Canada to fight in the Union army. His mother, who even in bondage had learned to read and write, was a strong influence on the poet's life and encouraged him in his literary efforts. Both parents furnished their son with firsthand information about slavery which Dunbar used brilliantly in his works.

Dunbar went to high school in Dayton and was elected editor of the school paper. Too poor to attend college, he became an elevator boy, wrote verses on the job, and peddled them to his riders. In 1893 he collected all of his poems and with a loan from a white friend published them under the title *Oak and Ivy*. Shortly after the publication of this work, another white friend, a judge, offered Dunbar a job as courthouse messenger with the opportunity to "read" law; but in the spring of 1893, when the Chicago World's Fair was opened, Dunbar, feeling that there would be more promising jobs there, elected to go to the Windy City. He was disappointed in his search for jobs, but he met Frederick Douglass, who was commissioner in charge of the Haitian exhibit. Douglass made the young poet his clerical assistant, paying him five dollars a week from his own funds.

In 1895 Dunbar, again with the help of other white friends, published his second collection of poems, *Majors and Minors*. It was this work which was reviewed by William Dean Howells for *Harper's Weekly* in 1896. Although 86 of the volume's 148 pages dealt with poems in standard English, Howells practically dismissed these poems and stressed the ones in dialect. In the same year, Dodd, Mead and Company published Dunbar's third volume, *Lyrics of Lowly Life*, and with it the famous introduction by Howells, which said: "[This] was the first instance of an American Negro who had evinced innate distinction in literature. . . . So far as I could remember, Paul Dunbar was the only man of pure African blood and of American civilization to feel the Negro life aesthetically and express it lyrically." It is easy to disagree strongly with the critic's statement, but its effect is hardly debatable. Howells's introduction made Dunbar the most popular black writer in America.

In 1897 the poet made a not-too-successful tour of England. On his return he was given, through the influence of Robert G. Ingersoll, a minor position in the Library of Congress, which he held for two years. In 1898 he married Alice Ruth Moore, a fairly well-known writer, but the marriage failed. A victim of overwork, of drink, and of tuberculosis, Paul Laurence Dunbar died in his birthplace in 1906, still in his thirties.

In addition to the poetical works mentioned previously, Dunbar published the following collections: *Lyrics of the Hearthside* (1899), *Lyrics of Love and Laughter* (1903), and *Lyrics of Sunshine and Shadow* (1905). He published four novels: *The Uncalled* (1898), *The Love of Landry* (1900), *The Fanatics* (1901), and *The Sport of the Gods* (1902), the only novel that had black major characters. It is also, most critics feel, Dunbar's best novel. He also published four collections of short stories: *Folks from Dixie* (1898), *The Strength of Gideon* (1900), *In Old Plantation Days* (1903), and *The Heart of Happy Hollow* (1904).

An accommodationist, Dunbar avoided almost entirely in his works any mention of racial injustice. Predominantly a pastoral poet, he wrote generally about the joys of plantation life both before and after the war, of contented slaves and untroubled freedom. Though he seldom mentioned the harshness of slavery and the viciousness of Reconstruction, he wrote a small number of poems which could be classified as protest poems, among them "We Wear the Mask" and "The Haunted Oak," an antilynching poem. These, however, are the exceptions. Although Dunbar felt it unfair to judge his standing as a poet by his "jingles in a broken tongue," his best poetry *is* written in dialect. Even though he paints only two aspects of black life— pathos and humor—his works show a deeper understanding and insight than the portrayal by any of his contemporaries, white or black. On the other hand, his poems in standard English are highly uneven, running the gamut from banal and sentimental verses to lyrics of undoubted excellence.

Like his dialect verse, Dunbar's short stories, with but few exceptions, present only the humorous or pathetic side of plantation life. He wrote for a white audience seemingly; he wrote the kind of stories found in the works of Thomas Nelson Page and other southern white apologists.

For biographical and critical comment on Dunbar's life and work, see the full-length study by Benjamin Brawley, *Paul Laurence Dunbar: Poet of His People* (1916). See also the following works: Victor Lawson's *Dunbar Critically Examined* (1941); Vernon Loggins's *The Negro Author* (1931); Sterling A. Brown's *Negro Poetry and Drama* (1937); Addison Gayle, Jr.'s *Oak and Ivy: A Biography of Paul Laurence Dunbar* (1971); and the entry in *Dictionary of American Negro Biography* by Arthur P. Davis. Bernard W. Bell's *The Afro-American Novel* (1987) should be consulted. Also useful for its exploration of the poet's psyche and its expression in Dunbar's poetry, see Jean Wagner's *Black Poets* (1973). The original source of much of the present-day knowledge of the poet's career is *The Life and Works of Paul Laurence Dunbar* (1907) by Lida Keck Wiggins.

The following poems are reprinted from *The Complete Poems of Paul Laurence Dunbar* (1913); the short story is from *The Best Stories of Paul Laurence Dunbar*, ed. Benjamin Brawley (1938).

AN ANTE-BELLUM SERMON

We is gathahed hyeah, my brothahs,
    In dis howlin' wildaness,
Fu' to speak some words of comfo't
    To each othah in distress.
An' we chooses fu' ouah subjic'
    Dis—we'll 'splain it by an' by;
"An' de Lawd said, 'Moses, Moses,'
    An' de man said, 'Hyeah am I.' "

Now ole Pher'oh, down in Egypt,
    Was de wuss man evah bo'n,
An' he had de Hebrew chillun
    Down dah wukin' in his co'n;
'T well de Lawd got tiahed o' his foolin',
    An' sez he: "I 'll let him know—
Look hyeah, Moses, go tell Pher'oh
    Fu' to let dem chillun go."

"An' ef he refuse to do it,
    I will make him rue de houah,
Fu' I 'll empty down on Egypt
    All de vials of my powah."
Yes, he did—an' Pher'oh's ahmy
    Was n't wuth a ha'f a dime;
Fu' de Lawd will he'p his chillun,
    You kin trust him evah time.

An' yo' enemies may 'sail you
    In de back an' in de front;
But de Lawd is all aroun' you,
    Fu' to ba' de battle's brunt.
Dey kin fo'ge yo' chains an' shackles
    F'om de mountains to de sea;
But de Lawd will sen' some Moses
    Fu' to set his chillun free.

An' de lan' shall hyeah his thundah,
    Lak a blas' f'om Gab'el's ho'n,
Fu' de Lawd of hosts is mighty
    When he girds his ahmor on.
But fu' feah some one mistakes me,
    I will pause right hyeah to say,
Dat I'm still a-preachin' ancient,
    I ain't talkin' 'bout to-day.

But I tell you, fellah christuns,
    Things 'll happen mighty strange;
Now, de Lawd done dis fu' Isrul,
    An' his ways don't nevah change,
An' de love he showed to Isrul
    Was n't all on Isrul spent;
Now don't run an' tell yo' mastahs
    Dat I 's preachin' discontent.

'Cause I is n't; I 'se a-judgin'
    Bible people by deir ac's;
I 'se a-givin' you de Scriptuah,
    I 'se a-handin' you de fac's.
Cose ole Pher'oh b'lieved in slav'ry,
    But de Lawd he let him see,
Dat de people he put bref in,—
    Evah mothah's son was free.

An' dahs othahs thinks lak Pher'oh,
    But dey calls de Scriptuah liar,
Fu' de Bible says "a servant
    Is a-worthy of his hire."
An' you cain't git roun' nor thoo dat,
    An' you cain't git ovah it,
Fu' whatevah place you git in,
    Dis hyeah Bible too 'll fit.

So you see de Lawd's intention,
    Evah sence de worl' began,
Was dat His almighty freedom
    Should belong to evah man,
But I think it would be bettah,
    Ef I 'd pause again to say,
Dat I 'm talkin' 'bout ouah freedom
    In a Bibleistic way.

But de Moses is a-comin',
    An' he 's comin', suah and fas'

We kin hyeah his feet a-trompin',
  We kin hyeah his trumpit blas'.
But I want to wa'n you people,
  Don't you git too brigity;
An' don't you git to braggin'
  'Bout dese things, you wait an' see.

But when Moses wif his powah
  Comes an' sets us chillun free,
We will praise de gracious Mastah
  Dat has gin us liberty;
An' we 'll shout ouah halleluyahs,
  On dat mighty reck'nin' day,
When we 'se reco'nised ez citiz'—
  Huh uh! Chillun, let us pray!

ODE TO ETHIOPIA

O Mother Race! to thee I bring
This pledge of faith unwavering,
  This tribute to thy glory.
I know the pangs which thou didst feel,
When Slavery crushed thee with its heel,
  With thy dear blood all gory.

Sad days were those—ah, sad indeed!
But through the land the fruitful seed
  Of better times was growing.
The plant of freedom upward sprung,
And spread its leaves so fresh and young—
  Its blossoms now are blowing.

On every hand in this fair land,
Proud Ethiope's swarthy children stand
  Beside their fairer neighbor;
The forests flee before their stroke,
Their hammers ring, their forges smoke,—
  They stir in honest labour.

They tread the fields where honour calls;
Their voices sound through senate halls
  In majesty and power.
To right they cling; the hymns they sing
Up to the skies in beauty ring,
  And bolder grow each hour.

Be proud, my Race, in mind and soul;
Thy name is writ on Glory's scroll
   In characters of fire.
High 'mid the clouds of Fame's bright sky
Thy banner's blazoned folds now fly,
   And truth shall lift them higher.

Thou hast the right to noble pride,
Whose spotless robes were purified
   By blood's severe baptism.
Upon thy brow the cross was laid,
And labour's painful sweat-beads made
   A consecrating chrism.

No other race, or white or black,
When bound as thou wert, to the rack,
   So seldom stooped to grieving;
No other race, when free again,
Forgot the past and proved them men
   So noble in forgiving.

Go on and up! Our souls and eyes
Shall follow thy continuous rise;
   Our ears shall list thy story
From bards who from thy root shall spring,
And proudly tune their lyres to sing
   Of Ethiopia's glory.

WHEN DE CO'N PONE'S HOT

Dey is times in life when Nature
   Seems to slip a cog an' go,
Jes' a-rattlin' down creation,
   Lak an ocean's overflow;
When de worl' jes' stahts a-spinnin'
   Lak a picaninny's top,
An' yo' cup o' joy is brimmin'
   'Twell it seems about to slop,
An' you feel jes' lak a racah,
   Dat is trainin' fu' to trot—
When yo' mammy says de blessin'
   An' de co'n pone 's hot.

When you set down at de table,
　　Kin' o' weary lak an' sad,
An' you 'se jes' a little tiahed
　　An' purhaps a little mad;
How yo' gloom tu'ns into gladness,
　　How yo' joy drives out de doubt
When de oven do' is opened,
　　An' de smell comes po'in' out;
Why, de 'lectric light o' Heaven
　　Seems to settle on de spot,
When yo' mammy says de blessin'
　　An' de co'n pone 's hot.

When de cabbage pot is steamin'
　　An' de bacon good an' fat,
When de chittlins is a-sputter'n'
　　So 's to show you whah dey 's at;
Tek away yo' sody biscuit,
　　Tek away yo' cake an' pie,
Fu' de glory time is comin',
　　An' it 's 'proachin' mighty nigh,
An' you want to jump an' hollah,
　　Dough you know you 'd bettah not,
When yo' mammy says de blessin'
　　An' de co'n pone 's hot.

I have hyeahd o' lots o' sermons,
　　An' I 've hyeahd o' lots o' prayers,
An' I've listened to some singin'
　　Dat has tuck me up de stairs
Of de Glory-Lan' an' set me
　　Jes' below de Mastah's th'one,
An' have lef' my hea't a-singin'
　　In a happy aftah tone;
But dem wu'ds so sweetly murmured
　　Seem to tech de softes' spot,
When my mammy says de blessin',
　　An' de co'n pone 's hot.

SIGNS OF THE TIMES

Air a-gittin' cool an' coolah,
　　Frost a-comin' in de night,
Hicka' nuts an' wa'nuts fallin',

Possum keepin' out o' sight.
Tu'key struttin' in de ba'nya'd,
   Nary step so proud ez his;
Keep on struttin', Mistah Tu'key,
   Yo' do' know what time it is.

Cidah press commence a-squeakin'
   Eatin' apples sto'ed away,
Chillun swa'min' 'roun' lak ho'nets,
   Huntin' aigs ermung de hay.
Mistah Tu'key keep on gobblin'
   At de geese a-flyin' souf,
Oomph! dat bird do' know whut 's comin';
   Ef he did he 'd shet his mouf.

Pumpkin gittin' good an' yallah
   Mek me open up my eyes;
Seems lak it 's a-lookin' at me
   Jes' a-la'in' dah sayin' "Pies."
Tu'key gobbler gwine 'roun' blowin',
   Gwine 'roun' gibbin' sass an' slack;
Keep on talkin', Mistah Tu'key,
   You ain't seed no almanac.

Fa'mer walkin' th'oo de ba'nya'd
   Seein' how things is comin' on,
Sees ef all de fowls is fatt'nin'—
   Good times comin' sho 's you bo'n.
Hyeahs dat tu'key gobbler braggin',
   Den his face break in a smile—
Nebbah min', you sassy rascal,
   He 's gwine nab you atter while.

Choppin' suet in de kitchen,
   Stonin' raisins in de hall,
Beef a-cookin' fu' de mince meat,
   Spices groun'—I smell 'em all.
Look hyeah, Tu'key, stop dat gobblin',
   You ain' luned de sense ob feah,
You ol' fool, yo' naik 's in dangah,
   Do' you know Thanksgibbin 's hyeah!

WE WEAR THE MASK

We wear the mask that grins and lies,
It hides our cheeks and shades our eyes,—
This debt we pay to human guile;
With torn and bleeding hearts we smile,
And mouth with myriad subtleties.

Why should the world be overwise,
In counting all our tears and sighs?
Nay, let them only see us, while
   We wear the mask.

We smile, but, O great Christ, our cries
To thee from tortured souls arise.
We sing, but oh the clay is vile
Beneath our feet, and long the mile;
But let the world dream otherwise,
   We wear the mask!

CHRISMUS ON THE PLANTATION

It was Chrismus Eve, I mind hit fu' a mighty gloomy day—
Bofe de weathah an' de people—not a one of us was gay;
Cose you 'll t'ink dat 's mighty funny 'twell I try to mek hit cleah,
Fu' a da'ky 's allus happy when de holidays is neah.

But we was n't, fu' dat mo'nin' Mastah 'd tol' us we mus' go,
He 'd been payin' us sence freedom, but he could n't pay no mo';
He wa'n't nevah used to plannin' 'fo' he got so po' an' ol',
So he gwine to give up tryin', an' de homestead mus' be sol'.

I kin see him stan'in' now erpon de step ez cleah ez day,
Wid de win' a-kind o'fondlin' thoo his haih all thin an' gray;
An' I 'membah how he trimbled when he said, "It 's ha'd fu' me,
Not to make yo Chrismus brightah, but I 'low it wa'n't to be."

All de women was a-cryin', an' de men, too, on de sly,
An' I noticed somep'n shinin' even in ol' Mastah's eye.
But we all stood still to listen ez ol' Ben come f'om de crowd
An' spoke up, a-try'n' to steady down his voice and mek it loud:—

"Look hyeah, Mastah, I 's been servin' you' fu' lo! dese many yeahs,
An' now, sence we 's got freedom an' you 's kind o' po', hit 'pears

Dat you want us all to leave you 'cause you don't t'ink you can pay.
Ef my membry has n't fooled me, seem dat whut I hyead you say.

"Er in othah wo'ds, you wants us to fu'git dat you 's been kin',
An' ez soon ez you is he'pless, we 's to leave you hyeah behin'.
Well, ef dat 's de way dis freedom ac's on people, white er black,
You kin jes' tell Mistah Lincum fu' to tek his freedom back.

"We gwine wo'k dis ol' plantation fu' whatevah we kin git,
Fu' I know hit did suppo't us, an' de place kin do it yit.
Now de land is yo's, de hands is ouahs, an' I reckon we 'll be brave,
An' we 'll bah ez much ez you do w'en we has to scrape an' save."

Ol' Mastah stood dah trimblin', but a-smilin' thoo his teahs,
An' den hit seemed jes' nachullike, de place fah rung wid cheahs,
An' soon ez dey was quiet, some one sta'ted sof' an' low:
"Praise God," an' den we all jined in, "from whom all blessin's flow!"

Well, dey was n't no use tryin', ouah min's was sot to stay,
An' po' ol' Mastah could n't plead ner baig, ner drive us 'way,
An' all at once, hit seemed to us, de day was bright agin,
So evahone was gay dat night, an' watched de Chrismus in.

ANNER 'LIZER'S STUMBLIN' BLOCK

It was winter. The gray old mansion of Mr. Robert Selfridge, of Fay-
ette County, Kentucky, was wrapped in its usual mantle of winter
somberness, and the ample plantation stretching in every direction
thereabout was one level plain of unflecked whiteness. At a distance
from the house the cabins of the Negroes stretched away in a long,
broken black line that stood out in bold relief against the extreme
whiteness of their surroundings.

About the center of the line, as dark and uninviting as the rest,
with its wide chimney of scrap limestone turning clouds of dense
smoke into the air, stood a cabin.

There was nothing in its appearance to distinguish it from the
other huts clustered about. The logs that formed its sides were just
as seamy, the timbers of the roof had just the same abashed, brow-
beaten look; and the keenest eye could not have detected the slightest shade of difference between its front and the bare, unwhitewashed fronts of its scores of fellows. Indeed, it would not have
been mentioned at all, but for the fact that within its confines lived
and thrived the heroine of this story.

Of all the girls of the Selfridge estate, black, brown, or yellow, Anner 'Lizer was, without dispute, conceded to be the belle. Her black eyes were like glowing coals in their sparkling brightness; her teeth were like twin rows of shining ivories; her brown skin was as smooth and soft as silk, and the full lips that enclosed her gay and flexile tongue were tempting enough to make the heart of any dusky swain throb and his mouth water.

Was it any wonder, then, that Sam Merritt—strapping, big Sam, than whom there was not a more popular man on the place—should pay devoted court to her?

Do not gather from this that it was Sam alone who paid his *devoirs* to this brown beauty. Oh, no! Anner 'Lizer was the "bright particular star" of that plantation, and the most desired of all blessings by the young men thereabout. But Sam, with his smooth but fearless ways, Sam with his lightsome foot, so airy in the dance, Sam, handsome Sam, was the all-preferred. If there was a dance to go to, a corn-husking to attend, a social at the rude little log church, Sam was always the lucky man who was alert and *able* to possess himself of Anner 'Lizer's "comp'ny." And so, naturally, people began to connect their names, and the rumor went forth, as rumors will, that the two were engaged; and, as far as engagements went among the slaves in those days, I suppose it was true. Sam had never exactly prostrated himself at his sweetheart's feet and openly declared his passion; nor had she modestly snickered behind her fan and murmured Yes in the approved fashion of the present. But he had looked his feelings, and she had looked hers, while numerous little attentions bestowed on each other, too subtle to be detailed, and the attraction which kept them constantly together, were earnests of their intentions more weighty than words could give. And so, let me say, without further explanation, that Sam and Anner 'Lizer were engaged. But when did the course of true love ever run smooth?

There was never a time but there were some rocks in its channel around which the little stream had to glide or over which it had to bound and bubble; and thus it was with the loves of our young friends. But in this case the crystal stream seemed destined neither to bound over nor glide by the obstacle in its path, but rather to let its merry course be checked thereby.

It may, at first, seem a strange thing to say, but it was nevertheless true, that the whole sweep and torrent of the trouble had rise in the great religious revival that was being enthusiastically carried on at the little Baptist meeting-house. Interest, or perhaps, more correctly speaking, excitement ran high, and regularly as night came round, all the hands on the neighboring plantations flocked to the scene of their devotions.

There was no more regular attendant at these meetings, nor more deeply interested listener to the pastor's inflammatory exhortations, than Anner 'Lizer. The weirdness of the scene and the touch of mysticism in the services—though, of course, she did not analyze it thus—reached her emotional nature and stirred her being to its depths. Night after night found her in her pew, the third bench from the rude pulpit, her large eyes, dilated to their fullest capacity, following the minister through every motion, seeming at times in their steadiness to look him through and beyond to the regions he was describing—the harp-ringing heaven of bliss or the fire-filled home of the damned.

Now Sam, on the other hand, could not be induced to attend these meetings; and when his fellow-servants were at the little church praying, singing, and shouting, he was to be found sitting in one corner of his cabin, picking his banjo, or scouring the woods, carrying ax and taper, and, with a dog trotting at his heels, hunting for that venison of the Negro palate—'coon.

Of course this utter irreverence on the part of her lover shocked Anner 'Lizer; but she had not entered far enough into the regions of the ecstasy to be a proselyte; so she let Sam go his way, albeit with reluctance, while she went to church unattended. But she thought of Sam; and many a time when she secretly prayed to get religion she added a prayer that she might retain Sam.

He, the rogue, was an unconscious but pronounced skeptic; and day by day, as Anner 'Lizer became more and more possessed by religious fervor, the breach between them widened; still widening gradually until the one span that connected the two hearts was suddenly snapped asunder on the night when Anner 'Lizer went to the mourners' bench.

She had not gone to church with that intention; indeed not, although she had long been deeply moved by a consciousness of her lost estate. But that night, when the preacher had pictured the boundless joys of heaven, and then, leaning over the pulpit and stretching out his arms before him, had said in his softest tone, "Now come, won't you, sinnahs? De Lawd is jes' on de othah side; jes' one step away, waitin' to receibe you. Won't you come to him? Won't you tek de chance o' becomin' j'int 'ars o' dat beautiful city whar de streets is gol' an' de gates is pearl? Won't you come to him, sinnah? Don't you see de pityin' look he's a-givin' you, a-sayin' Come, come?" she lost herself. Some irresistible power seemed dominating her, and she rose and went forward, dropping at the altar amid a great shouting and clapping of hands and cries of "Bless de Lawd, one mo' recruit fu' de Gospel ahmy."

Someone started the hymn, "We'll bow around the altar," and the refrain was taken up by the congregation with a fervor that made the rafters of the little edifice ring again.

The conquest of Anner 'Lizer, the belle of that section of Kentucky, was an event of great moment; and, in spite of the concentration of the worshipers' minds on their devotions, the unexpected occurrence called forth a deal of discussion among the brothers and sisters. Aunt Hannah remarked to Aunt Maria, over the back of the seat, that she "nevah knowed de gal was unner c'nviction." And Aunt Maria answered solemnly, "You know, sistah, de Lawd wuks in a myste'ious way his wondahs to pu'fo'm."

Meanwhile the hymn went on, and above it rose the voice of the minister: "We want all de Christuns in de house to draw up aroun' de altah, whar de fiah is bu'nin': you know in de wintah time when hit's col' you crowds up clost to de fiahplace; so now, ef you wants to git spi'tually wa'm, you mus' be up whar de fiah is." There was a great scrambling and shuffling of feet as the members rose with one accord to crowd, singing, around the altar.

Two of the rude benches had been placed end to end before the pulpit, so that they extended nearly the full width of the little church; and at these knelt a dozen or more mourners, swaying and writhing under the burden of their sins.

The song being ended, the preacher said: "Br'er Adams, please tek up de cross." During the momentary lull that intervened between the end of the song and the prayer, the wails and supplications of the mourners sounded out with weird effect. Then Br'er Adams, a white-haired patriarch, knelt and "took up the cross."

Earnestly he besought the divine mercy in behalf of "de po' sinnahs, a-rollin' an' a-tossin' in de tempes' of dere sins." "Lawd," he prayed, "come down dis evenin' in Sperit's powah to seek an' to save-ah; let us heah de rumblin' of yo' cha'iot wheels-ah lak de thundah f'om Mount Sinai-ah; oh, Lawd-ah, convert mou'nahs an' convict sinnahs-ah; show 'em dat dey mus' die an' cain't lib an' atter death to judg-a-ment; tu'n 'em aroun' befo' it is evahlastin' an' eternally too late." Then, warming more and more, and swaying his form back and forth, as he pounded the seat in emphasis, he began to wail out in a sort of indescribable monotone: "O Lawd, save de mou'nah!"

"Save de mou'nah!" came the response from all over the church.

"He'p 'em out of de miah an' quicksan's of dere sins!"

"He'p, Lawd!"

"And place deir feet upon de evahlastin' an' eternal rock-ah!"

"Do, Lawd."

"O Lawd-ah, shake a dyin' sinnah ovah hell an' fo'bid his mighty fall-ah!"

"O Lawd, shake 'em!" came from the congregation.

By this time everyone was worked up to a high state of excitement, and the prayer came to an end amid great commotion. Then a rich, mellow voice led out with:

> "Sabe de mou'nah jes' now,
> Sabe de mou'nah jes' now,
> Sabe de mou'nah jes' now,
> Only trust Him jes' now,
> Only trust Him jes' now,
> He'p de sinnah jes' now;"

and so to indefinite length the mournful minor melody ran along like a sad brook flowing through autumn woods, trying to laugh and ripple through tears.

Every now and then some mourner would spring half up, with a shriek, and then sink down again trembling and jerking spasmodically. "He's a-doubtin', he's a-doubtin'!" the cry would fly around; "but I tell you he purt' nigh had it that time."

Finally the slender form of Anner 'Lizer began to sway backward and forward, like a sapling in the wind, and she began to mourn and weep aloud.

"Praise de Lawd!" shouted Aunt Hannah, "de po' soul's gittin' de evidence: keep on, honey, de Lawd ain't fa' off." The sudden change attracted considerable attention, and in a moment a dozen or more zealous altar-workers gathered around Anner 'Lizer and began to clap and sing with all their might, keeping time to the melodious cadence of their music with heavy foot-pats on the resounding floor.

> "Git on boa'd-ah, little childering,
> Git on boa'd-ah, little childering,
> Git on boa'd-ah, little childering,
>   Dere's room fo' many mo'.
>
> "De gospel ship is sailin',
> It's loaded down wid souls.
> If you want to mek heab'n yo' happy home,
> You mus' ketch it fo' it goes.
>   Git on boa'd, etc.
>
> "King Jesus at de hellum,
> Fu' to guide de ship erright.
> We gwine fu' to put into heab'n's po't
> Wid ouah sails all shinin' white.
>   Git on boa'd," etc.

With a long dwell on the last word of the chorus, the mellow cadence of the song died away.

"Let us bow down fu' a season of silent praar," said the minister.

"Lawd, he'p us to pray," responded Uncle Eben Adams.

The silence that ensued was continually broken by the wavering wail of the mourners. Suddenly one of them, a stalwart young man, near the opening of the aisle, began to writhe and twist himself into every possible contortion, crying, "O Lawd, de devil's a-ridin' me; tek him off—tek him off!"

"Tek him off, Lawd!" shouted the congregation.

Then suddenly, without warning, the mourner rose straight up into the air, shouting, "Hallelujah, hallelujah, hallelujah!"

"He's got it—he's got it!" cried a dozen eager worshipers, leaping to their feet and crowding around the happy convert; "bless de Lawd, he's got it." A voice was raised, and soon the church was ringing with

> "Loose him and let him go,
> Let him shout to glory."

On went the man, shouting "Hallelujah," shaking hands, and bounding over seats in the ecstasy of his bliss.

His conversion kindled the flame of the meeting and set the fire going. You have seen corn in the popper when the first kernel springs up and flares open, how quickly the rest follow, keeping up the steady pop, pop, pop; well, just so it was after this first conversion. The mourners popped up quickly and steadily as the strength of the spiritual fire seemed to reach their swelling souls. One by one they left the bench on which, figuratively speaking, they may be said to have laid down their sins and proclaimed themselves possessors of religion; until, finally, there was but one left, and that one—Anner 'Lizer. She had ceased from her violent activity, and seemed perfectly passive now.

The efforts of all were soon concentrated on her, and such stamping and clapping and singing was never heard before. Such cries of "Jes' look up, sistah, don't you see Him at yo' side? Jes' reach out yo' han' an' tech de hem of His ga'ment. Jes' listen, sistah, don't you heah de angels singin'? Don't you heah de rumblin' of de cha'iot wheels? He's a-comin', He's a-comin, He's a-comin'!"

But Anner 'Lizer was immovable; with her face lying against the hard bench, she moaned and prayed softly to herself. The congregation redoubled its exertions, but all to no effect; Anner 'Lizer wouldn't "come thoo."

It was a strange case.

Aunt Maria whispered to her bosom friend: "You min' me, Sistah Hannah, dere's sump'n' on dat gal's min'." And Aunt Hannah answered, "I believe you."

Josephine, or more commonly Phiny, a former belle whom Anner 'Lizer's superior charms had deposed, could not lose this opportunity to have a fling at her successful rival. Of course such cases of vindictiveness in women are rare, and Phiny was exceptional when she whispered to her fellow-servant, Lucy: "I reckon she'd git 'ligion if Sam Me'itt was heah to see her." Lucy snickered, as in duty bound, and whispered back, "I wisht you'd heish."

Well, after all their singing, in spite of all their efforts, the time came for closing the meeting, and Anner 'Lizer had not yet made a profession.

She was lifted tenderly up from the mourners' bench by a couple of solicitous sisters, and, after listening to the preacher's exhortation to "pray constantly, thoo de day an' thoo de night, in de highways an' de byways an' in yo' secret closet," she went home praying in her soul, leaving the rest of the congregation to loiter along the way and gossip over the night's events.

All the next day Anner 'Lizer, erstwhile so cheerful, went about her work sad and silent, every now and then stopping in the midst of her labors and burying her face in her heat white apron to sob violently. It was true, as Aunt Hannah expressed, that "de Sperit had sholy tuk holt of dat gal wid a powahful han'."

All of her fellow-servants knew that she was a mourner, and, with that characteristic reverence for religion which is common to all their race, and not lacking even in the most hardened sinner among them, they respected her feelings. Phiny alone, when she met her, tossed her head and giggled openly. But Phiny's actions never troubled Anner 'Lizer, for she felt herself so far above her. Once though, in the course of the day, she had been somewhat disturbed, when she had suddenly come upon her rival, standing in the spring-house talking and laughing with Sam. She noticed, too, with a pang, that Phiny had tied a bow of red ribbon on her hair. She shut her lips and only prayed the harder. But an hour later, somehow, a ribbon as red as Phiny's had miraculously attached itself to her thick black plaits. Was the temporal creeping in with the spiritual in Anner 'Lizer's mind? Who can tell? Perhaps she thought that, while cultivating the one, she need not utterly neglect the other; and who says but that she was right?

Uncle Eben, however, did not take this view of the matter when he came hobbling up in the afternoon to exhort her a little. He found Anner 'Lizer in the kitchen washing dishes. Engrossed in the contemplation of her spiritual state, or praying for deliverance from the same, through the whole day she had gone about without speaking to anyone. But with Uncle Eben it was, of course, different, for he was a man held in high respect by all the Negroes and, next to the minister, the greatest oracle in those parts; so Anner 'Lizer spoke to him.

"Howdy, Uncl' Eben," she said, in a lugubrious tone, as the old man hobbled in and settled down in a convenient corner.

"Howdy, honey, howdy," he replied, crossing one leg over the other, as he unwound his long bandanna, placed it in his hat, and then deposited his heavy cane on the white floor. "I jes' thought I'd drap in to ax you how do you do today?"

"Po' enough, Uncl' Eben, fu' sho.'"

"Ain't foun' no res' fu' yo' soul yit?"

"No res yit," answered Anner 'Lizer, again applying the apron to her already swollen eyes.

"Um-m," sighed the old man, meditatively tapping his foot; and then the gay flash of Anner 'Lizer's ribbon caught his eye and he gasped: "Bless de Lawd, Sis 'Lizer; you don't mean to tell me dat you's gwine 'bout heah seekin' wid yo' har tied up in ribbon? Whut! tek it off, honey, tek if off; ef yo' wants yo' soul saved, tek it off!"

Anner 'Lizer hesitated, and raised her eyes in momentary protest, but they met the horrified gaze of the old man, and she lowered them again as her hand went reluctantly up to her head to remove the offending bit of finery.

"You see, honey," Uncle Eben went on, "when you sta'ts out on de Christian jou'ney, you's got to lay aside ev'ry weight dat doth so easy beset you an' keeps you fom pergressin'; y' ain't got to think nothin' 'bout pussunal 'dornment; you's jes' got to shet yo' eyes an' open yo' hea't an' say, Lawd, come; you mustn't wait fu' to go to chu'ch to pray, nuther, you mus' pray anywhar an' ev'ry whar. Why, when I was seekin', I ust to go 'way off up in de big woods to pray, an' dere's whar de Lawd answered me, an' I'm a-rejoicin' today in de powah of de same salvation. Honey, you's got to pray, I tell you. You's got to brek de backbone of yo' pride an' pray in earnes'; an' ef you does dat, you'll git he'p, fu' de Lawd is a praar-heahin' Lawd an' plenteous in mussy."

Anner 'Lizer listened attentively to the exhortation and evidently profited by it, for soon after Uncle Eben's departure she changed her natty little dress for one less pretentious, and her dainty, frilled white muslin apron gave way to a broad dark calico one. If grace was to be found by self-abnegation in the matter of dress, Anner 'Lizer was bound to have it at any price.

As afternoon waned and night came on, she grew more and more serious, and more frequent recourse was had to the corner of her apron. She even failed to see Phiny when that enterprising young person passed her, decked out in the whitest of white cuffs and

collars setting off in pleasant contrast her neat dark dress. Phiny giggled again and put up her hand, ostensibly to brush some imaginary
dust from her bosom but really to show her pretty white cuffs with
their big bone buttons. But it was all lost on Anner 'Lizer; her gaze
was downcast and her thoughts far away. If anyone was ever "seekin'
" in earnest, this girl was.

Night came, and with it the usual services. Anner 'Lizer was one
of the earliest of the congregation to arrive, and she went immediately to the mourners' bench. In the language of the congregation,
"Eldah Johnsing sholy did preach a powahful sermon" that night.
More sinners were convicted and brought to their knees, and, as before, these recruits were converted and Anner 'Lizer left. What was
the matter?

That was the question which everyone asked, but there were
none found who could answer it. The circumstance was all the more
astounding from the fact that this unsuccessful mourner had not
been a very wicked girl. Indeed, it was to have been expected that
she might shake her sins from her shoulders as she would discard a
mantle, and step over on the Lord's side. But it was not so.

But when a third night came and passed with the same result, it
became the talk of three plantations. To be sure, cases were not
lacking where people had "mourned" a week, two weeks, or even a
month; but they were woeful sinners and those were times of less
spiritual interest; but under circumstances so favorable as were now
presented, that one could long refrain from "gittin' religion" was the
wonder of all. So, after the third night, everybody wondered and
talked, and not a few began to lean to Phiny's explanation, that "de
ole snek in de grass had been a'goin' on doin' all her dev'ment on de
sly, so's *people* wouldn't know it; but de *Lawd* he did, an' he payin'
her up fu' it now."

Sam Merritt alone did not talk, and seemed perfectly indifferent
to all that was said. When he was in Phiny's company and she rallied him about the actions of his "gal," he remained silent.

On the fourth night of Anner 'Lizer's mourning, the congregation
gathered as usual at the church. For the first half-hour all went on
as usual, and the fact that Anner 'Lizer was absent caused no remark,
for everyone thought she would come in later. But time passed and
she did not come. "Eldah Johnsing's" flock became agitated. Of
course there were other mourners, but the one particular one was
absent; hence the dissatisfaction. Every head in the house was turned
toward the door, whenever it was opened by some late comer; and
around flew the whisper, "I wunner ef she's quit mou'nin'; you aint'
heerd of her gittin' 'ligion, have you?" No one had.

Meanwhile the object of their solicitude was praying just the same, but in a far different place. Grasping, as she was, at everything that seemed to give her promise of relief, somehow Uncle Eben's words had had a deep effect upon her. So, when night fell and her work was over, she had gone up into the woods to pray. She had prayed long without success, and now she was crying aloud from the very fullness of her heart, "O Lawd, sen' de light—sen' de light!" Suddenly, as if in answer to her prayer, a light appeared before her some distance away.

The sudden attainment of one's desires often shocks one; so with our mourner. For a moment her heart stood still and the thought came to her to flee, but her mind flashed back over the words of one of the hymns she had heard down at church, "Let us walk in de light," and she knew that before she walked in the light she must walk toward it. So she rose and started in the direction of the light. How it flickered and flared, disappeared and reappeared, rose and fell, even as her spirits, as she stumbled and groped her way over fallen logs and through briers! Her limbs were bruised and her dress torn by the thorns. But she heeded it not; she had fixed her eye— physical and spiritual—on the light before her. It drew her with an irresistible fascination. Suddenly she stopped. An idea had occurred to her. Maybe this light was a Jack-o'-lantern! For a moment she hesitated, then promptly turned her pocket wrong side out, murmuring, "De Lawd'll tek keer o' me." On she started; but lo! the light had disappeared! What! had the turning of the pocket indeed worked so potent a charm?

But no! it reappeared as she got beyond the intervention of a brush pile which had obscured it. The light grew brighter as she grew fainter; but she clasped her hands and raised her eyes in un- wavering faith, for she found that the beacon did not recede, but glowed with a steady and stationary flame.

As she drew near, the sound of sharp strokes came to her ears, and she wondered. Then, as she slipped into the narrow circle of light, she saw that it was made by a taper which was set on a log. The strokes came from a man who was chopping down a tree in which a 'coon seemed to have taken refuge. It needed no second glance at the stalwart shoulders to tell her that the man was—Sam. Her step attracted his attention, and he turned.

"Sam!"

"Anner 'Lizer!"

And then they both stood still, too amazed to speak. Finally she walked across to where he was standing, and said: "Sam, I didn't come out heah to fin' you, but de Lawd has 'p'inted it so, 'ca'se he knowed I orter speak to you." Sam leaned hopelessly on his ax; he thought she was going to exhort him.

Anner 'Lizer went on: "Sam, you's my stumblin' block in de high-road to salvation. I's been tryin' to git 'ligion fu' fo' nights, an' I cain't do it jes' on you' 'count. I prays an' I prays, an' jes as I's a'mos' got it, jes as I begin to heah de cha'iot wheels a-rollin', yo' face comes right in 'tween an' drives it all away. Tell me now, Sam, so's to put me out of my 'spense, does you want to ma'y me, er is you goin' to ma'y Phiny? I jes' wants you to tell me, not dat I keers pussonally, but so's my min' kin be at res' spi'tu'lly, an' I kin git 'ligion. Jes' say yes er no; I wants to be settled one way er t' other."

"Anner 'Lizer," said Sam, reproachfully, "you know I wants to ma'y you jes' ez soon ez Mas' Rob'll let me."

"Dere now," said Anner 'Lizer, "bless de Lawd!" And somehow Sam had dropped the ax and was holding her in his arms.

It boots not whether the 'coon was caught that night or not, but it is a fact that Anner 'Lizer set the whole place afire by getting religion at home early the next morning. And the same night the minister announced that "de Lawd had foun' out de sistah's stumblin' block an' removed it f'om de path."

PART 4

The New Negro Renaissance and Beyond: 1910–1954

THE POLITICAL COMPROMISE that in 1877 brought an end to Reconstruction and led to the complete disfranchisement of the blacks in the South had consequences which, by 1908, extended far beyond the sphere of politics. It had cultural and psychological effects such as those epitomized in the life and works of Booker T. Washington, whose tremendous influence on racial thought helped to impose on millions of blacks the life-style and character image which the majority of whites judged to be not only acceptable but true.

And this white acceptance had literary consequences. It fixed the respectability of the "darky rhymes," "coon songs," and "nigger dialect" of the minstrel tradition. As long as black writers followed this tradition, they were certain of the approval of a white audience. Whites were amused and their racial beliefs were confirmed by the works of Paul Laurence Dunbar, James Edwin Campbell, and Daniel Webster Davis, and by such Negro theatrical productions as "A Trip to Coontown," "Bandanna Land," and "Clorindy—The Origin of the Cakewalk." These works, which were all written and staged between 1898 and 1903, were taken as positive proof of the African American's inherent inferiority; and his inferiority justified the treatment accorded him in ordinary rounds of civil life.

But there were some blacks who refused to accept the minstrel tradition, who rebelled against the idea of racial inferiority, and who were outraged by the accommodationist doctrine of Booker Washington. Because most blacks were illiterate and unaware of attitudes and opinions around them, these rebels were few in number. Their spokesman did not make himself heard until 1903, when the minstrel tradition already seemed indestructible.

With the publication of W. E. B. Du Bois's *The Souls of Black Folk*, another concept of black character and ethos struggled toward a viable existence. Du Bois's book was a potpourri of history and fantasy, fiction and autobiography, prophecy and scholarly perception. But an unmistakable integrity of purpose gave it the unity of a single statement of protest such as no black writer had ever made. Prophetically he stated, "The problem of the twentieth century is the problem of the color line." Although *The Souls of Black Folk* may now seem reasonable and temperate, it was severely criticized, particularly in the South. The *Atlanta Constitution* castigated it. The *Nashville Banner* declared, "This book is dangerous for the negro to read, for it will only excite discontent and fill his imagination with things that do not exist, or things that should not bear upon his mind."

The book did just that. James Weldon Johnson, who himself had contributed his share of coon songs and dialect poetry to the minstrel tradition, said that *The Souls of Black Folk* had "a greater effect upon and within the Negro race in America than any other single book published in this country since *Uncle Tom's Cabin*."

Du Bois had told the truth. If the telling caused sharp criticism and rejection by whites, this criticism of *The Souls of Black Folk* was mild when compared to that generated by the "Resolution" which Du Bois composed for the Niagara Movement two years later.

The Souls of Black Folk and the "Resolution" set the tone and suggested the themes that were to preoccupy most African American literature for nearly two decades. Although black authors were not very productive during this time, the writing they did was principally propaganda and protest. It appeared in the pages of *The Crisis*—the NAACP's official organ—and in those weekly black newspapers (the *Boston Guardian*, the *Chicago Defender*, the *Baltimore Afro-American*) which Booker Washington had not seduced, bribed, or threatened into silence on all aspects of the race question.

But these periodicals gave space to imaginative writing, too, and not all of it concerned social issues. Poetry by William Stanley Braithwaite occasionally appeared in *The Crisis*, as did the short fiction and essays of Effie Lee Newsome and, with increasing frequency, the verse of Jessie Fauset. Fenton Johnson published in the *Chicago Defender*, and the work of several writers of lesser talent cropped up in other weekly newspapers whose "literary" standards were more flexible than those set by Du Bois for publication in *The Crisis*. Indeed, these newspapers were the only outlets available to black writers, particularly the angry ones, and although most black writers certainly wanted to attract a white audience, few succeeded.

Because the white audience was the paying audience, and because the measure of success for any black endeavor was the degree of white attention or approval it attracted, it is not surprising that some imaginative black writers avoided racial themes and sought publication simply as "artists." The minstrel tradition was scorned by the blacks who wrote, and whites ignored black protest. Besides, unlike other protest, black protest had already accumulated those connotations that reduced such writing to a level below the creative, a level where black folk art—including folk tales, spirituals, blues, and jazz—was also relegated. Folk art was considered an element of the "low culture," as distinct from the "high culture" of white middle-class America. Some black writers tried to overcome this situation by meeting the standards of craft and of "universality" that the white audience seemed to demand of its own creative artists. No one of the black writers who tried was a complete failure. No one of them, either, was an unqualified success.

William Braithwaite did earn a reputation as a critic. From 1913 to 1928 he annually published anthologies of magazine verse, which were the gleanings from white periodicals and demonstrated his critical sensibilities and perceptions. But Braithwaite's poetry, avoiding all consciousness of race, is strained. The poetry of James Weldon Johnson, who also strove for universality, is mediocre at best, but his innocuous, sentimental nonblack poems achieved publication in such white magazines as *Century* and *Outlook*.

It can be said that the black women poets who eschewed racial themes were generally better poets than the men. Most were middle-class housewives, and their men—husbands, fathers, brothers, and friends—sheltered them from the grosser realities of black life. The facts of wife- and motherhood were "universal" experiences upon which these poets could draw, and which excused them for avoiding the theme of protest. Their poetry was no better and no worse than that of most of their white female contemporaries.

This coterie of "raceless" writers represent Du Bois's "talented tenth" of Negroes who "through their knowledge of modern culture . . . could guide the American Negro into a higher civilization." Du Bois's earlier promotion of this idea had earned him the reputation of being class- and color-conscious, of being concerned only for the interest of the small "dickty" middle class of blacks. But by 1910 the idea of a "talented tenth" no longer seemed defensible or viable even to some members of the talented tenth. Other attitudes were developing.

James Weldon Johnson published *The Autobiography of An Ex-Coloured Man* in 1912, and the novel showed changes from Charles Chesnutt's tragic mulatto theme: to all appearances the protagonist is white, but the representation of his weaknesses contradicts the racial myth implicit in Chesnutt's thesis and denies the notion that more white blood makes a better and stronger person. Five years later came Johnson's *Fifty Years and Other Poems*, a revelation of true black consciousness. Even its strongest pieces are mild in comparison with today's black poetry, but they are never conciliatory or pleading.

At about the same time Fenton Johnson (no relation to James Weldon) published *Visions of the Dusk* (1915) and *Songs of the Soil* (1916). Influenced by the Chicago School, *Visions* helped free black poets from their enslavement to conventional verse forms and showed them that sophisticated poetry could deal realistically, and on a fairly high level, with the degradation and disillusionment of the typical African American's urban life. Ballads and the blues, of course, also dealt with these matters, but these modes of expression were folk in origin, idiom, and theme. Stripped of all sentiment, the realism and cynicism of the ballads and the blues spoke only to blacks, as did the earliest jazz; and like jazz, ballads and blues did not begin to enter the mainstream of American culture until the end of the second decade of the twentieth century.

But at that time many changes took place. With the First World War in its second year, the flow of European immigrant labor was suddenly cut off, and the industrial North was faced with a manpower shortage. It turned south for replenishment. Blacks were eager to go north and escape poverty, peonage, and lynching. Two million fled the South in less than four years. They crowded into the industrial cities of the North and Midwest, and the density of black ghettos increased twenty- and thirty-fold. Unaccustomed to urban living, to weekly wages that amounted to more than most had previously made in a year, and to the restricted freedom of the North, these blacks created problems and protested the absence of solutions. When black men were drafted, they protested discrimination and segregation in training camps. Overseas, where some were sent as combat troops (but most as stevedores and food handlers), their experiences with the French gave them a notion of what equality was. They liked it. As Alain Locke, one of the most perceptive observers, said, when the war ended "America had to reckon with a fundamentally changed Negro, a new Negro." This new African American tended to react defiantly. Cursed, he cursed back. Struck, he struck back. A dozen race riots in the "red summer" of 1919 proved his new mettle.

Defiance, then, was the new temper. It was also the organizing mode of Marcus Garvey's Universal Negro Improvement Association. Under such slogans as "A Place in the Sun" and "Back to Africa," Garvey marshalled thousands of lower-class urban blacks. His newspaper, The Negro World, inspired his followers with fiery editorials on black nationalism, with slanted news, and with stories—sometimes mythic and apocryphal, but often true— of black peoples' contributions to world culture. In 1922 Garvey claimed for UNIA a worldwide membership of four million.

Defiance was also the temper of more sophisticated publications for more sophisticated blacks. Du Bois's The Crisis editorials constantly challenged the vagaries of the white man's concept of democracy and how it should work. A. Philip Randolph's editorials in The Messenger, the magazine which he founded just after the war, were cited as "dangerous to the comfort and security" of white people. The Messenger, a congressman from South Carolina declared, "is antagonistic to the United States. . . . It pays tribute to [Eugene] Debs and every other convicted enemy of the Government."

But perhaps no expression of the new spirit had such impact as a poem entitled "If We Must Die." Written by Claude McKay, the poem was first published in *The Liberator*, which, unlike the magazines cited previously, was edited by whites for whites.

A complex of forces seemed suddenly to arouse a tremendous interest in black people and black life. If whites were caught up in this interest, they also contributed to it. The dramatists Eugene O'Neill, Ridgely Torrence, and Paul Green wrote plays about black life. White novelists, including Sherwood Anderson, Waldo Frank, Carl Van Vechten, and DuBose Heyward, produced fiction in which the major characters were black. Jazz music and the dances it inspired, the blues (called "torch songs" by white singers like Ruth Etting and Helen Morgan), and basic black ballads at last emerged from underground black life. John Charles Thomas and Ada May, Irene and Vernon Castle, Ziegfeld and his imitators were suddenly old hat. The sentimental plays, the melodramas, and the romantic musical shows gradually yielded to new modes and to a mood, generated by blacks, that was at once romantic and realistic, sentimental and cynical, abrasive and bland, profound and superficial, humorous and sad. And perhaps, above all, it was primitive.

The mood was primitive in what it expressed and often in the manner of expression. It was primitive in the sense of stripping experience—the experience of blackness as interpreted by black poets and novelists, essayists and editors, singers and composers—down to the quivering marrow of emotional content, psychological relevance, and racial insight. Black writers and artists wanted to make clear the meaning of being black in America. They were no longer afraid or ashamed. Indeed, black writers took an arrogant pride in their blackness. They flaunted it. They stood naked before whites and—sometimes in anger, sometimes in scorn, sometimes in satirical amusement—said, "Look at me! It will help you the better to see and know yourself."

Of course all the writers of the New Negro Renaissance did not have the same quality or kind of talent, nor were they all committed in the same degree to revelation. Some had great talent and versatility, and perhaps first among these was Langston Hughes. But Jean Toomer and, at their best, Claude McKay, Countee Cullen, Arna Bontemps, Sterling Brown, Nella Larsen, and Zora Hurston were of top rank. Most writers, however, were merely competent, and—like Wallace Thurman, George Schuyler (who wrote *Black No More*, the only sustained satirical novel by a black), Eric Walrond, Frank Marshall Davis, Rudolph Fisher, and Walter White—rode the great wave of popularity until it waned. Black critics showed a constant development from the formal pedantry of Benjamin Brawley to the cultural insights of Alain Locke to the sensitive understanding of Sterling Brown.

The Renaissance lacked a notable dramatist. Although many plays were written during the period, especially one-act dramas, few were produced. Garland Anderson's *Appearances* had a brief Broadway run, as did Hall Johnson's *Run, Little Chillun*; Wallace Thurman's *Harlem* (done in collaboration with William Rapp) was a Broadway success, and Angelina Grimké's *Rachel*, which was written in 1916, published in 1920, was among the first black plays to have professional production. By and large, however, during the Renaissance black drama was the weakest of the disciplines, and this is understandable. Up to that period, and beyond, blacks had little access to the legitimate theater (in the South not even as spectators) and therefore were not able to experience the kind of apprenticeship necessary to produce professional playwrights. It could be said that prior to the Renaissance blacks had practically no *significant* theater tradition. Few as they were, the Renaissance efforts showed signs of a new birth of interest in this field.

Several forces acted to produce this change. The little theater movement of the 1920s brought forth a new interest in folk plays and found white dramatists like Ridgely Torrence, Paul Green, Eugene O'Neill, and others using black characters in their plays. Black dramatists were influenced by the works of these men and by the little theater movement itself. A second influence was that of the *Crisis-Opportunity* literary contests of the period. These projects encouraged budding dramatists to write and in many cases led to publication of their best work. For instance, in 1927 Alain Locke and Montgomery Gregory edited *Plays of Negro Life*, a volume which contained twenty one-act offerings, ten by white writers, ten by black; among the latter, four were *Opportunity* prize plays.

Locke and Gregory's anthology was not the only collection of plays the period produced. In 1930 Willis Richardson, a Washington, D.C., postal worker, published *Plays and Pageants from the Life of the Negro* and in 1935, collaborating with May Miller, brought out *Negro History in Thirteen Plays*. Carter G. Woodson authenticated the historical data involved in the latter work. A competent dramatist as well as editor, Willis Richardson, though not as well known as others, contributed a great deal to New Negro drama.

The most versatile, the most experimental, and probably the outstanding dramatist of the Renaissance years, Langston Hughes made a great contribution to black drama, not only through his many well-known plays—folk and "social" dramas—but also through his establishment of people's theaters like the Suitcase Theatre in Harlem, the Negro Art Theatre of Los Angeles, and the Skyloft Players in Chicago. Hughes gave black drama a shot in the arm when it needed it most.

Another boost to Renaissance drama came from black colleges. Reflecting the new interest in little theater, many of these schools organized drama clubs and gave plays on their respective campuses. They also encouraged the writing of plays, particularly folk plays of black life. Randolph Edmonds played an important role in this college dramatic upsurge. During the Renaissance, Edmonds, then at Morgan College in Baltimore (now Morgan State University), was the prime mover in organizing the first Negro Intercollegiate Drama Association (NIDA). The association consisted originally of five colleges: Morgan, Howard, Virginia Union, Virginia State, and Hampton. Other schools have since been added and other associations formed.

Though the New Negro Renaissance produced no outstanding dramatic work, it did rejuvenate the black theater and prepared blacks for the opportunities they now have in the American theater as actors and playwrights.

The great outpouring of serious creative effort during the twenties did not attract a sizable black audience or patronage, and most blacks were ignorant of the novels, the poems, the plays, the essays. The measure of success for black artists and writers was still the degree of white interest and approval. The New Negro Renaissance was sustained by a white audience, and white entrepreneurs reaped the rewards. While race and racial experiences were (and are) the most compelling forces for the serious black artists, most of the white audience was looking for entertainment. "Fast-buck boys," mostly white, made a mockery of black artists' efforts to project their unhappy truths. The fast-buck boys made Harlem, which Carl Van Vechten called "nigger heaven," the mecca of the exotic, the savage, and the strange. The fad for things black soon began to die: by 1928 the end was in sight. Publishers no longer competed for black manuscripts. Black writers, including Hughes, McKay, Cullen, and Toomer, began to desert Harlem for Paris, Rome, Moscow, Lagos, Havana, and the all-black town Eatonville, Florida. The Great Depression brought the absolute end, and for the next ten years scarcely a black voice was heard above a whisper.

The Depression, however, provided a valuable apprentice period for a group of young writers who were employed on projects of the WPA and many of whom came under the watchful eye of the teacher-critic Sterling Brown, who served as a project director. Among these young black men were Frank Yerby, Willard Motley, Richard Wright, and Ralph Ellison. Yerby and Motley soon renounced the black consciousness. After the publication of *The Foxes of Harrow*, Yerby could no longer be called a black writer. Motley, who died in 1966, was not a black writer either, although there is at least one sketchily drawn black character in both *Knock on Any Door* and *We Fished All Night*.

When Richard Wright's four novellas, collectively called *Uncle Tom's Children* (1938), were followed by *Native Son* (1940), readers knew that a powerful talent had found itself. The stories in the first book showed promise; the novel fulfilled that promise. Although *Native Son* had social importance, its skillful structure, characterization, dramatic intensity, and subtly woven threads of symbolism made it a novel to be reckoned with aesthetically. As both a novel and a "social document," *Native Son* was by far the best work done by a black writer up to that time.

In 1946 Wright moved permanently to Paris, where he was no longer faced with the everyday reality of his blackness. But his departure did not leave the world of American black letters altogether impoverished. Ann Petry published her first novel, *The Street*, which was soon followed by *Country Place*. Dorothy West's *The Living Is Easy* appeared in 1948, three years prior to Owen Dodson's *Boy at the Window*. After the publication of *Native Son*, no truly major black novel appeared until Ralph Ellison's *Invisible Man* was published in 1952. Although it had taken seven years to write, it showed itself to be not a labored work but the work of a consummate artist. Ellison is also a brilliant critic and personal essayist. *Shadow and Act* (1964) is proof of it. James Baldwin published brilliant essays, and *Go Tell It on the Mountain*, his first and best novel, came out in 1953. There were poets, too, three of them of top rank. Margaret Walker was awarded the Yale Younger Poet's Prize for *For My People*. Gwendolyn Brooks won the Pulitzer Prize for her second volume, *Annie Allen* (1949). And Robert Hayden, before his untimely death in 1980, was becoming recognized as a major poet. Among his many honors was the Grand Prize for Poetry at the First World African Festival of Arts held in Dakar. Hayden was appointed consultant in poetry to the Library of Congress for an unprecedented two terms, 1976–78.

Until recently, criticism has been one of the weaker areas in black American literature. This is understandable because literature has to reach a certain maturity before criticism can flourish. We are reaching that maturity, and as a consequence there has been an upsurge in that field (see volume 2, introductions). Up to roughly the sixties, however, a small number of scholars kept alive the weak but continuing line of criticism which may be said to begin with William Stanley Braithwaite, the first professional black critic, and which moved through New Negro critics like Du Bois and James Weldon Johnson on to Alain Locke and Benjamin Brawley. The last-named two were teacher-critics, men who stayed in the classroom but whose influence extended beyond the walls of their respective schools.

Several of the *older* critics found in this section follow the teacher-critic tradition established by Locke and Brawley. These and others in this tradition, given in alphabetical order, along with representative publications are Sterling A. Brown (*The Negro in American Fiction; Negro Poetry and Drama*), Philip Butcher (*George Washington Cable*), Arthur P. Davis (*From the Dark Tower*), William Edward Farrison (*William Wells Brown, Author and Reformer*), Nick Aaron Ford (*The Contemporary Negro Novel*), Hugh M. Gloster (*Negro Voices in American Fiction*), Blyden Jackson (*The Waiting Years*), Therman B. O'Daniel (*Langston Hughes: Black Genius, An Evaluation*), and J. Saunders Redding (*To Make a Poet Black*). Without exception these teacher-critics were "integrationist" in their training and in their aesthetic beliefs. They had but one aim in mind: to direct their students and readers to the mainstream.

One thing seems perfectly clear about black writing in the period from 1910 to mid-century, and that is its steady development in two directions: from propaganda and the literature of knowledge toward artistry and the literature of power; and from the concept of the African American as a sort of imitation white man toward the concept of the Negro as a black man whose experiences are not simply a variety of sociological constructions.

W. E. B. Du Bois

(1868–1963)

AMONG THE BLACK INTELLECTUAL leaders and social activists of the first six decades of the present century, William Edward Burghardt Du Bois was by far the most distinguished and the most influential. Brilliant, highly educated, creative, a dedicated man of vision, Du Bois anticipated the New Negro Renaissance, was the driving force in the founding of the NAACP, was an early Pan-Africanist, prepared the ground for the black revolution of the sixties and edited for many years *The Crisis*, one of America's most effective protest periodicals. History will find this authentic American radical one of the great figures of this age.

Born in Great Barrington, Massachusetts, of mixed Dutch, French, and African ancestry, Du Bois was educated in that city's high school; at Fisk University, taking there his first A.B. degree; at Harvard, receiving there his second A.B. (cum laude) in 1890 and his M.A. in 1891; at the University of Berlin, where he studied for two years; and again at Harvard, taking there his Ph.D. in 1895—he was the first American black to receive the doctorate from that great school. His dissertation, *The Suppression of the African Slave Trade, 1638–1870,* became the first volume issued in the Harvard Historical Studies series.

A highlight résumé of Du Bois's career shows him first a teacher at Wilberforce University, subsequently the director of a study of the Philadelphia Negro, a professor at the original Atlanta University, secretary of the Pan-African Conference in London (1900), founder of the Niagara Movement in 1905, editor-founder of *Moon* magazine, chief founder of the newspaper *Horizon*, editor of *The Crisis* (1910–1934), editor-founder of the *Brownies' Book* (1920–1921), investigator in 1919 for the NAACP of the treatment of Negro troops in Europe, chief organizer of the First Pan-African Congress in Paris (1919), also of the second, third, and fourth. In 1934 he left *The Crisis* and returned to Atlanta University; he consulted for the NAACP at the founding of the United Nations, joined the Communist party (1961), and in 1963 became a citizen of Ghana, where he died the same year.

A prolific writer, Dr. Du Bois published the following major works: *The Philadelphia Negro* (1899); *The Souls of Black Folks* (1903), perhaps his greatest literary work; *Darkwater: Voices from within the Veil* (1920); *Black Folks, Then and Now* (1939); *Black Reconstruction* (1935); *Dusk of Dawn* (1940, 1975), his best autobiographical work; and *The World and*

Africa (1947, 1965, 1976). He published five novels: *The Quest of the Silver Fleece* (1911), *Dark Princess* (1928), and *The Black Flame: A Trilogy*, consisting of *The Ordeal of Mansart, Mansart Builds a School*, and *Worlds of Color* (1957–61). Du Bois was not a great novelist. His basic themes in this fiction—the economics of the cotton South, the unification of the darker races, or the evolution of an African American family—are more important than the craftsmanship used to present the themes.

W. E. B. Du Bois grew and changed with the years; he was often far ahead of his own generation in the stands he took. Beginning as the exponent of the undemocratic, middle-class "talented tenth" theory, he ended his life as an expatriate and a communist. "He was a man, take him for all in all" as Hamlet said of his father.

For comment on Du Bois's life, works, and place in history, see the full and authoritative article on him in *Dictionary of American Negro Biography*, written jointly by Rayford W. Logan and Michael R. Winston. This entry is valuable not only for the in-depth information it provides but also for the bibliography and leads it provides for the many different aspects of Du Bois's complex career. See also *W. E. B. Du Bois: A Profile* (1971), edited by Rayford W. Logan; *Critical Essays on W. E. B. Du Bois* (1985), edited by William L. Andrews; *W. E. B. Du Bois, Black Radical Democrat* by Manning Marable (1986); and Arnold Rampersad's *The Art and Imagination of W. E. B. Du Bois* (1976). Du Bois is one of several major twentieth-century writers whose impact upon the development of an African-American "sound" or "voice" is examined by Houston A. Baker, Jr., in his *Modernism and the Harlem Renaissance* (1987). Insight into the mind of Du Bois is found in Herbert Aptheker's many editions of the published correspondence and collected works of Du Bois.

The following selections come from *Dusk of Dawn* and *The Autobiography of W. E. B. Du Bois*.

A NEW ENGLAND BOY AND RECONSTRUCTION

As I have written elsewhere, "I was born by a golden river and in the shadow of two great hills." My birthplace was Great Barrington, a little town in western Massachusetts in the valley of the Housatonic, flanked by the Berkshire hills. Physically and socially our community belonged to the Dutch valley of the Hudson rather than to Puritan New England, and travel went south to New York more often

From W. E. B. Du Bois, *Dusk of Dawn*. New York: Harcourt, Brace, 1940, pp. 8–24. Reprint: Millwood, N.Y., Kraus-Thomson Organization Limited, 1974. Reproduced with permission of The Kraus Organization Limited.

and more easily than east to Boston. But my birthplace was less important than my birth-time. The Civil War had closed but three years earlier, and 1868 was the year in which the freedmen of the South were enfranchised and for the first time as a mass took part in government. Conventions with black delegates voted new constitutions all over the South; and two groups of laborers—freed slaves and poor whites—dominated the former slave states. It was an extraordinary experiment in democracy. Thaddeus Stevens, the clearest-headed leader of this attempt at industrial democracy, made his last speech impeaching Andrew Johnson on February sixteenth and on February twenty-third I was born.

Less than a month after my birth Andrew Johnson passed from the scene and Ulysses Grant became President of the United States. The Fifteenth Amendment enfranchising the Negro as a race became law and the work of abolishing slavery and making Negroes men was accomplished, so far as law could do it. Meanwhile elsewhere in the world there were stirring and change which were to mean much in my life: in Japan the Meiji Emperors rose to power the year I was born; in China the intrepid Empress Dowager was fighting strangulation by England and France; Prussia had fought with Austria and France, and the German Empire arose in 1871. In England, Victoria opened her eighth parliament; the duel of Disraeli and Gladstone began; while in Africa came the Abyssinian expedition and opening of the Suez Canal, so fateful for all my people.

My town was shut in by its mountains and provincialism; but it was a beautiful place, a little New England town nestled shyly in its valley with something of Dutch cleanliness and English reticence. The Housatonic yellowed by the paper mills, rolled slowly through its center; while Green River, clear and beautiful, joined in to the south. Main Street was lined with ancient elms; the hills held white pines and orchards and then faded up to magnificient rocks and caves which shut out the neighboring world. The people were mainly of English descent with much Dutch blood and with a large migration of Irish and German workers to the mills as laborers.

The social classes of the town were built partly on land-holding farmers and more especially on manufacturers and merchants, whose prosperity was due in no little degree to the new and high tariff. The rich people of the town were not very rich nor many in number. The middle class were farmers, merchants and artisans; and beneath these was a small proletariat of Irish and German mill workers. They lived in slums near the woolen mills and across the river clustering about the Catholic Church. The number of colored people in the town and county was small. They were all, save directly after the war, old families, well-known to the old settlers among the whites.

The color line was manifest and yet not absolutely drawn. I remember a cousin of mine who brought home a white wife. The chief objection was that he was not able to support her and nobody knew about her family; and knowledge of family history was counted as highly important. Most of the colored people had some white blood from unions several generations past. That they congregated together in their own social life was natural because that was the rule in the town: there were little social knots of people, but not much that today would be called social life, save that which centered about the churches; and there the colored folk often took part. My grandmother was Episcopalian and my mother, Congregational. I grew up in the Congregational Sunday school.

In Great Barrington there were perhaps twenty-five, certainly not more than fifty, colored folk in a population of five thousand. My family was among the oldest inhabitants of the valley. The family had spread slowly through the county intermarrying among cousins and other black folk with some but limited infiltration of white blood. Other dark families had come in and there was some intermingling with local Indians. In one or two cases there were groups of apparently later black immigrants, near Sheffield for instance. There survives there even to this day an isolated group of black folk whose origin is obscure. We knew little of them but felt above them because of our education and economic status.

The economic status was not high. The early members of the family supported themselves on little farms of a few acres; then drifted to town as laborers and servants, but did not go into the mills. Most of them rented homes, but some owned little homes and pieces of land; a few had very pleasant and well-furnished homes, but none had anything like wealth.

My immediate family, which I remember as a young child, consisted of a very dark grandfather, Othello Burghardt, sitting beside the fireplace in a high chair, because of an injured hip. He was good-natured but not energetic. The energy was in my grandmother, Sally, a thin, tall, yellow and hawk-faced woman, certainly beautiful in her youth, and efficient and managing in her age. My mother, Mary Sylvina, was born at Great Barrington, January 14, 1831, and died there in 1885 at the age of fifty-four years. She had at the age of thirty a son, Idelbert, born of her and her cousin, John Burghardt. The circumstances of this romance I never knew. No one talked of it in the family. Perhaps there was an actual marriage. If so, it was not recorded in the family Bible. Perhaps the mating was broken up on account of the consanguinity of the cousins by a family tradition which had a New England strictness in its sex morals. So far as I ever knew there was only one illegitimate child throughout the family in my grandfather's and the two succeeding generations. My mother was brown and rather small with smooth skin and lovely eyes, and hair that curled and crinkled down each side her forehead from the part in the middle. She was rather silent but very determined and very patient. My father, a light mulatto, died in my infancy so that I do not remember him. I shall later speak more intimately of him.

I was born in a rather nice little cottage which belonged to a black South Carolinian, whose own house stood next, at the lower end of one of the pleasant streets of the town. Then for a time I lived in the country at the house of my grandfather, Othello, one of three farming brothers. It was sturdy, small and old-fashioned. Later we moved back to town and lived in quarters over the woodshed of one of the town's better mansions. After that we lived awhile over a store by the railway and during my high school years in a little four room tenement house on the same street where I was born, but farther up, down a lane and in the rear of a home owned by the widow of a New York physician. None of these homes had modern conveniences but they were weatherproof, fairly warm in winter and furnished with some comfort.

For several generations my people had attended schools for longer or shorter periods so most of them could read and write. I was brought up from earliest years with the idea of regular attendance at school. This was partly because the schools of Great Barrington were near at hand, simple but good, well-taught, and truant laws were enforced. I started on one school ground, which I remember vividly, at the age of five or six years, and continued there in school until I was graduated from high school at sixteen. I was seldom absent or tardy, and the school ran regularly ten months in the year with a few vacations. The curriculum was simple: reading, writing, spelling and arithmetic; grammar, geography and history. We learned the alphabet; we were drilled rigorously on the multiplication tables and we drew accurate maps. We could spell correctly and read clearly.

By the time I neared the high school, economic problems and questions of the future began to loom. These were partly settled by my own activities. My mother was then a widow with limited resources of income through boarding the barber, my uncle; supplemented infrequently by day's work, and by some kindly but unobstrusive charity. But I was keen and eager to eke out this income by various jobs: splitting kindling, mowing lawns, doing chores. My first regular wage began as I entered the high school: I went early of mornings and filled with coal one or two of the new so-called "base-burning" stoves in the millinery shop of Madame

L'Hommedieu. From then on, all through my high school course, I worked after school and on Saturdays; I sold papers, distributed tea from the new A & P stores in New York; and for a few months, through the good will of Johnny Morgan, actually rose to be local correspondent of the *Springfield Republican*.

Meantime the town and its surroundings were a boy's paradise: there were mountains to climb and rivers to wade and swim; lakes to freeze and hills for coasting. There were orchards and caves and wide green fields; and all of it was apparently property of the children of the town. My earlier contacts with playmates and other human beings were normal and pleasant. Sometimes there was a dearth of available playmates but that was peculiar to the conventions of the town where families were small and children must go to bed early and not loaf on the streets or congregate in miscellaneous crowds. Later, in the high school, there came some rather puzzling distinctions which I can see now were social and racial; but the racial angle was more clearly defined against the Irish than against me. It was a matter of income and ancestry more than color. I have written elsewhere of the case of exchanging visiting cards where one girl, a stranger, did not seem to want mine to my vast surprise.

I presume I was saved evidences of a good deal of actual discrimination by my own keen sensitiveness. My companions did not have a chance to refuse me invitations; they must seek me out and urge me to come as indeed they often did. When my presence was not wanted they had only to refrain from asking. But in the ordinary social affairs of the village—the Sunday school with its picnics and festivals; the temporary skating rink in the town hall; the coasting in crowds on all the hills—in all these, I took part with no thought of discrimination on the part of my fellows, for that I would have been the first to notice.

Later, I was protected in part by the fact that there was little social activity in the high school; there were no fraternities; there were no school dances; there were no honor societies. Whatever of racial feeling gradually crept into my life, its effect upon me in these earlier days was rather one of exaltation and high disdain. They were the losers who did not ardently court me and not I, which seemed to be proven by the fact that I had no difficulty in outdoing them in nearly all competition, especially intellectual. In athletics I was not outstanding. I was only moderately good at baseball and football; but at running, exploring, story-telling and planning of intricate games, I was often if not always the leader. This made discrimination all the more difficult.

When, however, during my high school course the matter of my future career began to loom, there were difficulties. The colored population of the town had been increased a little by "contrabands," who on the whole were well received by the colored group; although the older group held some of its social distinctions and the newcomers astonished us by forming a little Negro Methodist Zion Church, which we sometimes attended. The work open to colored folk was limited. There was day labor; there was farming; there was house-service, particularly work in summer hotels; but for a young, educated and ambitious colored man, what were the possibilities? And the practical answer to this inquiry was: Why encourage a young colored man toward such higher training? I imagine this matter was discussed considerably among my friends, white and black, and in a way it was settled partially before I realized it.

My high school principal was Frank Hosmer, afterward president of Oahu College, Hawaii. He suggested, quite as a matter of fact, that I ought to take the college preparatory course which involved algebra, geometry, Latin and Greek. If Hosmer had been another sort of man, with definite ideas as to a Negro's "place," and had recommended agricultural "science" or domestic economy, I would doubtless have followed his advice, had such "courses" been available. I did not then realize that Hosmer was quietly opening college doors for me, for in those days they were barred with ancient tongues. This meant a considerable expenditure for books which were not free in those days—more than my folk could afford; but the wife of one of the mill-owners, or rather I ought to describe her as the mother of one of my playmates, after some hesitation offered to furnish all the necessary school books. I became therefore a high school student preparing for college and thus occupying an unusual position in the town even among whites, although there had been one or two other colored boys in the past who had gotten at least part of a high school education. In this way I was thrown with the upper rather than the lower social classes and protected in many ways. I came in touch with rich folk, summer boarders, who made yearly incursions from New York. Their beautiful clothes impressed me tremendously but otherwise I found them quite ordinary. The children did not have much sense or training; they were not very strong and rather too well dressed to have a good time playing.

I had little contact with crime and degradation. The slums in the town were not bad and repelled me, partly because they were inhabited by the foreign-born. There was one house among colored folk, where I now realize there must have been a good deal of gambling, drinking and other looseness. The inmates were pleasant to me but I was never asked to enter and of course had no desire. In the whole town, colored and white, there was not much crime. The one excess was drunkenness and there my mother quietly took a firm stand. I was never to enter a liquor saloon. I never did. I donned a Murphy "blue ribbon." And yet perhaps, as I now see, the one solace that this pleasant but spiritually rather drab little town had against the monotony of life was liquor; and rich and poor got drunk more or less regularly. I have seen one of the mill owners staggering home, and my very respectable uncle used to come home now and then walking exceedingly straight.

I was born in a community which conceived itself as having helped put down a wicked rebellion for the purpose of freeing four million slaves. All respectable people belonged to the Republican Party, but Democrats were tolerated, although regarded with some surprise and hint of motive. Most of the older men had been soldiers, including members of my own family. The town approached in politics a pure democracy with annual town meeting and elections of well-known and fairly qualified officials. We were placidly religious. The bulk of the well-to-do people belonged to the Episcopal and Congregational churches, a small number of farmers and artisans to the Methodist Church and the Irish workers to the Catholic Church across the river. The marriage laws and family relations were fairly firm. The chief delinquency was drunkenness and the major social problem of the better classes was the status of women who had little or no opportunity to marry.

My ideas of property and work during my boyhood were vague. They did not present themselves to me as problems. As a family we owned little property and our income was always small. Spending money for me came first as small gifts of pennies or a nickel from relatives; once I received a silver dollar, a huge fortune. Later I earned all my spending funds. I can see now that my mother must have struggled pretty desperately on very narrow resources and that the problem of shoes and clothes for me must have been at times staggering. But these matters seldom bothered me because they were not brought to my attention. My general attitude toward property and income was that all who were willing to work could easily earn a living; that those who had property had earned it and deserved it and could use it as they wished; that poverty was the shadow of crime and connoted lack of thrift and shiftlessness. These were the current patterns of economic thought of the town in my boyhood.

In Great Barrington the first glimpse of the outer and wider world I got, was through Johnny Morgan's news shop which occupied the front end of the post office. There newspapers and books were on display and I remember very early seeing pictures of "U. S." Grant, and of "Bill" Tweed who was beginning his extraordinary career in New York City; and later I saw pictures of Hayes and of the smooth and rather cruel face of Tilden. Of the great things happening in the United States at that time, we were actually touched only by the Panic of 1873. When my uncle came home from a little town east of us where he was the leading barber, he brought me, I remember, a silver dollar which was an extraordinary thing: up to that time I had seen nothing but paper money. I was six when Charles Sumner died and the Freedmen's Bank closed; and when I was eight there came the revolution of 1876 in the South, and Victoria of England became Empress of India; but I did not know the meaning of these events until long after.

In general thought and conduct I became quite thoroughly New England. It was not good form in Great Barrington to express one's thought volubly, or to give way to excessive emotion. We were even sparing in our daily greetings. I am quite sure that in a less restrained and conventional atmosphere I should have easily learned to express my emotions with far greater and more unrestrained intensity; but as it was I had the social heritage not only of a New England clan but Dutch taciturnity. This was later reinforced and strengthened by inner withdrawals in the face of real and imagined discriminations. The result was that I was early thrown in upon myself. I found it difficult and even unnecessary to approach other people and by that same token my own inner life perhaps grew the richer; but the habit of repression often returned to plague me in after years, for so early a habit could not easily be unlearned. The Negroes in the South, when I came to know them, could never understand why I did not naturally greet everyone I passed on the street or slap my friends on the back.

During my high school career I had a chance for the first time to step beyond the shadow of the hills which hemmed in my little valley. My father's father was living in New Bedford and his third wife who had greatly loved my own father wanted my grandfather to know and recognize me. The grandfather, a short thick-set man, "colored" but quite white in appearance, with austere face, was hard and set in his ways, proud and bitter. My father and grandfather had not been able to get along together. Of them, I shall speak more intimately later. I went to New Bedford in 1883 at the age of fifteen. On the way I saw Hartford and Providence. I called on my uncle in Amherst and received a new navy-blue suit. Grandfather was a gentleman in manner, precise and formal. He looked at me coolly, but in the end he was not unpleasant. I went down across the water to Martha's Vineyard and saw what was then "Cottage City" and came home by way of Springfield and Albany where I was a guest of my older half-brother and saw my first electric street light blink and sputter.

I was graduated from high school in 1884 and was of course the only colored student. Once during my course another young dark man had attended the school for a short time but I was very much ashamed of him because he did not excel the whites as I was quite used to doing. All thirteen of us had orations and mine was on "Wendell Phillips." The great anti-slavery agitator had just died in February and I presume that some of my teachers must have suggested the subject, although it is quite possible that I chose it myself. But I was fascinated by his life and his work and took a long step toward a wider conception of what I was going to do. I spoke in June and then came face to face with the problem of my future life.

My mother lived proudly to see me graduate but died in the fall and I went to live with an aunt. I was strongly advised that I was too young to enter college. Williams had been suggested, because most of our few high school graduates who went to college had attended there; but my heart was set on Harvard. It was the greatest and oldest college and I therefore quite naturally thought it was the one I must attend. Of course I did not realize the difficulties; some difficulties in entrance examinations because our high school was not quite up to the Harvard standard; but a major difficulty of money. There must have been in my family and among my friends a good deal of anxious discussion as to my future but finally it was temporarily postponed when I was offered a job and promised that the next fall I should begin my college work.

The job brought me in unexpected touch with the world. There had been a great-uncle of mine, Tom Burghardt, whose tombstone I had seen often in the town graveyard. My family used to say in undertones that the money of Tom Burghardt helped to build the Pacific Railroad and that this came about in this wise: nearly all his life Tom Burghardt had been a servant in the Kellogg family, only the family usually forgot to pay him; but finally they did give him a handsome burial. Then Mark Hopkins, a son or relative of the great Mark, appeared on the scene and married a daughter of the Kelloggs. He became one of the Huntington-Stanford-Crocker Pacific Associates who built, manipulated and cornered the Pacific railroads and with the help of the Kellogg nest-egg, Hopkins made nineteen million dollars in the West by methods not to be inquired into. His widow came back to Great Barrington in the eighties and planned a mansion out of the beautiful blue granite which formed our hills. A host of workmen, masons, stone-cutters and carpenters were assembled, and in the summer of 1884 I was made time-keeper for the contractors who carried on this job. I received the fabulous wage of a dollar a day. It was a most interesting experience and had new and

intriguing bits of reality and romance. As time-keeper and the obviously young and inexperienced agent of superiors, I was the one
who handed the discharged workers their last wage envelopes. I
talked with contractors and saw the problems of employers. I pored
over the plans and specifications and even came in contact with the
elegant English architect Searles who finally came to direct the work.

The widow had a steward, a fine, young educated colored fellow
who had come to be her right-hand man; but the architect sup-
planted him. He had the glamour of an English gentleman. The
steward was gradually pushed aside and down into his place. The
architect eventually married the widow and her wealth and the steward killed himself. So the Hopkins millions passed strangely into foreign hands and gave me my first problem of inheritance. But in the
meantime the fabrication and growth of this marvelous palace, beautiful beyond anything that Great Barrington had seen, went slowly
and majestically on, and always I could sit and watch it grow.

Finally in the fall of 1885, the difficulty of my future education
was solved. The whole subtlety of the plan was clear neither to me
nor my relatives at the time. Merely I was offered through the Reverend C. C. Painter, once excellent Federal Indian Agent, a scholarship
to attend Fisk University in Nashville, Tennessee; the funds were to
be furnished by four Connecticut churches which Mr. Painter had
formerly pastored. Disappointed though I was at not being able to go
to Harvard, I merely regarded this as a temporary change of plan; I
would of course go to Harvard in the end. But here and immediately
was adventure. I was going into the South; the South of slavery, rebellion and black folk; and above all I going to meet colored people
of my own age and education, of my own ambitions. Once or twice
already I had had swift glimpses of the colored world: at Rocky
Point on Narragansett Bay, I had attended an annual picnic beside
the sea, and had seen in open-mouthed astonishment the whole gorgeous color gamut of the American Negro world; the swaggering
men, the beautiful girls, the laughter and gaiety, the unhampered
self-expression. I was astonished and inspired. I became aware, once
a chance to go to a group of such young people was opened up for
me, of the spiritual isolation in which I was living. I heard too in
these days for the first time the Negro folk songs. A Hampton Quartet had sung them in the Congregational Church. I was thrilled and
moved to tears and seemed to recognize something inherently and
deeply my own. I was glad to go to Fisk.

On the other hand my people had undoubtedly a more discrimi-
nating and unromantic view of the situation. They said frankly that
it was a shame to send me South. I was Northern born and bred and
instead of preparing me for work and giving me an opportunity right

there in my own town and state, they were bundling me off to the South. This was undoubtedly true. The educated young white folk of Great Barrington became clerks in stores, bookkeepers and teachers, while a few went into professions. Great Barrington was not able to conceive of me in such local position. It was not so much that they were opposed to it, but it did not occur to them as a possibility.

On the other hand there was the call of the black South; teachers were needed. The crusade of the New England schoolmarm was in full swing. The freed slaves, if properly led, had a great future. Temporarily deprived of their full voting privileges, this was but a passing set-back. Black folk were bound in time to dominate the South. They needed trained leadership. I was sent to help furnish it.

I started out and went into Tennessee at the age of seventeen to be a sophomore at Fisk University. It was to me an extraordinary experience. I was thrilled to be for the first time among so many people of my own color or rather of such various and such extraordinary colors, which I had only glimpsed before, but who it seemed were bound to me by new and exciting and eternal ties. Never before had I seen young men so self-assured and who gave themselves such airs, and colored men at that; and above all for the first time I saw beautiful girls. At my home among my white school mates there were a few pretty girls; but either they were not entrancing or because I had known them all my life I did not notice them; but at Fisk at the first dinner I saw opposite me a girl of whom I have often said, no human being could possibly have been as beautiful as she seemed to my young eyes that far-off September night of 1885.

FROM **THE AUTOBIOGRAPHY OF W. E. B. DU BOIS**

. . . In 1950 the month of February had for me special meaning. I was a widower. The wife of 53 years lay buried in the New England hills beside her first-born boy. I was lonesome because so many boyhood friends had died, and because a certain illogical reticence on

From *The Autobiography of W. E. B. Du Bois*. Reprinted by permission of International Publishers Co., Inc.

The omitted material which precedes in this chapter deals with Du Bois's campaign as the American Labor party candidate for U.S. senator from New York; it also presents the trouble between the Department of Justice and the Peace Information Center, a Communist organization in which Du Bois was involved and which worked toward informing Americans of worldwide efforts for peace: the Peace Information Center and its officers were indicted for "failure to register as agents of a foreign principal."

my part had never brought me many intimate friends. But there was a young woman, a minister's daughter, to whom I had been a sort of father confessor in literary affairs and difficulties of life for many years, especially after her father's death 15 years before. I knew her hardships and I had rejoiced in her successes. Shirley Graham, with her beautiful martyr complex, finally persuaded herself that I needed her help and companionship, as I certainly did; so we decided to get married a few days after my next birthday, when I would be 83 years old.

Preparations for a birthday dinner to be held at the Essex House, New York City, were being made at the request of the Council on African Affairs of which I had become vice-chairman after leaving the NAACP. The list of sponsors was imposing and growing daily. Before the indictment about 300 people had made reservations and paid over $2,000.

Then came a strange series of events: on February 8 I was indicted for an alleged crime; on February 14, I was married secretly to Shirley, lest if I were found guilty she might have no right to visit me in jail; February 16 I was arraigned in Washington and on February 19, four days before the dinner, the hotel at which the dinner was planned cancelled our contract by telegram saying:

"Pursuant to our rules and regulations and for other sufficient reasons we hereby advise you that reservations of our facilities for Friday evening, February 23 for the W. E. B. Du Bois testimonial dinner is cancelled. Deposit is being returned. Vincent J. Coyle, Vice-President and Managing Director, Essex House Hotel, Inc."

We had five days before the dinner to find a place to entertain our 300 guests. In addition to this, three of our speakers, Charlotte Hawkins Brown, Mordecai Johnson and Rabbi Hillel Silver, hastily declined to appear. Some of the sponsors withdrew, but I do not know how many of the original list remained.

I can stand a good deal, and have done so during my life; but this experience was rather more than I felt like bearing, especially as the blows continued to fall. I had meantime been finger-printed, handcuffed, bailed and remanded for trial. I was more than ready to drop all thought of the birthday dinner.

But my remaining friends said No! I could do no less than stand beside them, although without Shirley's faith and strength I probably would not have allowed the dinner to take place. Franklin Frazier, the chairman, stood firm. He said the dinner must and would go on.

There ensued a period of wild search for a place of meeting; of securing other speakers and notifying participants. Subtly the whole picture changed; instead of a polite, friendly social gesture, this dinner became a fight for civil rights, and into the seats of timid and withdrawing guests slipped a new set of firmer men and women who were willing to face even the United States government in my defense and for the preservation of American freedom. They carried on the battle while I sat uneasily in the background.

The program was hastily rearranged. No white downtown hotel would harbor us, and turning to Harlem we found Small's Paradise, well-known to the cabaret world, much too small but with a proprietor willing and eager even to lose money by the venture. At the dinner Belford Lawson, head of the Alpha Phi Alpha fraternity, volunteered and made a fighting speech; Paul Robeson spoke courageously and feelingly. A strong letter from Judge Hubert Delany was read. Franklin Frazier presided and spoke. The room was crowded to suffocation, and many could not get to their seats. But the spirit was what the Germans call *feierlich* [festive]! Finally, amid cheers, birthday cakes and flowers, I made my speech. There were about 700 persons present who paid $6,557 in dinner fees and donations.

In this indictment of the Peace Information Center, I received a severe jolt, because in fact I found myself being punished before I was tried. In the first place, the Department of Justice allowed the impression to spread that my colleagues and I had in some way betrayed our country. Although the charge was not treason, it was widely understood and said that the Peace Information Center had been discovered to be an agent of the Soviet Union.

When we were arraigned in Washington February 16, the proceedings were brusque and unsympathetic. We were not treated as innocent people whose guilt was to be inquired into, but distinctly as criminals whose innocence was to be proven, which was assumed to be doubtful.

The white commercial press treated our case either with silence or violent condemnation. The New York *Herald-Tribune* had this editorial, February 11:

"The Du Bois outfit was set up to promote a tricky appeal of Soviet origin, poisonous in its surface innocence, which made it appear that a signature against the use of atomic weapons would forthwith insure world peace. It was, in short, an attempt to disarm America and yet ignore every form of Communist aggression. A lot of 'men and women of good will through the world,' to quote the petition's bland phrasing, were snared into signing without quite realizing that this thing came straight out of the Cominform."

So far as the nation was concerned, Alice Barrows secured 220 leaders of the arts, sciences, clergy and other professions in 33 states, including 35 universities, to sign "A Statement to the American People," released June 27, calling for the withdrawal of the prosecution. The statement, initiated by the National Council of the Arts,

Sciences and Professions, described the indictment as "but one of
numerous recent actions against individuals and organizations that
advocate peaceful solutions to the world's crisis. In this time of hysteria, the attempted labeling of 'foreign agent' on a distinguished
scholar and leader of a peace movement can fairly be interpreted as
an effort to intimidate and silence all advocates of peace."

The response of Negroes in general was slow. At first many Negroes were puzzled. They did not understand the indictment and assumed that I had let myself be drawn into some treasonable acts or
movements in retaliation for continued discrimination in this land,
which I had long fought. They understood this and forgave it, but
thought my action ill-advised. The Norfolk *Journal and Guide* expressed this clearly. The *Chicago Defender* said:

"Dr. Du Bois has earned many honors and it is a supreme tragedy
that he should have become embroiled in activities that have been
exposed as subversive in the twilight of his years." But on the other
hand, editors like Percival Prattis of the *Pittsburgh Courier*, Carl
Murphy of the *Afro-American*, and columnists like Marjorie Mc-
Kenzie, J. A. Rogers, and others, showed a courage and real intellectual leadership which was lacking elsewhere. The reaction of
Negroes revealed a distinct cleavage not hitherto clear in American
Negro opinion. The intelligentsia, the "Talented Tenth," the successful business and professional men, were not, for the most part, outspoken in my defense. There were many and notable exceptions, but
as a group this class was either silent or actually antagonistic. The
reasons were clear; many believed that the government had actual
proof of subversive activities on our part; until the very end they
awaited their disclosure.

Other Negroes of intelligence and prosperity had become American in their acceptance of exploitation as defensible, and in their imitation of American "conspicuous expenditure." They proposed to
make money and spend it as pleased them. They had beautiful
homes, large and expensive cars and fur coats. They hated "communism" and "socialism" as much as any white American. Their reaction toward Paul Robeson was typical; they simply could not
understand his surrendering a thousand dollars a night for a moral
conviction.

This dichotomy in the Negro group, this development of class
structure, was to be expected, and will be more manifest in the future, as discrimination against Negroes as such decreases. There will
gradually arise among American Negroes a separation according to
their attitudes toward labor, wealth and work. It is still my hope that
the Negro's experience in the past will, in the end, lead the majority

of his intelligentsia into the ranks of those advocating social control of wealth, abolition of exploitation of labor, and equality of opportunity for all.

I have belonged to a Negro graduate fraternity for 45 years—indeed helped its first formation. Today it contains in its membership a large number of leading business and professional Negroes in the United States. Yet of its 30 or more chapters covering the nation, only one expressed any sympathy with me, and none offered aid. It is probable that individual members of the fraternity gave my cause support, but no official action was taken save in one case. In my own New York chapter I was bitterly criticized.

Another of our projects was to secure the names of a dozen nationally prominent Negroes to this statement:

". . . We are not here concerned with the political or social beliefs of Dr. Du Bois. Many of us do not agree with him on these and other matters. But we are concerned with the right of a man to say within the law what he thinks without being subject to threat and intimidation. Especially we are concerned with Dr. Du Bois as a leader of the Negro American for 50 years. In that time until now his integrity and absolute sincerity has never been questioned. . . ."

We did not, however, succeed in getting enough such signatures to this statement to warrant its circulation. I recognized the fear in the Negro group, especially among the educated and well-to-do. One said to me sadly, "I have a son in government employ; he has a well-paid position and is in line for promotion. He has worked long for this start and has had many disappointments. I am sorry but I dare not sign this."

I served the NAACP for 28 years in all. When this case came up, although I was no longer officially connected with the organization, branches and members all over the nation wanted to help me and urged the main office to join in. The president of the Board of Directors said frankly to Shirley Graham that undoubtedly the Peace Information Center was supported by funds from the Soviet Union. He admitted that it was possible that I did not know this. At a meeting, March 12, of the Board of Directors, it was urged that the Board take a position on the indictment, and as one branch said, "give active, tangible aid to Dr. Du Bois in his present plight." However, the secretary, Walter White, reported that he had talked with Peyton Ford, assistant to the Attorney-General in Washington, and was told that there was definite evidence of guilt in the hands of the Department of Justice and that the four associates of Dr. Du Bois could not be prosecuted without prosecuting Dr. Du Bois.

A white member of the Board had offered to take up the matter of asking the legal department of the NAACP to join in our defense. After this member heard our "certain guilt" stated he made no further effort.

The Board finally passed this resolution:

"Without passing on the merits of the recent indictment of Dr. Du Bois, the board of directors of the NAACP expresses the opinion that this action against one of the great champions of civil rights lends color to the charge that efforts are being made to silence spokesmen for full equality of Negroes. The board also reaffirms its determination to continue its aggressive fight for full citizenship rights for all Americans."

Even this resolution was not given much publicity, and the main office advised the branches strongly "not to touch" this case. Some branches vigorously complained, and despite the attitude of the New York office, many branches of the NAACP supported our campaign.

Our appeal to the officials of the World Defenders of Peace resulted in wide publicity for our case all over the world. Messages began to pour in to us from Europe, Asia and Africa; from the West Indies and South America. We received letters from England, Scotland, and France; from Belgium, Holland, Luxembourg, and Scandinavia; from Germany, the Union of Socialist Soviet Republics, Austria, Czechoslovakia, Poland, Rumania, Albania, Hungary, Trieste, and Switzerland; from Canada, Cuba, Martinique, Jamaica, British Guiana and Brazil; from West Africa, South Africa, Southeast Asia, China, Viet Nam, Indonesia, India and Australia. International bodies sent their support, including the International Union of Students, the World Federation of Teachers' Unions, the International Federation of Women, the World Federation of Scientific Workers, and others.

An "International Committee in Defense of Dr. W. E. B. Du Bois and his Colleagues" was formed. The original signers included a university professor from Holland; two professors from Switzerland; a judge of the Court of Appeals and a federal judge in Brazil; two magistrates from Colombia and Iran; an Italian senator; and the president of the French Court of Cassation; together with ten Americans, eight white and two Negro. Eventually this committee grew to 200 with 33 Frenchmen, 30 Poles, 12 Belgians, 11 Germans, seven Englishmen, six Italians, five Brazilians, four each from Switzerland, the Soviet Union, Hungary and China; one to three each from Rumania, Bulgaria, Iran, Lebanon, Martinique, Holland, Austria; and 59 from the United States, of whom six were colored. Isabelle Blume of Belgium was chairman.

Articles were published in Austria, India, the Soviet Union, the Shanghai *China News* and Edinburgh *Review* in Scotland. The story

was told in at least a dozen different languages. From the West Indies came letters, from the professors of the University of Havana
and outstanding Cubans like Dr. Fernando Ortiz, Latin America's
most famous sociologist; Dr. Domingo Villamil, eminent Catholic ju-
rist; and Juan Marinello, senator and poet.

The International Union of Students wrote to the Department of
Justice:

"On behalf of over 5,000,000 students in 71 countries, the International Union of Students expresses indignation at the prosecution
of Dr. Du Bois and associates. Du Bois is an internationally known
scholar and spokesman for peace. His work for peace is in best traditions of the American people. Prosecution is an attack upon peace
supporters, upon Negro people and upon right of professors and students to act for peace. We join with peace-loving people throughout
the world in demanding that you dismiss Du Bois' indictment and
end persecution of United States peace supporters."

Despite the difficulty of securing meeting places in New York
where we could defend our cause, we succeeded late in September
in organizing a meeting in Town Hall. The National Council of the
Arts, Sciences and Professions put on an interesting program, with
Professor Henry Pratt Fairchild presiding. Here Bishop Wright, Cor-
liss Lamont and Lawrence D. Reddick, former curator of the Schomburg Collection and then Librarian of Atlanta University, spoke. Dr.
Reddick said in part:

"I have just come from a part of our country where the flag of
the Confederacy is more popular than the flag of the United States
of America; where Robert E. Lee is not only more of a hero than
Ulysses S. Grant but also more than George Washington; and where
the Governor threatens to close down the State's entire system of education if the courts should compel the public, tax-supported institutions that are presently maintained for whites only to admit a
single Negro."

I wrote this statement for the defendants:

"This case is a blow at civilization: by instituting thought control;
by seeking to stop the circulation of ideas; by seeking to shut off the
free flow of culture around the world and reducing all American culture to the level of Mississippi and Nevada; by making it a crime to
think as others think, if your thought is against the prejudices or
graft or barbarism of some backwoods partisan; by making it treason
to brand the hoary lie that War is the path to Peace; by crucifying
fathers and mothers who do not want their sons raised to murder
men, women and children . . .

"The Government can put into absolute control of our thinking,
feeling and culture any set of half-educated fanatics from Southern

rotten boroughs or western mining camps or Missouri gang politics
in order to: curtail and misdirect education in America; limit
thought and twist ambition; send school children hiding under desks
instead of learning to read and write; make saints of spies, informers
and professional liars; make a prisoned nation call Freedom that
which is slavery and to change a Democracy into a police state!

"Wake up, America. Your liberties are being stolen before your
very eyes. What Washington, Jefferson and Lincoln fought for, Truman, Acheson, and McGrath are striving desperately to nullify. Wake
up, Americans, and dare to think and say and do. Dare to cry: No
More War!"

This brought forward the whole question of costs. It had not occurred to us how costly justice in the United States is. It is not
enough to be innocent in order to escape punishment. You must
have money and a lot of it. In the end it cost us $35,150 to prose-
cute this case to a successful end, not counting the fee refused by
the Chief Counsel. If, as we had confidently expected, the case had
gone to higher courts to determine the constitutionality of this foreign agents Act, it might have cost us $100,000. Before this prospect
of sheer cost, we stood for many weeks appalled and discouraged.
We realized more than ever that this trial was not going to be simply
a legal process, but a political persecution, the outcome of which
would depend on public opinion; and that to raise the funds necessary for our defense, we would need the contributions of large numbers of poor people and need have no hope for gifts from the
rich. . . .

The government not only went to trouble and large expense,
risked its own reputation, but also forced us to extraordinary and
worldwide effort, to escape punishment. Personally, I had no funds
for such a case. I was retired from work, with a pension too small
for normal expenses of living. My wife's work and income were seriously curtailed by her complete immersion in this case. We had no
rich friends. None of the defendants were able personally to finance
this case. Had it not been for the almost miraculous rise of American
friends, we would have gone to jail by default. Not a cent of money
for the trial came from abroad. Even had this been possible, it would
have been used to convict us. But in this nation by popular appeal
to poor and middle-class folk, Negroes and white, trade unions and
other groups, we raised funds for these purposes:

Legal fees, $18,400; publicity, $5,600; office, $5,250; salaries,
$3,600; travel, $2,365.

To this should be added additional legal fees of at least $13,000;
$3,000 paid to an attorney hired by one of the defendants and not
paid for by the Committee, and at least $10,000 which Marcantonio

earned but would not accept. This amounts to a total of $40,215. To this should be added at least $2,000 in travel expenses paid by localities. How much the case cost the government we cannot know, but it could not have been less than $100,000 and it might have been much more.

I have faced during my life many unpleasant experiences; the growl of a mob; the personal threat of murder; the scowling distaste of an audience. But nothing has so cowed me as that day, November 8, 1951, when I took my seat in a Washington courtroom as an indicted criminal. I was not a criminal. I had broken no law, consciously or unwittingly. Yet I sat with four other American citizens of unblemished character, never before accused even of misdemeanor, in the seats often occupied by murderers, forgers and thieves; accused of a felony and liable to be sentenced before leaving this court to five years of imprisonment, a fine of $10,000 and loss of my civil and political rights as a citizen, representing five generations of Americans.

William Stanley Braithwaite

(1878–1962)

POET, CRITIC, and nationally known anthologist, William Stanley Beaumont Braithwaite was born in Boston and lived there most of his life. His father, William Smith Braithwaite, was a native of British Guiana who studied medicine in England but never obtained a degree. In Boston he became a physician's assistant. He married an American black who could pass for white, and he tried to keep the five children they had from as much contact as possible with American blacks. Braithwaite, for example, never went to a public school. He was taught at home by his father, who tried to rear all of his children like upper-class Britishers. In his literary career, the poet and critic Braithwaite inherited much of his father's racial snobbery, although during the last years of his life he became a part of black life in Atlanta. Largely self-educated, Braithwaite had honorary degrees from two black colleges, and during the forties held a chair as professor of literature at Atlanta University.

Associated with such national poets and critics as Robert Frost, Harriet Monroe, Edgar Lee Masters, Carl Sandburg, and others, Braithwaite was a one-time editor of the *New Poetry Review*, a regular contributor of literary criticism to the old *Boston Transcript*, and a contributor of essays to *Forum, Century, Scribner's, Atlantic Monthly*, and others. He is probably best known for his annual anthologies of magazine verse, which introduced to the American public several of the nation's best-known poets. He also compiled several anthologies of period verse, among them *The Book of Elizabethan Verse* (1906) and *The Book of Modern British Verse* (1919).

Braithwaite's own poetry fills three volumes: *Lyrics of Life and Love* (1904), *The House of Falling Leaves* (1908), and *Selected Poems* (1948). His prose works are his uncompleted *The House under Arcturus: An Autobiography*, published in three parts in *Phylon* in 1941, and *The Bewitched Parsonage* (1950), a biography of the Brontës.

In his poetry Braithwaite exemplified to an extreme degree an assimilationist attitude held from time to time by a few of his black contemporaries. Refusing to write as a "Negro poet" or to use racial themes, he elected to fight for equality by competing with white writers on their terms. This is a kind of literary "passing" which contemporary blacks find hard to understand, but the position is tenable. It is easy to criticize Braithwaite's refusal to be a race poet; it is not so easy to match his performance as a lyrical poet.

Braithwaite lived until 1962, but his best and most representative work as a poet was done by 1910. For his excellence in literature, he was awarded the Spingarn Medal in 1918.

For comment on Braithwaite's life and his position as poet and critic, see the article by Saunders Redding in *Dictionary of American Negro Biography*. The *Dictionary of Literary Biography* entry by Kenny J. Williams is quite comprehensive in its treatment; see also Benjamin Brawley, *The Negro in Literature and Art* (1929); Philip Butcher, "W. S. Braithwaite's Southern Exposure: Résumé and Revelation," *Southern Literary Journal* 3 (Spring 1971); and Butcher's introduction to *The William Stanley Braithwaite Reader* (1972), which he edited.

The following poems are reprinted from Braithwaite's *Selected Poems* (1948).

DEL CASCAR

Del Cascar, Del Cascar,
Sat upon a flaming star,
Sat, and let his feet hang down
Till in China the toes turned brown.

And he reached his fingers over
The rim of the sea, like sails from Dover,
And caught a Mandarin at prayer,
And tickled his nose in Orion's hair.

The sun went down through crimson bars,
And left his blind face battered with stars,
But the brown toes in China kept
Hot the tears Del Cascar wept!

TURN ME TO MY YELLOW LEAVES

Turn me to my yellow leaves,
I am better satisfied;
There is nothing in me grieves—
That was never born—and died.

Let me be a scarlet flame
On a windy autumn morn,
I, who never had a name,
Nor from a breathing image born.
From the margin let me fall
Where the farthest stars sink down.
And the void consume me,—all
Into nothingness to drown.
Let me dream my dream entire,
Withered as an autumn leaf—
Let me have my vain desire,
Vain—as it is brief!

SIC VITA

Heart free, hand free,
    Blue above, brown under,
All the world to me
    Is a place of wonder.
Sun shine, moon shine,
    Stars, and winds a-blowing,
All into this heart of mine
    Flowing, flowing, flowing!

Mind free, step free,
    Days to follow after,
Joys of life sold to me
    For the price of laughter.
Girl's love, man's love,
    Love of work and duty,
Just a will of God's to prove
    Beauty, beauty, beauty!

SCINTILLA

I kissed a kiss in youth
    Upon a dead man's brow;
And that was long ago—
    And I'm a grown man now.

It's lain there in the dust,
  Thirty years and more—
My lips that set a light
  At a dead man's door!

THE WATCHERS

Two women on the lone wet strand
  (*The wind's out with a will to roam*)
The waves wage war on rocks and sand,
  (*And a ship is long due home!*)

The sea spray's in the women's eyes—
  (*Hearts can writhe like the sea's wild foam*)
Lower descend the tempestuous skies,
  (*For the wind's out with a will to roam.*)

"O daughter, thine eyes be better than mine,"
  (*The waves ascend high as yonder dome*)
"North or south is there never a sign?"
  (*And a ship is long due home!*)

They watch there all the long night through—
  (*The wind's out with a will to roam*)
Wind and rain and sorrow for two,—
  (*And heaven on the long reach home!*)

QUIET HAS A HIDDEN SOUND
Beacon Hill

Quiet has a hidden sound
Best upon a hillside street,
When the sunlight on the ground
Is luminous with heat.

Something teases one to peek
Behind the summer afternoon
And watch the shadowy legends leak
Off Time's unscalèd tune.

Just a common city street
Running up a city hill,

Filled with nothing but the heat
And houses standing still!

But where is silence castlèd,
Or stranger, the sunlight magic,
Than on this hillside, where the tread
Of summertime is tragic!

Fenton Johnson

(1888–1958)

PLAYWRIGHT, EDITOR, short story writer, and would-be social reformer, Fenton Johnson is now remembered primarily as a poet, a disillusioned modern poet. His verses, like those of James Weldon Johnson, reflect the change in poetic climate brought about by two American movements: the "new poetry," usually associated with Harriet Monroe, and the "new Negro." Johnson's first publications deal largely with sentimental themes and folk material—spirituals and dialect verse; his later works show the influence of Sandburg and Masters.

Born in Chicago in 1888, Fenton Johnson was educated at the University of Chicago, Northwestern University, and the Columbia University School of Journalism. He taught in the South for about a year, returned to his birthplace, and when he was nineteen years old had several of his plays performed in Chicago's famed Pekin Theatre.

Johnson, however, was basically a poet and not a playwright. During his lifetime he published three volumes of verse: *A Little Dreaming* (1913), *Visions of the Dusk* (1915), and *Songs of the Soil* (1916). He left two unpublished volumes of verse, one of them written when he worked with the Federal Writers' Project. Johnson is known largely through two frequently anthologized poems: "The Scarlet Woman" and "Tired." These poems express a kind of futilitarian position seldom found in Negro writing up to Johnson's time. They helped to label him as a modern Negro, disillusioned by his race and his times. The label is not wholly justified. For most of his life, Johnson was a confirmed optimist about social reform.

As a short story writer, Fenton Johnson published in *The Crisis* and other periodicals. In 1920 he brought out *Tales of Darkest America*, a collection of short stories written for *The Favorite Magazine*, a magazine he had founded in 1918.

Johnson tried desperately to be a crusading social reformer, and to help his cause he founded in 1916 *The Champion Magazine*, a monthly survey of Negro achievement in various fields. According to Bernard W. Bell, its mission was to reconcile the races and "to impress upon the world that it is not a disgrace to be a Negro, but a privilege." The magazine folded in 1917; and the Reconciliation Movement, which he launched in 1921, also failed.

Fenton Johnson died in Chicago in 1958. Biographical and critical material may be found in Bernard Bell's article in *Dictionary of American*

Negro Biography; in Hammett Worthington Smith's article in *Dictionary of Literary Biography, Volume 50*; in Johnson's "The Story of Myself" from *Tales of Darkest America* (1920); and in numerous references to him in Eugene B. Redmond's *Drumvoices* (1976). In *Negro Poetry and Drama* (1937), Sterling Brown states that Fenton Johnson's works are "striking departures in Negro poetry." See also Jean Wagner's *Black Poets of the United States, from Paul Laurence Dunbar to Langston Hughes* (1973).

The following selections come from *The Book of Negro Poetry* (1922), edited by James Weldon Johnson.

CHILDREN OF THE SUN

We are children of the sun,
        Rising sun!
Weaving Southern destiny,
Waiting for the mighty hour
When our Shiloh shall appear
With the flaming sword of right,
With the steel of brotherhood,
And emboss in crimson die
Liberty! Fraternity!

We are the star-dust folk,
        Striving folk!
Sorrow songs have lulled to rest;
Seething passions wrought through wrongs,
Led us where the moon rays dip
In the night of dull despair,
Showed us where the star gleams shine,
And the mystic symbols glow—
Liberty! Fraternity!

We have come through cloud and mist,
        Mighty men!
Dusk has kissed our sleep-born eyes,
Reared for us a mystic throne
In the splendor of the skies,
That shall always be for us,
Children of the Nazarene,
Children who shall ever sing
Liberty! Fraternity!

From James Weldon Johnson's *The Book of Negro Poetry*, Harcourt, Brace and Co., © 1922.

THE NEW DAY

From a vision red with war I awoke and saw the Prince
    of Peace hovering over No Man's Land.
Loud the whistles blew and the thunder of cannon was
    drowned by the happy shouting of the people.
From the Sinai that faces Armageddon I heard this chant
    from the throats of white-robed angels:

    Blow your trumpets, little children!
    From the East and from the West,
    From the cities in the valley,
    From God's dwelling on the mountain,
    Blow your blast that Peace might know
    She is Queen of God's great army.
    With the crying blood of millions
    We have written deep her name
    In the Book of all the Ages;
    With the lilies in the valley,
    With the roses by the Mersey,
    With the golden flower of Jersey
    We have crowned her smooth young temples.
    Where her footsteps cease to falter
    Golden grain will greet the morning,
    Where her chariot descends
    Shall be broken down the altars
    Of the gods of dark disturbance.
    Nevermore shall men know suffering,
    Nevermore shall women wailing
    Shake to grief the God of Heaven.
    From the East and from the West,
    From the cities in the valley,
    From God's dwelling on the mountain,
    Little children, blow your trumpets!

From Ethiopia, groaning 'neath her heavy burdens, I
    heard the music of the old slave songs.
I heard the wail of warriors, dusk brown, who grimly
    fought the fight of others in the trenches of Mars.
I heard the plea of blood-stained men of dusk and the
    crimson in my veins leapt furiously.

    Forget not, O my brothers, how we fought
    In No Man's Land that peace might come again!
    Forget not, O my brothers, how we gave
    Red blood to save the freedom of the world!

We were not free, our tawny hands were tied;
But Belgium's plight and Serbia's woes we shared
Each rise of sun or setting of the moon.
So when the bugle blast had called us forth
We went not like the surly brute of yore
But, as the Spartan, proud to give the world
The freedom that we never knew nor shared.
These chains, O brothers mine, have weighed us down
As Samson in the temple of the gods;
Unloosen them and let us breathe the air
That makes the goldenrod the flower of Christ.
For we have been with thee in No Man's Land,
Through lake of fire and down to Hell itself;
And now we ask of thee our liberty,
Our freedom in the land of Stars and Stripes.

I am glad that the Prince of Peace is hovering over No
    Man's Land.

TIRED

I am tired of work; I am tired of building up somebody
    else's civilization.
Let us take a rest, M'Lissy Jane.
I will go down to the Last Chance Saloon, drink a gallon
    or two of gin, shoot a game or two of dice and
    sleep the rest of the night on one of Mike's barrels.
You will let the old shanty go to rot, the white people's
    clothes turn to dust, and the Calvary Baptist Church
    sink to the bottomless pit.
You will spend your days forgetting you married me and
    your nights hunting the warm gin Mike serves the
    ladies in the rear of the Last Chance Saloon.
Throw the children into the river; civilization has given
    us too many. It is better to die than it is to grow
    up and find out that you are colored.
Pluck the stars out of the heavens. The stars mark our
    destiny. The stars marked my destiny.
I am tired of civilization.

THE BANJO PLAYER

There is music in me, the music of a peasant people.
I wander through the levee, picking my banjo and sing-
      ing my songs of the cabin and the field. At the
      Last Chance Saloon I am as welcome as the violets
      in March; there is always food and drink for me
      there, and the dimes of those who love honest music.
      Behind the railroad tracks the little children clap
      their hands and love me as they love Kris Kringle.
But I fear that I am a failure. Last night a woman
      called me a troubadour. What is a troubadour?

THE SCARLET WOMAN

Once I was good like the Virgin Mary and the Minis-
      ter's wife.
My father worked for Mr. Pullman and white people's
      tips; but he died two days after his insurance ex-
      pired.
I had nothing, so I had to go to work.
All the stock I had was a white girl's education and a
      face that enchanted the men of both races.
Starvation danced with me.
So when Big Lizzie, who kept a house for white men,
      came to me with tales of fortune that I could reap
      from the sale of my virtue I bowed my head to Vice.
Now I can drink more gin than any man for miles
      around.
Gin is better than all the water in Lethe.

Alain Locke

(1886–1954)

ALAIN LEROY LOCKE played an important role, perhaps the most important role, in the development of the New Negro Renaissance (now generally called the Harlem Renaissance). In his "Harlem Issue" of the *Survey Graphic* (May 1925), which enlarged became in December of the same year *The New Negro*, he brought to America's attention a vast artistic storehouse of folklore and other materials from the culture of the nation's black population. *The New Negro* became not only a landmark publication in the history of black literature, but also the manifesto of the New Negro movement. The Harlem Renaissance was by no means one man's cause— Du Bois, James Weldon Johnson, Benjamin Brawley, and Charles S. Johnson appreciated this upsurge in Negro literature and art and contributed to its development—but Locke was the prime mover, the gadfly, the catalyst.

Born in Philadelphia, Pennsylvania, of genteel parents, Alain Locke was educated at that city's famous Central High School, graduating in 1902 as second in his class and with a B.A. degree with honors. (When Locke was a student at Central, the school awarded B.A. degrees.) He next attended the Philadelphia School of Pedagogy, where he was first in his class and received his second B.A. in 1904. He then went to Harvard, where he finished a four-year course in three years, was elected to Phi Beta Kappa, and received his third bachelor's degree magna cum laude. He also won the college's most prestigious prize, the Bowdoin, in 1907 for an English essay. In the same year he became America's first black Rhodes Scholar; he studied at Oxford from 1907 to 1910 and at the University of Berlin from 1910 to 1911.

In 1912 Locke was appointed to Howard University's Teachers College faculty as an assistant professor. Almost from the beginning of his tenure, he felt that Howard should be a center for Negro and African culture, and joining forces with Kelly Miller and others, he planted the seeds which have blossomed into the university's present standing as a major resource center for the study of black, African, and Caribbean literature and art.

In 1924 Howard faced a crisis brought on by the efforts of students and certain faculty members to oust the school's last white president, J. Stanley Durkee. Alain Locke joined the opposition and was dismissed by Durkee in 1925. From that year until 1928 Locke was away from the university, and during that period he published *The New Negro* (reprinted in 1968) and became the recognized leader of the New Negro Renaissance.

Though trained in philosophy and a distinguished professor in that field, Locke considered himself "more of a philosophical mid-wife to a generation of younger poets, writers, and artists than a professional philosopher," and he certainly made possible the development of many talents. For several of the Renaissance's most talented young writers, including McKay, Toomer, Cullen, and Hughes, Alain Locke was a combination literary adviser and sponsor. For a gentle satire of Locke (as Dr. Parkes) in this role and on certain themes which Locke emphasized, see Wallace Thurman's *Infants of the Spring* (1932).

Possessing an encyclopedic mind, Dr. Locke published works on art (*The Negro Art: Past and Present*, 1936); on black music (*The Negro and His Music*, 1936); and on African art ("A Note on African Art," *Opportunity*, May 1924). He was a pioneer motivator of interest in black drama, then the least developed of all Negro artistic disciplines. He and Montgomery Gregory, a Howard colleague, organized the Howard Players, one of the oldest little theater groups among Negroes. The two of them also published the first Negro drama anthology, *Plays of Negro Life* (1927). During the 1930s, Locke was editor-in-chief of the Bronze Booklet Series, a publishing venture which gave black writers a chance to bring to the average reader basic facts and "progressive views about Negro life." From 1929 to 1953 Locke wrote literary reviews for *Opportunity* and *Phylon*. He was granted a leave of absence in 1951/52 to write a volume, *The Negro in American Culture*, but he died in 1954 before finishing the study (it was completed by Margaret Just Butcher in 1956).

In summary and of necessity simplified, Alain LeRoy Locke's critical position stated in effect that although the American Negro had experienced a major social and spiritual transformation, he was still in his adolescence as a literary artist, but fortunately was approaching maturity; that the Negro possessed a "primitive tropical inheritance," a sense of "remembered beauty"; that the black writer should use fully his folk materials and legacy to rejuvenate American literature, but at the same time keep in step with the best offerings of Western literature and culture. To the modern critic, these tenets may seem naive, but whatever one thinks of them, Locke has a sure place in the history of black literature.

For comment on the life, works, and influence of Alain Locke, see Michael Winston's entry in *Dictionary of American Negro Biography*; Eugene C. Holmes's "Alain Locke: Philosopher, Critic, and Spokesman," *Journal of Philosophy* (February 28, 1957); Rayford W. Logan, ed., *The New Negro Thirty Years Afterward* (1955); Arthur P. Davis's *From the Dark Tower* (1974); Lillian Avon Midgette, "A Bio-bibliography of Alain LeRoy Locke," 1963 M.A. thesis, Atlanta University; and Johnny Washington's *Alain Locke and Philosophy: A Quest for Cultural Pluralism* (1986). A facsimile edition of the May 1925 *Survey Graphic* was issued in 1980.

The following selection comes from *The New Negro: An Interpretation.*

FROM **THE NEW NEGRO**

In the last decade something beyond the watch and guard of statistics has happened in the life of the American Negro and the three Norns who have traditionally presided over the Negro problem have a changeling in their laps. The Sociologist, the Philanthropist, the Race-leader are not unaware of the New Negro, but they are at a loss to account for him. He simply cannot be swathed in their formulae. For the younger generation is vibrant with a new psychology; the new spirit is awake in the masses, and under the very eyes of the professional observers is transforming what has been a perennial problem into the progressive phases of contemporary Negro life.

Could such a metamorphosis have taken place as suddenly as it has appeared to? The answer is no; not because the New Negro is not here, but because the Old Negro had long become more of a myth than a man. The Old Negro, we must remember, was a creature of moral debate and historical controversy. His has been a stock figure perpetuated as an historical fiction partly in innocent sentimentalism, partly in deliberate reactionism. The Negro himself has contributed his share to this through a sort of protective social mimicry forced upon him by the adverse circumstances of dependence. So for generations in the mind of America, the Negro has been more of a formula than a human being—a something to be argued about, condemned or defended, to be "kept down," or "in his place," or "helped up," to be worried with or worried over, harassed or patronized, a social bogey or a social burden. The thinking Negro even has been induced to share this same general attitude, to focus his attention on controversial issues, to see himself in the distorted perspective of a social problem. His shadow, so to speak, has been more real to him than his personality. Through having had to appeal from the unjust stereotypes of his oppressors and traducers to those of his liberators, friends and benefactors he has had to subscribe to the traditional positions from which his case has been viewed. Little true social or self-understanding has or could come from such a situation.

But while the minds of most of us, black and white, have thus

Alain LeRoy Locke (ed.), *The New Negro; An Interpretation*, Albert and Charles Boni, 1925; New York: Arno, 1968.

burrowed in the trenches of the Civil War and Reconstruction, the actual march of development has simply flanked these positions, necessitating a sudden reorientation of view. We have not been watching in the right direction; set North and South on a sectional axis, we have not noticed the East till the sun has us blinking.

Recall how suddenly the Negro spirituals revealed themselves; suppressed for generations under the stereotypes of Wesleyan hymn harmony, secretive, half-ashamed, until the courage of being natural brought them out—and behold, there was folk-music. Similarly the mind of the Negro seems suddenly to have slipped from under the tyranny of social intimidation and to be shaking off the psychology of imitation and implied inferiority. By shedding the old chrysalis of the Negro problem we are achieving something like a spiritual emancipation. Until recently, lacking self-understanding, we have been almost as much of a problem to ourselves as we still are to others. But the decade that found us with a problem has left us with only a task. The multitude perhaps feels as yet only a strange relief and a new vague urge, but the thinking few know that in the reaction the vital inner grip of prejudice has been broken.

With this renewed self-respect and self-dependence, the life of the Negro community is bound to enter a new dynamic phase, the buoyancy from within compensating for whatever pressure there may be of conditions from without. The migrant masses, shifting from countryside to city, hurdle several generations of experience at a leap, but more important, the same thing happens spiritually in the life-attitudes and self-expression of the Young Negro, in his poetry, his art, his education and his new outlook, with the additional advantage, of course, of the poise and greater certainty of knowing what it is all about. From this comes the promise and warrant of a new leadership. As one of them has discerningly put it:

> We have tomorrow
> Bright before us
> Like a flame.
>
> Yesterday, a night-gone thing
> A sun-down name.
>
> And dawn today
> Broad arch above the road we came.
> We march!

This is what, even more than any "most creditable record of fifty years of freedom," requires that the Negro of to-day be seen through other than the dusty spectacles of past controversy. The day of "aunties," "uncles" and "mammies" is equally gone. Uncle Tom and

Sambo have passed on, and even the "Colonel" and "George" play barnstorm rôles from which they escape with relief when the public spotlight is off. The popular melodrama has about played itself out, and it is time to scrap the fictions, garret the bogeys and settle down to a realistic facing of facts.

First we must observe some of the changes which since the traditional lines of opinion were drawn have rendered these quite obsolete. A main change has been, of course, that shifting of the Negro population which has made the Negro problem no longer exclusively or even predominantly Southern. Why should our minds remain sectionalized, when the problem itself no longer is? Then the trend of migration has not only been toward the North and the Central Midwest, but city-ward and to the great centers of industry—the problems of adjustment are new, practical, local and not peculiarly racial. Rather they are an integral part of the large industrial and social problems of our present-day democracy. And finally, with the Negro rapidly in process of class differentiation, if it ever was warrantable to regard and treat the Negro *en masse* it is becoming with every day less possible, more unjust and more ridiculous.

In the very process of being transplanted, the Negro is becoming transformed.

The tide of Negro migration, northward and city-ward, is not to be fully explained as a blind flood started by the demands of war industry coupled with the shutting off of foreign migration, or by the pressure of poor crops coupled with increased social terrorism in certain sections of the South and Southwest. Neither labor demand, the boll-weevil nor the Ku Klux Klan is a basic factor, however contributory any or all of them may have been. The wash and rush of this human tide on the beach line of the northern city centers is to be explained primarily in terms of a new vision of opportunity, of social and economic freedom, of a spirit to seize, even in the face of an extortionate and heavy toll, a chance for the improvement of conditions. With each successive wave of it, the movement of the Negro becomes more and more a mass movement toward the larger and the more democratic chance—in the Negro's case a deliberate flight not only from countryside to city, but from medieval America to modern.

Take Harlem as an instance of this. Here in Manhattan is not merely the largest Negro community in the world, but the first concentration in history of so many diverse elements of Negro life. It has attracted the African, the West Indian, the Negro American; has brought together the Negro of the North and the Negro of the South; the man from the city and the man from the town and village; the peasant, the student, the business man, the professional man, artist, poet, musician, adventurer and worker, preacher and criminal, exploiter and social outcast. Each group has come with its own separate motives and for its own special ends, but their greatest experience has been the finding of one another. Proscription and prejudice have thrown these dissimilar elements into a common area of contact and interaction. Within this area, race sympathy and unity have determined a further fusing of sentiment and experience. So what began in terms of segregation becomes more and more, as its elements mix and react, the laboratory of a great race-welding. Hitherto, it must be admitted that American Negroes have been a race more in name than in fact, or to be exact, more in sentiment than in experience. The chief bond between them has been that of a common condition rather than a common consciousness; a problem in common rather than a life in common. In Harlem, Negro life is seizing upon its first chances for group expression and self-determination. It is—or promises at least to be—a race capital. That is why our comparison is taken with those nascent centers of folk-expression and self-determination which are playing a creative part in the world to-day. Without pretense to their political significance, Harlem has the same rôle to play for the New Negro as Dublin has had for the New Ireland or Prague for the New Czechoslovakia.

Harlem, I grant you, isn't typical—but it is significant, it is prophetic. No sane observer, however sympathetic to the new trend, would contend that the great masses are articulate as yet, but they stir, they move, they are more than physically restless. The challenge of the new intellectuals among them is clear enough—the "race radicals" and realists who have broken with the old epoch of philanthropic guidance, sentimental appeal and protest. But are we after all only reading into the stirrings of a sleeping giant the dreams of an agitator? The answer is in the migrating peasant. It is the "man farthest down" who is most active in getting up. One of the most characteristic symptoms of this is the professional man, himself migrating to recapture his constituency after a vain effort to maintain in some Southern corner what for years back seemed an established living and clientele. The clergyman following his errant flock, the physician or lawyer trailing his clients, supply the true clues. In a real sense it is the rank and file who are leading, and the leaders who are following. A transformed and transforming psychology permeates the masses.

When the racial leaders of twenty years ago spoke of developing race-pride and stimulating race-consciousness, and of the desirability of race solidarity, they could not in any accurate degree have anticipated the abrupt feeling that has surged up and now pervades the awakened centers. Some of the recognized Negro leaders and a powerful section of white opinion identified with "race work" of the older order have indeed attempted to discount this feeling as a "passing phase," an attack of "race nerves" so to speak, an "aftermath of the war," and the like. It has not abated, however, if we are to gauge by the present tone and temper of the Negro press, or by the shift in popular support from the officially recognized and orthodox spokesman to those of the independent, popular, and often radical type who are unmistakable symptoms of a new order. It is a social disservice to blunt the fact that the Negro of the Northern centers has reached a stage where tutelage, even of the most interested and well-intentioned sort, must give place to new relationships, where positive self-direction must be reckoned with in ever increasing measure. The American mind must reckon with a fundamentally changed Negro.

The Negro too, for his part, has idols of the tribe to smash. If on the one hand the white man has erred in making the Negro appear to be that which would excuse or extenuate his treatment of him, the Negro, in turn, has too often unnecessarily excused himself because of the way he has been treated. The intelligent Negro of to-day is resolved not to make discrimination an extenuation for his shortcomings in performance, individual or collective; he is trying to hold himself at par, neither inflated by sentimental allowances nor depreciated by current social discounts. For this he must know himself and be known for precisely what he is, and for that reason he welcomes the new scientific rather than the old sentimental interest. Sentimental interest in the Negro has ebbed. We used to lament this as the falling off of our friends; now we rejoice and pray to be delivered both from self-pity and condescension. The mind of each racial group has had a bitter weaning, apathy or hatred on one side matching disillusionment or resentment on the other; but they face each other to-day with the possibility at least of entirely new mutual attitudes.

It does not follow that if the Negro were better known, he would be better liked or better treated. But mutual understanding is basic for any subsequent cooperation and adjustment. The effort toward this will at least have the effect of remedying in large part what has been the most unsatisfactory feature of our present stage of race relationships in America, namely the fact that the more intelligent and representative elements of the two race groups have at so many points got quite out of vital touch with one another.

The fiction is that the life of the races is separate, and increasingly so. The fact is that they have touched too closely at the unfavorable and too lightly at the favorable levels.

While inter-racial councils have sprung up in the South, drawing on forward elements of both races, in the Northern cities manual laborers may brush elbows in their everyday work, but the community and business leaders have experienced no such interplay or far too little of it. These segments must achieve contact or the race situation in America becomes desperate. Fortunately this is happening. There is a growing realization that in social effort the co-operative basis must supplant long-distance philanthropy, and that the only safeguard for mass relations in the future must be provided in the carefuly maintained contacts of the enlightened minorities of both race groups. In the intellectual realm a renewed and keen curiosity is replacing the recent apathy; the Negro is being carefully studied, not just talked about and discussed. In art and letters, instead of being wholly caricatured, he is being seriously portrayed and painted.

To all of this the New Negro is keenly responsive as an augury of a new democracy in American culture. He is contributing his share to the new social understanding. But the desire to be understood would never in itself have been sufficient to have opened so completely the protectively closed portals of the thinking Negro's mind. There is still too much possibility of being snubbed or patronized for that. It was rather the necessity for fuller, truer self-expression, the realization of the unwisdom of allowing social discrimination to segregate him mentally, and a counter-attitude to cramp and fetter his own living—and so the "spite-wall" that the intellectuals built over the "color-line" has happily been taken down. Much of this reopening of intellectual contacts has centered in New York and has been richly fruitful not merely in the enlarging of personal experience, but in the definite enrichment of American art and letters and in the clarifying of our common vision of the social tasks ahead.

The particular significance in the re-establishment of contact between the more advanced and representative classes is that it promises to offset some of the unfavorable reactions of the past, or at least to re-surface race contacts somewhat for the future. Subtly the conditions that are molding a New Negro are molding a new American attitude.

However, this new phase of things is delicate; it will call for less charity but more justice; less help, but infinitely closer understanding. This is indeed a critical stage of race relationships because of the likelihood, if the new temper is not understood, of engendering sharp group antagonism and a second crop of more calculated prejudice. In some quarters, it has already done so. Having weaned the Negro, public opinion cannot continue to paternalize. The Negro today is inevitably moving forward under the control largely of his own objectives. What are these objectives? Those of his outer life are happily already well and finally formulated, for they are none other than the ideals of American institutions and democracy. Those of his inner life are yet in process of formation, for the new psychology at present is more of a consensus of feeling than of opinion, of attitude rather than of program. Still some points seem to have crystallized.

Up to the present one may adequately describe the Negro's "inner objectives" as an attempt to repair a damaged group psychology and reshape a warped social perspective. Their realization has required a new mentality for the American Negro. And as it matures we begin to see its effects; at first, negative, iconoclastic, and then positive and constructive. In this new group psychology we note the lapse of sentimental appeal, then the development of a more positive self-respect and self-reliance; the repudiation of social dependence, and then the gradual recovery from hyper-sensitiveness and "touchy" nerves, the repudiation of the double standard of judgment with its special philanthropic allowances and then the sturdier desire for objective and scientific appraisal; and finally the rise from social disillusionment to race pride, from the sense of social debt to the responsibilities of social contribution, and offsetting the necessary working and common-sense acceptance of restricted conditions, the belief in ultimate esteem and recognition. Therefore the Negro to-day wishes to be known for what he is, even in his faults and shortcomings, and scorns a craven and precarious survival at the price of seeming to be what he is not. He resents being spoken of as a social ward or minor, even by his own, and to being regarded a chronic patient for the sociological clinic, the sick man of American Democracy. For the same reasons, he himself is through with those social nostrums and panaceas, the so-called "solutions" of his "problem," with which he and the country have been so liberally dosed in the past. Religion, freedom, education, money—in turn, he has ardently hoped for and peculiarly trusted these things; he still believes in them, but not in blind trust that they alone will solve his life-problem.

Each generation, however, will have its creed, and that of the present is the belief in the efficacy of collective effort, in race cooperation. This deep feeling of race is at present the mainspring of Negro life. It seems to be the outcome of the reaction to proscription and prejudice; an attempt, fairly successful on the whole, to convert a defensive into an offensive position, a handicap into an incentive. It is radical in tone, but not in purpose and only the most stupid forms of opposition, misunderstanding or persecution could make it otherwise. Of course, the thinking Negro has shifted a little toward the left with the world-trend, and there is an increasing group who affiliate with radical and liberal movements. But fundamentally for the present the Negro is radical on race matters, conservative on others, in other words, a "forced radical," a social protestant rather than a genuine radical. Yet under further pressure and injustice iconoclastic thought and motives will inevitably increase. Harlem's quix-otic radicalisms call for their ounce of democracy to-day lest to-mor-row they be beyond cure.

The Negro mind reaches out as yet to nothing but American wants, American ideas. But this forced attempt to build his Ameri-canism on race values is a unique social experiment, and its ultimate success is impossible except through the fullest sharing of American culture and institutions. There should be no delusion about this. American nerves in sections unstrung with race hysteria are often fed the opiate that the trend of Negro advance is wholly separatist, and that the effect of its operation will be to encyst the Negro as a benign foreign body in the body politic. This cannot be—even if it were desirable. The racialism of the Negro is no limitation or reser-vation with respect to American life; it is only a constructive effort to build the obstructions in the stream of his progress into an effi-cient dam of social energy and power. Democracy itself is obstructed and stagnated to the extent that any of its channels are closed. In-deed they cannot be selectively closed. So the choice is not between one way for the Negro and another way for the rest, but between American institutions frustrated on the one hand and American ideals progressively fulfilled and realized on the other.

There is, of course, a warrantably comfortable feeling in being on the right side of the country's professed ideals. We realize that we cannot be undone without America's undoing. It is within the gamut of this attitude that the thinking Negro faces America, but with vari-ations of mood that are if anything more significant than the attitude itself. Sometimes we have it taken with the defiant ironic challenge of McKay:

> Mine is the future grinding down to-day
> Like a great landslip moving to the sea,
> Bearing its freight of débris far away
> Where the green hungry waters restlessly
> Heave mammoth pyramids, and break and roar
> Their eerie challenge to the crumbling shore.

Sometimes, perhaps more frequently as yet, it is taken in the fervent and almost filial appeal and counsel of Weldon Johnson's:

> O Southland, dear Southland!
> Then why do you still cling
> To an idle age and musty page,
> To a dead and useless thing?

But between defiance and appeal, midway almost between cynicism and hope, the prevailing mind stands in the mood of the same au-thor's *To America*, an attitude of sober query and stoical challenge:

How would you have us, as we are?
    Or sinking 'neath the load we bear,
Our eyes fixed forward on a star,
    Or gazing empty at despair?

Rising or falling? Men or things?
    With dragging pace or footsteps fleet?
Strong, willing sinews in your wings,
    Or tightening chains about your feet?

More and more, however, an intelligent realization of the great
discrepancy between the American social creed and the American social practice forces upon the Negro the taking of the moral advantage that is his. Only the steadying and sobering effect of a truly
characteristic gentleness of spirit prevents the rapid rise of a definite
cynicism and counter-hate and a defiant superiority feeling. Human
as this reaction would be, the majority still deprecate its advent, and
would gladly see it forestalled by the speedy amelioration of its
causes. We wish our race pride to be a healthier, more positive
achievement than a feeling based upon a realization of the shortcomings of others. But all paths toward the attainment of a sound social
attitude have been difficult; only a relatively few enlightened minds
have been able as the phrase puts it "to rise above" prejudice. The
ordinary man has had until recently only a hard choice between the
alternatives of supine and humiliating submission and stimulating
but hurtful counter-prejudice. Fortunately from some inner, desperate resourcefulness has recently sprung up the simple expedient of
fighting prejudice by mental passive resistance, in other words by
trying to ignore it. For the few, this manna may perhaps be effective,
but the masses cannot thrive upon it.

Fortunately there are constructive channels opening out into
which the balked social feelings of the American Negro can flow
freely.

Without them there would be much more pressure and danger
than there is. These compensating interests are racial but in a new
and enlarged way. One is the consciousness of acting as the advance-
guard of the African peoples in their contact with Twentieth Century
civilization; the other, the sense of a mission of rehabilitating the
race in world esteem from that loss of prestige for which the fate
and conditions of slavery have so largely been responsible. Harlem,
as we shall see, is the center of both these movements; she is the
home of the Negro's "Zionism." The pulse of the Negro world has
begun to beat in Harlem. A Negro newspaper carrying news material
in English, French and Spanish, gathered from all quarters of America, the West Indies and Africa has maintained itself in Harlem for

over five years. Two important magazines, both edited from New York, maintain their news and circulation consistently on a cosmopolitan scale. Under American auspices and backing, three pan-African congresses have been held abroad for the discussion of common interests, colonial questions and the future co-operative development of Africa. In terms of the race question as a world problem, the Negro mind has leapt, so to speak, upon the parapets of prejudice and extended its cramped horizons. In so doing it has linked up with the growing group consciousness of the dark-peoples and is gradually learning their common interests. As one of our writers has recently put it: "It is imperative that we understand the white world in its relations to the non-white world." As with the Jew, persecution is making the Negro international.

As a world phenomenon this wider race consciousness is a different thing from the much asserted rising tide of color. Its inevitable causes are not of our making. The consequences are not necessarily damaging to the best interests of civilization. Whether it actually brings into being new Armadas of conflict or argosies of cultural exchange and enlightenment can only be decided by the attitude of the dominant races in an era of critical change. With the American Negro, his new internationalism is primarily an effort to recapture contact with the scattered peoples of African derivation. Garveyism may be a transient, if spectacular, phenomenon, but the possible rôle of the American Negro in the future development of Africa is one of the most constructive and universally helpful missions that any modern people can lay claim to.

Constructive participation in such causes cannot help giving the Negro valuable group incentives, as well as increased prestige at home and abroad. Our greatest rehabilitation may possibly come through such channels, but for the present, more immediate hope rests in the revaluation by white and black alike of the Negro in terms of his artistic endowments and cultural contributions, past and prospective. It must be increasingly recognized that the Negro has already made very substantial contributions, not only in his folk-art, music especially, which has always found appreciation, but in larger, though humbler and less acknowledged ways. For generations the Negro has been the peasant matrix of that section of America which has most undervalued him, and here he has contributed not only materially in labor and in social patience, but spiritually as well. The South has unconsciously absorbed the gift of his folk-temperament. In less than half a generation it will be easier to recognize this, but the fact remains that a leaven of humor, sentiment, imagination and tropic nonchalance has gone into the making of the South from a humble, unacknowledged source. A second crop of the Negro's gifts promises still more largely. He now becomes a conscious contributor and lays aside the status of a beneficiary and ward for that of a collaborator and participant in American civilization. The great social gain in this is the releasing of our talented group from the arid fields of controversy and debate to the productive fields of creative expression. The especially cultural recognition they win should in turn prove the key to that revaluation of the Negro which must precede or accompany any considerable futher betterment of race relationships. But whatever the general effect, the present generation will have added the motives of self-expression and spiritual development to the old and still unfinished task of making material headway and progress. No one who understandingly faces the situation with its substantial accomplishment or views the new scene with its still more abundant promise can be entirely without hope. And certainly, if in our lifetime the Negro should not be able to celebrate his full initiation into American democracy, he can at least, on the warrant of these things, celebrate the attainment of a significant and satisfying new phase of group development, and with it a spiritual Coming of Age.

Benjamin Brawley

(1882–1939)

SCHOLAR, LEGENDARY TEACHER, and pioneer critic, Benjamin Griffith Brawley was one of the most prolific Negro authors of his generation. The son of a Baptist minister, Brawley was educated in schools in Nashville, Tennessee, and Petersburg, Virginia, before entering the preparatory college where he took his first A.B. in 1901. He received a second baccalaureate from the University of Chicago, and an M.A. from Harvard. Brawley taught in several Negro colleges including his alma mater Atlanta Baptist, Shaw University, and Howard University.

From 1913, when he published *A Short History of the American Negro*, until his death, Brawley produced a stream of works, including numerous cultural, biographical, historical, and literary essays for several of America's most prestigious journals. His wide-ranging book-length publications, in addition to his first, include *A Short History of the English Drama* (1921); *A Social History of the American Negro* (1921); *A New Survey of English Literature* (1925); *The Negro in Literature and Art in the United States* (1929), later revised as *The Negro Genius* (1937); *A History of the English Hymm* (1932); and *Paul Laurence Dunbar: Poet of His People* (1936).

Several of Brawley's works on the Negro are still scholarly, sound, and useful. Brawley, however, failed to see the full significance of the works of New Negro (Harlem) Renaissance poets like Langston Hughes, Sterling Brown, and other poets who stressed the significance of jazz, the blues, and other folk materials of black people.

The best bibliographical sources for Brawley are *National Cyclopedia of American Biography: the North Carolina Historical Review* (vol. 34); and John W. Parker's memoir in *Phylon* (vol. 10, no. 1). See also the *Dictionary of America Negro Biography* entry by J. Saunders Redding.

The following selection comes from *The Negro in Literature and Art in the United States* (1929), revised and republished as *The Negro Genuis* (1937).

THE NEGRO IN AMERICAN FICTION

Ever since Sydney Smith sneered at American books a hundred years ago, honest critics have asked themselves if the literature of the United States was not really open to the charge of provincialism. Within the last year or two the argument has been very much revived; and an English critic, Mr. Edward Garnett, writing in *The Atlantic Monthly*, has pointed out that with our predigested ideas and made-to-order fiction we not only discourage individual genius, but make it possible for the multitude to think only such thoughts as have passed through a sieve. Our most popular novelists, and sometimes our most respectable writers, see only the sensation that is uppermost for the moment in the mind of the crowd—divorce, graft, tainted meat or money—and they proceed to cut the cloth of their fiction accordingly. Mr. Owen Wister, a "regular practitioner" of the novelist's art, in substance admitting the weight of these charges, lays the blame on our crass democracy which utterly refuses to do its own thinking and which is satisfied only with the tinsel and gewgaws and hobbyhorses of literature. And no theme has suffered so much from the coarseness of the mob-spirit in literature as that of the Negro.

As a matter of fact, the Negro in his problems and strivings offers to American writers the greatest opportunity that could possibly be given to them to-day. It is commonly agreed that only one other large question, that of the relations of capital and labor, is of as much interest to the American public; and even this great issue fails to possess quite the appeal offered by the Negro from the social standpoint. One can only imagine what a Victor Hugo, detached and philosophical, would have done with such a theme in a novel. When we see what actually has been done—how often in the guise of fiction a writer has preached a sermon or shouted a political creed, or vented his spleen—we are not exactly proud of the art of novel-writing as it has been developed in the United States of America. Here was opportunity for tragedy, for comedy, for the subtle portrayal of all the relations of man with his fellow man, for faith and hope and love and sorrow. And yet, with the Civil War fifty years in the distance, not one novel or one short story of the first rank has found its inspiration in this great theme. Instead of such work we have consistently had traditional tales, political tracts, and lurid melodramas.

From *The Negro in Literature and Art in the United States* by Benjamin Brawley. Originally published in 1929 by Duffield and Company, New York. Reprinted from the third edition (New York, 1930) in 1970 by AMS Press, New York.

Let us see who have approached the theme, and just what they have done with it, for the present leaving out of account all efforts put forth by Negro writers themselves.

The names of four exponents of Southern life come at once to mind—George W. Cable, Joel Chandler Harris, Thomas Nelson Page, and Thomas Dixon; and at once, in their outlook and method of work, the first two become separate from the last two. Cable and Harris have looked toward the past, and have embalmed vanished or vanishing types. Mr. Page and Mr. Dixon, with their thought on the present (though for the most part they portray the recent past), have used the novel as a vehicle for political propaganda.

It was in 1879 that "Old Creole Days" evidenced the advent of a new force in American literature; and on the basis of this work, and of "The Grandissimes" which followed, Mr. Cable at once took his place as the foremost portrayer of life in old New Orleans. By birth, by temperament, and by training he was thoroughly fitted for the task to which he set himself. His mother was from New England, his father of the stock of colonial Virginia; and the stern Puritanism of the North was mellowed by the gentler influences of the South. Moreover, from his long apprenticeship in newspaper work in New Orleans he had received abundantly the knowledge and training necessary for his work. Setting himself to a study of the Negro of the old régime, he made a specialty of the famous—and infamous— quadroon society of Louisiana of the third and fourth decades of the last century. And excellent as was his work, turning his face to the past in manner as well as in matter, from the very first he raised the question propounded by this paper. In his earliest volume there was a story entitled " 'Tite Poulette," the heroine of which was a girl amazingly fair, the supposed daughter of one Madame John. A young Dutchman fell in love with 'Tite Poulette, championed her cause at all times, suffered a beating and stabbing for her, and was by her nursed back to life and love. In the midst of his perplexity about joining himself to a member of another race, came the word from Madame John that the girl was not her daughter, but the child of yellow fever patients whom she had nursed until they died, leaving their infant in her care. Immediately upon the publication of this story, the author received a letter from a young woman who had actually lived in very much the same situation as that portrayed in " 'Tite Poulette," telling him that his story was not true to life and that he knew it was not, for Madame John really *was* the mother of the heroine. Accepting the criticism, Mr. Cable set about the composition of "Madame Delphine," in which the situation is somewhat similar, but in which at the end the mother tamely makes a confession to a priest. What is the trouble? The artist is so bound by cir-

cumstances and hemmed in by tradition that he simply has not the
courage to launch out into the deep and work out his human problems for himself. Take a representative portrait from "The Grandissimes":

> Clemence had come through ages of African savagery, through fires
> that do not refine, but that blunt and blast and blacken and char; starva-
> tion, gluttony, drunkenness, thirst, drowning, nakedness, dirt, fetichism,
> debauchery, slaughter, pestilence, and the rest—she was their heiress;
> they left her the cinders of human feelings. . . . She had had children of
> assorted colors—had one with her now, the black boy that brought the
> basil to Joseph; the others were here and there, some in the Grandissime
> households or field-gangs, some elsewhere within occasional sight, some
> dead, some not accounted for. Husbands—like the Samaritan woman's.
> We know she was a constant singer and laugher.

Very brilliant of course; and yet Clemence is a relic, not a prophecy.

Still more of a relic is Uncle Remus. For decades now, this
charming old Negro has been held up to the children of the South
as the perfect expression of the beauty of life in the glorious times
"befo' de wah," when every Southern gentleman was suckled at the
bosom of a "black mammy." Why should we not occasionally attempt to paint the Negro of the new day—intelligent, ambitious,
thrifty, manly? Perhaps he is not so poetic; but certainly the human
element is greater.

To the school of Cable and Harris belong also of course Miss
Grace King and Mrs. Ruth McEnery Stuart, a thoroughly representative piece of work being Mrs. Stuart's "Uncle 'Riah's Christmas Eve."
Other more popular writers of the day, Miss Mary Johnston and
Miss Ellen Glasgow for instance, attempt no special analysis of the
Negro. They simply take him for granted as an institution that always has existed and always will exist, as a hewer of wood and
drawer of water, from the first flush of creation to the sounding of
the trump of doom.

But more serious is the tone when we come to Thomas Nelson
Page and Thomas Dixon. We might tarry for a few minutes with Mr.
Page to listen to more such tales as those of Uncle Remus; but we
must turn to living issues. Times have changed. The grandson of
Uncle Remus does not feel that he must stand with his hat in his
hand when he is in our presence, and he even presumes to help us
in the running of our government. This will never do; so in "Red
Rock" and "The Leopard's Spots" it must be shown that he should
never have been allowed to vote anyway, and those honorable gentlemen in the Congress of the United States in the year 1865 did not
know at all what they were about. Though we are given the charac-

ters and setting of a novel, the real business is to show that the Negro has been the "sentimental pet" of the nation all too long. By all means let us have an innocent white girl, a burly Negro, and a burning at the stake, or the story would be incomplete.

We have the same thing in "The Clansman," a "drama of fierce revenge." But here we are concerned very largely with the blackening of a man's character. Stoneman (Thaddeus Stevens very thinly disguised) is himself the whole Congress of the United States. He is a gambler, and "spends a part of almost every night at Hall & Pemberton's Faro Place on Pennsylvania Avenue." He is hysterical, "drunk with the joy of a triumphant vengeance." "The South is conquered soil," he says to the President (a mere figure-head, by the way), "I mean to blot it from the map." Further: "It is but the justice and wisdom of heaven that the Negro shall rule the land of his bondage. It is the only solution of the race problem. Wait until I put a ballot in the hand of every Negro, and a bayonet at the breast of every white man from the James to the Rio Grande." Stoneman, moreover, has a mistress, a mulatto woman, a "yellow vampire" who dominates him completely. "Senators, representatives, politicians of low and high degree, artists, correspondents, foreign ministers, and cabinet officers hurried to acknowledge their fealty to the uncrowned king, and hail the strange brown woman who held the keys of his house as the first lady of the land." This, let us remember, was for some months the best-selling book in the United States. A slightly altered version of it has very recently commanded such prices as were never before paid for seats at a moving-picture entertainment; and with "The Traitor" and "The Southerner" it represents our most popular treatment of the gravest social question in American life! "The Clansman" is to American literature exactly what a Louisiana mob is to American democracy. Only too frequently, of course, the mob represents us all too well.

Turning from the longer works of fiction to the short story, I have been interested to see how the matter has been dealt with here. For purposes of comparison I have selected from ten representative periodicals as many distinct stories, no one of which was published more than ten years ago; and as these are in almost every case those stories that first strike the eye in a periodical index, we may assume that they are thoroughly typical. The ten are: "Shadow," by Harry Stillwell Edwards, in the *Century* (December, 1906); "Callum's Co'tin': A Plantation Idyl," by Frank H. Sweet, in the *Craftsman* (March, 1907); "His Excellency the Governor," by L. M. Cooke, in *Putnam's* (February, 1908); "The Black Drop," by Margaret Deland, in *Collier's Weekly* (May 2 and 9, 1908); "Jungle Blood," by Elmore Elliott Peake, in *McClure's* (September, 1908); "The Race-Rioter," by Harris Merton Lyon, in the *American* (February, 1910); "Shadow," by

Grace MacGowan Cooke and Alice MacGowan, in *Everybody's*
(March, 1910); "Abram's Freedom," by Edna Turpin, in the *Atlantic*
(September, 1912); "A Hypothetical Case," by Norman Duncan, in
Harper's (June, 1915); and "The Chalk Game," by L. B. Yates, in the
Saturday Evening Post (June 5, 1915). For high standards of fiction I
think we may safely say that, all in all, the periodicals here mentioned are representative of the best that America has to offer. In
some cases the story cited is the only one on the Negro question
that a magazine has published within the decade.

"Shadow" (in the *Century*) is the story of a Negro convict who
for a robbery committed at the age of fourteen was sentenced to
twenty years of hard labor in the mines of Alabama. An accident disabled him, however, and prevented his doing the regular work for
the full period of his imprisonment. At twenty he was a hostler,
looking forward in despair to the fourteen years of confinement still
waiting for him. But the three little girls of the prison commissioner
visit the prison. Shadow performs many little acts of kindness for
them, and their hearts go out to him. They storm the governor and
the judge for his pardon, and present the Negro with his freedom as
a Christmas gift. The story is not long, but it strikes a note of genuine pathos.

"Callum's Co'tin" is concerned with a hard-working Negro, a
blacksmith, nearly forty, who goes courting the girl who called at his
shop to get a trinket mended for her mistress. At first he makes himself ridiculous by his finery; later he makes the mistake of coming to
a crowd of merrymakers in his working clothes. More and more,
however, he storms the heart of the girl, who eventually capitulates.
From the standpoint simply of craftsmanship, the story is an excellent piece of work.

"His Excellency the Governor" deals with the custom on Southern plantations of having, in imitation of the white people, a Negro
"governor" whose duty it was to settle minor disputes. At the death
of old Uncle Caleb, who for years had held this position of responsibility, his son Jubal should have been the next in order. He was
likely to be superseded, however, by loud-mouthed Sambo, though
urged to assert himself by Maria, his wife, an old house-servant who
had no desire whatever to be defeated for the place of honor among
the women by Sue, a former field-hand. At the meeting where all
was to be decided, however, Jubal with the aid of his fiddle completely confounded his rival and won. There are some excellent
touches in the story; but, on the whole, the composition is hardly
more than fair in literary quality.

"The Black Drop," throughout which we see the hand of an experienced writer, analyzes the heart of a white boy who is in love with
a girl who is almost white, and who when the test confronts him

suffers the tradition that binds him to get the better of his heart. "But you will still believe that I love you?" he asks, ill at ease as they separate. "No, of course I can not believe that," replies the girl.

"Jungle Blood" is the story of a simple-minded, simple-hearted Negro of gigantic size who in a moment of fury kills his pretty wife and the white man who has seduced her. The tone of the whole may be gleaned from the description of Moss Harper's father: "An old darky sat drowsing on the stoop. There was something ape-like about his long arms, his flat, wide-nostriled nose, and the mat of gray wool which crept down his forehead to within two inches of his eyebrows."

"The Race-Rioter" sets forth the stand of a brave young sheriff to protect his prisoner, a Negro boy, accused of the assault and murder of a little white girl. Hank Egge tries by every possible subterfuge to defeat the plans of a lynching party, and finally dies riddled with bullets as he is defending his prisoner. The story is especially remarkable for the strong and sympathetic characterization of such contrasting figures as young Egge and old Dikeson, the father of the dead girl.

"Shadow" (in *Everybody's*) is a story that depends for its force very largely upon incident. It studies the friendship of a white boy, Ranny, and a black boy, Shadow, a relationship that is opposed by both the Northern white mother and the ambitious and independent Negro mother. In a fight, Shad breaks a collar-bone for Ranny; later he saves him from drowning. In the face of Ranny's white friends, all the harsher side of the problem is seen; and yet the human element is strong beneath it all. The story, not without considerable merit as it is, would have been infinitely stronger if the friendship of the two boys had been pitched on a higher plane. As it is, Shad is very much like a dog following his master.

"Abram's Freedom" is at the same time one of the most clever and one of the most provoking stories with which we have to deal. It is a perfect example of how one may walk directly up to the light and then deliberately turn his back upon it. The story is set just before the Civil War. It deals with the love of the slave Abram for a free young woman, Emmeline. "All his life he had heard and used the phrase 'free nigger' as a term of contempt. What, then, was this vague feeling, not definite enough yet to be a wish or even a longing?" So far, so good. Emmeline inspires within her lover the highest ideals of manhood, and he becomes a hostler in a livery-stable, paying to his master so much a year for his freedom. Then comes the astounding and forced conclusion. At the very moment when, after years of effort, Emmeline has helped her husband to gain his freedom (and when all the slaves are free as a matter of fact by virtue of the Emancipation Proclamation), Emmeline, whose husband has special reason to be grateful to his former master, says to the lady of the house; "Me an' Abram ain't got nothin' to do in dis worl' but to wait on you an' master."

In "A Hypothetical Case" we again see the hand of a master-crafts-man. Is a white boy justified in shooting a Negro who has offended him? The white father is not quite at ease, quibbles a good deal, but finally says Yes. The story, however, makes it clear that the Negro did not strike the boy. He was a hermit living on the Florida coast and perfectly abased when he met Mercer and his two companions. When the three boys pursued him and finally overtook him, the Negro simply held the hands of Mercer until the boy had recovered his temper. Mer-cer in his rage really struck himself.

"The Chalk Game" is the story of a little Negro jockey who wins a race in Louisville only to be drugged and robbed by some "flash-light" Negroes who send him to Chicago. There he recovers his for-tunes by giving to a group of gamblers the correct "tip" on another race, and he makes his way back to Louisville much richer by his visit. Throughout the story emphasis is placed upon the superstitious element in the Negro race, an element readily considered by men who believe in luck.

Of these ten stories, only five strike out with even the slightest degree of independence. "Shadow" (In the *Century*) is not a powerful piece of work, but it is written in tender and beautiful spirit. "The Black Drop" is a bold handling of a strong situation. "The Race-Rioter" also rings true, and in spite of the tragedy there is optimism in this story of a man who is not afraid to do his duty. "Shadow" (in *Everybody's*) awakens all sorts of discussion, but at least attempts to deal honestly with a situation that might arise in any neighborhood at any time. "A Hypothetical Case" is the most tense and indepen-dent story in the list.

On the other hand, "Callum's Co'tin'" and "His Excellency the Governor," bright comedy though they are, belong, after all, to the school of Uncle Remus. "Jungle Blood" and "The Chalk Game" be-long to the class that always regards the Negro as an animal, a mi-nor, a plaything—but never as a man. "Abram's Freedom," exceed-ingly well written for two-thirds of the way, falls down hopelessly at the end. Many old Negroes after the Civil War preferred to remain with their former masters; but certainly no young woman of the type of Emmeline would sell her birthright for a mess of pottage.

Just there is the point. That the Negro is ever to be taken seri-ously is incomprehensible to some people. It is the story of "The Man that Laughs" over again. The more Gwynplaine protests, the more outlandish he becomes to the House of Lords.

We are simply asking that those writers of fiction who deal with the Negro shall be thoroughly honest with themselves, and not remain forever content to embalm old types and work over outworn ideas. Rather should they sift the present and forecast the future. But of course the editors must be considered. The editors must give their readers what the readers want; and when we consider the populace, of course we have to reckon with the mob. And the mob does not find anything very attractive about a Negro who is intelligent, cultured, manly, and who does not smile. It will be observed that in no one of the ten stories above mentioned, not even in one of the five remarked most favorably, is there a Negro of this type. Yet he is obliged to come. America has yet to reckon with him. The day of Uncle Remus as well as of Uncle Tom is over.

Even now, however, there are signs of better things. Such an artist as Mr. Howells, for instance, has once or twice dealt with the problem in excellent spirit. Then there is the work of the Negro writers themselves. The numerous attempts in fiction made by them have most frequently been open to the charge of crassness already considered; but Paul Laurence Dunbar, Charles W. Chesnutt, and W. E. Burghardt Du Bois have risen above the crowd. Mr. Dunbar, of course, was better in poetry than in prose. Such a short story as "Jimsella," however, exhibited considerable technique. "The Uncalled" used a living topic treated with only partial success. But for the most part, Mr. Dunbar's work looked toward the past. Somewhat stronger in prose is Mr. Chesnutt. "The Marrow of Tradition" is not much more than a political tract, and "The Colonel's Dream" contains a good deal of preaching; but "The House Behind the Cedars" is a real novel. Among his short stories, "The Bouquet" may be remarked for technical excellence, and "The Wife of His Youth" for a situation of unusual power. Dr. Du Bois's "The Quest of the Silver Fleece" contains at least one strong dramatic situation, that in which Bles probes the heart of Zora; but the author is a sociologist and essayist rather than a novelist. The grand epic of the race is yet to be produced.

Some day we shall work out the problems of our great country. Some day we shall not have a state government set at defiance, and the massacre of Ludlow. Some day our little children will not slave in mines and mills, but will have some chance at the glory of God's creation; and some day the Negro will cease to be a problem and become a human being. Then, in truth, we shall have the Promised Land. But until that day comes let those who mold our ideals and set the standards of our art in fiction at least be honest with themselves and independent. Ignorance we may for a time forgive; but a man has only himself to blame if he insists on not seeing the sunrise in the new day.

Walter White

(1893–1955)

DYNAMIC CHIEF EXECUTIVE of the NAACP, literary counselor of young black writers, and authority on lynching, Walter Francis White too often has been overlooked as both a creative and a journalistic writer of the Harlem Renaissance. Because of the importance of his NAACP connection, this neglect is only natural. Nevertheless, as the author of two novels, an autobiography, many articles in the nation's leading journals, as a war correspondent, and as a columnist for the *Chicago Defender* and the *New York Herald-Tribune*, Walter White definitely deserves consideration of the "writing" side of his many-sided career.

A "volunteer Negro," blue-eyed and blond, Walter White could easily "pass" and did so often when his investigations called for this strategy. The son of middle-class parents, he was born in Atlanta, Georgia, in 1893. He was educated at Atlanta University, graduating in 1916. His great speaking and organizing ability in leading a fight against Atlanta's board of education attracted the attention of the NAACP. In 1918 he joined the staff of that organization as assistant to James Weldon Johnson. The two made an excellent team and they helped to make the NAACP the great organization it finally became. When Johnson stepped down in 1931, White became the chief executive and held this position through several changes in the association's purpose and structure until his death in 1955.

During the intervening years, he was, among many other things, delegate to the Second Pan-African Congress; consultant for the U. S. delegation at the organizing of the United Nations in 1945; war correspondent in the European, African, and Pacific war zones; and a participant in the Round the World Town Meeting of the Air, visiting India, Japan, and countries in Europe, the Middle East, Africa, and the Caribbean. In 1937 he was awarded the Spingarn Medal for his outstanding work in lobbying for the antilynching bill and investigating lynchings.

White published the following major works: *Rope and Faggot* (1920), *Fire in the Flint* (1924), *Flight* (1926), *A Rising Wind* (1945), and *A Man Called White* (1948). The second and third listed are novels, and like the fiction of Jesse Fauset, Nella Larsen, and others, they deal with three themes: the black middle class, passing for white, and lynching. *Fire in the Flint* is a lynching novel and *Flight* deals with the passing theme. Because he knew both subjects thoroughly, he gives a realistic picture in both works, but he is not a great novelist. His finest work is *Rope and*

Faggot, an authoritative study of lynching. *A Rising Wind* is a journalistic record of his experiences as a correspondent in the European, North African, and Italian theaters of war. The autobiography, *A Man Called White*, is not a good work artistically, but it is a fascinating work because the life of Walter White was that of a principal warrior in an important period of the American Negro's fight for decency and equality.

For comment on Walter White's literary place as an author and as an adviser to young black writers, see Edward E. Waldron's *Walter White and the Harlem Renaissance* (1978). For comment on White's overall career, see the excellent article by August Meier and Elliott Rudwick in *Dictionary of American Negro Biography*. See also White's autobiography, *A Man Called White* (1948), and Walter C. Daniel's entry in *Dictionary of Literary Biography, Volume 51*.

The following selection comes from *Rope and Faggot*.

SEX AND LYNCHING

With the most intransigent Negrophobe it is possible to conduct a conversation on certain phases of the race question and do so with a measured calmness of manner. But when one approaches, however delicately or remotely, the question of sex or "social equality," reason and judicial calm promptly take flight. Berserk rage usually siezes one's conversational *vis-à-vis*. One can count with mathematical certainty upon the appearance of the fiercely challenging: "How should *you* like to have your daughter marry a nigger?" as the answer to any attempt at sane discussion of this phase of the race question. It is of no avail to point out that there is but a tenuous connexion between sex relations or intermarriages on the one hand and ordinary justice and decency on the other. Sex with all its connotations so muddies the waters of reason that it is impossible to bring the conversation back to its more unimpassioned state.

Of all the emotional determinants of lynching none is more potent in blocking approach to a solution than sex, and of all the factors, emotional or otherwise, none is less openly and honestly discussed. Even the most fair-minded Southerner keeps away from the topic, fearing the tempest which follows its introduction as a topic of discussion. As a result, this element in the race problem and specifically in lynching is distorted by the conspiracy of semi-silence into an importance infinitely greater than the actual facts concerning it would justify. From the time of its introduction as a defense of

From Walter White, *Rope and Faggot: A Biography of Judge Lynch*, New York: Arno Press and The New York Times, 1969. Reprinted by permission of Jane White Viazzi.

lynching, which, as we shall see, was simultaneous with the elevation of cotton through inventions to one of the premier crops of the world, sex and alleged sex crimes have served as the great bulwark of the lyncher.

Some years ago in a novel I ventured to put into the mouth of one of my characters, a Southern white lawyer, what seemed to me a simple and truthful statement to the effect that not in all the lynchings where rape or attempted rape was alleged had such a crime actually occurred. Down upon me tumbled an amazing volume of abuse from small-town newspapers of the South. One of them, a Georgia daily, indignantly asserted that the South is the most law-abiding section of the United States, and, a few paragraphs later, invited me to visit Georgia and see what "Southern gentlemen do to those who slander the fair name of Southern womanhood."

This Southern excitability over so universal a fact as sex has many causes. It is impossible to trace them all to their source. But a few of them can be separated from the fabric of many patterns and weavings which is the race problem. Perhaps statement of these may serve to bring some light where there has been little but heat.

There are at least a half-dozen reasons why sex harasses the South, and especially the rural South and the anti-Negro South. The first is one that is common to most regions which are predominantly rural—the dullness of life and the lack of such diversions as theatres, moving-pictures, parties, concerts, shop-windows, and the like, which in the city leave less time for concupiscent desires and thoughts. The South has suffered more than other sections because of the fact noted in the preceding chapter—the preponderance of Methodists and Baptists to whom such diversions as card-playing, dancing, and theatre attendance are forbidden. In many parts of the South this circumstance has elevated attendance at church, sex escapades, and lynching into the principal escapes from the grim and sordid reality of work.

A second reason for over-emphasis on sex in the lynching states is that the creation of the bogy of sex crimes as a defence of lynching has made the South the terrified victim of the fears of its own conjuring. Despite the evidence of the figures showing that only a small percentage of lynched Negroes were even accused of rape, the vast majority of whites in the states where lynchings are most frequently staged really believe that most mob murders are the results of sex crimes. Having created the Frankenstein monster (and it is no less terrifying because it is largely illusory), the lyncher lives in constant fear of his own creation and, at the same time, has by means of his creation caused more crimes against the women of his race than there would have been in a more sane and normal environment.

The vast amount of advertising which lynchings have given to allegations of sex crimes has induced subnormal Negroes to attempt crimes of rape, the power of suggestion being as potent as it is. Such an aftermath to lynchings has been noted in certain instances—the idea of successfully consummating sex crimes having been implanted by the news of a lynching. The mentally deficient individual who would thus be impregnated with the thought of being able to escape punishment would obviously not be deterred by fear of a horrible death in expiation of his crime. Thus it is not at all improbable that lynching has added to sex crimes or attempts at such crimes. There is some foundation for such a surmise when one considers how infrequently Negroes are charged with such crimes in the states where lynchings have been very infrequent.

Third in the list of causes of sex-obsession in the South is the Southern white woman's proneness to hysteria where Negroes are concerned; and this is an aspect of the question of lynching which needs investigation by a competent psychologist. It is appropriate here only to report observations and conclusions based upon a fairly extensive experience with the statistics and literature of lynching. My own experience in investigating forty-one lynchings and the study of several thousand others reveals that in the great majority of cases where rape or attempted rape was alleged, the women can be divided into four classes: young girls ranging from the ages of twelve or thirteen to nineteen or twenty years of age, passing through the difficult period of adolescence; second (and this includes a considerable percentage of the alleged victims of attacks), women who range in age from the middle forties upwards; third, women who have been married for many years and usually to rather unattractive husbands; fourth, spinsters.

Fourth among the reasons is the intense religiosity of the lynching states and the primitiveness of their religion. Psychologists have long since established the intimate relation between the emotions of sex and of religion, and that the more primitive the religion, the greater is the part played by sex. Critics of the American scene from Frances Trollope to H. L. Mencken have observed in the frenzy of Methodist revivals what comes dangerously close to being a species of sex indulgence. Certainly one can find in many parts of the South numerous counterparts, male and female, white and Negro, of the woman William James describes in his *Varieties of Religious Experience* who could induce a state of rapture by dwelling upon the thought that "she could always cuddle up to God."

It is also a familiar phenomenon that the sex instinct figures in religious ecstasy in somewhat the same proportions that illiteracy and ignorance afflict the religious-minded. Given an elaborate system of taboos that label as "sinful" even relatively innocent diversions, which would absorb at least a part of the time otherwise given to erotic thoughts and desires, subjected to the explosive experiences attendant upon religious experiences, deprived by ignorance, geographical isolation, and poverty from books and other intellectual releases, and victims of a bogy of the Negro as a *bête noire*—all these handicaps reveal vividly the state of mind which turns devout Christians into lynchers, especially when sex enters the equation.

Maynard Shipley, in his *The War on Modern Science*, quotes the observations of a Southern observer on the connexion between illiteracy among native-born whites and the preponderance of Baptists in the total church population of certain Southern states. "The U.S. Census report for 1920 shows that the percentage of illiteracy is highest in those states where Baptists are more numerous. Among the native-born whites alone the percentage of illiteracy runs as follows; Alabama, 6.3; Georgia, 5.4; Kentucky, 7; Louisiana, 11.4; Mississippi, 3.6; North Carolina, 6.8; South Carolina, 6.5; Tennessee, 7.3; Texas, 3; Virginia, 5.9; West Virginia, 4.6." Cochran compares these figures with those of such states as Connecticut, New York, the Dakotas, and others in the North and West where there are fewer communicants of the evangelical churches and where also the illiteracy rate of native-born whites is one-half of one per cent. He paints a depressing picture of the relations between the poverty of ministers and their congregations, the ignorance of the clergy, the extent of Fundamentalism and opposition of scientific advancement among them, which seem amply to justify the pessimistic declaration of J. R. King of South Carolina that the common people of his state are "fast losing their thinking faculty for lack of use. Generations of religion have produced a generation of religious fanatics. . . . Unless there is help from the outside, the South is headed for a darker period than the Dark Ages."

When the student of human behaviour views the Southern scene and especially the rural sections of the South and sees the extent of religious bigotry of which the Ku Klux Klan, the Bible Crusaders, and the Supreme Kingdom are the organized forms; when he sees such catch-phrases as "Back to the Rock of Ages and forget the ages of Rocks" raised to the dignity of a supreme rallying-cry of fanaticism; when he watches the resolute efforts of the embattled Fundamentalists "who are making dogma into a statute and are driving out all who preach and teach the modern view of the Bible and religion" and thereby make even more primitive the religion of the South; when he sees all these and other forms of religious intolerance gripping the lynching states, then he can understand one of the most potent reasons for the enormous emphasis on sex in these states.

Even a superficial knowledge of the history of early and primitive religions will cause him to understand the insane fury of the residents of rural Mississippi and Georgia and Texas and the extent of their sadism when real or alleged sex crimes are perpetrated.

Dr. A. A. Brill, the distinguished psychiatrist, even more definitely links propensity to mob violence to abnormal sex instincts. "The torture which is an accompaniment of modern lynching," he declares, "shows that it is an act of perversion only found in those suffering from extreme forms of sexual perversion. Of course, not all lynchings are conducted in this fashion, but it is not uncommon to read accounts telling that the victim was tortured with hot irons, that his eyes were burned out, and that other monstrous cruelties were inflicted upon him. Such bestiality can be recognized only as a form of perversion. Lynching is a distinct menace to the community. It allows primitive brutality to assert itself and thus destroys the strongest fabric of civilization. Anyone taking part in or witnessing a lynching cannot remain a civilized person," (quoted from *Tenth Annual Report* of the NAACP).

A fifth reason for preoccupation with sex in the lynching states is the traditional attitude towards coloured women and the price now being paid for that attitude. For two and a half centuries of slavery slave women had no control over or defence of their bodies. As chattels, their bodies were their own only in so far as their owners were men of moral integrity. In codes and practices these owners ranged from those who permitted neither themselves, their overseers, nor male members of their families to tamper with the persons of their female slaves, down to owners who deliberately used slave women as breeders of half-white slaves—combining, as it were, pleasure with business. Midway between these poles of conduct were those who permitted and even urged their sons to take Negro mistresses and thus protect the chastity of white women, a somewhat analogous practice to that of ancient Rome when Solon caused female slaves "to be brought to the city and exposed to save other women from assaults on their virtue."

Whatever may be the current interpretation of virtue, it is axiomatic that an individual or society cannot maintain for any great length of time dual standards of personal conduct which are diametrically opposed to each other. The man who attempts to maintain a fixed respect towards one group of women and indulges meanwhile in all manner of immoralities with another group may seek ever so hard to maintain such a balanced dual standard. Inevitably and imperceptibly he finds it impossible, to the detriment of his respect for the first group. And that is precisely what has happened to the South, the white South, both male and female. For more than two hundred years this moral deterioration has affected the Southern states, and from that decay arises the most terrifying of all the aspects of the race problem to the white man.

As far back as 1691 the number of children born of slave fathers and white women had increased so alarmingly that Virginia, which seems to have been usually the state to legislate against what appeared to be evils arising from slavery, sought to end this intermixture by means of a law which prohibited *marriage* between a white man or woman with "a Negro, mulatto, or Indian man or woman, bond or free," on pain of banishment; and which prohibited *sexual relations* between a *white woman* and a *Negro* or *mulatto*. The care exercised not to interfere with sexual relations between *white men* and *Negro* or *mulatto women* will be noted. Any white woman who bore a Negro's child was liable to be fined or, in default of payment of that fine, to be sold into service for five years; the child was "bound in sevitude to the Church wardens until thirty years of age."

Maryland even earlier (in 1663), faced with the same problem, passed a law declaring that any free-born (i.e., white) woman marrying a Negro slave should serve the slave's owner as long as her husband lived; children born of the union should also be slaves, the property of the owner of the father of those children. The effect of this law was dismaying to its framers. Slave-owners, with eyes solely upon profits, utilized the measure to secure slaves free of all cost and urged their Negro male slaves to marry white women—thus securing the wives as slaves and the children they bore to their husbands free of all cost.

Even a later law, passed in 1715, making any free Negro and white woman who married each other servants for seven years and their children servants until thirty-one years of age did not put a stop to this type of marriage. North and South—wherever there was slavery—the loose conduct of white men towards coloured women was finding its counterpart in relations between white women and coloured men. Neither legislation nor public condemnation seemed appreciably to check intermixture of this sort. As the Northern states for economic reasons abandoned slavery, the practice and the problem seemed to dwindle in extent, but upon the states of the South, which, also for economic reasons clung to and extended slavery, there was placed a social heritage—and a fear—which have not yet been shaken off.

That the white women involved in this intermixture were not always of the humbler sort is revealed in an interesting decision of the South Carolina Supreme Court rendered in 1831 (*The State* v. *Thos. D. Davis* and *The State* v. *William Hanna*; 2 Bailey, 558). These cases are to this day the leading ones in South Carolina on the question involved and have been subsequently cited and followed in such cases as *Blake* v. *Tisdale* (14 *Rich Equity*, 100); *State* v. *Cantey* (2 *Hill*, 615); *Johnson* v. *Boon* (1 *Speers*, 270); *Waite* v. *Tax Col. of Kenshaw District* (3 *Rich.*, 140); and *Davenport* v. *Caldwell* (10 *S. C.*, 335). The issue involved in the two cases first cited was the credibility as a witness of a mulatto and the Supreme Court decision defined a mulatto, quadroon, person of colour, and a person with so little Negro blood as to be deemed in law a white person. In the course of its opinion the South Carolina Supreme Court made two interesting statements bearing upon the nature of intermixture in that state, which read: "In each case the jury found the mother to be a white woman and she was accordingly admitted to be sworn as a witness. . . . It is certainly true, as laid down by the presiding judge, that 'every admixture of African blood with the European, or white, is not be be referred to the degraded class.' "

In some states the idea of a child of a white woman being a slave was so repugnant that laws were passed defining such a child born of a Negro father as "Free Issue" and decreeing that such offspring should be free. In brief, the type of Southern white who was not above taking a Negro mistress was saddling upon himself and others a fear which to this day is the most serious menace to peace and amicable settlement of the race problems. Tannenbaum in *Darker Phases of the South* says of this class: "You cannot indulge in certain relations toward colored women and expect to escape free from influence in your attitude toward white women. The idealization of the white women in the South is thus partly the unconscious self-protection on the part of the white man from their own bad habits, notions, beliefs, attitudes, and practices. This helps to give the facts of sex in the South their peculiar quality of sensitiveness. It is not insinuated that all white men in the South are habituated to practices suggested here, but there are enough of these men to give the atmosphere its requisite tensity."

This defensive mechanism of which Tannenbaum speaks finds expression as well in the derogatory attitude towards coloured women of which a classic example was a Southern office-holder who declared that there was no such thing as a virtuous coloured girl of more than fourteen years of age; and who at the time possessed a considerable family by a Negro mistress as well as one by his white wife. In truth, there would be considerable amusement in the attitude thus expressed if it were not so tragic—a member of a supposedly "superior" race explaining and excusing his own moral derelictions by emphasizing the "immorality" of the women of the "inferior" race.

This type of Southerner is largely responsible for the sixth and by far most vexing cause of sensitiveness on the subject of sex in the lynching states. There is probably no single statement more frequently or more vehemently made in the South than that there is an ineradicable repulsion between the races which will keep the two races eternally separated. Even if there were not the evidence of possession of white blood by so large a percentage of Negroes, the very violence of this assertion and the frequency with which it is repeated would cause an unbiased observer to wonder why the statement is worthy of being made at all if those who make it believe it. Professor André Siegfried, of the Paris École des Sciences Politiques, in *America Comes of Age* gives the reason for the vehemence of the assertions. He says that "although the whites declare that the Negro is physically repulsive to them, you know that it simply is not true."

Though Professor Siegfried refers particularly to lack of physical repulsion of white men towards coloured women, much more disturbing is the suspicion that the absence of repulsion applies to both sexes of both races. There is no doubt that most of the intermixture has come from relations between white men and coloured women. But the suspicion that it is not confined to that class motivates to a large extent the sadistic features of many lynchings and burnings. It has caused the enactment in twenty-nine states of anti-intermarriage laws—legislation which would be most unnecessary if the boasted repulsion were really true. It has led—human curiosity overriding as it does laws, conventions, customs, and edicts of all sorts—to experimentation, most of which might not have been thought of had there not been the challenge of a barrier. It has caused the surreptitious spreading of stories of Negro superiority in sex relations and it did not matter whether or not that rumoured superiority existed in fact or fancy—the very violence of opposition by the mobbist seemed to lend credence to the truth of the assertion. Once again the lyncher brought into being a condition diametrically opposite to that which he sought to attain.

Though this terrifying thought is kept as a sort of racial secret, there are those who occasionally commit the indiscretion of saying what they think. There is, for example, the Rev. C. A. Owens, an eminent white Baptist minister of North Carolina, who, according to the Winston-Salem, North Carolina, *Journal*, preached a sermon in that city in 1925 in which he gave his reasons for believing in and supporting the Ku Klux Klan. The *Journal* quoted Mr. Owens in part as follows: "With the present movement northward of Negroes and in the absence of a race prejudice that has protected the Southerners, there is the greatest possible danger of the mingling of the races, so that in the future it may come to pass that you will send your daughter to the North for culture and she will come back with a little Negro."

Seldom if ever has there been a greater "slur upon the fair name of Southern womanhood" than this intimation by the Reverend Mr. Owens that only Southern race prejudice is keeping white women from sex affairs with Negroes. Perhaps it is fortunate for Mr. Owens that he is neither a Northerner nor a Negro—he most certainly would have been threatened with violence if not with lynching for such a statement had he not been a Southerner and a Klansman.

ᏣᎳᎦᏔ

All of these reasons for the dominance of sex as a factor in lynching, with all their other complications, centre in one objective—the economic ascendancy over Negro labour. William Pickens, the brilliant Negro scholar, rightly terms it "simply the shrewdest battle cry of the forces seeking the economic domination of the Negro. . . . The average man, even the most brainless, may be moved by it," and thus sex is used as "a red herring . . . whenever one discusses the economic, political or civic advancement of the Negro." In an address before the Sunrise Club of New York in 1926 Mr. Pickens laid down four propositions in the relation of "the sex-bogey to the real interests of society." They are (1) that the sex cry is always associated with economic greed and is loudest wherever the oppression and robbery are the worst; (2) that race or colour antagonism is not "instinctive," as is evidenced by little children and by unspoiled races, and as is often amusingly shown by the relationships of the dominant race to its servants from among the dominated race; (3) that there are no biological barriers between any two of the so-called human "races" and that pseudo-scientific demonstrations of the subject could be used in one direction as well as in another, and could be made to prove anything; and (4) that while sex, or "racial integrity" is very convenient publicity material for the leaders of American lynchings, sex-attachment is in fact one of the smallest causes, among even the alleged causes of this most barbarous form of repression. In these four concise statements is included as complete a statement as is possible within such limits of the relationship between sex and lynching.

If those who commit and defend lynchings on the score of its necessity as protection of womanhood were sincere and intelligent, there are certain immediate steps possible for them which would do more towards ending racial intermixture than ten thousand burnings.

The first of these would be the repeal of the laws forbidding intermarriage which today are on the statute books of twenty-nine states.* To dispose of the disadvantages of such laws to Negroes they deprive coloured women of legal protection of their persons or redress should a white man seduce one of them; they place upon coloured people the implication of inferiority which self-respecting Negroes resent; they give legal sanction to belief by a certain type of white man that despoilment of a coloured girl is not so reprehensible as a similar offense against a white girl. Such laws severely handicap the struggle which Negroes are making—it is they more than anything else that is checking intermixture. In many smaller towns of the South protection of women of their race from the unwelcome advances of white men can and sometimes does mean lynching for the protectors. Governor Hugh M. Dorsey of Georgia in 1921 gave an example of such conditions which is not unusual. He had called together a group of prominent citizens of that state to place before them a hundred and thirty-five cases of mistreatment of Negroes within the state which had come to him unsolicited during the preceding two years. Case No. 1 reads:

"July, 1919, two white men, drunk, went to the Negro section of a town in this county at night. An elderly Negro got his gun and went into the streets, it is claimed, to protect the women of his race. In the shooting, which followed, one of the white men was killed.

"The Negro was placed in the jail. The sheriff left him there, *with no guard*, to go to another place to get a prisoner. A county commissioner hearing that a mob was coming went to the jail to remove the prisoner, but could find no key to unlock the door. *The mob had the key.* They lynched the Negro." (Italics ours.)

So much for the disadvantages to Negroes of anti-intermarriage laws. For whites there are many harmful aspects. It obviously is not best for the moral stamina of any race to grant legal immunity to its men when they commit sex crimes against the members of another group. It is especially bad to grant such immunity to the men of a section that has had so bad a moral career as has the South. It is true beyond all doubt that there are many men and women in the South who not only are bitterly opposed to the victimization of coloured women, but are themselves morally clean. It is likewise true

---

*These states, according to the 1927 *World Almanac* are: Alabama, Arkansas, Arizona, California, Colorado, Delaware, Florida, Georgia, Idaho, Indiana, Kentucky, Louisiana, Maryland, Mississippi, Missouri, Montana, Nebraska, Nevada, North Carolina, North Dakota, Oklahoma, Oregon, South Carolina, South Dakota, Tennessee, Texas, Utah, Virginia, and West Virginia.

that their number is infinitely small when compared with white Southerners who, while innocent of such offences, do not feel that there is as great turpitude attached to seduction or rape of a coloured girl as of a white girl. Double standards of this sort have a most vicious effect upon morals, and anti-intermarriage laws perpetuate and protect such double standards.

There is no scientifically exact method of determining precisely the effect of anti-intermarriage laws upon the number of mixed bloods born in states where there are such laws and in states where there are not. The figures of the United States Census Bureau are not taken seriously by careful students because the term "mulatto" as used by that bureau is not a biological classification, but only a convenience for the use of the enumerators. There is also the factor of interstate migration, which plays a considerable part in nullifying the value of the census figures.

For lack, however, of more accurate figures, the decennial reports of the Census Bureau offer interesting data on the effect of laws prohibiting intermarriage between whites and Negroes. Even after most liberal allowances are made for the interpretations given by the individual enumerators to the departmental definition of mulattos, whites, and pure-blooded Negroes; even after making further allowance for interstate migration; even with due allowance for the reluctance of some Negroes to admit the possession of white blood, a significant circumstance emerges from these reports. The increase of mixed bloods in relation to the total of unmixed Negroes is considerably higher in those states which forbid intermarriage by law between whites and Negroes than in the other states, where no such prohibition exists. "Shot-gun weddings" or seduction and bastardy prosecutions have an extraordinarily salutary and moral effect upon certain types of men. On the score of efficiency anti-intermarriage laws have been a failure.

Such laws also actually compel and increase bastards. Powell, in his story of the girl and man into whose hearts "God put love," is not the only one who knows of such cases. These states, by banning marriage in such instances, force sordid, clandestine affairs and the bearing of illegitimate children with all the disadvantages which such offspring suffer in modern society. The only humane, sensible, and decent thing to do is to remove the barriers to marriage, and thus insure proper care of the children born of such unions.

Over and above all these immediate results is the psychology which such laws induce. There will never be any lasting solution of the race problem so long as laws and custom permit and sanction notions of superiority and inferiority which exist only in the imaginations of the self-elected "superior" group. To these states one feels inclined to give unsolicited advice—that instead of fuming and fretting over sex they should cast aside petty fears, realize that neither laws nor customs are of much avail where two individuals are drawn to each other, and that their frantic efforts to prevent intermixture, are doing more than any other thing to cause intermixture, usually upon the lowest plane.

James Weldon Johnson

(1871–1938)

EDUCATOR, SONG WRITER, POET and novelist, diplomat, and distinguished executive secretary of the NAACP, James Weldon Johnson was a rare combination of creative artist and man of affairs. Born of middle-class African American and West Indian parents in Jacksonville, Florida, he attended Atlanta University's Preparatory School and College, graduating in 1894. He became principal of a Negro public school in Jacksonville, founded and published the short-lived *Daily American* in 1895, studied law and passed the Florida bar in 1897.

In the summers from 1899 to 1901 Johnson went to New York and there collaborated with his brother, Rosamond, in writing light operas, musical comedies, and such popular songs as "Under the Bamboo Tree," "Oh Didn't He Ramble," and others. The two also wrote at this time "Lift Every Voice and Sing," now known as the Negro national anthem. In 1900 the brothers joined the famous Bob Cole in a very successful vaudeville act. By 1901 James Weldon Johnson had moved to New York to do two things: to devote more time to show business and to study literature at Columbia University. In 1904 Johnson was American consul at Puerto Cobello, Venezuela; from 1909 to 1912 he was consul at Corinta, Nicaragua. During these years as consul he wrote and published anonymously *The Autobiography of an Ex-Coloured Man* (1912). Leaving the consular service in 1913, he returned to New York, became contributing editor to the *New York Age*, and in 1915 wrote the libretto for the Spanish opera *Goyescas*, which was produced at the Metropolitan Opera House that same year.

From 1916 to 1931 Johnson was associated with the NAACP, first as field secretary and subsequently as executive secretary. During his tenure with the NAACP he lobbied for the Dyer antilynching bill, which the Senate defeated; he also investigated America's intervention in Haiti. Resigning from the NAACP in 1931, he became the Adam K. Spence Professor of Creative Literature at Fisk University, and after 1934 he gave an annual series of lectures at New York University—a pioneer effort in opening the doors of American white colleges and universities to black professors. James Weldon Johnson was killed in an automobile accident in Massachusetts in 1938.

Johnson's major literary works are *The Autobiography of an Ex-Coloured Man* (1912); *Fifty Years and Other Poems* (1917); (ed.) *The Book of American*

Negro Poetry, with an Essay on the Negro's Creative Genius (1922, 1931); *God's Trombones: Seven Negro Sermons in Verse* (1927); *Black Manhattan* (1930); *Saint Peter Relates an Incident of the Resurrection Day: Selected Poems* (1930, 1935); and *Along This Way: The Autobiography of James Weldon Johnson* (1933, 1968).

Johnson, along with Locke, Du Bois, and others, is an important "seed-planter" of the New Negro Renaissance. His poetry shows dramatically the change in tone between pre-Renaissance and Renaissance verse. Johnson began as a writer of dialect poetry, coon songs, sentimental verse, and old-fashioned protest poems. His last two poetic volumes show the new attitude toward folk material later seen in the works of Sterling Brown and Langston Hughes and the irony which characterized much of Renaissance protest literature. In addition, his "Essay on the Negro's Creative Genius," found in *The Book of American Negro Poetry*, is a valuable critical assessment which anticipates the New Negro Renaissance. His only novel, *Autobiography of an Ex-Coloured Man*, deals with "passing," a popular theme in Renaissance fiction. Johnson's *Black Manhattan* gives an excellent picture of pioneer blacks in the theater.

For information and comment on James Weldon Johnson's life and works, see first of all his own revealing autobiography, *Along This Way* (1933). See also Eugene Levy's *James Weldon Johnson: Black Leader, Black Voice* (1973); Jean Wagner's *Black Poets of the United States* (1973); Rayford Logan's entry in *Dictionary of American Negro Biography*; and Keneth Kinnamon's article in *Dictionary of Literary Biography, Volume 51*. There are James Weldon Johnson papers in Yale University's Beinecke Rare Book and Manuscript Library and at Fisk University.

"The Prodigal Son" is from *God's Trombones* (1927, 1955); the prose selections are from Johnson's *Black Manhattan* (1930, 1958), a valuable sourcebook on the Negro in New York City.

THE PRODIGAL SON

Young man—
Young man—
Your arm's too short to box with God.

But Jesus spake in a parable, and he said:
A certain man had two sons.
Jesus didn't give this man a name,
But his name is God Almighty.

And Jesus didn't call these sons by name,
But ev'ry young man,
Ev'rywhere,
Is one of these two sons.

And the younger son said to his father,
He said: Father, divide up the property,
And give me my portion now.

And the father with tears in his eyes said: Son,
Don't leave your father's house.
But the boy was stubborn in his head,
And haughty in his heart,
And he took his share of his father's goods,
And went into a far-off country.

There comes a time,
There comes a time
When ev'ry young man looks out from his father's house,
Longing for that far-off country.

And the young man journeyed on his way,
And he said to himself as he travelled along:
This sure is an easy road,
Nothing like the rough furrows behind my father's plow.

Young man—
Young man—
Smooth and easy is the road
That leads to hell and destruction.
Down grade all the way,
The further you travel, the faster you go.
No need to trudge and sweat and toil,
Just slip and slide and slip and slide
Till you bang up against hell's iron gate.

And the younger son kept travelling along,
Till at night-time he came to a city.
And the city was bright in the night-time like day,
The streets all crowded with people,
Brass bands and string bands a-playing,
And ev'rywhere the young man turned
There was singing and laughing and dancing.
And he stopped a passer-by and he said:
Tell me what city is this?
And the passer-by laughed and said: Don't you know?
This is Babylon, Babylon,
That great city of Babylon.

Come on, my friend, and go along with me.
And the young man joined the crowd.

Young man—
Young man—
You're never lonesome in Babylon.
You can always join a crowd in Babylon.
Young man—
Young man—
You can never be alone in Babylon,
Alone with your Jesus in Babylon.
You can never find a place, a lonesome place,
A lonesome place to go down on your knees,
And talk with your God, in Babylon.
You're always in a crowd in Babylon.

And the young man went with his new-found friend,
And bought himself some brand new clothes,
And he spent his days in the drinking dens,
Swallowing the fires of hell.
And he spent his nights in the gambling dens,
Throwing dice with the devil for his soul.
And he met up with the women of Babylon.
Oh, the women of Babylon!
Dressed in yellow and purple and scarlet,
Loaded with rings and earrings and bracelets,
Their lips like a honeycomb dripping with honey,
Perfumed and sweet-smelling like a jasmine flower;
And the jasmine smell of the Babylon women
Got in his nostrils and went to his head,
And he wasted his substance in riotous living,
In the evening, in the black and dark of night,
With the sweet-sinning women of Babylon.
And they stripped him of his money,
And they stripped him of his clothes,
And they left him broke and ragged
In the streets of Babylon.

Then the young man joined another crowd—
The beggars and lepers of Babylon.
And he went to feeding swine,
And he was hungrier than the hogs;
He got down on his belly in the mire and mud
And ate the husks with the hogs.
And not a hog was too low to turn up his nose
At the man in the mire of Babylon.

Then the young man came to himself—
He came to himself and said:
In my father's house are many mansions,
Ev'ry servant in his house has bread to eat,
Ev'ry servant in his house has a place to sleep;
I will arise and go to my father.

And his father saw him afar off,
And he ran up the road to meet him.
He put clean clothes upon his back,
And a golden chain around his neck,
He made a feast and killed the fatted calf,
And invited the neighbors in.

Oh-o-oh, sinner,
When you're mingling with the crowd in Babylon—
Drinking the wine of Babylon—
Running with the women of Babylon—
You forget about God, and you laugh at Death.
Today you've got the strength of a bull in your neck
And the strength of a bear in your arms,
But some o' these days, some o' these days,
You'll have a hand-to-hand struggle with bony Death,
And Death is bound to win.

Young man, come away from Babylon,
That hell-border city of Babylon.
Leave the dancing and gambling of Babylon,
The wine and whiskey of Babylon,
The hot-mouthed women of Babylon;
Fall down on your knees,
And say in your heart:
I will arise and go to my Father.

FROM **BLACK MANHATTAN**

New York's black Bohemia constituted a part of the famous old Ten-
derloin; and, naturally, it nourished a number of the ever present
vices; chief among them, gambling and prostitution. But it nourished
other things; and one of these things was artistic effort. It is in the
growth of this artistic effort that we are here interested; the rest of

---

the manifestations were commonplaces. This black Bohemia had its physical being in a number of clubs—a dozen or more of them well established and well known. There were gambling-clubs, honky-tonks, and professional clubs. The gambling-clubs need not be explained. The honky-tonks were places with paid and volunteer entertainers where both sexes met to drink, dance, and have a good time; they were the prototype of the modern night-club. The professional clubs were particularly the rendezvous of the professionals, their satellites and admirers. Several of these clubs were famous in their day and were frequented not only by blacks, but also by whites. Among the best-known were Joe Stewart's Criterion, the Douglass Club, the Anderson Club, the Waldorf, Johnny Johnson's, Ike Hines's, and later, and a little higher up, Barron Wilkins's Little Savoy, in West Thirty-fifth Street. The border line between the honky-tonks and some of the professional clubs was very thin. One of the latter that stood out as exclusively professional was Ike Hines's. A description of a club—really Ike Hines's—is given in *The Autobiography of an Ex-Coloured Man*.* That will furnish, perhaps, a fresher picture of these places and the times than anything I might now write:

> I have already stated that in the basement of the house there was a Chinese restaurant. The Chinaman who kept it did an exceptionally good business; for chop-suey was a favourite dish among the frequenters of the place. . . . On the main floor there were two large rooms: a parlour about thirty feet in length, and a large, square back room into which the parlour opened. The floor of the parlour was carpeted; small tables and chairs were arranged about the room; the windows were draped with lace curtains, and the walls were literally covered with photographs or lithographs of every coloured man in America who had ever "done anything." There were pictures of Frederick Douglass and of Peter Jackson, of all the lesser lights of the prize-ring, of all the famous jockeys and the stage celebrities, down to the newest song and dance team. The most of these photographs were autographed and, in a sense, made a really valuable collection. In the back room there was a piano, and tables were placed round the wall. The floor was bare and the centre was left vacant for singers, dancers, and others who entertained the patrons. In a closet in this room which jutted out into the hall the proprietor kept his buffet. There was no open bar, because the place had no liquor licence [sic]. In this back room the tables were sometimes pushed aside, and the floor given over to general dancing. The front room on the next floor was a sort of private party room; a back room on the same floor contained no furniture and was devoted to the use of new

*From *The Autobiography of an Ex-Coloured Man* by James Weldon Johnson. Copyright 1927 by Alfred A. Knopf, Inc. Renewal copyright 1955 by Carl Van Vechten. Reprinted by permission of the publisher.

and ambitious performers. In this room song and dance teams practised their steps, acrobatic teams practised their tumbles, and many other kinds of "acts" rehearsed their "turns." The other rooms of the house were used as sleeping-apartments.

No gambling was allowed, and the conduct of the place was surprisingly orderly. It was, in short, a centre of coloured Bohemians and sports. Here the great prize-fighters were wont to come, the famous jockeys, the noted minstrels, whose names and faces were familiar on every bill-board in the country; and these drew a multitude of those who love to dwell in the shadow of greatness. There were then no organizations giving performances of such order as are now given by several coloured companies; that was because no manager could imagine that audiences would pay to see Negro performers in any other role than that of Mississippi River roustabouts; but there was lots of talent and ambition. I often heard the younger and brighter men discussing the time when they would compel the public to recognize that they could do something more than grin and cut pigeon-wings.

Sometimes one or two of the visiting stage-professionals, after being sufficiently urged, would go into the back room and take the places of the regular amateur entertainers, but they were very sparing with their favours, and the patrons regarded them as special treats. There was one man, a minstrel, who, whenever he responded to a request to "do something," never essayed anything below a reading from Shakespeare. How well he read I do not know, but he greatly impressed me; and I can say that at least he had a voice which strangely stirred those who heard it. Here was a man who made people laugh at the size of his mouth, while he carried in his heart a burning ambition to be a tragedian; and so after all he did play a part in a tragedy.

These notables of the ring, the turf, and the stage, drew to the place crowds of admirers, both white and coloured. Whenever one of them came in, there were awe-inspired whispers from those who knew him by sight, in which they enlightened those round them as to his identity, and hinted darkly at their great intimacy with the noted one. Those who were on terms of approach showed their privilege by gathering round their divinity. . . .

A great deal of money was spent here, so many of the patrons were men who earned large sums. I remember one night a dapper little brown-skin fellow was pointed out to me and I was told that he was the most popular jockey of the day, and that he earned $12,000 a year. This latter statement I couldn't doubt, for with my own eyes I saw him spending at about thirty times that rate. For his friends and those who were introduced to him he bought nothing but wine—in sporting circles, "wine" means champagne—and paid for it at five dollars a quart. . . . This jockey had won a great race that day, and he was rewarding his admirers for the homage they paid him, all of which he accepted with a fine air of condescension.

Besides the people I have just been describing, there were at the place almost every night one or two parties of white people, men and women, who were out sight-seeing, or slumming. They generally came in cabs; some of them would stay only for a few minutes, while others sometimes stayed until morning. There was also another set of white people that came frequently; it was made up of variety performers and others who delineated "darky characters"; they came to get their imitations first-hand from the Negro entertainers they saw there.

⊙⟨∭⟩⊙

. . . In the midst of the period we are now considering, another shift in the Negro population took place; and by 1900 there was a new centre established in West Fifty-third Street. In this new centre there sprang up a new phase of life among coloured New Yorkers. Two well-appointed hotels, the Marshall and the Maceo, run by coloured men, were opened in the street and became the centres of a fashionable sort of life that hitherto had not existed. These hotels served dinner to music and attracted crowds of well-dressed people. On Sunday evenings the crowd became a crush; and to be sure of service one had to book a table in advance. This new centre also brought about a revolutionary change in Negro artistic life. Those engaged in artistic effort deserted almost completely the old clubs farther downtown, and the Marshall, run by Jimmie Marshall, an accomplished Boniface, became famous as the headquarters of Negro talent. There gathered the actors, the musicians, the composers, the writers, and the better-paid vaudevillians; and there one went to get a close-up of Cole and Johnson, Williams and Walker, Ernest Hogan, Will Marion Cook, Jim Europe, Ada Overton, Abbie Mitchell, Al Johns, Theodore Drury, Will Dixon, and Ford Dabney. Paul Laurence Dunbar was often there. A good many white actors and musicians also frequented the Marshall, and it was no unusual thing for some among the biggest Broadway stars to run up there for an evening. So there were always present numbers of those who love to be in the light reflected from celebrities. Indeed, the Marshall for nearly ten years was one of the sights of New York, for it was gay, entertaining, and interesting. To be a visitor there, without at the same time being a rank outsider, was a distinction. The Maceo run by Benjamin F. Thomas had the more staid clientele.

In the brightest days of the Marshall the temporary blight had not yet fallen on the Negro in the theatre. Williams and Walker and Cole and Johnson were at their height; there were several good Negro road companies touring the country, and a considerable number of coloured performers were on the big time in vaudeville. In the early 1900's there came to the Marshall two young fellows, Ford Dabney and James Reese Europe, both of them from Washington, who were to play an important part in the artistic development of the Negro in a field that was, in a sense, new. It was they who first formed the coloured New York entertainers who played instruments into trained, organized bands, and thereby became not only the daddies of the Negro jazz orchestras, but the grand-daddies of the unnumbered jazz orchestras that have followed. Ford Dabney organized and directed a jazz orchestra which for a number of years was a feature of Florenz Ziegfeld's roof-garden shows. Jim Europe organized the Clef Club. Joe Jordan also became an important factor in the development of Negro bands.

How long Negro jazz bands throughout the country had been playing jazz at dances and in honky-tonks cannot be precisely stated, but the first modern jazz band ever heard on a New York stage, and probably on any other stage, was organized at the Marshall and made its début at Proctor's Twenty-third Street Theatre in the early spring of 1905. It was a playing-singing-dancing orchestra, making dominant use of banjos, mandolins, guitars, saxophones, and drums in combination, and was called the Memphis Students—a very good name, overlooking the fact that the performers were not students and were not from Memphis. There was also a violin, a couple of brass instruments, and a double-bass. The band was made up of about twenty of the best performers on the instruments mentioned above that could be got together in New York. They had all been musicians and entertainers for private parties, and as such had played together in groups varying in size, according to the amount the employing host wished to spend. Will Marion Cook gave a hand in whipping them into shape for their opening. They scored an immediate success. After the Proctor engagement they went to Hammerstein's Victoria, playing on the vaudeville bill in the day, and on the roof-garden at night. In the latter part of the same year they opened at Olympia in Paris; from Paris they went to the Palace Theatre in London, and then to the Schumann Circus in Berlin. They played all the important cities in Europe and were abroad a year.

At the opening in New York the performers who were being counted on to carry the stellar honours were: Ernest Hogan, comedian; Abbie Mitchell, soprano; and Ida Forsyne, dancer; but while they made good, the band proved to be the thing. The instrumentalists were the novelty. There was one thing they did quite unconsciously; which, however, caused musicians who heard them to marvel at the feat. When the band played and sang, there were men who played one part while singing another. That is, for example, some of them while playing the lead, sang bass, and some while playing an alto part sang tenor; and so on, in accordance with the instrument each man played and his natural voice. The Memphis

Students deserve the credit that should go to pioneers. They were the beginners of several things that still persist as jazz-band features. They introduced the dancing conductor. Will Dixon, himself a composer of some note, conducted the band here and on its European tour. All through a number he would keep his men together by dancing out the rhythm, generally in graceful, sometimes in grotesque, steps. Often an easy shuffle would take him across the whole front of the band. This style of directing not only got the fullest possible response from the men, but kept them in just the right humour for the sort of music they were playing. Another innovation they introduced was the trick trap-drummer. "Buddy" Gilmore was the drummer with the band, and it is doubtful if he has been surpassed as a performer of juggling and acrobatic stunts while manipulating a dozen noise-making devices aside from the drums. He made this style of drumming so popular that not only was it adopted by white professionals, but many white amateurs undertook to learn it as a social accomplishment, just as they might learn to do card tricks. The whole band, with the exception, of course, of the players of wind-instruments, was a singing band; and it seems safe to say that they introduced the singing band—that is, a band singing in four-part harmony and playing at the same time.

One of the original members of the Memphis Students was Jim Europe. Afterwards he went for a season or two as musical director with the Cole and Johnson shows; and then in the same capacity with Bert Williams's *Mr. Lode of Kole*. In 1910 he carried out an idea he had, an idea that had a business as well as an artistic reason behind it, and organized the Clef Club. He gathered all the coloured professional instrumental musicians into a chartered organization and systematized the whole business of "entertaining." The organization purchased a house in West Fifty-third Street and fitted it up as a club, and also as booking-offices. Bands of from three to thirty men could be furnished at any time, day or night. The Clef Club for quite a while held a monopoly of the business of "entertaining" private parties and furnishing music for the dance craze, which was then just beginning to sweep the country. One year the amount of business done amounted to $120,000.

The crowning artistic achievement of the Clef Club was a concert given at Carnegie Hall in May 1912. The orchestra for the occasion consisted of one hundred and twenty-five performers. It was an unorthodox combination—as is every true jazz orchestra. There were a few strings proper, the most of them being 'cellos and double-basses; the few wind-instruments consisted of cornets, saxophones, clarinets, and trombones; there were a battery of drums; but the main part of the orchestra was composed of banjos, mandolins, and guitars. On this night all these instruments were massed against a background of ten upright pianos. In certain parts the instrumentation was augmented by the voices. New York had not yet become accustomed to jazz; so when the Clef Club opened its concert with a syncopated march, playing it with a biting attack and an infectious rhythm, and on the finale bursting into singing, the effect can be imagined. The applause became a tumult. It is possible that such a band as that could produce a similar effect even today.

Later Jim Europe with his orchestra helped to make Vernon and Irene Castle famous. When the World War came, he assembled the men for the band of the Fifteenth, New York's noted Negro regiment. He was with this band giving a concert in a Boston theatre, after their return from the War, when he met his tragic end.

1912 was also the year in which there came up out of the South an entirely new genre of Negro songs, one that was to make an immediate and lasting effect upon American popular music; namely, the blues. These songs are as truly folk-songs as the Spirituals, or as the original plantation songs, levee songs, and rag-time songs that had already been made the foundation of our national popular music. The blues were first set down and published by William C. Handy, a coloured composer and for a while a bandleader in Memphis, Tennessee. He put out the famous "Memphis Blues" and the still more famous "St. Louis Blues" and followed them by blues of many localities and kinds. It was not long before the New York song-writers were turning out blues of every variety and every shade. Handy followed the blues to New York and has been a Harlemite ever since, where he is known as the "Father of the Blues." It is from the blues that all that may be called *American music* derives its most distinctive characteristic.

It was during the period we have just been discussing that the earliest attempt at rendering opera was made by Negroes in New York. Beginning in the first half of the decade 1900–10 and continuing for four or five years, the Theodore Drury Opera Company gave annually one night of grand opera at the Lexington Opera House. Among the operas sung were *Carmen, Aida*, and *Faust*. These nights of grand opera were, at least, great social affairs and were looked forward to months ahead. In September 1928 H. Lawrence Freeman, a Negro musician and the composer of six grand operas, produced his opera *Voodoo* at the Fifty-second Street Theatre. Mr. Freeman's operas are *The Martyr, The Prophecy, The Octoroon, Plantation, Vendetta*, and *Voodoo*. In the spring of the present year he presented scenes from various of his works in Steinway Hall. He was the winner of the 1929 Harmon Award and Medal for musical composition.

❧❦❧

. . . These journals[†] shook up the Negroes of New York and the country and effected some changes that have not been lost; but able as were most of the men behind them, as radicals, they failed almost wholly in bringing about any co-ordination of the forces they were dealing with; perhaps that was to be expected. This post-war radical movement gradually waned—as it waned among whites—and the organs of the movement, one by one, withered and died. *The Messenger*, which continued to be published up to last year, was the longest-lived of them all. The *Negro World* is still being published; but it falls in a classification distinctly its own.

The Harlem radicals failed to bring about a correlation of the forces they had called into action, to have those forces work through a practical medium to a definite objective; but they did much to prepare the ground for a man who could and did do that, a man who was one of the most remarkable and picturesque figures that have appeared on the American scene—Marcus Garvey.

Marcus Garvey is a full-blooded black man, born, and born poor, in Jamaica, British West Indies, in 1887. He grew up under the triple race scheme that prevails in many of the West Indian islands—white, mulatto, and black. The conditions of this system aroused in him, even as a boy, a deep resentment, which increased as he grew older. His resentment against the mulattos was, perhaps, deeper than his resentment against the whites. At about the time he became of age, he left Jamaica and travelled in South America. He next went to England, where he stayed for several years. All the while he was seeking some escape from the terrible pressure of the colour bar. In England he met one or two African agitators. He became intimate with Duse Muhamed Effendi, an African political writer, who was running a small revolutionary newspaper in London, and from him learned something about world politics, especially with relation to Africa. It was probably then that he began to dream of a land where black men ruled. England was a disappointment. In 1914 he returned to Jamaica, determined to do something to raise the status of the black masses of the island. He began his public career by organizing the Universal Negro Improvement Association. He was discouraged by the fact that he aroused more interest and gained more

---

[†]"These journals" refers to a group of radical Negro periodicals, ranging in policy from "left centre to extreme left," that sprang up in Harlem around 1919. Among them were *The Messenger, Challenge, The Voice, The Crusader, The Emancipator*, and *The Negro World*. They were cited in a Department of Justice report in 1919 under the caption "Radicalism and Sedition among Negroes as Reflected in Their Publications." [Eds.]

support among the whites than among the blacks. He wrote Booker T. Washington about his plans—plans probably for establishing industrial training for the natives of Jamaica—and received a reply encouraging him to come to the United States. Before he could perfect arrangements to come, Booker T. Washington had died. But on March 23, 1916 Garvey landed in Harlem.

In some way or other he got about the country, visiting, as he says, thirty-eight states, studying the condition of the Negro in America, and then returned to New York. On June 12, 1917 a large mass meeting, called by Hubert Harrison, was held in Bethel A. M. E. Church in Harlem for the purpose of organizing the Liberty League. Some two thousand people were present, and among them was Marcus Garvey. Mr. Harrison introduced him to the audience and asked him to say a few words. This was Harlem's first real sight of Garvey, and his first real chance at Harlem. The man spoke, and his magnetic personality, torrential eloquence, and intuitive knowledge of crowd psychology were all brought into play. He swept the audience along with him. He made his speech an endorsement of the new movement and a pledge of his hearty support of it; but Garvey was not of the kidney to support anybody's movement. He had seen the United States and he had seen Harlem. He had doubtless been the keenest observer at the Liberty League organization meeting; and it may be that it was then he decided upon New York as the centre for his activities.

He soon organized and incorporated the Universal Negro Improvement Association in the United States, with New York as headquarters. He made his first appeal to the West Indian elements, not only to British, but to Spanish and French, and they flocked to him. He established the *Negro World* as his organ and included in it Spanish and French sections. He built Liberty Hall, a great basement that held five or six thousand people. There the association held its first convention in 1919, during the whole month of August, with delegates from the various states and the West Indies. By this time the scheme of the organization had expanded from the idea of economic solution of the race problem through the establishment of "Universal" shops and factories and financial institutions to that of its solution through the redemption of Africa and the establishment of a Negro merchant marine. At the mass meeting held in Carnegie Hall during this convention, Garvey in his address said:

> We are striking homeward toward Africa to make her the big black republic. And in the making of Africa the big black republic, what is the barrier? The barrier is the white man; and we say to the white man who dominates Africa that it is to his interest to clear out now, because we are coming, not as in the time of Father Abraham, 200,000 strong, but

we are coming 400,000,000 strong and we mean to retake every square inch of the 12,000,000 square miles of African territory belonging to us by right Divine.

Money poured in; war-time prosperity made it possible. Three ships were bought and placed in commission. Garvey had grown to be High Potentate of the association and "Provisional President of Africa." Around him he had established a court of nobles and ladies. There were dukes and duchesses, knight commanders of the Distinguished Order of Ethiopia, and knight commanders of the Sublime Order of the Nile. There were gorgeous uniforms, regalia, decorations, and insignia. There was a strict court etiquette, and the constitution provided that "No lady below the age of eighteen shall be presented at the 'Court Reception' and no gentleman below the age of twenty-one." There was established the African Legion, with a full line of commissioned officers and a quartermaster staff and commissariat for each brigade. The Black Cross nurses were organized. In fact, an embryo army was set up with Marcus Garvey as commander-in-chief. A mission was sent to Liberia to negotiate an agreement whereby the Universal Improvement Association would establish a colony there and aid in the development of the country.

Garvey became a world figure, and his movements and utterances were watched by the great governmental powers. (Even today from his exile in Jamaica his actions and words are considered international news.) The U.N.I.A. grew in the United States and spread through the region of the Caribbean. The movement became more than a movement, it became a religion, its members became zealots. Meetings at Liberty Hall were conducted with an elaborate liturgy. The moment for the entry of the "Provisional President" into the auditorium was solemn; a hushed and expectant silence on the throng, the African Legion and Black Cross nurses flanking the long aisle and coming to attention, the band and audience joining in the hymn: "Long Live our President," and Garvey, surrounded by his guard of honour from the Legion, marching majestically through the double line and mounting the rostrum; it was impressive if for no other reason than the way in which it impressed the throng. Garvey made a four months' tour of the West Indies in a Black Star liner, gathering in many converts to the movement, but no freight for the vessel. Of course, the bubble burst. Neither Garvey nor anyone with him knew how to operate ships. And if they had known, they could not have succeeded at the very time when ships were the greatest drug on the market. So the Black Star Line, after swallowing up hundreds of thousands of dollars, collapsed in December 1921. The Federal Government investigated Garvey's share-selling scheme and he was indicted and convicted on a charge of using the mails to defraud. While out of the Tombs on bail, he made an unsuccessful attempt to revive his shipping venture as the Black Cross Line.

Within ten years after reaching New York Marcus Garvey had risen and fallen, been made a prisoner in the Atlanta Federal Penitentiary, and finally been deported to his native island. Within that brief period a black West Indian, here in the United States, in the twentieth century, had actually played an imperial role such as Eugene O'Neill never imagined in his *Emperor Jones*.

Garvey failed; yet he might have succeeded with more than moderate success. He had energy and daring and the Napoleonic personality, the personality that draws masses of followers. He stirred the imagination of the Negro masses as no Negro ever had. He raised more money in a few years than any other Negro organization had ever dreamed of. He had great power and great possibilities within his grasp. But his deficiencies as a leader outweighed his abilities. He is a supreme egotist, his egotism amounting to megalomania; and so the men surrounding him had to be for the most part cringing sycophants; and among them there were also cunning knaves. Upon them he now lays the entire blame for failure, taking no part of it to himself. As he grew in power, he fought every other Negro rights organization in the country, especially the National Association for the Advancement of Colored People, centering his attacks upon Dr. Du Bois.

Garvey made several vital blunders, which, with any intelligent advice, he might have avoided. He proceeded upon the assumption of a triple race scheme in the United States; whereas the facts are that the whites in the United States, unlike the whites of the West Indies, make no distinction between people of colour and blacks, nor do the Negroes. There may be places where a very flexible social line exists, but Negroes in the United States of every complexion have always maintained a solid front on the rights of the race. This policy of Garvey, going to the logical limit of calling upon his followers to conceive of God as black, did arouse a latent pride of the Negro in his blackness, but it wrought an overbalancing damage by the effort to drive a wedge between the blacks and the mixed bloods, an effort that might have brought on disaster had it been more successful.

He made the mistake of ignoring or looking with disdain upon the technique of the American Negro in dealing with his problems of race, a technique acquired through three hundred years of such experience as the West Indian has not had and never can have. If he had availed himself of the counsel and advice of an able and honest American Negro, he would have avoided many of the barbed wires against which he ran and many of the pits into which he fell.

But the main reason for Garvey's failure with thoughtful American Negroes was his African scheme. It was recognized at once by them to be impracticable and fantastic. Indeed, it is difficult to give the man credit for either honesty or sanity in these imperialistic designs, unless, as there are some reasons to suppose, his designs involved the purpose of going into Liberia as an agent of development and then by gradual steps or a coup taking over the government and making the country the centre of the activities and efforts for an Africa Redeemed. But thoughtful coloured Americans knew that, under existing political conditions in Africa, even that plan could ultimately meet with nothing but failure. Had there been every prospect of success, however, the scheme would not have appealed to them. It was simply a restatement of the Colonization Society scheme advanced just one hundred years before, which had occasioned the assembling of the first national convention of Negroes in America, called to oppose "the operations and misrepresentations of the American Colonization Society in these United States." The central idea of Garvey's scheme was absolute abdication and the recognition as facts of the assertions that this is a white man's country, a country in which the Negro has no place, no right, no chance, no future. To that idea the overwhelming majority of thoughtful American Negroes will not subscribe. And behind this attitude is the common-sense realization that as the world is at present, the United States, with all of its limitations, offers the millions of Negroes within its borders greater opportunities than any other land.

Garvey's last great mistake came about through his transcending egotism. He had as leading counsel for his trial Henry Lincoln Johnson, one of the shrewdest and ablest Negro lawyers in the country. But the temptation to strut and pose before a crowded court and on the front pages of the New York newspapers was too great for Garvey to resist; so he brushed his lawyers aside and handled his own case. He himself examined and cross-examined the witnesses; he himself harangued the judge and jury; and he was convicted.

Garvey, practically exiled on an island in the Caribbean, becomes a somewhat tragic figure. There arises a slight analogy between him and that former and greater dreamer in empires, exiled on another island. But the heart of the tragedy is that to this man came an opportunity such as comes to few men, and he clutched greedily at the glitter and let the substance slip from his fingers.

Anne Spencer

(1882–1975)

PARAPHRASING Joseph Addison, one could easily say that to have known Anne Spencer was a liberal education. Writing in 1937, Sterling Brown, who knew her well, said of this remarkable woman: "Anne Spencer is the most original of all Negro women poets . . . her vision and expression are those of a wise, ironic but gentle woman of her times."

Born in Henry County, Virginia, in 1882, Anne Spencer was educated at Virginia Seminary in Lynchburg, Virginia, a city in which she spent most of her long life. Until her retirement, Spencer was the librarian at the Negro Dunbar High School in Lynchburg. She was also a civic gadfly in that city.

Age did not dim the brilliance of Anne Spencer's mind. When past ninety she was still writing poetry, still commenting wittily and ironically on the contemporary scene, and still entertaining in her beautiful home. In her earlier years she had entertained such friends as W. E. B. Du Bois, James Weldon Johnson, and other well-known Negroes of the period.

Anne Spencer never published a volume of her verse. In 1977, however, J. Lee Greene published *Time's Unfading Garden: Anne Spencer's Life and Poetry*, a volume in which Greene gives, not only a full account of Mrs. Spencer's fascinating life, but also forty-two of the "fifty items now available as complete poems or significant fragments." Anne Spencer claimed that she produced over one thousand poems during her writing years. A documentary film, "Echoes from the Garden: The Anne Spencer Story," was produced in 1980 by the Anne Spencer Memorial Foundation and Byron Studios.

For the fullest and most authentic information—biographical, critical, and bibliographical—on Spencer, see J. Lee Greene's *Time's Unfading Garden: Anne Spencer's Life and Poetry* (1977). Also valuable are the essays in Ann Allen Shockley's *Afro-American Women Writers, 1746–1933: An Anthology and Critical Guide* (1988) and the article by J. Lee Greene in *Dictionary of Literary Biography, Volume 51*. Spencer is considered an impetus for female creativity in *The First Wave: Women Poets in America, 1915–1945* by William Drake (1987).

Much of Anne Spencer's poetry has appeared over the years in many periodicals and in practically every major anthology of black poetry since the 1920s. The selections given here come from J. Lee Greene's *Time's Unfading Garden*.

BEFORE THE FEAST OF SHUSHAN

Garden of Shushan!
After Eden, all terrace, pool, and flower recollect thee:
Ye weavers in saffron and haze and Tyrian purple,
Tell yet what range in color wakes the eye;
Sorcerer, release the dreams born here when
Drowsy, shifting palm-shade enspells the brain;
And sound! ye with harp and flute ne'er essay
Before these star-noted birds escaped from paradise awhile to
Stir all dark, and dear, and passionate desire, till mine
Arms go out to be mocked by the softly kissing body of the wind—
Slave, send Vashti to her King!

The fiery wattles of the sun startle into flame
The marbled towers of Shushan:
So at each day's wane, two peers—the one in
Heaven, the other on earth—welcome with their
Splendor the peerless beauty of the Queen.

Cushioned at the Queen's feet and upon her knee
Finding glory for mine head,—still, nearly shamed
Am I, the King, to bend and kiss with sharp
Breath the olive-pink of sandaled toes between;
Or lift me high to the magnet of a gaze, dusky,
Like the pool when but the moon-ray strikes to its depth;
Or closer press to crush a grape 'gainst lips redder
Than the grape, a rose in the night of her hair;
Then—Sharon's Rose in my arms.

And I am hard to force the petals wide;
And you are fast to suffer and be sad.
Is any prophet come to teach a new thing
Now in a more apt time?
Have him 'maze how you say love is sacrament;
How says Vashti, love is both bread and wine;
How to the altar may not come to break and drink,
Hulky flesh nor fleshly spirit!

I, thy lord, like not manna for meat as a Judahn;
I, thy master, drink, and red wine, plenty, and when
I thirst. Eat meat, and full, when I hunger.
I, thy King, teach you and leave you, when I list.

All poems reprinted by permission of Chauncey E. Spencer.

No woman in all Persia sets out strange action
To confuse Persia's lord—
Love is but desire and thy purpose fulfillment;
I, thy King, so say!

LETTER TO MY SISTER

It is dangerous for a woman to defy the gods;
To taunt them with the tongue's thin tip,
Or strut in the weakness of mere humanity,
Or draw a line daring them to cross;
The gods own the searing lightning,
The drowning waters, tormenting fears
And anger of red sins.

Oh, but worse still if you mince timidly—
Dodge this way or that, or kneel or pray,
Be kind, or sweat agony drops
Or lay your quick body over your feeble young;
If you have beauty or none, if celibate
Or vowed—the gods are Juggernaut,
Passing over . . . over . . .

This you may do:
Lock your heart, then, quietly,
And lest they peer within,
Light no lamp when dark comes down
Raise no shade for sun;
Breathless must your breath come through
If you'd die and dare deny
The gods their god-like fun.

AT THE CARNIVAL

Gay little Girl-of-the-Diving-Tank,
I desire a name for you,
Nice, as a right glove fits;
For you—who amid the malodorous
Mechanics of this unlovely thing,
Are darling of spirit and form.
I know you—a glance, and what you are

Sits-by-the-fire in my heart.
My Limousine-Lady knows you, or
Why does the slant-envy of her eye mark
Your straight air and radiant inclusive smile?
Guilt pins a fig-leaf; Innocence is its own adorning.
The bull-necked man knows you—this first time
His itching flesh sees from divine and vibrant health,
And thinks not of his avocation.
I came incuriously—
Set on no diversion save that my mind
Might safely nurse its brood of misdeeds
In the presence of a blind crowd.
The color of life was gray.
Everywhere the setting seemed right
For my mood!
Here the sausage and garlic booth
Sent unholy incense skyward;
There a quivering female-thing
Gestured assignations, and lied
To call it dancing;
There, too, were games of chance
With chances for none;
But oh! the Girl-of-the-Tank, at last!
Gleaming Girl, how intimately pure and free
The gaze you send the crowd,
As though you know the dearth of beauty
In its sordid life.
We need you—my Limousine-Lady,
The bull-necked man, and I.
Seeing you here brave and water-clean,
Leaven for the heavy ones of earth,
I am swift to feel that what makes
The plodder glad is good; and
Whatever is good is God.
The wonder is that you are here;
I have seen the queer in queer places,
But never before a heaven-fed
Naiad of the Carnival-Tank!
Little Diver, Destiny for you,
Like as for me, is shod in silence;
Years may seep into your soul
The bacilli of the usual and the expedient;
I implore Neptune to claim his child to-day!

LINES TO A NASTURTIUM
A Lover Muses

Flame-flower, Day-torch, Mauna Loa,
I saw a daring bee, today, pause, and soar,
  Into your flaming heart;
Then did I hear crisp crinkled laughter
As the furies after tore him apart?

  A bird, next, small and humming,
Looked into your startled depths and fled. . . .
Surely, some dread sight, and dafter
  Than human eyes as mine can see,
Set the stricken air waves drumming,
  In his flight.

Day-torch, Flame-flower; cool-hot Beauty,
I cannot see, I cannot hear your fluty
Voice lure your loving swain,
But I know one other to whom you are in beauty
Born in vain;
Hair like the setting sun,
Her eyes a rising star,
Motions gracious as reeds by Babylon, bar
All your competing;
Hands like, how like, brown lilies sweet,
Cloth of gold were fair enough to touch her feet. . . .
Ah, how the senses flood at my repeating,
As once in her fire-lit heart I felt the furies
Beating, beating.

Georgia Douglas Johnson

(1886–1966)

THE FIRST NEGRO WOMAN after Frances E. W. Harper to gain general recognition as a poet, Georgia Douglas Johnson was born in Atlanta, Georgia, in 1886. She was educated at Atlanta University and at the Oberlin Conservatory of Music. After her marriage to Henry Lincoln Johnson, a nationally known public figure in the early decades of this century, she made her home in Washington, D.C., and became a very active pioneer in women's, civic, and literary movements in the capital. She was a leading force in the Saturday Nighters, one of several Washington literary clubs during the twenties. The Saturday Nighters met at her home, and, according to Langston Hughes, had such well-known visitors as Claude McKay and Zora Neale Hurston. May Miller, who also visited the club's meetings, states that in addition to local writers, W. E. B. Du Bois, James Weldon Johnson, A. Philip Randolph, and other celebrities came to meetings when they were in the city.

Johnson is a member of that group of Negro women writers called the "genteel school" (Jessie Fauset, Anne Spencer, Angelina Grimké, et al.) and is known primarily for her poetry: *The Heart of a Woman* (1918), *Bronze* (1922), *An Autumn Cycle* (1928). She also wrote one-act plays: Her *Plumes—A Folk Tragedy*, which follows, won the *Opportunity* First Prize for Drama in 1927. Her sentimental poem "I Want to Die While You Love Me" was very popular for many years and appeared in most of the early anthologies of Negro verse.

Biographical and critical studies of Georgia Douglas Johnson are not as easily found as they should be. Yet she was one of the most productive and one of the best known of the genteel school of Renaissance writers. For a brief and early sketch of her life and works, see Countee Cullen's anthology *Caroling Dusk* (1927); see also the many references to her in Eugene B. Redmond's *Drumvoices* (1976). For Langston Hughes's association with Johnson, see Arnold Rampersad's *The Life of Langston Hughes—Volume I: 1902–1941* (1986). Important biographical information and critical commentary can be found in Ann Allen Shockley's *Afro-American Women Writers, 1746–1933* (1988); in Gloria T. Hull's *Color, Sex, and Poetry: Three Women Writers of the Harlem Renaissance* (1987); and in the comprehensive *Dictionary of Literary Biography, Volume 51* article by Winona Fletcher. A brief examination of Johnson's plays is provided by Doris E. Abramson in "Angelina Weld Grimké, Mary T. Burrill, Georgia Douglas

416

Johnson, and Arita Bonner: An Analysis of Their Plays," *Sage* 2, no. 1 (Spring 1985). See also Jeanne-Marie Miller's excellent article, "Georgia Douglas Johnson and May Miller: Forgotten Playwrights," *CLA Journal* (June 1990).

Plumes was orginally published in *Opportunity*. The poems are taken from *The Book of American Negro Poetry*.

PLUMES—A FOLK TRAGEDY

CHARACTERS

CHARITY BROWN, the mother
EMMERLINE BROWN, the daughter
TILDY, the friend
DOCTOR SCOTT, physician

Scene: A poor cottage in the South.
Time: Contemporary. [1927]

SCENE: *The kitchen of a two-room cottage. A window overlooking the street. A door leading to street, one leading to the back yard and one to the inner room. A stove, a table with shelf over it, a washtub. A rocking-chair, a cane-bottom chair. Needle, thread, scissors, etc. on table.*

Scene opens with Charity Brown heating a poultice over the stove. A groaning is heard from the inner room.

CHARITY. Yes, honey, mamma is fixing somethin' to do you good. Yes, my baby, jus' you wait—I'm a-coming. (*Knock is heard at door. It is gently pushed open and Tildy comes in cautiously.*)

TILDY. (*Whispering*) How is she?

CHARITY. Poorly, poorly. Didn't rest last night none hardly. Move that dress and set in th' rocker. I been trying to snatch a minute to finish it but don't seem like I can. She won't have nothing to wear if she— she——

TILDY. I understands. How near done is it?

CHARITY. Ain't so much more to do.

TILDY. (*Takes up dress from chair; looks at it*) I'll do some on it.

CHARITY. Thank you, sister Tildy. Whip that torshon on and turn down the hem in the skirt.

TILDY. (*Measuring dress against herself*) How deep?

CHARITY. Let me see, now (*Studies a minute with finger against lip*) I tell you—jus' baste it, 'cause you see—she wears 'em short, but—it might be—— (*Stops.*)

TILDY. (*Bowing her head comprehendingly*) Huh-uh, I see exzackly. (*Sighs*) You'd want it long—over her feet—then.

CHARITY. That's it, sister Tildy. (*Listening*) She's some easy now! (*Stirring poultice*) Jest can't get this poltis' hot enough somehow this morning.

TILDY. Put some red pepper in it. Got any?

CHARITY. Yes. There ought to be some in one of them boxes on the shelf there. (*Points.*)

TILDY. (*Goes to shelf, looks about and gets the pepper*) Here, put a-plenty of this in.

CHARITY. (*Groans are heard from the next room*) Good Lord, them pains got her again. She suffers so, when she's 'wake.

TILDY. Poor little thing. How old is she now, sister Charity?

CHARITY. Turning fourteen this coming July.

TILDY. (*Shaking her head dubiously*) I sho' hope she'll be mended by then.

CHARITY. It don't look much like it, but I trusts so—— (*Looking worried*) That doctor's mighty late this morning.

TILDY. I expects he'll be 'long in no time. Doctors is mighty onconcerned here lately.

CHARITY. (*Going toward inner room with poultice*) They surely is and I don't have too much confidence in none of 'em. (*You can hear her soothing the child.*)

TILDY. (*Listening*) Want me to help you put it on, sister Charity?

CHARITY. (*From inner room*) No, I can fix it. (*Coming back from sick room shaking her head rather dejectedly.*)

TILDY. How is she, sister Charity?

CHARITY. Mighty feeble. Gone back to sleep now. My poor little baby. (*Bracing herself*) I'm going to put on some coffee now.

TILDY. I'm sho' glad. I feel kinder low-spirited.

CHARITY. It's me that low-sperited. The doctor said last time he was here he might have to oparate—said, she mought have a chance then. But I tell you the truth, I've got no faith a-tall in 'em. They takes all your money for nothing.

TILDY. They sho' do and don't leave a cent for putting you away decent.

CHARITY. That's jest it. They takes all you got and then you dies jest the same. It ain't like they was sure.

TILDY. No, they ain't sure. That's it exzactly. But they takes your money jest the same, and leaves you flat.

CHARITY. I been thinking 'bout Zeke these last few days—how he was put away——

TILDY. I wouldn't worry 'bout him now. He's out of his troubles.

CHARITY. I know. But it worries me when I think about how he was put away . . . that ugly pine coffin, jest one shabby old hack and nothing else to show—to show—what we thought about him.

TILDY. Hush, sister! Don't you worry over him. He's happy now, anyhow.

CHARITY. I can't help it! Then little Bessie. We all jest scrooged in one hack and took her little coffin in our lap all the way out to the graveyard. (*Breaks out crying.*)

TILDY. Do hush, sister Charity. You done the best you could. Poor folks got to make the best of it. The Lord understands——

CHARITY. I know that—but I made up my mind the time Bessie went that the next one of us what died would have a shore nuff funeral, everything grand,—with plumes!—I saved and saved and now—this yah doctor——

TILDY. All they think about is cuttin' and killing and taking your money. I got nothin' to put 'em doing.

CHARITY. (*Goes over to washtub and rubs on clothes*) Me neither. These clothes got to get out somehow, I needs every cent.

TILDY. How much that washing bring you?

CHARITY. Dollar and a half. It's worth a whole lot more. But what can you do?

TILDY. You can't do nothing—Look there, sister Charity, ain't that coffee boiling?

CHARITY. (*Wipes hands on apron and goes to stove*) Yes it's boiling good fashioned. Come on, drink some.

TILDY. There ain't nothing I'd rather have than a good strong cup of coffee. (*Charity pours Tildy's cup.*) (*Sweetening and stirring hers*) Pour you some. (*Charity pours her own cup*) I'd been dead, too, long ago if it hadn't a been for my coffee.

CHARITY. I love it, but it don't love me—gives me the shortness of breath.

TILDY. (*Finishing her cup, taking up sugar with spoon*) Don't hurt me. I could drink a barrel.

CHARITY. (*Drinking more slowly—reaching for coffeepot*) Here, drink another cup.

TILDY. I shore will, that cup done me a lot of good.

CHARITY. (*Looking into her empty cup thoughtfully*) I wish Dinah Morris would drop in now. I'd ask her what these grounds mean.

TILDY. I can read 'em a little myself.

CHARITY. You can? Well, for the Lord's sake, look here and tell me what this cup says! (*Offers cup to Tildy. Tildy wards it off.*)

TILDY. You got to turn it 'round in your saucer three times first.

CHARITY. Yes, that's right, I forgot. (*Turns cup 'round, counting*) One, two, three. (*Starts to pick it up.*)

TILDY. Huhudh. (*Meaning no*) Let it set a minute. It might be watery. (*After a minute, while she finishes her own cup*) Now let me see. (*Takes cup and examines it very scrutinizingly.*)

CHARITY. What you see?

TILDY. (*Hesitatingly*) I ain't seen a cup like this one for many a year. Not since—not since——

CHARITY. When?

TILDY. Not since jest before ma died. I looked in the cup then and saw things and—I stopped looking . . .

CHARITY. Tell me what you see, I want to know.

TILDY. I don't like to tell no bad news——

CHARITY. Go on. I can stan' anything after all I been thru'.

TILDY. Since you're bound to know I'll tell you. (*Charity draws nearer*) I sees a big gethering!

CHARITY. Gethering, you say?

TILDY. Yes, a big gethering. People all crowded together. Then I see 'em going one by one and two by two. Long line stretching out and out and out!

CHARITY. (*In a whisper*) What you think it is?

TILDY. (*Awed like*) Looks like (*Hesitates*) a possession!

CHARITY. (*Shouting*) You sure!

TILDY. I know it is. (*Just then the toll of a church bell is heard and then the steady and slow tramp, tramp, of horses' hoofs. Both women look at each other.*)

TILDY. (*In a hushed voice*) That must be Bell Gibson's funeral coming 'way from Mt. Zion. (*Gets up and goes to window*) Yes, it sho' is.

CHARITY. (*Looking out of the window also*) Poor Bell suffered many a year; she's out of her pain now.

TILDY. Look, here comes the hearse now!

CHARITY. My Lord! ain't it grand! Look at them horses—look at their heads—plumes—how they shake 'em! Land o' mighty! It's a fine sight, sister Tildy.

TILDY. That must be Jer'miah in that first carriage, bending over like; he shorely is putting her away grand.

CHARITY. No mistake about it. That's Pickett's best funeral turnout he's got.

TILDY. I'll bet it cost a lot.

CHARITY. Fifty dollars, so Matilda Jenkins told me. She had it for Bud. The plumes is what cost.

TILDY. Look at the hacks—— (*Counts*) I believe to my soul there's eight.

CHARITY. Got somebody in all of 'em too—and flowers—She shore got a lot of 'em. (*Both women's eyes follow the tail end of the procession, horses' hoofs die away as they turn away from window. The two women look at each other significantly.*)

TILDY. (*Significantly*) Well!—— (*They look at each other without speaking for a minute. Charity goes to the washtub*) Want these cups washed up?

CHARITY. No don't mind 'em. I'd rather you get that dress done. I got to get these clothes out.

TILDY. (*Picking up dress*) Shore, there ain't so much more to do on it now. (*Knock is heard on the door. Charity answers knock and admits Dr. Scott.*)

DR. SCOTT. Good morning. How's the patient today?

CHARITY. Not so good, doctor. When she ain't 'sleep she suffers so; but she sleeps mostly.

DR. SCOTT. Well, let's see, let's see. Just hand me a pan of warm water and I'll soon find out just what's what.

CHARITY. All right, doctor. I'll bring it to you right away. (*Bustles about fixing water—looking toward dress Tildy is working on*) Poor little Emmerline's been wanting a white dress trimmed with torshon a long time—now she's got it and it looks like—well—— (*Hesitates*) t'warn't made to wear.

TILDY. Don't take on so, sister Charity—The Lord giveth and the Lord taketh.

CHARITY. I know—but it's hard—hard—— (*Goes into inner room with water. You can hear her talking with the doctor after a minute and the doctor expostulating with her—in a minute she appears at the door, being led from the room by the doctor.*)

DR. SCOTT. No, my dear Mrs. Brown. It will be much better for you to remain outside.

CHARITY. But, doctor——

DR. SCOTT. NO. You stay outside and get your mind on something else. You can't possibly be of any service. Now be calm, will you?

CHARITY. I'll try, doctor.

TILDY. The doctor's right. You can't do no good in there.

CHARITY. I knows, but I thought I could hold the pan or somethin'. (*Lowering her voice*) Says he got to see if her heart is all right or somethin'. I tell you—now a days——

TILDY. I know.

CHARITY. (*Softly to Tildy*) Hope he won't come out here saying he got to operate. (*Goes to washtub.*)

TILDY. I hope so, too. Won't it cost a lot?

CHARITY. That's jest it. It would take all I got saved up.

TILDY. Of course, if he's goin' to get her up—but I don't believe in 'em. I don't believe in 'em.

CHARITY. He didn't promise tho'—even if he did, he said maybe it wouldn't do no good.

TILDY. I'd think a long time before I'd let him operate on my chile. Taking all yuh money, promising nothing and ten to one killing her to boot.

CHARITY. This is a hard world.

TILDY. Don't you trus' him. Coffee grounds don't lie!

CHARITY. I don't trust him. I jest want to do what's right by her. I ought to put these clothes on the line while you're settin' in here, but I jes hate to go outdoors while he's in there.

TILDY. (*Getting up*) I'll hang 'em out. You stay here. Where your clothes-pins at?

CHARITY. Hanging right there by the back door in the bag. They ought to dry before dark and then I can iron to-night.

TILDY. (*Picking up tub*) They ought to blow dry in no time. (*Goes toward back door.*)

CHARITY. Then I can shore rub 'em over to-night. Say, sister Tildy, hist 'em up with that long saplin' prop leaning in the fence corner.

TILDY. (*Going out*) All right.

CHARITY. (*Standing by the table beating nervously on it with her fingers— listens—and then starts to bustling about the kitchen*) (*Enter Doctor from inner room.*)

DR. SCOTT. Well, Mrs. Brown, I've decided I'll have to operate.

CHARITY. MY Lord! Doctor—don't say that!

DR. SCOTT. It's the only chance.

CHARITY. You mean she'll get well if you do?

DR. SCOTT. No, I can't say that—— It's just a chance—a last chance. And I'll do just what I said, cut the price of the operation down to fifty dollars. I'm willing to do that for you. (*Charity throws up her hands in dismay.*)

CHARITY. Doctor, I was so in hopes you wouldn't operate—I—I—— And yo' say you ain't a bit sure she'll get well—even then?

DR. SCOTT. No. I can't be sure. We'll just have to take the chance. But I'm sure you want to do everything——

CHARITY. Sure, doctor, I do want to—do—everything I can do to—to—— Doctor, look at this cup. (*Picks up fortune cup and shows the doctor*) My fortune's jes been told this very morning—look at these grounds—they says—— (*Softly*) it ain't no use, no use a-tall.

DR. SCOTT. Why, my good woman, don't you believe in such senseless things! That cup of grounds can't show you anything. Wash them out and forget it.

CHARITY. I can't forget it. I feel like it ain't no use; I'd just be spendin' the money that I needs—for nothing—nothing.

DR. SCOTT. But you won't though—— You'll have a clear conscience. You'd know that you did everything you could.

CHARITY. I know that, doctor. But there's things you don't know 'bout— there's other things I got to think about. If she goes—if she must go . . . I had plans—I been getting ready—now—— Oh, doctor, I jest can't see how I can have this operation—you say you can't promise—nothing?

DR. SCOTT. I didn't think you'd hesitate about it—I imagined your love for your child——

CHARITY. (*Breaking in*) I do love my child. My God, I do love my child. You don't understand . . . but . . . but—can't I have a little time to think about it, doctor? It means so much—to her—and—me!

DR. SCOTT. I tell you. I'll go on over to the office. I'd have to get my— (*Hesitates*) my things, anyhow. And as soon as you make up your mind, get one of the neighbors to run over and tell me. I'll come right back. But don't waste any time now, Mrs. Brown, every minute counts.

CHARITY. Thank you, doctor, thank you. I'll shore send you word as soon as I can. I'm so upset and worried I'm half crazy.

DR. SCOTT. I know you are . . . but don't take too long to make up your mind. . . . It ought to be done to-day. Remember—it may save her. (*Exits.*)

CHARITY. (*Goes to door of sick room—looks inside for a few minutes, then starts walking up and down the little kitchen, first holding a hand up to her head and then wringing them. Enter Tildy from yard with tub under her arm.*)

TILDY. Well, they're all out, sister Charity—— (*Stops*) Why, what's the matter?

CHARITY. The doctor wants to operate.

TILDY. (*Softly*) Where he—gone?

CHARITY. Yes—he's gone, but he's coming back—if I send for him.

TILDY. You going to? (*Puts down tub and picks up white dress and begins sewing.*)

CHARITY. I dunno—I got to think.

TILDY. I can't see what's the use myself. He can't save her with no operation—— Coffee grounds don't lie.

CHARITY. It would take all the money I got for the operation and then what about puttin' her away? He can't save her—don't even promise ter. I know he can't—feel it . . . I feel it . . .

TILDY. It's in the air. . . . (*Both women sit tense in silence. Tildy has commenced sewing again. Just then a strange, strangling noise comes from the inner room.*)

TILDY. What's that?

CHARITY. (*Running toward and into inner room*) Oh, my God! (*From inside*) Sister Tildy—Come here—No, —Some water, quick. (*Tildy with dress in hand starts toward inner room. Stops at door, sighs and then goes hurriedly back for the water pitcher. Charity is heard moaning softly in the next room, then she appears at doorway and leans against jamb of door*) Rip the hem out, sister Tildy.

CURTAIN

THE HEART OF A WOMAN

The heart of a woman goes forth with the dawn,
As a lone bird, soft winging, so restlessly on,
Afar o'er life's turrets and vales does it roam
In the wake of those echoes the heart calls home.

The heart of a woman falls back with the night,
And enters some alien cage in its plight,
And tries to forget it has dreamed of the stars
While it breaks, breaks, breaks on the sheltering bars.

I WANT TO DIE WHILE YOU LOVE ME

I want to die while you love me,
    While yet you hold me fair,
While laughter lies upon my lips
    And lights are in my hair.

I want to die while you love me,
    And bear to that still bed,
Your kisses turbulent, unspent
    To warm me when I'm dead.

All of Georgia Johnson's poems in this anthology come from James Weldon Johnson's *The Book of American Negro Poetry*, New York: Harcourt Brace and Company, 1922; revised edition, 1931.

I want to die while you love me
   Oh, who would care to live
Till love has nothing more to ask
   And nothing more to give!

I want to die while you love me
   And never, never see
The glory of this perfect day
   Grow dim or cease to be.

WELT

Would I might mend the fabric of my youth
That daily flaunts its tatters to my eyes,
Would I might compromise awhile with truth
Until our moon now waxing, wanes and dies.

For I would go a further while with you,
And drain this cup so tantalant and fair
Which meets my parchèd lips like cooling dew,
Ere time has brushed cold fingers thru my hair!

MY LITTLE DREAMS

I'm folding up my little dreams
Within my heart to-night,
And praying I may soon forget
The torture of their sight.

For Time's deft fingers scroll my brow
With fell relentless art—
I'm folding up my little dreams
To-night, within my heart!

Jean Toomer

(1894–1967)

ALTHOUGH HE WAS the author of only one outstanding work, although he was a "volunteer" Negro (that is, one who could pass for white), although he tells us that he had "several blood mixtures" and wasn't certain that he had "any colored blood," and although he, according to Langston Hughes in *The Big Sea*, refused to allow his poems to appear in Johnson's *Book of American Negro Poetry*, Jean Toomer *is* an important "seed planter" of the New Negro Renaissance and his one important publication influenced the work of several Renaissance poets.

The grandson of P. B. S. Pinchback, the well-known former Reconstruction Negro lieutenant governor and for a while acting governor of Louisiana, Jean Toomer was born in Washington, D.C., attended that city's famous Dunbar High School, studied agriculture for a semester at the University of Wisconsin, stayed one week in the Massachusetts College for Agriculture, and then went to a physical training college in Chicago. He was turned down by the draft in World War I, after which he worked at many odd jobs, among them teaching physical education in Milwaukee, selling cars in Chicago, working as a ship fitter in New Jersey, and in 1921 serving as a temporary principal of a Negro industrial school in rural Georgia. It was here that he had experiences and found material which later appeared in *Cane*.

During the 1920s, Toomer wrote poems and sketches which appeared in *Broom, Crisis, Dial, Prairie Schooner, Nomad, Opportunity, Little Review*, and other magazines. He also belonged to a group of writers which included Kenneth Burke and Hart Crane. In 1923 he published *Cane*, which sold only five hundred copies the first printing, but was definitely a critical success, one that was praised by Sherwood Anderson, Waldo Frank, Gorham Munson, and other nationally known critics.

During the summer of 1926 (possibly earlier), he became a disciple of Gurdjieff, the briefly popular Russian mystic, and studied at the latter's institute in Fontainbleau. Toomer later taught the Gurdjieff philosophy when he returned to America. Some of his minor works show the influence of his newly acquired philosophy.

In 1931 Toomer married Margery Latimer, a novelist; after she died in childbirth a year later, he married Margery Content in 1934. Both wives were white; both came from well-to-do and well-known families. After his second marriage, Toomer moved to Bucks County, Pennsylvania, and during his last years became deeply interested in the Society of Friends (the Quaker organization). He remained in Pennsylvania until his death in 1967.

Toomer's *Cane* represented an approach to writing entirely new in Negro literature. It made a complete break with the then prevailing protest tradition in black fiction. Objective, experimental, the work is called a novel but in reality is a mélange of poems, prose sketches, short stories, and drama. On the surface it appears to be a mixture of unrelated elements, but it is definitely not that. It has a tonal unity—a unity effected in large measure through the contrast of Negro life in rural Georgia with that in sophisticated Washington, D.C. Rural Georgia and its black life deeply impressed Toomer. He tells us in an article in *The New Negro* (1925) that "Georgia opened me. . . . I received my initial impulse to an individual art form from my experience there. . . . There one finds soil . . . the soil every art and literature that is to live must be imbedded in." Throughout *Cane* there is a brooding sense of the "pain and beauty" the Negro finds in the soil of the South—a soil in which his roots are imbedded; there is no escape.

For an understanding of this truly difficult book and its seemingly mixed-up author, see the critical analysis found in Roger Rosenblatt's article in *Dictionary of American Negro Biography*. See also the comprehensive commentary found in *Jean Toomer: A Critical Evaluation* (1988), edited by Therman B. O'Daniel. See also Robert Bone's *The Negro Novel in America* (1965); Darwin Turner's *In a Minor Chord* (1971); Jean Wagner's *Black Poets of the United States* (1973); Darwin Turner's *The Wayward and the Seeking: A Collection of Writings by Jean Toomer* (1982); and Arthur P. Davis's *From the Dark Tower* (1974). Other recent studies include *Jean Toomer, Artist: A Study of His Literary Life and Work, 1894–1936* by Nellie Y. McKay (1984) and *Jean Toomer* by Brian Joseph Benson and Mabel Mayle Dillard (1980).

The following selections come from *Cane*.

SONG OF THE SON

Pour O pour that parting soul in song,
O pour it in the saw-dust glow of night,
Into the velvet pine-smoke air to-night,
And let the valley carry it along.
And let the valley carry it along.

O land and soil, red soil and sweet-gum tree,
So scant of grass, so profligate of pines,
Now just before an epoch's sun declines
Thy son, in time, I have returned to thee,
Thy son, I have, in time, returned to thee.

In time, for though the sun is setting on
A song-lit race of slaves, it has not set;
Though late, O soil, it is not too late yet
To catch thy plaintive soul, leaving, soon gone,
Leaving, to catch thy plaintive soul soon gone.

O Negro slaves, dark purple ripened plums,
Squeezed, and bursting in the pine-wood air,
Passing, before they strip the old tree bare
One plum was saved for me, one seed becomes

An everlasting song, a singing tree,
Caroling softly souls of slavery,
What they were, and what they are to me,
Caroling softly souls of slavery.

COTTON SONG

Come, brother, come. Lets lift it;
Come now, hewit! roll away!
Shackles fall upon the Judgment Day
But lets not wait for it.

God's body's got a soul,
Bodies like to roll the soul,
Cant blame God if we dont roll,
Come, brother, roll, roll!

Cotton bales are the fleecy way
Weary sinner's bare feet trod,
Softly, softly to the throne of God,
"We aint agwine t wait until th Judgment Day!

Nassur; nassur,
Hump.
Eoho, eoho, roll away!
We aint agwine t wait until th Judgment Day!"

God's body's got a soul,
Bodies like to roll the soul,
Cant blame God if we dont roll,
Come, brother, roll, roll!

ESTHER

1

Nine.

Esther's hair falls in soft curls about her high-cheek-boned chalk-white face. Esther's hair would be beautiful if there were more gloss to it. And if her face were not prematurely serious, one would call it pretty. Her cheeks are too flat and dead for a girl of nine. Esther looks like a little white child, starched, frilled, as she walks slowly from her home towards her father's grocery store. She is about to turn in Broad from Maple Street. White and black men loafing on the corner hold no interest for her. Then a strange thing happens. A clean-muscled, magnificent, black-skinned Negro, whom she had heard her father mention as King Barlo, suddenly drops to his knees on a spot called the Spittoon. White men, unaware of him, continue squirting tobacco juice in his direction. The saffron fluid splashes on his face. His smooth black face begins to glisten and to shine. Soon, people notice him, and gather round. His eyes are rapturous upon the heavens. Lips and nostrils quiver. Barlo is in a religious trance. Town folks know it. They are not startled. They are not afraid. They gather round. Some beg boxes from the grocery stores. From old McGregor's notion shop. A coffin-case is pressed into use. Folks line the curb-stones. Business men close shop. And Banker Warply parks his car close by. Silently, all await the prophet's voice. The sheriff, a great florid fellow whose leggings never meet around his bulging calves, swears in three deputies. "Wall, y cant never tell what a nigger like King Barlo might be up t." Soda bottles, five fingers full of shine, are passed to those who want them. A couple of stray dogs start a fight. Old Goodlow's cow comes flopping up the street. Barlo, still as an Indian fakir, has not moved. The town bell strikes six. The sun slips in behind a heavy mass of horizon cloud. The crowd is hushed and expectant. Barlo's under jaw relaxes, and his lips begin to move.

"Jesus has been awhisperin strange words deep down, O way down deep, deep in my ears."

Hums of awe and of excitement.

"He called me to His side an said, 'Git down on your knees beside me, son, Ise gwine t whisper in your ears.' "

An old sister cries, "Ah, Lord."

" 'Ise agwine t whisper in your ears,' he said, an I replied, 'Thy will be done on earth as it is in heaven.' "

"Ah, Lord. Amen. Amen."

"An Lord Jesus whispered strange good words deep down, O way down deep, deep in my ears. An He said, "Tell em till you feel your throat on fire.' I saw a vision. I saw a man arise, an he was big an black an powerful—"

Some one yells, "Preach it, preacher, preach it!"

"—but his head was caught up in th clouds. An while he was agazin at th heavens, heart filled up with th Lord, some little white-ant biddies came an tied his feet to chains. They led him t th coast, they led him t th sea, they led him across th ocean and they didnt set him free. The old coast didnt miss him, an th new coast wasnt free, he left the old-coast brothers, t give birth t you an me. O Lord, great God Almighty, t give birth t you an me."

Barlo pauses. Old gray mothers are in tears. Fragments of melodies are being hummed. White folks are touched and curiously awed. Off to themselves, white and black preachers confer as to how best to rid themselves of the vagrant, usurping fellow. Barlo looks as though he is struggling to continue. People are hushed. One can hear weevils work. Dusk is falling rapidly, and the customary store lights fail to throw their feeble glow across the gray dust and flagging of the Georgia town. Barlo rises to his full height. He is immense. To the people he assumes the outlines of his visioned African. In a mighty voice he bellows:

"Brothers an sisters, turn your faces t th sweet face of the Lord, an fill your hearts with glory. Open your eyes an see th dawnin of th mornin light. Open your ears—"

Years afterwards Esther was told that at that very moment a great, heavy, rumbling voice actually was heard. That hosts of angels and of demons paraded up and down the streets all night. That King Barlo rode out of town astride a pitch-black bull that had a glowing gold ring in its nose. And that old Limp Underwood, who hated niggers, woke up next morning to find that he held a black man in his arms. This much is certain: an inspired Negress, of wide reputation for being sanctified, drew a portrait of a black madonna on the court-house wall. And King Barlo left town. He left his image indelibly upon the mind of Esther. He became the starting point of the only living patterns that her mind was to know.

2

Sixteen.

Esther begins to dream. The low evening sun sets the windows of McGregor's notion shop aflame. Esther makes believe that they really are aflame. The town fire department rushes madly down the road. It ruthlessly shoves black and white idlers to one side. It whoops. It clangs. It rescues from the second-story window a dimpled infant which she claims for her own. How had she come by it? She thinks of it immaculately. It is a sin to think of it immaculately. She must dream no more. She must repent her sin. Another dream comes. There is no fire department. There are no heroic men. The fire starts. The loafers on the corner form a circle, chew their tobacco faster, and squirt juice just as fast as they can chew. Gallons on top of gallons they squirt upon the flames. The air reeks with the stench of scorched tobacco juice. Women, fat chunky Negro women, lean scrawny white women, pull their skirts up above their heads and display the most ludicrous underclothes. The women scoot in all directions from the danger zone. She alone is left to take the baby in her arms. But what a baby! Black, singed, woolly, tobacco-juice baby—ugly as sin. Once held to her breast, miraculous thing: its breath is sweet and its lips can nibble. She loves it frantically. Her joy in it changes the town folks' jeers to harmless jealousy, and she is left alone.

Twenty-two.

Esther's schooling is over. She works behind the counter of her father's grocery store. "To keep the money in the family," so he said. She is learning to make distinctions between the business and the social worlds. "Good business comes from remembering that the white folks dont divide the niggers, Esther. Be just as black as any man who has a silver dollar." Esther listlessly forgets that she is near white, and that her father is the richest colored man in town. Black folk who drift in to buy lard and snuff and flour of her, call her a sweet-natured, accommodating girl. She learns their names. She forgets them. She thinks about men. "I dont appeal to them. I wonder why." She recalls an affair she had with a little fair boy while still in school. It had ended in her shame when he as much as told her that for sweetness he preferred a lollipop. She remembers the salesman from the North who wanted to take her to the movies that first night he was in town. She refused, of course. And he never came back, having found out who she was. She thinks of Barlo. Barlo's image gives her a slightly stale thrill. She spices it by telling herself his glories. Black. Magnetically so. Best cotton picker in the county, in the state, in the whole world for that matter. Best man with his fists, best man with dice, with a razor. Promoter of church benefits. Of colored fairs. Vagrant preacher. Lover of all the women for miles and miles around. Esther decides that she loves him. And with a vague sense of life slipping by, she resolves that she will tell him so, whatever people say, the next time he comes to town. After the making of this resolution which becomes a sort of wedding cake for her to tuck beneath her pillow and go to sleep upon, she sees nothing of Barlo for five years. Her hair thins. It looks like the dull silk on puny corn ears. Her face pales until it is the color of the gray dust that dances with dead cotton leaves.

3

Esther is twenty-seven.

Esther sells lard and snuff and flour to vague black faces that drift in her store to ask for them. Her eyes hardly see the people to whom she gives change. Her body is lean and beaten. She rests listlessly against the counter, too weary to sit down. From the street some one shouts, "King Barlo has come back to town." He passes her window, driving a large new car. Cut-out open. He veers to the curb, and steps out. Barlo has made money on cotton during the war. He is as rich as anyone. Esther suddenly is animate. She goes to her door. She sees him at a distance, the center of a group of credulous men. She hears the deep-bass rumble of his talk. The sun swings low. McGregor's windows are aflame again. Pale flame. A sharply dressed white girl passes by. For a moment Esther wishes that she might be like her. Not white; she has no need for being that. But sharp, sporty, with get-up about her. Barlo is connected with that wish. She mustnt wish. Wishes only make you restless. Emptiness is a thing that grows by being moved. "I'll not think. Not wish. Just set my mind against it." Then the thought comes to her that those purposeless, easy-going men will possess him, if she doesnt. Purpose is not dead in her, now that she comes to think of it. That loose women will have their arms around him at Nat Bowle's place tonight. As if her veins are full of fired sun-bleached southern shanties, a swift heat sweeps them. Dead dreams, and a forgotten resolution are carried upward by the flames. Pale flames. "They shant have him. Oh, they shall not. Not if it kills me they shant have him." Jerky, aflutter, she closes the store and starts home. Folks lazing on store window-sills wonder what on earth can be the matter with Jim Crane's gal, as she passes them. "Come to remember, she always was a little off, a little crazy, I reckon." Esther seeks her own room, and locks the door. Her mind is a pink mesh-bag filled with baby toes.

Using the noise of the town clock striking twelve to cover the creaks of her departure, Esther slips into the quiet road. The town, her parents, most everyone is sound asleep. This fact is a stable thing that comforts her. After sundown a chill wind came up from the west. It is still blowing, but to her it is a steady, settled thing like the cold. She wants her mind to be like that. Solid, contained, and blank as a sheet of darkened ice. She will not permit herself to notice the peculiar phosphorescent glitter of the sweet-gum leaves. Their movement would excite her. Exciting too, the recession of the dull familiar homes she knows so well. She doesnt know them at all. She closes her eyes, and holds them tightly. Wont do. Her being aware that they are closed recalls her purpose. She does not want to think of it. She opens them. She turns now into the deserted business street. The corrugated iron canopies and mule- and horse-gnawed hitching posts bring her a strange composure. Ghosts of the commonplace of her daily life take stride with her and become her companions. And the echoes of her heels upon the flagging are rhythmically monotonous and soothing. Crossing the street at the corner of McGregor's notion shop, she thinks that the windows are a dull flame. Only a fancy. She walks faster. Then runs. A turn into a side street brings her abruptly to Nat Bowle's place. The house is squat and dark. It is always dark. Barlo is within. Quietly she opens the outside door and steps in. She passes through a small room. Pauses before a flight of stairs down which people's voices, muffled, come. The air is heavy with fresh tobacco smoke. It makes her sick. She wants to turn back. She goes up the steps. As if she were mounting to some great height, her head spins. She is violently dizzy. Blackness rushes to her eyes. And then she finds that she is in a large room. Barlo is before her.

"Well, I'm sholy damned—skuse me, but what, what brought you here, lil milk-white gal?"

"You." Her voice sounds like a frightened child's that calls homeward from some point miles away.

"Me?"

"Yes, you Barlo?"

"This aint th place fer y. This aint th place fer y."

"I know. I know. But I've come for you."

"For me for what?"

She manages to look deep and straight into his eyes. He is slow at understanding. Guffaws and giggles break out from all around the room. A coarse woman's voice remarks, "So that how th dictie niggers does it." Laughs. "Mus give em credit fo their gall."

Esther doesnt hear. Barlo does. His faculties are jogged. She sees a smile, ugly and repulsive to her, working upward through thick licker fumes. Barlo seems hideous. The thought comes suddenly, that conception with a drunken man must be a mighty sin. She draws away, frozen. Like a somnambulist she wheels around and walks stiffly to the stairs. Down them. Jeers and hoots pelter bluntly upon her back. She steps out. There is no air, no street, and the town has completely disappeared.

George S. Schuyler

(1895–1977)

JOURNALIST AND NOVELIST, George Samuel Schuyler for over a half century was one of the most successful and versatile newspaper men in the nation. As a young writer, he was considered a militant. In his later years, he became one of the most conservative journalists in America and a member of the John Birch Society. The editorial he wrote when Martin Luther King, Jr., received the Nobel Peace Prize was so reactionary that his own paper, the *Pittsburgh Courier*, refused to print it. It was published in William Loeb's *Manchester Union Leader*.

Born in Providence, Rhode Island, Schuyler grew up in Syracuse, New York, where he received his grammar and high school education. He did not attend college, but he was well read. When he was seventeen he joined the U.S. Army and during World War I he served as a first lieutenant. Before he began his career as a journalist, he worked at all kinds of jobs and gained a firsthand knowledge of the people lowest down.

Schuyler's journalistic career was varied: he started first with Randolph and Owens's *The Messenger*, the first black socialist magazine in America; he next moved to the *Pittsburgh Courier* as a columnist ("Views and Reviews"), subsequently as editorial writer and contributor in other capacities. As a journalist Schuyler traveled to and investigated conditions in the Deep South, Africa, Europe, South America, and the West Indies. His articles and essays have appeared in *The Crisis, Nation, Opportunity, The New Masses, American Mercury*, and many other nationally known periodicals.

In the dead center of the New Negro Renaissance, Schuyler stated in a *Nation* (June 16, 1926) article that talk about "racial differences" in America was sheer nonsense. "The Aframerican," he wrote, "is merely a lampblacked Anglo-Saxon." This position antagonized many "new Negroes" who believed in the African legacy and the Negro's peculiar endowment. Naturally it infuriated the 1960s advocates of black nationalism. Because of this stand and his almost fanatical espousal of conservatism, Schuyler lost a great deal of his former popularity among blacks, even those of his generation.

Schuyler published three full-length works. The first, *Black No More* (1931), is also the first significant satirical novel written by an African American. The plot centers on the discovery by a black scientist of a potion that turns a Negro white. With this basis, Schuyler hilariously attacks all American color shibboleths, Negro organizations like the NAACP, and

Negro leaders like Du Bois. It is an irreverent and "Juvenalian"-type satire that spares no one. The second novel, *Slaves Today* (1931), is a documentary-type work that attacks the slave trade that then existed in Liberia with the connivance of certain high officials of that black republic. The third book, *Black and Conservative* (1966), is an autobiography which could have been a most fascinating work because Schuyler had an unusual and exciting life. Unfortunately, he overplayed his anticommunism obsession. George Schuyler was a better journalist than a novelist. Fearless, hard-hitting, and relentlessly consistent, he won a grudging respect for his abilities if not for the causes in which he exerted them.

Materials on Schuyler's life and works are understandably not plentiful. For a brief but comprehensive summary of his activities up to 1950, see G. James Fleming and Christian E. Burckel's *Who's Who in Colored America* (1950). For the most recent critical and biographical commentary, see Norma R. Jenes's article in *Dictionary of Literary Biography, Volume 51*. For an example of his early work, see his contribution to Brown, Davis, and Lee's *The Negro Caravan* (1941). See also "George S. Schuyler, Iconoclast," *The Crisis* (October 1965), an editorial; Melvin B. Tolson's "George S. Schuyler," *American Mercury* (March 1933); and *George S. Schuyler* by Michael W. Peplow (1980). Also see Arthur P. Davis's *From the Dark Tower* (1974).

The following essay is reprinted from the first Modern Library edition of *Anthology of American Negro Literature* (1929), edited by V. F. Calverton.

OUR GREATEST GIFT TO AMERICA

On divers occasions some eloquent Ethiop arises to tell this enlightened nation about the marvelous contributions of his people to our incomparable civilization. With glib tongue or trenchant pen, he starts from the arrival of the nineteen unfortunate dinges at Jamestown in 1619, or perhaps with the coming of the celebrated Columbus to these sacred shores with his Negro mate in 1492, and traces the multiple gifts of the black brethren to the present day. He will tell us of the vast amount of cotton picked by the Negro, of the hundreds of roads and levees the black laborers have constructed, of the miles of floors Negro women have scrubbed, and the acres of clothes they have washed, of the numerous wars in which, for some unknown reason, the Sambo participated, of the dances and cookery he invented, or of the spirituals and work songs composed by the sons of Ham and given to a none too grateful nation. The more erudite of these self-appointed spokesmen of the race will even go back to the Garden of Eden, the walls of Babylon, the pyramids of Egypt and the palaces of Ethiopia by way of introduction, and during their prefatory remarks they will not fail, often, to claim for the Negro race every person of importance that has ever resided on the face of the earth. Ending with a forceful and fervent plea for justice, equality, righteousness, humanitarianism, and other such things conspicuous in the world by their absence, they close amid a storm of applause from their sable auditors—and watch the collection plate.

This sort of thing has been going on regularly for the last century. No Negro meeting is a success without one or more such encouraging addresses, and no Negro publication that fails to carry one such article in almost every issue is considered worthy of purchase. So general has the practice become that even white audiences and magazines are no longer immune. It has become not unusual in the past few years for the Tired Society Women's Club of Keokuk, Iowa, or the Delicatessen Proprietors' Chamber of Commerce or the Hot Dog Venders' Social Club to have literary afternoons devoted exclusively to the subject of the lowly smoke. On such occasions there will be some notable Aframerican speakers as Prof. Hambone of Moronia Institute or Dr. Lampblack of the Federal Society for the Exploitation of Lynching, who will eloquently hold forth for the better part of an hour on the blackamoor's gifts to the Great Republic and why, therefore, he should not be kept down. Following him there will usually be a soulful rendition by the Charcoal Singers of their selected repertoire of genuine spirituals, and then, mayhap one of the younger Negro poets will recite one of his inspiring verses anent a ragged black prostitute gnawing out her soul in the dismal shadows of Hog Maw Alley.

It was not so many years ago that Negro writers used to chew their fingernails and tear as much of their hair as they could get hold of, because the adamantine editors of white magazines and journals invariably returned unread their impassioned manuscripts in which they sought to tell how valuable the Aframerican had always been to his country and what a dirty shame it was to incinerate a spade without benefit of jury. Not so today, my friends. The swarms of Negro hacks and their more learned associates have at last come into their own. They have ridden into popular demand on the waves of jazz music, the Charleston, Mammy Songs and the ubiquitous, if intricate, Black Bottom. Pick up almost any of the better class periodicals of national note nowadays and you are almost sure to find a lengthy paper by some sable literatus on the Negro's gifts to America, on his amazing progress in becoming just like other Americans in habit and thought, or on the horrible injustice of Jim Crow cars. The cracker editors are paying generously for the stuff (which is more than the Negro editors did in the old days), and as a result, the black scribblers, along with the race orators, are now wallowing in the luxury of four-room apartments, expensive radios, Chickering pianos, Bond Street habiliments, canvas-back duck, pre-war Scotch and high yellow mistresses.

All of which is very well and good. It is only natural that the peckerwoods, having become bored to death with their uninteresting lives, should turn to the crows for inspiration and entertainment. It is probably part of their widespread rationalization of the urge they possess to mix with the virile blacks. One marvels, however, that the principal contribution of our zigaboos to the nation has been entirely overlooked by our dusky literati and peripatetic platform prancers. None of them, apparently, has ever thought of it. While they have been ransacking their brains and the shelves of the public libraries for new Negro gifts of which to inform their eager listeners at so much per word or per engagement, they have ignored the principal gift sprawling everywhere about them. They had but to lift their eyes from the pages of their musty tome and glance around. But they didn't.

"And what," I can hear these propagandists feverishly inquiring with poised fountain pens and notebooks, "is this unchronicled contribution to the worth of our nation?" Well, I am not unwilling to divulge this "secret" that has been all too apparent to the observing. And though the brownish intelligentsia are now able to pay for the information—and probably willing to do so—I modestly ask nothing, save perhaps a quart of decent rye or possibly one of the numerous medals shoveled out every year to deserving coons. Hence, like all of the others, I now arise, flick a speck off my dinner jacket, adjust my horn-rimmed nose glasses, and, striking an attitude, declaim the magic word: Flattery!

Yes folks, the greatest gift we have made to America is flattery. Flattery, if you please, of the buckra majority; inflation of the racial ego of the dominant group by our mere proximity, by our actions and by our aspirations. "How come?" I am belligerently and skeptically quizzed, and very indulgently I elucidate. Imitation, some one has said, is the sincerest flattery. It is quite human to be pleased and feel very important when we are aped and imitated. Consider how we Negroes shove out our chests when an article appears in an enterprising darky newspaper from the pen of some prominent African chief saying that his dingy colleagues on the Dark Continent look to their American brethren, with their amazing progress, for inspiration. How sweet is flattery, the mother of pride. And pride, we have been told, is absolutely essential to progress and achievement. If all of this be true of the dark American, how much truer must it be of the pink American? By constant exposure to his energetic propagandists in press, on platform and in pulpit, the colored brother has forged ahead—to borrow an expression from the *Uplift*—until he can now eat with Rogers silver off Haviland china, sprawl on over-stuffed couches and read spicy literature under the glow of ornate floor lamps, while the strains of "Beer Bucket Blues" are wafted over the radio. This is generally known as progress. Now if the downtrodden Negro, under the influence of his flattering propagandists, has been able to attain such heights of material well-being, is it any wonder that the noble rednecks have leaped so much farther up the scale of living when surrounded by millions of black flatterers, both mute and vocal? Most certainly not.

Look, for example, at Isadore Shankersoff. By hook or by crook (probably the latter) he grabbed off enough coin of his native land to pay his passage to America. In Russia he was a nobody—hoofed by everybody—the mudsill of society. Quite naturally his inferiority complex was Brobdingnagian. Arriving under the shadow of the Statue of Liberty, he is still Isadore Shankersoff, the prey of sharpers and cheap grafters, but now he has moved considerably higher in the social scale. Though remaining mentally adolescent, he is no longer at the bottom; he is a white man! Over night he has become a member of the superior race. Ellis Island marked his metamorphosis. For the first time in his life he is better than somebody. Without the presence of the blackamoor in these wonderfully United States, he would still know himself for the thick-pated underling that he is, but how can he go on believing that when America is screaming to him on every hand that he is a white man, and as such entitled to certain rights and privileges forbidden to Negro scientists, artists, clergymen, journalists, and merchants. One can understand why Isadore walks with firmer tread.

Or glance at Cyrus Leviticus Dumbell. He is of Anglo-Saxon stock that is so old that it has very largely gone to seed. In the fastnesses of the Blue Ridge Mountains his racial strain has been safely preserved from pollution by black and red men, for over two hundred years. Thus he is a stalwart fellow untouched by thrift or education. Cy finally tires of the bushes and descends to one of the nearby towns. There he finds employment in a mill on a twelve-hour shift. The company paternalistically furnishes him everything he needs and thoughtfully deducts the cost regularly from his slender pay envelope, leaving him about two dollars for corn liquor and moving pictures. Cy has never had cause to think himself of any particular importance in the scheme of things, but his fellow workers tell him differently. He is a white man, they say, and therefore divinely appointed to "keep the nigger down." He must, they insist, protect white womanhood and preserve white supremacy. This country, he learns, is a white man's country, and although he owns none of it, the information strikes him not unpleasantly. Shortly he scrapes together ten dollars, buys Klan regalia, and is soon engaged in attending midnight meetings, burning crosses, repeating ritual from the Koran, flogging erring white womanhood for the greater purity of Anglo-Saxondom, and keeping vigilantly on the lookout for uppish and offensive zigaboos to lynch. Like the ancient Greeks and Romans, he now believes himself superior to everybody different from him. Nor does the presence of Jim Crow institutions on every hand contribute anything toward lessening that belief. Whatever his troubles may be, he has learned from his colleagues and the politicians, to blame it all on the dark folks, who are, he is now positive, without exception his inferiors.

Think, also, of demure little Dorothy Dunce. For twelve years she attended the palatial public school. Now, at eighteen, having graduated, she is about to apply her Latin, Greek, English literature, ancient history, geometry and botany to her everyday work as packer in a spaghetti factory. When she was very young, before she entered the kindergarten, her indulgent parents used to scare her by issuing a solemn warning that a big, black nigger would kidnap her if she wasn't a good little girl. Now that she has had American popular education turned loose upon her, she naturally believes differently: *i.e.*, that every big, burly, black nigger she meets on a dark street is ready to relieve her by force of what remains of her virtue. A value is placed upon her that she would not have in Roumania, Scotland, Denmark, or Montenegro. She is now a member of that exalted aggregation known as pure, white womanhood. She is also confident of her general superiority because education has taught her that Negroes are inferior, immoral, diseased, lazy, unprogressive, ugly, odoriferous, and should be firmly kept in their place at the bottom of the social and industrial scale. Quite naturally she swells with race pride, for no matter how low she falls, she will always be a white woman.

But enough of such examples. It is fairly well established, I think, that our presence in the Great Republic has been of incalculable psychological value to the masses of white citizens. Descendants of convicts, serfs and half-wits, with the rest have been buoyed up and greatly exalted by being constantly assured of their superiority to all other races and their equality with each other. On the stages of a thousand music halls, they have had their vanity tickled by blackface performers parading the idiocies of mythical black roustabouts and rustics. Between belly-cracking guffaws they have secretly congratulated themselves on the fact that they are not like these buffoons. Their books and magazines have told them, or insinuated, that morality, beauty, refinement and culture are restricted to Caucasians. On every hand they have seen smokes endeavoring to change from black to white, and from kinky hair to straight, by means of deleterious chemicals, and constantly they hear the Negroes urging each other to do this and that "like white folks." Nor do the crackers fail to observe, either, that pink epidermis is as highly treasured among blacks as in Nordic America, and that the most devastating charge that one Negro can make against another is that "he acs just like a nigger." Anything excellent they hear labeled by the race conscious Negroes as "like white folks," nor is it unusual for them, while loitering in the Negro ghetto, to hear black women compared to Fords, mulatto women to Cadillacs and white women to Packards. With so much flattery it is no wonder that the Caucasians have a very high opinion of themselves and attempt to live up to the lofty niche in which the Negroes have placed them. We should not marvel that every white elevator operator, school teacher and bricklayer identifies himself with Shakespeare, Julius Caesar, Napoleon, Newton, Edison, Wagner, Tennyson, and Rembrandt as creators of this great civilization. As a result we have our American society, where everybody who sports a pink color believes himself to be the equal of all other whites by virtue of his lack of skin pigmentation, and his classic Caucasian features.

It is not surprising, then, that democracy has worked better in this country than elsewhere. This belief in the equality of all white folks—making skin color the gauge of worth and the measure of citizenship rights—has caused the lowest to strive to become among the highest. Because of this great ferment, America has become the Utopia of the material world; the land of hope and opportunity. Without the transplanted African in their midst to bolster up the illusion, America would have unquestionably been a very different place; but instead the shine has served as a mudsill upon which all white people alike can stand and reach toward the stars. I submit that here is the gift par excellence of the Negro to America. To spur ten times our number on to great heights of achievement; to spare the nation the enervating presence of a destructive social caste system, such as exists elsewhere, by substituting a color caste system that roused the hope and pride of teeming millions of ofays—this indeed is a gift of which we can well be proud.

Claude McKay

(1889–1948)

"CLAUDE McKAY was one of the great forces bringing about what is now called the 'Negro Literary Renaissance'. . . . He is a poet and writer of genius." This evaluation, written by James Weldon Johnson in the *Reader's Guide* (September 1928), is higher than critics now give McKay. He did, however, contribute much to the Harlem Renaissance, and this in spite of several factors that would have denied a less gifted writer this superlative praise.

First of all, McKay was not born in America and he spent the first twenty-three years of his life in his native West Indies, not becoming a U.S. citizen until 1940. During many of the crucial years of the Renaissance, he lived abroad. For many of his years here and abroad, he had pro-leftist connections (except for W. E. B. Du Bois, Langston Hughes, and Frank Marshall Davis, most of the outstanding New Negro writers kept away from such connections). And he was seemingly contemptuous of certain Renaissance leaders, among them Du Bois.

On the positive side, however, this must be said: his militant sonnets inaugurated a new era in black protest poetry; he gave to Renaissance poetry the alien-and-exile theme used by Countee Cullen and several other poets; he emphasized for the first time in black fiction the seamier side of Negro life; and he brought to African American fiction several exotic and unusual themes culled from his island background and his experiences in Harlem and Marseilles—experiences which enriched the literature of the New Negro movement.

Born in Jamaica, British West Indies, Claude McKay was taught first by his free-thinking, schoolteacher brother, U'theo McKay, and by an English scholar, Edward Jekyll, who was interested in Jamaican folklore and who aided McKay in writing dialect poetry. A well-known island poet before he came to America, McKay published in 1912 two works: *Constab Ballads* and *Songs from Jamaica* (most of them in dialect). He came to the United States in the same year and studied at Tuskegee Institute for three months; becoming dissatisfied, he transferred to Kansas State College, where he remained for two years. Finally deciding that he wanted to pursue a literary career, he moved to Harlem, where he supported himself by working at odd jobs.

In 1917, using the pseudonym Eli Edwards, he published two (his first in America) poems in *The Seven Arts Magazine*—"Harlem Dancer" and "Invocation." He subsequently contributed regularly to *Pearson's Magazine* and Max Eastman's *The Liberator.* From 1919 to 1921 McKay lived in England, writing there for a Communist weekly called *The Worker's Dreadnought.* He went to Russia in 1920 and though not a Communist was lionized by the leaders then in power. McKay stayed abroad until 1934, when he returned to America, spending his last days as a seemingly devout Catholic. He died in 1948.

Claude McKay published, after leaving Jamaica, the following major poetical works: *Spring in New Hampshire and Other Poems* (1920), and *Harlem Shadows* (1922). He also published four works of fiction—*Home to Harlem* (1928), *Banjo, a Story without a Plot* (1929), *Gingertown* (1932), and *Banana Bottom* (1933). In addition he brought out an autobiography, *A Long Way from Home* (1937), and *Harlem: Negro Metropolis* (1940).

Several themes run through the poetical works of McKay. The most common is not racial as one would expect, but nostalgic, a longing for his tropical homeland. The best of these nostalgic poems is "Flame Heart." A second theme is the city. McKay seems to be fascinated by the bustling life of a metropolis like New York, but it is a love-hate affair. A third theme is that of the challenge of America to an alien Negro. The two best-known poems on this theme are "America" and "Baptism." Two minor themes for McKay became major for later Renaissance poets like Hughes and Cullen— the Harlem theme and the alien-and-exile theme. Two of McKay's best-known poems are racial in theme: "The Lynching" and "If We Must Die." The latter became a sort of rallying cry for the young defiant writers of the Harlem Renaissance.

Of McKay's fiction, the best known is *Home to Harlem*, in which, unlike the middle-class novels of Du Bois, Fauset, and others, the underclass are delineated. His best is perhaps *Banana Bottom*, in which he plays up, perhaps too much, the seamy side of Harlem.

The first full-length biographies of McKay have been published only recently: *Claude McKay: Rebel to Sojourner in the Harlem Renaissance* by Wayne F. Cooper (1987) and *Claude McKay* by James R. Giles (1976). An English translation from the Russian of McKay's *The Negro in America* was produced in 1979 and edited by Alan L. McLeod. McKay's life and works are also discussed in Melvin Dixon's *Ride Out the Wilderness: Geography and Identity in Afro-American Literature* (1987). Useful materials may also be found in the following works: Stephen H. Bronz's *Roots of Negro Racial Consciousness* (1964); Hugh M. Gloster's *Negro Voices in American Fiction* (1948); Robert A. Bone's *The Negro Novel in America* (1965); Jean Wagner's *Black Poets of the United States* (1973); and Arthur P. Davis's *From the Dark Tower: Afro-American Writers 1900–1960* (1974). Also see Arthur P. Davis's entry in *Dictionary of American Negro Biography* and the entry in *Dictionary of Literary Biography, Volume 51.*

The following poems are taken from *Selected Poems of Claude McKay* (1981); "Myrtle Avenue" is from *Home to Harlem* (1928, 1956).

HARLEM SHADOWS

I hear the halting footsteps of a lass
  In Negro Harlem when the night lets fall
Its veil. I see the shapes of girls who pass
  To bend and barter at desire's call.
Ah, little dark girls who in slippered feet
Go prowling through the night from street to street!

Through the long night until the silver break
  Of day the little gray feet know no rest;
Through the lone night until the last snow-flake
  Has dropped from heaven upon the earth's
      white breast,
The dusky, half-clad girls of tired feet
Are trudging, thinly shod, from street to street.

Ah, stern harsh world, that in the wretched way
  Of poverty, dishonor and disgrace,
Has pushed the timid little feet of clay,
  The sacred brown feet of my fallen race!
Ah, heart of me, the weary, weary feet
In Harlem wandering from street to street.

SPRING IN NEW HAMPSHIRE

(To J. L. J. F. E.)

Too green the springing April grass,
  Too blue the silver-speckled sky,
For me to linger here, alas,
  While happy winds go laughing by,
Wasting the golden hours indoors,
Washing windows and scrubbing floors.

Too wonderful the April night,
  Too faintly sweet the first May flowers,
The stars too gloriously bright,
  For me to spend the evening hours,
When fields are fresh and streams are leaping,
Wearied, exhausted, dully sleeping.

From *The Selected Poems of Claude McKay*, Harcourt Brace and Company, 1981.
Reprinted by permission of The Archives of Claude McKay, Carl Cowl, Administrator.

IF WE MUST DIE

If we must die, let it not be like hogs
Hunted and penned in an inglorious spot,
While round us bark the mad and hungry dogs,
Making their mock at our accurséd lot.
If we must die, O let us nobly die,
So that our precious blood may not be shed
In vain; then even the monsters we defy
Shall be constrained to honor us though dead!
O kinsmen! we must meet the common foe!
Though far outnumbered let us show us brave,
And for their thousand blows deal one deathblow!
What though before us lies the open grave?
Like men we'll face the murderous, cowardly pack,
Pressed to the wall, dying, but fighting back!

THE WHITE HOUSE

Your door is shut against my tightened face,
And I am sharp as steel with discontent;
But I possess the courage and the grace
To bear my anger proudly and unbent.
The pavement slabs burn loose beneath my feet,
A chafing savage, down the decent street;
And passion rends my vitals as I pass,
Where boldly shines your shuttered door of glass.
Oh, I must search for wisdom every hour,
Deep in my wrathful bosom sore and raw,
And find in it the superhuman power
To hold me to the letter of your law!
Oh, I must keep my heart inviolate
Against the potent poison of your hate.

AMERICA

Although she feeds me bread of bitterness,
And sinks into my throat her tiger's tooth,
Stealing my breath of life, I will confess
I love this cultured hell that tests my youth!

Her vigor flows like tides into my blood,
Giving me strength against her hate.
Her bigness sweeps my being like a flood.
Yet as a rebel fronts a king in state,
I stand within her walls with not a shred
Of terror, malice, not a word of jeer.
Darkly I gaze into the days ahead,
And see her might and granite wonders there,
Beneath the touch of Time's unerring hand,
Like priceless treasures sinking in the sand.

MYRTLE AVENUE

Zeddy was excited over Jake's success in love. He thought how often he had tried to make up to Rose, without succeeding. He was crazy about finding a woman to love him for himself.

He had been married when he was quite a lad to a crust-yellow girl in Petersburg. Zeddy's wife, after deceiving him with white men, had run away from him to live an easier life. That was before Zeddy came North. Since then he had had many other alliances. But none had been successful.

It was true that no Black Belt beauty would ever call Zeddy "mah han'some brown." But there were sweetmen of the Belt more repulsive than he, that women would fight and murder each other for. Zeddy did not seem to possess any of that magic that charms and holds women for a long time. All his attempts at home-making had failed. The women left him when he could not furnish the cash to meet the bills. They never saw his wages. For it was gobbled up by his voracious passion for poker and crap games. Zeddy gambled in Harlem. He gambled with white men down by the piers. And he was always losing.

"If only I could get those kinda gals that falls foh Jake," Zeddy mused. "And Jake is such a fool spade. Don't know how to handle the womens."

Zeddy's chance came at last. One Saturday a yellow-skinned youth, whose days and nights were wholly spent between pool-rooms and Negro speakeasies, invited Zeddy to a sociable at a grass-

"Myrtle Avenue" in *Home to Harlem* by Claude McKay. Copyright 1928 by Harper & Brothers; renewed 1956 by Hope McKay Virtue. Republished in 1987 by Northeastern University Press, Boston, Massachusetts. Reprinted by permission of The Archives of Claude McKay, Carl Cowl, Administrator.

widow's who lived in Brooklyn and worked as a cook downtown in
New York. She was called Gin-head Susy. She had a little apartment
in Myrtle Avenue near Prince Street.

Susy was wonderfully created. She was of the complexion known
among Negroes as spade or chocolate-to-the-bone. Her eyes shone
like big white stars. Her chest was majestic and the general effect
like a mountain. And that mountain was overgrand because Susy
never wore any other but extremely French-heeled shoes. Even over
the range she always stood poised in them and blazing in bright-
hued clothes.

The burning passion of Susy's life was the yellow youth of her
race. Susy came from South Carolina. A yellow youngster married
her when she was fifteen and left her before she was eighteen. Since
then she had lived with a yellow complex at the core of her heart.

Civilization had brought strikingly exotic types into Susy's race.
And like many, many Negroes, she was a victim to that. . . . Ancient
black life rooted upon its base with all its fascinating new layers of
brown, low-brown, high-brown, nut-brown, lemon, maroon, olive,
mauve, gold. Yellow balancing between black and white. Black
reaching out beyond yellow. Almost-white on the brink of a change.
Sucked back down into the current of black by the terribly sweet
rhythm of black blood. . . .

Susy's life of yellow complexity was surcharged with gin. There
were whisky and beer also at her sociable evenings, but gin was the
drink of drinks. Except for herself, her parties were all-male. Like so
many of her sex, she had a congenital contempt for women. All-male
were her parties and as yellow as she could make them. A lemon-
colored or paper-brown pool-room youngster from Harlem's Fifth
Avenue or from Prince Street. A bell-boy or railroad waiter or porter.
Sometimes a chocolate who was a quick, nondiscriminating lover
and not remote of attitude like the pampered high-browns. But choc-
olates were always a rarity among Susy's front-roomful of gin-lovers.

Yet for all of her wages drowned in gin, Susy carried a hive of
discontents in her majestic breast. She desired a lover, something
like her undutiful husband, but she desired in vain. Her guests consumed her gin and listened to the phonograph, exchanged rakish
stories, and when they felt fruit-ripe to dropping, left her place in
pursuit of pleasures elsewhere.

Sometimes Susy managed to lay hold of a yellow one for some
time. Something all a piece of dirty rags and stench picked up in the
street. Cleansed, clothed, and booted it. But so soon as he got his
curly hair straightened by the process of Harlem's Ambrozine Palace
of Beauty, and started in strutting the pavement of Lenox Avenue,
feeling smart as a moving-picture dandy, he would leave Susy.

Apart from Susy's repellent person, no youthful sweetmen at-
tempting to love her could hold out under the ridicule of his pals.
Over their games of pool and craps the boys had their cracks at
Susy.

"What about Gin-head Susy tonight?"

"Sure, let's go and look the crazy old broad over."

"I'll go anywheres foh swilling of good booze."

"She's sho one ugly spade, but she's right there with her Gordon
Dry."

"She ain't got 'em from creeps to crown and her trotters is B flat,
but her gin is regal."

But now, after all the years of gin sociables and unsatisfactory
lemons, Susy was changing just a little. She was changing under the
influence of her newly-acquired friend, Lavinia Curdy, the only
woman whom she tolerated at her parties. That was not so difficult,
as Miss Curdy was less attractive than Susy. Miss Curdy was a putty-
skinned mulattress with purple streaks on her face. Two of her upper front teeth had been knocked out and her lower lip slanted pa-
thetically leftward. She was skinny and when she laughed she resembled an old braying jenny.

When Susy came to know Miss Curdy, she unloaded a quantity
of the stuff of her breast upon her. Her drab childhood in a South
Carolina town. Her early marriage. No girlhood. Her husband leaving her. And all the yellow men that had beaten her, stolen from
her, and pawned her things.

Miss Curdy had been very emphatic to Susy about "yaller men."
"I know them from long experience. They never want to work.
They're a lazy and shiftless lot. Want to be kept like women. I found
that out a long, long time ago. And that's why when I wanted a man
foh keeps I took me a black plug-ugly one, mah dear."

It wouldn't have supported the plausibility of Miss Curdy's advice
if she had mentioned that more than one black plug-ugly had ruthlessly cut loose from her. As the black woman had had her entangle-
ments in yellow, so had the mulattress hers of black. But, perhaps,
Miss Curdy did not realize that she could not help desiring black. In
her salad days as a business girl her purse was controlled by many a
black man. Now, however, her old problems did not arise in exactly
the same way,—her purse was old and worn and flat and attracted
no attention.

"A black man is as good to me as a yaller when I finds a real
one." Susy lied a little to Miss Curdy from a feeling that she ought
to show some pride in her own complexion.

"But all these sociables—and you spend so much coin on gin,"
Miss Curdy had said.

"Well, that's the trute, but we all of us drinks it. And I loves to have company in mah house, plenty of company."

But when Susy came home from work one evening and found that her latest "yaller" sweetie had stolen her suitcase and best dresses and pawned even her gas range, she resolved never to keep another of his kind as a "steady." At least she made that resolve to Miss Curdy. But the sociables went on and the same types came to drink the Saturday evenings away, leaving the two women at the finish to their empty bottles and glasses. Once Susy did make a show of a black lover. He was the house man at the boarding-house where she cooked. But the arrangement did not hold any time, for Susy demanded of the chocolate extremely more than she ever got from her yellows.

"Well, boh, we's Brooklyn bound tonight," said Zeddy to Jake.

"You got to show me that Brooklyn's got any life to it," replied Jake.

"Theah's life anywheres theah's booze and jazz, and theah's cases o' gin and gramophone whar we's going."

"Has we got to pay foh it, buddy?"

"No, boh, eve'ything is f.o.c. ef the lady likes you."

"Blimey!" A cockney phrase stole Jake's tongue. "Don't bull me."

"I aint. Honest-to-Gawd Gordon Dry, and moh—ef you're the goods, all f.o.c."

"Well, I'll be browned!" exclaimed Jake.

Zeddy also took along Strawberry Lips, a new pal, burnt-cork black, who was thus nick-named from the peculiar stage-red color of his mouth. Strawberry Lips was typically the stage Negro. He was proof that a generalization has some foundation in truth. . . . You might live your life in many black belts and arrive at the conclusion that there is no such thing as a typical Negro—no minstrel coon off the stage, no Thomas Nelson Page's nigger, no Octavus Roy Cohen's porter, no lineal descendant of Uncle Tom. Then one day your theory may be upset through meeting with a type by far more perfect than any created counterpart.

"Myrtle Avenue used to be a be-be itching of a place," said Strawberry Lips, "when Doc Giles had his gambling house on there and Elijah Bowers was running his cabaret. H'm. But Bowers was some big guy. He knew swell white folks in politics, and had a grand automobile and a high-yaller wife that hadn't no need of painting to pass. His cabaret was running neck and neck with Marshall's in Fifty-third Street. Then one night he killed a man in his cabaret, and that finished him. The lawyers got him off. But they cleaned him out dry. Done broke him, that case did. And today he's plumb down and out."

Jake, Zeddy, and Strawberry Lips had left the subway train at Borough Hall and were walking down Myrtle Avenue.

"Bowers' cabaret was some place for the teasing-brown pick-me-up then, brother—and the snow. The stuff was cheap then. You sniff, boh?" Strawberry Lips asked Jake and Zeddy.

"I wouldn't know befoh I sees it," Jake laughed.

"I ain't no habitual prisoner," said Zeddy, "but I does any little thing for a change. Keep going and active with anything, says I."

The phonograph was discharging its brassy jazz notes when they entered the apartment. Susy was jerking herself from one side to the other with a potato-skinned boy. Miss Curdy was half-hopping up and down with the only chocolate that was there. Five lads, ranging from brown to yellow in complexion, sat drinking with jaded sneering expressions on their faces. The one that had invited Zeddy was among them. He waved to him to come over with his friends.

"Sit down and try some gin," he said. . . .

Zeddy dipped his hand in his pocket and sent two bones rolling on the table.

"Ise with you, chappie," his yellow friend said. The others crowded around. The gramophone stopped and Susy, hugging a bottle, came jerking on her French heels over to the group. She filled the glasses and everybody guzzled gin.

Miss Curdy looked the newcomers over, paying particular attention to Jake. A sure-enough eye-filling chocolate, she thought. I would like to make a steady thing of him.

Over by the door two light-brown lads began arguing about an actress of the leading theater of the Black Belt.

"I tell you I knows Gertie Kendall. I know her more'n I know you."

"Know her mah granny. You knows her just like I do, from the balcony of the Lafayette. Don't hand me none o' that fairy stuff, for I ain't gwine to swallow it."

"Youse an aching pain. I knows her, I tell you. I even danced with her at Madame Mulberry's apartment. You thinks I only hangs out with low-down trash becassin Ise in a place like this, eh? I done met mos'n all our big niggers: Jack Johnson, James Reese Europe, Adah Walker, Buddy, who used to play that theah drum for them Castle Walkers, and Madame Walker."

"Yaller, it 'pears to me that youse jest a nacherally-born story-teller. You really spec's me to believe youse been associating with the mucty-mucks of the race? Gwan with you. You'll be telling me next you done speaks with Charlie Chaplin and John D. Rockefeller—"

Miss Curdy had tuned her ears to the conversation and broke in: "Why, what is that to make so much fuss about? Sure he can dance with Gertie Kendall and know the dickty niggers. In my sporting days I knew Bert Williams and Walker and Adah Overton and Editor Tukslack and all that upstage race gang that wouldn't touch Jack Johnson with a ten-foot pole. I lived in Washington and had Congressmen for my friends—foop! Why you can get in with the top-crust crowd at any swell ball in Harlem. All you need is clothes and the coin. I know them all, yet I don't feel a bit haughty mixing here with Susy and you all."

"I guess you don't now," somebody said.

Gin went round . . . and round . . . and round. . . . Desultory dancing. . . . Dice. . . . Blackjack. . . . Poker. . . . The room became a close, live, intense place. Tight-faced, the men seemed interested only in drinking and gaming, while Susy and Miss Curdy, guzzling hard, grew uglier. A jungle atmosphere pervaded the room, and, like shameless wild animals hungry for raw meat, the females savagely searched the eyes of the males. Susy's eyes always came back to settle upon the lad that had invited Zeddy. He was her real object. And Miss Curdy was ginned up with high hopes of Jake.

Jake threw up the dice and Miss Curdy seized her chance to get him alone for a little while.

"The cards do get so tiresome," she said. "I wonder how you men can go on and on all night long poking around with poker."

"Better than worser things," retored Jake. Disgusted by the purple streaks, he averted his eyes from the face of the mulattress.

"I don't know about that," Miss Curdy bridled. "There's many nice ways of spending a sociable evening between ladies and gentlemen."

"Got to show me," said Jake, simply because the popular phrase intrigued his tongue.

"*And that I can.*"

Irritated, Jake turned to move away.

"Where you going? Scared of a lady?"

Jake recoiled from the challenge, and shuffled away from the hideous mulattress. From experience in seaport towns in America, in France, in England, he had concluded that a woman could always go farther than a man in coarseness, depravity, and sheer cupidity. Men were ugly and brutal. But beside women they were merely vicious children. Ignorant about the aim and meaning and fulfillment of life; uncertain and indeterminate; weak. Rude children who loved excelling in spectacular acts to win the applause of women.

But women were so realistic and straight-going. *They* were the real controlling force of life. Jake remembered the bal-musette fights between colored and white soldiers in France. Blacks, browns, yellows, whites. . . . He remembered the interracial sex skirmishes in

England. Men fought, hurt, wounded, killed each other. Women, like blazing torches, egged them on or denounced them. Victims of sex, the men seemed foolish, ape-like blunderers in their pools of blood. Didn't know what they were fighting for, except it was to gratify some vague feeling about women. . . .

Jake's thoughts went roaming after his little lost brown of the Baltimore. The difference! She, in one night, had revealed a fine different world to him. Mystery again. A little stray girl. Finer than the finest!

Some of the fellows were going. In a vexed spirit, Susy had turned away from her unresponsive mulatto toward Zeddy. Relieved, the mulatto yawned, threw his hands backwards and said: "I guess mah broad is home from Broadway by now. Got to final on home to her. Harlem, lemme see you."

Miss Curdy was sitting against the mantel-piece, charming Strawberry Lips. Marvellous lips. Salmon-pink and planky. She had hoisted herself upon his knees, her arm around his thick neck.

Jake went over to the mantelpiece to pour a large chaser of beer and Miss Curdy leered at him. She disgusted him. His life was a free coarse thing, but he detested nastiness and ugliness. Guess I'll haul bottom to Harlem, he thought. Congo Rose was a rearing wild animal, all right, but these women, these boys. . . . Skunks, tame skunks, all of them!

He was just going out when a chocolate lad pointed at a light-brown and said: "The pot calls foh four bits, chappie. Come across or stay out."

"Lemme a quarter!"

"Ain't got it. Staying out?"

Biff! Square on the mouth. The chocolate leaped up like a tiger-cat at his assailant, carrying over card table, little pile of money, and half-filled gin glasses with a crash. Like an enraged ram goat, he held and butted the light-brown boy twice, straight on the forehead. The victim crumpled with a thud to the floor. Susy jerked over to the felled boy and hauled him, his body leaving a liquid trail, to the door. She flung him out in the corridor and slammed the door.

"Sarves him right, pulling off that crap in mah place. And you, Mis'er Jack Johnson," she said to the chocolate youth, "lemme miss you quick."

"He done hits me first," the chocolate said.

"I knows it, but I ain't gwina stand foh no rough-house in mah place. Ise got a dawg heah wif me all ready foh bawking."

"K-hhhhh, K-hhhhh," laughed Strawberry Lips. "Oh, boh, I know it's the trute, but—"

The chocolate lad slunk out of the flat.

"Lavinia," said Susy to Miss Curdy, "put on that theah 'Tickling Blues' on the victroly."

The phonograph began its scraping and Miss Curdy started jig-jagging with Strawberry Lips. Jake gloomed with disgust against the door.

"Getting outa this, buddy?" he asked Zeddy.

"Nobody's chasing *us*, boh." Zeddy commenced stepping with Susy to the "Tickling Blues."

Outside, Jake found the light-brown boy still half-stunned against the wall.

"Aint' you gwine at home?" Jake asked him.

"I can't find a nickel foh car fare," said the boy.

Jake took him into a saloon and bought him a lemon squash. "Drink that to clear you' haid," he said. "And heah's car fare." He gave the boy a dollar. "Whar you living at?"

"San Juan Hill."

"Come on, le's git the subway, then."

The Myrtle Avenue Elevated train passed with a high raucous rumble over their heads.

"Myrtle Avenue," murmured Jake. "Pretty name, all right, but it stinks like a sewer. Legs and feets! Come take me outa it back home to Harlem."

Countee Cullen

(1903–1946)

A "DISCIPLE" of John Keats, Countee Cullen did not relish being called a "Negro poet." He strongly objected to being forced as a Negro to write of "nothing but the old atavistic urges" and the "none too beautiful aspects" of Negro lives. Because of our English-speaking culture, he felt that Negro writers had "more to gain from the rich background of English and American poetry than from any nebulous atavistic yearnings toward an African inheritance." And yet, he later confessed, "I find my poetry of itself treating of the Negro," and he could have added that his best poems treated "of the Negro."

Born Countee Porter in New York City, he lived with his grandmother until she died. He was then adopted by the Reverend Frederick A. Cullen, a very popular Harlem minister. Countee Cullen had a very successful career in the New York public schools: his first poem was published in 1918 in the *Modern School Magazine*; at DeWitt Clinton High School, he was editor of the weekly newspaper, became vice-president of his senior class, and graduated with top honors. He attended New York University, earning there Phi Beta Kappa honors. His first volume of verse, *Color* (1925), was published when he was a college senior (he had already published poems in *Harper's, Century, American Mercury, Nation*, and other prestigious magazines). In 1926, he received an M.A. from Harvard, and for a short while thereafter was an assistant editor of *Opportunity*.

In 1927 *Color* received the first award in literature from the William Harmon Foundation. During the same fruitful year Cullen published *Copper Sun* and *The Ballad of the Brown Girl* and edited *Caroling Dusk*, a poetry anthology. In 1928 he was awarded a Guggenheim Fellowship for study in Paris. Also in 1928, he married in a highly played-up society wedding Nina Yolande Du Bois, the daughter of W. E. B. Du Bois. The marriage ended in divorce a year later. His second marriage was to Ida Mae Roberson, the sister of Orlando Roberson, the singer. It was a highly successful union. Cullen taught in the New York public schools from 1919 to 1946; he died in New York City in 1946, still a relatively young man.

Cullen published the following major works in poetry, children's verse, and poetry anthologies: *Color* (1925, 1969); *Copper Sun* (1927); *The Medea and Some Poems* (1935); *The Lost Zoo (A Rhyme for the Young . . .)* (1940); and *On These I Stand: An Anthology of the Best Poems of Countee Cullen*

(1947).This last work, published posthumously, included poems he selected himself and six new poems never before published. Cullen's single novel, *One Way to Heaven*, was published in 1932. He collaborated with Arna Bontemps in writing a play, *St. Louis Woman* (based on Bontemp's *God Sends Sunday*), which became a successful Broadway musical in 1946. In addition to the fellowship and awards mentioned previously, Cullen won the Witter Bynner Poetry Prize three times, the John Reed Memorial Award, and the Spingarn Medal.

Not an experimental poet like Hughes, Cullen is preeminently a conventional lyrical poet; he admits to being "a rank conservative, loving the measured line and the skillful rhyme," and he was a master of such lines in all of his verse. In his racial poems, which he put in each volume under the rubric "color," Cullen emphasizes the alien-and-exile theme—a theme which says in effect that the American Negro is an unwanted, unhappy, and nonassimilated foreigner here, permanently deprived of his beautiful homeland in Africa. Although many New Negro poets used the same theme, Cullen's "Heritage" is the best known and most brilliant expression of it. Another major theme in Cullen's works is his own religious convictions, which run the gamut from the "pagan inclination" of the poems in *Color* (1925) to the strong affirmation of Christian faith found in *The Black Christ* (1929). He also makes another strong statement in this volume on the question of being a "Negro poet." In effect, he says, I have no more to say on racial matters—"content that silence hold her sway, / My tongue not rolling futile sounds / After my heart has had its say."

McKay's *Home to Harlem* and Cullen's *One Way to Heaven* are both delineations of Harlem life and are often compared. Of the two, Cullen's novel is closer to the *real* Harlem than McKay's. McKay emphasized the exotic and the primitive, giving a white folks' view of the black city. Cullen's work is an "inside view"—one geared to a black audience. Cullen, because he was a part of it, knew the life in a conventional black church, knew the relationship between middle class and underclass, and could laugh at the foibles of both classes as he did in his only novel. McKay's work is far better known than Cullen's and is probably artistically a better work.

For comments on the life and works of Countee Cullen, see the *Dictionary of American Negro Biography* entry by Arthur P. Davis. See also Margaret Perry's *A Bio-Bibliography of Countee P. Cullen, 1903–1946* (1971); Alan R. Shucard's *Countee Cullen* (1984); Houston A. Baker, Jr.'s *A Many-Colored Coat of Dreams: The Poetry of Countee Cullen* (1974); Jean Wagner's *Black Poets of the United States* (1973); Blanche E. Ferguson's *Countee Cullen and the Negro Renaissance* (1966); and Stephen H. Bronz's *Roots of Negro Racial Consciousness* (1964).

The following selections are reprinted from *On These I Stand* (1925, 1953).

YET DO I MARVEL

I doubt not God is good, well-meaning, kind,
And did He stoop to quibble could tell why
The little buried mole continues blind,
Why flesh that mirrors Him must some day die,
Make plain the reason tortured Tantalus
Is baited by the fickle fruit, declare
If merely brute caprice dooms Sisyphus
To struggle up a never-ending stair.
Inscrutable His ways are, and immune
To catechism by a mind too strewn
With petty cares to slightly understand
What awful brain compels His awful hand.
Yet do I marvel at this curious thing:
To make a poet black, and bid him sing!

INCIDENT

(For Eric Walrond)

Once riding in old Baltimore,
    Heart-filled, head-filled with glee,
I saw a Baltimorean
    Keep looking straight at me.

Now I was eight and very small,
    And he was no whit bigger,
And so I smiled, but he poked out
    His tongue, and called me, "Nigger."

I saw the whole of Baltimore
    From May until December;
Of all the things that happened there
    That's all that I remember.

PAGAN PRAYER

Not for myself I make this prayer,
　But for this race of mine
That stretches forth from shadowed places
　Dark hands for bread and wine.

For me, my heart is pagan mad,
　My feet are never still,
But give them hearths to keep them warm
　In homes high on a hill.

For me, my faith lies fallowing,
　I bow not till I see,
But these are humble and believe;
　Bless their credulity.

For me, I pay my debts in kind,
　And see no better way,
Bless these who turn the other cheek
　For love of you, and pray.

Our Father, God, our Brother, Christ—
　So are we taught to pray;
Their kinship seems a little thing
　Who sorrow all the day.

Our Father, God; our Brother, Christ,
　Or are we bastard kin,
That to our plaints your ears are closed,
　Your doors barred from within?

Our Father, God; our Brother, Christ,
　Retrieve my race again;
So shall you compass this black sheep,
　The pagan heart. Amen.

TRIBUTE

(To My Mother)

Because man is not virtuous in himself,
Nor kind, nor given to sweet charities,
Save goaded by the little kindling elf
Of some dear face it pleasures him to please;

Some men who else were humbled to the dust,
Have marveled that the chastening hand should stay
And never dreamed they held their lives in trust
To one the victor loved a world away.

So I, least noble of a churlish race,
Least kind of those by nature rough and crude,
Have at the intervention of your face
Spared him with whom was my most bitter feud
One moment, and the next, a deed more grand,
The helpless fly imprisoned in my hand.

FOR A LADY I KNOW

She even thinks that up in heaven
    Her class lies late and snores,
While poor black cherubs rise at seven
    To do celestial chores.

HERITAGE

What is Africa to me:
Copper sun or scarlet sea,
Jungle star or jungle track,
Strong bronzed men, or regal black
Women from whose loins I sprang
When the birds of Eden sang?
One three centuries removed
From the scenes his fathers loved,
Spicy grove, cinnamon tree,
What is Africa to me?

So I lie, who all day long
Want no sound except the song
Sung by wild barbaric birds
Goading massive jungle herds,
Juggernauts of flesh that pass
Trampling tall defiant grass
Where young forest lovers lie
Plighting troth beneath the sky.

So I lie, who always hear
Though I cram against my ear
Both my thumbs, and keep them there,
Great drums beating through the air.
So I lie, whose fount of pride,
Dear distress, and joy allied,
Is my sombre flesh and skin,
With the dark blood dammed within
Like great pulsing tides of wine
That, I fear, must burst the fine
Channels of the chafing net
Where they surge and foam and fret.

Africa? A book one thumbs
Listlessly, till slumber comes.
Unremembered are her bats
Circling through the night, her cats
Crouching in the river reeds,
Stalking gentle flesh that feeds
By the river brink; no more
Does the bugle-throated roar
Cry that monarch claws have leapt
From the scabbards where they slept.
Silver snakes that once a year
Doff the lovely coats you wear,
Seek no covert in your fear
Lest a mortal eye should see;
What's your nakedness to me?
Here no leprous flowers rear
Fierce corollas in the air;
Here no bodies sleek and wet,
Dripping mingled rain and sweat,
Tread the savage measures of
Jungle boys and girls in love.
What is last year's snow to me,
Last year's anything? The tree
Budding yearly must forget
How its past arose or set—
Bough and blossom, flower, fruit,
Even what shy bird with mute
Wonder at her travail there,
Meekly labored in its hair.
One three centuries removed
From the scenes his fathers loved,

Spicy grove, cinnamon tree,
What is Africa to me?

So I lie, who find no peace
Night or day, no slight release
From the unremittent beat
Made by cruel padded feet
Walking through my body's street.
Up and down they go, and back,
Treading out a jungle track.
So I lie, who never quite
Safely sleep from rain at night—
I can never rest at all
When the rain begins to fall;
Like a soul gone mad with pain
I must match its weird refrain;
Ever must I twist and squirm,
Writhing like a baited worm,
While its primal measures drip
Through my body, crying, "Strip!
Doff this new exuberance.
Come and dance the Lover's Dance!"
In an old remembered way
Rain works on me night and day.

Quaint, outlandish heathen gods
Black men fashion out of rods,
Clay, and brittle bits of stone,
In a likeness like their own,
My conversion came high-priced;
I belong to Jesus Christ,
Preacher of humility;
Heathen gods are naught to me.

Father, Son, and Holy Ghost,
So I make an idle boast,
Jesus of the twice turned cheek,
Lamb of God, although I speak
With my mouth thus, in my heart
Do I play a double part.
Ever at thy glowing altar
Must my heart grow sick and falter,
Wishing He I served were black,
Thinking then it would not lack
Precedent of pain to guide it,

Let who would or might deride it;
Surely then this flesh would know
Yours had borne a kindred woe.
Lord, I fashion dark gods, too,
Daring even to give to You
Dark despairing features where,
Crowned with dark rebellious hair,
Patience wavers just so much as
Mortal grief compels, while touches
Quick and hot, of anger, rise
To smitten cheek and weary eyes.
Lord, forgive me if my need
Sometimes shapes a human creed.

All day long and all night through,
One thing only must I do:
Quench my pride and cool my blood,
Lest I perish in the flood.
Lest a hidden ember set
Timber that I thought was wet
Burning like the dryest flax,
Melting like the merest wax,
Lest the grave restore its dead.
Not yet has my heart or head
In the least way realized
They and I are civilized.

TO JOHN KEATS, POET. AT SPRINGTIME

I cannot hold my peace, John Keats;
There never was a spring like this;
It is an echo, that repeats
My last year's song and next year's bliss.
I know, in spite of all men say
Of Beauty, you have felt her most.
Yea, even in your grave her way
Is laid. Poor, troubled, lyric ghost,
Spring never was so fair and dear
As Beauty makes her seem this year.

I cannot hold my peace, John Keats,
I am as helpless in the toil
Of Spring as any lamb that bleats

To feel the solid earth recoil
Beneath his puny legs. Spring beats
Her tocsin call to those who love her,
And lo! the dogwood petals cover
Her breasts with drifts of snow, and sleek
White gulls fly screaming to her, and hover
About her shoulders, and kiss her cheek,
While white and purple lilacs muster
A strength that bears them to a cluster
Of color and odor; for her sake
All things that slept are now awake.

And you and I, shall we lie still,
John Keats, while Beauty summons us?
Somehow I feel your sensitive will
Is pulsing up some tremulous
Sap road of a maple tree, whose leaves
Grow music as they grow, since your
Wild voice is in them, a harp that grieves
For life that opens death's dark door.
Though dust, your fingers still can push
The Vision Splendid to a birth,
Though now they work as grass in the hush
Of the night on the broad sweet page of the earth.

"John Keats is dead," they say, but I
Who hear your full insistent cry
In bud and blossom, leaf and tree,
Know John Keats still writes poetry.
And while my head is earthward bowed
To read new life sprung from your shroud,
Folks seeing me must think it strange
That merely spring should so derange
My mind. They do not know that you,
John Keats, keep revel with me, too.

TO CERTAIN CRITICS

Then call me traitor if you must,
Shout treason and default!
Say I betray a sacred trust
Aching beyond this vault.
I'll bear your censure as your praise,

For never shall the clan
Confine my singing to its ways
Beyond the ways of man.

No racial option narrows grief,
Pain is no patriot,
And sorrow plaits her dismal leaf
For all as lief as not.
With blind sheep groping every hill,
Searching an oriflamme,
How shall the shepherd heart then thrill
To only the darker lamb?

Wallace Thurman

(1902–1934)

ALTHOUGH WALLACE THURMAN was very much a part of the Negro Renaissance, he was a severe critic of that movement. One of the most versatile of the Renaissance writers, Thurman was a journalist, novelist, playwright, ghost writer, and a gadfly for several literary ventures.

Born in Salt Lake City, Utah, in 1902, Thurman finished high school in his native city. According to the *Dictionary of American Negro Biography*, he was a medical student for two quarters in 1919/20 at the University of Utah. Earlier scholars, however, following Langston Hughes's comments on Thurman in *The Big Sea*, state that Thurman's alma mater was the University of Southern California. Wherever he studied, all who knew him were impressed by his brilliant mind and his comprehensive knowledge of literature.

When Wallace Thurman arrived in Harlem in 1925, bringing with him some experience as a West Coast journalist, Theophilus Lewis helped him to gain a position first on *The Looking Glass*, a short-lived periodical, and subsequently with the well-known monthly magazine *The Messenger*. Thurman left *The Messenger* in 1926 and became the circulation manager of a liberal, white monthly, *The World Tomorrow*.

In the summer of 1926 Thurman, along with Langston Hughes, Zora Neale Hurston, Aaron Douglas, John P. Davis, Bruce Nugent, and Gwendolyn Bennett, founded the short-lived "little magazine" *Fire*. He also helped to establish another little magazine, *Harlem*, which was equally short lived. In 1929, according to Hughes, Thurman got a job as "reader" with Macaulay's—making him "the only Negro holding such a position in a big publishing company." He had also worked on the editorial staff of McFadden Publications, and was a ghost writer for *True Story*, often writing "true" confessions for this pulp magazine in Irish and Jewish dialects. He also wrote articles for the *Independent Bookman* and the *New Republic*.

Wallace Thurman actually lived in two worlds: the downtown white world of the Macaulay and McFadden publishing houses and the uptown world of the Harlem Renaissance. He was unhappy, however, in both worlds. He wanted to be, Hughes tells us, "a *very* great writer like Gorki or Thomas Mann, and he felt that he was merely a journalist writer." As a result of this kind of neurotic brooding, he became melancholy and suicide-prone. He was also not a well person. In December of 1934, he died of tuberculosis in the charity ward of Bellevue Hospital, still a young man.

Thurman's first widely acclaimed work was a sensational and successful Broadway play, *Harlem* (1929), written in collaboration with William Jourdan Rapp, the editor of *True Story*. The play dealt with a subject used by Rudolph Fisher: the often tragic impact of Harlem on southern Negroes who come North looking for the promised land. *Harlem* ran for over ninety performances in New York and had in addition a good reception in Los Angeles and Chicago.

In his first novel, *The Blacker the Berry*, also written in 1929, Thurman launched a frontal attack on a wrong perpetrated on dark-skinned Negro women, not by whites but by Negroes themselves, especially Negro men. In much of the folk literature, in a great deal of the street-corner-type joking among black men, the dark-skinned woman was often the butt of a coarse, vulgar, cruel, and humiliating humor aimed at her color. Moreover, practically all novels written by Negroes from the first, *Clotel*, written in 1853, down to those written in the sixties had light-colored heroines. Black was not considered beautiful until the black revolution. *The Blacker the Berry* is not a well-written novel, but it drove home a lesson that should have been learned long before Thurman wrote. The prejudice he attacked, though nowhere now as prevalent as it once was, is still with us, in subtle ways. *Infants of the Spring* (1932), Thurman's second novel, is a biting commentary on the failure (in the author's opinion) of the New Negro movement. The action of the novel takes place in Niggerati Manor (*nigger* plus *literati*), and it deals with a representative group of black creative artists and would-be artists plus two white men and a Jewish girl. Under thinly disguised and appropriate pseudonyms, Thurman brings to the manor for satirical treatment some of Harlem's best-known writers: Langston Hughes, Countee Cullen, Eric Walrond, Rudolph Fisher, Zora Neale Hurston, and Alain Locke. *Infants of the Spring* is more criticism than fiction, but it gives an appraisal of the phony side of the Renaissance that very much needed to be given.

Biographical material on Wallace Thurman is not plentiful. Langston Hughes's *The Big Sea: An Autobiography* (1940) and the "Portrait" by Mae Gwendolyn Henderson in *The Harlem Renaissance Remembered* (1972), edited by Arna Bontemps, are among the best. See also Doris E. Abramson's *Negro Playwrights in the American Theater, 1929–1959* (1969); Ernest B. Boynton, Jr.'s article in *Dictionary of American Negro Biography* and Phyllis R. Klotman's article in *Dictionary of Literary Biography, Volume 51*.

The following selection comes from *The Blacker the Berry*.

FROM **THE BLACKER THE BERRY**

More acutely than ever before Emma Lou began to feel that her luscious black complexion was somewhat of a liability, and that her marked color variation from the other people in her environment was a decided curse. Not that she minded being black, being a Negro necessitated having a colored skin, but she did mind being too black. She couldn't understand why such should be the case, couldn't comprehend the cruelty of the natal attenders who had allowed her to be dipped, as it were, in indigo ink when there were so many more pleasing colors on nature's palette. Biologically, it wasn't necessary either; her mother was quite fair, so was her mother's mother, and her mother's brother, and her mother's brother's son; but then none of them had had a black man for a father. Why *had* her mother married a black man? Surely there had been some eligible brown-skin men around. She didn't particularly desire to have had a "high yaller" father, but for her sake certainly some more happy medium could have been found.

She wasn't the only person who regretted her darkness either. It was an acquired family characteristic, this moaning and grieving over the color of her skin. Everything possible had been done to alleviate the unhappy condition, every suggested agent had been employed, but her skin, despite bleachings, scourgings, and powderings, had remained black—fast black—as nature had planned and effected.

She should have been a boy, then color of skin wouldn't have mattered so much, for wasn't her mother always saying that a black boy could get along, but that a black girl would never know anything but sorrow and disappointment? But she wasn't a boy; she was a girl, and color did matter, mattered so much that she would rather have missed receiving her high school diploma than have to sit as she now sat, the only odd and conspicuous figure on the auditorium platform of the Boise high school. Why had she allowed them to place her in the center of the first row, and why had they insisted upon her dressing entirely in white so that surrounded as she was by similarly attired pale-faced fellow graduates she resembled, not at all remotely, that comic picture her Uncle Joe had hung in his bedroom? The picture wherein the black, kinky head of a little red-lipped pickaninny lay like a fly in a pan of milk amid a white expanse of bedclothes.

But of course she couldn't have worn blue or black when the call was for the wearing of white, even if white was not complementary to her complexion. She would have been odd-looking anyway no matter what she wore and she would also have been conspicuous, for not only was she the only dark-skinned person on the platform, she was also the only Negro pupil in the entire school, and had been for the past four years. Well, thank goodness, the principal would soon be through with his monotonous farewell address, and she and the other members of her class would advance to the platform center as their names were called and receive the documents which would signify their unconditional release from public school.

As she thought of these things, Emma Lou glanced at those who sat to the right and to the left of her. She envied them their obvious elation, yet felt a strange sense of superiority because of her immunity for the moment from an ephemeral mob emotion. Get a diploma?—What did it mean to her? College?—Perhaps. A job?—Perhaps again. She was going to have a high school diploma, but it would mean nothing to her whatsoever. The tragedy of her life was that she was too black. Her face and not a slender roll of ribbon-bound parchment was to be her future identification tag in society. High school diploma indeed! What she needed was an efficient bleaching agent, a magic cream that would remove this unwelcome black mask from her face and make her more like her fellow men.

"Emma Lou Morgan."

She came to with a start. The principal had called her name and stood smiling down at her benevolently. Some one—she knew it was her Cousin Buddie, stupid imp—applauded, very faintly, very provokingly. Some one else snickered.

"Emma Lou Morgan."

The principal had called her name again, more sharply than before and his smile was less benevolent. The girl who sat to the left of her nudged her. There was nothing else for her to do but to get out of that anchoring chair and march forward to receive her diploma. But why did the people in the audience have to stare so? Didn't they all know that Emma Lou Morgan was Boise high school's only nigger student? Didn't they all know—but what was the use. She had to go get that diploma, so summoning her most insouciant manner, she advanced to the platform center, brought every muscle of her lithe limbs into play, haughtily extended her shiny black arm to receive the proffered diploma, bowed a chilly thanks, then holding her arms stiffly at her sides, insolently returned to her seat in that foreboding white line, insolently returned once more to splotch its pale purity and to mock it with her dark, outlandish difference.

Emma Lou had been born in a semi-white world, totally surrounded by an all-white one, and those few dark elements that had forced their way in had either been shooed away or else greeted with derisive laughter. It was the custom always of those with whom she came into most frequent contact to ridicule or revile any black person or object. A black cat was a harbinger of bad luck, black crepe was the insignia of mourning, and black people were either evil niggers with poisonous blue gums or else typical vaudeville darkies. It seemed as if the people in her world never went half-way in their recognition or reception of things black, for these things seemed always to call forth only the most extreme emotional reactions. They never provoked mere smiles or mere melancholy, rather they were the signal either for boisterous guffaws or pain-induced and tear-attended grief.

Emma Lou had been becoming increasingly aware of this for a long time, but her immature mind had never completely grasped its full, and to her, tragic significance. First there had been the case of her father, old black Jim Morgan they called him, and Emma Lou had often wondered why it was that he of all the people she heard discussed by her family should always be referred to as if his very blackness condemned him to receive no respect from his fellow men.

She had also begun to wonder if it was because of his blackness that he had never been in evidence as far as she knew. Inquiries netted very unsatisfactory answers. "Your father is no good." "He left your mother, deserted her shortly after you were born." And these statements were always prefixed or followed by some epithet such as "dirty black nogooder" or "durn his onery black hide." There was in fact only one member of the family who did not speak of her father in this manner, and that was her Uncle Joe, who was also the only person in the family to whom she really felt akin, because he alone never seemed to regret, to bemoan, or to ridicule her blackness of skin. It was her grandmother who did all the regretting, her mother who did the bemoaning, her Cousin Buddie and her playmates, both white and colored, who did the ridiculing.

Emma Lou's maternal grandparents, Samuel and Maria Lightfoot, were both mulatto products of slave-day promiscuity between male masters and female chattel. Neither had been slaves, their own parents having been granted their freedom because of their close connections with the white branch of the family tree. These freedmen had migrated into Kansas with their children, and when these children had grown up they in turn had joined the westward-ho parade of that current era, and finally settled in Boise, Idaho.

Samuel and Maria, like many others of their kind and antecedents, had had only one compelling desire, which motivated their every activity and dictated their every thought. They wished to put as much physical and mental space between them and the former home of their parents as was possible. That was why they had left Kansas, for in Kansas there were too many reminders of that which their parents had escaped and from which they wished to flee. Kansas was too near the former slave belt, too accessible to disgruntled southerners, who, deprived of their slaves, were inculcated with an easily communicable virus, nigger hatred.

Then, too, in Kansas all Negroes were considered as belonging to one class. It didn't matter if you and your parents had been freedmen before the Emancipation Proclamation, nor did it matter that you were almost three-quarters white. You were, nevertheless, classed with those hordes of hungry, ragged, ignorant black folk arriving from the South in such great numbers, packed like so many stampeding cattle in dirty, manure-littered box cars.

From all of this these maternal grandparents of Emma Lou fled, fled to the Rocky Mountain states which were too far away for the recently freed slaves to reach, especially since most of them believed that the world ended just a few miles north of the Mason-Dixon line. Then, too, not only were the Rocky Mountain states beyond the reach of this raucous and smelly rabble of recently freed cotton pickers and plantation hands, but they were also peopled by pioneers, sturdy land and gold seekers from the East, marching westward, always westward in search of El Dorado, and being too busy in this respect to be violently aroused by problems of race unless economic factors precipitated matters.

So Samuel and Maria went into the fast farness of a little known Rocky Mountain territory and settled in Boise, at the time nothing more than a trading station for the Indians and whites, and a red light center for the cowboys and sheepherders and miners in the neighboring vicinity. Samuel went into the saloon business and grew prosperous. Maria raised a family and began to mother nuclear elements for a future select Negro social group.

There was of course in such a small and haphazardly populated community some social intermixture between whites and blacks. White and black gamblers rolled the dice together, played tricks on one another while dealing faro, and became allies in their attempts to outfigure the roulette wheel. White and black men amicably frequented the saloons and dancehalls together. White and black women leaned out of the doorways and windows of the jerry-built frame houses and log cabins of "Whore Row." White and black housewives gossiped over back fences and lent one another needed household commodities. But there was little social intercourse on a higher scale. Sluefoot Sal, the most popular high yaller on "Whore Row," might be a buddy to Irish Peg and Blond Liz, but Mrs. Amos James, whose husband owned the town's only drygoods store, could certainly not become too familiar with Mrs. Samuel Lightfoot, colored, whose husband owned a saloon. And it was not a matter

of the difference in their respective husband's businesses. Mrs.
Amos James did associate with Mrs. Arthur Emory, white, whose
husband also owned a saloon. It was purely a matter of color.

Emma Lou's grandmother then, holding herself aloof from the inmates of "Whore Row," and not wishing to associate with such as
old Mammy Lewis' daughters, who did most of the town wash, and
others of their ilk, was forced to choose her social equals slowly and
carefully. This was hard, for there were so few Negroes in Boise anyway that there wasn't much cream to skim off. But as the years
passed, others, who, like Maria and her husband, were mulatto off-
springs of mulatto freedmen seeking a freer land, moved in, and
were soon initiated into what was later to be known as the blue vein
circle, so named because all of its members were fair-skinned
enough for their blood to be seen pulsing purple through the veins
of their wrists.

Emma Lou's grandmother was the founder and the acknowledged
leader of Boise's blue veins, and she guarded its exclusiveness passionately and jealously. Were they not a superior class? Were they
not a very high type of Negro, comparable to the persons of color
groups in the West Indies? And were they not entitled, ipso facto, to
more respect and opportunity and social acceptance than the more
pure blooded Negroes? In their veins was some of the best blood of
the South. They were closely akin to the only true aristocrats in the
United States. Even the slave masters had been aware of and acknowledged in some measure their superiority. Having some of
Marse George's blood in their veins set them apart from ordinary
Negroes at birth. These mulattoes as a rule were not ordered to
work in the fields beneath the broiling sun at the urge of a Simon
Legree lash. They were saved and trained for the more gentle jobs,
saved and trained to be ladies' maids and butlers. Therefore, let them
continue this natural division of Negro society. Let them also guard
against unwelcome and degenerating encroachments. Their motto
must be "Whiter and whiter every generation," until the grandchil-
dren of the blue veins could easily go over into the white race and
become assimilated so that problems of race would plague them no
more.

Maria had preached this doctrine to her two children, Jane and
Joe, throughout their apprentice years, and can therefore be forgiven
for having a physical collapse when they both, first Joe, then Emma
Lou's mother, married not mulattoes, but a copper brown and a blue
black. This had been somewhat of a necessity, for, when the mating
call had made itself heard to them, there had been no eligible blue
veins around. Most of their youthful companions had been sent
away to school or else to seek careers in eastern cities, and those few
who had remained had already found their chosen life's companions.

Maria had sensed that something of the kind might happen and had urged Samuel to send Jane and Joe away to some eastern boarding school, but Samuel had very stubbornly refused. He had his own notions of the sort of things one's children learned in boarding school, and of the greater opportunities they had to apply that learning. True, they might acquire the same knowledge in the public schools of Boise, but then there would be some limit to the extent to which they could apply this knowledge, seeing that they lived at home and perforce must submit to some parental supervision. A cot in the attic at home was to Samuel a much safer place for a growing child to sleep than an iron four poster in a boarding school dormitory.

So Samuel had remained adamant and the two carefully reared scions of Boise's first blue vein family had of necessity sought their mates among the lower orders. However, Joe's wife was not as undesirable as Emma Lou's father, for she was almost three-quarters Indian, and there was scant possibility that her children would have revolting dark skins, thick lips, spreading nostrils, and kinky hair. But in the case of Emma Lou's father, there were no such extenuating characteristics, for his physical properties undeniably stamped him as a full blooded Negro. In fact, it seemed as if he had come from one of the few families originally from Africa, who could not boast of having been seduced by some member of southern aristocracy, or befriended by some member of a strolling band of Indians.

No one could understand why Emma Lou's mother had married Jim Morgan, least of all Jane herself. In fact she hadn't thought much about it until Emma Lou had been born. She had first met Jim at a church picnic, given in a woodlawn meadow on the outskirts of the city, and almost before she had realized what was happening she had found herself slipping away from home, night after night, to stroll down a well shaded street, known as Lover's Lane, with the man her mother had forbidden her to see. And it hadn't been long before they had decided that an elopement would be the only thing to assure themselves the pleasure of being together without worrying about Mama Lightfoot's wrath, talkative neighbors, prying town marshals, and grass stains.

Despite the rancor of her mother and the whispering of her mother's friends, Jane hadn't really found anything to regret in her choice of a husband until Emma Lou had been born. Then all the fears her mother had instilled in her about the penalties inflicted by society upon black Negroes, especially upon black Negro girls, came to the fore. She was abysmally stunned by the color of her child, for she had been certain that since she herself was so fair that her child could not possibly be as dark as its father. She had been certain that it would be a luscious admixture, a golden brown with all its mother's desirable facial features and its mother's hair. But she hadn't reck-

oned with nature's perversity, nor had she taken under consideration
the inescapable fact that some of her ancestors too had been black,
and that some of their color chromosomes were still imbedded
within her. Emma Lou had been fortunate enough to have hair like
her mother's, a thick, curly black mass of hair, rich and easily controlled, but she had also been unfortunate enough to have a face as
black as her father's, and a nose which, while not exactly flat, was as
distinctly negroid as her too thick lips.

Her birth had served no good purpose. It had driven her mother
back to seek the confidence and aid of Maria, and it had given Maria
the chance she had been seeking to break up the undesirable union
of her daughter with what she termed an ordinary black nigger. But
Jim's departure hadn't solved matters at all, rather it had complicated
them, for although he was gone, his child remained, a tragic mistake
which could not be stamped out or eradicated even after Jane, by
getting a divorce from Jim and marrying a red-haired Irish Negro,
had been accepted back into blue vein grace.

Emma Lou had always been the alien member of the family and
of the family's social circle. Her grandmother, now a widow, made
her feel it. Her mother made her feel it. And her Cousin Buddie
made her feel it, to say nothing of the way she was regarded by out-
siders. As early as she could remember, people had been saying to
her mother, "What an extraordinarily black child! Where did you
adopt it?" or else, "Such lovely unniggerish hair on such a niggerish-
looking child." Some had even been facetious and made suggestions
like, "Try some lye, Jane, it may eat it out. She can't look any
worse. . . ."

જ✕✕✓

Summer vacation was nearly over and it had not yet been decided what to do with Emma Lou now that she had graduated from
high school. She herself gave no help nor offered any suggestions.
As it was, she really did not care what became of her. After all it
didn't seem to matter. There was no place in the world for a girl as
black as she anyway. Her grandmother had assured her that she
would never find a husband worth a dime, and her mother had said
again and again, "Oh, if you had only been a boy!" until Emma Lou
had often wondered why it was that people were not able to effect a
change of sex or at least a change of complexion.

It was her Uncle Joe who finally prevailed upon her mother to
send her to the University of Southern California in Los Angeles.
There, he reasoned, she would find a larger and more intelligent social circle. In a city the size of Los Angeles there were Negroes of

every class, color, and social position. Let Emma Lou go there where she would not be as far away from home as if she were to go to some eastern college.

$\mathbb{CWO}$

On registration day, Emma Lou rushed out to the campus of the University of Southern California one hour before the registrar's office was scheduled to open. She spent the time roaming around, familiarizing herself with the layout of the campus and learning the names of the various buildings, some old and vineclad, others new and shiny in the sun, and watching the crowds of laughing students, rushing to and fro, greeting one another and talking over their plans for the coming school year. But her main reason for such an early arrival on the campus had been to find some of her fellow Negro students. She had heard that there were to be quite a number enrolled, but in all her hour's stroll she saw not one, and finally somewhat disheartened she got into the line stretched out in front of the registrar's office, and, for the moment, became engrossed in becoming a college freshman.

All the while, though, she kept searching for a colored face, but it was not until she had been duly signed up as a student and sent in search of her advisor that she saw one. Then three colored girls had sauntered into the room where she was having a conference with her advisor, sauntered in, arms interlocked, greeted her advisor, then sauntered out again. Emma Lou had wanted to rush after them—to introduce herself, but of course it had been impossible under the circumstances. She had immediately taken a liking to all three, each of whom was what is known in the parlance of the black belt as high brown, with modishly-shingled bobbed hair and well formed bodies, fashionably attired in flashy sport garments. From then on Emma Lou paid little attention to the business of choosing subjects and class hours, so little attention in fact that the advisor thought her exceptionally tractable and somewhat dumb. But she liked students to come that way. It made the task of being advisor easy. One just made out the program to suit oneself, and had no tedious explanations to make as to why the student could not have such and such a subject at such and such an hour, and why such and such a professor's class was already full.

After her program had been made out, Emma Lou was directed to the bursar's office to pay her fees. While going down the stairs she almost bumped into two dark-brown-skinned boys, obviously brothers if not twins, arguing as to where they should go next. One insisted that they should go back to the registrar's office. The other was being equally insistent that they should go to the gymnasium and make an appointment for their required physical examination. Emma Lou boldly stopped when she saw them, hoping they would speak, but they merely glanced up at her and continued their argument, bringing cards and pamphlets out of their pockets for reference and guidance. Emma Lou wanted to introduce herself to them, but she was too bashful to do so. She wasn't yet used to going to school with other Negro students, and she wasn't exactly certain how one went about becoming acquainted. But she finally decided that she had better let the advances come from the others, especially if they were men. There was nothing forward about her, and since she was a stranger it was no more than right that the old-timers should make her welcome. Still, if these had been girls . . . , but they weren't, so she continued her way down the stairs.

In the bursar's office, she was somewhat overjoyed at first to find that she had fallen into line behind another colored girl who had turned around immediately, and, after saying hello, announced in a loud, harsh voice:

"My feet are sure some tired!"

Emma Lou was so taken aback that she couldn't answer. People in college didn't talk that way. But meanwhile the girl was continuing:

"Ain't this registration a mess?"

Two white girls who had fallen into line behind Emma Lou snickered. Emma Lou answered by shaking her head. The girl continued:

"I've been standin' in line and climbin' stairs and talkin' and a-signin' till I'm just 'bout done for."

"It is tiresome," Emma Lou returned softly, hoping the girl would take a hint and lower her own strident voice. But she didn't.

"Tiresome ain't no name for it," she declared more loudly than ever before, then, "Is you a new student?"

"I am," answered Emma Lou, putting much emphasis on the "I am."

She wanted the white people who were listening to know that she knew her grammar if this other person didn't. "Is you," indeed! If this girl was a specimen of the Negro students with whom she was to associate, she most certainly did not want to meet another one. But it couldn't be possible that all of them—those three girls and those two boys for instance—were like this girl. Emma Lou was unable to imagine how such a person had ever gotten out of high school. . . .

. . . But despite her vulgarity, the girl was not all bad. Her good nature was infectious, and Emma Lou had surmised from her monologue on the day before how utterly unselfish a person she could be and was. All of her store of the world's goods were at hand to be used and enjoyed by her friends. There was not, as she had said, "a selfish bone in her body." But even that did not alter the disgusting fact that she was not one who would be welcome by the "right sort of people." Her flamboyant style of dress, her loud voice, her raucous laughter, and her flagrant disregard or ignorance of English grammar seemed inexcusable to Emma Lou, who was unable to understand how such a person could stray so far from the environment in which she rightfully belonged to enter a first class university. Now Hazel, according to Emma Lou, was the type of Negro who should go to a Negro college. There were plenty of them in the South whose standard of scholarship was not beyond her ability. And, then, in one of those schools, her darky-like clownishness would not have to be paraded in front of white people, thereby causing discomfort and embarrassment to others of her race, more civilized and circumspect than she.

The problem irritated Emma Lou. She didn't see why it had to be. She had looked forward so anxiously, and so happily to her introductory days on the campus, and now her first experience with one of her fellow colored students had been an unpleasant one. But she didn't intend to let that make her unhappy. She was determined to return to the campus alone, seek out other companions, see whether they accepted or ignored the offending Hazel, and govern herself accordingly.

It was early and there were few people on the campus. The grass was still wet from a heavy overnight dew, and the sun had not yet dispelled the coolness of the early morning. Emma Lou's dress was of thin material and she shivered as she walked or stood in the shade. She had no school business to attend to; there was nothing for her to do but to walk aimlessly about the campus.

In another hour, Emma Lou was pleased to see that the campus walks were becoming crowded, and that the side streets surrounding the campus were now heavy with student traffic. Things were beginning to awaken. Emma Lou became jubilant and walked with jaunty step from path to path, from building to building. It then occurred to her that she had been told that there were more Negro students enrolled in the School of Pharmacy than in any other department of the university, so finding the Pharmacy building she began to wander through its crowded hallways.

Almost immediately, she saw a group of five Negro students, three boys and two girls, standing near a water fountain. She was both excited and perplexed, excited over the fact that she was so close to those she wished to find, and perplexed because she did not know how to approach them. Had there been only one person standing there, the matter would have been comparatively easy. She could have approached with a smile and said, "Good morning." The person would have returned her greeting, and it would then have been a simple matter to get acquainted.

But five people in one bunch all known to one another and all chatting intimately together!—it would seem too much like an intrusion to go bursting into their gathering—too forward and too vulgar. Then, there was nothing she could say after having said "good morning." One just didn't break into a group of five and say, "I'm Emma Lou Morgan, a new student, and I want to make friends with you." No, she couldn't do that. She would just smile as she passed, smile graciously and friendly. They would know that she was a stranger, and her smile would assure them that she was anxious to make friends, anxious to become a welcome addition to their group.

One of the group of five had sighted Emma Lou as soon as she had sighted them:

"Who's this?" queried Helen Wheaton, a senior in the College of Law.

"Some new 'pick,' I guess," answered Bob Armstrong, who was Helen's fiance and a senior in the School of Architecture.

"I bet she's going to take Pharmacy," whispered Amos Blaine.

"She's hottentot enough to take something," mumbled Tommy Brown. "Thank God, she won't be in any of our classes, eh Amos?"

Emma Lou was almost abreast of them now. They lowered their voices, and made a pretense of mumbled conversation among themselves. Only Verne Davis looked directly at her and it was she alone who returned Emma Lou's smile.

"Whatcha grinnin' at?" Bob chided Verne as Emma Lou passed out of earshot.

"At the little frosh, of course. She grinned at me. I couldn't stare at her without returning it."

"I don't see how anybody could even look at her without grinning."

"Oh, she's not so bad," said Verne.

"Well, she's bad enough."

"That makes two of them."

"Two of what, Amos?"

"Hottentots, Bob."

"Good grief," exclaimed Tommy, "why don't you recruit some good-looking co-eds out here?"

"We don't choose them." Helen returned.

"I'm going out to the Southern Branch where the sight of my fellow female students won't give me dyspepsia."

"Ta-ta, Amos," said Verne, "and you needn't bother to sit in my car any more if you think us so terrible." She and Helen walked away, leaving the boys to discuss the sad days which had fallen upon the campus.

Arna Bontemps

(1902–1973)

POET, NOVELIST, CHILDREN'S AUTHOR, anthologist, essayist, and playwright, Arna Wendell Bontemps was a talented, prolific, and many-sided writer—almost as many-sided as Langston Hughes, his friend and collaborator. In spite of his contribution to New Negro literature and his creative ability, Bontemps has never received the recognition he deserves. One reason for this neglect may be that, because approximately one-half of his published books are for juveniles, critics tended to think of Bontemps as a children's writer.

Another reason for the critics' attitude may have been Bontemps's early feeling about writing poetry. In *The Crisis* (April 27, 1927), he tells us that when he was twenty he felt the "writing of poetry" was both "immoral and vicious" and he burned all of his early verse. Unlike Hughes, Cullen, and McKay, he didn't publish his first collection (*Personals*, a thin volume of twenty-three poems) until late in his life (1963).

Born in Alexandria, Louisiana, Bontemps moved with his family to Los Angeles when only three. He attended high school at San Fernando Academy and college at Pacific Union, from which he graduated in 1923. Going to Harlem, he taught during the 1920s in private schools, and in 1926 and 1927 won several poetry prizes: "The Return" and "Golgotha Is a Mountain" both won Pushkin Awards from *Opportunity* and "Nocturne at Bethesda" won first prize in *The Crisis* poetry contest.

During the 1930s Bontemps wrote three novels, two children's books, and several short stories. He also taught at schools in Alabama and Chicago. During the 1940s he studied at Columbia and at the University of Chicago, and began his twenty-two-year tenure as head librarian at Fisk University. In 1956 he won the Jane Addam's Children's Book Award for his *Story of the Negro*, and in 1967 he won the James L. Dow Award of the Society of Midland Authors for *Anyplace But Here* (written in collaboration with Jack Conroy). He worked at the University of Illinois's Chicago Circle Campus and at Yale, where he was curator of the James Weldon Johnson Collection. He died in Nashville, Tennessee in 1973.

The poetry of Arna Bontemps contains several recurring themes, among them the alien-and-exile comparison found in several New Negro poems; religious belief, which is presented in an unusual number of poems; and the "return" theme, the going back to a former time, a former love, and a remembered place. He naturally wrote protest poems, as did most New

Negro poets, but his protest tends to be subtle and suggestive rather than frontal. In all of Bontemps's poetry one finds a sad, brooding quality, a meditative cast. He was an excellent craftsman and wrote several of the most popular Renaissance poems, among them: "Nocturne at Bethesda," "Golgotha Is a Mountain," "The Return," and "A Black Man Talks of Reaping."

The first of Bontemps's three novels, *God Sends Sunday* (1931), is a beginner's work and shows it. However, it deals with a fascinating subject, an unusual subject in black literature—the life of Little Augie, a jockey, his rise and fall in the "fast life" of the "fast" towns of New Orleans and St. Louis at the turn of the century, when Negro jockeys were popular in America. *God Sends Sunday* was made into a successful musical under the name *St. Louis Woman*. With the help of Countee Cullen, Bontemps turned the novel into a play; Johnny Mercer with Harold Alden wrote the music and lyrics.

Bontemps's second novel, *Black Thunder* (1936), is definitely his best. A historical work, it deals with the 1800 insurrection of Black Gabriel (Prosser), a slave uprising which occurred in and around Richmond, Virginia. Bontemps makes his central character into a heroic and convincing black. The work was reprinted in 1968.

The third novel, *Drums at Dusk* (1939), also a historical novel, deals with the uprising in Haiti, which Toussaint L'Ouverture would finally lead. More of a "costume piece" than a convincing example of historical fiction, the work suffers when compared with *Black Thunder*.

Among Bontemps's numerous publications for children, the best known are probably *Popo and Fifina, Children of Haiti* (1932), done in collaboration with Langston Hughes and with illustrations by E. Sims Campbell; *Golden Slippers* (1941), an "anthology of Negro poems for young readers"; *The Fast Sooner Hound* (1942), done in collaboration with Jack Conroy; and *Chariot in the Sky* (1951), which retells for young readers the story of the Fisk Jubilee Singers.

For comments on the life and works of Arna Bontemps, see Robert A. Bone's *The Negro Novel in America* (rev. ed., 1965); Hugh M. Gloster's *Negro Voices in American Fiction* (1948); Sterling A. Brown's *The Negro in American Fiction* (1937, 1969); and Arthur P. Davis's *From the Dark Tower* (1974). See also *Arna Bontemps–Langston Hughes Letters, 1925–67*, selected and edited by Charles H. Nichols (1980), which includes a bibliography and index; and *James Weldon Johnson and Arna W. Bontemps: A Reference Guide* by Robert E. Fleming (1978), which includes references up to 1976. John O'Brien's *Interviews with Black Writers* (1973) includes Bontemps among its distinguished subjects. See also Bernard W. Bell, *The Afro-American Novel and Its Tradition* (1987).

The following poems are from *Personals* (1963).

A BLACK MAN TALKS OF REAPING

I have sown beside all waters in my day.
I planted deep, within my heart the fear
That wind or fowl would take the grain away.
I planted safe against this stark, lean year.

I scattered seed enough to plant the land
In rows from Canada to Mexico,
But for my reaping only what the hand
Can hold at once is all that I can show.

Yet what I sowed and what the orchard yields
My brother's sons are gathering stalk and root,
Small wonder then my children glean in fields
They have not sown, and feed on bitter fruit.

MIRACLES

Doubt no longer miracles,
This spring day makes it plain
A man may crumble into dust
And straightway live again

A jug of water in the sun
Will easy turn to wine
If love is stopping at the well
And love's brown arms entwine.

And you who think him only man,
I tell you faithfully
That I have seen Christ clothed in rain
Walking on the sea.

NOCTURNE AT BETHESDA

I thought I saw an angel flying low,
I thought I saw the flicker of a wing
Above the mulberry trees; but not again.

Bethesda sleeps. This ancient pool that healed
A host of bearded Jews does not awake.

This pool that once the angels troubled does not move
No angel stirs it now, no Saviour comes
With healing in His hands to raise the sick
And bid the lame man leap upon the ground.

The golden days are gone. Why do we wait
So long upon the marble steps, blood
Falling from our open wounds? and why
Do our black faces search the empty sky?
Is there something we have forgotten? some precious thing
We have lost, wandering in strange lands?

There was a day, I remember now,
I beat my breast and cried, "Wash me God,
Wash me with a wave of wind upon
The barley; O quiet One, draw near, draw near!
Walk upon the hills with lovely feet
And in the waterfall stand and speak.

"Dip white hands in the lily pool and mourn
Upon the harps still hanging in the trees
Near Babylon along the river's edge,
But oh, remember me, I pray, before
The summer goes and rose leaves lose their red."

The old terror takes my heart, the fear
Of quiet waters and of faint twilights.
There will be better days when I am gone
And healing pools where I cannot be healed.
Fragrant stars will gleam forever and ever
Above the place where I lie desolate.

Yet I hope, still I long to live.
And if there can be returning after death
I shall come back. But it will not be here;
If you want me you must search for me
Beneath the palms of Africa. Or if
I am not there then you may call to me
Across the shining dunes, perhaps I shall
Be following a desert caravan.

I may pass through centuries of death
With quiet eyes, but I'll remember still
A jungle tree with burning scarlet birds.
There is something I have forgotten, some precious thing.

I shall be seeking ornaments of ivory,
I shall be dying for a jungle fruit.

　　　You do not hear, Bethesda.
O still green water in a stagnant pool!
Love abandoned you and me alike.
There was a day you held a rich full moon
Upon your heart and listened to the words
Of men now dead and saw the angels fly.
There is a simple story on your face;
Years have wrinkled you. I know, Bethesda!
You are sad. It is the same with me.

SOUTHERN MANSION

Poplars are standing there still as death
And ghosts of dead men
Meet their ladies walking
Two by two beneath the shade
And standing on the marble steps.

There is a sound of music echoing
Through the open door
And in the field there is
Another sound tinkling in the cotton:
Chains of bondmen dragging on the ground.

The years go back with an iron clank,
A hand is on the gate,
A dry leaf trembles on the wall.
Ghosts are walking.
They have broken roses down
And poplars stand there still as death.

THE RETURN

Once more, listening to the wind and rain,
Once more, you and I, and above the hurting sound
Of these comes back the throbbing of remembered rain,
Treasured rain falling on dark ground.
Once more, huddling birds upon the leaves
And summer trembling on a withered vine.

And once more, returning out of pain,
The friendly ghost that was your love and mine.

2

Darkness brings the jungle to our room:
The throb of rain is the throb of muffled drums.
Darkness hangs our room with pendulums
Of vine and in the gathering gloom
Our walls recede into a denseness of
Surrounding trees. This is a night of love
Retained from those lost nights our fathers slept
In huts; this is a night that must not die.
Let us keep the dance of rain our fathers kept
And tread our dreams beneath the jungle sky.

3

And now the downpour ceases.
Let us go back once more upon the glimmering leaves
And as the throbbing of the drums increases
Shake the grass and dripping boughs of trees.
A dry wind stirs the palm; the old tree grieves.

Time has charged the years: the old days have returned.

Let us dance by metal waters burned
With gold of moon, let us dance
With naked feet beneath the young spice trees.
What was that light, that radiance
On your face?—something I saw when first
You passed beneath the jungle tapestries?

A moment we pause to quench our thirst
Kneeling at the water's edge, the gleam
Upon your face is plain: you have wanted this.
Let us go back and search the tangled dream
And as the muffled drum-beats throb and miss
Remember again how early darkness comes
To dreams and silence to the drums.

Let us go back into the dusk again,
Slow and sad-like following the track
Of blowing leaves and cool white rain
Into the old gray dream, let us go back.
Our walls close about us we lie and listen
To the noise of the street, the storm and the driven birds.
A question shapes your lips, your eyes glisten
Retaining tears, but there are no more words.

Jessie Redmon Fauset

(1882–1961)

THE FICTION of the New Negro (Harlem) Renaissance was predominantly a middle-class fiction. Even though a few novelists, McKay among them, played up the primitive and exotic side of underclass life, and even though writers like Thurman and Cullen satirized some of the foibles of the middle class, by far the largest number of fictional works published during the Renaissance reflect the thinking and the objectives of the middle-class black. The authors of these middle-class-oriented works produced a best-foot-forward type of fiction which, among other things, praised black progress and protested America's failure to recognize that there was progress. The message these novelists sent to white America was this: except for color, we middle-class blacks are just like you, *the best of you*, and should be treated accordingly. The best-known and one of the most prolific of these "talented tenth" fiction writers was Jessie Redmon Fauset.

Born in Philadelphia, Pennsylvania, in 1882, Fauset came from an old and highly respected family, the kind of middle-class blacks she writes about in her novels. She was educated in the public schools of her native city; at Cornell University, where she received her A.B. with Phi Beta Kappa honors; at the University of Pennsylvania, where she took her M.A. degree; and at the Sorbonne.

In 1906 Fauset was appointed teacher of Latin and French in the famous "M" Street High School in Washington, D.C. (which became in 1916 Dunbar High School). In 1919 she left Washington and joined the staff of *The Crisis* as literary editor, and in 1926 she assumed the less exacting duties of contributing editor. While with *The Crisis*, Fauset was also the first literary editor of *The Brownies' Book*, later the managing editor. In 1921 she attended the Second Pan African Congress and wrote two articles for *The Crisis* (November and December 1921) on this historic event. After leaving *The Crisis*, Fauset returned to teaching, first in a Harlem junior high school, later at DeWitt Clinton High School, one of New York's finest secondary schools. In later life, she married Herbert Harris, a businessman. According to the *New York Times* (May 3, 1961) obituary, she was about seventy-six at her death. Jessie Redmon Fauset seemingly never revealed her birth date, although scholars now cite 1882 as her year of birth.

One of the New Negro Renaissance's most prolific fiction writers, Fauset published four full-length novels: *There Is Confusion* (1924); *Plum Bun: A Novel without a Moral* (1928, 1929); *The Chinaberry Tree: A Novel of American Life* (1931, 1969); and *Comedy: American Style* (1933, 1969). In these works she tried to show that the lives of middle-class Negroes can be just as exciting as those of the underclass found in McKay's works. Even though her novels don't actually uphold her thesis, many of her Negro contemporaries, including William Stanley Braithwaite, agreed with her (*The Crisis*, September 1924). Braithwaite considered *There Is Confusion* "an outstanding achievement in the entire range of fiction," and added that Jessie Fauset had also created "something entirely new in the treatment of race fiction," but he contended that it is not "race" but "universal" fiction that finally emerges, and he refers to Fauset as "the potential Jane Austen of Negro literature."

Writers of Fauset's "school" of middle-class novelists—Nella Larsen, Walter White, and others—tend to use the same themes over and over again. Among these overworked subjects are passing for white, color differences within a family, interracial families, loyalty to America and the nation's unfair treatment in return, lynching, the call of race and the promise of future equality achieved by blacks' superior achievement. Several of the themes used in Fauset's novels were based on actual incidents known to her readers. Part of the material used in *There Is Confusion* could have been based on the well-known biracial Grimké family; the color tragedy in *Comedy: American Style* could easily have been a fictional account of an actual situation in a prominent black family.

Also a minor poet, Fauset may be placed in the so-called genteel school of New Negro writers along with Georgia Douglas Johnson, Anne Spencer, and Angelina Grimké. These poets wrote largely on the themes found in lyrical poetry rather than on racial themes. Among her best-known verses are "La Vie C'est la Vie," "Noblesse Oblige," "Christmas Eve in France," and "Rondeau."

For biographical and critical material on Jessie Redmon Fauset, see Hugh M. Gloster's *Negro Voices in American Fiction* (1948); Saunders Redding's *To Make a Poet Black* (1939); Robert A. Bone's *The Negro Novel in America* (rev. ed., 1965); Benjamin Brawley's *The Negro in Literature and Art in the United States* (1930); Robert Hemenway's *The Black Novelist* (1970); and William Braithwaite's "The Novels of Jessie Fauset," *Opportunity* 12 (1934). A full-length study devoted to this exceptional writer is Carolyn Wedin Sylvander's *Jessie Redmon Fauset, Black American Writer* (1981). Ann Allen Shockley in her *Afro-American Women Writers* (1988) includes a comprehensive essay on Fauset. See also Deborah E. McDowell's article, "The Neglected Dimension of Jessie Redmon Fauset," in *Conjuring: Black Women, Fiction, and Literary Tradition*, edited by Marjorie Pryse and Hortense J. Spillers (1985). See also the articles on Fauset in *From the Dark Tower* and *Dictionary of American Negro Biography* by Arthur P. Davis, in Bernard W. Bell's *The Afro-American Novel and Its Tradition* (1987) and *Dictionary of Literary Biography*, Volume 51.

The selection that follows comes from *There Is Confusion* (1924, 1952).

FROM **THERE IS CONFUSION**

It was Joanna who first acquainted Peter with himself. But neither of the children knew this at the time. And although Peter came to realize it later it was many years before he told her so. For, though he went through many changes and though these two came to speak of many things, he kept a certain inarticulateness all his lifetime.

Joanna and all the older Marshalls went to a school in West Fifty-second Street, one after another like little steps, with Joanna at first quite some distance behind. They were known throughout the school. "Those Marshall children, you know those colored children that always dress so well and as though they had someone to take care of them. Pretty nice looking children, too, if only they weren't colored. Their father is a caterer, has that place over there on Fifty-ninth Street. Makes a lot of money for a colored man."

Peter, unlike Joanna, had gone to school, one might almost say, all over New York, and nowhere for any great length of time. Meriwether had stayed longest at Mrs. Reading's but as, in later years, he more and more went off on his runs without paying his bills, Mrs. Reading frequently refused to let Peter leave the house until his father's return.

"For all I know he may be joinin' his father on the outside and the two of them go off together. Then where'd I be? For them few rags that Mr. Bye keeps in his room wouldn't be no good to nobody."

This enforced truancy was the least of Peter's troubles. He did not like school,—too many white people and consequently, as he saw it, too much chance for petty injustice. The result of this was that Peter at twelve, possessed it is true of a large assortment of really useful facts, lacked the fine precision, if the doubtful usefulness, of Joanna's knowledge at ten. When Miss Susan settled in the Marshalls' neighborhood and brought Peter to the school in Fifty-second Street he was found to be lacking and yet curiously in advance. "We'll try him," said the principal doubtfully, "in the fifth grade. I'll take him to Miss Shanley's room."

Miss Shanley was Joanna's teacher. She greeted Peter without enthusiasm, not because he was colored but because he was clearly a problem. Joanna spied him immediately. He was too handsome with his brown-red skin, his black silky hair that curled alluringly, his dark, almost almond-shaped eyes, to escape her notice. But she for-

got about him, too, almost immediately, for the first time Miss Shanley called on him he failed rather ignominiously. Joanna did not like
stupid people and thereafter to her he simply was not.

On the contrary, Joanna had caught and retained Peter's attention. She was the only other colored person in the room and therefore to him the only one worth considering. And though at that time
Joanna was still rather plain, she already had an air. Everything
about her was of an exquisite perfection. Her hair was brushed till it
shone, her skin glowed not only with health but obviously with
cleanliness, her shoes were brown and shiny, with perfectly level
heels. She wore that first week a very fine soft sage-green middy suit
with a wide buff tie. The nails which finished off the rather square-
tipped fingers of her small square hands, were even and rounded
and shining. Peter had seen little girls with this perfection and assurance on Chestnut Street in Philadelphia and on Fifth Avenue in New
York, but they had been white. He had not yet envisaged this sort of
thing for his own. Perhaps he inherited his great-grandfather Joshua's
spiritless acceptance of things as they are, and his belief that differences between people were not made, but had to be.

Joanna clearly stood for something in the class. Peter noted a little enviously the quality of the tone in which Miss Shanley addressed her. To other children she said, "Gertrude, can you tell me
about the Articles of Confederation?" Usually she implied a doubt,
which Gertrude usually justified. But she was sure of Joanna. The
tenseness of her attitude might be seen to relax; her mentality prepared momentarily for a rest. "Joanna will now tell us,—" she would
announce. For Joanna, having a purpose and having been drilled by
Joel to the effect that final perfection is built on small intermediate
perfections, got her lessons completely and in detail every day.

It was at this time and for many years thereafter characteristic of
Peter that he, too, wanted to shine, but did not realize that one
shone only as a result of much mental polishing personally applied.
Joanna's assurance, her air of purposefulness, her indifference intrigued him and piqued him. He sidled across to the blackboard
nearest her—if they were both sent to the board—cleaned hers off if
she gave him a chance, managed to speak a word to her now and
then. He even contrived to wait for her one day at the Girls' entrance. Joanna threw him a glance of recognition, swept by, returned.

His heart jumped within him.

"If you see my sister Sylvia,—you know her?—tell her not to
wait for me. I have to go early to my music-lesson. She'll be right
out."

Sylvia didn't appear for half an hour and Peter should have been at the butcher's, but he waited. Sylvia and Maggie Ellersley came out laughing and glowing. Peter gave the message.

"Thanks," said Sylvia prettily. Maggie stared after him. She was still the least bit bold in those days.

"Ain't he the best looker you ever saw, Sylvia? Such eyes! Who is he, anyway? Not ever Joanna's beau?"

"Imagine old Joanna with a beau." Sylvia laughed. "He's just a new boy in her class. He *is* good looking."

Some important examinations were to take place shortly and Miss Shanley planned extensive reviews. She was a thorough if somewhat unimaginative teacher and she meant to have no loose threads. So she devoted two days to geography, two more to grammar, another to history, one to the rather puzzling consideration of that mysterious study, physiology. Perhaps by now the class was a bit fed up with cramming, perhaps the children weren't really interested in physiological processes. Joanna wasn't, but she always got lessons like these doggedly, thinking "Soon we'll be past all this," or "I'm going to forget this old stuff as soon as I grow up." Poor Miss Shanley was in despair. She could not call on Joanna for everything. Pupil after pupil had failed. Her eye roved over the room and fell on Peter's black head.

She sighed. He had not even been a member of the class when she had taught this particular physiological phenomenon. "Can't anyone besides Joanna Marshall give me the 'Course of the Food'?"

Peter raised his hand. "He looks intelligent," she thought. "Well, Bye you may try it."

"I don't think I can give it to you the way the others say it,"—the children had been reciting by rote, "but I know what happens to the food."

She knew he would fail if he didn't know it her way, but she let him begin.

This was old ground for Peter. "Look, I can draw it. See, you take the food in your mouth," he drew a rough sketch of lips, mouth cavity and gullet, "then you must chew it, masticate it, I think you said." He went on varying from his own simplified interpretation of Meriwether Bye's early instructions, past difficult names like pancreatic juice and thoracic duct, and while he talked he drew, recalling pictures from those old anatomies; expounding, flourishing. Miss Shanley stared at him in amazement. This jewel, this undiscovered diamond!

"How'd you come to know it, Peter?"

"I read it, I studied it." He did not say when. "But it's so easy to learn things about the body. It's yourself."

She quizzed him then while the other children, Joanna among

them, stared open-eyed. But he knew all the simple ground which she had already covered, and much, much beyond.

"If all the children," said Miss Shanley, forgetting Peter's past, "would just get their lessons like Peter Bye and Joanna Marshall."

She had coupled their names together! And after school Joanna was waiting for him. He walked up the street with her, pleasantly conscious of her interest, her frank admiration.

"How wonderful," she breathed, "that you should know your physiology like that. What are you going to be when you grow up, a doctor?"

"A surgeon," said Peter forgetting his old formula and expressing a resolve which her question had engendered in him just that second. He saw himself on the instant, a tall distinguished-looking man, wielding scissors and knife with deft nervous fingers. Joanna would be hovering somewhere—he was not sure how—in the offing. And she would be looking at him with this same admiration.

"My, won't you have to study?" Joanna could have told an aspirant almost to the day and measure the amount of time and effort it would take him to become a surgeon, a dentist, a lawyer, an engineer. All these things Joel discussed about his table with the intense seriousness which colored men feel when they speak of their children's futures. Alexander and Philip were to have their choice of any calling within reason. They were seventeen and fifteen now and the house swarmed with college catalogues. Schools, terms, degrees of prejudice, fields of practice,—Joanna knew them all.

"Yes," said Peter, "I suppose I will have to study. How did you come to know so much—did your father tell you?"

"Why, I get it out of books, of course." Joanna was highly indignant: "I never go to bed without getting my lessons. In fact, all I do is to get lessons of some kind—school lessons or music. You know I'm to be a great singer."

"No, I didn't know that. Perhaps you'll sing in your choir?"

Then Joanna astonished him. "In my choir—I sing there already! No! Everywhere, anywhere, Carnegie Hall and in Boston and London. You see, I'm to be famous."

"But," Peter objected, "colored people don't get any chance at that kind of thing."

"Colored people," Joanna quoted from her extensive reading, "can do everything that anybody else can do. They've already done it. Some one colored person somewhere in the world does as good a job as anyone else,—perhaps a better one. They've been kings and queens and poets and teachers and doctors and everything. I'm going to be the one colored person who sings best in these days, and I never, never, never mean to let color interfere with anything I *really* want to do."

"I dance, too," she interrupted herself, "and I'll probably do that besides. Not ordinary dancing, you know, but queer beautiful things that are different from what we see around here; perhaps I'll make them up myself. You'll see! They'll have on the bill-board, 'Joanna Marshall, the famous artist,'—" She was almost dancing along the sidewalk now, her eyes and cheeks glowing.

Peter looked at her wistfully. His practical experience and the memory of his father inclined him to dubiousness. But her superb assurance carried away all his doubts.

"I don't suppose you'll ever think of just ordinary people like me?"

"But you'll be famous, too—you'll be a wonderful doctor. Do be. I can't stand stupid, common people."

"You'll always be able to stand me," said Peter with a fervor which made his statement a vow.

Nella Larsen

(1893–1963)

A CHILD of racially mixed parents—her mother a Dane, her father a Negro from the Virgin Islands (formerly the Danish West Indies)—Nella Larsen was born in Chicago in 1893. After her father died when she was two, her mother married again, this time to a Dane, by whom she had a second daughter. At age eight Larsen attended school for a while with her half-sister in a school in which most of the other pupils had German or Scandinavian backgrounds. When Larsen was sixteen, she visited her mother's relatives in Denmark, staying there three years.

On her return in 1911 she entered the nursing school connected with Harlem's Lincoln Hospital. Upon her graduation three years later, she was appointed assistant superintendent of nurses at the Tuskegee Hospital. After serving two years in Alabama, she went back to New York, and in 1918 joined the staff of the city's department of health. In 1922, she resigned and enrolled in the New York Public Library Training School and became eventually a children's librarian in the New York Public Library, working for a while in the 135th Street Branch. In her later years, Larsen lived in Greenwich Village, where, according to some of her friends, she passed for white. Leaving the Village, she moved to Brooklyn, where she died in 1963.

In 1928 she published *Quicksand*, her first novel. The work received the Harmon Foundation's second prize in literature given that year for "distinguished achievement among Negroes." An excellent first novel, it leaned heavily on Larsen's own life story; it also invited comparison with the novels of Jessie Fauset, Larsen's contemporary. Both writers used a middle-class background, both used passing as a major theme, and both possessed the talented tenth attitude, which characterized most of the New Negro fiction. *Quicksand* is different in one respect: unlike most Renaissance novels, it did not attribute the protagonist's tragic life solely to the racial attitude in America. Helga Crane is also the victim of her own neurotic personality, and as such she is one of the most intriguing and complex characters found in the literature of the Harlem Renaissance. The novel is aptly titled: Helga's "quicksand" is within—not racial, but human.

Larsen's second novel, *Passing*, is one of four major novels of the era using "passing for white" as a principal theme; the other three are Johnson's *Autobiography of an Ex-Coloured Man*, Fauset's *Plum Bun*, and Walter White's *Flight*. The subject appears in many other works of fiction, in poetry, and in drama, for lynching and passing are among the most popular themes of the 1920s black writers. When segregation and discrimination were nationwide (the law in the South and the custom in the North), literally thousands of Negroes left the race to escape this blanket of oppression. Passing was a traumatic and dramatic experience, and thus black fiction used and overused it.

In Larsen's novel, the two main characters, Irene and Clare, are childhood friends; both are pretty, both could pass. Irene, who comes from a solid middle-class black home and who married a Harlem black physician, passes only for convenience in shopping downtown and in other trivial situations. On the other hand, Clare comes from a racially mixed background, is reared by a drunken father, and after the father's death lives unhappily with white aunts who are ashamed of her black blood. Deciding to join the white world, she marries a brutish white man who discovers her race. A complex character, Clare joins the ranks of tragic mulattoes portrayed in the works of George Washington Cable and other late nineteenth- and early twentieth-century writers.

For critical comment on Nella Larsen's two works, see Robert A. Bone's *The Negro Novel in America* (rev. ed., 1965); Benjamin Brawley's *The Negro in Literature and Art in the United States* (1930); Hugh M. Gloster's *Negro Voices in American Fiction* (1948); Robert Hemenway's *The Black Novelist* (1970); Saunders Redding's *To Make a Poet Black* (1939); and Joyce Ann Joyce's "Nella Larsen's *Passing*: A Reflection of the American Dream," *Western Journal of Black Studies* 7, No. 2 (Summer 1983).

For additional comment on Larsen's life and works, see Thadious M. Davis's article in *Dictionary of Literary Biography, Volume 51*; Ann Allen Shockley's *Afro-American Women Writers, 1746–1933: An Anthology and Critical Guide* (1988); Mary Helen Washington's *Invented Lives: Narratives of Black Women, 1860–1960*; and Deborah McDowell's introduction to *Quicksand* and *Passing* (1986). Also useful is the introduction to the 1971 reprint of *Passing* written by Hoyt Fuller. See also Bernard W. Bell's *The Afro-American Novel and Its Tradition* (1987).

The selection that follows comes from chapters 20 and 21 in *Quicksand* (1928).

FROM **QUICKSAND**

Twenty

The day was a rainy one. Helga Crane, stretched out on her bed, felt herself so broken physically, mentally, that she had given up thinking. But back and forth in her staggered brain wavering, incoherent thoughts shot shuttle-like. Her pride would have shut out these humiliating thoughts and painful visions of herself. The effort was too great. She felt alone, isolated from all other human beings, separated even from her own anterior existence by the disaster of yesterday. Over and over, she repeated: "There's nothing left but to go now." Her anguish seemed unbearable.

For days, for weeks, voluptuous visions had haunted her. Desire had burned in her flesh with uncontrollable violence. The wish to give herself had been so intense that Dr. Anderson's surprising, trivial apology loomed as a direct refusal of the offering. Whatever outcome she had expected, it had been something else than this, this mortification, this feeling of ridicule and self-loathing, this knowledge that she had deluded herself. It was all, she told herself, as unpleasant as possible.

Almost she wished she could die. Not quite. It wasn't that she was afraid of death, which had, she thought, its picturesque aspects. It was rather that she knew she would not die. And death, after the debacle, would but intensify its absurdity. Also, it would reduce her, Helga Crane, to unimportance, to nothingness. Even in her unhappy present state, that did not appeal to her. Gradually, reluctantly, she began to know that the blow to her self-esteem, the certainty of having proved herself a silly fool, was perhaps the severest hurt which she had suffered. It was her self-assurance that had gone down in the crash. After all, what Dr. Anderson thought didn't matter. She could escape from the discomfort of his knowing gray eyes. But she couldn't escape from sure knowledge that she had made a fool of herself. This angered her further and she struck the wall with her hands and jumped up and began hastily to dress herself. She couldn't go on with the analysis. It was too hard. Why bother, when she could add nothing to the obvious fact that she had been a fool?

"I can't stay in this room any longer. I must get out or I'll choke." Her self-knowledge had increased her anguish. Distracted, agitated, incapable of containing herself, she tore open drawers and closets trying desperately to take some interest in the selection of her apparel.

It was evening and still raining. In the streets, unusually deserted, the electric lights cast dull glows. Helga Crane, walking rapidly, aimlessly, could decide on no definite destination. She had not thought to take umbrella or even rubbers. Rain and wind whipped cruelly about her, drenching her garments and chilling her body. Soon the foolish little satin shoes which she wore were sopping wet. Unheeding these physical discomforts, she went on, but at the open corner of One Hundred and Thirty-eighth Street a sudden more ruthless gust of wind ripped the small hat from her head. In the next minute the black clouds opened wider and spilled their water with unusual fury. The streets became swirling rivers. Helga Crane, forgetting her mental torment, looked about anxiously for a shelter-

ing taxi. A few taxis sped by, but inhabited, so she began desperately
to struggle through wind and rain toward one of the buildings,
where she could take shelter in a store or a doorway. But another
whirl of wind lashed her and, scornful of her slight strength, tossed
her into the swollen gutter.

Now she knew beyond all doubt that she had no desire to die,
and certainly not there nor then. Not in such a messy wet manner.
Death had lost all of its picturesque aspects to the girl lying soaked
and soiled in the flooded gutter. So, though she was very tired and
very weak, she dragged herself up and succeeded finally in making
her way to the store whose blurred light she had marked for her
destination.

She had opened the door and had entered before she was aware
that, inside, people were singing a song which she was conscious of
having heard years ago—hundreds of years it seemed. Repeated over
and over, she made out the words:

> . . . *Showers of blessings,*
> *Showers of blessings . . .*

She was conscious too of a hundred pairs of eyes upon her as
she stood there, drenched and disheveled, at the door of this improvised meeting-house.

> . . . *Showers of blessings . . .*

The appropriateness of the song, with its constant reference to
showers, the ridiculousness of herself in such surroundings, was too
much for Helga Crane's frayed nerves. She sat down on the floor, a
dripping heap, and laughed and laughed and laughed.

It was into a shocked silence that she laughed. For at the first
hysterical peal the words of the song had died in the singers' throats,
and the wheezy organ had lapsed into stillness. But in a moment
there were hushed solicitous voices; she was assisted to her feet and
led haltingly to a chair near the low platform at the far end of the
room. On one side of her a tall angular black woman under a queer
hat sat down, on the other a fattish yellow man with huge outstanding ears and long, nervous hands.

The singing began again, this time a low wailing thing:

> *Oh, the bitter shame and sorrow*
> *That a time could ever be,*
> *When I let the Savior's pity*
> *Plead in vain, and proudly answered:*
> *"All of self and none of Thee,*
> *All of self and none of Thee."*

> *Yet He found me, I beheld Him,*
> *Bleeding on the cursed tree;*
> *Heard Him pray: "Forgive them, Father."*
> *And my wistful heart said faintly,*
> *"Some of self and some of Thee,*
> *Some of self and some of Thee."*

There were, it appeared, endless moaning verses. Behind Helga a woman had begun to cry audibly, and soon, somewhere else, another. Outside, the wind still bellowed. The wailing singing went on:

> *. . . Less of self and more of Thee,*
> *Less of self and more of Thee.*

Helga too began to weep, at first silently, softly; then with great racking sobs. Her nerves were so torn, so aching, her body so wet, so cold! It was a relief to cry unrestrainedly, and she gave herself freely to soothing tears, not noticing that the groaning and sobbing of those about her had increased, unaware that the grotesque ebony figure at her side had begun gently to pat her arm to the rhythm of the singing and to croon softly: "Yes, chile, yes, chile." Nor did she notice the furtive glances that the man on her other side cast at her between his fervent shouts of "Amen!" and "Praise God for a sinner!"

She did notice, though, that the tempo, the atmosphere of the place, had changed, and gradually she ceased to weep and gave her attention to what was happening about her. Now they were singing:

> *. . . Jesus knows all about my troubles . . .*

Men and women were swaying and clapping their hands, shouting and stamping their feet to the frankly irreverent melody of the song. Without warning the woman at her side threw off her hat, leaped to her feet, waved her long arms, and shouted shrilly: "Glory! Hallelujah!" and then, in wild, ecstatic fury jumped up and down before Helga clutching at the girl's soaked coat, and screamed: "Come to Jesus, you pore los' sinner!" Alarmed for the fraction of a second, involuntarily Helga had shrunk from her grasp, wriggling out of the wet coat when she could not loosen the crazed creature's hold. At the sight of the bare arms and neck growing out of the clinging red dress, a shudder shook the swaying man at her right. On the face of the dancing woman before her a disapproving frown gathered. She shrieked: "A scarlet 'oman. Come to Jesus, you pore los' Jezebel!"

At this the short brown man on the platform raised a placating hand and sanctimoniously delivered himself of the words: "Remembah de words of our Mastah: 'Let him that is without sin cast de first stone.' Let us pray for our errin' sistah."

Helga Crane was amused, angry, disdainful, as she sat there, listening to the preacher praying for her soul. But though she was contemptuous, she was being too well entertained to leave. And it was, at least, warm and dry. So she stayed, listening to the fervent exhortation to God to save her and to the zealous shoutings and groanings of the congregation. Particularly she was interested in the writhings and weepings of the feminine portion, which seemed to predominate. Little by little the performance took on an almost Bacchic vehemence. Behind her, before her, beside her, frenzied women gesticulated, screamed, wept, and tottered to the praying of the preacher, which had gradually become a cadenced chant. When at last he ended, another took up the plea in the same moaning chant, and then another. It went on and on without pause with the persistence of some unconquerable faith exalted beyond time and reality.

Fascinated, Helga Crane watched until there crept upon her an indistinct horror of an unknown world. She felt herself in the presence of a nameless people, observing rites of a remote obscure origin. The faces of the men and women took on the aspect of a dim vision. "This," she whispered to herself, "is terrible. I must get out of here." But the horror held her. She remained motionless, watching, as if she lacked the strength to leave the place—foul, vile, and terrible, with its mixture of breaths, its contact of bodies, its concerted convulsions, all in wild appeal for a single soul. Her soul.

And as Helga watched and listened, gradually a curious influence penetrated her; she felt an echo of the weird orgy resound in her own heart; she felt herself possessed by the same madness; she too felt a brutal desire to shout and to sling herself about. Frightened at the strength of the obsession, she gathered herself for one last effort to escape, but vainly. In rising, weakness and nausea from last night's unsuccessful attempt to make herself drunk overcame her. She had eaten nothing since yesterday. She fell forward against the crude railing which enclosed the little platform. For a single moment she remained there in silent stillness, because she was afraid she was going to be sick. And in that moment she was lost—or saved. The yelling figures about her pressed forward, closing her in on all sides. Maddened, she grasped at the railing, and with no previous intention began to yell like one insane, drowning every other clamor, while torrents of tears streamed down her face. She was unconscious of the words she uttered, or their meaning: "Oh God, mercy, mercy. Have mercy on me!" but she repeated them over and over.

From those about her came a thunderclap of joy. Arms were stretched toward her with savage frenzy. The women dragged themselves upon their knees or crawled over the floor like reptiles, sobbing and pulling their hair and tearing off their clothing. Those who succeeded in getting near to her leaned forward to encourage the unfortunate sister, dropping hot tears and beads of sweat upon her bare arms and neck.

The thing became real. A miraculous calm came upon her. Life seemed to expand, and to become very easy. Helga Crane felt within her a supreme aspiration toward the regaining of simple happiness, a happiness unburdened by the complexities of the lives she had known. About her the tumult and the shouting continued, but in a lesser degree. Some of the more exuberant worshipers had fainted into inert masses, the voices of others were almost spent. Gradually the room grew quiet and almost solemn, and to the kneeling girl time seemed to sink back into the mysterious grandeur and holiness of far-off simpler centuries.

Twenty-one

On leaving the mission Helga Crane had started straight back to her room at the hotel. With her had gone the fattish yellow man who had sat beside her. He had introduced himself as the Reverend Mr. Pleasant Green in proffering his escort for which Helga had been grateful because she had still felt a little dizzy and much exhausted. So great had been this physical weariness that as she had walked beside him, without attention to his verbose information about his own "field," as he called it, she had been seized with a hateful feeling of vertigo and obliged to lay firm hold on his arm to keep herself from falling. The weakness had passed as suddenly as it had come. Silently they had walked on. And gradually Helga had recalled that the man beside her had himself swayed slightly at their close encounter, and that frantically for a fleeting moment he had gripped at a protruding fence railing. That man! Was it possible? As easy as that?

Instantly across her still half-hypnotized consciousness little burning darts of fancy had shot themselves. No. She couldn't. It would be too awful. Just the same, what or who was there to hold her back? Nothing. Simply nothing. Nobody. Nobody at all.

Her searching mind had become in a moment quite clear. She cast at the man a speculative glance, aware that for a tiny space she had looked into his mind, a mind striving to be calm. A mind that was certain that it was secure because it was concerned only with things of the soul, spiritual things, which to him meant religious things. But actually a mind by habit at home amongst the mere material aspect of things, and at that moment consumed by some longing for the ecstasy that might lurk behind the gleam of her cheek, the flying wave of her hair, the pressure of her slim fingers on his heavy arm. An instant's flashing vision it had been and it was gone at once. Escaped in the aching of her own senses and the sudden disturbing fear that she herself had perhaps missed the supreme secret of life.

After all, there was nothing to hold her back. Nobody to care. She stopped sharply, shocked at what she was on the verge of considering. Appalled at where it might lead her.

The man—what was his name?—thinking that she was almost about to fall again, had reached out his arms to her. Helga Crane had deliberately stopped thinking. She had only smiled, a faint provocative smile, and pressed her fingers deep into his arms until a wild look had come into his slightly bloodshot eyes.

The next morning she lay for a long while, scarcely breathing, while she reviewed the happenings of the night before. Curious. She couldn't be sure that it wasn't religion that had made her feel so utterly different from dreadful yesterday. And gradually she became a little sad, because she realized that with every hour she would get a little farther away from this soothing haziness, this rest from her long trouble of body and of spirit; back into the clear bareness of her own small life and being, from which happiness and serenity always faded just as they had shaped themselves. And slowly bitterness crept into her soul. Because, she thought, all I've ever had in life has been things—except just this one time. At that she closed her eyes, for even remembrance caused her to shiver a little.

Things, she realized, hadn't been, weren't, enough for her. She'd have to have something else besides. It all came back to that old question of happiness. Surely this was it. Just for a fleeting moment Helga Crane, her eyes watching the wind scattering the gray-white clouds and so clearing a speck of blue sky, questioned her ability to retain, to bear, this happiness at such cost as she must pay for it. There was, she knew, no getting round that. The man's agitation and sincere conviction of sin had been too evident, too illuminating. The question returned in a slightly new form. Was it worth the risk? Could she take it? Was she able? Though what did it matter—now?

And all the while she knew in one small corner of her mind that such thinking was useless. She had made her decision. Her resolution. It was a chance at stability, at permanent happiness, that she meant to take. She had let so many other things, other chances, escape her. And anyway there was God, He would perhaps make it come out all right. Still confused and not so sure that it wasn't the fact that she was "saved" that had contributed to this after feeling of well-being, she clutched the hope, the desire to believe that now at last she had found some One, some Power, who was interested in her. Would help her.

She meant, however, for once in her life to be practical. So she would make sure of both things, God and man.

Her glance caught the calendar over the little white desk. The tenth of November. The steamer *Oscar II* sailed today. Yesterday she had half thought of sailing with it. Yesterday. How far away!

With the thought of yesterday came the thought of Robert Anderson and a feeling of elation, revenge. She had put herself beyond the need of help from him. She had made it impossible for herself ever again to appeal to him. Instinctively she had the knowledge that he would be shocked. Grieved. Horribly hurt even. Well, let him!

The need to hurry suddenly obsessed her. She must. The morning was almost gone. And she meant, if she could manage it, to be married today. Rising, she was seized with a fear so acute that she had to lie down again. For the thought came to her that she might fail. Might not be able to confront the situation. That would be too dreadful. But she became calm again. How could he, a naïve creature like that, hold out against her? If she pretended to distress? To fear? To remorse? He couldn't. It would be useless for him even to try. She screwed up her face into a little grin, remembering that even if protestations were to fail, there were other ways.

And, too, there was God.

∽❦∼

And so in the confusion of seductive repentance Helga Crane was married to the grandiloquent Reverend Mr. Pleasant Green, that rattish yellow man, who had so kindly, so unctuously, proffered his escort to her hotel on the memorable night of her conversion. With him she willingly, even eagerly, left the sins and temptations of New York behind her to, as he put it, "labor in the vineyard of the Lord" in the tiny Alabama town where he was pastor to a scattered and primitive flock. And where, as the wife of the preacher, she was a person of relative importance. Only relative.

Helga did not hate him, the town, or the people. No. Not for a long time.

As always, at first the novelty of the thing, the change, fascinated her. There was a recurrence of the feeling that now, at last, she had found a place for herself, that she was really living. And she had her religion, which in her new status as a preacher's wife had of necessity become real to her. She believed in it. Because in its coming it had brought this other thing, this anæsthetic satisfaction for her senses. Hers was, she declared to herself, a truly spiritual union. This one time in her life, she was convinced, she had not clutched a shadow and missed the actuality. She felt compensated for all previous humiliations and disappointments and was glad. If she remembered that she had had something like this feeling before, she put the unwelcome memory from her with the thought: "This time I know I'm right. This time it will last."

Eagerly she accepted everything, even that bleak air of poverty which, in some curious way, regards itself as virtuous, for no other reason than that it is poor. And in her first hectic enthusiasm she intended and planned to do much good to her husband's parishioners. Her young joy and zest for the uplifting of her fellow men came back to her. She meant to subdue the cleanly scrubbed ugliness of her own surroundings to soft inoffensive beauty, and to help the other women to do likewise. Too, she would help them with their clothes, tactfully point out that sunbonnets, no matter how gay, and aprons, no matter how frilly, were not quite the proper things for Sunday church wear. There would be a sewing circle. She visualized herself instructing the children, who seemed most of the time to run wild, in ways of gentler deportment. She was anxious to be a true helpmate, for in her heart was a feeling of obligation, of humble gratitude.

In her ardor and sincerity Helga even made some small beginnings. True, she was not very successful in this matter of innovations. When she went about to try to interest the women in what she considered more appropriate clothing and in inexpensive ways of improving their homes according to her ideas of beauty, she was met, always, with smiling agreement and good-natured promises. "Yuh all is right, Mis' Green," and "Ah suttinly will, Mis' Green," fell courteously on her ear at each visit.

She was unaware that afterwards they would shake their heads sullenly over their wash-tubs and ironing-boards. And that among themselves they talked with amusement, or with anger, of "dat uppity, meddlin' No'the'nah," and "pore Reve'end," who in their opinion "would 'a done bettah to a ma'ied Clementine Richards." Knowing, as she did, nothing of this, Helga was unperturbed. But even had she known, she would not have been disheartened. The fact that it was difficult but increased her eagerness, and made the doing of it seem only the more worth while. Sometimes she would smile to think how changed she was.

And she was humble too. Even with Clementine Richards, a strapping black beauty of magnificent Amazon proportions and bold shining eyes of jet-like hardness. A person of awesome appearance. All chains, strings of beads, jingling bracelets, flying ribbons, feathery neck-pieces, and flowery hats. Clementine was inclined to treat Helga with an only partially concealed contemptuousness, considering her a poor thing without style, and without proper understanding of the worth and greatness of the man, Clementine's own adored pastor, whom Helga had somehow had the astounding good luck to

marry. Clementine's admiration of the Reverend Mr. Pleasant Green
was open. Helga was at first astonished. Until she learned that there
was really no reason why it should be concealed. Everybody was
aware of it. Besides, open adoration was the prerogative, the almost
religious duty, of the female portion of the flock. If this unhidden
and exaggerated approval contributed to his already oversized pom-
posity, so much the better. It was what they expected, liked, wanted.
The greater his own sense of superiority became, the more flattered
they were by his notice and small attentions, the more they cast at
him killing glances, the more they hung enraptured on his words.

In the days before her conversion, with its subsequent blurring of
her sense of humor, Helga might have amused herself by tracing the
relation of this constant ogling and flattering on the proverbially
large families of preachers; the often disastrous effect on their wives
of this constant stirring of the senses by extraneous women. Now,
however, she did not even think of it.

She was too busy. Every minute of the day was full. Necessarily.
And to Helga this was a new experience. She was charmed by it. To
be mistress in one's own house, to have a garden, and chickens, and
a pig; to have a husband—and to be "right with God"—what pleasure did that other world which she had left contain that could surpass these? Here, she had found, she was sure, the intangible thing
for which, indefinitely, always she had craved. It had received embodiment.

Everything contributed to her gladness in living. And so for a
time she loved everything and everyone. Or thought she did. Even
the weather. And it was truly lovely. By day a glittering gold sun
was set in an unbelievably bright sky. In the evening silver buds
sprouted in a Chinese blue sky, and the warm day was softly
soothed by a slight, cool breeze. And night! Night, when a languid
moon peeped through the wide-opened windows of her little house,
a little mockingly, it may be. Always at night's approach Helga was
bewildered by a disturbing medley of feelings. Challenge. Anticipa-
tion. And a small fear.

In the morning she was serene again. Peace had returned. And
she could go happily, inexpertly, about the humble tasks of her
household, cooking, dish-washing, sweeping, dusting, mending, and
darning. And there was the garden. When she worked there, she felt
that life was utterly filled with the glory and the marvel of God.

Helga did not reason about this feeling, as she did not at that
time reason about anything. It was enough that it was there, coloring
all her thoughts and acts. It endowed the four rooms of her ugly
brown house with a kindly radiance, obliterating the stark bareness
of its white plaster walls and the nakedness of its uncovered painted

floors. It even softened the choppy lines of the shiny oak furniture and subdued the awesome horribleness of the religious pictures.

And all the other houses and cabins shared in this illumination. And the people. The dark undecorated women unceasingly concerned with the actual business of life, its rounds of births and christenings, of loves and marriages, of deaths and funerals, were to Helga miraculously beautiful. The smallest, dirtiest, brown child, barefooted in the fields or muddy roads, was to her an emblem of the wonder of life, of love, and of God's goodness.

For the preacher, her husband, she had a feeling of gratitude, amounting almost to sin. Beyond that, she thought of him not at all. But she was not conscious that she had shut him out from her mind. Besides, what need to think of him? He was there. She was at peace, and secure. Surely their two lives were one, and the companionship in the Lord's grace so perfect that to think about it would be tempting providence. She had done with soul-searching.

What did it matter that he consumed his food, even the softest varieties, audibly? What did it matter that, though he did no work with his hands, not even in the garden, his fingernails were always rimmed with black? What did it matter that he failed to wash his fat body, or to shift his clothing, as often as Helga herself did? There were things that more than outweighed these. In the certainty of his goodness, his righteousness, his holiness, Helga somehow overcame her first disgust at the odor of sweat and stale garments. She was even able to be unaware of it. Herself, Helga had come to look upon as a finicky, showy thing of unnecessary prejudices and fripperies. And when she sat in the dreary structure, which had once been a stable belonging to the estate of a wealthy horse-racing man and about which the odor of manure still clung, now the church and social center of the Negroes of the town, and heard him expound with verbal extravagance the gospel of blood and love, of hell and heaven, of fire and gold streets, pounding with clenched fists the frail table before him or shaking those fists in the faces of the congregation like direct personal threats, or pacing wildly back and forth and even sometimes shedding great tears as he besought them to repent, she was, she told herself, proud and gratified that he belonged to her. In some strange way she was able to ignore the atmosphere of self-satisfaction which poured from him like gas from a leaking pipe.

And night came at the end of every day. Emotional, palpitating, amorous, all that was living in her sprang like rank weeds at the tingling thought of night, with a vitality so strong that it devoured all shoots of reason.

Rudolph Fisher

(1897–1934)

HARLEM PHYSICIAN and roentgenologist, author, musician, scholar, and witty raconteur, Rudolph Fisher in his fiction gives one of the fullest and most realistic pictures of the black ghetto found in Harlem Renaissance literature. He knew the city intimately, and he wrote about its diverse classes and nationalities with a kind of good-natured understanding and fondness. One of his often-used themes concerns the impact of Harlem on the recent migrant from the South. His best work deals with this theme.

Born in Washington, D.C., in 1897, Rudolph Fisher was reared in Providence, Rhode Island. He was educated at that city's Classical High School and Brown University, where he had a brilliant record. With a major in English and in biology, he received his A.B. in 1919 and was elected to three honor fraternities: Phi Beta Kappa, Sigma Xi, and Delta Sigma Rho. He also won the Caesar Misch Prize in German and the Carpenter Prize in public speaking, was a James Manning Scholar and a Francis Wagland Scholar. Fisher was chosen by his classmates to be class-day orator and by the faculty to be commencement-day speaker. In 1920 he received his M.D. degree from the Howard University Medical School. After interning at Freedman's Hospital, he became a fellow of the research council of the Columbia University College of Physicians and Surgeons, where he stayed for two years, doing research in biology. In addition to his x-ray work and medical practice, he served as superintendent of the then International Hospital in Harlem. He died when only thirty-seven years old.

Rudolph Fisher published two full-length novels—*The Walls of Jericho* (1928, 1969, 1971) and *The Conjure-Man Dies: A Mystery Tale of Dark Harlem* (1932). However, his best work in fiction is found in his many short stories, published in *Atlantic Monthly, The Crisis, Survey Graphic, McClure's, Opportunity, Story*, and other periodicals. Fisher was also a musician, and he wrote arrangements for several Negro spirituals, including some especially for Paul Robeson. He also published articles in leading medical journals.

Fisher's first novel, *The Walls of Jericho*, was written to show that an author could treat the Harlem social extremes in one work. In this book he not only satirizes the pretensions of the elites, but also the white observers who came to Harlem. As in many other Harlem novels, there is a "passing" character; there is also a comedy team that speaks a special kind of Harlemese, which was funnier in 1920 than it is today. This is not a great novel, but Fisher tried and succeeded in looking at Harlem steadily and seeing it whole.

The second novel, *The Conjure-Man Dies*, is probably the first mystery in America written by an African American. A conventional thriller, it has all of the trappings found in a detective story of the 1930s, with this difference: it has for its main character a Harlem conjure-man who is also an African king; it has in addition the numbers racket, the superstitions, and the other colorful activities of Harlem life. A light work, yes, but it is not dull, and it has at least two unforgettable characters.

Of Rudolph Fisher's short fiction, the following stories are perhaps his best: "Miss Cynthia," "City of Refuge," and "The South Lingers On" (five sketches). All of them use the theme mentioned previously, the impact of Harlem on the recent migrant. Among Fisher's other popular short stories are "High Yaller," "Blades of Steel," "Ring Tail," and "The Promised Land." Two of his stories are found in the-best-of-the-year anthologies—one in Foley's, the other in O'Brien's. Still another won first prize in *The Crisis* 1925 short story contest.

For additional critical and biographical comment on Fisher, see Robert Hemenway's *The Black Novelist* (1970); Robert A. Bone's *The Negro Novel in America* (rev. ed., 1965); Claudette Brown's entry in *Dictionary of American Negro Biography*; and Eleanor Q. Tignor's entry in *Dictionary of Literary Biography: Volume 51*. See especially Dennis Poupard, ed., *Twentieth-Century Literary Criticism—Vol. II* (1983). See also the article on Fisher in Arthur P. Davis's *From the Dark Tower* (1974). Two very welcome collections of Fisher's stories appeared in 1987, both of which offer critical commentary and other useful information: *The Short Fiction of Rudolph Fisher*, edited by Margaret Perry, and *The City of Refuge: The Collected Stories of Rudolph Fisher*, edited by John McCluskey, Jr.

The following story, "High Yaller," originally appeared in *The Crisis* in two parts, in October and November 1925.

HIGH YALLER

1

The timekeeper's venomous whistle killed the ball in its flight, half-way to the basket. There was a triumphant bedlam. From the walls of Manhattan Casino impatient multitudes swarmed on to the immense floor, congratulating, consoling, gibing; pouring endlessly from the surrounding terrace, like long restrained torrents at last transcending a dam; sweeping tumultuously in from all sides, till the dance floor sank beneath a sounding flood of dark-skinned people, submerged to its furthest corners save the distant platform that gave the orchestra refuge, like a raft. A sudden blare of music cut the uproar. The turbulence gradually ordered itself into dense, crawling currents, sluggish as jammed traffic, while the din of voices at length reluctantly surrendered to the rhythmic swish-swash of shuffling feet.

Looking down from a balcony on that dark mass of heads, close together as buckshot, Evelyn Brown wondered how they all managed to enjoy it. Why must they always follow a basket-ball game with a dance?—the one pleasurable enough, the other mob-torture, she knew.

"Game?" challenged MacLoed.

She couldn't refuse her escort, of course. "If you are."

They descended and struck out like swimmers in the sea. MacLoed surrounded her as closely as a lifesaver. She knew that he had to, but she hated it—this mere hugging to music, this acute consciousness of her partner's body. The air was vile—hot, full of breath and choking perfume. You were forever avoiding, colliding, marking time on the same spot. So insulating was the crush that you might sway for several minutes near a familiar couple, even recognize their voices, yet catch only the merest glimpse of their vanishing faces.

Something of the sort was happening now. Evelyn heard someone say her name, and the mordant intonation with the succeeding spiteful snatch-phrases made her forget the physical unpleasantness of the moment.

"Evelyn Brown?—Hmph!—got yellow fever—I know better—color struck, I tell you—girls she goes around with—all lily whites—even the fellows—Mac to-day—pass for white anywhere—Jeff, Rickmond, Stanley Hall, all of 'em—You? Shoot! You don't count—you're crazy 'bout high yallers anyhow."

The words were engulfed. Evelyn had not needed to look. Mayme Jackson's voice was unmistakable.

The dance number ended on an unresolved, interrogative chord that set off an explosion of applause. Jay Martin, who had just been defending Evelyn against Mayme's charge, spied the former's fluff of fair hair through several intervening thicknesses of straight and straightened black, and, dragging Mayme by the arm, he made for the other couple.

"Now say what you said about Evelyn!" he dared Mayme, mock-maliciously, quite unaware that Evelyn already knew.

"Sweetest old thing in the world," came Mayme's tranquil purr.

"Rake in the chips," gasped Jay. "Your pot." He addressed Evelyn. "How about the next wrestle?"

There was a ready exchange of partners. The orchestra struck up an air from a popular Negro comedy: "Yaller Gal's Gone Out o' Style." Soon the two couples were urged apart in increasingly divergent currents.

"Black sea," commented Jay.

But Evelyn was thoughtful. "Jay?"

"Nobody else."

"I heard what Mayme said."

"You did? Aw, heck—don't pay any attention to that kid. She's a nut."

"I'm not so sure she isn't right, Jay."

"Right? About what?"

"I've been thinking over my best friends. They're practically all 'passing' fair. Any one of them could pass—for a foreigner, anyway."

"Me, for instance," he grinned. "Prince Woogy-boogy of Abyssinia."

"I'm afraid you prove the rule."

He was serious. "Well, what of it?"

"Oh, I don't mean I've done it intentionally. I never realized it till just now. But, just as Mayme says, it looks bad."

"Hang what Mayme says. She's kind o' gone on yaller men, herself. See the way she melted into Mac's shirtfront! Hung round his neck like a chest-protector. Didn't drape herself over *me* that way."

"Jay! You're as bad as she is."

"That's what she said."

"What do you mean?"

"Claims I fall only for pinks."

"Oh. I didn't mean that."

"Neither did she. Point is, there aren't any more dark girls. Skin bleach and rouge have wiped out the strain. The blacks have turned sealskin, the sealskins are high-brown, the high-browns are all yaller, and the yallers are pink. How's a bird going to fall for what ain't?"

They jazzed on a while in noisy silence. Evelyn's tone was surprisingly bitter when at last she spoke again:

"I wish I looked like Mayme." Astonished, Jay stared at her as she went on: "A washerwoman can make half a million dollars turning dark skins light. Why doesn't someone learn how to turn light skins dark?"

And now, in addition to staring, he saw her: the averted blue eyes, the fine lips about to quiver, the delicate, high-bridged nose, the white cheeks, colorless save for the faintest touch, the incredible tawny, yellow-flecked, scintillant hair,—an almost crystalline creature, as odd in this dark company as a single sapphire in jet. He was quick to comprehend. "I know a corner—let's sit out the rest," he suggested.

When they achieved their place in a far end of the terrace, the orchestra was outdoing itself in the encore. One of the members sang through a megaphone in a smoky, half-talking voice:

> *"Oh Miss Pink thought she knew her stuff,*
> *But Miss High Brown has called her bluff."*

When the encore ended, the dancers demanded yet another. The rasp of syncopation and the ceaseless stridor of soles mingled, rose about the two refugees, seeming to wall them in, so that presently they felt alone together.

"Jay, can you imagine what it's like to be colored and look white?"

He tried to be trivial. "Very convenient at times, I should think."

"But oftener unbearable. That song—imagine—everyone looking at you—laughing at you. And Mayme Jackson—'yellow fever'! Can I help it?—Jeff—Rickmond—Stanley Hall—yes, they're light. But what can I do? I like the others. I'd be glad to go places with them. But they positively avoid me."

"I don't, Ev."

"No, you don't, Jay." But her bitterness recaptured her. "Oh, I've heard them talking: "There goes Evelyn Brown—queen of the lily-whites—nothing brown about her but her name'!" A swiftly matured determination rendered her suddenly so grim that it seemed, fragile as she was, something about her must break. "Jay, no one's going to accuse me of jim-crowing again!"

"Shucks. What do you care as long as you don't mean to?"

"I'm not only not going to mean to. I'm not going to. I'm going to see to it that I don't."

"What the deuce—by cutting your gang?"

"No. By cultivating the others."

"Oh."

"Jay—will you help me?"

"Help you? Sure. How?"

"Come to see me oftener."

"Good night! Don't you see enough of me at the office every day?"

"Come oftener. Take me places when you're not too broke. Rush me!"

He grinned as he perceived her purpose. "Doggone good stunt!" he said slowly, with increasingly enthusiastic approval. "Blessed if I wouldn't like to see you put it over, Ev. It'll show Mayme something, anyhow."

"It'll show me something, too."

"You? What?"

She was about to answer when a sharp, indecent epithet rent the wall of noise that had until then isolated them. Looking involuntarily up, Jay saw two youngsters, quarreling vituperatively. They were too close to be ignored, and, since dancing was at its height, no one else was about.

"Excuse me a second," he said, rising before Evelyn could protest. The pair were but a few feet away. The evident aggressor was a hard-looking little black youth of indefinite age,—perhaps sixteen actual years, plus the accumulated bonus of worldly wisdom which New York pays its children. He grew worse, word by word. Approaching, Jay spoke sharply, in a low voice so that Evelyn might not hear:

"Cut out that gutter-talk, boy!"

"Aw, go to hell!"

Jay stopped, less amazed than aggravated. He knew his Harlem adolescent, but he was not quite sure what to do with it. Meanwhile he was being advised: "This is a horse-race, big boy. No jackasses allowed!"

He seized the lad firmly by the shoulder and said, "Son, if you don't cover that garbage-trap of yours——" but the boy flung away and defied him in a phrase both loud and ugly. Thoroughly angered, Jay clapped one hand over the offending mouth and, catching the youngster around the waist with the other, forcibly propelled him through a tangle of empty, spindle-legged chairs to a place where two big policemen, one black and one red, were complacently watching the dancers. Here he released him with "Now—talk."

The boy scowled with wrath and impotence. So outraged in the street, he would have found a stone to throw. Now only a retaliative speech was left him, and the nearness of the law attenuated even that:

"Aw 'ight! Showin' off before 'at ole 'fay gal, huh? Aw 'ight, y' pink-chaser, Ah'm goan put y' both in." And he sidled darkly off, pulling at his disadjusted collar.

Evelyn, out of earshot, followed it all with her eyes. "Mac wouldn't have done that," she mused as she saw Jay turn from the boy and start back toward her. "Mac would have pretended he didn't hear." And before Jay reached her, she had decided something: "I certainly like Jay Martin. He's so—white."

2

Over One Hundred and Thirty-fourth Street's sidewalks between Fifth and Lenox Avenues Jay Martin's roller-skates had rattled and

whirred in the days when that was the northern boundary of Negro
Harlem. He had grown as the colony grew, and now he could just
recall the time when his father, a pioneer preacher, had been forever
warning him never to cross Lenox Avenue and never to go beyond
One Hundred and Thirty-fifth Street; a time when no Negroes lived
on or near Seventh Avenue and when it would have been almost
suicidal for one to appear unarmed on Irish Eighth.

School had been a succession of fist-fights with white boys who
called him nigger, until, when he reached the upper grades, the colored boys began to outnumber the white; from that time until high
school, pitched battles superseded individual contests, and he ran
home bruised less often. His high school record had been good, and
his father, anxious to make a physician of him, had sent him on to
college. At the end of his third year, however, the looming draft menace, combined with the chance of a commission in the army, had
urged him into a training camp at Des Moines.

He had gone to France as a lieutenant. When he returned, un-
harmed, he found his father fatally ill and his mother helpless. Further study out of the question, he had taken his opportunity with a
Negro real estate firm, and for five years now he had been actively
concerned in black Harlem's extension, the spread whose beginnings
his earlier years had witnessed.

About Evelyn, of course, there had been hypothesis:

"Looks might funny to me when a woman Jennie Brown's color
has a yaller-headed young one white as Evelyn."

"Daddy was white, so I understan'."

"Huh. An' her mammy, too, mos' likely. 'At's de way dese rich
white folks do. Comes a wile oat dey doan want, dey ups an' gives it
to one de servants—to adopt."

"Oh, I dunno. How come she couldn't been married to some
white man 'nuther? Dey's plenty sich, right hyeh in Harlem."

"Plenty whut? Plenty common law, maybe. You know d' ain' no
se'f-respectin' white man gonna——"

"Well, doan make no diff'nce. Cain' none of us go but so fur
back in our fam'ly hist'ry 'fo we stops. An' doan nobody have t' ask
us why we stops. We jes' stops. Evelyn's a good girl. Smart—works
regular an' makes mo' out o' dem real estate niggers 'n she'd make in
Miss Ann's kitchen. Bad 's her mother's asthma's gittin', no tellin'
whut they'd do if 'twasn't f' Evelyn's job an' dem two women lodgers."

"Oh, I ain' sayin' nuthin' 'gins 'em. Only seem like to me—dey's a
white man in de woodpile somewha'."

Her own singularity had become conscious early in Evelyn's life.
There crept often into her mind of late an old, persistent recollection. She and Sookie Johnson, seven-year-old playmates, had been

playing jacks on the front stoop. There arose a dispute as to whose turn it was. Sookie owned the ball and Evelyn the jacks; neither would surrender her possession to the other, and the game was deadlocked. Whereupon, the spiteful Sookie had resorted to abuse:

"Y' ole yaller thing, you! My mother say y' cain't 'speck nuthin' f'm yaller niggers nohow!"

Evelyn had thrown the jacks into Sookie's face and ran heartbroken to her mother. Why didn't she have kinky hair and dark brown skin like Sookie's? "Why, honey, you're beautiful," her mother had comforted her. "Folks 'll call you names long as you live. They're just jealous, that's all."

Thus fortified, Evelyn had come to maturity, finding her mother's prophecy ever and again true. "They're just jealous" was but a fortification, however; within it Evelyn's spirit was still vulnerable, and she knew that under constant fire this stronghold could not stand forever. Mayme Jackson's thrust-in-the-back culminated what Sookie's sneer had begun. Evelyn felt her mother's defence crumbling rapidly and alarmingly, and her appeal to Jay Martin was a rather desperate effort to establish a defence of her own.

They sat now in the front room of her flat; a room too full of mock-mahogany furniture about to collapse; a room with gas light and a tacked-down carpet, with flower-figured wall-paper and a marble-topped walnut table in one corner, bearing a big brown morocco-bound Bible.

"Jay, will you?"

"Remember the time I pulled your hair in Sunday-School?"

"I'm going to pull your ears if you don't answer me!"

"Did you say something?"

"You make me tired."

"Aw, for Pete's sake, Ev, I can't take you to that dump."

"Have the last two weeks frozen your nerve?"

"No—but——"

"Well, this isn't like the others, you know. This is a colored place."

"But why go there? Let's go to Broadway's or Happy's."

"No. I want to see something new. Why isn't Hank's decent, anyway? It can't be any worse than the Hole in the Wall."

"Much worse. Regular rat-trap. No gentleman would take a lady——"

"You flatter us. Let's don't be a gentleman and lady tonight. I want to see the rat-trap."

"Why, Ev, the place was raided only last week!"

"You can't scare me that way. If it was it'll be all the safer this week."

"Lord! You girls know it all."

"I don't know anything about Hank's."

"But I'm trying to tell you——"

"Seeing is believing."

"There's nothing to see."

She introduced strategy. "All right. I guess Mac won't be so hard to persuade."

"Ev—please—for Pete's sake don't let anybody take you to that——"

"Jay, I'd really hate to have to go with anybody but you." He was growing helpless. "Just the tiniest peep into the place, Jay. We won't stay—cross my liver."

"Your mother wouldn't like it."

"Come here." She led him by the arm down the long hallway to the dining-room, where her mother was sewing.

"You may go any place you please, if you go with Jay," smiled Mrs. Brown.

Hank's at first glance, presented nothing unique: a sedate old house in an elderly row of houses with high entrances, several steps above the sidewalk; houses that had once been private, but now, trapped in an extending matrix of business, stoically accepted their fates as real estate offices, printing shops and law rooms. Here and there a card peeped around the corner of a window and whispered, "Rooms"; but not the most suspicious eye would have associated those timid invitations with the bold vertical electric sign projecting over the doorway of the one lighted building in the row. Great letters, one above another, blazed the word "Café"; smaller horizontal ones across the top read "Hank's," others across the bottom "Cabaret."

"This doesn't look so bad," commented Evelyn as they approached. "Police station right in the same block."

"Yes—convenient."

Several men stood about on the sidewalk, smoking and talking. One of these, a white man, looked sharply at Jay and Evelyn as they mounted the steps and entered.

"Why, this is like any restaurant," said Evelyn. "Just a lot of tables and folks eating."

"Only a blind," explained Jay. "The real thing is downstairs."

A dinner-coated attendant came toward them, "I'm sorry. Everything's gone in the cabaret. Would you care to wait a few minutes?"

Jay, eager for an excuse to flee, looked at Evelyn; but the blue eyes said, "Please," and he nodded. "Very well."

"This way, then."

They were led up a narrow flight of padded stairs, along a carpeted hallway with several mysterious closed doors on either side, and finally into a little room near the end. Against one wall of the room was a table with two chairs, and against the opposite a flat couch with two or three cushions. Curtains draped the one window, facing the door. The table was bare except for a small lamp with a parchment shade of orange and black, yielding a warm, dim light.

"M—m!" exclaimed Evelyn. "Cozy!"

"We can serve you here if you like," suggested the attendant.

"No, thanks," Jay answered quickly. "We'll wait."

The attendant seemed to hesitate a moment. Then, "All right," he said. "I'll let you know as soon as there's space in the cabaret." He went out and closed the door.

Evelyn was alive with interest. "Spiffy, isn't it?" She sat down on one of the chairs and looked about. "Couldn't get lost, could you?"

Jay thoughtfully took the other chair.

"You might," he said absently.

"What are you talking about? Goodness, what a lot of fun you're having!"

"I don't like this, that's a fact."

"What's wrong?"

Jay looked and noted that the door locked from within. He went over to the window, pulled the shade aside a crack, and made out the skeleton of a fire-escape in the darkness outside.

"Oh, nothing," he said, returning to his seat. "Not a thing."

"Heavens, you give me the shivers! What is it?"

He was not eager to answer. "I'm not sure but—I believe—that bird thinks you're ofay."

"White? What difference would that make?"

"Well, I'll tell you, Ev. This place, like some you already know about, has a mixed patronage, see? Part jigs, part ofays. That's perfectly all right as long as the jigs keep to their own parties and the ofays to theirs. But as soon as they begin to come mixed, trouble starts. The colored men don't like to see white men with colored women and the white men don't like to see colored men with white women. So the management avoids it. I don't believe that house-man was telling the truth when he said there was no room in the cabaret. It's too early in the evening and it's not a busy night. Fact is, the place is probably half full of ofays, and he figured that if we went down there together some drunk would get fly and I'd bounce him on the nose and right away there'd be a hullabaloo. So he took a chance that maybe we were more interested in each other than in the cabaret anyhow, and sidetracked us off up here."

"But he said he'd let us know—"

"Of course. He thought we'd be tickled silly to be in one of these rooms alone; but after I refused to be served up here, what else could he say? I don't think he has any more idea of coming back than Jack Johnson."

"Then what does he expect you to do?"

"Get tired waiting and beat it."

"Oh." A depressed silence. Then a tragic diminuendo: "Lord, what a misfit I am!"

He was contrite at once. "I'm a bum. I shouldn't have told you. I don't know—maybe I'm wrong. We're here, so let's wait awhile and see."

"Jay, if only I were one thing or the other! You can't imagine—"

He absolutely could not answer. From somewhere below a thin strain drifted to their ears, like a snicker: "Yaller Gal's Gone Out o' Style."

Jay rose. "Let's breeze. That shine isn't coming back."

"All right. I'm sorry to be such a nuisance."

"You're not the nuisance. It's—folks."

They went down the soft-carpeted hallway. Strange, low sounds behind the closed doors seemed to hush apprehensively as they approached and revive after they passed. Once a shrill laugh was abruptly cut off as if by a stifling hand. There was a thick atmosphere of suppression, a sense of unspoken fears and half-drawn breaths and whispers.

As they reached the head of the padded stairs they saw someone hurrying up and drew aside to let him pass. It was a youth in a white coat, bent on some errand. He looked at them as he went by. They resumed their course and proceeded down the stairs; but the boy halted in his, and turned to look again. Immediately, he left off his errand, and waiting until he heard the front door close behind them, retraversed the staircase. A minute later he was on the sidewalk talking in an undertone to the white man who had so sharply observed Evelyn and Jay when they entered, and who now stood smoking still, following their departure with his eyes.

"Ah know 'at sucker", scowled the little black youth. "Collects rents f' Hale an' Barker. See 'at 'fay wid 'im? Seen 'im pick 'uh up pre' near two weeks ago at Manhattan Casino."

The white man puffed a minute, while the boy looked up at him, side-long, expectant. "Hale and Barker, huh?—Hmph! All right, Shorty. I'll keep my eye on 'im. If you're on, I'll fix y' up as usual."

" 'At's the time papa." And the boy too stood eyeing the disappearing pair, an imp of malice and satisfaction.

3

A young man leaned nonchalantly on the high foot of Jay's wooden bed, grinning goodnaturedly at him; a young man who looked exactly like Jay, feature for feature, with one important exception: his skin was white.

"Who in hell are you?" asked Jay.

"What you would be if you could," came the prompt, pleasant response.

"Liar."

"Straight stuff, brother. Think of the heights you might rise to if you were I."

"Hell!" grunted Jay.

"Eventually, of course. But I mean meanwhile. Why, now you'd be in a big firm downtown, on your way to wealth. Or you might be a practicing physician—your old man could have kept you out of the draft."

"Oh, well, I'm not doing so worse."

"No, nor so better. And then there's Evelyn."

"What about Evelyn? Why, I wouldn't even know her."

"You'd know somebody like her. Don't kid yourself, boy. You like 'em pink. Remember Paris?"

"You lie like a bookmaker. I like 'em intelligent. If they happen to be bright on the outside, too, why of course, I don't bar 'em."

"No—of course not." The sarcastic caller paused a thoughtful moment. "I've got a jawful of advice for you, old-timer."

"Swallow it and choke."

"Now listen. Don't you get to liking Evelyn, see. She's too damned white."

"What of it?"

"Be yourself, son. You ask me that, after these last two weeks?"

Jay reached up and wiped a mosquito from his forehead and smacked at another singing into his ear. They irritated him. "I'll like whoever I damn please!" he flared.

"Don't get high, now," soothed the other. "I'm only warning you. Pull up on the emergency before something hits you. That girl's too fair for comfort."

"But I like her."

The other disregarded this. "You're too dark, buddy. You're ultra-violet anyhow, alone. Beside her you become absolute black—invisible. The lady couldn't see you with an arc-lamp."

"Shucks! Evelyn doesn't care."

"You're wrong there. She does. She can't help it. But she doesn't want to, so she tries hard to make herself believe she doesn't. She takes up with you, tells herself how much she likes you, invites all sorts of embarrassments upon both of you. She might even marry you. It's like taking bad medicine she thinks she's got to take and telling herself it's sweet. She figures it's better to gulp it down than to sip it, and it's better to say it's sweet than to make faces."

"Well, maybe. But I'm just conceited enough to think she likes me."

"Of course she does. I'm not talking about you. I'm talking about your color. If you were I, now, she'd jump at you."

"Humph! I don't see her jumping at MacLoed."

"Mac isn't either of us, buddy. He hasn't got a thing but his looks, and Evelyn's too wise to fall for that alone."

"There are others."

"None who can make her forget what she's trying to do. She thinks it's a sort of duty to be colored, so she's going to make a thorough job of it—do it up brown, you might say. See? The only man that could unscramble her would be a real white man. She's not going to compromise."

"You're too deep for me. But I don't believe she cares about the color of a fellow's skin."

"You don't? Well, stay away from her anyhow."

"How come?"

"To save her feelings. Every time you two go out together you're in torture. Everybody stares at you—jigs and ofays both. You've tried it now for two weeks. What's happened? The first night you went to Coney Island and nearly got yourself mobbed. A couple of days later you went into a ice-cream parlor on One Hundred and Twenty-Fifth Street, a place where Evelyn goes anytime she likes, and the proprietor had the nerve to tell you *your* presence hurt his business. Then how about that crowd of jigs on the subway? And last night, when you wanted to get up and punch that shine waiter in the ear because he gave Evelyn the once over and then rolled his eyes at you behind her back, as much as to say, 'Oh, boy! How I envy you!'—and she looking at him all the time in the mirror! To-night caps it all. You go out to enjoy yourself in a 'colored' place, and get jim-crowed by a man of your own color who's afraid to let the two of you be seen. Do you think Evelyn enjoys a string of things like that?"

"She enjoys 'em as much as I do."

"But it isn't the same. When people look at you, it's just with surprise. All their look says is, 'Wonder what that nigger is doing with a white woman?' But when they look at her, it's with contempt. They say, 'Humph! What a cheap drab she must be to tag around with a nigger!' No matter whether it's true or not. Do you suppose she enjoys being looked at like that?"

Jay was silent. Sounds came from the street below into his open window; an empty Coney Island bus, rumbling, clattering, shrieking, eager to get in before daybreak; gay singing of a joy-riding chorus, swelling, consummating, dying away; the night-clear whistle of a lone, late straggler—"Yaller Gal's Gone Out o' Style."

"What do you expect me to do about it?" he finally asked.

"Ease out. See less and less of her. When you breeze away for your vacation, forget to write."

"Simple, ain't it?"

"Quite." The devil straightened up. "And now that that's settled, suppose you go to sleep a while."

"Suppose you go to hell," suggested Jay glumly.

"With pleasure. See you again."

Jay closed his smarting eyes. His caller departed into the clothes-press or the hall or up the airshaft, he wasn't sure where; he knew only that when again he looked about, he was alone.

Evelyn Brown, too, lay in bed, debating with a visitor—a sophisticated young woman who sat familiarly on the edge of the counterpane and hugged her knees as she talked, and who might have been Evelyn over again, save for a certain bearing of self-assurance which the latter entirely lacked.

"Well, you've tried it," said this visitor. "See what a mess you've made of it."

"I wish you'd let me alone."

"I think too much of you, dear. And you're thinking too much of Jay. Surely the last two weeks have shown you how impossible that is."

"Two weeks isn't a long enough test."

"Quite long enough. The only place you and Jay could be happy together would be on a desert island that nobody could find. You can't go to a single place together without sooner or later wishing the ground would swallow you."

"Oh, I'd get hardened to it."

"Would that be happiness? And even if you did, he wouldn't. You don't think he enjoys all this, do you?"

"No, I suppose not."

"No. And don't think he's dumb enough to put himself into it for life, either."

"He cares enough to, I think."

"Then you've got to care enough not to let him."

"How?"

"Drop him."

"I can't."

"You must. Don't you see now why you lily-whites seek each other? It's self-protection. Whether you do it consciously or not, you're really trying to prevent painful embarrassment."

"But I can't just shut myself away from everyone who happens to be a little darker than I am. If I did it before I didn't realize it, and I wasn't to blame. But if I do it now, intentionally, I'm just drawing the color-line, and that wouldn't be right. What can I do?"

Her visitor smiled. "Do? Get out. Pass. What else?"

"That's impossible. There's mother. Wherever I'd go I'd have to take her, and she couldn't pass for anything but American Negro—"

Her protest was drowned in her visitor's laughter. It was harsh, strident laughter, like the suddenly stifled outburst she'd heard at Hank's that night. It was long, loud laughter that left the visitor breathless, panting pitiably.

Of a sudden Evelyn sat upright, fearfully aware that the laughter of her dream had merged into something real and close. She listened a moment. It was her mother in the next room. Asthma again.

She met both the women lodgers in the hall, frightened, helpless. "Did you hear her?"

Shortly Evelyn hurried from her mother's room, leaving the two women with her. She slipt on as little as she dared and sped out to get a physician.

A half hour passed before she returned with one. She noted a bright light in the front room and hastened to it thinking the two women had taken her mother there for air; but she found only the two of them, huddled together on the sofa, shivering in their bathrobes, with something close to panic in their eyes.

4

Jimmy MacLoed, red-eyed, stretchy, disconsolate, and broke, all the event of a prolonged and fatal night of stud-poker, got up at noon-time, dressed, and strolled languidly into the street, wondering from whom he could bum four bits for breakfast. At the corner of One Hundred and Thirty-fifth Street and the Avenue he encountered Jay Martin, hurrying to lunch. This was luck, for Jay always had bucks.

"See me go for breakfast?" he asked.

"No," grinned Jay, "but I'll add it to the five I'm by you already."

Dick's lunchroom seemed to have been designed so that the two waitresses could serve everybody without moving from where they stood. You could pass from the little front door to your stool before the counter without colliding with someone only when there was no one else there. Many a patron had unexpectedly thrust his knife further into his mouth than he intended because some damn fool, rushing out, squeezed between him and the wall. But one of the waitresses was pretty; and the ham with your eggs was cut thick, not shaved; and the French fried potatoes were really French fried, not boiled ones warmed over in grease. Jay and MacLoed considered themselves lucky to find two of the dozen stools still unoccupied.

They gave their orders and rested their elbows on the counter while the waitress that wasn't pretty threw down some pewter implements before them.

"Too bad about Evelyn's old lady, huh?" said MacLoed.

Jay became grave. "Too bad about Evelyn."

"Evelyn? Wha' d' y' mean?"

"Nobody's seen her since the funeral."

"No? Only three days. Maybe she's gone off for a rest."

"Didn't leave any notice at the office."

"Think she went dippy and jumped in the river or somethin'?"

"No. But I think she's jumped out of Harlem."

"You mean—passin'?"

"I don't know. The last time I saw her she was sick enough to do anything. Those two women roomers wouldn't stay in the house another night. None of her friends would either, even after her mother was safe in the undertaker's. She had three rotten days of it, except when my mother was there. Nobody much went to the funeral. I sent the only flowers. Next day, my mother went around to see how she was making out and found nobody home.—There hasn't been, since."

"Didn't leave word with nobody, huh?"

"Nope."

" 'S funny. 'D she have any relations?"

"Nope."

"Hm! Then that's what she's doin' all right."

"Passing?"

"Yea." Mac contemplated the ham and eggs that the homely waitress had just slid between his elbows. "Don't blame her. I'd do the same thing if I didn't have so damn much brownskin family."

"Why?"

"Why?—Why not? Wouldn't you?"

"Be white if I could?" Jay paid the waitress. "I don't know."

"The hell you don't. What would you be afraid of? Meetin' somebody? Hell! Don't see 'em. If they jump you, freeze 'em.—But you'd never meet anybody you knew. S'posin' you looked white and didn't have anything to stop you, what would be the hold-back?"

Jay chewed a minute thoughtfully. Then he looked at MacLoed as if wondering whether he was worth a reply. Finally he answered:

"Kids."

"Kids?" Mac ingested this with two pieces of the real French fried potatoes well swabbed in ham gravy. "You mean you might get married and have a little pickaninny to account for, huh? Well, you could get out o' that all right. Just tell her she'd been runnin' around with a nigger and quit."

Jay knew MacLoed too well to be shocked. "You might not want to quit," he said. "You might like her. Or you might have a conscience."

"Humph! Conscience and kids. Old stuff, buddy."

"And even if your scheme worked with a man who was passing, it wouldn't with a woman. She couldn't tell her white husband he'd been running around with a colored girl. That wouldn't explain the pickaninny."

"No.—The woman catches hell both ways, don't she?"

"It's a damned shame." Jay was speaking rather to himself than to MacLoed. "I know. I took her—places. That girl was white—as white as anybody could be. Lord only knows what she'll be now."

Three or four men had come in, standing in what little space they could find and reading the menu signs while they awaited seats. No one paid any particular attention to one of these who was "ofay." White patrons were not infrequent in Dick's. This one had moved close enough to Jay to hear his last statement. He touched him on the shoulder. As Jay turned the white drew aside his coat, and Jay glimpsed a badge. When the officer motioned him to step outside, there was nothing else to do, and with an "Excuse me a minute, Mac—be right back," he preceded the other to the sidewalk.

Outside, Jay asked, "What's the idea?"

"Didn't want to start a row in that dump. Somebody might 'a had a gun."

"What's the idea?"

"Let's walk down this way." Jay knew better than to refuse, though "this way" led toward the police station. "So you think it's a damned shame, do you? Well, I think it's a damned shame, too."

"What the devil are you talking about?"

"Come down out o' that tree, son. I'm talking about you and the white girl you picked up at Manhattan Casino a while back. You y'self said just now she's white. That about settles it."

"White? Why, I only meant——"

"I heard you. You said 'white.' White's white, ain't it?"

Presently: "What's the charge?"

"Don't play dumb, bud. There's been too damn much of this thing goin' on here. We're goin' to stop it."

Suddenly Jay Martin laughed.

The two walked on in silence.

5

From a point in the wide, deep balcony's dimness, Jay followed the quick-shifting scenes; not those on the screen at which he stared, but others, flashing out from his mind.

Coney Island. He and Evelyn arm in arm, inconsequent, hilarious, eating sticky popcorn out of the same bag, dipping in at the same time, gaily disputing the last piece. Their laughter suddenly chilled by an intentionally audible remark: "Look at that white girl with a nigger." A half-dozen lowering rowdies. Evelyn urging him away. People staring.

An ice-cream parlor. A rackety mechanical piano, tables with white tops and dappled wire legs; outside One Hundred and Twenty-fifth Street traffic shadowing past; Evelyn and he, wilted with the heat, waiting a couple of eternities for a waitress; he finally looking about impatiently, beckoning to one, who leers through him. The proprietor. "Of course we don't mind serving the lady, sir; but while we can't actually refuse, why—er—frankly your presence is unprofitable to us, sir." People staring.

The subway. He and Evelyn in a corner of the car. Above the rattle and bump of doors and clang of signal-gong, wild laughter, coarse, loud. Different. Negro laughter. Headlong into the car, stumbling over one another, a group of hilarious young colored people. Men contesting seats with women, and winning; women flouncing defiantly down on the men's knees. Conscious of the attention attracted by their loudness; pleased with it. Train starting, accelerating. Train-din rising. Negro-noise rising through and above it, like sharp pain through and above dull ache. "Oh, you high yaller!" Evelyn ashamed. People staring.

Finally a back room in the police station. Two or three red-faced ruffians in brass-buttoned uniforms, sneering, menacing, quite like those Coney Island rowdies. Himself, outraged, at bay, demanding to know on just what score he was there. Surly accusation, hot denial, scalding epithet—flame. A blow. Swift, violent struggle. "Now mebbe y'll leave white women alone!" Emptiness. After a time release; release raw with bodily anguish, raw with the recurrent sting of that cover-all charge of policemen, "resisting an officer."

What an enormity, blackness! From the demons and ogres and ravens of fairy tales on; storm-clouds, eclipses, night, the valley of the shadow, gloom, hell. White, the standard of goodness and perfection. Christ himself, white. All the angels. Imagine a black angel! A black angel with a flat nose and thick lips, laughing loudly. The devil! Standards, of course; but beneath the standards, what? An instinctive shrinking from the dark? He'd seen a little white child run in terror from his father once, the first black man the child had ever seen. Instinctive? He looked about. All this balcony full of fellow creatures instinctively shrinking from him. No help for it? Awful idea. Unbearable.

A general murmur of amusement refocussed his attention for a moment on the screen. Two chubby infants sat side by side on a doorstep; the one shiny black, with a head full of kinks and eyes of twinkling midnight; the other white, with eyes of gray and the noon-day sun in its hair; both dimpled and grinning and happy. Kids. Old stuff, buddy. Evelyn—would she dare?

The thoughts that gathered and throbbed like an abscess were suddenly incised. Off to one side, a row or two ahead, he had caught sight of an oddly familiar face. The dimness seemed to lift mock-ingly, so that he should have no doubt. Evelyn, like an answer. Dif-ferent, but—Evelyn. The attitude of the young man beside her was that of an escort, and something in his profile, in the fairness of his hair and skin, discernible even through the dusk, marked him to the staring Jay as unmistakably white. Watching with quickened pulse Jay saw the young man's hand move forward over Evelyn's arm, lying on the elbow-rest between them; move forward till it reached her own hand, which turned palm-upward to clasp it. Saw one white hand close firmly over the other.

He rose abruptly and made his way past stubborn knees to the aisle. The orchestra struck up a popular bit of Negro jazz. It fell on his ears like a guffaw: the familiar refrain of "Yaller Gal's Gone Out o' Style."

May Miller

(1899–   )

THE DAUGHTER of the legendary Dean Kelly Miller, May Miller (Mrs. John L. Sullivan) was born in Washington, D.C., and reared in the Howard University community. A graduate of Howard, she has done advanced work at American and Columbia universities, specializing in drama and poetry. For twenty years May Miller taught English and speech in the Frederick Douglass High School of Baltimore, Maryland, and supervised that city's junior high school English program.

On her return to the Capital, she entered fully into a literary career, devoting her major energies to writing poetry and to helping create in her native city an atmosphere which encouraged literary effort on the part of all the people. When the D.C. Commission on the Arts and Humanities was established, she was appointed as a literary member. While chairperson, she did outstanding work in poetry with the children of the District's public schools. As one critic has said, "May Miller is a Washington institution as well as a Washington poet."

May Miller's last volume of verse shows the kind of growth from volume to volume we have come to expect from her. Quietly philosophical and religious, her verses are the expression of a mature, sophisticated woman who has looked at life steadily and sees it whole.

Her poetry is a fusion of yesterday and today. Still using the classical and biblical allusions of an earlier poetry, she has made them an unobtrusive part of her current verse. She has put old wine in new bottles, and the result is a sensitive, modern poetry. *The Ransomed Wait* is an impressive example of this mixture of the old and new.

Among May Miller's many honors are the Institute for the Preservation and Study of African American Writing Award for 1986, the New York African Company's award for excellence in the theater, and the Howard University Distinguished Graduate Award for 1987.

For the past two decades Miller has served as poet-in-residence in the following institutions: Monmouth College, the University of Wisconsin, Bluefield State College (Bluefield, West Virginia), Exeter Academy, Southern University, and Wellesley. She has given numerous readings of her poetry over radio and television and in many public institutions, including the Smithsonian, the Martin Luther King, Jr., Library, the Folger Library, and the Library of Congress.

In addition to the numerous poems that have appeared in anthologies and outstanding periodicals, May Miller's major publications have been *Negro History in Thirteen Plays*, with Willis Richardson (1935); *Into the Clearing* (1959); *Poems* (1962); *Lyrics of Three Women*, with Katie Lyle and Maude Rubin (1964); *Not That Far* (1973); *The Clearing and Beyond* (1974); *Dust of Uncertain Journey* (1975); *Halfway to the Sun* (1981); and *The Ransomed Wait* (1983).

For an excellent study of May Miller's life and works, see *Dictionary of Literary Biography, Volume 41: Afro-American Poets since 1955* (1985). This account, written by Winifred L. Soelting, discusses Miller's dramatic contributions and career as well as her poetry. See also *Afro-American Women Writers* (1988) by Ann Allen Shockley, which contains biographical and critical commentary, and Claudia Tate's "The Pondered Moment: May Miller's Meditative Poetry" in *New Directions* (January 1985). See also Jeanne-Marie A. Miller's recent article, "Georgia Douglas Johnson and May Miller: Forgotten Playwrights of the New Negro Renaissance," in *CLA Journal* (June 1990).

Of the poems by May Miller that appear in this anthology, "Blazing Accusation," "Alain LeRoy Locke," "A Closing," and "For Robert Hayden" come from her volume *The Ransomed Wait*, published by the Lotus Press in 1983. "Anemones" comes from *The Federal Poet* (Winter, 1984–85).

GIFT FROM KENYA

Within the day a seventh time
I touch the pale wood antelope.
Forever squat on spindle legs
He tips his head to danger.
(But O to see the pronghorn herd
Run the ridge of a blunted hill
With the skyline copper-red).
It is too late to hear the axe
Which, in the ruined cedar grove,
Shivered down like a death drum note
To fell the trees that would become
The multi-hundred antelopes.

Some fluid centuries ago
My ancient father knew the tree;
Then young and bending in a wind,
Played near the sapling
While the hours of morning whipped

Singing round his loins.
When dark came down and the vultures slept,
In the fragrance of dew-heavy bark
He watched determined stars in course.
As man, in a glittering night of power
He traced with others curving paths
Leading out from the sheltering boughs.

The cedar carved to figurine,
And to all its counterparts,
Is hunched upon the years to come.
The man and his way are old in me,
Old in the unborn who wait
To hold the ice-aged heritage
That has no end in single flesh
However wound in death.

ALAIN LEROY LOCKE
(Teacher of Aesthetics)

He has gone from the tower,
one who led others in the climb
to realize tall spaces.
He spoke of truth and beauty
as if walking with companions.
Once looking beyond young faces
to the campus green with spring
he returned to smaller stature
sharing with gaping students awe
of phenomena of reason and being.

His casual mention of Leonardo Da Vinci's
left-hand angel and the Artist's dream
of helicopter wings and submarines
stunned us awake to our ignorance.
Side by side with Michael Angelo
he seemed to hang from
the Great Cathedral dome
to will humanity an ageless renaissance.

We shared with him a flow of knowledge
drowning sometime in his esoteric phrase
as clipped words polished Benin bronze
to a glowing heritage.

Responding to new imagery and impulse
we probed the dark world origin
of the Picasso riddle and romped
in a bacchanal of our own.

Recalling now we fit his tenets
to nuances, the rationale of living
only half-sensed in the early day.
Though late, we reassess the life
he assigned the abstract,
the continuum of reason he believed to be.
So remembering, we vision the tower
urged by echoes of a learned man.

ANEMONES

Prologue:
> Sun lifted morning
> to the embrace of light
> falling captured on the page:
> "Our universe created from nothing,
> to nothing may return."

> Give back the æons passed—
> the ten, the twenty billion years
> before time and space.
> Thought of it ends hysteria:
> the second of creation,
> a universe of other suns,
> the billions of speeding galaxies,
> the realm of stars hung somewhere
> between expansion and collapse.
> All this by chance?
> Isn't the questioning the answer?

> Innocent we probe backward
> to appraise nature's course
> from nothing to nothing
> as determined we chart
> a calculated path to doom.
> Only count ten fingers, ten toes
> and grasp the chill we face:
> the cold stare of the last child,

the stilled arms of lovers
stretched to emptiness.

Epilogue:
In this threatened room
a bright china bird stands tall
in a bowl of fading blossoms
which, for the sake of poetry,
we'll call anemones.

A CLOSING

In a house of empty rooms
I thought I heard a door close
down the long hall.
I couldn't know
whether someone had entered,
whether someone had left.
No further step,
simply the closing of a door—
an absence of other defined stir,
more like the hum of water
in a hidden spring,
like a starved echo
from an exacting hill
I could not measure.
I reached for the reassuring hand.
It was not there.
He had gone ahead.

BLAZING ACCUSATION

(In racial upheaval in Birmingham, Alabama, 1963,
four young girls died in the blasting of a church.)

Too early a death for those who young
have lost prophecy in blast and flame.
The broken have been assembled
as best could be to pose for burial.
The man in bleak authority intones
the word that cannot tell

when last the girls stood singing
under the sweetest tree,
how remote from nightmare
they giggled secrets believing
death was the end for the old.

After the moans are choked
and the flowers gone petalless,
the girls will be with greatgrandparents,
themselves not long in that last room.
Mothers and fathers,
grandfathers and grandmothers
still pace the waking street
though few are the footfalls
that echo where the children lie.

But walk they will
the sixty-odd more years they're due.
Beyond allotted time and self
the four of them will go
down red gullies of guilt
and alleys of dark memories,
through snagging fields of scarecrows,
and up an unforgetting hill
to blazon accusation of an age.

FOR ROBERT HAYDEN

He extended to truths
he believed abide
and called to comrades,
those faltering in the run
(the hopeless and the doomed)
and to those who, gifted,
lighted their flares
at his larger flame.
He had known them all,
had lived their stories
(the defeats, the acclaim)
while tracking the path
to a high green garden
where honor etches
a crystalline goal:
love of all mankind and art.

Melvin B. Tolson

(1898–1966)

MELVIN BEAUNORUS TOLSON seems to have taken all vocations to be his province. In an interview he tells us that he was, among other things, a "shoeshine boy, stevedore, soldier, janitor, packinghouse worker, cook on a railroad, waiter in beachfront hotels, boxer, actor, football coach, director of drama, lecturer for the NAACP, organizer of sharecroppers' unions, teacher, father of Ph.D.s, poet laureate of a foreign country, painter, newspaper columnist, fourtime mayor of a town, facer of mobs."[1] He could have added that he read everything and remembered everything he read.

The son of a self-taught but scholarly Methodist minister father and a musically talented mother, Tolson was born in Moberly, Missouri, in 1898. He attended elementary schools in Missouri and Iowa, where his father had churches, and finished high school in Kansas City, Missouri. He was class poet, captain of the football team, and both actor and director of the Greek Club's little theater. In 1919 he went to Fisk University but transferred the following year to Lincoln University (Pennsylvania), where he graduated with honors in 1923. He earned an M.A. in English from Columbia University in 1940. During his years of graduate study, Tolson received a fellowship in literature from the Rockefeller Foundation.

Melvin Tolson taught for many years at two schools: Wiley College in Texas and Langston University in Oklahoma. While in the latter institution, he served four terms as mayor of the town of Langston. He also wrote for many years a witty column for the *Washington, D.C. Tribune* called "Caviar and Cabbage." At the time of his death, Tolson was Avalon Professor of the Humanities at Tuskegee.

Although he had written a great deal before, Tolson did not receive national attention until he won the National Poetry Contest sponsored by the American Negro Exposition in Chicago for his long poem "Dark Symphony"—a work which was published in *Atlantic Monthly* (September 1941). Divided into six sections, each with a musical name, "Dark Symphony" was typical of most of the black poetry written at the time. A mixture of the usual parade of black heroes, of protest elements, and the loyalty-in-spite-of theme, the poem ends on an optimistic note: international brotherhood. The poem was published in Tolson's first collection

---

[1] Herbert Hill, ed., *Anger and Beyond*, (New York: Harper and Row, 1966), 184.

of verse, *Rendezvous with America* (1944). The same themes appear throughout this collection. It is not a great first collection, and it contains most of the themes expected of an African American at the time.

The second collection, *Libretto for the Republic of Liberia* (1953), however, is sensationally different. In 1947 Liberia commissioned Tolson as poet laureate of the republic's centennial celebration. The complete poem was not published until 1953, but a section of it, "Ti," appeared in *Poetry* (July 1950). It was this segment that attracted Allen Tate, who eventually wrote the laudatory preface to the 1953 publication. Tolson, Tate tells us, shows "a great gift for language, a profound historical sense, and a first-rate intelligence at work." After asserting that Tolson was the first black poet to assimilate "completely the full poetic language of the Anglo-Saxon tradition," Tate makes derogatory remarks about the materials and idiom of other black poets. Needless to say, black critics have never taken seriously Tate's comments. These comments, however, served to make Tolson a nationally known figure. The poem itself is a very difficult work. Even though it has sixteen pages of scholarly notes (in several different languages), it is still hard to understand. In addition, the work makes a complete break with Tolson's former conventional style, and this compounds the difficulty with the poem.

Tolson's last major publication, *Harlem Gallery, Book I: The Curator* (1965), also has an introduction by a distinguished critic, Karl Shapiro. His praise of the poem is just as extravagant as that of Tate. When he says, among other startling comments, that "Tolson writes in Negro," one can only wonder how such an outstanding critic could make such a bizarre statement. *Harlem Gallery*, though not quite as difficult to understand as *Libretto*, is also obscure in some sections. After reading the work, one may ask, What is Tolson trying to do? Whatever the answer, the reader will find *Harlem Gallery* a fascinating volume.

For comments on Tolson's life and poetry, see Joy Flasch's excellent study, *Melvin B. Tolson* (1972); see also Arthur P. Davis's *From the Dark Tower* (1974); Dudley Randall's "Melvin B. Tolson: Portrait of a Poet as Raconteur," *Negro Digest* (January 1966); and Maria K. Mootry's "The Step of Iron Feet: Creative Practice in the War Sonnets of Melvin B. Tolson and Gwendolyn Brooks," *Obsidian II: Black Literature in Review* 2 (Winter 1987).

Three book-length works on Tolson have appeared in recent years: Robert M. Farnsworth's *Melvin B. Tolson, 1898–1966: Plain Talk and Poetic Prophecy* (1984); *Caviar and Cabbage: Selected Columns by Melvin B. Tolson from the Washington Tribune, 1937–44*, which Farnsworth also edited (1982); and Mariann Russell's *Melvin B. Tolson's "Harlem Gallery": A Literary Analysis* (1980).

The following poem is the entire "Psi" section of *Harlem Gallery, Book I: The Curator*, originally published by Twayne Publishers, Inc. (1965).

PSI

Black Boy,
let me get up from the white man's Table of Fifty Sounds
in the kitchen; let me gather the crumbs and cracklings
of this autobio-fragment,
before the curtain with the skull and bones descends.

Many a *t* in the ms.
I've left without a cross,
many an *i* without a dot.
A dusky Lot
with a third degree and a second wind and a seventh turn
of pitch-and-toss,
my psyche escaped the Sodom of Gylt
and the Big White Boss.

Black Boy,
you stand before your heritage,
naked and agape;
cheated like a mockingbird
pecking at a Zuexian grape,
pressed like an awl to do
duty as a screw-
driver, you
ask the American Dilemma in you:
"If the trying plane
of Demos fail,
what will the trowel
of Uncle Tom avail?"

Black Boy,
in this race, at this time, in this place,
to be a Negro artist is to be
a flower of the gods, whose growth
is dwarfed at an early stage—
a Brazilian owl moth,
a giant among his own in an acreage
dark with the darkman's designs,
where the milieu moves back downward like the sloth.

Black Boy,
true—you

"Psi" by Melvin Tolson in *Harlem Gallery*. Copyright 1970 and reprinted with the permission of Twayne Publishers, a division of G.K. Hall & Co., Boston.

have not
dined and wined
(*ignoti nulla cupido*)
in the El Dorado of aeried Art,
for unreasoned reasons;
and your artists, not so lucky as the Buteo,
find themselves without a
skyscape sanctuary
in the
season of seasons:
in contempt of the contemptible,
refuse the herb of grace, the rue
of Job's comforter;
take no
lie-tea in lieu
of Broken Orange Pekoe.
Doctor Nkomo said: "*What* is he who smacks
his lips when dewrot eats away the golden grain
of self-respect exposed like flax
to the rigors of sun and rain?"

Black Boy,
every culture,
every caste,
every people,
every class,
facing the barbarians
with lips hubris-curled,
believes its death rattle omens
the *Dies Irae* of the world.

Black Boy,
summon Boas and Dephino,
Blumenbach and Koelreuter,
from their posts
around the gravestone of Bilbo,
who, with cancer in his mouth,
orated until he quaked the magnolias of the South,
while the pocketbooks of his weeping black serfs
shriveled in the drouth;
summon the ghosts
of scholars with rams' horns from Jericho
and facies in letters from Jerusalem,
so
we may ask them:
"What is a Negro?"

Black Boy,
what's in a people's name that wries the brain
like the neck of a barley bird?
Can sounding brass create
an ecotype with a word?

Black Boy,
beware of the thin-bladed mercy
stroke, for one drop of Negro blood
(V. *The Black Act of the F. F. V.*)
opens the flood-
gates of the rising tide of color
and jettisons
the D. A. R. in the Heraclitean flux
with Uncle Tom and
Crispus Attucks.
The Black Belt White,
painstaking as a bedbug in
a tenant farmer's truckle bed,
rabbit-punched old Darrow
because
he quoted Darwin's sacred laws
(instead of the Lord God Almighty's)
and gabbled that the Catarrhine ape
(the C from a Canada goose nobody knows)
appears,
after X's of years,
in the vestigial shape
of the Nordic's thin lips, his aquiline nose,
his straight hair,
orangutanish on legs and chest and head.
Doctor Nkomo, a votary of touch-and-go,
who can stand the gaff
of Negrophobes and, like Aramis,
parry a thrust with a laugh,
said:
"In spite of the pig in the python's coils,
in spite of Blake's lamb in the jaws of the tiger,
Nature is kind, even in the raw: she toils
. . . aeons and aeons and aeons . . .
gives the African a fleecy canopy
to protect the seven faculties of the brain
from the burning convex lens of the sun;
she foils
whiteness

(without disdain)
to bless the African
(as Herodotus marvels)
with the birthright of a burnt skin for work or fun;
she roils
the Aryan
(as his eye and ear repose)
to give the African an accommodation nose
that cools the drying-up air;
she entangles the epidermis in broils
that keep the African's body free from lice-infested hair.
As man to man,
the Logos is
Nature is on the square
with the African.
If a black man circles the rim
of the Great White World, he will find
(even if Adamness has made him half blind)
the bitter waters of Marah *and*
the fresh fountains of Elim."

Although his transition
was a far cry
from Shakespeare to Sardou,
the old Africanist's byplay gave
no soothing feverfew
to the Dogs in the Zulu Club;
said he:
"A Hardyesque artistry
of circumstance
divides the Whites and Blacks in life,
like the bodies of the dead
eaten by vultures
in a Tower of Silence.
Let, then, the man with a maggot in his head
lean . . . lean . . . lean
on race or caste or class,
for the wingless worms of blowflies shall grub,
dry and clean,
the stinking skeletons of these,
when the face of the macabre weather-
cock turns to the torrid wind of misanthropy;
and later their bones shall be swept together
(like the Parsees')
in the Sepulchre of Anonymity."

A Zulu Wit cleared away his unsunned
mood with dark laughter;
but I sensed the thoughts of Doctor Nkomo
pacing nervously to and fro
like Asscher's, after
he'd cleaved the giant Cullinan Diamond.

Black Boy,
the vineyard is the fittest place
in which to booze (with Omar) and study
soil and time and integrity—
the telltale triad of grape and race.

Palates that can read the italics
of *salt* and *sugar* know
a grapevine
transplanted from Bordeaux
to Pleasant Valley
cannot give grapes that make a Bordeaux wine.

Like the sons of the lone mother of dead empires,
who boasted their ancestors,
page after page—
wines are peacocky
in their vintage and their age,
disdaining the dark ways of those engaging
in the profits
of chemical aging.
When the bluebirds sing
their perennial anthem
a capriccio, in the Spring,
the sap begins to move up the stem
of the vine, and the wine in the bed of the deep
cask stirs in its winter sleep.
Its bouquet
comes with the years, dry or wet;
so the connoisseurs say:
"The history of the wine
is repeated by the vine."

Black Boy,
beware of wine labels,
for the Republic does not guarantee
what the phrase "Château Bottled" means—
the estate, the proprietor, the quality.
This ignominy will baffle you, Black Boy,

because the white man's law
has raked your butt many a time
with fang and claw.
Beware of the waiter who wraps
a napkin around your Clos Saint Thierry,
if Chance takes you into high-hat places
open to all creeds and races
born to be or not to be.
Beware of the pop
of a champagne cork:
like the flatted fifth and octave jump in Bebop,
it is theatrical
in Vicksburg or New York.
Beware of the champagne cork
that does not swell up like your ma when she had you—*that*
comes out flat,
because the bottle of wine
is dead . . . dead
like Uncle Tom and the Jim Crow Sign.
Beware . . . yet
your dreams in the Great White World
shall be unthrottled
by pigmented and unpigmented lionhearts,
for we know *without no*
every people, by and by, produces its "Château Bottled."

White Boy,
as regards the ethnic origin
of Black Boy and me,
the *What* in Socrates' *"Tò tí"*
is for the musk-ox habitat of anthropologists;
but there is another question,
dangerous as a moutaba tick,
secreted in the house
of every Anglo-Saxon sophist and hick:

Who is a Negro?
(I am a White in deah ole Norfolk.)
Who is a White?
(I am a Negro in little old New York.)
Since my mongrelization is invisible
and my Negroness a state of mind conjured up
by Stereotypus, I am a chameleon
on *that* side of the Mason-Dixon
that a white man's conscience
is not on.

My skin is as white
as a Roman's toga when he sought an office on the sly;
my hair is as blond
as xanthein;
my eyes are as blue
as the hawk's-eye.
At the Olympian powwow of curators,
when I revealed my Negroness,
my peers became shocked like virgins in a house
where satyrs tattooed on female thighs heralds of success.

White Boy,
counterfeit scholars have used
the newest brush-on Satinlac,
to make our ethnic identity
crystal clear for the lowest IQ
in every mansion and in every shack.
Therefore,
according to the myth that Negrophobes bequeath
to the Lost Gray Cause, since Black Boy is the color
of betel-stained teeth,
he and I
(from ocular proof
that cannot goof)
belong to races
whose dust-of-the-earth progenitors
the Lord God Almighty created
of different bloods,
in antipodal places.
However,
even the F. F. V. pate
is aware that laws defining a Negro
blackjack each other within and without a state.
The Great White World, White Boy, leaves you in a sweat
like a pitcher with three runners on the bases;
and, like Kant, you seldom get
your grammar straight—yet,
you are the wick that absorbs the oil in my lamp,
in all kinds of weather;
and we are teeth in the pitch wheel
that work together.

White Boy,
when I hear the word *Negro* defined,
why does it bring to mind
the chef, the gourmand, the belly-god

the disease of kings, the culinary art
in alien lands, Black Mammy in a Dixie big house,
and the dietitian's chart?
Now, look at Black Boy scratch his head!
It's a stereotypic gesture of Uncle Tom,
a learned Gentleman of Color said
in his monumental tome,
The *Etiquette of the New Negro*,
which,
the publishers say,
by the way,
should be in every black man's home.

The Negro is a dish in the white man's kitchen—
a potpourri,
an ola-podrida,
a mixie-maxie,
a hotchpotch of lineal ingredients;
with UN guests at his table,
the host finds himself a Hamlet on the spot,
for, in spite of his catholic pose,
the Negro dish is a dish nobody knows:
to some . . . tasty,
like an exotic condiment—
to others . . . unsavory
and inelegant.

White Boy,
the Negro dish is a mix
like . . . and *un*like
pimiento brisque, chop suey,
eggs à la Goldenrod, and eggaroni;
tongue-and-corn casserole, mulligan stew,
baked fillets of halibut, and cheese fondue;
macaroni milanaise, egg-milk shake,
mullagatawny soup, and sour-milk cake.

Just as the Chinese lack
an ideogram for "to be,"
our lexicon has no definition
for an ethnic amalgam like Black Boy and me.

Behold a Gordian knot without
the *beau geste* of an Alexander's sword!
Water, O Modern Mariner, water, everywhere,
unfit for *vitro di trina* glass
or the old-oaken-bucket's gourd!

For dark hymens on the auction block,
the lord of the mansion knew the macabre score:
not a dog moved his tongue,
not a lamb lost a drop of blood to protect the door.
O
Xenos of Xanthos,
what midnight-to-dawn lecheries,
in cabin and big house,
produced these brown hybrids and yellow motleys?

White Boy,
Buchenwald is a melismatic song
whose single syllable is sung to blues notes
to dark wayfarers who listen for the gong
at the crack of doom along
. . . that Lonesome Road . . .
before they travel on.

A Pelagian with the *raison d'être* of a Negro,
I cannot say I have outwitted dread,
for I am conscious of the noiseless tread
of the Yazoo tiger's ball-like pads behind me
in the dark
as I trudge ahead,
up and up . . . that Lonesome Road . . . up and up.

In a Vision in a Dream,
from the frigid seaport of the proud Xanthochroid,
the good ship *Défineznegro*
sailed fine, under an unabridged moon,
to reach the archipelago
Nigeridentité.
In the Strait of Octoroon,
off black Scylla,
after the typhoon Phobos, out of the Stereotypus Sea,
had rived her hull and sail to a T,
the *Défineznegro* sank the rock
and disappeared in the abyss
(*Vanitas vanitatum!*)
of white Charybdis.

Zora Neale Hurston

(1891–1960)

A COLORFUL AND UNPREDICTABLE FIGURE, Zora Neale Hurston was a popular member of that group of young writers whom we now think of as the "Harlem School." Wallace Thurman (*Infants of the Spring*) and Langston Hughes (*The Big Sea*) wrote amusing anecdotes about her. They and others thought she was a little too cosy with white folks (during the last decade of her life she became a rank conservative), but they all considered her very talented, and she was. Zora Neale Hurston contributed to the Harlem Renaissance as a fiction writer, as a dramatist, as an initiator of literary ventures (she was one of the editors of *Fire*), and above all else as an excellent folklorist.

Born in 1891, in Eatonville, Florida, an all-Negro town, which she used fully in two of her novels, Hurston was educated at Morgan Academy (now Morgan State University), Howard University, and Barnard College, receiving from the last-named institution her B.A. in 1927. At Barnard she studied anthropology under Franz Boas, who subsequently recommended her for several important research projects and fellowships in the field. In 1936/37, Hurston received a Guggenheim grant for the study of folklore in the West Indies, which included the study of voodoo in Haiti and Louisiana. Although she lived until 1960, her last publication was in 1948. She died poverty-stricken and half-forgotten.

Zora Neale Hurston wrote the following major works: *Jonah's Gourd Vine* (1934); *Mules and Men* (1935), based on folk material; *Their Eyes Were Watching God* (1937), now her best-known novel for reasons that follow; *Tell My Horse* (1938), also based on folk material; *Moses, Man of the Mountain* (1939), a retelling of the biblical story which makes Moses an Egyptian prince, not a Jew; *Dust Tracks on a Road: An Autobiography* (1942, 1984); and *Seraph on the Sewanee* (1948), a novel whose major characters are white.

Far more highly regarded by present-day critics than she was when alive, Zora Neale Hurston in recent years has come into her own. Today's black writers, particularly female authors, look upon Hurston as a pioneer creator of the "new" black woman. Her main character in *Their Eyes Were Watching God* is an independent, unconventional woman who finally decides to live on her terms rather than on those imposed by custom, and hence Janie is the ancestor of many characters in contemporary black novels.

One of the fullest and most scholarly studies on Zora Neale Hurston is Robert Hemenway's *Zora Neale Hurston: A Literary Biography* (1977). See also Darwin Turner's *In a Minor Chord: Three Afro-American Writers and Their Search for Identity* (1971) and *I Love Myself When I Am Laughing . . . and Then Again When I Am Looking Mean and Impressive: A Zora Neale Hurston Reader* (1979), edited by Alice Walker, with an introduction by Mary Helen Washington. Bernice Johnson Reagon's entry in *Dictionary of American Negro Biography* is an illuminating and sympathetic analysis of Hurston's life. See also Arthur P. Davis's, *From the Dark Tower* (1974), and Ann Allen Shockley's *Afro-American Women Writers* (1988). Three other studies on Hurston have been published in recent years. They are Lillie P. Howard's biography, *Zora Neale Hurston* (1980), and *Zora Neale Hurston*, a collection of critical essays and lectures edited by Harold Bloom (1986) and Karla Holloway's *The Character of the Word: The Texts of Zora Neale Hurston* (1987). The renewed interest in Hurston is also reflected in the republication of *Tell My Horse* (1985) and the 1981 collection of her short stories, *Spunk*, with a foreword by Bob Callahan.

Of the two excerpts that follow, the first comes from *Mules and Men*. As a trained anthropologist, Hurston knew folk speech thoroughly and wrote it poetically. Very few authors of her day could write or tell a "tall tale" as well as Zora Neale Hurston, or knew as many. The second selection comes from *Their Eyes Were Watching God*.

THE GILDED SIX-BITS

It was a Negro yard around a Negro house in a Negro settlement that looked to the payroll of the G. and G. Fertilizer works for its support.

But there was something happy about the place. The front yard was parted in the middle by a sidewalk from gate to doorstep, a sidewalk edged on either side by quart bottles driven neck down into the ground on a slant. A mess of homey flowers planted without a plan but blooming cheerily from their helter-skelter places. The fence and house were whitewashed. The porch and steps scrubbed white.

The front door stood open to the sunshine so that the floor of the front room could finish drying after its weekly scouring. It was Saturday. Everything clean from the front gate to the privy house.

Yard raked so that the strokes of the rake would make a pattern. Fresh newspaper cut in fancy edge on the kitchen shelves.

Missie May was bathing herself in the galvanized washtub in the bedroom. Her dark-brown skin glistened under the soapsuds that skittered down from her washrag. Her stiff young breasts thrust forward aggressively, like broad-based cones with the tips lacquered in black.

She heard men's voices in the distance and glanced at the dollar clock on the dresser.

"Humph! Ah'm way behind time t'day! Joe gointer be heah 'fore Ah get mah clothes on if Ah don't make haste."

She grabbed the clean meal sack at hand and dried herself hurriedly and began to dress. But before she could tie her slippers, there came the ring of singing metal on wood. Nine times.

Missie May grinned with delight. She had not seen the big tall man come stealing in the gate and creep up the walk grinning happily at the joyful mischief he was about to commit. But she knew that it was her husband throwing silver dollars in the door for her to pick up and pile beside her plate at dinner. It was this way every Saturday afternoon. The nine dollars hurled into the open door, he scurried to a hiding place behind the Cape jasmine bush and waited.

Missie May promptly appeared at the door in mock alarm.

"Who dat chunkin' money in mah do'way?" she demanded. No answer from the yard. She leaped off the porch and began to search the shrubbery. She peeped under the porch and hung over the gate to look up and down the road. While she did this, the man behind the jasmine darted to the chinaberry tree. She spied him and gave chase.

"Nobody ain't gointer be chunkin' money at me and Ah not do 'em nothin'," she shouted in mock anger. He ran around the house with Missie May at his heels. She overtook him at the kitchen door. He ran inside but could not close it after him before she crowded in and locked with him in a rough-and-tumble. For several minutes the two were a furious mass of male and female energy. Shouting, laughing, twisting, turning, tussling, tickling each other in the ribs; Missie May clutching onto Joe and Joe trying, but not too hard, to get away.

"Missie May, take yo' hand out mah pocket!" Joe shouted out between laughs.

"Ah ain't, Joe, not lessen you gwine gimme whateve' it is good you got in yo' pocket. Turn it go, Joe, do Ah'll tear yo' clothes."

"Go on tear 'em. You de one dat pushes de needles round heah. Move yo' hand, Missie May."

"Lemme git dat paper sack out yo' pocket. Ah bet it's candy kisses."

"Tain't. Move yo' hand. Woman ain't got no business in a man's clothes nohow. Go way."

Missie May gouged way down and gave an upward jerk and triumphed.

"Unhhunh! Ah got it! It 'tis so candy kisses. Ah knowed you had somethin' for me in yo' clothes. Now Ah got to see whut's in every pocket you got."

Joe smiled indulgently and let his wife go through all of his pockets and take out the things that he had hidden there for her to find. She bore off the chewing gum, the cake of sweet soap, the pocket handkerchief as if she had wrested them from him, as if they had not been bought for the sake of this friendly battle.

"Whew! dat play-fight done got me all warmed up!" Joe exclaimed. "Got me some water in de kittle?"

"Yo' water is on de fire and yo' clean things is cross de bed. Hurry up and wash yo'self and get changed so we kin eat. Ah'm hongry." As Missie said this, she bore the steaming kettle into the bedroom.

"You ain't hongry, sugar," Joe contradicted her. "Youse jes' a little empty. Ah'm de one whut's hongry. Ah could eat up camp meetin', back off 'ssociation, and drink Jurdan dry. Have it on de table when Ah git out de tub."

"Don't you mess wid mah business, man. You git in yo' clothes. Ah'm a real wife, not no dress and breath. Ah might not look lak one, but if you burn me, you won't git a thing but wife ashes."

Joe splashed in the bedroom and Missie May fanned around in the kitchen. A fresh red-and-white checked cloth on the table. Big pitcher of buttermilk beaded with pale drops of butter from the churn. Hot fried mullet, crackling bread, ham hock atop a mound of string beans and new potatoes, and perched on the windowsill a pone of spicy potato pudding.

Very little talk during the meal but that little consisted of banter that pretended to deny affection but in reality flaunted it. Like when Missie May reached for a second helping of the tater pone. Joe snatched it out of her reach.

After Missie May had made two or three unsuccessful grabs at the pan, she begged, "Aw, Joe, gimme some mo' dat tater pone."

"Nope, sweetenin' is for us menfolks. Y'all pritty lil frail eels don't need nothin' lak dis. You too sweet already."

"Please, Joe."

"Naw, naw. Ah don't want you to git no sweeter than whut you is already. We goin' down de road a lil piece t'night so you go put on yo' Sunday-go-to-meetin' things."

Missie May looked at her husband to see if he was playing some prank. "Sho nuff, Joe?"

"Yeah. We goin' to de ice cream parlor."

"Where de ice cream parlor at, Joe?"

"A new man done come heah from Chicago and he done got a place and took and opened it up for a ice cream parlor, and bein' as it's real swell, Ah wants you to be one de first ladies to walk in dere and have some set down."

"Do Jesus, Ah ain't knowed nothin' 'bout it. Who de man done it?"

"Mister Otis D. Slemmons, of spots and places—Memphis, Chicago, Jacksonville, Philadelphia and so on."

"Dat heavyset man wid his mouth full of gold teeths?"

"Yeah. Where did you see 'im at?"

"Ah went down to de sto' tuh git a box of lye and Ah seen 'im standin' on de corner talkin' to some of de mens, and Ah come on back and went to scrubbin' de floor, and he passed and tipped his hat whilst Ah was scourin' de steps. Ah thought Ah never seen *him* befo'."

Joe smiled pleasantly. "Yeah, he's up-to-date. He got de finest clothes Ah ever seen on a colored man's back."

"Aw, he don't look no better in his clothes than you do in yourn. He got a puzzlegut on 'im and he so chuckleheaded he got a pone behind his neck."

Joe looked down at his own abdomen and said wistfully: "Wisht Ah had a build on me lak he got. He ain't puzzlegutted, honey. He jes' got a corperation. Dat make 'm look lak a rich white man. All rich mens is got some belly on 'em."

"Ah seen de pitchers of Henry Ford and he's a spare-built man and Rockefeller look lak he ain't got but one gut. But Ford and Rockefeller and dis Slemmons and all de rest kin be as many-gutted as dey please, Ah's satisfied wid you jes' lak you is, baby. God took pattern after a pine tree and built you noble. Youse a pritty man, and if Ah knowed any way to make you mo' pritty still Ah'd take and do it."

Joe reached over gently and toyed with Missie May's ear. "You jes' say dat cause you love me, but Ah know Ah can't hold no light to Otis D. Slemmons. Ah ain't never been nowhere and Ah ain't got nothin' but you."

Missie May got on his lap and kissed him and he kissed back in kind. Then he went on. "All de womens is crazy 'bout 'im everywhere he go."

"How you know dat, Joe?"

"He tole us so hisself."

"Dat don't make it so. His mouf is cut crossways, ain't it? Well, he kin lie jes' lak anybody else."

"Good Lawd, Missie! You womens sho is hard to sense into

things. He's got a five-dollar gold piece for a stickpin and he got a ten-dollar gold piece on his watch chain and his mouf is jes' crammed full of gold teeths. Sho wisht it wuz mine. And whut make it so cool, he got money 'cumulated. And womens give it all to 'im."

"Ah don't see whut de womens see on 'im. Ah wouldn't give 'im a wink if de sheriff wuz after 'im."

"Well, he tole us how de white womens in Chicago give 'im all dat gold money. Se he don't 'low nobody to touch it at all. Not even put dey finger on it. Dey tole 'im not to. You kin make 'miration at it, but don't tetch it."

"Whyn't he stay up dere where dey so crazy 'bout 'im?"

"Ah reckon dey done made 'im vast-rich and he wants to travel some. He says dey wouldn't leave 'im hit a lick of work. He got mo' lady people crazy 'bout him than he kin shake a stick at."

"Joe, Ah hates to see you so dumb. Dat stray nigger jes' tell y'all anything and y'all b'lieve it."

"Go 'head on now, honey, and put on yo' clothes. He talkin' 'bout his pritty womens—Ah want 'im to see *mine*."

Missie May went off to dress and Joe spent the time trying to make his stomach punch out like Slemmons's middle. He tried the rolling swagger of the stranger, but found that his tall bone-and-muscle stride fitted ill with it. He just had time to drop back into his seat before Missie May came in dressed to go.

On the way home that night Joe was exultant. "Didn't Ah say ole Otis was swell? Can't he talk Chicago talk? Wuzn't dat funny whut he said when great big fat ole Ida Armstrong come in? He asted me, 'Who is dat broad wid de forte shake?' Dat's a new word. Us always thought forty was a set of figgers but he showed us where it means a whole heap of things. Sometimes he don't say forty, he jes' say thirty-eight and two and dat mean de same thing. Know whut he tole me when Ah wuz payin' for our ice cream? He say, 'Ah have to hand it to you, Joe. Dat wife of yours is jes' thirty-eight and two. Yes suh, she's forte!' Ain't he killin'?"

"He'll do in case of a rush. But he sho is got uh heap uh gold on 'im. Dat's de first time Ah ever seed gold money. It lookted good on him sho nuff, but it'd look a whole heap better on you."

"Who, me? Missie May, youse crazy! Where would a po' man lak me git gold money from?"

Missie May was silent for a minute, then she said, "Us might find some goin' long de road some time. Us could."

"Who would be losin' gold money round heah? We ain't even seen none dese white folks wearin' no gold money on dey watch chain. You must be figgerin' Mister Packard or Mister Cadillac goin' pass through heah."

"You don't know whut been lost 'round heah. Maybe somebody

way back in memorial times lost they gold money and went on off and it ain't never been found. An then if we wuz to find it, you could wear some 'thout havin' no gang of womens lak dat Slemmons say he got."

Joe laughed and hugged her. "Don't be so wishful 'bout me. Ah'm satisfied de way Ah is. So long as Ah be yo' husband, Ah don't keer 'bout nothin' else. Ah'd ruther all de other womens in de world to be dead than for you to have de toothache. Less we go to bed and git our night rest."

It was Saturday night once more before Joe could parade his wife in Slemmons's ice cream parlor again. He worked the night shift and Saturday was his only night off. Every other evening around six o'clock he left home, and dying dawn saw him hustling home around the lake, where the challenging sun flung a flaming sword from east to west across the trembling water.

That was the best part of life—going home to Missie May. Their whitewashed house, the mock battle on Saturday, the dinner and ice cream parlor afterwards, church on Sunday nights when Missie out-dressed any woman in town—all, everything, was right.

One night around eleven the acid ran out at the G. and G. The foreman knocked off the crew and let the steam die down. As Joe rounded the lake on his way home, a lean moon rode the lake in a silver boat. If anybody had asked Joe about the moon on the lake, he would have said he hadn't paid it any attention. But he saw it with his feelings. It made him yearn painfully for Missie. Creation ob-sessed him. He thought about children. They had been married more than a year now. They had money put away. They ought to be mak-ing little feet for shoes. A little boy child would be about right.

He saw a dim light in the bedroom and decided to come in through the kitchen door. He could wash the fertilizer dust off him-self before presenting himself to Missie May. It would be nice for her not to know that he was there until he slipped into his place in bed and hugged her back. She always liked that.

He eased the kitchen door open slowly and silently, but when he went to set his dinner bucket on the table he bumped it into a pile of dishes, and something crashed to the floor. He heard his wife gasp in fright and hurried to reassure her.

"Iss me, honey. Don't get skeered."

There was a quick, large movement in the bedroom. A rustle, a thud, and a stealthy silence. The light went out.

What? Robbers? Murderers? Some varmint attacking his helpless wife, perhaps. He struck a match, threw himself on guard and stepped over the doorsill into the bedroom.

The great belt on the wheel of Time slipped and eternity stood still. By the match light he could see the man's legs fighting with his breeches in his frantic desire to get them on. He had both chance and time to kill the intruder in his helpless condition—half in and half out of his pants—but he was too weak to take action. The shapeless enemies of humanity that live in the hours of Time had waylaid Joe. He was assaulted in his weakness. Like Samson awakening after his haircut. So he just opened his mouth and laughed.

The match went out and he struck another and lit the lamp. A howling wind raced across his heart, but underneath its fury he heard his wife sobbing and Slemmons pleading for his life. Offering to buy it with all that he had. "Please, suh, don't kill me. Sixty-two dollars at de sto'. Gold money."

Joe just stood. Slemmons looked at the window, but it was screened. Joe stood out like a rough-backed mountain between him and the door. Barring him from escape, from sunrise, from life.

He considered a surprise attack upon the big clown that stood there laughing like a chessy cat. But before his fist could travel an inch, Joe's own rushed out to crush him like a battering ram. Then Joe stood over him.

"Git into yo' damn rags, Slemmons, and dat quick."

Slemmons scrambled to his feet and into his vest and coat. As he grabbed his hat, Joe's fury overrode his intentions and he grabbed at Slemmons with his left hand and struck at him with his right. The right landed. The left grazed the front of his vest. Slemmons was knocked a somersault into the kitchen and fled through the open door. Joe found himself alone with Missie May, with the golden watch charm clutched in his left fist. A short bit of broken chain dangled between his fingers.

Missie May was sobbing. Wails of weeping without words. Joe stood, and after a while he found out that he had something in his hand. And then he stood and felt without thinking and without seeing with his natural eyes. Missie May kept on crying and Joe kept on feeling so much, and not knowing what to do with all his feelings, he put Slemmons's watch charm in his pants pocket and took a good laugh and went to bed.

"Missie May, whut you cryin' for?"

"Cause Ah love you so hard and Ah know you don't love *me* no mo'."

Joe sank his face into the pillow for a spell, then he said huskily, "You don't know de feelings of dat yet, Missie May."

"Oh Joe, honey, he said he wuz gointer give me dat gold money and he jes' kept on after me—"

Joe was very still and silent for a long time. Then he said, "Well, don't cry no mo', Missie May. Ah got yo' gold piece for you."

The hours went past on their rusty ankles. Joe still and quiet on one bed rail and Missie May wrung dry of sobs on the other. Finally the sun's tide crept upon the shore of night and drowned all its hours. Missie May with her face stiff and streaked towards the window saw the dawn come into her yard. It was day. Nothing more. Joe wouldn't be coming home as usual. No need to fling open the front door and sweep off the porch, making it nice for Joe. Never no more breakfast to cook; no more washing and starching of Joe's jumper-jackets and pants. No more nothing. So why get up?

With this strange man in her bed, she felt embarrassed to get up and dress. She decided to wait till he had dressed and gone. Then she would get up, dress quickly and be gone forever beyond reach of Joe's looks and laughs. But he never moved. Red light turned to yellow, then white.

From beyond the no-man's land between them came a voice. A strange voice that yesterday had been Joe's.

"Missie May, ain't you gonna fix me no breakfus'?"

She sprang out of bed. "Yeah, Joe. Ah didn't reckon you wuz hongry."

No need to die today. Joe needed her for a few more minutes anyhow.

Soon there was a roaring fire in the cookstove. Water bucket full and two chickens killed. Joe loved fried chicken and rice. She didn't deserve a thing and good Joe was letting her cook him some breakfast. She rushed hot biscuits to the table as Joe took his seat.

He ate with his eyes in his plate. No laughter, no banter.

"Missie May, you ain't eatin' yo' breakfus'."

"Ah don't choose none, Ah thank yuh."

His coffee cup was empty. She sprang to refill it. When she turned from the stove and bent to set the cup beside Joe's plate, she saw the yellow coin on the table between them.

She slumped into her seat and wept into her arms.

Presently Joe said calmly, "Missie May, you cry too much. Don't look back lak Lot's wife and turn to salt."

The sun, the hero of every day, the impersonal old man that beams as brightly on death as on birth, came up every morning and raced across the blue dome and dipped into the sea of fire every morning. Water ran downhill and birds nested.

Missie knew why she didn't leave Joe. She couldn't. She loved him too much, but she could not understand why Joe didn't leave her. He was polite, even kind at times, but aloof.

There were no more Saturday romps. No ringing silver dollars to stack beside her plate. No pockets to rifle. In fact, the yellow coin in his trousers was like a monster hiding in the cave of his pockets to destroy her.

She often wondered if he still had it, but nothing could have induced her to ask nor yet to explore his pockets to see for herself. Its shadow was in the house whether or no.

One night Joe came home around midnight and complained of pains in the back. He asked Missie to rub him down with liniment. It had been three months since Missie had touched his body and it all seemed strange. But she rubbed him. Grateful for the chance. Before morning youth triumphed and Missie exulted. But the next day, as she joyfully made up their bed, beneath her pillow she found the piece of money with the bit of chain attached.

Alone to herself, she looked at the thing with loathing, but look she must. She took it into her hands with trembling and saw first thing that it was no gold piece. It was a gilded half dollar. Then she knew why Slemmons had forbidden anyone to touch his gold. He trusted village eyes at a distance not to recognize his stickpin as a gilded quarter, and his watch charm as a four-bit piece.

She was glad at first that Joe had left it there. Perhaps he was through with her punishment. They were man and wife again. Then another thought came clawing at her. He had come home to buy from her as if she were any woman in the longhouse. Fifty cents for her love. As if to say that he could pay as well as Slemmons. She slid the coin into his Sunday pants pocket and dressed herself and left his house.

Halfway between her house and the quarters she met her husband's mother, and after a short talk she turned and went back home. Never would she admit defeat to that woman who prayed for it nightly. If she had not the substance of marriage she had the outside show. Joe must leave *her*. She let him see she didn't want his old gold four-bits, too.

She saw no more of the coin for some time though she knew that Joe could not help finding it in his pocket. But his health kept poor, and he came home at least every ten days to be rubbed.

The sun swept around the horizon, trailing its robes of weeks and days. One morning as Joe came in from work, he found Missie May chopping wood. Without a word he took the ax and chopped a huge pile before he stopped.

"You ain't got no business choppin' wood, and you know it."

"How come? Ah been choppin' it for de last longest."

"Ah ain't blind. You makin' feet for shoes."

"Won't you be glad to have a lil baby chile, Joe?"

"You know dat 'thout astin' me."

"Iss gointer be a boy chile and de very spit of you."

"You reckon, Missie May?"

"Who else could it look lak?"

Joe said nothing, but he thrust his hand deep into his pocket and fingered something there.

It was almost six months later Missie May took to bed and Joe went and got his mother to come wait on the house.

Missie May was delivered of a fine boy. Her travail was over when Joe came in from work one morning. His mother and the old women were drinking great bowls of coffee around the fire in the kitchen.

The minute Joe came into the room his mother called him aside.

"How did Missie May make out?" he asked quickly.

"Who, dat gal? She strong as a ox. She gointer have plenty mo'. We done fixed her wid de sugar and lard to sweeten her for de nex' one."

Joe stood silent awhile.

"You ain't ask 'bout de baby, Joe. You oughter be mighty proud cause he sho is de spittin' image of yuh, son. Dat's yourn all right, if you never git another one, dat un is yourn. And you know Ah'm mighty proud too, son, cause Ah never thought well of you marryin' Missie May cause her ma used tuh fan her foot round right smart and Ah been mighty skeered dat Missie May wuz gointer git misput on her road."

Joe said nothing. He fooled around the house till late in the day, then, just before he went to work, he went and stood at the foot of the bed and asked his wife how she felt. He did this every day during the week.

On Saturday he went to Orlando to make his market. It had been a long time since he had done that.

Meat and lard, meal and flour, soap and starch. Cans of corn and tomatoes. All the staples. He fooled around town for a while and bought bananas and apples. Way after while he went around to the candy store.

"Hello, Joe," the clerk greeted him. "Ain't seen you in a long time."

"Nope, Ah ain't been heah. Been round in spots and places."

"Want some of them molasses kisses you always buy?"

"Yessuh." He threw the gilded half dollar on the counter. "Will dat spend?"

"Whut is it, Joe? Well, I'll be doggone! A gold-plated four-bit piece. Where'd you git it, Joe?"

"Offen a stray nigger dat come through Eatonville. He had it on his watch chain for a charm—goin' round making out iss gold money. Ha ha! He had a quarter on his tiepin and it wuz all golded up too. Tryin' to fool people. Makin' out he so rich and everything. Ha! Ha! Tryin' to tole off folkses wives from home."

"How did you git it, Joe? Did he fool you, too?"

"Who, me? Naw suh! He ain't fooled me none. Know whut Ah done? He come round me wid his smart talk. Ah hauled off and knocked 'im down and took his old four-bits away from 'im. Gointer buy my wife some good ole lasses kisses wid it. Gimme fifty cents worth of dem candy kisses."

"Fifty cents buys a mighty lot of candy kisses, Joe. Why don't you split it up and take some chocolate bars, too? They eat good, too."

"Yessuh, dey do, but Ah wants all dat in kisses. Ah got a lil boy chile home now. Tain't a week old yet, but he kin suck a sugar tit and maybe eat one them kisses hisself."

Joe got his candy and left the store. The clerk turned to the next customer. "Wisht I could be like these darkies. Laughin' all the time. Nothin' worries 'em."

Back in Eatonville, Joe reached his own front door. There was the ring of singing metal on wood. Fifteen times. Missie May couldn't run to the door, but she crept there as quickly as she could.

"Joe Banks, Ah hear you chunkin' money in mah do'way. You wait till Ah got mah strength back and Ah'm gointer fix you for dat."

FROM **THEIR EYES WERE WATCHING GOD**

It was after the picnic that the town began to notice things and got mad. Tea Cake and Mrs. Mayor Starks! All the men that she could get, and fooling with somebody like Tea Cake! Another thing. Joe Starks hadn't been dead but nine months and here she goes sashaying off to a picnic in pink linen. Done quit attending church, like she used to. Gone off to Sanford in a car with Tea Cake and her all dressed in blue! It was a shame. Done took to high heel slippers and a ten dollar hat! Looking like some young girl, always in blue because Tea Cake told her to wear it. Poor Joe Starks. Bet he turns over in his grave every day. Tea Cake and Janie gone hunting. Tea Cake and Janie gone fishing. Tea Cake and Janie gone to Orlando to the movies. Tea Cake and Janie gone to a dance. Tea Cake making flower beds in Janie's yard and seeding the garden for her. Chopping down that tree she never did like by the dining room window. All those signs of possession. Tea Cake in a borrowed car teaching Janie to drive. Tea Cake and Janie playing checkers; playing coon-can; playing Florida flip on the store porch all afternoon as if nobody else was there. Day after day and week after week.

"Pheoby," Sam Watson said one night as he got in the bed, "Ah b'lieve yo' buddy is all tied up with dat Tea Cake shonough. Didn't b'lieve it at first."

"Aw she don't mean nothin' by it. Ah think she's sort of stuck on dat undertaker up at Sanford."

"It's somebody 'cause she looks mighty good dese days. New dresses and her hair combed a different way nearly every day. You got to have something to comb hair over. When you see uh woman doin' so much rakin' in her head, she's combin' at some man or 'nother."

" 'Course she kin do as she please, but dat's uh good chance she got up at Sanford. De man's wife died and he got uh lovely place tuh take her to—already furnished. Better'n her house Joe left her."

"You better sense her intuh things then 'cause Tea Cake can't do nothing' but help her spend whut she got. Ah reckon dat's whut he's after. Throwin' away whut Joe Starks worked hard tuh git tuh gether."

"Dat's de way it looks. Still and all, she's her own woman. She oughta know by now whut she wants tuh do."

"De men wuz talkin' 'bout it in de grove tuhday and givin' her and Tea Cake both de devil. Dey figger he's spendin' on her now in order tuh make her spend on him later."

"Umph! Umph! Umph!"

"Oh dey got it all figgered out. Maybe it ain't as bad as they say, but they talk it and make it sound real bad on her part."

"Dat's jealousy and malice. Some uh dem very mens wants tuh do whut dey claim deys skeered Tea Cake is doin'."

"De Pastor claim Tea Cake don't 'low her tuh come tuh church only once in awhile 'cause he want dat change tuh buy gas wid. Just draggin' de woman away from church. But anyhow, she's yo' bosom friend, so you better go see 'bout her. Drop uh lil hint here and dere and if Tea Cake is tryin' tuh rob her she kin see and know. Ah laks de woman and Ah sho would hate tuh see her come up lak Mis' Tyler."

"Aw mah God, naw! Reckon Ah better step over dere tomorrow and have some chat wid Janie. She jus' ain't thinkin' whut she doin', dat's all."

The next morning Pheoby picked her way over to Janie's house like a hen to a neighbor's garden. Stopped and talked a little with everyone she met, turned aside momentarily to pause at a porch or two—going straight by walking crooked. So her firm intention looked like an accident and she didn't have to give her opinion to folks along the way.

Janie acted glad to see her and after a while Pheoby broached her with, "Janie, everybody's talkin' 'bout how dat Tea Cake is draggin' you round tuh places you ain't used tuh. Baseball games and huntin' and fishin'. He don't know you'se useter uh more high time crowd than dat. You always did class off."

"Jody classed me off. Ah didn't. Naw, Pheoby, Tea Cake ain't draggin' me off nowhere Ah don't want tuh go. Ah always did want tuh git round uh whole heap, but Jody wouldn't 'low me tuh. When Ah wasn't in de store he wanted me tuh jes sit wid folded hands and sit dere. And Ah'd sit dere wid de walls creepin' up on me and squeezin' all de life outa me. Pheoby, dese educated women got uh heap of things to sit down and consider. Somebody done tole 'em what to set down for. Nobody ain't told poor me, so sittin' still worries me. Ah wants tuh utilize mahself all over."

"But, Janie, Tea Cake, whilst he ain't no jail-bird, he ain't got uh dime tuh cry. Ain't you skeered he's jes after yo' money—him bein' younger than you?"

"He ain't never ast de first penny from me yet, and if he love property he ain't no different from all de rest of us. All dese ole men dat's settin' round me is after de same thing. They's three mo' widder women in town, how come dey don't break dey neck after dem? 'Cause dey ain't got nothin', dat's why."

"Folks seen you out in colors and dey thinks you ain't payin' de right amount uh respect tuh yo' dead husband."

"Ah ain't grievin' so why do Ah hafta mourn? Tea Cake love me in blue, so Ah wears it. Jody ain't never in his life picked out no color for me. De world picked out black and white for mournin', Joe didn't. So Ah wasn't wearin' it for him. Ah was wearin' it for de rest of y'all."

"But anyhow, watch yo'self, Janie, and don't be took advantage of. You know how dese young men is wid older women. Most of de time dey's after whut dey kin git, then dey's gone lak uh turkey through de corn."

"Tea Cake don't talk dat way. He's aimin' tuh make hisself permanent wid me. We done made up our mind tuh marry."

"Janie, you'se yo' own woman, and Ah hope you know whut you doin'. Ah sho hope you ain't lak uh possum—de older you gits, de less sense yuh got. Ah'd feel uh whole heap better 'bout yuh if you wuz marryin' dat man up dere in Sanford. He got somethin' tuh put long side uh whut you got and dat make it more better. He's endurable."

"Still and all Ah'd ruther be wid Tea Cake."

"Well, if yo' mind is already made up, 'tain't nothin' nobody kin do. But you'se takin' uh awful chance."

"No mo' than Ah took befo' and no mo' than anybody else takes when dey gits married. It always changes folks, and sometimes it brings out dirt and meanness dat even de person didn't know they had in 'em theyselves. You know dat. Maybe Tea Cake might turn out lak dat. Maybe not. Anyhow Ah'm ready and willin' tuh try 'im."

"Well, when you aim tuh step off?"

"Dat we don't know. De store is got tuh be sold and then we'se goin' off somewhere tuh git married."

"How come you sellin' out de store?"

" 'Cause Tea Cake ain't no Jody Starks, and if he tried tuh be, it would be uh complete flommuck. But de minute Ah marries 'im everybody is gointuh be makin' comparisons. So us is goin' off somewhere and start all over in Tea Cake's way. Dis ain't no business proposition, and no race after property and titles. Dis is uh love game. Ah done lived Grandma's way, now Ah means tuh live mine."

"What you mean by dat, Janie?"

"She was borned in slavery time when folks, dat is black folks, didn't sit down anytime dey felt lak it. So sittin' on porches lak de white madam looked lak uh mighty fine thing tuh her. Dat's whut she wanted for me—don't keer whut it cost. Git up on uh high chair and sit dere. She didn't have time tuh think whut tuh do after you got up on de stool uh do nothin'. De object wuz tuh git dere. So Ah got up on de high stool lak she told me, but Pheoby, Ah done nearly languished tuh death up dere. Ah felt like de world wuz cryin' extry and Ah ain't read de common news yet."

"Maybe so, Janie. Still and all Ah'd love tuh experience it for just one year. It look lak heben tuh me from where Ah'm at."

"Ah reckon so."

"But anyhow, Janie, you be keerful 'bout dis sellin' out and goin' off wid strange men. Look whut happened tuh Annie Tyler. Took whut little she had and went off tuh Tampa wid dat boy dey call Who Flung. It's somethin' tuh think about."

"It sho is. Still Ah ain't Mis' Tyler and Tea Cake ain't no Who Flung, and he ain't no stranger tuh me. We'se just as good as married already. But Ah ain't puttin' it in de street. Ah'm tellin' *you*."

"Ah just lak uh chicken. Chicken drink water, but he don't pee-pee."

"Oh, Ah know you don't talk. We ain't shame faced. We jus' ain't ready tuh make no big kerflommuck as yet."

"You doin' right not tuh talk it, but Janie, you'se takin' uh mighty big chance."

" 'Tain't so big uh chance as it seem lak, Pheoby. Ah'm older than Tea Cake, yes. But he done showed me where it's de thought dat makes de difference in ages. If people thinks de same they can make it all right. So in the beginnin' new thoughts had tuh be thought and new words said. After Ah got used tuh dat, we gits 'long jus' fine. He done taught me de maiden language all over. Wait till you see de new blue satin Tea Cake done picked out for me tuh stand up wid him in. High heel slippers, necklace, earrings, *everything* he wants tuh see me in. Some of dese mornin's and it won't be long, you gointuh wake up callin' me and Ah'll be gone."

Langston Hughes

(1902–1967)

POET, NOVELIST, short story writer, dramatist, newspaper columnist, anthologist, founder of theaters, librettist, translator, song writer, author of children's works, and writer of autobiographies, James Mercer Langston Hughes was by far the most innovative, the most versatile, and in all probability the most talented writer of the Harlem Renaissance.

Born in Joplin, Missouri, in 1902, Langston Hughes, because his parents separated early, lived and attended grammar schools in seven cities. After his graduation from high school in 1919, he joined his father who was an engineer and lawyer in Mexico. The two did not get along, and after about a year he refused his father's offer to finance his study in Europe; he came back to America and registered at Columbia University. This was in 1921/22; by this time his poems were being published in such black magazines as *Brownies' Book* and *The Crisis*. Hughes did not return to Columbia, but later attended Lincoln University (Pennsylvania), graduating in 1929.

Between 1922 and 1924 he traveled as mess steward aboard freighters to the Azores, to Africa, to Paris, and to other places in Europe. Returning home in 1924, he joined his mother in Washington, D.C., where he allowed himself to be "discovered as a bus boy poet" by Vachel Lindsay. In 1926 he published *The Weary Blues*, his first volume of poems. In 1931–32 Hughes toured the South and West, reading his works. During the same period, he visited Haiti and subsequently the Soviet Union on an abortive moviemaking venture. In 1937 he reported on the Civil War in Spain for the *Afro-American*. From 1938 to 1940, Hughes founded three black theaters: one each in Harlem, Los Angeles, and Chicago.

In the years between 1943 and his death in 1967, Langston Hughes crowded in the following achievements: inaugurated the "Simple" columns for the *Chicago Defender*, was a visiting professor at Atlanta University, was a poet-in-residence at the University of Chicago's Laboratory School, lectured in Europe for the U.S. Information Agency, won the Spingarn Medal in 1960, and in 1966 attended the First World Festival of Negro Art in Dakar.

Langston Hughes was deeply involved in black life, which he loved and thoroughly understood. Although widely read by whites, he wrote for blacks; he used a language of beguiling simplicity to speak directly of simple things and common experience. He knew intimately the folklore of blacks, and very few writers have equaled his mastery in the use of blues, spirituals, ballads, jazz, and folk speech. Very few have his skill as a poet, and fewer still his sense of humor.

Space will not allow us to give here all of Hughes's works. The following titles are a partial list of publications which the editors consider major or significant. In poetry: *The Weary Blues* (1926); *Montage of a Dream Deferred* (1951), a brilliant poetic delineation of Harlem; and *The Panther and the Lash* (1967). In fiction: *Not without Laughter* (1930), *The Ways of White Folk* (1933), and the "Simple" series, published between 1950 and 1965. In drama: *Mulatto* (1935); *Little Ham* (1935); and *Don't You Want to Be Free?* (1936–37). In autobiography: *The Big Sea* (1940) and *I Wonder as I Wander* (1956).

For material on Langston Hughes's life and many publications, see Arnold Rampersad's *The Life of Langston Hughes—Volume I: 1902–1941* (1986) and *Volume II: 1941–1967* (1988); see also Faith Berry's *Langston Hughes Before and Beyond Harlem* (1983); Donald C. Dickinson's *A Bio-Bibliography of Langston Hughes, 1902–1967* (1967); James A. Emanuel's *Langston Hughes* (1967); the *CLA Journal's* special Hughes number (June 1968), edited by Therman B. O'Daniel; Arthur P. Davis's entry in *Dictionary of American Negro Biography*; and the entry in *Dictionary of Literary Biography, Volume 51*. Also of interest is the *Arna Bontemps–Langston Hughes Letters, 1925–1967*, selected and edited by Charles H. Nichols (1980). A novel approach to this key literary figure is *The World of Langston Hughes's Music*, a bibliography of musical settings of Hughes's work with recordings and other listings, by Kenneth P. Neilson (1982).

The works included here are from several sources.

NEGRO DANCERS

> "Me an' ma baby's
> Got two mo' ways,
> Two mo' ways to do de Charleston!
>   Da, da,
>   Da, da, da!
> Two mo' ways to do de Charleston!"
>
> Soft light on the tables,
> Music gay,
> Brown-skin steppers
> In a cabaret.

White folks, laugh!
White folks, pray!

"Me an' ma baby's
Got two mo' ways,
Two mo' ways to do de Charleston!"

THE CAT AND THE SAXOPHONE
2 A.M.

EVERYBODY
Half-pint,—
Gin?
No, make it
LOVES MY BABY
corn. You like
liquor,
don't you honey?
BUT MY BABY
Sure. Kiss me,
DON'T LOVE NOBODY
daddy.
BUT ME.
Say!
EVERYBODY
Yes?
WANTS MY BABY
I'm your
BUT MY BABY
sweetie, ain't I?
DON'T WANT NOBODY
Sure.
BUT
Then let's
ME,
do it!
SWEET ME.
Charleston,
mamma!
!

CROSS

My old man's a white old man
And my old mother's black.
If ever I cursed my white old man
I take my curses back.

If ever I cursed my black old mother
And wished she were in hell,
I'm sorry for that evil wish
And now I wish her well.

My old man died in a fine big house.
My ma died in a shack.
I wonder where I'm gonna die,
Being neither white nor black?

RUBY BROWN

She was young and beautiful
And golden like the sunshine
That warmed her body.
And because she was colored
Mayville had no place to offer her,
Nor fuel for the clean flame of joy
That tried to burn within her soul.

One day,
Sitting on old Mrs. Latham's back porch
Polishing the silver,
She asked herself two questions
And they ran something like this:
What can a colored girl do
On the money from a white woman's kitchen?
And ain't there any joy in this town?

Now the streets down by the river
Know more about this pretty Ruby Brown,

And the sinister shuttered houses of the bottoms
Hold a yellow girl
Seeking an answer to her questions.
The good church folk do not mention
Her name any more.

But the white men,
Habitués of the high shuttered houses,
Pay more money to her now
Than they ever did before,
When she worked in their kitchens.

THEME FOR ENGLISH B

The instructor said,

> *Go home and write*
> *a page tonight.*
> *And let that page come out of you—*
> *Then, it will be true.*

I wonder if it's that simple?

I am twenty-two, colored, born in Winston-Salem.
I went to school there, then Durham, then here
to this college on the hill above Harlem.
I am the only colored student in my class.
The steps from the hill lead down into Harlem,
through a park, then I cross St. Nicholas,
Eighth Avenue, Seventh, and I come to the Y.
the Harlem Branch Y, where I take the elevator
up to my room, sit down, and write this page:

It's not easy to know what is true for you or me
at twenty-two, my age. But I guess I'm what
I feel and see and hear. Harlem, I hear you:
hear you, hear me—we two—you, me, talk on this page.
(I hear New York, too.) Me—who?

Well, I like to eat, sleep, drink, and be in love.
I like to work, read, learn, and understand life.

"Theme For English B." From *Montage of a Dream Deferred*. Reprinted by permission of Harold Ober Associates Incorporated. Copyright 1951 by Langston Hughes. Copyright renewed 1979 by George Houston Bass.

I like a pipe for a Christmas present,
or records—Bessie, bop, or Bach.
I guess being colored doesn't make me *not* like
the same things other folks like who are other races.

So will my page be colored that I write?
Being me, it will not be white.
But it will be
a part of you, instructor.
You are white——
yet a part of me, as I am a part of you.
That's American.
Sometimes perhaps you don't want to be a part of me.
Nor do I often want to be a part of you.
But we are, that's true!
As I learn from you,
I guess you learn from me——
although you're older—and white——
and somewhat more free.

This is my page for English B.

MOTHER TO SON

Well, son, I'll tell you:
Life for me ain't been no crystal stair.
It's had tacks in it,
And splinters,
And boards torn up,
And places with no carpet on the floor—
Bare.
But all the time
I'se been a-climbin' on,
And reachin' landin's,
And turnin' corners,
And sometimes goin' in the dark
Where there ain't been no light.
So boy, don't you turn back.
Don't you set down on the steps

'Cause you finds it's kinder hard.
Don't you fall now—
For I'se still goin', honey,
I'se still climbin',
And life for me ain't been no crystal stair.

THE NEGRO SPEAKS OF RIVERS

To W. E. B. Du Bois

I've known rivers:
I've known rivers ancient as the world and older than the flow of
    human blood in human veins.

My soul has grown deep like the rivers.

I bathed in the Euphrates when dawns were young.
I built my hut near the Congo and it lulled me to sleep.
I looked upon the Nile and raised the pyramids above it.
I heard the singing of the Mississippi when Abe Lincoln went down
    to New Orleans, and I've seen its muddy bosom turn all golden
    in the sunset.

I've known rivers:
Ancient, dusky rivers.

My soul has grown deep like the rivers.

BOUND NO'TH BLUES

Goin' down the road, Lawd,
Goin' down the road.
Down the road, Lawd,
Way, way down the road.
Got to find somebody
To help me carry this load.

Road's in front o' me,
Nothin' to do but walk.
Road's in front o' me,
Walk . . . an' walk . . . an' walk.
I'd like to meet a good friend
To come along an' talk.

Hates to be lonely,
Lawd, I hates to be sad.
Says I hates to be lonely,
Hates to be lonely an' sad,
But ever' friend you finds seems
Like they try to do you bad.

Road, road, road, O!
Road, road . . . road . . . road, road!
Road, road, road, O!
On the no'thern road.
These Mississippi towns ain't
Fit fer a hoppin' toad.

PUZZLED

Here on the edge of hell
Stands Harlem—
Remembering the old lies,
The old kicks in the back,
The old, *Be patient*,
They told us before.

Sure, we remember.
Now, when the man at the corner store
Says sugar's gone up another two cents,
And bread one,
And there's a new tax on cigarettes—
We remember the job we never had,
Never could get,
And can't have now
Because we're colored.

So we stand here
On the edge of hell
In Harlem
And look out on the world
And wonder
What we're gonna do
In the face of
What we remember.

MOTTO

I play it cool
And dig all jive
That's the reason
I stay alive.

My motto,
As I live and learn,
            is:
Dig And Be Dug
In Return.

LOW TO HIGH

How can you forget me?
But you do!
You said you was gonna take me
Up with you—
Now you've got your Cadillac,
you done forgot that you are black.
How can you forget me
When I'm you?

But you do.

How can you forget me,
fellow, say?
How can you low-rate me
this way?
You treat me like you damn well please,
Ignore me—though I pay your fees.
How can you forget me?

But you do.

HIGH TO LOW

God knows
We have our troubles, too——
One trouble is you:
you talk too loud,
cuss too loud,
look too black,
don't get anywhere,
and sometimes it seems
you don't even care.
The way you send your kids to school
stockings down,
(not Ethical Culture)
the way you shout out loud in church,
(not St. Phillips)
and the way you lounge on doorsteps
just as if you were down South,
(not at 409)
the way you clown——
the way, in other words,
you let me down——
me, trying to uphold the race
and you——
well, you can see,
we have our problems
too, with you.

"High to Low." From *Montage of a Dream Deferred*. Reprinted by permission of Harold Ober Associates Incorporated. Copyright 1951 by Langston Hughes. Copyright renewed 1979 by George Houston Bass.

WHO'S PASSING FOR WHO?

One of the great difficulties about being a member of a minority race is that so many kindhearted, well-meaning bores gather around to help you. Usually, to tell the truth, they have nothing to help with, except their company—which is often appallingly dull.

Some members of the Negro race seem very well able to put up with it, though, in these uplifting years. Such was Caleb Johnson, colored social worker, who was always dragging around with him some nondescript white person or two, inviting them to dinner, showing them Harlem, ending up at the Savoy—much to the displeasure of whatever friends of his might be out that evening for fun, not sociology.

Friends are friends and, unfortunately, overearnest uplifters are uplifters—no matter what color they may be. If it were the white race that was ground down instead of Negroes, Caleb Johnson would be one of the first to offer Nordics the sympathy of his utterly inane society, under the impression that somehow he would be doing them a great deal of good.

You see, Caleb, and his white friends, too, were all bores. Or so we, who lived in Harlem's literary bohemia during the "Negro Renaissance," thought. We literary ones in those days considered ourselves too broad-minded to be bothered with questions of color. We liked people of any race who smoked incessantly, drank liberally, wore complexion and morality as loose garments, and made fun of anyone who didn't do likewise. We snubbed and high-hatted any Negro or white luckless enough not to understand Gertrude Stein, Ulysses, Man Ray, the theremin, Jean Toomer, or George Antheil. By the end of the 1920's Caleb was just catching up to Dos Passos. He thought H. G. Wells good.

We met Caleb one night in Small's. He had three assorted white folks in tow. We would have passed him by with but a nod had he not hailed us enthusiastically, risen, and introduced us with great acclaim to his friends, who turned out to be schoolteachers from Iowa, a woman and two men. They appeared amazed and delighted to meet all at once two Negro writers and a black painter in the flesh. They invited us to have a drink with them. Money being scarce with us, we deigned to sit down at their table.

The white lady said, "I've never met a Negro writer before."

The two men added, "Neither have we."

"Why, we know any number of *white* writers," we three dark bohemians declared with bored nonchalance.

"But Negro writers are much more rare," said the lady.

"There are plenty in Harlem," we said.

"But not in Iowa," said one of the men, shaking his mop of red
hair.

"There are no good *white* writers in Iowa either, are there?" we
asked superciliously.

"Oh yes, Ruth Suckow came from there."

Whereupon we proceeded to light in upon Ruth Suckow as old
hat and to annihilate her in favor of Kay Boyle. The way we flung
names around seemed to impress both Caleb and his white guests.
This, of course, delighted us, though we were too young and too
proud to admit it.

The drinks came and everything was going well, all of us drinking, and we three showing off in a high-brow manner, when suddenly at the table just behind us a man got up and knocked down a
woman. He was a brownskin man. The woman was blonde. As she
rose, he knocked her down again. Then the red-haired man from
Iowa got up and knocked the colored man down.

He said, "Keep your hands off that white woman."

The man got up and said, "She's not a white woman. She's my
wife."

One of the waiters added, "She's not white, sir, she's colored."

Whereupon the man from Iowa looked puzzled, dropped his
fists, and said, "I'm sorry."

The colored man said, "What are you doing up here in Harlem
anyway, interfering with my family affairs?"

The white man said, "I thought she was a white woman."

The woman who had been on the floor rose and said, "Well, I'm
not a white woman, I'm colored, and you leave my husband alone."

Then they both lit in on the gentleman from Iowa. It took all of
us and several waiters, too, to separate them. When it was over, the
manager requested us to kindly pay our bill and get out. He said we
were disturbing the peace. So we all left. We went to a fish restaurant down the street. Caleb was terribly apologetic to his white
friends. We artists were both mad and amused.

"Why did you say you were sorry," said the colored painter to
the visitor from Iowa, "after you'd hit that man—and then found out
it wasn't a white woman you were defending, but merely a light colored woman who looked white?"

"Well," answered the red-haired Iowan, "I didn't mean to be but-
ting in if they were all the same race."

"Don't you think a woman needs defending from a brute, no matter what race she may be?" asked the painter.

"Yes, but I think it's up to you to defend your own women."

"Oh, so you'd divide up a brawl according to races, no matter who was right?"

"Well, I wouldn't say that."

"You mean you wouldn't defend a colored woman whose husband was knocking her down?" asked the poet.

Before the visitor had time to answer, the painter said, "No! You just got mad because you thought a black man was hitting a *white* woman."

"But she *looked* like a white woman," countered the man.

"Maybe she was just passing for colored," I said.

"Like some Negroes pass for white," Caleb interposed.

"Anyhow, I don't like it," said the colored painter, "the way you stopped defending her when you found out she wasn't white."

"No, we don't like it," we all agreed except Caleb.

Caleb said in extenuation, "But Mr. Stubblefield is new to Harlem."

The red-haired white man said, "Yes, it's my first time here."

"Maybe Mr. Stubblefield ought to stay out of Harlem," we observed.

"I agree," Mr. Stubblefield said. "Good night."

He got up then and there and left the café. He stalked as he walked. His red head disappeared into the night.

"Oh, that's too bad," said the white couple who remained. "Stubby's temper just got the best of him. But explain to us, are many colored folks really as fair as that woman?"

"Sure, lots of them have more white blood than colored, and pass for white."

"Do they?" said the lady and gentleman from Iowa.

"You never read Nella Larsen?" we asked.

"She writes novels," Caleb explained. "She's part white herself."

"Read her," we advised. "Also read the *Autobiography of an Ex-Coloured Man*." Not that we had read it ourselves—because we paid but little attention to the older colored writers—but we knew it was about passing for white.

We all ordered fish and settled down comfortably to shocking our white friends with tales about how many Negroes there were passing for white all over America. We were determined to *épater le bourgeois* real good via this white couple we had cornered, when the woman leaned over the table in the midst of our dissertations and said, "Listen, gentlemen, you needn't spread the word, but me and my husband aren't white either. We've just been *passing* for white for the last fifteen years."

"What?"

"We're colored, too, just like you," said the husband. "But it's better passing for white because we make more money."

Well, that took the wind out of us. It took the wind out of Caleb, too. He thought all the time he was showing some fine white folks Harlem—and they were as colored as he was!

Caleb almost never cursed. But this time he said, "I'll be damned!"

Then everybody laughed. And laughed! We almost had hysterics. All at once we dropped our professionally self-conscious "Negro" manners, became natural, ate fish, and talked and kidded freely like colored folks do when there are no white folks around. We really had fun then, joking about that red-haired guy who mistook a fair colored woman for white. After the fish we went to two or three more night spots and drank until five o'clock in the morning.

Finally we put the light-colored people in a taxi heading downtown. They turned to shout a last good-by. The cab was just about to move off when the woman called to the driver to stop.

She leaned out the window and said with a grin, "Listen, boys! I hate to confuse you again. But, to tell the truth, my husband and I aren't really colored at all. We're white. We just thought we'd kid you by passing for colored a little while—just as you said Negroes sometimes pass for white."

She laughed as they sped off toward Central Park, waving, "Good-by!"

We didn't say a thing. We just stood there on the corner in Harlem dumbfounded—not knowing now *which* way we'd been fooled. Were they really white—passing for colored? Or colored—passing for white?

Whatever race they were, they had had too much fun at our expense—even if they did pay for the drinks.

PICTURE FOR HER DRESSER

It was a warm evening not yet dark when I stopped by Simple's. His landlady had the front door open airing the house, so I did not need to ring. I walked upstairs and knocked on his door. He was sitting on the bed, cutting his toenails, listening to a radio show, and frowning.

"Picture for Her Dresser" from *The Best of Simple* by Langston Hughes. Copyright © 1961 by Langston Hughes. Copyright renewed 1989 by Arna Bontemps and George Houston Bass. Reprinted by permission of Farrar, Straus & Giroux, Inc.

"Do you hear that?" he asked. "It's not about me, neither about you. All these plays, dramas, skits, sketches, and soap operas all day long and practically nothing about Negroes. You would think no Negroes lived in America except Amos and Andy. White folks have all kinds of plays on the radio about themselves, also on TV. But what have we got about us? Just now and then a song to sing. Am I right?"

"Just about right," I said.

"Come on, let's go take a walk." He put on his shoes first, his pants, then his shirt. "Is it cool enough for a coat?"

"You'd better wear one," I said. "It's not summer yet, and evening's coming on. You probably won't get back until midnight."

"Joyce is gone to a club meeting, so I won't be going to see her," he said. "She's expecting her sister-members to elect her a delegate to the regional which meets in Boston sometime soon. If they don't, she'll be a disappointed soul. She used to skip meetings, but that regional is why she goes regular now. Let's me and you stroll up Seventh Avenue to 145th, then curve toward Sugar Hill where the barmaids are beautiful and barflies are belles. I have not been on Sugar Hill in a coon's age."

It was dusk-dark when we reached the pavement. Taxis and pleasure cars sped by. The Avenue was alive with promenaders. On the way up the street we passed a photographer's shop with a big sign glowing in the window:

HARLEM DE-LUXE PHOTOGRAPHY STUDIO

IF YOU ARE NOT GOOD-LOOKING
WE WILL MAKE YOU SO
ENTER

"The last time I come by here," said Simple, "before my lady friend started acting like an iceberg, Joyce told me, 'Jess, why don't you go in and get your picture posed? I always did want a nice photograph of you to set on my dresser.'

"I said, 'Joyce, I don't want to take no picture.' But you know how womens is! So I went in.

"They got another big sign up on the wall inside that says:

RETOUCHING DONE

" 'I don't want them to *touch* me, let alone *retouch*,' I told Joyce.

"Joyce said, 'Be sweet, please, I do not wish no evil-looking Negro on my dresser.' So I submitted.

"Another sign states:

COLORED TO ORDER—EXPERT TINTING

"I asked, 'Joyce, what color do you want me to be?'

"Joyce said, 'A little lighter than natural. I will request the man how much he charges to make you chocolate.'

"About that time a long tall bushy-headed joker in a smock came dancing out of a booth and said, 'Next.'

"That were me next. There was a kind of sick green light blazing inside the booth. That light not only hurt my eyes, but turned my stomach before I even set down.

"The man said, 'Pay in advance.'

"My week's beer money went to turn me into chocolate to set on Joyce's dresser—providing I did not melt before I got out of there, it were so hot.

"The man said, 'Naturally, you want a retouching job?'

"I said, 'You know I *don't* want to look like I am.'

" 'That will be One Dollar extra,' he stated. 'Would you also wish to be tinted?'

" 'Gimme the works,' I said.

" 'We will add Three,' he additioned. 'And if you want more than one print, that will be Two Dollars each, after the negative.'

" 'One is enough,' I said. 'I would not want myself setting around on my *own* dresser. Just one print for the lady, that's all.'

" 'How about your mother?' asked the man. 'Or your sister down home?'

" 'Skip down home,' I said.

" 'Very well,' said the man. 'Now, look pleasant, please! You have observed the sign yonder which is the rule of the company:

IF YOU MOVE,
YOU LOSE.
IF YOU SHAKE—
NO RE-TAKE!

So kindly hold your position.'

" 'As much of my money as you've got,' I said, 'I will not bat a eye.'

" 'Tilt your head to one side and watch the birdie. Don't look like you have just et nails. . . . Smile! . . . Smile! . . . Smile! . . . Brightly, now! That's right!"

" 'I cannot grin all night,' I said, 'Neither can I set like a piece of iron much longer. If you don't take me as I am, *damn!*'

" 'No profanity in here, please,' says the man. 'Just hold it while I focus.'

"I held.

"He focussed.

"I sweated.

"He focussed.

"I said, 'Can't you see me?'

"He said, 'Shussh-ss-s! Now, a great big smile! . . . Hold it!'

"*F—L—A—S—H!*

"I were blind for the next ten minutes. Seven Dollars and a Half's worth of me to set on Joyce's dresser! When I go to get that picture out next week it better be good—also have a frame! As touchous as Joyce is these days, I want her to like that picture."

By that time we had reached the Woodside. The corner of 141st and Seventh was jumping. King Cole was coming cool off the juke box inside the bar.

"Daddy-o, let's turn in here and get a beer," said Simple. "I never was much on climbing hills and if I go any further, I'll have too far to walk back. Besides, I got to wake myself up in the morning. My Big Ben won't alarm, my wrist watch is broke, and my landlady is evil. She says I don't pay her to climb three flights of steps to wake me up—so I have got nobody to wake me in the morning. That is one reason why I wish I was married, so I would not have to worry about getting to work on time. Also I would have somebody to cook my breakfast. I am tired of coffee, crullers, coffee and crullers, which is all I can afford. Besides, I hate an alarm clock. . . . Two beers, bartender! . . . I like to be woke up gentle, some woman's hand shaking saying, 'Jess, honey, ain't you gonna make your shift?'

"And if I was to say, 'No,' she would say, 'Then all right, baby. You been working too hard lately anyhow. Sleep on. We will all get up about noon and go to the show.'

"That is the kind of woman I would like to have. Most womens is different. Most womens say, 'You better get up from there, Jess Semple, and go to work.' But even that would be better than a *brr-rrr-rr-r!* alarm clock every morning in your ears. I rather be woke up by a human than a clock."

"So you would make your wife get up before you, *just to wake you up*, would you?"

"Which is a woman's duty," said Simple. "He that earns the bread should be woke up, petted, fed, and got off to work in time. Then his wife can always go back to bed and get her beauty sleep—providing she is not working herself."

"No doubt a woman of yours would have to work."

"Only until we got a toe-holt," said Simple, "then Joyce could stay home and take care of the children."

"I haven't heard you speak of children before," I said. "You'll be too far along in age to start raising a family if you don't soon get married."

"You don't have to marry to have a family," said Simple.

"You wouldn't care to father children out of wedlock, surely?"

"A man slips up sometimes. But I don't need to worry about that. Joyce is a respectable woman—which is why I respects her. But she says as soon as we are wedlocked she wants a son that looks like me—which will be just as soon as that Negro in Baltimore pays for Isabel's divorce. So far that igaroot has only made one payment."

"I thought that man loved your wife so much he was willing to pay for the *whole* divorce. What happened?"

"I reckon inflation got him," said Simple. "Some things makes me sad to speak of. It takes three payments to get a decree. He made the down payment. Isabel writ that if I would make one, she would make one, then everybody could marry again. But I cannot meet a payment now with food up, rent up, phones up, cigarettes up, Lifebuoy up—everything up but my salary. Isabel wrote that divorces are liable to go up if I don't hurry up and pay up. I got a worried mind. Let's order one more beer—then I won't sleep restless. Have you got some change for this round?"

"I paid the last time."

"Except that *that* were not the last time. This round will be the last time. Just like a divorce in three installments, the last time is not the *last* time—if you still have to pay another time. Kindly order two beers."

"What do you take me for, a chump?"

"No, pal—a friend."

BOMBS IN BARCELONA

Nicolás Guillén went with me to Spain as a correspondent for a Cuban paper. Since everybody said food in that war-torn country was scarce, we took along with us an enormous basket of edibles. But we ate it all on the train. Guillén was a jovial companion with whom to travel and on the way to Barcelona he entertained me with Cubanismos and folk songs:

> Oyelo bien, encargada!
> Esta es la voz que retumba—
> Esta es la ultima rumba
> Que bailamos en tu morada.

At the border between France and Spain there is a tunnel, a long stretch of darkness through which the night express from Paris passes in the early morning. When the train comes out into the sunlight, on the Spanish side of the mountain, with a shining blue bay where children swim in the Mediterranean, you see the village of Port Bou. The town seemed bright and quiet that morning. But as I left the train, I noticed that almost all of the windows of the station were shattered. There were machine-gun marks on the walls of the custom-house and several nearby houses were in ruins, gutted by bombs. In the winding streets of Port Bou there were signs, REFUGIO, pointing to holes in the mountains to be used in case of air raids. And on old walls there were new Loyalist posters. One read: "It's better to be the tail of a lion than the head of a rat." This was my first view of war-time Spain, this little town by the blue sea where travelers changed trains.

In the country they were harvesting the wheat, and as we chugged southward, men and women were swinging primitive scythes in the fields. The Barcelona train was very crowded that day and all around me folks kept up a rapid fire of conversation in various accents. Guillén and I were the only Negroes on the train, so I thought, until at one of the stations when we got out to buy fruit, we noticed a dark face leaning from a window of the coach ahead of us. When the train started again, we went forward to investigate. He was a brownskin boy from the Canary Islands in a red shirt and a blue beret. He had escaped from the Canaries by the simple expedient of getting into his fishing boat with the rest of her crew and sailing toward French Morocco. From there he had gotten to France. The Canary Islands were a part of Spain, he said, but the fishermen did not like the men who had usurped power, so many of them sailed their boats away and came to fight with the Loyalists. This young man spoke a strange Spanish dialect that was hard for Guillén to understand, but he told us that many folks in the Canaries are colored, mixed with African and Spanish blood.

What should have been a short trip from the French border to Barcelona, took all day and well into the night. When our blacked-out train pulled into the blacked-out city near midnight, Nicolás Guillén was so tired that he had stopped talking or singing, and wanted nothing so much as a good bed. There were no lights whatsoever on the platform of the Barcelona station, so we followed the crowd moving slowly like shadows into the station where one lone lantern glimmered behind a ticket wicket. I was loaded down as usual with bags, books, records and a typewriter. Guillén had sense enough to travel light with mostly just his songs and himself. He helped me carry things, and clung to what little remained of our hamper of food. We took a bus through pitch-black streets to a hotel on the Ramblas—there was no gas for taxis and only one bus met each train. I was so tired that night that I slept right through an air-raid alert. Hotel instructions were that all guests were to assemble in the lobby when an alert sounded. Since the hotel had no basement, the ground floor was considered safest. But the so-called ground floor of this hotel was really several feet above street level. The lobby had enormous French doors and windows opening on a balcony. It did not look very safe to me. But I learned later that in a bombing no place was really safe, and that the Spaniards had two rather fatalistic theories about protection. One was during an air raid to go to the roof of a building and fall down with it if a bomb struck. The other was go to the ground floor and, in case of a hit, be buried at once under debris.

One could tell that Barcelona was jittery from the terrific bombing it had undergone the day before I arrived. But nothing happened during the first twenty-four hours I was there, so Guillén and I walked about, looking at the destruction and at the antiaircraft guns on most of the busy corners, the flower sellers on the tree-lined Ramblas, and the passing crowds everywhere, with folks clinging to the overcrowded street cars all day long. Sitting in the cafés, whenever the public radios started to blare out the latest war news, everybody would jump. Nerves were certainly on edge. But there were no planes overhead all day.

As Guillén and I sat at a sidewalk table on the Ramblas that afternoon, a dark young man passed, turned, looked back at me and spoke. He recognized me, he said, because he had heard me read my poems at the library in New York. He was a Puerto Rican named Roldan, who had come from Harlem to serve as an interpreter in Spain. At that moment he was on his way to a dance at a little club where the Cubans and other Spanish-speaking peoples from the Caribbean gathered. He invited us to come with him. The club had a beautiful courtyard and a little bar where rum drinks were mixed. The party that afternoon was in honor of the International Brigaders on leave, among them several Spanish-speaking Negroes and a colored Portugese. Catalonian soldiers and their girls mingled gaily with the Negro guests. And Guillén, lionized as Cuba's most famous poet, was in his element, surrounded by girls.

That night back at our hotel we knew it was wartime because, in the luxurious dining room with its tuxedoed waiters, there was only one fixed menu with no choice of food. The dinner was good, but not elaborate. Later we went to an outdoor café for coffee. Until midnight we sat watching the crowds strolling up and down the tiled sidewalks of the Ramblas. The fact that Barcelona was lightless did not keep people home on a warm evening. There was a wan bulb behind the bar inside to help the barman find his bottles, but other than that no visible light save for the stars shining brightly. The buildings were great grey shadows towering in the night, with windows shuttered everywhere and curtains drawn. There must be no visible lights in any windows to guide enemy aviators.

At midnight, the public radios on many corners began to blare the war news and people gathered in large groups to hear it. Then the café closed, and we went to the hotel. I had just barely gotten to my room and begun to undress when the low extended wail of a siren began, letting us know that Fascist planes were coming. They came, we had been told, from Mallorca across the sea at a terrific speed, dropped their bombs, then circled away into the night again. Quickly, I put on my shirt, passed Guillén's room, and together we started downstairs. Suddenly all the lights went out in the hotel. We heard people rushing down the stairs in the dark. A few had flashlights with them. Some were visibly frightened. In the lobby a single candle was burning, casting giantlike shadows on the walls. In an ever-increasing wail the siren sounded louder and louder, droning its deathly warning. Suddenly it stopped. By then the lobby was full of people, men, women and children, speaking in Spanish, English, French.

In the distance we heard a series of quick explosions.

"Bombs?" I asked.

"No, antiaircraft guns," a man explained.

Everyone became very quiet. Then we heard the guns go off again.

"Come here," a man called, leading the way. Several of us went out on the balcony where, in the dark, we could see the searchlights playing across the sky. Little round puffs of smoke from the antiaircraft shells floated against the stars. In the street a few women hurried along to public bomb-proof cellars.

Then for a long while nothing happened. No bombs fell. After about an hour, the lights suddenly came on in the hotel as a signal that the danger had ended. Evidently, the enemy planes had been driven away without having completed their mission. Everyone went back upstairs to bed. The night was quiet again. I put out my light, opened the window and, never being troubled with sleeplessness, I was soon sound asleep. The next thing I knew was that, with part of my clothes in my arms, I was running in the dark toward the stairs. A *terrific* explosion somewhere nearby had literally lifted me out of bed. Apparently I had slept through an alert, for almost all the other guests in the hotel had already assembled in the lobby, huddled in various stages of dress and undress. At the foot of the stairs I put my trousers on over my pajamas and sat down shaking like a leaf, evidently having been frightened to this dire extent while still asleep, because I had hardly realized I was afraid until I felt myself shaking. When I put one hand on the other, both hands were trembling. There were the sounds of what seemed like a major battle going on in the streets outside—but this was only the antiaircraft guns firing at the sky, so someone near me explained. Suddenly I developed the worst stomachache I've ever had in my life. I managed to find my way to a MEN'S ROOM about the time a distant explosion sounded, far away, yet near enough to cause the hotel to shake. When I came back, by the light of the single candle at the desk, I managed to find Guillén, sitting calmly like Buddha on a settee under a potted palm. He said, "*Ay, chico, eso es!*" Well, this is it! Which was of little comfort.

Gradually I began to be fully awake and less frightened, so I sat down, too, smoked a cigarette, and got acquainted with some of the other folks in the lobby. After perhaps a half hour, when the crackling of the antiaircraft batteries had died down, an all clear sounded, and the desk clerk said we might return to our beds. He blew out his candle before opening some of the French doors leading onto the balcony overlooking the Ramblas. Some of us went out on the balcony to see what was happening in the streets. An occasional military motor passed without lights, and a few people moved up and down—police and rescue workers, I supposed. As I stood there with the others a sudden crackle of shots rang out in our direction from across the corner square. Glass came down all over us from windows on the upper floors. A machine gun was firing directly at the hotel! We almost fell over each other getting back inside the lobby. Door and shutters were slammed again. Shortly some soldiers entered from the street and said that someone on an upper floor had turned on a light. (Their orders were to fire at any exposed light in any building.) Sternly they mounted the stairs in search of the offender. Later I learned that some foreigner (not knowing the rules) had turned on a bedside bulb after he had opened his window for air. So the guards simply blasted away at the lighted room. The frightened guest was severely reprimanded. And I had cause to quake all over again. It was quite a while before I went back to sleep that night.

Eventually, however, I got used to air raids in Spain—the Junkers, Heinkels, Savoias and Capronis going over—and the sound and the feel of bombs bursting. But I never got used to the alerts—those baleful, high, eerie, wailing sirens of warning.

Frank Marshall Davis

(1905–1987)

IN THE "FOREWARNING" to *I Am the American Negro*, Frank Marshall Davis tells us not to look for "fairy works" or a "Pollyanna Mind" in his works, but rather for "coarse victuals" and "companions who seldom smile." The last poem in the same work, entitled "Frank Marshall Davis: Writer" gives additional information concerning the author:

> "He is bitter
> A bitter bitter
> Cynic"
> They said
> "And his wine
> He brews from wormwood."

Davis felt that no "sensitive Negro" could live in America without finding his cup overflowing with "vinegar and his meat seasoned with gall." With this outlook, expressed often in Communist-line poetry, Davis produced a series of hard-biting social protest poems which, now a bit dated, were very impressive when they first appeared.

Born in Arkansas City, Kansas, in 1905, Frank Marshall Davis was educated at Friends University in Wichita and at the journalism school of Kansas State College, where he had a brilliant scholarly record. A well-known journalist as well as a poet, Davis helped to establish the *Atlanta Daily World* in 1931. He later became a feature writer in Chicago for the Associated Negro Press. His poetical works are found in the following volumes: *Black Man's Verse* (1935); *I Am the American Negro* (1937); *Through Sepia Eyes: Four Poems* (1938); and *47th Street Poems* (1948). These works and others established Davis as a popular "social minded poet." At one time he served as treasurer of the Chicago chapter of the League of American Writers.

Davis's poetry shows the influence of the "new poets" such as Masters and Sandburg. Several themes recur in his work: Chicago (the city itself *and* the black section), jazz and night life, and social criticism, which played up the issues generally popular at the time with leftist writers, particularly the American race problem. One of his strongest and most sensational protest poems is "Snapshots of the Cotton South" (*47th Street Poems*). A shocking piece, it presents seldom-told truths about the sex-and-racial relations in Dixie. Davis shows better than any other black poet of his generation, with the probable exception of Langston Hughes, the influence of Communism on black poetry.

Biographical and critical materials on Frank Marshall Davis are not plentiful, and this is unfortunate because he gives us an excellent picture of an aspect of New Negro life not found in many other works of the period. For brief comments on Davis, see Benjamin Brawley's *The Negro Genius* (1937, 1966); Stephen Henderson's *Understanding the New Black Poetry* (1973); Arthur P. Davis's *From the Dark Tower* (1974); and the several references in Eugene B. Redmond's *Drumvoices* (1976).

"Christ Is a Dixie Nigger" comes from *I Am the American Negro* (1937), the other poems from *Black Man's Verse* (1935).

CHRIST IS A DIXIE NIGGER

You tell me Christ was born nearly twenty centuries ago
    in a little one horse town called Bethlehem . . . your
    artists paint a man as fair as another New White Hope
Well, you got it all wrong . . . facts twisted as hell . . . see?

Let me tell you wise guys something
I've got my own ideas . . . I've got a better Christ and a
    bigger Christ . . . one you can put your hands on today
    or tomorrow.

My Christ is a Dixie nigger black as midnight, black as the
    roof of a cave's mouth
My Christ is a black bastard . . . maybe Joe did tell the
    neighbors God bigged Mary . . . but he fooled nobody
    . . . they all knew Christ's father was Mr. Jim who owns
    the big plantation . . . and when Christ started bawling
    out back in the cabins Mr. Jim made all three git
You see, I know   *
Christ studied medicine up North in Chicago then came
    back to Mississippi a good physician with ideas for gettin'
    the races together . . . he lectured in the little rundown
    schoolhouses awaiting Rosenwald money . . . he talked
    of the brotherhood and equality of man and of a Con-
    sitution giving everybody a right to vote and some of
    the nigger listeners told their white folks . . . then they

---

"Christ is a Dixie Nigger" is from *I Am the American Negro* (Chicago, Illinois: The Black Cat Press, 1937). Copyright 1937 by The Black Cat Press. The rest of Davis's poems printed here are from *Black Man's Verse* (Chicago, Illinois: The Black Cat Press, 1935). Copyright 1935 by The Black Cat Press.

found how Christ healed a white woman other doctors
gave up for lost . . . the two things together got him in
the calaboose

They called him a Communist and a menace to the Existing
   Relationship Between Black and White in the South
Sheriff and judge debated whether to open the hoosegow
   and tell reporters the mob stormed the jail or let the
   state lynch him on the gallows
Anyhow they got him
Maybe the rope was weak or Christ was too strong to die
   . . . I don't know
They cut him down and they patched him up . . . he hid
   in the swamps until he got well enough to get around
   again . . . then he lectured a little more . . . and faded out
Whether he went to heaven or Harlem or the white folks
   broke his neck and hid the corpse somewhere is a question they still ask—
See what I mean?

I don't want any of your stories about somebody running
   around too long ago to be anything but a highly public-
   ised memory
Your pink priests who whine about Pilate and Judas and
   Gethsemane I'd like to hogtie and dump into the stinking
   cells to write a New Testament around the Scottsboro
   Boys
Subdivide your million dollar temples into liquor taverns
   and high class whore-houses . . . my nigger Christ can't
   get past the door anyway

Remember this, you wise guys
Your tales about Jesus of Nazareth are no-go with me
   I've got a dozen Christs in Dixie all bloody and black . . .

REV. JOSEPH WILLIAMS

Being a Man of God
and a child of flesh and blood
my soul thirsting for truth
and my body hungering for eat and drink
realizing that the satisfaction of one
depended upon the survival of the other
and this could best be done

by preserving the Second Baptist Church
and that on the sisters
depended such preservation
you can understand
why the congregation stuck together
and why, when I died
the sisters mourned
and why so many children
will likewise search for truth
and have moles on their necks
like the Rev. Joseph Williams.

GOLDIE BLACKWELL

My three sisters and I
traded virginity
for comfort
my three sisters
got rings and Mrs.
and respectability
I got two dollars
and independence
and kept respectability
to myself.

ROBERT WHITMORE

Having attained success in business
possessing three cars
one wife and two mistresses
a home and furniture
talked of by the town
and thrice ruler
of the local Elks
Robert Whitmore
died of apoplexy
when a stranger from Georgia
mistook him
for a former Macon waiter.

GEORGE BROWN

For forty years in Mississippi
Voteless he watched white men swept into office
by a tidal wave of race hate
Powerless he saw the crooked politicians
eat the money he paid for taxes
at the table of Public Service
Voiceless he saw bigots who demanded
respect for the Constitution
stand with gun drawn if he tried
to exercise his Constitutional right
of the ballot
I say for forty years
he saw the majority vote given a winner
was less than a fraction of those taken
from his disfranchised people
So when he came North to Chicago
and a man blacker than he
sought a seat in Congress
was it so wrong for him to use
five of the votes
saved from Mississippi
even though it meant
the rest of his life
in the state penitentiary?

GILES JOHNSON, Ph.D.

Giles Johnson
had four college degrees
knew the whyfore of this
the wherefore of that
could orate in Latin
or cuss in Greek
and, having learned such things
he died of starvation
because he wouldn't teach
and he couldn't porter.

ROOSEVELT SMITH

You ask what happened to Roosevelt Smith

Well . . .

Conscience and the critics got him

Roosevelt Smith was the only dusky child born and bred
in the village of Pine City, Nebraska

At college they worshipped the novelty of a black poet and
predicted fame

At twenty-three he published his first book . . . the critics
said he imitated Carl Sandburg, Edgar Lee Masters
and Vachel Lindsay . . . they raved about a wealth of
racial material and the charm of darky dialect

So for two years Roosevelt worked and observed in Dixie

At twenty-five a second book . . . Negroes complained
about plantation scenes and said he dragged Aframer-
ica's good name in the mire for gold . . . "Europe,"
they said, "honors Dunbar for his 'Ships That Pass In
The Night' and not for his dialect which they don't
understand"

For another two years Roosevelt strove for a different medium of expression

At twenty-seven a third book . . . the critics said the density
of Gertrude Stein or T. S. Elliot hardly fitted the
simple material to which a Negro had access

For another two years Roosevelt worked

At twenty-nine his fourth book . . . the critics said a Negro
had no business imitating the classic forms of Keats,
Browning and Shakespeare . . . "Roosevelt Smith,"
they announced, "has nothing original and is merely
a blackface white. His African heritage is a rich source
should he use it"

So for another two years Roosevelt went into the interior
of Africa

At thirty-one his fifth book . . . interesting enough, the
critics said, but since it followed nothing done by any
white poet it was probably just a new kind of prose

Day after the reviews came out Roosevelt traded conscience
and critics for the leather pouch and bunions of a
mail carrier and read in the papers until his death
how little the American Negro had contributed to his
nation's literature . . .

Waring Cuney

(1906–1975)

THE SON of a well-known Washington, D.C., family, Waring Cuney was born in that city and educated in its public schools, including the famed Dunbar High School. He later studied at Howard University, Lincoln University (Pennsylvania), the New England Conservatory of Music, and in Rome, where he continued his voice training. During World War II Cuney served as an army technical sergeant in the South Pacific, winning there the Asiatic Pacific Theater Ribbon with three Bronze Battle Stars.

Waring Cuney first won recognition as a student poet at Lincoln. His poem "No Images" received first prize in the 1926 *Opportunity* poetry contest, and since then has become a classic. It has appeared in many national magazines and in most of the major anthologies of Negro literature. Some of his later protest poems sung by Joshua White were recorded and used in a very popular album entitled *Southern Exposure*. Several of Cuney's lyrics have also been recorded by Burl Ives.

In 1960 he published in the Netherlands a book of poems entitled *Puzzles*. In 1973 Cuney brought out a thin volume called *Storefront Church*. This work, which is volume twenty-three in the Heritage Series, was published in London by Paul Breman. Waring Cuney is also the editor (along with Langston Hughes and Bruce McM. Wright) of the *Lincoln University Poets: Centennial Anthology* (1954).

Cuney is not a prolific author; nor is he a writer of long poems. His forte is the short, meticulously carved poetic vignette, a type which often has the appeal of an aphorism. Like Langston Hughes and Sterling Brown, Cuney in many of his poems also makes effective use of the blues form.

Critical and biographical comment on Waring Cuney is not plentiful. Most of our information now comes from the brief notes found in the early anthologies in which he appeared; and he appeared in many, including: Countee Cullen's *Caroling Dusk* (1927); *Readings from Negro Authors* (1931), edited by Otelia Cromwell, Lorenzo Dow Turner, and Eva B. Dykes; and *The Negro Caravan* (1941), edited by Sterling A. Brown, Arthur P. Davis, and Ulysses Lee. *Lincoln University Poets* (1954), mentioned previously, contains thirteen of his poems; and Eugene B. Redmond's *Drumvoices* (1976) has seven references to Cuney's poetry.

The poems that follow come from *Puzzles* (1960) and *Storefront Church* (1973).

OLD WORKMAN

The old man sits on a bench in the sun,
A feeble frame of his youthful self.

How many years has it been—
A nine-pound sledge-hammer,
Made a rainbow around his shoulders?
Now the strength has gone from his hands.
A once powerful steel-driving man
Sits on a bench in the morning sun,
A shadow of the days of his youth.
He teases the children as they go to school.
As the children come and go he tells them,
John Henry said, "Don't cry until I cry."
The children ask, "Who was John Henry?"
The old man answers, "He was a steel-driving man."
The children ask, "What is a steel-driving man?"
Why did he say, "Don't cry until I cry?"
The old man says, "Run along, you'll be late for school."

COLORED

You want to know what it's like
Being colored?

Well,
It's like going to bat
With two strikes
Already called on you—

It's like playing pool
With your name
Written on the eight ball.

Did you ever say,
"Thank you, sir"—
For an umbrella full of holes?

"Old Workman," "Colored," "Beale Street," "Girl from Oklahoma," "Women and Kitchens," and "No Images" from *Puzzles* by Warring Cuney. Copyright for the Text 1960 by Waring Cuney. Permission granted by Stichting De Roos, Utrecht.

Did you ever dream
You had a million bucks,
And wake up with nothing to pawn?

You want to know what it's like
Being colored

Well,
The only way to know
Is to be born colored.

BEALE STREET

Did you know
That Beale Street
In Memphis,
Has a grave yard
At one end,
A river,
At the other?

No wonder
They say the blues
Began on Beale Street.
You could pick
A guitar,
You could make
A song about that:

Walkin' down
Beale Street
Sad an' low,
Nobody cares
If I stay or go.
Walkin' any which way down
Beale Street,
What do I see?
Nothin' but a
Grave yard,
Or a river,
In front of me.

GIRL FROM OKLAHOMA

I know a girl from Oklahoma.
She has a pretty face,
And a fine figure.
She has brains,
And money in the bank.
This girl from Oklahoma
Has the three B's,
Beauty, brains, and bucks.
She has what nine out of ten men
Are looking for.

This girl I know from Oklahoma
Talks to a psychiatrist
Three hours a week,
Because she is lonely.

WOMEN AND KITCHENS

No kitchen
Is big enough
For two women.

If you build
A kitchen
A city block long
By a city street wide,
It will be too small
For two women.
They can be sisters,
They can be friends,
They can be a girl
And her mother-in-law.
They can be strangers,
Or a servant
And the lady for whom she works.

It makes no difference.

A house with
Two women in it
Needs two kitchens.

A dance hall
Has room for many women.
So has a bargain basement.

Kitchens are different.

There should be a sign
Above all kitchen doors:
'Room For One Woman Only'.

NO IMAGES

She does not know
Her beauty,
She thinks her brown body
Has no glory.

If she could dance
Naked
Under palm trees,
And see her image in the river
She would know.

But there are no palm trees
On the street,
And dish water gives back no images.

PRAYER FOR A VISITOR

Lord—
this white man
here this evening—
may he be blessed by Thee.

Lord—
this white man
in our midst tonight—
may he see the light.

"Prayer For a Visitor" and "Hard-time Blues" from *Storefront Church*. Copyright 1973 by William Waring Cuney. Published by Paul Breman Limited.

Lord—
this white man
here in our church—
if he is a policeman
come to listen about
the sit-ins, and the sit-downs,
the meetings, and the picket lines—
Lord,
You tell him
that we have just begun.

Lord—
this white man
here this evening—
if he is a detective
come to find out
what we are about,
what our next move will be—
Lord, You tell him
that we do not know.

Pharaoh
rules so hard in the land
that God let Pharaoh feel
the strength of God's hand.

Lord—
this white man
here this evening—
may he be blessed by Thee.

Amen.

HARD-TIME BLUES

Went down home 'bout a year ago
things so bad, Lord, my heart was sore.
Folks had nothing was a sin and shame
every-body said hard time was the blame.
    Great-God-a-mighty folks feeling bad
    lost every thing they ever had.

Sun was shining fourteen days and no rain
hoeing and planting was all in vain.
Hard hard times, Lord, all around
meal barrels empty crops burnt to the ground.

Great-God-a-mighty folks feeling bad
lost every thing they ever had.

Skinny looking children bellies poking out
that old pellagra without a doubt.
Old folks hanging 'round the cabin door
ain't seen times this hard before.
Great-God-a-mighty folks feeling bad
lost every thing they ever had.

I went to the Boss at the Commissary store
folks all starving please don't close your door
want more food a little more time to pay
Boss Man laughed and walked away.
Great-God-a-mighty folks feeling bad
lost every thing they ever had.

Landlord coming 'round when the rent is due
you ain't got the money take your home from you
take your mule and horse even take your cow
get offa my land you ain't no good no how.
Great-God-a-mighty folks feeling bad
lost every thing they ever had.

William Attaway

(1912–   )

BORN IN MISSISSIPPI and educated in Chicago and at the University of Illinois, William Attaway left college to see the world, as a seaman, salesman, labor organizer, and actor (in the road company of *You Can't Take It with You*). A composer as well as a writer, Attaway has arranged songs for Harry Belafonte and is the author of *The Calypso Song Book*. He has also written television and film scripts, including the script for the screen version of Irving Wallace's novel *The Man*. His children's book *I Hear America Singing* was published in 1967.

The author of two provocative and unusual novels, William Attaway has not received the popularity and attention he deserves. His first novel, *Let Me Breathe Thunder* (1939; reprinted in 1969), is unusual in that it deals with white characters—white migrant workers. Though white, they are, like blacks, "outside" people, and Attaway treats them with great understanding. The second novel, *Blood on the Forge* (1941, reprinted in 1969 and 1970), is a perceptive analysis of the rural southern black's bewildering and occasionally tragic introduction to life in the alien industrial North. Edward Margolies feels that in this work Attaway has "rendered the usual subject matter of the proletarian novel into a work of art." Bonnie J. Barthold in *Black Time: Fiction of Africa, the Caribbean, and the United States* (1981) writes that Attaway "alone, among all black writers, makes the work the center of his sociological imagination."

For other critical comment on Attaway, see Edward Margolies, *Native Sons* (1968), and Margolies's introduction to the 1970 reprint of *Blood on the Forge*. See also Bernard W. Bell, *The Afro-American Novel and Its Tradition* (1987), and Cynthia Hamilton, "Work and Culture: The Evolution of Consciousness in Urban Industrial Society in the Fiction of William Attaway and Peter Abrahams," *Black American Literature Forum* (Spring/Summer 1987). Arthur P. Davis notes in *From the Dark Tower: Afro-American Writers 1900 to 1960* (1974) that "few novelists have explored this all important theme [the great migration] and none, of course, as sympathetically and artistically as William Attaway. Like too many other black artists, he stopped writing far too soon."

The following excerpt is from *Blood on the Forge* (1941).

FROM **BLOOD ON THE FORGE**

They hunched against one another, whispering and wondering, and big drops of rain, grayed with slag and soot, rolled on the long wooden bunkhouse. Passing the makings back and forth, they burned cigarettes until their tongues felt like flannel in their jaws. There was a crap game going on in the bunkhouse, but the newcomers didn't have any money to put on the wood. There was nothing for them to do that first day, except smoke and keep walking the rows of bunks. Windows stretched in the long wooden walls around them. And outside they could see the things that they would see for a long time to come.

A giant might have planted his foot on the heel of a great shovel and split the bare hills. Half buried in the earth where the great shovel had trenched were the mills. The mills were as big as creation when the new men had ridden by on the freight. From the bunkhouse they were just so much scrap iron, scattered carelessly, smoking lazily. In back of them ran a dirty-as-a-catfish-hole river with a beautiful name: the Monongahela. Its banks were lined with mountains of red ore, yellow limestone and black coke. None of this was good to the eyes of men accustomed to the pattern of fields.

Most of the crap shooters had been in the valley a long time. Some of them took time from the game to come back and talk with the green men.

"See them towers? That's where I works. The iron blast. Don't take the blast if you kin help it. It ain't the work—it's the head blower. Goddamn tough mick. Why, I seen the time when the keeper on my furnace mess up the blast, and the furnace freeze before you know it. That head blower don't stop to find who the fault go to. Naw, he run up and right quick lays out three men with a sow. One of the hunkies yanks a knife on him, but that hunky gits laid out too. I reckon somebody woulda got that mick 'fore this. Only a man ain't much fer a fight when he's makin' four hundred tons of fast iron from one sun to the other."

The men from the hills were not listening. They were not talking. Their attitude spoke. Like a refrain:

We have been tricked away from our poor, good-as-bad-ground-and-bad-white-men-will-let-'em-be hills. What men in their right minds would leave off tending green growing things to tend iron monsters?

"Lots of green guys git knocked out by the heat—'specially hunkies. They don't talk nothin' but gobbler talk. Don't understand nothin' else neither. Foreman tell one old feller who was workin' right next to me to put leather over his chest. Foreman might jest as well been whistlin', 'cause when the heat come down there that hunky lays with a chest like a scrambled egg."

Yes, them red-clay hills was what we call stripped ground, but there was growing things everywhere and crab-apple trees bunched—stunted but beautiful in the sun.

"Them old fellers hadn't oughta be put on a furnace. Course, a green man got to expect to git pitted up some. Lots o' young'uns got lead in their pants, and they gits tagged when the flame come jumpin' for their shovel. There always burns, too, when the furnace gits tapped and the slag spills over into the pit. But the quicker a man learn to move around on his feet the longer he stays livin'."

A man don't git to know what the place where he's born looks like until he goes someplace else. Then he begins to see with his mind things that his eyes had never been able to see. To us niggers who are seeing the red-clay hills with our minds this Allegheny County is an ugly, smoking hell out of a backwoods preacher's sermon.

"Mebbe they start you new boys out on the skull buster. That's a good way to git broke in. But jest keep minded that you got to be keerful o' that old devil, skull buster. Kill many a green man. How? Well, magnet lift the steel ball thirty feet up and drop her. Steel ball weigh nigh eight tons. That eight tons bust the hell out of old scrap metal. Got to be keerful not to git some of it in your skull. Yessir, many a green man long gone 'cause he couldn't keep old skull buster from aimin' at his head."

What's the good in strainin' our eyes out these windows? We can't see where nothin' grows around here but rusty iron towers and brick stacks, walled up like somebody's liable to try and steal them. Where are the trees? They so far away on the tops of the low mountains that they look like the fringe on a black wear-me-to-a-wake dress held upside down against the sky.

"Skull buster don't git as many as whores git. Roll mill help the gals out. Feller sees all that hot steel shooting along the runout tables, all them red-and-white tongues licking 'twixt them rollers. Feller go hog wild fer any gal what'll take his money. She don't have to work him up none—he's hot from that bakin' steel."

The sun on the red hillsides baked a man, but it was only a short walk to the bottoms and the mud that oozed up between his toes like a cool drink to hot black feet, steppin' easy, mindful of the cottonmouth.

"On the floor, under the Bessemers, you ain't got time to think what a gal's got 'tween her legs. . . ."

Melody and Chinatown went out into the wet. The door closed behind them. The rain had lessened to a drizzle. They could hear the clank of the mills over the steady swish of the rain. Melody led the way. He turned away from the river and walked toward the town.

"Boy, this here North don't seem like nothin' to me," complained Chinatown. "All this smoke and stuff in the air! How a man gonna breathe?"

The drizzle stopped. Thin clouds rolled. Melody looked up. "Sun liable to break through soon."

"Won't make no difference to us if the sun don't shine."

"How come?"

"There won't be no crop to make or take out."

"Sun make you feel better," said Melody.

"Couldn't shine through the smoke, nohow. Long time ago a fella told me a nigger need sun so's he kin keep black."

Melody kicked Chinatown with his knee. Chinatown kicked back. Soon they were kicking and dodging around the ash piles. They were laughing when they came to the weedy field at the edge of town. Both men stopped. The laughter died.

Quivering above the high weeds were the freckled white legs of a girl. She struggled with a small form—a little boy who wanted to be turned loose. Other children were peeping through the wet grass. They began to chant, "Shame, shame! Mary and her brother— shame!"

Chinatown and Melody wheeled and hurried away. They had no need to speak to each other. In both of them was the fear brought from Kentucky: that girl might scream. Back in the hills young Charley had been lynched because a girl screamed.

Breathing hard, they followed the path until it became a dirt street. In front of them was a long line of women waiting in front of a pump shed. A few boys crouched underneath one corner of the shelter, held by a game with a jackknife.

"Look—more hunkies!" breathed Chinatown.

"Keep shut," warned Melody.

The pump at the edge of town watered about fifty families. Every Saturday the women were here in line. This day they carried bathing water home. The rain had soaked into their shawl head coverings. They stood patiently.

Then one of the boys spied the three strangers. He was on his feet in a second.

"Ya-a-a . . ."

A rock whizzed between Melody and Chinatown. The two men halted, confused. In the eyes of all the Slavs was a hatred and con- tempt different from anything they had ever experienced in Kentucky. Another rock went past. Chinatown started to back away.

"We ain't done nothin'," cried Melody. He took a step toward the pump shed. The women covered their faces with their shawls.

"We ain't done nothin'," he cried again.

His words were lost in the shrill child voices: "Ya-a-a . . . ya-a-a . . . ya-a-a . . ."

Melody backed after his half brother. A little distance away they turned and trotted riverward.

"So this how the North different from the South," panted Chinatown.

"Musta mistook us for somebody," said Melody.

"When white folks git mad all niggers look alike," said Chinatown.

"Musta mistook us," insisted Melody.

It should have been easy for them to find the bunkhouse. The river was a sure landmark. But, in turning in among a series of knolls, they lost direction and found themselves back at the town. Before them a dirt road ran between rows of frame shacks. A large pile of garbage blocked the far end of the road.

"Oughta be somebody we kin ask where the bunkhouse," said Chinatown.

"Well, I ain't knockin' on nobody's door to ask nothing."

"All we got to do is start back to the river."

"Which way the river?" puzzled Melody, craning his neck around.

The light rain had started again. A mist had arisen through the rain. The low mountains were no longer visible. The mills along the water were blotted out. Their sound seemed to come from all directions.

"Maybe if I climbs that garbage . . ."

Chinatown started at a run down the road. At the top of the garbage pile he got his bearings. To the west the gray was tinged with faint streaks of orange.

"Over yonder apiece," he yelled, pointing westward.

At the cry, white faces appeared in the doorway opposite him. Nothing was said. Little faces grimaced between the overalled legs of the bearded father. With a movement of her hands beneath an apron, the mother fanned the breadth of her hips at him. An old Slav bent like a burned weed out of the window. Great handle-bar mustaches dripped below his chin. With eyes a snow-washed blue, he looked contempt at Chinatown. Then he wrinkled his nose and spat.

Chinatown slid down the pile of wet garbage. Hardly daring to hurry, he walked the middle of the road to the place where Melody waited.

"These here folks ain't mistook nobody."

They made quick tracks in the mud to the west.

At the river they did not stop to rest or look around. They wanted the shelter of the bunkhouse. This new place was full of hatreds that they did not understand. Melody led the way down-river. They had been going ten minutes when he stopped. There was no sign of the bunkhouse. Nothing but the river looked familiar.

"You reckon we been goin' wrong?" asked Chinatown.

"Got to be one way or the other," said Melody. He turned and looked behind him.

A fat-cheeked black girl moved along the river-front road. Bright red lipstick had turned to purple on her lips. A man's hat was pulled down over her ears. She wore an old overall coat over a stained satin dress.

Melody stared at her. She drew the coat tight around her hips and began to swagger. He was drawn by her eyes. They were cold pieces of wet glass.

"Wish I knowed what the way to Kentucky," Chinatown was moaning. He turned and saw the woman. "Man! Man! Kentucky kin wait."

The girl passed them. Her swimming eyes invited. They caught a heavy scent of perfume. Under the perfume was a rot stink. The stink sickened them. They were unnerved.

"Howdy, boys. Green, huh?"

They whirled and faced a small, dark man. He shifted from one foot to the other. His movements were like a squirrel's.

"Howdy," said Chinatown.

"How come you know we green?" asked Melody.

"They give all green niggers the same clothes," said the man.

"Oh . . ." Melody's gaze followed the woman.

"Beside, only a green man stop to look at that there gal."

They questioned him with their eyes.

"Her left breast 'bout rotted off." The man laughed. "You kin smell it a mile away."

"What you know!" Chinatown laughed.

Melody was stunned. He could not get the wet eyes out of his mind. All he could think to say was, "We lost from the bunkhouse."

"You been goin' wrong," said the man. "Back the other way a piece."

"Obliged," said Melody.

"I got to pass by there. Point it out."

"Obliged."

They walked along together.

"You work around here?" Chinatown asked.

"Blast. Boss of stove gang," said the man.

"Oh," said Chinatown. He looked at the old overalls.

"Sparks," explained the little man. "They'll git you too."

"Oh."

A group of Slav workmen came out of a gate in front of one of the mills. They moved with a slow stiffness, hardly shaking their drooping mustaches. There was dignity in the way they walked.

"Uh-uh," groaned Chinatown.

The workmen paused at the gate. One of them turned and waved at the little black man.

"Hallo, Bo."

The little man waved back. That greeting was the easy familiarity of men who had known each other over a period of years.

Chinatown voiced what was in his mind: "That there's the first white guy we seen don't hate niggers."

Bo asked, "You been havin' trouble?"

"Everybody treat us like poison," said Chinatown.

"Everythin' be smooth in a coupla weeks," said Bo. "Always hate new niggers round here."

"How come?"

"Well, company bring them in when there strike talk. Keep the old men in line."

"Oh . . ." said Chinatown. They walked a little. "There strike talk now?"

Bo looked him in the eye. "Looka here, boy. I don't know nothin' but my job."

"Yessir," said Chinatown.

"Don't mean nothin' by talkin' short," said Bo, "only it ain't a good thing for a feller to go spoutin' off."

"That's like Kentucky," said Chinatown.

Within sight of the bunkhouse, Bo stopped in the open to let water.

"Good idea," he said. "The outhouse always full of flies. Smells because nobody sprinkle ashes like they supposed to." He laughed. "Sometime a lizard use your behind for a bridge when you on the hole."

The men from the hills had always let water in the open. It made a feller feel free—space around him and the warm water running in the weeds. Nothing overhead but what God first put there. This touch of the past relaxed them. Their recent experiences became the unreality. This was the reality. They felt for a minute like Bo was an old friend.

Sterling A. Brown

(1901–1989)

POET, CRITIC, scholar, folklorist, and legendary teacher, Sterling A. Brown, through his publications, his lectures, his presence on various influential boards, institutes, and projects, and his direct contact with young Negro scholars and writers, had a tremendous influence on the course of African American literature. In his twilight years, Americans, old and young, black and white, integrationists and black nationalists, heaped upon him highly deserved awards, honors, and degrees. In all probability, Brown at the time of his death in 1989 was the most highly respected living figure in Afro-American letters.

Born in Washington, D.C., in 1901, Sterling Brown was educated at the famous Dunbar High School, at Williams College, where he earned his bachelor's degree and was elected to Phi Beta Kappa, and at Harvard, where he received an M.A. in English.

Sterling Brown taught at many American colleges, among them Virginia Seminary and College (Lynchburg), Lincoln University (Missouri), Fisk University, and from 1929 until his retirement in 1969 at Howard University. As a visiting professor, he taught at Atlanta University, New York University, Vassar College, the University of Minnesota, the New School, and the University of Illinois (Chicago Circle). The projects and organizations with which he was associated include the Carnegie Myrdal Study, the American Folklore Society, the Institute of Jazz Studies, the editorial board of *The Crisis*, the Federal Writers' Project, and the Committee on Negro Studies of the American Council of Learned Societies.

Professor Brown was not a prolific writer, but he made up in excellence what, because of his perfectionist tendencies, he lacked in volume. His major book publications include *Southern Road* (1932), a first volume of poetry which takes its place beside *Color* and *The Weary Blues; The Negro in American Literature* and *Negro Poetry and Drama*, two excellent pioneering critical works which appeared in 1938; *The Negro Caravan* (1941), with Arthur P. Davis and Ulysses Lee, a seminal anthology of black American writings; *The Reader's Companion to World Literature* (1956), edited by Lillian D. Horstein, and G. D. Percy, to which Brown contributed eighteen entries; *The Last Ride of Wild Bill and Eleven Narrative Poems* (1975); and *The Collected Poems of Sterling A. Brown* (1980). In addition, Brown over many years wrote literally hundreds of scholarly reviews, essays, and articles on literature, jazz, folklore, and Afro-American life.

For a recent and most impressive work on this author, see Joanne V. Gabbin's *Sterling A. Brown: Building the Black Aesthetic Tradition* (1985); it has excellent bibliographies. See also the following works: Jean Wagner's *Black Poets of the United States: From Paul Laurence Dunbar to Langston Hughes* (1973); Sherley Anne Williams's *Give Birth to Brightness: A Thematic Study in Neo-Black Literature* (1972); and Arthur P. Davis's *From the Dark Tower* (1974). *The Collected Poems of Sterling A. Brown* (National Poetry Series, 1980) has a valuable introduction by Sterling Stuckey.

The poems that follow are from *The Collected Poems of Sterling A. Brown*, which were selected by Michael S. Harper. The essay that follows appeared originally in *The Journal of Negro Education* (April 1933).

ODYSSEY OF BIG BOY

Lemme be wid Casey Jones,
   Lemme be wid Stagolee,
Lemme be wid such like men
   When Death takes hol' on me,
      When Death takes hol' on me. . . .

Done skinned as a boy in Kentucky hills,
   Druv steel dere as a man,
Done stripped tobacco in Virginia fiel's
   Alongst de River Dan,
      Alongst de River Dan;

Done mined de coal in West Virginia,
   Liked dat job jes' fine,
Till a load o' slate curved roun' my head,
   Won't work in no mo' mine,
      Won't work in no mo' mine;

Done shocked de corn in Marylan',
   In Georgia done cut cane,
Done planted rice in South Caline,
   But won't do dat again,
      Do dat no mo' again.

Been roustabout in Memphis,
   Dockhand in Baltimore,

Done smashed up freight on Norfolk wharves,
  A fust class stevedore,
    A fust class stevedore. . . .

Done slung hash yonder in de North
  On de ole Fall River Line,
Done busted suds in li'l New York
  Which ain't no work o' mine—
    Lawd, ain't no work o' mine.

Done worked and loafed on such like jobs,
  Seen what dey is to see,
Done had my time wid a pint on my hip
  An' a sweet gal on my knee,
    Sweet mommer on my knee:

Had stovepipe blond in Macon,
  Yaller gal in Marylan',
In Richmond had a choklit brown,
  Called me huh monkey man—
    Huh big fool monkey man.

Had two fair browns in Arkansaw
  And three in Tennessee,
Had Creole gal in New Orleans,
  Sho Gawd did two time me—
    Lawd two time, fo' time me—
But best gal what I evah had
  Done put it over dem,
A gal in Southwest Washington
  At Four'n half and M—
    Four'n half and M. . . .

Done took my livin' as it came,
  Done grabbed my joy, done risked my life;
Train done caught me on de trestle,
  Man done caught me wid his wife,
    His doggone purty wife. . . .

I done had my women,
  I done had my fun;
Cain't do much complainin'
  When my jag is done,
    Lawd, Lawd, my jag is done.

An' all dat Big Boy axes
  When time comes fo' to go,

Lemme be wid John Henry, steel drivin' man,
Lemme be wid old Jazzbo,
Lemme be wid ole Jazzbo. . . .

OLD LEM

I talked to old Lem
And old Lem said,
  "They weigh the cotton
  They store the corn
    We only good enough
    To work the rows;
  They run the commissary
  They keep the books
    We gotta be grateful
    For being cheated;
  Whippersnapper clerks
  Call us out of our name
    We got to say mister
    To spindling boys
  They make our figgers
  Turn somersets
  We buck in the middle
    Say, "Thankyuh, sah."
    They don't come by ones
    They don't come by twos
    But they come by tens.

"They got the judges
They got the lawyers
They got the jury-rolls
They got the law
    They don't come by ones
They got the sheriffs
They got the deputies
    They don't come by twos

They got the shotguns
They got the rope
  We git the justice
  In the end
    And they come by tens.

"Their fists stay closed
Their eyes look straight
  Our hands stay open
  Our eyes must fall
    They don't come by ones
They got the manhood
They got the courage
    They don't come by twos
  We got to slink around,
  Hangtailed hounds.
They burn us when we dogs
They burn us when we men
    They come by tens. . . .

"I had a buddy
Six foot of man
Muscled up perfect
Game to the heart
    They don't come by ones
Outworked and outfought
Any man or two men
    They don't come by twos
He spoke out of turn
At the commissary
They gave him a day
To git out the county.
He didn't take it.
He said "Come and get me."
They came and got him.
    And they came by tens.
He stayed in the county—
He lays there dead.

    They don't come by ones
    They don't come by twos
    But they come by tens."

SISTER LOU

Honey
When de man
Calls out de las' train
You're gonna ride,
Tell him howdy.

Gather up yo' basket
An' yo' knittin' an' yo' things,
An' go on up an' visit
Wid frien' Jesus fo' a spell.

Show Marfa
How to make yo' greengrape jellies
An' give po' Lazarus
A passel of them Golden Biscuits.

Scald some meal
Fo' some rightdown good spoonbread
Fo' li'l box-plunkin' David.

An' sit aroun'
An' tell them Hebrew Chillen
All yo' stories. . . .

Honey
Don't be feared of them pearly gates,
Don't go 'round to de back,
No mo' dataway
Not evah no mo'.

Let Michael tote yo' burden
An' yo' pocketbook an' evahthing
'Cept yo' Bible,
While Gabriel blows somp'n
Solemn but loudsome
On dat horn of his'n.

Honey
Go straight on to de Big House,
An' speak to yo' God
Widout no fear an' tremblin'.

Then sit down
An' pass de time of day awhile.

Give a good talkin' to
To yo' favorite 'postle Peter,
An' rub the po' head
Of mixed-up Judas,
An' joke awhile wid Jonah.

Then, when you gits de chance,
Always rememberin' yo' raisin',
Let 'em know youse tired
Jest a mite tired.

Jesus will find yo' bed fo' you
Won't no servant evah bother wid yo' room.
Jesus will lead you
To a room wid windows
Openin' on cherry trees an' plum trees
Bloomin' everlastin'.

An' dat will be yours
Fo' keeps.

Den take yo' time. . . .
Honey, take yo' bressed time.

MEMPHIS BLUES

1

Nineveh, Tyre,
Babylon,
Not much lef'
Of either one.
All dese cities
Ashes and rust,
De win' sing sperrichals
Through deir dus' . . .
Was another Memphis
Mongst de olden days,
Done been destroyed
In many ways. . . .
Dis here Memphis
It may go;
Floods may drown it;
Tornado blow;
Mississippi wash it
Down to sea—
Like de other Memphis in
History.

2

Watcha gonna do when Memphis on fire,
    Memphis on fire, Mistah Preachin' Man?
Gonna pray to Jesus and nebber tire,
    Gonna pray to Jesus, loud as I can,
        Gonna pray to my Jesus, oh, my Lawd!

Watcha gonna do when de tall flames roar,
    Tall flames roar, Mistah Lovin' Man?
Gonna love my brownskin better'n before—
    Gonna love my baby lak a do right man,
        Gonna love my brown baby, oh, my Lawd!

Watcha gonna do when Memphis falls down,
    Memphis falls down, Mistah Music Man?
Gonna plunk on dat box as long as it soun',
    Gonna plunk dat box fo' to beat de ban',
        Gonna tickle dem ivories, oh, my Lawd!

Watcha gonna do in de hurricane,
    In de hurricane, Mistah Workin' Man?
Gonna put dem buildings up again,
    Gonna put em up dis time to stan',
        Gonna push a wicked wheelbarrow, oh, my Lawd!

Watcha gonna do when Memphis near gone,
    Memphis near gone, Mistah Drinkin' Man?
Gonna grab a pint bottle of Mountain Corn,
    Gonna keep de stopper in my han',
        Gonna get a mean jag on, oh, my Lawd!

Watcha gonna do when de flood roll fas',
    Flood roll fas', Mistah Gamblin' Man?
Gonna pick up my dice fo' one las' pass—
    Gonna fade my way to de lucky lan',
        Gonna throw my las' seven—oh, my Lawd!

3

Memphis go
By Flood or Flame;
Nigger won't worry
All de same—
Memphis go
Memphis come back,
Ain' no skin
Off de nigger's back.
All dese cities
Ashes, rust. . . .
De win' sing sperrichals
Through deir dus'.

SLIM IN ATLANTA

Down in Atlanta,
  De whitefolks got laws
For to keep all de niggers
  From laughin' outdoors.

    Hope to Gawd I may die
      If I ain't speakin' truth
    Make de niggers do deir laughin'
      In a telefoam booth.

Slim Greer hit de town
  An' de rebs got him told,—
"Dontcha laugh on de street,
  If you want to die old."

    Den dey showed him de booth,
      An' a hundred shines
    In front of it, waitin'
      In double lines.

Slim thought his sides
  Would bust in two,
Yelled, "Lookout, everybody,
  I'm coming through!"

    Pulled de other man out,
      An' bust in de box,
    An' laughed four hours
      By de Georgia clocks.

Den he peeked through de door,
  An' what did he see?
Three hundred niggers there
  In misery.—

    Some holdin' deir sides,
      Some holdin' deir jaws,
    To keep from breakin'
      De Georgia laws.

An' Slim gave a holler,
  An' started again;
An' from three hundred throats
  Come a moan of pain.

An' everytime Slim
   Saw what was outside,
Got to whoopin' again
   Till he nearly died.

An' while de poor critters
   Was waitin' deir chance,
Slim laughed till dey sent
   Fo' de ambulance.

   De state paid de railroad
      To take him away;
   Den, things was as usural
      In Atlanta, Gee A.

REMEMBERING NAT TURNER

We saw a bloody sunset over Courtland, once Jerusalem,
As we followed the trail that old Nat took
When he came out of Cross Keys down upon Jerusalem,
In his angry stab for freedom a hundred years ago.
The land was quiet, and the mist was rising,
Out of the woods and the Nottaway swamp,
Over Southampton the still night fell,
As we rode down to Cross Keys where the march began.

When we got to Cross Keys, they could tell us little of him,
The Negroes had only the faintest recollections:
   "I ain't been here so long, I come from up roun' Newsome;
   Yassah, a town a few miles up de road,
   The old folks who coulda told you is all dead an' gone.
   I heard something, sometime; I doan jis remember what.
   'Pears lak I heard that name somewheres or other.
   So he fought to be free. Well. You doan say."

An old white woman recalled exactly
How Nat crept down the steps, axe in his hand,
After murdering a woman and child in bed,
"Right in this house at the head of these stairs."
(In a house built long after Nat was dead.)
She pointed to a brick store where Nat was captured,
(Nat was taken in a swamp, three miles away)
With his men around him, shooting from the windows
(She was thinking of Harper's Ferry and old John Brown.)

She cackled as she told how they riddled Nat with bullets
(Nat was tried and hanged at Courtland, ten miles away)
She wanted to know why folks would come miles
Just to ask about an old nigger fool.
> "Ain't no slavery no more, things is going all right,
> Pervided thar's a good goober market this year.
> We had a sign post here with printing on it,
> But it rotted in the hole and thar it lays;
> And the nigger tenants split the marker for kindling.
> Things is all right, naow, ain't no trouble with the niggers.
> Why they make this big to-do over Nat?"

As we drove from Cross Keys back to Courtland,
Along the way that Nat came down from Jerusalem,
A watery moon was high in the cloud-filled heavens,
The same moon he dreaded a hundred years ago.
The tree they hanged Nat on is long gone to ashes,
The trees he dodged behind have rotted in the swamps.

The bus for Miami and the trucks boomed by,
And touring cars, their heavy tires snarling on the pavement.
Frogs piped in the marshes, and a hound bayed long,
And yellow lights glowed from the cabin windows.

As we came back the way that Nat led his army,
Down from Cross Keys, down to Jerusalem,
We wondered if his troubled spirit still roamed the Nottaway,
Or if it fled with the cock-crow at daylight,
Or lay at peace with the bones in Jerusalem,
Its restlessness stifled by Southampton clay.

We remembered the poster rotted through and falling,
The marker split for kindling a kitchen fire.

NEGRO CHARACTER AS SEEN BY WHITE AUTHORS

Introduction

There are three types of Negroes, says Roark Bradford, in his
sprightly manner: "the nigger, the 'colored person,' and the Negro—
upper case N." In his foreword to *Ol' Man Adam an' His Chillun*, the

"Negro Character as Seen by White Authors" by Sterling Brown from *The Journal of
Negro Education* (April 1933). Washington, D.C.: Howard University. Copyright © 1933 by
Howard University.

source from which Marc Connelly drew the *Green Pastures*, and a book causing the author to be considered, in some circles, a valid interpreter of *the* Negro, Roark Bradford defines *the* Negro's character and potentialities. The Negro, he says, is the race leader, not too militant, concerned more with economic independence than with civil equality. The colored person, "frequently of mixed blood, loathes the blacks and despises the whites. . . . Generally he inherits the weaknesses of both races and seldom inherits the strength of either. He has the black man's emotions and the white man's inhibitions."[1] Together with the "poor white trash" it is the "colored persons" who perpetuate racial hatreds and incite race riots and lynchings. "The nigger" interests Mr. Bradford more than the rest. He is indolent, entirely irresponsible, shiftless, the bugaboo of Anglo-Saxon ideals, a poor fighter and a poor hater, primitively emotional and uproariously funny.

Such are the "original" contributions of Mr. Bradford, who states modestly that, in spite of the Negro's penchant to lying:

> I believe I know them pretty well. I was born on a plantation that was worked by them; I was nursed by one as an infant and I played with one when I was growing up. I have watched them at work in the fields, in the levee camps, and on the river. I have watched them at home, in church, at their picnics and their funerals.[2]

All of this, he believes, gives him license to step forth as their interpreter and repeat stereotypes time-hallowed in the South. It doesn't. Mr. Bradford's stories remain highly amusing; his generalizations about *the* Negro remain a far better analysis of a white man than of *the* Negro. We see that, even in pontifical moments, one white Southerner cannot escape being influenced by current folk-beliefs.

Mr. Bradford's views have been restated at some length to show how obviously dangerous it is to rely upon literary artists when they advance themselves as sociologists and ethnologists. Mr. Bradford's easy pigeon-holing of an entire race into three small compartments is a familiar phenomenon in American literature, where the Indian, the Mexican, the Irishman, and the Jew have been similarly treated. Authors are too anxious to have it said, "Here is *the* Negro," rather than here are a few Negroes whom I have seen. If one wishes to learn of Negro individuals observed from very specialized points of view, American literature can help him out. Some books will shed a

---

[1] Roark Bradford, *Ol' Man Adam an' His Chillun*, New York: Harper and Bros., 1928, p. xi.

[2] *Ibid.*, p. ix.

great deal of light upon Negro experience. But if one wishes to learn of *the* Negro, it would be best to study *the* Negro himself; a study that might result in the discovery that *the* Negro is more difficult to find than the countless human beings called Negroes.

The Negro has met with as great injustice in American literature as he has in American life. The majority of books about Negroes merely stereotype Negro character. It is the purpose of this paper to point out the prevalence and history of these stereotypes. Those considered important enough for separate classification, although overlappings *do* occur, are seven in number: (1) The Contented Slave, (2) The Wretched Freeman, (3) The Comic Negro, (4) The Brute Negro, (5) The Tragic Mulatto, (6) The Local Color Negro, and (7) The Exotic Primitive.

A detailed evaluation of each of these is impracticable because of limitations of space. It can be said, however, that all of these stereotypes are marked either by exaggeration or omissions; that they all agree in stressing the Negro's divergence from an Anglo-Saxon norm to the flattery of the latter; they could all be used, as they probably are, as justification of racial proscription; they all illustrate dangerous specious generalizing from a few particulars recorded by a single observer from a restricted point of view—which is itself generally dictated by the desire to perpetuate a stereotype. All of these stereotypes are abundantly to be found in American literature, and are generally accepted as contributions to true racial understanding. Thus one critic, setting out imposingly to discuss "the Negro character" in American literature, can still say, unabashedly, that "*The whole range of the Negro character is revealed thoroughly,*"[3] in one twenty-six-line sketch by Joel Chandler Harris of Br'er Fox and Br'er Mud Turtle.

The writer of this essay does not consider everything a stereotype that shows up the weaknesses of Negro character; sometimes the stereotype makes the Negro appear too virtuous. Nor does he believe the stereotypes of contented slaves and buffoons are to be successfully balanced by pictures of Negroes who are unbelievably intellectual, noble, self-sacrificial, and faultless. Any stereotyping is fatal to great, or even to convincing literature. Furthermore, he believes that he has considered to be stereotypes only those patterns whose frequent and tedious recurrence can be demonstrably proved by even a cursory acquaintance with the literature of the subject.

---

[3]John Herbert Nelson, *The Negro Character in American Literature,* Lawrence, Kansas: The Department of Journalism Press, 1926, p. 118.

The Contented Slave

"Massa make de darkies lub him
'Case he was so kind. . . ."
                    (Stephen Foster)

The first lukewarm stirrings of abolitionary sentiment in the South were chilled with Eli Whitney's invention of the cotton gin at the close of the 18th Century. Up until this time the *raison d'être* of slavery had not been so powerful. But now there was a way open to quick wealth; Cotton was crowned King, and a huge army of black servitors was necessary to keep him upon the throne; considerations of abstract justice had to give way before economic expediency. A complete rationale of slavery was evolved.

One of the most influential of the authorities defending slavery was President Dew of William and Mary College, who stated, in 1832,

> . . . slavery had been the condition of all ancient culture, that Christianity approved servitude, and that the law of Moses had both assumed and positively established slavery. . . . It is the order of nature and of God that the being of superior faculties and knowledge, and therefore of superior power, should control and dispose of those who are inferior. It is as much in the order of nature that men should enslave each other as that other animals should prey upon each other.[4]

The pamphlet of this young teacher was extensively circulated, and was substantiated by Chancellor Harper of the University of South Carolina in 1838:

> Man is born to subjection. . . . The proclivity of the natural man is to domineer or to be subservient. . . . If there are sordid, servile, and laborious offices to be performed, is it not better that there should be sordid, servile, and laborious beings to perform them?[5]

The economic argument had frequent proponents; an ex-governor of Virginia showed that, although Virginia was denied the tremendous prosperity accruing from cotton raising, it was still granted the opportunity to profit from selling Negroes to the far South. Sociologists and anthropologists hastened forward with proof of the Negro's three-fold inferiority: physically (except for his adaptability to cotton fields and rice swamps), mentally, and morally. Theologists advanced the invulnerable arguments from the Bible; in one of the "Bible Def-

---

[4] William E. Dodd, *The Cotton Kingdom*, Chapter III, Philosophy of the Cotton Planter, p. 53.

[5] *Ibid.*, p. 57.

ences of Slavery" we read: "The curse of Noah upon *Ham*, had a *general* and *interminable* application to the whole Hamite race, in placing them under a *peculiar* liability of being enslaved by the races of the two other brothers."[6]

The expressions of these dominant ideas in the fiction and poetry of the period did not lag far behind. In fact, one influential novel was among the leaders of the van, for in 1832, the year in which Professor Dew stated the argument that was to elevate him to the presidency of William and Mary College, John P. Kennedy published a work that was to make him one of the most widely read and praised authors of the Southland. His ideas of the character of the Negro and of slavery are in fundamental agreement with those of Dew and Harper. According to F. P. Gaines, in *The Southern Plantation*, Kennedy's *Swallow Barn* has the historical significance of starting the plantation tradition, a tradition hoary and mildewed in our own day, but by no means moribund.

Swallow Barn is an idyllic picture of slavery on a tidewater plantation. The narrator, imagined to be from the North (Kennedy himself was from Tidewater Maryland), comes to Virginia, expecting to see a drastic state of affairs. Instead, he finds a kindly patriarchy and grateful, happy slaves. After vignettes of the Negro's laziness, mirth, vanity, improvidence, done with some charm and, for a Southern audience, considerable persuasiveness, the "Northern" narrator concludes:

> I am quite sure they never could become a happier people than I find them here. . . . No tribe of people has ever passed from barbarism to civilization whose . . . progress has been more secure from harm, more genial to their character, or better supplied with mild and beneficent guardianship, adapted to the actual state of their intellectual feebleness, than the Negroes of *Swallow Barn*. And, from what I can gather, it is pretty much the same on the other estates in this region.[7]

Shortly after the publication of *Swallow Barn*, Edgar Allan Poe wrote:

> . . . .we must take into consideration the peculiar character (I may say the peculiar nature) of the Negro . . . [Some believe that Negroes] are, like ourselves, the sons of Adam and must, therefore, have like passions and wants and feelings and tempers in all respects. This we deny and appeal to the knowledge of all who know. . . . We shall take leave to speak as of things *in esse*, in a degree of loyal devotion on the part of the slave to which the white man's heart is a stranger, and of the mas-

---

[6]Josiah Priest, *Bible Defence of Slavery*, Glasgow, Ky.: W. S. Brown, 1851, p. 52.
[7]John P. Kennedy, *Swallow Barn*, p. 453.

ter's reciprocal feeling of parental attachment to his humble dependent. . . . That these sentiments in the breast of the Negro and his
master are stronger than they would be under like circumstances between individuals of the white race, we believe.[8]

In *The Gold-Bug*, Poe shows this reciprocal relationship between
Jupiter, a slave, and his master. Southern fiction of the thirties and
forties supported the thesis of Kennedy and Poe without being so
explicit. The mutual affection of the races, the slave's happiness with
his status, and his refusal to accept freedom appear here and there,
but the books were dedicated less to the defense of the peculiar institution than to entertainment. William Gilmore Simms, for instance, includes in *The Yemassee*, a novel published in the same year
as *Swallow Barn*, the typical pro-slavery situation of a slave's refusing
freedom: "I d—n to h—ll, maussa, ef I guine to be free!" roared the
adhesive black, in a tone of unrestrainable determination.[9] But the
burden of this book is not pro-slavery; Hector earns his freedom by
the unslavish qualities of physical prowess, foresight, and courage in
battle.

In 1853, Simms, in joining forces with Dew and Harper in the
Pro-Slavery Argument, writes: "Slavery has elevated the Negro from
savagery. The black man's finer traits of fidelity and docility were encouraged in his servile position. . . ."[10] Simms turned from cursory
references to slavery to ardent pro-slavery defense, in company with
other novelists of the South, for a perfectly definite reason. The
abolitionary attacks made by men like Garrison had taken the form
of pamphlets, and these had been answered in kind. The publication
of *Uncle Tom's Cabin* in 1851, however, showed that the abolitionists
had converted the novel into a powerful weapon. Pro-slavery authors
were quick to take up this weapon, although their wielding of it was
without the power of Harriet Beecher Stowe. *Swallow Barn* was reissued in 1851, and "besides the numerous controversial pamphlets
and articles in periodicals there were no fewer than fourteen pro-
slavery novels and one long poem published in the three years
(1852–54) following the appearance of *Uncle Tom's Cabin*."[11]

These novels are all cut out of the same cloth. Like *Swallow
Barn*, they omit the economic basis of slavery, and minimize "the
sordid, servile and laborious offices" which Chancellor Harper had

---

[8]Edgar Allan Poe, *Literary Criticism*, Vol. 1, "Slavery in the United States," p. 271.
[9]William Gilmore Simms, *The Yemassee*. Richmond: B. F. Johnson Publishing Co., 1911,
p. 423. The italics are mine but not the omissions.
[10]Jeanette Reid Tandy, "Pro-Slavery Propaganda in American Fiction of the Fifties,"
South Atlantic Quarterly, Vol. XXI, No. 1, p. 41.
[11]*Ibid.*, p. 41.

considered the due of "sordid, servile, and laborious beings." The pro-slavery authors use the first adjective only in considering free Negroes, or those who, by some quirk of nature, are disobedient; admit the second completely; and deny the third. Slavery to all of them is a beneficent guardianship, the natural and inevitable state for a childish people.

There is very little reference to Negroes working in the fields; even then they are assigned to easy tasks which they lazily perform to the tune of slave melodies. They are generally described as "leaving the fields." They are allowed to have, for additional provisions and huckstering, their own garden-plots, which they attend in their abundant leisure. Their holidays are described at full length: the corn huskings, barbecuing, Yuletide parties, and hunting the possum by the light of a kindly moon.

In *Life at the South, or Uncle Tom's Cabin As It Is* (1852), Uncle Tom, out of hurt vanity, but not for any more grievous cause, runs away. His wife, Aunt Dinah, although loving Tom, realizes that her greater loyalty is due to her master, and not to her errant spouse, and refuses to escape with him. Tom, after experiencing the harshness of the unfeeling North, begs to return to slavery. In *The Planter's Northern Bride*, the bride, having come to the slave South with misgivings, is quickly converted to an enthusiast for slavery, since it presents "an aspect so tender and affectionate." One fears that the bride is not unpartisan, however, since her appearance on the plantation elicited wild cries of worship, and her beloved husband is a great ethnologist, proving that the Negro's peculiar skull and skin were decreed by the divine fiat so that he could pick cotton. In *The Yankee Slave Dealer*, the meddling abolitionist cannot persuade any slaves to run off with him except a half-witted rogue. One slave recited to him *verbatim* a miniature *Bible Defence of Slavery*, citing the book of the Bible, the chapter, and the verse. In *The Hireling and The Slave*, William J. Grayson, "poet laureate" of South Carolina, contrasts the lot of the industrial worker of the North with that of the slave. Gems of this widely read poetical disquisition follow:

> And yet the life, so unassailed by care,
> So blessed with moderate work, with ample fare,
> With all the good the starving pauper needs,
> The happier slave on each plantation leads. . . .(p. 50)
> And Christian slaves may challenge as their own,
> The blessings claimed in fabled states alone. . . .(p. 50)

This pattern of the joyous contentment of the slave in a paradisaical bondage persisted and was strongly reenforced in Reconstruction days. If it was no longer needed for the defense of a tottering institu-

tion, it was needed for reasons nearly as exigent. Ancestor worshippers, the sons of a fighting generation, remembering bitterly the
deaths or suffering of their fathers, became elegists of a lost cause
and cast a golden glow over the plantation past; unreconstructed
"fire-eaters," determined to resurrect slavery as far as they were able,
needed as a cardinal principle the belief that Negroes were happy as
slaves, and hopelessly unequipped for freedom. Both types were persuasive, the first because the romantic idealizing of the past will always be seductive to a certain large group of readers, and the second
because the sincere unremitting harping upon one argument will finally make it seem plausible. We find, therefore, that whereas *Uncle
Tom's Cabin* had triumphed in the antebellum controversy, the pro-
slavery works of Page, Russell, and Harris swept the field in Reconstruction days. It is from these last skillful authors, undeniably acquainted with Negro folk-life, and affectionate toward certain aspects
of it, that the American reading public as a whole has accepted the
delusion of the Negro as contented slave, entertaining child, and
docile ward.

Mutual affection between the races is a dominant theme. Thus,
Irwin Russell, the first American poet to treat Negro life in folk
speech, has his ex-slave rhapsodizing about his "Mahsr John."
"Washintum an' Franklum . . . wuzn't nar a one . . . come up to
Mahsr John":

> Well times is changed. De war it come an' sot de niggers free
> An' now ol' Mahsr John ain't hardly wuf as much as me;
> He had to pay his debts, an' so his lan' is mos'ly gone—
> An' I declar' I's sorry for my pore ol' Mahsr John.[12]

The volume has many other references to the slave's docility toward,
and worship of his master.

Irwin Russell implies throughout that the Southern white best
understands how to treat the Negro. Perhaps this is one reason for
Joel Chandler Harris's praise:

> But the most wonderful thing about the dialect poetry of Irwin Russell
> is his accurate conception of the negro character. . . . I do not know
> where could be found today a happier or a more perfect representation
> of negro character.

On reading Russell's few poems, one is struck by the limited gamut
of characteristics allowed to Negroes. Inclined to the peccadilloes of
cheating, lying easily; a good teller of comic stories, a child of mirth,

---

[12]Irwin Russell, *Christmas Night in the Quarters*, New York: The Century Co., 1917, pp.
63 ff.

his greatest hardship that of being kicked about by refractory mules, and his deepest emotion, compassion for his master's lost estate— surely this is hardly a "perfect" representation of even Negro folk character?

Thomas Nelson Page followed Russell's lead in poetry. In the poems of *Befo' De War*, Page puts into the mouths of his Negroes yearnings for the old days and expressions of the greatest love for old marster. One old slave welcomes death if it will replace him in old "Marster's service." Old Jack entrusts his life-earnings to his son to give to young "Marster," since the latter can't work and needs them more.[13]

In most of Page's widely influential stories, there is the stock situation of the lifelong devotion of master and body-servant. In *Marse Chan*, old "Marse" is blinded in rescuing a slave from a burning barn. Sam accompanies his young Marse Chan to the war, his devotion overcoming "racial cowardice" to such a degree that he rides to the very cannon's mouth with him, and brings back his master's body. Of slavery, Sam speaks thus:

> Dem wuz good old times, marster—de bes' Sam ever see! Dey wuz, in fac'! Niggers didn't hed nothin 't all to do—jes' hed to 'ten to de feedin' an' cleanin' de hosses, an' doin' what de marster tell 'em to do; an' when dey wuz sick, dey had things sont 'em out de house, an' de same doctor come to see 'em whar ten' do de white folks when dey wuz po'ly. D'yar warn' no trouble nor nothin.[14]

Over all his fiction there is the reminiscent melancholy of an exiled Adam, banished by a flaming sword—wielded not by Michael but by a Yankee devil, from what was truly an Eden. In *The Negro: The Southerner's Problem*, we read:

> In fact, the ties of pride were such that it was often remarked that the affection of the slaves was stronger toward the whites than toward their own offspring.[15]

And in the same book there is an apostrophe to the "mammy" that is a worthy forerunner of the bids so many orators make for interracial good-will, and of the many remunerative songs that emerge from Tin Pan Alley.

Joel Chandler Harris is better known for his valuable contribution to literature and folk-lore in recording the Uncle Remus stories

---

[13]Thomas Nelson Page, *Befo' De War*. New York: Chas. Scribner's Sons, 1906, "Little Jack."

[14]Thomas Nelson Page, *In Ole Virginia*. New York: Chas. Scribner's Sons, 1889.

[15]Thomas Nelson Page, *The Negro: The Southerner's Problem*. New York: Chas. Scribner's Sons, 1904, p. 174.

than for his aid in perpetuation of the "plantation Negro" stereotype. Nevertheless, a merely cursory study of Uncle Remus's character would reveal his close relationship to the "Caesars," "Hectors," "Pompeys," *et al.* of the pro-slavery novel, and to Page's "Uncle Jack" and "Uncle Billy." In Uncle Remus's philosophizing about the old days of slavery there is still the wistful nostalgia. Harris comments, "In Middle Georgia the relations between master and slave were as perfect as they could be under the circumstances." This might mean a great deal, or nothing, but it is obvious from other words of Harris that, fundamentally, slavery was to him a kindly institution, and the Negro was contented. Slavery was:

> . . . in some of its aspects far more beautiful and inspiring than *any* of the relations between employers and the employed in this day.[16]

George Washington Cable, although more liberal in his views upon the Negro than his Southern contemporaries, gives an example of the self-abnegating servant in *Posson Jone'*. This slave uses his wits to safeguard his master. A goodly proportion of the Negro servants are used to solve the complications of their "white-folks." They are in a long literary tradition—that of the faithful, clever servant—and they probably are just as true to Latin prototypes as to real Negroes. In the works of F. Hopkinson Smith, Harry Stilwell Edwards, and in Maurice Thompson's *Balance of Power*, we have this appearance of a black *deus ex machina*.

To deal adequately with the numerous books of elegiac reminiscence of days "befo' de war" would be beyond the scope and purpose of this essay. The tone of them all is to be found in such sad sentences as these:

> Aunt Phebe, Uncle Tom, Black Mammy, Uncle Gus, Aunt Jonas, Uncle Isom, and all the rest—who shall speak all your virtues or enshrine your simple faith and fidelity? It is as impossible as it is to describe the affection showered upon you by those whom you called "Marster" and "Mistis."[17]

Ambrose Gonzales grieves that "the old black folk are going fast" with the passing of the "strict but kindly discipline of slavery," yearning, in Tennysonian accents, "for the tender grace of a day that is dead."[18]

---

[16]Julia Collier Harris, *Joel Chandler Harris, Editor and Essayist*. Chapel Hill: University of North Carolina Press, 1931, "The Old-Time Darky," p. 129.

[17]Essie Collins Matthews, *Aunt Phebe, Uncle Tom and Others*. Columbus, Ohio: The Champlin Press, 1915, p. 13.

[18]Ambrose Gonzales, *With Aesop Along the Black Border*. Columbia, S.C.: The State Co., 1924, p. xiv.

Although the realism of today is successfully discounting the sentimentalizing of the Old South, there are still many contemporary manifestations of the tradition. Hergesheimer, arch-romanticist that he is, writes that he would be happy to pay with everything the wasted present holds for the return of the pastoral civilization based on slavery.[19]

Donald Davidson, a Tennessee poet, has written this:

> Black man, when you and I were young together,
> We knew each other's hearts. Though I am no longer
> A child, and you perhaps unfortunately
> Are no longer a child, we still understand
> Better maybe than others. There is the wall
> Between us, anciently erected. Once
> It might have been crossed, men say. But now I cannot
> Forget that I was master, and you can hardly
> Forget that you were slave. We did not build
> The ancient wall, but there it painfully is.
> Let us not bruise our foreheads on the wall.[20]

Ol' Massa's People, by Orlando Kay Armstrong, is one of the most recent of the books in which ex-slaves speak—as in Page apparently with their master's voice—their praise of slavery. The theme seems inexhaustible; in the February issue of the *Atlantic Monthly* [1933] it is restated in nearly the words that have already been quoted. Designed originally to defend slavery, it is now a convenient argument for those wishing to keep "the Negro in his place"—out of great love for him, naturally—believing that he would be happier so.

The Wretched Freeman

"Go tell Marse Linkum, to tek his freedom back."

As a foil to the contented slave, pro-slavery authors set up another puppet—the wretched free Negro. He was necessary for the argument. Most of the pro-slavery novels paid a good deal of attention to his degradation. Either the novelist interpolated a long disquisition on the disadvantages of his state both to the country and to himself, or had his happy slaves fear contact with him as with a plague.

In *Life at The South, or Uncle Tom's Cabin as It Is*, Uncle Tom experiences harsh treatment from unfeeling Northern employers, sees Negroes frozen to death in snow storms, and all in all learns

---

[19]Joseph Hergesheimer, *Quiet Cities*. New York: Alfred A. Knopf, 1928, pp. 14 ff.
[20]Donald Davidson, *The Tall Men*. New York: Houghton Mifflin Co., 1927, p. 39.

that the North and freedom is no stopping place for him. In *The
Yankee Slave Dealer*, the slaves are insistent upon the poor lot of free
Negroes. In *The Planter's Northern Bride*, Crissy runs away from freedom in order to be happy again in servitude. Grayson in *The Hireling and Slave* prophesies thus:

> Such, too, the fate the Negro must deplore
> If slavery guards his subject race no more,
> If by weak friends or vicious counsels led
> To change his blessings for the hireling's bread. . . .
> There in the North in surburban dens and human sties,
> In foul excesses sung, the Negro lies;
> A moral pestilence to taint and stain.
> His life a curse, his death a social gain,
> Debased, despised, the Northern pariah knows
> He shares no good that liberty bestows;
> Spurned from her gifts, with each successive year,
> In drunken want his numbers disappear.[21]

There was a carry-over of these ideas in the Reconstruction. Harris, in one of his most moving stories, *Free Joe*, showed the tragedy
of a free Negro in a slave-holding South, where he was considered a
bad model by slave-owners, an economic rival by poor whites, and
something to be avoided by the slaves. The story might be considered as a condemnation of a system, but in all probability was taken
to be another proof of the Negro's incapacity for freedom. Although
Harris wrote generously of Negro advancement since emancipation,
there is little doubt that the implications of many passages furthered
the stereotype under consideration.

Page, a bourbon "fire-eater," for all of his yearnings for his old
mammy, saw nothing of good for Negroes in emancipation:

> Universally, they [Southerners] will tell you that while the old-time Ne-
> groes were industrious, saving, and, when not misled, well-behaved,
> kindly, respectful, and self-respecting, and while the remnant of them
> who remain still retain generally these characteristics, the "new issue,"
> for the most part, are lazy, thriftless, intemperate, insolent, dishonest,
> and without the most rudimentary elements of morality. . . . Universally,
> they report a general depravity and retrogression of the Negroes at large,
> in sections in which they are left to themselves, closely resembling a re-
> version to barbarism.[22]

The notion of the Negro's being doomed to extinction was
sounded by a chorus of pseudo-scientists, bringing forth a formida-

---

[21]William J. Grayson, *The Hireling and the Slave*. Charleston, S.C., McCarter and Co.,
1856, pp. 68 ff.

[22]Thomas Nelson Page, *The Negro: The Southerner's Problem, op. cit.*, p. 80.

ble (?) array of proofs. Lafcadio Hearn yielded to the lure of posing
as a prophet:

> As for the black man, he must disappear with the years. Dependent like
> the ivy, he needs some strong oak-like friend to cling to. His support
> has been cut from him, and his life must wither in its prostrate helpless-
> ness. Will he leave no trace of his past? . . . Ah, yes! . . . the weird and
> beautiful melodies born in the hearts of the poor, child-like people to
> whom freedom was destruction.[23]

Many were the stories ringing changes on the theme: "Go tell Marse
Linkum, to tek his freedom back." Thus, in *The Carolina Low Country*, Mr. Sass writes of Old Aleck, who, on being freed, spoke his
little piece: "Miss, I don't want no wagis." "God bless you, old
Aleck," sighs Mr. Sass.

Modern neo-Confederates repeat the stereotype. Allen Tate, co-
member with Donald Davidson of the Nashville saviors of the South,
implies in *Jefferson Davis, His Rise and Fall*, that to educate a Negro
beyond his station brings him unhappiness. One of the chief points
of agreement in the neo-Confederate *I'll Take My Stand* by Davidson,
Tate and ten others is that freedom has proved to be a perilous state
for the Negro. Joseph Hergesheimer agrees: "A free Negro is more
often wretched than not."[24] "Slavery was gone, the old serene days
were gone. Negroes were bad because they were neither slave nor
free."[25] And finally, a modern illustration must suffice. Eleanor Mer-
cein Kelly in an elegy for the vanishing South, called *Monkey Motions*, pities "the helplessness of a simple jungle folk, a bandar-log,
set down in the life of cities and expected to be men."[26]

It is, all in all, a sad picture that these savants give. What concerns us here, however, is its persistence, a thing inexpressibly more
sad.

The Comic Negro

*"That Reminds Me of a Story. There Were Once
Two Ethiopians, Sambo and Rastus . . . ."*
(1,001 After-Dinner Speakers.)

The stereotype of the "comic Negro" is about as ancient as the
"contented slave." Indeed, they might be considered complementary,

---

[23]Lafcadio Hearn, *Letters from the Raven*. New York: A. & C. Boni, 1930, p. 168.
[24]Joseph Hergesheimer, *op. cit.*, p. 137.
[25]*Ibid.*, p. 293.
[26]Blanche Colton Williams, *O. Henry Memorial Award Prize Stories of 1927*. Garden
City: Doubleday, Doran & Co., p. 207.

since, if the Negro could be shown as perpetually mirthful, his state could not be so wretched. This is, of course, the familiar procedure when conquerors depict a subject people. English authors at the time of Ireland's greatest persecution built up the stereotype of the comic Irishman, who fascinated English audiences, and unfortunately, in a manner known to literary historians, influenced even Irish authors.[27] Thus, we find, in a melodrama about Irish life, an English officer soliloquizing:

> I swear, the Irish nature is beyond my comprehension. A strange people!—merry 'mid their misery—laughing through their tears, like the sun shining through the rain. Yet what simple philosophers they! They tread life's path as if 'twere strewn with roses devoid of thorns, and make the most of life with natures of sunshine and song.[28]

Any American not reading the words "Irish nature" could be forgiven for taking the characterization to refer to American Negroes. Natures of sunshine and song, whose wretchedness becomes nothing since theirs is a simple philosophy of mirth! So runs the pattern.

In her excellent book, *American Humor*, Constance Rourke points out the Negro as one of the chief ingredients of the potpourri of American humor. She traces him as far back as the early '20's when Edwin Forrest made up as a Southern plantation Negro to excite the risibilities of Cincinnati. In *The Spy*, Cooper belabors the grotesqueness of Caesar's appearance, although Caesar is not purely and simply the buffoon:

> . . . . But it was in his legs that nature had indulged her most capricious humor. There was an abundance of material injudiciously used. The calves were neither before nor behind, but rather on the outer side of the limb, inclining forward. . . . The leg was placed so near the center (of the foot) as to make it sometimes a matter of dispute whether he was not walking backward.[29]

Kennedy in his *Swallow Barn* not only reveals the Negro as delighted by the master's benevolence, but also as delighting the master by his ludicrous departure from the Anglo-Saxon norm. Kennedy revels in such descriptions as the following:

> His face . . . was principally composed of a pair of protuberant lips, whose luxuriance seemed intended as an indemnity for a pair of crushed

---

[27] Vide: George Bernard Shaw's *John Bull's Other Island*, Daniel Corkery's *Synge and Anglo-Irish Literature*, Yeat's *Plays and Controversies*, Lady Gregory's *Our Irish Theatre*, for attacks upon the "comic" Irishman stereotype.

[28] John Fitzgerald Murphy, *The Shamrock and The Rose*. Boston: Walter H. Baker Co., n. d., p. 25.

[29] James Fenimore Cooper, *The Spy*. New York: Scott, Foresman Co., 1927, p. 45.

nostrils. . . . Two bony feet occupied shoes, each of the superfices and figure of a hoe. . . . Wrinkled, decrepit old men, with faces shortened as if with drawing strings, noses that seemed to have run all to nostril, and with feet of the configuration of a mattock. . . .[30]

It was in the early '30's, however, that T. D. Rice first jumped "Jim Crow" in the theaters along the Ohio River and set upon the stage the "minstrel Negro." Apparently immortal, this stereotype was to involve in its perpetuation such famous actors as Joseph Jefferson and David Belasco, to make Amos 'n' Andy as essential to American domesticity as a car in every garage, and to mean affluence for a Jewish comedian of whom only one gesture was asked: that he sink upon one knee, extend his white-gloved hands, and cry out "Mammy."

In pro-slavery fiction the authors seemed to agree on the two aspects of the comic Negro—that he was ludicrous to others, and forever laughing himself. Grayson writes in *The Hireling and The Slave:*

> The long, loud laugh, that freemen seldom share,
> Heaven's boon to bosoms unapproached by care;
> And boisterous jest and humor unrefined. . . .[31]

To introduce comic relief, perhaps, in stories that might defeat their own purposes if confined only to the harrowing details of slavery, anti-slavery authors had their comic characters. Topsy is the classic example; it is noteworthy that in contemporary acting versions of "Uncle Tom's Cabin," Topsy and the minstrel show note, if not dominant, are at least of equal importance to the melodrama of Eliza and the bloodhounds.

Reconstruction literature developed the stereotype. Russell's Negroes give side-splitting versions of the Biblical story (foreshadowing Bradford's *Ol' Man Adam An' His Chillun*), or have a fatal fondness for propinquity to a mule's rear end. Page's Negroes punctuate their worship of "ole Marse" with "Kyah-kyahs," generally directed at themselves. The humor of Uncle Remus is nearer to genuine folk-humor, which—it might be said in passing—is *not* the same as the "comic Negro" humor. Negroes in general, in the Reconstruction stories, are seen as creatures of mirth—who wouldn't suffer from hardship, even if they had to undergo it. Thus a Negro, sentenced to the chain-gang for stealing a pair of breeches, is made the theme of a comic poem.[32] This is illustrative. There may be random jokes in

---

[30]Kennedy, *op. cit., passim.*

[31]Grayson, *op. cit.*, p. 51.

[32]Belle Richardson Harrison, *Poetry of the Southern States*, Edited by Clement Wood, Girard, Kansas: Haldeman-Julius Co., 1924, p. 36.

Southern court rooms, but joking about the Negroes' experiences with Southern "justice" and with the chain-gang is rather ghastly—like laughter at the mouth of hell. Creatures of sunshine and of song!

The "comic Negro" came into his own in the present century, and brought his creators into theirs. Octavius Cohen, who looks upon the idea of Negro doctors and lawyers and society belles as the height of the ridiculous, served such clienteles as that of *The Saturday Evening Post* for a long time with the antics of Florian Slappey. His work is amusing at its best, but is pseudo-Negro. Instead of being a handicap, however, that seems a recommendation to his audience. Trusting to most moth-eaten devices of farce, and interlarding a Negro dialect never heard on land or sea—compounded more of Dogberry and Mrs. Malaprop than of Birmingham Negroes,[33] he has proved to the whites that all along they have known the real Negro—"Isn't he funny, now!"—and has shown to Negroes what whites wanted them to resemble. Mrs. Octavius Roy Cohen follows in the wake of her illustrious husband in *Our Darktown Press*, a gleaning of "boners" from Aframerican newspapers. Editorial carelessness is sadly enough familiar in race journals; every item in the book is vouched for, but the total effect is the reenforcing of a stereotype that America loves to believe in.

Arthur E. Akers, with a following in another widely read magazine, is another farceur. He uses the situation of the domestic difficulty, as old as medieval fabliaux and farces—and places it in a Southern Negro community, and has his characters speak an approximation to Negro dialect—but too slick and "literary" for conviction. Irate shrews and "Milquetoast" husbands, with razors wielded at departing parts of the anatomy, are Akers's stock-in-trade. Hugh Wiley with his Wildcat, inseparable from his goat, Lady Luck, unsavory but a talisman, is another creator of the farce that Negro life is too generally believed to be. E. K. Means, with obvious knowledge of Southern Negro life, is concerned to show in the main its ludicrous side, and Irvin Cobb, with a reputation of after-dinner wit to uphold, is similarly confined.

The case of Roark Bradford is different. An undoubted humorist, in the great line of Twain and the tall tales of the Southwest, he gleans from a rich store of Negro speech and folkways undeniably

---

[33]"Yeh, an' was he to git one good bite at a cullud man like me, he'd exterminate me so quick I wouldn't even have a chance to notrify my heirs," "I ain't hahdly sawn her right recent," are examples of his inimitable (fortunately so, although Amos an' Andy try it in "I'se regusted," etc.) dialect; "Drastic" "Unit" "Quinine" "Midnight," and "Sons and Daughters of I Will Arise" are examples of his nomenclature.

amusing tales. But as his belief about the Negro (cf. Introduction) might attest, he has a definite attitude to the Negro to uphold. His stories of the easy loves of the levee (frequently found in *Collier's*) concentrate upon the comic aspect of Negro life, although another observer might well see the tragic. In *Ol' Man Adam an' His Chillun* we have farce manufactured out of the Negro's religious beliefs. It seems to the writer that the weakest sections of *Green Pastures* stick closest to Bradford's stories, and that the majesty and reverence that can be found in the play must come from Marc Connelly. In *John Henry*, Bradford has definitely weakened his material by making over a folk-hero into a clown.

Although the situations in which the comic Negro finds himself range from the fantastic as in Cohen, to the possible as in "The Two Black Crows" and in "Amos 'n' Andy," his characteristics are fairly stable. The "comic Negro" is created for the delectation of a white audience, condescending and convinced that any departure from the Anglo-Saxon norm is amusing, and that any attempt to enter the special provinces of whites, such as wearing a dress suit, is doubly so. The "comic Negro" with certain physical attributes exaggerated— with his razor (generally harmless), his love for watermelon and gin, for craps, his haunting of chicken roosts, use of big words he doesn't understand, grandiloquent names and titles, "loud" clothes, bluster, hysterical cowardice, and manufactured word-play—has pranced his way by means of books, vaudeville skits, shows, radio programs, advertisements, and after-dinner speeches, into the folklore of the nation. As Guy B. Johnson urges there is a sort of—

> . . . folk attitude of the white man toward the Negro. . . . One cannot help noticing that the white man must have his fun out of the Negro, even when writing serious novels about him. This is partly conscious, indeed a necessity, if one is to portray Negro life as it is, for Negroes are human and behave like other human beings. Sometimes it is unconscious, rising out of our old habit of associating the Negro with the comical.[34]

In pointing out the stereotype, one does not deny the rich comedy to be found in Negro life. One is insisting, however, that any picture concentrating upon this to the exclusion of all else is entirely inadequate, that many of the most popular creators of the "comic Negro," "doctor" their material, and are far from accurate in depicting even the small area of Negro experience they select, and that too often they exceed the prerogative of comedy by making copy out of persecution and injustice.

---

[34]Guy B. Johnson, "Folk Values in Recent Literature on the Negro" in *Folk-Say*, edited by B. A. Botkin, Norman, Oklahoma, 1930, p. 371.

The Brute Negro

"All Scientific Investigation of the
Subject Proves the Negro to Be An Ape."
(Chas. Carroll, *The Negro a Beast*.)

Because the pro-slavery authors were anxious to prove that slavery had been a benefit to the Negro in removing him from savagery to Christianity, the stereotype of the "brute Negro" was relatively insignificant in antebellum days. There were references to vicious criminal Negroes in fiction (vicious and criminal being synonymous to discontented and refractory), but these were considered as exceptional cases of half-wits led astray by abolitionists. *The Bible Defence of Slavery,* however, in which the Rev. Priest in a most unclerical manner waxes wrathful at abolitionists, sets forth with a great array of theological argument and as much ridiculousness, proofs of the Negro's extreme lewdness. Sodom and Gomorrah were destroyed because these were strongholds of *Negro* vice. The book of Leviticus proved that *Negroes*

> outraged all order and decency of human society. Lewdness of the most hideous description was the crime of which they were guilty, blended with idolatry in their adoration of the gods, who were carved out of wood, painted and otherwise made, so as to represent the wild passions of lascivious desires. . . . The baleful fire of unchaste amour rages through the negro's blood more fiercely than in the blood of any other people . . . on which account they are a people who are suspected of being but little acquainted with the virtue of chastity, and of regarding very little the marriage oath. . . .[35]

H. R. Helper, foe of slavery, was no friend of the Negro, writing, in 1867, *Nojoque,* a lurid condemnation of the Negro, setting up black and beastly as exact synonyms. Van Evrie's *White Supremacy and Negro Subordination, or Negroes A Subordinate Race, and (so-called) Slavery Its Normal Condition* gave "anthropological" support to the figment of the "beastly Negro," and *The Negro A Beast* (1900) gave theological support. The title page of this book runs:

> The Reasoner of the Age, the Revelator of the Century! The Bible As It Is! The Negro and his Relation to the Human Family! The Negro a beast, but created with articulate speech, and hands, that he may be of service to his master—the White Man. . . . by Chas. Carroll, who has spent 15 years of his life and $20,000.00 in its compilation. . . .

---

[35]Josiah Priest, *op. cit.,* Eighth Section, *passim.*

Who could ask for anything more?

Authors stressing the mutual affection between the races looked upon the Negro as a docile mastiff. In the Reconstruction this mastiff turned into a mad dog. "Damyanks," carpetbaggers, scalawags, and New England schoolmarms affected him with the rabies. The works of Thomas Nelson Page are good examples of this metamorphosis. When his Negro characters are in their place, loyally serving and worshipping ole Marse, they are admirable creatures, but in freedom they are beasts, as his novel *Red Rock* attests. *The Negro: The Southerner's Problem* says that the state of the Negro since emancipation is one of minimum progress and maximum regress.

> [This] is borne out by the increase of crime among them, by the increase of superstition, with its black trail of unnamable immorality and vice; by the homicides and murders, and by the outbreak and growth of that brutal crime which has chiefly brought about the frightful crime of lynching which stains the *good name of the South* and has spread northward with the spread of the ravisher.... The Crime of rape ... is the fatal product of new conditions.... The Negro's passion, always his controlling force, is now, since the new teaching, for the white woman. [Lynching is justifiable] for it has its root deep in the basic passions of humanity; the determination to put an end to the *ravishing of their women by an inferior race*, or by any race, no matter what the consequence.... A crusade has been preached against lynching, even as far as England; but none has been attempted against the ravishing and tearing to pieces of white women and children.[36]

The best known author of Ku Klux Klan fiction after Page is Thomas Dixon. Such works as *The Clansman*, and *The Leopard's Spots*, because of their sensationalism and chapter titles (e.g., "The Black Peril," "The Unspoken Terror," "A Thousand Legged Beast," "The Hunt for the Animal"), seemed just made for the mentality of Hollywood, where D. W. Griffith in *The Birth of a Nation* made for Thomas Dixon a dubious sort of immortality, and finally fixed the stereotype in the mass-mind. The stock Negro in Dixon's books, unless the shuffling hat-in-hand servitor, is a gorilla-like imbecile, who "springs like a tiger" and has the "black claws of a beast." In both books there is a terrible rape, and a glorious ride of the Knights on a Holy Crusade to avenge Southern civilization. Dixon enables his white geniuses to discover the identity of the rapist by using "a microscope of sufficient power [to] reveal on the retina of the dead eyes the image of this devil as if etched there by fire." ... The doctor sees "The bestial figure of a negro—his huge black hand plainly defined. ... It was Gus." Will the wonders of science never cease?

---

[36]Page, *The Negro: The Southerner's Problem, passim* (Italics mine).

But, perhaps, after all, Negroes have been convicted on even flimsier evidence. Fortunately for the self-respect of American authors, this kind of writing is in abeyance today. Perhaps it fell because of the weight of its own absurdity. But it would be unwise to underestimate this stereotype. It is probably of great potency in certain benighted sections where Dixon, if he could be read, would be applauded—and it certainly serves as a convenient self-justification for a mob about to uphold white supremacy by a lynching.

The Tragic Mulatto

"The gods bestow on me
A life of hate,
The white man's gift to see
A nigger's fate."
("The Mulatto Addresses his
    Savior on Christmas Morning,"
        Seymour Gordden Link.)

Stereotyping was by no means the monopoly of pro-slavery authors defending their type of commerce, or justifying their ancestors. Anti-slavery authors, too, fell into the easy habit, but with a striking difference. Where pro-slavery authors had predicated a different set of characteristics for the Negroes, a distinctive sub-human nature, and had stereotyped in accordance with such a comforting hypothesis, anti-slavery authors insisted that the Negro had a common humanity with the whites, that in given circumstances a typically human type of response was to be expected, unless certain other powerful influences were present. The stereotyping in abolitionary literature, therefore, is not stereotyping of *character*, but of *situation*. Since the novels were propagandistic, they concentrated upon abuses: floggings, the slave mart, the domestic slave trade, forced concubinage, runaways, slave hunts, and persecuted freemen—all of these were frequently repeated. Stereotyped or not, heightened if you will, the anti-slavery novel has been supported by the verdict of history—whether recorded by Southern or Northern historians. Facts, after all, are abolitionist. Especially the fact that the Colonel's lady and old Aunt Dinah are sisters under the skin.

Anti-slavery authors did at times help to perpetuate certain pro-slavery stereotypes. Probably the novelists knew that harping upon the gruesome, to the exclusion of all else, would repel readers, who—like their present-day descendants—yearn for happy endings and do not wish their quick consciences to be harrowed. At any rate, comic relief, kindly masters (in contrast to the many brutes), loyal and submissive slaves (to accentuate the wrongs inflicted upon them) were scattered throughout the books. Such tempering of the attacks was turned to pro-slavery uses. Thus, Harris writes:

> It seems to me to be impossible for any unprejudiced person to read Mrs. Stowe's book and fail to see in it a defence of American slavery as she found it in Kentucky. . . . The real moral that Mrs. Stowe's book teaches is that the possibilities of slavery . . . are shocking to the imagination, while the realities, under the best and happiest conditions, possess a romantic beauty and a tenderness all their own. . . .[37]

Anti-slavery fiction did proffer one sterotype, doomed to unfortunate longevity. This is the tragic mulatto. Pro-slavery apologists had almost entirely omitted (with so many other omissions) mention of concubinage. If anti-slavery authors, in accordance with Victorian gentility, were wary of illustrating the practice, they made great use nevertheless of the offspring of illicit unions. Generally the heroes and heroines of their books are near-whites. These are the intransigent, the resentful, the mentally alert, the proofs of the Negro's possibilities. John Herbert Nelson says with some point:

> Abolitionists tried, by making many of their characters almost white, to work on racial feeling as well. This was a curious piece of inconsistency on their part, an indirect admission that a white man in chains was more pitiful to behold than the African similarly placed. Their most impassioned plea was in behalf of a person little resembling their swarthy protegés, the quadroon or octoroon.[38]

Nelson himself, however, shows similar inconsistency, as he infers that the "true African—essentially gay, happy-go-lucky, rarely ambitious or idealistic, the eternal child of the present moment, able to leave trouble behind—is unsuited for such portrayal. . . . Only the mulattoes and others of mixed blood have, so far, furnished us with material for convincing tragedy."[39]

The tragic mulatoo appears in both of Mrs. Stowe's abolitionary novels. In *Uncle Tom's Cabin*, the fugitives Liza and George Harris and the rebellious Cassy are mulattoes. Uncle Tom, the pure black, remains the paragon of Christian submissiveness. In *Dred*, Harry Gordon and his wife are nearly white. Harry is an excellent manager, and a proud, unsubmissive type:

> Mr. Jekyl, that humbug don't go down with me! I'm no more of the race of Ham than you are! I'm Colonel Gordon's oldest son—as white as my

---

[37]Julia Collier Harris, *op. cit.,* p. 117.
[38]John Herbert Nelson, *op. cit.,* p. 84.
[39]*Ibid.,* p. 136.

brother, who you say owns me! Look at my eyes, and my hair, and say if any of the rules about Ham pertain to me.[40]

The implication that there are "rules about Ham" that do pertain to blacks is to be found in other works. Richard Hildreth's *Archy Moore, or The White Slave*, has as its leading character a fearless, educated mulatto, indistinguishable from whites; Boucicault's *The Octoroon* sentimentalizes the hardships of a slave girl; both make the mixed blood the chief victim of slavery.

Cable, in the *Grandissimes*, shows a Creole mulatto educated beyond his means, and suffering ignominy, but he likewise shows in the character of Bras-Coupè that he does not consider intrepidity and vindictiveness the monopoly of mixed-bloods. In *Old Creole Days*, however, he discusses the beautiful octoroons, whose best fortune in life was to become the mistress of some New Orleans dandy. He shows the tragedy of their lives, but undoubtedly contributed to the modern stereotype that the greatest yearning of the girl of mixed life is for a white lover. Harriet Martineau, giving a contemporary portrait of old New Orleans, wrote:

> The quadroon girls . . . are brought up by their mothers to be what they have been; the mistresses of white gentlemen. The boys are some of them sent to France; some placed on land in the back of the State. . . . The women of their own color object to them, *"ils sont si degoutants!"*[41]

Lyle Saxon says that "the free men of color are always in the background; to use the Southern phrase, 'they know their place.' "

The novelists have kept them in the background. Many recent novels show this: *White Girl, The No-Nation Girl, A Study in Bronze, Gulf Stream, Dark Lustre*—all of these show luridly the melodrama of the lovely octoroon girl. Indeed "octoroon" has come to be a feminine noun in popular usage.

The stereotype that demands attention, however, is the notion of mulatto character, whether shown in male or female. This character works itself out with mathematical symmetry. The older theses ran: First, the mulatto inherits the vices of both races and none of the virtues; second, any achievement of a Negro is to be attributed to the white blood in his veins. The logic runs that even inheriting the worst from whites is sufficient for achieving among Negroes. The present theses are based upon these: The mulatto is a victim of a divided inheritance; from his white blood come his intellectual striv-

---

[40]Harriet Beecher Stowe, *Nina Gordon, or Dred*. Boston: Houghton, Mifflin and Co., 1881, p. 142.

[41]Quoted in Lyle Saxon, *Fabulous New Orleans*. New York: The Century Co., 1928, p. 182.

ings, his unwillingness to be a slave; from his Negro blood come his baser emotional urges, his indolence, his savagery.

Thus, in *The No-Nation Girl*, Evans Wall writes of his tragic heroine, Précieuse:

> Her dual nature had not developed its points of difference. The warring qualities, her double inheritance of Caucasian and black mingled in her blood, had not yet begun to disturb, and torture, and set her apart from either race. . . .
>
> [As a child,] Précieuse had learned to dance as soon as she could toddle about on her shapely little legs; half-savage little steps with strange movements of her body, exotic gestures and movements that had originated among the remote ancestors of her mother's people in some hot African jungle.
>
> . . . the wailing cry of the guitar was as primitive and disturbing as the beat of a tom-tom to dusky savages gathered for an orgy of dancing and passion in some moonflooded jungle. . . . Self-control reached its limit. The girl's half-heritage of savagery rose in a flood that washed away all trace of her father's people except the supersensitiveness imparted to her taut nerves. She must dance or scream to relieve the rising torrent of response to the wild, monotonous rhythm.

It is not long before the girl is unable to repress, what Wall calls, the lust inherited from her mother's people; the environment of debauchery, violence, and rapine is exchanged for concubinage with a white paragon, which ends, of course, in the inevitable tragedy. The girl "had no right to be born."

Dark Lustre, by Geoffrey Barnes, transfers the main essentials of the foregoing plot to Harlem. Aline, of the darkly lustrous body, thus analyzes herself in accordance with the old clichés: "The black half of me is ashamed of itself for being there, and every now and then crawls back into itself and tries to let the white go ahead and pass. . . ." Says the author: "There was too much of the nigger in her to let her follow a line of reasoning when the black cloud of her emotions settled over it." Half-white equals reason; half-black equals emotion. She too finds her ideal knight in a white man, and death comes again to the tragic octoroon who should never have been born. *White Girl, Gulf Stream, A Study in Bronze* are in substance very similar to these.

Roark Bradford in *This Side of Jordan* gives an unconscious *reductio ad absurdum* of this stereotype.

> The blade of a razor flashed through the air. Scrap has concealed it in the folds of her dress. Her Negro blood sent it unerringly between two ribs. Her Indian blood sent it back for an unnecessary second and third slash.

It might be advanced that Esquimaux blood probably would have kept her from being chilled with horror. The strangest items are attributed to different racial strains: In *No-Nation Girl* a woman cries out in childbirth because of her Negro expressiveness; from the back of Précieuse's "ankles down to her heels, the flesh was slightly thicker"—due to her Negro blood; Lessie in Welbourn Kelley's *Inchin' Along* "strongly felt the urge to see people, to talk to people. . . . That was the white in her maybe. Or maybe it was the mixture of white and black."

This kind of writing should be discredited by its patent absurdity. It is generalizing of the wildest sort, without support from scientific authorities. And yet it has set these *idées fixés* in the mob mind: The Negro of unmixed blood is no theme for tragedy; rebellion and vindictiveness are to be expected only from the mulatto; the mulatto is victim of a divided inheritance and therefore miserable; he is a "man without a race" worshipping the whites and despised by them, despising and despised by Negroes, perplexed by his struggle to unite a white intellect with black sensuousness. The fate of the octoroon girl is intensified—the whole desire of her life is to find a white lover, and then go down, accompanied by slow music, to a tragic end. Her fate is so severe that in some works disclosure of "the single drop of midnight" in her veins makes her commit suicide.

The stereotype is very flattering to a race which, for all its self-assurance, seems to stand in great need of flattery. But merely looking at one of its particulars—that white blood means asceticism and Negro blood means unbridled lust—will reveal how flimsy the whole structure is. It is ingenious that mathematical computation of the amount of white blood in a mulatto's veins will explain his character. And it is a widely held belief. But it is nonsense, all the same.

The Local Color Negro

> *"The defects of local color inhere in*
> *the constitution of the cult itself, which,*
> *as its name suggests, thought . . .*
> *first of the piquant surfaces and then—*
> *if at all—of the stubborn deeps of*
> *human life."*
>
> (Carl Van Doren:
> *Contemporary American Novelists.*)

Local color stresses the quaint, the odd, the picturesque, the different. It is an attempt to convey the peculiar quality of a locality. Good realistic practice would insist upon the localizing of speech, garb, and customs; great art upon the revelation of the universal beneath these local characteristics. Local color is now in disrepute because of its being contented with merely the peculiarity of dialect and manners. As B. A. Botkin, editor of *Folk-Say*, has stated: "In the past [local consciousness] has been narrowly sectional rather than broadly human, superficially picturesque rather than deeply interpretative, provincial without being indigenous."[42]

The "local color Negro" is important in any study of the Negro character in American literature. But, since the local colorists of the Negro were more concerned with fidelity to speech and custom, with revelation of his difference in song and dance and story, than with revelation of Negro character, they accepted at face valuation the current moulds into which Negro character had been forced. Therefore, local colorists have been and will be considered under other heads. Page and Russell were local colorists in that they paid close attention to Negro speech, but the Negro they portrayed was the same old contented slave. Their study of Negro speech, however, was fruitful and needed—for pro-slavery authors had been as false in recording Negro speech as they were in picturing Negro experience. Kennedy, for instance, forces a confessedly wretched dialect into the mouths of poor Negroes, and W. L. G. Smith has his Shenandoah Negroes speak Gullah, because his master, Simms, had written of South Carolina Negroes.

Cable, one of the best of the local colorists, in *The Grandissimes,* goes a step beyond the mere local color formula; *Old Creole Days* is local color, but has been considered under the "Tragic Mulatto." The Negroes in Lyle Saxon's old and new New Orleans, E. Larocque Tinker's old New Orleans, R. Emmett Kennedy's Gretna Green, are in the main kinsfolk to the contented slave; in Evans Wall's Mississippi canebrakes are exotic primitives, or tragic mulattoes; on Roark Bradford's levees are primitives; and those on Julia Peterkin's Blue Brook plantation, in Heyward's Catfish Row, and in John Vandercook's Surinam, Liberia, and Haiti, usually surmount, in the writer's opinion, the deficiencies of local color. Stereotyped, or genuinely interpreted, however, they all agree in one respect; they show the peculiar differences of certain Negroes in well-defined localities.

John B. Sale in *The Tree Named John* records with sympathy the dialect, superstitions, folk-ways of Mississippi Negroes. He is meticulous, perhaps to a fault, in his dialectal accuracy; the milieu is correspondingly convincing. His Negroes do carry on the pattern of mutual affection between the races—and yet they are far nearer flesh and blood than those of Page. Samuel Stoney and Gertrude Shelby, in *Black Genesis*, give the peculiarities of the Gullah Negro's cosmogony. Care is paid to fidelity in recording the dialect, but the authors'

---

[42]B. A. Botkin, *Folk-Say, A Regional Miscellany*. Norman: The Oklahoma Folk-Lore Society, 1929, p. 12.

comments reveal a certain condescension toward quaintness which is the usual bane of local colorists. In *Po' Buckra* the authors revealed the localized tragedy of the "brass-ankle"—the Croatan-Negro-near-white caste. Much of the "tragic mulatto" theme is in this book, as well as the purely local color interest. Ambrose Gonzales in his Gullah renditions of Aesop, and in his tales of the "black border," reveals for the curious the intricacies of a little known Negro dialect, following the lead of Harris, and C. C. Jones, who recorded the Br'er Rabbit tales in the dialect of the Georgia coast.

Although most of these authors who dwell upon quaint and picturesque divergencies are discussed under other headings, it will not do to underestimate this local color Negro. The showing of Negro peculiarities in speech, superstitions, and customs has been popular for many years, and is likely to be for a long while yet. It undoubtedly has its artistic uses; but being an end in itself is surely not the chief of them.

The Exotic Primitive

"Then I saw the Congo, cutting through the black. . . ."
(Vachel Lindsay)

This stereotype grew up with America's post-war revolt against Puritanism and Babbittry. Literary critics urged a return to spontaneity, to unrestrained emotions; American literature had been too long conventional, drab, without music and color. Human nature had been viewed with too great a reticence. Sex, which the Victorians had considered unmentionable, was pronounced by the school of Freud to have an overwhelming importance in motivating our conduct. So the pendulum swung from the extreme of Victorian prudishness to that of modern expressiveness.

To authors seaching "for life in the raw," Negro life and character seemed to beg for exploitation. There was the Negro's savage inheritance, as they conceived it: hot jungle nights, the tom-tom calling to esoteric orgies. There were the frankness and violence to be found in any underprivileged group, or on any frontier. There were the traditional beliefs of the Negro being a creature of his appetites, and although pro-slavery fiction had usually (because of Victorianism) limited these to his yearnings for hog meat and greens, 'possum and yams, and for whiskey on holidays, Reconstruction fiction had stressed his lustfulness. He seemed to be cut out for the hands of certain authors. They promptly rushed to Harlem for color. In Harlem dives and cabarets they found what they believed to be *the* Negro, *au naturel*.

The figure who emerges from their pages is a Negro synchronized to a savage rhythm, living a life of ecstasy, superinduced by jazz (repetition of the tom-tom, awakening vestigial memories of Africa) and gin, that lifted him over antebellum slavery, and contemporary economic slavery, and placed him in the comforting fastnesses of their "mother-land." A kinship exists between this stereotype and that of the contented slave; one is merely a "jazzed-up" version of the other, with cabarets supplanting cabins, and Harlemized "blues," instead of the spirituals and slave reels. Few were the observers who saw in the Negroes' abandon a release from the troubles of this world similar to that afforded in slavery by their singing. Many there were, however, who urged that the Harlem Negro's state was that of an inexhaustible *joie de vivre*.

Carl Van Vechten was one of the pioneers of the hegira from downtown to Harlem; he was one of the early discoverers of the cabaret; and his novel, *Nigger Heaven*, is to the exotic pattern what *Swallow Barn* was to the contented slave. All of the possibilities of the development of the type are inherent in the book. In the prologue we have the portrait of the "creeper," Don Juan of Seventh Avenue, whose amatory prowess causes him to be sought by women unknown to him. We feel that this prologue sets the tone of the work: we are going to see the Harlem of gin mills and cabarets, of kept men and loose ladies, of all-day sleepers and all-night roisterers. Van Vechten, who was already famed as a sophisticated romantic novelist, writes graphically of this Harlem. His style invited emulation from young men desiring to be men-about-town first and then novelists, just as Kennedy invited emulation from young Southerners desiring to defend slavery first. Van Vechten's novel does more than present the local color of Harlem; there is as well the character study of a young Negro intellectual who cannot withstand the dissipations of the "great Negro city." But the Bohemian life in Harlem is the main thing, even in this youngster's life. According to the publisher's blurb, "Herein is caught the fascination and tortured ecstasies of Harlem. . . . The author tells the story of modern Negro life." The blurb claims too much. There is another, there are many other Harlems. And *the* story of modern Negro life will never be found in one volume, or in a thousand.

Lasca Sartoris, exquisite, gorgeous, golden-brown Messalina of Seventh Avenue, is one of the chief characters of the book. On seeing her one of the characters comments: "Whew! She'll make a dent in Harlem." She does. She causes the young hero, Byron, in a drunken rage, to empty his gun in the body of one of her lovers, although the man was already dead, and a policeman was approaching.

Van Vechten has a noted magazine editor comment pontifically on the possibilities of Negro Literature:

> Nobody has yet written a good gambling story; nobody has gone into the curious subject of the divers tribes of the region. . . . There's the servant-girl, for instance. Nobody has ever done the Negro servant-girl, who refuses to 'live in.' Washing dishes in the day-time, she returns at night to her home in Harlem where she smacks her daddy in the jaw or else dances and makes love. On the whole I should say she has the best time of any domestic servant in the world. . . . The Negro fast set does everything the Long Island fast set does, plays bridge, keeps the bootlegger busy, drives around in Rolls-Royces and commits adultery, but it is vastly more amusing than the Long Island set for the simple reason that it is *amused.* . . . Why, Roy McKain visited Harlem just once and then brought me in a cabaret yarn about a Negro pimp. I don't suppose he even saw the fellow. Probably just made him up, imagined him, but his imagination was based on a background of observation. The milieu is correct. . . .[43]

Although these are merely the offhand comments of an editor, and not to be taken too seriously as final critical pronouncements on *the* Negro, still certain implications are obvious. The best Negro characters for literary purposes are suggested: gamblers, fast set, servant-girl-sweet-mamma, etc. All are similar in their great capacity for enjoyment—and it is that side that must be shown. The eternal playboys of the Western hemisphere! Why even one trip to Harlem will reveal the secret of their mystery. The connection of all of this to the contented slave, comic, local color Negro is patent. Another thing to be noticed is the statement issued by the literary market: Stereotypes wanted.

In *Black Sadie*, T. Bowyer Campbell, whose preference is for the stereotype of the contented slave of the South, ironically accounts for the Harlem fad by the desire of jaded sophisticates for a new thrill. But Campbell does agree in some degree with the Harlem stereotype: "Colored people demand nothing but easy happiness, good nature." Black Sadie, child of a man hanged for raping an old white woman, having become the toast of artistic New York, remaining a kleptomaniac—"it was in her blood"—even in affluence, causing a murder, returns—in the best tradition of minstrel songs—to happy Virginia. "Easy come, easy go, niggers," Campbell closes his book, philosophically.

Sherwood Anderson, in *Dark Laughter*, expresses a genuine Rousseauism. Hostile toward the routine of industrialism and Puritanism,

---

[43]Carl Van Vechten, *Nigger Heaven*. New York: Grosset and Dunlap, 1928, pp. 225 ff.

Anderson sets up as a foil the happy-go-lucky sensuality of river-front Negroes, who laugh, with genial cynicism, at the self-lacerations of hypersensitive Nordics. His "dark laughter" lacks the sinister undertone of Llwellyn Powys' "black laughter" heard in Africa. Anderson's Negroes are too formalized a chorus, however, for conviction, and are more the dream-children of a romanticist than actual flesh-and-blood creations. Anderson has drawn some excellent Negro characters; in *Dark Laughter*, however, he characterizes the Negroes too straitly. That the chief response of the Negro to his experience is a series of deep rounds of laughter at white sex-tangles is difficult of credence.

William Seabrook in *Magic Island* and *Jungle Ways* writes sensational travel tales—according to some, in the tradition of Munchausen and Marco Polo. He exploits the exotic and primitive, recording voodoo rites, black magic, strange sexual practices, weird superstitions, and cannibalism. His work brings a sort of vicarious satisfaction to Main Street, and advances the stereotype. He traces back to original sources what downtown playboys come up to Harlem to see.

The stereotype of the exotic-primitive would require more than a dogmatic refutation. Not so patently a "wish-fulfillment," as the "contented slave" stereotype was, nor an expression of unreasoning hatred, as the "brute Negro," it is advanced by novelists realistic in technique and rather convincing, although demonstrably "romantic" in their choice of the sensational. But it would be pertinent to question the three basic assumptions—either insinuated or expressed—underlying the stereotype: that the "natural" Negro is to be found in Harlem cabarets; that the life and character depicted there are representative of Negro life in general; and that the Negro is "himself," and startlingly different in the sensational aspects of his life.

It is strange that the "natural" Negro should be looked for in the most sophisticated of environment. Even the names "Cotton Club," "Plantation Revue," the lavish, though inaccurate, cotton bolls decorating the walls, the choruses in silken overalls and bandanas do not disguise but rather enforce the fact that Negro entertainers, like entertainers everywhere, give the public what clever managers, generally Caucasian, believe the public wants. Unwise as it is to generalize about America, or New York State, or even Queens from the Great White Way, it is no less unwise to generalize about Negro life and character from Harlem. It is even unwise to generalize about Harlem, from *the* Harlem shown in books. Strange to say, there is a Harlem that can be observed by the cold glare of daylight.

The exotic primitives of Mississippi levees and cane-brakes, of Catfish Row and Blue Brook Plantation are more convincing, as examples of frontier communities, and of underprivileged groups who are known to live violent lives. It is surely not impossible, however, to believe that observers with an eye for environmental factors might see an entirely different picture from the one presented by searchers for exotic-primitive innate tendencies.

Harvey Wickham in *The Impuritans* writes:

> On Pacific Street, San Francisco, there used to be, and probably still is, a Negro dance hall called the So-Different Cafe. The name was deceptive. It was not so different from any other slum-hole. [A slum hole] is tediously the same, whether it be in Harlem, lower Manhattan, London, Paris, Berlin, Rome, Athens, Pekin, or Timbuctoo. There is no possible variety in degradation. . . .[44]

Such a comment surely deserves as careful attention as the sterotype of the exotic-primitive.

Attempts at Realization

> *"John Henry said to his captain,*
> *A man ain't nothin' but a man . . . ."*
>   (Ballad of John Henry.)

It would be a mistake to believe that the works of all white authors bear out these stereotypes. Some of the best attacks upon stereotyping have come from white authors, and from Southerners, just as some of the strongest upholding of the stereotypes has come from Negroes. Moreover, the writer of this essay hopes that he will not be accused of calling everything a stereotype that does not flatter Negro character, or of insisting that the stereotypes have no basis in reality. Few of the most apologistic of "race" orators could deny the presence of contented slaves, of wretched freemen, in our past; nor of comic Negroes (even in the joke-book tradition), of self-pitying mulattoes, of brutes, of exotic primitives in our present. Negro life does have its local color, and a rich, glowing color it can be at times. What this essay has aimed to point out is the obvious unfairness of hardening racial character into fixed moulds. True in some particulars, each of these popular generalizations is dangerous when applied to the entire group. Furthermore, most of these generalizations spring from a desire to support what is considered social expediency rather than from a sincere attempt at interpretation, and are therefore bad art.

Attempts at sincere "realization" rather than imitation of set patterns can be found in the early works of Eugene O'Neill, whose plays first brought a tragic Negro to Broadway. Ridgeley Torrence

---

[44]Harvey Wickham, *The Impuritans*. New York: The Dial Press, 1929, p. 284.

saw another side to the familiar guitar playing clown—showing him to be a dreamer of dreams like the other Playboy of the Western World—and saw dignity in his long suffering, hard-working wife. *The Rider of Dreams*, in its quiet way, did much to demolish the old stereotypes.

Julia Peterkin, for all of her tendency to local color (*Bright April* is a storehouse of Negro superstitions and folk customs) and her emphasis on sex and violence,[45] is still of importance in her departure from the stereotypes.

In a simple, effective manner, she reveals the winning humanity of the Gullah people, whom she obviously loves and respects. If critics would refuse to call her the interpreter of *the* Negro, and realize that she writes of a very limited segment of life from a very personal point of view, they would do a service to her and to their own reputations. She has well-nigh surmounted the difficulty of being a plantation owner.

Du Bose Heyward has given us some of the best Negro characterizations in *Porgy* and *Mamba's Daughters*. Though the first is naturalistic with a flair for the exotic-primitive, Heyward does show in it essential humanity: Porgy reveals himself as capable of essential fineness, and even Bess is not completely past reclaiming. *Mamba's Daughters* reveals that Negroes, too, can be provident as Mamba was, or heroic as Hagar was, for the sake of the young. The travesty of Southern justice toward the Negro, the difficulties of the aspiring Negro, the artistic potentialities and actualities of Negroes, receive ample attention. Except for certain forgivable slips into the "comic," the book is an excellent illustration of the dignity and beauty that can be found in some aspects of lowly Negro life.

E. C. L. Adams, because he seems to let Negro characters speak for themselves, in their own idiom, and as if no white man was overhearing, has been very successful in his interpretation of Negro folklife. Here the humor expressed by the Negro is miles away from Cohen's buffoonery. There is a sharp, acid flavor to it; in the Negroes' condemnation of the Ben Bess case there is the bitterness that has been stored up for so very long. These folk are not happy-go-lucky, nor contented; they are shrewd, realistic philosophers, viewing white pretense and injustice with cynicism—though not with Sherwood Anderson's "Dark Laughter." Illiterate they may be, but they are not being fooled.

Howard Odum, by letting the Negro speak for himself, presents a similarly convincing folk-Negro, in this case, the rambling man, who

---

[45]*Vide: Black April, Scarlet Sister Mary* for examples of extreme promiscuity, and *Bright Skin* for violent deaths.

has been everywhere, and seen everybody. Many of the stereotypes are overthrown in *Rainbow Round My Shoulder*, although comic, and brutal, and submissive Negroes may be seen there. These are viewed, however, "in the round," not as walking generalizations about *the* Negro, and Odum is intent on making us understand how they got to be what they are.

Evelyn Scott and T. S. Stribling, historical novelists of the Civil War, as different as may be in technique, agree in giving us rounded pictures of antebellum Negroes. Slavery is not a perpetual Mardi Gras in their novels, nor are Negroes cast in the old, rigid moulds. They are characterized as human beings, not as representatives of a peculiar species. Paul Green's *In Abraham's Bosom* shows the Negro's handicapped struggles for education during the Reconstruction; Green has brought great dramatic power to bear upon revealing that the Negro is a figure worthy of tragic dignity. In *The House of Connelly* he has disclosed aspects of the so-called "contented slave" that antebellum authors were either ignorant of, or afraid to show.

Erskine Caldwell, George Milburn, William Faulkner, and Thomas Wolfe, while their métier is the portraiture of poor whites, help in undermining the stereotypes by showing that what have been considered Negro characteristics, such as dialect, illiteracy, superstitions, sexual looseness, violence, etc., are to be found as frequently among poor whites. When they do show Negro characters, they frequently show them to be burdened by economic pressure, the playthings of Southern justice, and the catspaws for sadistic "superiors."

A recent novel, *Amber Satyr*, shows a lynching that follows a white woman's relentless and frenzied pursuit of her hired man, a good-looking Negro. Welbourne Kelley's *Inchin' Along*, although influenced by some stereotypes (his mulatto wife, true to type, is the easy prey of the first white man who rides along), does show the hard-working, provident, stoical Negro. James Knox Millen wrote a powerful attack upon lynching in *Never No More*, showing the precarious hold the Southern Negro has upon peace and happiness. Scott Nearing, with a proletarian emphasis, has presented graphically the new slavery, peonage, in the South, with its horrible concomitant lynchings, and the bitter prejudice of organized labor in the North. And finally, John L. Spivak, in *Georgia Nigger*, has written a second *Uncle Tom's Cabin*, an indictment of peonage, and convict-labor in Georgia, powerful enough to put to shame all the rhapsodists of the folk Negro's happy state.

To trace the frequency with which the Negro author has stepped out of his conventional picture frame, from the spirituals and satiric folk-rhymes down to Langston Hughes, would exceed the bounds of this paper, and for present purposes is not needed. A reading of only a few of the white authors just mentioned (many of whom are from the South) would effectively illustrate the inadequacy of the familiar stereotypes.

It is likely that, in spite of the willingness of some Negro authors to accept at face value some of these stereotypes, the exploration of Negro life and character rather than its exploitation must come from Negro authors themselves. This, of course, runs counter to the American conviction that the Southern white man knows the Negro best, and can best interpret him. Nan Bagby Stephens states what other Southern authors have insinuated:

> Maybe it was because my slave-owning ancestors were fond of their darkies and treated them as individuals that I see them like that. It seems to me that no one, not even the negroes themselves, can get the perspective reached through generations of understanding such as we inherited.[46]

The writer of this essay holds to the contrary opinion, agreeing with another Southerner, F. P. Gaines,[47] that when a white man says that he knows the Negro he generally means that he knows the Negro of the joke-book tradition. Stephen Vincent Benet has written:

> Oh, blackskinned epic, epic with the black spear,
> I cannot sing you, having too white a heart,
> And yet, some day a poet will rise to sing you
> And sing you with such truth and mellowness. . . .
> That you will be a match for any song. . . .[48]

But whether Negro life and character are to be best interpreted from without or within is an interesting by-path that we had better not enter here. One manifest truth, however, is this: the sincere, sensitive artist, willing to go beneath the clichés of popular belief to get at an underlying reality, will be wary of confining a race's entire character to a half-dozen narrow grooves. He will hardly have the temerity to say that his necessarily limited observation of a few Negroes in a restricted environment can be taken as the last word about some mythical *the* Negro. He will hesitate to do this, even though he had a Negro mammy, or spent a night in Harlem, or has been a Negro all his life. The writer submits that such an artist is the only one worth listening to, although the rest are legion.

---

[46]*Contempo*, Volume II, No. 2, p. 3.

[47]F. P. Gaines, *op. cit.*, p. 17.

[48]Stephen Vincent Benet, *John Brown's Body*. Garden City, New York: Doubleday, Doran and Co., 1928, p. 347.

Owen Dodson

(1914–1983)

POET, NOVELIST, ESSAYIST, DRAMATIST, librettist, director, and educator, Owen Dodson was a prolific writer acclaimed as a standard-bearer and inspiration for a generation of black performing artists. He was for twenty years head of the Department of Drama, College of Fine Arts, at Howard University. There, he was a palpable influence upon scores of students, including many who today number among the best-known black performing artists and playwrights.

Born in Brooklyn, New York, Dodson was educated at Bates College and Yale University. He was a member of Phi Beta Kappa; and in 1967 he received a Doctor of Letters from Bates. Best known for his work in poetry and drama, Dodson was a recipient of the Rosenwald Fellowship, the General Education Board Fellowship, and the coveted Guggenheim Fellowship (1953–54) for study in Italy. He conducted numerous lectures and seminars at many American universities and colleges, including Vassar, Kenyon, Cornell, Rutgers, Iowa, and UCLA. During the spring of 1969, he was poet-in-residence at the University of Arizona.

Owen Dodson taught and directed dramatic groups in Atlanta, Hampton, and, during World War II, in the U.S. Navy. In 1949, with Ann Cook, he took the Howard Players to Denmark, Sweden, and Germany on America's first international undergraduate cultural exchange.

Dodson's plays have been presented by little theater groups all over the country, as well as off-Broadway and in England. His short story "The Summer Fire" received a prize in an international short story contest conducted by the *Paris Review*.

Among his publications are a book of poems, *Powerful Long Ladder* (1946), and a novel, *Boy at the Window* (1951; reprinted in 1972). The novel was also reprinted in 1967 as *When Trees Were Green*. A Japanese edition of *Boy at the Window* was published in 1961.

The summer 1980 volume of *Black American Literature Forum* features a comprehensive bibliography of works by or about Dodson and includes critical reviews of his poetry. An essay by Dodson, evaluating the work of three young playwrights, is also featured. The spring 1984 *Black American Literature Forum* issue, one of two that year devoted to poetry, was dedicated to the memory of Owen Dodson.

For additional commentary, see John O'Brien's *Interviews with Black Writers* (1973); Noel Schraufnagel, *From Apology to Protest* (1973); Theressa G. Rush, et al., *Black American Writers: Past and Present, Vol. 1* (1975); and Jane A. Bowden, ed., *Contemporary Authors, Vols.* 65–68 (1977).

The following poems come from *Powerful Long Ladder* (1946) and *The Promethean* (Howard University Art and Literary Magazine, May 1967). The narrative selection is an excerpt from *Boy at the Window* (1951); the play, *Everybody Join Hands,* is reprinted from *Theatre Arts* (September, 1943) and was dedicated to Pearl Buck.

MISS PACKARD AND MISS GILES
(Who founded Spelman College for Negro women in Georgia)

Two women, here in April, prayed alone
And saw again their vision of an altar
Built for mind and spirit, flesh and bone.

They never turned away, they never said
This dream is air, let us go back to our New England spring
And cultivate an earth that is not dead;
Let dark mothers weep, dark children bleed,
This land is barren land
Incapable of seed.

They made their crucifix far more
Than ornament; they wrestled with denial
And pinned him to the floor.

They made defeat an exile.
And year by year their vision shed its mist,
And still they smiled their Noah smile

Certain they had no death to fear,
Certain their future would be now
And all the Aprils we assemble here.

TELL RACHEL, HE WHISPERED

Tonight I talked to Jesus,
And Jesus spoke to me.
No, I don't remember

If His hair was long
Or if He wore a bible dress
Or had a halo on.
I know He spoke to me;
There were no trouble
In His eyes but I
Saw the gospels there.
When the morning stars
Sang bright together:
That were His voice.
He said He had heard of me,
Heard of long labours
In the vineyards of the city;
This city here, bless God
He asked after sister this
And brother that and The President.
Then it were time to speak:
I spoke 'bout Pastor Moss
Near working his bones to death
Trying to call the children home.
'Bout Sister Seneatha bakin,
Bakin' biscuits for the poor;
'Bout how hard I scrubbed to get
The education for Sarah
And put some pride in Freddie's heart.
Finally I told Him 'bout cramps in my lungs.
'That's why I'm here,'
He reached out to me, yes He did,
'My Father caused me
To journey down';
—Tell Rachel—, He whispered,
—Tell her to cease that scrubbin,
To get off the apron,
Smooth the calice
And wait for the chariot
Waiting by the curbstone.—
That's what Jesus said
Through His Father.
He meant it too.

FROM **BOY AT THE WINDOW**

"CHESTER, CHESTER, the next stop is CHESTER," the conductor rolled the word out. He made Chester seem like a capital. When the train stopped, it was at an old station. A red sign announced Chester again and that was all except a lot of colored people got on there and most of them pushed right into the car where Coin was. They were dressed up and laughing to beat the band. One great bosom lady sat across from him with her son. He was peaked and looked like the last rose of summer. Kept on calling her Ma. Kept hugging her up. A fat old boy was in the seat in front of the woman. He called her Mama. Others took seats here and there and commenced to yelling and waving and passing bottles and sandwiches. It was a picnic on the train. When the conductor came by for the tickets, there was such a digging into pockets and paper bags and wallets, looking under seats and acting the fool until all the tickets were handed in to screaming laughter. Coin began to laugh, too, whenever someone said anything funny. They kept on saying funny things and he kept on laughing. The train heated up until you could hardly breathe. Smelled like outing flannel and asafoetida. You weren't supposed to open the windows. Coin got himself cold water three times. When he was coming back the last time the talking and jokes and eating was louder and whooped-up more than ever. A man at the front of the car rose up out of his seat a little and called back, "Why don't you darkies shut up so we kin hear ourselves think."

What did he want to say that for? The happy confusion died down to a silence like an axe was hanging overhead by a thread. It stayed that way for a long time. Only the train wheels still raced: why don't you darkies shut up, why don't you darkies shut up.

The bosom woman's bosom panted up and down. She took three long puffs of her cigarette letting the smoke out of her nose in straight clouds, then she stood up, scrubbing the butt into the floor carefully. This woman, who had talked so hard and eaten more chicken than six, who had a laugh like a ten-gun salute, began walking down the aisle toward the man who had asked for silence. As she trod, she seemed to grow tall and furious as one of Popa's Bible prophets, Moses maybe or Genesis. You could see it in her back, in the way she threw her shoulders and lifted her head. People around buzzed low like the sound of bees with special stings. She reached her destination, leaned over the seat and pointed one dagger finger.

"If you don't know what you're talking about, you'd better ask somebody." Her voice filled the car and drowned the sound of the wheels.

"Nuts," came out of the seat, "nuts, you folks keeping up enough racket to drive a man crazy."

"You don't need to be driv crazy. You crazy already, that's what you are. Don't you come calling me no darkie."

"Aw, lady."

"Don't you be calling me no lady either. I been bringing up your children and scrubbing your nasty houses until my bones fair ache inside me. I ain't no lady, I'm a truck horse. Been a truck horse for you for too many years and I'm too tired to listen to you shutting me up. You hear that."

A voice from somewhere said, "NIGGERS, niggers," and that was all.

"Who said that!" She shot around and her eyes blazed fire even to where Coin sat. "You ain't afraid to say it again, is you? Cowards. That's what you is, a coward. Niggers, niggers. My boy is lying in the fields of Europe on the Kaiser's acres, that's where he is and I got a medal from the government. Cowards. It's too bad they didn't get your ass, that's what's too bad." She looked left and right, high and low. Only the train wheels dared to make a noise. Finally she strode back to her seat. Her heavy body seemed to shake the train. When she took her seat again, the boy who called her Mama turned around.

"Keep quiet, Mama, keep your big mouth shut."

She faced him like the wrath of God.

"Keep quiet, keep quiet! Why you shoulda been down there instead of me. Keep quiet, you chicken, that's what you is. Nobody's gonna call me out of my name. You hear me!" She worked herself up again. She walked up the aisle and down the aisle being bumped first to one side and then the other. Her voice sounded the hallelujah Sister Maudesta Lee shouted in church.

"All the planes that were fallen, and the ships rammed into, the bombs splitting the ocean apart, poison gas. God has a way."

The train wheels sang between her silences. People looked down.

"Don't give us nothing. Stepping all over us. Calling us darkies and niggers. God has a way. Colored boys working in the manholes of the streets in Philadelphia 'cause a white boy got his head rammed off by a trolley car. God has a way. They put colored on after that. Colored boys crawling about like cats under the streets and don't look out of them holes lessen they look both ways. They smart. God has a way. Trying to spoil my holiday. Don't give but the one day and you calling me outta my name. I hope there comes a

next war. I hope they knocks hell outta this country. That's what I
hopes. You can't think. Well, you better think. The end of the world
is scheduled to be by fire. Now, if you don't know what you're talking about, you'd better keep quiet." She paused. The sweat was running off of her forehead in beads. She sat down again like on a
throne. The train wheels sounded but didn't say any words.

When the train pulled into Baltimore, the bosom woman and her
friends got off. They stood at the window where the man who had
asked them to keep quiet sat, gazed in long like at an animal in the
zoo. As the train started again, they all laughed at him; laughed pure
and long and solid. The train wheels took up the laughter. It lasted
almost until Washington.

Coin knew something was wrong with the way every one had
acted but he didn't know where to place the blame. One thing he
had learned: what nobody would tell him. He knew now what a nigger was. His mother really had been right. A bad person. What confused him was that it meant much more than that. Maybe you
weren't a bad person but you were colored and they called you
nigger.

Walking with the rest of the people toward the exit, Coin spied
Uncle Troy at the gate. He was so happy to see him that he broke
into a trot calling his name.

"Uncle Troy."

"Coin, Coin!"

"Uncle Troy."

Coin rushed to him and his uncle felt his face, measured his
height with his stick.

"Lord, boy, I thought a baby was coming here to me but you're
almost grown. Must have grown several inches since I saw you. Let
me look at you." His hands felt Coin's face, and the old laughter
Coin remembered from Pennsylvania Station surrounded them.
"Well, you might as well begin working now. Mrs. Walker brought
me here but you gotta lead me there." He was still laughing as Coin
took his hand. The porter brought Coin's bag and hailed a taxi for
them.

In the cab Uncle Troy began to laugh again.

"What's this I feel on your chest?"

"Agnes put a tag on me."

"Now isn't that just like Agnes, sending you like freight."

EVERYBODY JOIN HANDS

(This play should, if possible, be played in the middle of the hall on a platform with the audience gathered about on all sides. The house lights go down slowly, and a chorus begins to sing "Everybody Join Hands.")

CHORUS

Everybody join hands
Our China must be free
Gather from field and mountain
Defend our liberty.

We'll fight to make the future
Shining, eternally brave.
Surround our walls with lasting peace
Let freedom's banners wave.

Mothers gather your children
Send them to clean the earth
To wash away all tyranny,
Send the sons you've given birth.

Everybody join hands,
Defend our liberty.
Gather from field and mountain.
Our China will be free.

SPEAKER

This play is about the Chinese people and their fight for freedom. It is not a realistic play, but it is true as the imagination is true—as ideas and ideals are true. The Chinese people are protecting their land against tyrants, the whole Chinese people. They scratched the Burma Road out with their finger-nails, they bury their thousand-a-day dead in common graves along the fighting fronts of China.

A rim of the dead protecting still their Chinese earth,
The people cry again not for deliverers for they are delivering themselves;
They cry again not for martyrs, for scores of martyrs have sainted their earth;
They cry again not for prophets, for their future is simple and clear;

"Everybody Join Hands" by Owen Dodson from *Theatre Arts* (September 1943). Reprinted by permission of the Estate of Owen Dodson.

They cry to all the others fighting for freedom to join hands
And symbol the earth again with Christ;
They cry for the whole world to save itself
From the revelation that free men can ever be tyrants again.
The whole Chinese people have bled for six years:
They require that their winter trees hanging with frozen blood
Be melted by spring and pass away;
They require that the hearts of free men all over the world
Be humble and be ready for that spring.

(The song fades. A gong sounds three times, light and delicate. Out of the darkness a SPEECH CHOIR *begins to speak and on the platform there are a dozen lighted Chinese lanterns held high by peasants in coolie hats. They chant a gay Chinese holiday song as they move across the platform rhythmically, stylized.)*

SPEECH CHOIR

There are no lovely Chinese lanterns any more—
They are blown out by war.
The kites are grounded,
Along the streets of Canton and Peiping and Lanchow
All the lovely paper dragon festivals are dead—
They are blown out by war.
Where is the China we read about, we saw pictures of,
The China I visited when I was a child?
It is blown out by war!

(The lantern carriers form single file and trot off with their lanterns and there is darkness again.)

SPEECH CHOIR

The good earth is fertilized with ammunition, *(low rumble)*
Planted with the bones and flesh of the Chinese people, *(larger rumble)*
Watered with the blood of the Chinese people. *(largest rumbling)*
From this earth the people will harvest freedom.

(Enter the movers. A lonesome and slow beat of a tom-tom. Their hands on their bellies, they move to the ideas in the lines that follow. On "They ran to the war lords that ruled them crying . . ." they move to one end of the platform crying their desperation. The war lords appear in stiff, jewelled gowns with long treacherous swords to cut the people down.)

SPEAKER

Before this war the people were ruled not by a central government,
But by war lords who preyed on the people.

They were terrible and unjust and the people remained
In their worm-low poverty.

SPEECH CHOIR
When famine concentrated its skeleton strength on their bellies,

SPEAKER
When yearly the rains came like the Biblical flood,

SPEECH CHOIR
When locusts shadowed the land and picked their harvest meatless,

SPEAKER
When the foreign leeches came and sucked the good of their earth,

SPEECH CHOIR
When the people no longer could bear their oppressors,

SPEAKER
They rose up and cried in desperate confusion;
They ran to the war lords that ruled them, crying:

SPEECH CHOIR
Where are the martyrs?
Where are the saints?
We are deserted!

Where are the deliverers?
Where are the miracles?
We are deserted!

SPEAKER
They rushed to the war lords but they were denied—
The lords walked stiffly with drawn swords,
And they sent bandits to rob the people
And cut down the defiant;
They left the weak to eat the dirt of their earth.
They left them there worming in the earth for food.
These people had no land of their own, no unity.
They were divided.
There was the knuckle of oppression always on their necks.

SPEECH CHOIR
Civil war and foreign leeches sucking the good of their land.

SPEAKER
Opium they were given to smoke,
Drugs of fantastic smell and poison,
Poison that destroyed the people's spirit and the people's bone.

SPEECH CHOIR

The opium of death!
The opium of compromised justice!
The opium of money!
The opium of flattery!
The opium of religion!

SPEAKER

The people were divided—

SPEECH CHOIR

The people were alone.

SINGERS

All over the land, desolation—
All over the land, division—
The Chinese earth moved with despair—
Life was mosquito cheap—
There was nothing to plant—
There was nothing to reap.

(The movers begin to go off with sorrow riding their backs and death hanging from their hands. They move low and chant deep and dark. Just as they are nearly off, a leader appears. They about face. He forms them into straight lines and, headed by him standing upright, they follow him off, moving rhythmically.)

SPEAKER

A leader appeared.
Inch by inch he had climbed to the people.
He had heard in his deep night sleep the voices,
And they pinched his heart,
They scarred his mind.
He came to the people not through peace,
But by fighting little civil wars.
He stood before them not as himself,
But as compassion and strength.
He was unity.
He was not too soon,
But he was early enough.
He had heard them cry!

SPEECH CHOIR (*whispering*)

Give us martyrs;
Give us deliverers;
What are the prophecies?
Where is hope?

Where is freedom?
Food?
Hope?
Death is a blue light, and
   it never blows out!
Our earth is swallowed up,
Help us!

(Gongs strike like terror; movers rush off; lights out sharply.)

SPEAKER

The dwarf men from Eastern Islands seized Manchuria,
Invaded Chahar and Jehal.

(Lights shine up again. A lone singer begins:)

SINGER

Please be brave my darling
I'm going out to meet the foe.
Please be brave my darling
You'll follow wherever I go.
Please be brave my darling
Remember you'll always know.
Wipe your tears my darling
I wanted our children to grow
In a world without any foe.
Please be brave my darling
You'll follow wherever I go.

(A coolie trots in waving a Chinese flag rhythmically and as he gets center there is a terrific explosion. Another coolie trots in with a bamboo pole across his shoulders and a pail at each end. He trots up to his fallen brother to pick up the flag. The enemy bombs get him also. Then there is silence and cautiously the movers creep toward the fallen coolies and carry them off. This action takes place during the following speech.)

SPEAKER

In North China in a village west of Peiping
Bombs whirled down blasting Chinese earth,
And the peasants couldn't understand.
They dragged their dead off their fields and were bewildered
By the death that shot down from shining birds flying in the sky.
Oh the hatchets of war cleaved the Chinese earth;
War was official now as weather bulletins.
But the Chinese people led by their leader sang
Chee Lai—which means *arise!*
Now they must defend their mountains and their plains,

Their cities and their dragons of faith.
The whole people gathered together by a whirlwind of freedom.

(The movers proceed to build the Burma Road with precise move-
ment—fast and mechanical, like an old movie. But it is not funny. The
song bursts out and continues as the road is built.)

CHORUS
Building are we a road to freedom,
Shovel out the dirt,
Scratch the mountains for freedom,
Dig the road,
Dig the road.

All the women and children for freedom,
All the brave young men,
Dig the road to freedom,
Dig the road,
Dig the road.

This blood and death for freedom
Now we sacrifice
Digging the road to freedom
Dig the road,
Dig the road.

SPEAKERS
The dwarf men from the East can never conquer this land,
With cunning tricks or complicated philosophy,
Or new machines—
This people is gathered together by a whirlwind of freedom.
They cried:

SPEECH CHOIR
Connect China—
Make our land one—
We will build a road across our plains
And through our mountains.

SPEAKER
The Burma Road came into the world a legend.
Out of every village and hamlet eight days journey,
On either side of the road went the summons for workers
To connect China with the Burma Road.
No modern machines—only human toil scratched this road from the
   earth.
Two hundred thousand men built the Burma Road
And three hundred bridges to span the road.

Two hundred thousand Chinese workers scratched the road out with
    their fingernails.
The road is a road and also symbol of what a people can accomplish
When the whirlwind of freedom blows them together.
Nightmare days—
Nerve-draining determination,
Rains came like Biblical floods,
And washed their toil away,
Dust and chills and fever,
But the people worked on,
Lack of food—the people scratched on.
From Lashio through Yunnan,
The Tibetan plateau,
Across deep canyons, past the jungle-fringed Mekong,
And the green faces of the Salween rivers to Kunming
They scratched out their road of freedom.

SPEECH CHOIR
>   Oh the days
>   When men died from malaria.
>   Oh the days
>   When truck wheels slipped on the mud
>   And men slipped into death.
>   Oh the days
>   When showers of rock shot up
>   And then shot down.
>   Oh the dead
>   And oh the days.
>   The dynamite and the deep canyons,
>   Oh the dead!

SPEAKER
The people sang as they worked
And the earth favored their rhythm
And where Marco Polo led cargoes
Of silk and jade and gold leaf, amber and ivory,
    (*Movers move across completed road with ammunition, rifles, etc.*)
Now the people lead convoys of ammunition,
Guns, tanks, food, courage, hope.
The Burma Road came into the world a legend
Of the people's strength when they fight for their freedom.

SPEECH CHOIR
The Chinese people moved their universities to the hills;
They took their factories apart and put them together in the hills;
They removed their ancient culture to the hills;
They executed their traitors;

They buried their treasures in the hills of free China,
And they will go back again when their whole land is theirs again.

SPEAKER

Once the people moaned for martyrs and saints,
For peace, for death, for freedom.
Now they know that they are these,
The whole Chinese people are these.

(The leader appears again and the people join hands in a triple circle about him.)

LEADER

Oh my people we work together,
We fight together against exhaustion within
And the leeches without.
Oh my people remember the opium that killed you.
The rape of your women and their agony.
Remember the rape of your land and the threadbare hope.
Remember how the leeches sucked your earth of oil,
Stripped your land of treasure,
Plugged your rivers with strange boats,
Raided your good name and laughed out loud.
Oh my people, forgive, only forgive forever.
Remember also the fighters for freedom
In Russia, England, France, Greece, Czechoslovakia,
Poland, Africa, Australia, America, Holland, Belgium,
And countries already conquered but unconquerable,
The living and the dead who fight the dwarf men from the East,
And the Frankenstein men from the West.
Oh my people
The hands of all good people are joined together
To rid the earth of tyrants and leeches.
Oh my people remember, remember,
That these war years are starvation years worse than before,
But that you plant freedom each time you plant your dead,
You redeem the earth with each razed hut,
With each devastation and each momentary defeat.
Oh my people remember
You fight to make a clean and beautiful earth out of a ruined one.
When freedom gathers a people together,
No show of arms can tear them asunder.
Oh my people, oh, my Chinese land, oh my world.

(The people begin to sing and, holding hands, they follow the leader, moving in a triple circle that unwinds itself as they move off one by one singing, "Everybody Join Hands." The house lights up.)

J. Saunders Redding

(1906–1988)

CRITIC, EDUCATOR, SCHOLAR, novelist, newspaper columnist, and auto-biographer, J. Saunders Redding had a long and fruitful career in the educational and literary worlds of both black and white America. A cultured, wise, and moderate man of letters, he observed and evaluated America's treatment of the black citizen and wrote about it brilliantly. His works include criticism, biography and autobiography, fiction, history, and journalistic articles.

Born in Wilmington, Delaware, in 1906, the son of middle-class parents, he attended Lincoln University (Pennsylvania) for one year, then went to Brown University, where he received his A.B. in 1928 and M.A. in 1932. He taught at Morehouse, Louisville Municipal College, Southern University, Elizabeth City, Hampton Institute (now Hampton University), Brown, Duke, the University of North Carolina, Grinnell College, George Washington, and Cornell University, where he was the Newman I. White Professor of American Studies and Humane Letters. He died in Ithaca, New York, in 1988.

During his professional career he was on the editorial board of *The American Scholar* and was published in *Atlantic Monthly*, *Harper's*, *American Mercury*, *Transition*, *Nation*, *Saturday Review*, *New Republic*, *Survey Graphic*, and other periodicals.

In addition to six honorary degrees, Professor Redding received the following awards and honors: the Mayflower Award from the North Carolina Historical Society for his *No Day of Triumph* (1942), a Rockefeller Foundation Fellowship, and a Guggenheim Fellowship. He traveled to India for the State Department and lectured in Africa for the American Society of African Culture. Throughout his life as teacher and writer, Saunders Redding gave numerous lectures at many American colleges and universities.

The major publications of Redding are *To Make a Poet Black* (1939), *No Day of Triumph* (1942), *Stranger and Alone* (1950), *They Came in Chains* (1950), *On Being Negro in America* (1951), *The Lonesome Road* (1958), *Cavalcade: Negro Writing from 1760 to the Present*, edited with Arthur P. Davis (1971), and the present work, *The New Cavalcade: African American Writing from 1760 to the Present*, edited with Arthur P. Davis and Joyce A. Joyce (1991).

As stated previously, *No Day of Triumph* won the North Carolina Historical Award for the best work by a resident of the state in 1942. Most critics consider it Redding's best work. Part autobiography, part travelogue, part social observation, the work is a series of dramatic episodes which gives the reader an unforgettable picture of black life, high and low, in the South from Virginia to Texas. *To Make a Poet Black* has also been a popular study. Published in 1939, it is an early critical work in Harlem Renaissance literature, and it is still a useful source. *They Came in Chains*, a part of Lippincott's People of America Series, and *The Lonesome Road*, a part of Doubleday's Mainstream of America Series, both show Redding's skill at bringing to life the drama of American history. *On Being Negro in America* is a very personal work, but in it Redding expresses the black intellectual's attitude toward the "deep sickness" found in American living.

For an excellent analysis of Saunders Redding's works and ideological position see Maria K. Mootry's "J. Saunders Redding: A Case Study of the Black Intellectual," *Western Journal of Black Studies*, 7, No. 2 (Summer 1983). See also the following works: Arna Bontemps's "Facing a Dilemma," *Saturday Review* (February 16, 1952); Arthur P. Davis's *From the Dark Tower* (1974); editor Darwin Turner's *Black American Literature Essays* (1969); and Henry F. Winslow's "Beyond the Seas—An Uneasy World," *Crisis* (February 1955).

The selections that follow come from *The American Negro Writer and His Roots*, which contains selected papers read at the 1959 First Conference of Negro Writers; and from *The Lonesome Road* (1958).

FROM **THE AMERICAN NEGRO WRITER AND HIS ROOTS**

I do not feel in the least controversial or argumentative about the announced subject. Indeed, I have touched upon it so often in one way or another that I long ago exhausted my store of arguments, and if I now revert to a kind of expressionistic way of talking, my excuse for it is patent. "The American Negro Writer and His Roots" is the kind of subject which, if one talked directly on it for more than twenty minutes, he would have to talk at least a year. I shan't talk directly on it, and I shan't talk a year. An exhaustive treatment? Heaven forbid—or anything near it. Suggestive? Well, I can only hope.

And anyway, I realize now that my position here is that of the boy who, through native disability, cannot himself play but is perfectly willing to furnish the ball for others to play in exchange for the pleasure of watching the game.

Since my theme is that the American situation has complex and multifarious sources and that these sources sustain the emotional and intellectual life of American Negro writers, let me take as my starting point a classic oversimplification. This is that the meaning of American society and of the American situation to the Negro is summed up in such works as *Native Son, Invisible Man*, and the *Ordeal of Mansart*, and in two or three volumes of poetry, notably *Harlem Shadows, The Black Christ*, and *The Weary Blues*, and that the American Negro writer's entire spirit is represented by such writers as Richard Wright, Ralph Ellison and William Burghardt Du Bois— by realists, surrealists, and romantic idealists.

Please understand me. Wright, Ellison and Du Bois are not mendacious men, and they are doing what writers must always do. They are telling the truth as they see it, which happens to be largely what it is, and they are producing from the examined, or at least the observed causes, the predictable effects; and no one should blame them if the impression they give of the American situation is deplorable. They have been blamed, you know. But let those who blame these writers blame themselves for forgetting that fiction is fiction, and that no novel can pretend to be an exact photographic copy of a country or of the people in a country.

Moreover, dishonor, bigotry, hatred, degradation, injustice, arrogance and obscenity do flourish in American life, and especially in the prescribed and proscriptive American Negro life; and it is the right and the duty of the Negro writer to say so—to complain. He has cause. The temptation of the moral enthusiast is not only strong in him; it is inevitable. He never suspends social and moral judgment. Few actions and events that touch him as a man fail to set in motion his machinery an as artist. History is as personal to him as the woman he loves; and he is caught in the flux of its events, the currents of its opinion and the tides of its emotion; and he believes that the mood is weak which tolerates an impartial presentment of these, and that this weak mood cannot be indulged in a world where the consequences of the actions of a few men produce insupportable calamities for millions of humble folk. He is one of the humble folk. He forages in the cause of righteousness. He forgets that he is also one of Apollo's company.

On the one hand, the jungle; on the other, the resourceful hunter to clear it. The jungle, where lurk the beasts, nourishes the hunter. It is there that he has that sum of relationships that make him what he is. It is where he lives. It is precisely because the jungle is there and is terrible and dangerous that the Negro writer writes and lives at all.

But first, I suppose you must grant me, if only for the sake of this brief exposition, that the American Negro writer is not just an American with a dark skin. If he were, I take it, the theme of this conference would be mighty silly and the conference itself superfluous. This granted, you want to know what the frame of reference is, and about this I shall be dogmatic.

Neither the simplest nor the subtlest scrutiny reveals to an honest man that he has two utterly diverse kinds of experience, that of sense data and that of purpose. Psychology seems to have no difficulty establishing the natural gradation of impulse to purpose. In varying degrees, all our experiences are complications of physical processes.

Shifting from the dogmatic to the apologetic, I must eliminate from view a period of nearly three hundred years from 1619 to 1900. It was the period that saw the solid establishment here in America of a tradition of race relations and of the concepts that supported the tradition. It was a period that need not be rehearsed. Within the frame of reference thus established, let us look at a certain chain of events.

In 1902 came Thomas Dixon's *The Leopard's Spots*, and three years later *The Clansman*. Both were tremendously popular, and both were included in the repertoires of traveling theatrical companies; and I think it is significant—though we will only imply how—that even a colored company, The Lafayette Players, undertook an adaptation of *The Leopard's Spots*. In 1903 there was a race riot in New York. In 1906 race riots occurred in Georgia and Texas; in 1908 in Illinois. By this latter year, too, all the Southern states had disfranchised the Negro, and color caste was legalized or had legal status everywhere. The Negro's talent for monkeyshines had been exploited on the stage, and some of the music that accompanied the monkeyshines was created by James Weldon Johnson and his brother Rosamond. Meantime, in 1904, Thomas Nelson Page had written the one true canonical book of the law and the prophets, *The Negro, The Southerner's Problem*. And, most cogent fact of all, Booker Washington, having sworn on this bible of reactionism, had been made the undisputed leader of American Negroes because, as he had pledged to do, he advocated a race policy strictly in line with the tradition and the supporting concepts of race relations.

If there had been a time when this tradition seemed to promise the Negro a way out, that time was not now. He had been laughed at, tolerated, amusingly despaired of, but all his own efforts were vain. All the instruments of social progress—schools, churches, lodges—adopted by colored people were the subjects of ribald jokes and derisive laughter. "Mandy, has you studied yo' Greek?" "I'se sewing, Ma." "Go naked, Gal. Git Dat Greek!"

Any objective judgment of Booker Washington's basic notion must be that it was an extension of the old tradition framed in new terms. Under the impact of social change, the concept was modified to include the stereotype of the Negro as a happy peasant, a docile and satisfied laborer under the stern but kindly eye of the white boss, a creature who had a place and knew it and loved it and would keep it unless he got bad notions from somewhere. The once merely laughable coon had become now also the cheap farm grub or city laborer who could be righteously exploited for his own good and for the greater glory of America. By this addition to the concept, the Negro-white status quo, the condition of inferior-superior race and caste could be maintained in the face of profound changes in the general society.

What this meant to the Negro writer was that he must, if he wished an audience, adhere to the old forms and the acceptable patterns. It meant that he must create within the limitations of the concept, or that he must dissemble completely, or that he must ignore his racial kinship altogether and leave unsounded the profoundest depths of the peculiar experiences which were his by reason of that kinship. Some chose the first course; at least one—Dunbar—chose the second (as witness his sickly, sticky novels of white love life and his sad epithalamium to death); and a good many chose the third: Braithwaite's anthologies of magazine verse, James Weldon Johnson's contributions to the *Century Magazine*, and the writing of Alice Dunbar, Anne Spencer, and Angelina Grimké.

But given the whole web of circumstances—empirical, historic, psychological—these writers must have realized that they could not go on and that the damps and fevers, chills and blights, terrors and dangers of the jungle could not be ignored. They must have realized that, with a full tide of race-consciousness bearing in upon them, they could not go on forever denying their racehood and that to try to do this at all was a symptom of psychotic strain. Rather perish now than escape only to die of slow starvation.

What had happened was that Booker Washington, with the help of the historic situation and the old concepts, had so thoroughly captured the minds of white people that his was the only Negro voice that could be heard in the jungle. Negro schools needing help could get it only through Booker Washington. Negro social thought wanting a sounding board could have it only on Washington's say-so. Negro political action was weak and ineffective without his strength. Many Negro writers fell silent, and for the writer, silence is death.

Many, but not all. There were stubborn souls and courageous, and the frankly mad among them. There was the Boston *Guardian*, and the Chicago *Defender*, and the Atlanta University Pamphlets, and *The Souls of Black Folk*, and finally the *Crisis*; and this latter quickly developed a voice of multi-range and many tones. It roared like a lion and cooed like a dove and screamed like a monkey and laughed like a hyena. And always it protested. Always the sounds it made were the sounds of revolt in the jungle, and protestation and revolt were becoming—forgive me for changing my figure—powerful re-agents in the social chemistry that produced the "new" Negro.

Other factors contributed to this generation too. The breath of academic scholarship was just beginning to blow hot and steadily enough to wither some of the myths about the Negro. The changes occurring with the onset of war in Europe sloughed off other emotional and intellectual accretions. The Negro might be a creature of "moral debate," but he was also something more. "I ain't a problem," a Negro character was made to say, "I's a person." And that person turned out to be a seeker after the realities in the American dream. When he was called upon to protect that dream with his blood, he asked questions and demanded answers. Whose dream was he protecting, he wanted to know, and why and wherefore? There followed such promises as only the less scrupulous politicians had made to him before. Then came the fighting and the dying, and finally came a thing called peace.

By this time, the Negro was already stirring massively along many fronts. He cracked Broadway wide open. The Garvey movement swept the country like wildfire. *Harlem Shadows, The Gift of Black Folk, Color, Fire in the Flint, The Autobiography of an Ex-Coloured Man*. The writers of these and other works were declared to be irresponsible. A polemical offensive was launched against them, and against such non-artist writers as Philip Randolph, Theophilus Lewis, William Patterson, Angelo Herndon. They were accused of negativism; they were called un-American. Cultural nationalism raised its head and demanded that literature be patriotic, optimistic, positive, uncritical, like *Americans All*, and *American Ideals*, and *America is Promises*, and *It Takes a Heap O' Living*, which were all written and published in the period of which I speak. But democracy encourages criticism, and it is true that even negative criticism implies certain positive values like veracity, for instance, and these Negro writers had positive allegiances. Their sensibilities were violently irritated, but their faith and imaginations were wonderfully nourished by the very environment which they saw to be and depicted as being bad.

Fortunately there was more than faith and fat imagination in some of these works. There was also talent. Had this not been so, Negro writing would have come to nothing for perhaps another quarter century, for the ground would not have been plowed for the seeds of later talents. But Du Bois, Johnson, McKay, Fisher, Cullen, Hughes knew what they were about. Their work considerably furthered the interest of white writers and critics. Whatever else O'Neill, Rosenfeld, Connolley, Calverton and Heyward did, they gave validity to the notion that the Negro was material for serious literary treatment.

Beginning then and continuing into the forties, Negro writing had two distinct aspects. The first of these was arty, self-conscious, somewhat precious, experimental, and not truly concerned with the condition of man. Some of the "little reviews" printed a lot of nonsense by Negro writers, including the first chapter of a novel which was to be entirely constructed of elliptical sentences. Then there was *Cane*: sensibility, inwardness, but much of it for the purpose of being absorbed into the universal oneness. Nirvana. Oblivion. Transcendence over one's own personality through the practice of art for art's sake. The appropriate way of feeling and thinking growing out of a particular system of living. And so eventually Gurdjieff.

But the second aspect was more important. The pathos of man is that he hungers for personal fulfillment and for a sense of community with others. And these writers hungered. There is no American national character. There is only an American situation, and within this situation these writers sought to find themselves. They had always been alienated, not only because they were Negroes, but because democracy in America decisively separates the intellectual from everyone else. The intellectual in America is a radically alienated personality, the Negro in common with the white, and both were hungry and seeking, and some of the best of both found food and an identity in communism. But the identity was only partial and, the way things turned out, further emphasized their alienation. So—at least for the Negro writers among them—back into the American situation, the jungle where they could find themselves. A reflex of the natural gradation of impulse to purpose.

Surely this is the meaning of *Native Son*. "Bigger Thomas was not black all the time," his creator says. "He was white too, and there were literally millions of him . . . Modern experiences were creating types of personalities whose existence ignored racial . . . lines." Identity. Community. Surely this is the meaning of *Invisible Man* and the poignant, pain-filled, pain-relieving humor of simple Jesse B. It is the meaning of *Go Tell It On The Mountain*, and it is explicitly the meaning of four brilliant essays in part three of a little book of essays called *Notes of a Native Son*. (How often that word "native" appears, and how meaningful its implications!) Let me quote a short, concluding passage from one of these essays.

"Since I no longer felt that I could stay in this cell forever, I was beginning to be able to make peace with it for a time. On the 27th . . . I went again to trial . . . and the case . . . was dismissed. The story of the *Drap De Lit,* . . . caused great merriment in the court-room. . . . I was chilled by their merriment, even though it was meant to warm me. It could only remind me of the laughter I had often heard at home. . . . This laughter is the laughter of those who consider themselves to be at a safe remove from all the wretched, for whom the pain of living is not real. I had heard it so often in my native land that I had resolved to find a place where I would never hear it anymore. In some deep, black, stony and liberating way, my life, in my own eyes, began during that first year in Paris, when it was borne in on me that this laughter is universal and never can be stilled." Explicit.

The human condition, the discovery of self. Community. Identity. Surely this must be achieved before it can be seen that a particular identity has a relation to a common identity, commonly described as human. This is the ultimate that the honest writer seeks. He knows that the dilemmas, the perils, the likelihood of catastrophe in the human situation are real and that they have to do not only with whether men understand each other but with the quality of man himself. The writer's ultimate purpose is to use his gifts to develop man's awareness of himself so that he, man, can become a better instrument for living together with other men. This sense of identity is the root by which all honest creative effort is fed, and the writer's relation to it is the relation of the infant to the breast of the mother.

FROM **THE LONESOME ROAD**

Robert Sengstacke Abbott was an altogether different breed. Though he was described as shrewd, calculating, and "tight with guile," the facts dispute the estimate. His mind was not equipped to deal with subtleties. The formal education he managed to acquire was not of much use to him. In middle life he was called a demagogue and dangerous—"like a monkey with a shotgun," Julius Rosenwald said, "who will hurt anybody." But he was more hurt than hurting, and his demagoguery, if this is what it can be called, had in it more of pathos than of calculating sense. He was not the son of his father.

Born in a cabin on the crummy edge of a Georgia plantation, Robert Abbott spent much of his life trying to live down the opprobrious term "Geechee." It was an epithet that conjured up in the Negro mind the storied attributes of the lowest slave type, the ignorant "field nigger," with a dull and stupid mind, gross habits, and primitive passions beyond control. And it was unfair. Robert's father, Tom, had been Charles Stevens's trusted boss house slave, the envy of other slaves for miles around. The esteem in which the Stevenses held him is attested by the fact that when freedom came they gave him a cabin and a plot of ground, and when he died in 1869 they buried him in their own graveyard.

And by that time, in the common opinion, Tom had deserved less. He had gone off to Savannah and abused his freedom. Nearly fifty years old and still unmarried, he had played city sport, lived by his wits and on his gracious white-folks manners, which attracted, among others, Flora Butler, a hairdresser and ladies' maid at the Savannah theater. But Flora was not a frivolous, easy woman. She would settle for nothing less than marriage to a man who had a job and "common decency." Tom pled and promised and, when they were married, took Flora to his cabin and plot of ground on St. Simon's Island. Farming, however, was beneath him. He converted the front room of his cabin into a store. In the room behind it Robert was born only five months before Tom died of "galloping consumption."

Flora was more durable. Free since childhood, she had become a skilled hairdresser and an expert seamstress, but no one on St. Simon's had a need for her services, and after the death of Tom she took her infant son and returned to Savannah, where she readily found employment among the wives of the German shopkeepers with whom she became a favorite by picking up a speaking knowledge of their language. This favoritism proved timely. She had been settled in the city only a few months when Tom Abbott's sister, alleging Flora to be an unfit mother, brought suit for the custody of the child. The Germans came to Flora's support, and one of them, John H. H. Sengstacke, engaged a lawyer who successfully defended her.

Sengstacke had had dealings with lawyers and lawsuits. His short history in America was thorny with legal tangles. White to all appearances, and German-reared, he was born the son of an immigrant father and a slave girl. When the mother died at the birth of a second child, his father took his two mulatto children to Germany to be reared by his sister. The father himself returned to the States in 1850, prospered in the mercantile trade, regularly remitted money for the support of his children, and died in 1862. He left a will that amply secured his offspring, but his white executors ignored it, for after his death no money from the estate, estimated at fifty thousand dollars, ever reached Germany. The son came to America to investigate in 1869.

John H. Hermann Sengstacke was an educated man, fluent in five languages—just the man for the job of translator for the Savannah *Morning News*. But in the course of pushing his claim to his father's estate he had to reveal the fact of his Negro blood. He was fired. Thereafter some of his father's old friends treated him with contempt. Completely unprepared for this betrayal of old loyalties and this ravishment of his personal dignity, by the time he was financially able to escape to Germany he had perforce identified himself with the Negro race, and he decided to remain. The experience of his Negroness left deep scars. Already there was something of the messiah in him, and something of the masochist. When the dwindled estate was finally settled he came to the conclusion—at once bitter torment and solace—that since he was a Negro he was lucky to salvage two or three thousand dollars, a small frame house, and a store-front building on a bluff in the western section of Savannah.

This was the man who married Flora Abbott in 1874 and gave his name not only to the seven children he begot but to his stepson as well. This was the man who, with the burning ardor of the ancient Christian convert, embraced with passion the scabrous cross of his Negroness and staggered under it with mad delight.

Ordained a minister of the Congregational Church and appointed a teacher in a rural Negro school, he also undertook to publish, edit, and sustain a Negro newspaper. As a preacher-teacher he earned altogether forty dollars a month. His church had few members, and these were so poor that they "could pay," he reported, "only one dollar towards his whole year's salary." Yet he alienated some of these and expelled others for belonging to secret societies. His school had no books, no blackboards, no pencils, no stove. He wrote his newspaper copy in longhand—all of it. "We labor under great disadvantages," he informed a friend. And indeed he did. Eventually the disadvantages became willful malignities offered to him personally. He saw the grim red finger of malice pointing at him from every quarter. He saw himself as a Negro persecuted not only by society but by individuals. The world was against the Sengstackes. The world was against him.

If this was the spirit of Robert's training at home and in his father's school, it was given substance by his earliest experiences at Beach Institute. This was a day school founded by the Freedmen's Bureau but supported by the American Missionary Society. In Savannah, as in other urban centers in those days, there was a Negro color caste as rigid as iron. Mulattoes, as we have seen, were generally the privileged and the exclusive. They had their own churches, their own social clubs. Only mulattoes were normally expected to go to school beyond the second or third grade.

Robert was as black as tar. The prejudice of his light-skinned schoolmates at Beach was cruel to an extreme possible only to adolescents. They dubbed him "Liver Lips," "Tar Baby," and "Crow." Their malevolence undoubtedly generated the unconscious self-hatred that was one of the twisted, ruling passions of Abbott's life— that made him shun the color black even in clothes and cars; that made him dun Negro fraternal organizations to use the whiteball as the symbol of rejection, and plaster black Chicago with slogans urging Negroes to "Go to a White Church on Sunday."

Only Joseph and Catharine Scarborough were not unkind to him at Beach, and if this was more out of respect for their father's friendship with the Reverend John H. H. Sengstacke than friendly regard for Robert, the latter did not sense it. Indeed, he fell in love with Catharine—he was seventeen at the time—and courted her for nearly thirty years. In 1897 he asked her to marry him, but her father was "outraged" at the black man's presumption, and Catharine declined the honor. In 1918, when she had twice been widowed by ne'er-do-well mulatto husbands, Catharine finally agreed to marry him. He was by then a millionaire, but even as he prepared to go to her in Savannah she wrote that she had changed her mind.

But all this was in the future in 1886. What was in the present was the intolerable weight of obloquy and the crushing blows to his self-esteem. He did not cry out aloud. Instead he adopted a system of attitudes—not principles of conduct or principles of ethics—informed only by a defensive spirit, which served him the rest of his life. And the chief of these was patient meekness. In some ways it was as false as Uriah Heep's—and to much the same purpose.

To the disappointment of his stepfather, Robert retreated from Beach after less than two full terms. He dreamed of Hampton, in Virginia, but when his stepfather suggested Claflin University, a hundred miles from his home, he pretended enthusiasm for that place and agreed to work his way through that institution's equivalent of high school. He stayed six months. He was nineteen and still separated from his future by a vast ignorance. Another year went by before Hampton accepted him "conditionally" to study the printing craft.

At Hampton, it is reported, "everybody always picked on him." His hangdog mien and his genuine feelings of inferiority invited it. He was the butt of crude, practical, and sometimes vicious jokes. He probably resented them, but he was too patient, too hungry for acceptance, and too cowardly to protest. Driven to the other extreme at times, he tried to bluster through class recitations, but his dull mind was no help to him, and he invariably made a fool of himself.

He did no better socially. The same prejudice, though degrees milder, that plagued him at Beach prevailed at Hampton, and, inept to begin with, Robert had no success in the highly formalized and rigidly controlled social life of the campus. He was not asked to join the intimate bull sessions. He got no invitations to parties. Girls ignored him, and one of his classmates told him, half in jest, that he was "too black to associate with fair women."

Ironically enough, his black skin did bring him one distinction. Toward the end of his first year he was chosen as a member of the Hampton Quartet. But this was not because his tenor voice was the best that could be found. It was because "white people resented seeing light-complexioned boys in the group"; because Hampton's white administrators knew the emotional impact that "four black boys forlornly singing spirituals" had on white audiences; and because white audiences were the targets of the school's financial appeals. Abbott had a good voice, and he sang the sorrow songs with feeling, but not even the distinction of becoming a member of the quartet in his first year suggested that, next to Booker T. Washington, he would one day be the school's best-known graduate. It took some students five years to complete the four-year course. Abbott required seven.

He was twenty-seven when he graduated and accepted a teaching post in a school on the outskirts of Savannah. Soon he was supplementing his income with part-time work as a printer. He was not very good in either job, and both together did not provide enough for him to court Catharine Scarborough in the manner he thought she deserved. Rivalry for that lady's attentions was keen, and when she rejected his first proposal Abbott felt that the odds were against him. His rivals, though scarcely more affluent than he, were light-skinned. Perhaps if he could get money he could overcome the handicap of his color, equalize the competition. But how get money? His stepfather's example proved that money was not in teaching or preaching. Even the printer's craft offered scant returns to a black man in Georgia. Perhaps in another state—a city in the North—he could use his vocation as a steppingstone "to higher things." After presenting Miss Scarborough with a handsome gold watch in the summer of 1897, he still had enough money to support himself while he explored.

He went to Chicago. When the Hampton Quartet had sung there at the World's Fair four years earlier, Abbott had been awed by the conspicuous display of Negro wealth and achievement. Now almost at once he wrote home, "I will stay out west and try to make a fortune."

But fortunes were not easily made, and he did not know how to begin. He managed to obtain part-time employment as a printer, but earning "real money" at his trade looked no more promising in Chicago than it had in Savannah. It did not take him long to discover that the men to emulate, the men whose names were spoken with deference along State Street and Dearborn Street, were either independent businessmen or professionals. Daniel Hale Williams was a physician and surgeon, Charles Smiley a caterer, Edward Morris a lawyer, and John Jones, who was still remembered as the first Negro to hold public office in Chicago, had been a wealthy merchant tailor. These men were of the status to which Abbott aspired. His ambition was uninformed by any idea of service or any dedication to large purposes. He wanted simply to "accomplish *something* noteworthy"; he wanted—as a later phrase had it—to be a big shot.

He tried to find ways into the closed circle of the elite. He joined the Grace Presbyterian Church where the elite went. He sacrificed necessities to buy admission to the charity balls given for the benefit of Provident Hospital and the Institutional Social Settlement. No one paid the slightest attention to him. For all that he had been a member of the Hampton Quartet and had a better than passable tenor voice, his bid to join the choir of Grace Presbyterian Church was rejected. He was black, and his speech gave him away as one of those "new-come Southern darkies" who were "spoiling things" for long-time residents of the North. Every rebuff fed his passion to "show them" and increased his torment to "make his mark," no matter how. He wrote his mother, "Tell father if he will back me, I will . . . run a paper. . . . Let me know his intentions before I begin to make up my mind as to what steps to take."

The Reverend Mr. Sengstacke, undoubtedly recalling his own costly experience, advised against the newspaper but seemed willing enough to back his stepson in another line, for in the fall of 1898 Robert enrolled in the evening classes of the Kent College of Law. Now for the first time he dropped Sengstacke as a surname and put himself on record as Robert S. Abbott. It is reported that when his stepfather heard of this he wept.

If Robert S. Abbott also wept, it was for other reasons. He had a better than average capacity for self-pity, and later he was to write of this period that he "probably would have starved to death but for the generosity of some folk who would loan me a dime now and then. Even when I did work I did not earn enough to pay back rent, repay loans and eat. . . ."

weekly bundles of the *Defender* east to New York and Boston, south to Atlanta and Birmigham, and west to Seattle and Los Angeles.

But the editorial page belonged to Abbott, and much of the credit for the *Defender's* growth must go to the editorials. This is not to say that Abbott wrote them. He seldom wrote them in their final form, for his prose was often ungrammatical and clumsy; but his ideas informed the editorials, and in them his consciousness, it might be said, prevailed.

It was a consciousness that was cunning without being the least subtle. It did not work from design but through instinct, and often, therefore, it plunged—like a man falling through space—past all the levels of logic to plop at last against the bedrock of personal experience. Whatever position he took, he took on this bedrock ground, and whatever position he took, he held tenaciously. He was almost never known to change his mind, even when he was demonstrably in error.

For instance, when he was a member of the Chicago Commission on Race Relations it was brought forcibly home to him that the *Defender's* campaign to lure Negroes from the South was doing more harm than good. The facts with which the commission dealt showed clearly that the hysterical South–North migration caused a great leap in all the depressing statistics—unemployment, delinquency, crime—and a tragic upsurge of anti-Negro feeling North and South. Mentioning the *Defender* by name, the commission itself urged "greater care and accuracy in reporting incidents involving whites and Negroes, the abandonment of sensational headlines and articles on racial questions, and more attention to means and opportunities of [Negroes] adjusting themselves and their fellows into more harmonious relations with their white neighbors. . . ." But, in 1914, Abbott had taken the position that migration to the North was the Negro's salvation, and in 1919 he refused to abandon it. When disastrous riots flared up all the summer and fall of the latter year, Abbott "did not view them as unmitigated evil."

If he seldom changed his mind, even more rarely did he change his heart. He was emotionally rigid and complex. He felt his black skin to be not only a severe handicap in the Negro world—which, of course, it was—but a source of personal shame. In spite of the most concrete evidence to the contrary—his wealth, prestige, and influence—he was convinced that his intrinsic worth as a person could be certified only by the acceptance of mulattoes. Nevertheless, he felt an obsessive loyalty to blackskin people per se. He reflected their moods instinctively and their minds so perfectly that they saw their composite image in the pages of the *Defender*. He was "for the masses, not the classes." He wanted them to "solidify, throw off the shackels. Rise!" and any small instance of rising—a high school graduation, a black boy on a white athletic team, a Negro victory in the prize ring or in any other contest against a white opponent—any immaterial instance was enough for columns of praise and joy.

Yet—strange duality!—no instance whatever was testimony to his own intrinsic worth. Only intimate social concourse with mulattoes could provide that; only, say, a light-skinned wife could make him worth while and respectable in his own eyes. When finally he married at the age of fifty he took to wife a woman whom he did not love but who was indistinguishable from white. When this unhappy affair ended in divorce he took a second wife who was "white in fact," and who, accompanying him to "white" places of entertainment, did not seem to mind the ridiculous gibberish he spoke in the impossible hope of being mistaken for a foreigner. It is strangely characteristic that, though he gave only casual and token assistance to the black Abbotts and completely ignored them in his will, he contributed regularly to the mulatto Sengstackes, was for years a dependable source of income for their white relatives in Germany, and saw to it that some of the white direct descendants of his father's master were educated.

Though these abiding indices to his character were evident in 1912, Abbott had at that time made up his mind on no public issues and on only one policy for his paper. The *Defender* would not fight Negroes and the editor's own private enemies. It would concentrate its fire on the common foe, the whites. Abbott wanted to unify "the black population for aggressive counter-action," and if this required him to vilify even well-meaning whites, then he would vilify. Of course this was wrong on the face of it, but "give the skunks hell," Abbott would say, and in his book of rules nearly every white man was a skunk, including the good philanthropist friend of the Negro, Julius Rosenwald, who was not the only white man to think that Abbott was a mindless "monkey with a shotgun, who will hurt anybody."

Anybody, that is, except Negroes—who certainly were hurt enough by the white press; and anything except the struggle in which even the semiliterate masses believed themselves engaged. Week after endless week the *Defender's* slogan for that struggle was "American Race Prejudice Must Be Destroyed." The proof of its destruction would rest, Abbott himself wrote (with a habitually greater regard for sense than syntax), in "the opening of all trades and trade unions to blacks. . . . Representation in the President's Cabinet. Engineers, firemen and conductors on all American railroads, and all jobs in government. Representation in all departments of the police forces over the entire United States; Federal legislation to abolish lynching and full enfranchisement of all American citizens."

Though Du Bois probably had the *Defender* in mind when he said that "some of the best colored papers are so wretchedly careless in their use of the English language . . . that when they see English they are apt to mistake it for something else," it is highly unlikely that he also included the *Defender* in his condemnation of those colored weeklies that did not "stand staunch for *principle*." That year, 1914, nearly every Negro paper in the country blasted Du Bois at one time or another, but not the *Defender*. Abbott hated and feared divisive argument among Negroes, and Abbott realized that he and Du Bois were fighting the same war on the same side.

Many Negroes did not realize, except sporadically, that Du Bois was on their side. The man had an unhappy predilection for making enemies. He was impatient, especially of ignorance; he was temperamentally unsuited to mingling with the masses. He was called "race traitor" more than once because it was thought he sounded like one. He was as caustically critical of Negroes as of whites. "Jeremiads were needed to redeem [the Negro] people," he said, and jeremiads he gave them. Abbott on the other hand gave them panegyrics and made excuses for their wrongdoing. Neither man realized that he reflected a deepening mood of frustration and despair.

There were reasons for this mood.

Arthur P. Davis

(1904–   )

VETERAN TEACHER, ANTHOLOGIST, critic, and one-time newspaper columnist, Arthur Paul Davis has worked in black schools for more than sixty years, and he finds that the most rewarding experience of his old age is the respect and affection which many of his former students still have for him.

Born in Hampton, Virginia, in 1904, Davis comes from a large family, several of whom have also spent their working lives in the field of education. He was educated at Hampton Institute (then a high school), at Howard University (freshman year), and at Columbia University, from which he received his A.B. (1927), M.A. (1929), and Ph.D. (1942). Davis has taught at North Carolina College for Negroes (now North Carolina Central), Hampton Institute Summer School, Virginia Union University, and since 1944 at Howard University, where he is at this writing university professor emeritus. Though trained in eighteenth-century literature, he has, during the past two decades, worked in black literature.

He is the author of *Isaac Watts: His Life and Works*, 1943 (a study of the father of English hymnology), and *From the Dark Tower: Afro-American Writers, 1900 to 1960* (1974). Davis is also co-editor (with the late Sterling A. Brown and Ulysses Lee) of *The Negro Caravan* (1941); co-editor with the late Saunders Redding of *Cavalcade: Negro American Writing from 1760 to the Present* (1971); co-editor with Michael Peplow of *The New Negro Renaissance: An Anthology* (1975); and co-editor with Saunders Redding and Joyce A. Joyce of the present volume, *The New Cavalcade: African American Writing from 1760 to the Present* (1991). In addition, Davis has published literally hundreds of scholarly essays and newspaper articles which have appeared in *Crisis, Opportunity, Phylon, CLA Journal, Norfolk Journal and Guide, Journal of Negro Education, Journal of Negro History*, and in many anthologies.

Davis, like most critics and writers of his generation, is an integrationist, not a black nationalist. He feels that black literature is American literature and should be judged by the critical standards of the Anglo-American tradition of which it is a part. This belief does not diminish his appreciation of the many contributions the writers of the Black Arts movement have made to American literature.

Among the honors and awards which Davis has received are the 1975 College Language Association's award for "Distinguished Contribution to

Literary Scholarship," the Howard University College of Liberal Arts award in 1979 for "singular contributions to the humanities," General Education Board Fellowships (1932/33; 1936/37), and the Doctor of Letters honorary degree conferred by Howard University in 1984. In 1982 Davis was given the Middle Atlantic Writers Association, Inc.'s Distinguished Literary Critic Award, and in 1988 the same association gave him the first Therman B. O'Daniel Distinguished Educator Award.

For recent comment on Arthur P. Davis's career, see the *Washington Post Magazine* (July 5, 1987) and *New Directions* for July 1980 and January 1988. See also Ann Allen Shockley and Sue P. Chandler, *Living Black American Authors: A Biographical Dictionary* (1973).

"Survival Techniques as Expressed in Afro-American Literature" was presented as a part of the "Distinguished Senior Scholars Lecture Series," University of the District of Columbia on September 1, 1983.

SURVIVAL TECHNIQUES AS EXPRESSED IN AFRO-AMERICAN LITERATURE

All minority groups employ survival techniques of one kind or another. Those of the American Negro have been expressed in our literature and folklore beginning in the eighteenth century down to the present. There are many survival techniques—those ways in which our forebears felt they could find the greatest fulfillment for themselves, both individually and collectively, in a racist society; or, to be more specific, how they could achieve full manhood and full citizenship, how they could ease the burden of daily living in such a society. Here I am not discussing survival techniques per se; that is, I am not treating them as a sociologist or political scientist would treat them. My emphasis is on these techniques as they appear in literature. I believe that the writings of a people give a better picture of that people's struggles, failures, and triumphs than any kind of

---

This lecture, given September 1, 1983, at the University of the District of Columbia, was part of the "Distinguished Senior Scholars Lecture Series." It was designed to commemorate the outstanding and inspiring career of Anna J. Cooper (1858–1964). Born in Raleigh, North Carolina, Mrs. Cooper was educated at St. Augustine's Normal and Collegiate Institute; at Oberlin, taking there her A.B. (1884) and M.A. (1887); and at the University of Paris, from which she received her Ph.D (1925). Best known for her work as principal of the old M Street High School (which became the famous Dunbar High School), she was a crusader for secondary training for Negro high school students which would prepare them for entrance to Ivy League colleges and universities. On her 100th birthday, she told *The Washington Post* proudly, "Our two boys accepted at Harvard were the first Negro high school graduates to enter without having to study at an academy first."

statistical analysis. In literature, one gets the group-soul, the collective reaction, the spiritual feel of a group or nation. One gets the *real* people, not the abstractions that a scientific investigation gives. The scientific investigation, of course, is also necessary; the literary picture complements the scientific.

The picture that emerges is that of the changing status of the American Negro. Through significant examples from Afro-American literature, the story may be pieced together of the change from the eighteenth-century status, when the Negro fought to be accepted as a part of the Western tradition, down to the present, when black nationalists are trying to repudiate Western culture and all for which it stands. Survival techniques have changed from stage to stage; some abide.

America's first significant black writer was Phillis Wheatley, a West African captured when she was around seven or eight years old. Her story is well known. A little genius, she learned to read and write and compose poetry in an incredibly short time. And through her poetry she became a recognized literary person in New England and in London. She became a member of Boston's most prestigious church. She gained her freedom. She corresponded with George Washington. She was commented on by the Western world's two best-known personalities: Thomas Jefferson and Voltaire. In terms of acceptance, she became the most successful Negro of her day.

How did she do it? What did survival mean to Phillis Wheatley? How did she think of herself in terms of self-fulfillment? For her the answer was found in one word: *Christianity.* That was her way out. Note the following poem, the only one in which she wrote wholly about herself: "On Being Brought from Africa to America."

> 'Twas mercy brought me from my *Pagan* land,
> Taught my benighted soul to understand
> That there's a God, that there's a Saviour too:
> Once I redemption neither sought nor knew.
> Some view our sable race with scornful eye,
> "Their colour is a diabolic die."
> Remember, *Christians, Negroes,* black as *Cain,*
> May be *refin'd,* and join th' angelic train.

Note the word *refin'd*—it means here to be renewed by Christianity, and to become one of the saints both here and in the next world. Christianity is the key to the door. A Negro turned Christian could better himself here and now and, most important, join the "angelic train."

In order to understand Wheatley's poem, we must bear in mind that during the seventeenth and early eighteenth centuries in Europe, scholars raised questions concerning the Negro's ability to be educated, and several experiments were made by rulers and noblemen to find the answer. The best known was that made by Peter the Great—with Ibrahim Petrovich Hannibal, who became a lieutenant-general in the czar's army and the great grandfather of Aleksandr Pushkin. Two other questions were also raised—could a Negro become a poet, then considered the highest and most intellectual calling in the literary arts; and could a Negro become a Christian and remain a slave? Poet Phillis Wheatley answered all three doubts. Christianity made her a member of Boston's finest church and won her freedom. Through the whole of the eighteenth century and into the early nineteenth Christianity in its several phases was the dominant survival technique for African Americans. For Wheatley, it was the matter of becoming assimilated. And as Richard Wright has pointed out, she was more a part of the world in which she lived than has been any other Negro writer since.

Our second writer approached Christianity in a way quite the opposite of that pursued by Wheatley. His name is David Walker, and he was born free in Wilmington, North Carolina. Walker traveled throughout the South and somehow acquired an education as well as a great hatred of slavery. When we come to know him, he is in Boston, where he had a shop in Brattle Street, near wharves, and was involved in writing for the abolition press and speaking for the cause. To reach a larger audience, in 1829 he published at his own expense *An Appeal . . . to the Coloured Citizens of the World, but in Particular and Very Expressly, to Those of the United States of America*, the most violent and incendiary antislavery document written in America up to that time.

Walker's *Appeal* gave new life to the young antislavery crusade in America. It was smuggled out of Boston by sailors and carried to southern seaports. This work brought forth many southern defenses of slavery, the best known that of Thomas R. Dew of Virginia. The mayor of Savannah, after discovering sixty copies in his city, wrote to the mayor of Boston, demanding that he suppress the work. The South offered $1,000 for Walker dead, and $10,000 alive. The book revitalized the abolition movement in the North, touching William Lloyd Garrison, John Brown, and others. In the South it was accused of causing Nat Turner's insurrection in 1831.

What was the message of Walker's *Appeal*? What did Walker advise as a means or technique of survival? The work, fashioned ironically on the U.S. Constitution, has a preamble and four articles. The third concerns "Our Wretchedness in Consequence of the Preachers of the Religion of Jesus Christ." Note that Walker also uses Christianity as a survival technique, but his is a militant use. He in short advocates insurrection based on an Old Testament concept concerning the Jews in Egypt: "Rebellion to Tyrants is obedience to God." This motto is found on the Seal of the United States, put there by Thomas Jefferson.

For Walker, *slavery* was the tyrant, and if Negroes didn't resist that tyrant in every way possible, they would be disobeying God. It was, therefore, the black man's *religious duty* to overthrow such a system. This was militancy—but militancy based on a Christian concept. Walker believed firmly that God would punish America, if it did not get rid of slavery. God made all men of one flesh. He made all men brothers. When America goes against God's will, it mocks God—and God, Walker says over and over—God will *not* be mocked.

Walker also has another Christian belief held by many Negroes of his generation, namely, that God would send a leader to American slaves, just as he sent Moses to the Hebrews in slavery. These pioneers believed in the Bible literally and made many comparisons between the Jewish captivity and American Negro slavery.

Walker begins his *Appeal* by stating that of all the slavery in history, America's slavery—practiced by Christians—was "the most wretched, degrading and cruel," far worse than that in any heathen nation. He then talks about the *hypocrisy* of American Christianity. There are no creatures in all the world more wretched than the Negroes in the southern and western parts of this country under "tyrants and devils." And yet the Christian preachers send out missionaries to convert the heathen in various parts of the globe. How foolish can these preachers be! Do they think they can mock God? God will not be mocked. Repent, America, Walker thunders; if you don't, God will tear up the face of this nation! Walker writes like an Old Testament prophet. His message is: slavery is sinful in the eyes of God. It must be uprooted, if this nation is to survive. This was a strong stand to take in 1829. Walker was found dead in 1830. He seemed to have been poisoned, but we don't really know. His friends had urged him to flee to Canada after he published the *Appeal*, but he stated publicly that he would never run. Walker was not only an early hero; he may have been a martyr to the abolition cause.

In the matter of using Christianity as a survival technique, Walker had a fiery disciple in Henry Highland Garnet. Born in Maryland, Garnet and his family escaped to the North early in his life. He was educated at the famous abolition school, Oneida Institute, and became a Baptist minister. In 1843 Garnet published a work that was even more incendiary than the *Appeal*. Garnet's revolutionary message was called "An Address to the Slaves of the United States of America." It said in effect: God puts the seeds of liberty in every man's heart. It is the duty of the Christian to live free. This is God's command. If you disobey, no matter the circumstances, you are sinning. If slavery causes you to disobey God's wishes, it is your Christian duty to rise up in rebellion and overthrow slavery. Garnet then adds: "Neither God nor angels, or just men, command you to suffer for a single moment. *Therefore, it is* your solemn and imperative duty to use every means, both *moral, intellectual and physical that promises success.*" And he further adds: "You had far better all die— *die immediately,* than live slaves, and entail your wretchedness upon your posterity." Here for the first time was a direct appeal to slaves *themselves* to rise up and throw off their shackles. The work was too strong even for Frederick Douglass, who felt that it spoke "too much of physical force."

Another variation of this theme of Christianity as a survival technique was one that was popular up to the first decades of this century. This was a belief held by many devout black Christians that God had a divine plan for them just as he had for the oppressed Jews in Egypt. They believed that God would appear at the proper time to help Negroes. Note James Weldon Johnson's lines from the poem "Fifty Years (1863–1913)":

> Full well I know, the hour when hope
> Sinks dead and 'round us everywhere
> Hangs stifling darkness, and we grope
> With hand uplifted in despair.

> Courage! Look out beyond, and see
> The far horizon's beckoning span!
> *Faith in your God-known destiny!*
> *We are part of some great plan!*

A variant of this belief that upheld and consoled the slave was the conviction that God would make amends in the next world for what Negroes had to suffer in this. Christianity as a guarantee of a better world to come was perhaps the most popular of all survival techniques for the slave. The Christian message is ideally suited for the poor and oppressed of the world, and American slaves seized it eagerly and enthusiastically. The overriding thesis for slaves was that God was a just God and He would make up in the world to come for the inequity in this world. Literally hundreds of lines in the spirituals have this theme:

> "Gonna tell God all my troubles . . ."

> "You take the world and give me Jesus"

> "I got shoes . . . Strut all over God's heaven"

And there are many, many others.

David Walker and Henry Highland Garnet advocated insurrection based on Christian concepts. Our third writer in this group advocated insurrection as an unequaled technique for obtaining freedom. His name was Martin R. Delany, and he should be known by black nationalists, because he is really the father of the "black is beautiful" concept. A colorful and militant leader of the abolition and post–Civil War eras, Martin R. Delany was born in Charlestown, then in Virginia, of a free mother. The family moved to Pittsburgh, where Delany got his early education. He subsequently attended Harvard Medical School, and practiced for a while in Pittsburgh. Delany published his own newspaper, called the *Mystery*, but gave that up and joined forces with Douglass on *The North Star*. Douglass said of Delany: "When I, Fred Douglass, pray to God I thank him for making me a man; Delany thanks God for making him a *black* man." And this was literally true. Delany gloried in blackness. He believed that black blood was superior to white blood, and had a so-called scientific theory for this stand. Delany was the first leader to advocate industrial education for Negroes, the first American Negro to explore Africa, the first Negro to be given a field rank in the U.S. Army. Lincoln made him a major in the Union army.

A fearless man, Delany, armed with a butcher knife and hatchet, stood a proslavery mob at bay in northern Ohio. When the Fugitive Slave Bill passed, Delany spoke to the mayor of Pittsburgh in a public address:

> If any man approaches that house in search of a slave—I care not who he may be, whether constable or sheriff, magistrate or even judge of the Supreme Court—Nay, let it be *he who sanctioned this act to become a law*, surrounded by his cabinet as his body guard . . . if he crosses the threshold of my door, and I do not lay him a lifeless corpse at my feet, I hope the grave may refuse my body a resting place, and righteous Heaven my spirit a home.

Delany was the third Negro to write a novel, and the first to make armed insurrection the theme of a novel. In 1859, he published *Blake; or, The Huts of America*. In this work he makes his protagonist what we now call a "heroic black" and shows him going from plantation to plantation up and down the Mississippi Valley, organizing slaves for an armed uprising. In the latter part of the work, the hero does the same thing in Cuba. All of this is fiction, of course, but it shows that Negroes thought seriously about insurrection as a survival technique.

It should be noted that the theme of black insurrection has run through African American writings down to the present. In 1899, Sutton Griggs, a Baptist minister who should be better known than he is, wrote a novel, *Imperium in Imperio*, whose plot had Negroes rising up in rebellion and seizing Texas and Louisiana. The first would be a home for all American Negroes, the second they would sell to a foreign government to raise money. In 1938, Arna Bontemps wrote an insurrection novel, *Black Thunder*, which was based on Gabriel Prosser's historic uprising in 1800 in Richmond, Virginia. The hero of the work, Gabriel, was a heroic black. In 1969, Sam Greenlee, in *The Spook Who Sat by the Door*, depicted the Chicago Negro gangs, trained by the hero, a black graduate of the FBI training school, as they rise up and take over the city. As late as 1973, John Wideman, a black Rhodes Scholar, wrote *The Lynchers*, an insurrection novel which showed Negroes lynching a white cop on Boston Common in order to start a riot, then fighting a race war, and finally establishing black nationhood.

Another technique often used by Negroes, especially during the abolition period is *irony*—a technique which make the oppressed feel superior to the oppressor by showing the difference between the latter's highfalutin ideas and his actual practice. Note the following poem "And What Shall You Say?" by Joseph Cotter, Jr.:

> Brother, come
>   And let us go unto our God
> And when we stand before him
>   I shall say—
> "Lord, I do not hate,
>   I am hated.
> I scourge no one,
>   I am scourged.
> I covet no lands,
>   My lands are coveted.
> I mock no peoples,
>   My people are mocked."
> And, brother, what shall you say?

This ironic approach consisted oftentimes of comparing the pious and grand rhetoric of official documents like the Declaration of Independence and the Constitution, and the parables of Christianity, with the harsh facts of slavery. David Walker used irony in modeling his *Appeal* on the U.S. Constitution. A well-known slave narrative by Lewis and Milton Clark pointed out that they were the sons of a veteran of the Revolution and still slaves. Many of these slave narratives and other works pointed out that the worst kind of slave overseer or master was one who boasted about being a Christian. Preachers, of course, made the cruelest of all masters. The greatest master of irony was Frederick Douglass, who attacked both Christian and political hyprocrisy. In his 1845 *Narrative*, he was so hard on Christianity, he added a postscript to the work stating that he was not attacking Christianity per se but southern Christianity, slave-holding Christianity. In one of his greatest orations, "The Meaning of the Fourth of July" (Rochester, 1852), Douglass made a dynamic contrast between the meaning of this day to whites and blacks:

> What, to the American slave, is *your* Fourth of July? I answer; a day that reveals to him, more than all other days in the year, the gross injustice and cruelty to which he is the constant victim. To him, your celebration is a sham; your boasted liberty, an unholy license; your national greatness, swelling vanity; your sounds of rejoicing are empty and heartless; your denunciation of tyrants, brass-fronted impudence; your shouts of liberty and equality, hollow mockery; your prayers and hymns, your sermons and thanksgivings, with all your religious parade and solemnity, are to Him, mere bombast, fraud, deception, impiety and hypocrisy—a thin veil to cover up crimes which would disgrace a nation of savages. There is not a nation on the earth guilty of practices more shocking and bloody than are the people of these United States, at this very hour.

The next two survival techniques existed together—accommodation and protest. They have always been with us and of course are still with us. In order to understand fully the clash between these two ways out for the Negro, it is necessary to know something of the period in which these two programs came to a dramatic climax involving two great leaders, Booker T. Washington and W. E. B. Du Bois. After the Tilden-Hayes Compromise of 1876, the Negroes were returned to the tender care of their former masters. Union troops were withdrawn, the Ku Klux Klan flourished, segregation became the law of the South and the custom of the North. Southern senators and southern popular writers ridiculed the Negro openly; lynchings became almost daily occurrences. In short, from 1876 down, roughly, to World War I was one of the worst periods for Negroes in our history. The Negro reacted to these conditions in two broad ways—accommodation and protest. The first, and by far the more popular, was based on the old saying, if your head is in the lion's mouth, don't twist his tail. It advocated gradualism, the long haul. The arch-exponent of accommodation was Booker T. Washington, and the best and most dramatic statement of his theory was expressed at the Cotton States Exposition in 1895. There he said, holding up his hand in a famous gesture: "In all things that are purely social, we can be as *separate* as the fingers, yet *one* as the hand in all things essential to mutual progress." He then added: "The wisest among my race understand that the agitation of questions of social equality, is the extremist folly."

For the literary creator who followed this type of accommodationist philosophy, certain rules had to be followed. He had to eliminate all open protest, all writing about voting rights, civil rights, and social equality. He had to emphasize *humor* because the Negro was always a funny or pathetic, never a tragic or even a serious character. In short, the black accommodation writer had to give the white reader only those aspects of the Negro the whites liked to hear about. Many Negro writers complied. *Up from Slavery*, by Booker T. Washington, was one of the masterpieces of accommodationist literature.

The outstanding exponent of literary accommodationism, however, is Paul Laurence Dunbar, particularly in his short stories and in his dialect poems. In both, Dunbar was imitating southern white writers of his day. His themes generally and his characters were either happy-go-lucky, soul-food eating, dancing peasants or faithful retainers. They are either funny or pathetic, seldom serious or tragic. A good example of Dunbar's faithful retainer short stories is "The Strength of Gideon" which shows old, loyal Gideon, refusing his own freedom to "keep his promise to the Master to protect the 'missus.' " Dunbar has a few poems of protest, but only a few. The following lines from "Chrismus on the Plantation" are typical of much of Dunbar.

"Look hyeah, Mastah, I 's been servin' you' fu' lo! dese many yeahs,
An' now, sence we 's got freedom an' you 's kind o' po', hit 'pears
Dat you want us all to leave you 'cause you don't t'ink you can pay.
Ef my membry has n't fooled me, seem dat whut I hyead you say.

"Er in othah wo'ds, you wants us to fu'git dat you 's been kin',
An' ez soon ez you is he'pless, we 's to leave you hyeah behin'.
Well, ef dat 's de way dis freedom ac's on people, white er black,
You kin jes' tell Mistah Lincum fu' to tek his freedom back.

The second of the two reactions to post-slavery servitude was that of protest, which says in effect, give us all here and now. As Washington headed the first type, Du Bois headed the second. Out of this movement, the NAACP and *The Crisis* were founded in 1909–1910. The chief protest writer, aside from Du Bois, was Charles W. Chesnutt. Among the things that writers like Chesnutt did was to offset or *try* to offset the stereotypes of the Negroes which southern white writers like Thomas Nelson Page, Joel Chandler Harris, and Thomas Dixon gave to America. These three were the most popular southern writers of their time, and they were popular in the North as well. Dunbar, an accommodationist, in his short stories imitated Harris and Page; on the other hand, the protest writer fought *against* the stereotypes of these men in *his* short stories. In *Conjure Woman*, Chesnutt created a character called Uncle Julius who was a "smart nigger" type, one who fooled the white folks, and not a "Tom" like Uncle Remus. Chesnutt's short stories, unlike those of Dunbar, were satirical and often bitter. Note his "Web of Circumstance." Moreover, in *The Marrow of Tradition* and *The Colonel's Dream*, Chesnutt answered Thomas Dixon's characterization of Negroes as rapists and brutes by showing that no people on earth were worse than the southern poor whites, who did the dirty work of the aristocrats.

This brings us to the New Negro Renaissance of the 1920s—essentially a protest movement. The New Negro (Harlem) Renaissance emphasized several survival techniques, all of them examples of protest against the nation's treatment of Negroes. One of the first was the so-called Talented Tenth theory, which said in effect that one tenth of any people are superior. Take those among us who fall into this category and give us our full rights on that basis. This, of course, was not only an undemocratic stand, but also essentially a totally impracticable position, one that was never taken literally. Nevertheless, most of the Negro novels during the Renaissance (especially those of Jessie Fauset) were based on this position. They said in effect, "we are like you, the best of you, like you in every respect except color; why not accept us?" These novels were best-foot-foremost works, dealing with middle-class Negro life. One should compare Claude McKay's *Home to Harlem* (depraved tenth) and Jesse Fauset's *There Is Confusion* to get the full message. Du Bois at first sponsored the Talented Tenth survival technique, but soon abandoned it.

As part of the Talented Tenth theory, passing for white played a part in these New Negro novels. Of course, it was a limited technique, because only a few Negroes could pass. The thing one notes first is that no Negro novelist *condoned* passing as a way out. The novelists used it to laugh at the white man, who put so much emphasis on keeping the Negro down—when he really couldn't tell who was a Negro. Between roughly 1890 and 1940, I estimate that more than a million Negroes left the race. I am sure that now there are millions of white Americans who don't realize they are black. This, I suppose, could be survival by integration.

Another technique which came to the fore during the Harlem Renaissance was the return to Africa movement. It was not really new; it was a new emphasis on an an old movement which came into being during the eighteenth and early nineteenth centuries in the form of the American Colonization Society, which was a white effort to get rid of America's free Negroes. Most of the early black American leaders—Douglass, David Walker, Bishop Allen, and others—rejected the movement on the following grounds: that this was the black American's country, one that he had helped to build; that Africa was pagan, whereas this was a Christian nation; and that it was a southern effort headed by Henry Clay, John Randolph, and others, an effort designed not to get rid of slavery but to get rid of free Negroes who were the troublemakers and the enemies of slavery.

Only two well-known leaders believed in the colonization cause: one was our first black capitalist, Paul Cuffee, and the other Martin R. Delany. Cuffee financed and himself carried a boat load of Negroes to Sierra Leone. Delany personally explored the Niger Valley in Africa, looking for places to grow cotton. These were the best known believers in the return to Africa movement. The movement died out and remained dormant for almost one hundred years. It was revived, however, during the New Negro Renaissance, when a West Indian visionary and charismatic figure named Marcus Garvey came to Harlem. Although his program was totally impracticable, it brought hope to thousands of people who needed it most—the black underclass. Though it was customary in those days to laugh at Garvey and his flamboyant uniforms, Black Cross, Black Star Line, and black Christ—Garvey's movement was the most successful proletarian movement in America up to that time. When he was deported in 1927, he had over half a million followers.

Garvey's preamble to the UNIA (Universal Negro Improvement Association) Declaration of Rights (1920) has this central theme: "We believe in the freedom of Africa for the Negro people of the world, and by the principle of Europe for the Europeans and Asia for the Asiatics, we also demand Africa for the Africans at home and abroad."

Although most of the middle-class New Negro Renaissance writers laughed at Garvey, his movement had a definite influence on the literature of the period. Much of the poetry of the Harlem Renaissance concerned Africa. It was a kind of literary Garveyism, featuring what is called the alien-and-exile theme, a theme which says that the Negro, an exile from his native land, will always be an alien here in the white man's world. Hughes, McKay, Cullen, and many other lesser poets used the theme, among them Lewis Alexander in his poem "Africa":

> Thou art not dead, altho the spoiler's hand
> Lies heavy as death upon thee; . . .
> Thou art not dead, but sleeping,—Motherland
> A mighty country, valorous and free,
> Thou shalt outlive this terror and this pain;
> *Shalt call thy scattered children back to thee,*
> Strong with the memory of their brothers slain;

> And rise from out thy charnel house to be
> Thy own immortal brilliant self again!

One of the great poems of the Harlem Renaissance, one too long to give here, is Countee Cullen's "Heritage." The return to Africa movement was also reflected in several articles in *The New Negro* by Alain Locke and others, and in Carter Woodson's *Journal of Negro History*. Though lasting only a short while, Garvey's influence was strong; it soon faded, only to have a rebirth, as we shall see, in the sixties.

Another time-honored technique of survival reflected in our literature and in our folk material is plain old-fashioned, stubborn endurance—the black man's ability to keep inching along in spite of bad crops, bad laws, injustice, lynchings, and every other kind of oppression. This ability has been his salvation. Sterling Brown's poem "Strong Men" expresses this trait in this excerpt:

> They dragged you from homeland,
> They chained you in coffles,
> They huddled you spoon-fashion in filthy hatches,
> They sold you to give a few gentlemen ease.
>
> They broke you in like oxen
> They scourged you,
> They branded you,
> They made your women breeders,
> They swelled your numbers with bastards . . .
> They taught you the religion they disgraced.
>
> You sang:
>   Keep a-inchin' along
>   Lak a po' inch worm. . . .
>
> You sang:
>   Bye and bye
>   I'm gonna lay down dis heaby load. . . .
>
> You sang:
>   Walk togedder, chillen,
>   Dontcha git weary. . . .
>
> The strong men keep a-coming' on
> The strong men git stronger.

The same type of endurance is exemplified in that excellent novel by Ernest Gaines, *The Autobiography of Miss Jane Pittman*. Miss Jane, born in slavery, *endured* to see the civil rights marches. For one hundred years, she inched along with dignity and with understanding, accommodating when necessary, standing firm when she could. This tough quality in Negroes guaranteed survival.

There were, however, southern white apologists who felt that the Negro couldn't stand alone without slavery to support him. A certain proslavery southern writer, Lafcadio Hearn, once wrote that the Negro is like the mistletoe, a childlike parasitic race, that needed to plant its roots in the oak tree of slavery in order to survive. Cut down the oak, and the mistletoe Negro will wither and pass away, leaving only the faint plaintive echoes of his beautiful slave songs. The Negro, somehow, didn't act as he should; he kept getting stronger and a-coming on.

A survival technique that the black man has always used has been trickery, or as it was called when I was a boy—fooling Cap'n Charlie. Folk literature is full of this kind of stories: Ol' John (the "smart nigger") always outsmarts and outwits Cap'n Charlie because the underdog has to be smarter than the top dog in order to survive. Cap'n Charlie's weakness, which the Negro exploits, is that Cap'n Charlie has fixed in his mind certain conceptions of the Negro, and one of these is that John is always dumb. He must cleave to this conception because he needs it to feel racially superior. John knows it and takes advantage of Cap'n Charlie's weakness.

In *The Outsider*, Richard Wright has a fascinating episode based on this weakness. Cross Damon needs a new birth certificate in order to change his image and identity. He gets it from two court clerks, just by playing dumb. Deep down these clerks realize that no person could be as stupid as Cross Damon acts, but this stupidity satisfies their concept of the Negro, and of course they give him the birth certificate.

Ralph Ellison in *Invisible Man* makes use of this fooling and tricking Cap'n Charlie. The young student protagonist takes the white trustee to the Golden Day, a house of assignation. When asked by the principal (Bledsoe) why he did it, the boy answers that he was trying to *please* Norton when he took him to the Golden Day.

> "Please him?" shouts Bledsoe. "And here you are a junior in college! Why, the dumbest black bastard in the cotton patch knows that the only way to please a white man is to tell him a lie!"

Another example of this survival technique is found in the grandfather's dying remarks in Ellison's great work:

> "Son, after I'm gone I want you to keep up the good fight. I never told you, but our life is a war and I have been a traitor all my born days, a spy in the enemy's country. . . . Live with your head in the lion's mouth. I want you to overcome 'em with yesses, undermine 'em with grins, agree 'em to death and destruction, let 'em swoller you—till they vomit or bust wide open."

Many Negroes in the old days went through life acting on this principle. Some still do.

One of the obvious survival techniques offered to Negroes during the twenties and thirties was communism. There was, I know from personal experience, a concerted drive to enlist Negroes in the cause because we were the most obvious victims of capitalistic exploitation. On the surface and theoretically, Marxism seemed the obvious and ideal answer to our problem. Supposedly egalitarian, or rather, classless, in nature, international in scope, making all men brothers, communism seemed the ideal answer for poor, exploited, oppressed, and predominantly working-class Negroes, and many black intellectuals became interested; a few became Party members.

But communism was ideal for Negroes only on the surface. First of all, it was too intellectual to appeal to black workers; it was too abstract. Second, any movement which scoffed at religion couldn't get very far with Negro masses. Third, it ignored the needs of an individual, and fourth, it ignored the nationalist tendencies always present among us, and by nationalist here I mean the sense of race. Whatever they promised, communists were still white, and that of course was the major obstacle.

Communism, however, for a short while did influence Negro literature. One of our truly great literary works, Richard Wright's *Native Son*, was a communist-based novel. Wright, however, repudiated the movement, and his novel *The Outsider* attacks communism. Wright's earlier attitude is given in the following stanza, and it summed up the feelings of many young black intellectuals at the time:

> I am black and I have seen black hands
> Raised in fists of revolt, side by side,
> With the white fists of white workers,
> And some day—and it is only this which sustains me
> And some day there shall be millions and millions of them,
> On some red day in a burst of fists on a new horizon!

Another one of our outstanding writers who felt for a while that communism was the way out, the best survival technique for Negroes, was Langston Hughes. Although Hughes never became a Party member, some of his best poems were inspired by the movement. The following short piece shows again the attitude, not only of Hughes but also of many young Negro intellectuals of his day.

> Goodmorning, Stalingrad
>   Where I live down in Dixie
> Things is bad—
>   But they're not so bad

I still can't say,
     Goodmorning, Stalingrad!
And I'm not so dumb
     I still don't know
That as long as your red star
     Lights the sky
We won't die.

But in spite of its influence on the literature of the period, communism never made any great progress among African Americans, and by the time we get to Ralph Ellison, we find in *Invisible Man* a strong and effective attack on Marxism. When we reach Ellison, we have also come down to the time of the so-called black revolution of the sixties. This *political* black revolution found its *literary* expression in the Black Arts movement. Until the sixties, practically all American Negroes considered the aim of all their various survival techniques to be integration, that is, that we become a part of the mainstream of American life with no restrictions. Nearly all of black literature up until the sixties was based on this ultimate goal. In some respects our literature has reached that goal—and to a lesser extent our life. The works of Richard Wright, James Baldwin, Ralph Ellison, Robert Hayden, and a few others are not just *Negro* works; they are outstanding American works—American works in the same way that John O'Hara's, Saul Bellow's, and other works of ethnic Americans have become American. Using the black experience, these black authors express it in the forms and techniques of the great Western tradition which is our inheritance. Wright's Bigger Thomas in *Native Son* is a ghetto Negro, but he represents the underprivileged and the dispossessed of the entire world. The protagonist of *Invisible Man* speaks not only for Negroes, but for all modern men seeking their identity. To the integrationist, this is what Negro literature should do. It makes black Americans a part of the mainstream.

To the black nationalist, this is the worst thing that could happen. For the black nationalist movement, headed by Amiri Baraka, Haki Madhubuti, and many others, survival means black nationhood; it means a complete break with the whole Western tradition of literature and life. It means the establishment of Africa as a cultural and spiritual homeland. It means having a literature of blacks for blacks based on black mythology, black imagery, and black experience. It means a black literature that should be all political, all of it designed to liberate. It means no more art for art's sake. In the words of Baraka from his poem "Black Art":

We want a black poem, and a
black world

> Let the world be a black poem
> and let all black people
> Speak this poem
> Silently or aloud.

Or in the words of Madhubuti:

> We must destroy Faulkner, dick, jane, and other perpetuators of evil.
> It's time for Du Bois, Nat Turner, and Kwame Nkrumah. As Frantz
> Fanon points out: destroy the culture and you destroy the people. This
> must not happen. Black artists are culture stabilizers; bringing back old
> values, and introducing new ones. Black art will talk to the people and
> with the will of the people stop impending "protective custody."

The integrationists felt that our survival depended on merging
with the mainstream, on becoming a part of the Western tradition.
The black nationalists say, let us destroy the Western tradition, get
rid of the "white bitch." Let us burn, burn, burn, and from the
ashes, phoenixlike, a new black culture and literature will arise. Unfortunately they included middle-class Negroes as a part of the old
order to be destroyed along with "honkey." Moreover, this theory for
survival is even more impracticable than was Garvey's. You can't
overthrow four hundred years of a culture with mere rhetoric.

I have not mentioned two of the most important survival techniques of recent times: Martin Luther King's nonviolent crusade and
Malcolm X's stirring black nationhood movement. Both, it seems to
me, are too close to us and our time to be adequately reflected in
black literature. There is, however, one all-important technique
which Negroes have used, over the years; that is, not all of us but a
chosen few. This technique I shall call the Anna J. Cooper technique,
the one that she used when she insisted on her students receiving
the same preparation the whites received in Washington at the time.
This technique may be labeled equality through superiority. It says
in effect give us an equal break and we'll take care of the rest. We
don't need special consideration—all we need is an equal chance to
get what others get. We know how well that technique worked for
the graduates of the old M Street High School (which became the
famous Dunbar High School), of which Anna J. Cooper was principal. It is a technique that won many of us honors in America's best
universities and furnished us with the best leadership we have had
over the years. It could be called the ultimate survival technique. I
wish there were more present-day Anna J. Coopers working with
and inspiring young blacks through this technique. If black Americans continue this pursuit, the promised land is ours. "Walk togedder chillen, dontcha git weary, dontcha git weary."

Therman B. O'Daniel

(1908–1986)

EDITOR, SCHOLAR, CRITIC, and educator (in the broadest sense of the term), Therman Benjamin O'Daniel was born in Wilson, North Carolina, July 8, 1908, the son of middle-class parents. He was educated in the public schools of Greensboro, North Carolina; at Lincoln University (Pennsylvania), taking there his B.A.; at the University of Pennsylvania, where he received his M.A.; and at the University of Ottawa (Canada), where he earned his Ph.D. in 1956. He also did post-doctoral work in English and American literature in the following schools: Harvard, University of Pennsylvania, University of Chicago (on a General Education Board Fellowship), Pennsylvania State University, and at the University of Ottawa (on a Ford Foundation Fellowship).

O'Daniel's professional career as teacher and administrator took him to the following centers of learning: Fort Valley State College, Allen, Dillard, and Morgan State universities. A many-sided educator, Professor O'Daniel served for more than forty-five years in African American colleges and universities in various positions including department head, chairman of key committees, summer school director, dean, and acting president.

His outstanding contributions to black literature were made as critic and editor. He was cofounder and editor of the *CLA Journal*, which under his guidance became a first-class literary periodical. O'Daniel also cofounded the Langston Hughes Society and was the first editor of *The Langston Hughes Review*, which he designed; he was an active and helpful worker in the Zora Neale Hurston Society and on the editorial board of the *MAWA Review*. O'Daniel's major works in his chosen field of critical-editing were the scholarly and impressive *Twenty-Five Year Cumulative Author-Title Index to the College Language Association Journal*; the Langston Hughes issue of *The CLA Journal* (June 1968); *Langston Hughes, Black Genius: A Critical Evaluation* (1971); *James Baldwin: A Critical Evaluation* (1977); and *Jean Toomer: A Critical Evaluation* (1988). Professor O'Daniel died before finishing the last-named volume. It was completed by Ann Venture Young of Morgan State and Cason Hill of Morehouse College, the two collaborating with Howard University Press.

As cofounder and editor of the *CLA Journal*, O'Daniel made a low-keyed but vastly important contribution to the young black writers of his generation; he gave them an opportunity to publish their works in an important literary journal. And he inspired them in many other ways.

There was nothing fancy about Therman O'Daniel. He did not follow any ideological or ethnic line or any avant-garde critical movement. A conventional scholar, teacher, editor, and critic, he knew his field thoroughly and carried out with scholarly precision any project he undertook. In short, he was a perfectionist, interested in a "fit audience . . . though few."

Among the many honors and awards he received during his long and distinguished career are the following: in New York City in 1972, the Black Academy of Arts and Letters gave him the Alice E. Johnson Memorial Fund Award; in 1978, he received an official citation from the state of Maryland for his work on James Baldwin; in 1974 and 1978, the College Language Association honored him for "meritorious service"; and in 1980, the General Alumni Association of Lincoln University gave him the university's "Highest Honor." The June 1986 issue of the *CLA Journal* has two commemorative tributes to O'Daniel: one by Dr. Ruth Sheffey of Morgan State, the other by Professor Mae Frances Alston, representing the Zora Neale Hurston Society. At the Fiftieth Anniversary Celebration of the College Language Association meeting in Washington, D.C., in 1987, Professor Leonard A. Slade, now of the State University of New York, read his "Elegy for Therman O'Daniel." On June 23, 1986, the Middle-Atlantic Writers Association Board of Directors conferred upon Therman B. O'Daniel officially the title "Dean-Editor of Afro-American Literary Criticism." The association also established in his memory the Therman B. O'Daniel Memorial Award for Literary Scholarship. Biographical material on Therman B. O'Daniel's early life will be found in G. James Fleming and Christian E. Burckel's *Who's Who in Colored America* (1950). Because of the nature of his contribution to African American literature—critical-editing, rather than creative writing—O'Daniel does not have the extensive biographical recognition he deserves.

The selection that follows, "Jean Toomer and Mae Wright: An Interview with Mae Wright Peck," shows a side of Toomer's life and character seldom portrayed today—that of a young black enjoying the decorous and conventional pleasures of middle-class life during the 1920s in vacation spots like Harper's Ferry and Highland Beach. The Toomer we now know best lived in a sophisticated white world of two rich wives, of association with the avant-garde literary circle of Waldo Frank, and of flirtation with the mystic teachings of the then-popular Gurdjieff Institute.

O'Daniel conducted the following interview with Mae Wright Peck over a period of time in 1980. The interview can be found in *Jean Toomer: A Critical Evaluation* (1988).

JEAN TOOMER AND MAE WRIGHT
An Interview with Mae Wright Peck

It was purely by chance that I learned that my good friend Mae Wright Peck of Baltimore, Maryland, was the same beautiful May[1] Wright with whom Jean Toomer was romantically involved during the early 1920s. At a 1979 Christmas party, given by Mae for her Washington cousins, our lively conversation on many topics eventually became centered on a discussion of early Negro writers, to whom some of those present were related; and, from this, we proceeded to talk about some of the younger writers of the Harlem Renaissance—Langston Hughes, Arna Bontemps, Countee Cullen, and others—whom some of us had known personally, when Mae informed us that she had also known Jean Toomer.

This announcement was particularly interesting to me because, at the moment, I was working on a collection of critical studies on Toomer, and, at various times, I had run across brief references to Mae Wright in the Toomer literature. Naturally, I wished immediately to pursue this topic further but thought that I should wait for a more opportune time. Just before my wife and I left the Christmas party, and as we were thanking Mae for her hospitality, I told her about the Toomer book which I had in progress and asked her if she would be willing, at some time soon, to talk with me about Toomer. Without hesitation, she said that she would.[2]

Several weeks later, after the busy Christmas and New Year holiday season had passed, we invited Mae to our home for dinner and

---

Reprinted by permission of the College Language Association.

---

[1] May Wright changed the spelling of her first name to *Mae* during her first year at Tufts University. There was a classmate whose name was *Amy* Wright, and though different from *May*, there was always confusion. Mae Wright hoped that the slight change would be helpful in solving the problem.

[2] Three formal meetings, a number of informal meetings, and many telephone conversations went into the preparation of this interview. The formal meetings were specifically arranged to discuss the subject; the informal meetings refer to times when Mrs. Peck and I saw each other at various events and chatted briefly about new information she had thought of or anything else pertinent to the subject; and the many telephone conversations were used to verify or clarify innumerable details. All of this was conveniently possible because Mrs. Peck and I both live in Baltimore, we are good personal friends, and she was very cooperative at all times. The formal meetings were held on Wednesday, January 30, 1980 (a dinner meeting at the O'Daniel home); on Friday, June 6, 1980 (a second dinner meeting at the O'Daniel home); and on Sunday, June 22, 1980, at Mrs. Peck's home. In between these formal meetings, the many informal meetings and telephone conversations occurred, and several drafts were prepared, corrected, and revised. The final manuscript was completed on Wednesday, July 2, 1980.

for the promised discussion of Toomer. Mae came and brought with her three books that had been gifts from Toomer. Two of them bore inscriptions, and one book, of course, was a first edition of *Cane*:

> *To*
> *May*
> *with love*
> *Jean*

Another was *New Hampshire: A Poem with Notes and Grace Notes*, by Robert Frost, with woodcuts by J. J. Lankes, published by Henry Holt and Company (New York, 1923). It was identically inscribed, but with an added date—*Christmas: 1923*. The third book was an unautographed copy of Waldo Frank's *Holiday*.

Mae said she thought I might be interested in seeing these books, and, indeed, I was; and, as we engaged in some general conversation, I gave them a brief examination. However, the time came to talk specifically about Toomer, and, without further ado, we began.

INTERVIEWER: Was it in Washington, D.C., that you first met Jean Toomer?

MAE: No, he and I met for the first time at Harper's Ferry, West Virginia.[3]

INTERVIEWER: Oh, I knew that Washington was Toomer's home, and thought perhaps that you had once lived there too, or had met Toomer there while visiting that city.

MAE: No. Baltimore is my home; I was born here and finished high school here.

INTERVIEWER: Douglass High School?

MAE: It was named Frederick Douglass High School a little later, but it was just called the Baltimore Colored High School when I graduated.

INTERVIEWER: Then you have spent most of your life in this city.

MAE: In a way, you might say so. However, I have traveled, of course, to many parts of the world. Also, I attended preparatory

---

[3]Harper's Ferry, West Virginia, is a small, mountain town, located in the extreme Eastern part of West Virginia. It is situated on bluffs overlooking the place where the Potomac and Shenandoah Rivers meet and flow together. The town was incorporated in 1763, but in 1747 Robert Harper established and operated a ferry there—thus, the name. The United States located an arsenal there in 1796, which John Brown seized in his raid of October 16, 1859. Storer College, now closed, was founded there in 1867.

school and college away from Baltimore; then lived and taught elsewhere for a few years before returning here to teach in the public school system, and later, to work for the State of Maryland in instructional television.

INTERVIEWER: That is very interesting, but somehow, I had associated you with Washington to some extent, as well as with Baltimore.

MAE: Well, that is true to the extent that I always had relatives in Washington. Before my mother and father were married, she lived there with her parents. It was her home at that time. She was a graduate of the Miner Normal School and taught for one year in one of the elementary schools. She met my father there. He was a graduate of the Yale Medical School and had gone to Washington to serve his internship at Freedmen's Hospital. After this, he moved to the nearby city of Baltimore to begin the practice of medicine, and in five years he had purchased and furnished a home and an office. Thus, when he married my mother in 1905, it was to Baltimore that he brought his bride, and later it was here that I was born. In a way, Washington was a second home for me during my childhood. I was very fond of my grandparents and other relatives there and was a frequent visitor to their homes.

INTERVIEWER: Now tell me about Harper's Ferry and how it happened that you met Jean Toomer there?

MAE: It was in the month of June, during the summer of 1922, and I had gone to Harper's Ferry on vacation with my family. The YMCA, that year, had taken over Storer College for its summer conferences, and it had invited some Baltimore and Washington families and, perhaps, some persons from other places to spend their vacations there. As a matter of fact, the YMCA needed the participation of these families in order to keep the facilities of the college open during the summer and provide funds to support the conference. Because of its elevation, Harper's Ferry was very pleasant in the summer, and it was reasonably close to Baltimore and Washington. Therefore, it was convenient for professional men, who had to attend to business during the week, to commute and spend their weekends with their families.

INTERVIEWER: Were there many families there?

MAE: Yes, a goodly number, I should say, including Attorney and Mrs. Perry Howard of Washington and their two young sons; Attorney and Mrs. William C. McCard from Baltimore; Mr. Clyde McDuffy, a latin teacher at Washington's Dunbar High School: Mr. and Mrs. John Nalle of Washington, and their daughter, Blanche, who later became Mrs. Clyde McDuffy, and others. Then there were many who seemed to come for a few days or a week at a time, rather than for the entire summer. I remember Mordecai Johnson being there for about a week on one vacation. This was before he became president of Howard University.

INTERVIEWER: And Jean Toomer?

MAE: Yes, and Jean Toomer, of course, was there. A Mr. Hamlin and a Mr. McGrew were the YMCA officials in charge of the conferences and were the persons who managed the entire operation. They assigned the families to rooms in the dormitories and to tables in the dining hall where we all ate our meals. The girls in our group were assigned a table together, and, there being no vacancy at the tables for the older persons, Toomer was assigned to our table. I remember that we young girls gave him a hard time, at first, trying to get enough to eat. He was playing the gentleman's role and held back until all of us were served. This amused us very much.

INTERVIEWER: What kind of person was Toomer? What did he look like?

MAE: Physically, Jean was a man over six feet tall, slender with a light olive complexion and a full head of black or very dark-brown hair. He had an athletic build, but he was not heavy—more the physique of a runner, I would say.

INTERVIEWER: By looking at him, could one identify him as a Negro?

MAE: No. If one had not been told that he had Negro blood in him, one never would have known it. He would have had no trouble whatever passing for white.

INTERVIEWER: What about his personality?

MAE: He was an excellent conversationalist and was very sociable and charming when he wanted to be, but at times he was withdrawn and stayed to himself.

INTERVIEWER: Did he ever discuss color with you?

MAE: No, he never did.

INTERVIEWER: What was the program at Harper's Ferry?

MAE: The YMCA had a program for its conferences, but the vacationers had nothing to do unless they made their own entertainment.

INTERVIEWER: How did Toomer fit in with this?

MAE: At first, I suppose that it was difficult for him, especially when one considers his age.

INTERVIEWER: What do you mean?

MAE: Well, I have mentioned the fact that Harper's Ferry, that summer, was somewhat of an improvised summer resort for the families in our group. The grown-up people were much older than Jean, and their children were many years younger. Except for its beautiful scenery and delightful climate—the cool, pleasant nights for sleeping, in contrast to the extremely hot and humid weather of Baltimore and Washington—Harper's Ferry had absolutely nothing else to offer the vacationers in our group. For company for me, since I was an only child, my mother had invited my younger cousin, Catherine Baker, from Washington, and a friend from Wilmington, Delaware, Alice Banton, daughter of Dr. and Mrs. Conwell Banton. Also, there was another friend, Elizabeth "Chita" McCard, of Baltimore, who was there for the summer with her uncle and aunt, Attorney and Mrs. William C. McCard. Her father, Dr. Harry S. McCard, was the attorney's brother. The three of us—Alice, "Chita," and I—often spent our vacations together, as we were the only children of families that had been friendly for years.

INTERVIEWER: Were you about the same age?

MAE: Yes, just about; Alice was a year older, and "Chita," about two years younger than I.

INTERVIEWER: Toomer must have been twenty-seven years old, going on twenty-eight.

MAE: Yes, he was twenty-seven at the time, and I was sixteen. I had just finished high school in three and a half years and was looking forward to entering college in the fall, or a preparatory school, for one year, before going on to college.

INTERVIEWER: How did the older people spend their time at Harper's Ferry?

MAE: Mostly resting and relaxing, and taking short walks to enjoy the beautiful scenery and the mountain air. Also, card playing, reading, and needlework were other forms of entertainment in which they engaged. Often, having much to talk about, they just sat on the campus and conversed with each other. At other times, after dinner, they arranged their chairs in a big circle and sang many of their favorite and well-known songs. Also, there were tennis courts, and some of them played and enjoyed the game of tennis. On the weekends there were plenty of good players on hand, and sometimes the spectators saw some good matches.

INTERVIEWER: What happened on rainy days?

MAE: In inclement weather, all of us used a large recreation room in the main dormitory, which also housed the dining hall. There, such games as whist, checkers, and dominoes were engaged in, along with the group singing.

INTERVIEWER: It is said that Toomer was fond of music; did he join in?

MAE: No, he never did.

INTERVIEWER: How did he spend his time? Had he come to Harper's Ferry to write?

MAE: If so, he did not, at first, discuss his writing with me, and after we got to know each other, we spent most of each day together. He could have been doing some writing when he was alone in his room, but in the beginning, he was not always talking about it to me or to my mother. As far as I could tell, he had just come to Harper's Ferry for a vacation.

INTERVIEWER: In other words, he did not seem to have a writing schedule while he was there?

MAE: No. But, as I have said, if so, he was very private about it, when we first met. Later on, however, my mother and I did come to know that Jean had written a few pieces and that he did aspire to become a professional writer. At this time, of course, he had done very little and was saying little or nothing about it. As a matter of fact, he did more talking about my writing than he did about his own.

INTERVIEWER: Had you written something?

MAE: Not really. I had just won a city-wide essay contest while in school, and Jean read the piece and favorably commented on it. He told me that he thought I had literary promise, if I would apply myself. At a later time, he sent me a list of authors to read and said that he would discuss them with me after I had read them. Also later, he sent me Waldo Frank's *Holiday* and some other books to read.

INTERVIEWER: Did you ever meet Waldo Frank?

MAE: Yes, and I saw him briefly on one or two occasions with Jean. Once he accompanied Jean when he visited my home in Balti-

more. Also, because of his friendship with Jean, when I was applying for admittance to a preparatory school, Frank wrote a letter of
recommendation in my behalf to Cushing Academy. However,
going back to your earlier question, I do recall Jean having quoted
a line or phrase from a poem that he could have been writing at
the time: "Ephemerally immolating hills,"[4] but, other than this, he
was not one to talk about what he was writing, if anything, at that
time—at least, not to me when we were together. I suppose that
the reason I remember this line is because I had to look up the
words to understand it.

INTERVIEWER: How did Toomer get along with your cousin and your
girlfriends?

MAE: Quite often we were all together, and he got along fine with
them and they with him, when he felt like being sociable. When
he wished to be alone with me, he was very good at planning
things for them to do. He organized them into, what he called, his
squad, like an army unit, and whenever he wished to do so, he
assigned them well-conceived tasks to execute and told them to
return in an hour or so and report to him.

INTERVIEWER: How did they react?

MAE: It is surprising how cooperative they were and how faithfully
they carried out his orders. Regarding my young cousin, Catherine, Jean told me that since her father was dead and my parents
kept Catherine with them so much, I had the responsibility to
help her mature into a lovely woman.

INTERVIEWER: Did Toomer ever discuss his college experiences with
you, or his teaching experiences in Sparta, Georgia?

MAE: No, he never did. The only thing that he mentioned about a
past experience that might have been remotely connected with
one of these, was that one time when he was out West, there was
a forest fire and he had helped to fight it. And the only reason,
perhaps, that he mentioned this was that he was wearing a sweater
that was partly burned, and when my mother asked him about it,
that is what he told her.

INTERVIEWER: Did you and Toomer take hikes together?

MAE: Not hikes as such, but we did take long walks together, almost
daily. Two of the spots frequented by us on these walks are fa-

---

[4]The first line of Toomer's poem "Glaciers of Dusk." See John C. Griffin, "Two Jean
Toomer Poems: 'For M.W.' and 'Glaciers of Dusk'," *Pembroke Magazine* 6 (January 1975).

mous and dear to the hearts of most visitors to Harper's Ferry: the legendary projecting rock, high above and overlooking the rivers called "Lover's Leap";[5] and the place where one can stand and look into three states—Maryland, Virginia, and West Virginia. Jean was a lover of nature and was very observant of the natural wonders in the beautiful Harper's Ferry environment. After he had been at Harper's Ferry for approximately a month, I guess, he returned to Washington for a week's visit. When he came back, Catherine, "Chita" McCard, Alice Banton, and I met him at the station, and he offered to engage the only taxicab there to take us up the hill to the college. I was in favor of that idea, but "Chita" and Alice took me aside and reminded me of the cost of such an expedition; so we all walked back to Storer College together. After returning from the Washington trip, he alluded, on one occasion, to the fact that he had had something published but said nothing that was specific, nor did he elaborate.

INTERVIEWER: Other than this brief trip to Washington, did Toomer spend the whole summer at Harper's Ferry?

MAE: Yes, I think so, at least most of it. He was still there when my family and I returned to Baltimore in August, but he must have left very soon afterwards because the YMCA program was coming to an end. Later on he told my mother that when our car left, it was like the empire leaving the czar.

INTERVIEWER: Did you see him anymore before you left for school?

MAE: Yes, he visited our home in Baltimore, from time to time, until I left for Cushing Academy. Having finished high school in three and a half years, I discovered that, although I had the required units for graduation, I was minus certain specific units needed for entrance to one of the New England colleges. Therefore, I spent one year in Cushing Academy, a preparatory school. After I went away, I did not see Jean anymore until Thanksgiving, but we wrote letters frequently to each other. In one of his letters, he told me that Miss Burrell, an outstanding teacher of English and dramatics at Washington's Dunbar High School, had told him that she had heard that he had fallen in love with a Baltimore girl.

INTERVIEWER: What was Toomer's reaction to this?

MAE: He said that, "being the diplomat that I am," he evaded the subject and gave her no satisfaction; just passed over it and continued talking to her on another topic.

---

[5]Lover's Leap is described by Toomer in his story "Avey" and is used as the setting for one of his scenes. Toomer, *Cane* (New York: Boni & Liveright, 1923).

INTERVIEWER: But it was true, was it not?

MAE: I suppose so. I think, at the time, we both thought that we were very much in love. When I came home for the Thanksgiving vacation, we saw each other frequently, and he took me to the Howard-Lincoln football game in Washington. After the game, we went dancing at the Lincoln-Colonnade. Jean was a marvelous dancer, and we had great fun.

INTERVIEWER: Yes, but the vacation period was short.

MAE: That is true, but the Christmas vacation period was longer, and we saw a great deal of each other at that time, and again during the Easter vacation. My friend Anne DeBerry of Springfield, Massachusetts, visited me during the Christmas holidays, and at times, my home was full of girlfriends of our own ages. On one such occasion, Jean told my mother that he felt like a grandfather among such a youthful group. He never, however, expressed such sentiments to me.

INTERVIEWER: Were you two ever engaged?

MAE: Yes, in an informal manner. What I mean by this is that my mother knew about it, but it had not reached the point where my father was informed and his consent was requested.

INTERVIEWER: But your father knew him, of course?

MAE: Certainly; he met Jean and knew him quite well at Harper's Ferry and saw him on many occasions when he visited me and had dinner with the family in Baltimore. But my father was busy with his profession, while my mother was always around when Jean came and got to know him very well. As a matter of fact, he sometimes wrote to my mother about our romance and about his hopes to become a writer of fame and fortune. In other words, they were very fond of each other, and she seemed to encourage our courtship, or at least did not oppose it. Thus, as Jean and I talked of marriage, we shared this hope with my mother. However, all three of us realized that marriage, in that day, required that the man have money or an income, and Jean had neither. He did have confidence in the success of the book he was writing[6] and expected that its sale would launch him as a serious member of the writing profession. Also, he expected money from the book's sale, as well as from the sale of other writings later. Then, and only then, would he be in a position to approach my father and ask for a formal engagement. Unfortunately, you and I both

---

[6]Toomer, *Cane* (New York: Boni & Liveright, 1923).

know that he did not get the merited acceptance that he expected; that recognition did not come until many years later; and that he never did realize substantive money from his writings.

INTERVIEWER: So, with fated circumstance working against it, the engagement really got bogged down, did it not?

MAE: It certainly did. I should state here, however, that although my father was a very loving and indulgent parent in other ways, he was adamant in regard to my finishing college. For this reason, the subject of an engagement was never discussed with him, and from what he had always emphatically told me—even before I met Jean—I knew there was no use talking to him at that time. Uppermost in my father's mind was a good education for his daughter at one of the better New England colleges, and he had always stressed the fact that he would support me as long as I stayed in school, but should I decide to leave school, all support would be withdrawn immediately. I knew that he meant this. As for Jean, at that time, as has already been stated, he had no visible means nor any very promising prospects of being able to support the two of us.

INTERVIEWER: And yet, he still remained hopeful?

MAE: At that time, yes. I have spoken to you of Jean's letters to my mother. In them, he constantly reassured her of his love and respect for me, and his hopes for our happy future together. Indeed, there had to have been some sort of *understanding* if he were to continue to see me after the summer of 1922. My mother and her family came from a culture in which it was customary for a young man to *state his intentions* after he had come calling on a girl enough times to indicate a serious interest. Yet, because of my youth, Jean's impecunious circumstances, and my parents' desire that I get an education, a formal engagement was not encouraged.

INTERVIEWER: Let me ask you a few questions about Toomer's family. Did he have much to say about his family?

MAE: No, it was not his practice to talk about the members of his family when we were together. I know that he was very fond of his grandmother, and occasionally she would be mentioned by him as he talked, but he never began a conversation specifically about her or any other family member.

INTERVIEWER: He dedicated the first two parts of *Cane* to his grandmother, which might indicate his deep affection for her.[7] His

---

[7]Toomer dedicated the third part of *Cane*, "Kabnis," to his friend Waldo Frank.

grandfather, however, died in December of 1921, some six months before you met Toomer. Did your family know his family?

MAE: My mother and her family, having lived in Washington, knew of the Pinchbacks, of course, but they were not personal friends of theirs.

INTERVIEWER: What about Toomer's Uncle Bismarck? Did you ever meet him?

MAE: No, nor did Jean ever discuss him with me, but I did hear the name somewhere without any particulars. I guess the reason that I remember this at all is that, at the time, I thought *Bismarck* to be a rather odd name for an uncle.

INTERVIEWER: Did Toomer ever discuss his theories about physical exercise and body building with you?

MAE: No, but he was a great believer in taking long walks, and there could have been a connection between this and whatever he might have believed on the subject.

INTERVIEWER: What, if anything, did Toomer have to say about the moral and social codes of behavior? Did he consider these codes repressive and damaging to one's effort to find fulfillment and self-realization?

MAE: No, he did not discuss any of this with me. If he had such ideas in mind, perhaps he thought he should discuss more interesting topics when we were together.

INTERVIEWER: You will pardon me for mentioning this, but I think that it should be discussed to some extent, to prevent false conclusions from being drawn about it.

MAE: What is it that you have in mind?

INTERVIEWER: I am thinking about the story "Avey," in which a very important scene is laid at Harper's Ferry. Since it is known that you met Toomer in Harper's Ferry, that he spent the summer there while you and your family were vacationing there, and that your romance began there, it is very likely that some interpreters of this story, not having all of the facts, might conclude that Toomer was thinking of you when he drew his portrait of the character Avey. If this were to occur what would be your comment on it?

MAE: I would say, first of all, that such an interpretation would certainly be a false one. The narrator of the story had met Avey the year before. She was a grown woman and already a teacher. He saw her the next year in Harper's Ferry, and five years later, he met her in Washington, and they went to the grounds of Soldiers' Home at night. The only similarity to my life with Jean is the description of Harper's Ferry, which is a good and accurate description: Lover's Leap . . . the river and a railroad track beneath . . . other vivid details presented with an economy of words—certainly a beautiful description which makes the setting real and the character Avey realistic, but who, in no way, resembles me. Talented writers of fiction frequently use a snatch of a situation here and another snatch there to create a background for a scene or an incident; or they may create a character that is a composite of many persons. There is no telling what the creative mind will do. For instance, regarding a poem that Jean sent to me, he said that he was dedicating the poem to me and to our meeting at Harper's Ferry but that the poem itself had nothing to do with Harper's Ferry. At the time that I knew Jean, I had never even heard of Soldiers' Home, and to this day I have never been on the grounds of the place. Also, there is no way that I could have been out past nine o'clock at night—that was my curfew time at home. When I went to Cushing Academy and during my first year at Tufts University, the school rule deadline, imposed by the student government, was eight o'clock at night for all at the academy and for freshmen at college. Thus, I was never out at night with a boy or man past eight or nine o'clock unless there was a chaperone. I attended my first dance in June of 1922—my high school commencement dance—and went with my escort, Charlie Drew, a friend since childhood, and my father, who came in and sat with the other fathers who had accompanied their daughters and escorts. It is difficult, perhaps, with today's relaxed standards, to understand the world in which I grew up more than a half century ago. In "Avey" there is an incident on a pleasure steamer, the *Jane Mosely*, that "puffed up the Potomac." I never went with Jean on any steamer either on the Potomac River or the Chesapeake Bay. In my younger days I went to Brown's Grove just about every Sunday. Captain Brown, a black man who owned *The Starlight*, and my maternal grandfather were very close friends, and my grandfather came to Baltimore every Sunday, in the summer, when we were not out of the city, and took us on the cruise at Captain Brown's invitation. It was a delightful cruise on *The Starlight*, but Jean and I never went on that boat (if the excursions were still running in 1922) nor on any other excursion boat. The male character in the story is supposed to have tried to teach Avey to swim. Jean never tried to teach me to swim. I was an expert swimmer. Having spent several of my summers at Highland Beach right on the Chesapeake Bay, I was soon thrown into the water by some of the older kids and learned what a sink-or-swim experience was like. Also, though I am not sure of the year, we went to Colton one summer, where, there being no beach, the guests were taken out into deep water in a yacht. We jumped off into deep water and swam near the boat until time to return to the hotel. Jean and I never went to the seashore together, but had we gone, he would not have needed to teach me to swim. Finally, Avey is described as being lazy, too lazy to write, sloppy, and indolent. I was certainly not lazy. I was a good swimmer, a fair basketball player, and played guard on the freshman team at college. I was extremely studious, having lopped off two and a half years of the normal twelve-year public education stint by "skipping" grades in elementary school and finishing high school a half year early. While at Harper's Ferry, I studied advanced Latin for one hour daily with Mr. McDuffy, whom I mentioned earlier. I had already read Caesar, Cicero, and Vergil in high school. My grades in college remained high, and I was elected to Phi Beta Kappa. These are not the hallmarks of a lazy person.

INTERVIEWER: I should say not; and likewise, there is no way possible, realistically or imaginatively, that Avey could have been a portrayal of Mae Wright.

MAE: After reading some of Jean's stories, my mother asked him why he always wrote about the sordid, seamy side of life.

INTERVIEWER: How did he respond to this?

MAE: I am very sorry that I cannot remember what she said his reply was, but I seem to remember that his answer did not satisfy her.

INTERVIEWER: By the way, I have seen several photographs of Toomer; do you have a picture of him?

MAE: No, not a picture of Jean himself, except of him in group snapshots taken at Harper's Ferry, but I do have a photograph of a bust of him.

INTERVIEWER: Are you speaking of a photograph of a sculptured likeness of Toomer?

MAE: I am not surprised that this amazes you, but that is exactly what I am talking about, and you might find the story of my connection with this picture both interesting and amusing.

INTERVIEWER: I am sure that I would.

MAE: Well, when I went away to school, I found it customary for the girls to display pictures of their boyfriends in their dormitory rooms. Naturally, I wished to be in vogue, so I wrote to Jean and asked him to send me a picture. He replied that he did not have a regular picture but he did have this photograph of his bust, which he would get to me.

INTERVIEWER: And that is what he sent?

MAE: Well, he did not send it, for it must have been near a holiday period, and I got it while I was home on vacation. He and Waldo Frank were leaving on a trip, so he sent me the following undated letter:

> Saturday Evening

Dear Mae:
>   Waldo is just in. He wants to push ahead, so we're leaving on the 10:25 train.
>   I haven't a picture. I'm leaving this one of my bust for you. I'll write as soon as we reach Spartanburg.

>   Love —
>   Jean.

If you don't come to the house Sunday, I'll have Ken mail this to you.

I learned that the bust of Jean, of which the photograph was taken, was executed by May Howard Johnson, a sculptor who was born and educated in Philadelphia. Later, she moved to Washington, where she taught at Howard University but also had her own studio. When I got back to school and the students saw my picture of Jean's bust, they said it looked like a bust of Milton.

INTERVIEWER: I must agree, that is certainly an interesting and humorous story. Now tell me what happened during the year of 1923.

MAE: That was a very busy year for me and for Jean. After a year at Cushing Academy, I entered Tufts University, in September, as a college freshman. Jean was busy getting his book published and was moving about a good bit in a new environment, associating with new friends who were writers and creative artists of various types.

INTERVIEWER: Did you keep in touch with each other?

MAE: Yes, to some extent, but we did not see each other often, nor did we correspond as regularly as in the past. However, he sent me a poem that was mainly descriptive of the natural beauties of Harper's Ferry and which he said was reminiscent of our summer there, and when *Cane* was published, he sent me a copy of it immediately. Later, when I saw him, he wondered why I had not written to him about the book.

INTERVIEWER: Do you have the letters that he wrote to you?

MAE: Sometimes now, I wish that I had saved them, but I did not. You know how it is in early life, such things as letters are kept only for a short time. I do remember keeping one more of them, in addition to the one about the photographed bust, and finally putting it away somewhere—the one in which he sent the poem. I was really looking for it, when the other one turned up.

INTERVIEWER: What did you think of *Cane*?

MAE: Well, that was my problem. I thoroughly enjoyed parts of the book, and yet I found it rather confusing. I had not written to him about it because, really, I had been groping for something to say. You see, I had been accustomed to reading literary works that were more structured, or let me say, structured in a more conventional manner, and *Cane* was in a new vein unfamiliar to me at that time.

INTERVIEWER: What happened then?

MAE: Well, nothing really that had anything seriously to do with *Cane*. It was natural that he should be curious to know my opinion of his book, even though he was not expecting any weighty appraisal from me, and he was a bit disappointed when I failed to respond. However, no major issue occurred because of this incident. It was just coincidental that about this time our correspondence became less frequent, and we gradually began to drift apart. Both of us suddenly were facing new and exciting experiences. All at once our horizons were widening on separate frontiers, and all of our associates were new and different. I was in college with students and new friends of my own age, enjoying each and every challenging new experience and looking forward to my life ahead. The highly intellectual and talented Jean Toomer, as we know him today, was among his more mature peers, an energetic avant-garde group of creative artists and thinkers of new ideas and theories, and our paths were destined not to meet again.

Richard Wright

(1908–1960)

WITH EVERY CONCEIVABLE ODD against him—racial prejudice, poverty-stricken background, broken family, lack of formal education, and all of the indignities that a black boy in Mississippi would know—Richard Wright was able to rise above these handicaps and become one of the great American writers of this century. Two of his many works—*Native Son* and *Black Boy*—are landmark publications, ones that will meet Samuel Johnson's definition of a classic.

With the first, *Native Son* (1940), Negro American literature came of age, according to many critics. A modern novel, using modern literary techniques, the work shocked America with its bitterness and its violence. It showed dramatically the revolutionary potential arising from the nation's treatment of blacks, and it influenced several young black authors to write abrasive naturalistic novels like *Native Son*. Among these "disciples" of Richard Wright were William Attaway (*Blood on the Forge*, 1941), Charles R. Offord (*The White Face*, 1943), Chester Himes (*If He Hollers Let Him Go*, 1945), and Ann Petry (*The Street*, 1946). Wright's second work, *Black Boy: A Record of Childhood and Youth* (1945), is a great American autobiography, written in the militant spirit of Frederick Douglass's 1845 *Narrative*, one that broke completely with the race-praising, name-dropping, best-foot-forward tradition of most of the black autobiographies written before *Black Boy*.

Born on a farm near Natchez, Mississippi, in 1908, Wright lived during his early childhood in Memphis, Tennessee. When his parents separated and his mother became seriously ill, he spent a short time in an orphanage and later lived in the homes of several relatives in Arkansas and Mississippi. After finishing high school in 1925 in Jackson, Mississippi, he went to Memphis seeking employment. In 1927 he moved to Chicago, where he worked at many kinds of odd jobs, was often hungry, and was occasionally on relief; in 1932 he joined the Communist party. He was soon thereafter appointed to the Federal Writers' Project, then went to New York in 1937 and took a position as Harlem editor of *The Daily Worker*; he also edited a Communist literary journal called *New Challenge*. After winning a $500 first prize from *Story* magazine for his novella "Fire and Cloud," Wright spent several months working on the WPA *American Guide*; he also wrote critical essays and short stories for such periodicals as *New Republic, New Masses, Left Front,* and *Partisan Review*.

In 1939 he received a Guggenheim Fellowship, and in 1940 he published *Native Son* and married Ellen Poplar from Brooklyn (he had been married before for a short while; both wives were white). In 1941 he wrote the photo essay *12 Million Black Voices: A Folk History of the Negro in the United States*, and in that year received the Spingarn Medal. Wright severed his connection with the Communist party in 1942, published *Black Boy* in 1945, and after World War II became an expatriate in France. In 1949 he went to Argentina to play the role of Bigger Thomas in the film version of *Native Son*. After visiting Ghana in 1953, he published *Black Power*, an account of his trip, the following year. In 1956 and 1957, respectively, he published two more travel-comment volumes—*The Color Curtain* (concerning Asia) and *Pagan Spain*. Richard Wright died in Paris in 1960.

In addition to the works mentioned previously, Wright, who was a prolific writer, published the following major volumes: *Uncle Tom's Children: Four Novellas* (1938), one of them the prize-winning "Fire and Cloud," mentioned previously; *The Outsider* (1953), in which he dramatized existentialist doctrines; *Savage Holiday* (1954), in which he used white characters; *White Man Listen!* (1957); and *The Long Dream* (1958), a novel. *Lawd Today* (1963), a novel, and *Eight Men* (1969), a collection of short stories, were published posthumously.

For biographical and critical comment on Richard Wright, see the perceptive article by Michel Fabré in *Dictionary of American Negro Biography*; see also Fabré's *The Unfinished Quest of Richard Wright: A Critical Biography* (1973); Edward L. Margolies's *Native Sons: A Critical Study of Twentieth-Century Negro American Authors* (1968); Robert A. Bone's *The Negro Novel in America* (rev. ed., 1965); John A. Williams's *The Most Native of Sons* (1970); Russell C. Brignano's *Richard Wright: An Introduction to the Man and His Works* (1970); and Joyce A. Joyce's *Richard Wright's Art of Tragedy* (1986). The most recent volumes on Wright are Margaret Walker's *The Daemonic Genius of Richard Wright* (1988) and Eugene Miller's *Voice of a Native Son: The Poetics of Richard Wright* (1990).

The following selections are an excerpt from *Black Boy*, chapter 9, (1937, 1965) and "Bright and Morning Star," one of the novellas in *Uncle Tom's Children* (1938).

FROM **BLACK BOY**

My life now depended upon my finding work, and I was so anxious that I accepted the first offer, a job as a porter in a clothing store selling cheap goods to Negroes on credit. The shop was always crowded with black men and women pawing over cheap suits and dresses. And they paid whatever price the white man asked. The boss, his son, and the clerk treated the Negroes with open contempt, pushing, kicking, or slapping them. No matter how often I witnessed it, I could not get used to it. How can they accept it? I asked myself. I kept on edge, trying to stifle my feelings and never quite succeeding, a prey to guilt and fear because I felt that the boss suspected that I resented what I saw.

One morning, while I was polishing brass out front, the boss and his son drove up in their car. A frightened black woman sat between them. They got out and half dragged and half kicked the woman into the store. White people passed and looked on without expression. A white policeman watched from the corner, twirling his night stick; but he made no move. I watched out of the corner of my eyes, but I never slackened the strokes of my chamois upon the brass. After a moment or two I heard shrill screams coming from the rear room of the store; later the woman stumbled out, bleeding, crying, holding her stomach, her clothing torn. When she reached the sidewalk, the policeman met her, grabbed her, accused her of being drunk, called a patrol wagon and carted her away.

When I went to the rear of the store, the boss and his son were washing their hands at the sink. They looked at me and laughed uneasily. The floor was bloody, strewn with wisps of hair and clothing. My face must have reflected my shock, for the boss slapped me reassuringly on the back.

"Boy, that's what we do to niggers when they don't pay their bills," he said.

His son looked at me and grinned.

"Here, hava cigarette," he said.

Not knowing what to do, I took it. He lit his and held the match for me. This was a gesture of kindness, indicating that, even if they had beaten the black woman, they would not beat me if I knew enough to keep my mouth shut.

"Yes, sir," I said.

Excerpt from *Black Boy* by Richard Wright. Copyright 1937, 1942, 1944, and 1945 by Richard Wright. Copyright © renewed. Reprinted by permission of HarperCollins Publishers, Inc.

After they had gone, I sat on the edge of a packing box and stared at the bloody floor until the cigarette went out.

The store owned a bicycle which I used in delivering purchases. One day, while returning from the suburbs, my bicycle tire was punctured. I walked along the hot, dusty road, sweating and leading the bicycle by the handle bars.

A car slowed at my side.

"What's the matter there, boy?" a white man called.

I told him that my bicycle was broken and that I was walking back to town.

"That's too bad," he said. "Hop on the running board."

He stopped the car. I clutched hard at my bicycle with one hand and clung to the side of the car with the other.

"All set?"

"Yes, sir."

The car started. It was full of young white men. They were drinking. I watched the flask pass from mouth to mouth.

"Wanna drink, boy?" one asked.

The memory of my six-year-old drinking came back and filled me with caution. But I laughed, the wind whipping my face.

"Oh, no!" I said.

The words were barely out of my mouth before I felt something hard and cold smash me between the eyes. It was an empty whisky bottle. I saw stars, and fell backwards from the speeding car into the dust of the road, my feet becoming entangled in the steel spokes of the bicycle. The car stopped and the white men piled out and stood over me.

"Nigger, ain't you learned no better sense'n that yet?" asked the man who hit me. "Ain't you learned to say *sir* to a white man yet?"

Dazed, I pulled to my feet. My elbows and legs were bleeding. Fists doubled, the white man advanced, kicking the bicycle out of the way.

"Aw, leave the bastard alone. He's got enough," said one.

They stood looking at me. I rubbed my shins, trying to stop the flow of blood. No doubt they felt a sort of contemptuous pity, for one asked:

"You wanna ride to town now, nigger? You reckon you know enough to ride now?"

"I wanna walk," I said simply.

Maybe I sounded funny. They laughed.

"Well, walk, you black sonofabitch!"

Before they got back into their car, they comforted me with:

"Nigger, you sure ought to be glad it was us you talked to that way. You're a lucky bastard, 'cause if you'd said that to some other white man, you might've been a dead nigger now."

I was learning rapidly how to watch white people, to observe their every move, every fleeting expression, how to interpret what was said and what left unsaid.

Late one Saturday night I made some deliveries in a white neighborhood. I was pedaling my bicycle back to the store as fast as I could when a police car, swerving toward me, jammed me into the curbing.

"Get down, nigger, and put up your hands!" they ordered.

I did. They climbed out of the car, guns drawn, faces set, and advanced slowly.

"Keep still!" they ordered.

I reached my hands higher. They searched my pockets and packages. They seemed dissatisfied when they could find nothing incriminating. Finally, one of them said:

"Boy, tell your boss not to send you out in white neighborhoods at this time of night."

"Yes, sir," I said.

I rode off, feeling that they might shoot at me, feeling that the pavement might disappear. It was like living in a dream, the reality of which might change at any moment.

Each day in the store I watched the brutality with growing hate, yet trying to keep my feelings from registering in my face. When the boss looked at me I would avoid his eyes. Finally the boss's son cornered me one morning.

"Say, nigger, look here," he began.

"Yes, sir."

"What's on your mind?"

"Nothing, sir," I said, trying to look amazed, trying to fool him.

"Why don't you laugh and talk like the other niggers?" he asked.

"Well, sir, there's nothing much to say or smile about," I said, smiling.

His face was hard, baffled; I knew that I had not convinced him. He whirled from me and went to the front of the store; he came back a moment later, his face red. He tossed a few green bills at me.

"I don't like your looks, nigger. Now, get!" he snapped.

I picked up the money and did not count it. I grabbed my hat and left.

I held a series of petty jobs for short periods, quitting some to work elsewhere, being driven off others because of my attitude, my speech, the look in my eyes. I was no nearer than ever to my goal of saving enough money to leave. At times I doubted if I could ever do it.

One jobless morning I went to my old classmate, Griggs, who worked for a Capitol Street jeweler. He was washing the windows of the store when I came upon him.

"Do you know where I can find a job?" I asked.

He looked at me with scorn.

"Yes, I know where you can find a job," he said, laughing.

"Where?"

"But I wonder if you can hold it," he said.

"What do you mean?" I asked. "Where's the job?"

"Take your time," he said. "You know, Dick, I know you. You've been trying to hold a job all summer, and you can't. Why? Because you're impatient. That's your big fault."

I said nothing, because he was repeating what I had already heard him say. He lit a cigarette and blew out smoke leisurely.

"Well," I said, egging him on to speak.

"I wish to hell I could talk to you," he said.

"I think I know what you want to tell me," I said.

He clapped me on the shoulder; his face was full of fear, hate, concern for me.

"Do you want to get killed?" he asked me.

"Hell, no!"

"Then, for God's sake, learn how to live in the South!"

"What do you mean?" I demanded. "Let white people tell me that. Why should you?"

"See?" he said triumphantly, pointing his finger at me. "There it is, *now!* It's in your face. You won't let people tell you things. You rush too much. I'm trying to help you and you won't let me." He paused and looked about; the streets were filled with white people. He spoke to me in a low, full tone. "Dick, look, you're black, black, *black*, see? Can't you understand that?"

"Sure. I understand it," I said.

"You don't act a damn bit like it," he spat.

He then reeled off an account of my actions on every job I had held that summer.

"How did you know that?" I asked.

"White people make it their business to watch niggers," he explained. "And they pass the word around. Now, my boss is a Yankee and he tells me things. You're marked already."

Could I believe him? Was it true? How could I ever learn this strange world of white people?

"Then tell me how must I act?" I asked humbly. "I just want to make enough money to leave."

"Wait and I'll tell you," he said.

At that moment a woman and two men stepped from the jewelry store; I moved to one side to let them pass, my mind intent upon

Griggs's words. Suddenly Griggs reached for my arm and jerked me violently, sending me stumbling three or four feet across the pavement. I whirled.

"What's the matter with you?" I asked.

Griggs glared at me, then laughed.

"I'm teaching you how to get out of white people's way," he said.

I looked at the people who come out of the store; yes, they were *white*, but I had not noticed it.

"Do you see what I mean?" he asked. "White people want you out of their way." He pronounced the words slowly so that they would sink into my mind.

"I know what you mean," I breathed.

"Dick, I'm treating you like a brother," he said. "You act around white people as if you didn't know that they were white. And they see it."

"Oh, Christ, I can't be a slave," I said hopelessly.

"But you've got to eat," he said.

"Yes, I got to eat."

"Then start acting like it," he hammered at me, pounding his fist in his palm. "When you're in front of white people, *think* before you act, *think* before you speak. Your way of doing things is all right among *our* people, but not for *white* people. They won't stand for it."

I stared bleakly into the morning sun. I was nearing my seventeenth birthday and I was wondering if I would ever be free of this plague. What Griggs was saying was true, but it was simply utterly impossible for me to calculate, to scheme, to act, to plot all the time. I would remember to dissemble for short periods, then I would forget and act straight and human again, not with the desire to harm anybody, but merely forgetting the artificial status of race and class. It was the same with whites as with blacks; it was my way with everybody. I sighed, looking at the glittering diamonds in the store window, the rings and the neat rows of golden watches.

"I guess you're right," I said at last. "I've got to watch myself, break myself . . ."

"No," he said quickly, feeling guilty now. Someone—a white man—went into the store and we paused in our talk. "You know, Dick, you may think I'm an Uncle Tom, but I'm not. I hate these white people, hate 'em with all my heart. But I can't show it; if I did, they'd kill me." He paused and looked around to see if there were any white people within hearing distance. "Once I heard an old drunk nigger say:

> All these white folks dressed so fine
> Their ass-holes smell just like mine . . ."

I laughed uneasily, looking at the white faces that passed me. But Griggs, when he laughed, covered his mouth with his hand and bent at the knees, a gesture which was unconsciously meant to conceal his excessive joy in the presence of whites.

"That's how I feel about 'em," he said proudly after he had finished his spasm of glee. He grew sober. "There's an optical company upstairs and the boss is a Yankee from Illinois. Now, he wants a boy to work all day in summer, mornings and evenings in winter. He wants to break a colored boy into the optical trade. You know algebra and you're just cut out for the work. I'll tell Mr. Crane about you and I'll get in touch with you."

"Do you suppose I could see him now?" I asked.

"For God's sake, take your *time!*" he thundered at me.

"Maybe that's what's wrong with Negroes," I said. "They take too much time."

I laughed, but he was disturbed. I thanked him and left. For a week I did not hear from him and I gave up hope. Then one afternoon Griggs came to my house.

"It looks like you've got a job," he said. "You're going to have a chance to learn a trade. But remember to keep your head. Remember you're black. You start tomorrow."

"What will I get?"

"Five dollars a week to start with; they'll raise you if they like you," he explained.

My hopes soared. Things were not quite so bad, after all. I would have a chance to learn a trade. And I need not give up school. I told him that I would take the job, that I would be humble.

"You'll be working for a Yankee and you ought to get along," he said.

The next morning I was outside the office of the optical company long before it opened. I was reminding myself that I must be polite, must think before I spoke, must think before I acted, must say "yes sir, no sir," that I must so conduct myself that white people would not think that I thought I was as good as they. Suddenly a white man came up to me.

"What do you want?" he asked me.

"I'm reporting for a job, sir," I said.

"O.K. Come on."

I followed him up a flight of steps and he unlocked the door of the office. I was a little tense, but the young white man's manner put me at ease and I sat and held my hat in my hand. A white girl came and began punching the typewriter. Soon another white man, thin and gray, entered and went into the rear room. Finally a tall, red-faced white man arrived, shot me a quick glance and sat at his desk.

His brisk manner branded him a Yankee.

"You're the new boy, eh?"

"Yes, sir."

"Let me get my mail out of the way and I'll talk with you," he said pleasantly.

"Yes, sir."

I even pitched my voice to a low plane, trying to rob it of any suggestion or overtone of aggressiveness.

Half an hour later Mr. Crane called me to his desk and questioned me closely about my schooling, about how much mathematics I had had. He seemed pleased when I told him that I had had two years of algebra.

"How would you like to learn this trade?" he asked.

"I'd like it fine, sir. I'd like nothing better," I said.

He told me that he wanted to train a Negro boy in the optical trade; he wanted to help him, guide him. I tried to answer in a way that would let him know that I would try to be worthy of what he was doing. He took me to the stenographer and said:

"This is Richard. He's going to be with us."

He then led me into the rear room of the office, which turned out to be a tiny factory filled with many strange machines smeared with red dust.

"Reynolds," he said to a young white man, "this is Richard."

"What you saying there, boy!" Reynolds grinned and boomed at me.

Mr. Crane took me to the older man.

"Pease, this is Richard, who'll work with us."

Pease looked at me and nodded. Mr. Crane then held forth to the two white men about my duties; he told them to break me in gradually to the workings of the shop, to instruct me in the mechanics of grinding and polishing lenses. They nodded their assent.

"Now, boy, let's see how clean you can get this place," Mr. Crane said.

"Yes, sir."

I swept, mopped, dusted, and soon had the office and the shop clean. In the afternoons, when I had caught up with my work, I ran errands. In an idle moment I would stand and watch the two white men grinding lenses on the machines. They said nothing to me and I said nothing to them. The first day passed, the second, the third, a week passed and I received my five dollars. A month passed. But I was not learning anything and nobody had volunteered to help me. One afternoon I walked up to Reynolds and asked him to tell me about the work.

"What are you trying to do, get smart, nigger?" he asked me.

"No sir," I said.

I was baffled. Perhaps he just did not want to help me. I went to Pease, reminding him that the boss had said that I was to be given a chance to learn the trade.

"Nigger, you think you're white, don't you?"

"No, sir."

"You're acting mighty like it," he said.

"I was only doing what the boss told me to do," I said.

Pease shook his fist in my face.

"This is a *white* man's work around here," he said.

From then on they changed toward me; they said good morning no more. When I was just a bit slow in performing some duty, I was called a lazy black sonofabitch. I kept silent, striving to offer no excuse for worsening of relations. But one day Reynolds called me to his machine.

"Nigger, you think you'll ever amount to anything?" he asked in a slow, sadistic voice.

"I don't know, sir," I answered, turning my head away.

"What do niggers think about?" he asked.

"I don't know, sir," I said, my head still averted.

"If I was a nigger, I'd kill myself," he said.

I said nothing. I was angry.

"You know why?" he asked.

I still said nothing.

"But I don't reckon niggers mind being niggers," he said suddenly and laughed.

I ignored him. Mr. Pease was watching me closely; then I saw them exchange glances. My job was not leading to what Mr. Crane had said it would. I had been humble, and now I was reaping the wages of humility.

"Come here, boy," Pease said.

I walked to his bench.

"You didn't like what Reynolds just said, did you?" he asked.

"Oh, it's all right," I said smiling.

"You didn't like it. I could see it on your face," he said.

I stared at him and backed away.

"Did you ever get into any trouble?" he asked.

"No, sir."

"What would you do if you got into trouble?"

"I don't know, sir."

"Well, watch yourself and don't get into trouble," he warned.

I wanted to report these clashes to Mr. Crane, but the thought of what Pease or Reynolds would do to me if they learned that I had "snitched" stopped me. I worked through the days and tried to hide my resentment under a nervous, cryptic smile.

The climax came at noon one summer day. Pease called me to his workbench; to get to him I had to go between two narrow benches and stand with my back against a wall.

"Richard, I want to ask you something," Pease began pleasantly, not looking up from his work.

"Yes, sir."

Reynolds came over and stood blocking the narrow passage between the benches; he folded his arms and stared at me solemnly. I looked from one to the other, sensing trouble. Pease looked up and spoke slowly, so there would be no possibility of my not understanding.

"Richard, Reynolds here tells me that you called me Pease," he said.

I stiffened. A void opened up in me. I knew that this was the showdown.

He meant that I had failed to call him Mr. Pease. I looked at Reynolds; he was gripping a steel bar in his hand. I opened my mouth to speak, to protest, to assure Pease that I had never called him simply *Pease*, and that I had never had any intention of doing so, when Reynolds grabbed me by the collar, ramming my head against a wall.

"Now, be careful, nigger," snarled Reynolds, baring his teeth. "I heard you call 'im *Pease*. And if you say you didn't, you're calling me a liar, see?" He waved the steel bar threateningly.

If I had said: No, sir, Mr. Pease, I never called you *Pease*, I would by inference having been calling Reynolds a liar; and if I had said: Yes, sir, Mr. Pease, I called you *Pease*, I would have been pleading guilty to the worst insult that a Negro can offer to a southern white man. I stood trying to think of a neutral course that would resolve this quickly risen nightmare, but my tongue would not move.

"Richard, I asked you a question!" Pease said. Anger was creeping into his voice.

"I don't remember calling you *Pease*, Mr. Pease," I said cautiously. "And if I did, I sure didn't mean . . ."

"You black sonofabitch! You called me *Pease*, then!" he spat, rising and slapping me till I bent sideways over a bench.

Reynolds was up on top of me demanding:

"Didn't you call him *Pease*? If you say you didn't, I'll rip your gut string loose with this f–k–g bar, you black granny dodger! You can't call a white man a liar and get away with it!"

I wilted, I begged them not to hit me. I knew what they wanted. They wanted me to leave the job.

"I'll leave," I promised. "I'll leave right now!"

They gave me a minute to get out of the factory, and warned me not to show up again or tell the boss. Reynolds loosened his hand on my collar and I ducked out of the room. I did not see Mr. Crane or the stenographer in the office. Pease and Reynolds had so timed it that Mr. Crane and the stenographer would be out when they turned on the terror. I went to the street and waited for the boss to return. I saw Griggs wiping glass shelves in the jewelry store and I beckoned to him. He came out and I told him what had happened.

"Then what are you standing there like a fool for?" he demanded. "Won't you ever learn? Get home! They might come down!"

I walked down Capitol Street feeling that the sidewalk was unreal, that I was unreal, that the people were unreal, yet expecting somebody to demand to know what right I had to be on the streets. My wound went deep; I felt that I had been slapped out of the human race. When I reached home, I did not tell the family what had happened; I merely told them that I had quit, that I was not making enough money, that I was seeking another job.

That night Griggs came to my house; we went for a walk.

"You got a goddamn tough break," he said.

"Can you say it was my fault?" I asked.

He shook his head.

"Well, what about your goddamn philosophy of meekness?" I asked him bitterly.

"These things just happen," he said, shrugging.

"They owe me money," I said.

"That's what I came about," he said. "Mr. Crane wants you to come in at ten in the morning. Ten sharp, now, mind you, because he'll be there and those guys won't gang up on you again."

The next morning at ten I crept up the stairs and peered into the office of the optical shop to make sure that Mr. Crane was in. He was at his desk. Pease and Reynolds were at their machines in the rear.

"Come in, Richard," Mr. Crane said.

I pulled off my hat and walked into the office; I stood before him.

"Sit down," he said.

I sat. He stared at me and shook his head.

"Tell me, what happened?"

An impulse to speak rose in me and died with the realization that I was facing a wall that I would never breach. I tried to speak several times and could make no sounds. I grew tense and tears burnt my cheeks.

"Now, just keep control of yourself," Mr. Crane said.

I clenched my fists and managed to talk.

"I tried to do my best here," I said.

"I believe you," he said. "But I want to know what happened. Which one bothered you?"

"Both of 'em," I said.

Reynolds came running to the door and I rose. Mr. Crane jumped to his feet.

"Get back in there," he told Reynolds.

"That nigger's lying!" Reynolds said. "I'll kill 'im if he lies on me!"

"Get back in there or get out," Mr. Crane said.

Reynolds backed away, keeping his eyes on me.

"Go ahead," Mr. Crane said. "Tell me what happened."

Then again I could not speak. What could I accomplish by telling him? I was black; I lived in the South. I would never learn to operate those machines as long as those two white men in there stood by them. Anger and fear welled in me as I felt what I had missed; I leaned forward and clapped my hands to my face.

"No, no, now," Mr. Crane said. "Keep control of yourself. No matter what happens, keep control . . ."

"I know," I said in a voice not my own. "There's no use of my saying anything."

"Do you want to work here?" he asked me.

I looked at the white faces of Pease and Reynolds; I imagined their waylaying me, killing me. I was remembering what had happened to Ned's brother.

"No, sir," I breathed.

"Why?"

"I'm scared," I said. "They would kill me."

Mr. Crane turned and called Pease and Reynolds into the office.

"Now, tell me which one bothered you. Don't be afraid. Nobody's going to hurt you," Mr. Crane said.

I stared ahead of me and did not answer. He waved the men inside. The white stenographer looked at me with wide eyes and I felt drenched in shame, naked to my soul. The whole of my being felt violated, and I knew that my own fear had helped to violate it. I was breathing hard and struggling to master my feelings.

"Can I get my money, sir?" I asked at last.

"Just sit a minute and take hold of yourself," he said.

I waited and my roused senses grew slowly calm.

"I'm awfully sorry about this," he said.

"I had hoped for a lot from this job," I said. "I'd wanted to go to school, to college . . ."

"I know," he said. "But what are you going to do now?"

My eyes traveled over the office, but I was not seeing.

"I'm going away," I said.

"What do you mean?"

"I'm going to get out of the South," I breathed.

"Maybe that's best," he said. "I'm from Illinois. Even for me, it's hard here. I can do just so much."

He handed me my money, more than I had earned for the week. I thanked him and rose to leave. He rose. I went into the hallway and he followed me. He reached out his hand.

"It's tough for you down here," he said.

I barely touched his hand. I walked swiftly down the hall, fighting against crying again. I ran down the steps, then paused and looked back up. He was standing at the head of the stairs, shaking his head. I went into the sunshine and walked home like a blind man.

BRIGHT AND MORNING STAR

She stood with her black face some six inches from the moist windowpane and wondered when on earth would it ever stop raining. It might keep up like this all week, she thought. She heard rain droning upon the roof and high up in the wet sky her eyes followed the silent rush of a bright shaft of yellow that swung from the airplane beacon in far off Memphis. Momently she could see it cutting through the rainy dark; it would hover a second like a gleaming sword above her head, then vanish. She sighed, troubling, Johnny-Boys been trampin in this slop all day wid no decent shoes on his feet. . . . Through the window she could see the rich black earth sprawling outside in the night. There was more rain than the clay could soak up; pools stood everywhere. She yawned and mumbled: "Rains good n bad. It kin make seeds bus up thu the groun er it kin bog things down lika watah-soaked coffin." Her hands were folded loosely over her stomach and the hot air of the kitchen traced a filmy veil of sweat on her forehead. From the cook stove came the soft singing of burning wood and now and then a throaty bubble rose from a pot of simmering greens.

"Shucks, Johnny-Boy coulda let somebody else do all tha runnin in the rain. Theres others bettah fixed fer it than he is. But, naw!

Johnny-Boy ain the one t trust nobody t do nothin. Hes gotta do it *all* hisself. . . ."

She glanced at a pile of damp clothes in a zinc tub. Waal, Ah bettah git t work. She turned, lifted a smoothing iron with a thick pad of cloth, touched a spit-wet finger to it with a quick, jerking motion: *smiiitz!* Yeah, its hot! Stooping, she took a blue work-shirt from the tub and shook it out. With a deft twist of her shoulders she caught the iron in her right hand; the fingers of her left hand took a piece of wax from a tin box and a frying sizzle came as she smeared the bottom. She was thinking of nothing now; her hands followed a life-long ritual of toil. Spreading a sleeve, she ran the hot iron to and fro until the wet cloth became stiff. She was deep in the midst of her work when a song rose up out of the far off days of her childhood and broke through half-parted lips:

> Hes the Lily of the Valley, the Bright n Mawnin Star
> Hes the Fairest of Ten Thousin t mah soul . . .

A gust of wind dashed rain against the window. Johnny-Boy oughta c mon home n eat his suppah. Aw, Lawd! Itd be fine ef Sug could eat wid us tonight! Itd be like ol times! Mabbe aftah all it wont be long fo he comes back. Tha lettah Ah got from im las week said *Don give up hope.* . . . Yeah; we gotta live in hope. Then both of her sons, Sug and Johnny-Boy, would be back with her.

With an involuntary nervous gesture, she stopped and stood still, listening. But the only sound was the lulling fall of rain. Shucks, ain no usa me ackin this way, she thought. Ever time they gits ready to hol them meetings Ah gits jumpity. Ah been a lil scared ever since Sug went t jail. She heard the clock ticking and looked. Johnny-Boys a *hour* late! He sho mus be havin a time doin all tha trampin, trampin thu the mud. . . . But her fear was a quiet one; it was more like an intense brooding than a fear; it was a sort of hugging of hated facts so closely that she could feel their grain, like letting cold water run over her hand from a faucet on a winter morning.

She ironed again, faster now, as if she felt the more she engaged her body in work the less she would think. But how could she forget Johnny-Boy out there on those wet fields rounding up white and black Communists for a meeting tomorrow? And that was just what Sug had been doing when the sheriff had caught him, beat him, and tried to make him tell who and where his comrades were. Po Sug! They sho musta beat the boy somethin awful! But, thank Gawd, he didnt talk! He ain no weaklin, Sug ain! Hes been lion-hearted all his life long.

That had happened a year ago. And now each time those meetings came around the old terror surged back. While shoving the iron

a cluster of toiling days returned; days of washing and ironing to
feed Johnny-Boy and Sug so they could do party work; days of carrying a hundred pounds of white folks' clothes upon her head across
fields sometimes wet and sometimes dry. But in those days a
hundred pounds was nothing to carry carefully balanced upon her
head while stepping by instinct over the corn and cotton rows. The
only time it had seemed heavy was when she had heard of Sug's arrest. She had been coming home one morning with a bundle upon
her head, her hands swinging idly by her sides, walking slowly with
her eyes in front of her, when Bob, Johnny-Boy's pal, had called
from across the fields and had come and told her that the sheriff had
got Sug. That morning the bundle had become heavier than she
could ever remember.

And with each passing week now, though she spoke of it to no
one, things were becoming heavier. The tubs of water and the
smoothing iron and the bundle of clothes were becoming harder to
lift, with her back aching so; and her work was taking longer, all
because Sug was gone and she didn't known just when Johnny-Boy
would be taken too. To ease the ache of anxiety that was swelling
her heart, she hummed, then sang softly:

> He walks wid me, He talks wid me
> He tells me Ahm His Own. . . .

Guiltily, she stopped and smiled. Looks like Ah jus cant seem t
fergit them ol songs, no mattah how hard Ah tries. . . . She had
learned them when she was a little girl living and working on a
farm. Every Monday morning from the corn and cotton fields the
slow strains had floated from her mother's lips, lonely and haunting;
and later, as the years had filled with gall, she had learned their deep
meaning. Long hours of scrubbing floors for a few cents a day had
taught her who Jesus was, what a great boon it was to cling to Him,
to be like Him and suffer without a mumbling word. She had
poured the yearning of her life into the songs, feeling buoyed with a
faith beyond this world. The figure of the Man nailed in agony to
the Cross, His burial in a cold grave, His transfigured Resurrection,
His being breath and clay, God and Man—all had focused her feelings upon an imagery which had swept her life into a wondrous
vision.

But as she had grown older, a cold white mountain, the white
folks and their laws, had swum into her vision and shattered her
songs and their spell of peace. To her that white mountain was
temptation, something to lure her from her Lord, a part of the world
God had made in order that she might endure it and come through
all the stronger, just as Christ had risen with greater glory from the

tomb. The days crowded with trouble had enhanced her faith and she had grown to love hardship with a bitter pride; she had obeyed the laws of the white folks with a soft smile of secret knowing.

After her mother had been snatched up to heaven in a chariot of fire, the years had brought her a rough workingman and two black babies, Sug and Johnny-Boy, all three of whom she had wrapped in the charm and magic of her vision. Then she was tested by no less than God; her man died, a trial which she bore with the strength shed by the grace of her vision; finally even the memory of her man faded into the vision itself, leaving her with two black boys growing tall, slowly into manhood.

Then one day grief had come to her heart when Johnny-Boy and Sug had walked forth demanding their lives. She had sought to fill their eyes with her vision, but they would have none of it. And she had wept when they began to boast of the strength shed by a new and terrible vision.

But she had loved them, even as she loved them now; bleeding, her heart had followed them. She could have done no less, being an old woman in a strange world. And day by day her sons had ripped from her startled eyes her old vision, and image by image had given her a new one, different, but great and strong enough to fling her into the light of another grace. The wrongs and sufferings of black men had taken the place of Him nailed to the Cross; the meager beginnings of the party had become another Resurrection; and the hate of those who would destroy her new faith had quickened in her a hunger to feel how deeply her new strength went.

"Lawd, Johnny-Boy," she would sometimes say, "Ah just wan them white folks t try t make me tell *who* is *in* the party n who *ain!* Ah just wan em t try, n Ahll show em somethin they never thought a black woman could have!"

But sometimes like tonight, while lost in the forgetfulness of work, the past and the present would become mixed in her; while toiling under a strange star for a new freedom the old songs would slip from her lips with their beguiling sweetness.

The iron was getting cold. She put more wood into the fire, stood again at the window and watched the yellow blade of light cut through the wet darkeness. Johnny-Boy ain here yit. . . . Then, before she was aware of it, she was still, listening for sounds. Under the drone of rain she heard the slosh of feet in mud. Tha ain Johnny-Boy. She knew his long, heavy footsteps in a million. She heard feet come on the porch. Some woman. . . . She heard bare knuckles knock three times, then once. Thas some of them comrades! She unbarred the door, cracked it a few inches, and flinched from the cold rush of damp wind.

"Whos tha?"

"Its me!"

"Who?"

"Me, Reva!"

She flung the door open.

"Lawd, chile c mon in!"

She stepped to one side and a thin, blond-haired white girl ran through the door; as she slid the bolt she heard the girl gasping and shaking her wet clothes. Somethings wrong! Reva wauldna walked a mile t mah house in all this slop fer nothin! Tha gals stuck onto Johnny-Boy. Ah wondah ef anything happened t im?

"Git on inter the kitchen, Reva, where its warm."

"Lawd, Ah sho is wet!"

"How yah reckon yuhd be, in all tha rain?"

"Johnny-Boy ain here *yit*?" asked Reva.

"Naw! N ain no usa yuh worryin bout im. Jus yuh git them shoes off! Yuh wanna ketch yo deatha col?" She stood looking absently. Yeah; its somethin about the party er Johnny-Boy thas gone wrong. Lawd, Ah wondah ef her pa knows how she feels bout Johnny-Boy? "Honey, yuh hadnt oughta come out in sloppy weather like this."

"Ah had t come, An Sue."

She led Reva to the kitchen.

"Git them shoes off n git close t the stove so yuhll git dry!"

"An Sue, Ah got somethin t tell yuh . . ."

The words made her hold her breath. Ah bet its somethin bout Johnny-Boy!

"Whut, honey?"

"The sheriff wuz by our house tonight. He come to see pa."

"Yeah?"

"He done got word from somewheres bout tha meetin tomorrow."

"Is it Johnny-Boy, Reva?"

"Aw, naw, An Sue! Ah ain hearda word bout im. Ain yuh seen im tonight?"

"He ain come home t eat yit."

"Where kin he be?"

"Lawd knows, chile."

"Somebodys gotta tell them comrades tha meetings off," said Reva. "The sheriffs got men watchin our house. Ah had to slip out t git here widout em followin me."

"Reva?"

"Hunh?"

"Ahma ol woman n Ah wans yuh t tell me the truth."

"Whut, An Sue?"

"Yuh ain tryin t fool me, is yuh?"

"*Fool* yuh?"

"Bout Johnny-Boy?"

"Lawd, naw, An Sue!"

"Ef theres anythin wrong jus tell me, chile. Ah kin stan it."

She stood by the ironing board, her hands as usual folded loosely over her stomach, watching Reva pull off her water-clogged shoe. She was feeling that Johnny-Boy was already lost to her; she was feeling the pain that would come when she knew it for certain; and she was feeling that she would have to be brave and bear it. She was like a person caught in a swift current of water and knew where the water was sweeping her and did not want to go on but had to go on to the end.

"It ain nothin bout Johnny-Boy, An Sue," said Reva. "But we gotta do somethin er we'll all git inter trouble."

"How the sheriff know about tha meetin?"

"Thas whut pa wans t know."

"Somebody done turned Judas."

"Sho looks like it."

"Ah bet it wuz some of them new ones," she said.

"Its hard t tell," said Reva.

"Lissen, Reva, yuh oughta stay her n git dry, but yuh bettah git back n tell yo pa Johnny-Boy ain here n Ah don know when hes gonna show up. *Some*bodys gotta tell them comrades t stay erway from yo pas house."

She stood with her back to the window, looking at Reva's wide, blue eyes. Po critter! Gotta go back thu all tha slop! Though she felt sorry for Reva, not once did she think that it would not have to be done. Being a woman, Reva was not suspect; she would *have* to go. It was just as natural for Reva to go back through the cold rain as it was for her to iron night and day, or for Sug to be in jail. Right now, Johnny-Boy was out there on those dark fields trying to get home. Lawd, don let em git im tonight! In spite of herself her feelings became torn. She loved her son and, loving him, she loved what he was trying to do. Johnny-Boy was happiest when he was working for the party, and her love for him was for his happiness. She frowned, trying hard to fit something together in her feelings: for her to try to stop Johnny-Boy was to admit that all the toil of years meant nothing; and to let him go meant that sometime or other he would be caught, like Sug. In facing it this way she felt a little stunned, as though she had come suddenly upon a blank wall in the dark. But outside in the rain were people, white and black, whom she had known all her life. Those people depended upon Johnny-Boy, loved him and looked to him as a man and leader. Yeah; hes gotta keep on; he cant stop now. . . . She looked at Reva; she was crying and pulling her shoes back on with reluctant fingers.

"Whut yuh carryin on tha way fer, chile?"

"Yuh done los Sug, now yuh sendin Johnny-Boy . . ."

"Ah got t, honey."

She was glad she could say that. Reva believed in black folks and not for anything in the world would she falter before her. In Reva's trust and acceptance of her she had found her first feelings of humanity; Reva's love was her refuge from shame and degradation. If in the early days of her life the white mountain had driven her back from the earth, then in her last days Reva's love was drawing her toward it, like the beacon that swung through the night outside. She heard Reva sobbing.

"Hush, honey!"

"Mah brothers in jail too! Ma cries ever day . . ."

"Ah knows, honey."

She helped Reva with her coat; her fingers felt the scant flesh of the girl's shoulders. She don git ernuff t eat, she thought. She slipped her arms around Reva's waist and held her close for a moment.

"Now, yuh stop that cryin."

"A-a-ah, c—c—cant hep it. . . ."

"Everythingll be awright; Johnny-Boyll be back."

"Yuh think so?"

"Sho, chile. Cos he will."

Neither of them spoke again until they stood in the doorway. Outside they could hear water washing through the ruts of the street.

"Be sho n send Johnny-Boy t tell the folks t stay erway from pas house," said Reva.

"Ahll tell im. Don yuh worry."

"Good-bye!"

"Good-bye!"

Leaning against the door jamb, she shook her head slowly and watched Reva vanish through the falling rain.

II

She was back at her board, ironing, when she heard feet sucking in the mud of the back yard; feet she knew from long years of listening were Johnny-Boy's. But tonight, with all the rain and fear, his coming was like a leaving, was almost more than she could bear. Tears welled to her eyes and she blinked them away. She felt that he was coming so that she could give him up; to see him now was to say good-bye. But it was a good-bye she knew she could never say; they were not that way toward each other. All day long they could sit in the same room and not speak; she was his mother and he was her son. Most of the time a nod or a grunt would carry all the meaning that she wanted to convey to him, or he to her. She did not even turn her head when he heard him come stomping into the kitchen. She heard him pull up a chair, sit, sigh, and draw off his muddy shoes; they fell to the floor with heavy thuds. Soon the kitchen was full of the scent of his drying socks and his burning pipe. Tha boys hongry! She paused and looked at him over her shoulder; he was puffing at his pipe with his head tilted back and his feet propped up on the edge of the stove; his eyelids drooped and his wet clothes steamed from the heat of the fire. Lawd, that boy gits mo like his pa every day he lives, she mused, her lips breaking in a slow faint smile. Hols tha pipe in his mouth just like his pa usta hol his. Wondah how they woulda got erlong ef his pa hada lived? They oughta liked each other, they so mucha like. She wished there could have been other children besides Sug, so Johnny-Boy would not have to be so much alone. A man needs a woman by his side. . . . She thought of Reva; she liked Reva; the brightest glow her heart had ever known was when she had learned that Reva loved Johnny-Boy. But beyond Reva were cold white faces. Ef theys caught it means *death*. . . . She jerked around when she heard Johnny-Boy's pipe clatter to the floor. She saw him pick it up, smile sheepishly at her, and wag his head.

"Gawd, Ahm sleepy," he mumbled.

She got a pillow from her room and gave it to him.

"Here," she said.

"Hunh," he said, putting the pillow between his head and the back of the chair.

They were silent again. Yes, she would have to tell him to go back out into the cold rain and slop; maybe to get caught; maybe for the last time; she didn't know. But she would let him eat and get dry before telling him that the sheriff knew of the meeting to be held at Lem's tomorrow. And she would make him take a big dose of soda before he went out; soda always helped to stave off a cold. She looked at the clock. It was eleven. Theres time yit. Spreading a newspaper on the apron of the stove, she placed a heaping plate of greens upon it, a knife, a fork, a cup of coffee, a slab of cornbread, and a dish of peach cobbler.

"Yo suppahs ready," she said.

"Yeah," he said.

He did not move. She ironed again. Presently, she heard him eating. When she could no longer hear his knife tinkling against the edge of the plate, she knew he was through. It was almost twelve now. She would let him rest a little while longer before she told him. Till one er'clock, mabbe. Hes so tired. . . . She finished her ironing, put away the board, and stacked the clothes in her dresser drawer. She poured herself a cup of black coffee, drew up a chair, sat down and drank.

"Yuh almos dry," she said, not looking around.

"Yeah," he said, turning sharply to her.

The tone of voice in which she had spoken had let him know that more was coming. She drained her cup and waited a moment longer.

"Reva wuz here."

"Yeah?"

"She lef bout an hour ergo."

"Whut she say?"

"She said ol man Lem hada visit from the sheriff today."

"Bout the meetin?"

"Yeah."

She saw him stare at the coals glowing red through the crevices of the stove and run his fingers nervously through his hair. She knew he was wondering how the sheriff had found out. In the silence he would ask a wordless question and in the silence she would answer wordlessly. Johnny-Boys too trustin, she thought. Hes trying t make the party big n hes takin in folks fastern he kin git t know em. You cant trust ever white man yuh meet. . . .

"Yuh know, Johnny-Boy, yuh been takin in a lotta them white folks lately . . ."

"Aw, ma!"

"But, Johnny-Boy . . ."

"Please, don talk t me bout tha now, ma."

Yuh ain t ol t lissen n learn, son," she said.

"Ah know whut yuh gonna say, ma. N yuh wrong. Yuh cant judge folks jus by how yuh feel bount em n by how long yuh done knowed em. Ef we start tha we wouldnt have *no*body in the party. When folks pledge they word t be with us, then we gotta take em in. Wes too weak t be choosy."

He rose abruptly, rammed his hands into his pockets, and stood facing the window; she looked at his back in a long silence. She knew his faith; it was deep. He had always said that black men could not fight the rich bosses alone; a man could not fight with every hand against him. But he believes so hard hes blind, she thought. At odd times they had had these arguments before; always she would be pitting her feelings against the hard necessity of his thinking, and always she would lose. She shook her head. Po Johnny-Boy he don know . . .

"But ain nona our folks tol, Johnny-Boy," she said.

"How yuh know?" he asked. His voice came low and with a tinge of anger. He still faced the window and now and then the yellow blade of light flicked across the sharp outine of his black face.

"Cause Ah know em," she said.

"*Anybody* mighta tol," he said.

"It wuznt nona *our* folks," she said again.

She saw his hand sweep in a swift arc of disgust.

"*Our* folks! Ma, who in Gawd's name is *our* folks?"

"The folks we wuz born n raised wid, son. The folks we *know!*"

"We can't make the party grow tha way, ma."

"It mighta been Booker," she said.

"Yuh don know."

". . . er Blattberg . . ."

"Fer Chrissakes!"

". . . er any of the fo-five others whut joined las week."

"Ma, yuh jus don wan me t go out tonight," he said.

"Yo ol ma wans yuh t be careful, son."

"Ma, when yuh start doubtin folks in the party, then there ain no end."

"Son, Ah knows ever black man n woman in this parta the county," she said, standing too. "Ah watched em grow up; Ah even helped birth n nurse some of em; Ah knows em *all* from way back. There ain none of em that *coulda* tol! The folks Ah know jus don open they dos n ast death t walk in! Son, it wuz some of them *white* folks! Yuh jus mark mah word n wait n see!"

"Why is it gotta be *white* folks?" he asked. "Ef they tol, then theys jus Judases, thas all."

"Son, look at whuts befo yuh."

He shook his head and sighed.

"Ma, Ah done tol yuh a hundred times. Ah can't see white n Ah cant see black," he said. "Ah sees rich men n Ah sees po men."

She picked up his dirty dishes and piled them in a pan. Out of the corners of her eyes she saw him sit and pull on his wet shoes. Hes goin! When she put the last dish away he was standing fully dressed, warming his hands over the stove. Jus a few mo minutes now n he'll be gone, like Sug, mabbe. Her throat tightened. This black man's fight takes *ever*thin! Looks like Gawd put us in this worl jus t beat us down!

"Keep this, ma," he said.

She saw a crumpled wad of money in his outstretched fingers.

"Naw; yuh keep it. Yuh might need it."

"It ain mine, ma. It berlongs t the party."

"But, Johnny-Boy, yuh might hafta go erway!"

"Ah kin make out."

"Don fergit yosef too much son."

"Ef Ah don come back theyll need it."

He was looking at her face and she was looking at the money.

"Yuh keep tha," she said slowly. "Ahll give em the money."

"From where?"

"Ah got some."

"Where yuh git it from?"

She sighed.

"Ah been savin a dollah a week fer Sug ever since hes been in jail."

"Lawd, ma!"

She saw the look of puzzled love and wonder in his eyes. Clumsily, he put the money back into his pocket.

"Ahm gone," he said.

"Here; drink this glass of soda watah."

She watched him drink, then put the glass away.

"Waal," she said. "Take the stuff outta ya pockets!"

She lifted the lid of the stove and he dumped all the papers from his pocket into the fire. She followed him to the door and made him turn round.

"Lawd, yuh tryin to maka revolution n yuh cant even keep yo coat buttoned." Her nimble fingers fastened his collar high around his throat. "There!"

He pulled the brim of his hat low over his eyes. She opened the door and with the suddenness of the cold gust of wind that struck her face, he was gone. She watched the black fields and the rain take him, her eyes burning. When the last faint footstep could no longer be heard, she closed the door, went to her bed, lay down, and pulled the cover over her while fully dressed. Her feelings coursed with the rhythm of the rain: Hes gone! Lawd, Ah *know* hes gone! Her blood felt cold.

III

She was floating in a grey void somewhere between sleeping and dreaming and then suddenly she was wide awake, hearing and feeling in the same instant the thunder of the door crashing in and a cold wind filling the room. It was pitch black and she stared, resting on her elbows, her mouth open, not breathing, her ears full of the sound of tramping feet and booming voices. She knew at once: They lookin fer im! Then, filled with her will, she was on her feet, rigid, waiting, listening

"The lamps burnin!"

"Yuh see her?"

"Naw!"

"Look in the kitchen!"

"Gee, this place smells like niggers!"

"Say, somebody's here er been here!"

"Yeah; theres fire in the stove!"

"Mabbe hes been here n gone?"

"Boy, look at these jars of jam!"

"Niggers make good jam!"

"Git some bread!"

"Heres some cornbread!"

"Say, lemme git some!"

"Take it easy! There plenty here!"

"Ahma take some of this stuff home!"

"Look, heres a pota greens!"

"N some hot cawffee!"

"Say, yuh guys! C mon! Cut it out! We didn't come here for a feas!"

She walked slowly down the hall. They lookin fer im, but they ain got im yit! She stopped in the doorway, her gnarled, black hands as always folded over her stomach, but tight now, so tightly the veins bulged. The kitchen was crowded with white men in glistening raincoats. Though the lamp burned, their flashlights still glowed in red fists. Across her floor she saw the muddy tracks of their boots.

"Yuh white folks git outta mah house!"

There was quick silence; every face turned toward her. She saw a sudden movement, but did not know what it meant until something hot and wet slammed her squarely in the face. She gasped, but did not move. Calmly, she wiped the warm greasy liquor of greens from her eyes with her left hand. One of the white men had thrown a handful of greens out of the pot at her.

"How they taste, ol bitch?"

"Ah ast yuh t git outta mah house!"

She saw the sheriff detach himself from the crowd and walk toward her.

"Now, Anty . . ."

"White man, don yuh *Anty* me!"

"Yuh ain got the right sperit!"

"Sperit hell! Yuh git these men outta mah house!"

"Yuh ack like yuh don like it!"

"Naw, Ah don like it, n yuh knows dam wall Ah don!"

"Whut yuh gonna do bout it?"

"Ahm tellin yuh t git outta mah house!"

"Gittin sassy?"

"Ef telling yuh t git outta mah house is sass, then Ahm sassy!"

Her words came in a tense whisper; but beyond, back of them, she was watching, thinking, judging the men.

"Listen, Anty," the sheriff's voice came soft and low. "Ahm here t hep yuh. How come yuh wanna ack this way?"

"Yuh ain never heped yo *own* sef since yuh been born," she flared. "How kin the likes of yuh hep me?"

One of the white men came forward and stood directly in front of her.

"Lissen, nigger woman, yuh talkin t *white* men!"

"Ah don care who Ahm talkin t!"

"Yuhll wish some day yuh did!"

"Not t the likes of yuh!"

"Yuh need somebody t teach yuh how t be a good nigger!"

"*Yuh* cant teach it t me!"

"Yuh gonna change yo tune."

"Not longs mah bloods warm!"

"Don git smart now!"

"Yuh git outta mah house!"

"Spose we don go?" the sheriff asked.

They were crowded around her. She had not moved since she had taken her place in the doorway. She was thinking only of Johnny-Boy as she stood there giving and taking words; and she knew that they, too, were thinking of Johnny-Boy. She knew they wanted him, and her heart was daring them to take him from her.

"Spose we don go?" the sheriff asked again.

"Twenty of yuh runnin over one ol woman! Now, ain yuh white men glad yuh so brave?"

The sheriff grabbed her arm.

"C mon, now! Yuh done did ernuff sass for one night. Wheres tha nigger son of yos?"

"Don yuh wished yuh knowed?"

"Yuh wanna git slapped?"

"Ah ain never seen one of yo kind tha wuznt too low fer . . ."

The sheriff slapped her straight across her face with this open palm. She fell back against a wall and sank to her knees.

"Is tha whut white men do t nigger women?"

She rose slowly and stood again, not even touching the place that ached from his blow, her hands folded over her stomach.

"Ah ain never seen one of yo kind tha wuznt too low fer . . ."

He slapped her again; she reeled backward several feet and fell on her side.

"Is tha whut we too low t do?"

She stood before him again, dry-eyed, as though she had not been struck. Her lips were numb and her chin was wet with blood.

"Aw, let her go! Its the nigger we wan!" said one.

"Wheres that nigger son of yos?" the sheriff asked.

"Find im," she said.

"By Gawd, ef we hafta find im we'll kill im!"

"He wont be the only nigger yuh ever killed," she said.

She was consumed with a bitter pride. There was nothing on this earth, she felt then, that they could not do to her but that she could take. She stood on a narrow plot of ground from which she would die before she was pushed. And then it was, while standing there feeling warm blood seeping down her throat, that she gave up Johnny-Boy, gave him up to the white folks. She gave him up because they had come tramping into her heart demanding him, thinking they could get him by beating her, thinking they could scare her into making her tell where he was. She gave him up because she wanted them to know that they could not get what they wanted by bluffing and killing.

"Wheres this meetin gonna be?" the sheriff asked.

"Don yuh wish yuh knowed?"

"Ain there gonna be a meetin?"

"How come yuh astin me?"

"There *is* gonna be a meeting," said the sheriff.

"Is it?"

"Ah gotta great mind t choke it outta yuh!"

"Yuh so smart," she said.

"We ain playin wid yuh!"

"Did Ah say yuh wuz?"

"Tha nigger son of yos is erroun here somewheres n we aim t find him," said the sheriff. "Ef yuh tell us where he is n ef he talks, mabbe he'll git off easy. But eff we hafta find im, we'll kill im! Ef we hafta find im, then yuh git a sheet t put over im in the mawnin, see? Git yuh a sheet, cause hes gonna be dead!"

"He won't be the only nigger yuh ever killed," she said again.

The sheriff walked past her. The others followed. Yuh didn't git whut yuh wanted! she thought exultingly. N yuh ain gonna *never* git it! Hotly, something ached in her to make them feel the intensity of her pride and freedom; her heart groped to turn the bitter hours of her life into words of a kind that would make them feel that she had taken all they had done to her in her stride and could still take more. Her faith surged so strongly in her she was all but blinded. She walked behind them to the door, knotting and twisting her fingers. She saw them step to the muddy ground. Each whirl of the yellow beacon revealed glimpses of slanting rain. Her lips moved, then she shouted:

"Yuh didnt git whut yuh wanted! N yuh ain gonna nevah git it!"

The sheriff stopped and turned; his voice came low and hard.

"Now, by Gawd, thas ernuff outta yuh!"

"Ah know when Ah done said ernuff!"

"Aw, naw, yuh don!" he said. "Yuh don known when yuh done said ernuff, but Ahma teach yuh ternight!"

He was up the steps and across the porch with one bound. She backed into the hall, her eyes full on his face.

"Tell me when yuh gonna stop talkin!" he said, swinging his fist.

The blow caught her high on the cheek; her eyes went blank; she fell flat on her face. She felt the hard heel of his wet shoes coming into her temple and stomach.

"Lemme hear yuh talk some mo!"

She wanted to, but could not; pain numbed and choked her. She lay still and somewhere out of the grey void of unconsciousness she heard someone say: *aw fer chrissakes leave her erlone its the nigger we wan. . . .*

IV

She never knew how long she had lain huddled in the dark hallway. Her first returning feeling was of a nameless fear crowding the inside of her, then a deep pain spreading from her temple downward over her body. Her ears were filled with the drone of rain and she shuddered from the cold wind blowing through the door. She opened her eyes and at first saw nothing. As if she were imagining it, she knew she was half-lying and half-sitting in a corner against a wall. With difficulty she twisted her neck and what she saw made her hold her breath—a vast white blur was suspended directly above her. For a moment she could not tell if her fear was from the blur or if the blur was from her fear. Gradually the blur resolved itself into a huge white face that slowly filled her vision. She was stone still, conscious really of the effort to breathe, feeling somehow that she existed only by the mercy of that white face. She had seen it before; its fear had gripped her many times; it had for her the fear of all the white faces she had ever seen in her life. *Sue . . .* As from a great distance, she heard her name being called. She was regaining consciousness now, but the fear was coming with her. She looked into the face of a white man, wanting to scream out for him to go; yet accepting his presence because she felt she had to. Though some remote part of her mind was active, her limbs were powerless. It was as if an invisible knife had split her in two, leaving one half of her lying there helpless, while the other half shrank in dread from a forgotten but familiar enemy. *Sue its me Sue its me . . .* Then all at once the voice came clearly.

"Sue, its me! Its Booker!"

And she heard an answering voice speaking inside of her, Yeah, its Booker . . . The one whut jus joined . . . She roused herself, struggling for full consciousness; and as she did so she transferred to the person of Booker the nameless fear she felt. It seemed that Booker towered above her as a challenge to her right to exist upon the earth.

"Yuh awright?"

She did not answer; she started violently to her feet and fell.

"Sue, yuh hurt!"

"Yah," she breathed.

"Where they hit yuh?"

"Its mah head," she whispered.

She was speaking even though she did not want to; the fear that had hold of her compelled her.

"They beat yuh?"

"Yeah."

"Them bastards! Them Gawddam bastards!"

She heard him saying it over and over; then she felt herself being lifted.

"Naw!" she gasped.

"Ahma take yuh t the kitchen!"

"Put me down!"

"But yuh cant stay here like this!"

She shrank in his arms and pushed her hands against his body; when she was in the kitchen she freed herself, sank into a chair, and held tightly to its back. She looked wonderingly at Booker. There was nothing about him that should frighten her so, but even that did not ease her tension. She saw him go to the water bucket, wet his handkerchief, wring it, and offer it to her. Distrustfully, she stared at the damp cloth.

"Here; put this on yo forehead . . ."

"Naw!"

"C mon; itll make yuh feel bettah!"

She hesitated in confusion. What right had she to be afraid when someone was acting kindly as this toward her? Reluctantly, she leaned forward and pressed the damp cloth to her head. It helped. With each passing minute she was catching hold of herself, yet wondering why she felt as she did.

"What happened?"

"Ah don know."

"Yuh feel bettah?"

"Yeah."

"Who all wuz here?"

"Ah don know," she said again.

"Yo head still hurt?"

"Yeah."

"Gee, Ahm sorry."

"Ahm awright," she sighed and buried her face in her hands.
She felt him touch her shoulder.

"Sue, Ah got some bad news fer yuh . . ."

She knew; she stiffened and grew cold. It had happened; she
stared dry-eyed, with compressed lips.

"Its mah Johnny-Boy," she said.

"Yeah; Ahm awful sorry t hafta tell yuh this way. But Ah thought
yuh oughta know . . ."

Her tension eased and a vacant place opened up inside of her. A
voice whispered, Jesus, hep me!

"W-w-where is he?"

"They got im out to Foleys Woods tryin t make im tell who the
others is."

"He ain gonna tell," she said. "They just as wall kill im, cause he
ain gonna nevah tell,"

"Ah hope he don," said Booker. "But he didnt hava chance t tell
the others. They grabbed im jus as he got t the woods."

Then all the horror of it flashed upon her; she saw flung out over
the rainy countryside an array of shacks where white and black comrades were sleeping; in the morning they would be rising and going
to Lem's; then they would be caught. And that meant terror, prison,
and death. The comrades would have to be told; she would have to
tell them; she could not entrust Johnny-Boy's work to another, and
especially not to Booker as long as she felt toward him as she did.
Gripping the bottom of the chair with both hands, she tried to rise;
the room blurred and swayed. She found herself resting in Booker's
arms.

"Lemme go!"

"Sue, yuh too weak t walk!"

"Ah gotta tell em!" she said.

"Set down, Sue! Yuh hurt! Yuh sick!"

When seated, she looked at him helplessly.

"Sue, lissen! Johnny-Boys caught. Ahm here. Yuh tell me who
they is n Ahll tell em."

She stared at the floor and did not answer. Yes; she was too weak
to go. There was no way for her to tramp all those miles through the
rain tonight. But should she tell Booker? If only she had somebody
like Reva to talk to! She did not want to decide alone; she must
make no mistake about this. She felt Booker's fingers pressing on her
arm and it was as though the white mountain was pushing her to
the edge of a sheer height; she again exclaimed inwardly, Jesus, hep
me! Booker's white face was at her side, waiting. Would she be

doing right to tell him? Suppose she did not tell and then the comrades were caught? She could not ever forgive herself for doing a thing like that. But maybe she was wrong; maybe her fear was what Johnny-Boy had always called "jus foolishness." She remembered his saying, Ma we can't make the party grow ef we start doubtin everbody. . . .

"Tell me who they is, Sue, n Ahll tell em. Ah jus joined n Ah don know who they is."

"Ah don know who they is," she said.

"Yuh *gotta* tell me who they is, Sue!"

"Ah told yuh Ah don know."

"Yuh *do* know! C mon! Set up n talk!"

"Naw!"

"Yuh wan em all t git *killed*?"

She shook her head and swallowed. Lawd, Ah don blieve in this man!

"Lissen, Ahll call the names n yuh tell me which ones is in the party n which ones ain, see?"

"Naw!"

"Please, Sue!"

"Ah don know," she said.

"Sue, yuh ain doin right by em. Johnny-Boy wouldn't wan yuh t be this way. Hes out there holdin up his end. Les hol up ours . . ."

"Lawd, Ah don know . . ."

"Is yuh scareda me cause Ahm *white*? Johnny-Boy ain like tha. Don let all the work we done go fer nothin."

She gave up and bowed her head in her hands.

"Is it Johnson? Tell me, Sue?"

"Yeah," she whispered in horror; a mounting horror of feeling herself being undone.

"Is it Green?"

"Yeah."

"Murphy?"

"Lawd, Ah don know!"

"Yuh gotta tell me, Sue!"

"Mistah Booker, please leave me erlone . . ."

"Is it Murphy?"

She answered yes to the names of Johnny-Boy's comrades; she answered until he asked her no more. Then she thought, How he know the sheriffs men is watchin Lems house? She stood up and held onto her chair, feeling something sure and firm within her.

"How yuh know about Lem?"

"Why . . . How Ah know?"

"Whut yuh doin here this tima night? How yuh know the sheriff got Johnny-Boy?"

"Sue, don yuh blieve in me?"

She did not, but she could not answer. She stared at him until her lips hung open; she was searching deep within herself for certainty.

"You meet Reva?" she asked.

"Reva?"

"Yeah; Lems gal?"

"Oh, yeah. Sho, Ah met Reva."

"She tell yuh?"

She asked the question more of herself than of him; she longed to believe.

"Yeah," he said softly. "Ah reckon Ah oughta be goin t tell em now."

"Who?" she asked. "Tell *who?*"

The muscles of her body were stiff as she waited for his answer; she felt as though life depended upon it.

"The comrades," he said.

"Yeah," she sighed.

She did not know when he left; she was not looking or listening. She just suddenly saw the room empty and from her the thing that had made her fearful was gone.

V

For a space of time that seemed to her as long as she had been upon the earth, she sat huddled over the cold stove. One minute she would say to herself, They both gone now; Johnny-Boy n Sug . . . Mabbe Ahll never see em ergin. Then a surge of guilt would blot out her longing. "Lawd, Ah shouldna tol!" she mumbled. "But no man kin be so lowdown as t do a thing like tha . . ." Several times she had an impulse to try to tell the comrades herself; she was feeling a little better now. But what good would that do? She had told Booker the names. He jus couldnt be a Judas t po folks like us . . . He *couldnt!*

"An Sue!"

Thas Reva! Her heart leaped with an anxious gladness. She rose without answering and limped down the dark hallway. Through the open door, against the background of rain, she saw Reva's face lit now and then to whiteness by the whirling beams of the beacon. She was about to call, but a thought checked her. Jesus, hep me! Ah gotta tell her bout Johnny-Boy . . . Lawd, Ah can't!

"An Sue, yuh there?"

"C mon in, chile!"

She caught Reva and held her close for a moment without speaking.

"Lawd, Ahm sho glad yuh here," she said at last.

"Ah thought somethin had happened t yuh," said Reva, pulling away. "Ah saw the do open . . . Pa told me to come back n stay wid yuh tonight . . ." Reva paused and started. "W-w-whuts the mattah?"

She was so full of having Reva with her that she did not understand what the question meant.

"Hunh?"

"Yo neck . . ."

"Aw, it ain nothin, chile. C mon in the kitchen.'"

"But theres blood on yo neck!"

"The sheriff wuz here . . ."

"Them fools! Whut they wanna bother yuh fer? Ah could kill em! So hep me Gawd, Ah could!"

"It ain nothin," she said.

She was wondering how to tell Reva about Johnny-Boy and Booker. Ahll wait a lil while longer, she thought. Now that Reva was here, her fear did not seem as awful as before.

"C mon, lemme fix yo head, An Sue. Yoh hurt."

They went to the kitchen. She sat silent while Reva dressed her scalp. She was feeling better now; in just a little while she would tell Reva. She felt the girl's finger pressing gently upon her head.

"Tha hurt?"

"A lil, chile."

"Yuh po thing!"

"It ain nothin."

"Did Johnny-Boy come?"

She hesitated.

"Yeah."

"He done gone t tell the others?"

Reva's voice sounded so clear and confident that it mocked her. Lawd, Ah cant tell this chile . . .

"Yuh told im, didn't yuh, An Sue?"

"Y-y-yeah . . ."

"Gee! Thas good! Ah told pa he didnt hafta worry ef Johnny-Boy got the news. Mabbe thingsll come out awright."

"Ah hope . . ."

She could not go on; she had gone as far as she could. For the first time that night she began to cry.

"Hush, An Sue! Yuh awways been brave. Itll be awwright!"

"Ain nothin awwright, chile. The worls jus too much fer us, Ah reckon."

"Ef you cry that way itll make me cry."

She forced herself to stop. Naw; Ah cant carry on tha way in fronta Reva . . . Right now she had a deep need for Reva to believe in her. She watched the girl get pine-knots from behind the stove, rekindle the fire, and put on the coffee pot.

"Yuh wan some cawffee?" Reva asked.

"Naw, honey."

"Aw, c mon, An Sue."

"Jusa lil, honey."

"Thas the way to be. Oh, say, Ah fergot," said Reva, measuring out spoonsful of coffee. "Pa told me t tell yuh t watch out fer tha Booker man. Hes a stool."

She showed not one sign of outward movement or expression, but as the words fell from Reva's lips she went limp inside.

"Pa tol me soon as Ah got back home. He got word from town . . ."

She stopped listening. She felt as though she had been slapped to the extreme outer edge of life, into a cold darkness. She knew now what she had felt when she had looked up out of her fog of pain and had seen Booker. It was the image of all the white folks, and the fear that went with them, that she had seen and felt during her life-time. And again, for the second time that night, something she had felt had come true. All she could say to herself was, Ah didnt like im! Gawd knows, Ah didn't! Ah told Johnny-Boy it wuz some of them white folks . . .

"Here; drink yo cawffee . . ."

She took the cup; her fingers trembled, and the steaming liquid spilt onto her dress and leg.

"Ahm sorry, An Sue!"

Her leg was scalded, but the pain did not bother her.

"Its awright," she said.

"Wait; lemme put some lard on tha burn!"

"It don hurt."

"Yuh worried bout somethin."

"Naw, honey."

"Lemme fix yuh so mo cawffee."

"Ah don wan nothin now, Reva."

"Waal, buck up. Don be tha way . . ."

They were silent. She heard Reva drinking. No; she would not tell Reva; Reva was all she had left. But she had to do something, some way, somehow. She was undone too much as it was; and to tell Reva about Booker or Johnny-Boy was more than she was equal to; it would be too coldly shameful. She wanted to be alone and fight this thing out with herself.

"Go t bed, honey. Yuh tired."

"Naw; Ahm awright, An Sue."

She heard the bottom of Reva's empty cup clank against the top of the stove. Ah *got* t make her go t bed! Yes; Booker would tell the names of the comrades to the sheriff. If she could only stop him some way! That was the answer, the point, the star that grew bright in the morning of new hope. Soon, maybe half an hour from now, Booker would reach Foleys Woods. Hes boun t go the long way, cause he don know no short cut, she thought. Ah could wade the creek n beat im there. . . . But what would she do after that?

"Reva, honey, go t bed. Ahm awright. Yuh need res."

"Ah ain sleepy, An Sue!"

"Ah knows whuts bes fer yuh, chile. Yuh tired n wet."

"A wanna stay up wid yuh."

She forced a smile and said:

"Ah don think they gonna hurt Johnny-Boy . . ."

"Fer *real*, An Sue?"

"Sho, honey."

"But Ah wanna wait up wid yuh."

"Thas mah job, honey. Thas whut a mas fer, t wait up fer her chullun."

"Good night, An Sue."

"Good night, honey."

She watched Reva pull up and leave the kitchen; presently she heard the shucks in the mattress whispering, and she knew that Reva had gone to bed. She was alone. Through the cracks of the stove she saw the fire dying to grey ashes; the room was growing cold again. The yellow beacon continued to flit past the window and the rain still drummed. Yes; she was alone; she had done this awful thing alone; she must find some way out, alone. Like touching a festering sore, she put her finger upon that moment when she had shouted her defiance to the sheriff, when she had shouted to feel her strength. She had lost Sug to save others; she had let Johnny-Boy go to save others; and then in a moment of weakness that came from too much strength she had lost all. If she had not shouted to the sheriff, she would have been strong enough to have resisted Booker; she would have been able to tell the comrades herself. Something tightened in her as she remembered and understood the fit of fear she had felt on coming to herself in the dark hallway. A part of her life she thought she had done away with forever had had hold of her then. She had thought the soft, warm past was over; she had thought that it did not mean much when now she sang: *"Hes the Lily of the Valley, the Bright n Mawnin Star . . ."* The days when she had sung that song were the days when she had not hoped for anything

on this earth, the days when the cold mountain had driven her into
the arms of Jesus. She had thought that Sug and Johnny-Boy had
taught her to forget Him, to fix her hope upon the fight of black
men for freedom. Through the gradual years she had believed and
worked with them, had felt strength shed from the grace of their terrible vision. That grace had been upon her when she had let the
sheriff slap her down; it had been upon her when she had risen time
and again from the floor and faced him. But she had trapped herself
with her own hunger; to water the long dry thirst of her faith her
pride had made a bargain which her flesh could not keep. Her having told the names of Johnny-Boy's comrades was but an incident in
a deeper horror. She stood up and looked at the floor while call and
counter-call, loyalty and counter-loyalty struggled in her soul. Mired
she was between two abandoned worlds, living, but dying without
the strength of the grace that either gave. The clearer she felt it the
fuller did something well up from the depth of her for release; the
more urgent did she feel the need to fling into her black sky another
star, another hope, one more terrible vision to give her the strength
to live and act. Softly and restlessly she walked about the kitchen,
feeling herself naked against the night, the rain, the world; and
shamed whenever the thought of Reva's love crossed her mind. She
lifted her empty hands and looked at her writhing fingers. Lawd,
whut kin Ah do now? She could still wade the creek and get to Foley's Woods before Booker. And then what? How could she manage
to see Johnny-Boy or Booker? Again she heard the sheriff's threatening voice: Git yuh a sheet, cause hes gonna be dead! The sheet! Thas
it, the *sheet!* Her whole being leaped with will; the long years of her
life bent toward a moment of focus, a point. Ah kin go wid mah
sheet! Ahll be doin whut he said! Lawd Gawd in Heaven, Ahma go
lika nigger woman wid mah windin sheet t git mah dead son! But
then what? She stood straight and smiled grimly; she had in her
heart the whole meaning of her life; her entire personality was
poised on the brink of a total act. Ah know! Ah *know!* She thought
of Johnny-Boy's gun in the dresser drawer. Ahll hide the gun in the
sheet n go aftah Johnny-Boy's body. . . . She tiptoed to her room,
eased out the dresser drawer, and got a sheet. Reva was sleeping; the
darkness was filled with her quiet breathing. She groped in the
drawer and found the gun. She wound the gun in the sheet and held
them both under her apron. Then she stole to the bedside and
watched Reva. Lawd, hep her! But mabbe shes bettah off. This had t
happen sometimes . . . She n Johnny-Boy couldna been together in
this here South . . . N Ah couldn't tell her bout Booker. Itll come out
awright n she wont nevah know. Reva's trust would never be
shaken. She caught her breath as the shucks in the mattress rustled

dryly; then all was quiet and she breathed easily again. She tiptoed
to the door, down the hall, and stood on the porch. Above her the
yellow beacon whirled through the rain. She went over muddy
ground, mounted a slope, stopped and looked back at her house.
The lamp glowed in her window, and the yellow beacon that swung
every few seconds seemed to feed it with light. She turned and
started across the fields, holding the gun and sheet tightly, thinking,
Po Reva . . . Po critter . . . Shes fas ersleep . . .

VI

For the most part she walked with her eyes half shut, her lips
tightly compressed, leaning her body against the wind and the driving rain, feeling the pistol in the sheet sagging cold and heavy in her
fingers. Already she was getting wet; it seemed that her feet found
every puddle of water that stood between the corn rows.

She came to the edge of the creek and paused, wondering at
what point was it low. Taking the sheet from under her apron, she
wrapped the gun in it so that her finger could be upon the trigger.
Ahll cross here, she thought. At first she did not feel the water; her
feet were already wet. But the water grew cold as it came up to her
knees; she gasped when it reached her waist. Lawd, this creeks high!
When she had passed the middle, she knew that she was out of danger. She came out of the water, climbed a grassy hill, walked on,
turned a bend and saw the lights of autos gleaming ahead. Yeah;
theys still there! She hurried with her head down. Wonda did Ah
beat im here? Lawd, Ah *hope* so! A vivid image of Booker's white
face hovered a moment before her eyes and a surging will rose up in
her so hard and strong that it vanished. She was among the autos
now. From nearby came the hoarse voices of the men.

"Hey, yuh!"

She stopped, nervously clutching the sheet. Two white men with
shotguns came toward her.

"Whut in hell yuh doin out here?"

She did not answer.

"Didn't yuh hear somebody speak t yuh?"

"Ahm comin aftah mah son," she said humbly.

"Yo *son*?"

"Yessuh."

"Whut yo son doin out here?"

"The sheriff's got im."

"Holy Scott! Jim, its the niggers ma!"

"What yuh got there?" asked one.

"A sheet."

"A *sheet*?"

"Yessuh."

"Fer whut?"

"The sheriff tol me t bring a sheet t git his body."

"Waal, waal . . ."

"Now, ain tha somethin?"

The white men looked at each other.

"These niggers sho love one ernother," said one.

"N tha ain no lie," said the other.

"Take me t the sheriff," she begged.

"Yuh ain givin us *orders*, is yuh?"

"Nawsuh."

"We'll take yuh when wes good n ready."

"Yessuh."

"So yuh wan his body?"

"Yessuh."

"Waal, he ain dead yit."

"They gonna kill im," she said.

"Ef he talks they wont."

"He ain gonna talk," she said.

"How yuh know?"

"Cause he ain."

"We got ways of makin niggers talk."

"Yuh ain got no way fer im."

"You thinka lot of that black Red, don yuh?"

"Hes mah son."

"Why don yuh teach im some sense?"

"Hes mah son," she said again.

"Lissen, ol nigger woman, yuh stand there wid yo hair white. Yuh got bettah sense than t blieve tha niggers kin make a revolution . . ."

"A black republic," said the other one, laughing.

"Take me t the sheriff," she begged.

"Yuh his ma," said one. "Yuh kin make im talk n tell whos in this thing wid im."

"He ain gonna talk," she said.

"Don yuh wan im t live?"

She did not answer.

"C mon, les take her t Bradley."

They grabbed her arms and she clutched hard at the sheet and gun; they led her toward the crowd in the woods. Her feelings were simple; Booker would not tell; she was there with the gun to see to that. The louder became the voices of the men the deeper became her feeling of wanting to right the mistake she had made; of wanting to fight her way back to solid ground. She would stall for time until Booker showed up. Oh, ef theyll only lemme git close t Johnny-Boy! As they led her near the crowd she saw white faces turning and looking at her and heard a rising clamor of voices.

"Whos tha?"

"A nigger woman!"

"Whut she doin out here?"

"This is his ma!" called one of the men.

"Whut she want?"

"She brought a sheet t cover his body!"

"He ain dead yit!"

"They tryin t make im talk!"

"But he will be dead soon ef he don open up!"

"Say, look! The niggers ma brought a sheet t cover up his body!"

"Now, ain tha sweet?"

"Mabbe she wans t hol a prayer meetin!"

"Did she git a preacher?"

"Say, go git Bradley!"

"O.K.!"

The crowd grew quiet. They looked at her curiously; she felt their cold eyes trying to detect some weakness in her. Humbly, she stood with the sheet covering the gun. She had already accepted all that they could do to her.

The sheriff came.

"So yuh brought yo sheet, hunh?"

"Yessuh," she whispered.

"Looks like them slaps we gave yuh learned yuh some sense, didnt they?"

She did not answer.

"Yuh don need tha sheet. Yo son ain dead yit," he said, reaching toward her.

She backed away, her eyes wide.

"Naw!"

"Now, lissen, Anty!" he said. "There ain no use in yuh ackin a fool! Go in there n tell tha nigger son of yos t tell us whos in this wid im, see? Ah promise we wont kill im ef he talks. We'll let him git outta town."

"There ain nothin Ah kin tell im," she said.

"Yuh wan us t kill im?"

She did not answer. She saw someone lean toward the sheriff and whisper.

"Bring her erlong," the sheriff said.

They led her to a muddy clearing. The rain streamed down through the ghostly glare of the flashlights. As the men formed a semi-circle she saw Johnny-Boy lying in a trough of mud. He was tied with rope; he lay hunched and one side of his face rested in a pool of black water. His eyes were staring questioningly at her.

"Speak t im," said the sheriff.

If she could only tell him why she was here! But that was impossible; she was close to what she wanted and she stared straight before her with compressed lips.

"Say, nigger!" called the sheriff, kicking Johnny-Boy. "Here's yo ma!"

Johnny-Boy did not move or speak. The sheriff faced her again.

"Lissen, Anty," he said. "Yu got mo say wid im than anybody. Tell im t talk n hava chance. Whut he wanna pertect the other niggers n white folks fer?"

She slid her finger about the trigger of the gun and looked stonily at the mud.

"Go t him," said the sheriff.

She did not move. Her heart was crying out to answer the amazed question in Johnny-Boy's eyes. But there was no way now.

"Wall, yuhre astin fer it. By Gawd, we gotta way to *make* yuh talk t im," he said, turning away. "Say, Tim, git one of them logs n turn that nigger upside-down n put his legs on it!"

A murmur of assent ran through the crowd. She bit her lips; she knew what that meant.

"Yuh wan yo nigger son crippled?" she heard the sheriff ask.

She did not answer. She saw them roll the log up; they lifted Johnny-Boy and laid him on his face and stomach, then they pulled his legs over the log. His knee-caps rested on the sheer top of the log's back and the toes of his shoes pointed groundward. So absorbed was she in watching that she felt that it was she who was being lifted and made ready for torture.

"Git a crowbar!" said the sheriff.

A tall, lank man got a crowbar from a nearby auto and stood over the log. His jaws worked slowly on a wad of tobacco.

"Now, its up t yuh Anty," the sheriff said. "Tell the man what t do!"

She looked into the rain. The sheriff turned.

"Mabbe she think wes playin. Ef she don say nothin, then break em at the knee-caps!"

"O.K., Sheriff!"

She stood waiting for Booker. Her legs felt weak; she wondered if she would be able to wait much longer. Over and over she said to herself, Ef he come now Ahd kill em both!

"She ain saying nothin, Sheriff!"

"Waal, Gawddammit, let im have it!"

The crowbar came down and Johnny-Boy's body lunged in the mud and water. There was a scream. She swayed, holding tight to the gun and sheet.

"Hol im! Git the other leg!"

The crowbar fell again. There was another scream.

"Yuh break em?" asked the sheriff.

The tall man lifted Johnny-Boy's legs and let them drop limply again, dropping rearward from the knee-caps. Johnny-Boy's body lay still. His head had rolled to one side and she could not see his face.

"Jus lika broke sparrow wing," said the man, laughing softly.

Then Johnny-Boy's face turned to her; he screamed.

"Go way, ma! Go way!"

It was the first time she had heard his voice since she had come out to the woods; she all but lost control of herself. She started violently forward, but the sheriff's arm checked her.

"Aw naw! Yuh had yo chance!" He turned to Johnny-Boy. "She kin go ef yuh talk."

"Mistah, he ain gonna talk," she said.

"Go way, ma!" said Johnny-Boy.

"Shoot im! Don make im suffah so," she begged.

"He'll either talk or he'll never hear yuh ergin," the sheriff said. "Theres other things we kin do t im."

She said nothing.

"What yuh come here fer, ma?" Johnny-Boy sobbed.

"Ahm gonna split his eardrums," the sheriff said. "Ef yuh got anything t say t im yuh bettah say it *now!*"

She closed her eyes. She heard the sheriff's feet sucking in mud. Ah could save im! She opened her eyes; there were shouts of eagerness from the crowd as it pushed in closer.

"Bus em, Sheriff!"

"Fix im so he can't hear!"

"He knows how t do it, too!"

"He busted a Jew boy tha way once!"

She saw the sheriff stoop over Johnny-Boy, place his flat palm over one ear and strike his fist against it with all his might. He placed his palm over the other ear and struck again. Johnny-Boy moaned, his head rolling from side to side, his eyes showing white amazement in a world without sound.

"Yuh wouldn't talk t im when yuh had the chance," said the sheriff. "Try n talk now."

She felt warm tears on her checks. She longed to shoot Johnny-Boy and let him go. But if she did that they would take the gun from her, and Booker would tell who the others were. Lawd, hep me! The men were talking loudly now, as though the main business was over. It seemed ages that she stood there watching Johnny-Boy roll and whimper in his world of silence.

"Say, Sheriff, heres somebody lookin fer yuh!"

"Who is it?"

"Ah don know!"

"Bring em in!"

She stiffened and looked around wildly, holding the gun tight. Is tha Booker? Then she held still, feeling that her excitement might betray her. Mabbe Ah kin shoot em both; Mabbe Ah kin shoot *twice!* The sheriff stood in front of her, waiting. The crowd parted and she saw Booker hurrying forward.

"Ah know em all, Sheriff!" he called.

He came full into the muddy clearing where Johnny-Boy lay.

"Yuh mean yuh got the names?"

"Sho! The ol nigger . . ."

She saw his lips hang open and silent when he saw her. She stepped forward and raised the sheet.

"Whut . . ."

She fired, once; then, without pausing, she turned, hearing them yell. She aimed at Johnny-Boy, but they had their arms around her, bearing her to the ground, clawing at the sheet in her hand. She glimpsed Booker lying sprawled in the mud, on his face, his hands stretched out before him; then a cluster of yelling men blotted him out. She lay without struggling, looking upward through the rain at the white faces above her. And she was suddenly at peace; they were not a white mountain now; they were not pushing her any longer to the edge of life. Its awright . . .

"She shot Booker!"

"She hada gun in the sheet!"

"Whut she shoot im fer?"

"Kill the bitch!"

"Ah *thought* somethin wuz wrong bout her!"

"Ah wuz fer givin it t her from the firs!"

"Thas whut yuh git fer treatin a nigger nice!"

"Say, Bookers dead!"

She stopped looking into the white faces, stopped listening. She waited, giving up her life before they took it from her; she had done what she wanted. Ef only Johnny-Boy . . . She looked at him, he lay looking at her with tired eyes. Ef she could only tell im! But he lay already buried in a grave of silence.

"Whut yuh kill im fer, hunh?"

It was the sheriff's voice; she did not answer.

"Mabbe she wuz shootin at yuh, Sheriff?"

"Whut yuh kill im fer?"

She felt the sheriff's foot come into her side; she closed her eyes.

"Yuh black bitch!"

"Let her have it!"

"Yuh reckon she foun out bout Booker?"

"She mighta."

"Jesus Chris, whut yuh dummies *waitin* on!"

"Yeah; kill her!"

"Kill em *both*!"

"Let her know her nigger sons dead firs!"

She turned her head toward Johnny-Boy; he lay looking puzzled in a world beyond the reach of voices. At leas he can't hear, she thought.

"C mon, let im have it!"

She listened to hear what Johnny-Boy could not. They came, two of them, one right behind the other; so close together that they sounded like one shot. She did not look at Johnny-Boy now; she looked at the white faces of the men, hard and wet in the glare of the flashlights.

"Yuh hear tha, nigger woman?"

"Did tha surprise im? Hes in hell now wonderin whut hit im!"

"C mon! Give it t her, Sheriff!"

"Lemme shoot her, Sheriff! It wuz mah pal she shot!"

"Awright, Pete! Thas fair ernuff!"

She gave up as much of her life as she could before they took it from her. But the sound of the shot and the streak of fire that tore its way through her chest forced her to live again, intensely. She had not moved, save for the slight jarring impact of the bullet. She felt the heat of her own blood warming her cold, wet back. She yearned suddenly to talk. "Yuh didn't git whut yuh wanted! N yuh ain gonna nevah git it! Yuh didn't kill me; Ah come here by mahsef . . ." She felt rain falling into her wide-open, dimming eyes and heard faint voices. Her lips moved soundlessly. *Yuh didnt git yuh didnt yuh didnt* . . . Focused and pointed she was, buried in the depths of her star, swallowed in its peace and strength; and not feeling her flesh growing cold, cold as the rain that fell from the invisible sky upon the doomed living and the dead that never dies.

Pauli Murray

(1910–1985)

AUTHOR, ATTORNEY, LAW PROFESSOR, first black woman to become an ordained priest in the Episcopal church, theology teacher, poet, and civil rights activist, Pauli Murray led a varied and fascinating life and wrote about it in an exciting autobiography.

Born in Baltimore, Maryland, in 1910, she was reared in Durham, North Carolina, in the home of her grandparents—proud, middle-class blacks, both of them mulattoes. Her grandfather was a Civil War veteran; her grandmother was related to a prominent white family of Chapel Hill. Murray was educated in Durham's public schools, and at New York City's Hunter College, graduating in 1933. This meant that she was in Harlem during the Renaissance and knew several of its major figures. She took her first law degree at Howard University in 1944, graduating as head of her class and winning a fellowship to the Harvard Law School. Rejected at Harvard because of her sex, she took her master's degree in law from the University of California at Berkeley, became a tutor in Yale's law school, and received her doctorate there in 1965. Murray taught law at Boston University, at Brandeis, and in Ghana. During the 1940s she was a civil rights activist, advocating the passive resistance doctrine of Gandhi. She was also a strong worker in the women's rights movement. In 1977, after she had practiced law in New York and California, had turned to theology, and had attended New York's General Theological Seminary, she was ordained as a priest in the Episcopal church.

Murray's major work, *Proud Shoes: The Story of an American Family* (1956), may be loosely defined as a memoir, the principal subjects of which are the historical facts, the stories (some apocryphal), and the collective memories of her ancestral family's oldest members—stories and memories which helped to shape her life. The work also gives insight into the complex relationships among members of a racially mixed family. *Proud Shoes* is a worthy addition to that line of classic black autobiographies in which one finds *Narrative of the Life of Frederick Douglass, Up from Slavery, Black Boy*, and others. When *Proud Shoes* was first published, three of New York City's most important dailies praised it highly—the *Times*, the *Post*, and the *Herald-Tribune*.

Murray's second major publication, *Dark Testament and Other Poems* (1970), contains a mixture of different types of verse, treating varying themes—racial protest, social comment, philosophical subjects, and love.

749

Her title poem, and the volume itself, owes much to her association with Stephen Vincent Benét, who inspired and encouraged her. A few of Murray's poems have appeared in well-known anthologies, among them: Langston Hughes and Arna Bontemps, eds., *The Poetry of the Negro, 1746–1970* (1970), and Lindsay Patterson, ed., *A Rock against the Wind: Black Love Poems* (1973). She also published many articles on civil liberty and legal issues.

For comment on Pauli Murray's life and publications, see the article by Nellie McKay in *Dictionary of Literary Biography, Volume 41* (1985). For details of her early activities, see *Who's Who in Colored America* (1950), edited by G. James Fleming and Christian E. Burckel.

The selection that follows comes from *Proud Shoes* (1956, 1978).

FROM **PROUD SHOES**

As I look back on those years at Grandfather's house, I see that I inhabited a world of unbelievable contradictions. There were the disciplines of study, of doing one's duty at all costs, of walking up to fear and conquering it. Against these were the imagined terrors of the cemetery and its dead and the equally disconcerting fear of the living—that unknown white world with which I had little or no contact but which surrounded and stifled me, a great amorphous mass without personality about which I had much curiosity but dared not investigate in the interests of maintaining my dignity and pride. There were the exhortations of Grandfather and my aunts as teachers to bring out the best in people and there were Grandmother's gloomy prophecies warning of the worst. There were competing prides and loyalties—Grandfather's loyalty to his Union cause and Grandmother's to her Smiths—and while each sprang from widely different sources, both, it seemed to me, in the long run ended up in near poverty and isolation between the Bottoms and the cemetery.

For me all this could only end in rebellion. I do not know which generated the greater revolt in me: the talk I heard about the Smiths or stories of the Fitzgeralds. Each played its part. Listening to my elders tell of the old days in North Carolina, it sometimes appeared that the world my aunts and mother grew up in bore little resemblance to the one in which I lived only a few decades later.

When the Fitzgeralds had gone south, there were no rigid Jim Crow laws as I knew them in my time and there was still room to breathe. Durham was a village without pre-Civil War history or strong ante-bellum traditions. In some ways it was like a frontier town. There was considerable prejudice, of course, but there were recognition of individual worth and bridges of mutual respect between the older white and colored families of the town which persisted into the twentieth century. Robert and Richard Fitzgerald were respected as builders of this tobacco center and their families were held in high esteem.

Everyone knew the Fitzgerald daughters and what their families stood for. Uncle Richard Fitzgerald was known as the town's leading brick manufacturer and was considered wealthy. He owned a great deal of property all over town and was president of the first Negro bank organized in Durham. He and his family lived in a fine eighteen-room slate-roofed house of many turrets and gables and a wide piazza, set in a large maple-and-magnolia grove and surrounded by white sandy drives and terraced lawns. Grandfather lived in much humbler surroundings but was equally respected for his integrity and stubbornness in the face of many odds. People sometimes distinguished the two families as the "rich Fitzgeralds" and "poor Fitzgeralds," but treated them all with deference and courtesy. When my aunts went to town men of good breeding tipped their hats and used courtesy titles in their business transactions. They went where they pleased with little restraint and were all grown women before the first law requiring separation on trains and streetcars appeared in North Carolina.

They regarded these laws disdainfully as a temporary evil, perhaps, and often ignored them, but they were never crushed by them. They had known better times and were closer to the triumphs of Grandfather's youth. I could only look forward to a time when I could complete Grandfather's work, which had been so violently interrupted during Reconstruction.

Mary Ruffin Smith had sown seeds of rebellion in disposing of her wealth. She had done what she thought was best according to her lights, but we thought differently. She gave the balance of her estate, which consisted mostly of heavily wooded land worth around $50,000, to the Western Diocese of the Protestant Episcopal Church in the state and to the University of North Carolina. The University got the Jones's Grove tract with the stipulation that it be converted into a permanent trust fund in memory of her late brother who once owned it. The fund was to be used for the education of students at the University and is known as the Francis Jones Smith Scholarships.

Grandmother and her children owned property almost in the shadow of the University with whose history and traditions they were well acquainted. It did not take her daughters long to ask why she must pay taxes to support an institution which they could not attend. It was a burning issue in our family, kindled as much by feelings of personal injustice as by group discrimination. I heard it so often at home that it was only natural that I should be among the first to hammer on the doors of the University and demand the right to enter.

Then there was the fact of Grandfather's pension check and what it symbolized. I used to lead him to town each month when he went to cash it. He seemed to walk straighter on those days. He was the Robert Fitzgerald of old before blindness and infirmity had slowed his steps and interrupted his work. His check was his government's recognition of honored service and of the disability he had suffered in his country's cause.

But I saw the things which Grandfather could not see—in fact had never seen—the signs which literally screamed at me from every side—on streetcars, over drinking fountains, on doorways: FOR WHITE ONLY, FOR COLORED ONLY, WHITE LADIES, COLORED WOMEN, WHITE, COLORED. If I missed the signs I had only to follow my nose to the dirtiest, smelliest, most neglected accommodations or they were pointed out to me by a heavily armed, invariably mountainous red-faced policeman who to me seemed more a signal of calamity than of protection. I saw the names of telephone subscribers conspicuously starred "(C)" in the telephone directory and the equally conspicuous space given to crimes of Negroes by the newspapers, the inconspicuous space given to public recognition and always with the ignominious and insulting "negro" or "negress."

When Grandfather came south to teach, the little Negro freedmen and the poor white children were more or less on an equal footing, shared an abysmal ignorance and went to log cabin schools. A half century later the crusade against starving the colored schools was a feeble whimper. Each morning I passed white children as poor as I going in the opposite direction on their way to school. We never had fights; I don't recall their ever having called me a single insulting name. It was worse than that. They passed me as if I weren't there! They looked through me and beyond me with unseeing eyes. Their school was a beautiful red-and-white brick building on a wide paved street. Its lawn was large and green and watered every day and flower beds were everywhere. Their playground, a wonderland of iron swings, sand slides, see-saws, crossbars and a basketball court, was barred from us by a strong eight-foot-high fence topped by barbed wire. We could only press our noses against the wire and watch them playing on the other side.

I went to West End where Aunt Pauline taught, on Ferrell Street, a dirt road which began at a lumberyard and ended in a dump. On one side of this road were long low warehouses where huge barrels of tobacco shavings and tobacco dust were stored. All day long our nostrils sucked in the brown silt like fine snuff in the air. West End looked more like a warehouse than a school. It was a dilapidated, rickety, two-story wooden building which creaked and swayed in the wind as if it might collapse. Outside it was scarred with peeling paint from many winters of rain and snow. Inside the floors were bare and splintery, the plumbing was leaky, the drinking fountains broken and the toilets in the basement smelly and constantly out of order. We'd have to wade through pools of foul water to get to them. At recess we herded into a yard of cracked clay, barren of tree or bush, and played what games we could improvise like hopscotch or springboard, which we contrived by pulling rotted palings off the wooden fence and placing them on brickbats.

It was never the hardship which hurt so much as the contrast between what we had and what the white children had. We got the greasy, torn, dog-eared books; they got the new ones. They had field day in the city park; we had it on a furrowed stubbly hillside. They got wide mention in the newspaper; we got a paragraph at the bottom. The entire city officialdom from the mayor down turned out to review their pageantry; we got a solitary official.

Our seedy run-down school told us that if we had any place at all in the scheme of things it was a separate place, marked off, proscribed and unwanted by the white people. We were bottled up and labeled and set aside—sent to the Jim Crow car, the back of the bus, the side door of the theater, the side window of a restaurant. We came to know that whatever we had was always inferior. We came to understand that no matter how neat and clean, how law abiding, submissive and polite, how studious in school, how churchgoing and moral, how scrupulous in paying our bills and taxes we were, it made no essential difference in our place.

It seemed as if there were only two kinds of people in the world —*They* and *We*—*White* and *Colored*. The world revolved on color and variations in color. It pervaded the air I breathed. I learned it in hundreds of ways. I picked it up from grown folks around me. I heard it in the house, on the playground, in the streets, everywhere. The tide of color beat upon me ceaselessly, relentlessly.

Always the same tune, played like a broken record, robbing one of personal identity. Always the shifting sands of color so that there was no solid ground under one's feet. It was color, color, color all the time, color, features and hair. Folks were never just folks. They were white folks! Black folks! Poor white crackers! No-count niggers! Red necks! Darkies! Peckerwoods! Coons!

Two shades lighter! Two shades darker! Dead white! Coal black! High yaller! Mariny! Good hair! Bad hair! Stringy hair! Nappy hair! Thin lips! Thick lips! Red lips! Liver lips! Blue veined! Blue gummed! Straight nosed! Flat nosed!

Brush your hair, child, don't let it get kinky! Cold-cream your face, child, don't let it get sunburned! Don't suck your lips, child, you'll make them too niggerish! Black is evil, don't mix with mean niggers! Black is honest, you half-white bastard. I always said a little black and a little white sure do make a pretty sight! He's black as sin and evil in the bargain. The blacker the berry, the sweeter the juice!

To hear people talk, color, features and hair were the most important things to know about a person, a yardstick by which everyone measured everybody else. From the looks of my family I could never tell where white folks left off and colored folks began, but it made little difference as far as I was concerned. In a world of black-white opposites, I had no place. Being neither very dark nor very fair, I was a nobody without identity. I was too dark at home and too light at school. The pride I learned at home was almost canceled out by the cloak of shame I wore at school, especially when my schoolmates got angry and yelled at me, "You half-white bastard! You dirty-faced Jew baby! Black is honest! Yaller is dishonest!"

I was a minority within a minority, shoved down by inexorable pressures from without, thrust up by intolerable frustrations from within. Black ancestry brought the shame of slavery; white ancestry was condemned as bastardy and brought another kind of shame. Since there was no middle ground between these two extremes, I sought neutral territory in my American Indian ancestry, a group nonexistent in my community and which could not challenge my asserted kinship. I fell back on Great-Grandmother Harriet and her Cherokee blood. That she too had been a slave subject to all the evils of slavery was submerged in the more significant fact that the American Indians at least had preferred annihilation to enslavement. This seemed to me a worthier trait than acceptance of bondage as the price of survival.

It is little wonder, then, perhaps, that I was strongly anti-American at six, that I hated George Washington, mumbled the oath of allegiance to the American flag which we children were taught in the second grade and was reluctant to stand up when we sang "The Star-Spangled Banner." I was unmoved by the story of Washington's crossing the Delaware, nor was I inspired by his truthfulness and valor. My thin knowledge of history told me that the George Washingtons and their kind had stolen the country from the American Indians, and I could lodge all my protests against this unforgivable piece of thievery.

Every February the lower grades buzzed with activities commemorating the birthdays of George Washington and Abraham Lincoln. I dutifully cut out log cabins to symbolize Lincoln's birth but I invariably messed up the hatchets and bunches of cherries. My folks would have been horrified at my private seditious thoughts if they had known of them. Grandfather and my aunts considered themselves part of the noblest of professions—schoolteaching—a profession allied with feelings of deepest patriotism. Aunt Pauline's classroom walls were full of American flags, pictures of American Presidents, and a print of the famous Spirit of '76. I regularly attended church every Sunday where prayers were offered for the "President of the United States and all others in civil authority." Yet, for all their patriotism, the somber fact remained that until the three Negro schools of Durham in my childhood—West End, East End and Whitted—all burned to the ground mysteriously one after the other, the colored children got no new buildings.

I do not know how long this lack of patriotism might have kept up if Grandfather Fitzgerald had not died the summer I was nearly nine. His last illness came upon him while Aunt Pauline and I were in Baltimore and we had to cut short our trip and come home immediately. It was the first time I had ever seen Grandfather helpless. He looked so still and pale in the big iron bed upstairs. His eyes were fixed upon the ceiling, his lips were dry and cracked and his breath came in quick gasps. At first he could talk to us but he got so he couldn't speak and his lips made soundless movements.

Uncle Richard had died a year earlier but I had not felt his death. It was the first time in those years of living close to the symbols of death I was aware of it approaching. Grandmother was like a wild animal. I had never seen her like that before. She yelled and stormed so that Grandfather's sisters, Aunt Mary and Aunt Agnes, did not dare come into the house. They stood at the back fence and asked how Grandfather was, then went away again.

Aunt Pauline woke me on Monday morning, August 4, while it was still dark.

"Your grandfather took a turn for the worse during the night. I don't think he'll last until morning and I've got to send for Aunt Mary and Aunt Agnes. You're the only one to go. If I stand in the back door and watch you till you get up the hill, do you think you could run through the cemetery and get them?"

I was terrified. I had never been through the cemetery alone after dark, but Grandfather was dying and it seemed that in death he was to give me the courage I had never found during his life. I put on my clothes and went out into the crisp cool blackness of early morning. I climbed the fence while Aunt Pauline took her post in the doorway. I sped up the little bricked alleyways, past the ominous Confederate gun, past crazy-leaning tombstones, vaults and marble angels, past the shadowy trees rustling slightly in an early morning breeze, past the mausoleum at the top of the hill where Aunt Pauline could no longer see me and I was on my own.

I outran death that morning and arrived at Aunt Agnes's house in a state of collapse. She was ill and only Aunt Mary could go back with me. It was still twilight and as we started back through the cemetery she took my hand, but I was no longer afraid. I had taken the first step toward walking in Grandfather's shoes. Aunt Pauline took Aunt Mary straight upstairs to Grandfather's room when we got home, but she made me stay outside and I sat on the stair landing feeling lost and alone and wondering about death. When Aunt Pauline came out and started down the stairs crying I knew that Grandfather was gone.

Then the strangest thing happened. Grandmother, who had been like a raging volcano, took charge. She made everybody leave Grandfather's room and locked herself inside. When she came out again some time later she was quiet and calm as if some terrible storm had gone out of her. She had cleaned Grandfather's body, bathed him all over and put on his burial underclothes. She wanted the undertaker to find him as he had lived—everything in order.

I did not see Grandfather again until after the undertaker came and left and a black crepe was hung on our door. He was lying on a bier in front of the fireplace, dressed in his salt-and-pepper-gray broadcloth suit and covered from his chest down with a long dark drape. Out of childish curiosity I slipped into the parlor and looked underneath the drape. Grandfather, who had always been my symbol of strength and authority, now looked tiny and shrunken. He was fully dressed except for his shoes, and his white-stockinged feet turned upward and curled over a bit. I remember wondering why a person was buried without his shoes on. For years I could not go into the parlor without still seeing the image of Grandfather lying in his dark suit before the fireplace with his white-stockinged feet curled up and over.

The family patriarch had gone down in death, and it was like the shock of a great landmark tree crashing in the forest. It was the signal for the gathering of all the relatives from near and far. Most of our blood kinsfolk came together for a three-day period of mourning. The ban on exiles was lifted temporarily, old associations were renewed, family stories embellished by collective memories were re-told, and sometimes new business ventures were started. The wake had the solemnity of a high religious observance with an undertone of family reunion. There was subdued merriment among the more distant relatives while the chief mourners stayed in a special room surrounded by only the closest of friends. The atmosphere was hushed most of the time except for the occasional irreverent laughter of children. It seemed to me that I had more visitors and playmates during those three days than I had had in my entire life at Grand-father's house.

But when the day of the funeral came, the only sign of grief among Grandmother and my aunts was their pale, tight-lipped ap-pearance in their long black dresses and flowing black veils. They marched—not walked— in the funeral procession, as Grandfather had always marched before them, and they all sang his favorite hymns as if they were the choir instead of the bereaved. It was a family custom to sing a loved one on his way to the other side and it has been followed to this day.

Once the family patriarch was lowered into his grave, however, and the long black funeral veils were laid away for the future, his mantle of authority fell naturally and wordlessly upon that next member of the clan, man or woman, who had been emerging through the years. Every family must have such a head, it seemed; otherwise it became rudderless and scattered, losing its strength and identity. For the Fitzgerald clan of Fitzgeralds and Cleggs, that day it became Great-Aunt Mary, the oldest survivor of those who had come south in 1869. In our immediate family it was Aunt Pauline.

Grandfather was buried in the Fitzgerald family graveyard where Great-Grandfather Thomas, Great-Grandmother Sarah Ann, Uncle Richard and other relatives already rested. It was on the west side of Chapel Hill Road next to the old section of Maplewood Cemetery. Only an iron picket fence separated the Fitzgeralds from their white contemporaries who had been early settlers in Durham, but a far wider gulf separated the living descendants. And it was in Grand-father's death that I found a symbol which would somehow sustain me until I grew older and found other ways of balancing loyalty with revolt.

Grandfather died in 1919 and it would be a number of years be-fore the graves of World War I veterans appeared. Meanwhile the white cemetery from our back door to Chapel Hill Road and beyond was filled with Confederate dead. Every Memorial Day or Decoration Day, the cemetery hillside was dotted with crossbarred Confederate flags. As a Union veteran, Grandfather was entitled to a United States flag for his grave, so every May I walked proudly through a field of Confederate flags hugging my gold-pointed replica of Old Glory. I crossed Chapel Hill Road to the Fitzgerald family burial ground and planted it at the head of Grandfather's grave.

This solitary American flag just outside the iron fence which separated it from the Confederate banners waving on the other side was an act of hunger and defiance. It tied me and my family to something bigger than the Rebel atmosphere in which we found ourselves. In time Grandfather would be joined by Grandmother here and we would sell Grandmother's farm and the family homeplace. We would scatter and there would not be one Robert and Cornelia Fitzgerald descendant left in the South. We would become city folk in stifling little apartments in northern cities, far from the land and rootless, and the Fitzgerald name would die out leaving only the Fitzgerald mark here and there. We younger ones would search for something we had lost or perhaps had never had.

But for that moment upon this lone flag I hung my nativity and the right to claim my heritage. It bore mute testimony to the irrefutable fact that I was an American and it helped to negate in my mind the signs and symbols of inferiority and apartness. In those early years there was little identity in my mind between the Union flag which waved over my grandfather's grave and the United States flag upon which I looked with so much skepticism at West End School. It would be a while yet before I realized that the two were the same.

I spent many hours digging up weeds, cutting grass and tending the family plot. It was only a few feet from the main highway between Durham and Chapel Hill. I wanted the white people who drove by to be sure to see this banner and me standing by it. Whatever else they denied me, they could not take from me this right and the undiminished stature it gave me. For there at least at Grandfather's grave with the American flag in my hands, I could stand very tall and in proud shoes.

Chester Himes

(1909–1984)

NOVELIST, WRITER OF SHORT FICTION and detective stories, and autobiographer, Chester Bomar Himes lived a long, prolific, and highly varied life, much of it spent abroad, principally in France and Spain. His writing career had two major phases: the first, lasting roughly from 1945 to 1955, produced five novels, all of them influenced in varying degrees by the Richard Wright school of harsh naturalism. The second phase, running roughly from 1957 until his death, brought forth a series of detective stories or mysteries, as they are now called, which became quite popular, particularly in France. Because of this popularity Himes was given the Grand Prix Policier, the mystery writers' award, for 1958. In America, the best-known and most popular of these mysteries, *Cotton Comes to Harlem* (1965), was made into a successful film. It features a fascinating pair of black detectives—Coffin Ed Smith and Gravedigger Jones. During this second phase, Himes also wrote two other very popular works: *Pinktoes* (1965), a hilarious satire on sex-and-race relations, and his autobiography, *The Quality of Hurt* (1972), which tells about the life of this many-sided and talented, but troubled writer.

Born in Jefferson City, Missouri, of middle-class parents (his father was a trade school teacher in several black institutions), Himes spent his early life in several states as his parents moved from school to school. Two tragedies touched and made an indelible mark on the character of young Himes. The first occurred about 1922 when he and his brother, Joseph, were preparing a chemistry demonstration for their high school. Chester accidentally set off an explosion which permanently blinded his brother. The second occurred while he was a third-year student at Ohio State University, when he was found guilty of armed robbery and sentenced to twenty years in the Ohio State Penitentiary. Like O. Henry, Malcolm X, and other talented prisoners, he learned a great deal from that unfortunate experience. While in prison, he published short stories which appeared in *Abbott's Monthly* and *Esquire*. After his release in 1936, Himes set out on an odyssey which took him to Cleveland, New York, San Francisco, and to other cities. He worked in shipyards on the West Coast, flirted with communism, worked for the Ohio Writers' Project, and made the acquaintance of several well-known writers, among them Langston Hughes. Gaining material for his writing from all of these experiences, he wrote stories which appeared in *The Crisis*, *Opportunity*, *Commentary*, and in other periodicals. Getting tired of America and its characteristic "violence," Himes became an expatriate in 1955. He died in Spain in 1984.

Certain themes tend to recur in the novels of Himes's early years as a writer, among them: the emasculation of the black male by the black middle-class female, as in *Third Generation* (1954); the white female as the enemy and destroyer of black manhood, as in *Lonely Crusade* (1947); and the never-lifting fog of white oppression which hangs over American blacks, as in *If He Hollers Let Him Go* (1945). The black-man-white-woman liaison occurs again in *The Primitive* (1955). *Cast the First Stone* (1955), probably based on Himes's prison experience, is a protest novel which pleads for a greater understanding of and a greater tolerance for homosexuals.

Chester Himes is not a great novelist. He lacks both the stylistic technique and the profound social understanding of his friend Richard Wright. He is, however, like Wright in his eye for the sensational and in his ability to dramatize the black man's position in America.

For comment on Chester Himes's life and works, see Edward Margolies's *Native Sons: A Critical Study of Twentieth-Century Negro American Authors* (1968); see also Margolies's "The Thrillers of Chester Himes" in *Studies in Black Literature* (June 1970). "My Man Himes" is a lengthy and informative interview found in *Amistad I* (1970), edited by John A. Williams and Charles F. Harris. In addition, see the following works: Robert A. Bone's *The Negro Novel in America* (1958); Arthur P. Davis's *From the Dark Tower* (1974); "Chester Himes" in the *Encyclopedia International* (2nd ed., 1968); and an unpublished M.A. thesis by Archie D. Sanders in Howard University's Moorland-Spingarn Research Center, entitled "The Image of the Negro in Five Novels by Chester Himes" (1965). The "Postscript" to Hime's *A Case of Rape* (1980 and 1984), written by Calvin Hernton, gives some excellent biographical material on Himes.

The following selections are, first, an excerpt from *Third Generation* (1954) and, second, chapter 2 from *The Quality of Hurt* (1972, 1977).

FROM **THIRD GENERATION**

It was late at night when the train pulled into the old stone station. A short black man wearing a black derby hat, dark suit and black, box-toed shoes alighted from a Pullman car. The conductor looked away. The short black man stood at the bottom of the steps and extended his hand to a woman. She wore a linen duster over a pale-blue silk jersey dress, and a large pink hat with feathers. Her face was white and strained; her deep-set eyes fixed in an unseeing stare.

The short black man touched her arm. She looked at him. A smile flickered in her stiff white face, flickered out. The short black man helped her down the steps. The conductor's mouth pursed in a grim, straight line; his face reddened slowly.

A Pullman porter followed, carrying two heavy valises and a woman's straw traveling case. The short black man tipped him and hailed a station porter. Then he took the woman's arm and, preening with self-importance, followed the porter through the huge, dimly lit South Station to a dark side street.

"We'll just go straight to the hotel, honey, unless you want to stop for a bowl of hot milk or a glass of wine," he said.

"No," she said.

He looked at her, undecided, as if to interpret her meaning. She seemed passive, acquiescent. He smiled indulgently and patted her arm.

The porter hailed a horse cab and put the luggage aboard, and the short black man, tipping him generously, helped the woman to enter and climbed in beside her. His actions were slightly erratic. He seemed laboring under great emotion, tautened with excitement.

The old cab went clattering through the drab cobbled streets, past row after row of gray stone houses interlocked and identical as peas, in the dim light like prison walls enclosing the tunnel down which she went to her doom. She couldn't help the distortions of her imagination. She was frightened, lonely, homesick. The man beside her, whom she had married that morning, now seemed a stranger. And this seemed a monstrously wrong thing they were doing.

He sensed her need for reassurance and patted her hand comfortingly. But tremors of his excitement passed down through his touch into her skin and she shuddered.

He'd gone to great pains to arrange everything so there would be no embarrassment or anxiety, and her attitude puzzled and angered him.

"It's a big city," he said. "More people here than in all the state of North Carolina."

She looked out at the depressing sameness of the gloomy streets. "Yes," she replied.

They lapsed into silence . . .

. . . as if she were that kind of woman, she was thinking . . .

. . . she'll be all right, he reassured himself doubtfully . . .

The clop-clop of the horses' hoofs hammered on the silence. The neighborhood changed. Smell of city slums pressed into the cab.

Strident Negroid laughter shattered on the night. The horse cab pulled up before an old dilapidated stone-faced building which carried the faded legend, HOTEL, atop a dingy door.

The short black man alighted and helped the woman down. He paid the driver and struggled with the luggage. She opened the door for him and followed across the dusty foyer to the scarred and littered desk. A few moth-eaten chairs sat here and there in the dim light of turned-down lamps and in one a fat black man sat slumped, asleep and snoring slightly. The smell of damp decay hung in the air.

The short black man put down his luggage and smiled at the woman reassuringly. "It's the best colored hotel in town. I thought it'd be better than to try to . . ." his voice petered out, leaving the thought unspoken.

She didn't answer.

The night clerk came from somewhere out of the shadows, hitching up his suspenders.

"I reserved the bridal suite," the short black man said.

"Yas suh," the night clerk said, and teeth came alive in his face as he slanted a glance at the strained white face of the waiting woman. "Yas *suh!*"

The short black man signed the register and the night clerk picked up the luggage and preceded them up the narrow, bending stairs, his footsteps muffled on the threadbare carpet. The night clerk opened a door at the front of the narrow corridor, entered the darkness and lit a lamp, lit the grate, carried the luggage within, and stood to one side, his big white teeth winking at them like an electric sign. The woman looked at him with a shudder of distaste.

Impulsively the short black man lifted the woman across the threshold. Her body was stiff and unyielding. Gingerly he stood her erect, then turned and tipped the servant.

"Thankee-suh, thankee-suh. Ah knows y'all gonna have uh good time," the night clerk said as if it was a dirty joke.

The short black man quickly closed the door. He turned and went across to the woman, who hadn't moved, and tried to put his arm around her. She pulled away and went over and sat on the moth-eaten sofa. The same smell of decay encountered below was in the room, but here it was dry, mingled with the vague scent of countless assignations. Again the woman shuddered as her thoughts were assailed by a sickening recollection. Once, as a little girl, when cutting through a vulgar street in niggertown, Atlanta, she had heard an obscene reference to her vagina. She had not known then what it had meant, only that it was vulgar and dirty and had filled her with a horrible shame. She had never told anyone, but the feeling of shame had lingered in her thoughts like a drop of pus, poisoning her conception of sex. As she had approached womanhood, she had resolved to make her marriage immaculate. And now it seemed dirtied at the very start by this cloying scent.

The fire sputtered cheerfully in the grate. Beyond was the door into the bedroom. The short black man went and lit the bedroom lamp, then came back and turned down the living-room lamp and went over and sat beside her.

"You go to bed, honey," he said gently. "You must be tired."

She turned and for the first time gave him a grateful smile. "I'm not tired." She groped for words. She spread her hands slightly, inclusively. "It's so squalid."

"It's the best they have," he said defensively.

She arose and started toward the bedroom, then impulsively bent down and kissed him on the lips and, laughing girlishly, went into the bedroom and closed the door. Slowly she undressed before the mirror, glancing furtively, a little ashamedly at her nude figure, letting the realization that she was married come to her.

She was a tiny woman with soft milk-white skin and tiny breasts as round and hard as oranges. Her face was slightly longish and her expression a little austere. Laughing at herself, she slipped into her nightgown and, putting out the light, crawled quickly into bed. She lay looking into the dark, her thoughts pounding, listening to the movements of her husband as he undressed in the other room. The latch clicked, the door slowly opened. She tensed beneath the covers, watching him enter the room.

His short muscular body, seemingly blacker than the night, was silhouetted against the faint luminescence of the doorway. *He's naked!* she thought, horrified as by some startling obscenity. And then as he came toward her, his naked body assumed a sinister aspect, its very blackness the embodiment of evil. She felt a cold shock of terror.

"William," she whimpered.

"I'm right here, honey," he said reassuringly.

She felt his hand pulling back the cover. She could scarcely breathe.

He lay down beside her with infinite gentleness. For a time he lay still. Then his hand moved and he touched her breasts. Her body became instantly taut. She could not analyze her fear of him, but she dreaded the feel of his touch. She was still caught in a state of shock. She feared him as something inhuman.

He turned over and kissed her on the throat. She lay rigid in terror. His hand went down over the smooth satin nightgown and rested on her stomach. Then, abruptly, he reached down and drew the gown up about her waist and his hand searched frantically. His breathing shortened and thickened.

"Don't!" she gasped. "Don't! Not now! Not here! Not in this hovel!" Her arms had stretched out, gripping the sheets in the classic posture of crucifixion.

He scrambled over her. His hot breath licked at her face.

"Don't!" she cried again. "Don't!" And then she screamed in terror, "Light the lamp so I can see you!"

But he had gone out of himself and was panting uncontrollably, unaware, unhearing, his head filled with the roaring fire of his lust. He mounted her like a stud. The penetration chilled her body like death. For an instant the vision of her father's kindly white face with its long silky beard flickered through her consciousness. Then her mind closed against reality as it filled with a sense of outrage; her organs tightened as she stiffened to the pain and degradation.

He struggled brutally and savagely and blindly and then desperately to overcome her, conquer her, win her. She fought to hold herself back. He could not control himself; his muscles jerked with frenzy, the vague pallor of her face floating through the red haze of his vision. When she felt her virginity go bleedingly to this vile and bestial man she hated him.

He threw back the covers, leaped from the bed and lit the lamp, unaware of his reason for doing so. Standing naked, the shadow of his black, knotty body with the muscular bowed legs, darker than the night, he trembled with frustration and dissatisfaction, not knowing what was wrong with him.

She lay rigid in the posture of crucifixion, her stiff white face as still as if in death, looking at him through pools of horror. The sight of his black body was incalculably repulsive. Finally she closed her eyes. She felt as if she had been raped, victimized, debased by an animal. "You beast," she said.

He was shocked out of his daze. He groped for reason, sucking at his lower lip, trying to frame in simple thought the basis for her attitude.

"But, honey, we're married now," he said in a soft, placating voice.

"You rapist," she said through clenched teeth. "You don't know what marriage is."

Had it not been for the prospect of facing the night alone in a strange and terrifying city, she would have left him then. But she realized she had no place to go. Her family wouldn't have welcomed her home, she knew. There would have been a scandal. No one would have understood. In view of all the hardships and travail her parents had experienced during their marriage, they would have

been appalled by her attitude. So she steeled herself to stay with
him.

Vaguely aware that he was losing her, he tried to win her back.
Afterwards, he was infinitely gentle. But she never became recon-
ciled. Each time, she received him with horror and revulsion. Although a child was conceived, she never got over that first night.
She was never able to separate the blackness of his skin from the
brutality of his act; the two were irrevocably bound together in all
her thoughts of him.

After they returned to the college in Georgia where he taught, he
discovered she hated him. She was cold and distant and shuddered
at his touch. He thought it was due to her condition; many women
hated their husbands during pregnancy. To lighten the burden of
housekeeping for her he brought his sister to live with them and do
the housework. Beatrice was a thin, black girl with short, kinky hair.
It was her first time away from home. And she stood in such awe of
her forbidding, white-faced sister-in-law she was painfully self-conscious and stupid. Mrs. Taylor was ill and unhappy and very impatient with the girl. She thought her mean and sullen, and took out
her spleen toward her husband on her.

One day Beatrice burst into tears and begged Professor Taylor to
send her home. He turned on his wife and shouted, "Confound you,
quit picking on my sister!"

"Then get her out of my house," she retorted. "I can't help it if
she feels inferior because she's black."

"Inferior? Because she's black?"

"Yes, that's why she's so sullen and slovenly. It's no crime to be
black." For the first time she had revealed her attitude toward color.

He was shocked. Then suddenly it all came clear, the source of
her unhappiness, the reason she hated him. "Confound it, who do
you think you are, a white woman!" he raved, turning ashy with
fury. "You're a colored woman, too, just like my sister. The only difference is my sister and I aren't bastards." It was an epithet black
people hurled at light-complexioned Negroes, challenging their legit-
imacy.

Her face blanched. "You'll live to see the day you regret that vile
calumny," she vowed.

"Yes, and you'll live to see the day you'll wish you were black as
me," he replied cuttingly.

She pursed her lips and turned away. He knew that he had
scored a hit and felt a sense of triumph. But he little knew how
deeply he had wounded her, nor how relentlessly she'd seek vengeance. Added to the shock and horror of her wedding night, it
completed the destruction of their marriage.

For years she punished him in every conceivable manner. She left his bed and for four years forbade him to touch her. She wasted his salary on expensive luxuries and ran him into debt to embarrass him. All her love and tenderness were spent on her child. She treated her husband with unwavering contempt and made enemies of all his associates. She whipped him with her color at every turn, and whipped all those about him. There came the time when she was not welcome in a single house. Yet her scorn and fury continued unabated. Eventually he was asked to leave the college.

When they came to this college in Missouri, he was beaten. Only then did she feel avenged. After Thomas became of school age she relented and accepted him again as the father of her children. She had resigned herself to marital unhappiness, but now she longed for a family. It was the beginning of her bitter struggle for security, for possessions and prestige and a home, and for opportunities for her children.

By then Professor Taylor had lost all hope and confidence. He refused to share in her plans and seemed only interested in earning his salary. When William was born she became desperate. She tried to fire him with ambition again. But he seemed dead inside. For a time she was sorry for him. She knew she had destroyed him. And she wanted to remake him with her love and devotion. She forgave him for all that he had done to her. When he seemed most despondent and forlorn she responded to him most passionately. Charles came as the result of this tender interlude. She often thought that was the reason she loved him best. All the while she carried him she felt devoted to his father. She thought she was mending him with her love.

When it finally became evident that he was unchanged, her love reverted to hate. She became more disillusioned than ever. She was chagrined as much as infuriated. She hated him for leading her on. All waste, she thought. All her efforts to fire his ambition and spur him on—nothing but waste. Nothing had changed.

Even now, after twelve years, she was still as revolted by him as she had been on their wedding night, she reflected as she went bitterly about her chores. Twelve years of nothing but waste. He had the same type of job he'd had when they were married, with scarcely any more salary. They didn't even own the house in which they lived. Her own parents had owned their home in less than twelve years of freedom, she thought bitterly. But her husband had given up. It filled her with rage and frustration.

Even with all his other faults, including his apishness and carnality, she could respect him if he had kept fighting to advance. She could make allowances if he were a success. But he couldn't even succeed at teaching, for which he had been trained.

None was better educated. He was a fine blacksmith and wheelwright. His students had built some of the best carriages and wagons seen in that city. He could make the most elaborate andirons and coal tongs and gates and lampposts imaginable. He had made jewelry and lamps and dishes from gold and silver. He was an artist at the forge and anvil. There was practically nothing he couldn't forge from metal. Many prominent white people from all over the city commissioned him for jobs. He had made the wrought-iron gate for the governor's mansion, and a pair of ornamental silver bridles for the district attorney. All of the school's metal work was done in his shop. He made cedar chests and brass lockers and all manner of things for the faculty members; he shod their horses and repaired their harnesses. Nor could she accuse him of neglecting his own home in this manner. Their house contained numerous fine pieces that he'd made—marble-topped tables with intricately wrought iron legs, hat racks, stools, fenders, footscrapers, chests, cabinets.

And the children loved him too. He made most of their Christmas toys—little wagons, the exact replicas of large expensive ones, with hickory axles and iron-bound hubs, spoked wheels with iron tires, solid oak beds with removable sides, and seats with real springs. They were the joy and wonder of the neighborhood. And he had made sleds with fine iron runners, rocking horses, and miniature garden tools for them.

No one could deny he had the ability. That was what enraged her most. He could if he tried. But when opportunity knocked he seemed to shrink within himself. Often she wondered if his being black had anything to do with it; if in some way he was racially incapable of doing great things. During moments of despondency she regretted having married a black man. She should have known better. Had she married a man her own color at least she would not have to worry about her children being black.

She had long since concluded that he was not going to get anywhere. And regretting it was just a waste of time, she told herself. But she was tied to him by her children. And she would never let him hold back her children.

For a moment she wondered where it was all going to end. Now she was not so certain of anything. But as she worked, a strange set came over her face and her actions became forceful. It was as if she stood with clenched fists, drawing on her heritage, and said over and over again, "I will! I will! I will!"

FROM **THE QUALITY OF HURT**

I was late getting my boat train ticket and all those for the first boat train had been sold out, and that was the cause of all the trouble. Since I had to take the second boat train I decided I may as well take first class and ride in comfort because I was very tired and my broken toe ached. Being ignorant of Continental trains, I assumed that first class would be roomy and luxurious and provide an opportunity for me to stretch out and have a nap during the ride. My first altercation was with the porter. He wanted five hundred old francs to take my suitcase and tape recorder—I carried my typewriter—from the ship to the nearby train. The franc was then 348 to the dollar, and I thought that was damn exorbitant for what I had heard of the poor starving French. I hadn't come over to France to be an ambassador of good will; I was as argumentative, bad-tempered, and unsympathetic as I had been in the United States. I didn't want any sympathy from the French, but I didn't want to be over-charged by them. However, the porter had his way, chiefly because I would have either had to pay what he charged or carry them myself.

Secondly, the first-class compartment to which I had been assigned didn't give any hope of a nap. Eight of us, myself and seven strangers, most of them either oversized or bundled up so voluminously as to appear so, sat across from each other in a small compartment on faded purple plush seats, so close to those we faced that we had to maneuver sharply for foot space. And all of our hand luggage was packed tightly to the ceiling in overhead racks that didn't inspire any confidence. A fat, talkative South American couple sat next to me, in the center on my side, squashing me into the ice-cold window, and these, I must confess, were the only occupants of that compartment whom I remembered, because they had so much trouble with the douaniers, I suppose. She was wearing a fur coat and had three others of unrecognizable furs stuffed atop their two immense leather suitcases on the rack over their heads. Once the man had to take down both cases and lug them into the passage and open them for inspection, and the woman had to try on each of the fur coats to establish herself as the owner. And then the husband disappeared in the company of two douaniers for a long time and it was assumed he had to open some luggage in the baggage room.

It was about 9 P.M. on April 11 when we left Le Havre. The train plodded through a cold black dark night and I looked out the window at the vague passing silhouettes, with here and there a dimly lit cluster of huddled gray-stone buildings springing from the gloom, and thought of all the wars that had been fought on French soil and the bodies of all the dead that fertilized the darkness and wondered what I had let myself in for. Once a flaming-red neon sign appeared in the black sky reading FORD, and I felt vaguely reassured, although back in the United States there had been nothing in the name to afford me any assurance. After what seemed hours the train pulled into a gloomy cavernous structure that was a smaller, older, grimier likeness of New York City's old Thirty-fifth Street Pennsylvania Railroad Station. According to the French course I had studied in Vermont, a railway porter was called *facteur*. A few porters rushed toward the first-class coaches and passengers began handing them luggage through the windows. While the other passengers in my compartment were taking down their luggage and squeezing into the passage, I pushed down the window and leaned out and shouted, "*Facteur!*" No one paid me the slightest attention. I craned my neck, looking for Richard Wright or a Frenchman carrying a copy of *La Croisade de Lee Gordon* in his arms, but there was no sign of either. Finally, when my coach had cleared out a little, I took down my luggage and carried it out onto the platform in two trips. Still no sign of Dick or Yves Malartic.

My coach was the first coach on the train next to the exit; the train had backed into the station. Crowds waited outside the ticket booths beyond the railing, greeting friends and relatives. I gathered up my luggage, carrying my suitcase and tape recorder in each hand and my portable typewriter under my arm, and followed the others out into the big gloomy station. I didn't see any sign of a waiting room, and I wouldn't have recognized one if I had seen it, so I stood in what I thought was a conspicuous place in the big cavernous lobby, thinking surely that one of my friends would see me. But after a considerable time, in which the train seemed to have completely emptied, I concluded they had met the first train as they had promised and had returned to their respective homes, no doubt expecting me to telephone. I had their telephone numbers but I didn't know how to use the telephone, and I decided it would be simpler if I took a taxi out to Dick's. There was a big neon sign over the side exit reading TAXI. I picked up my luggage and staggered in that direction. There were no taxis. I put my luggage on the sidewalk and waited. It was cold. I buttoned my coat about my neck and turned up the collar. Finally one of the huge old-fashioned box-shaped Renault taxis pulled to the curb beside me and the driver looked in my direction. I walked over and gave him the number in French, "*Quatorze rue Monsieur le Prince.*"

He shrugged. "*Pas compris.*"

I unbuttoned my coat and took out the two letters from Dick and Dan Levin I had placed in my inside pocket for just such an emergency and pointed to the letterhead of Dick's letter. His face lit up. "*Ah, m'suh luh Prance.*" He waited patiently while I loaded my luggage into the back seat, which seemed about the size of the railway compartment I had just quit.

By then it must have been midnight. The lighting seemed abnormally dim for a big city and there was scarcely a sign of life on the streets. My taxi was the only car moving. When we passed through the Louvre in the black dark, I though we were entering a walled city.

"*Louvre,*" the driver threw over his shoulder as the big hearselike taxi curved perilously on cobblestones. I saw the vague silhouette of what seemed like an ancient fortress.

"*Ah oui,*" I said.

After traversing a succession of dark narrow streets that could have been taken from the Hollywood film of *The Hunchback of Notre Dame,* we passed the first lighted and inhabited café I had seen and a short distance further drew up before the huge green carriage doors of a low brick building with a single lighted window on the fourth floor. I gave the driver a thousand-franc note and he gave me two dirty one hundreds in return, of which I gave him one hundred for a tip and he sat patiently and watched me struggle with my luggage. When I had dragged it before the doors across the wet sidewalk, I looked about for a pedestrian entrance. Fortunately the driver had remained on hand for a moment to see what I would do next, for with a great performance he condescended to get from his cab and cross the sidewalk to press the button that released the lock on the carriage doors, which, it became suddenly apparent, were the only doors. Through the crack I had a glimpse of a black dark cavern beyond. With an air of strained patience the driver reached inside and pressed the light switch and a cobblestone carriageway, flanked by a paved sidewalk leading back to wide curved stairs on one side, sprang into view. I saluted the driver and dragged my luggage inside. While looking about for a directory of tenants, I heard the door click locked behind me. I felt locked in a prison and suffered a brief moment of panic, but I had taken a number of my tranquilizers and the panic vanished almost instantly. I realized that I must climb the stairs until I found a door bearing Dick's nameplate. The wall opposite the staircase contained only dark, curtained glass windows of what might have been a café closed for the night.

I picked up my luggage as best I could and started up the stairs. I hadn't progressed more than a few steps before the lights went out. I cursed and lowered my luggage onto the stairs and searched for my lighter. I was groping my way back toward the switch beside the entrance, holding the lighter before me like a torch, when a light appeared suddenly behind the curtained windows and a monster charged forth, the likes of which I had never seen. She looked like some prehistoric species of the human race; obviously female, judging from the huge drooping breasts topping a squarish big-hipped body beneath a flagging purple robe and the things in her hair, and she seemed in a rage. My first impulse was to run, but the door was closed and locked and I couldn't find out how to open it before she was upon me. I began reaching desperately for my letter from Dick, hoping she wouldn't mistake the gesture, and held it before her face.

"*Allez!*" she screamed. "*Allez! Allez! Vite! Vite! Vite!*"

I gathered the general meaning but I had then begun to get angry myself and I shouted at her in English that Mister Wright was expecting me. She pressed the button that unlocked the door and attempted to push me onto the sidewalk. I resisted and for a moment we tussled in the carriageway and the sour rancid smell of a sweaty body and unwashed hair nauseated me. "*Mes bagages!*" I had the presence of mind to shout. "*Mes bagages!*"

I noticed another vague shape behind the curtained door as she rushed back to the stairway, swept up my three pieces of luggage as though they had no weight, and rushed back to the entrance and flung them onto the sidewalk. As I heard my tape recorder and typewriter hitting the pavement, I suffered a moment of fury. She didn't know what she was doing. If she had been in Harlem, throwing a soul brother's fine possessions around like that, she'd have gotten her head cut off. But I didn't resist when she pushed me out behind them and slammed and locked the door. I felt as though I had inadvertently entered the cage of a raving lunatic. Disconsolately I gathered up my luggage once again and headed down the street in the direction of the one lighted café. I discovered it was crammed full of drunken Americans. I had a distinct and sudden conviction that I was having a nightmare.

Someone told me in a southern United States accent that I might find a taxi around the corner a half block away. I carried my luggage to a sign that read TAXIS, and after standing in the dark and the cold for another half hour one of those huge hearselike taxis pulled up and I told him to take me back to the Gare Saint-Lazare.

I discovered the waiting room that time. It was called *salle d'attente, première classe.* But it looked so dark, gloomy, and unattended that I didn't care to use it, and in fact I wasn't certain it was open for use, so I stood in the now almost deserted lobby, surrounded by my luggage, hoping against hope that some English-speaking station official might notice my predicament and offer assistance. But the few uniformed personnel who passed didn't even look about at my tentative "Pardon me, sir," but hurried on as though the open arms of Danielle Darrieux awaited them, and if any gendarmes were about they watched over me unseen. But shortly a number of prostitutes gathered, buzzing about me like green flies. They came and went in a silent spectacle which might have been entitled *The Night the Whores of Saint-Lazare Came Out to Tempt le Nègre de New York*, but there was one in bare legs and a belted coat who stood her ground, waiting for the others to clear off perhaps, and might have even won me by her persistence until I remembered the letter from Dan Levin giving me the name of Hôtel de la Vigne, which was run by a retired American Army officer, where I could apply for a room in an emergency. I had spent all of my French money and only had a few American dollar bills, but somehow I managed to reach an agreement with the last taxi driver left, an old man in the smallest car that I had ever seen—I later learned it was the smallest Citroën ever made—with a dog huddled up beside him, to take me for a dollar, giving him the letter to read the address. He took me there and left me in the taxi while he went in to ask if they had a room. After a moment he returned, beaming, and helped me in with my luggage. The housekeeper, who had been awakened, said in fluent English that the taxi fare was five hundred francs. I told her I didn't have any French money but I was a friend of Mr. Richard Wright and she could trust me, pulling Dick's letter from my pocket to substantiate my claim.

"Oh, you're Mr. Chester Himes," she said. "Mr. Wright has reserved a room for tonight for you."

It was all I could do to keep down the hysterics. She paid the taxi driver and took me to my room. As it didn't have a telephone, I decided to postpone calling Dick until morning. After drinking the half pint of whiskey I had left, I climbed into the big cold double bed and went to sleep.

In the meantime Dick and Malartic had met the first train, and, positively ascertaining I was not aboard, had retired to a café across the street on rue Saint-Lazare and had awaited the second. Stationing themselves at either end of the second-class coaches on the second train so as not to miss me, they waited. But as I was in the first-class section, in the first coach, I had alighted unseen by them, while they had still been looking for me at the other end of the train. I had grown impatient in a perfectly natural American fashion and had taken a taxi to his house. Dick's youngest daughter, Rachel, had been ill, and not being aware that I would appear alone, Dick had left instructions with the concierge not to let anyone up to his apartment. Dick was alarmed by my disappearance, and Yves Malartic was not the kind of Frenchman to spoil any American's good alarm, and had filled him with gruesome accounts of persons who had been known to disappear in the Paris *gares* and had not been found until months, even years, afterward, destitute and penniless if they were men, or sold into white slavery somewhere in North Africa if they were women.

As all his friends knew, Dick had an excitable temperament and was given to such self-indulgent exaggeration that the buzzing of a blowfly could range like a typhoon in his imagination. He rushed back to Ellen in a state of extreme concern and declared that something dreadful must have happened to me for I had completely disappeared and he must notify the police at once. Ellen took the more mundane view that some woman lay at the center of the mystery and cautioned him against undue haste lest the unraveling cause great embarrassment. At just about that time Alva telephoned from some place in Belgium, instantly justifying Ellen's suspicions, to ask if I had arrived. Ellen said accusingly that I seemed to have disappeared and asked if she could shed any light on the mystery. No doubt if Ellen could have read Alva's mind, she would have discovered they shared the same suspicions, but Alva expressed a concern equal to Dick's. Then Ellen asked the question for which Alva never forgave her, "Was Chester drunk?"

Early next morning I was awakened by a hammering on the door. Dick had stopped by on his way to the police to cancel the reservation until further notice, and the proprietor had informed him that I was upstairs in the room he had reserved for me sleeping. I could see he was alive with curiosity; he had always been extremely curious about me. He knew of my prison record and he had known Jean, and he suspected I had lived a life of wild and raging fury. I think I am one of the tamest men he ever knew, but he never came to know me well enough to know this. After we had sorted out the mixup, he invited me to lunch, saying Ollie Harrington would be there, and for some reason seemed called upon to apologize for Ollie's not coming down to the station the night before to pick me up in his car. But I saw no reason why Ollie should have felt obligated, or that Dick should have felt he thought so, for I didn't know Ollie that well. I had seen him in officer's uniform around Harlem at the end of the war, always in the company of high-society blacks whom I had met during the short time I lived with my cousin Henry Moon and his wife Molly. Most of the time Ollie had been escorting his blond wife, who I thought was Norwegian, and whom I remember best for her thick ankles and unshapely legs.

I dressed and went with Dick down the street to the Café Monaco for a French breakfast (*petit-déjeuner*) of chicory-tasting coffee

and a croissant; it was the café I had seen the night before filled
with drunken Americans, but in the morning it was filled only with
hung-over Americans. Dick greeted everyone with boisterous condescension; it was obvious he was the king thereabouts. His apartment
was only half a block up the street, which was adjacent to the street
of my hotel, and at that time the Café Monaco was the most notorious hangout for Americans in the Latin Quarter, and naturally that
entire section between the Odéon and Place de l'Odéon was a honeycomb of brothels, bistros, caves, and the favorite cafés of homosexuals, male and female. Later I learned that it was the custom of
my fellow countrymen to sleep with a French prostitute the first
night of their arrival and spend the following week or two trying to
get cured of VD. I seemed to have been one of the few exceptions;
but I noticed that all the girls, both amateur and professional, having
their morning coffee, were giving me the once-over, trying to assess
whether I was a man worthy of their attention or a fairy trying to
latch onto Dick.

Dick expected a gathering of our soul brother compatriots, all of
whom knew I was to arrive the night before, but not one of them
appeared, an eccentricity which I was later to learn was the natural
reaction of the envious and jealous American blacks who lived in
Paris—or anywhere else in Europe, for that matter. They did not
want any arriving brother to get the idea they thought he was important.

So we spent the remainder of the morning looking for a permanent hotel room for me—a chore for which Dick had expected help
from the other brothers. Dick was very anxious for me to get my
trunk from customs so he could get his copies of *The Outsider*. Before noon we had found a front room on the second floor of the
Hôtel Scandinavie, on the rue de Tournon, across from the Café
Tournon, a favorite hangout for Jewish war refugees, which was also
patronized by some of the brothers.

Ollie had arrived by the time we got back to his house for lunch,
and explanations were in order. I was surprised to find Ellen had
become thin and blond with lots of make-up and a harried, dissatisfied look. One of the first things she said to me was that she and
Dick had gone completely French. I noticed Dick look sort of sheepish but he offered no comment, and Ollie looked wise and indulgent
and his eyes twinkled knowingly. I didn't know what to say, so I
said nothing.

The lunch consisted of spaghetti and meatballs, which didn't
seem very French to me, and Ellen told me of Alva's call and asked
me who she was and I said I would call her back without answering

her question. I scarcely recognized Ollie—he had grown stout, and looked more like a Balkan character out of an Eric Ambler spy story in his neat salt-and-pepper tweed than a black refugee from the United States. In a conversational lull, I told Dick I had seen the film of *Native Son*, for which he had written the screenplay, co-produced, and acted the role of Bigger Thomas; and that when I had left it was showing in a chain of twenty or more neighborhood theaters. He immediately brightened up and rubbed his hands jubilantly, and said maybe he would get his money back. He confessed he had spent more than a year in its making and had initially lost a great deal of money in the production. Then his agent called and I could hear him talking about an advance from Gallimard for one of his books, which they were publishing. At the same time Ellen was talking away about the great expense of having her hair dyed weekly and she had learned to do it with a rinse of Clorox, which served just as well. I could believe the Clorox part, anyway. Then when Dick returned, they both asked if I would like to go to a writers' colony in La Ciotat, on the Mediterranean sea, run by a friend of theirs named Daniel Guerin; he was quite interested in having me as one of their guests. I said I'd have to think it over.

Julia and Rachel came in to say hello. I remembered Julia as a tiny tot in New York, but she had grown to be the spit and image of her father. But I had never seen Rachel before; she was like a dark-blond doll and spoiled, and it was immediately apparent that she was her father's pet.

When Ollie left, Ellen asked me if I wanted to call Alva from there—she had the number—but I thanked her and said I would call later. I have always abhorred being overhead in my love talk.

Dick helped me move my luggage to the Hôtel Scandinavie and he was so impatient for me to get my trunk that I went with him to get his car from the garage where it was being repaired. He had taken a big American Oldsmobile with him to France and found it terribly difficult to drive through the old narrow streets of the Latin Quarter. But what made him give it up was a typical traffic incident. The Parisian police were impatient with big American cars blocking traffic in the congested centers, and once when circling on the Place de la Concorde, Dick had stopped to let the traffic open up ahead of him. However, there was a narrow space in the congested cars, and the traffic cop was impatient for him to move his car to make room for traffic flowing in another direction. He waved Dick forward into the narrow space ahead. Dick hesitated; it did not seem there was space for his wide Olds. The cop bore down on him gesturing to him to proceed, shouting, "*Vite! Vite! Allez-y!*"

Dick stepped on the accelerator and the big car with its hydro-matic drive leaped forward into the narrow opening and crushed the fenders on both sides and on each side of the adjoining cars.

The traffic cop shook his head sadly and said, "Tch! Tch! Tch!"

So Dick had sold his Olds and bought a reconditioned Citroën *traction avant*. But late one night, several days before I had arrived, turning a corner into a dark narrow street he had hit a man on a bicycle and had knocked him a number of yards through the air and run over his bicycle. His insurance was paying all the costs; fortunately the man had not been killed, but at that time he was still in the hospital, and Dick's car had been in the garage.

But it had been repaired and as it was getting late in the day and nearing the time customs would close, we drove straight from the garage to the customs shed in the Gare Saint-Lazare. It was not until we were standing at the counter and I had presented my baggage check that I discovered that I had left my trunk keys in my suitcase at the hotel. There was insufficient time for us to return for them and get back before customs closed, and the douanier was approaching from the shed with my big green wardrobe trunk with its impregnable lock on a handcart.

Dick explained that I had lost my key but I would swear there was nothing in the trunk for me to declare. One could see the douanier was sympathetic, but it was such a big trunk and weighed more than a hundred kilos, which is a lot of trunk for France, and he wasn't much more than a porter himself, so he couldn't permit it to pass. Dick said that he would send for a locksmith to open the trunk and that I would gladly pay for it; and in desperation he said they could pry the trunk open with a crowbar. I wasn't having my good trunk pried open with a crowbar, or even opened by a locksmith, for all Dick's books, and he knew damn well I wasn't, but I didn't say anything. The douanier said he'd have to ask his superior and went and fetched him from his office in the rear. Then Dick began putting on his act. Beside us on the counter were several big cartons of Kleenex and one of toilet tissue, still in the factory packing, being collected by a uniformed chauffeur apparently from the United States Embassy. Dick pointed to the cartons and said to the chief douanier in his bad French, "They can't even wipe their ass on French paper." There was a great animosity against the remnants of the United States occupation forces still stationed in and about Paris at the time, and signs were scribbled on every wall in the Latin Quarter reading: "U.S. GO HOME."

The chief douanier laughed at Dick's crack and passed my trunk unopened. For which I was damn grateful, for I had my own share of American toiletries, which Dick himself had suggested I bring, including Kleenex, American soap, toothpaste, toilet paper, etc.

The trunk fitted on the back seat in Dick's car, which was an *onze chevaux*, much to my surprise, for the Citroën, although one of the biggest and fastest cars of France, looked very small in comparison to the American land cruisers of that year. Together, blowing and panting, we got it up to my second-floor hotel room. Before we could get our breath, Dick insisted on my opening it so he could get his books, and without stopping for another thing, he took me through the dark narrow streets (it was already black dark by that time) to the English Book Store, run by a young blond Frenchwoman named Gaite, for her to put on display in her window. I noticed at the time that she paid far more attention to me as a male than to Dick's valued copies of *The Outsider*, but nevertheless the three of us stood outside the shop on the sidewalk for the next half hour listening to Dick discuss how the books could be displayed to their best advantage. Gaite spoke English, and was reputed to have had an immoderate curiosity about black writers, although I was never able to verify this; at first I was unable to find my way back to her store and later I didn't have time.

I ate alone that first night, not having yet met any of the other brothers, and later Dick took me to a nightclub down the street from him called La Romance, run by a Frenchwoman in her fifties with dyed red hair who was acquainted with him, as was everyone in the Latin Quarter, and perhaps in all of Paris, and who dominated the conversation, declaring loudly in broken English how much more destructive and uncouth and undisciplined and bestial the United States Army had been than the Nazis. "If the war had lasted, the Americans would have burned Paris to the ground!" she exclaimed.

I soon tired of her bullshit and said good night to Dick and went wandering off alone and was soon lost among the myriad of bistros and students on the boulevard Saint Michel and day was breaking before I found my way home.

Thereafter I found my first week in Paris exceedingly dull. I had dinner with Yves Malartic and his wife Yvonne and about a dozen of his acquaintances, including a couple of editors, an opera singer and her lover, and several others whose chief aim in life seemed to belittle Americans. I met them by appointment at the Deux Magots on Saint-Germain-des-Prés, looking elegant, I thought, in my Oxford blue suit, black shoes, and gray burberry (for it was cold), and greeted Yves, "Je suis très content de vous avoir," trying out my French. Yves was a little man, slightly over five feet, but we had corresponded a great deal while he had been translating *Lonely Crusade* and he was very friendly, but upon hearing my carefully rehearsed speech he looked puzzled and said, "Himes, you must forgive an uncultured Frenchman such as myself, but I do not understand English so well." I didn't try my French any more that night.

We all went to a restaurant nearby and I was presented with a menu written in French script, of which I did not understand a single thing, so I let Yves order for me. A young American white man sitting across the aisle from us said, "It's written in English on the back," but I didn't turn it over for fear of spoiling the obvious joke.

For a time they made fun of the existentialists, including *le roi* Sartre and *le dauphin* Camus; and then they started making fun of me in a sly fashion. First they started on my cigarette lighter, a nine-dollar stainless-steel Dunhill I had bought in New York. I told them it was English. Then they said I had greeted them in such strange English; did all *américains noires* speak such English? I said I had thought I was speaking French. At that they thawed and began on the food. They said the steak we had eaten had been horseflesh; had I ever eaten horseflesh before? I said in Harlem we not only ate horseflesh but ate hamburgers made of cat and stews made of dog, and that I had read that during the French Revolution the Parisians had eaten ragout made of rat. It was all in good fun and we parted on good terms and I promised to visit Yves soon. He lived on the seventh and top floor of a walkup on rue Montparnasse, near the corner of Boulevard Montparnasse, and advised that if I should call, it would be best to stand on the sidewalk across the street and shout up to him before attempting to climb nine flights of stairs.

I spent some afternoons at the Café Monaco outside on the terrace, which caught the sun when it shone, but it was mostly cold and rainy that April. I saw Ollie there and some of the other soul brothers, but I had little to say to them for somehow we didn't speak the same language and we weren't interested in the same women; I never visited any of them in their hotels or wherever they lived, and the most I knew of any of them except Dick was from chatting a few moments about nonsense in cafés. One day Dick asked me if I knew William Gardner Smith. I knew of William Gardner Smith—his book *The Last of the Conquerors* had been advertised across the front cover of the Signet edition of *If He Hollers Let Him Go*, much to my displeasure—and I said I would like to meet him. Dick took me over to the Café Tournon, across the street from my hotel, and introduced me to a moderately tall, pleasant looking brown-skinned young man who talked very rapidly in choppy, broken sentences, and said how glad he was to meet me, but it was very obvious that he and Dick did not like each other at all. *The Last of the Conquerors* had not been published in France, and I don't think it ever was, I don't know why; I think it is a fine book and compares favorably with Hemingway's *A Farewell to Arms*, to which it is very similar, both being intense love stories about very young people under conditions of war, and both giving the impression of being written by very young people with strong and subtle talents. But Bill had written another book of which I had not heard, *Anger at Innocence*, which had been selected by a book club in France, and since none of Dick's books had ever received that doubtful distinction, I think Bill felt a little superior about the matter, which was very normal for one so young, and he was young. Youth was the most outstanding characteristic of William Gardner Smith—youth and a naïveté.

One day, very much to my surprise, I received a note at my hotel from a French journalist named Annie Brierre, asking if I would care to come to her house to be interviewed for the newspaper *France-U.S.A.*, giving an address in Square du Roule. It was a private square not far from the Etoile, and Mme. Brierre's apartment was what I had always thought the apartments of the French minor aristocracy would be like. She was a big-boned woman in her fifties with the imposingly strong face and big nose of the old French, but somehow, looking even more masculine than many men, and with a straightforward, unaffected manner, she gave the impression of being entirely feminine.

Every morning either Dick or Ellen came by the hotel between seven and eight and got me out of bed so we could go across to the Café Tournon and have coffee. I had always been attracted to Ellen, ever since I had first met her in 1944, when she had been a plump, pleasant, brown-haired young woman with a very sweet disposition. I often imagined she felt some vague attraction for me also. But I couldn't understand why Dick felt called upon to come around so early, unless he wanted to beat Ellen there, which of course was silly, for I respected Dick more than anyone else I knew and would certainly never have done anything to embarrass him. At that time the Scandinavie was filled with homosexuals and a large number of young American girls who wished to cram a lifetime of sexual escapades into the short time they would have before they had to return home and marry. Dick once said, "Chester, when it gets warm these American girls go down the street, flinging open their arms, and cry, 'Take me! Take me! I'm young and good in bed.' " As I have said before, Dick always exaggerated. But anyway, the residents in the hotel began to wonder what sort of arrangement we had—were Dick and I lovers, or Ellen and me, or did they take turns with me?

But generally I wouldn't see them again for the rest of the day. Ellen had the supervising of the household chores—they had a maid, of course—and tending to Rachel, and taking Julia back and forth to school, as is required of French mothers. So I spent most of my days at the Café Monaco and my nights at the Café Tournon. I met the black painter Walter Coleman at the Monaco. He was living with a short, hefty, redheaded, loudmouthed Texan girl at that time; and they would have knock-down-drag-out fights on occasion. She would stand up to him and fight like a man, and when they started cursing each other, "motherfucking" each other, you couldn't tell the white woman from Texas from the black man from Baltimore. But Walter had a highly volatile and rather likable personality and he and his girl began coming around to my room selling me bottles of gin and whiskey at half the price they cost in the stores: I never learned what they paid for them or how they got them.

I met other soul brothers: Ish Kelly, whom Dick wrote about in his book *The Long Dream*, calling him Fish Belly; Mercer Cook's son, who was attending the Sorbonne; Dr. E. Franklin Frazier, who was living in Paris at the time as head of the Mutual Security Agency and I visited him and his wife Marie, whom I had known from the period I lived with Henry and Molly Moon in Harlem. I had always liked Dr. Frazier and Marie; he was an extraordinary raconteur, and Marie also had a sharp sense of humor. She was a large, formidable-looking woman, with a face like an eagle's, and people who didn't know her thought she had a fierce temper. She told me that she always rode in the first-class coaches of the Paris subway on second-class tickets, and when the conductors asked her to move back into second class she would look at them fiercely and say in English, "I don't speak French." They would shrug and move off. This worked excellently until one day when she had said to the conductor, "I don't speak French," a kindly white American woman sitting next to her volunteered, "Oh, I'll translate for you. I speak English." Marie glared at the woman and said, "I don't speak English either."

I met a young black couple named Hines at their house who had worked for some United States government agency in Monrovia, Liberia, and another single girl, Ruth, who had worked for the embassy in Monrovia. Ruth had been transferred to the Paris embassy as a secretary while the Hineses were on their way home. She was very kind to me, she took me to Leroy and Gaby Haynes' barbecue restaurant on rue Manuel for the first time, and bought whiskey from the embassy commissary for me at $1.65 per bottle for the finest scotch and $1.75 per bottle for the famous American bourbons, and cartons of my favorite cigarettes, Lucky Strikes, for nine cents a pack. She had a studio on the rez-de-chaussée of a nice apartment house up the hill from Place du Trocadero, equipped with all the modern conveniences—bath, built-in closets, etc. The proprietor had had it built for his daughter, who had gone off to live in Mexico. I used to visit her to pick up the whiskey and cigarettes and take baths, but she never let me make love to her. Black women can say no and mean it with such good humor that you aren't offended and will remain friends.

And then one night at the Café Tournon, in his abrupt jerky way, Bill Smith asked me if I wanted to take a walk down to the Seine with him. I said all right, and a big-busted redheaded girl named Rory Calhoun said she'd come along with us. I got to looking at Rory's breasts, aimed at me like howitzers, and suggested to Bill that he could leave us. Bill said he couldn't do that, she was married to a Dutch boy who was a good friend of his. Rory looked from one to the other of us and grinned like an idiot.

All Bill wanted was to borrow twenty-five hundred francs to go to Ringside, the jazz joint in fashion at that time which had become famous from the singing of Eartha Kitt and the visits of Ava Gardner. I went along with Bill, but nothing interesting happened that night and I got cornered by a middle-aged black couple who wanted to discuss the race problem and I left. The joint is called the Blue Note now, famous for Bud Powell and Kenny Clarke.

I didn't know about the American Hospital at the time, and Dick had recommended a doctor in the quarter—J. Schiller, I think his name was—to treat my broken toe. Dr. Schiller had several spayed Siamese cats in his dreary dark apartment where his office was located, and I held them responsible for the nauseating odor of his office until I learned he was the VD specialist of the quarter. He injected my toe with cortisone and gave me a shot of penicillin, after which I could scarcely walk at all.

I had only been in Paris for one week when Vandi arrived. She had booked into the Hôtel Saints-Pères on rue des Saints-Pères, off the boulevard Saint-Germain, and I returned to my hotel to find her telegram from the ship just about the time she arrived, "COME QUICKLY: FOR YOU KNOW WHAT . . ." She was in her bath when I got to the hotel and I waited for her in the garden, which had by then been opened. She was just the same; she demanded that we first go to my hotel and go to bed. It was afternoon, but I had learned by then that that was the correct time for extracurricular assignations in Paris. Afterward she said my body was just like the statues in the Tuileries, and I wondered suddenly what had happened to the men in New York during the short time since I had left.

She was there for a week and spent most of her leisure time with me—chiefly, I think, because she didn't feel like breaking in a new lover. We were more affectionate than we had been at any time. I found it amusing the way American women instantly dropped all their sexual inhibitions on arriving in Paris. I took her by Dick and Ellen's—she had known them both from her days with the Rosenwald Foundation—and we found Dick typing industriously on his novel, which was later published as *Savage Holiday*, on the paper he had asked me to bring. Dick told us that the plot for the story had come to him suddenly several months previously when he had been in bed with a high fever. Later, when he had let me read the finished manuscript, I believed him. One morning I went and climbed the nine flights of stairs to Yves Malartic's penthouse to fetch him and Yvonne to join Vandi and me for petit-déjeuner. It was a lovely little place with huge French windows letting out on small terraces back and front, offering a breathtaking view of practically all of Paris; but, as is customary with these pleasant little top-floor rooms constructed primarily for the maids, it had no bath, and the "water closet" was in the corridor shared by the adjoining apartment.

⌾✕⌾

I never ceased to regard Dick's apartment with envy and amazement. It occupied the entire fourth floor of the building, and to me it appeared sumptuously furnished. The first room to the right of the entrance foyer was his book-lined study, with two large modernistic paintings, dozens of copies of his own books, several typewriters, his desk, a tape recorder, and overstuffed leather armchairs—all the paraphernalia of a working writer. It was the inner sanctum to which only selected visitors were ever invited. Beyond it were the dining room, the living room, the master bedroom, and at the back the bath, all overlooking the street. On the other side were a storeroom, pantry, kitchen, and the children's bedroom and nursery—eight rooms, exclusive of the bath and water closets. For this he was paying about thirty-five dollars a month for taxes and upkeep on an arrangement whereby he had put up a down payment against the price of the apartment which would become his in the course of time. But he had made many expensive improvements, including central heating and a hot water system, which was then considered a luxury in Paris houses.

Among the paintings he had acquired were a number by an artist who was then becoming fashionable in art circles. One day when Dick and I were sitting on the terrace of the Deux Magots, Mrs. Putnam came over to invite us to a cocktail party at the atelier of this artist the following Sunday afternoon. Dick phoned me right after lunch that Sunday, saying he was alone, and asked me to come over and pass the time until the cocktail party. While we were sitting in his study, the doorbell rang and he ushered in a surprise visitor, a tall, slender, blond man, whom he introduced as Mr. Schine. At that time David Schine and Roy Cohn were the investigators for the Senate committee on un-American activities, headed by Senator Joe McCarthy. Schine was gathering information about a man named Jarrel, who had been appointed to a position in the State Department, and he wanted Dick to give a statement that Jarrel had been a member of the John Walter Reed Club in Chicago at the same time as himself. Dick said that he himself had never been a member of the club, that he did not know any of the members, and that he did not remember ever meeting anyone named Jarrel. Schine seemed infuriated by Dick's reply, and he told Dick how he and Cohn pressured Langston Hughes into stating before the committee that he regretted some of his un-American political activities and writings. Suddenly Dick asked Schine if he had read my novel, *Lonely Crusade*. Schine said he had never heard of me or my book. Dick advised him to read it. After advising Dick to refresh his memory about Jarrel, Schine left. Afterward Dick said, "That stupid son of a bitch thinks he can threaten me; I'll never testify. I've written everything I have to say about my communist affiliations." I had nothing to say.

Later, as we were preparing to leave for the party, the telephone rang. When Dick returned from answering it, he wore that look of malicious satisfaction which his close friends had come to know so well. He asked if I knew James Baldwin. I said no, but I had heard a great deal about him from an old college friend named Jesse Jackson who some years ago had left his wife and daughter in Columbus, Ohio, and had gone to live in Greenwich Village, as the protégé of a German Jewish refugee couple, to write children's books. Jesse had praised Baldwin as a genius. And I had read a review of *Lonely Crusade* that Baldwin had published in the Socialist Party's newspaper, the *New Leader*, but I had never met him.

Dick said that he had been instrumental in getting Baldwin an award for eighteen hundred dollars and a renewal for nine hundred from Harper & Brothers to enable him to write his first novel, which was eventually rejected by Harper's editor-in-chief, Edward Aswell, Dick's editor. The book had finally been published by Beacon Press as *Go Tell It on the Mountain*. He said Baldwin had "repaid his generosity" by "attacking him" in a number of published articles, the most recent of which had appeared in a new Ford Foundation quarterly called *New Directions*, if memory serves me right. I admitted having read the article, which had been published back to back with an article by a young Negro writer named Richard Gibson, in which I was mentioned derogatorily. "Now Baldwin has the nerve to call me to borrow five thousand francs (ten dollars)," he said gleefully.

He had made an appointment to meet him at the Deux Magots, and insisted that I go with him. I remember thinking at the time that he sounded as though he wanted a witness. I reminded him of our invitation to the cocktail party, but he had no intention of missing this confrontation with Baldwin. He persuaded me to call Mrs. Putnam and tell her we were held up by some changes he was making in his new manuscript, which had to be in the mail in the morning, and wouldn't be able to leave the house.

Then we hurried to the Deux Magots and found Baldwin waiting for us at a table on the terrace across from the Église Saint-Germain. I was somewhat surprised to find Baldwin a small, intense young man of great excitability. Dick sat down in lordly fashion and started right off needling Baldwin, who defended himself with such intensity that he stammered, his body trembled, and his face quivered. I sat and looked from one to the other, Dick playing the fat cat and forcing Baldwin into the role of the quivering mouse. It wasn't particularly funny, but then Dick wasn't a funny man. I never found it easy to laugh with Dick; it was far easier to laugh at him on occasion. Dick accused Baldwin of showing his gratitude for all he had done for him by his scurrilous attacks. Baldwin defended himself by saying that Dick had written his story and hadn't left him, or any other American black writer, anything to write about. I confess at this point they lost me. Then suddenly a large group of people approached us. I looked up and was startled to find Mrs. Putnam among them. They turned out to be the artist and his wife who had given the cocktail party and several of their guests. I started off saying we had just that moment finished work, but Dick and Baldwin kept on going at one another and no one paid me any attention. It wasn't long before Mrs. Putnam and all of her friends had gotten to the heart of the argument and taken sides. All of the women and the majority of the men, including the artist, took Baldwin's side— chiefly, I think, because he looked so small and intense and vulnerable and Dick appeared so secure and condescending and cruel. But in the course of time they left us to go to dinner, and still Baldwin and Dick carried on while I sat and watched the people come and go. Later we went down the boulevard to a Martiniquan café. It had grown late, close to midnight, and we had not eaten, but still the discussion went on. It seemed that Baldwin was wearing Dick down and I was getting quite drunk. The last I remember before I left them at it was Baldwin saying, "The sons must slay their fathers." At the time I though he had taken leave of his senses, but in recent years I've come to better understand what he meant. Much later, while traveling in Crete, I read Mary Renault's book *The King Must Die*, and I was reminded of Baldwin's remark that night, "The sons must slay their fathers." And I realized suddenly that he was right. On the American literary scene, the powers that be have never admitted but one black at a time into the arena of fame, and to gain the coveted admission, the young writer must unseat the reigning diety. It's a pity but a reality as well.

In time I came to realize that Dick had been correct in accusing so many various people of attacking him: they *were* attacking him. American blacks must always get ahead in American society by walking over each other.

But afterward I used to tease Dick by referring to Baldwin as his son.

Dorothy West

(1912–   )

NOVELIST, JOURNALIST, founder-editor of literary magazines, and graduate of the Harlem Renaissance, Dorothy West, after a varied and exciting career, now lives quietly on Martha's Vineyard. During her earlier years in New York she was a friend and associate of many of that outstanding group of writers and artists who were a part of the New Negro Movement (the Harlem Renaissance), among them: Hughes, Cullen, Thurman, Barthe, Hurston, and the Robesons. To these nationally known writers and artists, practically all of them older, she was the talented, charming ingenuous "child" from Boston; and they loved and admired her.

Born in Boston in 1912, the daughter of a successful middle class family, she grew up a typical Bostonian (a Negro Brahmin), living on Brookline Avenue and attending Girls Latin School. As a young girl, she joined the Saturday Evening Quill Club, a literary club founded in 1925 by twenty black men and women interested in writing. Two of Dorothy West's short stories appeared in the *Annuals* of this group, one in the first issue (1928), another in the 1929 second *Annual*. Also in 1929, she won a prize in the *Opportunity* Contest for that year. She was only seventeen at the time.

For three months in 1929 (a fruitful year for her), she was in London as an extra in the cast of *Porgy*. In 1932 she became one of a group of blacks who went on a wild-goose-chase to Russia to make a film. Her father died while she was abroad; she returned to Boston and eventually went to New York, where for two years she worked in the public welfare department of that city.

Believing that a new magazine was needed to take up the unfinished business of the Harlem Renaissance, West financed, founded, and edited a literary journal called *Challenge*. She received contributions to the new magazine from several of her literary friends—James Weldon Johnson, Claude McKay, Zora Neale Hurston, Countee Cullen, and others. She wrote under the pseudonym, Mary Christopher. Although Wallace Thurman harshly criticized the project, calling it "schoolgirlish," Mrs. West published by 1937 five issues of *Challenge*.

With her friend, Marian Minus, as co-editor, she then published *New Challenge*. Among the writers appearing in this venture were Richard Wright, Alain Locke, Frank Marshall Davis, Sterling A. Brown, and Margaret Walker, appearing in print for the first time. According to Adelaide Cromwell (see bibliography), West gave up *New Challenge* because some of her community-influenced associates wished to control the journal. West then joined the Writers Project of WPA, and in the late sixties moved to Martha's Vineyard to work for the *Vineyard Gazette* and to write *The Living is Easy*.

The Living is Easy is not an outstanding novel; its plot is too melo-dramatic; its characters are not convincing. It is hard to conceive of a real life woman as money-grabbing, as domineering, and as consistently chur-lish as Cleo; it is equally as hard to conceive of a man as patient, as long-suffering, and as limited as Bart Judson. Family allegiance among southern blacks has always been strong, but in this work West exaggerates it beyond credibility. And there are other stylistic and structural shortcomings. The novel, however, is highly readable; and it gives, among other things, an inside view of life among middle class black Bostonians—their snobbish-ness, their color prejudice, their contempt for the peasant African American migrants brought to *their* city by World War I; and above all else, their failure to see that the North, including Boston, in its treatment of African Americans is different from the South, not in kind but only in degree, if that. The fact that a few of West's fictional characters are based on persons well known during the era depicted in the novel adds to the value of the work.

For the best comment on the life, background, and writings of Dorothy West, see the 1982 reprint of *The Living is Easy*, which has an afterword by Adelaide M. Cromwell. (Most of the facts given in the headnote come from Cromwell's addition.) See also "Part V" of Mary Helen Washington's *Invented Lives: Narratives of Black Women, 1860–1960* (1987). Arnold Ram-persad's *The Life of Langston Hughes, Vol. I: 1902–1941* (1986) contains several references to Dorothy West and her Harlem Renaissance friends.

FROM **THE LIVING IS EASY**

Simeon Binney bent over his desk. Behind him, in the dingy back room, the two small presses were noisily clattering. But his ear was turned inward. He was writing his father's obituary. The doctor had said that his father would die before morning. He had felt no shock nor sorrow, and he had come away as soon as Thea returned to re-lieve him. She would give their father her tears, as he could not.

Simeon had been born in this house when the neighborhood was wholly Caucasian, except for the Binneys, who, according to their neighbors' praise, represented the best in the colored race. They be-haved as if they were white. Simeon played with the neighborhood children and sat beside them in Sunday school. But his brownness made him seem different to them, just as Thea's fair skin made her seem the same.

He was darker than either parent, a throwback to a paternal grandfather. He was not an undesirable shade by the standards of his parents' set. Indeed, he was considered the handsomest colored child in Boston. In the usual way, most people made the unamusing witticism that it was a pity that a boy should be prettier than his sister. He was tan, with fine features, great black eyes, and black curls. He was tall for his age and strongly built, in every way giving a manly appearance. Nobody guessed the extent of his sensitiveness, his insecurity in what was considered his safe and happy world.

He felt that he lived in two worlds. There was the world outside, peopled with whites, whites everywhere. He couldn't understand why his parents were proud that he and Thea were always the only colored children in school, in church, in their block. Didn't they know that made him feel lonely? It was good to come into the other world, the narrow nursery world, and play with Thea, and pretend that this was the whole, that he and she alone existed.

He hadn't had any inherent dislike of white children. He hadn't known there was anything special about them at first. For Thea and his father were fair, his mother was very light. He had never noticed that he was darker. Nor had he known that their skin shades were preferable to darker ones.

The five-year-old boy, big enough now to play outside without his Irish nurse's supervision, approached the children on the block with vulnerable innocence. He had never heard any discussions about the difference in man. All that he knew was that there was a favored race of people called Bostonians, and that he was fortunate enough to be one of them.

The group of children he approached stared at him open-mouthed. They were also five-year-olds, and their world had been as prescribed as his. They, too, knew they were little Bostonians, and they thought all little Bostonians looked alike. They were unprepared for the exotic appearance of this brown boy. He might have stepped out of one of their picture books of strange boys in strange lands.

"Hello," Simeon said.

"Hello," they said soberly, somewhat surprised that he spoke their tongue.

"I'm Simeon Binney," he offered cheerfully.

They were silent. They did not know whether they wanted to tell this odd boy their names or not.

Simeon stuck out his hand. He had been taught to do that. And he was used to hearing delighted murmurs at this charming display of grown-up manners.

The boys backed away. They had never seen a brown hand extended. Then one asked shyly, "Will it come off?"

"What?" asked Simeon blankly.

"The brown on your hand," the boy explained.

"It isn't dirt," he said indignantly. Then he felt surprised. What was it?

"Where do you come from?" a pink-cheeked boy asked.

"Over there." He pointed to his house, the corner house, the finest in the block of brownstone dwellings.

"No," the pink-cheeked child said patiently, "I mean, what country?"

"Boston," Simeon answered in a shocked tone, for he had supposed that all Bostonians recognized Bostonians. Certainly he had known without question that these children, whose dress, whose accent, whose houses were identical with his, were his fellow countrymen.

One of the boys drew a sputtering breath. "I think you're a colored boy," he said. It frightened him a little to make this pronouncement, for he didn't know whether it was good or bad.

"I'm a Boston boy," Simeon said with a sob. "Same as you."

Plainly this didn't make sense to them. They looked at each other, shifted self-consciously, and began to sidle away. This was something they wanted explained by a grown-up as soon as they could reach one. They chorused Good-bye, for, after all, he was a small person like themselves, and the inherent humanity of children evoked this gesture of brotherhood.

Simeon played by himself. He could not go in to his mother. He felt ashamed, though he could not explain his feeling. When a reasonable time had passed, he mounted the stone steps quietly and scooted up the back stairs. In the bathroom he scrubbed his hands vigorously, but it was just as he had known it would be, there was no whiteness under the brown. He was not like the other boys. He was not a Bostonian.

He waited for his father to come home and explain to him what a colored boy was. He was reluctant to ask his mother. He knew that she was modest, and did not speak of unseemly things. His father failed him. He was prepared for this moment, and said deftly: "Everybody is colored, Simeon. Some skins are colored lighter than others. Like Thea's. Some look as if they were not colored at all. Like those boys. But put them beside a sheet of white paper, and you will see that they look pale gray. Those boys had never seen a brown boy. Had you been red-haired, they would have asked you if your

hair was on fire." Simeon was supposed to smile at this, but his face
stayed solemn. For he knew that a red-haired boy wouldn't have
smiled either. "You're the color of an Indian, Simeon, and the Indians are the oldest Americans. If any boy ever asks you again why
you're brown, you may say it's because your grandfather was a full-
blooded Indian."

Simeon accepted this half-truth without enthusiasm. No matter
how long the Indians had lived in America, they hadn't lived in Boston. No wonder those boys had asked him what country he came
from. He couldn't understand why his father had let the doctor leave
a boy who looked like an Indian instead of a boy who looked like a
Bostonian.

The next day, when Simeon unwillingly went out to play, the little boys rushed to greet him and vigorously pumped his hand. They,
too, had had instructions in correct demeanor from their fathers,
who had been preparing for their questions as soon as they saw that
the Binney boy looked old enough to come out to play. Their fathers
had explained to them that you did not speak of color to colored
persons. It hurt their feelings. You must always act as if they had no
color at all. God made everybody, and in His infinite wisdom He had
made some people brown. It was as rude to ask a colored boy why
he was brown as it was to ask a lame boy why he limped. The way
for a well-bred Boston boy to behave was with generosity toward
those with fewer blessings.

Through the long afternoon Simeon waited to return to the subject of race. He had decided not to say he was an Indian. He was
going to stand pat on being a Bostonian. He was going to fight about
it if he had to. But the subject was never reopened.

The boys had set out to be bountiful. From that day on, he was
never left out of anything. To all outward appearances he was the
most popular boy in the block. Yet no boy ever fought him, though
they fought each other, no boy called him by a nickname, though
they were Fatty and Skinny and Shorty as soon as they left their
stoops, and no boy ever contradicted him, though they shouted each
other down with "You did!" "I didn't!"

He was never their equal. He was their charge, whom they were
honor-bound to treat with charity. They never knew whether they
liked him or not. They only knew it was something of a bother to be
with him, for the feelings of a colored boy had to be coddled.

When Thea was old enough to go out alone to play, these boys
and their sisters treated her as one of themselves, for her pink
cheeks and chestnut hair were close enough in color to theirs not to
distract them. Their easy acceptance established a loyalty in her that
made her unable to understand Simeon's distrust. With Thea, as

with Simeon, the first ten years of her life left a profound impression. She was never quite at ease with her own group. Her very fair
skin and chestnnut hair singled her out, accorded her a special treatment that she was unused to, that pointed out to her how preferable
was the status of whites, since even a near-white was made an idol.

When Simeon was twelve and Thea nine, the poorer streets surrounding theirs began to be populated by the black newcomers to
the North. They soon learned of the rich colored family living right
alongside rich white folks on a near-by street. They took to strolling
down this street to see if they could espy their own kind and color
riding fat and sassy behind a bang-up coachman. They would stand
and gape at the windows, their voices loud and approving and
proud. Some would even go so far as to start a conversation with
Thea and Simeon.

Thea would toss her chestnut hair and skip away. She was a little
bit scared. These people smelled, they wore queer clothes, they
spoke a strange tongue, and their blood was black, while hers was
blue.

But Simeon sensed that their blood was the same, and he was
ashamed. Because he was ashamed, he could not run away like
Thea. He had to face them for his own pride. He had to believe that
he could stand in the company of these people and still feel confident of the wall of culture between them.

Mr. Binney was completely outraged by the ever-increasing concourse of dark faces within the sacred precincts of his street. He
didn't feel at all like a king with worshiping subjects. He felt like a
criminal who had been found and tracked down. In his wildest
nightmare he had never imagined that his house would be a mecca
for lower-class Negroes. They were ruining the character of the
street. They were making it a big road. The worst thing of all was
that Simeon, who was being so carefully brought up, who scarcely
knew the difference between white and colored, whose closest
friends had always been white, was making friends with the little
black urchins who boldly hung around the back door in the hope of
enticing him away from his playmates on the front stoop.

The day Mr. Binney made up his mind to move was the unforgettable Sunday that he heard sounds of battle, rushed to the back
window to find Simeon in his new suit engaged in strife. Simeon,
who had never fought in his life, was rolling all over the alley with a
ruffian who had never worn shoes until he came North. It was
spring. Windows were open. Neighbors were witnessing this unholy
spectacle of young Binney so demeaning himself as to fight with a
boy beneath his station. It put them both in the same class.

Mr. Binney so far forgot himself as to bellow for his son. Simeon disentangled himself, shock his opponent's hand, and bounded into the house. He felt wonderfully elated, and he was scared but happy that his father had witnessed the fight. His father had never seen him fight in his life.

"Come in, sir!" his father commanded, leading him into his den. He turned and faced Simeon. "I have never been so ashamed in my life. My son behaving like an alley rat. I've never known you to raise your hand to one of the boys in the block. You've had the reputation of being a perfect young gentleman. Then the whole street sees you and that dirty black imp sprawled all over the alley. Do you know what they said to themselves?" Mr. Binney took a deep breath. He was going to say the worst thing he had ever said to Simeon. But Simeon had to be roundly shocked into full realization of his unpardonable breach of conduct. "They said, 'Isn't that just like niggers?' "

The word had never been used in Simeon's household. Its effect was not explosive. As a matter of fact, Mr. Binney had the uncomfortable feeling that Simeon accepted the ugly word as if he supposed it was part of his father's vocabulary.

"I know," said Simeon quietly. "I suppose they said 'colored' instead of 'nigger,' but that doesn't matter. I've always known they've never seen me as like themselves. They fight with each other, Father. Not in the alley, and not on Sunday. But I have to fight when I can. It mayn't make sense to you, Father, but Scipio Johnson"—Mr. Binney visibly winced—"is the first boy who ever fought me man to man."

It didn't make sense to Mr. Binney. "It is time you learned a hard-and-fast rule, Simeon. A colored man can never afford to forget himself, no matter what the provocation. He must always be superior to a white man if he wants to be that white man's equal. We are better fixed financially than any family on this street. You and Thea attend private schools. The other children go to public school. Your manners are superior. Your mother has more help. We set a finer table. If our manner of living was exactly like theirs, we would not be considered good enough to live on this street."

Simeon thought that he and his father had met on common ground. He, too, had something to say that was better said now. "I don't like white people, Father. I think I hate them."

His father was shocked and disturbed. "Never say such an unreasonable thing again. You get that from those wretched black boys. Do you know why they hate white people? Because they're lazy and shiftless and poor. They hate them because they envy them. You are Simeon Binney. You will never have to envy anyone. You are being raised like a white man's son. Pay me the courtesy, sir, of thinking like one."

The Binneys moved to to Cambridge. They were the first family on their street to move away because of the rapid encroachment of Negroes. They began the general exodus. Mr. Binney could say with pride, right up to the day of his death, that he had never lived on a street where other colored people resided.

Simeon went to Harvard. He ranked among the top ten in all his classes, because colored men must be among the first in any field if they are not to be forever lost among the mediocre millions.

He took the classical courses. Mr. Binney was disappointed that Simeon didn't want to specialize in law or medicine or dentistry. All of the sons of his friends were aspiring to the professions. They were the gentlemen that meant to be titled. Their fathers were gentlemen without higher education. They had learned their manners and mode of living in service to the rich. They were ambitious for their sons and instilled in them the Boston tradition that knowledge has no equal. That there would be a surfeit of professional men in a city where the majority of Negroes were too poor and ignorant to seek professional services did not deter them. In his heart each hopeful student supposed that he would be the one to establish a practice among whites. This was Boston, where a man was appraised for his worth, and paid in New England currency accordingly. What they did not know was that the whites, whom they dreamed of doctoring and advising, were confidently expecting them to attend their own, thereby effecting a painless segregation.

Mr. Binney was somewhat mollified when Simeon explained that he intended to work for a doctorate. At least Simeon would have a title even if he would never be able to hang out a shingle on which to display it. Still, he was worried about the boy. He hoped he did not think he could be a rich man's idle son. He had the elegance for it, but now there was not going to be the money. He, Mr. Binney, could not hold on to his business another year. The ten-thousand-dollar rent alone was far in excess of last year's profits. He was already drawing heavily on his capital. There was just enough left to see Thea through finishing school and Simeon through college.

Simeon would have to work for his living. Perhaps he would elect to teach. Perhaps it was not too fantastic to imagine, he might even teach at Harvard. They thought the world and all of him there. The faculty had the highest praise for him. His class respected him. He was even putting away a fair sum tutoring undergraduates. If Simeon would just make up his mind to teach, a position at Harvard should be his for the asking.

Simeon elected to edit a Negro newspaper. It was a sudden decision arrived at a few weeks before he received his doctorate. Thea was just home from school. She and Simeon were out for an eve-

ning's stroll in the vicinity of the Yard. She was holding his arm, and
her face, full of lively affection, was upturned to his. A group of
young men, in freshman caps, approached them. They were not very
steady. They did not know Simeon, nor he them. They stopped in
front of him and Thea and would not let them pass.

"Watch your step, nigger. Let go that white girl," one of them
said.

"Move out of our away," said Simeon quietly.

"Who's going to make us?"

Simeon said quickly to Thea, "Run home and don't look back."
Then he hunched his shoulders and gave a little prancing step. "Put
up your dukes," he said.

It was not a fair fight. There were three of them, and they attacked from all sides. But it didn't matter to Simeon. It was what
he'd been wanting since he was five. A fight with white men. That
there were three of them, that his fists could smash three faces, that
his wild, tortured curses could befoul three pairs of ears, that he
could smell the hated blood that flowed in three hot streams, made
it the moment in his life that satisfied the long waiting.

He was found unconscious a few minutes later by a passing pa-
trolman. His watch, his wallet were on him. He was carted off to jail
as a drunk and thrown into a cell to sleep it off.

When he roused he didn't mind being where he was. His head
was throbbing, there were bruises on his face, and blood in his
mouth. But it wasn't important. This would wake these sleeping colored Bostonians. They would see they were not a privileged group,
that no Negro was immune from a white man's anger when he did
not watch his step. These self-styled better Negroes were standing
still, sticking their heads in the sand, pretending that liberalism was
still alive in Boston. They were using the transplanted Southerner for
their scapegoat. It was he, they insisted, who was causing the
changed attitude, if one existed, not the changing times. The colored
problem began with their coming. It was no wonder. They were
coming in such droves. These upper-class Negroes, Simeon argued
to himself, didn't have the sense to see that a minority group was
never a problem until its numerical strength threatened the dominant race at the polls. What power had the Old Colored Families,
sparsely scattered by preference in the many suburbs of Boston?
They had none, and they did not know it was desirable. To them the
Irish were pushing, and they were proud that they were not. They
would have been outraged and astounded if they had been told that
they knew their place, and kept it.

All of these things Simeon expected to say in a rousing speech to
the press when it was discovered that a Harvard graduate had been

beaten by brother Harvardites for no other crime than walking with his sister in the neighborhood of his own house.

Toward midnight he was summoned to the sergeant's desk. His father was there, looking distressed. There was somebody from the dean's office, looking uncomfortable. There were three bloodied freshmen, looking sober and sheepish. The policeman who had made the arrest, looking red-faced. And the sergeant and two reporters, looking bored.

A solution had been arrived at by everyone concerned except Simeon. The unfortunate happening was to be considered a freshman prank, prompted by an overindulgence in strong drink. The freshmen were to apologize, which they did easily and earnestly, thrusting out their well-kept hands, which Simeon ignored until he heard his father's embarrassed plea, "Simeon, remember you are as much a gentleman as these young men," and felt that he would look foolish and childish if he continued to stand on what his father and the others did not recognize as his dignity. The Irish policeman apologized next. He did it gruffly, because he was upset by all the formality and fine English. It made him feel inferior to everybody present, and that was ridiculous since two of them were niggers.

In a few brief minutes it was over. There was general handshaking, with Simeon's hand feeling cold as a clam to whoever touched it. The young men and the dean's representative bowed themselves out, not with obsequiousness, but with the graciousness befitting those who have transgressed against the rule of *noblesse oblige*.

Simeon turned to his father. "I thought you would bring your lawyer," he said.

Mr. Binney looked scandalized. "Fineberg's crudity would have been out of place in a delicate situation like this. He would have made a race issue out of it, and taken it to court."

"It was a race issue," said Simeon stolidly. "They said, 'Nigger, let go that white woman.' "

His father looked racked. Everybody had been carefully avoiding any reference to those unhappy words. "They were drunk, Simeon. They forgot themselves. As soon as they sobered, they were Harvard gentlemen."

"And when they get drunk again, they'll insult some other couple whose juxtaposition doesn't suit them."

"Simeon, be reasonable. You and your sister have walked together through the streets of Cambridge half your lives. Have you ever been insulted before? It isn't likely that you'll be insulted again. They made a very natural mistake. Thea is fair enough to appear white. You must face facts, Simeon. Since that riffraff has come up from the South, their men have run after white women. You see them all over the South End, the worst elements of colored men walking with low-type white women."

"Thea and I are hardly comparable," said Simeon stiffly. He disliked having to say that. It weakened the point of the argument. But his pride could not let that observation pass.

"Of course, you're not," said his father soothingly. "Those young men were the first to say so when they sobered." He patted Simeon's shoulder. "Let's go home now. Your face needs attention. You need rest. You will get your degree in a few weeks. It will be a wonderful occasion for me. Don't spoil it by making a mountain out of a molehill. I want you to look and feel your best."

"I'll be ready in a moment," said Simeon wearily. "I want a word with the reporters. Will you wait for me outside?"

His father's patience broke. "They're not going to print anything, Simeon. They promised. They know how the better class of colored people feel about any story that is derogatory to the race. You're young and headstrong. I won't let you do anything tonight that you'll regret tomorrow. Rest assured that your name will appear in every paper in Boston when you receive your Ph.D. That will be a proud day. Don't do anything to take away from its glory. Give me your promise."

Simeon promised. He supposed he owed his father that much for his education. They walked toward home. Simeon was silent. He knew what he meant to do. He would publish a newspaper for colored people and make them face the facts of their second-class citizenship. He had enough savings to make a down payment on a printing press. His father would not deny him the use of the unoccupied South End house when he convinced him that he would either edit a paper for Negroes or harangue on Boston Common before audiences largely composed of whites.

For two years now Simeon had struggled to keep the paper in circulation. The people who read it were not the people who could pay for subscriptions. There were only occasional ads for church socials and rooms for rent. His bills were mounting. His single helper was underpaid. He himself never had a decent meal unless he ran over to Cleo's. Cambridge was too far away, and there was the carfare, and poor Thea was a rotten cook, with little enough to cook anyway.

If he could not keep the six-page sheet alive, at least he had established the need for a Negro newspaper. It passed around from hand to hand in the South End. On the day of its appearance there were little clusters of shabby people with nickels in their hands, waiting for the shabby newsboy to appear.

Thea did the social column. It was the only thing that kept the better Bostonians even mildly interested. It satisfied their curiosity as to who might have had a party to which they had not been invited, or what person of social prominence from New York, Philadelphia, or Washington was visiting what socially prominent Bostonian at his beautiful home in the suburbs.

Nothing else in the paper met with their approval. Every other word was *colored*. That this was Simeon's concession to their sensibilities did not make it any more palatable. Had he used the word *Negro*, they would have refused to read the paper altogether.

There was far too much, they complained, about the happenings below the Mason-Dixon line. They could be resolved quite easily. The nice colored people should come North. They needn't all come to Boston. There were many other large cities among which they could disperse themselves without dispossessing the already established families. As for the other elements, their extermination was the best thing possible. Every locality had its thieves and cutthroats. In the South they happened to be black. That Simeon should waste his time and talent writing long editorials protesting their punishments, urging the improvement of their conditions, was the folly of hotheaded youth. It was thoughtless cruelty to call attention to the dregs of the colored race.

Simeon, they concluded, was much too race-conscious for a young man who had been brought up exactly as if he were white. His persistence in identifying himself with anybody and everybody who happened to be black just showed what lasting effect those few months of contact with common colored children had had on a growing boy.

Simeon picked up his pencil. "Carter Burrows Binney was born in Boston in the year this once abolitionist city sent its son to liberate the enslaved black souls of the South . . ."

Across the sea England was writing the obit of a Kaiser. The world was at war.

Ann Petry

(1911–   )

THE WINNER of the 1946 Houghton Mifflin Literary Fellowship for her first novel, *The Street*, Ann Lane Petry has been, among other interesting things, a writer of children's plays; an actress in the American Negro theater; a pharmacist for fourteen years in her family's drugstore; a journalist, working at first on the *Amsterdam News*, subsequently on *The People's Voice*; and a sociological investigator for the New York Foundation, studying the effect of segregation on ghetto children. These experiences helped to prepare her for the writing of her first novel.

A native of Old Saybrook, Connecticut, and a member of a family that had been pharmacists in that town for several generations, Ann Petry received her education at two schools: the College of Pharmacy (University of Connecticut), where she took her professional degree, and at Columbia University. Petry has known intimately two worlds, the provincial but highly fascinating world of an old New England small town and the harsh world of Harlem. She has written with understanding of both worlds—in *Country Place* of the former, in *The Street* of the latter.

Ann Petry's publications include *The Street* (1946); *Country Place* (1947); *The Drugstore Cat* (1949); *The Narrows* (1953); *Harriet Tubman: Conductor on the Underground Railroad* (1955); *Tituba of Salem Village* (1963); *Legends of the Saints* (1970); and *Miss Muriel and Other Stories* (1971).

For comment on Ann Petry's life and works, see Robert A. Bone's *The Negro Novel in America* (rev. ed., 1965); James Toy's "Mrs. Petry's Harlem," *The Crisis* (May 1946); Arthur P. Davis's *From the Dark Tower* (1974); Ben Richardson's *Great American Negroes* (1956); and Gloria Wade-Gayles's *No Crystal Stair: Visions of Race and Sex in Black Women's Fiction* (1984). See also Calvin C. Hernton's comparison of *The Street* to Richard Wright's *Native Son* in *The Sexual Mountain and Black Women Writers* (1987); John O'Brien's *Interviews with Black Writers* (1973); and Mary Helen Washington's *Invented Lives: Narratives of Black Women, 1860–1960* (1987); and Marilyn Mobley's essay in the recent Scribner's collection entitled *Black American Writers*.

"Like a Winding Sheet," appeared in Martha Foley's *Best American Short Stories of 1946*. Foley dedicated the volume to Ann Petry.

LIKE A WINDING SHEET

He had planned to get up before Mae did and surprise her by fixing breakfast. Instead he went back to sleep and she got out of bed so quietly he didn't know she wasn't there beside him until he woke up and heard the queer soft gurgle of water running out of the sink in the bathroom.

He knew he ought to get up but instead he put his arms across his forehead to shut the afternoon sunlight out of his eyes, pulled his legs up close to his body, testing them to see if the ache was still in them.

Mae had finished in the bathroom. He could tell because she never closed the door when she was in there and now the sweet smell of talcum powder was drifting down the hall and into the bedroom. Then he heard her coming down the hall.

"Hi, babe," she said affectionately.

"Hum," he grunted, and moved his arms away from his head, opened one eye.

"It's a nice morning."

"Yeah," he rolled over and the sheet twisted around him, outlining his thighs, his chest. "You mean afternoon, don't ya?"

Mae looked at the twisted sheet and giggled.

"Looks like a winding sheet," she said. "A shroud—." Laughter tangled with her words and she had to pause for a moment before she could continue. "You look like a huckleberry—in a winding sheet—"

"That's no way to talk. Early in the day like this," he protested.

He looked at his arms silhouetted against the white of the sheets. They were inky black by contrast and he had to smile in spite of himself and he lay there smiling and savouring the sweet sound of Mae's giggling.

"Early?" She pointed a finger at the alarm clock on the table near the bed, and giggled again. "It's almost four o'clock. And if you don't spring up out of there you're going to be late again."

"What do you mean 'again'?"

"Twice last week. Three times the week before. And once the week before and—"

"I can't get used to sleeping in the day time," he said fretfully. He pushed his legs out from under the covers experimentally. Some of

"Like a Winding Sheet," published in *The Crisis* (November 1945); and in *Best American Short Stories of 1946* by Houghton Mifflin, 1946. Reprinted by permission of Russell & Volkening as agents for the author. Copyright 1946 by Ann Petry, renewed in 1974 by Ann Petry.

the ache had gone out of them but they weren't really rested yet. "It's too light for good sleeping. And all that standing beats the hell out of my legs."

"After two years you oughtta be used to it," Mae said.

He watched her as she fixed her hair, powdered her face, slipping into a pair of blue denim overalls. She moved quickly and yet she didn't seem to hurry.

"You look like you'd had plenty of sleep," he said lazily. He had to get up but he kept putting the moment off, not wanting to move, yet he didn't dare let his legs go completely limp because if he did he'd go back to sleep. It was getting later and later but the thought of putting his weight on his legs kept him lying there.

When he finally got up he had to hurry and he gulped his break-fast so fast that he wondered if his stomach could possibly use food thrown at it at such a rate of speed. He was still wondering about it as he and Mae were putting their coats on in the hall.

Mae paused to look at the calendar. "It's the thirteenth," she said. Then a faint excitement in her voice. "Why it's Friday the thir-teenth." She had one arm in her coat sleeve and she held it there while she stared at the calendar. "I oughtta stay home," she said. "I shouldn't go otta the house."

"Aw don't be a fool," he said. "To-day's payday. And payday is a good luck day everywhere, any way you look at it." And as she stood hesitating he said, "Aw, come on."

And he was late for work again because they spent fifteen min-utes arguing before he could convince her she ought to go to work just the same. He had to talk persuasively, urging her gently and it took time. But he couldn't bring himself to talk to her roughly or threaten to strike her like a lot of men might have done. He wasn't made that way.

So when he reached the plant he was late and he had to wait to punch the time clock because the day shift workers were streaming out in long lines, in groups and bunches that impeded his progress.

Even now just starting his work-day his legs ached. He had to force himself to struggle past the out-going workers, punch the time clock, and get the little cart he pushed around all night because he kept toying with the idea of going home and getting back in bed.

He pushed the cart out on the concrete floor, thinking that if this was his plant he'd make a lot of changes in it. There were too many standing up jobs for one thing. He'd figure out some way most of 'em could be done sitting down and he'd put a lot more benches around. And this job he had—this job that forced him to walk ten hours a night, pushing this little cart, well, he'd turn it into a sittin-down job. One of those little trucks they used around railroad stations would be good for a job like this. Guys sat on a seat and the thing moved easily, taking up little room and turning in hardly any space at all, like on a dime.

He pushed the cart near the foreman. He never could remember to refer to her as the forelady even in his mind. It was funny to have a woman for a boss in a plant like this one.

She was sore about something. He could tell by the way her face was red and her eyes were half shut until they were slits. Probably been out late and didn't get enough sleep. He avoided looking at her and hurried a little, head down, as he passed her though he couldn't resist stealing a glance at her out of the corner of his eyes. He saw the edge of the light colored slacks she wore and the tip end of a big tan shoe.

"Hey, Johnson!" the woman said.

The machines had started full blast. The whirr and the grinding made the building shake, made it impossible to hear conversations. The men and women at the machines talked to each other but looking at them from just a little distance away they appeared to be simply moving their lips because you couldn't hear what they were saying. Yet the woman's voice cut across the machine sounds— harsh, angry.

He turned his head slowly. "Good Evenin', Mrs. Scott," he said and waited.

"You're late again."

"That's right. My legs were bothering me."

The woman's face grew redder, angrier looking. "Half this shift comes in late," she said. "And you're the worst one of all. You're always late. Whatsa matter with ya?"

"It's my legs," he said. "Somehow they don't ever get rested. I don't seem to get used to sleeping days. And I just can't get started."

"Excuses. You guys always got excuses," her anger grew and spread. "Every guy comes in here late always has an excuse. His wife's sick or his grandmother died or somebody in the family had to go to the hospital," she paused, drew a deep breath. "And the niggers are the worse. I don't care what's wrong with your legs. You get in here on time. I'm sick of you niggers—"

"You got the right to get mad," he interrupted softly. "You got the right to cuss me four ways to Sunday but I ain't letting nobody call me a nigger."

He stepped closer to her. His fists were doubled. His lips were drawn back in a thin narrow line. A vein in his forehead stood out swollen, thick.

And the woman backed away from him, not hurriedly but slowly—two, three steps back.

"Aw, forget it," she said. "I didn't mean nothing by it. It slipped out. It was a accident." The red of her face deepened until the small blood vessels in her cheeks were purple. "Go on and get to work," she urged. And she took three more slow backward steps.

He stood motionless for a moment and then turned away from the red lipstick on her mouth that made him remember that the foreman was a woman. And he couldn't bring himself to hit a woman. He felt a curious tingling in his fingers and he looked down at his hands. They were clenched tight, hard, ready to smash some of those small purple veins in her face.

He pushed the cart ahead of him, walking slowly. When he turned his head, she was staring in his direction, mopping her forehead with a dark blue handkerchief. Their eyes met and then they both looked away.

He didn't glance in her direction again but moved past the long work benches, carefully collecting the finished parts, going slowly and steadily up and down, back and forth the length of the building and as he walked he forced himself to swallow his anger, get rid of it.

And he succeeded so that he was able to think about what had happened without getting upset about it. An hour went by but the tension stayed in his hands. They were clenched and knotted on the handles of the cart as though ready to aim a blow.

And he thought he should have hit her anyway, smacked her hard in the face, felt the soft flesh of her face give under the hardness of his hands. He tried to make his hands relax by offering them a description of what it would have been like to strike her because he had the queer feeling that his hands were not exactly a part of him any more—they had developed a separate life of their own over which he had no control. So he dwelt on the pleasure his hands would have felt—both of them cracking at her, first one and then the other. If he had done that his hands would have felt good now— relaxed, rested.

And he decided that even if he'd lost his job for it he should have let her have it and it would have been a long time, maybe the rest of her life before she called anybody else a nigger.

The only trouble was he couldn't hit a woman. A woman couldn't hit back the same way a man did. But it would have been a deeply satisfying thing to have cracked her narrow lips wide open with just one blow, beautifully timed and with all his weight in back of it. That way he would have gotten rid of all the energy and tension his anger had created in him. He kept remembering how his heart had started pumping blood so fast he had felt it tingle even in the tips of his fingers.

With the approach of night fatigue nibbled at him. The corners of his mouth dropped, the frown between his eyes deepened, his shoulders sagged; but his hands stayed tight and tense. As the hours dragged by he noticed that the women workers had started to snap and snarl at each other. He couldn't hear what they said because of the sound of machines but he could see the quick lip movements that sent words tumbling from the sides of their mouths. They gestured irritably with their hands and scowled as their mouths moved.

Their violent jerky motions told him that it was getting close on to quitting time but somehow he felt that the night still stretched ahead of him, composed of endless hours of steady walking on his aching legs. When the whistle finally blew he went on pushing the cart, unable to believe that it had sounded. The whirring of the machines died away to a murmur and he knew then that he'd really heard the whistle. He stood still for a moment filled with a relief that made him sigh.

Then he moved briskly, putting the cart in the store room, hurrying to take his place in the line forming before the paymaster. That was another thing he'd change, he thought. He'd have the pay envelopes handed to the people right at their benches so there wouldn't be ten or fifteen minutes lost waiting for the pay. He always got home about fifteen minutes late on payday. They did it better in the plant where Mae worked, brought the money right to them at their benches.

He stuck his pay envelope in his pants' pocket and followed the line of workers heading for the subway in a slow moving stream. He glanced up at the sky. It was a nice night, the sky looked packed full to running over with stars. And he thought if he and Mae would go right to bed when they got home from work they'd catch a few hours of darkness for sleeping. But they never did. They fooled around—cooking and eating and listening to the radio and he always stayed in a big chair in the living room and went almost but not quite to sleep and when they finally got to bed it was five or six in the morning and daylight was already seeping around the edges of the sky.

He walked slowly, putting off the moment when he would have to plunge into the crowd hurrying toward the subway. It was a long ride to Harlem and to-night the thought of it appalled him. He paused outside an all-night restaurant to kill time, so that some of the first rush of workers would be gone when he reached the subway.

The lights in the restaurant were brilliant, enticing. There was life and motion inside. And as he looked through the window he thought that everything within range of his eyes gleamed—the long imitation marble counter, the tall stools, the white porcelain topped tables and especially the big metal coffee urn right near the window.

Steam issued from its top and a gas flame flickered under it—a lively, dancing, blue flame.

A lot of the workers from his shift—men and women—were lining up near the coffee urn. He watched them walk to the porcelain topped tables carrying steaming cups of coffee and he saw that just the smell of the coffee lessened the fatigue lines in their faces. After the first sip their faces softened, they smiled, they began to talk and laugh.

On a sudden impulse he shoved the door open and joined the line in front of the coffee urn. The line moved slowly. And as he stood there the smell of the coffee, the sound of the laughter and of the voices, helped dull the sharp ache in his legs.

He didn't pay any attention to the girl who was serving the coffee at the urn. He kept looking at the cups in the hands of the men who had been ahead of him. Each time a man stepped out of the line with one of the thick white cups the fragrant steam got in his nostrils. He saw that they walked carefully so as not to spill a single drop. There was a froth of bubbles at the top of each cup and he thought about how he would let the bubbles break against his lips before he actually took a big deep swallow.

Then it was his turn. "A cup of coffee," he said, just as he had heard the others say.

The girl looked past him, put her hands up to her head and gently lifted her hair away from the back of her neck, tossing her head back a little. "No more coffee for awhile," she said.

He wasn't certain he'd heard her correctly and he said, "What?" blankly.

"No more coffee for awhile," she repeated.

There was silence behind him and then uneasy movement. He thought someone would say something, ask why or protest, but there was only silence and then a faint shuffling sound as though the men standing behind him had simultaneously shifted their weight from one foot to the other.

He looked at her without saying anything. He felt his hands begin to tingle and the tingling went all the way down to his finger tips so that he glanced down at them. They were clenched tight, hard, into fists. Then he looked at the girl again. What he wanted to do was hit her so hard that the scarlet lipstick on her mouth would smear and spread over her nose, her chin, out toward her cheeks; so hard that she would never toss her head again and refuse a man a cup of coffee because he was black.

He estimated the distance across the counter and reached forward, balancing his weight on the balls of his feet, ready to let the blow go. And then his hands fell back down to his sides because he forced himself to lower them, to unclench them and make them dangle loose. The effort took his breath away because his hands fought against him. But he couldn't hit her. He couldn't even now bring himself to hit a woman, not even this one, who had refused him a cup of coffee with a toss of her head. He kept seeing the gesture with which she had lifted the length of her blond hair from the back of her neck as expressive of her contempt for him.

When he went out the door he didn't look back. If he had he would have seen the flickering blue flame under the shiny coffee urn being extinguished. The line of men who had stood behind him lingered a moment to watch the people drinking coffee at the tables and then they left just as he had without having had the coffee they wanted so badly. The girl behind the counter poured water in the urn and swabbed it out and as she waited for the water to run out she lifted her hair gently from the back of her neck and tossed her head before she began making a fresh lot of coffee.

But he walked away without a backward look, his head down, his hands in his pockets, raging at himself and whatever it was inside of him that had forced him to stand quiet and still when he wanted to strike out.

The subway was crowded and he had to stand. He tried grasping an overhead strap and his hands were too tense to grip it. So he moved near the train door and stood there swaying back and forth with the rocking of the train. The roar of the train beat inside his head, making it ache and throb, and the pain in his legs clawed up into his groin so that he seemed to be bursting with pain and he told himself that it was due to all that anger-born energy that had piled up in him and not been used and so it had spread through him like a poison—from his feet and legs all the way up to his head.

Mae was in the house before he was. He knew she was home before he put the key in the door of the apartment. The radio was going. She had it tuned up loud and she was singing along with it.

"Hello, Babe," she called out as soon as he opened the door.

He tried to say "hello" and it came out half a grunt and half sigh.

"Your sure sound cheerful," she said.

She was in the bedroom and he went and leaned against the door jamb. The denim overalls she wore to work were carefully draped over the back of a chair by the bed. She was standing in front of the dresser, tying the sash of a yellow housecoat around her waist and chewing gum vigorously as she admired her reflection in the mirror over the dresser.

"Whatsa matter?" she said. "You get bawled out by the boss or somep'n?"

"Just tired," he said slowly. "For God's sake do you have to crack that gum like that?"

"You don't have to lissen to me," she said complacently. She patted a curl in place near the side of her head and then lifted her hair away from the back of her neck, ducking her head forward and then back.

He winced away from the gesture. "What you got to be always fooling with your hair for?" he protested.

"Say, what's the matter with you, anyway?" she turned away from the mirror to face him, put her hands on her hips. "You ain't been in the house two minutes and you're picking on me."

He didn't answer her because her eyes were angry and he didn't want to quarrel with her. They'd been married too long and got along too well and so he walked all the way into the room and sat down in the chair by the bed and stretched his legs out in front of him, putting his weight on the heels of his shoes, leaning way back in the chair, not saying anything.

"Lissen," she said sharply. "I've got to wear those overalls again tomorrow. You're going to get them all wrinkled up leaning against them like that."

He didn't move. He was too tired and his legs were throbbing now that he had sat down. Besides the overalls were already wrinkled and dirty, he thought. They couldn't help but be for she'd worn them all week. He leaned further back in the chair.

"Come on, get up," she ordered.

"Oh, what the hell," he said wearily and got up from the chair. "I'd just as soon live in a subway. There'd be just as much place to sit down."

He saw that her sense of humor was struggling with her anger. But her sense of humor won because she giggled.

"Aw, come on and eat," she said. There was a coaxing note in her voice. "You're nothing but a old hungry nigger trying to act tough and—" she paused to giggle and then continued, "You—"

He had always found her giggling pleasant and deliberately said things that might amuse her and then waited, listening for the delicate sound to emerge from her throat. This time he didn't even hear the giggle. He didn't let her finish what she was saying. She was standing close to him and that funny tingling started in his finger tips, went fast up his arms and sent his fist shooting straight for her face.

There was the smacking sound of soft flesh being struck by a hard object and it wasn't until she screamed that he realized he had hit her in the mouth—so hard that the dark red lipstick had blurred and spread over her full lips, reaching up toward the tip of her nose, down toward her chin, out toward her cheeks.

The knowledge that he had struck her seeped through him slowly and he was appalled but he couldn't drag his hands away from her face. He kept striking her and he thought with horror that something inside him was holding him, binding him to this act, wrapping and twisting about him so that he had to continue it. He had lost all control over his hands. And he groped for a phrase, a word, something to describe what this thing was like that was happening to him and he thought it was like being enmeshed in a winding sheet—that was it—like a winding sheet. And even as the thought formed in his mind his hands reached for her face again and yet again.

Elma Stuckey

(1907–1988)

THE GRANDDAUGHTER of former slaves, Elma Stuckey was born in Memphis, Tennessee, in 1907. She attended Manassas High School in Memphis and for a year Lane College in Jackson, Tennessee. With her husband and two children—one of them now the well-known scholar Sterling Stuckey of Northwestern University—she moved to Chicago in 1945. Elma Stuckey did many things in her long and full life: she worked as a maid, a hat check girl, a rural school teacher, a nursery school head teacher, and a supervisor for the Illinois Department of Labor; she was also writer-in-residence at the University of Illinois. Until her death, she was a full-time writer and lecturer appearing before audiences, black and white, at many high schools, community organizations, colleges, and universities, including Harvard and Wisconsin.

Her first major work, *The Big Gate* (1975), gives voice to the harsh and bitter attitude which many slaves—more than we now realize—took toward their masters and the "peculiar institution." Stuckey learned about slavery firsthand from her grandparents; her anecdotes and narratives have the ring of authority, and she has presented them to us with a wealth of sardonic wit. As Stephen E. Henderson has written concerning this work, "Elma Stuckey's vital voice comes alive in these lines. Read them and hear it. Hear it and hear the voices of the people who created the spirituals and the blues." For E. D. Hirsch, Jr., commenting on *The Big Gate*, Elma Stuckey is the A. E. Housman of slavery: "Her gem-like pieces have Housman's humor, irony, and cadence plus a vitality of their own." Stuckey's second volume, *The Collected Poems of Elma Stuckey*, was published in 1987. It contains *The Big Gate* plus additional poems. Henderson, professor of English at Howard University, wrote the introduction to *The Big Gate*; Hirsch, Kenan Professor of English at the University of Virginia, wrote the introduction to the *Collected Poems*. At the time of her death, Mrs. Stuckey, though eighty-one and seriously handicapped, was hard at work on her third volume of poems.

The works that follow come from *The Collected Poems of Elma Stuckey* (1987).

HOUSE NIGGERS

Two times they call us from the field
And tell us Marse is dying,
Two times house niggers huddle up
And all of them is crying.

I'se sick of looking at that sight
And ask them why they cry,
They say they tired of waiting,
Marse take too long to die.

JIM

He's gonna chop his way into Heaven,
He was buried with the hoe in his hand,
And he knows just how to swing it
'cause Jim was a cotton choppin' man.

Now Jim was big and powerful,
Yeah, Jim was a six-foot man,
He's gonna chop the door wide open,
Means to get in the promised land.

Old Jim didn't say no prayers,
Bare-foot he sung them blues,
He don't like no milk and honey,
Won't wear no silvery shoes.

He swo' when he chopped the cotton,
He swo' caused he worked so hard,
Old Jim had a tough time livin',
He got a crow for to pick with God.

He's sho gonna get into Heaven,
He was buried with the hoe in his hand,
And he knows just how to swing it
'cause Jim was a cotton choppin' man.

From *The Collected Poems of Elma Stuckey* (1987). All poems are reprinted by permission of Sterling Stuckey.

SOUTHERN BELLE

Ole Missus is a vile one,
Got everything, she rich!
But walk around house niggers
Buck naked, not a stitch.

I don't know what she provin',
Ole Marsa love the shacks,
There's something in them quarters
That his Ole Missus lacks.

MR. BODY

It was on a Sunday morning
That she shot him dead.
After an all night drinking bout,
She shot him in the head.

The police came and asked her
What time did he die?
"Police, I am telling you,
I ain't got no cause to lie.

"I pulled his gold watch from him
And looked at its face,
It said nine o'clock a.m.
I put it back in place."

Strange, ironic is it not,
He will never drink a toddy.
Like his name, oh what a shame,
He really is a body.

NO FLOWERS

She was black and sold moonshine
For a white man she called Joe,
She was a bootleg woman,
Yeah, she was that for sho'.

She had a daughter, name of Lil,
And the night that mamma died

Lil took a swig of moonshine
And they say she never cried,
They say she never cried.

She got on the phone and talked to Joe,
"Have you heard that mamma's dead?
Bring two gallons of moonshine—
One for the foot of the casket
And one for to set at the head,
Yeah, one for the foot of the casket
And one for to set at the head."

And Joe brought the moonshine,
Two gallons, like Lil said,
One for the foot of the casket
And one for to set at the head,
Yeah, one for the foot of the casket
And one for to set at the head.

MOURNERS BENCH

The sinners were coaxed to sit up front.
There were gamblers and a wench,
There were whoremongers and drunkards
And backsliders on the bench.

The preacher sweated and hollered,
"He'll forgive, don't care what you do.
Just trust Him tonight, Oh trust Him,
For Jesus loves all of you."

He screamed, "Trust in Jesus,
Just listen to His teaching."
Those on the bench were saved
By his pleading and his preaching.

The wench went right back to whoring,
The gamblers went right back to gambling,
The drunkard went right back to drinking,
The whoremonger right back to rambling.

They all had one thing in common,
They felt they had nothing to fear.
They'd keep on sinning since He forgives,
And return to the bench next year.

LILL

Lill was lying paralyzed
On her left side.
Before I could say a word,
She ordered me to take
A tissue off the top
Of a kleenex box,
To lay aside a pork sandwich
And to take a half-pint of whiskey
From the bottom of the box.

"Take the top off the bottle and hold
The sheet up so the nurse can't
See me drinking."
She drank—glugger, lugger, lugger
Glugger, lugger, lugger—
Until half the whiskey was gone.
I put the bottle back in the kleenex box,
Put the pork sandwich on top of it
And put the tissue back on top.

"How are things on the outside?" Lill asked
"Any man out there got a dollar?"
She raised herself on her good elbow,
Attempted to shake her behind and shoulders
And said, "If a man out there got
A dollar, I git that dollar."

Eventually she walked out of the hospital
As well as anyone:
What led her to walk again
Is a question that boggles my mind.
Was it the pork or whiskey
Or was it the two combined?

TENEMENT

She kept half-pints of
Corn whiskey hidden in her flour barrel
And sold them for a quarter
To the others in the Tenement.

Miss Sue and her husband
Were always a little bit tipsy

And on Saturday nights would fight
Until daybreak on Sunday.

She would complain, "John don't blongst
To nothin',
No church, no club,
He just blongst to me."

One Saturday, two big white police
Went to Miss Sue's apartment.
"You Sue White?"
"I'm Sue White but I'm black."

"We can see that.
Where's the corn whiskey?"
"Police, I ain't got none."
Pushing her aside, they searched and found nothing.

When they left, she came out with
A half-pint completely covered with flour.
"Somebody done snitched on me; somebody
Done snitched on me but when God is with you,
The devil can't do you no harm."

That night, she and John started fighting.
His mouth was bleeding and there were bruises
On his face and bald head.
A next door neighbor took him to the county hospital.

Later Miss Sue said, "My snuff don't taste right,
My snuff don't taste right."
She hooked her finger and raked around in her mouth
And out came a piece of John's lip.

She rinsed it off and
Laid it on the mantlepiece.
When the doctors asked if it could be found,
A neighbor took it to them.

Miss Sue said they didn't sew it back on right:
"But one thing, he can't cuss me like he used to.
When he try to call me goddamn bitch,
All he can say is, "You ga da bish!"

SACRILEGIOUS

She said she felt sorry for Jesus
And said he was little and poor.
If she had her way and had her say,
He would never cross her door.

I told her He felt sorry for us,
That's why He was crucified.
She got angry and began to scream,
Claiming that the Bible lied.

She said He was a lil' ole sissy
And had twelve men after Him,
Talking in riddles and parables
And doing it at His whim.

"There's one thing He never counted on,
When He was leading His flock.
Lil' ole sissy, letting men kiss Him,
Well, Judas fixed His clock."

REBEL

I break the hoe, I break the plow
And here he come, that hellion.
I say right then unto myself,
This a one-man rebellion.

I stand foursquare and face Ole Marse,
He call me crazy nigger,
I rush him and I take his gun
And then I pull the trigger.

My time is come and I don't care
If they hang me from a tree,
By bein' crazy like a fox
I sent Marse 'head of me.

Gwendolyn Brooks

(1917–)

GWENDOLYN BROOKS (Blakely) has been writing since she was thirteen, when she published her first verses in a children's magazine. She is now a major American poet, and her work has appeared in many of the nation's outstanding periodicals and anthologies. Her poetry is principally concerned with the nuances—tragic and comic—of the black person's experience in a world where color counts, heavily. A keen and sympathetic observer, Gwendolyn Brooks knows thoroughly the ghetto people about whom she writes. She is a brilliant wordsmith and her insights have deepened and sharpened as she progressed from a relatively simple style (*A Street in Bronzeville*) to a decidedly complex style (*In the Mecca*).

Born in Topeka, Kansas, Gwendolyn Brooks was reared in Chicago, where she learned from her own neighborhood many facts of ghetto life. She was educated at Wilson Junior College and has been a teacher of creative writing at Chicago's Columbia College at Elmhurst and at Northeastern Illinois State College; she has also served as visiting Rennebohn Professor of Creative Writing at the University of Wisconsin, and as a poetry consultant at the Library of Congress.

Brooks has received many distinguished honors and awards. She was the first black to win the Pulitzer Prize for Poetry (in 1950 for *Annie Allen*). In 1945 she received the *Mademoiselle* Merit Award; in 1946, the American Academy of Letters Award; in 1946 and 1947, Guggenheim Fellowships; in 1949, the Eunice Tietjens Memorial Award, from *Poetry* magazine; and in 1964, the Friends Literary Award for Poetry. Columbia College (Chicago) awarded her a Doctor of Humane Letters degree, and Illinois made her a member of its art council and poet laureate of the state.

Gwendolyn Brooks's major publications include: *A Street in Bronzeville* (1945); *Annie Allen* (1949); *Maud Martha*, a short novel (1953); *The Bean Eaters* (1960); *Selected Poems* (1963); *In the Mecca* (1968); *Riot* (1969); *Aloneness*—a children's book (1971); *The Tiger Who Wore White Gloves*—also a children's book (1974); *Becomings* (1975); *Primer for Blacks* (1980); *To Disembark* (1981); and *Blacks* (1987).

With the publication of *In the Mecca* (1968), Gwendolyn Brooks, until then an integrationist, began her change to a strong Black Arts approach to literature. She attributes the beginning of her "conversion" to a black writers' conference she attended at Fisk University in 1967. She also admits that "Haki (Don L. Lee) . . . has had a great influence on my thinking."

For comments on the life and works of Gwendolyn Brooks, see *Contemporary Authors*, Vol. I (1962); *Current Biography* (1950); George Kent, "The Poetry of Gwendolyn Brooks," Part 1, *Black World* (September 1971), Part 2 (October 1971); Houston A. Baker, "The Achievement of Gwendolyn Brooks," *CLA Journal* (September 1972); Arthur P. Davis, *From the Dark Tower* (1974); and Marsha Jones, "Poetry in Motion: The Prose of Gwendolyn Brooks," *About Time* (June 1988).

Important recent studies include a collection of essays, *A Life Distilled: Gwendolyn Brooks, Her Poetry and Fiction*, by Maria K. Mootry and Gary Smith (1987), and *Invented Lives: Narratives of Black Women, 1860–1960* (1987) by Mary Helen Washington. See also *Black Women Writers, 1950–1980: A Critical Evaluation* (1984), edited by Mari Evans; *No Crystal Stair: Visions of Race and Sex in Black Women's Fiction* (1984) by Gloria Wade-Gayles; *Black Feminist Criticism: Perspectives on Black Women Writers* by Barbara Christian (1985); D. H. Melhem's *Gwendolyn Brooks: Poetry and the Heroic Voice* (1987); and George Kent's *A Life of Gwendolyn Brooks* (1990).

The poems given below constitute an attempt to represent all of Gwendolyn Brooks's major poetical works from *A Street in Bronzeville* to *In the Mecca*. The poems are taken from *Blacks* and *Children Coming Home*.

OF DE WITT WILLIAMS ON HIS WAY TO LINCOLN CEMETERY

He was born in Alabama.
He was bred in Illinois.
He was nothing but a
Plain black boy.

Swing low swing low sweet sweet chariot.
Nothing but a plain black boy.

Drive him past the Pool Hall.
Drive him past the Show.
Blind within his casket,
But maybe he will know.

Down through Forty-seventh Street:
Underneath the L,
And Northwest Corner, Prairie,
That he loved so well.

Don't forget the Dance Halls—
Warwick and Savoy,
Where he picked his women, where
He drank his liquid joy.

Born in Alabama.
Bred in Illinois.
He was nothing but a
Plain black boy.

Swing low swing low sweet sweet chariot.
Nothing but a plain black boy.

THE SUNDAYS OF SATIN-LEGS SMITH

Inamoratas, with an approbation,
Bestowed his title. Blessed his inclination.

He wakes, unwinds, elaborately: a cat
Tawny, reluctant, royal. He is fat
And fine this morning. Definite. Reimbursed.

He waits a moment, he designs his reign,
That no performance may be plain or vain.
Then rises in a clear delirium.

He sheds, with his pajamas, shabby days.
And his desertedness, his intricate fear, the
Postponed resentments and the prim precautions.

Now, at his bath, would you deny him lavender
Or take away the power of his pine?
What smelly substitute, heady as wine,
Would you provide? life must be aromatic.
There must be scent, somehow there must be some.
Would you have flowers in his life? suggest
Asters? a Really Good geranium?
A white carnation? would you prescribe a Show
With the cold lilies, formal chrysanthemum
Magnificence, poinsettias, and emphatic
Red of prize roses? might his happiest
Alternative (you muse) be, after all,
A bit of gentle garden in the best
Of taste and straight tradition? Maybe so.
But you forget, or did you ever know,

His heritage of cabbage and pigtails,
Old intimacy with alleys, garbage pails,
Down in the deep (but always beautiful) South
Where roses blush their blithest (it is said)
And sweet magnolias put Chanel to shame.

No! He has not a flower to his name.
Except a feather one, for his lapel.
Apart from that, if he should think of flowers
It is in terms of dandelions or death.
Ah, there is little hope. You might as well—
Unless you care to set the world a-boil
And do a lot of equalizing things,
Remove a little ermine, say, from kings,
Shake hands with paupers and appoint them men,
For instance—certainly you might as well
Leave him his lotion, lavender and oil.

Let us proceed. Let us inspect, together
With his meticulous and serious love,
The innards of this closet. Which is a vault
Whose glory is not diamonds, not pearls,
Not silver plate with just enough dull shine.
But wonder-suits in yellow and in wine,
Sarcastic green and zebra-striped cobalt.
With shoulder padding that is wide
And cocky and determined as his pride;
Ballooning pants that taper off to ends
Scheduled to choke precisely.

                             Here are hats
Like bright umbrellas; and hysterical ties
Like narrow banners for some gathering war.

People are so in need, in need of help.
People want so much that they do not know.

Below the tinkling trade of little coins
The gold impulse not possible to show
Or spend. Promise piled over and betrayed.

These kneaded limbs receive the kiss of silk.
Then they receive the brave and beautiful
Embrace of some of that equivocal wool.
He looks into his mirror, loves himself—
The neat curve here, the angularity

That is appropriate at just its place;
The technique of a variegated grace.

Here is all his sculpture and his art
And all his architectural design.
Perhaps you would prefer to this a fine
Value of marble, complicated stone.
Would have him think with horror of baroque,
Rococo. You forget and you forget.

He dances down the hotel steps that keep
Remnants of last night's high life and distress.
As spat-out purchased kisses and spilled beer.
He swallows sunshine with a secret yelp.
Passes to coffee and a roll or two.
Has breakfasted.

          Out. Sounds about him smear,
Become a unit. He hears and does not hear
The alarm clock meddling in somebody's sleep;

Children's governed Sunday happiness;
The dry tone of a plane; a woman's oath;
Consumption's spiritless expectoration;
An indignant robin's resolute donation
Pinching a track through apathy and din;
Restaurant vendors weeping; and the L
That comes on like a slightly horrible thought.

Pictures, too, as usual, are blurred.
He sees and does not see the broken windows
Hiding their shame with newsprint; little girl
With ribbons decking wornness, little boy
Wearing the trousers with the decentest patch,
To honor Sunday; women on their way
From "service," temperate holiness arranged
Ably on asking faces; men estranged
From music and from wonder and from joy
But far familiar with the guiding awe
Of foodlessness.
          He loiters.

                Restaurant vendors
Weep, or out of them rolls a restless glee.
The Lonesome Blues, the Long-lost Blues, I Want A
Big Fat Mama. Down these sore avenues

Comes no Saint-Saëns, no piquant elusive Grieg,
And not Tschaikovsky's wayward eloquence
And not the shapely tender drift of Brahms.
But could he love them? Since a man must bring
To music what his mother spanked him for
When he was two: bits of forgotten hate,
Devotion: whether or not his mattress hurts:
The little dream his father humored: the thing
His sister did for money: what he ate
For breakfast—and for dinner twenty years
Ago last autumn: all his skipped desserts.

The pasts of his ancestors lean against
Him. Crowd him. Fog out his identity.
Hundreds of hungers mingle with his own,
Hundreds of voices advise so dexterously
He quite considers his reactions his,
Judges he walks most powerfully alone,
That everything is—simply what it is.

But movie-time approaches, time to boo
The hero's kiss, and boo the heroine
Whose ivory and yellow it is sin
For his eye to eat of. The Mickey Mouse,
However, is for everyone in the house.

Squires his lady to dinner at Joe's Eats.
His lady alters as to leg and eye,
Thickness and height, such minor points as these,
From Sunday to Sunday. But no matter what
Her name or body positively she's
In Queen Lace stockings with ambitious heels
That strain to kiss the calves, and vivid shoes
Frontless and backless, Chinese fingernails,
Earrings, three layers of lipstick, intense hat
Dripping with the most voluble of veils.
Her affable extremes are like sweet bombs
About him, whom no middle grace or good
Could gratify. He had no education
In quiet arts of compromise. He would
Not understand your counsels on control, nor
Thank you for your late trouble.

At Joe's Eats

You get your fish or chicken on meat platters.
With coleslaw, macaroni, candied sweets,
Coffee and apple pie. You go out full.
(The end is—isn't it?—all that really matters.)

And even and intrepid come
The tender boots of night to home.

Her body is like new brown bread
Under the Woolworth mignonette.
Her body is a honey bowl
Whose waiting honey is deep and hot.
Her body is like summer earth,
Receptive, soft, and absolute . . .

THE RITES FOR COUSIN VIT

Carried her unprotesting out the door.
Kicked back the casket-stand. But it can't hold her.
That stuff and satin aiming to enfold her,
The lid's contrition nor the bolts before.
Oh oh. Too much. Too much. Even now, surmise,
She rises in the sunshine. There she goes,
Back to the bars she knew and the repose
In love-rooms and the things in people's eyes.
Too vital and too squeaking. Must emerge.
Even now she does the snake-hips with a hiss,
Slops the bad wine across her shantung, talks
Of pregnancy, guitars and bridgework, walks
In parks or alleys, comes haply on the verge
Of happiness, haply hysterics. Is.

WE REAL COOL

The Pool Players.
Seven at the Golden Shovel.

We real cool. We
Left school. We

Lurk late. We
Strike straight. We

Sing sin. We
Thin gin. We

Jazz June. We
Die soon.

THE CHICAGO DEFENDER SENDS A MAN TO LITTLE ROCK
Fall, 1957

In Little Rock the people bear
Babes, and comb and part their hair
And watch the want ads, put repair
To roof and latch. While wheat toast burns
A woman waters multiferns.

Time upholds or overturns
The many, tight, and small concerns.

In Little Rock the people sing
Sunday hymns like anything,
Through Sunday pomp and polishing.

And after testament and tunes,
Some soften Sunday afternoons
With lemon tea and Lorna Doones.

I forecast
And I believe
Come Christmas Little Rock will cleave
To Christmas tree and trifle, weave,
From laugh and tinsel, texture fast.

In Little Rock is baseball; Barcarolle.
That hotness in July . . . the uniformed figures raw and implacable
And not intellectual,
Batting the hotness or clawing the suffering dust.

The Open Air Concert, on the special twilight green. . . .
When Beethoven is brutal or whispers to lady-like air.
Blanket-sitters are solemn, as Johann troubles to lean
To tell them what to mean. . . .

There is love, too, in Little Rock. Soft women softly
Opening themselves in kindness,
Or, pitying one's blindness,
Awaiting one's pleasure
In azure
Glory with anguished rose at the root. . . .
To wash away old semi-discomfitures.
They re-teach purple and unsullen blue.

The wispy soils go. And uncertain
Half-havings have they clarified to sures.

In Little Rock they know
Not answering the telephone is a way of rejecting life,
That it is our business to be bothered, is our business
To cherish bores or boredom, be polite
To lies and love and many-faceted fuzziness.
I scratch my head, massage the hate-I-had.
I blink across my prim and pencilled pad.
The saga I was sent for is not down.
Because there is a puzzle in this town.
The biggest News I do not dare
Telegraph to the Editor's chair:
"They are like people everywhere."

The angry Editor would reply
In hundred harryings of Why.

And true, they are hurling spittle, rock,
Garbage and fruit in Little Rock.
And I saw coiling storm a-writhe
On bright madonnas. And a scythe
Of men harassing brownish girls.
(The bows and barrettes in the curls
And braids declined away from joy.)

I saw a bleeding brownish boy. . . .

The lariat lynch-wise I deplored.

The lovelist lynchee was our Lord.

MALCOLM X

For Dudley Randall

Original.
Ragged-round.
Rich-robust.

He had the hawk-man's eyes.
We gasped. We saw the maleness.
The maleness raking out and making guttural the air
and pushing us to walls.

And in a soft and fundamental hour
a sorcery devout and vertical
beguiled the world.
He opened us—
who was a key,

who was a man.

THE WALL
August 27, 1967

For Edward Christmas
"The side wall of a typical slum building on the
corner of 43rd and Langley became a mural com-
municating black dignity. . . ."
—Ebony

A drumdrumdrum.
Humbly we come.
South of success and east of gloss and glass are
sandals;
flowercloth;
grave hoops of wood or gold, pendant
from black ears, brown ears, reddish-brown
and ivory ears;

black boy-men.
Black
boy-men on roofs fist out "Black Power!" Val,
a little black stampede
in African
images of brass and flowerswirl,

fists out "Black Power!"—tightens pretty eyes,
leans back on mothercountry and is tract,
is treatise through her perfect and tight teeth.

Women in wool hair chant their poetry.
Phil Cohran gives us messages and music
made of developed bone and polished and honed cult.
It is the Hour of tribe and of vibration,
the day-long Hour. It is the Hour
of ringing, rouse, of ferment-festival.
On Forty-third and Langley
black furnaces resent ancient
legislatures
of ploy and scruple and practical gelatin.
They keep the fever in,
fondle the fever.

All
worship the Wall.

I mount the rattling wood. Walter
says, "She is good." Says, "She
our Sister is." In front of me
hundreds of faces, red-brown, brown, black, ivory,
yield me hot trust, their yea and their Announcement
that they are ready to rile the high-flung ground.
Behind me, Paint.
Heroes.
No child has defiled
the Heroes of this Wall this serious Appointment
this still Wing
this Scald this Flute this heavy Light this Hinge.

An emphasis is paroled.
The old decapitations are revised,
the dispossessions beakless.

And we sing.

UNCLE SEAGRAM

My uncle likes me too much.

I am five and a half years old, and in kindergarten.
In kindergarten everything is clean.

My uncle is six feet tall with seven bumps on his chin.
My uncle is six feet tall, and he stumbles.
He stumbles because of his Wonderful Medicine
packed in his pocket all times.

Family is ma and pa and my uncle,
three brothers, three sisters, and me.

Every night at my house we play checkers and dominoes.
My uncle sits *close*.
There aren't any shoes or socks on his feet.
Under the table a big toe tickles my ankle.
Under the oilcloth his thin knee beats into mine.
And mashes. And mashes.

When we look at TV
my uncle picks *me* to sit on his lap.
As I sit, he gets hard in the middle.
I squirm, but he keeps me, and kisses my ear.

I am not even a girl.

Once, when I went to the bathroom,
my uncle noticed, came in, shut the door,
put his long white tongue in my ear,
and whispered "We're Best Friends, and Family,
and we know how to keep Secrets."

My uncle likes me too much. I am worried.

I do not like my uncle anymore.

Margaret Walker

(1915–   )

THE AUTHOR of two major, prize-winning works, Margaret Walker has done outstanding work in both poetry and fiction. Her first important publication, *For My People* (1942), won a place in the Yale Series of Younger Poets; *Jubilee* (1966), a novel, won a Houghton Mifflin literary award.

Born in Birmingham, Alabama, in 1915, the daughter of a Methodist minister and a music teacher, both university graduates, Margaret Abigail Walker received her early education in church schools in Meridian, Mississippi, Birmingham, and in New Orleans, where she grew up. She took her A.B. degree at Northwestern University, her M.A. in creative writing at the University of Iowa, and her Ph.D. in creative writing also from Iowa, which accepted her novel, *Jubilee*, in lieu of the usual dissertation.

Margaret Walker (Mrs. Firnish James Alexander in private life) has had a full and varied life. Among other things she has been a typist, newspaper reporter, editor of a magazine, a social worker, and a member of the Chicago Federal Writers' Project. She has taught at Livingston College in North Carolina, West Virginia State College, and Jackson State College in Mississippi. She has been a visiting professor at Northwestern University. Now retired, she continues to lecture extensively.

In addition to the two works mentioned above, Walker has published the following volumes: *Ballad of the Free* (1966); *Prophets for a New Day* (1966); *How I Wrote Jubilee* (1972); *October Journey* (1973); *A Poetic Equation: Conversations Between Nikki Giovanni and Margaret Walker*, with Nikki Giovanni (1974); and *The Daemonic Genius of Richard Wright* (1989), *This Is My Century: New and Collected Poems* (1989), and *How I Wrote Jubilee and Other Essays on Life and Literature*, ed. Maryemma Graham (1990).

Jubilee is the fictionalized treatment of Walkers' maternal great-grandmother's experiences during slavery and Reconstruction. In it she makes use of that fascinating treasure house of fact, fiction, legend, and folk material coming from the Negro's slave background. Walker also uses brilliantly other folk material in part 2 of *For My People*.

Several themes are used repeatedly in the poetry of Margaret Walker, among them: the poet's love of the South ("My roots are deep in Southern Life"); a subdued strain of militancy ("Let the martial songs be written . . . / Let a race of men rise up and take control"); and a sense of brotherhood ("There is a journey from me to you").

For recent comment on the life and works of Margaret Walker, see

Eleanor Traylor's article, "Bolder Measures Crashing Through: Margaret Walker's Poem of the Century," in *Callaloo* 10 (Fall 1987). This essay serves as introduction to Walker's complete poems, *This Is My Century: New and Collected Poems.* See also Mari Evans's *Black Women Writers, 1950–1980* (articles by Eugenia Collier and Eleanor Traylor), published in 1984; Claudia Tates's *Black Women at Work* (1983); and Addison Gale, Jr.'s *The Black Aesthetic* (1971).

The two selections that follow come from *For My People* and *Jubilee*, chapters 17 and 18.

FOR MY PEOPLE

For my people everywhere singing their slave songs repeatedly: their
    dirges and their ditties and their blues and jubilees, praying their
    prayers nightly to an unknown god, bending their knees humbly
    to an unseen power;

For my people lending their strength to the years, to the gone years and
    the now years and the maybe years, washing ironing cooking scrub-
    bing sewing mending hoeing plowing digging planting pruning
    patching dragging along never gaining never reaping never knowing
    and never understanding;

For my playmates in the clay and dust and sand of Alabama backyards
    playing baptizing and preaching and doctor and jail and soldier
    and school and mama and cooking and playhouse and concert and
    store and hair and Miss Choomby and company;

For the cramped bewildered years we went to school to learn to know
    the reasons why and the answers to and the people who and the
    places where and the days when, in memory of the bitter hours
    when we discovered we were black and poor and small and dif-
    ferent and nobody cared and nobody wondered and nobody under-
    stood;

For the boys and girls who grew in spite of these things to be man and
    woman, to laugh and dance and sing and play and drink their wine
    and religion and success, to marry their playmates and bear chil-
    dren and then die of consumption and anemia and lynching;

For my people thronging 47th Street in Chicago and Lenox Avenue in
New York and Rampart Street in New Orleans, lost disinherited
dispossessed and happy people filling the cabarets and taverns and
other people's pockets needing bread and shoes and milk and land
and money and something—something all our own;

For my people walking blindly spreading joy, losing time being lazy,
sleeping when hungry, shouting when burdened, drinking when
hopeless, tied and shackled and tangled among ourselves by the
unseen creatures who tower over us omnisciently and laugh;

For my people blundering and groping and floundering in the dark of
churches and schools and clubs and societies, associations and
councils and committees and conventions, distressed and disturbed
and deceived and devoured by money-hungry glory-craving leeches,
preyed on by facile force of state and fad and novelty, by false
prophet and holy believer;

For my people standing staring trying to fashion a better way from
confusion, from hypocrisy and misunderstanding, trying to fashion
a world that will hold all the people, all the faces, all the adams
and eves and their countless generations;

Let a new earth rise. Let another world be born. Let a bloody peace
be written in the sky. Let a second generation full of courage issue
forth; let a people loving freedom come to growth. Let a beauty
full of healing and a strength of final clenching be the pulsing in
our spirits and our blood. Let the martial songs be written, let the
dirges disappear. Let a race of men now rise and take control.

POPPA CHICKEN

Poppa was a sugah daddy
Pimping in his prime;
All the gals for miles around
Walked to Poppa's time.

Poppa Chicken owned the town,
Give his women hell;
All the gals on Poppa's time
Said that he was swell.

Poppa's face was long and black;
Poppa's grin was broad.
When Poppa Chicken walked the streets
The gals cried Lawdy! Lawd!

Poppa Chicken made his gals
Toe his special line:
"Treat 'em rough and make 'em say
Poppa Chicken's fine!"

Poppa Chicken toted guns;
Poppa wore a knife.
One night Poppa shot a guy
Threat'ning Poppa's life.

Poppa done his time in jail
Though he got off light;
Bought his pardon in a year;
Come back out in might.

Poppa walked the streets this time,
Gals around his neck.
And everybody said the jail
Hurt him nary speck.

Poppa smoked his long cigars—
Special Poppa brands—
Rocks all glist'ning in his tie;
On his long black hands.

Poppa lived without a fear;
Walked without a rod.
Poppa cussed the coppers out;
Talked like he was God.

Poppa met a pretty gal;
Heard her name was Rose;
Took one look at her and soon
Bought her pretty clothes.

One night she was in his arms,
In walked her man Joe.
All he done was look and say,
"Poppa's got to go."

Poppa Chicken still is hot
Though he's old and gray,
Walking round here with his gals
Pimping every day.

WE HAVE BEEN BELIEVERS

We have been believers believing in the black gods of an old land,
  believing in the secrets of the seeress and the magic of the charmers
  and the power of the devil's evil ones.

And in the white gods of a new land we have been believers believing
  in the mercy of our masters and the beauty of our brothers, believing
  in the conjure of the humble and the faithful and the pure.

Neither the slavers' whip nor the lynchers' rope nor the bayonet could
  kill our black belief. In our hunger we beheld the welcome table and
  in our nakedness the glory of a long white robe. We have been believers in the new Jerusalem.

We have been believers feeding greedy grinning gods, like a Moloch
  demanding our sons and our daughters, our strength and our wills
  and our spirits of pain. We have been believers, silent and stolid
  and stubborn and strong.

We have been believers yielding substance for the world. With our
  hands have we fed a people and out of our strength have they wrung
  the necessities of a nation. Our song has filled the twilight and our
  hope has heralded the dawn.

Now we stand ready for the touch of one fiery iron, for the cleansing
  breath of many molten truths, that the eyes of the blind may see and
  the ears of the deaf may hear and the tongues of the people be filled
  with living fire.

Where are our gods that they leave us asleep? Surely the priests and
  the preachers and the powers will hear. Surely now that our hands
  are empty and our hearts too full to pray they will understand.
  Surely the sires of the people will send us a sign.

We have been believers believing in our burdens and our demigods too
  long. Now the needy no longer weep and pray; the long-suffering
  arise, and our fists bleed against the bars with a strange insistency.

HARRIET TUBMAN

Dark is the face of Harriet,
Darker still her fate
Deep in the dark of Southern wilds
Deep in the slavers' hate.

Fiery the eye of Harriet,
Fiery, dark, and wild;
Bitter, bleak, and hopeless
Is the bonded child.

Stand in the fields, Harriet,
Stand alone and still
Stand before the overseer
Mad enough to kill.

This is slavery, Harriet,
Bend beneath the lash;
This is Maryland, Harriet,
Bow to poor white trash.

You're a field hand, Harriet,
Working in the corn;
You're a grubber with the hoe
And a slave child born.

You're just sixteen, Harriet,
And never had a beau;
Your mother's dead long time ago,
Your daddy you don't know.

This piece of iron's not hard enough
To kill you with a blow,
This piece of iron can't hurt you,
Just let you slaves all know.

I'm still the overseer,
Old marster'll believe my tale;
I know that he will keep me
From going to the jail.

Get up, bleeding Harriet,
I didn't hit you hard;
Get up, bleeding Harriet,
And grease your head with lard.

Get up, sullen Harriet,
Get up and bind your head.
Remember this is Maryland
And I can beat you dead.

How far is the road to Canada?
How far do I have to go?
How far is the road from Maryland
And the hatred that I know?

I stabbed that overseer;
I took his rusty knife;
I killed that overseer;
I took his lowdown life.

For three long years I waited,
Three years I kept my hate,
Three years before I killed him,
Three years I had to wait.

Done shook the dust of Maryland
Clean off my weary feet;
I'm on my way to Canada
And Freedom's golden street.

I'm bound to git to Canada
Before another week;
I come through swamps and mountains,
I waded many a creek.

Now tell my brothers yonder
That Harriet is free;
Yes, tell my brothers yonder
No more auction block for me.

Come down from the mountain, Harriet,
Come down to the valley at night,
Come down to your weeping people
And be their guiding light.

Sing Deep Dark River of Jordan,
Don't you want to cross over today?
Sing Deep Wide River of Jordan,
Don't you want to walk Freedom's way?

I stole down in the night time,
I come back in the day,
I stole back to my Maryland
To guide the slaves away.

I met old marster yonder
A-coming down the road,
And right past me in Maryland
My old marster strode.

I passed beside my marster
And covered up my head;
My marster didn't know me
I guess he heard I'm dead.

I wonder if he thought about
That overseer's dead;
I wondered if he figured out
He ought to know this head?

You'd better run, brave Harriet,
There's ransom on your head;
You better run, Miss Harriet,
They want you live or dead.

Been down in valleys yonder
And searching round the stills,
They got the posse after you,
A-riding through the hills.

They got the blood hounds smelling,
They got their guns cocked too;
You better run, bold Harriet,
The white man's after you.

They got ten thousand dollars
Put on your coal-black head;
They'll give ten thousand dollars;
They're mad because you fled.

I wager they'll be riding
A long, long time for you.
Yes, Lord, they'll look a long time
Till Judgment Day is due.

I'm Harriet Tubman, people,
I'm Harriet the slave,
I'm Harriet, free woman,
And I'm free within my grave.

Come along, children, with Harriet
Come along, children, come along
Uncle Sam is rich enough
To give you all a farm.

I killed the overseer.
I fooled old marster's eyes,
I found my way to Canada
With hundreds more besides.

Come along to Harpers Ferry
Come along to brave John Brown
Come along Harriet, children,
Come along ten million strong.

I met the mighty John Brown,
I know Fred Douglass too
Enlisted Abolitionists
Beneath the Union Blue.

I heard the mighty trumpet
That sent the land to war;
I mourned for Mister Lincoln
And saw his funeral car.

Come along with Harriet, children,
Come along to Canada.
Come down to the river, children,
And follow the northern star.

I'm Harriet Tubman, people,
I'm Harriet, the slave,
I'm Harriet, free woman,
And I'm free beyond my grave.

Come along to freedom, children,
Come along ten million strong;
Come along with Harriet, children,
Come along ten million strong.

FROM **JUBILEE**

Put on Men's Clothes and a Man's Old Cap

Early in the next week Randall Ware came to visit Vyry. He came as usual, at night, after the regular run of the patter-roller. Vyry was

---

listening for the second call of the whippoorwill when suddenly she heard the crackling sound of a shot distinctly ring out in the autumn night. When Randall Ware reached her cabin he was bleeding profusely, although the bullet had only grazed her arm.

"It's only a scratch," he said, but she was shaking with fear.

He was also somewhat shaken and truly alarmed despite his attempted bravado. While she washed and dressed the flesh wound, they talked.

"This means I got to go."

"Go where?"

"Go away from here; get out of Georgia, maybe get clean outen the South."

Vyry began to cry.

"Don't cry. I can take you with me, if you've got the will to go."

"What you mean?"

"I mean run away."

"How I'm gwine run away with two children?"

"Leave them here."

"Leave my younguns? Is you done lost your senses?"

"Naw. If you'll just trust me and do like I say, you'll get your babies back again, but you can't run far with them pulling on you."

"If I leave my children, I'll never see them no more in this life. Sho's you born to die, I'll never see them no more."

"Do you want to be free?"

"You know I wants my freedom, but I ain't leaving my younguns."

"I keep telling you they'll be safe. Leave them like I say, and you'll get your freedom and your babies."

"Naw. Big Missy'll sell them. She'll sell 'em sho's you born. I knows that woman. She hates me worser than poison."

"She won't do no such thing. They too young to bring a price. I got plans to see they are taken care of. We'll have them again as soon as we get out the South and out of danger."

"What kinda plans you got now?"

"If I can just get you to Maryland, there's a woman there to take you straight into Canady. I know the road all the way to Maryland. I know every underground stop."

"Underground? Underground where?"

"Underground railroad. Don't you know the secret road slaves use to escape up North? Lucy went that way, and if you do like I say, as milk white-skinned as you are anyhow, you won't have a speck of trouble."

"What kinda plans you got for my younguns?"

"I'm begging you to trust me; believe me when I say they'll be safe. And we won't lose them. You will surely see them again."

"I knows I is, cause I ain't leaving them."

"All right, you be stubborn and stay here. They'll be worse off here with you than they'll be if you do like I say. And anyways they just ain't no ifs and buts about it, I gotta go. If they catch me again out here they liable to kill me. This here bullet tonight ain't nothing but a warning. I thought you wanted your freedom. I wants you and the younguns with me but if you ain't coming . . ."

"What you want me to do?"

"Wait till Friday night. Don't tell nobody nothing; but start getting ready tomorrow. Put on men's clothes, a pair of britches and a coat, and a man's old cap. Be sure you dress good and warm, and dress the younguns too. Dress them good and warm and give the baby a sugar tit. Then lie down till midnight. Wait till you see the moon riding straight up overhead and then leave. Be sure you leave the younguns. They'll be sleeping and they won't know when you leave. Then make it to the swamp. But don't walk the log across the creek. You know where the lowest part of the water is?"

She nodded her head for yes.

"Wade through the low water. That'll kill the scent of your tracks, cause bloodhounds lose the scent in the water, and they won't come across."

"Bloodhounds?" Her eyes widened.

"Well, when they miss you, they liable to sic the dogs on you. You know that as well as I do. That's why I say leave by midnight and come by yourself. There'll be somebody waiting for you on the other side of the creek."

"Don't you reckon they can pick up my scent across the crick quick as they do here?"

"If you do like I say, you'll be a long ways off when they start to look for you."

"I don't like it. I don't like it, at all. Supposen something go wrong?"

"Something's already done gone wrong."

"What you mean?"

"That boy you sent that note by mixed it with the pass. That's how come they wouldn't sell. They knowed I had a man set to buy you."

"Was the man there?"

"Of course he was. I got old man Bob Qualls, but I reckon they getting on to him, his buying slaves and setting them free, and they suspecting he's a abolitionist, too."

"You think that's how come they wouldn't sell?"

"I told him not to let nobody outbid him, don't care how high they go, and I know he done what I said, but before they would sell to him, they quit."

"Stead of me, they sold the boy."

"That's what I'm talking about. That's what I know. They watching me. They been watching me, and now they may be watching you. I gotta go. You can see tonight how come I gotta go, but I don't wanta leave you here."

"I wants to go with you. I wants to go bad."

"Do like I say and I won't have to slip here no more."

"What I'm gwine do with Jim and Minna?"

"Leave them to me. Do like I say. I'll meet you Friday night, and mind, don't you fail to come alone!"

Friday was a rainy day. It rained all day until nearly ten o'clock that night and the ground was soaked and muddy. Vyry was tense and desperate. She was so jumpy and nervous and so fearful she could scarcely control herself. She seemed to sense, however, that this night might be the last break she could make for freedom. Everything else had failed. If once her little family became separated they might never be together again. She knew how slave families were constantly sold one by one to different masters in faraway places. If Randall Ware were caught or killed here Marse John could claim his property, all his land as well as the family he owned. He could even say her free man was a slave and belonged to him. When the rain poured down all day she began to give up hope of going, but at last it ended and the moon came out again quite clear and bright in the sky.

Her baby, Minna, was teething. She was feverish and fretful; cried easily, and was wakeful. Vyry nursed her and gave her water, but she slept fitfully until late in the night. Vyry would look at Minna and her heart would turn over in loving anguish at the thought of leaving a helpless nursing baby. After the rain ceased and the moon came out, she felt it was getting late, so she put on her clothes to go. She had so much under the breeches they felt tight. They were very unfamiliar anyway since she had borrowed them without asking anyone's permission. Suddenly the baby slept. She stood and looked at her children a long time, and then she stood in the door of her cabin and watched the moon climb high in the sky. Just as she turned to kiss the children once more goodbye, Jim woke up. He wanted to get up and she helped him, but when he saw her strange clothes he whimpered drowsily and asked here where she was going. She answered him, "Nowhere," so he went back to sleep.

The moon went in and out of the clouds in the sky, weaving back and forth through darkness into light. She still hesitated. Each time the baby cried out in her fretful sleep, Vyry winced as if someone had touched her. She turned again to the door and seeing the moon moving across the top of the sky, sailing through the middle, she steeled her inner resolve, and then taking the knapsack she had prepared with food and water, she started from the cabin. This time Minna cried loudly and Jim opened his eyes wide. Vyry trembled in desperation. She grabbed the baby and told Jim to get up, too. He was so sleepy he could not move fast, but since he was already dressed in all his clothes she only paused long enough to wrap the baby again. Then, with the baby in her arms and Jim pulling on her stuffed pantsleg, she started out to make it to the swamp.

Whenever it had rained as much as it had rained that day, the packed clay around the quarters was thick and gooey. Every step Vyry and Jim took, they could feel the mud sucking their feet down and fighting them as they withdrew their feet from its elastic hold. Jim was so sleepy and so little and so scared of the night that he whimpered and whined and cried with each step. The baby still slept fitfully while Vyry pressed her way doggedly to the swamps. She knew Randall Ware would be angry. "But I couldn't leave my children; I just couldn't. I knows if I leave my baby she will die."

They were leaving a tell-tale trail of footsteps behind them with no accompanying rain to wash away the tracks. She heard hoot owls, night noises of small creatures—birds and insects, a distant dog's baying at the moon, but no whippoorwill. They had gone no more than a mile and she had nearly three-quarters of a mile to go farther, when day began to break and roosters began to crow for morning. Desperately, Vyry tried to hurry. The baby sucked on the sugar tit and slept quietly, but poor Jim was still stumbling along, crying and whimpering and whining to himself. At last they were in sight of the swamps. Feeling sorry for little Jim she decided to rest a few minutes before trying to wade the creek. She would have to take both her children in her arms and then balance them on her hips with the small knapsack slung across her back in order to wade the creek. She sat down on an old log, meaning to rest only a few minutes.

The morning was foggy and over the creek the fog hung like a thick gray cloud, but despite its density she began to discern figures moving. A bad spasm clutched her stomach instinctively. She tensed her body with the sure intuition that she was not only being watched but that the watchful figures would soon surround her. Impassively she saw the patter-roller and guards, together with Grimes, emerge from the shadows and walk toward her. Fervently she prayed that Randall Ware was no longer waiting for her across the creek, but had gone on his way. As for herself, she was too tired and bleak to care. Exhausted and hopeless she sat and waited for the men who surrounded her to capture her and her children. She could not have run one step if her very life had depended on it. Despite everything, she felt glad the children were still with her and they were safe. She

looked into little Minna's sleeping face and smiled, and she patted
Jim's hand softly to reassure him of her nearness. Then she pulled
him closer to her in a warm embrace.

> *I look up at the stars,*
> *and I look at my scars,*
> *and I look at my children*
> *and I wonder . . .*

Seventy-five Lashes on Her Naked Back

That morning going back to the plantation everything around her
seemed unreal. The fog lifted slowly and through the misty morning
she moved steadily toward what she knew would be her punishment. The children were not alarmed, and for that she was glad. Little Jim trotted homeward without a whimper while the baby sleeping
in her arms was soundless. Grimes and his men did not speak to her
but she knew that they were ruthless and there would be no compassion. It was a well-known fact that if a slave ran away and was
caught in the act, flogging was the punishment. She could expect a
whipping. She did not let herself think ahead beyond each step.
Once she thought about Marse John. Perhaps he would interfere and
not let them beat her. But she knew this was not possible because he
was never at home whenever anything happened. He had been gone
three days and might be gone two or three more; supposedly, he had
gone to town on business. Maybe they can put it off until he comes
home. No, she also knew better than that. Big Missy would want to
get this over with before Marster's return. It was always easier for
Miss Salina to explain things later and justify them most after they
had occurred. Vyry was not at all surprised, therefore, when Grimes
took her children from her on entering Marster's backyard. He led
her to the whipping post not far from the wet fields where the field
hands were not working this morning because the ground was too
wet.

Two of Grimes's men tied her hands together as if she were folding them to pray, and then stretched them high above her head.
They tied her to the post so that her feet were tied together and
crossed above the ground. It seemed as if she were hanging on the
post in mid-air, her feet stretched as far as they could stretch without touching the earth beneath her and her hands stretched as far
above her head without reaching beyond the post. Her body was naked to the waist, and she braced herself to bear the lash of the whip
upon her naked flesh.

Grimes did not choose to beat her. One of the guards who was
generally hired to whip slaves was now ready to flog Vyry.

He took the whip in his hands. It was a raw-hide coach-whip used to spur the horses. He twirled it up high over his head, and when he came down with it he wrapped it all the way around her body and cut neatly into her breast and across her back all at the same time with one motion while the whip was a-singing in the air. It cut the air and her flesh and cried "zing" and Vyry saw stars that were red and black and silver, and there were a thousand of those stars in the midnight sky and her head felt as if it would split open and the whip cut her like a red-hot poke iron or a knife that was razor sharp and cut both ways. The whip burned like fire and cut the blood out of her and stung like red-hot pins sticking in her flesh while her head was reeling and whirling. It hurt so badly she felt as if her flesh were a single molten flame, and before she could catch her breath and brace herself again, he had wrapped the whip around her the second time. When she heard the whip go "zing" the second time and felt the stars rocking in her head, she opened her mouth to scream, but her throat was too dry to holler and she gritted her teeth and smashed her head hard against the post in order to steel herself once more to bear the pain. When he wrapped her all around with the whip the third time she thought she heard a roaring noise like thunder rumbling and a forest of trees falling in a flood. Everything went black; she was caught up in the blackness of a storm. She was whirling around in a cutting, fiery wind while the fire was burning her flesh like a tormenting fever and she kept sinking down in the fire and fighting the blackness until every light went out like a candle and she fainted.

She never did know how many lashes he gave her, whether he cut her the required seventy-five times as he was told to do, or whether he quit short of that number, thinking she was already dead and further beating was useless.

When she came to she heard a buzzing in her ears and everything still looked black though it wasn't yet evening. It must have been afternoon but there was no sunlight. Somebody had cut her loose from the post and left her huddled in a heap on the ground at the bottom of the whipping post. At first she thought it was night because all she could see looked black. She looked at her hands and her arms and she pulled at the shreds of rags on her legs and all her flesh looked black. She was as black as a man's hat and she was black like that all over. She looked around her on the ground and saw blood splattered and clotted around her while something glistened white like salt. Although her mind was still dazed she knew now why her back was still on fire and she felt as if she were lying on a bed of red-hot needles and iron. It was the salt somebody had thrown on her bleeding raw back. She was too weak to move. She wondered why she was still living, because they must have meant to kill her. "Why has God let me live?" *All the black people must be scared to come and get me till it is black dark. Maybe they think I'm dead. Lawd, have mercy, Jesus! Send somebody to get me soon, please Jesus!* The flies were making the buzzing sound and she felt her body throbbing in a rhythm with the flies. Fever parched her lips and eyes and her bruised hands and ran through her brutalized flesh.

After dark the other house servants came and got her and took her to her cabin. Caline and May Liza poured warm oil on her back and washed it free of salt. Then they put her on a soft pallet of rags and let her sleep. When the fever had parched its course through Vyry and the raw bruises began to form healing scars, the cloud in her mind began to lift. She could remember deep waves and complete inundation in the dark waters that threatened to take her under. She could not remember her own children and when they were brought to her she did not know them. Once she thought she saw Marse John standing over her and thought she heard him cursing terrible oaths, but even his face was vague in her memory. Caline and May Liza brought her hot broth to drink and coaxed her to swallow but she did not know them either or remember what they had done. After three days the fever seemed to be leaving her and her mind began to clear. She was too weak to speak above a whisper, and when she was able to examine herself she saw where one of the lashes had left a loose flap of flesh over her breast like a tuck in a dress. It healed that way.

Robert Hayden

(1913–1980)

THE FIRST NEGRO to be appointed consultant in poetry to the Library of Congress, a position he held for two years, Robert Hayden is definitely one of the outstanding American poets of our generation. Although Hayden lived through the Black Arts revolution in poetry, he was not touched by it to any appreciable extent. Unlike Gwendolyn Brooks, he did not become converted to "blackness." He believed that black poetry in spite of its specialized content was "essentially American"; he also believed that "any poet's most clearly defined task is to create with honesty and sincerity poems that will illuminate human experience—not exclusively *Negro experience.*"

Born in Detroit, Michigan, Robert Hayden was educated at Wayne State University, taking there his A.B. in 1936. After working for two years with the Federal Writers' Project, where he directed research in local black history and folklore, he attended the University of Michigan, receiving from that school his M.A. in English. He taught English for two years at the University of Michigan, twice winning there the university's prestigious Avery Hopgood Award for Poetry (in 1938 and in 1942).

Hayden's professional career was not confined wholly to teaching, although, outside of writing, that was his major pursuit. After leaving the University of Michigan, he worked as music and drama critic for the *Michigan Chronicle*, leaving this position in 1946 to join the faculty of Fisk University as a professor of English. He stayed at Fisk until 1968, returning then to Michigan. A prominent follower of the Baha'i faith, Hayden was an editor of *World Order*, the Baha'i magazine.

In addition to the Avery Hopgood Poetry awards mentioned previously, Hayden received a Rosenwald Fellowship in 1947, a Ford Foundation grant in 1954, and the Grand Prize for Poetry at the First World Festival of Negro Arts in Dakar, Senegal, in 1965 for *A Ballad of Remembrance.*

A superb craftsman and a perfectionist, Hayden grew with the years. His verses became more sensitive, subtle, and provocative as his insights deepened. Throughout his life, he wrote for a "fit audience though few."

Among Robert Hayden's publications are the following works: *Heart-shape in the Dust* (1940); *The Lion and the Archer*, with Myron O'Higgins (1949); *Figure of Time: Poems* (1955); *A Ballad of Remembrance* (1962); *Selected Poems* (1966); *Words in the Mourning Time* (1970); *The Night-Blooming Cereus* (1972); *Angle of Ascent: New and Selected Poems* (1975);

and *American Journal* (1978). Hayden also edited two anthologies: *Kaleidoscope: Poems by American Negro Poets* (1967) and (with David J. Burroughs and Frederick R. Lapides) *Afro-American Literature: An Introduction* (1970). Hayden's *Collected Prose*, edited by Frederick Glaysher, appeared in 1984, followed by *Collected Poetry*, also edited by Glaysher, in 1985.

For biographical and critical comment on Robert Hayden, see the following works: Arthur P. Davis's *From the Dark Tower* (1974); Stephen Henderson's *Understanding the New Black Poetry* (1973); Richard Barksdale and Keneth Kinnamon's *Black Writers of America* (1972); Julius Lester's comment on *Words in the Mourning Time* in the *New York Times Book Review* (January 24, 1971); and the excellent recent study, Pontheolla T. Williams's *Robert Hayden: A Critical Analysis of His Poetry* (1987). Additional recent comment may be found in two 1984 critical biographies, *From the Auroral Darkness: The Life and Poetry of Robert Hayden*, by John Hatcher, and *Robert Hayden*, by Fred M. Fetrow.

The following selections are from *Selected Poems* (1966).

THE DIVER

Sank through easeful
azure. Flower
creatures flashed and
shimmered there—
lost images
fadingly remembered.
Swiftly descended
into canyon of cold
nightgreen emptiness.
Freefalling, weightless
as in dreams of
wingless flight,
plunged through infra-
space and came to
the dead ship,
carcass that swarmed with
voracious life.
Angelfish, their
lively blue and
yellow prised from

darkness by the
flashlight's beam,
thronged her portholes
Moss of bryozoans
blurred, obscured her
metal. Snappers,
gold groupers explored her,
fearless of bubbling
manfish. I entered
the wreck, awed by her silence,
feeling more keenly
the iron cold.
With flashlight probing
fogs of water
saw the sad slow
dance of gilded
chairs, the ectoplasmic
swirl of garments,
drowned instruments
of buoyancy,
drunken shoes. Then
livid gesturings,
eldritch hide and
seek of laughing
faces. I yearned to
find those hidden
ones, to fling aside
the mask and call to them,
yield to rapturous
whisperings, have
done with self and
every dinning
vain complexity.
Yet in languid
frenzy strove, as
one freezing fights off
sleep desiring sleep;
strove against the
cancelling arms that
suddenly surrounded
me, fled the numbing
kisses that I craved.
Reflex of life-wish?
Respirator's brittle

belling? Swam from
the ship somehow;
somehow began the
measured rise.

HOMAGE TO THE EMPRESS OF THE BLUES

Because there was a man somewhere in a candystripe silk shirt,
gracile and dangerous as a jaguar and because a woman moaned
for him in sixty-watt gloom and mourned him Faithless Love
Twotiming Love Oh Love Oh Careless Aggravating Love,

>She came out on the stage in yards of pearls, emerging like
>a favorite scenic view, flashed her golden smile and sang.

Because grey laths began somewhere to show from underneath
torn hurdygurdy lithographs of dollfaced heaven;
and because there were those who feared alarming fists of snow
on the door and those who feared the riot-squad of statistics,

>She came out on the stage in ostrich feathers, beaded satin,
>and shone that smile on us and sang.

MIDDLE PASSAGE

1

Jesús, Estrella, Esperanza, Mercy:

>Sails flashing to the wind like weapons,
>sharks following the moans the fever and the dying;
>horror the corposant and compass rose.

Middle Passage:
>>voyage through death
>>>to life upon these shores.

>>"10 April 1800—
>>Blacks rebellious. Crew uneasy. Our linguist says
>>their moaning is a prayer for death,

ours and their own. Some try to starve themselves.
Lost three this morning leaped with crazy laughter
to the waiting sharks, sang as they went under."

Desire, Adventure, Tartar, Ann:

Standing to America, bringing home
black gold, black ivory, black seed.

> *Deep in the festering hold thy father lies,*
> *of his bones New England pews are made,*
> *those are altar lights that were his eyes.*

Jesus Saviour Pilot Me
Over Life's Tempestuous Sea

We pray that Thou wilt grant, O Lord,
safe passage to our vessels bringing
heathen souls unto Thy chastening.

Jesus Saviour

"8 bells. I cannot sleep, for I am sick
with fear, but writing eases fear a little
since still my eyes can see these words take shape
upon the page & so I write, as one
would turn to exorcism. 4 days scudding,
but now the sea is calm again. Misfortune
follows in our wake like sharks (our grinning
tutelary gods). Which one of us
has killed an albatross? A plague among
our blacks—Ophthalmia: blindness—& we
have jettisoned the blind to no avail.
It spreads, the terrifying sickness spreads.
Its claws have scratched sight from the Capt.'s eyes
& there is blindness in the fo'c'sle
& we must sail 3 weeks before we come
to port."

> *What port awaits us, Davy Jones'*
> *or home? I've heard of slavers drifting, drifting,*
> *playthings of wind and storm and chance, their crews*
> *gone blind, the jungle hatred*
> *crawling up on deck.*

Thou Who Walked On Galilee

"Deponent further sayeth *The Bella J*
left the Guinea Coast

with cargo of five hundred blacks and odd
for the barracoons of Florida:

"That there was hardly room 'tween-decks for half
the sweltering cattle stowed spoon-fashion there;
that some went mad of thirst and tore their flesh
and sucked the blood:

"That Crew and Captain lusted with the comeliest
of the savage girls kept naked in the cabins;
that there was one they called The Guinea Rose
and they cast lots and fought to lie with her:

"That when the Bo's'n piped all hands, the flames
spreading from starboard already were beyond
control, the negroes howling and their chains
entangled with the flames:

"That the burning blacks could not be reached,
that the Crew abandoned ship,
leaving their shrieking negresses behind,
that the Captain perished drunken with the wenches:

"Further Deponent sayeth not."

Pilot Oh Pilot Me

2

Aye, lad, and I have seen those factories,
Gambia, Rio Pongo, Calabar;
have watched the artful mongos baiting traps
of war wherein the victor and the vanquished

Were caught as prizes for our barracoons.
Have seen the nigger kings whose vanity
and greed turned wild black hides of Fellatah,
Mandingo, Ibo, Kru to gold for us.

And there was one—King Anthracite we named him—
fetish face beneath French parasols
of brass and orange velvet, impudent mouth
whose cups were carven skulls of enemies:

He'd honor us with drum and feast and conjo
and palm-oil-glistening wenches deft in love,
and for tin crowns that shone with paste,
red calico and German-silver trinkets

Would have the drums talk war and send
his warriors to burn the sleeping villages

and kill the sick and old and lead the young
in coffles to our factories.

Twenty years a trader, twenty years,
for there was wealth aplenty to be harvested
from those black fields, and I'd be trading still
but for the fevers melting down my bones.

3

Shuttles in the rocking loom of history,
the dark ships move, the dark ships move,
their bright ironical names
like jests of kindness on a murderer's mouth;
plough through thrashing glister toward
fata morgana's lucent melting shore,
weave toward New World littorals that are
mirage and myth and actual shore.

Voyage through death,
                             voyage whose chartings are unlove.
A charnel stench, effluvium of living death
spreads outward from the hold,
where the living and the dead, the horribly dying,
lie interlocked, lie foul with blood and excrement.

> *Deep in the festering hold thy father lies,*
> *the corpse of mercy rots with him,*
> *rats eat love's rotten gelid eyes.*

> *But, oh, the living look at you*
> *with human eyes whose suffering accuses you,*
> *whose hatred reaches through the swill of dark*
> *to strike you like a leper's claw.*

> *You cannot stare that hatred down*
> *or chain the fear that stalks the watches*
> *and breathes on you its fetid scorching breath;*
> *cannot kill the deep immortal human wish,*
> *the timeless will.*

"But for the storm that flung up barriers
of wind and wave, *The Amistad*, señores,
would have reached the port of Príncipe in two,
three days at most; but for the storm we should
have been prepared for what befell.
Swift as the puma's leap it came. There was
that interval of moonless calm filled only
with the water's and the rigging's usual sounds,

then sudden movement, blows and snarling cries
and they had fallen on us with machete
and marlinspike. It was as though the very
air, the night itself were striking us.
Exhausted by the rigors of the storm,
we were no match for them. Our men went down
before the murderous Africans. Our loyal
Celestino ran from below with gun
and lantern and I saw, before the cane-
knife's wounding flash, Cinquez,
that surly brute who calls himself a prince,
directing, urging on the ghastly work.
He hacked the poor mulatto down, and then
he turned on me. The decks were slippery
when daylight finally came. It sickens me
to think of what I saw, of how these apes
threw overboard the butchered bodies of
our men, true Christians all, like so much jetsam.
Enough, enough. The rest is quickly told:
Cinquez was forced to spare the two of us
you see to steer the ship to Africa,
and we like phantoms doomed to rove the sea
voyaged east by day and west by night,
deceiving them, hoping for rescue,
prisoners on our own vessel, till
at length we drifted to the shores of this
your land, America, where we were freed
from our unspeakable misery. Now we
demand, good sirs, the extradition of
Cinquez and his accomplices to La
Havana. And it distresses us to know
there are so many here who seem inclined
to justify the mutiny of these blacks.
We find it paradoxical indeed
that you whose wealth, whose tree of liberty
are rooted in the labor of your slaves
should suffer the august John Quincy Adams
to speak with so much passion of the right
of chattel slaves to kill their lawful masters
and with his Roman rhetoric weave a hero's
garland for Cinquez. I tell you that
we are determined to return to Cuba
with our slaves and there see justice done. Cinquez—
or let us say 'the Prince'—Cinquez shall die."

The deep immortal human wish,
the timeless will:

    Cinquez its deathless primaveral image,
    life that transfigures many lives.

Voyage through death
                to life upon these shores.

FREDERICK DOUGLASS

When it is finally ours, this freedom, this liberty, this beautiful
and terrible thing, needful to man as air,
usable as earth; when it belongs at last to all,
when it is truly instinct, brain matter, diastole, systole,
reflex action; when it is finally won; when it is more
than the gaudy mumbo jumbo of politicians:
this man, this Douglass, this former slave, this Negro
beaten to his knees, exiled, visioning a world
where none is lonely, none hunted, alien,
this man, superb in love and logic, this man
shall be remembered. Oh, not with statues' rhetoric,
not with legends and poems and wreaths of bronze alone,
but with the lives grown out of his life, the lives
fleshing his dream of the beautiful, needful thing.

O DAEDALUS, FLY AWAY HOME

Drifting night in the Georgia pines,
coonskin drum and jubilee banjo.
    Pretty Malinda, dance with me.

Night is juba, night is conjo.
    Pretty Malinda, dance with me.

Night is an African juju man
weaving a wish and a weariness together
    to make two wings.

    O fly away home fly away

Do you remember Africa?

    O cleave the air fly away home

My gran, he flew back to Africa,
just spread his arms and
   flew away home.

Drifting night in the windy pines;
night is a laughing, night is a longing.
   Pretty Malinda, come to me.

Night is a mourning juju man
weaving a wish and a weariness together
   to make two wings.

   O fly away home fly away

Ulysses Lee

(1913–1969)

COLLEGE PROFESSOR, editor, army officer, scholar, and historian, Ulysses Grant Lee, Jr., was born in Washington, D.C., the son of middle-class parents. His father owned a grocery store in nearby Maryland, but in his earlier days had been a cavalry sergeant in the United States Army.

Lee was educated at the District's famed Dunbar High School, at Howard University, where he received his A.B., *summa cum laude*, and his M.A. He spent a year at the University of Pennsylvania and then moved to the University of Chicago, where he earned his Ph.D., "with honors." A brilliant and many-sided scholar, Lee's major field was the history of culture, with a concentration in American literature, history, church history, philosophy, and art.

His professional life was as varied as his academic. Beginning as a graduate assistant at Howard, he subsequently taught at Lincoln University (Missouri), moved from there to teach at Morgan State College (now University), and during the year of his death, he was concurrently a professor at Morgan and at the University of Pennsylvania.

Lee's professional life outside the academic world included several important editing assignments, among them the Federal Writers' Project, where he worked on two of the project's outstanding publications: *Washington: City and Capital* and *The Negro in Virginia*. He was associate editor of *The Midwest Journal*, an editor for the Arno Press, a member of the editorial board of *CLA Journal*, and associate editor of the *Journal of Negro History*. At the time of his death, he was the editor-designate of the last-named work.

Ulysses Lee had two careers, one in the academic world, another in the military. He started the second career as a commissioned graduate of Howard's ROTC program and a reservist. Called up in 1942, he was among the first officers to be assigned to the Information and Education Division of the Amy. During World War II, he served as an education officer and editorial analyst both in the field and at the headquarters of Army Service Forces. From 1946 to 1952 (he was given the rank of major in the latter year), he was staff historian of the Office of the Chief of Military History, Department of the Army. It was also during this period that Major Lee, as a specialist on all phases of the Negro's connection with the United States Army, wrote his major work, *The Employment of Negro Troops* (*United States Army in World War II*), a scholarly and history-making study.

Lee produced two major works; in addition to the one mentioned previously, he edited (with Sterling A. Brown and Arthur P. Davis) *The Negro Caravan*, a pioneering anthology of Negro writings. He also wrote a number of scholarly articles for the *1944 Army Service Manual*, the *Journal of Negro History, Présence Africaine, Current History*, and other periodicals.

Throughout Dr. Lee's entire academic life, he won awards and honors for achievement. The first came in his high school years, when he won the Harvard Club Award. During his later years, he was given the Rosenwald, the Alvia Kay Brown (University of Chicago), and the Rockefeller fellowships. He received the Army Commendation Medal in 1946, and in 1958 was elected an alumni member of Howard's chapter of Phi Beta Kappa.

Very little biographical material on Lee has been published. The entry in *Dictionary of American Negro Biography*, written by Arthur P. Davis, is perhaps the fullest account. See also Robert Ewell Greene's *Black Defenders of America, 1775–1973: A Reference and Pictorial History* (1974), which has a brief sketch of Ulysses Lee's life. The Lee Papers are found in Howard University's Moorland-Spingarn Research Center.

The selection that follows comes from *Current History* (July, 1968). Some of the findings in this essay throw light on the place of blacks even in conflicts that followed Vietnam, such as the crisis in the Persian Gulf (1990–91).

THE DRAFT AND THE NEGRO

Pick up any metropolitan newspaper and look at the photographs from the front in Vietnam; read the obituaries of men killed in action; observe the video-tapes and the picture essays in *Life* and *Look* and *The New York Times Magazine*. One fact is clear: there are proportionately more Negroes in the United States combat forces and on the battle lines today than there were in any other military action in American history. The reasons lie in the past and in the present; in the nature of the American societal fabric; and in the nature and operation of the draft laws and enlistment regulations. The effects of disproportionate Negro participation alter the nature of armed forces and of our society and, more especially, the lives and attitudes of Negroes in the United States today.

In a more nearly perfect democracy, there would be little reason to discuss Negroes and the draft, for Negroes would be affected and they would react in consonance with the rest of the national population. But despite the massive alteration of the terms of Negroes' service in the armed forces and in the position of Negroes in American life since the close of World War II, no one can seriously argue in 1968 that Negroes do not constitute a special, still "unfinished business" for the American democracy. The intensive civil rights activities of the 1960's, followed by a series of disastrous riots, summer after summer, in the great American cities, culminated in the arson and looting which followed the assassination of Dr. Martin Luther King, Jr., in April, 1968.

The nation's continuing failure to come to grips with the poverty of the rural South as well as that of the great city ghettos overshadows the simultaneously increasing integration of Negroes into many phases of American life, including the economic, on the managerial level, and the political, on the decision-making level. The increase of serious studies of "the Negro in American life" and the greater exposure of Negroes in the entertainment, sports, and intellectual worlds do not alter the essentials of the present situation. Not even a set of legally nondiscriminatory draft regulations, nor legally nondiscriminatory armed services (which are probably closer in fact to this ideal than any other discernible American institution) can alter the fact that in the pursuit of their daily and even their presumably patriotic duties Negroes face problems different from those of the population at large.

They also differ from those of our smaller, less widely distributed, and therefore less visibly distinctive minorities. For although Puerto Ricans, American Indians, Mexican-Americans, and Orientals face problems analogous to those of American Negroes in particular parts of the nation, they can still expect an approach different in kind and manner in the rest of the country. Though there have been separate and special Puerto Rican and Japanese-American—and even Filipino and Norwegian-American—units in the armed forces in the past, these proceeded from a different social and military philosophy from that which provided segregated Negro units in the armed forces from the Civil War (and, in some instances, from the American Revolution) through World War II. On the surface, today, the draft operates without discrimination; Selective Service no longer keeps records by race; the prospective Negro draftee takes the same chances as anyone else. But, in reality, for a variety of reasons, this is not yet the case.

Historical Position of the Negro

The services of Negroes in the land and naval forces of the United States from the days of the colonial militia to the present have been well documented. Up to the Civil War, the nation relied largely upon volunteers with state militia forces at their core. Distinguished personages in their own communities raised companies and regiments; these, in turn, entered the service of the nation and were counted against the quotas levied against each state. During the Revolution, local units might contain a varying number of Negroes, some of them free volunteers, some of them slaves serving in the hope of obtaining their freedom thereby, some serving in the places of their masters. In some cases, full companies of Negroes, such as Connecticut's "Attucks Guards" and Boston's "Massasoit Guards," were organized. Virginia's navy of 40 vessels had Negroes aboard each ship.

But by the time of the Civil War, and for 80 years thereafter, it was true that "Negroes must fight for the right to fight." Early in the war, free Negroes volunteered their services to the Union forces, only to be rejected as a matter of political as well as social policy. By the middle of 1862, when volunteers for the Union forces were becoming scarce, Union generals, like David Hunter in South Carolina and J. H. Lane in Kansas, began to form Negro regiments without full authorization; and, in New Orleans, B. F. Butler organized the Louisiana "Native Guards." On March 3, 1863, in response to the growing manpower problems of the Northern armies, Congress passed the first national draft law in the nation's history. Subsequently states (including Rhode Island and Massachusetts) raised volunteer Negro units whose enlistees counted against state quotas even when the units were recruited in the South.

Draft–Race Riots

The new draft law and the reaction of white Northern workingmen to the formal Emancipation Proclamation issued on January 1, 1863, precipitated the New York draft riots, the bloodiest race riots in American history. The draft law provided that a drafted man might purchase his release for a payment of $300. Working men, often recent immigrants, already believing that freed slaves would migrate north and usurp their jobs, saw the new draft law as a measure discriminating against them in favor of the rich. Anti-war Copperhead orators and newspapers declared that Northern workingmen were being forced to fight and risk death for the freedom of slaves who would soon take their jobs. Riots began when the names of the first draftees appeared in the New York papers on Sunday, July 12, 1863. Draft headquarters, saloons and newspapers were the mob's first targets; then they attacked any Negro found on the streets. By the second day, the homes and businesses of those employing or sympathizing with Negroes were looted and burned. What began as anti-draft riots ended as anti-Negro riots, with the Colored Orphan Asylum one of the main targets. The riot lasted four days, and Negro bodies were left hanging from the trees and lampposts on the streets of New York.

Thus, the first American draft law had an immediate social effect upon Negroes. The Bureau of Colored Troops, established in May, 1863, to recruit and supervise Negro units in the South as well as the North, recruited and organized 185,000 Negroes into the United States Colored Troops after August, 1863. If Negroes in independent and state units are added, it is estimated that the number of Negroes serving in the Civil War reached 390,000.

After the Civil War, the congressionally authorized reorganization of the Army (in 1866) provided for the organization of Negro infantry and cavalry regiments within the regular Army and the Act of 1869 fixed their number at two regiments in each branch of the service. The four regular regiments (the 24th and 25th Infantry and the 9th and 10th Cavalry) remained the core of Negro regular Army strength until World War II for the cavalry, and until the Korean War for the infantry units. But while these units guaranteed a role for Negroes in the Army, they also placed a limit on the nature of his service. They were all-Negro units with white officers, except for the chaplain and an occasional Negro graduate of West Point. They became famed Indian fighters—the Buffalo soldiers of the plains— but their existence meant that no Negroes served in other branches of the military service except in time of war.

In the Spanish-American War, Negro volunteer regiments were called "Immunes" because of the belief that they would not be subject to the yellow fever that proved as dangerous to American troops as Spanish arms. Negro state militia units became National Guard units, though only those in Illinois, New York, Massachusetts, Ohio, Maryland, and the District of Columbia remained by World War I. The Navy continued to enlist Negroes, in small numbers, for general service until the end of World War I. These men served throughout the fleet; when the Navy banned Negro enlistments after World War I, Negro opponents of the new policy recalled that it was a Negro, Chief Gunner's Mate John Christopher Jordan, who fired the first shot at Manila Bay, from the cruiser *Olympia*, Admiral George Dewey's flagship.

The Draft: World War I

The Selective Service draft of World War I was designed to spread service in the armed forces through all segments of the population. Negroes were about 10.7 percent of the population, and about that proportion of the 3,464,296 Americans serving in World War I, or 371,710, were Negroes. But this did not mean that Negroes served on an equal basis. Most Negroes were draftees, since few of them were able to enlist; most of the draftees served in supply trains and in port, engineer and pioneer (labor) battalions. Of the two Negro combat divisions, one, the 93d, made up of National Guard units and a draft regiment largely from South Carolina, was never completely organized for it had neither artillery nor trains. The other division, the 92d, was composed completely of draftees. While there were Negro officers and enlisted men in the former National Guard units, no provision was made for training Negro officers until public protests from Negroes and concerned whites, including the officials of the then young National Association for the Advancement of Colored People (N.A.A.C.P.), gained the concession of a segregated officers' training camp (the 17th Provisional ROTC) located at Des Moines, Iowa. Only infantry officers were trained; of the 1,200 who volunteered, about 700 were commissioned.

Ironically, in the Civil War and the Spanish-American War, Negro officers had been commissioned without the bitterness that preceded the establishment of the Des Moines center and without the problems that followed. Most of the problems were a direct result of the continuation of segregation not only in the form of separate units, but also within units where most officers, including all senior officers, were white; even when Negroes were commissioned, they did not serve in grades higher than captain. Accusations of morale-destroying discrimination on the part of commanders against their troops were frequent and counter-accusations on the efficiency of the troops and their newly-commissioned Negro officers were as frequent.

In the aftermath of World War I, the Navy stopped Negro enlistments altogether until 1932, when it permitted enlistments in the messmen's branch only. At the same time, as a concomitant of the general reduction of the size of the regular Army, the statutory Negro regiments were only partially filled and were broken into detachments performing a variety of tasks as garrison troops at a number of posts and stations. And despite vigorous efforts, no Negroes were permitted to enlist in the Air Force.

The Draft: World War II

With this in mind, on the eve of World War II, Negro and liberal organizations, leading Negro newspapers and political figures launched a vigorous campaign to guarantee that any new Selective

Service Act would prohibit discrimination against Negroes in the operation of the draft.

The Selective Training and Service Act of 1940 contained two provisions intended to prevent racial discrimination. The first, Section 3 (a) dealt with volunteering through the draft: "That within the limit of the quota determined—for the subdivision in which he resides, any person, regardless of race or color, between the ages of eighteen and forty-five, shall be afforded an opportunity to volunteer for induction into the land or naval forces of the United States for the training and service prescribed. . . ." The second, Section 4 (a) dealt with the selection and training of draftees: "In the selection and training of men under this Act, and in the interpretation and execution of the provisions of this Act, there shall be no discrimination against any person on account of race or color."

With this provision in the Act, the newly mobilizing armed forces of 1940 could have become a revolutionary force. But they did not, and their leaders had no such intention. The Navy and the Marine Corps avoided the entire problem by accepting only volunteers; not needing to use the draft in the first years of the war, they were not affected by the Act. Within the Army, the Air Corps, which could rely on volunteers, sought to evade the problem as long as possible. The Army itself was forced to rely upon the draft, since it was both the largest and the least glamorous of the military services. It looked at the wording of the act and decided that it could live with it. The Army declared that separate units were not in themselves discriminatory and that if the training of Negro and white draftees were kept at the same level, there would be no discrimination. Army apologists stated that the Army was not a sociological laboratory, that it reflected and did not mold social attitudes.

Nevertheless, prodded by President Franklin D. Roosevelt, the Army announced on October 9, 1940, that its Negro personnel would be "maintained on the general basis of the proportion of the Negro population of the country" despite the fact that its policy was "not to intermingle colored and white enlisted personnel in the same regimental organizations." When carried out literally, this meant that because it received most of the Negro draftees, the Army had to find troop and station units for them. Initially, each arm and service and eventually each type of unit was to have a proportionate number of Negroes, averaging ten per cent. This eventually proved impossible: if the Army activated 100 infantry divisions, ten would have had to be Negro; if there were seven locomotive repair companies, seven-tenths of a company would have to be Negro.

But since the Army as a whole had to receive a fixed percentage of Negroes, these branches which had been traditionally closed to

Negro soldiers, including the Air Force and the Signal Corps, were forced by the pressures generated by the other branches, especially the Infantry and the Engineers, to accept their share of the quotas. This led to a great waste of manpower as unneeded units, often created especially for the purpose, were organized to receive the otherwise unwanted Negroes. Thus there were units such as medical sanitary companies and airbase security battalions for which no use could be predicted.

Further, the in-flow of Negro draftees never managed to maintain an even 10 per cent of all draftees. It never embraced at any one time and in any one place a full cross-section of Negro skills and abilities. Few Negro units, therefore, could be guaranteed the men that they needed; few units could be guaranteed the replacements they needed; no white unit could receive a Negro replacement, no matter how well prepared, and no Negro unit could receive a white specialist, no matter how great the need. Individuals could be temporarily assigned, at times, but this procedure was seldom resorted to even in times of great need.

The quota system, though it failed, did open the other armed services to Negroes. After the tightening of the manpower supply midway through the war, in February, 1943, the Army succeeded in forcing the Navy to accept its men through the draft; the War Manpower Commission then directed the Navy to accept Negroes proportionately with the other services.

The Navy and the Marine Corps were thereafter reluctant users of the draft, which made them subject to the provisions of the Selective Service Act. But the Navy and the Marine Corps are not pluralistic, multi-branched services. The Navy soon ran out of billets for Negroes in shore stations, ordnance units and construction battalions. In late 1943, it manned a destroyer escort and a patrol boat with mainly Negro seamen and white officers. This was hardly a successful venture; moreover, its logical extension would have been a cruiser or battleship manned by a Negro crew. Cartoons in the Negro press poked fun at the experiment, showing tiny black tugboats bringing up the rear in flotillas of giant white battleships and carriers. In August, 1944, the Navy assigned Negroes to 25 auxiliary vessels, limiting the Negroes to 10 per cent of the crew of each vessel.

The two fleet experiments demonstrated that Negroes could handle a wider variety of tasks aboard ship than had been believed and that the mixed crews had no real problems. In April, 1945, the Navy announced that Negroes were eligible for assignment, at up to 10 per cent of crew strength, to all auxiliary fleet vessels; in December, all ships were instructed that "In the administration of naval personnel no differentiation shall be made because of race or color"; and, on February 27, 1946, the Navy announced that Negroes were eligible for "all types of assignments in all ratings in all activities and all ships of the naval service" and that in "housing, messing and other facilities, no special or unusual provisions will be made for the accommodation of Negroes." The Navy thus became the first major American institution to declare a non-discriminatory, non-segregational policy for all of its activities.

The Army, in the meantime, had conducted its own experiment, under somewhat different circumstances and auspices. In the Battle of the Bulge, at Bastogne, Belgium, in December, 1944, Negroes from supply and support units fought with the white riflemen of the besieged combat units. When the European Theater's Services of Supply offered Negroes the chance to retrain as riflemen, over 2,500 volunteered. Original plans to use these men as individual replacements were countermanded and the men were sent out in platoons to Third Army units along the Rhine and in companies to Seventh Army units in Southeastern France. Reports of performance were good, with the edge going to the smaller units. Since the one Negro division then in combat, the 92d, in Italy, had suffered continuing problems since its commitment as a division, the performance of the infantry replacements seemed to indicate the direction which the Army should take. Nonetheless, Army boards created after the war, while proposing increased opportunities for Negroes within the service, continued to support separate units and a quota system.

Finally, President Harry S Truman, in Executive Order 9981, July 26, 1948, declared it to be the policy of the President that "there shall be equality of treatment and opportunity for all persons in the armed services without regard to race, color, religion or national origin." A committee was established in the same directive with authorization to examine the policies of the armed services with a view to determining how this order should be effected. The committee reported to the President in 1950, just as the Korean War was beginning, saying that it had found, "in fact, that inequality had contributed to inefficiency." The Korean War hastened the implementation of the committee's findings. Informal and on-the-spot integration produced results similar to those of the infantry-replacement platoon integration at the close of World War II. The last of the large Negro combat units, the venerable but now shaken 24th Infantry, disappeared during the Korean War. By the close of the war in 1953, young Negro recruits serving in Korea found it hard to believe that an all-Negro infantry regiment had ever existed.

The Draft Today

A selective service or draft act exists to provide manpower for military forces. An equitable Selective Service Act is intended to spread the requirements for military service over the population's entire group of mentally and physically able men as fairly as possible and in accordance with the needs of the armed forces. All reports from Vietnam and from armed forces installations around the world point to circumstances within the armed forces which are markedly different from those at home.

> There, [one observer reports] for the first time in history, an element of American society has fully accepted the Negro, with potentially great repercussions . . . the integration is as complete as any we are likely to see in our lifetimes. Whites take orders from Negroes or save Negro lives in combat. Negro and white soldiers eat, sleep, travel, and fight side by side. They even trade dirty jokes, something no one would have believed possible in 1950.[1]

Other dispatches and reports, such as those of Whitney Young of the Urban League and of Thomas A. Johnson of *The New York Times*, support this view. So do reenlistment figures, which show that Negroes reenlist in a ratio of two to one for whites.

Why, then, should there be any opposition to the draft at all among Negroes if Negroes in general feel that the biggest national failing is a refusal to count them in on the benefits of the mainstream of American life?

The operation of the draft and the relative positions of the armed forces are themselves discriminatory. Of the services, the Army takes approximately 97 per cent of all draftees; the Marine Corps takes the remainder, for the Navy and the Air Force rely on volunteers. The result is that Negroes constitute approximately 13 per cent of the Army, 10 per cent of the Air Force, 5.6 per cent of the Navy, and 8 per cent of the Marines. Moreover, the proportion of Negroes in the combat forces, especially in Vietnam, is higher by far than their proportion in the Army and the number of Negro fatalities is higher still.

The National Advisory Commission on Selective Service reported in the spring of 1967 that Negroes constituted 11 per cent of the total enlisted strength in Vietnam, 14.5 per cent of the Army, and 22.4 per cent of all Army troops killed in action.

---

[1]Stephen E. Ambrose, "The Negro in the Army," Baltimore *Evening Sun*, April 19, 1968.

Current estimates are that Negroes constitute nearly 20 per cent of the combat forces, about 25 per cent of the front-line non-commissioned officers, about 2 per cent of the commissioned officers, and over 14 per cent of those killed in action.

The reduction in the current figures reflects the efforts of the Department of Defense to reduce criticism and to combat the notion, held by many Negroes, that the disproportionate combat death rate is intentional.

The figures on enlistments and reenlistments indicate that many Negroes feel that the armed services offer a better way of life for them and their families, at higher incomes and with better facilities for living, than the civilian society. This in itself is regarded as a strong, indirect criticism of American society, though the situation is not new. For most of their existence, the four Negro regiments of the old Army had waiting lists and, at times, when it was possible to enlist only by going to Fort Huachuchua in Arizona where one of the regiments was stationed, eager applicants showed up from as far away as New York and the Philippines.

The draft process itself reveals other rankling inequities. An often stated reason for the high proportion of Negroes in the combat forces is that relatively few Negroes enter the Army with a reasonably high level of education or with acquired skills, so that they are less readily eligible than whites for specialized, technical assignments and schools. This is an unfavorable reflection on the public educational system available to Negroes and on an industrial economy that fails to train the Negro potential in our society.

Moreover, in the matter of deferrable classes and occupations, Negro youths are at a distinct disadvantage. Relatively fewer Negroes are attending colleges and graduate schools; most Negroes have not therefore been eligible for student deferments. Few are in critical occupations and those who are so employed are seldom the sole physicians or specialists upon whom an entire community depends.

Nor can Negroes rush to join the National Guard as a means of avoiding—even if temporarily—combat assignments; Negroes in the Guard today represent only 1.15 per cent of the total and only 0.6 per cent of the Air National Guard.

For these and other reasons, some 30.2 per cent of qualified Negroes are drafted, while 18.8 per cent of the qualified whites are drafted. The constitution of local draft boards may also play a part in this picture; they certainly share the criticism levelled against the Selective Service System as it has operated in the immediate past. Many draft boards, until 1967, retained most of their World War II and Korean War members. In mid-1966, only 1.3 per cent of all draft board members were Negroes, although the national Negro population is about 12 per cent. During 1967, at least 316 Negroes were added to the nation's 4,080 local draft boards, making approximately 600 in mid-1968.

To overcome the inequities of the present system of selection and deferments, many Negroes, including members of the National Association for the Advancement of Colored People, support a return to a lottery system.

Obviously affecting attitudes towards the draft is the conviction, held by a rapidly growing number of Negroes and many whites, that the war in Vietnam is not only an unjust war but one whose enormous budget prevents adequate attention to problems at home, especially to the reconstruction of cities and the war on poverty. College students of the Society of African and Afro-American Students have been especially vocal in their opposition to the "racist war in Vietnam." In the spring of 1967, their New England Regional meeting, attended by 200 students from 14 colleges, declared that "We believe that America is the black man's battlefield and that the black man must not join the atrocities of this war." Upon his return to the mainland from Bimini, Representative Adam Clayton Powell (D., N.Y.) gave college audiences an updated version of a saying frequently repeated by Negro soldiers in the Pacific during World War II "Hence lies a black man killed fighting a colored man for the white man." (In World War II the second term was usually "yellow man" while the first was "colored man.") For a year before he was slain, Dr. Martin Luther King, Jr., had opposed the Vietnamese War as "a blasphemy against all that America stands for," a war in which Negroes are "dying in disproportionate numbers in Vietnam. Twice as many Negroes as whites are in combat." This he saw as a "reflection of the Negro's position in America." While the N.A.A.C.P. deplored a merger of the civil rights and peace movement, CORE (Congress of Racial Equality) and SNCC (Student Nonviolent Coordinating Committee) agreed, along with most of the locally-based Black Power and separatist movements.

A number of Negroes, primarily from the college and intellectual groups, have applied for conscientious objector status from their local boards because of moral objections to the Vietnamese War, nor is it possible to know how much further the pitifully small number of Negro commissioned officers will be reduced by the reluctance of young Negroes of college age to enter Reserve Officer Training Corps units because of their opposition to what they see as a colonial or racist war.

In service, there are clear advantages for Negroes noted by most observers and many participants; thus there is a high rate of enlistment and reenlistment "generated largely by the superiority of opportunity for training and advancement in the military sector as compared with civilian life" (as Mahlon T. Puryear, executive director of the Urban League, phrased it when announcing the establishment of an Office of Veterans Affairs by his organization in the late summer of 1967). Yet it is unlikely that the Negro of the ghetto, whose whole encounter with his environment produces anger, anxiety and hostility growing out of his sense of entrapment, will find the draft an inviting solution. If he does, he does not wait to be drafted: he volunteers instead and looks ahead to an assignment in Germany or Hawaii or even in Vietnam.

Samuel W. Allen (Paul Vesey)

(1917–   )

POET, SCHOLAR, EDITOR, translator, and lecturer, Samuel W. Allen (Paul Vesey) was strongly influenced by the negritude movement and by expatriates Richard Wright and James Baldwin. Throughout his writings, Allen explores the rich culture of blacks—their survival and struggle against oppression and their African heritage.

Allen was born in Columbus, Ohio, in 1917, the second of four sons. He was not sheltered from the "true situation" of the African American nor was his spirit dampened by the racial climate of the early 1900s. He grew up in a home that stressed the importance of family and fostered the will and determination to succeed.

Majoring in sociology, Allen received his bachelor's degree from Fisk University where he graduated magna cum laude in 1938. He received a law degree from Harvard Law School in 1941. Drafted into the U. S. Army, Allen spent four years in the armed services. In 1947, he took advantage of the GI Bill and took some humanity courses at the New School for Social Research until 1948. Allen also studied in Paris at the Alliance Française (1948) and at the Sorbonne (1948–50). Between 1956 and 1981, he practiced law, and worked as a writer-in-residence at two universities. Currently he is devoting his time to writing.

Allen's first poems were published in 1949 in *Présence Africaine*. He later became an editor, translator, and recruiter for the magazine. Allen also became a well-known critic while in Paris and later published several essays, including "Negritude and Its Relevance to the American Negro Writer" (1960) in the *American Negro Writer and His Roots* and "Tendencies in African Poetry" (1963) in *Africa Seen by American Negro Scholars*. He also translated the introduction to Senghor's *Anthologie de la Nouvelle Poesie Negre* (1948), "Black Orpheus" by Sartre, so non-French-speaking people could read it.

Elfenbein Zahne (Ivory Tusks) (1956) was Allen's first published collection of poems. The United States, however, did not have much access to Allen's poems until he published *Ivory Tusks and Other Poems* in 1968. Another book of poetry, *Paul Vesey's Ledger*, was published in 1975. According to Ruth L. Brittin's article in *Dictionary of Literary Biography*, *Paul Vesey's Ledger* leads the reader down a chronological and thematic road to the culture of black people. *Every Round and Other Poems* was published in 1987.

Allen's poems have been published in more than one hundred anthologies, such as Langston Hughes's *New Negro Poets: USA* (1964) and Woodie King, Jr.'s *The Forerunners: Black Poets in America* (1981). He has received several fellowships and grants: two from the Wurlitzer Foundation of Taos, New Mexico (1979 and 1980–81); a NEA Creative Writing Fellowship Award for poetry in 1979; and a Rockefeller Foundation Grant to the Bellagio Conference and Study Center in Italy in 1981.

For further readings on Allen, see Wilfred Cartey's "Dark Voices" in *Présence Africaine*; George Dickenberger's "Paul Vesey" in *Black Orpheus*, 4 (Oct. 1958); Ezekial Mphahlele's "Roots" in *The African Image*; Mphahlele's *Voices in the Whirlwind and Other Essays* (1972); and Eugene Redmond's *Drumvoices: The Mission of Afro-American Poetry, A Critical History* (1976).

The following poems are taken from *Every Round and Other Poems*.

IN MY FATHER'S HOUSE
A Reverie

In my father's house when dusk had fallen
I was alone on the dim first floor
I knew there was someone some power desirous
Of forcing the outer door.

How shall I explain—

I bolted it securely
And was locking the inner when
Somehow I was constrained to turn
To see it silently again.

Transfixed before the panther night
My heart gave one tremendous bound
Paralyzed, my feet refused
The intervening ground.

How shall I say—

I was in the house and dusk had fallen
I was alone on the earthen floor
I knew there was a power
Lurking beyond the door.

I bolted the outside door
And was closing the inner when
I noticed the first had swung open again
My heart bound and I knew it would be upon me
        I rushed to the door
It came on me out of the night and I rushed to the yard
If I could throw the ball the stone the spear in my hand
Against the wall my father would be warned but now
Their hands had fallen on me and they had taken me and
        I tried
To cry out but O I could not cry out and the cold gray waves
Came over me O stifling me and drowning me . . .

IVORY TUSKS

Pale and uncertain
lost in the distance
the ivory tusks they do not want.
The bleached sands sweep my eyelids,
heavy with revolving doors
I turn and reeling, turn again
but I am yet not comforted.

I seek the solace of the circling fangs
but I cannot be comforted
I drink huge vats of blood

I devour houses gleaming in the sun
twining green with vine
and I am yet not comforted.

Inconsolable inconsolable
all that matters lost
ice ages of days
and I will not be comforted.

SPRINGTIME, GHETTO, USA

Two pairs of eyes peered face to face
  in the soft moonlight.
The Ides had passed, again the Spring had come
The lucent shaft glowed through the window
Etching dimly the quiet room
  in the moon's light.

Outside, beyond, the April winds
Pillaged the frail clouds
Slashing them about
Stirring the window boxes
Now urging lovers toward each other
  on the grasses
    in the soft light.

Inside the shadowed tenement
One pair of eyes looked up
The rodent's down
  into the crib
    in the moon's light.

Albert L. Murray

(1916–   )

ALBERT MURRAY'S fiction and nonfiction explore black culture from a perspective somewhat different from that of other black artists and essayists. Like many of his contemporaries, Murray sees the strength and diversity of African American culture as arising out of blacks' triumph over the difficulties imposed by white oppression. He takes this viewpoint a little further, however, by saying that the elements that bespeak the courage, complexity, and creativity of the black community owe something of their origins to the very fact that black people were forced to struggle for centuries to attain a sense of solidarity and independence. His work examines the nature of the hero who must cooperate with hostile forces in order to achieve his goal. Within this framework, Murray also discusses the blues as a musical form that embodies this kind of "antagonistic cooperation" by synthesizing disparate elements into a unique and harmonious whole.

Murray was born in 1916 in Nokomis, Alabama, and received his B.S. in 1939 from Tuskegee Institute. He served in the Air Force from 1943 to 1962. While in the Air Force he received his M.A. from New York University; he also studied at various times at the University of Michigan, Ohio State University, and the University of Paris, among other institutions. He taught composition and literature at Tuskegee Institute and directed the college theater from 1940 to 1943 and from 1946 to 1951. He has also taught at Columbia University (1968), Colgate University (1970 and 1973), and the University of Massachusetts at Boston (1971) and served as writer-in-residence at Emory University (1978).

Murray's first published work, *The Omni-Americans: New Perspectives on Black Experience and American Culture* (1970), is a collection of essays all of which treat the theme of blacks' "antagonistic cooperation" with white society to forge a self-identified culture. His second book of nonfiction, *The Hero and the Blues* (1973), contains the texts of three lectures that he delivered in 1972 for the ninth Paul Anthony Brick Lecture series at the University of Missouri. Here Murray explores among other issues the significance of black music, most particularly the blues, in the emergence and survival of the black community. His most recent published work, *Stomping the Blues* (1976), continues his exploration of the blues and its function in black consciousness. Murray has also published two works of fiction, both of which are semi-autobiographical: *South to a Very Old Place* (1971) and *Train Whistle Guitar* (1974) reprinted in 1989.

For an in-depth survey of Murray's works, see Elizabeth Schultz' article in *Dictionary of Literary Biography*. Also see James Alan McPherson, "The View from the Chinaberry Tree," *Atlantic* (December 1974) and John Wideman, "*Stomping the Blues*: Ritual in Black Music and Speech," *American Poetry Review*, no. 4 (1978).

The following selection is taken from the 1989 edition of *Train Whistle Guitar*.

FROM **TRAIN WHISTLE GUITAR**

The color you almost always remember when you remember Little Buddy Marshall is sky-blue. Because that shimmering summer sunshine blueness in which neighborhood hens used to cackle while distant yard dogs used to bark and mosquito hawks used to flit and float along nearby barbwire fences, was a boy's color. Because such blueness also meant that it was whistling time and rambling time. And also baseball time. Because that silver bright midafternoon sky above outfields was the main thing Little Buddy Marshall and I were almost always most likely to be wishing for back in those days when we used to make up our own dirty verses for that old song about it ain't gonna rain no more no more.

But the shade of blue and blueness you always remember whenever and for whatever reason you remember Luzana Cholly is steel blue, which is also the clean, oil-smelling color of gunmetal and the gray-purple patina of freight train engines and railroad slag. Because in those days, that was a man's color (even as tobacco plus black coffee was a man's smell), and Luzana Cholly also carried a blue steel .32-20 on a .44 frame in his underarm holster. His face and hands were leather brown like dark rawhide. But blue steel is the color you always remember when you remember how his guitar used to sound.

Sometimes he used to smell like coffee plus Prince Albert cigarettes, which he rolled himself, and sometimes it was a White Owl Cigar, and sometimes it was Brown's Mule Chewing Tobacco. But when he was wearing slick starched wash-faded blue denim overalls

plus tucked in jumper plus his black and white houndstooth-
checked cap plus high top, glove-soft banker-style Stacey Adams,
which was what he almost always traveled in, he also smelled like
green oak steam. And when he was dressed up in his tailor-made
black broadcloth boxback plus pegtop hickory-striped pants plus either a silk candy-striped or silk pongee shirt plus knitted tie and diamond stickpin plus an always brand new gingerly blocked black
John B. Stetson hat because he was on his way somewhere either to
gamble or to play his guitar, what he smelled like was barbershop
talcum and crisp new folding money.

I can remember being aware of Luzana Cholly all the way back
there in the blue meshes of that wee winking blinking and nod web
of bedtime story time when I couldn't yet follow the thread of the
yarns I was to realize later on that somebody was forever spinning
about something he had done, back when all of that was mainly
grown folks talking among themselves by the fireside or on the
swingporch as if you were not even there: saying Luzana and old
Luzana and old Luze, and I didn't know what, to say nothing of
where Louisiana was.

But I already knew who he himself was even then, and I could
see him very clearly whenever they said his name because I still can't
remember any point in time when I had not already seen him coming up that road from around the bend and down in the L & N railroad bottom. Nor can I remember when I had not yet heard him
playing the blues on his guitar as if he were also an engineer telling
tall tales on a train whistle, his left hand doing most of the talking
including the laughing and signifying as well as the moaning and
crying and even the whining, while his right hand thumped the
wheels going somewhere.

Then there was also his notorious holler, the sound of which was
always far away and long coming as if from somewhere way down
under. Most of the time (but not always) it started low like it was
going to be a moan or even a song, and then it jumped all the way
to the very top of his voice and suddenly broke off. Then it came
back, and this time it was already at the top. Then as often as not he
would make three or four, or sometimes three followed by four,
bark-like squalls and let it die away in the darkness (you remember
it mostly as a nighttime sound); and Mama always used to say he
was whooping and hollering like somebody back on the old plantations and back in the old turpentine woods, and one time Papa said
maybe so but it was more like one of them old Luzana swamp hollers the Cajuns did in the shrimp bayous. But I myself always
thought of it as being something else that was like a train, a bad
express train saying Look out this me and here I come and I'm on
my way one more time.

I knew that much about Luzana Cholly even before I was big enough to climb the chinaberry tree. Then finally I could climb all the way to the top, and I also knew how to box the compass; so I also knew what Louisiana was as well as where, or at least which way, it was from where I was.

At first he was somebody I used to see and hear playing the guitar when he was back in town once more. I hadn't yet found out very much about him. Nor was I ever to find out very much that can actually be documented. But it is as if I have always known that he was as rough and ready as rawhide and as hard and weather worthy as blue steel, and that he was always either going somewhere or coming back from somewhere and that he had the best walk in the world, barring none (until Stagolee Dupas (*fils*) came to town).

Anyway I had already learned to do my version of that walk and was doing the stew out of it long before Little Buddy Marshall first saw it, because he probably saw me doing it and asked me about it before he saw Luzana Cholly himself and that is probably how he found out about Luzana Cholly and rawhide and blue steel in the first place.

During that time before Little Buddy came was also when I was first called Mister. Miss Tee, who was the one I had always regarded as being without doubt the best of all Big Auntees, had always called me My Mister; and Mama had always called me Little Man and My Little Man and Mama's Little Man; but some time after Little Buddy Marshall came she used to drop the *Little* part off and that is how they started calling me Mister Man before my nickname became Scooter. But long before Little Buddy Marshall came I had been telling myself that Luzana Cholly was the Man I wanted to be like.

Then Little Buddy Marshall was there and it was as if time itself were sky-blue; and every day was for whistling secret signals and going somewhere to do something you had to have nerves as strong as rawhide to get away with. Luzana Cholly was the one we always used to try to do everything like in those days. Even when you were about to do something that had nothing whatsoever to do with anything you had ever heard about him, as often as not when your turn came you said Watch old Luze. Here come old Luze. This old Luze. If Luze can't ain't nobody can.

And then not only had we come to know as much as we did about what he was like when he was there in the flesh and blood, we also knew how to talk to him, because by that time he also knew who we were. Sometimes we would come upon him sitting somewhere by himself tuning and strumming his guitar and he would let us stay and listen as long as we wanted to, and sometimes he would sneak our names into some very well known ballad just to signify at us about something, and sometimes he would make up new ballads right on the spot just to tell us stories.

We found out that the best time to signify at him because you needed some spending change was when he was on his way to the Skin Game Jungles. (Also: as far as you could tell, gambling and playing the guitar and riding the rails to and from far away places were the only steady things he ever had done or ever would do, except during the time he was in the Army and the times he had been in jail—and not only had he been to jail and the county farm, he had done time in the penitentiary!)

We were supposed to bring him good luck by woofing at him when he was headed for a skin game. So most of the time we used to try to catch him late Saturday afternoon as he came across the oil road from Gins Alley coming from Miss Pauline Anderson's Cookshop. Sometimes he would have his guitar slung across his back even then, and that he was wearing his .32-20 in his underarm holster goes without saying.

Say now hey now Mister Luzana Cholly.

Mister Luzana Cholly one time.

(Watch out because here come old Luzana goddamn Cholly one more goddamn time and one goddamn time more and don't give a goddamn who the hell knows it.)

Mister Luzana Cholly all night long.

Yeah me, ain't nobody else but.

The one and only Mister Luzana Cholly from Bogaluzana bolly.

(Not because he was born and raised in Bogalusa, Louisiana; because he once told us he was bred and born in Alabama, and was brought up here and there to root hog or die poor. Somebody had started calling him Luzana because that was where he had just come back in town from when he made his first reputation as a twelve-string guitar player second to none, including Leadbelly. Then it also kept people from confusing him with Choctaw Cholly, who was part Indian and Chastang Cholly the Cajun.)

Got the world in a jug.

And the stopper in you hand.

Y'all tell em, 'cause I ain't got the heart.

A man among men.

And Lord God among women!

Well tell the dy ya.

He would be standing wide legged and laughing and holding a wad of Brown's Mule Chewing Tobacco in with his tongue at the same time. Then he skeet a spat of amber juice to one side like some clutch hitters do when they step up to the plate, and then he would wipe the back of his leathery hand across his mouth and squint his eyess the way some batters sight out at the pitcher's mound.

Tell the goddamn dyyyy ya! He leveled and aimed his finger and then jerked it up like a pistol firing and recoiling.

Can't tell no more though.

How come, little sooner, how the goddamn hell come?

B'cause money talks.

Well shut my mouth. Shut my big wide mouth and call me suitcase.

Ain't nobody can do that.

Not nobody that got to eat and sleep.

I knowed y'all could tell em. I always did know good and damn well y'all could tell em. And y'all done just told em.

But we ain't go'n tell no more.

We sure ain't.

Talk don't mean a thing in the world if you ain't got nothing to back it up with.

He would laugh again then and we would stand waiting because we knew he was going to run his hand deep down into his pocket and come up not with the two customary nickels but two quarters between his fingers. He would flick them into the air as if they were jacks and catch them again, one in each hand; and then he would close and cross his hand, making as if to look elsewhere, flip one to me and one to Little Buddy Marshall.

Now talk. But don't talk too loud and don't tell too much, and handle your money like the whitefolks does.

Mama used to say he was don't-carified, and Little Buddy Marshall used to call him hellfied Mister Goddamn hellfied Luzana ass-kicking Cholly; and he didn't mean hell-defying, or hell-fired either. Because you couldn't say he was hell-defying because you couldn't even say he ever really went for bad, not even when he was whooping that holler he was so notorious for. Perhaps that was *somewhat* hell-defying to some folks, but even so what it really meant as much as anything else was I don't give a goddamn if I *am* hell-defying, which is something nobody driven by hell fire ever had time to say.

As for going for bad, that was the last thing he needed to do, since everybody, black or white, who knew anything at all about him already knew that when he made a promise he meant if it's the last thing I do, if it's the last thing I'm able to do on this earth. Which everybody also knew meant if you cross me I'll kill you and pay for you, as much as it meant anything else. Because the idea of going to jail didn't scare him at all, and the idea of getting lynch-mobbed didn't faze him either. All I can remember him ever saying about that was: If they shoot at me they sure better not miss me they sure better get me that first time. Whitefolks used to say he was a crazy nigger, but what they really meant or should have meant was that he was confusing to them. Because if they knew him well enough to call him crazy they also had to know enough about him to realize that he wasn't foolhardy, or even careless, not even what they wanted to mean when they used to call somebody biggity. Somehow or other it was as if they respected him precisely because he didn't seem to care anything about them one way or the other. They certainly respected the fact that he wasn't going to take any foolishness off of them.

Gasoline Point folks also said he was crazy. But they meant their own meaning. Because when they said crazy they really meant something else, they meant exactly the same thing as when they called him a fool. At some point some time ago (probably when my favorite teacher was Miss Lexine Metcalf) I decided that what they were talking about was something like poetic madness, and that was their way of saying that he was forever doing something unheard of if not downright outrageous, doing the hell out of it, and not only getting away with whatever it was, but making you like it to boot. You could tell that was the way they felt by the way they almost always shook their heads laughing even as they said it, and sometimes even before they said it: Old crazy Luzana Cholly can sure play the fool out of that guitar. Old crazy Luzana Cholly is a guitar playing fool and a card playing fool and a pistol packing fool and a freight train snagging fool, and don't care who knows it.

I still cannot remember ever having heard anybody saying anything about Luzana Cholly's mother and father. Most of the time you forgot all about that part of his existence just as most people had probably long since forgotten whether they had ever heard his family name. Nobody I know ever heard him use it, and no sooner had you thought about it than you suddenly realized that he didn't seem ever to have had or to have needed any family at all. Nor did he seem to need a wife or steady woman either. But that was because he was not yet ready to quit the trail and settle down. Because he had lived with more women from time to time and place to place than the average man could or would even try to shake a stick at.

The more I think about all of that the more I realize that you never could tell which part of what you heard about something he had done had actually happened and which part somebody else had probably made up. Nor did it ever really matter which was which. Not to anybody I ever knew in Gasoline Point, Alabama, in any case, to most of whom all you had to do was mention his name and they were ready to believe any claim you made for him, the more outrageously improbable the better. All you had to do was say Luzana

Cholly old Luzana Cholly old Luze. All you had to do was see that sporty limp walk. Not to mention his voice, which was as smoke-blue sounding as the Philamayork-skyline-blue mist beyond blue steel railroad bridges. Not to mention how he was forever turning guitar strings into train whistles which were not only the once-upon-a-time voices of storytellers but of all the voices saying what was being said in the stories as well.

Not that I who have always been told that I was born to be somebody did not always know on my deepest levels of comprehension that the somebody-ness of Luzana Cholly was of its very nature nothing if not legendary. Which no doubt also has something to do with why I almost always used to feel so numb and strange when somebody other than kinfolks called out the name that Mama had given me and Miss Tee had taught me how to spell and write. I always jumped, even when I didn't move. And in school I wanted to hide, but you had to answer because it was the teacher calling the roll so I said Present and it didn't sound like myself at all. It was not until Uncle Jerome nicknamed me Scooter that I could say That's me, that's who I am and what I am and what I do.

Anyway, such somehow has always been the nature of legends and legendary men (which probably exist to beget other lengends and would-be lengendary men in the first place) that every time Little Buddy Marshall and I used to do that sporty-blue limp-walk (which told the whole world that you were ready for something because at worst you had only been ever so slightly sprained and bruised by all the terrible situations you had been through) we were also reminding ourselves of the inevitability of the day when we too would have to grab ourselves an expert armful of lightning special L & N freight train rolling north by east to the steel blue castles and patent leather avenues of Philamayork, which was the lodestone center of the universe.

That is why we had started practicing freight train hopping on the tanks and boxcars in the switchyard as soon as we had gained enough leeway to sneak that far away from the neighborhood. That was the first big step, and you were already running a double risk (of being caught and of getting maimed for life at the very least) as soon as you started playing with something as forbidden as that, which was what they told you everything you had ever heard about old Peg Leg Nat to keep you from doing. Old Peg Leg Nat Carver, who had a head as bald and shiny as the nickelplated radiator of the Packard Straight Eight and who prided himself on being able to butt like a billy goat, and who now spent most of his time fishing and selling fresh fish and shrimp and crabs from the greenness of his palm frond covered wheelbarrow. Somebody was always reminding

you of what had happened to him. Mama for instance, who could
never pass up a chance to say Here come old Peg Leg Nat and a peg
leg or something worse is just exactly what messing around with
freight trains will get you. And she had had me scared for a while,
but not for long. Because then Little Buddy Marshall and I found out
that what had happened probably never would have happened if Old
Nat, who was then known as old Butt Head Nat, had not been
drunk and trying to show everybody how fancy he was. And anyway
anybody could see that getting his leg cut off hadn't really stopped
old Nat for good, since not only did he still do it again every time
he got the itch to go somewhere, he also could still beat any two-
legged man except Luzana Cholly himself snagging anything rolling
through Gasoline Point.

Then Little Buddy found out that Luzana Cholly himself was getting ready to leave town again soon and I myself found out which
way he was going to be heading (but not where) and which day, so
we also knew which train; and that was when we got everything together and started waiting.

Then at long last after all the boy blue dreaming and scheming
and all the spyglass scanning it was that day and we were there in
that place because it was time to take the next step. I was wearing
my high top brogan shoes and I had on my corduroy pants and a
sweater under my overalls with my jumper tucked in. I was also
wearing my navy blue baseball cap and my rawhide wristband and I
had my pitcher's glove folded fingers up in my left hip pocket. And
Little Buddy was wearing and carrying the same amount of the very
same traveling gear except for his thin first base pad instead of big
thick Sears Roebuck catcher's mitt. Our other things plus something
to eat were rolled up in our expertly tied blanket rolls so that we
could maneuver with both arms free.

Little Buddy was also carrying Mister Big Buddy Marshall's pearl
handled .38 Smith & Wesson. And our standard equipment for any
trip outside that neighborhood in those days always included our all-
purpose jackknives, which we had learned to snap open like a
switchblade and could also flip like a Mexican dagger. Also, buck-
skin pioneers and wilderness scouts that we would always be, we
had not forgotten hooks and twine to fish with. Nor were we ever to
be caught in any root hog or die poor situation without our trusty
old Y-stock (plus inner tube rubber plus shoe tongue leather) sling-
shots and a drawstrip Bull Durham pouch of birdshot babbitt metal
plus at least a handfull of peewee sized gravel pebbles.

It was May but school was not out of session yet, so not only
were we running away from home we were also playing hooky, for

which the Truant Officer also known as the School Police could take you to Juvenile Court and have you detained and then sent to the Reformatory School. (Mt. Meigs and Wetumpka were where they used to send you in those days. No wonder I still remember them as being two of the ugliest place names in the whole state of Alabama. Not as ugly as Bay Minette, which I still remember as a prototype of all the rattlesnake nests of rawboned hawkeyed nigger-fearing lynch-happy peckerwoods I've ever seen or heard tell of. But ugly enough to offset most of the things you didn't like about grade school.)

It was hot even for that time of year, and with that many clothes on, we were already sweating. But you had to have them, and that was the best way to carry them. There was thin breeze coming across the railroad from the river, the marsh and Polecat Bay, but the sun was so hot and bright that the rail tracks were shimmering under the wide open sky as if it were the middle of summer.

We were waiting in the thicket under the hill between where the Dodge Mill Road came down and where the oil yard switching spurs began, and from where we were you could see up and down the clearing as far as you needed to.

I have now forgotten how long we had to stay there waiting and watching the place from where we had seen Luzana Cholly come running across the right of way to the tracks so many times. But there was nothing you could do but wait then, as we knew he was doing, probably strumming his guitar and humming to himself.

Man, I wish it would hurry up and come on, Little Buddy said all of a sudden.

Man, me too, I probably said without even having to think about it.

Man, got to get to goddamn splitting, he said and I heard his fingers touching the package of cigarettes in his bib pocket.

We were sitting on the blanket rolls with our legs crossed Indian fire circle fashion. Then he was smoking another One Eleven, holding it the way we both used to do in those days, letting it dangle from the corner of your curled lips while tilting you head to one side with one eye watching and the other squinted, like a card sharper.

Boy, goddammit, you just watch me nail the sapsucker, he said.

Man, and you just watch me.

You could smell the mid-May woods up the slope behind us then, the late late dogwoods, the early honeysuckles, and the warm earth-plus-green smell of the pre-summer undergrowth. I can't remember which birds you used to hear during each season, not like I used to; but I do remember hearing a woodpecker somewhere on a

dead hollow tree among all the other bird sounds that day because I
also remember thinking that woodpeckers always sounded as if they
were out in the open in the very brightest part of the sunshine.

Waiting and watching you were also aware of how damp and
cool the sandy soft ground was underneath you there in the gray
and green shade; and you could smell that smell too, even as the
Gulf Coast states breeze blew all of the maritime odors in to you
from the river and the marshlands. Little Buddy finished his cigarette
and flipped the stub out into the sunshine and then sat with his
back against a sapling and sucked his teeth. I looked out across the
railroad to where the gulls were circling over the reeds and the
water.

You know something? Goddammit, when I come back here to
this here little old granny-dodging burg, boy I'm going to be a goddamn man and a goddamn half, Little Buddy said, breaking the silence again.

As before, he was talking as much to himself as to me. But I said:
And don't give a goddamn who knows it. Then he said: Boy, Chicago. And I said: Man, Detroit. And he said: Man, St. Louis. And I
said: And Kansas City. Then: Hey, Los Angeles. Hey, San Francisco.
Hey, Denver, Colorado. Him calling one and me adding another until we had leapfrogged all the way back down to the Florida Coast
Line, with him doing that old section gang chant: Say I don't know
but I think I will make my home in Jacksonville (Hey big boy cain't
you line em).

Then I was the one, because that is when I said: Hey, you know
who the only other somebody else in the world I kinda wish was
here to be going too? And little Buddy said: Old Cateye Gander. Me
too. Old Big-toed Gander. Man, shit I reckon.

Man, old Gander Gallagher can steal lighting if he have to.

Man, who you telling?

Man, how about that time? You know that time getting them
wheels for that go-cart. That time from Buckshaw.

Right on out from under the nightwatchman's nose, man.

And everybody know they got some peckerwoods down there
subject to spray your ass with birdshot just for walking too close to
that fence after dark.

Man, shit I reckon. And tell you you lucky it wasn't that other
barrel, because that's the one with triple ought buckshot.

Hey man but old Luze though.

Man, you know you talking about somebody now.

Talking about somebody taking the cake.

Goddammit man, boy, just think. We going!

Me and you and old hard cutting Luze, buddy.

Boy, and then when we get back, I said that and I could see it. Coming back on that Pan American I would be carrying two leather suitcases, and have a money belt and an underarm holster for my special-made .38 Special. And I would be dressed in tailor-made clothes and handmade shoes from London, England by way of Phila- mayork.

Hey Lebo, I said, thinking about all that then. How long you think it might take us to get all fixed up to come back.

Man, shoot, I don't know and don't care.

You coming back when old Luze come back?

Man, I don't know. Just so we go. Man, me I just want to go.

I didn't say anything else then. Because I was trying to think about how it was actually going to be then. Because what I had been thinking about before was how I wanted it to be. I didn't say any- thing else because I was thinking about myself then. And then my stomach began to feel weak and I tried to think about something else. But I couldn't. Because what I suddenly remembered as soon as I closed my eyes that time was the barbershop and them talking about baseball and boxing and women and politics with the newspa- pers rattling and old King Oliver's band playing "Sugarfoot Stomp" on the Victrola in Papa Gumbo's cookshop next door, and I said I want to and I don't want to but I got to, then I won't have to any- more either and if I do I will be ready.

Then I looked over at Little Buddy again, who now was lying back against the tree with his hands behind his head and his eyes closed, whose legs were crossed, and who was resting as easy as some baseball players always seem able to do before gametime even with the band hot timing the music you always keep on hearing over and over when you lose. I wondered what he was really thinking. Did he really mean it when he said he didn't know and didn't even care? You couldn't tell what he was thinking, but if you knew him as well as I did it was easy enough to see that he was not about to back out now, no matter how he was feeling about it.

So I said to myself: Goddammit if Little Buddy Marshall can go goddammit I can too because goddammit ain't nothing he can do I cain't if I want to because he might be the expert catcher but I'm the ace pitcher and he can bat on both sides but I'm the all-round in- field flash and I'm the prizefighter and I'm also the swimmer.

But what I found myself thinking about again then was Mama and Papa, and that was when I suddenly realized as never before how worried and bothered and puzzled they were going to be when it was not only that many hours after school but also after dark and I still was not back home yet. So that was also when I found myself thinking about Miss Tee again. Because she was the one whose house would be the very first place I was absolutely certain Mama would go looking for me, even before asking Mister Big Buddy about Little Buddy.

Hey, Lebo.
Hey, Skebo.
Skipping city.
Man, you tell em.
Getting further.
Man, ain't no lie.
Getting long gone.
Man, ain't no dooky.

Goddammit to hell, Little Buddy said then, why don't it come on?

Son-of-a-bitch, I said.

Goddamn granny-dodging son-of-a-bitching mother-fucking motherfucker, he said lighting another One Eleven, come on here son-of-a-bitching motherfucking son-of-a-bitch.

I didn't say anything else because I didn't want him to say anything else. Then I was leaning back against my tree looking out across the sandy clearing at the sky beyond the railroad and the marsh territory again, where there were clean white pieces of clouds that looked like balled up sheets in a wash tub, and the sky itself was blue like rinse water with bluing in it; and I was thinking about Mama and Papa and Uncle Jerome and Miss Tee again, and I couldn't keep myself from hoping that it was all a dream.

That was when I heard the whistle blowing for Three Mile Creek Bridge and opened my eyes and saw Little Buddy already up and slinging his roll over his shoulder.

Hey, here that son-of-a-bitch come. Hey, come on, man.

I'm here, son, I said snatching my roll into place, Don't be worrying about me. I been ready.

The engine went by, and the whistle blew again, this time for the Chickasabogue, and we were running across then sandy crunch-spongy clearing. My ears were ringing then, and I was sweating and my neck was hot and sticky and my pants felt as if the seat had been ripped away. There was nothing but the noise of the chugging and steaming and the smell of coal smoke, and we were running into it, and then we were climbing up the fill and running along the high bed of crosstie slag and cinders.

We were trotting along in reach of it then, that close to the um chuckchuck um chuckchuck um chuckchuckchuck, catching our

breath and remembering to make sure to let at least one empty boxcar go by. Then when the next gondola came Little Buddy took the
front end, and I grabbed the back. I hit the hotbox with my right
foot and stepped onto the step and pulled up. The wind was in my
ears then, but I knew all about that from all the practice I had had
by that time. So I climbed on up the short ladder and got down on
the inside, and there was Little Buddy coming grinning back toward
me.

Man, what did I tell you!

Man, did you see me lam into that sucker?

Boy, we low more nailed it.

Hey, I bet old Luze be kicking it any minute now.

Man, I'm talking about cold hanging it, man.

Boy, you know it, man, I said. But I was thinking I hope so, I
hope old Luze didn't change his mind, I hope we don't have to start
out all by ourselves.

Hey going, boy, Little Buddy said.

Man, I done told you!

We crawled up into the left front corner out of the wind, and
there was nothing to do but wait again then. We knew that this was
the northbound freight that always had to pull into the hold for
Number Four once she was twelve miles out, and that was when we
were supposed to get to the open boxcar.

So we got the cigarettes out and lit up, and there was nothing
but the rumbling thunder-like noise the wide open gondola made
then, plus the far away sound of the engine and the low rolling pony
tail of gray smoke coming back. We were just sitting there then, and
after we began to get used to the vibration, nothing at all was happening except being there. You couldn't even see the scenery going
by.

You were just there in the hereness and nowness of the time
then, and I don't think you ever really remember very much about
being in situations like that except the way you felt, and all I can
remember now about that part is the nothingness of doing nothing,
and the feeling not of going but of being taken, as of being borne
away on a bare barge or even on the bare back of a storybeast.

All you could see after we went through the smokey gray lattice-
work of Chicasabogue Bridge was the now yellow blue sky and the
bare floor and the sides of the heavy rumbling gondola, and the only
other think I have ever remembered is how I wished something
would happen because I definitely did not want to be going anywhere at all then, and I already felt lost even though I knew good
and well that I was not yet twelve miles from home. Because although Little Buddy Marshall and I had certainly been many times

farther away and stayed longer, this already seem to be farther and longer than all the other times together!

Then finally you could tell it was beginning to slow down, and we stood up and started getting ready. Then it was stopping and we were ready and we climbed over the side and came down the ladder and struck out forward. We were still in the bayou country, and beyond the train-smell there was the sour-sweet snakey smell of the swampland. We were running on slag and cinders again then and with the train quiet and waiting for Number Four you could hear the double crunching of our brogans echoing through the water-logged moss-draped cypresses.

Along there the L & N causeway embankment was almost as high as the telegraph lines, and the poles were black with a fresh coat of creosote and there were water lilies floating on the slimy green ditch that separated the railroad right of way from the edge of the swamp. Hot-collared and hustling to get to where we estimated the empty boxcar to be, we came pumping on. And then at last we saw it and could slow down and catch our breath.

And that was when we also saw that old Luzana Cholly himself was already there. We had been so busy trying to get there that we had forgotten all about him for the time being. Not only that but this was also the part that both of us had completely forgotten to think about all along. so we hadn't even thought about what we were going to say, not to mention what he was going to say.

And there he was now standing looking down at us from the open door with an unlighted cigarette in his hand. We had already stopped without even realizing it, and suddenly everything was so quiet that you could hear your heart pounding inside your head. It was as if the spot where you were had been shut off from everything else in the world. I for my part knew exactly what was going to happen then, and I was so embarrassed that I could have sunk into the ground, because I also thought: Now he's going to call us a name. Now he just might never have anything to do with us anymore.

We were standing there not so much waiting as frozen then, and he just let us stay there and feel like two wet puppies shivering, their tails tucked between their legs. Then he lit his cigarette and finally said something.

Oh no you don't oh no you don't neither. Because it ain't like that aint like that ain't never been like that and ain't never going to be not if I can help it.

He said that as much to himself as to us, but at the same time he was shaking his head not only as if we couldn't understand him but also as if we couldn't even hear him.

Y'all know it ain't like this. I know y'all know good and well it *cain't* be nothing like *this*.

Neither one of us even moved an eye. Little Buddy didn't even dig his toe into the ground.

So this what y'all up to. Don't say a word. Don't you open your mouth.

I could have crawled into a hold. I could have sunk into a pond. I could have melted leaving only a greasy spot. I could have shriveled to nothing but an ash.

Just what y'all call y'allself doing? That's what I want to know. So tell me that. Just tell me that. Don't say a word. Don't you say one word. Don't you say a goddamn mumbling word to me. Neither one of you.

We weren't even about to make a sound.

What I got a good mind to do is whale the sawdust out of both you little crustbusters. That's what I ought to be doing right now instead of talking to somebody ain't got no better sense than that.

But he didn't move. He just stood where he was looking down.

Well, I'm a son-of-a-bitch. That's what I am. I'm a son-of-a-bitch. I'm a thick-headed son-of-a-bitch. Hell, I musta been deaf dumb and blind to boot not to know this. Goddamn!

That was all he said then, and then he jumped down and walked us to where the side spur for the southbound trains began, and all we did was sit there near the signal box and feel terrible until Number Four had come whistling by and was gone and we heard the next freight coming south. Then what he did when it finally got there was worse than any name he could ever have called us. He wouldn't let us hop it even though it was only a short haul and pickup local that was not much more than a switch engine with more cars than usual. He waited for it to slow down for the siding and then he picked me up (as they pick you up to put you in the saddle of a pony because you're not yet big enough to reach the stirrups from the ground on your own) and put me on the front end of the first gondola, and did the same thing to Little Buddy; and then he caught the next car and came forward to where we were.

So we came slow-poking it right back toward the Chickasaboque and were back in Gasoline Point before the sawmill whistles even started blowing the hands back to work from noontime. I could hardly believe that so little time had passed. But then such is the difference between legendary time and actuality, which is to say, the time you remember and the time you measure.

We came on until the train all but stopped for Three Mile Creek Bridge, and then he hopped down and took Little Buddy off first and then me, and we followed him down the steep, stubble covered em-

bankment and then to the place the hobos used under the bridge.
He unslung the guitar and sat down and lit another cigarette and
flipped the match stem into the water and watched it float away.
Then he sat back and looked at us again, and then he motioned for
us to sit down in front of him.

That was when we found out what we found out directly from
Luzana Cholly himself about hitting the road, which he (like every
fireside knee-pony uncle and shade tree uncle and tool shed uncle
and barbership uncle since Uncle Remus himself) said was a whole
lot more than just a notion. He was talking in his regular matter-of-
fact voice again then, so we knew he was not as exasperated with us
as he had been. But as for myself I was still too scandalized to face
him, and as for Little Buddy, he seldom if every looked anybody
straight in the eye anyway. Not that he was ever very likely to miss
any move you made.

That time was also when Luzana Cholly told me and Little Buddy
what he told us about the chain gang and the penitentiary: and as he
talked, his voice uncle-calm and his facts first-hand and fresh from
the getting-place, he kept reaching out every now and then to touch
the guitar. But only as you stroke your pet or touch a charm, or as
you finger a weapon or tool or your favorite piece of sports equipment. Because he did not play any tunes or even any chords, or
make up any verse for us that day. But even so, to this day I remember what he said precisely as if it had actually been another song
composed specifically for us.

Then, after he had asked us if it wasn't about time for two old
roustabouts like us to eat something and the two of us had shared a
can of sardines while he worked on a bite from his plug of Brown's
Mule Chewing Tobacco, the main thing he wanted to talk about was
going to school and learning to use your head like the smart, rich
and powerful whitefolks, (nor did he or anybody else I can remember mean whitefolks in general. So far as I know the only white people he thought of as being smart were precisely those who were
either rich and powerful or famous. The rest were peckerwoods,
about whom you had to be careful not because they were smart but
because so many of them were so mean and evil about not being
smart and powerful and famous). He said the young generation was
supposed to take what they were already born with and learn how to
put it with everything the civil engineers and inventors and doctors
and lawyers and bookkeepers had found out about the world and be
the one to bring about the day the old folks had always been pro-
phesying and praying for.

The three of us just sat looking across the water then. And then
we heard the next northbound freight coming, and he stood up and

got ready; and he said we could watch him but we better not try to follow him this time, and we promised, and we also promised to go to school the next morning.

So then we came back up the embankment, because the train was that close, and he stood looking at us, with the guitar slung across his back. Then he put his hands on our shoulders and looked straight down into our eyes, and you knew you had to look straight back into his, and we also knew that we were no longer supposed to be ashamed in front of him because of what we had done. He was not going to tell. And we were not going to let him down.

Make old Luze proud of you, he said then, and he was almost pleading. *Make old Luze glad to take his hat off to you some of these days. You going further than old Luze ever dreamed of. Old Luze ain't been nowhere. Old Luze don't know from nothing.*

And then the train was there and we watched him snag it and then he was waving goodbye.

Ralph Ellison

(1914–   )

BORN IN OKLAHOMA CITY, Ralph Ellison was the son of lower-middle class parents who encouraged their son's interest in literature, folk material, and music, especially jazz and the blues. They also instilled in him an independence which, in all probability, helped him to shun party lines—whether Marxian or nationalistic—which many black intellectuals of his generation embraced.

Winning a scholarship to Tuskegee Institute, Ellison went there to study music, hoping to become a composer of symphonies. After three years at the Alabama school, he went to New York in 1936 to earn money to return to Tuskegee, but never did. He met Richard Wright, worked with the WPA (Works Progress, later Works Projects Administration), and decided to give up his music studies for a writing career. Although he never joined the Communist party, he was intellectually interested in Marxism—as were many other young blacks at the time—and after 1937 wrote articles for *New Masses* and other leftist periodicals. He began his literary career writing reviews, essays, and short stories. In 1942 he served as managing editor of the *Negro Quarterly*. Four years later he married Fanny McConnell, his second wife with whom he still lives in New York City.

A Rosenwald grant in 1945 provided him with the time he needed to complete his famous novel *Invisible Man*, published in 1952. *Shadow and Act*, a collection of essays, was published in 1966. During the years since *Invisible Man* and *Shadow and Act* were published, Ellison has taught, lectured, and served as author-in-residence at a surprisingly large number of the nation's best colleges and universities. A brilliant critic of literature and jazz, he has written articles on both subjects for many of America's most prestigious literary journals.

Ralph Ellison has received a great number of awards and honors, national and international, among them: Fellow of the American Academy in Rome; for *Invisible Man*, he received in 1953 the National Book Award, the Russwurm Award, and the National Newspaper Publishers' Award. In 1965 the New York *Herald Tribune Book Review* poll named *Invisible Man* as the "most distinguished novel written between 1945 and 1965." He gave the Gertrude Clarke Whittal Lecture at the Library of Congress and the Ewing Lectures at the University of California.

To date, Ellison has published only three major works: *Invisible Man* (1952), *Shadow and Act* (1964), and *Going to the Territory* (1986). In addition, he has published many short works of fiction, a great number of critical reviews, and numerous authoritative articles on jazz and folklore. In 1944, Ellison published "Flying Home," a short story which is an early example of the techniques used in his great novel. "Flying Home" begins with realistic details about an airport in the South designed to train black pilots; it moves on to the Greek myth of Icarus and to a well-known African American folk story. With this mélange, he makes the story an extended metaphor of the black man's place in America. In technique, "Flying Home" is a microcosm of the macrocosm, which is *Invisible Man*.

Ellison's novel superbly blends several motifs, several levels of meanings, and several language styles to give us a work that moves from realism to surrealism; a work that makes masterful use of myth, dreams, symbolism, and other techniques taken from the Western literary tradition. To the Western heritage, he adds and skillfully blends that body of folk material which comes from the black man's experience in America. *Invisible Man* lends itself to many different readings and interpretations—almost as many as there are critics evaluating the novel, and they are legion.

Ellison's second major work, *Shadow and Act*, was published in 1964. The essays in this volume, the author tells the reader, are autobiographical in their "basic significance and are concerned with three general themes: "literature and folklore; Negro musical expression—especially jazz and the blues; and the complex relationship between the Negro American subculture and North American culture as a whole."[1] The work, in part, is a statement of his own position on race and criticism. Because of his background, his imagination could carry him beyond the "category of race," and he could think of himself as a potential "Renaissance man." The 1964 date of publication of *Shadow and Act* is significant because the Black Arts Movement was becoming more prominent.

Going to the Territory, Ellison's third major work, is a collection of essays, lectures, personal reminiscences, and interviews that tell us much about Ellison the man as well as Ellison the author. Nearly all of the selections included in *Going to the Territory* were written after the 1964 publication date of *Shadow and Act*, to which it serves as an excellent companion volume. One essay, "An Extravagance of Laughter," was written especially for the volume.

For recent critical comment on Ellison's works, see Bernard Bell, *The Afro-American Novel and Its Tradition* (1987); Kimberly W. Benston (ed.), *Speaking for You: The Vision of Ralph Ellison* (1987); and Robert G. O'Meally, *The Craft of Ralph Ellison* (1980).

The two selections that follow come from *Invisible Man* and *Shadow and Act*.

---

[1]Ralph Ellison, *Shadow and Act* (New York: Random House, 1953, 1964), xviii.

FROM **INVISIBLE MAN**

I saw them as we approached the short stretch that lay between the railroad tracks and the Golden Day. At first I failed to recognize them. They straggled down the highway in a loose body, blocking the way from the white line to the frazzled weeds that bordered the sun-heated concrete slab. I cursed them silently. They were blocking the road and Mr. Norton was gasping for breath. Ahead of the radiator's gleaming curve they looked like a chain gang on its way to make a road. But a chain gang marches single file and I saw no guards on horseback. As I drew nearer I recognized the loose gray shirts and pants worn by the veterans. Damn! They were heading for the Golden Day.

"A little stimulant," I heard behind me.

"In a few minutes, sir."

Up ahead I saw the one who thought he was a drum major strutting in front, giving orders as he moved energetically in long, hip-swinging strides, a cane held above his head, rising and falling as though in time to music. I slowed the car as I saw him turn to face the men, his cane held at chest level as he shortened the pace. The men continued to ignore him, walking along in a mass, some talking in groups and others talking and gesticulating to themselves.

Suddenly, the drum major saw the car and shook his cane-baton at me. I blow the horn, seeing the men move over to the side as I nosed the car slowly forward. He held his ground, his legs braced, hands on hips, and to keep from hitting him I slammed on the brakes.

The drum major rushed past the men toward the car, and I heard the cane bang down upon the hood as he rushed toward me.

"Who the hell you think you are, running down the army? Give the countersign. Who's in command of this outfit? You trucking bastards was always too big for your britches. Countersign me!"

"This is General Pershing's car, sir," I said, remembering hearing that he responded to the name of his wartime Commander-in-Chief. Suddenly the wild look changed in his eyes and he stepped back and saluted with stiff precision. Then looking suspiciously into the back seat, he barked,

"Where's the General?"

"There," I said, turning and seeing Mr. Norton raising himself, weak and white-faced, from the seat.

"What is it? Why have we stopped?"

"The sergeant stopped us, sir . . ."

"Sergeant? What sergeant?" He sat up.

"Is that you, General?" the vet said, saluting. "I didn't know you were inspecting the front lines today. I'm very sorry, sir."

"What . . .?" Mr. Norton said.

"The General's in a hurry," I said quickly.

"Sure is," the vet said. "He's got a lot to see. Discipline is bad. Artillery's shot to hell." Then he called to the men walking up the road, "Get the hell out of the General's road. General Pershing's coming through. Make way for General Pershing!"

He stepped aside and I shot the car across the line to avoid the men and stayed there on the wrong side as I headed for the Golden Day.

"Who was that man?" Mr. Norton gasped from the back seat.

"A former soldier, sir. A vet. They're all vets, a little shell-shocked."

"But where is the attendant?"

"I don't see one, sir. They're harmless though."

"Nevertheless, they should have an attendant."

I had to get him there and away before they arrived. This was their day to visit the girls, and the Golden Day would be pretty rowdy. I wondered where the rest of them were. There should have been about fifty. Well, I would rush in and get the whiskey and leave. What was wrong with Mr. Norton anyway, why should he get *that* upset over Trueblood? I had felt ashamed and several times I had wanted to laugh, but it had made him sick. Maybe he needed a doctor. Hell, he didn't ask for any doctor. Damn that bastard Trueblood.

I would run in, get a pint, and run out again, I thought. Then he wouldn't see the Golden Day. I seldom went there myself except with some of the fellows when word got out that a new bunch of girls had arrived from New Orleans. The school had tried to make the Golden Day respectable, but the local white folks had a hand in it somehow and they got nowhere. The best the school could do was to make it hot for any student caught going there.

He lay like a man asleep as I left the car and ran into the Golden Day. I wanted to ask him for money but decided to use my own. At the door I paused; the place was already full, jammed with vets in loose gray shirts and trousers and women in short, tight-fitting, stiffy starched gingham aprons. The stale beer smell struck like a club through the noise of voices and the juke box. Just as I got inside the door a stolid-faced man gripped me by the arm and looked stonily into my eyes.

"It will occur at 5:30," he said, looking straight through me.

"What?"

"The great all-embracing absolute Armistice, the end of the world!" he said.

Before I could answer, a small plump woman smiled into my face and pulled him away.

"It's your turn, Doc," she said. "Don't let it happen till after me and you done been upstairs. How come I always have to come get you?"

"No, it is true," he said. "They wirelessed me from Paris this morning."

"Then, baby, me an' you better hurry. There's lots of money I got to make in here before that thing happens. You hold it back a while, will you?"

She winked at me as she pulled him through the crowd toward the stairs. I elbowed my way nervously toward the bar.

Many of the men had been doctors, lawyers, teachers, Civil Service workers; there were several cooks, a preacher, a politician, and an artist. One very nutty one had been a psychiatrist. Whenever I saw them I felt uncomfortable. They were supposed to be members of the professions toward which at various times I vaguely aspired myself, and even though they never seemed to see me I could never believe that they were really patients. Sometimes it appeared as though they played some vast and complicated game with me and the rest of the school folk, a game whose goal was laughter and whose rules and subtleties I could never grasp.

Two men stood directly in front of me, one speaking with intense earnestness. ". . . and Johnson hit Jeffries at an angle of 45 degrees from his lower left lateral incisor, producing an instantaneous blocking of his entire thalamic rine, frosting it over like the freezing unit of a refrigerator, thus shattering his autonomous nervous system and rocking the big brick-laying creampuff with extreme hyperspasmic muscular tremors which dropped him dead on the extreme tip of his coccyx, which, in turn, produced a sharp traumatic reaction in his sphincter nerve and muscle, and then, my dear colleague, they swept him up, sprinkled him with quicklime and rolled him away in a barrow. Naturally, there was no other therapy possible."

"Excuse me," I said, pushing past.

Big Halley was behind the bar, his dark skin showing through his sweat-wet shirt.

"Whatcha saying, school-boy?"

"I want a double whiskey, Halley. Put it in something deep so I can get it out of here without spilling it. It's for somebody outside."

His mouth shot out, "Hell, naw!"

"Why?" I asked, surprised at the anger in his thyroid eyes.

"You still up at the school, ain't you?"

"Sure."

"Well, those bastards is trying to close me up agin, that's why. You can drink till you blue in the face in here, but I wouldn't sell you enough to spit through your teeth to take outside."

"But I've got a sick man out in the car."

"What car? You never had no car."

"The white man's car. I'm driving for him."

"Ain't you in school?"

"He's *from* the school."

"Well, who's sick?"

"He is."

"He too good to come in? Tell him we don't Jimcrow nobody."

"But he's sick."

"He can die!"

"He's important, Halley, a trustee. He's rich and sick and if anything happens to him, they'll have me packed and on my way home."

"Can't help it, school-boy. Bring him inside and he can buy enough to swim in. He can drink outa my own private bottle."

He sliced the white heads off a couple of beers with an ivory paddle and passed them up the bar. I felt sick inside. Mr. Norton wouldn't want to come in here. He was too sick. And besides I didn't want him to see the patients and the girls. Things were getting wilder as I made my way out. Supercargo, the white-uniformed attendant who usually kept the men quiet was nowhere to be seen. I didn't like it, for when he was upstairs they had absolutely no inhibitions. I made my way out to the car. What could I tell Mr. Norton? He was lying very still when I opened the door.

"Mr. Norton, sir. They refused to sell me whiskey to bring out."

He lay very still.

"Mr. Norton."

He lay like a figure of chalk. I shook him gently, feeling dread within me. He barely breathed. I shook him violently, seeing his head wobble grotesquely. His lips parted, bluish, revealing a row of long, slender amazingly animal-like teeth.

"SIR!"

In a panic I ran back into the Golden Day, bursting through the noise as through an invisible wall.

"Halley! Help me, he's dying!"

I tried to get through but no one seemed to have heard me, I was blocked on both sides. They were jammed together.

"Halley!"

Two patients turned and looked me in the face, their eyes two inches from my nose.

"What is wrong with this gentleman, Sylvester?" the tall one said.

"A man's dying outside!" I said.

"Someone is always dying," the other one said.

"Yes, and it's good to die beneath God's great tent of sky."

"He's got to have some whiskey!"

"Oh, that's different," one of them said and they began pushing a path to the bar. "A last bright drink to keep the anguish down. Step aside, please!"

"School-boy, you back already?" Halley said.

"Give me some whiskey. He's dying!"

"I done told you, school-boy, you better bring him in here. He can die, but I still got to pay the bills."

"Please, they'll put me in jail."

"You going to college, figure it out," he said.

"You'd better bring the gentleman inside," the one called Sylvester said. "Come, let us assist you."

We fought our way out of the crowd. He was just as I left him.

"Look, Sylvester, it's Thomas Jefferson!"

"I was just about to say, I've long wanted to discourse with him."

I looked at them speechlessly; they were both crazy. Or were they joking?

"Give me a hand," I said.

"Gladly."

I shook him. "Mr. Norton!"

"We'd better hurry if he's to enjoy his drink," one of them said thoughtfully.

We picked him up. He swung between us like a sack of old clothes.

"Hurry!"

As we carried him toward the Golden Day one of the men stopped suddenly and Mr. Norton's head hung down, his white hair dragging in the dust.

"Gentlemen, this man is my grandfather!"

"But he's *white*, his name's Norton."

"I should know my own grandfather! He's Thomas Jefferson and I'm his grandson—on the 'field-nigger' side," the tall man said.

"Sylvester, I do believe that you're right. I certainly do," he said, staring at Mr. Norton. "Look at those features. Exactly like yours— from the identical mold. Are you sure he didn't spit you upon the earth, fully clothed?"

"No, no, that was my father," the man said earnestly.

And he began to curse his father violently as we moved for the door. Halley was there waiting. Somehow he'd gotten the crowd to quieten down and a space was cleared in the center of the room. The men came close to look at Mr. Norton.

"Somebody bring a chair."

"Yeah, let Mister Eddy sit down."

"That ain't no Mister Eddy, man, that's John D. Rockefeller," someone said.

"Here's a chair for the Messiah."

"Stand back y'all," Halley ordered. "Give him some room."

Burnside, who had been a doctor, rushed forward and felt for Mr. Norton's pulse.

"It's solid! This man has a *solid* pulse! Instead of beating, it *vibrates*. That's very unusual. Very."

Someone pulled him away. Halley reappeard with a bottle and a glass. "Here, some of y'all tilt his head back."

And before I could move, a short, pock-marked man appeared and took Mr. Norton's head between his hands, tilting it at arm's length and then, pinching the chin gently like a barber about to apply a razor gave a sharp, swift movement.

"Pow!"

Mr. Norton's head jerked like a jabbed punching bag. Five pale red lines bloomed on the white cheek, glowing like fire beneath translucent stone. I could not believe my eyes. I wanted to run. A woman tittered, I saw several men rush for the door.

"Cut it out, you damn fool!"

"A case of hysteria," the pock-marked man said quietly.

"Git the hell out of the way," Halley said. "Somebody git that stool pigeon attendant from upstairs. Git him down here, quick!"

"A mere mild case of hysteria," the pock-marked man said as they pushed him away.

"Hurry with the drink, Halley!"

"Heah, school-boy, you hold the glass. This here's brandy I been saving for myself."

Someone whispered tonelessly into my ear, "You see, I told you that it would occur at 5:30. Already the Creator has come." It was the stolid-faced man.

I saw Halley tilt the bottle and the oily amber of brandy sloshing into the glass. Then tilting Mr. Norton's head back, I put the glass to his lips and poured. A fine brown stream ran from the corner of his mouth, down his delicate chin. The room was suddenly quiet. I felt a slight movement against my hand, like a child's breast when it whimpers at the end of a spell of crying. The fine-veined eyelids flickered. He coughed. I saw a slow red flush creep, then spurt, up his neck, spreading over his face.

"Hold it under his nose, school-boy. Let 'im smell it."

I waved the glass beneath Mr. Norton's nose. He opened his pale blue eyes. They seemed watery now in the red flush that bathed his face. He tried to sit up, his right hand fluttering to his chin. His eyes widened, moved quickly from face to face. Then coming to mine, the moist eyes focused with recognition.

"You were unconscious, sir," I said.

"Where am I, young man?" he asked wearily.

"This is the Golden Day, sir."

"What?"

"The Golden Day. It's a kind of sporting-and-gambling house," I added reluctantly.

"Now give him another drinka brandy," Halley said.

I poured a drink and handed it to him. He sniffed it, closed his eyes as in puzzlement, then drank; his cheeks filled out like small bellows; he was rinsing his mouth.

"Thank you," he said, a little stronger now. "What is this place?"

"The Golden Day," said several patients in unison.

He looked slowly around him, up to the balcony, with its scrolled and carved wood. A large flag hung lank above the floor. He frowned.

"What was this building used for in the past?" he said.

"It was a church, then a bank, then it was a restaurant and a fancy gambling house, and now *we* got it," Halley explained. "I think somebody said it used to be a jailhouse too."

"They let us come here once a week to raise a little hell," someone said.

"I couldn't buy a drink to take out, sir, so I had to bring you inside," I explained in dread.

He looked about him. I followed his eyes and was amazed to see the varied expressions on the patients' faces as they silently returned his gaze. Some were hostile, some cringing, some horrified; some, who when among themselves were most violent, now appeared as submissive as children. And some seemed strangely amused.

"Are all of you patients?" Mr. Norton asked.

"Me, I just runs this joint," Halley said. "These here other fellows . . ."

"We're patients sent here as therapy," a short, fat, very intelligent-looking man said. "But," he smiled, "they send along an attendant, a kind of censor, to see that the therapy fails."

"You're nuts. I'm a dynamo of energy. I come to charge my batteries," one of the vets insisted.

"I'm a student of history, sir," another interrupted with dramatic gestures. "The world moves in a circle like a roulette wheel. In the beginning, black is on top, in the middle epochs, white holds the odds, but soon Ethiopia shall stretch forth her noble wings! Then place your money on the black!" His voice throbbed with emotion. "Until then, the sun holds no heat, there's ice in the heart of the earth. Two years from now and I'll be old enough to give my mulatto mother a bath, the half-white bitch!" he added, beginning to leap up and down in an explosion of glassy-eyed fury.

Mr. Norton blinked his eyes and straightened up.

"I'm a physician, may I take your pulse?" Burnside said, seizing Mr. Norton's wrist.

"Don't pay him no mind, mister. He ain't been no doctor in ten years. They caught him trying to change some blood into money."

"I did too!" the man screamed. "I discovered it and John D. Rockefeller stole the formula from me."

"Mr. Rockefeller did you say?" Mr. Norton said. "I'm sure you must be mistaken."

"WHAT'S GOING ON DOWN THERE?" a voice shouted from the balcony. Everyone turned. I saw a huge black giant of a man, dressed only in white shorts, swaying on the stairs. It was Supercargo, the attendant. I hardly recognized him without his hard-starched white uniform. Usually he walked around threatening the men with a strait jacket which he always carried over his arm, and usually they were quiet and submissive in his presence. But now they seemed not to recognize him and began shouting curses.

"How you gon keep order in the place if you gon git drunk?" Halley shouted. "Charlene! Charlene!"

"Yeah?" a woman's voice, startling in its carrying power, answered sulkily from a room off the balcony.

"I want you to git that stool-pigeoning, joy-killing, nut-crushing bum back in there with you and sober him up. Then git him in his white suit and down here to keep order. We got white folks in the house."

A woman appeared on the balcony, drawing a woolly pink robe about her. "Now you lissen here, Halley," she drawled, "I'm a woman. If you want him dressed, you can do it yourself. I don't put on but one man's clothes and he's in N'Orleans."

"Never mind all that. Git that stool pigeon sober!"

"I want order down there," Supercargo boomed, "and if there's white folks down there, I wan's *double* order."

Suddenly there was an angry roar from the men back near the bar and I saw them rush the stairs.

"Get him!"

"Let's give him some order!"

"Out of my way."

Five men charged the stairs. I saw the giant bend and clutch the posts at the top of the stairs with both hands, bracing himself, his body gleaming bare in is white shorts. The little man who had slapped Mr. Norton was in front, and, as he sprang up the long flight, I saw the attendant set himself and kick, catching the little man just as he reached the top, hard in the chest, sending him backwards in a curving dive into the midst of the men behind him. Supercargo got set to swing his leg again. It was a narrow stair and only one man could get up at a time. As fast as they rushed up, the giant kicked them back. He swung his leg, kicking them down like a fungo-hitter batting out flies. Watching him, I forgot Mr. Norton. The Golden Day was in an uproar. Half-dressed women appeared from the rooms off the balcony. Men hooted and yelled as at a football game.

"I WANT ORDER!" the giant shouted as he sent a man flying down the flight of stairs.

"THEY THROWING BOTTLES OF LIQUOR!" a woman screamed. "REAL LIQUOR!"

"That's a order he don't want," someone said.

A shower of bottles and glasses splashing whiskey crashed against the balcony. I saw Supercargo snap suddenly erect and grab his forehead, his face bathed in whiskey, "Eeeee!" he cried, "Eeeee!" Then I saw him waver, rigid from his ankles upward. For a moment the men on the stairs were motionless, watching him. Then they sprang forward.

Supercargo grabbed wildly at the balustrade as they snatched his feet from beneath him and started down. His head bounced against the steps making a sound like a series of gunshots as they ran dragging him by his ankles, like volunteer firemen running with a hose. The crowd surged forward. Halley yelled near my ear. I saw the man being dragged toward the center of the room.

"Give the bastard some order!"

"Here I'm forty-five and he's been acting like he's my old man!"

"So you like to kick, huh?" a tall man said, aiming a shoe at the attendant's head. The flesh above his right eye jumped out as though it had been inflated.

Then I heard Mr. Norton beside me shouting, "No, no! Not when he's down!"

"Lissen at the white folks," someone said.

"He's the white folks' man!"

Men were jumping upon Supercargo with both feet now and I felt such an excitement that I wanted to join them. Even the girls were yelling, "Give it to him good!" "He never pays me!" "Kill him!"

"Please, y'all, not in here! Not in my place!"

"You can't speak your mind when he's on duty!"

"Hell, no!"

Somehow I got pushed away from Mr. Norton and found myself beside the man called Sylvester.

"Watch this, school-boy," he said. "See there, where his ribs are bleeding?"

I nodded my head.

"Now don't move your eyes."

I watched the spot as though compelled, just beneath the lower rib and above the hip-bone, as Sylvester measured carefully with his toe and kicked as though he were punting a football. Supercargo let out a groan like an injured horse.

"Try it, school-boy, it feels so good. It gives you relief," Sylvester said. "Sometimes I get so afraid of him I feel that he's inside my head. There!" he said, giving Supercargo another kick.

As I watched, a man sprang on Supercargo's chest with both feet and he lost consciousness. They began throwing cold beer on him, reviving him, only to kick him unconscious again. Soon he was drenched in blood and beer.

"The bastard's out cold."

"Throw him out."

"Naw, wait a minute. Give me a hand somebody."

They threw him upon the bar, stretching him out with his arms folded across his chest like a corpse.

"Now, let's have a drink!"

Halley was slow in getting behind the bar and they cursed him.

"Get back there and serve us, you big sack of fat!"

"Gimme a rye!"

"Up here, funk-buster!"

"Shake them sloppy hips!"

"Okay, okay, take it easy," Halley said, rushing to pour them drinks, "Just put y'all's money where your mouth is."

With Supercargo lying helpless upon the bar, the men whirled about like maniacs. The excitement seemed to have tilted some of the more delicately balanced ones too far. Some made hostile speeches at the top of their voices against the hospital, the state and the universe. The one who called himself a composer was banging away the one wild piece he seemed to know on the out-of-tune pi-ano, striking the key-board with fists and elbows and filling in other effects in a bass voice that moaned like a bear in agony. One of the most educated ones touched my arm. He was a former chemist who was never seen without his shining Phi Beta Kappa key.

"The men have lost control," he said through the uproar. "I think you'd better leave."

"I'm trying to," I said, "as soon as I can get over to Mr. Norton."

Mr. Norton was gone from where I had left him. I rushed here and there through the noisy men, calling his name.

When I found him he was under the stairs. Somehow he had been pushed there by the scuffling, reeling men and he lay sprawled in the chair like an aged doll. In the dim light his features were sharp and white and his closed eyes well-defined lines in a well-tooled face. I shouted his name above the roar of the men, and got no answer. He was out again. I shook him, gently, then roughly, but still no flicker of his wrinkled lids. Then some of the milling men pushed me up against him and suddenly a mass of whiteness was looming two inches from my eyes; it was only his face but I felt a shudder of nameless horror. I had never been so close to a white person before. In a panic I struggled to get away. With his eyes closed he seemed more threatening than with them open. He was like a formless white death, suddenly appeared before me, a death which had been there all the time and which had now revealed itself in the madness of the Golden Day.

"Stop screaming!" a voice commanded, and I felt myself pulled away. It was the short fat man.

I clamped my mouth shut, aware for the first time that the shrill sound was coming from my own throat. I saw the man's face relax as he gave me a wry smile.

"That's better," he shouted into my ear. "He's only a man. Remember that. He's only a man!"

I wanted to tell him that Mr. Norton was much more than that, that he was a rich white man and in my charge; but the very idea that I was responsible for him was too much for me to put into words.

"Let us take him to the balcony," the man said, pushing me toward Mr. Norton's feet. I moved automatically, grasping the thin ankles as he raised the white man by the armpits and backed from beneath the stairs. Mr. Norton's head lolled upon his chest as though he were drunk or dead.

The vet started up the steps still smiling, climbing backwards a step at a time. I had begun to worry about him, whether he was drunk like the rest, when I saw three of the girls who had been leaning over the balustrade watching the brawl come down to help us carry Mr. Norton up.

"Looks like pops couldn't take it," one of them shouted.

"He's high as a Georgia pine."

"Yeah, I tell you this stuff Halley got out here is too strong for white folks to drink."

"Not drunk, ill!" the fat man said. "Go find a bed that's not being used so he can stretch out awhile."

"Sho, daddy. Is there any other little favors I can do for you?"

"That'll be enough," he said.

One of the girls ran up ahead. "Mine's just been changed. Bring him down here," she said.

In a few minutes Mr. Norton was lying upon a three-quarter bed, faintly breathing. I watched the fat man bend over him very professionally and feel for his pulse.

"You a doctor?" a girl asked.

"Not now, I'm a patient. But I have a certain knowledge."

Another one, I thought, pushing him quickly aside. "He'll be all right. Let him come to so I can get him out of here."

"You needn't worry, I'm not like those down there, young fellow," he said. "I really was a doctor. I won't hurt him. He's had a mild shock of some kind."

We watched him bend over Mr. Norton again, feeling his pulse, pulling back his eyelid.

"It's a mild shock," he repeated.

"This here Golden Day is enough to shock anybody," a girl said, smoothing her apron over the smooth sensuous roll of her stomach.

Another brushed Mr. Norton's white hair away from his forehead and stroked it, smiling vacantly. "He's kinda cute," she said. "Just like a little white baby."

"What kinda ole baby?" the small skinney girl asked.

"That's the kind, an *ole* baby."

"You just like white men, Edna. That's all," the skinny one said.

Edna shook her head and smiled as though amused at herself. "I sho do. I just love 'em. Now this one, old as he is, he could put his shoes under my bed any night."

"Shucks, me I'd kill an old man like that."

"Kill him nothing," Edna said. "Girl, don't you know that all these rich ole white men got monkey glands and billy goat balls? These old bastards don't never git enough. They want to have the whole world."

The doctor looked at me and smiled. "See, now you're learning all about endocrinology," he said. "I was wrong when I told you that he was only a man; it seems now that he's either part goat or part ape. Maybe he's both."

"It's the truth," Edna said. "I used to have me one in Chicago—"

"Now you ain't never been to no Chicago, gal," the other one interrupted.

"How you know I ain't? Two years ago . . . Shucks, you don't know nothing. That ole white man right there might have him a coupla jackass balls!"

The fat man raised up with a quick grin. "As a scientist and a physician I'm forced to discount that," he said. "That is one operation that has yet to be performed." Then he managed to get the girls out of the room.

"If he should come around and hear that conversation," the vet said, "it would be enough to send him off again. Besides, their scientific curiosity might lead them to investigate whether he really does have a monkey gland. And that, I'm afraid, would be a bit obscene."

"I've got to get him back to the school," I said.

"All right," he said, "I'll do what I can to help you. Go see if you can find some ice. And don't worry."

I went out on the balcony, seeing the tops of their heads. They were still milling around, the juke box baying, the piano thumping, and over at the end of the room, drenched with beer, Supercargo lay like a spent horse upon the bar.

Starting down, I noticed a large piece of ice glinting in the remains of an abandoned drink and seized its coldness in my hot hand and hurried back to the room.

The vet sat staring at Mr. Norton, who now breathed with a slightly irregular sound.

"You were quick," the man said, as he stood and reached for the ice. "Swift with the speed of anxiety," he added, as if to himself. "Hand me that clean towel—there, from beside the basin."

I handed him one, seeing him fold the ice inside it and apply it to Mr. Norton's face.

"Is he all right?" I said.

"He will be in a few minutes. What happened to him?"

"I took him for a drive," I said.

"Did you have an accident or something?"

"No," I said. "He just talked to a farmer and the heat knocked him out . . . Then we got caught in the mob downstairs."

"How old is he?"

"I don't know, but he's one of the trustees . . ."

"One of the very first, no doubt," he said, dabbing at the blue-veined eyes. "A trustee of consciousness."

"What was that?" I asked.

"Nothing . . . There now, he's coming out of it."

I had an impulse to run out of the room. I feared what Mr. Norton would say to me, the expression that might come into his eyes.

And yet, I was afraid to leave. My eyes cold not leave the face with
its flickering lids. The head moved from side to side in the pale glow
of the light bulb, as though denying some insistent voice which I
could not hear. Then the lids opened, revealing pale pools of blue
vagueness that finally solidified into points that froze upon the vet,
who looked down unsmilingly.

Men like us did not look at a man like Mr. Norton in that manner, and I stepped hurriedly forward.

"He's a real doctor, sir," I said.

"I'll explain," the vet said. "Get a glass of water."

I hesitated. He looked at me firmly. "Get the water," he said,
turning to help Mr. Norton to sit up.

Outside I asked Edna for a glass of water and she led me down
the hall to a small kitchen, drawing it for me from a green old-fashioned cooler.

"I got some good liquor, baby, if you want to give him a drink,"
she said.

"This will do," I said. My hands trembled so that the water
spilled. When I returned, Mr. Norton was sitting up unaided, carrying on a conversation with the vet.

"Here's some water, sir," I said, extending the glass.

He took it. "Thank you," he said.

"Not too much," the vet cautioned.

"Your diagnosis is exactly that of my specialist," Mr. Norton said,
"and I went to several fine physicians before one could diagnose it.
How did you know?"

"I too was a specialist," the vet said.

"But how? Only a few men in the whole country possess the
knowledge—"

"Then one of them is an inmate of a semi-madhouse," the vet
said. "But there's nothing mysterious about it. I escaped for awhile—
I went to France with the Army Medical Corps and remained there
after the Armistice to study and practice."

"Oh yes, and how long were you in France?" Mr. Norton asked.

"Long enough," he said. "Long enough to forget some fundamentals which I should never have forgotten."

"What fundamentals?" Mr. Norton said. "What do you mean?"

The vet smiled and cocked his head. "Things about life. Such
things as most peasants and folk peoples almost always know
through experience, though seldom through conscious thought . . ."

"Pardon me, sir," I said to Mr. Norton, "but now that you feel
better, shouldn't we go?"

"Not just yet," he said. Then to the doctor, "I'm very interested.
What happened to you?" A drop of water caught in one of his eye-

brows glittered like a chip of active diamond. I went over and sat on a chair. Damn this vet to hell!

"Are you sure you would like to hear?" the vet asked.

"Why, of course."

"Then perhaps the young fellow should go downstairs and wait . . ."

The sound of shouting and destruction welled up from below as I opened the door.

"No, perhaps you should stay," the fat man said. "Perhaps had I overheard some of what I'm about to tell you when I was a student up there on the hill, I wouldn't be the casualty that I am."

"Sit down, young man," Mr. Norton ordered. "So you were a student at the college," he said to the vet.

I sat down again, worrying about Dr. Bledsoe as the fat man told Mr. Norton of his attending college, then becoming a physician and going to France during the World War.

"Were you a successful physician?" Mr. Norton said.

"Fairly so. I performed a few brain surgeries that won me some small attention."

"Then why did you return?"

"Nostalgia," the vet said.

"Then what on earth are you doing here in this . . .?" Mr. Norton said, "With your ability . . ."

"Ulcers," the fat man said.

"That's terribly unfortunate, but why should ulcers stop your career."

"Not really, but I learned along with the ulcers that my work could bring me no dignity," the vet said.

"Now you sound bitter," Mr. Norton said, just as the door flew open.

A brown-skinned woman with red hair looked in. "How's white-folks making out?" she said, staggering inside. "White-folks, baby, you done come to. You want a drink?"

"Not now, Hester," the vet said. "He's still a little weak."

"He sho looks it. That's how come he needs a drink. Put some iron in his blood."

"Now, now, Hester."

"Okay, okay . . . But what y'all doing looking like you at a funeral? Don't you know this is the Golden Day?" she staggered toward me, belching elegantly and reeling. "Just look at y'all. Here school-boy looks like he's scared to death. And white-folks here is acting like y'all two strange poodles. Be happy y'all! I'm going down and get Halley to send you up some drinks." She patted Mr. Norton's cheek as she went past and I saw him turn a glowing red. "Be happy, white-folks."

"Ah hah!" the vet laughed, "you're blushing, which means that you're better. Don't be embarrassed. Hester is a great humanitarian, a therapist of generous nature and great skill, and the possessor of a healing touch. Her catharsis is absolutely tremendous—ha, ha!"

"You do look better, sir," I said, anxious to get out of the place. I could understand the vet's words but not what they conveyed, and Mr. Norton looked as uncomfortable as I felt. The one thing which I did know was that the vet was acting toward the white man with a freedom which could only bring trouble. I wanted to tell Mr. Norton that the man was crazy and yet I received a fearful satisfaction from hearing him talk as he had to a white man. With the girl it was different. A woman usually got away with things a man never could.

I was wet with anxiety, but the vet talked on, ignoring the interruption.

"Rest, rest," he said, fixing Mr. Norton with his eyes. "The clocks are all set back and the forces of destruction are rampant down below. They might suddenly realize that you are what you are, and then your life wouldn't be worth a piece of bankrupt stock. You would be canceled, perforated, voided, become the recognized magnet attracting loose screws. Then what would you do? Such men are beyond money, and with Supercargo down, out like a felled ox, they know nothing of value. To some, you are the great white father, to others the lyncher of souls, but for all, you are confusion come even into the Golden Day."

"What are you talking about?" I said, thinking: *Lyncher?* He was getting wilder than the men downstairs. I didn't dare look at Mr. Norton, who made a sound of protest.

The vet frowned. "It is an issue which I can confront only by evading it. An utterly stupid proposition, and these hands so lovingly trained to master a scalpel yearn to caress a trigger. I returned to save life and I was refused," he said. "Ten men in masks drove me out from the city at midnight and beat me with whips for saving a human life. And I was forced to the utmost degradation because I possessed skilled hands and the belief that my knowledge could bring me dignity—not wealth, only dignity—and other men health!"

Then suddenly he fixed me with his eyes. "And now, do you understand?"

"What?" I said.

"What you've heard!"

"I don't know."

"Why?"

I said, "I really think it's time we left."

"You see," he said turning to Mr. Norton, "he has eyes and ears and a good distended African nose, but he fails to understand the

simple facts of life. *Understand.* Understand? It's worse than that. He
registers with his senses but short-circuits his brain. Nothing has
meaning. He takes it in but he doesn't digest it. Already he is—well,
bless my soul! Behold! a walking zombie! Already he's learned to
repress not only his emotions but his humanity. He's invisible, a
walking personification of the Negative, the most perfect achievement of your dreams, sir! The mechanical man!"

Mr. Norton looked amazed.

"Tell me," the vet said, suddenly calm. "Why have you been interested in the school, Mr. Norton?"

"Out of a sense of my destined role," Mr. Norton said shakily. "I
felt, and I still feel, that your people are in some important manner
tied to my destiny."

"What do you mean, destiny?" the vet said.

"Why, the success of my work, of course."

"I see. And would you recognize it if you saw it?"

"Why, of course I would," Mr. Norton said indignantly. "I've
watched it grow each year I've returned to the campus."

"Campus? Why the campus?"

"It is there that my destiny is being made."

The vet exploded with laughter. "The campus, what a destiny!"
He stood and walked around the narrow room, laughing. Then he
stopped as suddenly as he had begun.

"You will hardly recognize it, but it is very fitting that you came
to the Golden Day with the young fellow," he said.

"I came out of illness—or rather, he brought me," Mr. Norton
said.

"Of course, but you came, and it was fitting."

"What do you mean?" Mr. Norton said with irritation.

"A little child shall lead them," the vet said with a smile. "But
seriously, because you both fail to understand what is happening to
you. You cannot see or hear or smell the truth of what you see—
and you, looking for destiny! It's classic! And the boy, this automa-
ton, he was made of the very mud of the region and he sees far less
than you. Poor stumblers, neither of you can see the other. To you
he is a mark on the score-card of your achievement, a thing and not
a man; a child, or even less—a black amorphous thing. And you, for
all your power, are not a man to him, but a God, a force—"

Mr. Norton stood abruptly. "Let's us go, young man," he said an-
grily.

"No, listen. He believes in you as he believes in the beat of his
heart. He believes in that great false wisdom taught slaves and prag-
matists alike, that white is right. I can tell you *his* destiny. He'll do
your bidding, and for that his blindness is his chief asset. He's your

man, friend. Your man and your destiny. Now the two of you descend the stairs into chaos and get the hell out of here. I'm sick of both of you pitiful obscenities! Get out before I do you both the favor of bashing in your heads!"

I saw his motion toward the big white pitcher on the washstand and stepped between him and Mr. Norton, guiding Mr. Norton swiftly through the doorway. Looking back, I saw him leaning against the wall making a sound that was a blending of laughter and tears.

"Hurry, the man is as insane as the rest," Mr. Norton said.

"Yes, sir," I said, noticing a new note in his voice.

The balcony was now as noisy as the floor below. The girls and drunken vets were stumbling about with drinks in their hands. Just as we went past an open door Edna saw us and grabbed my arm.

"Where you taking white-folks?" she demanded.

"Back to school," I said, shaking her off.

"You don't want to go up there, white-folks, baby," she said. I tried to push past her. "I ain't lying," she said. "I'm the best little homemaker in the business."

"Okay, but please let us alone," I pleaded. "You'll get me into trouble."

We were going down the stairs into the milling men now and she started to scream, "Pay me then! If he's too good for me, let him pay!"

And before I could stop her she had pushed Mr. Norton, and both of us were stumbling swiftly down the stairs. I landed against a man who looked up with the anonymous familiarity of a drunk and shoved me hard away. I saw Mr. Norton spin past as I sank farther into the crowd. Somewhere I could hear the girl screaming and Halley's voice yelling, "Hey! Hey! Hey, now!" Then I was aware of fresh air and saw that I was near the door and pushed my way free and stood panting and preparing to plunge back for Mr. Norton—when I heard Halley calling, "Make way y'all!" and saw him piloting Mr. Norton to the door.

"Whew!" he said, releasing the white man and shaking his huge head.

"Thanks, Halley—" I said and got no further.

I saw Mr. Norton, his face pale again, his white suit rumpled, topple and fall, his head scraping against the screen of the door.

"Hey!"

I opened the door and raised him up.

"Goddamit, out agin," Halley said. "How come you bring this white man here, school-boy?"

"Is he dead?"

"DEAD!" he said, stepping back indignantly. "He *caint* die!"

"What'll I do, Halley?"

"Not in my place, he caint die," he said, kneeling.

Mr. Norton looked up. "No one is dead or dying," he said acidly. "Remove your hands!"

Halley fell away, surprised. "I sho am glad. You sho you all right? I thought sho you was dead this time."

"For God's sake, be quiet!" I exploded nervously. "You should be glad that he's all right."

Mr. Norton was visibly angry now, a raw place showing on his forehead, and I hurried ahead of him to the car. He climbed in un-aided, and I got under the wheel, smelling the heated odor of mints and cigar smoke. He was silent as I drove away.

HIDDEN NAME AND COMPLEX FATE
A Writer's Experience in the United States

In *Green Hills of Africa*, Ernest Hemingway reminds us that both Tolstoy and Stendhal had seen war, that Flaubert had seen a revolution and the Commune, that Dostoievsky had been sent to Siberia and that such experiences were important in shaping the art of these great masters. And he goes on to observe that "writers are forged in injustice as a sword is forged." He declined to describe the many personal forms which injustice may take in this chaotic world—who would be so mad as to try?—nor does he go into the personal wounds which each of these writers sustained. Now, however, thanks to his brother and sister, we do know something of the injustice in which he himself was forged, and this knowledge has been added to what we have long known of Hemingway's artistic temper.

In the end, however, it is the quality of his art which is primary. It is the art which allows the wars and revolutions which he knew, and the personal and social injustice which he suffered, to lay claims upon our attention; for it was through his art that they achieved their most enduring meaning. It is a matter of outrageous irony, per-haps, but in literature the great social clashes of history no less than the painful experience of the individual are secondary to the mean-ing which they take on through the skill, the talent, the imagination

Address sponsored by the Gertrude Clarke Whittall foundation, Library of Congress, January 6, 1964.

and personal vision of the writer who transforms them into art. Here they are reduced to more manageable proportions; here they are imbued with humane values; here, injustice and catastrophe become less important in themselves than what the writer makes of them. This is *not* true, however, of the writer's struggle with that recalcitrant angel called Art; and it was through *this* specific struggle that Ernest Hemingway became *Hemingway* (now refined to a total body of transcendent work, after forty years of being endlessly dismembered and resurrected, as it continues to be, in the styles, the themes, the sense of life and literature of countless other writers). And it was through this struggle with form that he became the master, the culture hero, whom we have come to know and admire.

It was suggested that it might be of interest if I discussed here this evening some of my notions of the writer's experience in the United States, hence I have evoked the name of Hemingway, not by way of inviting far-fetched comparisons but in order to establish a perspective, a set of assumptions from which I may speak, and in an attempt to avoid boring you by emphasizing those details of racial hardship which for some forty years now have been evoked whenever writers of my own cultural background have essayed their experience in public.

I do this *not* by way of denying totally the validity of these by now stylized recitals, for I have shared and still share many of their detailed injustices—what Negro can escape them?—but by way of suggesting that they are, at least in a discussion of a writer's experience, as *writer*, as artist, somewhat beside the point.

For we select neither our parents, our race nor our nation; these occur to us out of the love, the hate, the circumstances, the fate, of others. But we *do* become writers out of an act of will, out of an act of choice; a dim, confused and ofttimes regrettable choice, perhaps, but choice nevertheless. And what happens thereafter causes all those experiences which occurred before we began to function as writers to take on a special quality of uniqueness. If this does not happen then as far as writing goes, the experiences have been misused. If we do not make of them a value, if we do not transform them into forms and images of meaning which they did not possess before, then we have failed as artists.

Thus for a writer to insist that his personal suffering is of special interest in itself, or simply because he belongs to a particular racial or religious group, is to advance a claim for special privileges which members of his group who are not writers would be ashamed to demand. The kindest judgment one can make of this point of view is that it reveals a sad misunderstanding of the relationship between suffering and art. Thomas Mann and André Gide have told us much of this and there are critics, like Edmund Wilson, who have told of the connection between the wound and the bow.

As I see it, it is through the process of making artistic forms—plays, poems, novels—out of one's experience that one becomes a writer, and it is through this process, this struggle, that the writer helps give meaning to the experience of the group. And it is the process of mastering the discipline, the techniques, the fortitude, the culture, through which this is made possible that constitutes the writer's real experience as *writer*, as artist. If this sound like an argument for the artist's withdrawal from social struggles, I would recall to you W. H. Auden's comment to the effect that:

> In our age, the mere making of a work of art is itself a political act. So long as artists exist, making what they please, and think they ought to make, even if it is not terribly good, even if it appeals to only a handful of people, they remind the Management of something managers need to be reminded of, namely, that the managed are people with faces, not anonymous members, that *Homo Laborans* is also *Homo Ludens*. . . .

Without doubt, even the most *engagé* writer—and I refer to true artists, not to artists *manqués*—begin their careers in play and puzzlement, in dreaming over the details of the world in which they become conscious of themselves.

Let Tar Baby, that enigmatic figure from Negro folklore, stand for the world. He leans, black and gleaming, against the wall of life utterly noncommittal under our scrutiny, our questioning, starkly unmoving before our naïve attempts at intimidation. Then we touch him playfully and before we can say *Sonny Liston!* we find ourselves stuck. Our playful investigations become a labor, a fearful struggle, an *agon*. Slowly we perceive that our task is to learn the proper way of freeing ourselves to develop, in other words, technique.

Sensing this, we give him our sharpest attention, we question him carefully, we struggle with more subtlety; while he, in his silent way, holds on, demanding that we perceive the necessity of calling him by his true name as the price of our freedom. It is unfortunate that he has so many, many "true names"—all spelling chaos; and in order to discover even one of these we must first come into the possession of our own names. For it is through our names that we first place ourselves in the world. Our names, being the gift of others, must be made our own.

Once while listening to the play of a two-year-old girl who did not know she was under observation, I heard her saying over and over again, at first with questioning and then with sounds of growing satisfaction, "I am Mimi Livisay? . . .I am Mimi Livisay. I *am* Mimi Livisay . . . I am *Mimi* Li-vi-say! I am Mimi . . ."

And in deed and in fact she was—or became so soon thereafter, by working playfully to establish the unity between herself and her name.

For many of us this is far from easy. We must learn to wear our names within all the noise and confusion of the environment in which we find ourselves; make them the center of all of our associations with the world, with man and with nature. We must charge them with all our emotions, our hopes, hates, loves, aspirations. They must become our masks and our shields and the containers of all those values of our familial past.

And when we are reminded so constantly that we bear, as Negroes, names originally possessed by those who owned our enslaved grandparents, we are apt, especially if we are potential writers, to be more than ordinarily concerned with the veiled and mysterious events, the fusions of blood, the furtive couplings, the business transactions, the violations of faith and loyalty, the assaults; yes, and the unrecognized and unrecognizable loves through which our names were handed down unto us.

So charged with emotion does this concern become for some of us, that we have, earlier, the example of the followers of Father Divine and, now, the Black Muslims, discarding their original names in rejection of the bloodstained, the brutal, the sinful images of the past. Thus they would declare new identities, would clarify a new program of intention and destroy the verbal evidence of a willed and ritualized discontinuity of blood and human intercourse.

Not all of us, actually only a few, seek to deal with our names in this manner. We take what we have and make of them what we can. And there are even those who know where the old broken connections lie, who recognize their relatives across the chasm of historical denial and the artificial barriers of society, and who see themselves as bearers of many of the qualities which were admirable in the original sources of their common line (Faulkner has made much of this); and I speak here not of mere forgiveness, nor of obsequious insensitivity to the outrages symbolized by the denial and the division, but of the conscious acceptance of the harsh realities of the human condition, of the ambiguities and hypocrisies of human history as they have played themselves out in the United States.

Perhaps, taken in aggregate, these European names which (sometimes with irony, sometimes with pride, but always with personal investment) represent a certain triumph of the spirit, speaking to us of those who rallied, reassembled and transformed themselves and who under dismembering pressures refused to die. "Brothers and sisters," I once heard a Negro preacher exhort, "let us make up our faces before the world, and our names shall sound throughout the land with honor! For we ourselves are our *true* names, not their epithets! So let us, I say, Make Up Our Faces and Our Minds!"

Perhaps my preacher had read T. S. Eliot, although I doubt it. And in actuality, it was unnecessary that he do so, for a concern with names and naming was very much a part of that special area of American culture from which I come, and it is precisely for this reason that this example should come to mind in a discussion of my own experience as a writer.

Undoubtedly, writers begin their *conditioning* as manipulators of words long before they become aware of literature—certain Freudians would say at the breast. Perhaps. But if so, that is far too early to be of use at this moment. Of this, though, I am certain: that despite the misconceptions of those educators who trace the reading difficulties experienced by large numbers of Negro children in Northern schools to their Southern background, these children are, in *their* familiar South, facile manipulators of words. I know, too, that the Negro community is deadly in its ability to create nicknames and to spot all that is ludicrous in an unlikely name or that which is incongruous in conduct. Names are not qualities; nor are words, in this particular sense, actions. To assume that they are could cost one his life many times a day. Language skills depend to a large extent upon a knowledge of the details, the manners, the objects, the folkways, the psychological patterns, of a given environment. Humor and wit depend upon much the same awareness, and so does the suggestive power of names.

"A small brown bowlegged Negro with the name 'Franklin D. Roosevelt Jones' might sound like a clown to someone who looks at him from the outside," said my friend Albert Murray, "but on the other hand he just might turn out to be a hell of a fireside operator. He might just lie back in all of that comic juxtaposition of names and manipulate you deaf, dumb and blind—and you not even suspecting it, because you're thrown out of stance by his name! There you are, so dazzled by the F.D.R. image—which you *know* you can't see—and so delighted with your own superior position that you don't realize that it's *Jones* who must be confronted."

Well, as you must suspect, all of this speculation on the matter of names has a purpose, and now, because it is tied up so ironically with my own experience as a writer, I must turn to my own name.

For in the dim beginnings, before I ever thought consciously of writing, there was my own name, and there was, doubtless, a certain magic in it. From the start I was uncomfortable with it, and in my earliest years it caused me much puzzlement. Neither could I understand what a poet was, nor why, exactly, my father had chosen to name me after one. Perhaps I could have understood it perfectly well had he named me after his own father, but that name had been given to an older brother who died and thus was out of the question. But why hadn't he named me after a hero, such as Jack Johnson, or a soldier like Colonel Charles Young, or a great seaman like Admiral Dewey, or an educator like Booker T. Washington, or a great orator and abolitionist like Frederick Douglass? Or again, why hadn't he named me (as so many Negro parents had done) after President Teddy Roosevelt?

Instead, he named me after someone called Ralph Waldo Emerson, and then, when I was three, he died. It was too early for me to have understood his choice, although I'm sure he must have explained it many times, and it was also too soon for me to have made the connection between my name and my father's love for reading. Much later, after I began to write and work with words, I came to suspect that he was aware of the suggestive powers of names and of the magic involved in naming.

I recall an odd conversation with my mother during my early teens in which she mentioned their interest in, of all things, prenatal culture! But for a long time I actually knew only that my father read a lot, and that he admired this remote Mr. Emerson, who was something called a "poet and philosopher"—so much so that he named his second son after him.

I knew, also, that whatever his motives, the combination of names he'd given me caused me no end of trouble from the moment when I could talk well enough to respond to the ritualized question which grownups put to very young children. Emerson's name was quite familiar to Negroes in Oklahoma during those days when World War I was brewing, and adults, eager to show off their knowledge of literary figures, and obviously amused by the joke implicit in such a small brown nubbin of a boy carrying around such a heavy moniker, would invariably repeat my first two names and then to my great annoyance, they'd add "Emerson."

And I, in my confusion, would reply, "No, *no, I'm* not Emerson; he's the little boy who lives next door." Which only made them laugh all the louder. "Oh no," they'd say, *"you're* Ralph Waldo Emerson," while I had fantasies of blue murder.

For a while the presence next door of my little friend, Emerson, made it unnecessary for me to puzzle too often over this peculiar adult confusion. And since there were other Negro boys named Ralph in the city, I came to suspect that there was something about the combination of names which produced their laughter. Even today I know of only one other Ralph who had as much comedy made out of his name, a campus politician and deep-voiced orator whom I knew at Tuskegee, who was called in friendly ribbing, *Ralph Waldo*

Emerson Edgar Allan Poe, spelled Powe. This must have been quite a trial for him, but I had been initiated much earlier.

During my early school years the name continued to puzzle me, for it constantly evoked in the faces of others some secret. It was as though I possessed some treasure or some defect, which was invisible to my own eyes and ears; something which I had but did not *possess*, like a piece of property in South Carolina, which was mine but which I could not have until some future time. I recall finding, about this time, while seeking adventure in back alleys—which possess for boys a superiority over playgrounds like that which kitchen utensils possess over toys designed for infants—a large photographic lens. I remember nothing of its optical qualities, of its speed or color correction, but it gleamed with crystal mystery and it was beautiful.

Mounted handsomely in a tube of shiny brass, it spoke to me of distant worlds of possibility. I played with it, looking through it with squinted eyes, holding it in shafts of sunlight, and tried to use it for a magic lantern. But most of this was as unrewarding as my attempts to make the music come from a phonograph record by holding the needle in my fingers.

I could burn holes through newspapers with it, or I could pretend that it was a telescope, the barrel of a cannon, or the third eye of a monster—*I* being the monster—but I could do nothing at all about its proper function of making images; nothing to make it yield its secret. But I could not discard it.

Older boys sought to get it away from me by offering knives or tops, agate marbles or whole zoos of grass snakes and horned toads in trade, but I held on to it. No one, not even the white boys I knew, had such a lens, and it was my own good luck to have found it. Thus I would hold on to it until such time as I could acquire the parts needed to make it function. Finally I put it aside and it remained buried in my box of treasures, dusty and dull, to be lost and forgotten as I grew older and became interested in music.

I had reached by now the grades where it was necessary to learn something about Mr. Emerson and what he had written, such as the "Concord Hymn" and the essay "Self-Reliance," and in following his advice, I reduced the "Waldo" to a simple and, I hoped, mysterious "W," and in my own reading I avoided his works like the plague. I could no more deal with my name—I shall never really master it—than I could find a creative use for my lens. Fortunately there were other problems to occupy my mind. Not that I forgot my fascination with names, but more about that later.

Negro Oklahoma City was starkly lacking in writers. In fact, there was only Roscoe Dungee, the editor of the local Negro newspaper and a very fine editorialist in that valuable tradition of personal journalism which is now rapidly disappearing; a writer who in his emphasis upon the possibilities for justice offered by the Constitution anticipated the anti-segregation struggle by decades. There were also a few reporters who drifted in and out, but these were about all. On the level of *conscious* culture the Negro community was biased in the direction of music.

These were the middle and late twenties, remember, and the state was still a new frontier state. The capital city was one of the great centers for southwestern jazz, along with Dallas and Kansas City. Orchestras which were to become famous within a few years were constantly coming and going. As were the blues singers—Ma Rainey and Ida Cox, and the old bands like that of King Oliver. But best of all, thanks to Mrs. Zelia N. Breaux, there was an active and enthusiastic school music program through which any child who had the interest and the talent could learn to play an instrument and take part in the band, the orchestra, the brass quartet. And there was a yearly operetta and a chorus and a glee club. Harmony was taught for four years and the music appreciation program was imperative. European folk dances were taught throughout the Negro school system, and we were also taught complicated patterns of military drill.

I tell you this to point out that although there were no incentives to write, there was ample opportunity to receive an artistic discipline. Indeed, once one picked up an instrument it was difficult to escape. If you chafed at the many rehearsals of the school band or orchestra and were drawn to the many small jazz groups, you were likely to discover that the jazzmen were apt to rehearse far more than the school band; it was only that they seemed to enjoy themselves better and to possess a freedom of imagination which we were denied at school. And one soon learned that the wild, transcendent moments which occurred at dances or "battles of music," moments in which memorable improvisations were ignited, depended upon a dedication to a discipline which was observed even when rehearsals had to take place in the crowded quarters of Halley Richardson's shoeshine parlor. It was not the place which counted, although a large hall with good acoustics was preferred, but what one did to perfect one's performance.

If this talk of musical discipline gives the impression that there wee no forces working to nourish one who would one day blunder, after many a twist and turn, into writing, I am misleading you. And here I might give you a longish lecture on the Ironies and Uses of Segregation. When I was a small child there was no library for Negroes in our city; and not until a Negro minister invaded the main library did we get one. For it was discovered that there was no law, only custom, which held that we could not use these public facilities. The results were the quick renting of two large rooms in a Negro office building (the recent site of a pool hall), the hiring of a young Negro librarian, the installation of shelves and a hurried stocking of the walls with any and every book possible. It was, in those first days, something of a literary chaos.

But how fortunate for a boy who loved to read! I started with the fairy tales and quickly went through the junior fiction; then through the Westerns and the detective novels, and very soon I was reading the classics—only I didn't know it. There were also the Haldeman Julius Blue Books, which seem to have floated on the air down from Girard, Kansas; the syndicated columns of O. O. McIntyre, and the copies of *Vanity Fair* and the *Literary Digest* which my mother brought home from work—how could I ever join uncritically in the heavy-handed attacks on the so-called Big Media which have become so common today?

There were also the pulp magazines and, more important, that other library which I visited when I went to help my adopted grandfather, J. D. Randolph (my parents had been living in his rooming house when I was born), at his work as custodian of the law library of the Oklahoma State Capitol. Mr. Randolph had been one of the first teachers in what became Oklahoma City; and he'd also been one of the leaders of a group who walked from Gallatin, Tennessee, to the Oklahoma Territory. He was a tall man, as brown as smoked leather, who looked like the Indians with whom he'd herded horses in the early days.

And while his status was merely the custodian of the law library, I was to see the white legislators come down on many occasions to question him on points of law, and often I was to hear him answer without recourse to the uniform rows of books on the shelves. This was a thing to marvel at in itself, and the white lawmakers did so, but even more marvelous, ironic, intriguing, haunting—call it what you will—is the fact that the Negro who knew the answers was named after Jefferson Davis. What Tennessee lost, Oklahoma was to gain, and after gaining it (a gift of courage, intelligence, fortitude and grace), used it only in concealment and, one hopes, with embarrassment.

So, let us, I say make up our faces and our minds!

In the loosely structured community of that time, knowledge, news of other ways of living, ancient wisdom, the latest literary fads, hate literature—for years I kept a card warning Negroes away from the polls, which had been dropped by the thousands from a plane which circled over the Negro community—information of all kinds, found its level, catch-as-catch can, in the minds of those who were receptive to it. Not that there was no conscious structuring—I read my first Shaw and Maupassant, my first Harvard Classics in the home of a friend whose parents were products of that stream of New England education which had been brought to Negroes by the young and enthusiastic white teachers who staffed the schools set up for the freedmen after the Civil War. These parents were both teachers and there were others like them in our town.

But the places where a rich oral literature was truly functional were the churches, the schoolyards, the barbershops, the cotton-picking camps; places where folklore and gossip thrived. The drug store where I worked was such a place, where on days of bad weather the older men would sit with their pipes and tell tall tales, hunting yarns and homely versions of the classics. It was here that I heard stories of searching for buried treasure and of headless horse-men, which I was told were my own father's versions told long be-fore. There were even recitals of popular verse, "The Shooting of Dan McGrew," and, along with these, stories of Jesse James, of Ne-gro outlaws and black United States marshals, of slaves who became the chiefs of Indian tribes and of the exploits of Negro cowboys. There was both truth and fantasy in this, intermingled in the myste-rious fashion of literature.

Writers, in their formative period, absorb into their consciousness much that has no special value until much later, and often much which is of no special value even then—perhaps, beyond the fact that it throbs with affect and mystery and in it "time and pain and royalty in the blood" are suspended in imagery. So, long before I thought of writing, I was claimed by weather, by speech rhythms, by Negro voices and their different idioms, by husky male voices and by the high shrill singing voices of certain Negro women, by music; by tight spaces and by wide spaces in which the eyes could wander; by death, by newly born babies, by manners of various kinds, com-pany manners and street manners; the manners of white society and those of our own high society; and by interracial manners; by street fights, circuses and ministrel shows; by vaudeville and moving pic-tures, by prize fights and foot races, baseball games and football matches. By spring floods and blizzards, catalpa worms and jack rab-bits; honeysuckle and snapdragons (which smelled like old cigar butts); by sunflowers and hollyhocks, raw sugar cane and baked yams; pigs' feet, chili and blue haw ice cream. By parades, public dances and jam sessions, Easter sunrise ceremonies and large funer-als. By contests between fire-and-brimstone preachers and by presid-ing elders who go "laughing-happy" when moved by the spirit of God.

I was impressed by expert players of the "dozens" and certain notorious bootleggers of corn whiskey. By jazz musicians and fortune-tellers and by men who did anything well; by strange sicknesses and by interesting brick or razor scars; by expert cursing vocabularies as well as by exalted praying and terrifying shouting, and by transcendent playing or singing of the blues. I was fascinated by old ladies, those who had seen slavery and those who were defiant of white folk and black alike; by the enticing walks of prostitutes and by the limping walks affected by Negro hustlers, especially those who wore Stetson hats, expensive shoes with well-starched overalls, usually with a diamond stickpin (when not in hock) in their tieless collars as their gambling uniforms.

And there were the blind men who preached on corners, and the blind men who sang the blues to the accompaniment of washboard and guitar; and the white junkmen who sang mountain music and the famous hucksters of fruit and vegetables.

And there was the Indian-Negro confusion. There were Negroes who were part Indian and who lived on reservations, and Indians who had children who lived in towns as Negroes, and Negroes who were Indians and traveled back and forth between the groups with no trouble. And Indians who were as wild as wild Negroes and others who were as solid and as steady as bankers. There were the teachers, too, inspiring teachers and villainous teachers who chased after the girl students, and certain female teachers who one wished would chase after young male students. And a handsome old principal of military bearing who had been blemished by his classmates at West Point when they discovered on the eve of graduation that he was a Negro. There were certain Jews, Mexicans, Chinese cooks, a German orchestra conductor and an English grocer who owned a Franklin touring car. And certain Negro mechanics—"Cadillac Slim," "Sticks" Walker, Buddy Bunn and Oscar Pitman—who had so assimilated the automobile that they seemed to be behind a steering wheel even as they walked the streets or danced with girls. And there were the whites who despised us and the others who shared our hardships and our joys.

There is much more, but this is sufficient to indicate some of what was present even in a segregated community to form the background of my work, my sense of life.

And now comes the next step. I went to Tuskegee to study music, hoping to become a composer of symphonies and there, during my second year, I read *The Waste Land* and that, although I was then unaware of it, was the real transition to writing.

Mrs. L. C. McFarland had taught us much of Negro history in grade school and from her I'd learned of the New Negro Movement of the twenties, of Langston Hughes, Countee Cullen, Claude

McKay, James Weldon Johnson and the others. They had inspired
pride and had given me a closer identification with poetry (by now,
oddly enough, I seldom thought of my hidden name), but with music so much on my mind it never occurred to me to try to imitate
them. Still I read their work and was excited by the glamour of the
Harlem which emerged from their poems and it was good to know
that there were Negro writers.—Then came *The Waste Land.*

I was much more under the spell of literature than I realized at
the time. *Wuthering Heights* had caused me an agony of unexpressi-
ble emotion and the same was true of *Jude the Obscure,* but *The
Waste Land* seized my mind. I was intrigued by its power to move
me while eluding my understanding. Somehow its rhythms were often closer to those of jazz than were those of the Negro poets, and
even though I could not understand then, its range of allusion was
as mixed and as varied as that of Louis Armstrong. Yet there were its
discontinuities, its changes of pace and its hidden system of organization which escaped me.

There was nothing to do but look up the references in the foot-
notes to the poem, and thus began my conscious education in literature.

For this, the library at Tuskegee was quite adequate and I used it.
Soon I was reading a whole range of subjects drawn upon by the
poet, and this led, in turn, to criticism and to Pound and Ford Ma-
dox Ford, Sherwood Anderson and Gertrude Stein, Hemingway and
Fitzgerald and "round about 'til I was come" back to Melville and
Twain—the writers who are taught and doubtlessly overtaught to-
day. Perhaps it was my good luck that they were not taught at Tuskegee, I wouldn't know. But at the time I was playing, having an
intellectually interesting good time.

Having given so much attention to the techniques of music, the
process of learning something of the craft and intention of modern
poetry and fiction seemed quite familiar. Besides, it was absolutely
painless because it involved no deadlines or credits. Even then, however, a process which I described earlier had begun to operate. The
more I learned of literature in this conscious way, the more the details of my background became transformed. I heard undertones in
remembered conversations which had escaped me before, local customs took on a more universal meaning, values which I hadn't understood were revealed; some of the people whom I had known were
diminished while others were elevated in stature. More important, I
began to see my own possibilities with more objective, and in some
ways, more hopeful eyes.

The following summer I went to New York seeking work, which
I did not find, and remained there, but the personal transformation

continued. Reading had become a conscious process of growth and discovery, a method of reordering the world. And that world had widened considerably.

At Tuskegee I had handled manuscripts which Prokofiev had given to Hazel Harrison, a Negro concert pianist who taught there and who had known him in Europe, and through Miss Harrison I had become aware of Prokofiev's symphonies. I had also become aware of the radical movement in politics and art, and in New York had begun reading the work of André Malraux, not only the fiction but chapters published from his *Psychology of Art*. And in my search for an expression of modern sensibility in the works of Negro writers I discovered Richard Wright. Shortly thereafter I was to meet Wright, and it was at his suggestion that I wrote both my first book review and my first short story. These were fatal suggestions.

For although I had tried my hand at poetry while at Tuskegee, it hadn't occurred to me that I might write fiction, but once he suggested it, it seemed the most natural thing to try. Fortunately for me, Wright, then on the verge of his first success, was eager to talk with a beginner and I was able to save valuable time in searching out those works in which writing was discussed as a craft. He guided me to Henry James' prefaces, to Conrad, to Joseph Warren Beach and to the letters of Dostoievsky. There were other advisers and other books involved, of course, but what is important here is that I was consciously concerned with the art of fiction, that almost from the beginning I was grappling quite consciously with the art through which I wished to realize myself. And this was not done in isolation; the Spanish Civil War was now in progress and the Depression was still on. The world was being shaken up, and through one of those odd instances which occur to young provincials in New York, I was to hear Malraux make an appeal for the Spanish Loyalists at the same party where I first heard the folk singer Leadbelly perform. Wright and I were there seeking money for the magazine which he had come to New York to edit.

Art and politics; a great French novelist and a Negro folk singer; a young writer who was soon to publish *Uncle Tom's Children*; and I who had barely begun to study his craft. It is such accidents, such fortuitous meetings, which count for so much in our lives. I had never dreamed that I would be in the presence of Malraux, of whose work I became aware on my second day in Harlem when Langston Hughes suggested that I read *Man's Fate* and *Days of Wrath* before returning them to a friend of his. And it is this fortuitous circumstance which led to my selecting Malraux as a literary "ancestor," whom, unlike a relative, the artist is permitted to choose. There was in progress at the time all the agitation over the Scottsboro boys and the Herndon Case, and I was aware of both. I had to be; I myself had been taken off a freight train at Decatur, Alabama, only three years before while on my way to Tuskegee. But while I joined in the agitation for their release, my main energies went into learning to write.

I began to publish enough, and not too slowly, to justify my hopes for success, and as I continued, I made a most perplexing discovery; namely, that for all his conscious concern with technique, a writer did not so much create the novel as he was created *by* the novel. That is, one did not make an arbitrary gesture when one sought to write. And when I say that the novelist is created by the novel, I mean to remind you that fictional techniques are not a mere set of objective tools, but something much more intimate: a way of feeling, of seeing and of expressing one's sense of life. And the process of *acquiring* technique is a process of modifying one's responses, of learning to see and feel, to hear and observe, to evoke and evaluate the images of memory and of summoning up and directing the imagination; of learning to conceive of human values in the ways which have been established by the great writers who have developed and extended the art. And perhaps the writer's greatest freedom, as artist, lies precisely in his possession of technique; for it is through technique that he comes to possess and express the meaning of his life.

Perhaps at this point it would be useful to recapitulate the route—perhaps as mazelike as that of *Finnegan's Wake*—which I have been trying to describe; that which leads from the writer's discovery of a sense of purpose, which is that of becoming a writer, and then the involvement in the passionate struggle required to master a bit of technique, and then, as this begins to take shape, the disconcerting discovery that it is *technique* which transforms the individual before he is able in turn to transform it. And in that personal transformation he discovers something else: he discovers that he has taken on certain obligations, that he must not embarrass his chosen form, and that in order to avoid this he must develop taste. He learns—and this is most discouraging—that he is involved with values which turn in their own way, and not in the ways of politics, upon the central issues affecting his nation and his time. He learns that the American novel, from its first consciousness of itself as a literary form, has grappled with the meaning of the American experience; that it has been aware and has sought to define the nature of that experience by addressing itself to the specific details, the moods, the landscapes, the cityscapes, the tempo of American change. And that it has borne, at its best, the full weight of that burden of conscience and consciousness which Americans inherit as one of the results of the revolutionary circumstances of our national beginnings.

We began as a nation not through the accidents of race or religion or geography (Robert Penn Warren has dwelled on these circumstances) but when a group of men, *some* of them political philosophers, put down, upon what we now recognize as being quite sacred papers, their conception of the nation which they intended to establish on these shores. They described, as we know, the obligations of the state to the citizen, of the citizen to the state; they committed themselves to certain ideas of justice, just as they committed us to a system which would guarantee all of its citizens equality of opportunity.

I need not describe the problems which have arisen from these beginnings. I need only remind you that the contradiction between these noble ideals and the actualities of our conduct generated a guilt, an unease of spirit, from the very beginning, and that the American novel at its best has always been concerned with this basic moral predicament. During Melville's time and Twain's, it was an implicit aspect of their major themes; by the twentieth century and after the discouraging and traumatic effect of the Civil War and the Reconstruction it had gone underground, had become *understated*. Nevertheless it did not disappear completely and it is to be found operating in the work of Henry James as well as in that of Hemingway and Fitzgerald. And then (and as one who believes in the impelling moral function of the novel and who believes in the moral seriousness of the form) it pleases me no end that it comes into explicit statement again in the works of Richard Wright and William Faulkner, writers who lived close to moral and political problems which would not stay put underground.

I go into these details not to recapitulate the history of the American novel but to indicate the trend of thought which was set into motion when I began to discover the nature of that process with which I was actually involved. Whatever the opinions and decisions of critics, a novelist must arrive at his own conclusions as to the meaning and function of the form with which he is engaged, and these are, in all modesty, some of mine.

In order to orient myself I also began to learn that the American novel had long concerned itself with the puzzle of the one-and-the-many; the mystery of how each of us, despite his origin in diverse regions, without diverse racial, cultural, religious background, speaking his own diverse idiom of the American in his own accent, is, nevertheless, American. And with this concern with the implicit pluralism of the country and with the composite nature of the ideal character called "the American," there goes a concern with gauging the health of the American promise, with depicting the extent to which it was being achieved, being made manifest in our daily conduct.

And with all of this there still remained the specific concerns of literature. Among these is the need to keep literary standards high, the necessity of exploring new possibilities of language which would allow it to retain that flexibility and fidelity to the common speech which has been its glory since Mark Twain. For me this meant learning to add to it the wonderful resources of Negro American speech and idiom and to bring into range as fully and eloquently as possible the complex reality of the American experience as it shaped and was shaped by the lives of my own people.

Notice that I stress as "fully" as possible, because I would no more strive to write great novels by leaving out the complexity of circumstances which go to make up the Negro experience and which alone go to make the obvious injustice bearable, than I would think of preparing myself to become President of the United States simply by studying Negro American history or confining myself to studying those laws affecting civil rights.

For it seems to me that one of the obligations I took on when I committed myself to the art and form of the novel was that of striving for the broadest range, the discovery and articulation of the most exalted values. And I must squeeze these from the life which I know best. (A highly truncated impression of that life I attempted to convey to you earlier.)

If all this sounds a bit heady, remember that I did not destroy that troublesome middle name of mine, I only suppressed it. Sometimes it reminds me of my obligations to the man who named me.

It is our fate as human beings always to give up some good things for other good things, to throw off certain bad circumstances only to create others. Thus there is a value for the writer trying to give as thorough a report of social reality as possible. Only by doing so may we grasp and convey the cost of change. Only by considering the broadest accumulation of data may we make choices that are based upon our own hard-earned sense of reality. Speaking from my own special area of American culture, I feel that to embrace uncritically values which are extended to us by others is to reject the validity, even the sacredness, of our own experience. It is also to forget that the small share of reality which each of our diverse groups is able to snatch from the whirling chaos of history belongs not to the group alone, but to all of us. It is a property and a witness which can be ignored only to the danger of the entire nation.

I could suppress the name of my namesake out of respect for the achievements of its original bearer but I cannot escape the obligation of attempting to achieve some of the things which he asked of the American writer. As Henry James suggested, being an American is an arduous task, and for most of us, I suspect, the difficulty begins with the name.

SELECTED BIBLIOGRAPHY

I. ANTHOLOGIES AND COLLECTIONS
(Note: all authors in this section are editors.)

Abrahams, Roger D. *Afro-American Folktales: Stories from Black Traditions in the New World.* Pantheon, 1985.

Andrews, William L. *Six Women's Slave Narratives.* Oxford University Press (The Schomburg Library of Nineteenth-Century Black Women Writers), 1988.

Baker, Houston A., Jr. *A Many-Colored Coat of Dreams: The Poetry of Countee Cullen.* Broadside Press, 1974.

Bambara, Toni Cade. *The Black Woman: An Anthology.* New American Library, 1970.

————. *Tales and Stories for Black Folks.* Doubleday, 1971.

Baraka, Amiri, and Amina Baraka. *Confirmation: An Anthology of African American Women.* Quill, 1983.

Barksdale, Richard, and Keneth Kinnamon. *Black Writers of America: A Comprehensive Anthology.* Macmillan, 1972.

Barthelemy, Anthony G. *Collected Black Women's Narratives.* Oxford University Press (The Schomburg Library of Nineteenth-Century Black Women Writers), 1988.

Beam, Joseph. *In the Life: A Black Gay Anthology.* Alyson, 1986.

Bell, Bernard W. *Modern and Contemporary Afro-American Poetry.* Allyn & Bacon, 1972.

Berry, Faith. *Good Morning, Revolution: Uncollected Social Protest Writings of Langston Hughes.* Lawrence Hill, 1973.

Bontemps, Arna. *American Negro Poetry.* Hill & Wang, 1963.

————. *Great Slave Narratives.* Beacon Press, 1969.

Brasner, William, and Dominick Consolo. *Black Drama: An Anthology.* Merrill, 1970.

Brawley, Benjamin. *Early Negro American Writers.* University of North Carolina Press, 1935.

Brewer, J. Mason. *American Negro Folklore.* Quadrangle, 1968.

Brooks, Gwendolyn. *Jump Bad, A New Chicago Anthology.* Broadside Press, 1971.

————. *A Broadside Treasury, 1965–1970.* Broadside Press, 1971.

————. *The World of Gwendolyn Brooks.* Harper & Row, 1971.

————. *Blacks/Gwendolyn Brooks.* David, 1987.

925

Brown, Patricia L., Don L. Lee (a.k.a. Haki R. Madhubuti), and Francis Ward. *To Gwen, with Love: An Anthology Dedicated to Gwendolyn Brooks.* Johnson Publishing Co., 1971.

Brown, Sterling A., Arthur P. Davis, and Ulysses Lee. *The Negro Caravan: Writings by American Negroes.* Dryden, 1941; Arno, 1969.

Chapman, Abraham. *Black Voices: An Anthology of Afro-American Literature.* New American Library, 1968.

———. *Steal Away: Stories of the Runaway Slaves.* Preager, 1971.

———. *New Black Voices: An Anthology of Contemporary Afro-American Literature.* New American Library, 1972.

Clarke, John H. *American Negro Short Stories.* Hill & Wang, 1966.

Cooper, Wayne F. *The Passion of Claude McKay: Selected Prose and Poetry, 1912–1948.* Schocken Books, 1973.

Courlander, Harold. *A Treasury of Afro-American Folklore: The Oral Literature, Traditions, Recollections, Legends, Tales, Songs, Religious Beliefs, Customs, Sayings and Humor of Peoples of African Descent in the Americas.* Crown Publishers, 1976.

Cromwell, Otelia Lorenzo Turner, and Eva B. Dykes. *Readings from Negro Authors.* Harcourt, 1931.

Cullen, Countee. *Caroling Dusk: An Anthology of Verse by Negro Poets.* Harper, 1927.

Dance, Daryl Cumber. *Shuckin' and Jivin': Folklore from Contemporary Black Americans.* Indiana University Press, 1978.

Davis, Angela Y., and Other Political Prisoners. *If They Come in the Morning: Voices of Resistance by Angela Y. Davis and Others.* Third Press, 1971.

Davis, Arthur P., and Saunders Redding. *Cavalcade: Negro American Writing from 1760 to the Present.* Houghton Mifflin, 1971.

Davis, Arthur P., and Michael W. Peplow. *The New Negro Renaissance: An Anthology.* Holt, Rinehart and Winston, 1975.

Emanuel, James A., and Theodore Gross. *Dark Symphony: Negro Literature in America.* Free Press, 1968.

Exum, Pat Crutchfield. *Keeping the Faith: Writings by Contemporary Black American Women.* Fawcett, 1974.

Faggett, Harry Lee, and Nick Aaron Ford. *Best Short Stories by Afro-American Writers (1925–1950).* Meador, 1950; Krause Reprint, 1977.

Ford, Nick Aaron. *Black Insights: Significant Literature by Black Americans, 1760 to the Present.* Ginn, 1971.

Gibson, Donald B. *Black and White: Stories of American Life.* Washington Square Press, 1971.

Giovanni, Nikki. *Night Comes Softly: Anthology of Black Female Voices.* MEDIC Press, 1970.

Glaysher, Frederick. *Collected Prose/Robert Hayden.* University of Michigan Press, 1984.

———. *Collected Poems/Robert Hayden.* Liveright, 1985.

Graham, Maryemma. *The Complete Poems of Frances E. W. Harper.* Oxford University Press (The Schomburg Library of Nineteenth-Century Black Women Writers), 1988.

Greene, J. Lee. *Time's Unfading Garden: Ann Spencer's Life and Poetry.* Louisiana State University Press, 1977.

Hansberry, Lorraine. *To Be Young, Gifted and Black: Lorraine Hansberry in Her Own Words*. New American Library, 1969; Samuel French, 1971.

Harley, Sharon, and Rosalyn Terborg-Penn. *Afro-American Women: Struggles and Images*. Kennikat Press, 1978.

Harper, Michael S. *The Collected Poems of Sterling Brown*. Harper & Row, 1980.

Harper, Michael S., and Robert B. Stepto. *Chant of Saints: A Gathering of Afro-American Literature, Art, and Scholarship*. University of Illinois Press, 1979.

Harrison, Paul Carter. *Kuntu Drama: Plays of the African Continuum*. Grove Press, 1974.

Hayden, Robert E. *Kaleidoscope: Poems by American Negro Poets*. Harcourt, Brace & World, 1967.

———. *Afro-American Literature: An Introduction*. Harcourt, Brace, Jovanovich, 1971.

Hill, Herbert. *Soon, One Morning: New Writings by American Negroes, 1940–1962*. Knopf, 1963.

Himes, Chester. *Black on Black: Baby Sister and Selected Writings*. Doubleday, 1973.

Hopkins, Lee Burnett. *On Our Way: Poems of Pride and Love*. Knopf, 1974.

Houchins, Sue E. *Spiritual Narratives: Maria W. Stewart, Jarena Lee, Julia A. J. Foote, Virginia W. Broughton*. Oxford University Press (The Schomburg Library of Nineteenth-Century Black Women Writers), 1988.

Hudson, Theodore R. *From LeRoi Jones to Amiri Baraka: The Literary Works*. Duke University Press, 1973.

Huggins, Nathan I. *Voices from the Harlem Renaissance*. Oxford University Press, 1976.

Hughes, Langston. *New Negro Poets, U.S.A.* Indiana University Press, 1964.

———. *The Book of Negro Humor*. Dodd, Mead, 1966.

———. *The Best Short Stories by Negro Writers: An Anthology from 1899 to the Present*. Little, Brown, 1967.

Hughes, Langston, and Arna Bontemps. *The Poetry of the Negro*. Doubleday, 1949; rev. ed., *The Poetry of the Negro, 1746–1970*, 1970.

———. *The Book of Negro Folklore*. Dodd, Mead, 1958.

Hull, Gloria T. *The Works of Alice Dunbar-Nelson*. 3 vols. Oxford University Press (The Schomburg Library of Nineteenth-Century Black Women Writers), 1988.

Hurston, Zora Neale. *Spunk: The Selected Stories of Zora Neale Hurston*. Turtle Island Foundation, 1985.

Johnson, Charles S. *Ebony and Topaz: A Collectanea*. National Urban League, 1927.

Johnson, James Weldon. *The Book of American Negro Poetry*. Harcourt, 1922; rev. and enl., 1931.

Jones, LeRoi, and Larry Neal. *Black Fire: An Anthology of Afro-American Writing*. William Morrow, 1968.

Jones, Robert B., and Marjorie Toomer Latimer. *The Collected Poems of Jean Toomer*. University of North Carolina Press, 1988.

Kellner, Bruce. *"Keep A-Inchin Along": Selected Writings of Carl Van Vechten About Black Art and Letters*. Greenwood Press, 1979.

Kerlin, Robert T. *Negro Poets and Their Poems*. Associated Publishers, 1935.

Kinnamon, Keneth. *James Baldwin: A Collection of Critical Essays*. Prentice-Hall, 1974.

King, Woodie. *Black Short Story Anthology*. Columbia University Press, 1972.

———. *The Forerunners: Black Poets in America*. Howard University Press, 1976.

Locke, Alain L. *The New Negro: An Interpretation*. Boni, 1925; Atheneum, 1968.

Long, Richard A., and Eugenia W. Collier. *Afro-American Writing: An Anthology of Prose and Poetry*. 2 vols. New York University Press, 1972.

Major, Clarence. *The New Black Poetry*. International Publications, 1969.

Margolies, Edward. *A Native Sons Reader: Selections by Outstanding Black American Authors of the Twentieth-Century*. Lippincott, 1970.

Mberi, Antar S. K., and Cosmo Pieterse. *Speak Easy, Speak Free*. International Publishers, 1977.

McCluskey, John, Jr. *The City of Refuge: The Collected Stories of Rudolph Fisher*. University of Missouri Press, 1987.

Miller, E. Ethelbert. *Women Surviving Massacres and Men: Nine Women Poets, An Anthology*. Anemone Press, 1977.

Moon, Bucklin. *Primer for White Folks*. Doubleday, 1945.

Murphy, Beatrice M. *Today's Negro Voices: An Anthology by Young Negro Poets*. Messner, 1970.

Osofsky, Gilbert. *Puttin' on Ole Massa: The Slave Narratives of Henry Bibb, William W. Brown, and Solomon Northrop*. Harper, 1969.

Patterson, Lindsay. *A Rock Against the Wind: Black Love Poems, An Anthology*. Dodd, Mead, 1973.

Perry, Margaret. *The Short Fiction of Rudolph Fisher*. Greenwood Press, 1987.

Plato, Ann. *Essays: Including Biographies and Miscellaneous Pieces, in Prose and Poetry*. Introduction by Kenny J. Williams, Oxford University Press (The Schomburg Library of Nineteenth-Century Black Women Writers), 1988.

Plumpp, Sterling D. *Somehow We Survive: An Anthology of South African Writing*. Thunder's Mouth Press, 1982.

Randall, Dudley. *Black Poetry: A Supplement to Anthologies Which Exclude Black Poets*. Broadside Press, 1969.

———. *The Black Poets*. Bantam, 1971.

———. *Homage to Hoyt Fuller*. Broadside Press, 1984.

Randall, Dudley, and Margaret Burroughs. *For Malcolm: Poems on the Life and the Death of Malcolm X*. Broadside Press, 1967.

Redmond, Eugene B. *Rope of Wind and Other Stories/Henry Dumas*. Random House, 1979.

———. *Goodbye, Sweetwater: New and Selected Stories/Henry Dumas*. Thunder's Mouth Press, 1988.

Reed, Ishmael. *Yardbird Lives*. Grove Press, 1978.

Render, Sylvia Lyons. *The Short Fiction of Charles W. Chestnutt*. Howard University Press, 1974.

Robinson, William H. *Early Black American Poets*. Wm. C. Brown, 1969.

Sanchez, Sonia. *We Be Word Sorcerors: 25 Stories by Black Americans*. Bantam, 1973.

Sherman, Joan R. *Invisible Poets: Afro-Americans of the Nineteenth Century*. University of Illinois Press, 1974.

———. *Collected Black Women's Poetry*. 4 vols. Oxford University Press (The Schomburg Library of Nineteenth-Century Black Women Writers), 1988.

Shields, John C. *The Collected Works of Phillis Wheatley*. Oxford University Press (The Schomburg Library of Nineteenth-Century Black Women Writers), 1988.

Shuman, R. Baird. *Nine Black Poets*. Moore, 1968.

————. *A Galaxy of Black Writing.* Moore, 1970.

Smith, Arthur L. *Rhetoric of Black Revolution.* Allyn & Bacon, 1969.

Smith, Barbara. *Home Girls: A Black Feminist Anthology.* Kitchen Table: Women of Color Press, 1983.

Stadler, Quandra P. *Out of Our Lives: A Collection of Contemporary Black Fiction.* Howard University Press, 1975.

Troupe, Quincy, and Rainer Schulte. *Giant Talk: An Anthology of Third World Writers.* Random House, 1975.

Turner, Darwin T. *Black American Literature: Poetry.* Chas. E. Merrill, 1969.

————. *Black Drama in America: An Anthology.* Fawcett, 1971.

————. *The Wayward and the Seeking: A Collection of Writings by Jean Toomer.* Howard University Press, 1980.

Walker, Alice. *I Love Myself When I am Laughing. . . . And Then Again When I am Looking Mean and Impressive: A Zora Neale Hurston Reader.* The Feminist Press, 1979.

Washington, Mary Helen. *Black-Eyed Susans: Classic Stories By and About Black Women.* Anchor Press/Doubleday, 1975.

————. *Midnight Birds: Stories of Contemporary Black Women Writers.* Anchor Press/Doubleday, 1980.

————. *Invented Lives: Narratives of Black Women's Lives, 1860–1960.* Anchor Press/Doubleday, 1987.

Watkins, Sylvester C. *Anthology of American Negro Literature.* Random House, 1944.

Williams, John A., and Charles F. Harris. *Amistad I: Writings on Black History and Culture.* Vintage/Random House, 1970.

————. *Amistad II: Writings on Black History and Culture.* Vintage/Random House, 1971.

Woodson, Carter G. *Negro Orators and Their Orations.* Associated Publishers, 1925.

II. HISTORY, BIBLIOGRAPHY, CRITICISM, AND COMMENT

Allen, William G. *Wheatley, Banneker, and Horton.* Books for Libraries, 1970.

Baker, Houston A., Jr. *Black Literature in America.* McGraw-Hill, 1971.

————. *Long Black Song: Essays in Black American Literature and Culture.* University Press of Virginia, 1972.

————, ed. *Twentieth-Century Interpretations of Native Son: A Collection of Critical Essays.* Prentice-Hall, 1972.

————. *Singers of Daybreak: Studies in Black American Literature.* Howard University Press, 1975, 1983.

————, ed. *A Dark and Sudden Beauty: Two Essays in Black American Poetry by George Kent and Stephen Henderson.* Afro-American Studies Program, University of Pennsylvania, 1977.

————, ed. *Reading Black: Essays in the Criticism of African, Caribbean and Black American Literature.* Cornell University Press, 1978.

————. *The Journey Back: Issues in Black Literature and Criticism.* University of Chicago Press, 1980.

————. *Blues, Ideology, and Afro-American Literature: A Vernacular Theory.* University of Chicago Press, 1984.

————. *Modernism and the Harlem Renaissance.* University of Chicago Press, 1987.

————. *Afro-American Poetics: Revisions of Harlem and the Black Aesthetic.* University of Wisconsin Press, 1988.

Ball, Wendy A., ed. *Rare Afro-Americana: A Reconstruction of the Adger Library.* G. K. Hall, 1981.

Barthold, Bonnie J. *Black Time: Fiction of Africa, the Caribbean, and the United States.* Yale University Press, 1981.

Bell, Bernard W. *The Folk Roots of Contemporary Afro-American Poetry.* Broadside Press, 1974.

————. *The Afro-American Novel and its Traditions.* University of Massachusetts Press, 1987.

Bell, Roseann Pope, Bettye J. Parker, and Beverly Guy-Sheftall. *Sturdy Black Bridges: Visions of Black Women in Literature.* Anchor Press, 1979.

Benston, Kimberly W., ed. *Imamu Amiri Baraka (LeRoi Jones): A Collection of Critical Essays.* Prentice-Hall, 1978.

————, ed. *Speaking for You: The Vision of Ralph Ellison.* Howard University Press, 1987.

Berzon, Judith R. *Neither White Nor Black: The Mulatto Character in American Fiction.* New York University Press, 1978.

Bigsby, C. W. E. *The Second Black Renaissance: Essays in Black Literature.* Greenwood Press, 1980.

Bloom, Harold, ed. *Zora Neale Hurston's "Their Eyes Were Watching God."* Chelsea House, 1987.

Bogle, Donald. *Toms, Coons, Mulattoes, Mammies, and Bucks: An Interpretive History of Blacks in American Films.* Viking Press, 1973; Penguin, 1979; Continuum, 1989.

Bone, Robert A. *The Negro Novel in America.* Yale University Press, 1958, 1965.

Bontemps, Arna, ed. *The Harlem Renaissance Remembered.* Dodd, Mead, 1972.

Brawley, Benjamin. *The Negro in Literature and Art in the United States.* Atlanta, 1910; Duffield, 1918.

Brignano, Russell. *Richard Wright: An Introduction to the Man and His Works.* University of Pittsburgh Press, 1970.

Brown, Sterling A. *The Negro in American Fiction.* Associates in Negro Folk Education, 1937; Atheneum, 1969 (reissued with *Negro Poetry and Drama* in one volume).

————. *Negro Poetry and Drama.* Associates in Negro Folk Education, 1937; Atheneum, 1969 (reissued with *The Negro in American Fiction* in one volume).

Brown, Sterling A., Arthur P. Davis, and Ulysses Lee, eds. *The Negro Caravan: Writings by American Negroes.* Dryden, 1941; Arno, 1969.

Bruce, Dickson D., Jr. *Black American Writing from the Nadir: The Evolution of a Literary Tradition, 1877–1915.* Louisiana State University Press, 1989.

Bruck, Peter, ed. *The Black American Short Story in the 20th Century: A Collection of Critical Essays.* Humanities Press, 1977.

Butcher, Margaret J. *The Negro in American Culture: Based on Materials Left by Alain Locke.* Knopf, 1956, 1972.

Butcher, Philip, ed. *The Minority Presence in American Literature, 1600–1900.* 2 vols. Howard University Press, 1977.

Butler-Evans, Elliott. *Race, Gender, and Desire: Narrative Strategies in the Fiction of Toni Cade Bambara, Toni Morrison, and Alice Walker.* Temple University Press, 1989.

Callahan, John F. *In the Afro-American Grain: The Pursuit of Voice in Twentieth-Century Black Fiction.* University of Illinois Press, 1988.

Christian, Barbara. *Black Women Novelists: The Development of a Tradition, 1892–1976.* Greenwood Press, 1980.

———. *Black Feminist Criticism: Perspectives on Black Women Writers.* Pergamon, 1985.

Cobb, Martha. *Harlem, Haiti, and Havana: A Comparative Critical Study of Langston Hughes, Jacques Romain, and Nicolas Guillen.* Three Continents Press, 1979.

Coleman, James W. *Blackness and Modernism: The Literary Career of John Edgar Wideman.* University Press of Mississippi, 1989.

Cooke, Michael G., ed. *Afro-American Literature in the Twentieth Century: The Achievement of Intimacy.* Yale University Press, 1986.

Dance, Daryl Cumber. *Long Gone: The Mecklenburg Six and the Theme of Escape in Black Folklore.* University of Tennessee Press, 1987.

Davis, Arthur P. *From the Dark Tower: Afro-American Writers, 1900–1960.* Howard University Press, 1974.

Davis, Charles T., and Michel Fabre. *Richard Wright: A Primary Bibliography.* G. K. Hall, 1982.

———. *The Slave's Narrative.* Oxford University Press, 1985.

Deodene, Frank, and William P. French. *Black American Poetry Since 1952: A Preliminary Checklist.* Chatham Bookseller, 1970.

———. *Black American Poetry Since 1944: A Preliminary Checklist.* Chatham Bookseller, 1971.

Dixon, Melvin. *Ride Out the Wilderness: Geography and Identity in Afro-American Literature.* University of Illinois Press, 1987.

Dundes, Alan. *Mother Wit from the Laughing Barrel: Readings in the Interpretation of Afro-American Folklore.* Prentice-Hall, 1973.

Evans, Mari. *Black Women Writers, 1950–1980: A Critical Evaluation.* Doubleday, 1984.

Farrison, William E. *William Wells Brown, Author and Reformer.* University of Chicago Press, 1969.

Fisher, Dexter, and Robert B. Stepto, eds. *Afro-American Literature: The Reconstruction of Instruction.* Modern Language Association, 1979.

Fisher, Miles Mark. *Negro Slave Songs in the U.S.* (new edition). Russell and Russell, 1968.

Ford, Nick Aaron. *The Contemporary Negro Novel.* Meador, 1936; McGrath, 1968.

Fox, Robert E. *Conscientious Sorcerors: The Black Post-Modernist Fiction of LeRoi Jones-Amiri Baraka, Ishmael Reed, and Samuel R. Delany.* Greenwood Press, 1987.

French, William P., Michel Fabre, and Amrijit Singh, eds. *Afro-American Poetry and Drama, 1760–1975: A Guide to Information Sources.* Gale, 1979.

Gates, Henry Louis, Jr., ed. *Black Literature and Literary Theory.* Methuen, 1984.

———, ed. *Figures in Black: Words, Signs and the Racial Self.* Oxford University Press, 1987.

———, ed. *The Signifying Monkey: A Theory of Afro-American Literary Criticism.* Oxford University Press, 1988.

Gayle, Addison, Jr., ed. *Black Expression: Essays By and About Black Americans in the Creative Arts.* Weybright and Talley, 1969.

——, ed. *The Black Aesthetic.* Doubleday, 1971.

——. *The Way of the New World: The Black Novel in America.* Doubleday, 1975.

Gibson, Donald B., ed. *Five Black Writers: Essays on Wright, Ellison, Baldwin, Hughes, and LeRoi Jones.* New York University Press, 1970.

——. *The Politics of Literary Expression: A Study of Major Black Writers.* Greenwood Press, 1981.

Gloster, Hugh M. *Negro Voices in American Fiction.* University of North Carolina Press, 1948; Russell, 1965.

Gross, Seymour, and John E. Hardy, eds. *Images of the Negro in American Literature: Essays in Criticism.* University of Chicago Press, 1966.

Gubert, Betty Kaplan. *Early Black Bibliographies, 1863–1918.* Garland, 1982.

Gwaltney, John Langston. *Drylongso: A Self-Portrait of Black America.* Vintage, 1980.

Hansberry, Lorraine. *The Movement: Documentary of a Struggle for Equality.* Simon & Schuster, 1964.

Harris, Norman. *Connecting Times: The Sixties in Afro-American Fiction.* University Press of Mississippi, 1988.

Harris, Trudier. *From Mammies to Militants: Domestics in Black American Literature.* Temple University Press, 1982.

——. *Exorcising Blackness: Historical and Literary Lynching and Burning Rituals.* Indiana University Press, 1985.

Harris, William J. *The Poetry and Poetics of Amiri Baraka: The Jazz Aesthetic.* University of Missouri Press, 1985.

Hatch, James V. *Black Image on the American Stage: A Bibliography of Plays and Musicals, 1770–1970.* Drama Book Specialists, 1970.

Hatch, James V., and Omanii Abdullah, comps. and eds. *Black Playwrights, 1823–1977: An Annotated Bibliography of Plays.* R. R. Bowker, 1977.

Hatcher, John. *From the Auroral Darkness: The Life and Poetry of Robert Hayden.* G. Ronald, 1984.

Hemenway, Robert. *The Black Novelist.* Chas. E. Merrill, 1970.

Henderson, Stephen, ed. *Understanding the New Black Poetry: Black Speech and Black Music as Poetic References.* William Morrow, 1972.

Hernton, Calvin C. *The Sexual Mountain and Black Women Writers: Adventures in Sex, Literature, and Real Life.* Anchor Press/Doubleday, 1987.

Hersey, John, ed. *Ralph Ellison: A Collection of Critical Essays.* Prentice-Hall, 1974.

Hogue, W. Lawrence. *Discourse and the Other: The Production of the Afro-American Text.* Duke University Press, 1986.

Holloway, Karla F. C. *The Character of the Word: The Texts of Zora Neale Hurston.* Greenwood Press, 1987.

Houston, Helen R. *The Afro-American Novel, 1965–1975: A Descriptive Bibliography of Primary and Secondary Materials.* Whitson, 1977.

Howard, Lillie. *Zora Neale Hurston.* Twayne/G. K. Hall, 1980.

Hudson, Theodore R. *From LeRoi Jones to Amiri Baraka: The Literary Works.* Duke University Press, 1973.

Huggins, Nathan I. *Harlem Renaissance.* Oxford University Press, 1971.

Hughes, Carl Milton. *The Negro Novelist: A Discussion of the Writings of American Negro Novelists, 1940–50.* Citadel, 1953.

Jackson, Blyden. *The Waiting Years: Essays on American Negro Literature*. Louisiana State University Press, 1976.

Jackson, Blyden, and Louis D. Rubin, Jr. *Black Poetry in America: Two Essays in Historical Interpretation*. Louisiana State University Press, 1974.

Johnson, Charles. *Being and Race: Black Writing Since 1970*. Indiana University Press, 1988.

Johnson, James Weldon. *Black Manhattan*. Knopf, 1930.

Johnson, Lemuel. *The Devil, the Gargoyle, and the Buffoon: The Negro as Metaphor in Western Literature*. Kennikat Press, 1974.

Joyce, Joyce Ann. *Richard Wright's Art of Tragedy*. University of Iowa Press, 1986.

Kallenbach, Jessamine S. *Index to Black American Literary Anthologies*. G. K. Hall, 1979.

Kent, George E. *Blackness and the Adventure of Western Culture*. Third World Press, 1972.

Kinnamon, Keneth. *The Emergence of Richard Wright: A Study in Literature and Society*. University of Illinois Press, 1972.

Kinnamon, Keneth, Joseph Benson, Michel Fabre, and Craig Werner, eds. *A Richard Wright Bibliography: Fifty Years of Criticism and Commentary, 1933–1982*. Greenwood Press, 1988.

Klotman, Phyllis R. *Another Man Gone: The Black Runner in Contemporary Afro-American Literature*. Kennikat, 1976.

Kramer, Victor A., ed. *The Harlem Renaissance Re-examined*. AMS, 1987.

Lawson, Victor. *Dunbar Critically Examined*. Associated Publishers, 1941.

Locke, Alain L. *The New Negro: An Interpretation*. Boni, 1925; Atheneum, 1968.

Loggins, Vernon. *The Negro Author: His Development in America to 1900*. Columbia University Press, 1931; Kennikat, 1964.

Margolies, Edward. *The Art of Richard Wright*. Southern Illinois University Press, 1969.

———. *Native Sons: A Critical Study of Twentieth-Century Negro American Authors*. Lippincott, 1969.

Martin, Reginald. *Ishmael Reed and the New Black Aesthetic Critics*. St. Martin's Press, 1988.

Mason, Julian D., Jr., ed. *The Poems of Phillis Wheatley*. University of North Carolina Press, 1966, 1989.

McKay, Nellie Y., ed. *Critical Essays on Toni Morrison*. G. K. Hall, 1988.

Miller, R. Baxter. *Black American Literature and Humanism*. University Press of Kentucky, 1981.

———, ed. *Black American Poets Between Worlds, 1940–1960*. University of Tennessee Press, 1986.

Milliken, Stephen F. *Chester Himes: A Critical Appraisal*. University of Missouri Press, 1976.

Mitchell, Loften. *Black Drama: The Story of the American Negro in the Theatre*. Hawthorne Books, 1967.

Mootry, Maria K., and Gary Smith, eds. *A Life Distilled: Gwendolyn Brooks, Her Poetry and Fiction*. Univeristy of Illinois Press, 1987, 1989.

Murray, Albert. *The Omni-Americans: New Perspectives on the Black Experience and American Culture*. Outerbridge & Dienstfrey, 1970; rept. as *The Omni-Americans: Some Alterations to the Folklore of White Supremacy*, Vintage, 1983.

———. *The Hero and the Blues*. University of Missouri Press, 1973.

Newson, Adele S. *Zora Neale Hurston*. G. K. Hall, 1987.

Nichols, Charles H. *Many Thousand Gone*. Brill Adler, 1963; Indiana University Press, 1969.

Noble, Peter. *The Negro in Films*. Robinson Ltd. (London), 1948.

———. *The Cinema and the Negro, 1905–1948*. Gordon, 1980.

Null, Gary, *Black Hollywood: The Negro in Motion Pictures*. Citadel, 1977.

O'Daniel, Therman B., ed. *Langston Hughes, Black Genius: A Critical Evaluation*. William Morrow, 1971.

———. ed. *James Baldwin: A Critical Evaluation*. Howard University Press, 1977.

O'Daniel, Therman B., with Cason L. Hill. *Jean Toomer: A Critical Evaluation*. Howard University Press, 1988.

O'Meally, Robert G. *The Craft of Ralph Ellison*. Harvard University Press, 1980.

Peplow, Michael W. *George S. Schuyler*. Twayne/G. K. Hall, 1980.

Peplow, Michael W., and Robert S. Bravard. *Samuel R. Delany: A Primary and Secondary Bibliography, 1962–1979*. G. K. Hall, 1980.

Perry, Margaret. *A Bio-bibliography of Countee P. Cullen (1903–1946)*. Greenwood Press, 1971.

Porter, Dorothy B. *North American Negro Poets: A Bibliographical Checklist of Their Writings (1760–1944)*. The Book Farm, 1945.

———. *The Negro in the United States: A Selected Bibliography*. Library of Congress, 1970.

Pryse, Marjorie, and Hortense Spillers, eds. *Conjuring: Black Women, Fiction, and Literary Tradition*. Indiana University Press, 1985.

Rampersad, Arnold. *The Art and Imagination of W. E. B. DuBois*. Harvard University Press, 1976.

Rampersad, Arnold, and Deborah McDowell, eds. *Slavery and the Literary Imagination*. Johns Hopkins University Press, 1988.

Redding, J. Saunders. *To Make a Poet Black*. University of North Carolina Press, 1939; Core Collection, 1978; Cornell University Press, 1988.

———. *The Lonesome Road: The Story of the Negro in America*. Doubleday, 1958.

Redmond, Eugene B. *Drumvoices: The Mission of Afro-American Poetry, A Critical History*. Doubleday/Anchor Press, 1976.

Richmond, Merle A. *Bid the Vassal Soar: Interpretive Essays on the Life and Poetry of Phillis Wheatley (ca. 1753–1784) and George Moses Horton (ca. 1797–1883)*. Howard University Press, 1974.

Robinson, William H. *Phillis Wheatley: A Bio-Bibliography*. G. K. Hall, 1981.

———, ed. *Critical Essays on Phillis Wheatley*. G. K. Hall, 1982.

Rose, Alan H. *Demonic Vision: Racial Fantasy and Southern Fiction*. Shoe String Press, 1976.

Settle, Elizabeth A., and Thomas A. Settle, eds. *Ishmael Reed: A Primary and Secondary Bibliography*. G. K. Hall, 1982.

Shaw, Harry B., ed. *Gwendolyn Brooks*. Twayne, 1980.

Sheffey, Ruthe T., ed., *A Rainbow Round Her Shoulder: The Zora Neale Hurston Symposium Papers*. Morgan State University Press, 1982.

Sherman, Joan R. *Invisible Poets: Afro-Americans of the Nineteenth Century*. University of Illinois Press, 1974.

Sims, Janet L. *The Progress of Afro-American Women: A Selected Bibliography and Research Guide*. Greenwood Press, 1980.

Sims, Rudine. *Shadow and Substance: Afro-American Experience in Contemporary Children's Fiction.* American Library Association, 1982.

Starling, Marion Wilson. *The Slave Narrative: Its Place in American History.* G. K. Hall, 1981; Howard University Press, 1988.

Stepto, Robert B. *From Behind the Veil: A Study of Afro-American Narrative.* University of Illinois Press, 1979.

Tate, Claudia. *Black Women Writers at Work.* Continuum, 1983.

Turner, Darwin T. *In a Minor Chord: Three Afro-American Writers and Their Search for Identity.* Southern Illinois University Press, 1971.

Tyms, James D. *Spiritual (Religious) Values in the Black Poet.* University Press of America, 1977.

Waldron, Edward E. *Walter White and the Harlem Renaissance.* Kennikat Press, 1978.

Walker, Margaret. *Richard Wright, Daemonic Genius: A Portrait of the Man, A Critical Look at His Work.* Warner Books, 1988.

Walser, Richard, ed. *The Black Poet: Being the Remarkable Story (partly told by himself) of George Moses Horton, a North Carolina Slave.* Philosphical Library, 1966.

Wegelin, Oscar. *Jupiter Hammon, American Negro Poet: Selections from His Writings and a Bibliography.* Heartman, 1915.

Weixlmann, Joe, and Chester Fontenot. *Black American Prose Theory.* Penkevill, 1983.

Weixlmann, Joe, and Houston A. Baker, Jr., eds. *Belief versus Theory in Black American Literary Criticism.* Penkevill, 1985.

Whitlow, Roger. *The Darker Vision: A Socio-Historical Study of Nineteenth-Century Black American Literature.* Gordon Press, 1979.

Williams, George Washington. *The American Negro, from 1776 to 1876.* R. Clarke, 1876.

Williams, Pontheolla T. *Robert Hayden: A Critical Analysis of His Poetry.* University of Illinois Press, 1987.

Williams, Sherley A. *Give Birth to Brightness: A Thematic Study in Neo-Black Literature.* Dial Press, 1972.

Willis, Susan. *Specifying: Black Women Writing the American Experience.* University of Wisconsin Press, 1986.

Yellin, Jean Fagan. *Women and Sisters: The Anti-Slavery Feminists in American Culture.* Yale University Press, 1990.

Young, James O. *Black Writers of the Thirties.* Louisiana State University Press, 1973.

III. POETRY PUBLICATIONS

Allen, Samuel W. (Paul Vesey pseud.) *Elfenbein Zahne (Ivory Tusks).* Wolfgang Rothe (Heidelberg), 1956.

———. *Ivory Tusks and Other Poems.* Poets Press, 1968.

———. *Paul Vesey's Ledger.* Paul Breman, 1975.

Amini, Johari M. (a.k.a. Jewel C. Latimore). *Images in Black.* Third World Press, 1969.

————. *Let's Go Somewhere*. Third World Press, 1970.

Banks, C. Tillery. *Hello to Me With Love: Poems of Self-Discovery*. William Morrow, 1980.

Baraka, Imamu (a.k.a. LeRoi Jones). *Spirit Reach*. Jihad, 1972.

————. *In the Tradition (For Black Arthur Blythe)*. Jihad, 1980.

————. *Reggae or Not: Poems*. Contact II Publications, 1981.

Barrax, Gerald. *Another Kind of Rain: Poems*. University of Pittsburgh Press, 1970.

————. *An Audience of One*. University of Georgia Press, 1980.

Bontemps, Arna. *Personals*. Paul Breman, 1963.

————. *Hold Fast to Dreams: Poems Old and New*. Follet, 1969.

Brooks, Gwendolyn. *Blacks*. David, 1987.

————. *Gottschalk and the Grande Tarantelle/Gwendolyn Brooks*. David, 1988.

————. *Winnie*. David, 1988.

Brown, Sterling A. *Southern Road*. Harcourt, 1932.

————. *The Last Ride of Wild Bill, and Eleven Narrative Poems*. Broadside Press, 1975.

Burroughs, Margaret. *What Shall I Tell My Children Who Are Black?* M.A.A.H. Press, 1968.

————. *Africa, My Africa*. DuSable Museum, 1970.

Campbell, James E. *Echoes from the Cabin and Elsewhere*. Chicago, 1905.

Chase-Riboud, Barbara. *Portrait of a Nude Woman as Cleopatra*. William Morrow, 1987.

Clifton, Lucille. *Good Times*. Random House, 1969.

————. *Good News About the Earth*. Random House, 1972.

————. *An Ordinary Woman*. Random House, 1974.

————. *Two-Headed Woman*. University of Massachusetts, 1980.

————. *Next: New Poems*. BOA Editions, 1987.

————. *Good Woman: Poems and a Memoir, 1969–1980*. BOA Editions, 1987.

Coleman, Wanda. *Mad Dog Black Lady*. Black Sparrow Press, 1979.

————. *Heavy Daughter Blues*. Black Sparrow Press, 1987.

Cortez, Jayne. *Piss-stained Stairs and the Monkey Man's Wares*. Phrase Text, 1969.

————. *Scarifications*. Bola Press, 1973, 1978.

————. *Mouth on Paper*. Bola Press, 1977.

————. *Firespitter*. Bola Press, 1982.

————. *Coagulations*. Thunder's Mouth Press, 1984.

Cullen, Countee. *Color*. Harper, 1925.

————. *The Ballad of the Brown Girl*. Harper, 1927.

————. *Copper Sun*. Harper, 1927.

————. *The Black Christ and Other Poems*. Harper, 1929.

————. *The Medea and Some Poems*. Harper, 1935.

————. *The Lost Zoo*. Harper, 1940.

————. *On These I Stand*. Harper, 1947.

Cuney, Waring. *Puzzles*. Deroos (Utrecht), 1960.

————. *Storefront Church*. Paul Breman, 1973.

Danner, Margaret. *Impressions of African Art Forms*. Broadside Press, 1960.

————. *To Flower*. Hemphill Press, 1963.

————. *Iron Lace*. Kriya Press, 1968.

————. *Down of a Thistle*. Country Beautiful, 1976.

Danner, Margaret, and Dudley Randall. *Poem Counterpoem*. Broadside Press, 1966.

Davis, Frank Marshall. *Black Man's Verse*. Black Cat Press, 1935.

------. *I Am the American Negro*. Black Cat Press, 1937.

------. *47th Street*. Decker Press, 1948.

Davis, Thulani. *All the Renegade Ghosts Rise*. Anemone Press, 1978.

------. *playing the changes*. Wesleyan University Press, 1985.

Dent, Tom. *Magnolia Street*. Published by Author, 1976.

------. *Blue Lights and River Songs*. Lotus Press, 1982.

Derricote, Toi. *The Empress of the Death House*. Lotus Press, 1978.

Deveaux, Alexis. *Li Chen/Second Daughter First Son*. Ba Tone Press, 1975.

------. *Don't Explain: A Song of Billie Holiday*. Harper & Row, 1980; Writers & Readers, 1988.

Dodson, Owen. *Powerful Long Ladder*. Farrar, Straus & Giroux, 1946.

Dove, Rita. *Ten Poems*. Penumbra Press, 1977.

------. *Mandolin*. Ohio Review, 1982.

------. *Museum*. Carnegie-Mellon University Press, 1983.

------. *Thomas and Beulah*. Carnegie-Mellon University Press, 1986.

------. *Grace Notes*. W. W. Norton, 1989.

Dumas, Henry (edited by Eugene B. Redmond). *Play Ebony: Play Ivory*. Random House, 1975; originally published as *Poetry for my People*, Southern Illinois University Press, 1970.

Dunbar, Paul Laurence. *Oak and Ivy*. Dayton, Ohio, 1893.

------. *Majors and Minors*. Toledo, Ohio, 1895.

------. *Lyrics of Lowly Life*. New York, 1896; Citadel Press, 1984.

------. *Lyrics of the Hearthside*. New York, 1899; AMS Press, 1972.

------. *Lyrics of Love and Laughter*. New York, 1903.

------. *Lyrics of Sunshine and Shadow*. New York, 1905; AMS Press, 1972.

------. *The Complete Poems of Paul Laurence Dunbar*. Dodd, Mead, 1913; 1980.

Emanuel, James A. *The Treehouse and Other Poems*. Broadside Press, 1968.

------. *Panther Man*. Broadside Press, 1970.

------. *Black Man Abroad: The Toulouse Poems*. Lotus Press, 1978.

------. *A Chisel in the Dark (Poems, Selected and New)*. Lotus Press, 1980.

------. *The Broken Bowl (New and Uncollected Poems)*. Lotus Press, 1983.

Evans, Mari. *Where Is All the Music?* Paul Breman, 1968.

------. *I Am a Black Woman*. William Morrow, 1970.

------. *Singing Black*. Reed Visuals, 1976.

------. *Nightstar: 1973–1978*. Center for Afro-American Studies, UCLA, 1981.

Fair, Ronald. *Excerpts*. Paul Breman, 1975.

------. *Rufus*. Lotus Press, 1977.

Fields, Julia. *East of Moonlight*. Chatham Bookseller, 1973.

------. *Slow Coins: Minted by Julia Fields*. Three Continents Press, 1981.

Forbes, Calvin. *From the Book of Shine*. Burning Deck Press, 1979; Razorback Press, 1980.

Giovanni, Nikki. *Black Judgement*. Broadside Press, 1968.

------. *Black Feeling, Black Talk*. Broadside Press, 1970.

------. *Black Feeling Black Talk Black Judgement*. William Morrow, 1970.

------. *Re-Creation*. Broadside Press, 1970.

------. *My House: Poems*. William Morrow, 1972.

————. *The Women and The Men*. William Morrow, 1975, 1979.

————. *Cotton Candy on a Rainy Day*. William Morrow, 1978.

————. *Those Who Ride the Night Wind*. William Morrow, 1983.

Hammon, Jupiter. *An Evening Thought: Salvation by Christ, with Penetential Cries, A Broadside*. Long Island, NY, 1760.

————. *A Poetical Address to Phillis Wheatley, A Broadside*. Long Island, NY, 1779.

Harper, Frances E. W. *Poems on Miscellaneous Subjects*. Boston, 1854.

————. *Moses: A Story of the Nile*. Philadelphia, 1869.

————. *Poems*. Philadelphia, 1871.

————. *Poems*. Philadelphia, 1900.

Harper, Michael S. *Dear John, Dear Coltrane*. University of Pittsburgh Press, 1970; University of Illinois Press, 1985.

————. *History is Your Own Heartbeat*. University of Illinois Press, 1971.

————. *Photographs: Negatives; History As Apple Tree*. Scarab Press, 1972.

————. *Song: I Want a A Witness*. University of Pittsburgh Press, 1972.

————. *Debridement*. Doubleday, 1973.

————. *Nightmare Begins Responsibility*. University of Illinois Press, 1975.

————. *Images of Kin: New and Selected Poems*. University of Illinois Press, 1977.

————. *Rhode Island: Eight Poems*. Pym-Randall Press, 1981.

————. *Healing Song for the Inner Ear: Poems*. University of Illinois Press, 1984.

Hayden, Robert E. *Heart-Shape in the Dust*. Falcon Press, 1940.

————. *Figure of Time: Poems*. Hemphill Press, 1955.

————. *A Ballad of Remembrance*. Paul Breman, 1962.

————. *Selected Poems*. October House, 1966.

————. *Words in the Mourning Time*. October House, 1970.

————. *The Night-Blooming Cereus*. Paul Breman, 1972.

————. *Angle of Ascent: New and Selected Poems*. Liveright, 1975.

————. *American Journal: Poems*. Effendi Press, 1978; Liveright, 1982.

————. *The Legend of John Brown*. Detroit Institute of Art, 1978.

Horton, George Moses. *Hope of Liberty*. Raleigh, N.C., 1829.

————. *Naked Genius*. Raleigh, N.C., 1865; Chapel Hill Historical Society, 1982.

Hughes, Langston. *The Weary Blues*. Knopf, 1926.

————. *Fine Clothes for the Jew*. Knopf, 1927.

————. *Dear Lovely Death*. Troutbeck Press, 1931.

————. *The Dream Keeper*. Knopf, 1932.

————. *A New Song*. International Workers Order, 1938.

————. *Shakespeare in Harlem*. Knopf, 1942.

————. *In Freedom's Plow*. Musette, 1943.

————. *Fields of Wonder*. Knopf, 1947.

————. *One-Way Ticket*. Knopf, 1949.

————. *Montage of a Dream Deferred*. Henry Holt, 1951.

————. *Selected Poems*. Knopf, 1959.

————. *Ask Your Mama: Twelve Moods for Jazz*. Knopf, 1961.

————. *The Panther and the Lash*. Knopf, 1967.

Jeffers, Lance. *When I Know the Power of My Black Hand*. Broadside Press, 1974.

————. *O Africa, Where I Baked My Bread*. Lotus Press, 1977.

————. *Grandsire*. Lotus Press, 1979.

Joans, Ted. *Jazz Poems*. Rhino Review, 1959.

————. *All of Ted Joans and No More.* Excelsior, 1961.

————. *The Hipsters.* Corinth, 1961.

————. *Black Pow-Wow.* Hill & Wang, 1969; Calder & Boyars, 1973.

————. *Afrodisia; New Poems.* Hill & Wang 1970; Calder & Boyars, 1976.

————. *A Black Manifesto in Jazz Poetry and Prose.* Calder & Boyars, 1971.

————. *The Aardvark-Watcher (Der Erdferkelforscher).* Literarisches Colloquium (Berlin), 1980.

Johnson, Fenton. *A Little Dreaming.* Chicago, 1913.

————. *Visions of the Dusk.* New York, 1915.

————. *Songs of the Soil.* New York, 1916.

Johnson, Georgia Douglas. *Autumn Love Cycle.* H. Viral, 1928; Books for Libraries Press, 1971.

————. *Heart of a Woman and Other Poems.* The Cornhill Co., 1918.

Johnson, James Weldon. *Fifty Years, and Other Poems.* The Cornhill Co., 1917.

————. *God's Trombones: Seven Negro Sermons in Verse.* Viking, 1927, 1969.

————. *St. Peter Relates an Incident . . .* Viking, 1935.

Jones, LeRoi (a.k.a. Imamu Baraka). *Preface to a Twenty-Volume Suicide Note.* Totem-Corinth, 1961.

————. *The Dead Lecturer.* Grove, 1964.

————. *Black Arts.* Jihad, 1966.

————. *Black Magic Poetry: 1961–1967.* Bobbs-Merrill, 1969.

Jordan, June. *Who Look at Me.* Crowell, 1969.

————. *His Own Where.* Crowell, 1971.

————. *Some Changes.* Dutton, 1971.

————. *Dry Victories.* Holt, Rinehart and Winston, 1972.

————. *New Days: Poems of Exile and Return.* Emerson Hall, 1974.

————. *Things That I Do in the Dark: Selected Poems.* Random House, 1977.

————. *Passion: New Poems, 1977–1980.* Beacon Press, 1980.

————. *Civil Wars.* Beacon Press, 1981.

————. *Living Room.* Thunder's Mouth Press, 1985.

Knight, Etheridge. *Poems from Prison.* Broadside Press, 1968.

————. *Belly Song and Other Poems.* Broadside Press, 1973.

————. *The Essential Etheridge Knight.* University of Pittsburgh Press, 1986.

Lane, Pinkie Gordon. *Wind Thoughts.* South & West, 1972.

————. *The Mystic Female.* Bailey Press, 1978.

————. *I Never Scream: New and Selected Poems.* Lotus Press, 1985.

Lee, Don L. (a.k.a. Haki R. Madhubuti). *Think Black.* Broadside Press, 1967.

————. *Black Pride.* Broadside Press, 1968.

————. *Don't Cry, Scream.* Broadside Press, 1969.

————. *We Walk the Way of the New World.* Broadside Press, 1970.

Lester, Julius. *Who I Am; Poems.* Dial Press, 1974.

Lorde, Audre. *From a Land Where Other People Live.* Broadside Press, 1973.

————. *The New York Head Shop and Museum.* Broadside Press, 1975.

————. *Coal.* W. W. Norton, 1976.

————. *Between Ourselves.* Eidolon Editions, 1977.

————. *Chosen Poems—Old and New.* W. W. Norton, 1982.

————. *Our Dead Behind Us.* W. W. Norton, 1986.

Madgett, Naomi Long. *One and the Many.* Exposition, 1956.

————. *Star by Star*. Lotus Press, 1965; Evenill, 1970.

————. *Pink Ladies in the Afternoon*. Lotus Press, 1972.

————. *Exits and Entrances*. Lotus Press, 1978.

————. *Phantom Nightingale: Juvenilia: Poems, 1934–1943*. Lotus Press, 1981.

————. *Octavia and Other Poems*. Third World Press, 1988.

Madhubuti, Haki R. (a.k.a. Don L. Lee). *Earthquake & Sunrise Missions*. Third World Press, 1984.

————. *Killing Memory, Seeking Ancestors*. Lotus Press, 1987.

Major, Clarence. *Swallow the Lake*. Wesleyan University Press, 1970.

————. *Symptoms & Madness*. Corinth Books, 1971.

————. *The Cotton Club: New Poems*. Broadside Press, 1972.

————. *The Syncopated Cakewalk*. Barlenmir, 1974.

————. *Inside Diameter: The France Poems*. Permanent Press, 1985.

————. *Painted Turtle: Woman with Guitar*. Sun & Moon, 1988.

————. *Surfaces and Masks: A Poem*. Coffee House Press, 1988.

McClane, Kenneth A. *Out Beyond the Bay*. Ithaca House, 1975.

————. *Moons and Low Times*. Ithaca House, 1978.

————. *To Hear the River*. West End Press, 1981.

————. *These Halves are Whole*. Black Willow Press, 1983.

————. *A Tree Beyond Telling: Poems, Selected and New*. Black Scholar Press, 1983.

————. *Take Five: Collected Poems, 1972–1986*. Greenwood Press, 1987.

McKay, Claude. *Spring in New Hampshire*. Grant Richard (London), 1920.

————. *Harlem Shadows*. Harcourt, 1922.

————. *Selected Poems*. Bookman Associates, 1953.

Miller, E. Ethelbert. *Migrant Worker*. The Washington Writers' Publishing House, 1978.

————. *Season of Hunger—Cry of Rain*. Lotus Press, 1982.

————. *where are the love poems for dictators?* Open Hand, 1986.

Miller, May, *Into the Clearing*. Charioteer Press, 1959.

————. *The Clearing and Beyond*. The Charioteer Press, 1974.

Murray, Pauli. *Dark Testament and Other Poems*. Silvermine, 1970.

Neal, Larry. *Black Boogaloo*. Journal of Black Poetry Press, 1969.

————. *Hoodoo Hollerin' Bebop Ghosts*. Howard University Press, 1974.

Oden, Gloria. *Resurrections*. Olivant Press, 1978.

————. *The Tie That Binds*. Olivant Press, 1980.

Plumpp, Sterling D. *Portable Soul*. Third World Press, 1969.

————. *Half Black, Half Blacker*. Third World Press, 1970.

————. *Clinton*. Broadside Press, 1976.

————.*The Mojo Hands Call, I Must Go*. Thunder's Mouth Press, 1982.

Randall, Dudley. *Cities Burning*. Broadside Press, 1968.

————. *Love You*. Paul Breman, 1970.

————. *More to Remember: Poems for Four Decades*. Third World Press, 1971.

————. *After the Killing*. Third World Press, 1973.

————. *A Litany of Friends: New and Selected Poems*. Lotus Press, 1981, 1983.

————. *Golden Song*. Harlo, 1985.

Redmond, Eugene B. *Sentry of the Four Golden Pillars*. Black River Writers, 1970.

————. *River of Bones and Flesh and Blood: Poems*. Black River Writers, 1971.

————. *Songs from an Afro/Phone*. Black River Writers, 1972.

————. *Consider Loneliness as These Things.* Black River Writers, 1973.

————. *In a Time of Rain and Desire: New Love Poems.* Black River Writers, 1973.

Reed, Ishmael. *Conjure: Selected Poems, 1963–1970.* University of Massachusetts Press, 1973.

————. *Chattanooga: Poems.* Random House, 1974.

————. *A Secretary to the Spirits.* NOK Publishers, 1977.

————. *New and Collected Poems.* Atheneum, 1988.

Rivers, Conrad Kent. *The Black Bodies and This Sunburnt Face.* Free Lance Press, 1962.

Rodgers, Carolyn M. *Songs of a Black Bird.* Third World Press, 1969.

————. *The Heart As Ever Green.* Anchor Press/Doubleday, 1970.

————. *Now Ain't That Love.* Broadside Press, 1970.

————. *How I Got Ovah: New and Selected Poems.* Anchor Press/Doubleday, 1975.

Sanchez, Sonia. *Homecoming.* Broadside Press, 1970.

————. *A Blues Book for Blue Black Magical Women.* Broadside Press, 1973.

————. *Love Poems.* Third World Press, 1973.

————. *I've Been a Woman: New and Selected Poems.* Black Scholar Press, 1979.

————. *homegirls and handgrenades.* Thunder's Mouth Press, 1984.

————. *Under a Soprano Sky.* Africa World Press, 1987.

Scott-Heron, Gil. *Small Talk at 125th Street and Lenox.* World, 1970.

————. *So Far, So Good.* Third World Press, 1990.

Shange, Ntozake. *Melissa & Smith.* Bookslinger Editions, 1976.

————. *Nappy Edges.* St. Martin's Press, 1978.

————. *Three Pieces.* St. Martin's Press, 1981; Penguin, 1982.

————. *A Daughter's Geography.* St. Martin's Press, 1983.

————. *Ridin' the Moon in Texas: Word Paintings.* St. Martin's Press, 1987.

Spellman, A. B. *The Beautiful Days.* Poets Press, 1965.

Stuckey, Elma. *The Big Gate.* Precedent, 1976.

————. *The Collected Poems of Elma Stuckey.* Precedent, 1987.

Tolson, Melvin B. *Rendevous with America.* Dodd, Mead, 1944.

————. *Libretto for the Republic of Liberia.* Twayne, 1953.

————. *Harlem Gallery; Book I: The Curator.* Twayne, 1965.

————. *A Gallery of Harlem Portraits.* University of Missouri Press, 1979.

Troupe, Quincy. *Embryo Poems.* Barlenmir, 1972.

————. *Snake-Back Solos: Selected Poems, 1969–1977.* I. Reed Books, 1978.

————. *Skulls Along the River.* Reed & Cannon, 1984.

Van Der Zee, James (Photography), Owen Dodson (Poetry), and Camille Billops (Text). *The Harlem Book of the Dead.* Morgan & Morgan, 1979.

Walker, Margaret. *For My People.* Yale University Press, 1942; Ayer, 1969.

————. *Prophets for a New Day.* Broadside Press, 1970.

————. *October Journey.* Broadside Press, 1973.

————. *This is My Century: New and Collected Poems/Margaret Walker.* University of Georgia Press, 1989.

Wheatley, Phillis. *An Elegiac Poem, on the Death of the Rev. Mr. George Whitefield.* Boston, 1770.

————. *Poems on Various Subjects, Religious and Moral.* Bell (London), 1773.

Whitfield, James M. *America and Other Poems.* Buffalo, 1853.

————. *Not a Man, and Yet a Man.* Springfield, Ohio, 1877.

————. *The Rape of Florida.* St. Louis, 1884.

————. *Twasinta's Seminoles: or, The Rape of Florida.* St. Louis, 1885.

————. *An Idyl of the South: An Epic in Two Parts.* New York, 1901.

Williams, Sherley Anne. *The Peacock Poems.* Wesleyan University Press, 1978.

————. *Some One Sweet Angel Chile.* William Morrow, 1982.

Wright, Jay. *Death as History.* Kriya Press, 1967.

————. *Dimensions of History.* Kayak, 1976.

————. *Soothsayers and Omens.* Seven Woods Press, 1976.

————. *The Double Invention of Komo.* University of Texas Press, 1980.

————. *Explications/Interpretations.* University of Kentucky Press, 1984.

————. *Selected Poems of Jay Wright.* Princeton University Press, 1987.

————. *Elaine's Book.* University Press of Virginia, 1988.

Young, Al. *Dancing: Poems.* Corinth Books, 1969.

————. *The Song Turning Back into Itself: Poems.* Holt, Rinehart and Winston, 1971.

————. *The Geography of the Near Past.* Holt, Rinehart & Winston, 1976.

————. *The Blues Don't Change: New and Selected Poems.* Louisiana State University Press, 1982.

————. *Heaven: Collected Poems, 1958–1988.* Creative Arts, 1989.

IV. FICTION

Attaway, William. *Let Me Breathe Thunder.* Doubleday, 1939.

————. *Blood on the Forge.* Doubleday, 1941; Macmillan, 1970.

————. *Hear America Singing.* Lion, 1967.

Baldwin, James. *Go Tell It on the Mountain.* Knopf, 1953; Signet, 1954.

————. *Giovanni's Room.* Dial Press, 1956.

————. *Another Country.* Dell, 1960; Dial Press, 1962.

————. *Going to Meet the Man.* Dial Press, 1965.

————. *Tell Me How Long the Train's Been Gone.* Dial Press, 1968.

————. *If Beale Street Could Talk.* Dial Press, 1974.

————. *Just Above My Head.* Dial Press, 1978.

Bambara, Toni Cade. *Gorilla, My Love.* Bantam, 1972; Vintage, 1981.

————. *The Sea Birds are Still Alive.* Random House, 1977; Vintage, 1982.

————. *The Salt Eaters.* Random House, 1980.

Baraka, Imamu (a.k.a. LeRoi Jones) *Three Books.* Grove, 1975.

Barrax, Gerald William. *Another Kind of Rain.* University of Pittsburgh Press, 1970.

Bates, Arthenia J. *Seeds Beneath the Snow: Vignettes from the South.* Greenwich, 1969; Howard University Press, 1975.

Beckham, Barry. *My Main Mother.* Walker, 1969.

————. *Runner Mack.* William Morrow, 1972; Howard University Press, 1984.

————. *Double Dunk.* Holloway House, 1980.

Bontemps, Arna. *God Sends Sunday.* Harcourt, 1931.

————. *Black Thunder.* Macmillan, 1936; Beacon Press, 1968.

————. *Drums at Dusk.* Macmillan, 1939.

Bradley, David. *South Street.* Grossman/Viking, 1975.

————. *The Chaneysville Incident.* Harper and Row, 1981.

Brooks, Gwendolyn. *Maud Martha*. Harper, 1953; Farrar, Straus & Giroux, 1969.

Brown, Cecil. *The Life and Loves of Mr. Jiveass Nigger*. Fawcett World Library, 1969; Farrar, Straus & Giroux, 1970.

———. *Days Without Weather*. Farrar, Straus & Giroux, 1982.

Brown, William Wells. *Clotel; or, The President's Daughter: A Narrative of Slave Life in the United States*. London, 1853; Citadel, 1969; Macmillan, 1970.

Bullins, Ed. *The Reluctant Rapist*. Harper and Row, 1973.

Butler, Octavia. *Kindred*. Doubleday, 1979; Beacon Press, 1988.

———. *Survivor*. New American Library, 1979.

———. *Wild Seed*. Doubleday, 1980; Timescape, 1981.

———. *Dawn*. Warner Books, 1987; Popular Library, 1988.

———. *Adulthood Rites*. Warner Books, 1988.

Cain, George. *Blueschild Baby*. McGraw-Hill, 1971.

Chesnutt, Charles W. *The Conjure Woman*. Houghton Mifflin, 1899.

———. *The Wife of His Youth, and Other Stories of the Color Line*. Houghton Mifflin, 1899.

———. *The House Behind the Cedars*. Houghton Mifflin, 1900.

———. *The Marrow of Tradition*. Houghton Mifflin, 1901.

———. *The Colonel's Dream*. Doubleday, Page, 1905.

Childress, Alice. *Like One of the Family . . . Conversations from a Domestic's Life*. Independence Publishers, 1956; Beacon Press, 1986.

———. *Mojo*. Coward, McCann and Geoghegan, 1972.

———. *A Hero Ain't Nothin' But a Sandwich*. Coward, McCann and Geoghegan, 1973.

———. *A Short Walk*. Coward, McCann and Geoghegan, 1979.

Cooper, J. California. *A Piece of Mine: Short Stories*. Wild Trees Press, 1984.

———. *Homemade Love*. St. Martin's Press, 1987.

———. *Some Soul to Keep*. St. Martin's Press, 1987.

———. *Family*. Doubleday, 1991.

Cullen, Countee. *One Way to Heaven*. Harper, 1932.

Davis, George. *Coming Home*. Random House, 1971; Howard University Press, 1984.

Delany, Martin R. *Blake; or, The Huts of America* (This work originally appeared serially in seven installments of the *Anglo-African* magazine in 1859). Beacon Press, 1970.

Delany, Samuel R. *The Jewels of Aptor*. Ace, 1962; Gregg, 1971, 1972.

———. *Captives of the Flame*. Ace, 1963.

———. *The Towers of Toron*. Ace, 1964, 1977.

———. *The Einstein Intersection*. Ace, 1967; Garland Presss, 1979.

———. *Nova*. Doubleday, 1968; Bantam, 1975.

———. *Driftglass*. Ace, 1971; Gregg, 1977.

———. *Distant Stars*. Ultramarine, 1981.

———. *Neveryona; or The Tales of Signs and Cities*. Bantam, 1983.

Demby, William. *The Catacombs*. Pantheon, 1965.

———. *Love Story Black*. Reed, Cannon & Johnson, 1978; Dutton, 1986.

Deveaux, Alexis. *Spirits in the Streets*. Anchor Press/Doubleday, 1973.

Dodson, Owen. *Boy at the Window*. Farrar, Straus & Giroux, 1951; reissued as *When Trees Were Green*, Popular Library, 1967.

Du Bois, W. E. B., *The Quest of the Silver Fleece*. A. C. McClurg, 1911; Mnemosyne, 1969.

———. *The Dark Princess*. Harcourt, 1928.

———. *The Black Flame: A Trilogy—The Ordeal of Mansart, Mansart Builds a School; Worlds of Color*. Mainstream Publishers, 1957, 1959, 1961.

Dumas, Henry. *Ark of Bones, and Other Stories*. Southern Illinois University Press, 1974.

———. *Jonoah and the Green Stone*. Random House, 1976.

Dunbar, Paul Laurence. *Folks from Dixie*. Dodd, Mead, 1898.

———. *The Uncalled*. Dodd, Mead, 1898; Literature House, 1970; AMS Press, 1972.

———. *The Love of Landry*. Dodd, Mead, 1900; Literature House, 1970.

———. *The Strength of Gideon, and Other Stories*. Dodd, Mead, 1900.

———. *The Fanatics*. Dodd, Mead, 1901; Literature House, 1970.

———. *The Sport of the Gods*. Dodd, Mead, 1902, 1981; Collier, 1970.

———. *In Old Plantation Days*. Dodd, Mead, 1903.

———. *The Heart of Happy Hollow*. Dodd, Mead, 1904; Books for Libraries Press, 1970.

Ellison, Ralph. *Invisible Man*. Random House, 1952.

———. *Going to the Territory*. Vintage Books, 1987.

Fair, Ronald. *Many Thousand Gone*. Harcourt, 1965.

———. *Hog Butcher*. Harcourt, 1966.

———. *World of Nothing: Two Novellas*. Harper and Row, 1970.

———. *We Can't Breathe*. Harper and Row, 1972.

Fauset, Jessie R. *There is Confusion*. Boni & Liveright, 1924.

———. *Plum Bun*. Stokes, 1929.

———. *The Chinaberry Tree*. Stokes, 1931.

———. *Comedy American Style*. Stokes, 1933.

Fisher, Rudolph. *The Walls of Jericho*. Knopf, 1928.

———. *The Conjure Man Dies*. Covici, Friede, 1932.

Forrest, Leon. *There is a Tree More Ancient Than Eden*. Random House, 1973; rev. ed., Another Chicago Press, 1988.

———. *The Bloodworth Orphans*. Random House, 1977; rev. ed., Another Chicago Press, 1987.

———. *Two Wings to Veil My Face*. Random House, 1984.

Gaines, Ernest J. *Catherine Carmier*. Atheneum, 1964; Chatham Booksellers, 1972; North Point Press, 1981.

———. *Of Love and Dust*. Dial Press, 1967; W. W. Norton, 1979.

———. *Bloodline*. Dial Press, 1968; W. W. Norton, 1976.

———. *The Autobiography of Miss Jane Pittman*. Dial Press, 1971; Doubleday, 1987.

———. *A Long Day in November*. Dial Press, 1971.

———. *The Sky is Gray*. Zenith Books, 1971.

———. *In My Father's House*. Knopf, 1978; W. W. Norton, 1983.

———. *A Gathering of Old Men*. Knopf, 1983.

Greenlee, Sam. *The Spook Who Sat by the Door*. R. W. Baron, 1969.

———. *Blues for an African Princess*. Third World Press, 1970.

———. *Bagdad Blues*. Emerson Hall, 1973.

Griggs, Sutton E. *Imperium in Imperio*. Orion, 1899; Arno, 1969.

———. *Overshadowed*. Orion, 1901.

———. *Unfettered*. Orion, 1902.

———. *The Hindered Hand*. Orion, 1905.

———. *Pointing the Way*. Orion, 1908.

Guy, Rosa. *Bird at My Window*. Lippincott, 1966.

———. *Ruby*. Random House, 1976.

———. *Edith Jackson*. Viking, 1978.

———. *The Disappearance*. Delacorte, 1979.

———. *A Measure of Time*. Henry Holt, 1983.

———. *My Love, My Love; or, The Peasant Girl*. Henry Holt, 1985.

Haley, Alex. *Roots*. Doubleday, 1976.

Harper, Frances E. W. *Iola Leroy; or, Shadows Uplifted*. Philadelphia, 1893; Oxford University Press (The Schomburg Library of Nineteenth-Century Black Women Writers), 1988.

Himes, Chester. *If He Hollers Let Him Go*. Doubleday, 1945; Thunder's Mouth Press, 1986.

———. *Lonely Crusade*. Knopf, 1947; Thunder's Mouth Press, 1986.

———. *Cast the First Stone*. Coward-McCann, 1953.

———. *The Real Cool Killers*. Avon, 1959; Berkely Medallion Editions, 1966; Vintage, 1988.

———. *Cotton Comes to Harlem*. Putnam, 1965; Vintage, 1988.

———. *Pinktoes*. Putnam, 1965.

———. *A Rage in Harlem*. Avon, 1965.

———. *Run Man, Run*. Putnam, 1966.

———. *Blind Man with a Pistol*. William Morrow, 1969.

———. *Black on Black: Baby Sister and Selected Writings*. Doubleday, 1973.

———. *A Case of Rape*. Targ Editions, 1980; Howard University Press, 1984.

Hopkins, Pauline. *Contending Forces: A Romance Illustrative of Negro Life North and South*. The Colored Cooperative Publishing Co., 1900; Oxford University Press (The Schomburg Library of Nineteenth-Century Black Women Writers), 1988.

Hughes, Langston. *Not Without Laughter*. Knopf, 1930.

———. *The Ways of White Folks*. Knopf, 1934.

———. *Laughing to Keep from Crying*. Henry Holt, 1952.

———. *Simple Stakes a Claim*. Rinehart, 1957.

———. *Tambourines to Glory*. John Day, 1959.

———. *The Best of Simple*. Hill & Wang, 1961.

———. *Something in Common, and Other Stories*. Hill & Wang, 1963.

———. *Simple's Uncle Sam*. Hill & Wang, 1965.

Hunter, Kristin. *God Bless the Child*. Scribner's, 1964. Howard University Press, 1987.

———. *The Landlord*. Scribner's, 1966.

———. *Boss Cat*. Scribner's Sons, 1971.

———. *The Survivors*. Scribner's Sons, 1975.

———. *The Lakestown Rebellion*. Scribner's Sons, 1978.

Hurston, Zora Neale. *Jonah's Gourd Vine*. Lippincott, 1934, 1971.

———. *Their Eyes Were Watching God*. Lippincott, 1937; University of Illinois Press, 1978.

———. *Moses, Man of the Mountain*. Lippincott, 1939; University of Illinois Press, 1984.

———. *Seraph on the Suwanee*. Scribner's, 1948; AMS Press, 1974.

Jeffers, Lance. *Witherspoon*. Flippin Press, 1983.

Johnson, Charles. *Faith and the Good Thing*. Viking, 1974; Atheneum, 1987.

———. *Oxherding Tale*. Indiana University Press, 1982.

———. *The Sorceror's Apprentice*. Atheneum, 1986.

———. *Middle Passage*. Atheneum, 1990.

Jones, Gayl. *Corregidora: A Novel*. Random House, 1975; Beacon Press, 1986.

———. *Eva's Man*. Random House, 1976; Beacon Press, 1987.

———. *White Rat*. Random House, 1977.

Jones, LeRoi (a.k.a. Imamu Baraka). *The System of Dante's Hell*. Grove, 1965.

———. *Tales*. Grove, 1967.

Kelley, William Melvin. *Different Drummer*. Doubleday, 1962.

———. *Dancers on the Shore*. Doubleday, 1964; Howard University Press, 1984.

———. *A Drop of Patience*. Doubleday, 1965; Chatham Booksellers, 1973.

———. *dem*. Doubleday, 1967.

———. *Dunfords Travels Everywheres*. Doubleday, 1970.

Killens, John O. *Youngblood*. Dial Press, 1956.

———. *And Then We Heard the Thunder*. Knopf, 1963; Howard University Press, 1983.

———. *'Sippi*. Simon & Schuster, 1967; Thunder's Mouth Press, 1988.

———. *Slaves*. Pyramid Press, 1969.

———. *The Great Black Russian: A Novel on the Life and Times of Alexander Pushkin*. Wayne State University Press, 1988.

Larsen, Nella. *Quicksand*. Knopf, 1928; Negro Universities Press, 1969; Collier, 1971; reissued as one volume with *Passing*, Rutgers University Press, 1986.

———. *Passing*. Knopf, 1932; Arno, 1969; Negro Universities Press, 1969; Collier, 1971; reissued as one volume with *Quicksand*, Rutgers University Press, 1986.

Lester, Julius. *This Strange New Feeling*. Dial Press, 1982.

Major, Clarence. *All-Night Visitors*. Olympia, 1969.

———. *Emergency Exit*. Fiction Collective, 1972, 1979.

———. *No*. Emerson Hall, 1973.

———. *Reflex and Bone Structure*. Fiction Collective, 1975; Editions L'Age d'Homme, 1982.

———. *My Amputations: A Novel*. Fiction Collective, 1986.

———. *Such Was the Season*. Mercury House, 1987.

Marshall, Paule. *Brown Girl, Brownstones*. Random House, 1959; The Feminist Press, 1981.

———. *Soul Clap Hands and Sing*. Atheneum, 1961; Howard University Press, 1988.

———. *The Chosen Place, The Timeless People*. Harcourt, 1969.

———. *Praisong for the Widow*. Putnam's Sons, 1983.

———. *Reena and Other Stories*. The Feminist Press, 1983.

Mathis, Sharon Bell. *Teacup Full of Roses.* Viking Press, 1972.

Mayfield, Julian. *The Hit.* Vanguard, 1957.

——. *The Long Night.* Vanguard, 1958.

——. *The Grand Parade.* Vanguard, 1961.

——. *Nowhere Street.* Paper Back Library, 1963.

McKay, Claude. *Home to Harlem.* Harper, 1928.

——. *Banjo.* Harper, 1929.

——. *Gingertown.* Harper, 1932.

——. *Banana Bottom.* Harper, 1933.

McPherson, James Alan. *Hue and Cry.* Atlantic-Little, Brown, 1969; Fawcett, 1979.

——. *Railroad.* Random House, 1976.

——. *Elbow Room.* Little, Brown, 1977; Scribner, 1987.

Meriwether, Louise. *Daddy was a Number Runner.* Prentice-Hall, 1970; Feminist Press, 1986.

Michaux, Oscar. *The Conquest.* Woodruff Press, 1913.

——. *The Forged Note.* Western Book Supply Co., 1915.

——. *The Case of Mrs. Wingate.* Book Supply Co., 1944.

——. *The Story of Dorothy Stanfield.* Book Supply Co., 1946.

——. *The Masquerade: A Historical Novel.* Book Supply Co., 1947.

Morrison, Toni. *The Bluest Eye.* Holt, Rinehart and Winston, 1970.

——. *Sula.* Knopf, 1974.

——. *Song of Solomon.* Knopf, 1977.

——. *Tar Baby.* Knopf, 1981.

——. *Beloved.* Knopf, 1987.

Motley, Willard. *Knock on Any Door.* Appleton-Century, 1947.

——. *We Fished All Night.* Appleton-Century, 1951.

——. *Let No Man Write My Epitaph.* Random House, 1958.

——. *Tourist Town.* Putnam, 1965.

——. *Let Noon Be Fair.* Putnam, 1966.

Murray, Albert. *Train Whistle Guitar.* McGraw-Hill, 1974; Northeastern University Press, 1989.

Naylor, Gloria. *The Women of Brewster Place.* Penguin, 1983.

——. *Linden Hills.* Ticknor and Fields, 1985.

——. *Mama Day.* Ticknor and Fields, 1988.

Petry, Ann. *The Street.* Houghton Mifflin, 1946; Pyramid Books, 1961; Beacon Press, 1985.

——. *Country Place.* Houghton Mifflin, 1947.

——. *The Narrows.* Houghton Mifflin, 1953; Beacon Press, 1988.

——. *Tituba of Salem Village.* Crowell, 1964.

——. *Legend of the Saints.* Crowell, 1972.

——. *Giveadamn Brown.* Doubleday, 1978.

Polite, Carlene Hatcher, (tr. by Pierre Alien). *The Flagellants.* Farrar, Straus & Giroux, 1967; Beacon Press, 1987.

Redding, J. Saunders. *Stranger and Alone.* Harcourt, Brace, 1950.

Reed, Ishmael. *The Free-Lance Pallbearers.* Doubleday, 1967; Chatham Booksellers, 1975; Atheneum, 1988.

——. *Catechism of De Neoamerican Hoodoo Church.* Breman, 1970.

————. *19 Necromancers from Now*. Doubleday, 1970.

————. *Yellow Back Radio Broke-Down*. Doubleday, 1971; Chatham Booksellers, 1975.

————. *Mumbo Jumbo*. Doubleday, 1972; Atheneum, 1989.

————. *The Last Days of Louisiana Red*. Random House, 1974; Atheneum, 1989.

————. *Flight to Canada*. Random House, 1976.

————. *Shrovetide in Old New Orleans*. Doubleday, 1978.

————. *The Terrible Twos*. St. Martin's Press, 1982; Atheneum, 1988.

————. *Reckless Eyeballing*. St. Martin's Press, 1986; Atheneum, 1988.

————. *The Terrible Threes*. Atheneum, 1989.

Schuyler, George. *Black No More*. Macaulay, 1931.

————. *Slaves Today*. Harcourt, 1931.

Scott-Heron, Gil. *The Vulture*. World, 1970.

————. *The Nigger Factory*. Dial Press, 1972.

Shange, Ntozake. *Sassafrass: A Novella*. Shameless Hussy Press, 1977.

————. *Sassafrass, Cypress & Indigo*. St. Martin's Press, 1982.

————. *From Okra to Greens: A Different Love Story*. Coffee House Press, 1984.

Shockley, Ann Allen. *The Black and White of It*. Naiad, 1980, 1987.

Smith, William Gardner. *Last of the Conquerers*. Farrar, Straus & Giroux, 1948.

————. *Anger at Innocence*. Farrar, Straus & Giroux, 1950.

————. *South Street*. Farrar, Straus & Giroux, 1954.

————. *The Stone Face*. Farrar, Straus & Giroux, 1963.

Thurman, Wallace. *The Blacker the Berry*. Macaulay, 1929.

————. *Infants of the Spring*. Macaulay, 1932.

Toomer, Jean. *Cane*. Boni & Liveright, 1923; Harper, 1969.

Turpin, Waters E. *These Low Grounds*. Harper, 1937.

————. *O Canaan!* Doubleday, 1939.

————. *The Rootless*. Vantage, 1957.

Van Dyke, Henry. *Blood of Strawberries*. Farrar, Straus & Giroux, 1968.

————. *Dead Piano*. Farrar, Straus & Giroux, 1971.

Walker, Alice. *The Third Life of Grange Copeland*. Harcourt Brace Jovanovich, 1970.

————. *In Love and Trouble: Stories of Black Women*. Harcourt Brace Jovanovich, 1973.

————. *Meridian*. Harcourt Brace Jovanovich, 1976.

————. *You Can't Keep a Good Woman Down*. Harcourt Brace Jovanovich, 1981.

————. *The Color Purple*. Harcourt Brace Jovanovich, 1982.

————. *The Temple of My Familiar*. Harcourt Brace Jovanovich, 1989.

Walker, Margaret. *Jubilee*. Houghton Mifflin, 1966; Bantam, 1975.

Walrond, Eric. *Tropic Death*. Boni & Liveright, 1926.

Webb, Frank J. *The Garies and Their Friends*. London, 1857; Arno, 1969.

West, Dorothy. *The Living is Easy*. Houghton Mifflin, 1948; Arno, 1969; The Feminist Press, 1982.

West, John B. *Death on the Rocks*. New American Library, 1961.

————. *Never Kill a Cop*. New American Library, 1961.

White, Walter. *The Fire in the Flint*. Knopf, 1924.

————. *Flight*. Knopf, 1926.

Wideman, John Edgar. *A Glance Away*. Harcourt Brace and World, 1967; Chatham Booksellers, 1975; Henry Holt, 1985.

————. *Hurry Home*. Harcourt, 1969; Henry Holt, 1986.

————. *The Lynchers*. Harcourt Brace Jovanovich, 1973; Henry Holt, 1986.

————. *Damballah*. Schocken, 1981; Random House, 1988.

————. *Hiding Place*. Avon Books, 1981; Schocken, 1984; Random House, 1988.

————. *Sent for You Yesterday*. Bard/Avon Books, 1983.

————. *Reuben*. Henry Holt, 1987.

————. *Philadelphia Fire*. Henry Holt, 1990.

Williams, John A. *The Angry Ones*. Ace Books, 1960.

————. *Night Song*. Farrar, Straus & Giroux, 1961.

————. *Sissie*. Farrar, Straus & Giroux, 1963.

————. *The Man Who Cried I Am*. Little, Brown, 1967.

————. *Sons of Darkness, Sons of Light*. Little, Brown, 1969.

————. *Captain Blackman: A Novel*. Doubleday, 1972.

————. *Mothersill and the Foxes*. Doubleday, 1975.

————. *!Clicksong*. Houghton Mifflin, 1982.

————. *Jacob's Ladder*. Thunder's Mouth Press, 1987.

Williams, Sherley Anne. *Dessa Rose*. William Morrow, 1986.

Wilson, Harriet E. *Our Nig*. Rand and Avery, 1859; Vintage Books, 1983.

Wright, Charles, *The Wig, A Mirror Image*. Farrar, Straus & Giroux, 1966.

————. *Absolutely Nothing to Get Alarmed About*. Farrar, Straus & Giroux, 1973.

Wright, Jay. *Homecoming Singer*. Corinth Books, 1971.

Wright, Richard. *Uncle Tom's Children*. Harper, 1938, 1969.

————. *Native Son*. Harper, 1940.

————. *The Outsider*. Harper & Brothers, 1953.

————. *Savage Holiday*. Harper, 1954.

————. *The Long Dream*. Doubleday, 1958.

————. *Eight Men: Stories by Richard Wright*. World, 1961; Thunder's Mouth Press, 1987.

————. *Lawd Today*. Walker, 1963.

Wright, Sara E. *This Child's Gonna Live*. Dell, 1969.

Yerby, Frank. *The Foxes of Harrow*. Dial Press, 1946; Delta Diamond, 1986.

————. *Floodtide*. Dial Press, 1950; Thorndike Press, 1982.

————. *The Old Gods Laugh: A Modern Romance*. Dial Press, 1964.

————. *The Girl From Storyville*. Dial Press, 1972; Heinemann, 1972.

————. *The Voyage Unplanned*. Dial Press, 1974.

————. *Devilseed*. Doubleday, 1984.

————. *McKenzie's Hundred*. Doubleday, 1985.

Young, Al. *Snakes*. Holt, Rinehart & Winston, 1970.

————. *Who Is Angelina?* Holt, Rinehart & Winston, 1975.

————. *Ask Me Now*. McGraw-Hill, 1980.

————. *Seduction by Light*. Delta Fiction, 1988.

V. AUTOBIOGRAPHY

Andrews, William L., ed. *Six Women's Slave Narratives*. Oxford University Press (The Schomburg Library of Nineteenth-Century Black Women Writers), 1988.

Angelou, Maya. *I Know Why the Caged Bird Sings*. Random House, 1969.

————. *Gather Together in My Name*. Random House, 1974; Bantam 1975.

————. *Singin' & Swingin' & Gettin' Merry Like Christmas*. Random House, 1976; Bantam, 1977.

————. *The Heart of a Woman*. Random House, 1981; Bantam 1984.

Baraka, Amiri (a.k.a. LeRoi Jones). *The Autobiography of LeRoi Jones*. Freudlich Books, 1984.

Barthelemy, Anthony G., ed. *Collected Black Women's Narratives*. Oxford University Press (The Schomburg Library of Nineteenth-Century Black Women Writers), 1988.

Barton, Rebecca C. *Witnesses for Freedom: Negro Americans in Autobiography*. Harper, 1948.

Brooks, Gwendolyn Elizabeth. *Report from Part One*. Broadside Press, 1972.

Brown, Claude. *Manchild in the Promised Land*. Macmillan, 1965.

Brown, Hallie Q. *Homespun Heroines and Other Women of Distinction*. Ayer, 1926; Books for Libraries Press, 1971; with introduction by Randall K. Burkett, Oxford University Press (The Schomburg Library of Nineteenth-Century Black Women Writers), 1988.

Brown, Henry Box. *Narrative of Henry Box Brown*. Boston, 1849.

Brown, William Wells. *Narrative of William W. Brown, a Fugitive Slave*. Boston, 1847.

————. *Three Years in Europe: or, Places I Have Seen and People I Have Met*. London, 1852.

Clark, Lewis, and Milton Clark. *Narrative of the Sufferings of Lewis and Milton Clark*. Boston, 1846.

Clifton, Lucille. *Generations: A Memoir*. Random House, 1976.

Craft, William. *Running a Thousand Miles for Freedom; or, The Escape of William and Ellen Craft from Slavery*. London, 1860.

Davis, Angela Y. *Angela Davis: An Autobiography*. Random House, 1974; International Publishers, 1988.

Delany, Samuel R. *Heavenly Breakfast: An Essay on the Winter of Love*. Bantam, 1979.

————. *The Motion of Light in Water: Sex and Science Fiction Writing in the East Village, 1957–1965*. Arbor House, 1988.

Douglass, Frederick. *Narrative of the Life of Frederick Douglass, An American Slave*. Boston, 1845; New American Library and Harvard University Press, 1960.

————. *My Bondage and My Freedom*. New York, 1855.

————. *Life and Times of Frederick Douglass*. Hartford, 1881; Boston, 1892; Pathway Press, 1941; Collier Books, 1962.

Du Bois, W. E. B. *Dusk of Dawn: An Essay Toward an Autobiography of a Race Concept*. Harcourt, 1940; Schocken, 1968.

————. *The Autobiography of W. E. B. Du Bois*. International Publishers, 1968.

Gayle, Addison. *Wayward Child: A Personal Odyssey*. Anchor Press, 1977.

Giovanni, Nikki. *Gemini: An Extended Autobiographical Statement on My First Twenty-Five Years of Being a Black Poet*. Bobbs-Merrill, 1971; Penguin, 1976.

Golden, Marita. *Migrations of the Heart: A Personal Odyssey*. Anchor Press/Doubleday, 1983.

Hammon, Briton. *A Narrative of the Uncommon Sufferings and Surprising Deliverance of Briton Hammon, a Negro Man*. Boston, 1760.

Henson, Josiah. *The Life of Josiah Henson*. Boston, 1849.

———. *Truth Stranger than Fiction: Father Henson's Story of His Own Life*. Boston and Cleveland, 1858.

———. *An Autobiography of Josiah Henson (Mrs. Harriet Beecher Stowe's "Uncle Tom")*. London, 1876.

Herndon, Angelo. *Let Me Live*. Arno House, 1937, 1969.

Himes, Chester. *The Quality of Hurt: The Autobiography of Chester Himes* (vol. 1). Doubleday, 1972.

Houchins, Sue E., ed. *Spiritual Narratives: Maria W. Stewart, Jarena Lee, Julia A. J. Foote, Virginia W. Broughton*. Oxford University Press (The Schomburg Library of Nineteenth-Century Black Women Writers), 1988.

Hughes, Langston. *The Big Sea*. Hill & Wang, 1940.

———. *I Wonder as I Wander*. Hill & Wang, 1956.

Hurston, Zora Neale. *Dust Tracks on a Road*. Lippincott, 1942, 1971; University of Illinois Press, 1984.

Jacobs, Harriet (Jean Fagan Yellin, ed.). *Incidents in the Life of a Slave Girl*. Harvard University Press, 1987; Oxford University Press (The Schomburg Library of Nineteenth-Century Black Women Writers), 1988.

Johnson, James Weldon. *Along This Way: The Autobiography of James Weldon Johnson*. Viking, 1933, 1968.

Keckley, Elizabeth. *Behind the Scenes; or, Thirty Years a Slave, and Four Years in the White House*. New York, 1868; Oxford University Press (The Schomburg Library of Nineteenth-Century Black Women Writers), 1988.

Kennedy, Adrienne. *People Who Led to My Plays*. Knopf, 1987.

Lorde, Audre. *The Cancer Journals*. Spinster's Ink, 1980.

———. *Zami: A New Spelling of My Name*. The Crossing Press, 1982.

Marrant, John. *A Narrative of the Lord's Wonderful Dealings with J. Marrant, a Black*. London, 1785.

McKay, Claude. *A Long Way from Home*. Lee Furman, 1937.

Miller, Kelly. *Out of the House of Bondage*. Neale, 1914.

Murray, Pauli. *Proud Shoes*. Harper, 1956.

Nichols, Charles H. *Many Thousand Gone: The Ex-Slaves' Account of Their Bondage and Freedom*. Brill Adler, 1963; Indiana University Press, 1969.

———, comp. *Black Men in Chains: Narratives by Escaped Slaves*. Lawrence Hill, 1972.

Northrup, Solomon (Anonymous). *Twelve Years a Slave: The Narrative of Solomon Northrup*. Auburn, 1853.

Payne, Daniel A. *Recollections of Seventy Years*. Nashville, TN, 1888.

Redding, J. Saunders. *No Day of Triumph*. Harper, 1942.

Robeson, Paul. *Here I Stand*. Othello Associates, 1958.

Roper, Moses. *Narrative of the Adventures and Escapes of Moses Roper, From American Slavery*. London, 1837.

Schuyler, George S. *Black and Conservative*. Arlington House, 1966.

Seacole, Mary. *Wonderful Adventures of Mrs. Seacole in Many Lands*. With introduction by W. L. Andrews, Oxford University Press (The Schomburg Library of Nineteenth-Century Black Women Writers), 1988.

Smith, Amanda. *An Autobiography: The Story of the Lord's Dealings with Mrs. Amanda Smith, the Colored Evangelist*. With introduction by Jualynne E. Dodson, Oxford University Press (The Schomburg Library of Nineteenth-Century Black Women Writers), 1988.

Stevenson, Brenda, ed. *The Journals of Charlotte Forten Grimke*. Oxford University Press (The Schomburg Library of Nineteenth-Century Black Women Writers), 1988.

Truth, Sojourner (Anonymous). *Narrative of Sojourner Truth, Northern Slave*. Boston, 1850.

————. *Narrative of Sojourner Truth, a Bondswoman of Olden Times*. Boston, 1875.

Vassa, Gustavus. *The Interesting Narrative of the Life of Olaudah Equiano, or Gustavus Vassa, the African*. London, 1789.

Walser, Richard, ed. *The Black Poet; Being the Remarkable Story (partly told by himself) of George Moses Horton, a North Carolina Slave*. Philosophical Library, 1966.

Ward, Samuel Ringgold. *The Autobiography of a Fugitive Negro*. London, 1855.

Washington, Booker Taliaferro. *Up From Slavery; An Autobiography*. New York, 1901.

White, Walter. *A Man Called White*. Viking, 1948.

Wright, Richard. *Black Boy*. Harper, 1945.

X, Malcolm (with Alex Haley). *The Autobiography of Malcolm X*. Grove, 1965.

VI. BIOGRAPHY

Albert, Octavia V. Rogers. *The House of Bondage; or Charlotte Brooks and Other Slaves*. Hunt & Eaton, 1890; Books for Libraries Press, 1972; with introduction by Frances Smith Foster, Oxford University Press (The Schomburg Library of Nineteenth-Century Black Women Writers), 1988.

Benson, Brian Joseph, and Mabel M. Dilliard. *Jean Toomer*. Twayne/G. K. Hall, 1980.

Berry, Faith. *Langston Hughes: Before and Beyond Harlem*. Lawrence Hill & Co., 1983.

Brawley, Benjamin. *Women of Achievement*. Chicago, 1919.

————. *Paul Laurence Dunbar: Poet of His People*. University of North Carolina Press, 1936; Kennikat Press, 1967.

————. *Negro Builders and Heroes*. University of North Carolina Press, 1937.

————. *The Negro Genius*. Dodd, 1937.

Brown, Lloyd W. *Amiri Baraka*. Twayne/G. K. Hall, 1980.

Brown, William Wells. *The Black Man: His Antecedents, His Genius, and His Achievements*, New York and Boston, 1863.

————. *The Rising Sun; or the Antecedents and Advancement of the Colored Race*. Boston, 1874.

Butcher, Philip. *George W. Cable: The Northampton Years*. Columbia University Press, 1959.

————. *George W. Cable*. Twayne, 1962.

Cash, E. A. *John A. Williams: The Evolution of a Black Writer*. Okpaku Communications, 1974.

Chesnutt, Charles W. *Frederick Douglass*. Boston, 1899.

Cook, Mercer. *Five French Negro Authors*. Associated Publishers, 1943.

Cooper, Wayne F. *Claude McKay, Rebel Sojourner in the Harlem Renaissance: A Biography*. Louisiana State University Press, 1987.

Cunningham, Virginia. *Paul Laurence Dunbar and His Song*. Dodd, Mead, 1947; Biblo & Tannen, 1969.

Davis, Thadious, and Trudier Harris, eds. *Afro-American Fiction Writers After 1955*. (*Dictionary of Literary Biography*, vol. 33) Gale, 1984.

———. *Afro-American Writers After 1955: Dramatists and Prose Writers* (*Dictionary of Literary Biography*, vol. 38). Gale, 1985.

Dickinson, Donald C. *A Bio-bibliography of Langston Hughes, 1902–1967*. Archon, 1972.

Du Bois, W. E. B. *John Brown*. G. W. Jacobs, 1909; International Publishers, 1962; Metro Books, 1972.

Emanuel, James A. *Langston Hughes*. Twayne, 1967.

Fabre, Michel. *The Unfinished Quest of Richard Wright*. William Morrow, 1973.

Farrison, William E., *William Wells Brown: Author and Reformer*. University of Chicago Press, 1969.

Fauset, Arthur Huff. *Sojourner Truth, God's Faithful Pilgrim*. University of North Carolina Press, 1938.

Ferguson, Blanche E. *Countee Cullen and the Negro Renaissance*. Dodd, Mead, 1966.

Flasch, Joy. *Melvin B. Tolson*. Twayne/G. K. Hall, 1972.

Fleming, Robert E. *Williard Motley*. Twayne/G. K. Hall, 1978.

Franklin, John Hope. *Geroge Washington Williams, A Biography*. University of Chicago Press, 1985.

Gayle, Addison, Jr. *Oak and Ivy: A Biography of Paul Laurence Dunbar*. Doubleday, 1971.

———. *Richard Wright: The Ordeal of a Native Son*. Anchor Press/Doubleday, 1980.

Graham, Shirley. *There Was Once a Slave: The Heroic Story of Frederick Douglass*. Messner, 1947.

———. *Booker T. Washington*. Messner, 1955.

Greene, J. Lee. *Time's Unfading Garden: Ann Spencer's Life and Poetry*. Louisiana State University Press, 1977.

Handy, William C. *Negro Authors and Composers of the United States*. AMS Press, 1976.

Harris, Trudier, ed. *Afro-American Writers, 1940–1955* (*Dictionary of Literary Biography*, vol. 76). Gale, 1988.

Harris, Trudier, and Thadious Davis, eds. *Afro-American Poets Since 1955* (*Dictionary of Literary Biography*, vol. 41). Gale, 1985.

———. *Afro-American Writers Before the Harlem Renaissance* (*Dictionary of Literary Biography*, vol. 50). Gale, 1986.

———. *Afro-American Writers from the Harlem Renaissance to 1940* (*Dictionary of Literary Biography*, vol. 51). Gale, 1987.

Haskins, James. *Always Movin' On: The Life of Langston Hughes*. Watts, 1976.

Hatcher, John. *From the Auroral Darkness: The Life and Poetry of Robert Hayden*. G. Ronald, 1984.

Hemenway, Robert. *Zora Neale Hurston: A Literary Biography*. University of Illinois Press, 1980.

Hughes, Langston. *Famous American Negroes*. Dodd, Mead, 1954.

Hull, Gloria T. *Color, Sex and Poetry: Three Women Writers and the Harlem Renaissance.* Indiana University Press, 1987.

Keller, Frances Richardson. *An American Crusade: The Life of Charles Waddell Chesnutt.* Brigham, 1978.

Kent, George E. *A Life of Gwendolyn Brooks.* University Press of Kentucky, 1990.

Levy, Eugene. *James Weldon Johnson: Black Leader, Black Voice.* University of Chicago Press, 1973.

Linneman, Russell J., ed. *Alain Locke: Reflections on a Modern Renaissance Man.* Louisiana State University Press, 1983.

Longsworth, Polly. *I, Charlotte Forten, Black and Free.* Crowell, 1970.

McKay, Nellie Y. *Jean Toomer, Artist: A Study of His Literary Life and Work, 1894–1936.* University of North Carolina Press, 1984.

Melhem, D. H. *Gwendolyn Brooks: Poetry and the Heroic Voice.* University of Kentucky Press, 1987.

Moore, Jack B. *W. E. B. Du Bois.* Twayne/G. K. Hall, 1981.

Ofari, Earl. *Let Your Motto Be Resistance: The Life and Thought of Henry Highland Garnet.* Beacon Press, 1972.

Ottley, Roi. *The Lonely Warrior: The Life and Times of Robert S. Abbott.* Henry Regnery, 1955.

Peplow, Michael W. *George S. Schuyler.* Twayne/G. K. Hall, 1980.

Perry, Margaret. *A Bio-bibliography of Countee P. Cullen (1903–1946).* Greenwood Press, 1971.

Quarles, Benjamin. *Frederick Douglass.* Associated Publishers, 1948.

Rampersad, Arnold. *The Life of Langston Hughes, Volume I: I, Too, Sing America.* Oxford University Press, 1986.

———. *The Life of Langston Hughes, Volume II: I Dream a World.* Oxford University Press, 1988.

Reddick, Lawrence D. *Crusader Without Violence: A Biography of Martin Luther King, Jr.* Harper, 1959.

Redding, J. Saunders. *The Lonesome Road: The Story of the Negro's Part in America.* Doubleday, 1958.

Render, Sylvia Lyons. *Charles W. Chestnutt.* Twayne/G. K. Hall, 1980.

Robeson, Eslanda Goode. *Paul Robeson, Negro.* Harper, 1930.

Robinson, William H. *Phillis Wheatley in the Black American Beginnings.* Broadside Press, 1975.

Sheppard, Gladys B. *Mary Church Terrell, Respectable Person.* Human Relations Press, 1959.

Shockley, Ann Allen, and Sue P. Chandler. *Living Black American Authors: A Biographical Directory.* R. R. Bowker, 1973.

Simmons, William J. *Men of Mark: Eminent, Progressive & Rising.* Cleveland, 1887; Arno, 1968.

Still, William. *The Underground Rail Road: A Record of Facts, Authentic Narratives, Letters.* Philadelphia, 1872.

Sylvander, Carolyn W. *Jesse Redmon Fauset: Black American Writer.* Whitson, 1980.

Terry, Ellen. *Young Jim: The Early Years of James Weldon Johnson.* Dodd, Mead, 1967.

Troupe, Quincy, ed. *James Baldwin: The Legacy.* Simon & Schuster, 1989.

Turner, Darwin T. *Afro-American Writers.* Appleton-Century-Crofts, 1970.

Wagner, Jean. *Black Poets of the United States: From Paul Laurence Dunbar to Langston Hughes.* University of Illinois Press, 1973.

Walker, Alice. *Langston Hughes, American Poet.* Harper & Row, 1974.

Walker, Margaret. *Richard Wright, Daemonic Genius.* Warner/Amistad, 1988.

Washington, Booker T. *Frederick Douglass.* Philadelphia and London, 1907.

Wegelin, Oscar. *Jupiter Hammon, American Negro Poet: Selections from His Writings and a Bibliography.* Heartman, 1915.

Wideman, John Edgar. *Brothers and Keepers.* Holt, Rinehart & Winston, 1984; Penguin, 1985.

Wiggins, Lida Keck. *The Life and Works of Paul Laurence Dunbar.* Nichols, 1907.

Williams, John A. *The Most Native of Sons: A Biography of Richard Wright.* Doubleday, 1970.

Wright, Richard. *American Hunger.* Harper & Row, 1944, 1977; Thunder's Mouth Press, 1988.

Young, James O. *Black Writers of the Thirties.* Louisiana State University Press, 1973.

VII. ESSAYS

(Note: Book Publications only; for other essays see collections in I and II.)

Baker, Houston, ed. *Reading Black: Essays in the Criticism of African, Caribbean and Black American Literature.* Cornell University Press, 1978.

Baldwin, James. *The Fire Next Time.* Dial, 1955.

———. *Notes of a Native Son.* Beacon Press, 1955.

———. *Nobody Knows My Name.* Dial, 1961; Dell, 1963.

———. *No Name in the Street.* Dial, 1972.

———. *The Devil Finds Work: An Essay.* Dial, 1976.

Baraka, Imamu Amiri (a.k.a. LeRoi Jones). *Daggers and Javelins: Essays, 1974–1979.* William Morrow, 1984.

Benston, Kimberly W., ed. *Imamu Amiri Baraka (LeRoi Jones): A Collection of Critical Essays.* Prentice-Hall, 1978.

Bigsby, C. W. E. *The Second Black Renaissance: Essays in Black Literature.* Greenwood Press, 1980.

———. *The Negro Genius.* Dodd, 1937.

Brown, William Wells. *Three Years in Europe.* London, 1852.

———. *The American Fugitive in Europe.* Boston, Cleveland, and New York, 1855.

———. *My Southern Home; or, the South and Its People.* Boston, 1880.

Bruck, Peter, and Wolfgang Karrer, eds. *The Afro-American Novel Since 1960: A Collection of Critical Essays.* Benjamins North America, 1982.

Butcher, Margaret J. *The Negro in American Culture; Based on Materials Left by Alain Locke.* Knopf, 1956, 1972.

Clarke, John Henrik, ed. *William Styron's "Nat Turner": Ten Black Writers Respond.* Beacon Press, 1968.

Cleaver, Eldridge. *Soul on Ice.* McGraw-Hill, 1968.

Cooke, Michael G., ed. *Modern Black Novelists: A Collection of Critical Essays.* Prentice-Hall, 1971.

Cruse, Harold. *The Crisis of the Negro Intellectual.* William Morrow, 1967.

Davis, Charles T., and Henry Louis Gates, Jr., eds. *Black is the Color of the Cosmos: Essays on Afro-American Literature and Culture, 1942–1981.* Garland, 1982; Howard University Press, 1989.

Du Bois, W. E. B. *The Souls of Black Folk.* A. C. McClurg, 1903.

———. *Darkwater.* Harcourt, 1920.

———. *The Gifts of Black Folk.* Associated Publishers, 1924.

Ellison, Ralph. *Shadow and Act.* Random House, 1964.

Garnet, Henry Highland. *The Past and Present Condition and Destiny of the Colored Race, A Discourse Delivered at the Fifteenth Anniversary of the Female Benevolent Society of Troy, New York, February 14, 1848.* Mnemosyne, 1969.

Gayle, Addison, Jr., ed. *Black Expression: Essays By and About Black Americans in the Creative Arts.* Weybright and Talley, 1969.

———. *The Black Situation.* Horizon, 1970.

———, ed. *Modern Black Poets: A Collection of Critical Essays.* Prentice-Hall, 1973.

Giovanni, Nikki. *Sacred Cows and Other Edibles.* William Morrow, 1988.

Giovanni, Nikki, and Margaret Walker. *A Poetic Equation: Conversations Between Nikki Giovanni and Margaret Walker.* Howard University Press, 1974, 1983.

Goldwin, Robert A., ed. *Civil Disobedience: Five Essays by Martin Luther King, Jr., and Others.* Public Affairs Conference Center, Kenyon College, 1968.

Gross, Seymour, and John E. Hardy, eds. *Images of the Negro in American Literature: Essays in Criticism.* University of Chicago Press, 1966.

Hurston, Zora Neale. *Mules and Men.* Lippincott, 1935; Indiana University Press, 1978.

———. *Tell My Horse.* Lippincott, 1938.

———. *The Sanctified Church.* Turtle Island Foundation, 1983.

Inge, M. Thomas, Maurice Duke, and Jackson R. Bryer, eds. *Black American Writers: Bibliographical Essays.* 2 vols. St. Martin's Press, 1976.

Jackson, Blyden. *The Waiting Years: Essays on American Negro Literature.* Louisiana State University Press, 1976.

Jackson, Blyden, and Louis D. Rubin, Jr. *Black Poetry in America: Two Essays in Historical Interpretation.* Louisiana State University Press, 1974.

Jones, LeRoi (a.k.a. Amiri Baraka). *Home: Social Essays.* William Morrow, 1966.

———. *Raise, Race, Rays, Raze: Essays Since 1965.* Random House, 1971.

———, ed. *The Moderns: New Fiction in America.* Corinth, 1966.

Kaiser, Ernest. *Freedomways Reader: Afro-Americans in the Seventies.* International Publishers, 1977.

Killens, John Oliver. *Black Man's Burden.* Simon & Schuster, 1965.

King, Martin Luther, Jr. *Stride Toward Freedom: The Montgomery Story.* Harper & Row, 1958.

———. *Strength to Love.* Harper & Row, 1963; Fortress Press, 1981.

———. *Why We Can't Wait.* Harper & Row, 1964.

———. *Nobel Lecture by the Reverend Dr. Martin Luther King, Jr.* Harper & Row, 1965; Clarke & Way, 1965.

———. *Conscience for Change.* Canadian Broadcasting Company, 1967.

———. *The Measure of a Man.* Pilgrim Press, 1968; Fortress Press, 1988.

———. *The Trumpet of Conscience.* Harper & Row, 1968.

———. *Where Do We Go From Here?: Chaos or Community?* Hodder & Stoughton, 1968.

Lee, Don L. (a.k.a. Haki R. Madhubuti). *From Plan to Planet*. Broadside Press, 1973.

Lester, Julius. *Search for the New Land*. Dial, 1970.

———. *Look Out, Whitey! Black Power's Gonna Git Your Mama!* Dial, 1968.

———. *Lovesong: Becoming a Jew*. Henry Holt, 1988.

Lorde, Audre. *Sister Outsider: Essays and Speeches*. The Crossing Press, 1984.

———. *A Burst of Light*. Firebrand Books, 1988.

Madhubuti, Haki R. (a.k.a. Don L. Lee). *Black Men: Obsolete, Single, Dangerous?* Third World Press, 1989.

Miller, Kelly. *Race Adjustment*. Neal, 1908.

———. *The Everlasting Stain*. Associated Publishers, 1924.

Nichols, Charles, ed. *Arna Bontemps/Langston Hughes: Letters, 1925–1967*. Dodd, Mead, 1980.

O'Daniel, Therman B., ed. *Langston Hughes, Black Genius: A Critical Evaluation*. William Morrow, 1971.

Plato, Ann. *Essays: Including Biographies and Miscellaneous Pieces, in Prose and Poetry*. With introduction by Kenny J. Williams, Oxford University Press (The Schomburg Library of Nineteenth-Century Black Women Writers), 1988.

Pratt, Louis H., and Fred L. Standley, eds. *Conversation with James Baldwin*. University Press of Mississippi, 1989.

Redding, J. Saunders. *On Being Negro in America*. Bobbs-Merrill, 1951, 1962.

Reed, Ishmael. *Shrovetide in Old New Orleans*. Doubleday, 1978; Avon Books, 1979.

———. *God Made Alaska for the Indians: Selected Essays*. Garland, 1982.

———. *Writin' is Fightin': 37 Years of Boxing on Paper*. Atheneum, 1988.

Ro, Sigmund. *Rage and Celebration: Essays on Contemporary Afro-American Writing*. Humanities Press, 1984.

Robinson, William H., ed. *Critical Essays on Phillis Wheatley*. G. K. Hall, 1982.

Scott, Nathan A., Jr. *Modern Literature and the Religious Frontier*. Harper, 1958.

———. *The Broken Center: Studies in the Theological Horizon of Modern Literature*. Yale University Press, 1966.

———. *Craters of the Spirit: Studies in the Modern Novel*. Corpus, 1968.

———. *Negative Capability: Studies in the New Literature and the Religious Situation*. Yale University Press, 1969.

Shange, Ntozake. *See No Evil: Prefaces, Essays, & Accounts, 1976–1983*. Momo's Press, 1984.

Sheffey, Ruthe T. *Trajectory: Fueling the Future and Preserving the Black Literary Past, Essays in Criticism*. Morgan State University Press, 1986.

Turner, Darwin T., ed. *Black American Literature: Essays*. Charles E. Merrill, 1969.

Walker, Alice. *In Search of Our Mothers' Gardens: Womanist Prose*. Harcourt Brace Jovanovich, 1983.

———. *Living by the Word: Selected Writings, 1973–1987*. Harcourt Brace Jovanovich, 1988.

Walker, Margaret. *How I Wrote Jubilee*. Third World Press, 1977; reissued as *How I Wrote Jubilee, and Other Essays on Life and Literature*, The Feminist Press, 1989.

Washington, Booker T. *The Future of the American Negro*. New York, 1899.

———. (with W. E. B. Du Bois) *The Negro in the South*. G. W. Jacobs, 1907.

Williams, John A. *This Is My Country, Too*. New American Library, 1965; Signet, 1966.

Wright, Richard. *Black Power*. Harper, 1954.
————. *Pagan Spain*. Harper, 1957.
————. *White Man, Listen!* Doubleday, 1957.

VIII. DRAMA
(book publication only)

ANTHOLOGIES, COLLECTIONS, AND CRITICAL COMMENTARY

Abramson, Dorothy. *Negro Playwrights in the American Theatre: 1925–59*. Columbia University Press, 1969.
Adams, William et al., eds. *Afro-American Literature: Drama*. Houghton Mifflin, 1979.
Arata, Esther S. *More Black American Playwrights: A Bibliography*. Scarecrow, 1978.
Arata, Esther S., and Nicholas J. Rotoli. *Black American Playwrights, 1800 to Present: A Bibliography*. Scarecrow, 1976.
Archer, Leonard C. *Black Images in the American Theatre*. Pageant-Poseidon, 1973.
Benston, Kimberly. *Baraka: The Renegade and the Mask*. Yale University Press, 1976.
Bond, Frederick W. *The Negro and the Drama*. Associated Publishers, 1940; McGrath, 1969.
Brown, Sterling A. *Negro Poetry and Drama*. Associates in Negro Folk Education, 1937; Atheneum, 1969.
Brown-Guillory, Elizabeth. *Their Place on the Stage: Black Women Playwrights in America*. Greenwood Press, 1988.
Childress, Alice, ed. *Black Scenes*. Doubleday, 1971.
Couch, William, Jr., ed. *New Black Playwrights: An Anthology*. Louisiana State University Press, 1968; Avon, 1970.
Craig, E. Quita. *Black Drama of the Federal Theatre Era: Beyond the Formal Horizons*. University of Massachusetts Press, 1980.
Davis, Thadious M. and Trudier Harris, eds. *Afro-American Writers After 1955: Dramatists and Prose Writers* (*Dictionary of Literary Biography*, vol. 38). Gale Research, 1985.
Dent, Thomas, C., Gilbert Moses, and Richard Schechner. *The Free Southern Theatre by the Free Southern Theatre*. Bobbs-Merrill, 1969.
Fabre, Genevieve (Melvin Dixon, trans.). *Drumbeats, Masks, and Metaphor: Contemporary Afro-American Theatre*. Harvard University Press, 1983.
Fletcher, Tom. *100 Years of the Negro in Show Business*. Burdge, 1954.
French, William P., Michel J. Fabre, and Amritjit Singh. *Afro-American Poetry and Drama, 1760–1975*. Gale Research, 1979.
Harrison, Paul Carter. *The Drama of Nommo*. Grove, 1972.
Hatch, James V. *Black Image on the American Stage: A Bibliography of Plays and Musicals, 1770–1970*. Drama Book Specialists, 1970.
Hatch, James, and Ted Shine, eds. *Black Theatre, U.S.A.: Forty-five Plays by Black Americans, 1847–1974*. The Free Press, 1974.
Hatch, James, and Omanii Abdullah, comps. and eds. *Black Playwrights 1823–1977: An Annotated Bibliography of Plays*. R. R. Bowker, 1977.
Hill, Errol, ed. *The Theatre of Black Americans*. 2 vols. Prentice-Hall, 1980.
Isaacs, Edith. *The Negro in the American Theatre*. Theatre Arts, 1947.

Jerome, V. J. *The Negro in Hollywood Films.* Masses & Mainstream, 1950.

Kennedy, Adrienne. *People Who Lead to My Plays.* Knopf, 1987.

Keyssar, Helene. *The Curtain and the Veil: Strategies in Black Drama.* Franklin, 1980.

King, Woodie. *Black Theatre, Present Condition.* National Black Theatre Touring Circuit, 1981.

Locke, Alain LeRoy, and Montgomery Gregory, eds. *Plays of Negro Life.* Harper, 1927; Negro Universities Press, 1970.

Mitchell, Loften. *Black Drama: The Story of the American Negro in the Theatre.* Hawthorne Books, 1967.

Noble, Peter. *The Cinema and the Negro, 1905–1948.* Gordon, 1980.

Null, Gary. *Black Hollywood: The Negro in Motion Pictures.* Citadel, 1977.

Oliver, Clinton F., and Stephanie Sills, eds. *Contemporary Black Drama: From A Raisin in the Sun to No Place to Be Somebody.* Scribners, 1971.

Ostrow, Eileen Joyce, ed. *Center Stage: An Anthology of 21 Contemporary Black American Plays.* Sea Urchin, 1981.

Patterson, Lindsay, ed. *Anthology of the American Negro in the Theatre: A Critical Approach.* Publishers Co., 1967.

————, ed. *Black Theatre: A Twentieth-Century Collection of the Works of its Best Playwrights.* Dodd, Mead, 1971; New American Library, 1973.

TDR. *Black Theatre Issue: T-40, Summer.* TDR, 1968.

Turner, Darwin T., ed. *Black Drama in America: An Anthology.* Fawcett, 1971.

Wittke, Carl. *Tambo and Bones: A History of the American Minstrel Stage.* Duke University Press, 1930.

Woll, Allen. *Dictionary of the Black Theatre: Broadway, Off-Broadway, and Selected Harlem Theatre.* Greenwood Press, 1983.

PLAYS IN PRINT

Amis, Lola Jones. *Three Plays.* Exposition, 1965.

Baldwin, James. *Blues for Mr. Charlie.* Dial, 1964.

————. *The Amen Corner.* Dial, 1968.

————. *One Day When I Was Lost: A Scenario Based on The Autobiography of Malcolm X.* Michael Joseph, 1972.

Baraka, Amiri (a.k.a. LeRoi Jones). *Selected Plays and Prose of Amiri Baraka/LeRoi Jones.* William Morrow, 1979.

Brown, William Wells. *The Escape; or A Leap for Freedon—A Drama in Five Acts.* Boston, 1858; Historic Publications, 1969.

Bullins, Ed. *How Do You Do: A Nonsense Drama.* Illuminations Press, 1967.

————. *Five Plays by Ed Bullins.* Bobbs-Merrill, 1969; revised as *The Electronic Nigger and Other Plays,* Faber & Faber, 1970.

————. *The Duplex: A Black Love Fable in Four Movements.* William Morrow, 1971.

————. *Four Dynamite Plays.* William Morrow, 1972.

————. *The Theme is Blackness: The Corner and Other Plays.* William Morrow, 1972.

————, ed. *New Plays from the Black Theatre.* Bantam, 1969.

————, ed. *The New Lafayette Theatre Presents: Plays with Aesthetic Comments by Six Black Playwrights.* Doubleday, 1974.

Caldwell, Ben. *Prayer Meeting (Or, The First Militant Minister).* Jihad, 1967.

Carter, Steve. *Nevis Mountain Dew*. Dramatists Play Service, 1980.

Childress, Alice. *Wine in the Wilderness: A Comedy-Drama*. Dramatists Play Service, 1969.

———. *Mojo and String*. Dramatists Play Service, 1971.

———. *Wedding Band: A Love/Hate Story in Black and White*. Samuel French, 1973.

———. *Where the Rattlesnake Sounds: A Play about Harriet Tubman*. Coward, McCann & Geoghegan, 1975.

———. *Let's Hear It for the Queen*. Coward, 1976.

Cotter, Joseph Seamon, Sr. *Caleb, the Degenerate: A Play in Four Acts*. Bradley & Gilbert, 1903; New York, 1940.

Davis, Ossie. *Purlie Victorious: A Comedy in Three Acts*. Samuel French, 1961, 1971.

———. *Escape to Freedom: A Play About Young Frederick Douglass*. Viking, 1978.

———. *Langston: A Play*. Delacorte, 1982.

Dean, Darryl. *Family Reunion*. The Dramatic Publishing Co., 1979.

Dean, Phillip Hayes. *This Bird of Dawning Singeth All Night Long*. Dramatists Play Service, 1971.

———. *American Night Cry*. Dramatists Play Service, 1972.

———. *The Sty of the Blind Pig*. Dramatists Play Service, 1972.

———. *Freeman*. Dramatists Play Service, 1973.

———. *Every Night When the Sun Goes Down*. Dramatists Play Service, 1976.

———. *Paul Robeson*. Nelson Doubleday, 1978.

Edmonds, Randolph. *Shades and Shadows*. Meador, 1930.

———. *Six Plays for a Negro Theatre*. W. H. Baker, 1934.

———. *Land of Cotton and Other Plays*. Associated Publishers, 1942.

———. *Earth and Stars*. Florida A & M University, 1961.

Edwards, Gus. *The Offering*. Dramatists Play Service, 1978.

———. *Old Phantoms*. Dramatists Play Service, 1979.

Elder, Lonnie III. *Ceremonies in Dark Old Men*. Farrar, Straus & Giroux, 1969.

Evans, Don. *The Prodigals*. Dramatists Play Service, 1977.

Franklin, J. E. *Black Girl: From Genesis to Revelations*. Howard University Press, 1977.

Fuller, Charles. *A Soldier's Play*. Nelson Doubleday, 1982; Hill & Wang, 1982.

———. *Zooman and the Sign*. Nelson Doubleday, 1982; Samuel French, 1982.

Gordone, Charles. *No Place to Be Somebody*. Bobbs-Merrill, 1969.

Goss, Clay. *Homecookin': Five Plays*. Howard University Press, 1974.

Graham, Arthur. *The Nationals: A Black Happening of Many Minds*. Black Book Production, 1968.

Grimke, Angelina. *Rachel*. Cornhill, 1920.

Gunn, Bill. *Black Picture Show*. Reed, Cannon & Johnson, 1975.

Hansberry, Lorraine. *A Raisin in the Sun*. Signet/New American Library, 1959.

———. *The Sign in Sidney Brustein's Window*. Random House, 1965.

———. *Les Blancs and the Last Plays of Lorraine Hansberry*. Random House, 1972.

———. (Robert Nemiroff, ed.). *The Collected Last Plays of Lorraine Hansberry*. Random House, 1972; New American Library, 1983.

Harrison, Paul Carter, ed. *Kuntu Drama: Plays of the African Continuum*. Grove Press, 1974.

Hill, Leslie Pinckney. *Toussaint L'Ouverture*. Christopher, 1928.

Hughes, Langston. *Tambourines to Glory*. Day, 1958.

————. (W. Smalley, ed.). *Five Plays.* University of Indiana Press, 1963.

Johnson, Georgia Douglas. *Plumes.* Samuel French, 1927.

Jones, LeRoi (a.k.a. Imamu Baraka). *Dutchman; and the Slave.* William Morrow, 1964; Faber & Faber, 1965.

————. *The Baptism and The Toilet.* Grove, 1967.

————. *Four Black Revolutionary Plays.* Bobbs-Merrill, 1969.

————. *Slave Ship.* Jihad, 1969.

————. *J-E-L-L-O.* Third World Press, 1970.

————. *The Motion of History and Other Plays.* William Morrow, 1978.

————. *The Sidney Poet Heroical.* I. Reed Books, 1979.

Kennedy, Adrienne. *Cities in Bezique.* Samuel French, 1969.

————. *Funnyhouse of a Negro.* Samuel French, 1969.

King, Woodie, ed. *A Black Quartet: Four Plays by Amiri Baraka, Ed Bullins, Ben Caldwell, and Ron Milner.* New American Library, 1970.

Lee, Leslie. *The First Breeze of Summer.* Samuel French, 1975.

Mackey, William Wellington. *Behold: Cometh the Vanderkellans!* Azazel Books, 1966; Azakiel Press, 1967.

Milner, Ron. *What the Winesellers Buy.* Samuel French, 1974.

Mitchell, Loften. *A Land Beyond the River.* Pioneer Drama Service, 1963.

————. *Tell Pharaoh.* Negro Universities Press, 1970.

Molette, Carlton, and Barbara Molette. *Rosalee Prichett.* Dramatists Play Service, 1972.

O'Neal, Regina. *Three Television Plays.* Broadside Press, 1974.

Peterson, Louis S. *Take a Giant Step.* Samuel French, 1954.

Richardson, Willis. *Plays and Pageants from the Life of the Negro.* Associated Publishers, 1930.

Richardson, Willis, and May Miller. *Negro History in Thirteen Plays.* Associated Publishers, 1935.

Russell, Charles. *Five on the Black Hand Side.* Samuel French, 1970.

Shange, Ntozake. *For Colored Girls Who Have Considered Suicide When the Rainbow is Enuf: A Choreopoem.* Macmillan, 1977.

————. *From Okra to Greens: A Different Love Story.* Coffee House Press, 1984.

Shears, Carl S. (a.k.a Sagitarius). *I Am Ishmael, Son of Blackamoor.* Nuclassics and Science, 1975.

Shine, Ted. *Contributions.* Dramatists Play Service, 1970.

Spence, Eulalie. *Fool's Errand.* Samuel French, 1927.

————. *Foreign Mail.* Samuel French, 1927.

Stuart, Nuba-Harold. *Hunter!* (revised and rewritten). Samuel French, 1980.

Van Peebles, Melvin. *Sweet Sweetback's Baadasss Song.* Lancer Books, 1971.

————. *Don't Play Us Cheap.* Bantam Books, 1973.

Van Peebles, Melvin, in Collaboration with Paul Carter Harrison. *Ain't Supposed to Die a Natural Death.* Bantam Books, 1973.

Wadud, Ali. *Companions of the Fire.* Dramatists Play Service, 1980.

Walker, Joseph A. *The River Niger.* Hill & Wang, 1973.

Ward, Douglass Turner. *Happy Ending and Day of Absence: Two Plays.* Dramatists Play Service, 1966; Joseph Okpaku, 1966.

————. *The Reckoning.* Dramatists Play Service, 1970.

Wesley, Richard. *The Sirens.* Dramatists Play Service, 1975.

————. *The Mighty Gents*. Dramatists Play Service, 1979.

————. *The Past is the Past and Gettin' It Together*. Dramatists Play Service, 1979.

White, Edgar B. *Underground: Four Plays*. William Morrow, 1970.

————. *The Crucificado: Two Plays*. William Morrow, 1973.

————. *Lament for Rastafari and Other Plays*. Boyars, 1983.

Williams, Samm-Art. *Home*. Nelson Doubleday, 1978; Dramatists Play Service, 1980.

Wilson, August. *Fences*. New American Library/Plume, 1986.

————. *Ma Rainey's Black Bottom*. New American Library/Plume, 1985.

Wright, Jay. *Balloons: A Comedy in One Act*. Baker's Plays, 1968.

Wright, Richard (with Paul Green). *Native Son: A Play in Ten Scenes*. Harper, 1941; Samuel French, 1980.

INDEX